lonely planet

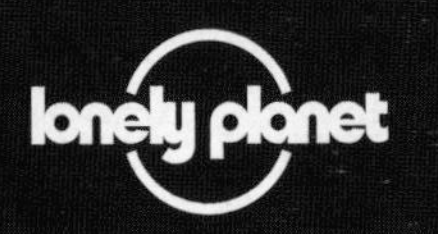

Portugal

Abigail Hole, Charlotte Beech

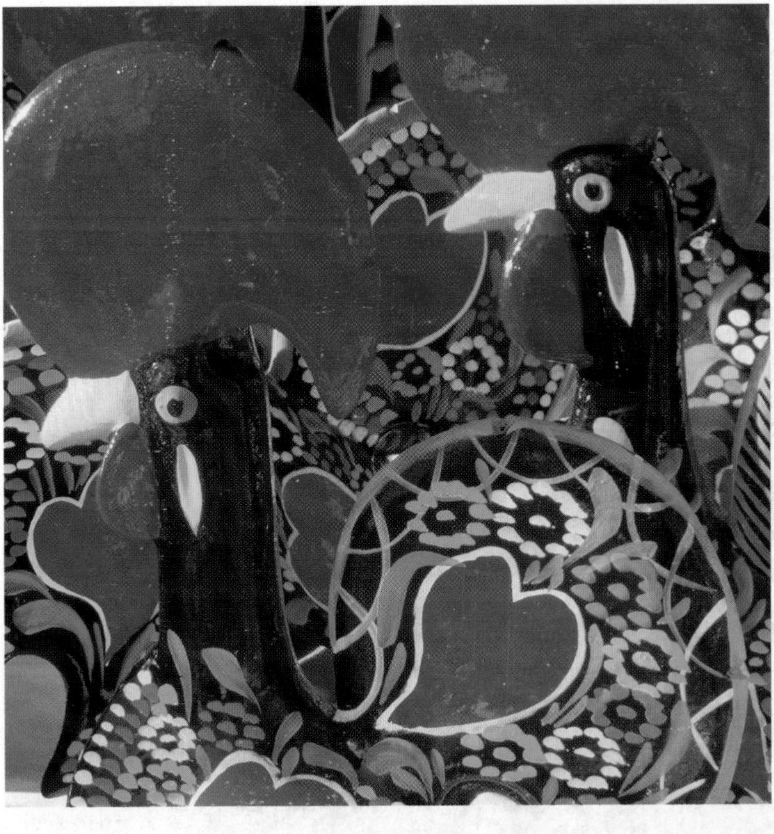

Contents

Lonely Planet books provide independent advice. Lonely Planet does not accept advertising in guidebooks, nor do we accept payment in exchange for listing or endorsing any place or business. Lonely Planet writers do not accept discounts or payments in exchange for positive coverage of any sort.

Os livros da Lonely Planet fornecem recomendação independente. A Lonely Planet não aceita fazer publicidade nos seus guias turísticos, nem tampouco aceita pagamento em troca da inclusão ou endosso de qualquer local ou negócio. Os autores da Lonely Planet não aceitam discontos ou pagamentos pela elaboração de uma reportagem vantajosa de qualquer tipo.

BETHUNE CARMICHAEL

Mosteiro dos Jerónimos (p92), Belém, Lisbon

ANDERS BLOMQVIST

Claustro Principal (p286), Convento de Cristo, Tomar

ANDERS BLOMQVIST

Cromeleque dos Almendres (p215)

Gare do Oriente (p91), Lisbon

CARLOS COSTA

MARTIN MOOS

Claustro Real (p272), Santa Maria da Vitória, Batalha

JULIA WILK

Palácio Nacional de Mafra (p133), Mafra

Mosteiro de Santa Maria de Alcobaça (p269), Alcobaça

ANDERS BLOM

Destination Portugal

Stunningly beautiful and sunny, Portugal is one of Europe's most fascinating nations. It's a huge country disguised as a small one, with a bewitching air of faded grandeur and exotic tendrils that are a reminder of when it was massive, a 16th-century global superpower, running territories in China, Brazil, India, Mozambique, Angola and Cape Verde.

The ocean has a powerful hold on Portugal. With 830km of coastline it's unsurprising that the Portuguese have spent a long time looking out to sea. The great blue expanse dominates its history, cuisine, economy and spare time. But it is surprising that the Portuguese were so passionate about exploration. Portugal itself is wonderful, with amazing beaches, glorious architecture, vast landscapes, rural hideaways, convents and monasteries, and an unfair share of natural beauty. And it's not only beautiful, but fantastically diverse: the south has burnished-gold cliffs and craggy streaked rocks meeting long beaches, lagoons and serene sandy islands, while the north rucks up into great wooded hillsides, gashed through with ravines and rivers. If all you ask from a holiday destination are sophisticated resorts, romantic cities, remote stuck-in-time whitewashed villages, palace hotels, farmhouse retreats, empty golden sands, great surf, fun nightlife, flavoursome, fruity, good-value wine and simple, delicious cuisine, Portugal is the place for you.

The cinnamon sprinkling on this custard-tart country is that the Portuguese are notably charming, courteous, good-humoured and know how to have fun – all reasons why the 2004 European Football Championships passed here with such ease (and so much excitement). It's also cheap – still one of Europe's biggest bargains. You will get more for your euro here than anywhere else.

GERRY REILLY

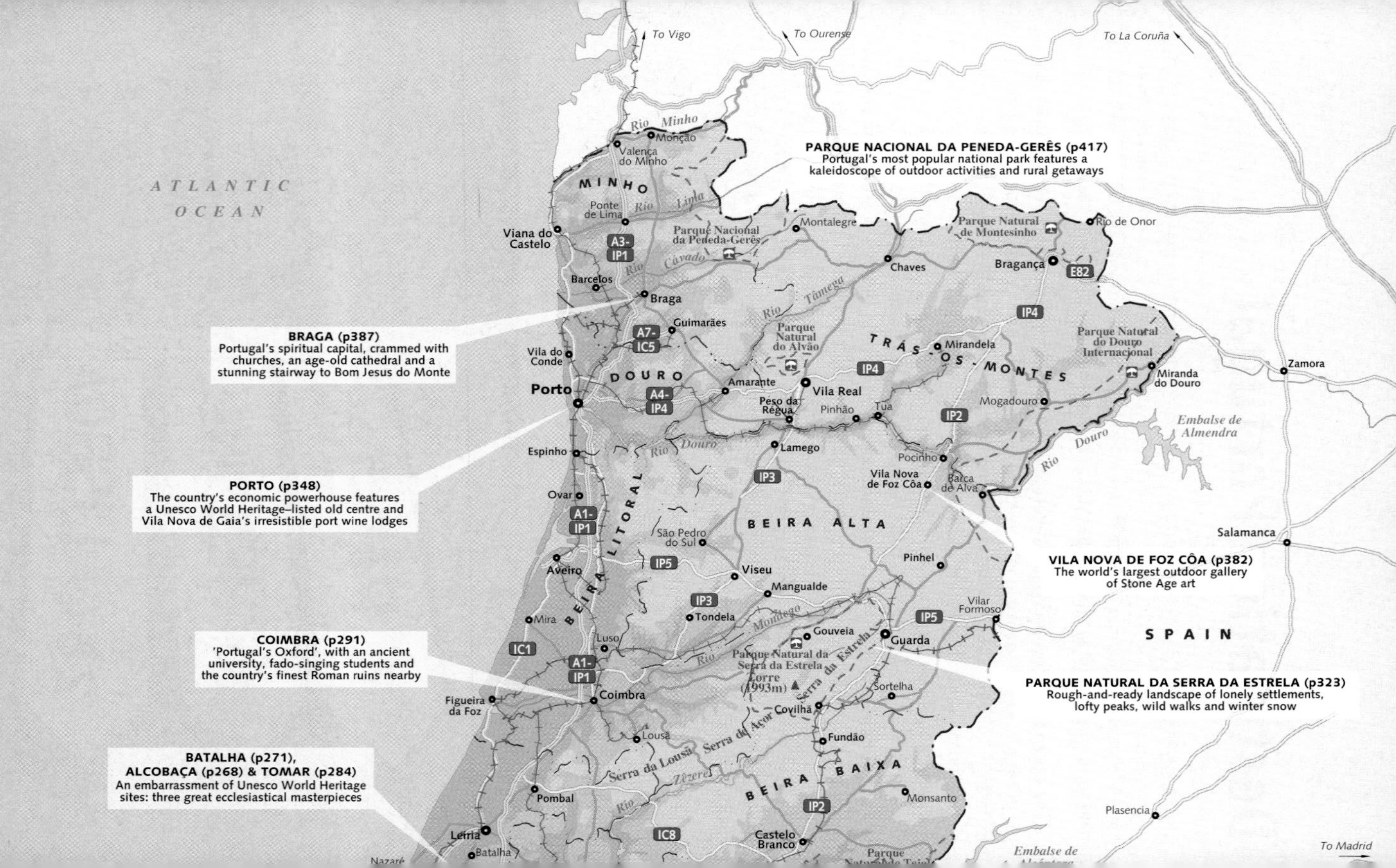

PARQUE NACIONAL DA PENEDA-GERÊS (p417)
Portugal's most popular national park features a kaleidoscope of outdoor activities and rural getaways
BRAGA (p387)
Portugal's spiritual capital, crammed with churches, an age-old cathedral and a stunning stairway to Bom Jesus do Monte
PORTO (p348)
The country's economic powerhouse features a Unesco World Heritage–listed old centre and Vila Nova de Gaia's irresistible port wine lodges
COIMBRA (p291)
'Portugal's Oxford', with an ancient university, fado-singing students and the country's finest Roman ruins nearby
BATALHA (p271), ALCOBAÇA (p268) & TOMAR (p284)
An embarrassment of Unesco World Heritage sites: three great ecclesiastical masterpieces
VILA NOVA DE FOZ CÔA (p382)
The world's largest outdoor gallery of Stone Age art
PARQUE NATURAL DA SERRA DA ESTRELA (p323)
Rough-and-ready landscape of lonely settlements, lofty peaks, wild walks and winter snow
ATLANTIC OCEAN
SPAIN
To Vigo
To Ourense
To La Coruña
To Madrid
MINHO
DOURO
TRÁS-OS-MONTES
BEIRA ALTA
BEIRA LITORAL
BEIRA BAIXA
Rio Minho
Rio Lima
Rio Cávado
Rio Tâmega
Rio Douro
Rio Mondego
Rio Zêzere
Serra da Lousã
Serra de Açor
Serra da Estrela
Embalse de Almendra
Parque Nacional da Peneda-Gerês
Parque Natural de Montesinho
Parque Natural do Alvão
Parque Natural do Douro Internacional
Parque Natural da Serra da Estrela
Torre (1993m)
Valença do Minho
Monção
Ponte de Lima
Viana do Castelo
Barcelos
Braga
Guimarães
Vila do Conde
Porto
Espinho
Ovar
Aveiro
Mira
Figueira da Foz
Luso
Coimbra
Lousã
Pombal
Leiria
Batalha
Nazaré
Montalegre
Chaves
Bragança
Rio de Onor
Mirandela
Miranda do Douro
Mogadouro
Amarante
Vila Real
Peso da Régua
Pinhão
Tua
Lamego
Pocinho
Vila Nova de Foz Côa
Barca de Alva
São Pedro do Sul
Viseu
Mangualde
Tondela
Gouveia
Guarda
Pinhel
Vilar Formoso
Sortelha
Covilhã
Fundão
Monsanto
Castelo Branco
Zamora
Salamanca
Plasencia
A3-IP1
A7-IC5
A4-IP4
A1-IP1
IC1
IP5
IP3
IP4
IP2
E82
IC8

SINTRA (p116)
Extraordinary, mountainous, wooded escape, filled with icing-sugar palaces and exotic gardens
LISBON (p71)
Entrancing multicultural capital with decadant buildings draped over seven hills, great monuments and charismatic nightlife
LAGOS (p182)
An Algarvian jewel: a pretty city, sea, sand, copper-streaked coves, water sports and fun, fun, fun
CASTELO DE VIDE (p232) & MARVÃO (p235)
Walled hilltop villages laden with brilliant flowers overlooking endless Alentejan plains
ÉVORA (p203)
Renaissance, Roman and Moorish legacies and fine food make this a must-see Unesco World Heritage city
MERTOLA (p237) & ALCOUTIM (p199)
Enchanting whitewashed, fortified outposts overlooking the lazy curve of the Rio Guadiana
TAVIRA (p160)
Elegant Algarve town, a boat trip away from long island beaches
ELEVATION
1500m
1000m
500m
200m
0
0
25
50km
0
15
30miles
ATLANTIC OCEAN
SPAIN
ESTREMADURA
RIBATEJO
ALTO ALENTEJO
BAIXO ALENTEJO
ALGARVE
LISBON
Caldas da Rainha
Peniche
Óbidos
Ericeira
Mafra
Vila Franca de Xira
Sintra
Cascais
Estoril
Santarém
Barreiro
Setúbal
Abrantes
Belver
Ponte de Sor
Coruche
Mora
Vendas Novas
Montemor-o-Novo
Évora
Arraiolos
Évoramonte
Estremoz
Borba
Vila Viçosa
Elvas
Caia
Castelo de Vide
Marvão
Portalegre
Badajoz
Mérida
Embalse de Orellana
Reguengos de Monsaraz
Monsaraz
Mourão
Alcácer do Sal
Santiago do Cacém
Sines
Ferreira
Beja
Moura
Barrancos
Serpa
Vila Verde de Ficalho
Aljustrel
Castro Verde
Ourique
Vila Nova de Milfontes
Zambujeira do Mar
Odemira
Odeceixe
Aljezur
Monchique
Silves
Portimão
Lagos
Sagres
Albufeira
Loulé
Faro
Tavira
Vila Real de Santo António
Ayamonte
Alcoutim
Mértola
Huelva
Seville
Utrera
To Córdoba
To Córdoba
To Malaga
Parque Natural das Serras de Aire e Candeeiros
Parque Natural de Sintra-Cascais
Parque Natural da Arrábida
Parque Natural da Serra de São Mamede
Parque Natural do Vale do Guadiana
Parque Natural do Sudoeste Alentejano e Costa Vicentina
Parque Natural da Ria Formosa
Serra de Monchique
Serra do Caldeirão
Rio Tejo
Rio Sado
Rio Guadiana
A1
A2
A5
A6-IP7
A8
A9
A12-IP1
E1
E52
E90
IC1
IC4
IP1
IP2
IP6
IP7
IP8

Coastal Getaways

The vast beach at **Figueira da Foz** (p307), dotted with candy-striped beach huts, is as popular with surfers and windsurfers as sun-seekers. **Costa da Caparica** (p135) is just a volleyball lob from Lisbon, a delightful surprise of long, golden sands backed by ochre cliffs and edged by turquoise sea. Wild surf-heaven is to be found in the west, with wonderful unspoilt beaches meeting the swelling Atlantic around **Vila Nova de Milfontes** (p249). Near **Tavira** (p160) are remote-feeling islands, with sand, sand and yet more sand disappearing far into the blue horizon.

PAUL BERNHARDT

Surf the Algarve at Carrapateira (p194)

Enjoy the views at Praia da Rainha, Cascais (p126)

ANDERS BLOMQVIST

Hire a boat and explore the Algarve beaches (p145)

GERRY RE

GERRY REILLY

Take in the twisted ochre-and-red rock faces and long gorgeous beaches of the Algarve at Lagos (p182)

CARLOS COSTA

Bliss out on the beach at Setúbal (p137)

Sunbathe on Carvoeiro's sandy shores (p175)

GERRY REILLY

Rural Escapes

You can't beat the **Parque Natural da Serra da Estrela** (p323) and the **Parque Nacional da Peneda-Gerês** (p417) for stunning views and picturesque hamlets and villages. If it's absolute peace and isolation you're craving, you'll find it in abundance at **Parque Natural de Montesinho** (p443). Alentejan hilltop, walled villages, overlooking the region's vast wheat seas, have a medieval atmosphere all of their own. Head for a hike around the inland **Serra de Monchique** (p197) for a thrilling contrast with the Algarve coast. Or for something more affordable, there are countless homely manors and farmhouses scattered throughout the country – for example, around **Sintra** (p116) and **Évora** (p203).

ANDERS BLOMQVIST

Discover the *espigueiros* (stone granaries) of Parque Nacional da Peneda-Gerês (p417)

Travel back in time to the Alentejan village of Monsaraz (p217)

BETHUNE CARMICHAEL

Explore the chilly heights and mountain vistas of Parque Natural da Serra da Estrela (p323)

CARLOS C

BETHUNE CARMICHAEL

Look west into Spain from the fortified hilltop village of Marvão (p235)

BETHUNE CARMICHAEL

Luxuriate in the Palace Hotel do Buçaco (p305)

Check out the unusual village of Rio de Onor (p444), entirely unfazed by the Spanish border splicing it in two

ANDERS BLOMQVIST

Unique boho nightlife throngs the streets of Lisbon's **Bairro Alto** (p84), while its waterside **Lux** (p107) is one of Europe's best clubs. **Belém** (p92) has incredible architecture, a fantastic design museum and heavenly custard tarts. **Museu Calouste Gulbenkian** (p90) is a cultural feast, with ancient Egypt the starter and Lalique the after-dinner mint. A top showcase for cutting-edge art is Porto's **Museu de Arte Contemporânea** (p355), surrounded by grounds that are a masterpiece in themselves. Vila Nova da Gaia's vast hillside of **port warehouses** (p368) and the opposite Ribeira district of Porto cast light on how the twin cities have grown around their port.

CHRISTOPHER GROENHOUT

Trundle through Lisbon's hilly cobbled streets on Tram 28 (p94)

Be enthralled by Lisbon's Moorish-medieval Alfama district (p86)

JULIA WILKINSON

Experience Porto's Rio Douro and Ribeira (p355), seen here from the Ponte de Dom Luís I

JOHN

Festival & Events

Minho's massive **Feira de Barcelos** (p394) is a market-goer's paradise. Viana do Castelo parties as if there's no tomorrow during both **Romaria de Nossa Senhora d'Agonia** and **Carnaval** (both p406). **Easter Week** (p391) in Braga is Portugal's grandest Semana Santa. Portugal's booziest bash has to be Coimbra University's **Queima das Fitas** (p299). **Festa de Santo António** (p97) in Lisbon is an all-night party for the capital's favourite saint. And then there's Amarante's **Festas de Junho** (p373), with a tradition of swapping phallic cakes, and Tomar's **Festa dos Tabuleiros** (p287) which means trays-on-heads for the town's virgins.

PAUL BERNHARDT

Throw yourself into the fun at Porto's merriest festival, the Festa de Sáo Joáo (p358)

Join in the vigil at Fátima, host of one of the Catholic world's biggest pilgrimages (p276)

PAUL BERNHARDT

Revel in the folk dancing at Ponte de Lima's Feiras Novas (p414), one of Portugal's most ancient events

JULIA WILKINSON

Monumental Portugal

Gaze on Stone Age ancient ibex and horses etched into al-fresco rock faces at **Vila Nova de Foz Côa** (p382). Found near Évora are myriad megaliths including the remote 95-stone **Cromeleque dos Almendres** (p215), as impressive as Stonehenge. One of the oldest cathedrals in Portugal stands plumb in the centre of **Braga** (p387). Stunning **Convento de Cristo** (p285) sums up the mystique of the Knights Templar, while **Mosteiro dos Jerónimos** (p92) epitomises the euphoria of the Age of Discoveries. The gloriously austere Alcobaça **church** (p269) is a Gothic masterpiece.

ANDERS BLOMQVIST

Examine the detail on the western doorway of Batalha's Mosteiro de Santa Maria da Vitória (p271)

Inspect the extraordinary mosaics found at the Roman ruins of Conimbriga (p303)

MARTIN MOOS

See history illuminated in Évora's complete Roman temple, Templo Romano (p203)

MARTIN

Getting Started

Portugal is a small and concentrated parcel of delights that is fortunate because, with so many alluring sights on offer, it can be difficult to decide exactly where to go. As well as being compact in size, there is good-value, efficient transport in most areas which enables you to experience a whole range of contrasts, even if you are only visiting for a short time. Balmy beaches, amazing architecture, fantastic museums, sophisticated clubbing, rural idylls – Portugal offers you the lot.

WHEN TO GO

See Climate Charts (p456) for more information.

Portugal's high season is mid-June to mid-September. The Atlantic tempers the Mediterranean climate down south, where summer temperatures regularly reach 30°. The Algarve has almost year-round sunshine. Spring and autumn are good for lush foliage. It gets hot everywhere in July and August, but particularly in the Algarve and Alentejo – where it climbs over 45° in some places – and the upper Douro valley. Bear in mind that most Portuguese take their holidays in August, which means accommodation along the coast is hard to find and resorts get very busy.

It's worth making a beeline to a Portuguese festival, particularly Carnaval (around February or March) and Easter Week (around March or April). Dates vary annually, so check with a turismo (tourist information office, p464).

COSTS & MONEY

Portugal remains excellent value for money, whether you're travelling on the cheap or trying to spend your inheritance. If you are scrimping, you could get by on around €20 to €30 per day, as long as you camp (€4 to €8 per person and tent) or stay in youth hostels (€8 to €14), buy your own food and do free stuff like lying on the beach. Travelling in low season will help, too.

Many museums are free on certain days (often Sunday) and note that in restaurants you can often share a *dose* (serving) – it doesn't have to be per person – or ask for a *meia dose* (half serving). Family tickets to attractions usually save a few euros and student or senior cards often get you discounts. If you want to get drunk on the cheap on the Algarve look out for drinks promotions – they're everywhere.

DON'T LEAVE HOME WITHOUT…

Most essentials you'll be able to find in Portugal, but it's worth packing certain things, to avoid hassle rather than anything else. A phrasebook will be a help both practically and socially. Sun lotion is available in towns and resorts, but you can avoid paying over the odds or trying to find some in a remote village on a Sunday if you take it with you. Tampons – these are available but can be expensive and you might have to find a pharmacy to buy them. If you wear contacts, take a large enough supply. If you wear glasses, take a spare pair. Sunglasses – again you can buy them in many places (Lisbon has a sector of touts specialising in overpriced shades and fake hash) – but you may want some that suit you. Electrical adaptors – these are available in small electrical shops, but it saves you having to look up 'small electrical shop' in your phrasebook. Even if you're not dreaming of trekking, a compass can be useful for getting your bearings. Finally you may want an umbrella if you're headed to the showery north.

TOP TENS

BOOKS

Get under the Portuguese skin with these page-turning reads:

- *Ballad of Dog's Beach* by José Cardoso Pires (p40)
- *Baltazar and Blimunda* by José Saramago (p53)
- *A God Strolling in the Cool of An Evening* by Mario de Carvalho (p40)
- *The Inquisitor's Manual* by António Lobo Antunes (p40)
- *The Night in Lisbon* by Erich Maria Remarque
- *The Portuguese: The Land & Its People* by Marion Kaplan (p36)
- *The Sin of Father Amaro* by Eça de Queirós (p39)
- *A Small Death in Lisbon* by Robert Wilson
- *Tales from the Mountain* by Miguel Torga (p40)
- *The Year of the Death of Ricardo Reis* by José Saramago (p41)

FILMS

Go on a trip without leaving the sofa:

- *Capitães de Abril* (p32)
- *The Convent* (p41)
- *A Foreign Land* (p39)
- *Ganhar a Vida* (p42)
- *A Lisbon Story* (p84)
- *Noite Escura* (p42)
- *O Delfim* (p45)
- *Ossos* (p38)
- *A Talking Picture* (p41)
- *Voyage to the Beginning of the World* (p41)

SCENIC & MONUMENTAL MARVELS

Laden with natural and architectural beauty, it's difficult to limit Portugal's finest to a top 10, but we've had a try.

- Alcobaça (p268)
- Batalha (p271)
- Braga (p387)
- Conimbriga (p303)
- Convento de Cristo (p285)
- Évora (p203)
- Vila Nova de Foz Côa (p382)
- Parque Natural da Serra da Estrela (p323)
- Sintra (p116)
- Porto's Ribeira District (p355)

Mid-range travellers are looking at around €20 to €30 for a room per person and €20 to €40 on food per day, depending on how much alcohol you drink.

TRAVEL LITERATURE

The entertaining, unique travelogue *Cork Boat* (2004) by journalist John Pollack recounts his quest to make a boat from cork stoppers (different strokes for different folks) and steer it along the Douro. And 165,321 corks and 15,000 rubber bands later he succeeds.

They went to Portugal (1947) and *They Went to Portugal, Too* (1991) form an entertaining historical hotchpotch of travelling glories and gripes, by Rose Macaulay, who also wrote *Fabled Shore: From the Pyrenees to Portugal* (1950).

For the full story, read Lord Byron's *Selected Letters and Journals* (1982) – mad, bad, dangerous to know, and a good read. The parts on Portugal are short, but trace an unintentionally comic trajectory: from honeymoon, via disillusionment, to disgust.

Nineteenth-century Gothic novelist William Beckford was not bad or dangerous, just mad, and his accounts of his stay in Portugal in his *Journals and Recollections of an Excursion to the Monasteries of Alcobaça and Batalha* (1835) are splendidly entertaining.

Almeida Garrett's *Travels in my Homeland* (1846) details the great 19th-century Portuguese writer's impressions of his country. Or you could dip into *Lisbon: What the Tourist Should See* (1962) by Fernando Pessoa. It seems Pessoa was better at adopting different literary personalities than travel writing, but this is still worth a look. *Journey to Portugal: A Pursuit of Portugal's History and Culture* (1981) is José Saramago's account of his travels in 1979. This musings-and-novel combination could just be for Saramago aficionados.

Many of these books are out of print, but you can find second-hand copies by browsing www.abebooks.com.

HOW MUCH?

Litre of gas/petrol (unleaded)
€1.06

Litre of bottled water
€0.50

Sagres and Super Bock beer
€1-3

Souvenir T-shirt
€5-10

Uma bica (short black)
€0.50

Pasteis de nata (custard tart)
€0.70

Ceramic tile
€2-100s

Sardinhas assadas (grilled sardines)
€4.50

Ticket to football
€20-50

Bottle of port
€5-1000s

INTERNET RESOURCES

Lonely Planet (www.lonelyplanet.com) Where else would you go for damn fine travel information, links, and advice from other travellers?

Lifecooler (lifecooler.sapo.pt) In Portuguese – excellent for insider up-to-the-minute reviews, restaurant, bar, club and hotel listings, and special offers.

Portugal Tourism (www.portugal.org) Portugal's official tourism site.

Portugal Virtual (www.portugalvirtual.pt) General information and good hotel, restaurant and practical listings.

Portugal's Yellow Pages (www.paginasamarelas.pt) Portugal's phone numbers at your fingertips.

Plateia (www.plateia.iol.pt) In Portuguese – for booking tickets for current events (including sports) and good for seeing what's on.

Itineraries

CLASSIC ROUTES

AN ATLANTIC STRETCH

Two Weeks / Lisbon to Porto

Take in faded grandeur, cutting-edge culture and fun nights in **Lisbon** (p72), then head north. It would be criminal not to linger in the hills and woods of **Sintra** (p116) on the way. Then make your way up to walled-village **Óbidos** (p260), so pretty it was a royal wedding gift. Next, **Alcobaça** (p268) and **Batalha** (p271) – a stunning partnership of Unesco World Heritage sites. After all that culture, go for a picnic in the 700-year-old coastal pinewood of **Pinhal de Leiria** (p275) before wending up to the university town of **Coimbra** (p291), where you can listen to *fado* (traditional Portuguese singing). Enjoy a few of the fabulous day trips on offer: marvel at myriad Roman mosaics in nearby **Conimbriga** (p303), indulge in a woodland walk to the gloriously over-the-top palace at **Buçaco** (p304), or snoop around the hilltop castle at **Montemor-o-Velho** (p311). Take your pick of seaside resorts west of Coimbra, including the surfing hotspot **Figueira da Foz** (p307), just beyond Montemor-o-Velho. Brush off the sand and make your way up to Portugal's second city, **Porto** (p348), for a celebratory tipple or two across the Rio Douro in port wine's warehouse wonderland **Vila Nova de Gaia** (p368).

It's around 320km from Lisbon to Porto, but bear in mind you'll be making some detours. Train connections are regular and cheap, and buses regularly plough the Lisbon–Coimbra–Porto route, as well as the suggested stop-offs on the way.

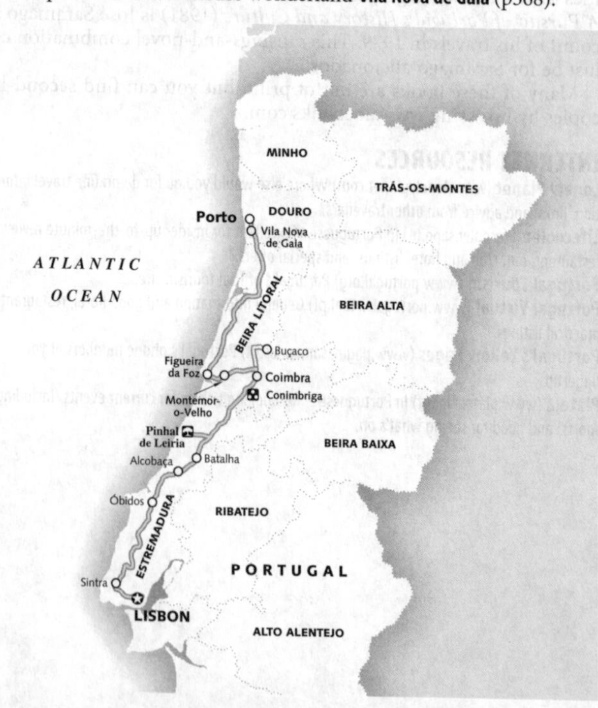

HILLTOP ADVENTURE

Two Weeks / Lisbon to Lisbon

Lisbon (p72), with its seven peaks topped by a castle, viewpoints and churches, is the ultimate in hilltop cities and a stunning place to start. From the capital dip down to **Beja** (p241), the sedate, pretty capital of Baixo Alentejo, to access **Mértola** (p237), one of Alentejo's most dramatic hilltop villages, an open-air museum with a Moorish legacy, set high above the snaking Rio Guadiana.

Next head north – stop at Unesco-listed **Évora** (p203) for high culture, slices of history, and Alentejan haute cuisine, then get yourself over to the magical hilltop village of **Monsaraz** (p217), overlooking ancient olive groves and land littered with Neolithic sites.

From here you can also visit the massive new lake created by the controversial Alqueva dam. You'll have to go back to Évora to reach the frontier, outback town of **Elvas** (p225), with its extraordinary zigzagging fortifications protecting narrow streets, only 14km from Spain.

From Elvas, head north to the charming, walled Alentejan capital, **Portalegre** (p229), again high up and excellent for excursions into the rugged **Parque Natural da Serra de São Mamede** (p230). Enjoy some adventures in the beautiful mountains – the area is a bird-watcher's paradise.

Finally head north again to flower-laden, stuck-in-time whitewashed and walled **Castelo de Vide** (p232) and tiny garrison village **Marvão** (p235), high on a rocky bluff, before returning to Lisbon.

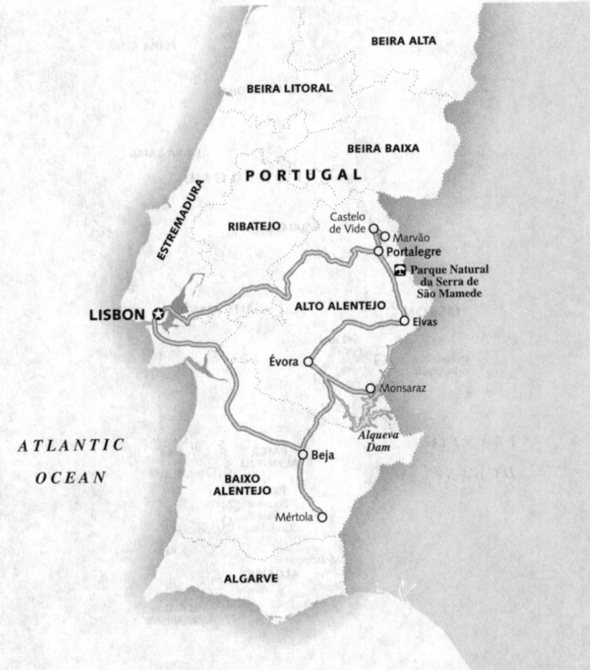

This route is around 700km. It's possible to cover it by public transport, though you'd spend a lot of time on buses, and transport to Monsaraz is somewhat hit and miss.

RIVER DEEP, MOUNTAIN HIGH

Two Weeks / Lisbon to Serpa

This trip will give you a chance to visit spectacular contrasts in scenery through following Portugal's southern rivers and ridges. Start in **Lisbon** (p72), on the banks of the Rio Tejo's gaping mouth. Then head to **Setúbal** (p137) at the end of the Rio Sado, visiting the beautiful protected area of the Parque Natural da Arrábida, near where the river meets the sea.

From here you will move on up to **Monchique** (p197), with densely wooded hills and the Algarve's highest point at 902m, around where there are stunning walking, biking and pony-trekking opportunities.

From here you can dive back down to the coast, making your way east to **Tavira** (p160), with its genteel 18th-century buildings straddling the Rio Gilão. From here take a boat trip across to the peaceful, sandy Ilha de Tavira (p165). Continuing east, you'll reach **Vila Real de Santo António** (p166), where the Rio Guadiana serves as the border between Portugal and Spain.

Now you can choose between following the river north by bike or cruising along it, chugging up to Alcoutim, then taking a road trip to **Mértola** (p237), from where you can explore the **Parque Natural do Vale do Guadiana** (p240). Following the river north, next stop at medieval-seeming **Serpa** (p245), close to the huge waters of the Alqueva lake – visit the huge dam to see the extraordinary drowned landscape.

This route is around 350km, and how long you take about it will depend how you travel – it will be slower, but a lot more rewarding, if you take some boat trips and time out to go hiking or biking. Allow two weeks.

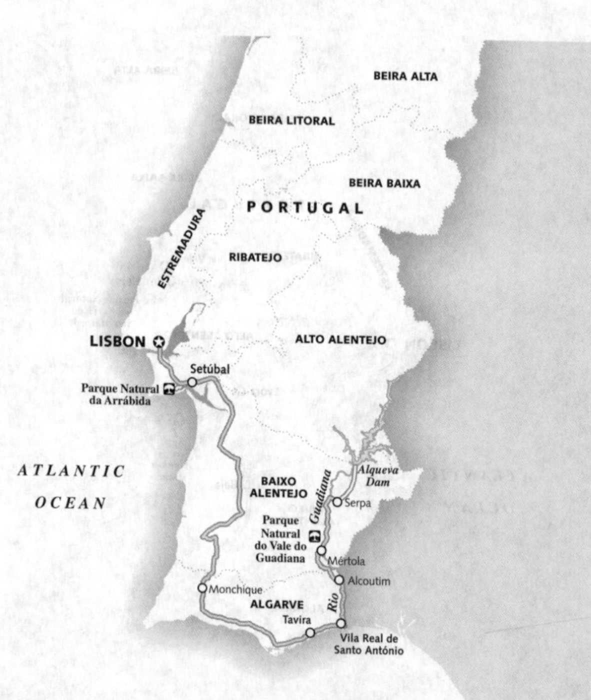

ROADS LESS TRAVELLED

A BEIRA BAIXA BASH

Two to Three Weeks / Coimbra to Monsanto

For rugged scenery, outdoor adventure and stunning sights off the all-too trodden trail near the coast, the remote Beiras region is the place to go – and the deeper you delve, the fewer travellers you'll see. You'll most likely approach this route from the cultural capital and ancient university town of **Coimbra** (p291), around which there are enough excellent day trips to keep you hooked for several days – especially the Roman remains at **Conimbriga** (p303), and photographer's paradise at royal retreat and spa at **Luso** and **Buçaco** (both p304).

But from here, lose the crowds – make a break west to pristine rural idylls such as **Piódão** (p306), or any of the traditional hamlets and villages in the beautiful **Parque Natural da Serra da Estrela** (p323), packed with exquisite scenery, outdoor pursuits and Portugal's highest point – **Torre** (p331), also home to the country's only ski resort. Base yourself bang in the middle at **Manteigas** (p329) to give you the run of the whole mountain range.

You could start the descent from these heady heights via the chilly highland towns of **Covilhã** (p332) or **Guarda** (p339), and then choose between one or all of the fabulous castles and fortified towns of lowland Beiras: northern **Almeida** (p344), far-flung **Sortelha** (p322) and the boulder-strewn **Monsanto** (p320) are all stunning destinations that see only a fraction of the tourist traffic of coastal Portugal.

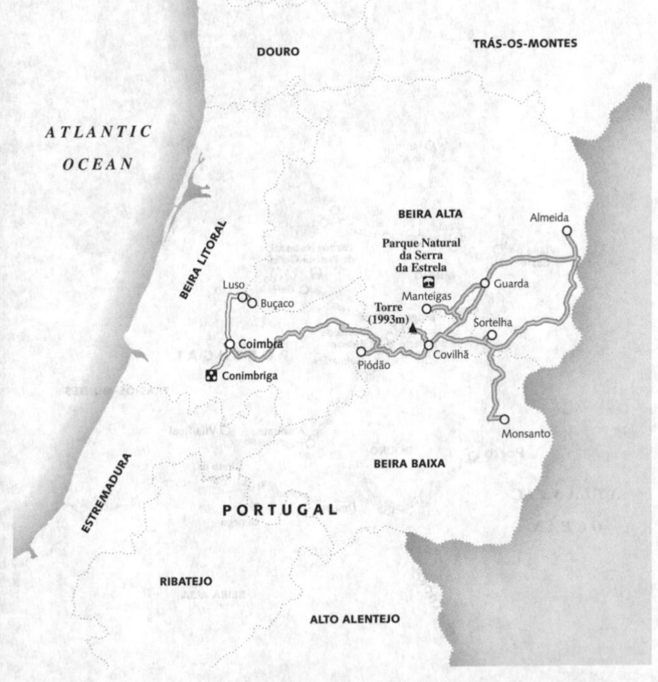

This off-the-beaten-track route rewards you with some of Portugal's most spectacular scenery and sights, but public transport is dire. If you've got your own wheels you could whiz around its 245km to 400km length in two weeks or less, but if you're reliant on buses, you'd have to skip several of the more remote villages.

MEANDERINGS IN THE MINHO

Two to Three Weeks / Porto to Porto

Outdoor adventures and rural getaways await you in Portugal's oft-ignored northern reaches – not to mention some of the country's most colourful markets, festivals and folklore. Starting from **Porto** (p348), you could travel up the coast to the north's festival capital – folklore-rich **Viana do Castelo** (p403) – and beyond to the border fortresses of **Valença do Minho** (p408) eye-balling the Spaniards across the river.

From here, beat it down to charming backwater **Ponte de Lima** (p411), and its dreamy Roman bridge. Nearby **Ponte da Barca** (p415) is a springboard to the remote villages of **Soajo** (p420) and **Lindoso** (p421), little changed for centuries.

From **Braga** (p387), the spiritual epicentre of Portugal, you could head back up north, into eastern **Parque Nacional da Peneda-Gerês** (p417), to spa town **Vila do Gerês** (p422) and nearby spots for canoeing, mountain biking and fantastic hiking. Alternatively, if you're passing on a Thursday – head the short distance west to **Barcelos** (p394) to catch its famous mid-week market.

Back in Braga, head down south via the pilgrimage site of **Bom Jesus do Monte** (p393) and Celtic ruins at **Citânia dos Briteiros** (p402)to the cradle of the nation in history-rich **Guimarães** (p397).

For the final stretch, work your way down to picturesque **Amarante** (p371), famous for its monastery and phallic cakes, and to Vila Real's must-see **Palácio de Mateus** (p430). The most scenic way to return to Porto to catch a river cruise from **Peso da Régua** (p379), perhaps with a quick trip down to **Lamego** (p375) first.

Apart from remote corners of Parque Nacional da Peneda-Gerês, this route isn't difficult to traverse by public transport. Covering the whole 540km length will take a long two weeks, or a leisurely three if you want to linger in Peneda-Gerês.

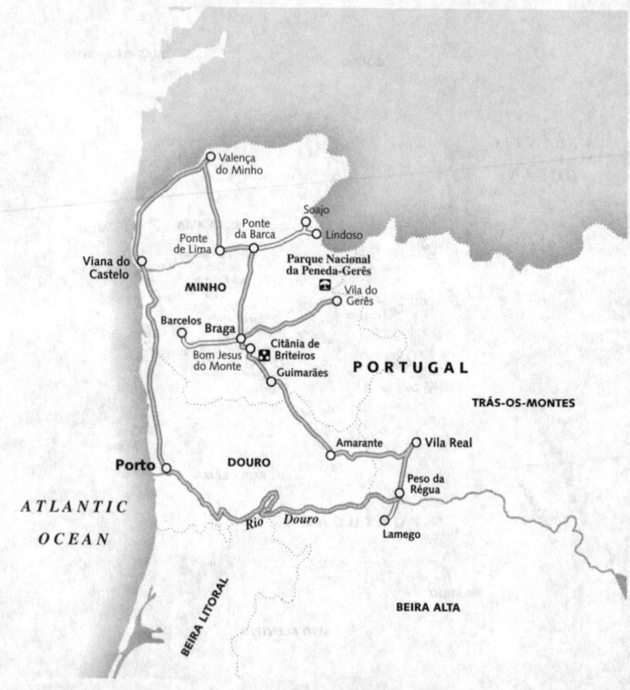

TAILORED TRIPS

THE GRAPE ESCAPE

Wandering wine-lovers flock to northern Portugal, and particularly the Douro region to soak up the fruits of its harvests. How quickly you cover this 360km route depends on how much wine you soak up along the way. You can cover the distance in just over a week, but that's no reason to rush when there are scores of delightful *quintas* (country houses, often taking guests) and small vineyards to welcome you along the way.

Almost any trip tailored to port wine will begin and end in **Porto** (p348) at the mouth of the Rio Douro, along which port wine has been shipped for centuries. And staring at Porto a short hop across the Douro is the wine's destination – **Vila Nova de Gaia** (p368).

Having seen where the wines end up, you can trace them back to their source by catching a slow Rio Douro cruise boat from Porto up the Douro valley to **Peso da Régua** (p379) and beyond to the very heart of vineyard country, the tiny village of **Pinhão** (p381). Asking locally will give you any number of different vineyards and *adegas* (wine cellars) to visit.

While you're in the vicinity, don't miss a trip to **Lamego** (p375), surrounded by beautiful architecture and home to one of Portugal's few sparkling wines. You could also nip up to **Vila Real** (p429), erstwhile home of its namesake rosé wine. If you fancy a break from all the tastings, at the end of the mainline railway is **Vila Nova de Foz Côa** (p382), famous for its ancient open-air rock art.

On your return along the Douro, catch the train back as far as Livração and change to the Linha da Tâmega narrow-gauge train up to the historic town of **Amarante** (p371). From here, it's an easy hop back to Porto to complete your crash course in port wines back in Vila Nova de Gaia.

PORTUGAL FOR KIDS

Looping down from Lisbon to the Algarve and back you'll cover roughly 360km. Transport in the Algarve is excellent. Start at Lisbon's **Parque das Nações** (p91) with its amazing **oceanarium** (p91). Moseying south, visit the beaches of **Costa da Caparica** (p135) or stop at **Setúbal** for dolphin spotting. Continue down the beautiful, wild western coast: **Vila Nova de Milfontes** (p249), via bus from Setúbal, or **Odeceixe** (p196), if you have a car. On the Algarve coast, you are spoilt for choice. Base yourself at vibrant **Lagos** (p182) or **Albufeira** (p171), or quieter **Carvoeiro** (p175) or **Tavira** (p160). Take time out from beach life with a day at one of the nearby water parks. Kids will enjoy the castle at **Silves** (p176), and the really excellent endangered-species zoo, which you will find near **Monchique** (p197).

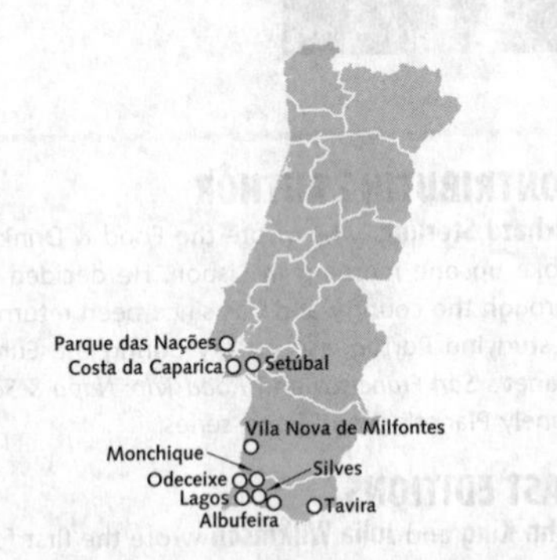

The Authors

ABIGAIL HOLE

Coordinating Author, Lisbon & Around, The Algarve, The Alentejo and Estremadura & Ribatejo

Abigail has been travelling around the Iberian Peninsula on and off since her childhood and she loves Portugal passionately. Inspired by her Iberian adventures she is now a freelance travel writer who delights in the exotic; further-flung assignments have taken her to Mali, Mauritania, Egypt, Tunisia and India. Abigail currently lives in Rome.

My Favourite Trip

I start on a high in Lisbon and stay for a week. My next stop is the hills and mansions of Sintra. I then head north to Tomar to visit the extraordinary Knights Templar headquarters before travelling to the ancient university town of Coimbra for some fado melancholia. Porto is next – high on my list for its old city and glinting port – and then Braga with its 35 churches. I then head southeast to Parque Natural da Serra da Estrela, before meandering down to the Alentejo, stopping in flower-laden Castelo de Vide and Marvão, the historic city of Évora, and the huddled hilltop villages of Monsaraz and Mértola. Magical Alcoutim is my first taste of the Algarve, followed by some basking on the sandbanks close to genteel Tavira. Finally I leg it to Lagos – the Algarve's party town.

CHARLOTTE BEECH

The Beiras, The Douro, The Minho and Trás-os-Montes

Charlotte first fell for the charms of Portugal's southern coast as a teenager, but as an adult she also became hooked by the country's underrated north – and not just for its addictive wines. She now returns at the slightest opportunity. Charlotte has written many Lonely Planet guidebooks – from *Peru* to *India* – and has also contributed to numerous guides as an editor. When not on the road, she lives in London with her South American partner.

CONTRIBUTING AUTHOR

Richard Sterling, who wrote the Food & Drink chapter, was a university student in Madrid when he woke up one morning in Lisbon. He decided to stay a while. He eventually ate and drank his way through the country and has since been returning to do it again and again. One of Richard's hobbies is studying Portuguese history during the European Age of Discoveries. He is the author of Lonely Planet's *San Francisco* and *Road Trip: Napa & Sonoma Wine Country*, and he is the principal author of Lonely Planet's World Food series.

LAST EDITIONS

John King and **Julia Wilkinson** wrote the first four editions of this book.

Snapshot

Europe's longest bridge strides out from Lisbon for 17km and bears the name of one of Portugal's hero-explorers who, 500 years ago, struck out to sea with equal confidence. The construction of the Vasco da Gama bridge was linked to the 1998 Expo, which attracted 10 million visitors. This big party was a good warm-up for the next one, hosting the huge-league 2004 European Football Championships. This is a country that's come a long way in 30 years. In 1974 it was still a dictatorship, the end of which saw 10 years of political chaos. Looking at the stable democracy of today it's hard to believe any of this really happened. However, stable it may be, uneventful it's not.

Portugal joined the EC in 1986, when its GDP was half the EU average – today it's more like 75%, an incredible leap in such a short time. EU membership had a fantastic impact on Portugal, with floods of foreign investment, big infrastructure developments and city-centre overhauls. In 1987 Portugal had 240km of highways; in 2003 1441km.

But the GDP is still three-quarters of the EU average. And in 2000 the carnival float began to slow. Since the late 1990s' boom, Portuguese buzz words have been 'slowdown' and 'unemployment', with people feeling the pinch that had been squeezing the rest of Europe. You can see the impact in the streets – less people in the restaurants and bars as Portuguese eat at home and take less holidays. In 2001, its budget deficit breached the EU limit of 3% of GDP. Cuts in public spending and rises in taxes helped, but they don't make for a happy population.

Euro2004 provided welcome sparkle amid the gloom, but even though football is on a close par with God, people grumbled: why 10 stadiums? Wouldn't the €500 million be better spent elsewhere? Who will use these echoing venues when the football circus has left town? But the fervent roar of the tournament, and its notable success, drowned out the chorus of disapproval.

Shortly after breezily hosting Euro2004, Portugal waved goodbye to their prime minister, José Manuel Durão Barroso, as he slid into his role as European Union President. Most see this as a great coup for Portugal, but they also shake their heads. It's a bewildering thing to have your prime minister quit for a better job. Rather than calling an election, President Jorge Sampaio appointed former Lisbon mayor Pedro Santana Lopes to steer the country through the downturn. The centre-right Social Democrats insist that continuity is necessary to get through the recession – but they're in power so they would say that, wouldn't they?

But all these events were a most welcome distraction from the Casa Pia orphanage scandal, in which prominent politicians, diplomats and TV talk show hosts were implicated as part of a paedophile ring. Revelations oozed out 30 years after the abuse began and sent shock waves across the country, shattering confidence in public figures – allegations spread faster than Portugal's devastating summer fires.

In the meantime, EU funds have dried up. When 10 mostly former communist countries joined the bloc in 2004, the average EU GDP decreased. Only countries whose GDP is less than 75% of the EU average receive aid from Brussels, so Portugal has lost out, while not being any richer.

The challenges ahead could even fluster Vasco da Gama. It's unsurprising at times like these you turn to the beautiful game to take your mind off things.

FAST FACTS

Population:
10.4 million

GDP:
US$18,990

Inflation:
3.2%

Unemployment rate:
6%

Bicas (espressos) per day:
22,000,000

Per capita cod consumption per annum:
10kg

History

PRE-ROMAN & ROMAN ERAS

The Iberian Peninsula has been inhabited for a whopping 500,000 years. If you want to see the earliest evidence of human habitation in Portugal, check out the ancient Palaeolithic inscriptions near Vila Nova de Foz Côa in the Alto Douro (p382). For Neolithic ghosts, head for the atmospheric fortified hilltop settlements, dating from 5500 BC, in the lower Tejo (Tagus) valley.

In the first millennium BC Celtic people started trickling into the Iberian Peninsula, settling northern and western Portugal around 700 BC. Dozens of *citânias* (fortified villages) popped up, such as the formidable Citânia of Briteiros (p402). Further south, Phoenician traders, followed by Greeks and Carthaginians, founded coastal stations and mined metals inland.

When the Romans swept into southern Portugal in 210 BC, they expected an easy victory. But they hadn't reckoned on the Lusitani, a Celtic warrior tribe based between the Rio Tejo and Rio Douro, which resisted ferociously for half a century. Only when its brilliant leader, Viriato (Viriathus), was tricked and assassinated in 139 BC did resistance collapse.

By 19 BC the Romans had eliminated all traces of Lusitanian independence. A capital was established at Olisipo (Lisbon) in 60 BC, and Christianity became firmly rooted in Portugal during the 3rd century AD. For a vivid glimpse into Roman Portugal, you won't see a better site than Conimbriga (p303), near Coimbra, or the monumental remains of the so-called Temple of Diana (p209), in Évora

A Concise History of Portugal (2003), by David Birmingham, is a readable, portable and thoroughly up-to-date history book to browse through.

By the 5th century, when the Roman Empire had all but collapsed, Portugal's inhabitants had been under Roman rule for 600 years. So what did the Romans ever do for them? Most usefully, roads and bridges. But also wheat, barley, olives and vines; large farming estates called *latifúndios* (still found in the Alentejo); a legal system; and, above all, a Latin-derived language. In fact, no other invader proved so useful.

MOORS & CHRISTIANS

The gap left by the Romans was filled by barbarian invaders from beyond the Pyrenees: Vandals, Alans, Visigoths and Suevi. At first, the Germanic Suevi had the greatest impact, then from 469 onwards Aryan Christian Visigoths had the upper hand.

Internal Visigoth disputes paved the way for Portugal's next great wave of invaders, the Moors – North African Muslims invited in 711 to help a Visigoth faction. They quickly occupied large chunks of Portugal's southern coast.

Southerners enjoyed peace and productivity under the Moors, who established a capital at Shelb (Silves). The new rulers were tolerant of Jews and Christians. Christian smallholding farmers, called Mozarabs, could keep their land and were encouraged to try new methods and crops, especially citrus and rice. Arabic words filtered into the Portuguese language, and locals became addicted to Moorish sweets.

TIMELINE

22,000 BC

A gallery of Palaeolithic art is scratched on rocks in the Alto Douro

5500 BC

Neolithic fortified hilltop settlements appear in the lower Tejo (Tagus) valley

Meanwhile in the north, Christian forces were gaining strength and reached as far as Porto in 868. But it was in the 11th century that the Reconquista (Christian reconquest) hotted up. In 1064 Coimbra was taken and, in 1085, Alfonso VI thrashed the Moors in their Spanish heartland of Toledo; he is said to have secured Seville by winning a game of chess with its emir. But in the following year, Alfonso's men were driven out by ruthless Moroccan Almoravids who answered the emir's distress call.

Alfonso cried for help and European crusaders came running – rallying against the 'infidels'. Among them were Henri of Burgundy and his cousin Raymond, who won not only battlefield glory but also the hand of Alfonso's daughter.

But on Alfonso's death in 1109 things got messy. Alfonso Raimúndez (later Alfonso VII), took control of León, while Teresa – regent for her son Afonso Henriques – favoured a union with Galicia, thanks to a dalliance with a Galician. But she didn't reckon with the nationalist ideas of her son.

In 1128 Afonso Henriques took arms against his mother, defeating her forces near his capital, at Guimarães. At first he bowed to his cousin Alfonso VII, but soon after a dramatic victory against the Moors in 1139 at Ourique (Alentejo), he named himself Dom – King of Portugal – a title confirmed in 1179 by the pope (after extra tribute was paid, naturally). He also retook Santarém and Lisbon from the Moors.

By the time he died in 1185, the Portuguese frontier was secure to the Rio Tejo. Yet despite the ruthless help of the crusaders, it was another century before the south was torn from the Moors.

In 1297, the boundaries of the Portuguese kingdom – much the same then as they are today – were formalised with neighbouring Castile. The kingdom of Portugal had arrived.

The Contemporary Portuguese Political History Research Centre's website (www.cphrc.org.uk) is a great resource – if a tad dense for bedtime reading.

THE BURGUNDIAN ERA

During the Reconquista, people faced more than just war and turmoil; in the wake of Christian victories came new rulers and settlers.

The Church and its wealthy clergy were the greediest landowners, followed by aristocratic fat cats. Though theoretically free, most common people remained subjects of the landowning class, with few rights. The first hint of democratic rule came with the establishment of the *cortes* (parliament). This assembly of nobles and clergy first met in 1211 at Coimbra, then capital. Commoners (mostly wealthy merchants) were permitted in 1254. Six years later, the capital moved to Lisbon.

Afonso III deserves credit for standing up to the Church, but it was his son 'The Poet King' Dinis (1279–1325) who really shook Portugal into shape. A far-sighted, cultured man, he took control of the judicial system, started progressive afforestation programmes and encouraged internal trade. He suppressed the dangerously powerful military order of the Knights Templar, refounding them as the Order of Christ (p285). He cultivated music, the arts and education, and founded a university in Lisbon in 1290, later transferred to Coimbra (p296).

Dom Dinis' foresight was spot-on when it came to defence: he built or rebuilt some 50 fortresses along the eastern frontier with Castile, and

210–139 BC

Invading Romans face fierce resistance by Lusitani, but their cunning eventually wins through

AD 400–500

Roman Empire crumbles, making way for the Vandals, Alans, Visigoths and Suevi signed a pact of friendship with England in 1308, the basis for a future long-lasting alliance.

It was none too soon. Within 60 years of Dinis' death, Portugal was at war with Castile. Fernando I helped provoke the clash by playing a game of alliances with both Castile and the English. He dangled promises of marriage to his daughter Beatriz in front of both nations, eventually marrying her off to Juan I of Castile, and thus throwing Portugal's future into Castilian hands.

On Fernando's death in 1383 his wife, Leonor Teles, ruled as regent. But she too was entangled with the Spanish, having long had a Galician lover. The merchant classes preferred unsullied Portuguese candidate João, son (albeit illegitimate) of Fernando's father. João assassinated Leonor's lover, Leonor fled to Castile and the Castilians duly invaded.

The Political Science Resources website (www.psr.keele.ac.uk /area/portugal.htm) has good links for politics and current events as well as history.

The showdown came in 1385 when João faced a mighty force of Castilians at Aljubarrota. Even with Nuno Álvares Pereira (the Holy Constable) as his military right-hand man and English archers at the ready, the odds were stacked against him. João vowed to build a monastery if he won – and he did.

The victory clinched independence and João made good his vow with Batalha's stunning Battle Abbey (see p271). It also sealed Portugal's alliance with England; and João wed John of Gaunt's daughter. Peace was finally concluded in 1411. Portugal was ready to look further afield for adventure.

THE AGE OF DISCOVERIES

João's success had whetted his appetite and, spurred on by his sons, he soon turned his military energies abroad. Morocco was the obvious target, and in 1415 Ceuta fell easily to his forces. It was a turning point in Portuguese history, a first step into their golden age.

It was João's third son, Henry, who focused the spirit of the age – a combination of crusading zeal, love of martial glory and lust for gold – into extraordinary explorations across the seas. These explorations were to transform the small kingdom into a great imperial power (see Beyond the Ends of the Earth, below).

BEYOND THE ENDS OF THE EARTH

By the time Prince Henry the Navigator (1394–1460) died, he had almost single-handedly set Portugal on course for its Age of Discoveries, turning it into a wealthy maritime power and transforming seaborne exploration from a groping process to a near science (p190).

As governor of the Algarve, he assembled the very best sailors, map-makers, shipbuilders, instrument-makers and astronomers, with the aim of getting explorers as far as humanly possible. His aim was as much religious as commercial – to sap Islamic power by siphoning off its trade and bypassing them by sea.

Madeira and the Azores were soon in the bag. Then in 1434 Gil Eanes sailed beyond Cape Bojador in West Africa, breaking a maritime superstition that this was the end of the world. In fact, Henry's sailors got at least as far as present-day Sierra Leone, and it wasn't long before ships began returning laden with West African gold and slaves.

The biggest breakthrough came in 1497 during the reign of Manuel I (who gave himself the ponderous title 'Lord of the Conquest, Navigation, and Commerce of India, Ethiopia, Arabia and Persia'), when Vasco da Gama reached southern India. With gold and slaves from Africa and spices from the East, Portugal was soon rolling in riches. Manuel I was so thrilled by the discoveries (and resultant cash injection) that he ordered a frenzied building spree in celebration. Top of his list was the extravagant Mosteiro dos Jerónimos in Belém (p92), which would later become his pantheon. Another brief boost to the Portuguese economy at this time came courtesy of an influx of around 150,000 financially savvy Jews expelled from Spain in 1492.

An ambitious and beautiful romance novel, *Distant Music* (2003) by Lee Langley spans no less than six centuries of Portugal's history since 1429, not to mention different classes and diverse regions.

Spain, however, had also jumped on the exploration bandwagon and was soon disputing Portuguese claims. Christopher Columbus' 1492 'discovery' of America for Spain led to a fresh outburst of jealous conflict. It was resolved by the pope in the bizarre 1494 Treaty of Tordesillas, by which the world was divided between the two great powers along a line 370 leagues west of the Cape Verde islands. Portugal won the lands to the east of the line, including Brazil, officially claimed in 1500.

The rivalry spurred the first circumnavigation of the world. In 1519 the Portuguese navigator Fernão Magalhães (Ferdinand Magellan), his allegiance transferred to Spain after a tiff with Manuel I, set off in an effort to prove that the Spice Islands lay in Spanish 'territory'. He reached the Philippines in 1521 but was killed in a skirmish there. One of his five ships, under the Basque navigator Juan Sebastián Elcano, reached the Spice Islands and then sailed home via the Cape of Good Hope, proving the earth was round.

As its explorers reached Timor, China and eventually Japan, Portugal cemented its power with garrison ports and trading posts. The monarchy, taking its 'royal fifth' of profits, became stinking rich – indeed the wealthiest monarchy in Europe, and the lavish Manueline architectural style symbolised the exuberance of the age. You only need witness the unabashedly triumphant Mosteiro dos Jerónimos to appreciate the monumental confidence of the age.

The Last Kabbalist of Lisbon (2000), by Richard Zimler, is a thriller cast as a long-lost manuscript about the murder of a 16th-century Jewish mystic. It reveals the harrowing life of secret Jews during Portugal's Inquisition.

It couldn't last, of course. By the 1570s the huge cost of expeditions and maintaining an empire was taking its toll. The expulsion of commercially minded refugee Spanish Jews in 1497 and the subsequent persecution of converted Jews – *marranos* (New Christians) – during the Inquisition only worsened the financial situation.

The final straw came in 1557 when young idealistic Prince Sebastião took the throne, determined to take Christianity to Morocco. He rallied an 18,000-strong force and set sail from Lagos (see p182) only to be disastrously defeated at the Battle of Alcácer-Quibir. Sebastião and 8000 others were killed, including much of the Portuguese nobility. His aged successor, Cardinal Henrique, drained the royal coffers ransoming those captured.

On Henrique's death in 1580, Sebastião's uncle, Felipe II of Spain (Felipe I of Portugal), fought for and won the throne. This marked the end of centuries of independence, Portugal's golden age and its glorious moment on the world stage.

1297
The whole country is finally wrested from the Moors and the kingdom of Portugal is complete

1385
João beats off the Castilians at Aljubarrota, sealing Portugal's independence and alliance with England

DELVING DOWN UNDER

Many historians believe that Portuguese explorers reached Australia in the 16th century, 250 years before its 'official' discoverer, Captain James Cook. At least one Australian historian, Kenneth McIntyre, is convinced that by 1536 the Portuguese had secretly mapped three-quarters of the island's coastline. In 1996 a 500-year-old Portuguese coin was found by a treasure hunter on Victoria's Mornington Peninsula, adding further weight to the theory.

SPAIN'S RULE & PORTUGAL'S REVIVAL

Spanish rule began promisingly – Felipe promised to preserve Portugal's autonomy and attend the long-ignored parliament. But commoners resented Spanish rule and held on to the dream that Sebastião was still alive; pretenders continued to pop up until 1600. Though Felipe was honourable, his successors were considerably less so, using Portugal to raise money and soldiers for Spain's wars overseas, and appointing Spaniards to govern Portugal.

Meanwhile, Portugal's empire was slipping out of its grasp. In 1622 the English seized Hormoz, and by the 1650s the Dutch had taken Malaka, Ceylon (Sri Lanka) and part of Brazil.

Resentment exploded in 1640 when nationalists drove the female governor of Portugal and her Spanish garrison from Lisbon. It was then the Duke of Bragança reluctantly stepped into the hot seat and was crowned João IV.

With a hostile Spain breathing down their necks, Portugal searched for allies. Two swift treaties with England led to Charles II's marriage to João's daughter, Catherine of Bragança, and the ceding of Tangier and Bombay to England. In return the English promised arms and soldiers: however, a preoccupied Spain made only half-hearted attempts to recapture Portugal, and recognised Portuguese independence in 1668.

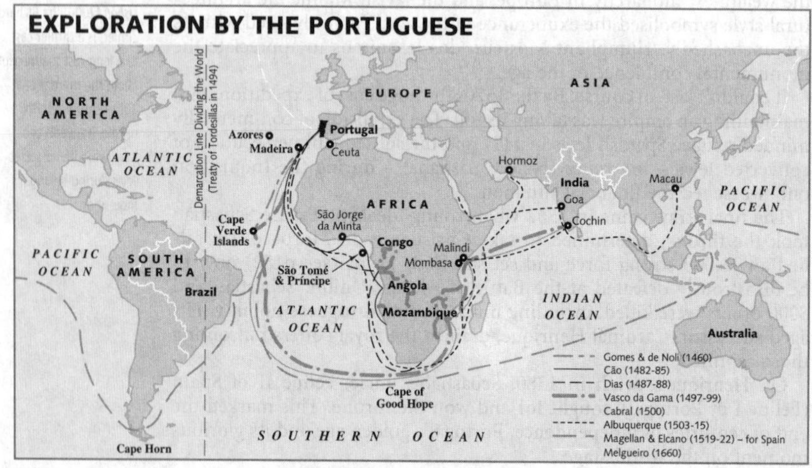

1415
Prince Henry the Navigator jump-starts the seaborne Portuguese Age of Discoveries

1497
Vasco da Gama reaches south India, and three years later Portugal claims Brazil

Moves towards democracy now stalled under João's successors. The Crown hardly bothered with parliament, thanks to renewed financial independence from gold and precious stones discovered in Brazil during the 17th century. Another era of profligate expenditure followed: the awesome monastery-palace in Mafra (see p133) exemplifies this over-the-top extravagance perfectly.

Meanwhile, the 1703 Methuen Treaty jacked up Anglo-Portuguese trade – especially import of English textiles and export of Portuguese wines. But this wasn't the boon it at first appeared, since it increased Portugal's dependence on Britain, hurt the local textile industry and stalled efforts to increase wheat production.

Into the looming chaos stepped a man for the moment – the Marquês de Pombal, chief minister to hedonistic Dom José I (the latter more interested in opera than affairs of state). Described as an enlightened despot, Pombal dragged Portugal into the modern era, crushing opposition with brutal efficiency.

Pombal set up state monopolies, curbed the power of British merchants and boosted agriculture and industry as Brazilian gold production declined. He abolished slavery and distinctions between traditional and New Christians, and overhauled education.

When Lisbon suffered a devastating earthquake in 1755 (see p72), Pombal swiftly rebuilt the city. He was by then at the height of his power, and succeeded in dispensing with his main enemies by implicating them in an attempt on the king's life.

He might have continued had it not been for the accession of the devout Dona Maria I in 1777. The anticlerical Pombal was promptly sacked, tried and charged with various offences, though never imprisoned. Although his religious legislation was repealed, his economic, agricultural and educational policies were largely maintained, helping the country back towards prosperity.

But turmoil was once again on the horizon, as Napoleon swept through Europe.

A hugely informative, if heavyweight, compilation of essays on the demise of Portugal's colonies is *The Last Empire: Thirty Years of Portuguese Decolonisation* (2003), edited by Stewart Lloyd Jones and António Costa Pinto.

It was the Portuguese who first began England's obsession with tea: their explorers introduced it to Europe in the mid-17th century and tea-enthusiast Catherine of Bragança did the rest.

THE DAWN OF A REPUBLIC

In 1793 Portugal found itself at war again when it joined England in sending naval forces against revolutionary France. Before long, Napoleon threw Portugal an ultimatum: close your ports to British shipping or be invaded.

There was no way Portugal could turn its back on Britain, upon which it depended for half its trade and protection of its sea routes. In 1807 Portugal's royal family fled to Brazil (where it stayed for 14 years), and Napoleon's forces marched into Lisbon, sweeping Portugal into the Peninsular War (France's invasion of Spain and Portugal, which lasted until 1814).

To the rescue came Sir Arthur Wellesley (later Duke of Wellington), Viscount Beresford, and their seasoned British troops. After a series of setbacks, the Portuguese–British army drove the French back across the Spanish border in 1811.

Free but weakened, Portugal was administered by Beresford while the royals dallied in Brazil. In 1810 Portugal lost a profitable intermediary role by giving Britain the right to trade directly with Brazil. The next humiliation was João's 1815 proclamation of Brazil as a kingdom united

1580–1640
The Spanish rule after Felipe II claims the throne, ending the Portuguese golden age

1755
Lisbon is destroyed by three major earthquakes, followed by tremors, a fire and a tidal wave

with Portugal. With soaring debts and dismal trade, Portugal was at one of the lowest points in its history, reduced to a de facto colony of Brazil and a protectorate of Britain.

From 1884 to 1963, almost five million Portuguese emigrated to Brazil. Compare that to the modern-day population of Portugal – just over 10 million!

Meanwhile, resentment simmered in the army. Rebel officers quietly convened parliament and draw up a new liberal constitution. Based on Enlightenment ideals, it abolished many rights of the nobility and clergy, and instituted a single-chamber parliament.

Faced with this *fait accompli*, João returned and accepted its terms – though his wife and son Miguel were bitterly opposed to it. João's elder son, Pedro, had other ideas; left behind to govern Brazil, he snubbed the constitutionalists by declaring Brazil independent in 1822 and himself its emperor. When João died in 1826, the stage was set for civil war.

Offered the crown, Pedro dashed out a new, less liberal charter and then abdicated in favour of his seven-year-old daughter Maria, provided she marry uncle Miguel, and uncle Miguel accepted the new constitution. Sure enough, Miguel took the oath, but promptly abolished Pedro's charter and proclaimed himself king. A livid Pedro rallied the equally furious Liberals and forced Miguel to surrender at Évoramonte in 1834.

Revolutionary zeal quickly led to the abolition of religious orders, at which timely point Pedro went to meet his maker. However, his daughter Maria, now Queen of Portugal at just 15, kept his flame alive with fanatical support of his 1826 charter. Radical supporters of the liberal 1822 constitution were even more vociferous – so much so that by 1846 the prospect of civil war again loomed.

However, the Duke of Saldanha called in the international big guns, and peace was happily restored. Saldanha steered the country into more stable waters by 1856. Pedro's charter was toned down and Portugal's infrastructure radically modernised.

However, the country remained in dire straits at the turn of the century. Industrial growth was minuscule, budgets rarely balanced and foreign (notably British) involvement left a quarter of Portugal's trade and industry outside its control. Rural areas were increasingly depopulated in favour of cities, and emigration (especially to Brazil) snowballed.

One of Portugal's best period dramas to date, *O Milagre Segundo Salomé* (2004), directed by Mário Barroso, is a tear-jerking romance film about a prostitute in early 20th-century Portugal.

Much was changing, but for many the changes weren't fast enough. As urban discontent grew, so did socialism and trade unions. Nationalist republicanism swept through the lower-middle classes, spurring an attempted coup in 1908. It failed, but the following month the king and crown prince were brutally assassinated in Lisbon.

Carlos' younger son, Manuel II, tried feebly to appease republicans, but it was too little, too late. On 5 October 1910, after an uprising by military officers, a republic was declared. Manuel, dubbed 'the Unfortunate', sailed into exile in Britain where he died in 1932.

THE RISE & FALL OF SALAZAR

Hopes were high among republicans after a landslide victory in the 1911 elections, but it became clear that the sentiments of the new national anthem ('Oh sea heroes, oh noble people…raise again the splendour of Portugal…!') were vain hopes. Under Afonso Augusto da Costa's leftist Democrat Party, power was maintained by a combination of patronage and anticlericalism bitterly opposed in rural areas.

1793–1811
French troops invade Portugal, but are fought off with help from British

1890–1910
Mass emigration to Brazil peaks

Meanwhile, the economy was in tatters, strained by an economically disastrous decision to join the Allies in WWI. In post-war years the chaos deepened: republican factions squabbled, unions led strikes and were repressed, and the military grew powerful. The new republic soon had a reputation as Europe's most unstable regime. Between 1910 and 1926 there were an astonishing 45 changes of government, often resulting from military intervention. Another coup in 1926 brought another round of new names and faces, but one rose above the others – António de Oliveira Salazar.

A renowned economics professor, Salazar was appointed finance minister and given sweeping powers to bring Portugal's economy to heel. This he did with such prowess that by 1932 he had the top job; he would remain prime minister for 36 years.

Salazar hastily enforced his 'New State' – a corporatist republic that was nationalistic, Catholic, authoritarian and essentially repressive. All political parties were banned except the loyalist National Union, which ran the show, and the National Assembly. Strikes were banned, and propaganda, censorship and brute force kept society in order. The sinister new secret police, Polícia Internacional e de Defesa do Estado (PIDE), inspired terror and suppressed opposition by imprisonment and torture. Various attempted coups during Salazar's rule came to nothing. For a chilling taste of life as a political prisoner under Salazar, you could visit the 16th-century Fortaleza at Peniche (p257) – used as a jail by the dictator.

A Small Death in Lisbon (1999), by Robert Wilson, is a vivid award-winning thriller that cuts between 1941 and a post-1974 murder investigation, showing the impacts of WWII and the Revolution of the Carnations on the Portuguese psyche.

The only good news was a dramatic economic turnaround. Through the 1950s and 1960s Portugal experienced an annual industrial growth rate of 7% to 9%.

Internationally, wily Salazar played two hands, unofficially supporting Franco's nationalists in the Spanish Civil War, and allowing British use of Azores airfields during WWII despite official neutrality (and illegal sales of tungsten to Germany). It was later discovered that Salazar authorised transfer of Nazi-looted gold to Portugal – 44 tonnes according to Allied records, some allegedly transferred to a Bank of Portugal account in New York.

But it was something else that finally brought bought the Salazarist era to a close – decolonisation. Refusing to relinquish the colonies, he was faced with ever more costly and unpopular military expeditions. In 1961 Goa was occupied by India and nationalists rose up in Angola. Guerrilla movements also appeared in Portuguese Guinea and Mozambique.

In the event, Salazar didn't have to face the consequences. In 1968 he had a stroke, and died two years later.

His successor, Marcelo Caetano, failed to ease unrest. Military officers sympathetic to African freedom fighters grew reluctant to fight colonial wars. Several hundred officers formed the Movimento das Forças Armadas (MFA), which on 25 April 1974, carried out a nearly bloodless coup later nicknamed the Revolution of the Carnations (after victorious soldiers stuck carnations in their rifle barrels). Carnations are still a national symbol of freedom.

FROM REVOLUTION TO DEMOCRACY

Despite the coup's popularity, the following year saw unprecedented chaos. It began where the revolution had begun – in the African colonies. Independence was granted immediately to Guinea-Bissau, followed by

1908

Portuguese King Carlos and son assassinated: Portugal is declared a republic within two years

1910–26

An astounding 45 governments are skittled in 16 years

> The big-budget Portuguese film *Capitães de Abril* (April Captains; 2000), directed by Maria de Medeiros, is a must-see for those interested in the events of 1974's Revolution of the Carnations.

speedy decolonisation of the Cape Verde islands, São Tomé e Príncipe, Mozambique and Angola.

The transition wasn't smooth: civil war racked Angola, and freshly liberated East Timor was invaded by Indonesia. Within Portugal, too, times were turbulent. Although suddenly swamped by almost a million refugees from African colonies, the country managed to ride out the social upheaval remarkably well.

However, Portugal was an economic mess, with widespread strikes and a tangle of political ideas and parties. The communists and a radical wing of the MFA launched a revolutionary movement, nationalising firms and services. Peasant farmers seized land to establish communal farms that were doomed to fail. While revolutionaries held sway in the south, the conservative north was led by Mário Soares and his Partido Socialista (PS; Socialist Party).

It took a more moderate government, formed in 1975, to unite the country after a coup by radical leftists was crushed. At last, the revolution had ended.

THE ROCKY ROAD TO STABILITY

Portugal was soon committed to a blend of socialism and democracy, with a powerful president, elected assembly and Council of the Revolution to control the armed forces.

Mário Soares' minority government soon faltered, prompting a series of attempts at government by coalitions and nonparty candidates, including Portugal's first woman prime minister, Maria de Lourdes Pintassilgo. In the 1980 parliamentary elections a new political force took the reins – the conservative Aliança Democrática (AD; Democratic Alliance), led by Francisco Sá Carneiro.

> The law allowing all Portuguese women to vote was only established as late as 1975.

After Carneiro's almost immediate death in a plane crash (of which evidence of foul play later surfaced), Francisco Pinto Balsemão stepped into his shoes. He began moves to join the European Community (EC).

It was partly to keep the EC and International Monetary Fund (IMF) happy that a new coalition government under Mário Soares implemented a strict programme of economic modernisation. Not surprisingly, the belt-tightening wasn't popular. Loudest critics were Soares' right-wing partners in the Partido Social Democrata (PSD; Social Democrat Party), led by the dynamic Aníbal Cavaco Silva. Communist trade unions also organised strikes, and the appearance of urban terrorism by the radical left-wing Forças Populares de 25 Abril (FP-25), deepened unrest.

By mid-1985 the government collapsed over labour-reform disagreements, and the PSD emerged a narrow winner in subsequent elections. But this wasn't the end of Soares. In the February 1986 presidential elections the veteran socialist became president – the country's first civilian head of state for 60 years. Another record was set the following year when parliamentary elections returned Cavaco Silva and the PSD with the first clear majority since 1974. With a repeat performance four years later, it looked as if the country had finally reached calm waters.

In 1986, after nine years of negotiations, Portugal joined the EC. Flush with new funds, it raced ahead of its neighbours with unprecedented economic growth. The new cash flow also gave Cavaco Silva the power to

1932–68
António de Oliveira Salazar hustles in repressive new state and rules with iron glove for 36 years

1974
Salazar's successor Marcelo Caetano overthrown by army officers in Revolution of the Carnations

push ahead with radical economic reforms. But workers gave a big thumbs down to – you guessed it – labour law reform. Thus the 1980s were crippled by strikes – including one involving 1.5 million workers – though all to no avail. The controversial legislation was eventually passed.

The PSD, now also stricken by corruption scandals, suffered massive losses in municipal elections. But canny Cavaco Silva fought back with a surprise reshuffle removing scandal-tainted ministers. Still-popular Soares won the presidential elections in 1991, and – amazingly – the PSD renewed its majority in subsequent legislative elections.

The electorate may have been disgusted by scandals, unemployment, inflation and public-sector shortcomings, but they were wooed nonetheless by the PSD's promises of growth.

Portugal only narrowly missed claiming Europe's first woman PM: in 1979 Margaret Thatcher snatched the honour just three months before Maria de Lourdes Pintassilgo (1930–2004).

PORTUGAL TODAY

It was soon obvious that these promises would be hard to fulfil. In 1992 EC trade barriers fell and Portugal suddenly faced new competition. Fortunes dwindled as recession set in, and disillusionment grew as Europe's single market revealed the backwardness of Portugal's agricultural sector.

Strikes, crippling corruption charges and student demonstrations over rising fees only undermined the PSD further, leading to Cavaco Silva's resignation in 1995.

Inevitably, the PS soon clinched power under a go-getting António Guterres. The presidential elections were then clinched by socialist Jorge Sampaio, marking the end of the PSD's decade in power, and the first time since 1974 that president and prime minister were both from the same party (SP).

Decades of an uneasy truce were over. Business was reassured by Guterres' budgetary rigour and unexpected success qualifying for the European and Monetary Union (EMU) in 1998. Indeed for a while, Portugal was a star EMU performer. Steady economic growth helped Guterres win a second term, although the party failed (by just one seat) to win an overall parliamentary majority.

But it couldn't last. Corruption scandals, rising inflation and a faltering economy soon spelt disaster. Once the darling of the EMU, Portugal plunged into an economic shambles. The 2001 local elections saw major towns swing to the centre-right, Guterres resigned and 2002 general elections saw his party squashed by the PSD.

Things were far from rosy for the new prime minister, José Manuel Durão Barroso, who had to form a coalition government with his former foe, the radically right-wing Centro Democrático Social-Partido Popular (CDS-PP; Popular Party). The government has since had the unenviable job of tackling Portugal's financial and budgetary crisis, for a time one of the worst in the EU.

But the uphill slog has been punctuated with surprises. In 2004, Barroso took Europe by surprise when he was appointed Portugal's first president of the European Commission, causing a flurry of political shuffling that saw Pedro Santana Lopes take the top job. Meanwhile, Portugal's success as host nation in the European Football Championships of 2004 did wonders for the country's morale, despite its 1–0 loss in the final to Greece, as it looks ahead to a hard economic and political future.

1974–75
Most Portuguese colonies gain independence, and Portugal floods with their refugees

2002
Hello euro, goodbye escudos

The Culture

THE NATIONAL PSYCHE

People tend to come to Portugal without a preconceived notion of its people. However, if any international image sticks, it is one from the Salazar years: of quiet resignation, of a people drowning their sorrows in smoky bars, with plenty of wine and nostalgic music. While this image is far behind the times, its legacy lingers.

In particular, the Portuguese like to indulge in a little *saudade*, a nostalgic, often deeply melancholic longing for better times. The idea is most eloquently expressed in bittersweet *fado* music (a traditional, melancholy Portuguese style of singing) – yearning laments that express fatalism and exquisite frustration about matters that cannot be changed. It's also partly thanks to repression under Salazar that Portugal – most especially in the north – remains a very traditional and conservative country. Extremism is definitely not encouraged. While people are friendly, honest, unhurried and gracious, they can also be extremely formal and polite – and religious festivals and pilgrimages are taken very seriously.

The in-depth Portuguese Culture Web (www.portcult.com) is an amusing personal look at Portuguese culture from an immigrant's perspective.

The Salazar years did nothing to wipe out Portugal's fierce sense of national identity – forged through a plucky history of expelling numerous invaders and a seafaring tradition in which Portugal once led the world. These days the national pride also finds expression through football – less a pastime than a countrywide narcotic.

However, the nation's huge outflow of emigrants and influx of immigrants has inevitably given the national character a certain fluidity. As has its geographical diversity; the colder northern reaches seem to breed a tougher and more reserved character, while the scorching plains in the south encourage an open, sunny-natured outlook. The Portuguese are not averse to mocking their countrymen with such blunt stereotypes either. For example, the sleeves-up people of Porto recite an old saying about the country's biggest cities: 'Coimbra sings, Braga prays, Lisbon shows off and Porto works' and call their southerner counterparts Moors.

However, it is the city–countryside divide that is most dramatic. It's easy to see Portugal as a dynamic, forward-looking nation in the cities – but the contrast in the countryside could not be bigger. As their young desert them, many tiny rural communities almost seem to intensify their adherence to the old ways.

SAUDADE

It's been described as nostalgia for a glorious past, a fathomless yearning and longing for home, but unless you're Portuguese you'll probably never really grasp the uniquely Portuguese passion for *saudade*. Its musical form is the aching sorrow of *fado* – a melancholic submission to the twists and turns of fate. In Portuguese and Brazilian poetry it's a mystical reference for nature, a brooding sense of loneliness, especially popular among certain 19th- and early 20th-century poets who fostered a cult of *saudosismo*. In tangible form it's the return of thousands of émigrés to their home villages every August, drawn not just by family ties but by something deeper – a longing for all that home and Portugal represents: the heroism of the past, the sorrows of the present and wistful hopes for the future.

RESPONSIBLE TRAVEL

In many popular destinations the summer tourist influx puts a real strain on local infrastructure. It's not uncommon for as many as 40,000 annual visitors to squeeze into villages with usual populations less than 2000 – stretching local services to the limit.

One way to minimise your impact is to visit outside the high season. Spending your money in less-visited areas also helps to even out tourism's financial impact, while simultaneously broadening your view of the country.

In traditionally minded rural areas, outlandish dress can also cause offence. While beachwear (and even nudity on some beaches) is fine in coastal tourist resorts, shorts and skimpy tops on a visit to a church are a definite no-no (as is intruding during church services).

Speaking Portuguese – however clumsily – will earn you lots of brownie points. Politeness is highly valued, so be sure to address people correctly (*senhor* for men, *senhora* for women, *senhora dona* followed by the Christian name for an elderly or respected woman).

LIFESTYLE

Portugal is a country that has undergone rapid transition. Held back for decades under Salazar, it has since been sprinting to catch up with the rest of Western Europe. Few other countries could claim to have urbanised so quickly, let alone set up a welfare state, reduced family sizes, improved employment for women, developed a middle class, changed consumer lifestyles and set an empire free – all in such a political blink of the eye.

Like any society changing at a frantic pace, it's inevitable that yawning chasms have opened up between the lifestyles of city-dwellers and rural folk, young and old. In urban centres you'll see many old houses shabby on the outside, but step inside and you'll find them packed with mod cons – shiny computers, modern kitchenware, and a widescreen TV.

The number of cars has almost tripled in the last decade – mostly in city and coastal areas. Even in the smaller settlements, you can see grandmas whizzing by on mopeds, a handbag swinging from one arm. But at the same time, these vehicles will flash past any number of donkey-drawn carts on country roads.

The Portuguese are the world's biggest drinkers, according to a survey by – we are assured unbiased – French researchers. Apparently the home of port imbibes 11.2 litres of pure alcohol per person every year.

Also, while the urban Portuguese are worrying increasingly about crime, their country compatriots frequently leave their doors unlocked and windows open. In smaller country towns, it's also common for two-thirds of the population to be aged 65 years or over. Partly as a result of this, Portugal's interior remains staunchly traditional, and pious *romarias* (religious festivals in honour of a patron saint), fairs and markets are a big part of life.

In terms of personal liberty, it's hard to imagine now that, only decades ago, the Portuguese could not vote freely, dress or write uninhibitedly, or even own a cigarette lighter without first having a state license. It's extraordinary then to consider the modern government's new softer drug laws (p461), its pioneering schemes for public access to the Internet, and the widespread tolerance shown towards hedonistic resorts of the southern coast.

Attitudes towards women and homosexuals are also changing, albeit at a snail's pace. There are still very few women in top posts, and although around two-thirds of women are employed they are paid significantly less than men. But times are changing. Already, two-thirds of university graduates are female. The government has even toyed with the idea of enforcing minimum quotas of women candidates in elections.

Meanwhile, acceptance of gay and lesbian lifestyles largely depends on your location (see p460).

PORTUGUESE BID FOR WORLD DOMINATION

Ever since gold and diamonds were discovered in Brazil in the 17th century, the Portuguese have sought their fortunes, or a better life, overseas. Most left during the 18th and 19th centuries (to Brazil) and in the 1950s and 1960s to France, Germany and elsewhere.

Portugal's emigration rate is still one of Europe's highest and its overseas population one of the largest. It's estimated that three million Portuguese live or work abroad (compare that to a population of little more than 10 million). Brazil, South Africa, the USA and Canada have all welcomed the influx, and France and Germany have huge numbers of temporary workers, who flock home in August and at Christmas.

POPULATION

Portugal's population breakdown has seen dramatic changes in the last few decades. The country's emigration rate has long been among Europe's highest (see above), but its immigration rate shot up during the mid-1970s when around one million African *retornados* (refugees) immigrated from former Portuguese colonies.

They later came from war-torn Angola and Mozambique, followed by others from Guinea-Bissau and São Tomé e Príncipe. Officially, there are now just over 100,000 Africans in Portugal (plus many illegal immigrants). They make up Portugal's major ethnic groups (the 54,000 Cape Verdeans are the biggest group), with especially big communities in Lisbon.

One of the finest all-round books about the Portuguese is Marion Kaplan's perceptive *The Portuguese: The Land & Its People* (1998). Ranging from literature to emigrants, its female perspective seems appropriate for a country whose men so often seem to be abroad.

Another influx resulting from Portugal's empire building is of Brazilians – some 26,600 have now put down roots here. There's a small resident Roma (Gypsy) population and there are also increasing numbers of immigrant workers from central and Eastern Europe. However, the biggest influx in recent years has been sun-seekers from Western Europe buying properties and settling in southern regions. Altogether, there are 225,000 foreign residents in Portugal.

Most native Portuguese share typically Mediterranean features, such as brown eyes and dark hair. The majority still live in rural areas, such as in the Minho, one of Portugal's poorest and most densely populated regions, and the ever more densely populated Algarve coast. But the urban population has increased dramatically since the 1960s, from 22% of the total to around 42%; smaller villages are fast disappearing as their youth move away and ageing populations fizzle out.

SPORT

Football

Football (soccer) is not a game here: it's a national obsession. Life – male life, at any rate – and often the national economy come to a near standstill during any big match, with bar and restaurant TVs showing nothing else.

Apart from Lisbon, the biggest single community of Portuguese is found in Paris.

Boozy post-match celebrations are a tradition in themselves, with fans taking to the streets, honking, setting off fireworks and gridlocking entire town centres until the wee hours.

The country was consumed with football hysteria in 2004 when it hosted the UEFA European Football Championships, the biggest sports event ever staged in Portugal.

Sports authorities were counting on the tournament to provide a big shot in the arm for Portuguese football, and they got it. Local clubs, with mounting debts and ageing stadiums, were watching the country's star players earn a fortune abroad (for example Luís Figo at Real Madrid and

FOOTBALL FEVER

Summer 2004 proved to be an agonising roller coaster ride for Portuguese football fanatics. It was always set to be an eventful year but few expected the extraordinary drama – not to mention nail-biting, hair-pulling, surprise twists and moments of blind ecstasy – that followed.

For five long years Portugal had been preparing to host the UEFA European Football Championships (Euro2004), and in May 2004, anticipation was reaching fever pitch. Nerves were jangling – would the country be ready for such a mammoth test of their infrastructure and security measures? Would they leave the world with a positive image of Portugal?

It was into this climate that an extraordinary scandal broke. On 1 May, 16 senior football officials and referees were detained in a corruption scandal that went right to the top – to the chairman of Portugal's football league, no less. Valentim Loureiro was accused of using his influence to secure sympathetic referees for matches – and he wasn't alone. Other top detainees included a deputy mayor and chairman of the Referees' Committee. Portuguese football was floored, mere weeks before Euro2004.

Nothing could have raised their flagging morale better than what happened next. FC Porto, Portugal's top league team, steamed past Monaco to pick up the European Champions League title – having battled past the like of Manchester United and Real Madrid on the way. José Mourinho's team also clinched the national title days afterwards.

So soccer hysteria could not have been higher when Euro2004 descended on an eager Portugal just two weeks later. Many supporters were jittery about Brazilian coach Luiz Felipe Scolari's Portuguese squad, but still went into the tournament with high hopes. Little did they know that the tournament would end almost exactly as it started.

On 12 June, the first match kicked off at Porto's new Estádio do Dragão, with Portugal suffering a stinging and surprise defeat by newcomers Greece. But Portugal sprang back with increasingly confident performances – battling past the likes of Spain, England and Holland to the final. It was like a dream come true. Could they pull off the biggest victory in the history of Portuguese football?

But their surprise opponents were again those dark-horse Greeks. And the final, on 4 July at Lisbon's Estádio da Luz and watched by 16.5 million viewers, saw Greece cause one of the biggest shocks in the championship's history by clinching the title 1–0.

It ended a summer which, for all its highs, lows, scandals and glory, Portuguese fans would never forget. And despite getting so close to the ultimate prize only to be denied it, the nation congratulated itself on hosting a virtually glitch-free championship.

Cristiano Ronaldo at Manchester United). But sure enough, the sports authorities set about building and sprucing up stadiums and building vital new transport links to the venues.

On a national level, the story of Portuguese football is mainly about Lisbon and Porto – who also took Europe by storm in 2004. The big three teams – Lisbon's Sporting Clube de Portugal and Sport Lisboa e Benfica and Porto's Futebol Clube do Porto – have among them won every national championship but two since the 1920s (Porto's upstart Boavista Futebol Club3 briefly broke the spell in 2001).

The season lasts from September to May, and almost every village and town finds enough players to field a team. Major teams and their stadiums are noted under bigger towns in this book.

The Portuguese were recently declared the laziest nation in the European Union by a study on sedentary lifestyles carried out by scientists at the University of Navarra in Spain.

Bullfighting

Love it or loathe it, bullfighting is a national institution. It was first recorded in Portugal a staggering 2000 years ago by a Roman historian. The sport was then honed in the 12th century, when the *tourada* became a way to maintain military fitness and prepare nobles for horseback battle. However, the gory death of a nobleman in 1799 resulted in a less bloodthirsty Portuguese bullfight, in which the bulls' horns are covered in leather or capped with metal balls and the animals are not killed publicly.

A typical *tourada* starts with an enraged bull charging into the ring towards a *cavaleiro,* a dashing horseman dressed in 18th-century finery and plumed tricorn hat. The *cavaleiro* sizes the animal up as his team of *peões de brega* (footmen) distract and provoke the bull with capes. Then, with superb horsemanship, he gallops within inches of the bull's horns and plants several barbed *bandarilha* (spears) in the angry creature's neck.

The next phase, the *pega,* features eight brave (read foolhardy) young *forcados* dressed in breeches, white stockings and short jackets, who face the weakened bull barehanded. The leader swaggers towards the bull, provoking it to charge. Bearing the brunt of the attack, he throws himself onto the animal's head and grabs the horns while his mates rush in to grab the beast, often being tossed in all directions. Their success wraps up the contest and the bull is led out. Though Portuguese bullfighting rules prohibit a public kill, they are killed after the show – you just don't witness the final blow.

Bullfighting remains popular here despite opposition from international animal-welfare organisations. Portugal's own anti-bullfighting lobby is vocal but small. If you feel strongly you can contact the **Liga Portuguesa dos Direitos dos Animais** (LPDA; Portuguese League for Animal Rights; ☎ 214 578 413; www.lpda.pt in Portuguese) for more information and suggestions of action.

The season runs from late April or March to October. The most traditional contests take place in bull-breeding Ribatejo province, especially in Santarém (p280) during the June fair, and in the otherwise unexceptional Vila Franca de Xira during the town's July and October festivals. Frequent *touradas* in the Algarve and Lisbon are more tourist-oriented.

There are around 200 million Portuguese speakers around the world today – not bad given that Portugal itself only has a population of just over 10 million.

MULTICULTURALISM

Portugal's emigration rate has long been one of Europe's highest, but in the 1970s the tables were turned and the country was flooded with *retornados* (p36). They generally integrated exceptionally well into Portuguese society, with many picking up work in the booming construction industry. Their culture and music has also helped to shape that of the Portuguese – most notably in the kicking African beats so popular in Lisbon clubs. Similarly, the big Brazilian population in Portugal has helped promote its mellow musical tastes here.

However, it's not all jazz and funk in Lisbon's multicultural society. While Portugal has one of the lowest percentages of avowed racists in the EU, at times racism does rear its ugly head in the capital. Gang-related tensions between Angolans and Cape Verdeans have exploded there. The slum living conditions of many immigrants is a depressing indication of the lack of government and national attention to this Afro-Portuguese community.

Ossos (Bones; 1998), directed by Pedro Costa, is a dark and disturbing film about life in a Creole Lisbon slum – not for the faint-hearted.

A lower-profile prejudice is sometimes present in rural Portugal, which can rail against outsiders – especially the Roma population, although some small-town folks can also be wary of tourists. The latest influx of immigrants, especially expats from Britain and Germany, has been to the southern Algarve, although locals often simply regard them as long-stay tourists.

But it's comforting to note that by international standards none of the teething troubles associated with Portuguese immigrant populations are serious. The country seems to take each new wave in its stride.

RELIGION

Christianity has been a pivotal force in shaping Portugal's history, and religion still plays a big part in the lives of its people. The country is famous for its impressive pilgrimages and *romarias* (religious festivals in honour of a plethora of patron saints), which continue unabated and are celebrated with a special fervour in the north. One of Europe's most important centres of pilgrimage is in Portugal at Fátima (p276), where up to 300,000 pilgrims congregate every May and October. See p459 for a list of Portugal's myriad *romarias*.

However, it's not just through rousing events and festivals that the Portuguese demonstrate their faith. Around half of northern Portugal's population still attends Sunday masses, as do more than a quarter in Lisbon – though there are noticeably fewer churchgoers on the southern coast.

In the more traditional north, Catholic traditions often mingle with curious folk practices. For example, there is wild and untamed dancing in Trás-os-Montes (p443), while Amarante's patron saint is associated with the swapping of phallic cakes (p373). In Tomar, the singular Festa dos Tabuleiros (p287) also has colourful pagan roots. And on a hill above Ponte de Lima (p413) is a chapel dedicated to St Ovido, patron saint of ears, with walls covered in votive offerings of wax ears. Similar chapels, adorned with wax limbs of all kinds, can be found even inside churches, revealing a pragmatic sort of tolerance by the Catholic Church.

According to statistics, around 95% of the population is Roman Catholic, although the number of practising Catholics is steadily dropping. Other Christian denominations make up much of the remaining population, as well as many Muslims and a small number of Jews.

Terra Estrangeira (A Foreign Land; 1995), directed by Walter Salles and Daniela Thomas, is a modern film noir thriller that jumps between Sao Paolo and Lisbon at a time when Brazilians were leaving the country in droves.

ARTS

Literature

Portuguese literature has long been moulded by foreign influences – notably that of Spain – but has retained its individuality throughout. Two major styles dominate: lyric poetry and realistic fiction. The country's most outstanding literary figure is Luís Vaz de Camões (1524–80), a poet who enjoyed little fame or fortune in his lifetime. Only after his death was his genius recognised, thanks largely to an epic poem, *Os Lusiadas* (The Lusiads; 1572). It tells of Vasco da Gama's 1497 sea voyage to India, but it's also a superbly lyrical paean to the Portuguese spirit, written when Portugal was still one of the most powerful countries in the Western world. Four centuries after its humble publication, it's considered the national epic, its poet a national hero.

In the 19th century a tide of romanticism flooded Portuguese literature. A prominent figure in this movement was poet, playwright and romantic novelist Almeida Garrett (1799–1854), who devoted his life to stimulating political awareness through his writings. Among his works is the novel *Viagens na Minha Terra* (Travels in My Homeland; 1846), an allegory of contemporary political events, presented as a home-grown travelogue. Despite being Portugal's most talented playwright since the 16th-century court dramatist Gil Vicente, he was exiled for his political liberalism.

The Sin of Father Amaro is a powerful 19th-century novel by Eça de Queirós. The book is set in Portugal, though it was recently relocated for a popular Mexican film, *El Crimen del padre Amaro* (2002).

Garrett's contemporary Alexandre Herculano (also exiled) was meanwhile continuing the long Portuguese tradition of historical literature (which flourished most strongly during the Age of Discoveries) with a vast body of work, most notably his magnum opus *História de Portugal* (1846). Towards the end of the 19th century several important writers emerged, among them the ever-popular José Maria Eça de Queirós, who introduced a stark realism to Portuguese literature with his powerful novels and more entertaining narratives, such as *Os Maias* (The Maias; 1888).

Fernando Pessoa (1888–1935), author of the 1934 *Mensagem* (Message), is posthumously regarded as the most extraordinary poet of his generation; his four different poet-personalities (which he referred to as heteronyms) created four distinct strains of poetry and prose. *A Centenary Pessoa* (1995), published in English, provides a fascinating insight into his work.

You won't get a better insider glimpse of the harsh life in 20th-century rural Portugal than *The Creation of the World* and *Tales from the Mountain* by Miguel Torga, a renowned writer from Trás-os-Montes.

However, Portugal's creative juices were soon to be stoppered. The Salazar dictatorship, spanning much of the early modern era, effectively buried the freedom of expression. Several writers suffered during this period, including the poet and storyteller Miguel Torga (1907–95), whose background in Trás-os-Montes brought a radical individualism to his writings – so much so that several of his writings were banned.

One of the most notable writers who survived and often documented this repressive era was José Cardoso Pires (1925–98), a popular novelist and playwright whose finest work, *Balada da Praia dos Cães* (Ballad of Dog's Beach; 1982), is a gripping thriller based on a real political assassination in the Salazar era. Prominent poets of the time were Jorge de Sena (1919–78), a humanist thinker who also wrote much fiction and criticism; and David Mourão-Ferreira (1927–97), whose works include the novel *Un Amor Feliz* (Lucky in Love; 1986). In Portugal's former colonies (particularly Brazil), writers such as Nobel prize–winner Jorge Amado (1912–2001) have also made their mark on modern Portuguese-language literature.

Today's literary scene is largely dominated by two names: José Saramago (opposite) and António Lobo Antunes. Antunes (1942–) produces magical, fast-paced prose, often with dark undertones and vast historical sweeps. His novel *O Regresso das Caravelas* (The Return of the Caravels; 2002) features a surreal time warp where 15th-century navigators meet 1970s soldiers and contemporary Lisboêtas. His *Manual dos Inquisidores* (The Inquisitor's Manual; 1996) is a dark look at the run-up and aftermath of the 1974 revolution.

The Anarchist Banker (1997), edited by Eugénio Lisboa, is a collection of late 19th- and 20th-century fiction from Portugal. Big names included are Eça de Queirós, Antonio Patricio, Fernando Pessoa, Irene Lisboa and José Rodrigues Migueis.

Hot names on the late 20th-century poetry front included Pedro Tamen and Sophia de Mello Breyner (awarded the Portuguese Camões Prize in 1999), who has found fame both as a poet and as a writer of children's stories, using the sea as her great theme. Up-and-coming novelists include Ana Gusmão, whose stories are set in urban landscapes and reflect conflicts in relationships, cultures and traditions; and José Riço Direitinho, whose haunting novel *Breviário das Más Inclinações* (The Book of Bad Habits; 1994) is peopled by folk memories, superstitious peasants and rural traditions. Also consider the work of Mario de Carvalho, who won the Pegasus Prize for Literature with his gripping novel *Deus Passeando Pela Brisa da Tarde* (A God Strolling in the Cool of an Evening; 1996), which is set in Roman Portugal.

Look out for the beautiful novels of Lídia Jorge, whose book *O Vale da Paixao* (The Painter of Birds; 1995), a tale about an Algarve family split by emigration, won her several Portuguese and international awards.

Cinema

Portugal has a distinguished history of film making, though poor foreign distribution has left the world largely ignorant of it. The only internationally famous director is Manoel de Oliveira, described by the British

JOSÉ SARAMAGO

When José Saramago (1922–) was awarded the 1998 Nobel prize for literature, the Vatican reacted as if bitten. Why? In 1991 Saramago had published *O Evangelho Segundo Jesus Cristo* (The Gospel According to Jesus Christ), a unique reinterpretation of the biblical gospels, in which Jesus is depicted as a human being of flesh and blood, complete with sexual feelings and doubt. Mary Magdalene appears as a strong, intelligent and loving woman and, up above, God and Satan argue about which of them embodies true evil, a fight God easily wins.

The Roman Catholic clergy was appalled and in response the government removed the book from a list of nominations for the EU's European Literary Award. Saramago, disgusted by this, went into self-imposed exile in Spain's Canary Islands.

A common thread in Saramago's stories is the inherent goodness of human nature, although humanity itself comes in for fierce criticism. See, for example, his apocalyptic novel *Ensaio sobre a Cegueira* (Blindness; 1995). And yet one of his most powerful novels is *Memorial do Convento* (Baltazar and Blimunda; 1982), set in the turbulent 18th century. With the construction of Mafra's giant convent as a backdrop, it is arguably one of the most empathic love stories ever written. One of his most readable novels is the captivating *Ano Da Morte De Ricardo Reis* (The Year of the Death of Ricardo Reis; 1984).

Now in his 80s, Saramago is still going strong and in 2004 published a heavy-going new novel *El Homen Duplicado* (The Double).

Guardian newspaper as 'the most eccentric and the most inspired of cinema's world masters'. The ex-racing driver has made over 20 films (all except three after he turned 60), including *The Convent* (1995) starring Catherine Deneuve and John Malkovich. *The Convent* is actually set in a Portuguese convent – Malkovich and Deneuve travel to Portugal to research the theory that Shakespeare is Spanish–Jewish. Also of gossipy interest, this Portugal connection has led to Malkovich being a player in several Lisbon businesses – Lux nightclub (p107) and Bica do Sapato restaurant (p104). Malkovich and Deneuve also appear in Olivieira's *Je Rentre à la Maison* (I'm Going Home; 2002), made in French and set in Paris. Olivieira's *Viagem ao Princípio do Mundo* (Voyage to the Beginning of the World; 1997) is a deceptively simple road movie that explores Portugal's rural past. It's a melancholy meditation on aging and also tells us a great deal about its filmmaker. *Um Filme Falado* (A Talking Picture; 2003) is a thought-provoking film exploring how Europe has been moulded by the past. It examines countries through a series of characters on a cruise from the Mediterranean to India. Slow, but well worth sticking with. Oliveira's latest offering is the period film *O Quinto Império* (The Fifth Empire; 2004), which follows the disastrous story of Sebastião. Oliveira's rather theatrical, fastidious films often feature long, silent takes and can be an acquired taste.

You can now find a wealth of information on Portuguese films, companies, directors and upcoming events on the Instituto de Cinema Audiovisual e Multimédia multilingual website (www.icam.pt).

Other well-established Portuguese film makers include João Botelho, Paulo Rocha and the maverick sexagenarian João Cesar Monteiro. His film *Vai e Vem* (Come and Go; 2002) has raised the usual international eyebrows.

Alongside the older film makers, a new generation of directors has now emerged, producing works that are often provocative and harrowing, exposing the darker side of Portugal. Ground-breaking films include those by Pedro Costa and Teresa Villaverde, whose 1999 film, *Os Mutantes* (The Mutants), is a disturbing work about unwanted youngsters.

The country's best-known actress is Maria de Medeiros who turned director with her *Capitães de Abril* (April Captains; 2000), based on the 1974 Revolution of the Carnations. Significantly, this was funded by the Instituto de Cinema Audiovisual e Multimédia (ICAM; Institute for Cinema Audiovisuals and Multimedia), which has grown more daring in its approach. Other up-and-coming female directors include Catarina Ruivo.

Portugal's talent for dark social commentaries has continued past the millennium. Another directorial name to emerge in this genre is João Canijo, whose films *Ganhar a Vida* (Get a Life; 2001), about a Portuguese émigré in France, and *Noite Escura* (In the Darkness of the Night; 2003), set around Portugal's seedy rural nightlife, have caused waves internationally. If you can track it down, the hard-hitting film *A Passagem da Noite* (Night Passage; 2003) by Luís Filipe Rocha, about a raped girl who discovers she is pregnant, is also good, if harrowing.

However, despite the growing confidence of the Portuguese film industry, cinemas still tend to favour subtitled European and American films. Cinema buffs will find international festivals in Porto in February, the Algarve and Viana do Castelo in May, Tróia in June and Figueira da Foz in September.

Music

Fundamental to Portugal's history of musical expression is its foot-tapping folk music, which you can hear at almost every festival. It traces its roots to the medieval troubadour, and is traditionally accompanied by a band of guitars, violins, clarinets, harmonicas and various wooden percussion instruments. In fact, the instruments are often more attractive than the singing, which could generously be described as a high-pitched, repetitive wail.

Instituto Camões' website (www.instituto-camoes.pt/cvc) is an English-language site with background information on Portuguese language, literature and theatre, plus potted biographies of the country's most important authors and poets.

Far more enigmatic is Portugal's most famous style of music, *fado* (Portuguese for 'fate'). These melancholic chants – performed as a set of three songs, each one lasting three minutes – are also said to have their roots in troubadour songs (although African slave songs have had an influence too). They're traditionally sung by one performer accompanied by a 12-string Portuguese *guitarra* (a pear-shaped guitar). Fado emerged in the 18th century in Lisbon's working-class districts of Alfama and Mouraria and gradually moved upmarket.

There are two styles of fado music, one from Lisbon (still considered the most genuine) and the other from the university town of Coimbra. The latter is traditionally sung by men only since it praises the beauty of women. In 1996 *fadista* Manuela Bravo caused an outcry when she recorded a CD of Coimbra fados – the entire issue of CDs mysteriously disappeared almost as soon as it had appeared (see p302).

The greatest modern *fadista* was Amália Rodrigues, who brought fado international recognition. She died in 1999 aged 79, after more than 60 years of extraordinary fado performances ('I don't sing fado,' she once said, 'it sings me'). Pick up a copy of her greatest hits to hear what fado should really sound like.

However, while fado brings to mind dark bars of the Salazar years, this is not a musical form stuck in time. Top-notch contemporary performers and exponents of a new fado style include the dynamic young *fadista* Mísia, who broke new ground by experimenting with instrumentation and commissioning lyrics by contemporary poets. She has since been followed by several excellent performers.

The current darling of the fado industry is Mariza, whose extraordinary voice and fresh contemporary image has struck a chord both at home and internationally. But the men aren't outdone: one of the great young male voices in traditional fado these days is Camané.

Venues for live fado include Lisbon (p110), Coimbra (p302), Porto (p364) and elsewhere. See p97 for details on an annual fado festival, and p87 for a museum dedicated to its history.

Both fado and traditional folk songs – and, increasingly, strains from Europe and Africa – have shaped Portugal's *música popular* (modern folk-music scene) Often censored during the Salazar years, its lyrics became overtly political after 1974, with singers using performances to support various revolutionary factions.

The Portuguese guitar, too, took on a new range of expression under masters such as Carlos Paredes and António Chaínho. Well-known folk groups include the venerable Madredeus. At the grass-roots level are student song groups, called *tunas académicas,* who give performances all over the country during March.

Jazz is also hugely popular in Portugal, which hosts several jazz festivals. One of the leading lights of Lisbon's lively African jazz scene is diva Maria João. If you spend time in Lisbon, and want a taster of Portuguese jazz, make a beeline for the Hot Clube (p108).

On the rock scene, don't miss the old masters Xutos & Pontapés, the quirky Gift and the popular Blind Zero. Or if fresh-faced pop is more your scene, you'll soon discover chart sensation David Fonseca, who sings in English.

African-influenced urban music is now all the rage. Dozens of Lisbon nightclubs resonate to the rhythms of the former colonies. African jazz was at the forefront of this trend, and big names include Cesaria Évora from Cape Verde and drum-maestro Guem from Angola.

However, the hottest urban clubs around the country are now dominated by DJ culture. You'll hear lots of hip-hop and funk, made popular by the likes of Hip-Hop Tuga and the hugely popular Da Weasel, and a new wave of Portuguese dance-floor music – increasingly being exported around Europe. Look out for names like Micro Audio Waves, Mike

Maria Velho da Costa is one of the three authors of *Novas Cartas Portuguesas* (The Three Marias: New Portuguese Letters; 1972) whose modern feminist interpretation of the 17th-century *Letters of a Portuguese Nun* (p241) so shocked the Salazar regime that its authors were put on trial. The story was made into a film by Jesus Franco in 1977.

MUSICAL TOP TEN

- *Fado em Mim* (2002) Mariza's entrancing voice is the success story of modern fado, and this is her most popular album to date. Her latest offering is *Fado Curvo*.
- *Amália Rodrigues* (1997) A collection of classics from Amália Rodrigues, Portugal's *grand dame* of fado music.
- *Ainda* (2001) Folk-group Madredeus, known for mesmerizing music accompanied by guitar, accordion and cello – this was the soundtrack for the film *A Lisbon Story*.
- *Afro-Portuguese Odyssey* (2002) Wide-ranging look at how the African colonies musically influenced Portugal, and vice versa.
- *A Golden Age of Portuguese Music* (2004) Devotional choral music, straight from the 17th-century court of Dom Joao IV.
- *Sonic Fiction* (2003) For a taste of Lisbon's Bairro Alto nightlife, try this languorous funk by the Spaceboys and designed for the dance floor.
- *Iniciação a Uma Vida Banal – O Manual* (1999) Take innovative hip-hop, mix in a dash of soul and Brazilian groove and you have the hugely popular Da Weasel.
- *Undercovers* (2003) Portuguese jazz at its best, performed by Maria João and Mario Laginha.
- *O Melhor* (1998) By Carlos Paredes – a masterclass in the Portuguese guitar.
- *Ritual* (2001) Misia is another of Portugal's brightest modern *fadistas*.

Stellar and the Space Cowboys. Plus the biggest names at the time of writing were house DJs Rui da Silva and Rui Vargas, who regularly play in Lisbon's hottest club venue – Lux (p107).

Visual Arts

The earliest visual arts to be found in Portugal are several treasure-troves of 20,000-year-old Palaeolithic carvings (see Rescuing Portugal's Rock Art, p383).

The cave-dwellers' modern successors were heavily influenced by French, Italian and Flemish styles. The first major exception was the 15th-century primitive painter Nuno Gonçalves, whose polyptych of the *Panels of São Vicente* (p89) is a unique tapestry-style revelation of contemporary Portuguese society.

The 16th-century Manueline school produced some uniquely Portuguese works, remarkable for their incredible delicacy, realism and luminous colours. The big names of this school are Vasco Fernandes (known as Grão Vasco) and Gaspar Vaz, who both worked from Viseu (their best works are in Viseu's first-rate Museu de Grão Vasco, see p337). In Lisbon, other outstanding Manueline artists were Jorge Afonso (court painter to Dom Manuel I), Cristóvão de Figueiredo and Gregório Lopes.

Hot on the heels of the Renaissance, the 17th century saw artist Josefa de Óbidos (p261) make waves with her rich still lifes. However, the fine arts waned somewhat until the 19th century saw an artistic echo of both the naturalist and romantic movements, expressed strongly in the works of Silva Porto and Marquês de Oliveira, while Sousa Pinto excelled as a pastel artist in the early 20th century.

Naturalism remained the dominant trend into the 20th century, although Amadeo de Souza-Cardoso (p373) struck out on his own path of cubism and expressionism, and Maria Helena Vieria da Silva came to be considered the country's finest abstract painter (although she lived in Paris for most of her life).

Other eminent figures in contemporary art include Almada Negreiros (often called the father of Portugal's modern art movement) and Guilherme Santa-Rita's shorter career in abstract art. Their works and others can be seen in Lisbon's Centro de Arte Moderna (p90) and Porto's Museu Nacional Soares dos Reis (p355).

'The 1974 revolution inspired a surge of artistic development'

The conservative Salazar years that followed didn't create the ideal environment to nurture contemporary creativity, and many artists left the country. These include Portugal's best known modern artist – Paula Rego, born in Lisbon in 1935 but a resident of the UK since 1951. Her colourful paintings and prints often use fables and fantasy to explore unsettling views of sexuality and staid old stereotypes.

Rego's contemporary Helena Almeida has had a particularly strong influence on Portugal's younger artists. Her large-scale often self-reflective photographic portraits combine drawing, photography and painting, challenging the relationship between illusion and reality.

Among the younger generation, born around the time of the 1974 revolution – an event which inspired a surge of artistic development – Miguel Branco is the link between the new and old eras. His small, evocative paintings bring to mind the Renaissance masters – despite being contemporary in style. Eduardo Batarda produces influential works in acrylic, often adapting paintings in comic-strip style. Other 20th-century stars to keep an eye out for are António Areal, Angelo de Sousa and Nadir Afonso. Graça Morais, a figurative artist from Trás-os-Montes, also paints moving scenes from her village life.

However, the biggest trend in Portuguese contemporary art is in innovative video and multimedia projects. Most notably, João Onofre's primitive grainy creations take a humorous look at social dynamics; Miguel Soares' futuristic, slightly unsettling works reflect Portugal's rapidly changing times; and João Penalva's musical video installations are well worth looking out for. Minimalist painter Julião Sarmento has also dabbled in video and photographic works to explore different ways of seeing.

Other exciting breaks with tradition include the work of young collectives such as the Tone Scientists (Carlos Roque, Rui Valério and Rui Toscano), which blend visual art with classical music, and offbeat events such as the Festival Internacional de Banda Desenhada da Amadora (www.amadorabd.com in Portuguese), held every November near Lisbon, showcasing the talents of Portugal's comic-strip artists.

One of José Cardoso Pires' novels, *O Delfim* (The Dauphin), set at the end of Salazar's reign, has been made into a great melodramatic film (2002); Fernando Lopez directed.

SCULPTURE

Sculptors have excelled throughout Portugal's history. Among the first masterpieces are the carved tombs of the 12th to 14th centuries, including the those of Inês de Castro and Dom Pedro in the Mosteiro de Santa Maria de Alcobaça (see p269).

During the Manueline era sculptors including Diogo de Boitaca went wild with Portuguese seafaring fantasies and exuberant decoration (p50). At the same time, foreign influences were seeping in, including Flemish, followed in the 16th century by the flamboyant Gothic and plateresque styles of Spanish Galicia and Biscay. During the Renaissance, several French artists settled in Portugal and excelled in architectural sculpting. The ornate pulpit in Coimbra's Igreja de Santa Cruz (see p297) is regarded as Chanterène's masterpiece.

Foreign schools continued to influence Portuguese sculptors in the 18th-century baroque era, when Dom João V took advantage of the assembly of foreign artists working on the Convento do Mafra to found an influential school of sculpture. Its most famous Portuguese teacher was Joaquim Machado de Castro.

A century later the work of António Soares dos Reis reflects similar influences. However, Soares also ties himself in knots trying to create something uniquely Portuguese (and impossibly intangible) by attempting to portray in sculpture the melancholic feeling of *saudade* (p34).

At the turn of the 20th century two names were prominent: Francisco Franco and the prolific sculptor António Teixeira Lopes, whose most famous work is his series of children's heads. These, along with work by Soares, are on display in the Museu Nacional Soares dos Reis in Porto (p355).

Leading lights on the contemporary scene include Noé Sendas, who creates life-size figures in thought-provoking poses and dress; Leonor Antunes, whose sculptural installations invite viewers to explore how they relate to their surroundings; and Lisbon's Pedro-Cabrita Reis, who also creates impressive architectural installations designed to stimulate memories. Also keep an eye out for the dramatic modern sculptures by Rui Chafes, influenced heavily by the Romantic period.

HANDICRAFTS & INDIGENOUS ARTS

You only have to visit the big weekly markets in Portugal to see the astounding range of traditional handicrafts available – from myriad forms of ceramics to baskets of rush, willow, cane or rye straw, from fabulously painted wooden furniture of the Alentejo to carved ox yokes of the Minho.

Long traditions of hand-embroidery and weaving are also found throughout Portugal – as is lace-making, mainly found along the coast ('where there are nets, there is lace,' goes the saying).

For more details of where to buy these crafts, see Shopping (p462).

Theatre & Dance

The theatre scene has finally cast out the demons of the Salazar years. The venerable Teatro Nacional Dona Maria II (p111) of Lisbon and Teatro Nacional de São João (p364) of Porto have now been joined by numerous private companies, boosted by increased funding from the Ministry of Culture. Portugal's biggest recent theatre success has been the musical *Amália* (about fado's greatest diva), seen by over a million people. Also keep an eye out for Tomar's innovative theatre company, Fatias de Cá, which tends to perform in amazing venues, such as castles and palaces.

'Their whirling, foot-stomping and finger-waggling routines make great watching'

The Gulbenkian Foundation, one of Portugal's most generous and wide-ranging private arts sponsors, also continues to support new theatre companies and dance. Indeed, Portuguese modern dance is capturing increased international acclaim; every November contemporary dance fans flock to Lisbon's Festival Internacional de Dança Contemporânea. One of the country's leading choreographers is Vera Mantero, previously a ballerina, now an exponent of cutting-edge experimental dance styles. Prestigious ballet performances also get palatial settings in Sintra (p116) during August.

However, it's good old folk dancing that you'll most frequently see in the north. Almost every village has its own dancers, all in flamboyant costumes, the women draped in jewellery. Their whirling, foot-stomping and finger-waggling routines make great watching and some, such as the flowery *pauliteiros* (stick dancers) of Miranda do Douro (p447), have gone professional, touring the country and abroad.

Architecture

Tiling covers Portugal like nowhere else, busy and dazzling against bee yellow, dusty blue and rosy pink walls. Also emblematically Portuguese are the churches – often deceptively plain outside, so that stepping inside is like entering another world, dripping with gold. Even more spectacular are the cathedrals and palaces, their sinuous curves a framework for seaweed-like carving. Many of these sumptuous buildings date from Portugal's most glorious era, its Age of Discoveries.

At the other end of the architectural scale are Portugal's medieval walled villages, their narrow streets, like those in Spain, preserving the pattern of their Arabic past, with thick walls glaring white against the summer heat.

Roman ruins, Visigothic remains, Gothic vaults and baroque façades are the icons of a rich heritage of churches and monasteries, palaces and mansions. But you can step outside time by exploring the rural landscape, where the evidently prosperous prehistoric inhabitants had time enough spare to erect numberless tombs, temples and lonely megaliths.

Time never stands still: contemporary architecture offers superb museums, soaring infrastructure and huge football stadiums like vast extraterrestrial insects.

At the well-produced panoramic creation 360° Portugal (www.360portugal.com) you can peer around castles, megaliths, churches, archaeological sites and more.

BIG STONES

A most mysterious group of 95 huge monoliths form a strange circle in an isolated clearing among Alentejan olive groves near Évora. It's one of Europe's most impressive prehistoric sites: the Cromeleque dos Almendres (p215).

All over Portugal, but especially in the Alentejo, you can visit such ancient funerary and religious structures, built during the Neolithic and Megalithic eras, about 6000 years ago. Most impressive are the dolmens: funerary chambers – rectangular, polygonal or round – reached by a corridor of stone slabs and covered with earth to create an artificial mound. King of these is the Anta Grande do Zambujeiro (p215), also near Évora, and Europe's largest dolmen, with six 6m-high stones forming a huge chamber. Single monoliths, or menhirs, often carved with phallic or religious symbols, also dot the countryside like an army of stone sentinels. Their relationship to promoting fertility seems obvious.

ARCHITECTURAL TOP TEN

- **Cromeleque dos Almendres** (p215) A ring of 95 prehistoric big stones.
- **Templo Romano** (p209) Roman columns in Évora's heart.
- **Mosteiro de Santa Maria de Alcobaça** (p269) Lean Gothic.
- **Palácio Nacional de Mafra** (p133) Vast, vast, vast extravagance.
- **Convento de Cristo** (p285) Mysterious Manueline, Gothic and Renaissance.
- **Mosteiro de Santa Maria da Vitória** (p271) Gothic grandeur.
- **Mosteiro dos Jerónimos** (p92) Manueline masterpiece.
- **Gare do Oriente** (p91) Skeletal Death Star architecture.
- **Ponte de Vasco da Gama** (p91) A 17km-long bridge.

With the arrival of the Celts (800–200 BC) came the first established hilltop settlements, called *castros*. The best-preserved example is the Citânia de Briteiros (p402), where you can literally step into Portugal's past. Stone dwellings were built on a circular or elliptical plan, and the complex was surrounded with a dry-stone defensive wall. In the *citânias* (fortified villages) further south, dwellings tended to be rectangular.

COLUMNS & CHRISTIANS

The Romans left their typical architectural and engineering feats – roads, bridges, towns complete with forums (marketplaces), villas, public baths and aqueducts. These have now largely disappeared from the surface of life, though the majority of Portugal's cities are built on Roman foundations and you can descend into dank foundations under new buildings in Lisbon and Évora. At the country's largest Roman site, at Conimbriga (p303), an entire Roman town is under excavation. Revealed so far are some spectacular mosaics, along with structural or decorative columns, carved entablatures and classical ornamentation, which give a sense of the Roman high life.

Portugal's most famous and complete Roman ruin is the Templo Romano, the so-called Temple of Diana in Évora (p209), with its flouncy-topped Corinthian columns, nowadays echoed by the complementary towers of Évora cathedral. This is the finest temple of its kind on the Iberian Peninsula, its preservation the result of having been walled up in the Middle Ages, and later used as a slaughterhouse.

Fires of Excellence: Spanish and Portuguese Oriental Architecture, by Miles Danby & Matthew Weinreb (1998), is a stunningly photographed exploration of Portugal's Arabian history and aesthetics.

The various Teutonic tribes who invaded after the fall of Rome in the early 5th century left little trace other than a few churches built by the Visigoths, a fierce bunch of Aryan Christians. Though heavily restored over the centuries, these ancient churches still reveal a Roman basilican outline, rectangular and divided by columns into a nave and two aisles. Two fine examples are the Capela de São Pedro de Balsemão (p378) and the Igreja de Santa Amaro (p243). Most unusual is the Capela de São Frutuoso (near Braga) – Byzantine (Graeco-Asiatic) in character, laid out in the shape of a Greek cross.

The Visigoths also rebuilt the Roman town of Idanha-a-Velha (p321), now a quiet hamlet near Castelo Branco; you can see their influence in parts of the cathedral here. Many other Visigothic churches were destroyed by the Moors after they kicked out the Visigoths in AD 711.

FEELING MOORISH

Unlike Spain, Portugal has no complete buildings left from the Moorish period. You will find the odd Moorish arch or wall, bits of fortresses, and the atmospheric remains of several *mourarias* (Moorish quarters), notably in Moura (p247), which retains a well and a Moorish tower as part of its castle. Nearby Mértola (p237) retained much of its Islamic characteristics (nothing like a bit of economic torpor to halt development) and includes a distinctive former mosque converted into a church.

SMOKE SIGNALS

Peculiar to the Algarve are cut-out diamond-shape-dotted whitewashed chimneys, rising minaret-like from buildings with a geometric nod to the region's Moorish past. Often buildings have two – one used regularly, above the kitchen, and a lacier version for special occasions. The cost was measured in construction time – the more intricate, the longer it took – so the stonemasons would ask how many days of chimney you wanted.

AZULEJOS

Portugal's favourite decorative art is easy to spot – polished painted tiles called *azulejos* (after the Arabic *al zulaycha*, meaning polished stone). These cover everything from churches to houses to train stations with the best examples being at Aveiro (p313), Pinhão (p381) and Porto's São Bento (p366). The Moors introduced the art, having picked it up from the Persians, but the Portuguese liked it so much they tiled anything that stayed still long enough.

Portugal's earliest 16th-century tiles are Moorish, from Seville. These were decorated with interlocking geometric or floral patterns (figurative representations aren't an option for Muslim artists for religious reasons). After the Portuguese captured Ceuta in Morocco in 1415, they began exploring the art themselves. The 16th-century Italian invention of majolica, in which colours are painted directly onto wet clay over a layer of white enamel, gave works a fresco-like brightness and kicked off the Portuguese azulejo love affair.

You can easily spot the earliest tiles, polychrome and geometric, either imported by the Moors or produced by the Portuguese. The earliest home-grown examples date from the 1580s, and may be seen in churches such as Lisbon's Igreja de São Roque (p85), providing an ideal counterbalance to fussy, gold-heavy baroque. Some of Portugal's earliest tiles adorn the Palácio Nacional da Sintra (p118).

The late 17th century saw a fashion for huge panels, depicting everything from cherubs to commerce, saints to seascapes. As demand grew, mass production became necessary and the Netherlands' blue-and-white Delft tiles started to run all over the walls.

Portuguese tile makers rose to the challenge of this influx, and the splendid work of virtuoso Portuguese masters António de Oliveira Bernardes and his son Policarpo in the 18th century springs from this competitive creativity. You can see their work in Évora, in the breathtaking Igreja de São João (p209).

Fantastic 17th and 18th century tiling also covers Igreja de São Vicente de Fora in Lisbon (p87). Rococo themes appeared, as at Lamego's Igreja de Nossa Senhora dos Remédios (p375), or Lisbon's Palácio Nacional de Queluz (p132) and Quinta dos Marquêses da Fronteira (p91), offering lots of buxom mythological ladies, and providing religious scenes with a chintzy garden-party look.

By the end of the century, industrial-scale manufacture began to affect quality, coupled with the massive demand for tiles after the 1755 Lisbon earthquake. Tiling answered the need for decoration, but was cheap and practical – a solution for a population that had felt the ground move beneath its feet.

From the late 19th century, the Art Nouveau and Art Deco movements took azulejos by storm, providing fantastic façades and interiors for shops, restaurants and residential buildings – notably by Rafael Bordalo Pinheiro (visit Caldas de Rainha, where there is a museum devoted to his work, p263), Jorge Colaço and Jorge Barradas, whose work you can see at the Museu da Cidade in Lisbon (p91).

Azulejos still coat contemporary life, and you can explore the latest in azulejos while going places on the Lisbon metro. Maria Keil designed 19 of the stations, from the 1950s onwards – look out for stunning block-type prints at Intendente (considered her masterpiece) and Anjos. Oriente (p91) also showcases extraordinary contemporary work. Artists from five continents were invited to contribute, including Austria's Hundertwasser. Look out also for public works by Júlio de Resende, responsible for Ribeira Negra, Porto (1987; p357).

For more information on this beautiful art, and a visual feast, visit Lisbon's Museu Nacional do Azulejo (p88). There are also many impressive pieces in Lisbon's Museu de Cidade. Lisbon and Porto have the best on-the-street examples.

Having seen all this, you might want to take some home: good places to buy are Lisbon (see p112 for recommended shops and factories), and any of the ceramic centres (see p463).

Portuguese Decorative Tiles, by Rioletta Sabo (1998), is an all-out wallow in the dazzling colours and diversity of Portugal's favourite wall-covering.

Silves (p176) was the Moorish capital of the Algarve, and retains an enormous well, now on display as part of the archaeological museum.

The Moors did, however, powerfully influence Portuguese architecture, no matter how hard the Christians tried to stamp out their mark. This is particularly noticeable in private homes, and especially in the south: terraces and horseshoe arches, wrought-iron work and whitewash, flat roofs and geometric ornamentation, and the use of water in decoration.

FORTRESS-CHURCHES

During the Christian recapture of Portugal from the Moors, completed by 1297, most mosques were torn down and replaced by a church or cathedral, often on the same site. These were in the simple, robust Romanesque style – with rounded arches, thick walls and heavy vaulting – originally introduced to Portugal by Burgundian monks. As in Lisbon and Coimbra, they often resembled fortifications – demonstrating concerns about the Moors wreaking revenge, and anticipating the Castilian threat.

More delicate Romanesque touches can be found in several small, lovely churches (notably the Igreja de São Salvador (p415) in Bravães, where portals often display fine animal or plant motifs in their archivolts. Only one complete example of a secular building remains from this time – Bragança's endearing five-sided Domus Municipalis (p441), Portugal's oldest town hall.

GOING GOTHIC

Cistercians introduced the Gothic trend, and this reached its pinnacle in Alcobaça, in one of Portugal's most ethereally beautiful buildings. The austere abbey church and cloister of the Mosteiro de Santa Maria de Alcobaça (p269), begun in 1178, has a lightness and simplicity strongly influenced by French Clairvaux Abbey. Its hauntingly simple Cloisters of Silence were a model for later cathedral cloisters at Coimbra, Lisbon, Évora, and many others. This was the birth of Portuguese Gothic, which flowered and transmuted over the coming years as the country gained more and more experience of the outside world. For centuries Portugal had been culturally dominated and restricted by Spain and the Moors.

By the 14th century, when the Mosteiro de Santa Maria da Vitória (commonly known as Mosteiro da Batalha or Battle Abbey, p271) was constructed, simplicity was a distant, vague memory. Portuguese, Irish and French architects worked on this breathtaking monument for more than two centuries. The combination of their skills and the changing architectural fashions of the times – from Flamboyant (late) Gothic to Gothic Renaissance to Manueline, turned the abbey into a seething mass of carving, organic decorations, lofty space, and slanting stained-glass light. It's a showcase of High Gothic art. It exults in the decorative (especially in its Gothic Royal Cloisters and Chapter House), while the flying buttresses tip their hat to English Perpendicular Gothic.

Secular architecture also enjoyed a Gothic boom, thanks to the need for fortifications against the Moors and to the castle-building fervour of the 13th-century ruler, Dom Dinis. Some of Portugal's most spectacular, huddled, thick-walled castles – for example, Estremoz (p219), Óbidos (p260) and Bragança (p438) – date from this time, many featuring massive double perimeter walls and an inner square tower.

MANUELINE MANIA

Manueline is a uniquely Portuguese style, a specific, crazed flavour of late-Gothic architecture. Ferociously decorative, it coincided roughly with the reign of Dom Manuel I (1495–1521) and is interesting not just because of its extraordinarily imaginative designs, burbling with life, but also because this dizzyingly creative architecture skipped hand in hand with the era's booming confidence.

During Dom Manuel's reign, Vasco da Gama and fellow explorers claimed new overseas lands and new wealth for Portugal. The Age of Discoveries was expressed in sculptural creations of eccentric inventiveness, drawing heavily on nautical themes: twisted ropes, coral and anchors in stone, topped by the ubiquitous armillary sphere (a navigational device, which became Dom Manuel's personal symbol) and the Cross of the Order of Christ (symbol of the religious military order that largely financed and inspired Portugal's explorations).

'Manueline architecture skipped hand in hand with the era's booming confidence'

Manueline first emerged in Setúbal's Igreja de Jesus (p139), designed in the 1490s by French expatriate Diogo de Boitaca, who gave it columns like trees growing into the ceiling, and ribbed vaulting like twisted ropes. The style soon caught on, and soon decorative carving was creeping, twisting and crawling over everything (aptly described by 19th-century English novelist William Beckford as 'scollops and twistifications').

Outstanding Manueline masterpieces are the Mosteiro dos Jerónimos (p92), masterminded largely by Diogo de Boitaca and João de Castilho and the Mosteiro de Santa Maria da Vitória's (p271), otherworldly Capelas Imperfeitas (Unfinished Chapels). Other famous creations include Belém's Torre de Belém (p93), a Manueline–Moorish cake crossed with a chesspiece by Diogo de Boitaca and his brother Francisco, and Diogo de Arruda's fantastical organic, seemingly barnacle-encrusted window in the Chapter House of Tomar's Convento de Cristo (p285), as well as its fantastical 16-sided charola – the Templar church, resembling an eerie *Star Wars* set. Many other churches sport a Manueline flourish against a plain façade.

The style was enormously resonant in Portugal, and reappeared in the early 20th-century in exercises in mystical Romanticism, such as Sintra's Quinta da Regaleira (p121) and Palácio Nacional da Pena (p120), and Luso's over-the-top and the extraordinary neo-Manueline Palace Hotel do Buçaco (p305).

RETICENTLY RENAISSANCE

After all that froth and fuss, the Portuguese were slow to take up the Renaissance style, a return to Roman classical design and proportion. One of its protagonists, the Italian Andrea Sansovino, is thought to have spent time in Portugal, though he made little impression. The Quinta da Bacalhoa, a 15th-century house at Vila Nogueira de Azeitão (near Setúbal) is his only notable contribution. The French sculptor Nicolas Chanterène was the main pioneer of Renaissance ideas here, and from around 1517 onwards, his influence abounds in sculpture and architectural decoration.

Portugal has few Renaissance buildings, but some examples of the style are the Great Cloisters in Tomar's Convento de Cristo (p285), designed by Spanish Diogo de Torralva in the late 16th century, the nearby Igreja de Nossa Senhora da Conceição (p281), and the Convento de Bom Jesus at Valverde (p215), outside Évora.

MOODY & MANNERIST

Sober and severe, the Mannerist style reflects the spirit of its time, coinciding with the years of Spanish rule (1580–1640) and the heavy influence of the Inquisition and the Jesuits. It persisted throughout much of the 17th century. Lisbon's marvellous Igreja de São Vicente de Fora (p87), built between 1582 and 1627 by Felipe Terzi, is a typical example of balanced Mannerist classicism. It served as a model for many other churches.

BRAZIL, BAROQUE & BUCKETS OF GOLD

With independence from Spain re-established and the influence of the Inquisition on the wane, Portugal burst out in baroque fever – an architectural style that was exuberant, theatrical and fired straight at the senses. Nothing could rival the Manueline flourish, but the baroque style – named after the Portuguese word for a rough pearl, *barroco* – cornered the market in flamboyance. At its height in the 18th century (almost a century later than in Italy), it was characterised by curvaceous forms, huge monuments, spatially complex schemes and lots and lots and lots of gold.

Financed by the 17th-century gold and diamond discoveries in Brazil, and encouraged by the extravagant Dom João V, local and foreign (particularly Italian) artists created mind-bogglingly opulent masterpieces. You'll see prodigious *talha dourada* (gilded woodwork) in church interiors all over the place, but it reached its most extreme in Aveiro's Convento de Jesus (p315), Lisbon's Igreja de São Roque (p85) and Porto's Igreja de São Francisco (p354).

Work on Palácio Nacional de Mafra was so lavish and expensive it nearly bankrupted the country.

The baroque of central and southern Portugal was more restrained. Examples include the chancel of Évora's cathedral (p208), and the massive Palácio Nacional de Mafra (p133). Designed by the German architect João Frederico Ludovice to rival the similar palace-monastery of San Lorenzo de El Escorial (near Madrid), the Mafra version is relatively sober, apart from its size – which is such that at one point it had a workforce of 45,000 working on it, looked after by a police force of 7000.

Meanwhile, the Tuscan painter and architect Nicolau Nasoni (who settled in Porto around 1725) introduced a more ornamental baroque style to the north. Nasoni is responsible for Porto's Torre dos Clérigos (p354) and Igreja da Misericórdia (p354), and the whimsical Palácio de Mateus (p430) near Vila Real (internationally famous as the image on Mateus rosé wine bottles).

In the mid-18th century a school of architecture evolved in Braga. Local artists such as André Soares built churches and palaces in a very decorative style, heavily influenced by Augsburg engravings from southern Germany. Soares' Casa do Raio (p391), in Braga, and much of the monumental staircase of the nearby Bom Jesus do Monte (p393), are typical examples of this period's ornamentation.

Only when the gold ran out did the baroque fad fade. At the end of the 18th century, architects flirted briefly with rococo (best exemplified by Mateus Vicente's Palácio de Queluz, p132), begun in 1747, or the palace at Estói (p158) before embracing neoclassicism.

POST-EARTHQUAKE SOBRIETY

Houses were tiled on the outside after the 1755 earthquake as a cheap and more expendable means of decoration.

After Lisbon's devastating 1755 earthquake, the autocratic Marquês de Pombal invited architect Eugenio dos Santos to rebuild the Baixa area in a plain style, using classical elements that could be easily built and repeated. This new 'Pombaline' style featured a grid pattern marked by unadorned houses and wide avenues. It had a knock-on effect and led to a reaction against the excesses of the baroque period in other parts of the country. In Porto, for instance, the Hospital de Santo António and the Feitoria Inglesa (Factory House), both designed by Englishmen, show a noticeable return to sober Palladian and classical designs. Lisbon's early-19th-century Palácio Nacional da Ajuda was also designed on neoclassical lines and served as the inspiration for the elegantly restrained Palácio de Brejoeira (near Monção, in the Minho).

NEO-EVERYTHING, ART NOUVEAU & THE NEW

In the early 19th century most new building of major monuments came to a halt. This was partly due to the aftereffects of the Peninsular War (1807–14) and partly because a liberal decree in 1834 dissolved the religious orders, allowing their many buildings to be appropriated by the state. Some former monasteries are still used by the government today – notably Lisbon's Benedictine Mosteiro de São Bento (p88), now the seat of parliament.

When new buildings did emerge they tended to draw on all the architectural styles of the past, from Moorish (as in Lisbon's Rossio station) to neoclassical (Porto's stock exchange, the Palácio da Bolsa, p354). A distinctly French influence can be seen in many grand apartment blocks and office buildings built at this time.

Towards the end of the 19th century the increased use of iron and steel reflected Portugal's emergence as an industrial nation. Train stations (eg Lisbon's Alcântara station) and other grand buildings were covered in iron and glass. Gustave Eiffel built iron bridges across the rivers Minho, Lima and Douro, and his followers were responsible for several Eiffel lookalikes, including Lisbon's wonderfully eccentric Elevador de Santa Justa (p86) (kind of Eiffel Tower crossed with a doily).

One of the most delightful movements during this period was Art Nouveau, a burst of carefree, decorative fancy that produced many beautifully decorated cafés and shops (check out Lisbon's Versailles (p106) and Pastelaria São Roque (p106), or Braga's Café Astória (p393).

The Salazar years favoured decidedly severe, Soviet-style, state commissions (eg Coimbra University's dull faculty buildings, which replaced elegant 18th-century neoclassical ones). Ugly buildings and apartment

Memorial do Convento (Baltazar and Blimunda; 1982) is José Saramago's Nobel prize-winning novel about the Mafra extravaganza – a convent-palace dreamed up by size-junkies and compulsive builders.

The Lisbon metro is not just about transport – it's an art gallery, showcasing the best of Portuguese contemporary art and architecture, with especially wonderful azulejos. Check out Metro Lisboa's website at www.metrolisboa.pt.

LOCAL PLACES FOR LOCAL PEOPLE

Local architecture varies according to building materials to hand and climate. Northern Portugal is packed with granite, a hard material perfect for constructing thick-walled, two-storey houses with slate roofs that keep out winter weather. In the coastal Beiras, local limestone is used for houses that are faced with painted stucco or, occasionally, azulejo.

On the coast near Aveiro, several villages are famous for their candy-striped houses built of wood from nearby pine forests. Brick houses in the Ribatejo and the Alentejo are long, single-storey structures, stuccoed and whitewashed, with a single colour (usually blue) outlining their architectural features. To keep out the summer heat these houses have few doors and windows; their huge fireplaces and chimneys provide both warmth and a place to smoke the meat and sausages typical of the region.

Perhaps most extraordinary are the marble towns in the Alentejo – Estremoz (p219), Vila Viçosa (p223) and Borba (p222) – where there is such a surfeit of fine marble that it is casually used everywhere, from kerbs to cobblestones, giving the towns a luminescent pinky-golden glow.

By contrast, the Algarve's clay or stone houses appear modest. Those with flat terraces (used for drying produce, catching rainwater and generally hanging out), instead of the usual red tile roofs, are a Moorish legacy. Such characteristics are a combination of the Arabic legacy and influences absorbed on long-distance travels abroad; for example, in Tavira, pagoda-like red-tiled roofs are a souvenir of visits east. Typical, too, of Mediterranean houses are the Algarve's shaded porches and arcaded verandas at ground level.

blocks rose on city outskirts. Notable exceptions dating from the 1960s are Lisbon's Palácio da Justiça in the Campolide district, and the gloriously sleek Museu Calouste Gulbenkian (p90). The beautiful wood-panelled Galeto (p105) café-restaurant is a time capsule from this era.

Check out OHM Design's website (www.ohmdesign.com) for designs, furniture, and essays by Alvora Siza, and news on his current work.

The tendency towards urban mediocrity continued after the 1974 revolution, although architects such as Fernando Távora and Eduardo Souto Moura have produced impressive schemes. Lisbon's postmodern Amoreiras shopping complex (p113), by Tomás Taveira, is another striking contribution.

Portugal's greatest contemporary architect is Alvaro Siza. A believer in clarity and simplicity, his expressionist approach is reflected in projects such as the Pavilhão de Portugal (p91) for Expo 98, Porto's splendid Museu de Arte Contemporânea (p355) and the Igreja de Santa Maria at Marco de Canavezes, south of Amarante. He has also restored central Lisbon's historic Chiado (p84) shopping district with notable sensitivity, following a major fire in 1988.

Spanish architect Santiago Calatrava designed the lean organic monster Gare do Oriente (p91) for the Expo 98, architecture that is complemented by the work of many renowned contemporary artists. The interior is more state-of-the-art spaceship than station. The longest bridge in Europe, the Ponte de Vasco da Gama built in 1998, stalks out across the river from nearby.

Alvara Siza, by Brigitte Fleck (2001), is a handy monograph on the great contemporary architect, whose nationwide projects include the clean cubism of Porto's Museu de Arte Contemporânea.

Most recent architectural spectacles are the stadiums for Euro2004. Near Porto, Manuel Salgado's Estádio do Dragão (p364) has a transparent roof, built from 280 tonnes of steel, and is as tall as a 14-storey building. In Braga, the stadium was carved into a granite mountain face – more than one million cubic metres of granite were blasted out of the hillside to make room for the venue, which is ringed by dramatic mountains.

Environment

THE LAND

Size isn't everything. Portugal is one of Europe's smallest countries, covering an area of just 92,389 sq km and measuring only 560km north to south and 220km east to west. But despite its pipsqueak size, its land is impressively diverse. A single day's travel could see you pass from dramatic mountain ranges in the north to undulating meadows in the south; meanwhile the coast switches its mood from wicked surf-crashing Atlantic waves to balmy Mediterranean beaches, perfect for paddlers.

Together with Ireland, Portugal dips its toes into the Atlantic at the westernmost extreme of Europe; and it's no accident that, with 830km of Atlantic coastline, Portugal is one of the greatest nations of seafarers and explorers in history. In many ways though, Portugal is at the mercy of its rivers, which bring precious water to its parched southern lands (p61).

One of Portugal's most important waterways, the Rio Tejo, slices the country almost perfectly in half, flowing northeast to southwest and spilling its contents into the Atlantic at Lisbon, one of Portugal's few natural harbours. The mountains loom mostly north of the Tejo, while vast plains spread to the south.

But let's take a step-by-step tour of the country. Topping the country, the heavily populated northwestern Minho is blessed by fertile rolling plateaus and by rivers flowing through deep gorges. Step down and neighbouring Beira Alta, Douro and Trás-os-Montes are all carved from high granite, schist and slate plateaus. This region, rising to 800m, is nicknamed the *terra fria* (cold country) for its winter chill.

Meanwhile the southern and eastern Alto Douro (in southern Trás-os-Montes) rightly scores the name *terra quente* (hot country), a scorched landscape of sheltered valleys with dark schists that trap the heat and create the perfect microclimate – described by locals as 'nine months of winter and three months of hell' – for pumping out Portugal's famous port wine.

However, for real mountains you need only look to the Serra da Estrela, which tops out at the 1993m Torre, the highest peak in mainland Portugal and even home to a winter ski resort. Rolling down further south, you'll reach the low-lying, often marshy Atlantic coastline of Beira Litoral and Estremadura, sprinkled with river-mouth lagoons and salt marshes.

Inland, between the Rio Tejo and the Rio Guadiana, the Alto Alentejo joins the Spanish tablelands in wide flat plateaus. Further south still, in northern Baixo Alentejo, are ridges of quartz and marble, and a vast undulating landscape of wheat, cork trees and olive trees – a large swathe of which is now submerged by the vast Alqueva Dam.

Only the eastern Serra do Caldeirão and western Serra de Monchique break the flatness of the south, and are a natural border between the Alentejo and the Algarve. They also act as a climatic buffer for the Algarve, which basks in a Mediterranean glow.

The islands of Madeira and the Azores, originally colonised in the 15th century, are also part of Portugal, although too far away to be considered in a peninsular visit: Madeira lies 900km to the southwest, off Africa's west coast; the nine-island Azores archipelago sprawls 1440km west of Lisbon.

Landscapes of Portugal, by Brian and Eileen Anderson (1993), and the more up-to-date *Landscapes of the Algarve* (2000) are great sources for country walks and car journeys in Portugal.

WILDLIFE

While few visitors come to Portugal specifically to track down its wildlife, the country is nonetheless home to some of the rarest and most interesting creatures in Europe. Northern Portugal has forests and hills rich in animal and bird life, while the south's parched plains and coastline also shelter their fair share of fauna.

The Algarve Tiger, by Eduardo Goncalves et al (2002), is a passionate book about the world's most endangered feline, the Iberian lynx.

Animals

When most of us think of Portuguese wildlife, we think of its rarest creatures: the shaggy-bearded Iberian lynx, now teetering on the brink of extinction, and the much maligned wolf (below). However, the fauna you're most likely to stumble across is rabbits, hares and bats. With luck, in more remote areas you might come across foxes, deer, otters or even foraging wild boars.

A few North African species have also sneaked into the picture. The most delightful settler is the Mediterranean chameleon, introduced to the eastern coastal Algarve about 70 years ago (see p167). Two more such species are the spotted, weasel-like genet that hides during the day, and the Egyptian mongoose, which you may stumble upon trotting across quieter Algarve roads.

Bird fanciers will also be kept busy. Portugal has a mixed bag of bird-life – from temperate to Mediterranean species, plus migrants too. You've an excellent chance of admiring wetland species – including flamingos, egrets, herons, spoonbills and many species of shore birds – in reserves, such as the Reserva Natural do Sapal de Castro Marim e Vila Real de Santo António (p168) and the Parque Natural da Ria Formosa (p159).

You may even score a glimpse of more unusual birds: nimble lesser kestrels and the shy black stork near Mértola (p237) and around Castro Verde. vividly coloured purple gallinules (p159) in the Parque Natural da Ria Formosa, hefty bustards and sandgrouse on the Alentejo plains, and Iberian species such as the great spotted cuckoo, red-winged nightjar, rufous bushchat and azure-winged magpie.

However, if it's birds of prey that ruffle your feathers, your best bet is in the Parque Natural do Douro Internacional (see p450), over which soar various species of eagles, kestrels and vultures.

Birdwatching Guide to the Algarve, by Kevin and Christine Carlson (1995), has all the information you'll need on south-coast birds.

Portugal's leading ornithological society is the **Sociedade Portuguesa para o Estudo de Aves** (SPEA; ☎ 213 220 430; www.spea.pt; Rua da Vitória 53, 1100-618 Lisbon), which runs government-funded projects to map the distribution of Portugal's breeding birds. **Naturetrek** (☎ 01962-733051; www.naturetrek.co.uk) run an eight-day bird-watching excursion around southern Portugal.

ENDANGERED SPECIES

The most high profile of Portugal's endangered animals is the fast-dwindling Iberian lynx (opposite). But this iconic species is not the only one set to disappear.

Moving from cats to dogs – the rusty-coloured Iberian wolf is also in serious decline. Shockingly, there are only around 200 left in Portugal (out of an estimated 1500 on the Iberian Peninsula). Most live in the Parque Natural de Montesinho in Trás-os-Montes (p443) and adjacent areas of Spain. But despite being protected by law, the wolf is still illegally shot, trapped or poisoned on a regular basis as it is blamed (often mistakenly) for attacking cattle and domestic animals. Also see p134 for details of a wolf sanctuary near Mafra.

Portugal is home to the most endangered big cat in the world.

Dog-lovers will be fascinated by the web-footed wonder, the Algarve water-dog. This little creature's unique webbed feet once made it the fish-

THE LYNX EFFECT

No endangered animal in Portugal plucks at the heartstrings quite like the tufty-eared Iberian lynx. Though not much bigger than the common house cat, this is the only big cat endemic in Europe and easily the world's most endangered feline. Just 135 Iberian lynx are now left in Spain and Portugal, its numbers decimated by disease, poachers, wildfires, dam- and road-building and scarcity of rabbits (its favourite food).

The last remaining hide-outs of the four dozen or so animals in Portugal are mostly in scattered, remote regions of the Algarve (see also p323). A network of protected areas, habitat corridors and captive breeding programmes are now being thrown together to save the species. For details of how to help, check the website of **SOS Lynx** (www.soslynx.org). It's alarming to think that if the species dies out, it may well be the first feline extinction since prehistoric times.

erman's best friend, able to dive down to depths of 6m to retrieve broken nets. Now practically extinct (dog fanciers in the USA have snapped up many in recent years) it's the subject of a special breeding programme at Parque Natural da Ria Formosa's Quinta de Marim headquarters (p159). The park is also home to the strictly protected Mediterranean chameleon (p167), though its shifting colours can make it hard to spot!

Portugal's protected areas also harbour several endangered birds, including the majestic Spanish imperial eagle, the tawny owl in the Parque Nacional da Peneda-Gerês (p417), and the purple gallinule in the Parque Natural da Ria Formosa. Outside the parks you can see endangered species in Mértola, which hosts the country's largest nesting colony of lesser kestrels between March and September, or in the Castro Verde region, a haunt of the great bustard, Europe's heaviest bird weighing in at a whopping 17kg! (This is one of the heaviest birds capable of flight.)

Grupo Lobo is a wolf-conservation organisation and runs volunteer programmes. For more information on the disappearing Iberian wolf, see its website (http://lobo.fc.ul.pt).

Plants

Like its climate, Portugal's flora is a potent cocktail of Mediterranean and Atlantic elements. In spring, Mediterranean flowers set the countryside ablaze in the Algarve and Alentejo; especially enchanting are the white and purple rockroses. The pretty Bermuda buttercup, a South African invader, also paints Algarve fields a brilliant yellow in the winter. Orchid lovers will also have a wild time. They thrive in the Algarve, especially around Faro. Meanwhile, in the rainier northern climes, gorse, heather and broom cloak the hillsides.

Early settlers in the south cultivated vines and citrus trees, while the Moors introduced almonds, carobs, figs, palms and the gorgeous white irises that decorate roadsides. Portuguese explorers and colonists also got in on the act, bringing back various exotics, including South African figs and American prickly pear cacti. In Sintra you'll see dozens of exotic species, planted as fashionable novelties in the 18th and 19th centuries. More recently, profitable plantations of Australian eucalyptus have engulfed vast areas with their thirsty monoculture.

Incredibly, up to a third of Portugal's species are of foreign origin.

PUT A CORK IN IT

Doggedly battling it out with commercial giants like the eucalyptus are two home-grown trees that have long crafted Portugal's landscape and lifestyle: the olive and the cork oak, the latter now a threatened species. Since Roman times both have been grown and harvested in harmony with the environment, providing not only income but protection for many other species.

Travel across the vast Alentejo plains and you'll see many thousands of cork oak trees: they're the tall, round-topped evergreens with glossy, holly-like leaves and wrinkled bark that's often stripped away, leaving a strangely naked, ochre trunk.

Every year around 15 billion natural cork bottle-stoppers are produced in Portugal.

Indeed the cork oak has long been one of the country's prize agricultural performers and Portugal is the biggest cork producer in the world. Treasured for its lightness, admired for its insulating and sealing qualities, more versatile than any synthetic alternative, cork is used for everything from footwear to floors, gaskets to girders. And – of course – for bottle stoppers. The absence of smell and taste make it the essential 'bung' for quality wines.

Cork is cultivated as carefully as port wine. Trees mature for at least 25 years before their first stripping; indeed, there are laws against debarking too early. After that they may only be shorn every ninth year. Cork cutters slice and snip by hand, as skilfully as barbers. Treated with such respect, a tree can produce cork for up to 200 years: moreover, the largest cork tree in Portugal produced over a tonne of raw cork last time it was harvested. Now that's a lot of bottles bunged!

But this exceptionally sustainable industry is now under threat. There have long been critics of cork stoppers – some 300 million bottles of wine a year do indeed end up 'corked', contaminated by an organic compound in the cork. Now there's growing worldwide use of a synthetic alternative: plastic.

And much is at stake if cork forests decline. These are areas of exceptional biological diversity on which various threatened species depend, including the Iberian lynx and Bonelli's eagle. An international campaign has been launched to promote 'real cork' and urge producers and retailers to publicise its importance. Check out the website www.corkqc.com for more on the natural cork campaign and the multimillion euro battle to improve the quality of organic bottle stoppers in the face of their synthetic competition.

NATIONAL PARKS

Portugal's myriad natural parks offer vast areas of unspoilt mountains, forests and coastal lagoons. And the reluctance of most Portuguese to go walking anywhere, let alone venture into remote areas, can be a huge bonus for travellers. Step even a short distance off the beaten track and you'll find that you have extraordinary landscapes all to yourself.

PORTUGAL'S WORLD HERITAGE SITES

- Mosteiro dos Jerónimos (1983; p92) and Torre de Belém, (1983; p93), Lisbon
- Mosteiro de Santa Maria da Vitória (1983; p271), Batalha
- Convento de Cristo (1983; p285), Tomar
- Historic Centre of Évora (1986; p203)
- Mosteiro de Santa Maria de Alcobaça (1989; p269), Alcobaça
- Cultural Landscape of Sintra (1995; p116)
- Historic Centre of Porto (1996; p348)
- Prehistoric Rock-Art Sites (1998; p382), Vale do Côa
- Historic Centre of Guimarães (2001; p397)
- Alto Douro Wine Region (2001; p381)

Parks & Reserves	Features	Activities	Page
Parque Nacional da Peneda-Gerês	lushly forested mountains, rock-strewn plateaus, hot springs, wolves, deer, birds of prey, long-horned cattle	spa, mountain biking, canoeing, hiking, horse riding, wildlife spotting	p417
Parque Natural da Arrábida	coastal mountain range, damaged in recent wildfires; birds of prey, diverse flora	horse & donkey riding, wildlife spotting	p144
Parque Natural da Ria Formosa	salty coastal lagoons, lakes, marshes & dunes; rich birdlife, Mediterranean chameleon	nature trails, bird-watching, beaches	p159
Parque Natural da Serra da Estrela	pristine mountains – Portugal's highest; rich bird life, rare herbs	exceptional hiking, skiing, paragliding, mountain biking	p323
Parque Natural da Serra de São Mamede	forest & brush covered mountains; rare plants	vultures, eagles, kites, black stork, wildlife spotting, walking	p230
Parque Natural das Serras de Aire e Candeeiros	limestone mountains, cave systems; covered in gorse & olive trees	caving, hiking, bird-watching, biking	p279
Parque Natural de Montesinho	remote oasis of peaceful grassland & forest; last wild refuge for Iberian wolf	wildlife spotting, mountain biking, hiking	p443
Parque Natural de Sintra-Cascais	rugged coastline & mountains; diverse flora	tours by jeep, walking, biking	p116
Parque Natural do Alvão	granite basin, pine forest, waterfalls; rich birdlife, deer, boar	hiking, biking, river trips, buying traditional handicrafts	p433
Parque Natural do Douro Internacional	canyon country with high cliffs & lakes; home to many endangered birds of prey	bird-watching, nature trails	p450
Parque Natural do Vale do Guadiana	gentle hills & plains, rivers; rare birds of prey, snakes, toads, prehistoric sites	wildlife spotting, walking, visiting prehistoric sites	p240
Parque Natural do Sudoeste Alentejano e Costa Vicentina	coastal cliffs & remote beaches; unique plants, otters, foxes, 200 bird types	wildlife spotting, 4WD trips	p194
Reserva Natural das Berlenga	remote islands in clear seas, rock formations, caves; seabirds	cruises, short walks	p259
Reserva Natural das Dunas de São Jacinto	thickly wooded coastal park; rich in bird life	bird-spotting, nature trails	p315
Reserva Natural do Estuário do Sado	estuary of mud, marshes, lagoons & dunes; birdlife incl flamingos, molluscs, bottlenose dolphins	wildlife spotting, canoeing, boat trips	p137
Reserva Natural do Sapal de Castro Marim e Vila Real de Santo António	marshland & salt pans; flamingo, spoonbills, avocet, caspian terns, white stork	bird-watching, botany	p168

The Parque Nacional da Peneda-Gerês (p417) is the only bona-fide *parque nacional* (national park) in Portugal, but there are also 24 other *parques naturais* (natural parks), *reservas naturais* (nature reserves) and *paisagens protegidas* (protected landscape areas). These areas total some 6500 sq km – just over 7% of Portugal's land area.

The Instituto da Conservação da Natureza (ICN; Map pp80–1) is the government agency responsible for the parks. Its **Divisão de Informática** (Information Division; ☎ 213 507 900; www.icn.pt; Rua de Santa Marta 55, Lisbon) has general information, but detailed maps and English-language material are surprisingly scant. Standards of maintenance and facilities vary wildly, and hopeful hikers may be disappointed by resources: 'trails' often turn out to be roads or nothing at all; the park 'map' a glossy leaflet for motorists; and 'park accommodation' a couple of huts, which are geared for school groups.

The Mediterranean chameleon, resident of the south coast, has a tongue longer than its body.

Nevertheless, exploring Portugal's mixed bag of natural parks is well worth the effort. Browse the table that shows Portugal's parks and nature reserves (p59) to get a picture of all the rich wildlife and diverse landscapes on offer.

ENVIRONMENTAL ISSUES

Portugal has been slow to wake up to its environmental problems, notably soil erosion, pollution, rubbish disposal and the effects of mass tourism on fragile coastal areas. Of growing concern, too, is the spread of huge, water-thirsty eucalyptus plantations that effectively destroy regional wildlife habitat and aggravate an already serious drought problem brought on by climatic change. While such intensively cultivated plantations continue to proliferate (now accounting for over one-fifth of the country's forest area), Portugal's traditional, sustainable cork plantations are under serious threat (p57).

Litter is a growing problem, but industrial development is to blame for Portugal's most polluted seasides – you'd be wise to avoid beaches near the industrial centre of Sines. Having said that, around 162 Portuguese beaches claim an international Blue Flag for cleanliness and some areas have undergone radical clean-ups in recent years.

However, disaster narrowly avoided Portugal's northwestern coast in November 2002 when the oil tanker *Prestige* spilled 6000 tonnes of oil off the Spanish Galician coast, causing one of the world's worst environmental catastrophes. The ship emptied its oily slick over much of the western Spanish and part of the French coastline. To keep up to date with water quality, get hold of the free, regularly updated map of coastal water, *Qualidade da Água em Zonas Balneares* from **Instituto da Água** (☎ 218 430 022; inforag@inag.pt).

RESPONSIBLE TOURISM

Every year around six million sun-seeking visitors cram into the overdeveloped beaches of the Algarve, permanently transforming the coastline and once-remote habitats. You can't halt the inexorable rise of hotel, villa and apartment-block complexes, but if you want to minimize your impact on the south's delicate landscapes, do beware of supposedly 'ecofriendly' tours such as jeep safaris that, though great fun, damage and disrupt natural habitats.

Instead you could choose organised walks, which are far less destructive plus you learn first-hand knowledge of environmental issues. Walks organised by Quercus, the country's leading environmental organisation (p61) are recommended, but we note other organisations offering guided walks in local listings in the regional chapters throughout this guide.

IT'S THOSE DARN DAMS AGAIN

Poor old Portugal faces a stark choice when it comes to water: go thirsty or be dammed. The country has built almost 100 dams to control its precious water supply, and in 2002 the government began filling the monstrous dam at Alqueva, near Beja (p205), creating the largest man-made lake in Europe.

The huge reservoir now submerges just over 100 sq miles of the arid Alentejo despite desperate environmental attempts to restrict its depth and size. Among its casualties are over a million oak and olive trees and the habitats of several endangered species, including Bonelli's eagle, the otter, black storks, bats and the Iberian lynx. And that's not even mentioning the stone-age art and Roman fortress now under water. Even the supposed beneficiaries – the farmers themselves – may increasingly find irrigation costs too high.

WATER SHORTAGES

It's water – or rather the lack of it – that is fast becoming Portugal's worst environmental nightmare. Years of terrible drought in the mid-1990s heralded an alarming trend that continues to grow. Every year around 3% of Portugal's forest goes up in flames, worsening soil erosion and devastating farmland. And matters have only got worse in recent years.

Brush and forest fires in northern and central Portugal in 2003 alone devastated around 2600 sq km of Portuguese land: that's an area roughly equivalent to Luxembourg. The summer of 2004 brought more calamity and caused irreparable damage to Parque Natural da Arrábida (p144) near Lisbon, among many other regions.

Portugal is not alone in its thirst. Squabbles with Spain continue over shared water sources. Unfortunately for Portugal, three of its major rivers – the Douro, the Tejo and the Guadiana – originate in Spain. And both countries desperately need this water for agriculture (which accounts for three-quarters of water use in Portugal), hydroelectricity and to counter their dire drought situation in the south. Despite water-sharing agreements with Portugal, Spain is increasing its withdrawals from the Guadiana in order to divert it to the dry south.

Meanwhile, Portugal's own answer to this water problem has been to erect a giant dam near Beja, causing enormous environmental damage and leaving activists foaming at the mouth (above).

An excellent general website on Portuguese environmental and nature-related topics is www.naturlink.pt.

ENVIRONMENTAL ORGANISATIONS

Almargem (☎ 289 412 959; Alto de São Domingos 14, 8100-536 Loulé) Active in the Algarve.

Associação Nacional de Conservação da Natureza (Quercus; National Association for the Conservation of Nature; ☎ 217 788 474; www.quercus.pt; Apartado 4333, 1503-003 Lisbon) Portugal's best and busiest environmental group is which has branch offices and education centres scattered around Portugal. In addition to churning out studies and publishing environmental guides, Quercus members are Portugal's most active campaigners for environmental causes. Some Quercus branches arrange field trips.

Grupo de Estudos de Ordenomento do Território e Ambiente (Geota; ☎ 213 956 120; www.geota.pt; Travessa do Moinho de Vento 17, 1200-727 Lisbon) This environment study group is also an activist organisation which arranges weekend trips.

Liga para a Proteção da Natureza (LPN; League for the Protection of Nature; ☎ 217 780 097; www.lpn.pt; Estrela do Calhariz de Benfica 187, 1500-124 Lisbon) This is Portugal's oldest conservation group and often publicises environmental issues.

Food & Drink

Richard Sterling

When we think of Portugal we tend to think famous seafarers like Prince Henry the Navigator or Vasco da Gama. We think of one of the earliest European empires with possessions in Africa, India and the Far East. And we think of the spice trade which Portugal dominated for 100 years. And we think of port wine. But most of us in the Anglophone world don't think of food. Let us all repent and be educated. Admittedly, there aren't many Portuguese restaurants in our sphere. And since the Portuguese are such enthusiastic bibbers there isn't much of their table wines left for export. So start your education here, then go to Portugal for your advanced studies.

Portuguese food has been likened to what we like to call 'comfort food'. Yet it isn't the quiet comfort food that fills us with a lazy sense of well being. The Portuguese version is full of zest and verve. It makes you feel happy. It makes you feel like singing. It is full of colour and rich aroma. It feels good in the mouth. And it is supremely approachable. French cooking might be grand, but you almost need to go to school to learn how to enjoy it. Not so the Portuguese! It beckons. The Portuguese table is generous, reflecting the abundance of its land and its people's heart. But, above all, Portuguese cookery is an endless series of acts of love, produced by a people who love to love.

Did Portuguese fishermen discover America, long before Columbus, while following the codfish? Could be.

STAPLES & SPECIALITIES

Take a drive along the coast in Viana do Castelo or Aveiro between March and June. What you will see is what the entire coast of Portugal used to look like until quite recently: miles and miles of fish gutted and splayed out to the open air, salted and drying in the sun. Most of it is codfish for the making of what we can rightly call Portugal's national dish, *bacalhau*. It is impossible to underestimate the gastronomic importance of *bacalhau* to these seafaring people. It keeps on long journeys, it's cheap and nutritious. It has sustained them for centuries and they seem to have an almost mystic relationship with it. It is often said that a Portuguese housewife has 365 recipes for *bacalhau,* and if she prepared all of them

TOP FIVE RESTAURANTS

People often ask which are the best restaurants. That's impossible to say. But we can say which ones we think are good representatives of their type or region.

- **Don Tonho** (p361) Set into the quayside arches on Porto's picturesque Ribeira waterfront, just below the towering Ponte Dom Luis I, is this elegant place for *bacalhau* (salt cod) and other traditional Portuguese favourites.
- **Palace Hotel do Buçaco** (p306) This ex-royal retreat hidden in the forest is as much about devouring your fairy-tale surroundings as the excellent food.
- **Adega Faustino** (p438) On a more earthy footing, this cavernous old wine warehouse offers a taste of Northern specialities passed through generation after generation.
- **Restaurante O Fialho** (p213) The kind of restaurant that people talk of in hushed, awed voices: it takes its Alentejan food seriously.
- **Restô** (p104) More about the views than the food (though it's Portuguese with an exotic twist), this restaurant seems to float above the twinkling city.

TRAVEL YOUR TASTE BUDS

Portuguese cuisine is not like the haute cuisine of France, the highly varied cuisine of China or the spicy fare of Malaysia. It's home-style cooking, but it's home-style cooking as art. It's also the art of individuality. Cooks are much given to putting their own twist on a traditional recipe or to combining ingredients that others might not. *Carne de porco à alentejana* is a dish of braised pork with baby clams, a sort of Portuguese surf and turf. Care for bacon as dessert? Try *pasteis de toucihno,* sweet bacon tartlets, a treat in the south. Few peoples in the world feast on *lapas* (limpets), but the Portuguese braise the tiny little conical molluscs with garlic and swoon for them. And in this land of carnivores you might be lucky to find *sopa de legumes* (vegetable soup).

We Dare You

When the Portuguese slaughter a pig for food then food it shall be, all of it. Not just hams and trotters and shoulders, but brains, organs, guts and all. They will eat everything but the oink. The blood will be made into sausage, rather like an English black pudding. The entrails will be fried or tossed into a stew. The stomach lining will be removed and consigned to soup. Bits of brain and hunks of heart and kilos of kidneys will find their way to market, and to the menu you'll soon be holding in your hand.

in the space of one year her family would not likely complain. The fish are caught in cold northern waters around Iceland, Newfoundland and Norway, but they are brought back to Portugal for the salting and drying. When you buy *bacalhau* from the shop it looks more like a fossil than a fish. It can be hard as a rock, and will often be dusted with fine salt. But soak it overnight and it comes back to life. The salt leaches out and the texture is tender yet firm, offering something to the teeth. It is delicious when simply cooked plain in a pan, or any of 364 other ways.

Cod: A Biography of the Fish That Changed the World (1998) by Mark Kurlansky is a fascinating account of how this simple yet crucial food affected the peoples whose lives it touched and the historic events that ensued.

Portuguese will eat anything else that swims in the sea. Grilled sardines are a favourite, especially when cooked over a wood fire. The Portuguese often cook them without cleaning them, cooking them head, guts and all. But they don't eat the guts. Compare them, though, with the gutted. You'll find that those 'unedited' fish are more flavourful. They go especially well with *vinho verde* (semisparkling young wine: more later). Another popular fish is tuna, served as a big fat steak. You'll often see *espada* (scabbard fish), not to be confused with *espadarte* (swordfish), also much in evidence. Squid, cuttlefish and octopus are so common you might stop being aware of them. But keep your eyes open for them and try them deep fried as a finger food, something to munch on during your walkabout.

Folk wisdom here says that when you need strength for your mighty labours you must resort to meat. Perhaps the most common meat is pork, and if you don't have at least one meal of roast suckling pig you just haven't been to Portugal. As for fowl, chicken is fire grilled all over the land and is superb.

In *Portuguese Homestyle Cooking,* by Ana Patuleia Ortins (2002), 'frugal cuisine' is made rich and satisfying with an ample collection of authentic recipes.

No Portuguese meal is complete without the holy trinity of bread, olive oil and wine. Bread is the most basic food of this land, and you'll usually find it dense, chewy and delicious. It's the main ingredient in *açorda* (bread soup). Olive oil is the preferred cooking medium, as well as condiment, sauce and gravy. And without wine it's not a meal, just a snack. While meat, fish and fowl are prized, humbler fare such as beans and rice find their way to the table daily. Rarely are they simply boiled plain. They are made into savoury soups and stews and casseroles, richly embellished with sausages or herbs or meat essences. Garlic is the herb par excellence, followed by parsley. And while black pepper is used sparingly, the Portuguese love the fiery chilli sauce *piri piri.* Sugar and eggs are the chief ingredients in Portuguese sweets. Rich and creamy custards and cakes come trooping gaily from every Portuguese kitchen. Perhaps the national dessert would be *pudim*, a deceptively light custard flavoured with Baileys Irish Cream.

Portuguese wild boar is fattened on an exclusive diet of acorns. Makes them yummy!

The Portuguese begin the day with a minuscule breakfast, perhaps a piece of toast, maybe with a small glass of wine. Then, of course, by lunch time they are ravenous and can think only of food and drink. Perhaps that's why they don't mind eating in smoke-filled rooms with TVs blaring and the occasional dog wandering in. A three-course lunch may sound small, but portions are huge. After two hours at the table they might return to work or enjoy a siesta. Dinner will be quite late, and somewhat lighter than lunch, but just as smoky. Get used to it.

DRINKS

Wine & Port

The Portuguese are among the most bibulous people in the world. They can start the day with a glass of wine, and will always end it with same, or with a glass of *aguardente* (distilled spirits). And yet it is rare to see a Portuguese falling down drunk, and alcoholism is almost unknown. Perhaps it's because they drink from small glasses. And they don't binge drink, preferring to have a tipple throughout the day.

Perhaps the best known table wine of Portugal is that innocuous pink stuff, Mateus Rose. But, then, that's about all the table wine Portugal exports. The people drink all the rest. And there is a staggering variety in Portugal. The great export of this land, though, is, of course, port. But this is not a purely Portuguese dram. The British were instrumental in its development into the wine as we know it, as they were always the chief market for it. This is why so many port labels bear British names such as Warre and Sandeman.

The Portuguese don't drink much port. It's more an English drop. Lucky for us.

Port begins as a rather unremarkable red wine. Although it is remarkable that port is still commonly trodden, by human foot, rather than crushed by machine. The purpose of this is to extract as much content from the grape skins as possible, adding to its rich character. While the wine is still fermenting and still has a high sugar content it is 'fortified' with brandy. This halts fermentation by killing the yeast, thus maintaining the sugar content. It also gives this unremarkable wine remarkable ageing ability. Even a relatively short time in cask produces a sweet yet balanced wine with a rich bouquet, a gem-like colour and a complex flavour that lingers long after it leaves your mouth.

There are several different kinds of port, but three are most common:

Ruby Taking its name for its colour, this is a young port, very fruity, aged up to three years in wood. It's generally the least expensive and you'll see it everywhere.

Tawny Taking its name for its colour, anywhere from gold to reddish brown, this is a blend of wines of different ages. The blending master seeks a balance of the fruit of a young wine and the complexity of a more mature wine.

Vintage This is the granddaddy of ports. All the wine used must be of the same year and of highest quality. Only about three years in ten qualify for the making of vintage port. It can be, and often is, aged for decades before being released. It is very complex, with a bouquet that often fills a room. Some of the best vintages of the 20th century include 1900, 1908, 1937 and 1963. 1970 is great but still finding its way to market.

Port has a cousin in Madeira, grown on the island of the same name. It begins as an unremarkable white wine that is fortified with brandy. What really sets it apart from its mainland cousin is that this wine is 'cooked'. It spends several months in an *estufa*, a heated vat. The effect is to slowly caramelize some of the sugars in the wine, giving it a richer, more complex taste. Madeira can take on colours from tawny to almost chocolate. The main varieties are Sercial (dry and light), Bual (medium sweet and golden) and Malmsey (quite sweet and dark).

As for table wines, you are about to enter the Land of Confusion. The astonishing variety of Portuguese wines is matched by their astonishing inconsistency in labeling. Wines of the same grape variety might be called something different depending on where they are grown. Wines of the same region might be called the same thing even though they are of different varieties. Portugal is a land of innumerable smallholdings. And, up until recent times, communication between regions was poor. Hence we have a case of great regional pride, and ignorance of what goes on in other regions. But the dichotomy doesn't bother the Portuguese, so don't let it bother you. If you never come to understand a Portuguese wine label, you'll be in the same boat as most of the Portuguese. Try a little of this, a little of that, wherever you happen to be. You'll soon find out what pleases you most. And very little of it is expensive: experimentation is quite affordable.

The world's only source of cork for closing wine bottles is Portugal.

There are, thankfully, a few constants of the Portuguese wine world. Throughout the country you should be able to find *vinho verde* (green wine), perhaps Portugal's signature wine. It takes its name from the fact that the grapes are harvested before full ripeness. This produces a light, crisp dry wine that goes especially well with what is often a cuisine high in fat and salt. While there are red *vinhos verdes,* most are white and usually made from the Alvarinho grape. If it is, it will say so on the label. It's not quite a sparkling wine, but it can have a slight 'schpritz'. If you see a wine with 'Estremadura' on the label you've found one from the region most heavily under vines, and with good reason. This is an excellent wine-growing region and the people here have been at it since at least medieval times. Watch especially for wines made by Bucelas and Colares. A very good red is Ramisco, and you won't be disappointed in white Malvasia.

Other Drinks

Beer is almost as popular as wine, but the Portuguese have a curious attitude towards it. It's a drink to be taken by itself, or with a light snack. Wine is the drink to take with food, and you will cause raised eyebrows if you ask for beer at table. You may, however, have it for breakfast, which is not considered a meal. On draught you may order *um imperial* (200mL), *um principe* (330mL), *uma caneca* (500mL) or, if you have a sailor's thirst, *um girafe* (1000mL). Sagres, a full-flavoured brew, is the biggest seller. Cristal is refreshing, and Super Bock is malty and is no small beer. *Aguardente* is the term for distilled spirits, not to be confused with brandy. Brandy is made from fruit or wine.

A good website for information on Portuguese wines, especially port, is www.vino.com/explore/explore.asp?CID=11&Cat=2. It also includes some recipes and words on cuisine.

Aguardente can be made from whatever is to hand. When it's good it's very very good, and when it's bad it's horrid. Good or horrid, this is what the Portuguese like to end a meal with.

As for nonalcoholic drinks, tea is very lacklustre. You'd do best to bring your own if you're used to drinking premium teas. Lipton's is about the best you'll get here. Aside from women drinking *cha com limao* (lemon tea) it's just not thought much of. Coffee, on the other hand, is superb. The Portuguese were among the first European coffee traders and they've had lots of practice. Ironically, they are not great consumers of the bean. They might have *uma bica* (short black) in the morning or as a midday pick-me-up, but they drink a lot more wine and beer than coffee.

Water is just as important as wine, and your water glass will be larger than your wine glass. The message is clear. Some waters are promoted as having medicinal qualities, and they are labelled as *água minero-medicinal.* For still water ask for *sem gas*; for sparkling *com gas.*

CELEBRATIONS

The Portuguese seem to live to celebrate. And their favourite way to celebrate is with food and drink. Throw in a little music and dancing and you've got the Portuguese meaning of life. Most celebrations stem from three sources and through their food and drink they imbibe those sources: the Christian calendar, the harvest, and important dates in Portuguese history. Ninety-seven per cent of the people are Roman Catholic, a large percentage are still attached to the land and its abundance, and all are keenly aware of their country's past. While most celebrations are observed nationwide, every community celebrates its own patron saint, and some celebrate a historic day for the community.

On the religious calendar Pascoa (Easter) is by far the most important date. Just as in the Anglophone world, eggs play a part in the festivities, though the Portuguese prefer to make omelettes rather than hide eggs. The eggs symbolise new life and rebirth and, in fact, have done so since before Christianity. Also on the Easter table are roast lamb, piglet or kid, again symbols of new life. And to mix their symbols (for greater symbolism one assumes) they will bake a pie of eggs and lamb.

For more information on Portugal's celebrations see www.portugal.org/tourism/calendar07.shtml.

Carnaval, which is the Latin for 'farewell to meat', marks the beginning of Lent, the 40 days before Easter during which the pious take no meat and vow to give up other goodies or vices. The Portuguese have goodies and vices in abundance, so they pull out all the stops the day before Lent. The signature dish of Carnaval is *cozida à portuguesa*, a soupy stew of sausages, meats and vegetables.

Sometimes the Portuguese don't need any excuse to celebrate. Witness Domingos Gastronomicos (Gastronomic Sundays). In many parts of the country from February to May every Sunday selected restaurants will prepare local regional dishes and publish their historical or social significance. Even schools get involved with children doing the cooking or learning from their parents.

WHERE TO EAT & DRINK

As a general rule, if you see a restaurant whose name includes the word 'internacional', walk on. Likewise if it's full of well-dressed people speaking English or German. And be suspicious of any place boasting 'regional' or 'genuine' *cozinha* (cuisine). But no matter what the name, if you see it full of locals looking happy, that's the best recommendation you can get. Whatever place you choose, the operating hours, as well as the name of the owner, will be plainly posted out front. Be aware that many eateries are closed on Sunday. Only very smart restaurants take bookings, so it's usually first come, first served. But if it looks like a long wait, just walk on. There is always another good choice just down the street.

Restaurants come by many names, but there is often little difference between them. Certainly one type that is distinct and should not be missed is the *churrasqueira*. Think of it as a place that raises the humble char-grilled chicken *(frango no churrasco)* to the level of fine art. Portuguese chickens are nothing like the pale, mass-produced fowl we are used to. These birds are raised in barnyards where they grow up fat, happy and tasty. At the *churrasqueira* they are so succulent and flavourful that they need no adornment, though you may like to dab on a little *piri piri.*

At the *grill restaurante* you'll find four-legged fare in abundance, grilling over flames. There may or may not be a printed menu, but the meat is on display in glass cases. Pork will be plentiful, but you'll also find excellent beef and lamb. Portions are large enough to have you staggering from the table with your plate still half full.

For fish, betake yourself to the *marisqueira* (seafood house). Here your dinner swims live in tanks or reposes on beds of ice on display. Not just fin fish but all manner of crustacea. So saunter in, pick your dinner and pay by weight. And be aware that this is pricey dining. The locals come here mainly for special occasions.

For snacking and socialising over a cold beer you'll want a *cervejaria* (beer hall). They are open all day and well into the night. They may offer as little as one beer on tap and a few in bottle, the one on tap being the local favourite. But it's very pleasant to stand at the bar nursing a cold one on a hot day and munching on the salty snacks that go so well with it. You simply must try the roasted pig ears. They're very chewy and last a long time. But you can also have a bit of ham, a fish cake or *chourico,* a spicy pork sausage.

The Portuguese still season fish with *garum*, a fermented fish sauce (like the Thai version) used by the ancient Romans.

A proper sit-down restaurant is the *restaurante*. Here you can find the best and the worst of Portuguese dining. When they are good they are very very good, but when they are bad the service is indifferent, the food forgettable, the linens old and dirty. These establishments are relatively new on the Portuguese culinary scene, and they simply haven't got it completely right yet. Remember that this is a land of home-style cookery, not a Parisian café society.

VEGETARIANS & VEGANS

Vegetarians and vegans, are you ever a long way from home! The very idea of avoiding meat is foreign to the Portuguese. This is partly due to the fact that until fairly recently meat was very dear for the average person, and the eating of meat was a status symbol. Many people still remember those days of poverty. And, besides, they just love their meat, fish and fowl. If you can eat eggs and dairy products you'll survive. If your dietary code is simply 'nothing with ears' you'll do all right on a diet of fish. But if your code is 'nothing with a face' you might want to pack a lunch. In a restaurant greenery is a rare sight. Salad is insipid, just a couple of leaves and a slice of tomato and onion. You can look for *caldo verde*, a kale and potato soup, but ask what the stock is made from. You can always ask for *tem alguma hortaliça,* a plate of vegetables, and you might get it. Beware of innocent-looking pastries. They are often made with lard. If you plan to stick to a strict code you're going to have to DIY. Betake yourself to the market to purchase your provender and eat it in exile. Or you could base yourself in an Algarve resort where they cater to a wider range of customers and diets. A little online research ahead of time will yield some results for places like Lisbon and Loulé.

GETTING TIPSY

Tipping can be a little confusing for the visitor. Often there is a service charge. Check your bill closely, and if there is a service charge then there is no need to tip. If there is no service charge then the customary tip is 5% to 10% depending on how well you enjoyed the meal. In many simple establishments the waiter may write out your tab next to your plate on the paper table covering, or even on your serviette. It is safe to assume then that there was no service charge levied.

There are still many places that don't accept credit cards. And they generally don't have any sign announcing it. Ask.

WHINING & DINING

The Portuguese are very family-oriented people and they love children more than anything. Yours will be welcome to all but places of adult entertainments. If it's not a busy time in a restaurant some of the staff will likely fuss over your kids, give them some candy or in some way entertain them. Children's menus are not common, but they are usually able to take a *meia dose* (half-portion) at half-price. (Adults have the same option in traditional places.) Or they can simply share your meal. Don't be surprised to see kids about 14 or 15 being given a little wine, usually mixed with water. The Portuguese are steady drinkers but they are responsible drinkers, cultivating habits of moderation from an early age. For between-meal snacks you can take the kids to the *minimercado* (a kind of convenience store) or the *hipermercado* (like an inexpensive supermarket). Keep in mind that Portuguese pastries can be very heavy, and can spoil an appetite easily if taken close to meal time. Consider giving them fruit for snacks. After all, they're going to see precious little plant food in the restaurant.

Check out www.palcus.org/network/food.html. It is a page of links to recipes, Portuguese restaurants worldwide and online suppliers of Portuguese foods and wines.

HABITS & CUSTOMS

Welcome to the most user-friendly tables of Europe. You'll usually get a plate, a knife, a fork, a wine glass and a paper serviette. None of these will be changed in the course of the meal unless you break one. If you ask for it you'll get a water glass. If you order a shot of spirits afterward, as the locals will likely do, you'll receive another glass for that. As for table manners, just try to show how much you are enjoying yourself. Talk boisterously and in a loud voice. Flail your hands about, pointing and gesticulating with your knife and fork, and pound the table once for emphasis. If you use tobacco feel free to light up a ciggie or a stogie and blow smoke in your neighbour's face. He's probably blowing smoke in your face already. If you see a wash basin in a *tasca* (a working-class restaurant or tavern), avail yourself of it before eating. It's the custom.

There is only one caveat at the Portuguese table: don't ask for salt and pepper. If *piri piri* is offered you are welcome to use it. But asking for any other kind of seasoning or condiment is to cast aspersions on the cook. And cooks are highly respected people in Portugal. You don't want to get on their bad side.

EAT YOUR WORDS

Want to know *piri piri* from *pimenta*? *Cachorro* from *cachucho*? Get behind the cuisine scene by getting to know the language. For pronunciation guidelines see p482.

Useful Phrases

Table for..., please. *Uma mesa para..., se faz favor.*
oo·ma *me*·za *pa*·ra..., se faz fa·*vorr*

Can I see the menu, please? *Posso ver o menu, por favor?*
po·so verr o me·*noo*, porr fa·*vorr*

Can I see the wine list, please? *Posso vera carta de vinhos, por favor?*
po·so *ve*·ra *kar*·ta de *vee*·nyozh, porr fa·*vorr*?

Can you recommend a good local wine? *Pode recomendar-me um bom vinho da regiao?*
po·de rre·ko·*meng*·darr-me oong bong *vee*·nyo da rre·*zheeow*?

Do you have a high chair for the baby? *Tem uma cadeira de bebe?*
teng *oo*·ma ka·*day*·ra de be·*be*?

I'll have a beer, please. *Vou tomar uma cervejar.*
vo to·*mar oo*·ma ser·ve·*zhar*

Can I have the bill/check, please. *A conta, se faz favor.*
a *kong*·ta, se faz fa·*vorr*

I'm vegetarian. *Sou vegetariano/a.*
so ve·zhe·ta·ree·*a*·no/a

Food & Drink Glossary

adega (a·*de*·ga) – cellar, usually wine cellar; also may denote a winery; also a traditional bar or bar-restaurant serving wine from the barrel
aguardente (a·gwar·*deng*·te) – strongly alcoholic 'firewater'
almôndegas (ow·*mong*·de·gazh) – meatball served in tomato gravy
cachorro (ka·*sho*·rro) – a tinned sausage usually served on a roll
cachucho (ka·*shoo*·sho) – sea bream
casa de pasto (*ka*·za de *pash*·to) – casual eatery
cervejaria (ser·ve·zha·*ree*·a) – beerhouse
chanfana (shang·*fa*·na) – mutton or goat stew cooked with red wine
churrasqueira (shoo·rrash·*kay*·ra) – grilled-chicken restaurant
confeitaria (kon·fay·ta·*ree*·a) – cake and pastry shop
dose (*do*·ze) – serving or portion
empada (eng·pa·*da*) – a little pot pie
escabeche (esh·ka·*besh*) – raw meat or fish marinated in vinegar and oil
espetada (esh·pe·*ta*·da) – kebab
favas (fa·*vazh*) – a dish of broad beans
gamba (gang·*ba*) – prawn
marisqueira (ma·reesh·*kay*·ra) – seafood house
meia dose (*may*·a *do*·ze) – half-portion
merenda (me·*reng*·da) – light snack
paio (pay·*oo*) – smoked pork sausage
pasteis de nata (*pash*·taysh de *na*·ta) – custard tart
pastelaria (pash·te·la·*ree*·a) – pastry and cake shop
pernil no forno (*per*·neel no *forr*·no) – roast leg of pork
pequeno almoço (pe·*ke*·no ow·*mo*·so) – breakfast, traditionally just coffee and a bread roll
pimenta (pee·*meng*·ta) – pepper
piri piri (*pee*·ree *pee*·ree) – fiery chili sauce; it is the signature condiment of Portugal
pudim (poo·*deeng*) – pudding
rota dos vinhos (*ro*·ta dozh *vee*·nyosh) – wine route
sardinhas assadas (sar·*dee*·nyazh a·*sa*·dash) – grilled sardines
simples (seeng·*plezh*) – plain, no filling or icing
tasca (*tash*·ka) – tavern
uma bica (*oo*·ma *bee*·ka) – short black
vindima (veeng·*dee*·ma) – grape harvest
vinho da casa (*vee*·nyo da *ka*·za) – house wine
vinho maduro (*vee*·nyo ma·*doo*·ro) – wine matured for more than a year
vinho verde (*vee*·nyo *ver*·de) – semisparkling young wine

Lisbon & Around

CONTENTS

As romantic as Paris, as fun as Madrid, as laid-back as Rome, but small enough to fit in their handbags – Lisbon is faded, beautiful and difficult to leave. It's aesthetically extraordinary, dipping and rising over seven hills, a twinkling palette of buildings resting on the Rio Tejo, overseen in an echo of Rio by the Cristo Rei statue on the opposite bank. The architecture has a *fin-de-siècle* decadence, snaked through with cobbled streets. Yellow trams and funiculars clunk over its hills, making picturesque work of the topography that splashes out shimmering views.

Lisbon is a city in thrall to the past: in the centre, low rents allow small, dusty shops specialising in hats, thread or dried cod to go strong; the city's latest (17.2km-long) bridge is named for its local hero, the 16th-century discoverer Vasco da Gama; Praça da Figueira – where Africans gather to chat – has been a meeting place since the cleric at a nearby church was African, around 300 years ago. Baroque cafés, 1960s diners, velvet-lined bars and Art Deco bakeries – all continue to bustle in Lisbon. It was suppression under Salazar that so preserved this rich fabric, which in other cities has been renovated into oblivion.

Over the last decade, EU membership, the enormous Expo 98 and the spotlight of the 2004 European Football championships have added some 21st-century polish, but this sprucing up hasn't shined away any charisma. And, hanging on to its outskirts, there is still more to explore: the out-there magic of Sintra, great, sweeping beaches and beautiful national parks.

HIGHLIGHTS

- **Indulgence**
  Pasteís de Belém – a secret-recipe custard tart (p106)
- **Old Town Stroll**
  The ancient Alfama district (p94)
- **Trundling Fun**
  Take tram No 28 from the Baixa (p94)
- **Boho au Go-Go**
  Bairro Alto – great nightlife, and Lux – one of Europe's best clubs (p107)
- **Matchless**
  Benfica vs Porto at Estádio da Luz (p111)
- **Tragic Magic**
  Fado – a shot of the Portuguese blues (p110)
- **Culture Vulture**
  The extraordinary collection of the Museu Calouste Gulbenkian (p89)
- **Fishy Business**
  The magical, under-the-sea world of the Oceanarió (p91)
- **Never-Never Land**
  Sintra's palaces and wooded hills (p116)

POPULATION (CITY): 564,660	AREA (CITY): 86.5 SQ KM

HISTORY

Immense riches, fires, plague, earthquakes, tidal waves, revolutions, coups and a dictatorship – Lisbon has certainly had a few ups and downs.

It's said that Ulysses was here first, but certainly the Phoenicians settled here 3000 years ago, calling the city Alis Ubbo (Delightful Shore). Others soon recognised its delightful qualities: the Greeks, then Carthaginians, then in 205 BC Romans, who stayed until the 5th century AD. After some tribal chaos, it was taken over by North African Moors in 714. They fortified the city they called Lissabona and fended off the Christians for 400 years.

But in 1147, after a four-month siege, Christian fighters (mainly British crusader-hooligan-pillagers) under Dom Afonso Henriques recaptured the city and, in 1260, Afonso III moved his capital here from Coimbra. Lisbon became the capital in 1256. Coimbra had been a fine capital while the Moors held sway in the centre of the country, but once they had been driven south, Lisbon's excellent port and the central position made it the ideal choice.

In the 15th and 16th centuries Lisbon boomed, the opulent centre of a vast empire after Vasco da Gama discovered a sea route to India. The party raged on into the 17th century, when gold was discovered in Brazil. Merchants flocked here, trading in gold, spices, silks and jewels. Frenziedly extravagant architecture held up a mirror to the era, with Manueline works such as Belém's Mosteiro dos Jerónimos.

But at 9.30am on All Saints' Day, 1 November 1755, everything changed. Three major earthquakes hit, as residents celebrated Mass. The tremors brought an even more devastating fire and tidal wave. Around 90,000 of the city's 270,000 inhabitants died and much of the city was ruined, never to recover its former status. Dom João I's chief minister, the redoubtable Marquês de Pombal, immediately coped with the crisis by rebuilding the city as quickly as possible, in a simple, cheap, easily managed style that created today's formal, gleaming grid. (Though it was the Marquês de Alorna who uttered the famous words, 'We must bury the dead, and feed the living'.)

In November 1807 Napoleon's forces occupied the city for the next four years and Lisbon slid with the rest of the country into chaos.

In 1908, at the height of the turbulent republican movement, Dom Carlos and his eldest son were assassinated in Praça da Comercio. The next 16 years saw 45 changes of government, and another high-profile assassination (President Sidónio Pais, at Rossio station in 1918). During WWII Lisbon (officially neutral) became packed with spies.

Two bloodless coups (in 1926 and 1974) rocked the city. In 1974–75 there was a massive influx of refugees from the former African colonies, changing the demographic of the city and adding to its richness culturally, if not financially.

After Portugal joined the European Community (EC) in 1986, massive EC funding started to boost redevelopment (welcome after a 1988 fire in Chiado). Streets became cleaner and investment improved facilities. Lisbon has spent the last decade dashing in and out of the limelight as 1994 European City of Culture, host of Expo 98 and the 2004 European Football Championships.

ORIENTATION

Lisbon's seven hills – Estrela, Santa Catarina, São Pedro de Alcântara, São Jorge, Graça, Senhora do Monte and Penha de França – sit on the northern side of Portugal's finest natural harbour, the wide mouth of the Rio Tejo. São Jorge is topped by the *castelo* (castle), and each of the others by a church or a stunning *miradouro* (viewpoint).

At the river's edge is the grand Praça do Comércio. Behind it march the streets of the Baixa (lower) district, up to Praça da Figueira and Praça Dom Pedro IV (aka Rossio).

Here the city forks along two arteries. Lisbon's splendid main street, Avenida da Liberdade, stretches 1.5km northwest from the Rossio and the adjacent Praça dos Restauradores to Praça Marquês de Pombal and the large Parque Eduardo VII. The other fork is the commercial strip of Avenida Almirante Reis, running north for almost 6km from Praça da Figueira (where it's called Rua da Palma) to the airport (p115), a bus or taxi ride away.

From the Baixa it's a steep climb west, through swanky shopping district Chiado, into the narrow-streeted nightlife-haven Bairro Alto. Eastwards from the Baixa it's another climb to the Castelo de São Jorge

LISBON IN…

Two Days

Start in the **Baixa** district, then explore **Alfama**, surveying the city from **Castelo St Jorge**. Have lunch in Alfama or Baixa, then take a tram to **Belém** in the afternoon, having a custard tart for tea. Thus fortified visit **Monasterio dos Jerominos** or spend the afternoon in the **Museu Calouste Gulbenkian**. In the evening eat in **Bairro Alto**, then pickle all that culture in its many bars. End the night at **Lux**, if you have the energy and inclination. On day two get a train out to **Sintra**. Head back to Lisbon, and a **fado** club.

Four Days

Explore **Alfama** and the **Museu Calouste Gulbenkian** the first day, finish up in **Bairro Alto** and **Lux**, then spend the second day in **Belém**. On the third day head out to **Sintra**, exploring the sights slowly and staying a night, before going back to Lisbon for a **fado** finale.

and the ancient, maze-like Alfama district around it.

River ferries depart from Praça do Comércio and from Cais do Sodré to the west. Lisbon's long-haul train stations are Santa Apolónia (1.5km east of Praça do Comércio), Rossio, Cais do Sodré, and Barreiro (across the Tejo). Gare do Oriente is the new kid on the transport block, combining bus, train and metro stations on the northeastern outskirts of town.

The city has two main long-distance bus terminals: Arco do Cego, on Avenida João Crisóstomo, near Saldanha metro station; and Gare do Oriente (see p113).

Besides metro and buses, there are ageing trams, with smart new ones running 6km west from Praça da Figueira to the waterfront suburb of Belém (see p116).

Lisbon is connected south across the Tejo to the Costa da Caparica and Setúbal Peninsula by the immense, 70m-high Ponte 25 de Abril, Europe's longest suspension bridge, which also carries trains to the suburbs. Vasco da Gama bridge – 17.2km long – reaches across the Tejo further north, from Sacavem (near Parque das Nações) to Montijo, speeding up north–south traffic.

Maps

Turismos dispense a small, free city map. Decent maps for sale in bookshops include the colourful 1:15,000 Falk *Lisboa*, and Michelin's regularly updated 1:10,000 *Lisboa Planta*. Kümmerly + Frey's 1:15,000 *Lisboa* includes bus and metro routes.

The 230-page *Guia Urbano* city atlas (€10), covers the city at 1:5000 (available at ICEP turismo, p83), though it's seldom updated.

Two government mapping agencies, the **Instituto Geográfico do Exército** (Map pp74–5) and **Instituto Gráfico Português** (Map pp80–1), supply excellent topographic maps. For details, see p461.

INFORMATION

Bookshops

Second-hand books are sold on Calçada do Carmo, behind Rossio station, and from some stalls in the arcades of Praça do Comércio at the end of Rua Augusta.

Librairie Française (Map pp80-1; ☎ 217 956 866; Avenida Marquês de Tomar 38) The city's only exclusively French bookshop.

Livraria Bertrand Chiado (Map pp76-8; ☎ 213 421 941; Rua Garrett 73); Greater Lisbon (Map p74-5; Centro Comercial Colombo shopping centre); Belém (Map p81; Centro Cultural de Belém) Dating to the 18th century, and Lisbon's biggest and best.

Livraria Buchholz (Map pp80-1; ☎ 213 170 580; Rua Duque de Palmela 4) Huge collection of literature in Portuguese, English, French and German.

Livraria Municipal (Map pp80-1; ☎ 213 530 522; Avenida da República 21A) A spacious, tiled bookshop, devoted entirely to Lisbon, with some titles in English.

Cultural Centres

British Council (Map p79; ☎ 213 214 595; Rua de São Marçal 174) In a palatial building; has a huge **library** (Rua Luís Fernandes 1-3; 🕑 2-6pm Mon-Fri), with the latest English newspapers.

Institut Franco-Portugais de Lisbonne (Map pp80-1; www.ifp-lisboa.com; Avenida Luís Bívar 91) Has regular cultural (including film) events, and a library called **Mediateca** (☎ 213 111 421).

(Continued on page 82)

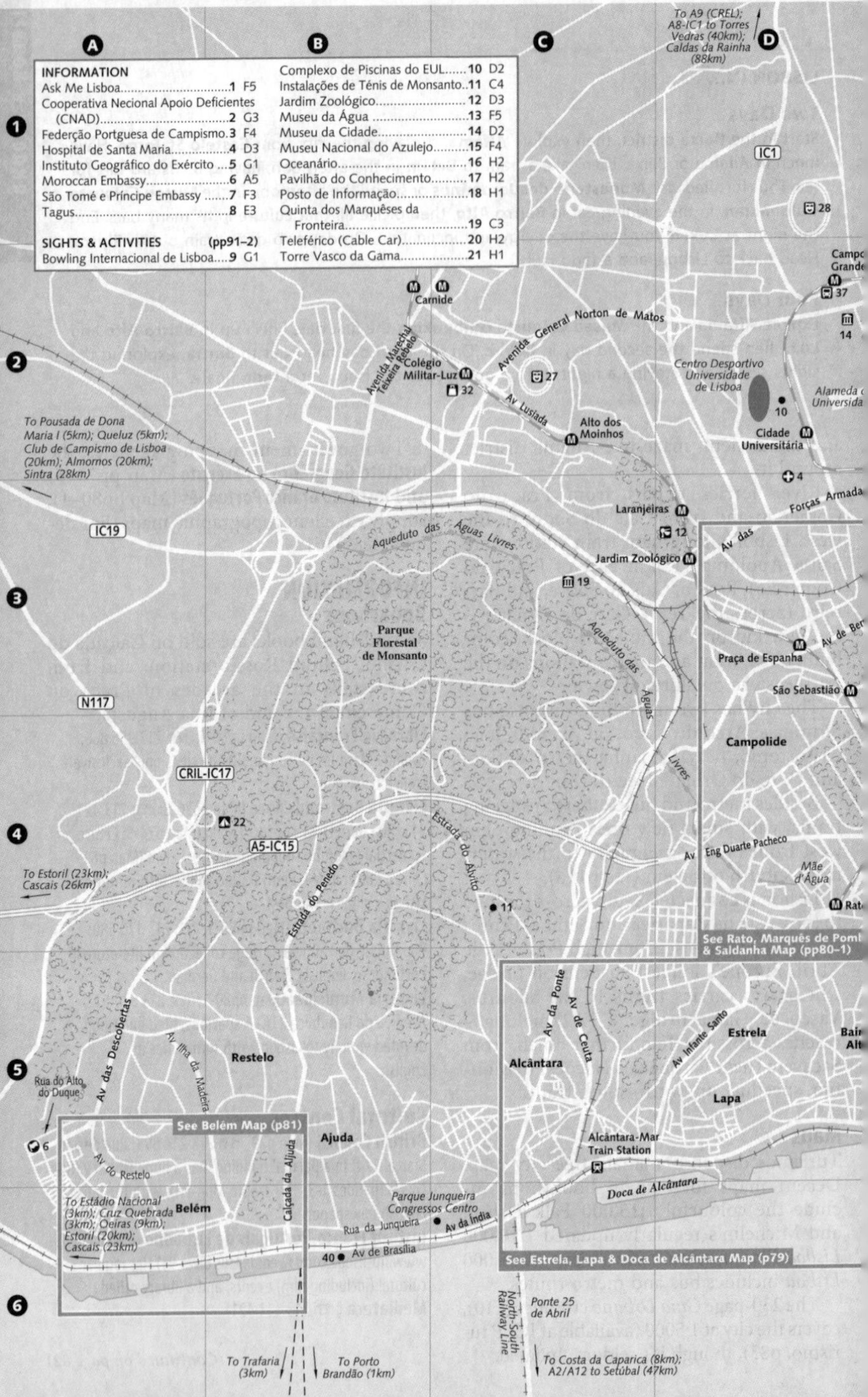

INFORMATION
Ask Me Lisboa 1 F5
Cooperativa Necional Apoio Deficientes (CNAD) 2 G3
Federção Portguesa de Campismo 3 F4
Hospital de Santa Maria 4 D3
Instituto Geográfico do Exército 5 G1
Moroccan Embassy 6 A5
São Tomé e Príncipe Embassy 7 F3
Tagus 8 E3
SIGHTS & ACTIVITIES (pp91–2)
Bowling Internacional de Lisboa 9 G1
Complexo de Piscinas do EUL 10 D2
Instalações de Ténis de Monsanto 11 C4
Jardim Zoológico 12 D3
Museu da Água 13 F5
Museu da Cidade 14 D2
Museu Nacional do Azulejo 15 F4
Oceanário 16 H2
Pavilhão do Conhecimento 17 H2
Posto de Informação 18 H1
Quinta dos Marquêses da Fronteira 19 C3
Teleférico (Cable Car) 20 H2
Torre Vasco da Gama 21 H1
To A9 (CREL); A8-IC1 to Torres Vedras (40km); Caldas da Rainha (88km)
IC1
Campo Grande
Carnide
Avenida Marechal Teixeira Rebelo
Colégio Militar-Luz
Avenida General Norton de Matos
Av Lusíada
Alto dos Moinhos
Centro Desportivo Universidade de Lisboa
Alameda da Universidade
Cidade Universitária
To Pousada de Dona Maria I (5km); Queluz (5km); Club de Campismo de Lisboa (20km); Almornos (20km); Sintra (28km)
IC19
Laranjeiras
Forças Armadas
Aqueduto das Águas Livres
Jardim Zoológico
Av das
Praça de Espanha
Av de Berna
São Sebastião
Parque Florestal de Monsanto
N117
Campolide
CRIL-IC17
A5-IC15
Estrada do Alvito
Av Eng Duarte Pacheco
Mãe d'Água
Rato
To Estoril (23km); Cascais (26km)
Estrada do Penedo
See Rato, Marquês de Pombal & Saldanha Map (pp80–1)
Av das Descobertas
Av Ilha da Madeira
Restelo
Av da Ponte
Av de Ceuta
Av Infante Santo
Estrela
Alcântara
Lapa
Rua do Alto do Duque
See Belém Map (p81)
Calçada da Ajuda
Ajuda
Alcântara-Mar Train Station
Av do Restelo
Doca de Alcântara
To Estádio Nacional (3km); Cruz Quebrada (3km); Oeiras (9km); Estoril (20km); Cascais (23km)
Belém
Parque Junqueira Congressos Centro
Rua da Junqueira
Av da Índia
Av de Brasília
See Estrela, Lapa & Doca de Alcântara Map (p79)
North-South Railway Line
Ponte 25 de Abril
To Trafaria (3km)
To Porto Brandão (1km)
To Costa da Caparica (8km); A2/A12 to Setúbal (47km)

0 1 km
0 0.5 miles

E
F
G
H
1
2
3
4
5
6

To A1-IP1 to Santarém (60km); Porto (305km)
To Ponte Vasco da Gama (1.5km); A12 to Setúbal (45km); A2-IP1 to the Algarve (240km)
Aeroporto de Lisboa
36
Av Dr Alfredo Bensaúde
5
Av Dom João II
23
Av de Boa Esperança
21
39
Parque das Nações
Fil; Lisbon Exhibition Centre
Av Cidade do Porto
Av de Berlim
Olivais Norte
Gare do Oriente
9
Oceanos
Rua da Pimenta
38
33
18
30
20
31
Avenida Marechal Craveiro Lopes
Av Marechal Gomes da Costa
Cabo Ruivo
Olivais
Doca dos Olivais
16
17
Alameda dos
Teatro Camões
26
Rua D Fuas Roupinho
Avenida Infante Dom Henrique
Avenida Almirante Gago Coutinho
Alvalade
Chelas
Av do Santo Condestável
Biblioteca Nacional
Av dos Estados Unidos da América
Roma
Entrecampos
2
Bela Vista
Entrecampos Poente Train Station
Entrecampos Train Station
7
Campo Pequeno
Areeiro
8
Av da República
Av 5 de Outubro
Olaias
Alameda
Estrada de Chelas
Av Infante Dom Henrique
Saldanha
Av Almirante Reis
Arroios
Picoas
Parque
Igreja de Penha de França
Av Dom Alfonso III
Av Mouzinho de Albuquerque
Anjos
3
Marquês de Pombal
de Campismo
Xabregas
Intendente
15
35
34
Avenida
Av Infante Dom Henrique
13
Martim Moniz
Rossio Train Station
Restauradores
Graça
Rossio
Castelo
1
29
24
25
Baixa-Chiado
Alfama
Santa Apolónia
Baixa
Cais do Sodré Train & Metro Station
Praça do Comércio
RIO TEJO

See Baixa, Alfama & Castelo Map (pp76–8)

To Cacilhas (2km); Almada (3km)
To Barreiro (9km)
To Montijo; Seixal; Reserva Natural do Estuário do Sado

SLEEPING (pp100–1)
Lisboa Camping – Parque Municipal......22 B4
Pousada da Juventude da Lisboa Parque Nações......23 G1

EATING (p104)
Bica do Sapato......24 F5
Casanova......25 F5

ENTERTAINMENT (pp106–12)
Bugix......26 H2
Estádio da Luz (SL Benfica)......27 C2
Estádio José de Alvalade......28 D1
Fnac......(see 32)
Lux......29 F5
Pavilhão Atlântico......30 H1
Pavilhão de Portugal......31 H2

SHOPPING (pp112–13)
Centro Comercial Colombo......32 C2
Centro Vasco da Gama......33 G1
Cerâmica Viúva Lamego......34 E4
Livraria Bertrand......(see 32)
Olaria do Desterros......35 E4
Sneakers Delight......(see 25)

TRANSPORT (pp113–16)
Airporto de Lisboa......36 E1
Bus Station for Ericeira, Mafra, Peniche, Torres Vedras & Malveira......37 D2
Eurolines Ticket Office......(see 38)
Gare do Oriente......38 G1
Tejo Bike......39 H1
Tejo Bike......40 B6

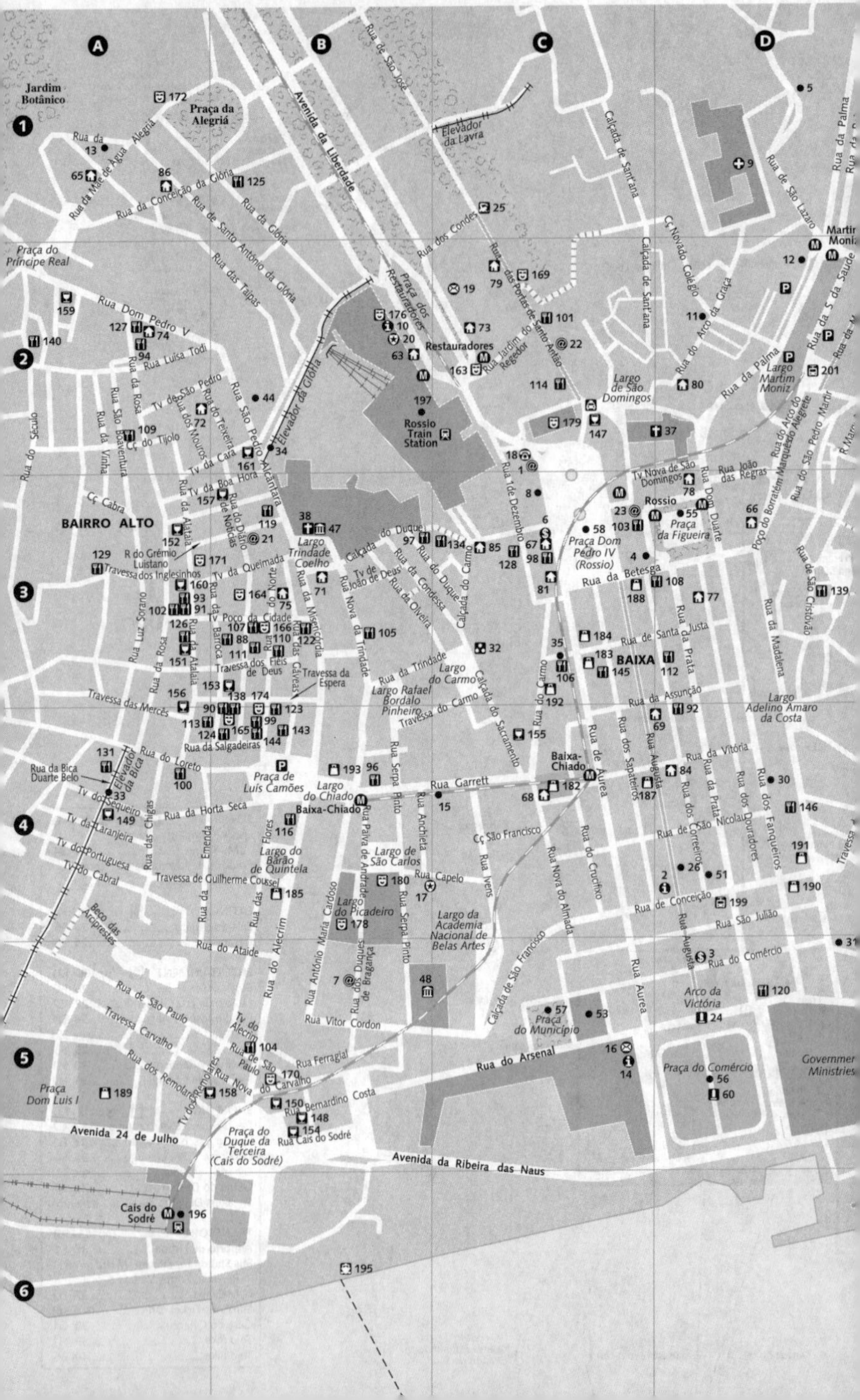
Jardim Botânico
Praça da Alegriá
Praça do Príncipe Real
BAIRRO ALTO
BAIXA
Avenida da Liberdade
Elevador da Lavra
Elevador da Glória
Restauradores
Rossio Train Station
Largo de São Domingos
Rossio
Praça da Figueira
Praça Dom Pedro IV (Rossio)
Largo Trindade Coelho
Largo do Carmo
Largo Rafael Bordalo Pinheiro
Baixa-Chiado
Praça de Luís Camões
Largo do Chiado
Largo de São Carlos
Largo do Picadeiro
Largo da Academia Nacional de Belas Artes
Largo do Barão de Quintela
Praça do Município
Arco da Victória
Praça do Comércio
Government Ministries
Praça Dom Luís I
Praça do Duque da Terceira (Cais do Sodré)
Cais do Sodré
Largo Martim Moniz
Largo Adelino Amaro da Costa
Rua do Arsenal
Avenida 24 de Julho
Avenida da Ribeira das Naus
Rua Garrett
Rua Augusta
Rua Áurea
Rua da Prata
Rua dos Fanqueiros
Rua Dom Pedro V
Rua da Misericórdia
Rua do Loreto
Rua da Horta Seca
Rua do Alecrim
Rua da Palma
Rua de São Lázaro
Calçada de Sant'ana
Rua das Portas de Santo Antão
Rua dos Condes
Rua de São José

0 200 m
0 0.1 miles
E
F
G
H
1
2
3
4
5
6
Rua do Benformoso
Rua das Olarias
Cç do Monte
Rua Damasceno Monteiro
Rua da Graça
Rua do Sol à Graça
Rua da Bela Vista
Rua da Senhora da Glória
GRAÇA
Rua Leite de Vasconcelos
Largo da Graça
Rua da Verónica
Rua de Entremuros do
Rua do Terreirinho
Largo das Olarias
Rua dos Lagares
Rua dos Cavaleiros
Largo do Terreirinho
Calçada de Santo André
Rua de Ponte do Lima
Calçada da Graça
Travessa das Mónicas
Rua da Voz do Operário
Campo de Santa Clara
Arco Grande da Cima
Costa do Castelo
Largo de Rodrigues de Freitas
Calçada de São Vincente
Largo do Outeirinho da Amendoeira
Campo de
Santa Clara
Rua do Paradiso
Santa Apolónia Train Station
Largo de Santa Marinha
Castelo de São Jorge
Santa Cruz
CASTELO
Rua de São Tomé
Rua das Escolas Gerais
Rua dos Corvos
Rua do Vigário
Rua do Museu de Artilharia
Rua Cruz do Castelo
Rua G ilherme
Esplanada do Castelo
R Santa
Rua do Chão da Feira
Tv de Santa Luzia
Largo das Portas do Sol
Santa
Beco de Helena
ALFAMA
Igreja de Santo Estêvão
Largo Contador Mor
Igreja de São Tiago
Igreja de Santa Luzia
Rua dos Remédios
Rua do Jardim do Tabaco
Avenida Infante Dom Henrique
Rv da Mata
Lg do Loios
Rua de São Tiago
Rua de São Miguel
Igreja de São Miguel
Rua de São Mamede
R do Limoeiro
Rua da Saudade
Largo das Alcaçarias
Rua Terreiro do Trigo
Largo do Chafariz de Dentro
Rua das Pedras Negras
Pátio do Aljube
Santo António
Rua Augusto Rosa
Largo de São Martinho
Doca do Jardim do Tabaco
Largo da Sé
Sé
Cruzes da Sé
Rua do Barão
Praça
Rua de São João da
Rua Afonso de Albuquerque
Arco de Jesu
Rua dos Bacalhoeiros
Rua da Alfândega
Campo das Cebolas
Avenida Infante Dom Henrique
Doca da Marinha
Santa Apolónia Train Station
(due to open 2005)
RIO TEJO
To Barreiro
To Montyo; Seixal
43
62
41
200
42
186
95
181
76
70
54
39
29
52
46
194
132
40
137
167
121
87
45
117
175
133
118
162
135
27
59
177
49
89
130
64
168
82
136
115
28
83
142
173
141
36
61
198

INFORMATION

Abracadabra 1 C2
Ask Me Lisboa 2 D4
ATM & Cash Exchange Machine 3 D5
Carris Ticket Kiosk 4 C3
Centro Comunitário Gay e Lésbico de Lisboa 5 D1
Cota Câmbios 6 C3
Cyber Bica 7 B5
Farmácia Estácio 8 C3
Hospital de São José 9 D1
ICEP Turismo 10 B2
International Telephone Service 11 D2
Lavandaria Lina 12 D2
Lave Neve 13 A1
Lisboa Welcome Centre 14 C5
Livraria Bertrand 15 C4
Main Post Office 16 C5
Police Headquarters 17 B4
Pontonet (see 14)
Portugal Telecom 18 C2
Post Office 19 C2
Tourist Police Post 20 B2
Web Café 21 B3
Western Union 22 C2
Western Union 23 C3

SIGHTS & ACTIVITIES (pp83–7)

Arco da Victória 24 D5
Ateneu Comercial Complexo de Piscinas 25 C1
Banco Comércial Portuguesa 26 D4
Casa do Fado e da Guitarra Portuguesa 27 G4
Casa dos Bicos 28 E5
Castelo de São Jorge 29 E3
CEM 30 D4
Conservia Lisboa 31 D5
Convento do Carmo Ruins 32 C3
Elevador da Bica 33 A4
Elevador da Glória 34 B2
Elevador de Santa Justa 35 C3
Igreja da Conceição Velha 36 E5
Igreja de São Domingos 37 D2
Igreja de São Roque 38 B3
Igreja de São Vicente de Fora 39 G3
Largo das Portas do Sol 40 F4
Military Barracks 41 F2
Miradouro da Graça 42 F2
Miradouro da Senhora do Monte 43 E1
Miradouro de Pedro de Alcântara 44 B2
Miradouro de Santa Luzia 45 F4
Miradouro de São Jorge 46 E3
Museu Arqueológico do Carmo (see 32)
Museu de São Roque 47 B3
Museu do Chiado 48 B5
Museu do Teatro Romano 49 E4
Museu Militar 50 H3
Nucleo Arqueologico 51 D4
Olisipónia 52 E3
Paços do Concelho 53 C5
Panteão Nacional (Igreja de Santa Engrácia) 54 H3
Praça da Figueira 55 D3
Praça do Comércio 56 D5
Praça do Município 57 C5
Praça Dom Pedro IV (Rossio) 58 C3
Ruins of Roman Theatre 59 E4
Statue of Dom José I 60 D5
Transtejo Cruises 61 E6

SLEEPING (pp97–8)

Albergaria Senhora do Monte 62 E1
Apartment VIP Eden 63 B2
Beira Mar 64 F4
Hospedaria Bons Dias (see 85)
Hotel Botânico 65 A1
Hotel Lisboa Tejo 66 D3
Hotel Métrópole 67 C3
Lisboa Regency Chiudo 68 C4
New Aljubarrota 69 D4
Olissipo Castelo 70 E2
Pensão Estrela de Ouro 71 B3
Pensão Globo 72 A2
Pensão Imperial 73 C2
Pensão Londres 74 A2
Pensão Lunar 75 B3
Pensão Ninho das Águias 76 E2
Pensão Norte 77 D3
Pensão Praça da Figueira 78 D3
Pensão Residencial Florescente 79 C2
Pensão Residencial Gerês 80 D2
Pensão Santo Tirso 81 C3
Pensão São João da Praça 82 E5
Pensão Varandas 83 E5
Residencial Duas Nações 84 D4
Residencial Estrela do Mondego 85 C3
Residencial Nova Avenida 86 A1
Sé Guest House (see 82)
Solar dos Mouros 87 E4

EATING (pp101–4)

A Baîuca 88 B3
A Tasca da Sé 89 E4
A Tasca do Manel 90 B4
A Toca 91 A3
Adega Regional da Beira 92 D4
Ali-a-Papa 93 A3
Bonsai 94 A2
C@fé Taborda 95 E2
Café A Brasileira 96 B4
Café Buenos Aires 97 B3
Café Nicola 98 C3
Calcuta 99 B4
Casa da India 100 A4
Casa do Alentejo 101 C2
Casa Nostra 102 A3
Casa Suiça 103 C3
Cervejaria Alemã 104 B5
Cervejaria da Trindade 105 B3
Chiadomel 106 C3
Cocheira Alentejana 107 B3
Confeitaria Nacional 108 D3
El Gordo I 109 A2
El Gordo II 110 B3
El Ultimo Tango 111 B3
Ena Pai 112 D3
Fidalgo 113 A4
Gambrinus 114 C2
Jardim do Marisco 115 G5
La Brasserie de l'Entrecôte 116 B4
Lautasco 117 F4
Malmequer Bemmequer 118 F4
Mamma Rosa 119 B3
Martinho da Arcada 120 D5
Mestre André 121 G4
O Cantinho das Gáveas 122 B3
O Cantinho do Bem Estar 123 B4
O Caracol 124 B4
O Fumeiro 125 B1
Pap'Açorda 126 A3
Pastelaria São Roque 127 A2
Pingo Doce Supermarket 128 C3
Ponte Picante 129 A3
Porte de Alfama 130 F4
Restaurante Alto Minho 131 A4
Restaurante Arço do Castelo 132 E3
Restaurante Cais d'Alfama 133 G4
Restaurante O Sol 134 C3
Restaurante Tipico Taverna d'El Rei 135 F4
Restaurante Viagems de Sabores 136 E5
Restô 137 E4
Sabor e Arte 138 B4
São Cristóvão 139 D3
Snob 140 A2
Solar do Vez 141 E5
Solar dos Bicos 142 E5
Stasha 143 B4
Sul 144 B4
UMA 145 C3
Velho Macedo 146 D4

DRINKING (pp106–9)

A Ginjinha 147 C2
Bar Americano 148 B5
Bicaense 149 A4
British Bar 150 B5
Capela 151 A3
Catacombas Jazz Bar 152 A3
Clube da Esquina 153 B3
Hennessy's 154 B5
Heróis 155 C4
Majong 156 A3
Mezcal 157 B3
O'Gilin's 158 A5
Pavilhão Chines 159 A2
Portas Largas 160 A3
Solar do Vinho do Porto 161 B2

ENTERTAINMENT (pp106–12)

A Baîuca 162 F4
ABEP Ticket Agency 163 C2
Adaga Mesquita 164 B3
Adega do Ribatejo 165 B4
Adega Machado 166 B3
Chapitô 167 E4
Clube de Fado 168 F4
Coliseu dos Recreios 169 C2
Discoteca Jamaica 170 B5
Fnac (see 182)
Fragil 171 A3
Hot Clube de Portugal 172 A1
MUSIcais 173 G5
Nono 174 B4
Parreirinha de Alfama 175 F4
Salão Foz 176 B2
Taverna do Embuçado 177 F4
Teatro Municipal de São Luís 178 B4
Teatro Nacional de Dona Maria II 179 C2
Teatro Nacional de São Carlos 180 B4
Teatro Taborda 181 E2

SHOPPING (pp112–13)

Armazens do Chiudo 182 C4
Arte Rustica 183 C3
Centro de Artesanato (see 189)
Discoteca Amália 184 C3
Fábrica Sant'Ana 185 B4
Feira da Ladra (Flea Market) 186 H2
Madeira House 187 C4
Manuel Tavares 188 C3
Mercado da Ribeira 189 A5
Napoleão 190 D4
Santos Oficios 191 D4
Valentim de Carvalho Megastore & Edifício Grandella 192 C3
Vista Alegre 193 B4

TRANSPORT (pp113–16)

Bus No 37 194 E3
Cais Do Sodré Ferry Terminal 195 B6
Cais do Sodré 196 A6
Rossio 197 B2
Terreiro do Paço Ferry Terminal 198 E6
Tram No 28/Baixa 199 D4
Tram No 28/Largo da Graça 200 F2
Tram No 28/Largo Martim Moniz 201 D2

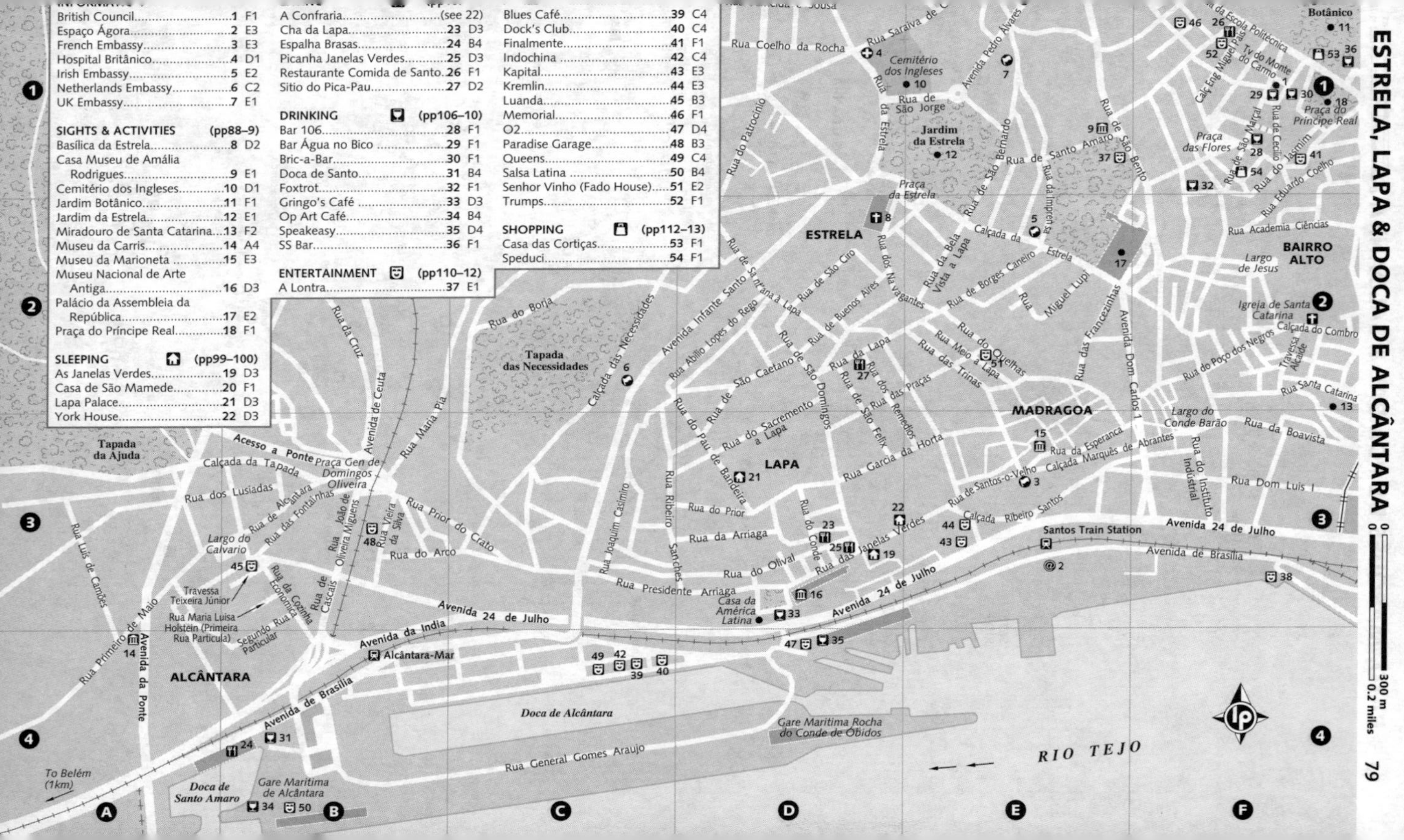
0 300 m
0 0.2 miles
British Council 1 F1
Espaço Ágora 2 E3
French Embassy 3 E3
Hospital Britânico 4 D1
Irish Embassy 5 E2
Netherlands Embassy 6 C2
UK Embassy 7 E1
SIGHTS & ACTIVITIES (pp88–9)
Basílica da Estrela 8 D2
Casa Museu de Amália Rodrigues 9 E1
Cemitério dos Ingleses 10 D1
Jardim Botânico 11 F1
Jardim da Estrela 12 E1
Miradouro de Santa Catarina 13 F2
Museu da Carris 14 A4
Museu da Marioneta 15 E3
Museu Nacional de Arte Antiga 16 D3
Palácio da Assembleia da República 17 E2
Praça do Príncipe Real 18 F1
SLEEPING (pp99–100)
As Janelas Verdes 19 D3
Casa de São Mamede 20 F1
Lapa Palace 21 D3
York House 22 D3
A Confraria (see 22)
Cha da Lapa 23 D3
Espalha Brasas 24 B4
Picanha Janelas Verdes 25 D3
Restaurante Comida de Santo 26 F1
Sitio do Pica-Pau 27 D2
DRINKING (pp106–10)
Bar 106 28 F1
Bar Água no Bico 29 F1
Bric-a-Bar 30 F1
Doca de Santo 31 B4
Foxtrot 32 F1
Gringo's Café 33 D3
Op Art Café 34 B4
Speakeasy 35 D4
SS Bar 36 F1
ENTERTAINMENT (pp110–12)
A Lontra 37 E1
Blues Café 39 C4
Dock's Club 40 C4
Finalmente 41 F1
Indochina 42 C4
Kapital 43 E3
Kremlin 44 E3
Luanda 45 B3
Memorial 46 F1
O2 47 D4
Paradise Garage 48 B3
Queens 49 C4
Salsa Latina 50 B4
Senhor Vinho (Fado House) 51 E2
Trumps 52 F1
SHOPPING (pp112–13)
Casa das Cortiças 53 F1
Speduci 54 F1
ESTRELA
LAPA
MADRAGOA
BAIRRO ALTO
ALCÂNTARA
RIO TEJO
Doca de Alcântara
Doca de Santo Amaro
Gare Maritima de Alcântara
Gare Maritima Rocha do Conde de Óbidos
Santos Train Station
Alcântara-Mar
Tapada das Necessidades
Tapada da Ajuda
Jardim da Estrela
Cemitério dos Ingleses
Casa da América Latina
Praça da Estrela
Praça das Flores
Praça do Príncipe Real
Largo do Conde Barão
Largo de Jesus
Largo do Calvario
Praça Gen de Domingos Oliveira
Igreja de Santa Catarina
Avenida 24 de Julho
Avenida de Brasília
Avenida da India
Avenida da Ponte
Avenida Dom Carlos 1
Avenida Infante Santo
Avenida de Ceuta
Avenida Pedro Álvares
Acesso a Ponte
Calçada da Tapada
Calçada das Necessidades
Calçada da Estrela
Calçada Ribeiro Santos
Calçada Marquês de Abrantes
Calçada do Combro
Rua General Gomes Araujo
Rua Presidente Arriaga
Rua Coelho da Rocha
Rua do Patrocinio
Rua de São Bento
Rua de Santo Amaro
Rua de São Domingos
Rua do Sacremento a Lapa
Rua do Pau de Bandeira
Rua Garcia da Horta
Rua de Santos-o-Velho
Rua das Janelas Verdes
Rua do Olival
Rua da Arriaga
Rua do Prior
Rua Ribeiro Sanches
Rua Joaquim Casimiro
Rua do Borja
Rua da Cruz
Rua Maria Pia
Rua Prior do Crato
Rua do Arco
Rua dos Lusiadas
Rua Luís de Camões
Rua Primeiro de Maio
Rua da Boavista
Rua Dom Luis I
Rua do Instituto Indústrial
Rua da Esperança
Rua das Francezinhas
Rua Miguel Lupi
Rua de Borges Caneiro
Rua da Bela Vista a Lapa
Rua dos Navagantes
Rua de Buenos Aires
Rua de São Ciro
Rua de Sant'ana à Lapa
Rua Abilio Lopes do Rego
Rua de São Caetano
Rua da Lapa
Rua de São Felix
Rua dos Remedios
Rua das Praças
Rua das Trinas
Rua Meio a Lapa
Rua do Quelhas
Rua de São Bernardo
Rua da Imprensa
Rua de São Jorge
Rua da Estrela
Rua Saraiva de Carvalho
Rua do Poço dos Negros
Rua Santa Catarina
Travessa Alcaide
Rua Academia Ciências
Rua Eduardo Coelho
Rua do Jasmim
Rua de Cecilio
Rua de São Marçal
Calç Eng Miguel Pais
Tv do Monte do Carmo
Rua da Escola Politécnica
Rua de Alcântara
Rua das Fontainhas
Rua João de Oliveira Miguens
Rua Vieira da Silva
Rua de Cascais
Rua da Cozinha Económica
Travessa Teixeira Júnior
Rua Maria Luisa Holstein (Primeira Rua Particula)
Segundo Rua Particular
Botânico
To Belém (1km)
A
B
C
D
E
F
1
2
3
4

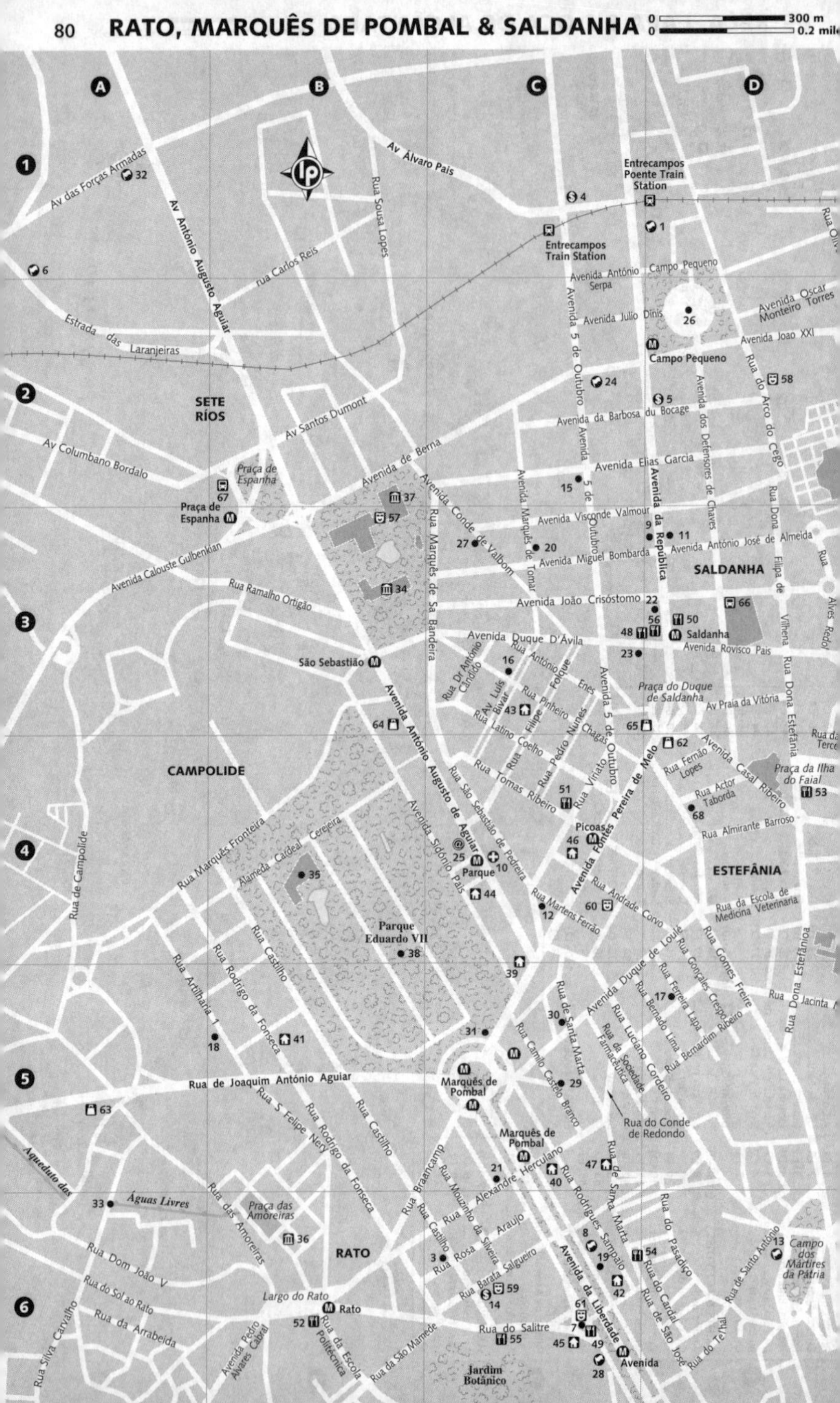
0 300 m
0 0.2 miles
A
B
C
D
1
2
3
4
5
6
Av das Forças Armadas
Av António Augusto Aguiar
Av Álvaro Pais
Rua Sousa Lopes
rua Carlos Reis
Estrada das Laranjeiras
Entrecampos Poente Train Station
Entrecampos Train Station
Avenida António Serpa
Campo Pequeno
Avenida Julio Dinis
Avenida Oscar Monteiro Torres
Avenida Joao XXI
Avenida 5 de Outubro
Rua do Arco do Cego
Avenida dos Defensores de Chaves
Avenida da Barbosa du Bocage
Avenida Elias Garcia
Avenida da República
SETE RÍOS
Av Santos Dumont
Av Columbano Bordalo
Praça de Espanha
Avenida de Berna
Avenida Conde de Valbom
Rua Marquês de Sa Bandeira
Avenida Marquês de Tomar
Avenida Visconde Valmour
Avenida Miguel Bombarda
Avenida António José de Almeida
SALDANHA
Avenida Calouste Gulbenkian
Rua Ramalho Ortigão
Avenida João Crisóstomo
Avenida Duque D'Ávila
Saldanha
Avenida Rovisco Pais
São Sebastião
Rua Dr António Cândido
Rua António Enes
Av Luís Bivar
Rua Pinheiro Chagas
Rua Filipe Folque
Rua Latino Coelho
Rua Pedro Nunes
Praça do Duque de Saldanha
Av Praia da Vitória
Rua Dona Filipa de Vilhena
Rua Dona Estefânia
Avenida Fontes Pereira de Melo
Rua Fernão Lopes
Avenida Casal Ribeiro
Praça da Ilha do Faial
CAMPOLIDE
Rua Tomas Ribeiro
Rua Viriato
Rua Actor Taborda
Rua Almirante Barroso
Rua São Sebastião de Pedreira
Avenida Sidónio Pais
Avenida António Augusto de Aguiar
Picoas
ESTEFÂNIA
Rua Marquês Fronteira
Alameda Cardeal Cerejeira
Rua de Campolide
Parque
Rua Martens Ferrão
Rua Andrade Corvo
Rua da Escola de Medicina Veterinaria
Parque Eduardo VII
Rua Artilharia 1
Rua Rodrigo da Fonseca
Rua Castilho
Avenida Duque de Loulé
Rua Gonçalves Crespo
Rua Gomes Freire
Rua Ferreira Lapa
Rua Bernardo Lima
Rua de Santa Marta
Rua Luciano Cordeiro
Rua da Sociedade Farmacêutica
Rua Bernardim Ribeiro
Rua Jacinta
Rua Camilo Castelo Branco
Rua de Joaquim António Aguiar
Marquês de Pombal
Rua S Felipe Nery
Rua do Conde de Redondo
Aqueduto das Águas Livres
Rua Braamcamp
Rua Alexandre Herculano
Rua Rodrigues Sampaio
Rua do Passadiço
Praça das Amoreiras
Rua das Amoreiras
Rua Mouzinho da Silveira
Rua Rosa Araujo
RATO
Rua Barata Salgueiro
Avenida da Liberdade
Rua do Cardal
Rua de Santo António
Campo dos Mártires da Pátria
Rua Dom João V
Rua do Sol ao Rato
Largo do Rato
Rato
Rua da Arrabeida
Rua Silva Carvalho
Avenida Pedro Alvares Cabral
Rua da Escola Politécnica
Rua da São Mamede
Rua do Salitre
Avenida
Rua de São José
Rua do Telhal
Jardim Botânico

INFORMATION
Angolan Embassy....1 D1
Associação Opus Gay....2 D3
Australian Embassy....(see 8)
Automóvel Club de Portugal (ACP)....3 C6
Banque Nationale de Paris....4 C1
Barclays Bank....5 D2
Brazilian Embassy....6 A1
Cambridge School....7 C6
Canadian Embassy....8 C6
Centro de Linguas....9 D3
Clínica Médica Internacional....10 C4
Comissão para a Igualdade e para os Direitos das Mulheres....11 D3
Foreigners' Registration Service....12 C4
German Embassy....13 D6
Grupo Deutsche Bank....14 C6
ICEP Head Office....15 C2
Institut Franco-Portugais de Lisbonne....16 C3
Instituto da Conservação da Natureza (ICN)....17 D5
Instituto Gráfico Português....18 B5
Instituto Português da Juventude (IPJ)....19 C6
Librairie Française....20 C3
Livraria Buchholz....21 C5
Livraria Municipal....22 D3
Luggagebox....(see 66)
Movijovem....23 C3
Mozambican Embassy....24 C2
Postnina....25 C4
Praça de Touros....26 D2
Secretariado Nacional de Rehabilitação....27 C3
Spanish Embassy & Consulate....28 C6
Tagus....29 C5
Top Atlântica....30 C5
Tour Bus Terminal....31 C5
US Embassy & Consulate....32 A1

SIGHTS & ACTIVITIES (pp89–91)
Aqueduto das Águas Livres....33 A6
Centro de Arte Moderna....34 B3
Estufas....35 B4
Mãe d'Água Reservoir....36 B6
Museu Calouste Gulbenkian....37 B2
Parque Eduardo VII....38 B4

SLEEPING (p100)
Best Western Hotel Eduardo VII....39 C5
Dom Carlos Liberty....40 C5
Four Seasons Ritz....41 B5
Hotel Britannia....42 C6
Hotel Impala....43 C3
Hotel Miraparque....44 C4
Pensão Residencial 13 da Sorte....45 C6
Pousada da Juventude de Lisboa....46 C4
Residência Dublin....47 C5

EATING (pp104–5)
Bella Italia III....48 C3
Cervejaria Ribadouro....49 C6
Galeto....50 D3
Li Yuan....51 C4
Real Fábrica....52 B6
Restaurante Espiral....53 D4
Restaurante Estrela de Santa Marta....54 C6
Restaurante Os Tibetanos....55 C6
Versailles....56 D3

ENTERTAINMENT (pp110–12)
Concert Halls (Fundaçio Calouste Gulbenkian)....57 B3
Culturgest....58 D2
Instituto do Cinemateca Portuguesa....59 C6
Mussulo....60 C4
São Jorge Cinema....61 C6

SHOPPING (pp112–13)
Atrium Saldanha....62 D4
Complexo das Amoreiras....63 A5
El Corte Inglés....64 B3
Galerias Monumental....65 D3

TRANSPORT (pp113–16)
Arco do Cego Bus Station....66 D3
Bus Station for Costa da Caparica & Sesimbra....67 B2
Eurolines (Intercentro) Ticket Office....68 D4
Eurolines (Intercentro) Ticket Office....(see 66)

BELÉM

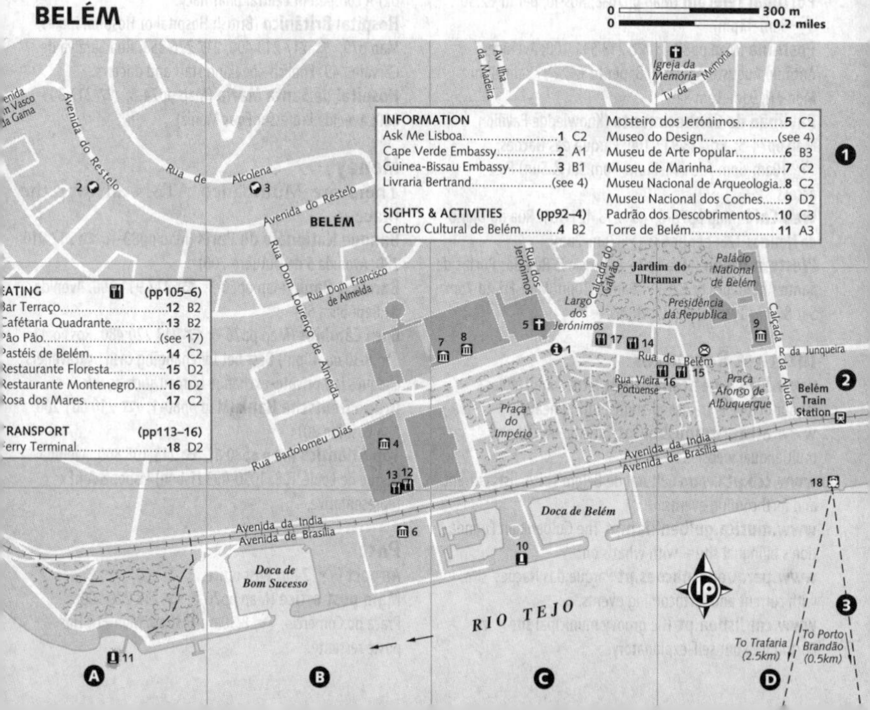

(Continued from page 73)

Emergency

Police headquarters (Map pp76-8; ☎ 217 654 242; Rua Capelo 13)

Tourist police post (Map pp76-8; ☎ 213 421 634; Palácio Foz, Praça dos Restauradores; 24hr) Next to the ICEP turismo.

Internet Access

Among many places to log on you will find the following:

Abracadabra (Map pp76-8; Rossio 65; per hr €2.50; 7am-10pm Mon-Fri, 8am-10am Sat & Sun)

Cyber Bica (Map pp76-8; ☎ 213 225 004; Rua Duques de Bragança; per hr €3; noon-2am Mon-Fri, 7pm-2am Sat) Groovy café-bar.

Espaço Ágora (Map p79; ☎ 213 940 170; Armazém 1, Avenida de Brasilia, Santos; per hr €2; 9am-12.30am Mon-Fri, to midnight Sat, 9.30am-9pm Sun) A youth hangout and café.

Instituto Português da Juventude (IPJ; Map pp80-1; ☎ 213 532 696; Rua Andrade Corvo, 46; 9am-7.30pm Mon-Fri, to 3pm Sat) Offers 30 minutes free access.

Pontonet (Map pp76-8; ☎ 210 312 810; 1st fl, Lisboa Welcome Center, Praça do Comércio; per hr €3.50; 9am-8pm)

Portugal Telecom (Map pp76-8; Rossio; per hr €2.50; 8am-11pm)

Postnina (Map pp80-1; ☎ 213 511 100; Avenida António Augusto Aguiar 17B; per hr €4; 8am-8pm Mon-Fri, 9am-1pm Sat)

Pavilhão do Conhecimento (Knowledge Pavilion; Map pp74-5; ☎ 218 917 100; Parque das Nações; 10am-6pm Tue-Fri, 11am-7pm Sat & Sun) Free access.

Web Café (Map pp76-8; ☎ 213 421 181; Rua do Diário de Notícias 126; per hr €3; 2pm-2am)

Western Union (Map pp76-8; Rossio & Rua das Portas de Santo Antão; per hr €2; 9am-9.30pm Mon-Fri, to 7pm Sat & Sun) Two central locations.

Internet Resources

www.luso.u-net.com/lisbon.htm John Laidlar's labour of love is train-and-tramspotting heaven.

www.atl-turismolisboa.pt Turismo de Lisboa's multilingual website.

www.ccb.pt Centro Cultural de Belém's site, lists current and forthcoming events.

www.musica.gulbenkian.pt The Gulbenkian Foundation's bilingual site – with what's on.

www.parquedasnacoes.pt Parque das Nações' site, with current and forthcoming events.

www.cm-lisboa.pt The groovy municipal site – in Portuguese but self-explanatory.

Laundry

Lave Neve (Map pp76-8; Rua da Alegria 37; per 5kg €8.50 ; 9am-1pm & 3-7pm Mon, 10am-1pm & 3-7pm Tue-Fri, 9am-1pm Sat) The only self-service place in Lisbon.

Lavandaria Lina (Map pp76-8; Ground fl, Martin Moniz Centre; per 4kg €6.50; 10am-12.30pm & 3-8pm Mon-Fri, to 6pm Sat) Not self-service.

Left Luggage

Airport (up to 10kg/30kg/over 30kg per day €2/3/5.80) By Level 2's car park P2.

Luggagebox (Map pp80-1; Arco do Cego bus terminal; per day per item €2.50; 8am-7pm Mon-Fri, to 1pm & 2-6pm Sat, 9am-1pm & 2-6pm Sun)

Train stations (Gare do Oriente, Rossio, Cais do Sodré & Santa Apolónia; per hr/max 24hr €1-3.50/5-11) Coin-operated lockers only.

Medical Services

The ICEP turismo has a list of private doctors and dentists who speak English or other languages.

Clinica Medica Internacional (Map pp80-1; ☎ 213 513 310; Ave Antonio Augusto de Aguiar 40) A quick, pricey, private clinic with English-speaking doctors.

Farmácia Estácio (Map pp76-8; ☎ 213 211 390; Rossio 62) A competent central pharmacy.

Hospital Britânico (British Hospital or Hospital Inglês; Map p79; ☎ 217 213 400, 217 276 353; Rua Saraiva de Carvalho 49) English-speaking staff and doctors.

Hospital de Santa Maria (Map pp74-5; ☎ 217 805 000; Avenida Professor Egas Moniz)

Money

There are Multibanco ATMs all over the place.

Banque Nationale de Paris (Map pp80-1; ☎ 217 910 200; Avenida 5 de Outubro 206)

Barclays Bank (Map pp80-1; ☎ 217 911 100; Avenida da República 50)

Cota Câmbios (Map pp76-8; ☎ 213 220 480; Rossio 41; 8.30am-10pm) Best bet for changing cash or travellers cheques is a private-exchange bureau such as this.

Grupo Deutsche Bank (Map pp80-1; ☎ 210 001 200; Rua Castilho 20)

Top Atlântica (Map pp80-1; ☎ 213 108 800; Avenida Duque de Loulé 108, 1050-093 Lisbon) Lisbon's AmEx representative.

Post

Airport (24hr) Post office.

Main post office (Map pp76-8; ☎ 213 220 900; Praça do Comércio; 8.30am-6.30pm Mon-Fri) Has poste restante.

Post office (Map pp76-8; ☎ 213 238 700; Praça dos Restauradores; 🕑 8am-10pm Mon-Fri, 9am-6pm Sat & Sun) Another central post office.

Telephone & Fax

With a phonecard, including the Portugal Telecom card, you can make international direct dial (IDD) calls from most payphones. At Portugal Telecom booths in post offices you can pay when you're done. Faxes can be sent from post offices or Postnina (see opposite).

International Telephone Service (Map pp76-8; Rua do Arço da Graça; 🕑 9am-midnight), You can make bargain-basement international calls here (€0.25 per minute to Europe).

Portugal Telecom (Map pp76-8; Rossio 68; 🕑 8am-11pm) Has rows of booths.

Tourist Information

Available at all Turismo de Lisboa outlets is the Lisboa Card (see below).

Ask Me Lisboa Rua Augusta (Map pp76-8; near Rua Conceição; 🕑 10am-1pm & 2-6pm); Santa Apolónia (Map pp74-5; door No 47, inside train station; 8am-4pm Tue-Sat); Belém (Map p81; 🕑 10am-1pm & 2-6pm Tue-Sat) Turismo de Lisboa's runs several of these information kiosks and these are the most useful.

ICEP turismo (Map pp76-8; ☎ 213 463 314; Palácio Foz, Praça dos Restauradores; 🕑 9am-8pm) For national inquiries try here, efficiently run by the state's tourism organisation. There's also a Turismo de Lisboa desk here.

Lisboa Welcome Center (Map pp76-8; ☎ 210 312 810; Praça do Comércio; 🕑 9am-8pm)

Turismo de Lisboa Information (☎ 210 312 810; atl@atl-turismolisboa.pt); Airport (☎ 218 450 660; 🕑 8am-midnight) Doles out maps, advises on taxis and other transport, and makes hotel reservations.

LISBOA CARD

With this discount card, you get free travel on the metro, buses, trams and lifts (plus the train to Belém); free admission to 26 museums and monuments (including some in Sintra); and discounts of up to 50% on sights, tours, cruises and other admission charges. The 24/48/72-hour versions cost €12.75/21.50/26.55 (children from five to 11 €5.70/8.55/11.40) – reasonable value if you are a tenacious tourist. You validate the card when you want to start it.

The card is sold at all Turismos de Lisboa and Carris ticket kiosks.

There are excellent free publications worth picking up at hotels and tourist offices include the followingg:

Follow Me Lisboa A fortnightly Portuguese/English leisure guide.

Guia Gay e Lésbico Gay and lesbian leaflet guide.

Lisboa Step by Step A quarterly tourist guide, produced by Turismo de Lisboa, featuring what's on in the city.

Tips An info-packed miniguide, usually found in hotels.

Your Guide: Lisboa Published by ANA, the airport authority, listing shops, restaurants and nightlife.

Travel Agencies

Tagus Rato (Map pp80-1; ☎ 213 525 986; www.viagenstagus.pt in Portuguese; Rua Camilo Castelo Branco 20); Arreiro (Map pp74-5; ☎ 218 491 531; Praça de Londres 9C; 🕑 9.30am-6pm Mon-Fri, 10am-1.30pm Sat) Leading youth-oriented travel agency, offering budget hotel, bus, train and air bookings (plus ISIC and ITIC cards).

Top Atlântica (Map pp80-1; ☎ 213 108 800; Avenida Duque de Loulé 108, 1050-093 Lisbon)

DANGERS & ANNOYANCES

Lisbon has a low crime rate, but take care as you would in most large cities. Most crime against foreigners involves car break-ins, pickpocketing or bag-snatching. Use a moneybelt and keep valuables hidden. If you do get challenged, it is far better to hand stuff over than take a risk. Park cars in guarded or locked garages.

Late at night (especially weekends), avoid wandering alone through the streets of Bairro Alto, Alfama and Cais do Sodré – take a taxi. Parks and gardens are best avoided once the sun has set. After dark, Interdente is a no-go area, a red-light and drug-user district that's contained by local police.

Rivalry between Cape Verdean and Angolan gangs may have led to attacks in African nightclubs: seven people died at the popular African nightclub Luanda in April 2000 when tear-gas canisters were set off. Security has tightened since the incident, but if you see any sign of trouble – make a move in the opposite direction.

SIGHTS

Baixa & the Riverfront **Map pp76–8**

Following the 1755 earthquake, when the autocratic Marquês de Pombal, Dom José I's chief minister, rebuilt the city centre the area from the riverside to Rossio was reborn. Wide, commercial streets (with footpaths)

A LISBON STORY

You can take a crash course in Lisbon's charms by watching Wim Wenders' sweet, meandering film *A Lisbon Story* (1994), in which a sound engineer goes in search of a missing director, discovering the city through footage he has left behind.

The great Portuguese director Manoel de Oliveira, who's been making movies since they were silent, also makes a cameo appearance.

were each dedicated to a trade, recalled by Baixa's street names – Áurea (formerly Ouro, gold), Sapateiros (shoemakers), Correeiros (saddlers), Prata (silver), Douradores (gilders) and Fanqueiros (cutlers).

This *baixa* (lower town) is still Lisbon's heartbeat. Down the middle runs pedestrianised Rua Augusta, the old street of the cloth merchants, now hosting cafés, shops and banks.

PRAÇA DO COMÉRCIO & AROUND

The city's grandest square is **Praça do Comércio**, an architectural fanfare of Portugal's wealth and might. Most visitors coming by river or sea once arrived here and the huge square still feels like the city's entrance, with Joaquim Machado de Castro's bronze **equestrian statue** of Dom José I; the 18th-century, arcaded **ministries** along three sides; and Verissimo da Costa's **Arco da Victória**, the arch opening onto Rua Augusta. The stock exchange was once on the southeastern corner. Before the earthquake, the *praça* (town square) was called Terreiro do Paço (Palace Square), after the royal Palácio da Ribeira that overlooked it until the morning of 1 November 1755. In 1908 the square witnessed the death knell of the monarchy, when King Carlos I and his son were assassinated by anarchists.

Just off the square's northwestern corner, the smaller **Praça do Município** is dominated on the eastern side by the 1874 **Paços do Concelho** (town hall) where the republic was proclaimed from its balcony on 5 October 1910, on the southern side by the former marine arsenal, and centrally a finely carved, 18th-century *pelourinho* (pillory).

To the west is the spike-domed **Mercado da Ribeira**, the city's former main food market, with an arts and crafts centre (p113).

CENTRAL BAIXA

Under the *baixa* is the **Núcleo Arqueológico** (☎ 213 211 700; admission free), a web of tunnels believed to be the remnants of a Roman spa (or a temple) and probably dating from the 1st century AD. You can descend into the dank depths – via the **Banco Comércial Portuguesa** (Rua dos Correeiros 9) – on a guided tour run by the Museu da Cidade (p91). There are three on Thursdays, two on Saturdays; you'll need to phone ahead to book.

From Largo Martim Moniz, the No 28 tram twists up into Alfama and Graça. At the Baixa's other end, the **Elevador de Santa Justa** – a charming, eccentric wrought-iron lift designed by Raul Mésnier du Ponsard (a follower of Gustave Eiffel) and completed in 1902 – hoists you 32m above Rua de Santa Justa to a viewing platform and café opposite Convento do Carmo.

ROSSIO & PRAÇA DA FIGUEIRA

The focus of the Baixa is this pair of squares, a meeting place for Lisbon's multicultural population, filled with hustle, bustle, cafés and fountains. You are bound to cross these squares repeatedly during your visit – all roads seem to lead here.

In the middle of the Rossio is a **statue**, allegedly of Dom Pedro IV, after whom the square is named (but everyone calls it Rossio). On the northern side of the square is the restored 1846 **Teatro Nacional de Dona Maria II**, topped by a statue of 16th-century playwright Gil Vicente.

Rossio was once the scene of animal markets, fairs and bullfights, and the theatre was built on the site of a palace in which the unholiest excesses of the 16th–19th-century Portuguese Inquisition took place. In the nearby **Igreja de São Domingos** (admission free; ⌚ 7.30am-7pm Mon-Fri, noon-6pm Sat) the Inquisition's judgments, or autos-da-fé, were pronounced. Inside it's imposing, with gashed pillars like a damaged rockface. The much-battered church has (just about) survived earthquakes in 1531 and 1755, and fire in 1959. The high altar, designed by the Mafra architect dates from 1748.

Chiado & Bairro Alto

The Chiado, a wedge of wide streets between Rua do Crucifixo and Rua da Misericórdia, is elegantly 18th century, with upmarket shops and cafés. It leads up to the

ROLLING MOTION SQUARE

This was the nickname given to the Rossio by early English visitors because of the undulating mosaic pattern of its footpaths. Such cobbled pavements – made of hard-cut white limestone and grey basalt cubes and originally installed by 19th-century prison labour gangs – are everywhere, painstakingly pounded by hand into a bed of sand.

contrastingly weblike Bairro Alto (upper district), a fashionable 17th-century residential quarter, now the Lisbon Soho with one-off designers, vintage boutiques, record shops, restaurants and boho bars and cafés. The following are on Map pp76–8 unless otherwise noted.

In the Chiado the graceful ruins of the **Convento do Carmo**, uphill from Rua Garrett, are Lisbon's only remaining Gothic architecture – mostly devoured by the 1755 earthquake. Now regularly used as an open-air theatre, just the tall slender pillars, arches, walls and flying buttresses remain of one of Lisbon's largest churches, built in 1423. The **Museu Arqueológico do Carmo** (☎ 213 478 629; adult/child under 14 €2.50/free, 10am-2pm Sun free; ⌚ 10am-6pm Apr-Sep, to 5pm Oct-Mar) was set up to safeguard religious treasures after the abolition of religious orders in 1834. It has an outstanding collection of 14th-century carved tombs, some prehistoric implements and a dishevelled trio of mummies – one battered Egyptian and two gruesome 16th-century Peruvians.

By contrast, the gutted buildings that pockmarked the Chiado after a massive fire in 1988 have been magnificently restored by architect Álvaro de Siza Vieira, most now housing elegant shopping malls. One survivor of the fire is **Teatro Nacional de São Carlos** (p111), Lisbon's opera house and well worth a visit – a delirious gold-and-red, cherub-and-garland extravaganza built in the 1790s.

Nearby, in the strikingly converted Convento de São Francisco, is the **Museu do Chiado** (☎ 213 432 148; www.museudochiado-ipmuseus.pt; Rua Serpa Pinto 4; adult/under 26/senior €3/1.50/1.50, 10am-2pm Sun free; ⌚ 2-6pm Tue, 10am-6pm Wed-Sun), beautifully lit and laid out with contemporary art exhibitions plus a permanent display of 19th- and 20th-century Portuguese and foreign art (including works by Rodin and Maillol). Highlights are the marvellous panels (1927–32) by José de Almada Negreiros from San Carlos Cinema.

From Praça dos Restauradores, the **Elevador da Glória** climbs up to a superb viewpoint atop one of Lisbon's seven hills, **Miradouro de São Pedro de Alcântara**, and is a less tiring way of getting to Bairro Alto. Across the road is the **Solar do Vinho do Porto** (p107), where you can tuck into some port.

A short walk southeast of the viewpoint is 16th-century Jesuit **Igreja de São Roque** (☎ 213 235 381; Largo Trindade Coelho; admission free; ⌚ 8.30am-5pm), whose plain façade, designed by the architect of São Vicente, is one of Lisbon's biggest deceptions. Bankrolled by Brazilian riches, the interior squirms with gold, marble and Florentine *azulejos* (hand-painted tiles).

Most spectacular is the **Capela de São João Baptista**, to the left of the altar, a stylistic tussle between classical austerity and decorative hysteria. Commissioned in 1742 by Portugal's most extravagant king, Dom João V (also responsible for Mafra, the convent that nearly bankrupted the country), this chapel was designed and built in Rome over eight years, using the most expensive materials possible including amethyst, alabaster, agate, jade, lapis lazuli and Carrara marble. The four representations of the saint's life are fine mosaics that imitate oil paintings. After its consecration by Pope Benedict XIV it was dismantled and shipped across to Lisbon for the staggering amount of UK£225,000.

The adjacent **Museu de São Roque** (☎ 213 235 381; adult/child €1/free, Sun free; ⌚ 10am-5pm Tue-Sun) contains more evidence of flash ecclesiastical cash, with lavish devotional items, weird reliquaries, and 16th- and 17th-century paintings.

If you carry on northwest of the viewpoint, you'll hit **Principe Real**, a relaxing shady square around which is Lisbon's principal gay area.

Near Principe Real is the venerable, 19th-century **Jardim Botânico** (Map p79; ☎ 213 921 802; www.jb.ul.pt; Rua da Escola Politécnica 58; adult/child €1.50/0.60; ⌚ 9am-6pm Mon-Fri, 10am-6pm Sat & Sun Oct-Apr, 9am-8pm Mon-Fri, 10am-8pm Sat & Sun May-Sep). Its diversity of international flora is a tribute to Portugal's worldwide tendrils at

FUNICULAR FUN

The city has three bee-yellow funiculars (*elevadors* or *ascensors*) – originally water-powered, which labour up and down some of the city centre's steepest hills – and a wonderful bit of 19th-century weirdness, the **Elevador de Santa Justa** (return €2.20, prepaid €1.30; 9am-9pm). It's a frilly, wrought-iron lift in the Baixa, which elevates you around 45m to a café with a superb view across the rooftop, ruins of Carmo and the river. Perhaps the most charming ride is on the **Elevador da Bica** (7am-9pm Mon-Sat, 9am-9pm Sun) through the Santa Catarina district, at the southwestern corner of Bairro Alto. The other two funiculars are the **Elevador da Glória** (7am- 9pm Mon-Sat, 9am-9pm Sun), from Praça dos Restauradores up to the São Pedro de Alcântara viewpoint, and the **Elevador do Lavra**, the first street funicular in the world, opening in 1884 and running from Largo de Anunciada, on the eastern side of Restauradores.

the time. It is a marvellous, exotic escape, shaded by magnificent old trees.

From the southern end of the Bairro Alto (walking distance from Cais do Sodré) the **Elevador da Bica** creeps up to Rua do Loreto, a few blocks west of Praça de Luís Camões. At the end of Rua Marechal Saldanha, on another of Lisbon's seven hills, is the **Miradouro de Santa Catarina** (Map p79) with a popular outdoor café, offering exhilarating views across the river and the Ponte 25 de Abril.

Alfama, Castelo & Graça

This area east and northeast of the Baixa is Lisbon's oldest district. Unlike anywhere else in the city, its tangled web of semimedieval, semi-Arabic steeply slanted streets leads up and up to outstanding views from three of Lisbon's seven hills – São Jorge, Graça and Senhora do Monte. The following are on Map pp76–8 unless otherwise noted.

ALFAMA

The haphazard, medinalike Alfama has a distinctively Arabic legacy, like its name: the Arabic *al-hama* means 'springs' or 'bath', a name perhaps inspired by hot springs found near Largo das Alcaçarias. Once an upper-class Moorish residential area, it reverted after earthquake damage to a working-class and fisherfolk quarter. The sharply stepped, rock-built hills meant it was one of the few districts to survive the big one in 1755.

Diving down from the castle to the river, the district's alleys (*becos* and *travessas*) and steep stairways are a world away from the Baixa's tidy European grid. By day a lively enclave of restaurants and thimble-sized grocery stores, the area retains a strong sense of community. For a real rough-and-tumble atmosphere, visit during the Festas dos Santos Populares in June (p97).

East from the Praça do Comércio is Campo das Cebolas (Field of the Onions), where there's the bizarre 16th-century **Casa dos Bicos** (House of Points) – a pincushion façade built by Afonso de Albuquerque, a former India viceroy. It is now the offices for the Comemorações dos Descobrimentos organisation; if the lobby is open you can see bits of the old Moorish city wall and brick streets.

Directly north is the **sé** (admission free; 9am-7pm Tue-Sat, to 5pm Mon & Sun). This Romanesque cathedral was built in 1150, on the site of a Moorish building (possibly a mosque), soon after the city was recaptured from the Moors by Afonso Henriques. The fortress-like appearance of the building shows that the Christians may have been victorious, but they weren't taking any chances. It was damaged in the 1755 earthquake, and extensively restored in the 1930s. Inside is largely baroque, with religious riches on display in the **treasury** (admission €2.50; 10am-5pm Mon-Sat). The Gothic **cloister** (admission €2.50; 10am-5pm Mon, to 6.30pm Tue-Sat May-Sep, to 5pm Mon-Sat Oct-Apr) dates from the 13th century, and holds intriguing archaeological excavations, with stonework from the 6th century BC, a medieval cistern and the Islamic foundations.

Nearby is the **Museu do Teatro Romano** (217 513 200; Pátio do Aljube 5; admission free; 10am-1pm & 2-6pm Tue-Sun), displaying the city's ruined Roman theatre. Built during Emperor Augustus' time, it was extended in AD 57 to seat up to 5000. Abandoned in the 4th century, its stones were snaffled to build the city. Not much is left but the museum cleverly recreates the scene.

Two stunning viewpoints lie northeast: the glorious **Miradouro de Santa Luzia** with a well-situated café, and **Largo das Portas do Sol** (the 'sun gateway', originally one of the seven Moorish gateways).

Fado (Portugal's traditional meloncholy singing) was born in Alfama. To learn more, visit the **Casa do Fado e da Guitarra Portuguesa** (☎ 218 823 470; Largo do Chafariz de Dentro; adult/child under 6/under 14/student/senior €2.50/free/0.75/1.25/1.25; 🕑 10am-12.30pm & 2-5.30pm), a vibrant museum tracing fado's history from its working-class roots to international fame and finishing at a recreated fado house.

CASTELO DE SÃO JORGE

The **castle** (☎ 218 877 244; admission free; 🕑 9am-9pm Mar-Oct, to 6pm Nov-Feb; bus 37 from Rossio) has stupendous views across the city. From its Visigothic beginnings in the 5th century, it was later fortified by the Moors in the 9th century, sacked by Christians in the 12th century and used as a royal residence from the 14th to 16th centuries – and as a prison in every century.

The building itself is a series of open courtyards, filled with trees and birdsong, and you can climb and walk around the battlements. Near the entrance is **Olisipónia** (Map pp76-8; ☎ 218 877 244; adult/under 26 €1.50/0.75; 🕑 10am-1pm & 2-5.30pm), an exhibition with multilingual commentary about Lisbon's history – it uses a video wall to jazz up the already exciting history, but glosses over anything unpalatable (did anyone say slave trade?).

Northwest of the castle is the former **Mouraria Quarter**, the Moorish district after the Christian reconquest.

GRAÇA

Northeast of the castle lies Graça. Following Rua de São Tomé up from Largo das Portas do Sol, you pass Largo de Rodrigues de Freitas and reach Calçada da Graça, which leads to the splendid **Miradouro da Graça** (with a café). To the right is a former Augustinian convent, now a military barracks, and about 700m beyond the convent is the area's third major viewpoint, on another of Lisbon's hills, the **Miradouro da Senhora do Monte**, the best in town for views of the castle, Mouraria and the centre.

Two cultural sites lie just to the east (tram No 28 also passes close by). Dominating the scene is the huge dome of the Igreja de Santa Engrácia. When work began on this in 1682, it was planned as one of Lisbon's grandest. After centuries of dithering and neglect, the sombre, domed marble edifice was inaugurated in 1966 (when the dome was completed!) as the **Panteão Nacional** (National Pantheon; ☎ 218 854 820; Campo de Santa Clara; adult/child under 14/under 26 €2/1/free, 10am-2pm Sun free; 🕑 10am-5pm Tue-Sun). It contains chilly marble cenotaphs to historic and literary figures – Vasco da Gama and Henry the Navigator in their usual pride of place, with new-kids-in-town tucked away in side chapels: General Humberto Delgado, the opposition leader assassinated by the secret police in 1965, and Amália, the famous fado singer.

Walk up to the rooftop (there is a lift for the disabled) for a sunbake and great views of Alfama, the river and almost the whole unreal length of the Vasco da Gama bridge.

Nearby is wonderful **Igreja de São Vicente de Fora** (☎ 218 824 400; adult/child under 12/under 25 €2.50/free/1.25; 🕑 10am-6pm Tue-Sun). Founded in 1147, this monastery – 'St Vincent of Outside', as it was outside the city walls – was built on the burial sites of foreign crusaders and later, between 1582 and 1627, reconstructed by the master of the Italian Renaissance, Felipe Terzi. In 1755's earthquake the roof and dome collapsed on worshippers. Building works continued till the early 18th century, when finally the canons got to live here in peace – until 1834 when religious orders were banished. Today it has a wide, strikingly stark nave and coffered vault.

Remarkable blue-and-white azulejos (14,521 of them) date from the 18th century. They dance across almost every wall, echoing the curves of the architecture – across the serene, white cloisters and up to the 1st floor, which features a unique collection of 38 panels depicting La Fontaine's fables (entertaining 17th-century moral tales), accompanied by excellent English and French background text.

Under the sacristy, decorated in eye-tiring polychrome marble, lie the crusaders' tombs. The former refectory holds a mausoleum containing the sombre marble tombs of most of the Braganças – a lone, weeping, cloaked woman holds stony vigil, to great dramatic impact.

The monastery rooftop has more fantastic views.

WHAT'S FREE

Many museums are free Sunday morning. The **Centro Cultural de Belém** (p93) presents regular free music and dance performances. Everything during its daylong Festa da Primavera (Spring Festival) in March is also free. The **Museu Calouste Gulbenkian** (p89) gives free musical recitals at noon some Sundays in the library foyer. In shopping venues, **Fnac** (p110) has a regular programme of free exhibitions, concerts and films. The **Mercado da Ribeira** (p113) also has free concerts and exhibitions.

The **BaixAnima Festival** puts the bizarre into Baixa on weekends from mid-July to end of September with flamboyant street performers, centred on Rua Augusta.

SANTA APOLÓNIA

Northeast of Santa Apolónia train station is Lisbon's most beautiful museum, the **Museu Nacional do Azulejo** (National Tile Museum; Map pp74-5; ☎ 218 147 747; Rua Madre de Deus 4; adult/under 26/senior €3/1.50/1.50, 10am-2pm Sun free; 🕒 2-6pm Tue, 10am-6pm Wed-Sun). It's housed in the 16th-century convent of Igreja de Nossa Senhora da Madre de Deus, with lovely small tiled courtyards, Manueline cloister and gold-smothered baroque chapel, set off with more blue-and-white tiles. Illustrating the history and development of the tile, the museum has many exquisite pieces, from early Ottoman geometry to zinging blue-and-yellow altars, and from chintzy religious scenes to Goan intricacies. Among the exhibits is a fascinating 36m-long panel with a rare depiction of pre-earthquake Lisbon. (For more on azulejos, see p49) There's also a lovely restaurant in the museum (p103) and disabled access.

West of Santa Apolónia train station, in a suitably florid building, is the **Museu Militar** (☎ 218 842 300; Largo do Museu de Artilharia; adult/child under 10/under 18 €2.50/free/1.80; 🕒 10am-5pm Tue-Sun), with the biggest collection of artillery in the world. It's a mind-blowing, if fusty, display of ways to do damage. One for Charlton Heston types.

The **Aqueduto das Águas Livres** (p90) and **Mãe d'Água** reservoir (p91) are part of the **Museu da Água** (Map pp74-5; ☎ 218 135 522; Rua do Alviela 12; admission €3; 🕒 10am-6pm Mon-Sat), in a restored 19th-century pump station, which explains the complex watering system and is run by Empresa Portuguesa das Águas Livres (EPAL), the municipal water company.

Estrela, Lapa & Doca de Alcâtara — Map p79

Estrela and Lapa, west of Bairro Alto, are wealthy districts with a discreet, moneyed look. Getting here on a westbound tram No 28 is fun (you can also take bus No 13 from Praça do Comércio).

In the Largo de São Bento is one of the area's most imposing sights, the **Palácio da Assembleia da República** (Palácio da Assembleia Nacional), Portugal's parliament, once the enormous 17th-century Benedictine Mosteiro de São Bento. The national assembly has convened here since 1833.

Nearby is **Casa Museu de Amália Rodrigues** (☎ 213 971 896; Rua de São Bento 17; admission €5; 🕒 10am-1pm & 2-6pm Tue-Sun). More of a pilgrimage site than a museum, this ochre house is where fado diva Amália lived – along the street you'll notice graffiti announcing it Rua Amália. The short tours include recordings of performances.

At the top of Calçada da Estrela bulge the dome and belfries of the **Basílica da Estrela** (☎ 213 960 915; admission free; 🕒 8am-1pm & 3-8pm). Completed in 1790 by order of Dona Maria I (whose tomb is here) in gratitude for a male heir, the church is all elegant neoclassicism outside and chilly, echoing baroque inside. The view from the dome could join the cut-throat competition for the city's best.

Across the road is an attractive public park, the **Jardim da Estrela**, with a good children's playground. Beyond this lies the unkempt Protestant **Cemitério dos Ingleses** (English Cemetery), founded in 1717. Among expats at rest here are novelist Henry Fielding (author of *Tom Jones*), who died during an unsuccessful visit to Lisbon to improve his health in 1754. At the far corner are the remains of Lisbon's old Jewish cemetery.

To the south of Estrela is **Lapa**, Lisbon's diplomatic quarter. Here is the fine **Museu Nacional de Arte Antiga** (National Museum of Ancient Art; ☎ 213 964 151; www.mnarteantiga-ipmuseus.pt; Rua das Janelas Verdes 9; adult/under 26/senior €3/1.50/1.50, 10am-2pm Sun free; 2-6pm Tue, 10am-6pm Wed-Sun). Housed in a grand 17th-century palace (take bus No 60 from Praça da Figueira or tram No 15 west from Praça do Comércio), this has an amazing European art collection, bursting with Portuguese works, including painting, sculpture, ceramics, textiles and furniture. There is also a superb collection of decorative art from Africa, India, China and Japan. You can buy a guide (€1) in Portuguese or English.

Masterpiece of the collection is the *Panels of São Vicente* by Nuno Gonçalves, most brilliant of the Flemish-influenced 15th-century Portuguese painters. His genius was to depict contemporary society with extraordinarily naturalistic portraits, so the centuries-old faces look like ones you might meet today. The six fabulously detailed panels show a social lucky dip (from fishermen, sailors and priests, to the Duke of Bragança and his family) paying homage to São Vicente, Portugal's patron saint. The frequently reproduced central panels include Prince Henry the Navigator, who apparently borrowed his hat from Benjamin Bunny.

Foreign highlights include Bosch's hallucinatory *Temptation of St Anthony*, populated by strange creatures and flying fish, a haunting, glowing *Salome* by Lucas Cranach, *St Jerome* (a self-portrait?) by Dürer, *Works of Mercy* by Brueghel, Poussin's *Philistines Attacked by the Plague*, Courbet's bleak *Snow* and *Danaide* by Rodin.

Artefacts from China and Japan form a fascinating collection, the highlight being Japanese *namban* screens. *Namban* ('southern barbarians'), the Japanese name for the Portuguese who landed on Tanegaxima island in 1543, now refers to all Japanese art inspired by this encounter. The 16th-century screens show the arrival of the huge-nosed Portuguese in absorbing detail. Vastly rich inlaid Goan furniture is another joy.

Gem-smothered religious treasures include the *Monstrance of Belém* (1506), a reliquary container made with gold brought back by Vasco da Gama on his second journey. There's also some amazing jewellery – mostly from convent collections – and a gleaming silverware collection, with dozens of masterpieces by the French silversmith Thomas Germain and his son François-Thomas, made in the late 18th century for the Portuguese court and royal family.

The wing integrates the beautiful baroque chapel – sole remnant of a Carmelite convent that adjoined the palace.

For something entirely different, head to charming **Museu da Carris** (☎ 213 613 000; Rua 1 de Maio; adult/child under 12/under 26 €2.50/0.50/1.30; 10am-5pm Mon-Fri, to 1pm & 2-5pm Sat), housed in the Carris headquarters, which tells the history of Lisbon's most endearing means of transport using the models-in-glass-cases method. Tram No 15 passes right by so you can have a holistic experience.

Museu da Marioneta (Puppet Museum; ☎ 213 942 810; Rua da Esperança 146; adult/under 26/senior €2.50/1.30/1.30; 10am-12.30pm & 2-5.30pm Wed-Sun), in the eastern part of the district, houses a bewitching collection of puppets in the splendid Convento das Bernardas. There's something of everything here, from shadow puppets and Punch and Judy, to Vietnamese water and elephant puppets and full-sized Portuguese creations. There's a surprisingly grand **restaurant** (dishes €16.50-32, lunch Wed-Sun).

Rato, Marquês de Pombal & Saldanha

Map pp80–1

Head north for hothouses and high culture.

Chief must-see is the eclectic, brilliant collection of the **Museu Calouste Gulbenkian** (☎ 217 823 461; www.museu.gulbenkian.pt; Avenida de Berna 45A; adult/child €3/free, Sun free; combined ticket with Centro de Arte Moderna €5; 10am-6pm Tue-Sun; metro São Sebastião). Calouste Sarkis Gulbenkian, born to Armenian parents in Istanbul in 1869, was one of the 20th century's wealthiest philanthropists, an astute and generous patron of the arts even before he struck it rich in Iraqi oil. His guiding tenet for this collection was 'Only the best is good enough for me' and he was advised by experts such as art historian Sir Kenneth Clark. His great artistic coup was buying from Leningrad's Hermitage between 1928 and 1930, when the young Soviet Union desperately needed hard currency. He fell out with the British in 1942, who declared him a 'technical enemy', waving his collection goodbye. Washington also had beady eyes on his loot but during the war years he plumped on Portugal as his safe haven. He lived in Lisbon's Hotel Aviz for 13 years until his death in 1955, when he bequeathed the nation the stupendous lot (some pieces had already gone to the Museu Antiga) along with a charitable foundation – Portugal's main cultural life force.

The museum is one of Europe's unsung treasures, housed in a sleek, specially designed 1960s building, with escape routes into surrounding restful gardens. The collection – over 6000 pieces, although only 1500 can be permanently exhibited – spans every major epoch of Western art and much Eastern art. It's interspersed with bilingual information touch-screens and you can follow two circuits: one Oriental and classical, one European. You'll need at least a full day – possibly two – so you can spend one day in the East, one in the West, taking frequent garden breathers.

Nearby is the foundation's other major museum, the **Centro de Arte Moderna** (Modern Art Centre; ☎ 217 823 474; admission €3, combined ticket €5, free Sun; ⏲ 2-6pm Tue-Sun), a white, warehouse-like space showing an unparalleled collection of modern Portuguese art, including influential Amadeo de Souza Cardoso, who caused a scandal with his experiments in cubism, expressionism and futurism; abstract works by iconic modernist José de Almada Negreiros; the haunting grotesque fairytales of Paula Rego, Portugal's best-known contemporary artist; and the geometric brilliance of Angelo de Souza. Works by modern British artists such as David Hockney, Bridget Riley, Anthony Gormley and Julien Opie serve as points of reference. The café is a Lisbon institution, and good for vegetarians.

Parque Eduardo VII (Avenida da Liberdade) is down the road. The huge park (named after England's Edward VII, who visited Lisbon in 1903) provides a fine escape, especially in its gorgeous **estufas** (greenhouses; adult/child under 12 €1.20/free), filled with brilliant exotic flowers. The **estufa fria** (cool greenhouse; ⏲ 9am-5pm Oct-Apr, to 6pm May-Sep) and **estufa quente** (hot greenhouse; ⏲ 9am-4.30pm Oct-Apr, to 5.30pm May-Sep) were built on an old quarry site – planting began in 1910. There's also an **outdoor area** (⏲ 9am-4.30pm Oct-Apr, to 5.30pm May-Sep), with a large pond. Access is from Rua Castilho on the western side of the park. There's a great playground nearby.

The 109 arches of the **Aqueduto das Águas Livres** lope across the hills into Lisbon from

MUSEU CALOUSTE GULBENKIAN HIGHLIGHTS

Among the classical and Oriental collections, some of the most memorable items are in the **Egyptian Room**: an exquisite 2700-year-old alabaster bowl, a gilded silver mummy mask, small female statuettes (each differently coiffed), and some naturalistic bronze cats. In the adjoining **Greek and Roman** section are a 2400-year-old Attic vase, luminescent Roman glassware and Hellenic coins with finely carved heads and figures.

Oriental Islamic treasures include some 16th- and 17th-century Turkish faïence glowing with brilliant greens and blues, Persian carpets and 14th-century mosque lamps from Syria, with strikingly sensuous shapes. The adjoining **Armenian** collection includes illuminated manuscripts from the 16th to 18th centuries.

In the **Chinese and Japanese** section, huge pieces of 18th-century Chinese porcelain contrast with small neat Japanese writing boxes and lacquered picnic sets of the same era.

Going west, **European Art** sweeps from medieval ivories and jewel-like manuscripts to 15th- to 19th-century masterpieces. All the big names are here, including Rembrandt *(Portrait of an Old Man)*, Van Dyck and Rubens (including the frantic *Loves of the Centaurs*). Particularly lovely is the 15th-century *Portrait of a Girl* by Ghirlandaio and a white marble *Diana* by Houdon.

Eighteenth- and 19th-century European art doesn't get skimped, with Aubusson tapestries, fabulously fussy furniture (including items from Versailles), Sèvres porcelain, and intricate clocks. Outstanding works include Gainsborough's *Mrs Lowndes*, two atmospheric La Tour portraits, turbulent Turners and a passionate *Spring Kiss* by Rodin. There are also Manets (*Boy Blowing Bubbles*), Monets *(Stilllife with Melon)* and a marvellously pretty Renoir.

Grand finale is the incredible collection of **René Lalique** glass and jewellery. Here are fabulous, unique fantasies, such as the outrageous, otherworldly *Dragonfly* pectoral glittering with gold, enamel, moonstones and diamonds, the dark-wood *Serpents Mirror* and the *Cats* choker – an extravaganza in rock crystal, gold, enamel and diamonds.

Caneças, over 18km away – most spectacularly at **Campolide**, where the tallest arch is an incredible 65m high (take any train from Rossio to the first stop). Built between 1728 and 1835, by order of Dom João V, it brought Lisbon its first clean drinking water.

The King laid the aqueduct's final stone at **Mãe d'Água** (Mother of Water; Praça das Amoreiras; adult €3; 10am-6pm Mon-Sat), the city's massive, 5500-cu-metre main reservoir. The reservoir's cool, echoing chamber (check out the start of the narrow aqueduct passage), completed in 1834, now hosts art exhibitions. See the Santa Apolónia section (p88) for details of the related museum.

Greater Lisbon — Map pp74–5

Quinta dos Marquêses da Fronteira (☎ 217 782 023; Largo de São Domingos de Benfica 1; admission €5; tours at 10.30am, 11am, 11.30am & noon Mon-Sat) is a charming, rundown, 17th-century mansion, with tiles covering any space that's not formal Renaissance garden. You must reserve ahead for a tour.

Two metro stops north of Parque Eduardo VII is the kid-pleasing but somewhat cooped-up **Jardim Zoológico** (Zoological Garden; ☎ 217 232 900; adult/child €11/8.30; 10am-6pm Oct-Apr, to 8pm May-Sep), in attractive gardens with more than 2000 animals. There's also a dolphin show and rowing boats.

Further north the **Museu da Cidade** (City Museum; ☎ 217 591 617; Campo Grande 245; admission €2, 10am-1pm Sun free; to 1pm & 2-6pm Tue-Sun; metro Campo Grande), in the Palácio Pimenta, careers through Lisbon's amazing rollercoaster history with an enormous model of pre-earthquake Lisbon and an excellent collection of tiles.

PARQUE DAS NAÇÕES

On the northeastern riverfront, the **Parque das Nações** (naz-*oish;* Nations Park) was built for Expo 98. The development includes a huge world-of-its-own aquarium – the Oceanarió – plus the Pavilhão do Conhecimento, a cable car, a landscaped riverside park with restaurants and bars, and some stunning modern architecture: the ribbed, organic, Death Star structure of **Gare do Oriente** designed by Spanish architect Santiago Calatrava, and the **Pavilhão de Portugal** by Portugal's leading architect, Álvaro Siza Vieira.

Designed by acclaimed Spanish architect Santiago Calatrava, Gare do Oriente station is an extraordinary vaulted, vented structure that creates spectacular, haunting, organic and skeletal shapes. The echoing interiors resemble the Star Wars Death Star while the outside features vast, angled fish scale-like ribbing. The metro station below features azulejo works by international artists from Hundertwasser to Zao Wo Ki. The other spectacular development born of the 1998 Expo was the Ponte de Vasco da Gama. This bridge is awesome – unbelievably long (17,185m long and 30m wide) – and vanishes into the distance. It's no surprise that it's Europe's longest bridge. The curvature of the earth had to be taken into account when building, so as to locate the piers evenly. The foundations go down to 85m below sea level and it's been built to withstand an earthquake 4.5 times stronger than the big one of 1755, and to cope with winds of up to 250kmph. The 2km-long site sometimes feels as if you have wandered into an architectural model, but is an entertaining place to visit, particularly for families. The Atlantic Pavilion hosts major concerts, such as Madonna in 2004.

Take the metro to Gare do Oriente and walk through the Centro Vasco da Gama to the park's main **Posto de Informação** (☎ 218 919 333; www.parquedasnacoes.pt; 10am-8pm Apr-Oct, to 7pm Nov-Mar), with free maps and information. The Cartão do Parque (adult/child €15.50/8.50) gives free admission to the Oceanarió, Pavilhão do Conhecimento, cable car and Vasco da Gama tower, as well as discounts on bikes, bowling and at some restaurants.

Children and adults alike will adore the superb **Oceanário** (Oceanarium; ☎ 218 917 002; www.oceanario.pt; adult/child under 4/under 12 €9/free/4.50; 10am-7pm Apr-Oct, to 6pm Nov-Mar). This magical seven-million-litre aquarium – the vast central tank contains five million litres – has 450 different species from the world's different seas, accompanied by loads of fascinating facts to wow your inner anorak (did you know the Pacific covers a third of the world?). Wonderful sea creatures include the 2.5m-wide giant manta, seemingly flying through the water, cuddly sea otters, endearing penguins, 3m-long sharks, plant-like seadragons, and Nemo from *Finding Nemo,* aka the clown anenomefish. There is disabled access.

Lie on a bed of nails or play an invisible harp at the **Pavilhão do Conhecimento** (Knowledge Pavilion; ☎ 218 917 100; www.pavconhecimento.pt; adult/child €5/2.50; ⏲ 10am-6pm Tue-Fri, 11am-7pm Sat & Sun), with lots of fun exhibits explaining scientific phenomena and pointing out how reality and perception often contradict. There's an indoor playground for three- to six-year olds, a free cybercafé and disabled access.

The 140m-high **Torre de Vasco da Gama** (☎ 218 918 000; adult/child 5-14 €2.50/1.50; ⏲ 10am-8pm Apr-Oct, to 6pm Nov-Mar) has panoramic views of the park, river and city, and an upmarket restaurant.

A riverside **teleférico** (cable car; adult/child 5-14 €5.50/3 return; ⏲ 11am-7pm), over 1km long and 20m high, gives stunning views of the river and the Vasco da Gama bridge.

Tejo Bike (☎ 218 871 976; ⏲ 10am-8pm Apr-Oct, noon-6pm Nov-Mar), at the northern end of the park, rents bikes (per hour adult/child/tandem €4/3/7) or karts (adult/child/family €6/5/12).

A **minitrain** (adult/child €2.50/1.50; ⏲ 10am-7pm Apr-Sep, to 5pm Nov-Mar) trundles around hourly, too.

For details about the park's bowling centre, see p94.

Belém

Map p81

Stately Belém, 6km west of the Rossio, has immense historical importance and architectural riches, and makes a great day trip. (Note: everything's closed Monday.) Most famously, this was the place from which the great explorer Vasco da Gama set sail on 8 July 1497 for the two-year voyage on which he discovered a sea route to India, shifting the world's balance of power and showering riches on the Portuguese.

When Vasco da Gama returned safely, Dom Manuel I ordered the construction of a monastery on the site of the riverside chapel (founded by Henry the Navigator) where Da Gama and his officers had kept an all-night vigil before departing.

The Jerónimos, like its predecessor, was dedicated to the Virgin Mary, St Mary of Bethlehem (Belém) – hence the district's name.

The fantastical monastery and an offshore watchtower (both Unesco World Heritage sites) are prime examples of splendidly over-excited Manueline architecture (p50).

The best way to get here is on the modern No 15 tram from Praça da Figueira or Praça do Comércio; alternatively take bus No 14 from Rossio or Praça da Figueira. Frequent trains from Cais do Sodré to Oeiras stop at Belém.

A miniature **tourist train** (☎ 213 582 334; ticket €3; ⏲ 10am-7pm Apr-Aug) makes a regular tour of the slightly spread-out sights.

MOSTEIRO DOS JERÓNIMOS

Vasco da Gama's discovery of a sea route to India inspired the glorious **Mosteiro dos Jerónimos**, (www.mosteirojeronimos.pt), a Unesco World Heritage site with an architectural exuberance that trumpets 'navigational triumph'. Killing two birds with one architectural edifice, it also became a pantheon for Manuel I and his royal descendants (many now entombed in its chancel and side chapels). Huge sums were funnelled into the project, including pepper money (a 5% tax on income from the spice trade with African and Far Eastern colonies).

Work began around 1501, following a Gothic design by architect Diogo de Boitaca, considered a Manueline originator. After his death in 1517, building resumed with a Renaissance flavour under Spaniard João de Castilho and, later, with classical overtones under Diogo de Torralva and Jérome de Rouen (Jerónimo de Ruão). The monastery was completed in 1541, a riverside masterpiece – the waters have since receded.

The huge neo-Manueline western wing and domed bell tower were added in the 19th century.

It was populated with monks of the Order of St Jerome, whose spiritual job for about four centuries was to give comfort and guidance to sailors – and to pray for the king's soul. When the order was dissolved in 1833 the monastery was used as a school and orphanage until about 1940.

The façade has a horizontal structure, to encourage a feeling of repose. It looks like no-one told João de Castilho about the repose idea – his fantastic southern portal is a filigree frenzy, dense with religious and secular significance.

You enter the **church** (☎ 213 620 034; Praça do Império; admission free; ⏲ 10am-6.30pm Tue-Sun May-Sep, to 5pm Tue-Sun Oct-Apr) through the western portal. The first thing you notice about the interior is its height, reaching up to an

JOHN KING

Elevador da Bica (p86), Bairro Alto, Lisbon

PAUL BERNHARDT

Lisbon nightlife (p106)

Lisbon (p71)

CARLOS COSTA

BRUCE YUAN-YUE BI

Sala das Armas (p120), Palácio Nacional de Sintra, Sintra

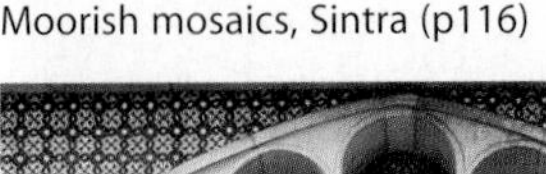

Moorish mosaics, Sintra (p116)

MARTIN MOOS

Rio Sado, Setúbal (p137)

CARLO

unsupported baroque transept vault 25m high. Tall, tree trunk-like columns seem to grow into the ceiling, which is itself a spider web of stone. Windows cast a lilting golden light over the church. Superstar Vasco da Gama is interred in the lower chancel, just to the left of the entrance, in a place of honour opposite literary big gun Luís de Camões, the 16th-century poet.

From the upper choir you get a superb view of the church, and the rows of seats are Portugal's first Renaissance woodcarvings.

Peaceful even when crowded, the monastery's golden-stone **cloisters** (adult/child under 15/under 26 €3/free/1.50, 10am-2pm Sun free; same as church) dance with Manueline organic detail and exotic influences from overseas. The simple tomb of renowned poet and writer Fernando Pessoa is here. One wall is lined with 12 confessionals – so monks could hear penitents who came to the church. The sarcophagus in the echoing chapterhouse on the northeastern corner belongs to the 19th-century Portuguese historian Alexandre Herculano (he of many street names).

TORRE DE BELÉM

Another Unesco World Heritage site, the **Torre de Belém** (Tower of Belém; ☎ 213 620 034; Avenida da Índia; admission 3.50; 10am-6pm Tue-Sun May-Sep, to 5pm Oct-Apr) has come to symbolise the Age of Discoveries. The pearly-grey chesspiece was designed by the brilliant Arruda brothers, Diogo and Francisco, in a shaken-not-stirred mix of early Gothic, Byzantine and Manueline styles. It's just offshore, about 1km from the monastery – before the shoreline shifted south, the tower sat right out in midstream. Manuel I built it around 1515 to guard the entrance to Lisbon's harbour, perhaps to catch invaders off guard.

PADRÃO DOS DESCOBRIMENTOS

The huge limestone **Padrão dos Descobrimentos** (Discoveries Monument; admission adult/child under 7/under 18 €2/free/1.50; 9am-5pm Tue-Sun), inaugurated in 1960 on the 500th anniversary of Prince Henry the Navigator's death, is shaped like a stylised caravel, chock-full of Portuguese bigwigs. At the prow is Henry himself; behind him are top-of-the-pops explorers Vasco da Gama, Diogo Cão and Fernão de Magalhães, poet Luís de Camões, painter Nuno Gonçalves and 27 other good-and-greats. Inside are exhibition rooms, an audiovisual show introducing the city – *The Lisbon Experience* – and a lift and stairs to the top, with its impressive monastery and river views.

CENTRO CULTURAL DE BELÉM & MUSEU DO DESIGN

One of Lisbon's most important cultural venues, **Centro Cultural de Belém** (CCB; ☎ 213 612 400; www.ccb.pt; Praça do Império) is a mottled grey-peach modern building with music, dance and exhibitions.

Inside is the world-class **Museu do Design** (☎ 213 612 934; adult/child under 12/under 15 €3/0.50/1.75; 11am-8pm, last admission 7.15pm). Financier Francisco Capelo started his collection in 1937. The wonderful array includes the lean lines of Charles and Ray Eames, the '60s bright excesses of Vernon Panton, late-'60s beanbags, Frank O Gehry's 1970s *Wiggle Side* chair, and Michael Graves' scary 1981 *Plaza* dressing table (an overgrown Barbie set). Not only are these beautiful, humorous pieces of design, but the museum also puts their development in a social context. The contest for the most uncomfortable-looking chair is also impressive, but we think Philippe Starck's *WW* stool has the edge.

Other halls feature changing modern art exhibitions. There's an excellent bookshop and disabled access.

OTHER MUSEUMS

The **Museu Nacional dos Coches** (National Coach Museum; ☎ 213 610 850; Praça Afonso de Albuquerque; adult/student €3/1.50; 10am-5.30pm Tue-Sun), in the former royal riding school, has a fairytale collection of 17th- to 19th-century coaches. The oldest is Phillip II's, used to visit Portugal in 1619. Cunningly plain on the outside, it has inside a suitably regal golden globular ceiling. Most spectacular are the three triumphal vehicles sent to Pope Clement by spendthrift king João V. Festooned with symbols of triumphant Portuguese navigation, they are so gold and heavy it's surprising they could move at all.

The **Museu de Arte Popular** (Folk Art Museum; ☎ 213 011 282; Avenida de Brasília; adult/child under 12 €2/free; 10am-12.30pm & 2-5pm Tue-Sun) should house a charming collection of regional folk art. The main museum has been closed long-term for refurbishment, but there are occasional temporary exhibitions.

Opened in 1893, the **Museu Nacional de Arqueologia** (National Museum of Archaeology; Praça do Império; ☎ 213 620 000; adult/child under 15/under 25 €3/free/1.50, 10am-2pm Sun free; 🕑 2-6pm Tue, 10am-6pm Wed-Sun), in the Mosteiro dos Jerónimos' western wing, has exhibits from prehistory to Moorish times, including reverentially lit Graeco-Roman antiquities, such as funerary masks, mummies, tiny mummified crocodiles, sandals and combs. The other highlight is the Treasures Room, with a great haul of gleaming, burnished antique gold jewellery, from massive Bronze Age torques to a delicate Roman snake bracelet.

Next door is the **Museu de Marinha** (Naval Museum; ☎ 213 620 019; adult/child under 6/under 17 €3/free/1.50; 🕑 10am-5pm Tue-Sun Oct-Mar, to 6pm Tue-Sun Apr-Sep). Among the armadas of model boats, this has gems such as Vasco da Gama's portable wooden altar and the rich, polished private quarters of the 1900 UK-built royal yacht *Amélia*. There are also ornate royal barges, the biggest a 1780 neo-Viking number, and a cute wooden 1917 seaplane that could've been made from a toy kit. A **children's museum** (🕑 weekends) offers brightly coloured creative activities.

ACTIVITIES

Bird-watching

The **Reserva Natural do Estuário do Tejo** (headquarters ☎ 212 341 742; Avenida dos Combatentes da Grande Guerra 1, Alcochete) is upriver from Lisbon. A vitally important wetland area, it hosts around 40,000 migrant wading birds during the winter, including avocets and teals. It's accessible from Montijo, a ferry ride from Lisbon's Terreiro do Paço (p113).

Bowling

Bowling Internacional de Lisboa (Map pp74-5; ☎ 218 922 521; www.bilbowling.com; Parque das Nações; 🕑 noon-2am Mon-Thu, to 4am Fri, 11am-4am Sat, to 2am Sun) is Portugal's biggest centre.

Golf

There are six major courses around (p131), plus the **Lisbon Sports Club** (☎ 214 310 077; Casal da Carregueira, Belas), which is located just north of Queluz.

Swimming

The handiest swimming pool is the small, rooftop (indoor) **Ateneu Comercial Complexo de Piscinas** (Map pp76-8; ☎ 213 430 947; Rua das Portas de Santo Antão 102; admission Mon-Fri €3.50, Sat €3.60; 🕑 9am-noon, 1.30-4.30pm & 9-10pm Mon, Wed & Fri, 7.30am-10am, 1.30-4pm & 9-10pm Tue & Thu, 3.30-7pm Sat). Professional-standard **Complexo de Piscinas do EUL** (Map pp74-5; ☎ 217 994 970; Avenida Professor Gama Pinto; admission €8; 🕑 6.45am-10pm Mon-Fri, to 7pm Sat) is part of the university's sports complex. (Head north 400m from Cidade-Universitária metro.)

Tennis

Also at the university sports complex are the university's **tennis courts** (☎ 217 932 895). More courts are at the **Instalações de Ténis de Monsanto** (Map pp74-5; ☎ 213 648 741; Parque Florestal de Monsanto); to get there take bus No 24 from Alcântara or 29 from Belém. You'll need to reserve at both places.

WALKING TOUR – TRAM 28 & ALFAMA

Start: Largo Martim Moniz or Baixa
Finish: Near Praça do Comercio
Distance: 2km
Duration: Two to three hours

This viewpoint-to-viewpoint route starts on tram No 28 from Largo Martim Moniz or Baixa, thus taking in the city's best tram route *and* avoiding uphill slogs. Take the tram up to Largo da Graça – just to the east of the huge barracks. From here you can walk northwards and turn left behind the barracks to pay a visit to the **Miradouro da Senhora do Monte** (**1**; p87). Otherwise, walk south and turn right in front of the barracks to **Miradouro da Graça** (**2**; p87). Then retrace your steps, walking eastwards to visit the tiled glories of **Igreja de São Vicente de Fora** (**3**; p87), then the cool, echoing **Panteão Nacional** (**4**; p87). If it's Saturday, make a detour to the **Thieves Market** (**5**; p96). Otherwise, walk directly west along Arco Grande da Cima till you reach Largo de Rodrigues de Freita. Take the Costa do Castelo fork, continuing west. This way you can walk right around the outskirts of the castle, along narrow cobbled streets, with some stunning views. Pass in front of **Hotel Solar dos Mouros** (**6**; p99), then turn left up to the **castelo** (**7**; p87) and a **viewpoint (8)**. Next head down the steep lanes to Largo das Portal do Sol,

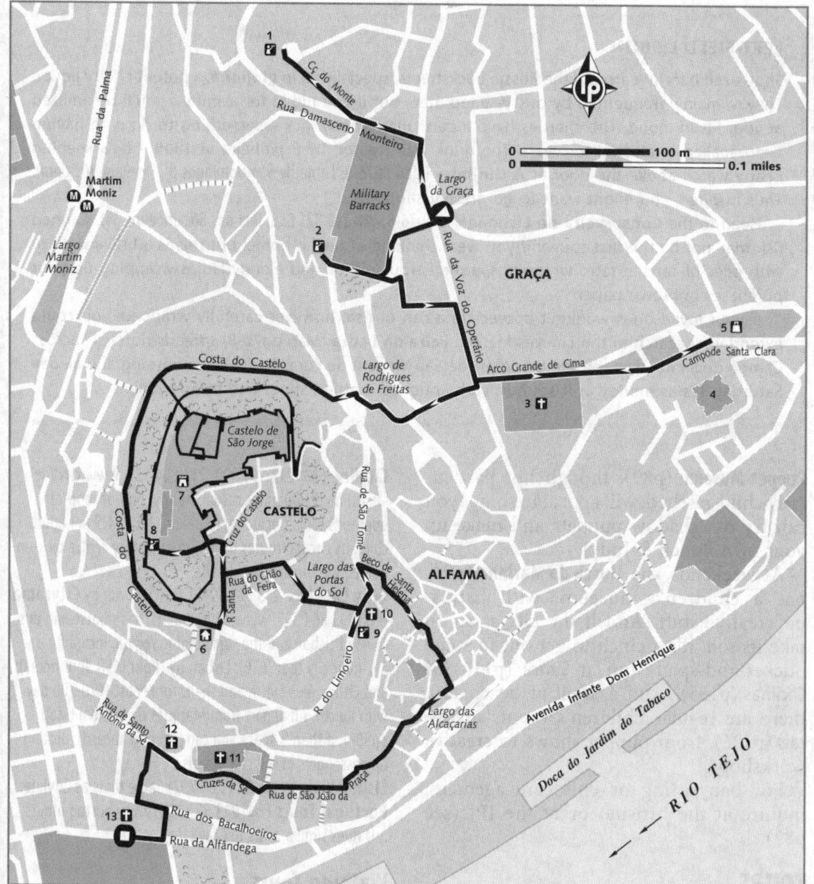

and another fine view from **Miradouro de Santa Luzia** (**9**; p87). From here walk northward, past **Igreja de Santa Luzia (10)** on your right, and turn right in the atmospheric lane of Beco de Santa Helena. This will take you through one of Alfama's most colourful neighbourhoods, to Largo das Alcaçarias, from where you can take Rua de São João westwards to the **sé** (**11**; p86) and the **Igreja de Santo António (12)**. Downhill from here, your final stop is a gaze at the amazing Manueline façade of **Igreja da Conceiça o Velha (13)**, just east of Praça do Comercio.

LISBON FOR CHILDREN

Prime kids' territory is **Parque das Nações** (p91). Hop-on hop-off **tours** (p96) are a good idea in short bursts as Lisbon's hills could prove even more tiring for small legs. Boat trips and tram rides, particularly **No 28** (p116) are fun for kids. Viewpoint lifts are often winners, from the *Charlie and the Chocolate Factory* absurdity of **Elevador Santa Justa** (p84) to the **Discoveries Monument** (p93) and **Cristo Rei** (p135). You can often entertain a child in a church if they get a chance to light a candle.

Most large squares and parks in Lisbon have children's playgrounds, with the star prize going to **Parque Eduardo VII** (p90), where there is also a busily bird-inhabited lake. The **zoo** (p91) is another kid-pleaser, and includes an Animax Fun Park which has a 3D cinema and remote-control boats. The

LEFT-FIELD LISBON

Shot-sized bars lurk around the Rossio backstreets, specialising in **ginjinha**, a potent cherry liquor. They're mainly frequented by dusty-suited men, but if you nip in for a snifter, you'll be amazed at your lift in mood. The cherries have a particularly zippy kick – something to do with having been soaked in alcohol for years. The drink was created by Espinheira in 1840 – he's keeping beady watch above the door at **A Ginjinha** (Map pp76-8; Largo de São Domingos 8; 9am-10.30pm). Thus inspired, you might want to go present-shopping.

Head to the **Conserveira de Lisboa** (Map pp76-8; 218 871 058; Rua dos Bacalhoeiros 34). Canned fish may not be the first souvenir you were thinking of taking home, but this is a brilliant place with piles of cans in retro wrappings, a monstrous old till and elderly ladies wrapping up your purchases in brown paper.

If your loved ones wouldn't appreciate a can of fish, however carefully wrapped, you could extend your search to the Thieves Market. **Feira da Ladra** (Map pp76-8) spreads riotously across Campo de Santa Clara, beside the Igreja de São Vincent de Fora, on Tuesday morning and all day Saturday. It's as motley as it sounds, with antiques, clothes, shoes and bizarre junk.

Puppet Museum (p89), though not particularly child-pitched, will appeal to some (you can try out shadow puppets and make up your own Punch & Judy).

At weekends, the **Museu do Marinha** (p94) has a children's museum, with hands-on creative stuff. And if the city starts to take its toll, it's a cinch to get out to some bucket-and-spade fun at **Sintra** (p116) or **Cacilhas** (p135). And as well as beach fun, there are regular children's events in **Cascais** (p126), from puppet shows to creative workshops.

For babysitting or childcare agencies, inquire at the turismo or at the IPJ (see p82).

TOURS

Bus & Tram Tours

Art Shuttle (toll-free 800 250 251; www.artshuttle.net; per person 3hr tour €35, 2-8 people) Runs minibus tours to most important museums, galleries and cultural sites. Also offers combined river and land tour (€50) and, if you're really pressed for time, a 30-minute helicopter tour (€800, max 5 people).

Carris (213 613 010, 966 298 558; carristur@carris.pt) The municipal transport company runs 1½-hour tram tours (adult/child €16/8): one around the Baixa and Alfama (13 to 18 daily); and one that continues to Belém (three daily). Carris also runs frequent open-top bus tours (€13/6.50) from Praça do Comércio: the Tagus Tour of the city and Belém; and the Orient Tour of northeast Lisbon, including Parque das Nações and the Tile Museum. It also offers a €30 two-day ticket for unlimited trips on Tagus, the tourist tram, the Orient and normal Carris service.

Cityline (213 191 090, 213 864 322; www.cityline-sightline.pt) Operates casual, hourly, hop-on-hop-off open-bus tours (including to Belém) for €14/9 per adult/child. Its circular routes have numerous city centre pick-up points; the turismo has details.

Gray Line (213 522 594) Gray Line, run by **Cityrama** (213 864 322; www.cityrama.pt), has sightseeing bus tours of Lisbon and the surrounding region, including a 5½-hour city tour (€30); Lisbon by Night (€58, four hours); and Lisbon plus Sintra and the Estoril coast (€70, full day with lunch). All depart from Marquês de Pombal (Map pp80-1; if there's space you can just hop aboard), picking up passengers at selected hotels.

Lisboa Vision (214 788 792) Same tours as Cityline.

Portugal Tours (213 522 902; www.portugaltours.pt) Runs similar tours to Gray Line.

Walking Tours

Centro Nacional de Cultura (CNC; 213 466 722; www.cnc.pt; Rua António Maria Cardoso 68; 3hr walk €25) Organises walks for groups of five or more people. Contact the CNC for details.

Papa-Léguas (218 452 689; www.papa-leguas.com in Portuguese; Rua Conde de Sabugosa 3F) Offers walks in Parque Florestal de Monsanto from May to October, costing €15 per person.

River Cruises

Gray Line (213 522 594) Minicruises on the Tagus, at 2.30pm (€27, Tue-Sun Apr-Oct) From Parque Eduardo VII.

Transtejo (218 820 348; www.transtejo.pt; Terreiro do Paço terminal) Runs 2½-hour, multilingual Rio Tejo cruises (adult/child €20/8) at 11am and 3pm from April to October, from the east of Praça do Comércio. These head to Parc das Nações, then Belém.

FESTIVALS & EVENTS

Lisbon loves an opportunity to parade, celebrate and munch, and has abundant festivals combining all the above.

February

Festival das Músicas e dos Portos (Harbour & Music Festival) 10 days in early February, features fado combined with music from another port city (previously Athens and New Orleans).

March

Super Bock Super Rock (www.superbock.pt) Lisbon shares its biggest rock event with Porto: a fortnight of 18 concerts in both cities.

Lisbon Arte (www.lisboarte.com) From mid-March to the end of April, open studios all over Lisbon show contemporary art.

April

Festa da Música At Centro Cultural de Belém (p93) Lots of classical concerts at the end of the month.

May

Encontros de Música Contemporânea (Contemporary Music Encounters) One of several annual international music festivals organised by the Fundação Calouste Gulbenkian (p89).

Festival Cantigas do Maio (Songs of May) The south-bank town of Seixal hosts this unusual festival in late May, with traditional international music.

June

Festival Internacional de Cinema de Tróia (☎ 265 539 120) Long-established, and taking place in early June.

Festas dos Santos Populares (Festivals of the Popular Saints) The city goes crazy in June with Christianised versions of the summer solstice, featuring Festa de São João, Festa de São Pedro and Festa de Santo António.

Festa de Santo António (St Anthony; 12–13 June, see 'St Anthony', right) This one is when Lisbon really lets its hair down. It's the climax of three weeks of partying known as the Festas de Lisboa, celebrated with particular intensity in Alfama and Madragoa, with some 50 *arraiais* (street parties). The highlight is the Marchas Populares on the evening of 12 June when dozens of communities march along Avenida da Liberdade, with the ultimate *arraial* in the Alfama on the same night.

Festa de São João (St John; 23–24 June)

Festa de São Pedro (St Peter; 28–29 June)

August

Jazz em Agosto (Jazz in August) Early August sees another music festival at the Fundação Calouste Gulbenkian (p89).

Festival dos Oceanos (Oceans Festival) For two weeks from mid-August, big shows and parades, concerts and gastronomic fairs all have a nautical theme.

September

Festival de Cinema Gay e Lésbico (Gay & Lesbian Film Festival) For two weeks in late September.

November

Festival Internacional de Dança Contemporânea Dance fans flock to Centro Cultural de Belém's alternative event.

> **ST ANTHONY**
>
> Although St Vincent is Lisbon's patron saint, Lisboêtas prefer St Anthony, born in Lisbon in 1195 (try not to mention he mainly lived in France and Italy).
>
> Revered in Italy as St Anthony of Padua, or simply Il Santo, his good deeds made him internationally famous, and he was canonised shortly after his death in 1231. He is best renowned in Portugal for being the saint of love – many single women apply for husband-finding help by leaving him notes, and newlyweds leave thank-you gifts at his church opposite the Sé. The city's affection for him really bubbles over during the Festa de Santo António (12–13 June).

SLEEPING

It's wise to reserve ahead during high season (July to mid-September), when prices are highest. July prices are listed here. Off-season they can drop considerably, and some places offer discounts for long stays.

Rossio, Praça dos Restauradores & Baixa — Map pp76–8

With the biggest range of places to stay, the central area is best for budget travellers, but also has well-heeled choices. This is where to stay if you want to be near the action, and is quieter than Bairro Alto.

BUDGET

Many cheap places in the Baixa are on upper floors of old residential flats.

Pensão Praça da Figueira (☎/fax 213 426 757; rrcoelho@clix.pt; 3rd fl, Travessa Nova de São Domingos 9; s/d €15/30, with shower €23/33; 💻) A well-run, super place with wooden floors and bright, well-kept rooms, small, communal kitchens with fridge, and laundry service. Some of the rooms have *praça* views.

Pensão Imperial (☎ 213 420 166; 4th fl, Praça dos Restauradores 78; s/d with shared bathroom €20/40) A cheery place with an irresistible location (but note no lift) and varnished wooden floors. Readers have enjoyed staying here; some rooms on the lower floor overlook the *praça*, but those on the upper floor are quieter.

Pensão Norte (☎ 218 878 941; fax 218 868 462; 2nd-4th fl, Rua dos Douradores 161; s/d with shower €30/60) Has a warren of small, nice functional rooms with telephone, which overlook the street.

Pensão Santo Tirso (☎ 213 470 428; fax 213 422 070; 3rd fl, Rossio 18; s/d with shared bathroom €20/40) This friendly, bright pension has nice plain rooms, some of which overlook the square. Singles are poky, but it's welcoming and the management speaks English well.

Pensão Estrela de Ouro (☎ 213 465 110; 3rd fl, Largo Trindade Coelho 6; d/tr €30/35) Conveniently near the centre, on a rundown quiet strip behind the station – a quick but steep walk to Bairro Alto – this has bright, clean rooms with flouncy curtains.

Residencial Estrela do Mondego (☎ 213 240 840; 2nd fl, Calçada do Carmo 25; d with/without bathroom from €25/30; ❄) Homely and popular, but brusque, with spacious, plain rooms (some with fridge, all with telephone), this also has flats for rent.

Hospedaria Bons Dias (☎ 213 471 918; 5th fl, Calçada do Carmo 25; d from €30) In the same building as Estrela de Ouro, behind Rossio, this is popular with brightly decorated rooms, some with a small balcony, and a lift.

MID-RANGE

Pensão Residencial Florescente (☎ 213 463 517; www.residencialflorescente.com; Rua das Portas de Santo Antão 99; s/d €40/60) On a pedestrianised street that has lots of tourist restaurants, in a nice old building, Florescente has comfortable, snug, mundanely decorated rooms with telephone. You'll need to book ahead.

Pensão Residencial Gerês (☎ 218 810 497; www.pensaogeres.web.pt; Calçada do Garcia 6; s/d €35/45 with shared bathroom, d/tr with shower €50/80; 💻) A small, clean, efficient guesthouse, with attractive rooms overlooking the narrow street down to the hustle of the Largo.

Residencial Duas Nações (☎ 213 460 710; fax 213 470 206; Rua da Vitória 41; s/d without bathroom €20/25, with bathroom €35/45) In the Baixa's pedestrianised district, this popular, good-deal 19th-century place has serviceable rooms with utility furniture and phone. Upper floors have views. Rooms with bathroom are best – others tend to be on the small side.

New Aljubarrota (☎/fax 213 460 112; p_aljubarrota@hotmail.com; 4th fl, Rua da Assunção 53; s/d with breakfast & shared bathroom €28/45) Friendly and family-style in the pedestrian area, readers have appreciated the warm welcome here, and it has clean, pretty rooms – some of which have balconies. Singles can be poky. The self-service breakfast is excellent and there are lots of nice homely touches.

TOP END

Unless stated otherwise, all the prices include breakfast.

Lisboa Regency Chiado (☎ 213 256 100; www.regency-hotels-resorts.com; Rua Nova do Almada 114; s/tw from €170/180) In an elegant building, this has sleek, plush rooms, neutrally decorated but with flashes of colour. Go for a top-floor one with terrace, taking in the castle, cathedral and river.

Hotel Metrópole (☎ 213 219 030; www.almeidahotels.com; Rossio 30; s/d €150/170) Built in the 1920s, this is a small, low-key hotel with spacious, renovated but endearingly old-fashioned rooms with antique furnishings. There are views over Baixa, Alfama and to the Castle.

Hotel Lisboa Tejo (☎ 218 866 182; www.hotellisboatejo.com; Poço do Borratém 4; s/d €100/110) In a fine old building, this has adventurously decorated doubles in dashing colours, and a selectively disdainful reception. There's an ancient *poço* (well) near the entrance – the spring was probably used from Roman times, and survived the 1755 earthquake.

Apartment VIP Eden (☎ 213 216 600; www.viphotels.com; Praça dos Restauradores 24; 2/4-person apt €90/130; ♿) Has nicely plain studios and apartments, with views across the square and CD players, satellite TV, telephone, kitchen with microwave and disabled access. The best thing is the small rooftop pool, which has a fantastic cityscape view – you can swim while eyeing up the castle.

Bairro Alto

Even closer to the heart of the action, Bairro Alto is perfect if you want to step out of your door into the city's nightlife. The following are on Map pp76–8 unless otherwise noted.

THE AUTHOR'S CHOICE

Pensão Londres (☎ 213 462 203; www.pensaolondres.com.pt; Rua Dom Pedro V 53; d with/without bathroom incl breakfast from €50/40) Helpful and with a great range of simple yet comfortable rooms with phone. Ask for a room with a view – the 4th floor has romantic views over the city. Book well ahead in summer.

BUDGET

Residência Nova Avenida (☎/fax 213 423 689; Rua de Santo António da Glória 87; s/d €18/25, s/d with shower €25/30) A high-ceilinged old house with chandeliers, this is tucked away, so quiet, and has varied rooms, many with balcony. Get a room on the upper floor for the views.

Pensão Globo (☎/fax 213 462 279; Rua do Teixeira 37; s/d/tr €23/30/45) This is a popular, 17-room, efficient, simple place, close to the nightlife district but on a quietish, narrow street. Laundry service available.

Pensão Luar (☎/fax 213 460 949; Rua do Teixeira 37; s without/d with bathroom €15/from 25) The single may be cheap, but has a coffin ambience. Other rooms, however, are spacious, clean and pleasant. Luar is nicely low key but can be noisy at night as it's in central Bairro Alto.

TOP END

Casa de São Mamede (Map p79; ☎ 213 963 166; Rua da Escola Politécnica 159; s/d with breakfast €70/80) In a former magistrate's elegant 1758 townhouse, this has rooms with grand, heavy wooden furniture. It has a good location near Bairro Alto nightlife, but be steeled for a staid reception if you stumble back in the early hours.

Hotel Botânico (☎ 213 420 392; Rua Mãe d'Água 16; s/d €80/85; ❄) Quiet, friendly and businesslike.

Alfama & Graça — Map pp76–8

Alfama has some of Lisbon's most charismatic hotels, and is a steep walk or short tram ride from the centre.

BUDGET

Pensão São João da Praça (☎ 218 862 591; fax 218 880 415; 2nd fl, Rua São João da Praça 97; r without/with bathroom €28/38) Next to the cathedral, this is in a characterful 19th-century house. Rooms are simple, small and nothing special but with good outlooks. Reception can be inefficient.

Pensão Varandas (☎ 218 870 519; 2nd fl, Rua Afonso de Albuquerque 7, Rua dos Bacalhoeiros 8; s/d with shower €20/25) The best among several waterfront cheapies, this is cheerfully run, sweet and friendly, and the best rooms have tiny balconies overlooking Campo das Cebolas.

Beira Mar (☎ 218 871 528; 4th fl, Largo Terreiro do Trigo 16; s/d with shared bathroom from €25/30) Also on the waterfront, the best room in this high-up place is room 4, with a balcony and river view.

MID-RANGE

Sé Guest House (☎/fax 218 864 400; 1st fl, Rua São João da Praça 97; d with shared bathroom €60) On the 1st floor of a 19th-century house is this charming guesthouse, filled with unusual knick-knacks. The doubles are romantic, some rooms look out onto the cathedral. Bathrooms are gleamingly clean.

TOP END

Albergaria Senhora do Monte (☎ 218 866 002; senhoradomonte@hotmail.com; Calçada do Monte 39; r €120, with terrace €145) Near the Miradouro da Senhora do Monte, with pale, comfortable rooms, this has top-of-the-world views. The ones with big terraces are a steal. Free car parking, and tram No 28 runs close by.

Solar dos Mouros (☎ 218 854 940; www.solardosmouros.pt; Rua do Milagre de Santo António 4; s/d from €106/156; ❄) Eight bright, hip rooms are hung with contemporary art, designed and decorated by painter Luís Lemos, inside a tangerine-coloured, characterful, traditional building. There are views of the river (more expensive) or up to the castle.

Olissipo Castelo (☎ 218 820 190; www.olissipohotels.com; Rua Casa do Castelo 112-126; s/d €240/50 Jun-Sep, r €135 Oct-May; ❄) Well located, this modern building built in a plain traditional style

THE AUTHOR'S CHOICE

Pensão Ninho das Águias (☎ 218 854 070; Costa do Castelo 74; s/tr without bathroom €25/60, d with bathroom €45) Just below the castle, this amazing bargain house-on-a-hill has stunning city views, elegant rooms and a garden terrace. Reserve months ahead.

has businesslike, bland, comfortable rooms, some with city-view terraces.

Lapa

Map p79

Lisbon's sleek and leafy diplomatic district has some beautiful top-notch places.

TOP END

York House (☎ 213 962 435; www.yorkhouselisboa.com; Rua das Janelas Verdes 32; s/d from €180/200) Hidden away among greenery, this former 17th-century convent with 34 antique-furnished rooms is beautiful and knows it. The restaurant spills into a sun-dappled courtyard. Expect a snooty reception if you don't look the part.

As Janelas Verdes (☎ 213 968 143; www.heritage.pt; Rua das Janelas Verdes 47; s/d/tr €170/182/210) In an 18th-century palace that novelist Eca de Queirós used as a model in his novel *Os Maias,* this has fine rooms (some with balcony), and a courtyard as well as a library with a terrace. Welcoming and lovely.

Lapa Palace (☎ 213 950 005; www.lapa-palace.com; Rua do Pau de Bandeira, 4; d from €325;) A 19th-century country mansion, this has glorious river views. Rooms evoke being put up by a head of state. There is disabled access.

Rato, Marquês de Pombal & Saldanha

Map pp80–1

Most of the city's top-end places are clustered in this area.

BUDGET

Pousada da Juventude de Lisboa (☎ 213 532 696; lisboa@movijovem.pt; Rua Andrade Corvo 46; dm/d €15/42; 24hr; metro Picoas, bus No 46 or 90 from Santa Apolónia or Rossio, or AeroBus from airport) Well located and well run, this is in a fine old building, near Parque Eduardo VII. Buses stop at the end of the road.

MID-RANGE

Hotel Impala (☎ 213 148 914; fax 213 575 362; Rua Filipe Folque 49; 2-/4-person apt €70/80) This offers bargain modern apartments in a peaceful area, with terrace and kitchen. They'll drop prices if it's quiet.

Pensão Residencial 13 da Sorte (☎ 213 539 746; fax 213 531 851; Rua do Salitre 13; d/tr €50/60;) With 22 rooms, this is a small-scale and popular establishment, thanks to attractive, spacious, smart rooms (with telephone and fridge), as well as good management.

Residência Dublin (☎ 213 555 489; fax 213 543 365; Rua de Santa Marta 45; d €45) Friendly, pleasant and run by a helpful Indian family, Dublin proffers small, old-fashioned, stucco-ceilinged rooms with telephone.

Also offering creature comforts:

Best Western Hotel Eduardo VII (☎ 213 568 822; www.hoteleduardovii.pt; Avenida Fontes Pereira de Melo 5; s/d €85/100;) Long-established, classic, modern but tired; panoramic rooftop restaurant.

Dom Carlos Liberty (☎ 213 173 570; Rua Alexandre Herculano 13; s/d €82/98;) Formerly Hotel Presidente; refurbished, small, bright rooms.

Hotel Miraparque (☎ 213 524 286; www.miraparque.com; Avenida Sidónio Pais 12; s/d €90/100;) Traditional, quiet, courteous. Overlooks park.

TOP END

These prices include breakfast unless otherwise stated.

Hotel Britannia (☎ 213 155 016; www.heritage.pt; Rua Rodrigues Sampaio 17; s/d €165/185;) Designed by Portuguese modernist architect Cassiano Branco in the 1940s, this was altered over the years but has been restored to its former glory, with original fittings uncovered. The entrance hall is the best of its Art Deco features, but it has large plush rooms, with marble bathrooms. Breakfast costs €12.50.

Four Seasons Ritz (☎ 213 811 400; www.fourseasons.com/lisbon; Rua da Fonseca 88; s/d €320/345;) Plush and lush, with 10 floors on top of a Lisbon hill, this has all the comforts and service you would expect from somewhere with such a name. Many of the large rooms overlook the city and most have terraces. Bathrooms are big and marble smothered.

Greater Lisbon

As well as the camp sites and a hostel, Lisbon's outskirts harbour a palatial *pousada* (guesthouse).

BUDGET

Pousada da Juventude de Lisboa Parque Nações (Map pp74-5; ☎ 218 920 890; lisboaparque@movijovem.pt; Via de Moscavide; dm/d €13/37; reception 8am-midnight) This is near Parque das Nações, 1km north of Gare do Oriente (take a metro to the centre). It has a restaurant, plus cooking and laundry facilities.

There are other **pousadas da juventude** across the Tejo at **Almada** (☎ 212 943 491; almada@movijovem.pt; Quinta do Bucelinho, Pragal), and near the beach at **Catalazete** (☎ 214 430 638;

catalazete@movijovem.pt; Estrada Marginal, Oeiras), 12km west of Lisbon, accessible by frequent trains from Cais do Sodré. Both these have bargain four-person apartments (€63) and dorms. Reservations are essential – at least a month ahead in summer.

Lisboa Camping – Parque Municipal (Map pp74-5; ☎ 217 623 100; fax 217 623 106; adult/tent/car €5.30/5.50/3;) In the huge, green, forested Parque Florestal de Monsanto, 6km west of the Rossio, this is big and well equipped, with tennis courts, playground, restaurant, bar and disabled access. Bungalows for two to six are also available. To get there, take bus No 43 from Cais do Sodré, No 50 from Gare do Oriente.

Clube de Campismo de Lisboa (☎ 219 623 960; fax 219 623 144; adult/tent/car €1/4.40/1;) Open to Camping Card International (CCI) cardholders only, and 20km northwest of Lisbon at Almornos, this is a shady, large site, with restaurant, bar, disabled access, playground and pool (admission fee).

There are other camp sites at Costa de Caparica (p136), Praia Grande (p125) and Praia do Guincho (p129).

TOP END

Pousada de Dona Maria I (☎ 214 356 158; recepcao.dmaria@pousadas.pt; s/d with breakfast €169/178;) The Royal Guard of the Court quarters in this ice-cream–pink rococo palace at Queluz (p132) have been converted to this beautiful *pousada,* with high-ceilinged, at-home-with-the-royals rooms.

EATING

From bargain to blowout, you can eat well in Lisbon.

Turismo de Lisboa's Restaurant Card (person/couple/family €5.80/7.80/10.30) offers discounts of 10% to 15% in over 40 restaurants – valid for 72 hours and available at turismos and some hotels. You can get great value here, especially at lunch when daily specials cost around €5.

Many places close on Sunday night or Monday.

Rossio, Praça dos Restauradores & Baixa

Restaurants throng the centre, offering traditional cuisine and popular with tourists and locals. Lots of places have outside tables on cobbled streets and squares. The following are on Map pp76–8 unless otherwise noted.

BUDGET

Restaurant O Sol (Calçado do Duque 21; dishes €2-5) A small vegie café with healthy food and outside tables on the stepped, cobbled lane.

Velho Macedo (Rua da Madalena; dishes €6; daily) An excellent, untouristy backstreet restaurant, with simple food cooked to perfection – try the delicious squid.

Rua dos Correeiros has lots of good-value places, catering to Portuguese at lunch time and tourists at night, with set menus and mains at around €6 including: **Ena Pai** (☎ 213 421 759; Rua dos Correeiros 182) and **Adega Regional da Beira** (☎ 213 467 014; Rua dos Correeiros 132).

There are supermarkets and **minimercados** (grocery shops) everywhere. There's a well-stocked **Pingo Doce supermarket** near Rossio.

MID-RANGE

UMA (☎ 213 427 425; Rua dos Sapateiros 177; dishes €7-10) With a delicious, award-winning *arroz de marisco* (rice and seafood stew), and other great dishes, this backstreet place is recommended by readers.

Martinho da Arcada (☎ 218 879 259; Praça do Comércio 3; dishes €11-18; breakfast, lunch & dinner) With outside tables under a colonnade, in business since 1782, this tiled, yellow-and-white tableclothed place was another haunt of Pessoa and a good spot for a drink, as well as traditional dishes.

Casa do Alentejo (☎ 213 469 231; Rua das Portas de Santo Antão 58; dishes €8-12) Has reasonable Alentejan cuisine (eg *carne de porco à alentejana,* pork and clams) and wines, but an extraordinary setting: a 19th-century Franco–Arabic cocktail, with a gloriously faded ballroom and two azulejo-adorned dining rooms.

O Fumeiro (☎ 213 474 203; Rua da Conceição da Glória 25; dishes €6-12; lunch & dinner) Devoted to the earthy, aromatic cuisine of the mountainous Beira Alta and Serra da Estrela region; even the walls are decked with sausages.

Cervejaria Ribadouro (Map pp80-1; ☎ 213 549 411; Rua do Salitre 2; dishes €7.50-17.50; Wed-Mon) A traditional, sleekly modernised beer hall, popular with locals, offering hearty fare such as the house special, beefsteak, and tempting seafood.

Rua das Portas de Santo Antão has loads of touristy cafés and restaurants, many with outdoor seating.

TOP END

Gambrinus (☎ 213 421 466; Rua das Portas de Santo Antão 25; dishes €12-54, most around €20; lunch & dinner) A top-notch, wood-panelled restaurant resembling a gentleman's club, serving treats such as caviar, truffles and partridge and English-style roast beef, as well as excellent seafood. You can also sit up at the bar.

Bairro Alto

Bairro Alto is Lisbon's trendiest eating district, with the most eclectic range of restaurants in the city – many of which are no bigger than your sitting room. The following are on Map pp76–8 unless otherwise noted.

BUDGET

Restaurante Alto Minho (☎ 213 468 183; Rua da Bica Duarte Belo 61; dishes €2.50-5.50; Sun-Fri lunch) Next to the Elevador da Bica, this traditional, cheery, tiled place does cheap, filling Portuguese staples such as *bacalhau* (dried salt cod), is the speciality with jugs of wine, and is popular with the locals.

Casa da India (☎ 213 423 661; Rua do Loreto 49; dishes €5-8; 9-2am Mon-Sat) Despite the name, this is a traditional joint with a Portuguese menu. It's popular and lively, always busy, with a clatter of TV. A good place to watch football, and you can sit at tables or at the bar (good for lone diners). The sardines are good and the *gambas á guilho* (garlic prawns) divine.

Ponte Picante (☎ 213 214 722; Travessa dos Inglesinhos 48; dishes €3-4; 11am-8pm Mon-Thu, to 2am Fri & Sat) Great, hip place for sitting out in the little courtyard outside, where music often floats over from nearby musicians practising. The food is snacky (salads, quiches) with mighty fine vegetarian choices.

O Cantinho do Bem Estar (☎ 213 464 265; Rua do Norte 46; dishes €7-12; lunch Tue-Sun, dinner Tue-Sat) Cheery, small and tiled, with crammed together tables, this does simple grilled dishes, or seafood and rice, in large portions.

Other belly fillers:

A Toca (☎ 213 467 160; Rua da Atalaia 85; dishes €5-8.50; lunch & dinner Mon-Sat) Basic, small and cheerful.

Cocheira Alentejana (☎ 213 464 868; Travessa Poço Cidade 19; dishes €8-11; lunch & dinner Mon-Sat) Rustic, popular and a *dose* (serving) will do for two.

Chiadomel (☎ 213 474 401; Rua de Santa Justa 105; mains €4.50-8.25; 7.30am-10pm) Simple, central café.

MID-RANGE

Snob (☎ 213 463 723; Rua do Seculo 178; dishes €2.50-13.25; 9pm-3.30am) This is where journalists come to huddle in brown-leather booths amid baize, brass, reading lamp–light, and walls comfortingly lined with whiskey bottles. It has a gentlemanly menu of things such as hot dogs and shrimp rissoles. The steaks are renowned. Food served till late.

Mamma Rosa (☎ 213 465 350; Rua do Gremio Lusitano 14; dishes €8-16.50; dinner) Small, buzzing, filling: this Italian bounces with ebullient waiters, a boho feel and big portions.

Fidalgo (☎ 213 422 900; Rua da Barroca 27; dishes €6.50-10; dinner Mon-Sat) Award-winning, sitting-room small, with bottle-lined walls, this is a lively, sophisticated, gay-friendly, buzzing choice. It offers interesting, well-executed fish and meat dishes and delicious desserts.

A Tasca do Manel (☎ 213 463 813; Rua da Barroca 24; dishes €7-12) Tiled and wooden, this is a hip *tasca* (tavern), always packed and lively and with tasty traditional fish and meat dishes.

Casa Nostra (☎ 213 425 931; Travessa do Poço da Cidade 60; dishes €9-15; lunch Tue-Fri, dinner Tue-Sat) An elegant Italian restaurant, low lit, with white tablecloths, Tiffany-coloured woodwork and impressive cuisine.

El Ultimo Tango (☎ 213 420 341; Rua Diário de Notícias 62; dishes €8.50-10.20; dinner Mon-Sat) Argentinian Tango serves big tasty steaks behind twee lace curtains, in a cosy arched place with open kitchen at the back.

Cervejaria da Trindade (☎ 213 423 506; Rua Nova da Trindade 20C; dishes €6.50-15) In a former convent building, this has a fine, tiled and bustling dining room; beef and seafood dishes are particularly popular but you can also pop in for a sandwich.

O Caracol (☎ 213 427 094; Rua da Barroca 14; dishes €7-17; lunch Tue-Fri, dinner Tue-Sat) Packed with locals, this is a traditional Portuguese, welcoming-and-cheerful, blue-and-white checked tablecloth restaurant. It's a good place to take kids.

Bonsai (☎ 213 462 515; Rua da Rosa 248; dishes €2.50-16.50; lunch & dinner Mon-Sat, lunch Tue-Fri only Nov-Mar) Surprisingly spacious: rush walls, black tables, tinkling music and good authentic Japanese food, with a regularly changing menu.

O Cantinho das Gáveas (☎ 216 426 460; Rua das Gáveas 82; dishes €7.50-9; lunch & dinner Mon-Fri, dinner Sat) This has excellent seafood-rice dishes.

Plain, traditional and classy, it's busy and lively yet low key – a charming choice.

Stasha (☎ 213 431 131; Rua das Gáveas 29; dishes €8-12; lunch Mon-Fri, dinner Tue-Sun) A funky, lively restaurant-bar, this has adventurous dishes with international flavours and good vegie choices. Inside is peachy and dim, brightened with paintings.

Restaurante Comida de Santo (Map p79; ☎ 213 963 339; Calçada Eng Miguel Pais 39; dishes €10-16) A small, bright, recommended Brazilian restaurant, with big tropical murals, big wooden carvings and big food.

Other atmospheric notions:

Sul (☎ 213 462 449; Rua do Norte 13; dishes €12-16; dinner) Romantic, candlelit and exotic, with mainly Italian dishes.

A Baîuca (☎ 213 423 813; Rua da Barroca 24; dishes €8-9; dinner) Small, cosy and garlicky; trad Portuguese grub.

Sabor e Arte (☎ 213 471 846; Travessa da Espera 29; dishes €5.50-11.50; lunch & dinner Mon-Sat) Intimate and relaxed; Italian, Portuguese and Mexican dishes.

Ali-a-Papa (☎ 213 472 116; Rua da Atalaia 95; dishes around €9) An exotic doll's house serving North African flavours.

Calcuta (☎ 213 428 295; Rua do Norte 17; dishes €5.50-10; lunch & dinner Mon-Sat) North Indian, nice, and good for vegies.

Café Buenos Aíres (☎ 213 420 739; Calçada do Duque 31B; dishes €6.50-12; dinner) Nominally Argentinian (serves steaks), candlelit and romantic.

TOP END

El Gordo II (☎ 213 426 372; Travessa dos Freis de Deus 28; dishes €3.25-28; dinner Tue-Sun) Lit with a rosy glow from cloth lanterns, and decorated with mirrors and carved wooden screens, this has excellent, though not cheap, Spanish tapas such as octopus in smoked paprika, or pimento peppers; there are outdoor tables on the cobbled steps. The other branch is **El Gordo I** (☎ 213 424 266; Rua S Boaventura 16; Fri-Wed).

Pap'Açorda (☎ 213 464 811; Rua da Atalaia 57; dishes €14-30; closed evening Sat & Sun) Hip, with a cool contrast between the chandeliers dripping with glass and the exposed brick walls. The speciality is sometime Alentejan peasants' staple *açorda* (a bread and shellfish soup served in a clay pot). The chocolate mousse is legendary.

La Brasserie de l'Entrecôte (☎ 213 428 344; Rua do Alecrim 117; menu €14; lunch & dinner) Here candlelight flickers across the high ceiling and plants, and a refined crowd tucks into a single-minded menu of French food – it concentrates on doing one thing well: entrecôte steak with superb herb and nut sauces. Don't take your vegan date.

Alfama & Graça

The following are on Map pp76–8 unless otherwise noted.

BUDGET

Restaurante Cais d'Alfama (☎ 218 873 274; Largo do Chafariz de Dentro 24; dishes €4-12; lunch Mon-Sat & dinner Thu-Sat Jun-Sep, lunch daily Apr & May, Mon-Sat Dec-Mar) Attracts locals with its cheerful atmosphere and extensive tasty choices, including fresh barbecued sardines. There are a few outside tables on the square.

A Tasca da Sé (☎ 218 875 551; Rua Augusto Rosa 62; dishes €5.50-11.50; lunch & dinner) Terracotta- and brown-tiled and handily near the cathedral, this small and welcoming family restaurant offers delicious home-cooked dishes.

São Cristóvão (☎ 218 885 578; Rua de São Cristóvão 30; mains around €6) A cheerful, tiny, family-run restaurant famous for its Cape Verdean dishes and other African fare, like a punchy *moamba de galinha* (Angolan chicken stew).

Museu Nacional do Azulejo (Map pp74-5; mains around €7) Bright courtyard-facing restaurant, lovely for a long lunch, with tiled walls and white tablecloths (for the museum, see p88).

Solar do Vez (☎ 218 870 794; Campo das Cebolas 48; dishes €4-6; lunch & dinner) Appealing, smaller and cheaper than its neighbours, this offers bargain *pratos do dia* (daily specials) and outdoor tables.

Porte de Alfama (☎ 218 864 536; Rua de São João da Praça 17; dishes €6-7; lunch & dinner) A tiny place with outdoor tables. Simple dishes – barbecued fish is good, though they sometimes have trouble with the barbecue. Free fado on Saturday.

MID-RANGE

Restaurante Viagems de Sabores (☎ 218 870 189; Rua São João da Praça 103; dishes €8.50-12.50; dinner) A superb, amazing-value international restaurant, small, with warm décor, offering a journey for your tastebuds from Thai to Indian. The tuna is delicious. You'll need to book.

Mestre André (☎ 218 871 487; Calçadinha de Santo Estevão; dishes €6.50-12.50; lunch Mon-Fri, dinner

Mon-Sat) A charming neighbourhood restaurant with small tables under a star-spangled ceiling, this has tasty *bacalhau con nata* (cod with cream) and delicious cheesecake made with Portuguese cheese.

Casanova (Map pp74-5; ☎ 218 877 532; Cais da Pedra á Bica do Sapato; dishes €6.50-13; lunch Wed-Sun, dinner Tue-Sun) Close to Bica do Sapato and under its wing, this is *the* place for authentic Italian pizza served in an airy modern space, as swinging as its lightbulbs. There is some riverside seating. No reservations, just turn up and wait.

C@fé Taborda (☎ 218 879 484; Costa do Castelo 75; mains from €7) Up near Castelo de São Jorge is this high-up vegetarian and fish restaurant with marvellous views through its large plate-glass windows.

Restaurante Arço do Castelo (☎ 218 876 598; Rua Chão Feira 25; dishes €7-11; lunch & dinner Mon-Sat) A small, relaxed Indian restaurant lined with bottles, this has good Goan dishes. Meatballs, coconut tiger-prawn curry and *piri piri* chicken are all recommended.

Malmequer Bemmequer (☎ 218 876 535; Rua de São Miguel 23; dishes €6-12.50; lunch & dinner Wed-Sun) This is bright restaurant adorned with murals on a small square, with an extensive menu of excellent charcoal-grilled dishes and blue-and-white cheery-check tablecloths.

Lautasco (☎ 218 860 173; Beco do Azinhal 7; dishes €8-15; lunch & dinner Mon-Sat) This has a wonderfully romantic location, tucked in a leafy, decorated courtyard. The food is good too.

Solar dos Bicos (☎ 218 869 447; Rua dos Bacalhoeiros 8; dishes €6-30; lunch & dinner) This touristy place offers pretty outside seating and reliable Portuguese dishes, but when the waiter says 'service not included' you might be inclined to agree. Good setting but overpriced.

THE AUTHOR'S CHOICE

Restô (☎ 218 867 334; Costa do Castelo 7; tapas €4-5, restaurant dishes around €10; dinner Tue-Sun) Part of the Chapitô arts cooperative, this place has an open-air terrace with amazing, sweeping city views – perfect for a sundowner – plus an arty tapas bar (open till 2am), also with good views. Plus there's a small, candlelit upstairs restaurant, lined by windows, which feels like you're floating above Lisbon. Food is unusual with lots of international flavours.

TOP END

Bica do Sapato (Map pp74-5; ☎ 218 810 320; Cais da Pedra, Avenida Infante Dom Henrique; sushi €2-7, café €14-22, restaurant €18-32; lunch Tue-Sat, dinner Mon-Sat) An uberhip minimalist dockside venue part-owned by actor John Malkovich, this comprises restaurant, café and sushi bar. Service is impeccable.

Jardim do Marisco (☎ 218 824 240; Doca do Jardim do Tabaco complex; dishes €6.50-14) This is in another revitalised dock. A spacious, open-plan, big-windowed restaurant, with a riverside terrace. Specialities are surf and turf.

Rato, Marquês de Pombal & Saldanha — Map pp80–1

BUDGET

Bella Italia III (☎ 213 528 636; Avenida Duque d'Ávila 40C; breakfast, lunch & dinner Mon-Sat) A bright and cheerful Portuguese pastry shop and restaurant pretending to be an Italian restaurant…well, it does serve pizza and pasta.

MID-RANGE

Real Fábrica (☎ 213 852 090; Rua da Escola Politécnica 275; dishes €7.25-14.50; lunch & dinner) A trendy converted 19th-century silk factory, Real Fábrica is thronged with people tucking into mighty fine meat and fish. There's a long bottle-lined bar, and big plate-glass windows onto the street. Eat inside or on the terrace. Service is brisk and efficient.

Restaurante Os Tibetanos (☎ 213 142 038; Rua do Salitre 117; dishes €4-7; lunch & dinner Mon-Fri) Part of a school of Tibetan Buddhism in an old house topped with prayer flags, this ever-popular vegetarian will fill you up with daily specials such as quiche or rice with vegetables. Desserts are delicious – try rose-petal ice cream with yogurt.

Li Yuan (☎ 213 577 740; Rua Viriato 23; dishes €5.10-16.10; lunch & dinner) With lots of rosewood and two-tone tiling, this is good for Chinese dishes.

Restaurante Estrela de Santa Marta (☎ 213 548 400; Rua de Santa Marta 14A; dishes €6.50-13.50; lunch & dinner) This is a smart, bright, low-key, classy restaurant serving typical Portuguese dishes such as fresh grilled fish and seafood rice. It gets busy with Portuguese at lunch time.

THE AUTHOR'S CHOICE

Galeto (☎ 213 544 444; Avenida da República 14; dishes €8.50-20.40) A Lisbon institution, preserved in a time capsule since 1968, this is a huge, where-it's-at diner, where you sit around long banquettes, designed for people-watching. The clientele changes throughout the night, from early-evening liaisons to late-night club casualties. Staff members are pensioned-off Woody Allen extras. Walls are panelled with geometric-patterned original wood. Food is simple and hearty; try the grilled squid. Tall pyramids of fruit are just asking to be knocked down.

Restaurante Espiral (☎ 213 573 585; Praça da Ilha do Faial 14A; €1-3; 🕑 10am-8.30pm Mon-Sat) A basement vegetarian place with an artificial garden, this has a worthy feel. Go early at lunch time to get a seat. There's a self-help bookstore upstairs if the vegetables don't do it for you and a café next door if all you want is a snack.

Centro de Arte Moderna (🕑 lunch Tue-Sun) At the museum (p90), this has a renowned self-service canteen; it's good for vegies.

Alcântara & Lapa — Map p79

MID-RANGE & TOP END

Picanha Janelas Verdes (☎ 213 975 401; Rua das Janelas Verdes 96; set-price dish €13.50-15; 🕑 lunch daily, dinner Mon-Sat) This concentrates on serving *picanha* (steak seasoned with garlic and olive oil) and *peito de pato grelhado*, both popular Brazilian dishes.

A Confraria (☎ 213 962 435; dishes €12-24) The upmarket restaurant at York House (p100) is renowned for its esoteric French delicacies (mainly more than €20). Sit outside in the sun-dappled courtyard.

Docas

There's a string of waterfront restaurants and bars around the Docas area, under the thundering, twinkling Ponte 24 de Abril, which gives the area some *On the Waterfront* cachet. See Drinking & Clubbing (p109) for more details.

It's worth wandering along the strip to see what takes your fancy, but one of the nicest, with delicious food and especially good salads (try the one with yoghurt and honey), is **Espalha Brasas** (Map p79; ☎ 213 962 059; dishes €9-15; 🕑 lunch & dinner Mon-Sat).

Parque das Nações

Centro Vasco da Gama (p113) has a supermarket for all your self-catering needs.

Torre Vasco da Gama (Map pp74-5; ☎ 218 951 687; mains around €15) Swish, swoosh and impress your friends at this 100m-high restaurant, with fantastic views over the city, river and Vasco da Gama bridge. Food is carefully arranged on big plates – delectable, if a bit uptight.

Greater Lisbon

Amoreiras (p113) and **Centro Comercial Colombo** (p113) are very big malls with useful supermarkets for the self-caterers.

Belém

The following are on Map p81 unless otherwise noted.

BUDGET

Pão Pão Queijo Queijo (Rua de Belém 126; dishes €1-6.25; 🕑 8am-midnight Mon-Fri, to 8pm Sat & Sun) A packed-out fast-food place, with some outside tables, this serves *schwarma* and great falafels.

MID-RANGE

Most tempting restaurants are on Rua Vieira Portuense, with outdoor seating overlooking the park.

Restaurante Floresta (☎ 213 636 307; Rua Vieira Portuense 2; dishes €4.90-8; 🕑 lunch & dinner Tue-Sun) The best value along this strip, this is cheerful and reliable, and has outside tables.

Restaurante Montenegro (☎ 213 638 279; Rua Vieira Portuense 44; dishes €6-11; 🕑 lunch Tue-Sun, dinner Tue-Sat) This is a lovely, friendly place to sit outside and linger over lunch. Has good shellfish-rice.

Rosa dos Mares (☎ 213 637 277; Rua de Belem 110; dishes €9-18; 🕑 lunch & dinner) This smart, bright 1st-floor restaurant is intimate, with craggy white walls and excellent seafood.

Cafétaria Quadrante (☎ 213 622 722; Centro Cultural de Belém; mains €4-10; 🕑 daily) For snacks (including Brazilian dishes) with a panoramic view, try the rooftop here.

Cervejaria Alemã (Map pp76-8; ☎ 213 422 916; Rua do Alecrim 23; dishes €7-12) Head here if you are yearning for bratwurst. This is a smart, unusual place, with a brightly lit

TOP TEN CAFÉS & PASTELARIAS

The Portuguese know a thing or two about cakes. Here is a tenaciously researched survey.

- **Pastéis de Belém** (Map p81; Rua de Belém 84; tart €0.75; daily) Sublime, divine traditional *pastéis de Belém* custard tarts, with the eggiest, lightest, crispiest tarts, served warm with a sprinkling of cinnamon and sugar. The recipe is secret – but they taste like they are made by angels. Yum. Founded in 1837, the traditional tiled tearoom is also pretty.
- **Café A Brasileira** (Map pp76-8; ☎ 213 469 547; Rua Garrett 120) With a wonderful original Art Deco interior, with lots of wood and tiled floors. This place has literary credentials – the bronze statue at a table outside is writer Fernando Pessoa, a former habitué. It's touristy but still a local favourite with lots of atmosphere. Good for late-night snacks.
- **Versailles** (Map pp80-1; ☎ 213 546 340; Avenida da República 15A; dishes €6.50-16.50) One of Lisbon's grandest *pastelarias,* this is a splendid marble, column, chandelier and icing-sugar stucco confection, matched by delicious cakes and desserts, and frequented by battalions of well-coiffed elderly ladies. It also serves good savoury food.
- **Café Nicola** (Map pp76-8; ☎ 213 460 579; Rossio 24; dishes €1.35-10; 8am-10pm Mon-Fri, 9am-10pm Sat, 10am-7pm Sun) The grande dame of Lisbon's cafés, this has shiny 1930s Art Deco features, and outside tables. The white-tableclothed restaurant at the back is a good place for lunch.
- **Pastelaria São Roque** (Map pp76-8; Rua Dom Pedro V; dishes €1-5; daily) A mirrored, temple-like café, with gold-topped columns and alcove tables for window-watching. It justifiably declares itself *catedral do pâo* (cathedral of bread) in tiles behind the counter. The homemade soup is delicious.
- **O Cha da Lapa** (Map p79; ☎ 213 957 029; Fritz Idr do Olival 6) A smart, English-feeling tearoom, refined and well mannered, with flock wallpaper, tea and scones.
- **Sitio do Pica-Pau** (Map p79; ☎ 213 978 267; Rua Rémed-Lapa; 8am-5.30pm Mon-Fri) A sweet café with a small, shrub-surrounded terrace looking down a steep, cobbled, pastel-painted street to the river.
- **Confeitaria Nacional** (Map pp76-8; ☎ 213 461 720; Praça da Figueira 18) A 170-year-old café with a dizzying array of pastries and sweets.
- **Casa Suiça** (Map pp76-8; ☎ 213 214 090; 2 entrances – Rossio 96-101 & Praça da Figueira) A long-established favourite doing a brisk trade with tourists outside and sedate elderly locals inside.
- **Bar Terraço** (Map p81; Centro Cultural de Belém; dishes €1-7.60; 12.30-9.30pm Mon-Fri, 12.30-7pm Sat & Sun) On the 3rd floor, this is a calm, spacious, modern café with battered armchairs, wooden tables and a terrace overlooking the river.

Many Lisbon viewpoints have café-kiosks – our tips are Alfama's **Largo das Portas do Sol** (p87), Bairro Alto's **Miradouro de Santa Catarina** (p86) and Graça's **Miradouro da Graça** (p87).

pine-lined interior, specialising in German cuisine.

DRINKING & CLUBBING

Lisbon has some really great nightlife, so don't miss a chance to get out on the town. It is relaxed and yet constantly evolving, with various focal districts that harbour small hole-in-the-wall one-offs and big brash-and-bouncy bars; huge, cool clubs; small, smoky jazz joints and some of Europe's most exciting African clubs.

Most bars open from around 10pm until 3am, do not charge for admission and have a relaxed dress code.

Clubs sometimes have an admission fee (particularly weekends – around €5 to €20, including a drink or two) and some operate a card-stamping system to ensure you spend a minimum amount.

Opening hours vary but clubs won't get going before 2am or 3am; the music dies when people leave – any time between 4am and 10am.

Bairro Alto

The following are on Map pp76–8 unless otherwise noted.

BARS

Visiting this web of narrow streets is like dying and going to bar heaven. The best approach is to wander and halt wherever takes your fancy. But you could also try these favourites.

Clube da Esquina (Rua da Barroca 30) Titchy, like most of the bars here, wooden-floored and decorated with old radios, this has a DJ spinning funky music but is quiet enough to have a good chat. It's like cool nightlife in a cardigan.

Catacombas Jazz Bar (Rua da Rosa 154) This has live jazz on Thursday night, and on other nights its small rooms, tables and chairs are packed – not as self-consciously trendy as some and a relaxed place to be.

Mezcal (20 Travessa Agua da Flor) A popular haunt with a vaguely Mexican theme (tequila), this attracts all sorts of weird and wonderful characters – the later it gets the freakier they get.

Portas Largas (Rua da Atalaia 105) A well-worn, well-loved linchpin of the Bairro Alto scene, this was once a *tasca* and retains its original fittings – the long bar, black-and-white tiled floor and a smattering of columns and porticos. People-wise it's a mishmash – gays, straights and not-sures linger around the bar and spindly marble tables.

Majong (Rua da Atalaia) Scruffy, with school chairs and deep-red walls, this is a cool hangout, somewhat boho, centred around some serious games of table football.

Capela (Rua da Atalaia 45) With no name outside and cheerful staff, this is a dark, busy, friendly bar that takes its music seriously and has nightly DJs. Good place to find out about what's on nightlife-wise.

Bicaense (Rua da Bica de Duarte Beló 42A) Out of the main action, this has so-hip-it-hurts clientele, is dimly lit and decked with old radios and projectors. The back room is used for occasional live music – sometimes plinky avant-garde taking itself sooo seriously.

Heróis (Calçada do Sacramento) A Chiado bar – packed with white Panton chairs (plastic retro classics), Perspex, and overseen by Kylie (in poster form) – this hosts a cool, largely gay crowd listening to laid-back house.

> **THE AUTHOR'S CHOICE**
>
> **Solar do Vinho do Porto** (☎ 213 475 707; Rua de São Pedro de Alcântara 45; 🕓 11am-midnight Mon-Sat; glass €1-24.50) In a suitably awed atmosphere, here is an excellent opportunity to taste over 200 varieties of port – dark and red or light and tangy – either upstairs, which does a genteel-tearoom impression, or downstairs in a cosy cavern. Bottles cost €6.50 to €1194. Top tip: taste here and buy at the supermarket later.

CLUBS

Fragil (Rua da Atalaia 126) Granddaddy to the Lisbon nightclub scene, this is not the happening place it once was now guru Marcel Reis has moved his attentions to Lux. But Fragil can be fun, with a small dance floor and a relaxed, mixed gay-straight crowd. At weekends it's mainly house, weekdays you are at the DJ's mercy.

A Lontra (Map p79; Rua de São Bento 155) Near Barrio Alto, this place hosts an eclectic, mainly African-Portuguese, clientele bumping and grinding to African sounds, R&B, hip-hop and house. It fills up about 3am and is open late.

Alfama

Map pp76–8

Alfama is perfect for a drink with a view.

BARS

Esplanada Igreja da Graça (🕓 10.30am-3am) Brilliant views from this terrace, with soothing

> **THE AUTHOR'S CHOICE**
>
> **Lux** (Map pp74-5; 218 820 890; Avenida Infante Dom Henrique) Near Santa Apolónia train station is Lisbon's ice-cool, must-see club. It's run by ex-Fragil maestro Marcel Reis and part-owned by John Malkovich and is lots of fun, with an oversized shoe, a mirrored tunnel, and violet light setting the scene. It's huge and airy, special but not snooty, and hosts the best big-name house DJs and live acts. Weekends are less hip but the music is still tip-top. Lux style policing is heartwarmingly lax but get here after 4am on a Friday or Saturday and you might have trouble getting in because of the crowds.

music during the day that gets heavier the later it gets. Weather permitting.

Chapitô and **Taborda**, both alternative theatres with fantastic views from their bars, are excellent choices for a sundowner or a late-night drink overlooking the twinkling city.

CLUBS

MUSIcais (Avenida Infante Dom Henrique, Pavilion A/B, Doca do Jardim do Tabaco) By day a great hangout for trendy Lisboêtas, with its waterside deck, by night good for live music and cheesy tunes.

Príncipe Real & São Bento

Centre of the Lisbon gay scene, this area also houses some unique drinking dens.

BARS

Pavilhão Chines (Map pp76-8; Rua Dom Pedro V 89-91) This was once a grocery, and the dates above the door mark its previous owner's lifespan. It's now the most fabulous bar in Lisbon, or perhaps anywhere, designed by Luís Pinto Coelho. The walls are lined with polished cabinets, full of carefully arranged kitsch, such as many-outfitted Action Men. A well-executed cocktail, a game of pool against a backdrop of Toby jugs and suspended model aircraft: what more could you want?

Foxtrot (Map p79; Travessa de Santa Teresa 28) By the same designer, this splendidly stately place feels like it has been here since the 1940s (actually only since the '80s), with low lighting, staid sofas, oriental silks and rambling rooms.

CLUBS

Hot Clube de Portugal (Map pp80-1; www.isa.utl.pt; Praça da Algeria 39; 🕑10pm-2am Tue-Sat) Here the masters play you jazz in a small, smoky setting, just the way it should be. Shows are at 11pm and 12.30am.

GAY & LESBIAN LISBON

Take a look at www.portugalgay.pt for more pink listings.

Bars

While no longer in the closet, gay and lesbian venues remain discreet; ring the bell.

Bar Água No Bico (Map p79; Rua de São Marçal 170) Translates curiously as 'water in the beak'; a pub-like, snug place.

Bric-a-Bar (Map p79; Rua Cecilio de Sousa 82-84) Popular with leathers.

Bar 106 (Map p79; Rua de São Marçal 106) Busy and popular.

SS Bar (Map p79; Calçada do Patriarcal, 38) The name is the owner's initials rather than anything more sinister.

Clubs

Finalmente (Map p79; Rua da Palmeira 38) This fun place, absurdly popular, offers a tiny dance floor, nightly drag shows, and so many people there's no way you could fall over.

Memorial (Map p79; Rua Gustavo de Matos Sequeira 42A) Mainly lesbian, this laid-back place attracts a mixed crowd, often men looking for women.

Trumps (Map p79; Rua da Imprensa Nacional 104B) With two bars and a sizable dance floor, more posy than Finalmente, while mysteriously hosting much the same crowd.

Organisations & Events

Gay Pride Festival is in June, and the Festival de Cinema Gay e Lésbico is late September.

Associação Opus Gay (Map pp80-1; ☎ 213 151 396, after hr 962 400 017; opus@opusgay association.com; 2nd fl, Rua da Ilha Terceira 34; 🕑5-8pm Wed-Sat) Also has a visitors centre, including Internet café.

Centro Comunitário Gay e Lésbico de Lisboa (Lisbon Gay & Lesbian Community Centre; Map pp76-8; ☎ 218 873 918; ilga-portugal@ilga.org; Rua de São Lazaro 88; 🕑4-8pm Mon-Sat Sep-Jul) Has a café, library, Internet and counselling facilities.

Grupo de Mulheres (Women's Group; ☎ /fax 218 873 918; gmulheres@yahoo.com) Part of ILGA-Portugal, it organises regular social gatherings and lesbian film screenings.

Cais do Sodré & Avenida 24 de Julho

Old favourites and large clubs cluster around this trendy nightlife area, where people come for a change from Bairro Alto. During the Salazar years, this area was the only place for a bit of night-time seed, and some areas retain this seedy feel – particularly tacky Rua Nova do Carvalho. The following are on Map pp76–8 unless otherwise noted.

BARS

Ó Gilíns (Rua dos Remolares 8-10) An Irish pub with live music evenings Thursday to Saturday; also offers Irish breakfast. Lots of homesick English speakers.

Hennessy's (Rua Cais do Sodré 32-38) A proper pub atmosphere and Guinness, of course. This is on two levels and serves snacks.

British Bar (Rua Bernardino Costa 52; Mon-Sat) Resembling an early-20th-century railway bar, this is old-fashioned and bottle-lined, with an old-fashioned clientele and a backwards clock. There's even a resident shoe shiner. Across the road is **Bar Americano** (Rua Bernardino Costa 35), similarly classic and dating back to the 1920s.

Gringo's Café (Map p79; Avenida 24 de Julho 116-118) On a desolate stretch, this has a Wild West theme to its dark interior and is popular with bikers.

Speakeasy (Map p79; www.speakeasy-bar.com; Armazém 115, Cais das Oficinas) On the other side of the tracks, this converted warehouse offers live music – mainly crowd-pleasing covers bands – attracting a wide range of ages. Weekends are packed. Food is Cajun and good.

CLUBS

Kapital (Map p79; Avenida 24 de Julho 68) For young, wealthy Lisboêtas (blazers, V-necks, big hair on the men, oh-so-casual glam on the women), this is nightclub nirvana. Expect a door policy, chrome, people so cool they're almost frozen and matching music. If it feels too much like a 1980s teen movie, there's an adjoining tunnel to next-door Kremlin.

Kremlin (Map p79; Escadinhas da Praia 5) Vaulted Kremlin used to be a monastery. Doubtless the BPM have the previous inhabitants turning in their graves, but acid and techno certainly seem to do the trick for the regulars. People head here after everything else has closed, so you can picture the scene at 7am.

> **THE AUTHOR'S CHOICE**
>
> **Discoteca Jamaica** (Map pp76-8; Rua Nova do Carvalho; 11pm-4am or 6am) At most of the clubs on this seedy street, dancing involves laps, but this is a gem. Everyone in the know (gay/straight, black/white, old/young) has a great affection for offbeat Jamaica, where weekends get busy with a mixture of mostly retro music and reggae. Packed from 3am from Thursday to Saturday; other nights you might just get 10 people propped up against the bar but they're characters.

Docas & Alcântara — Map p79

The Docas are the newest of the drinking-clubbing areas and at the other end of the spectrum from Bairro Alto. There are two separate areas: Doca de Alcântara, and to the west, Doca de Santo Amaro, which has a cool setting under the lit-up, rumbling Abril bridge. Vibe-wise, at both the finger is on the pop and hip-hop pulse. Good fun if you're after lively tunes and getting lucky. To get here, take the train from Cais do Sodré to Alcântara Mar and follow *maritima* signs, turning right to Doca de Santo Amaro; or catch tram No 15 from Praça da Figueira.

North of Santo Amaro is Lisbon's most popular African club, Luanda, bumping and grinding till late.

BARS

Doca de Santo (☎ 213 963 535, Doca de Santo Amaro) This is clatteringly large, but with style and lots of open-air, leafy seating – a glamorous yet relaxed place to settle with a cocktail. Serves good salads (among other things).

Op Art Café (Doca de Santo Amaro) This is a well-kept secret, on its own, on the water's edge away from the rest of the bars. A super place for a drink.

CLUBS

Salsa Latina (Gare Maritima de Alcântara, Doca de Santo Amaro) This big place is good fun, with a big, energetic live band playing salsa, merengue and Latino tunes and lots of people following the teacher's moves. Attracts all ages.

Luanda (Travessa Teixeira Júnior 6) This is a big, African club, Lisbon's favourite booty shaker, with a fantastically steamy, glitzy atmosphere. People dress to impress, but are all too cool to get on the floor before 3am when it really, really gets going.

Indochina (Rua Cintura do Porto) With Eastern décor through a colonial looking glass, this has a quirky charm and has a good atmosphere, but is as large and pop-pumping as the rest on the strip.

Queens (Avenida de Brasilia 226) Not as camp as the name, but is still the Docas place for disco divas – the glitziest on this stretch, with podium dancers to give it that sense of occasion.

Armazém F (Armazém 65, Avenida de Brasilia) By the riverside, an upmarket warehouselike bar, restaurant and club, home to varied rhythms from salsa to techno, and often hosts live music acts.

O2 (Armazém 113, Cais da Rocha Conde de Obidos) Light, spacey, cube-decked and minimal with lots of UV. Fills up with club-scene clubbers freaking out (as far as club-scene clubbers do) to house and techno from about 2am or 3am.

Dock's Club (Rua Cintura do Porto) This is another fun-packed, people-packed place, with mirrors and glitterballs, pop hits and a bit of a meat market.

Blues Café (Rua Cintura do Porto) One of the most popular on the strip, this is a happening place, playing mainstream pop, R&B and hip-hop. A place to pull.

Estefânia

Mussulo (Map pp80-1; Rua Sousa Martins 5D, Estefânia) Late-night, popular club, faithful to its Angolan roots with a mixture of soft rhythms and Afro-techno.

Parque das Nações

There are many interchangeable restaurant-bars along Rua da Pimenta, good for a riverside promenade with lots of weekend bustle.

Bugix (Map pp74-5; Rua dinner Fuas Roupinho, Parque das Nações) A club above a riverside restaurant, plays pop and is popular with young wealthy Lisboêtas.

ENTERTAINMENT

Lisbon has an entertainment spread worthy of a capital: classical concerts, dance, theatre, opera, frequent live bands and, of course, fado – the Portuguese blues.

Information & Tickets

For details of events during your stay, grab a copy of the monthly *Follow Me Lisboa* (free) from a turismo, or, if your Portuguese is up to it, call the **What's On** (☎ 217 901 062) hotline. The free monthly **Agenda Cultural Lisboa** (www.lisboacultural.pt) includes details of performances and screenings; cinema listings can also be found in the daily *Diário de Notícias*. Tickets are available from the following outlets:

ABEP Ticket Agency (Map pp76-8; ☎ 213 475 824; Praça dos Restauradores)

Fnac Greater Lisbon (Map pp74-5; ☎ 217 114 237; Centro Comercial Colombo); Baixa Chiado (Map pp76-8; ☎ 213 221 800; Armazéns do Chiado, Rua do Carmo 3)

NetParque (☎ 218 917 600; www.netparque.pt)

Ticket Line (☎ 217 120 300; www.ticketline.pt)

Fado

Bairro Alto and Alfama are where the dark melancholy of fado was born, and there are many places where you can indulge in a bit of dignified solemnity. Backed by the bright-toned 12-string Portuguese guitar, with Arabic influences that make it resemble flamenco, fado's fun-packed themes are love, *saudade* (p34), destiny, death, bullfighting, social injustice, and fado itself. If it's *fado vadio* (open fado), anyone can get up and sing. Most places mainly cater to tourists, but this means they often host the finest singers – although counterbalanced by the often overpriced, mediocre food and touristy feel. However, a fado concert depends entirely on the night in question – one night a singer might create an electric, tangible atmosphere, the next night, with the same ingredients, it can feel entirely different.

The following list is a smattering of fado venues available. It's a good idea to make a reservation, especially at weekends. Most require you to spend a minimum amount, which will include the cost of the fado. Although they open late if necessary, at many they'll empty out by midnight. For more information on fado, see p42.

BAIRRO ALTO **Map pp76–8**

Adega Machado (☎ 213 224 640; Rua do Norte 91; minimum €16; 🕓 8.30pm-3am Tue-Sun) Filipe de Arajo Machado runs this place, started by his *fadista* mother and father. Clientele is largely groups, but there is a good and lively atmosphere.

Adega do Ribatejo (☎ 213 468 343; Rua Diario de Noticias 23; minimum €15; 8.30pm-12.30am Mon-Sat) Small, with some professionals, some amateurs – can be very good.

Adega Mesquita (☎ 213 219 280, www.adegamesquita.com; Rua Diario de Noticias 107; 9pm-1am; minimum €15) A long-established fado house, with singers and folk dancers.

Nono (☎ 213 429 989; Rua do Norte 47; 9pm-2.30am Mon-Sat; minimum €10, tourist menu & cover €27.50; dishes €5-30) Smaller, less formal, more of a local atmosphere.

ALFAMA — Map pp76–8

A Baiuca (☎ 218 867 284; Rua de São Miguel 20; dishes €9-11) A special place with *fado vadio*, when anyone can take a turn. On a good night it's packed with locals, with hissing if people dare make noise during the singing. The food is simple and tasty – fado goes on till midnight, food stops around 10pm. Reserve ahead.

Clube de Fado (☎ 218 852 704; Rua de S João da Praça; dishes €5-23; minimum €10; 9pm-2.30am Mon-Sat) Overpriced, mediocre food and touristy feel; some fine artists in an arched, colonnaded hall. Popular with groups.

Parreirinha de Alfama (☎ 218 868 209; Beco do Espírito Santo 1; minimum €15; 8pm-3am) Renowned singers.

Taverna do Embuçado (☎ 218 865 088; Beco dos Cortumes 10; minimum €15; 9pm-2.30am Mon-Sat) At time of going to press had temporarily moved to Beco dos Armazéns do Linho. Well-known singers.

LAPA

Senhor Vinho (Map p79; ☎ 213 972 681; www.restsrvinho.com; Rua do Meio á Lapa; 8pm-2am; minimum spend €15) Small, with good singers, this has a dramatic atmosphere. The star is Maria da Fé or catch the marvellous Aldina Duarte.

Cinema

For the latest blockbusters try the multi plexes in the **Amoreiras** (☎ 213 878 752; p113) and **Centro Comercial Colombo** (☎ 217 113 222; p113) malls. More traditional cinemas are the grand **São Jorge** (Map pp80-1; ☎ 213 579 144; Avenida da Liberdade 175), and the **Instituto da Cinemateca Portuguesa** (Museu do Cinema; Map pp80-1; ☎ 213 596 200; www.cinemateca.pt; Rua Barata Salgueiro 39), which shows off-beat, art-house, world and old films – just around the corner. Tickets cost €3 to €5. The institute sometimes shows films at **Salão Foz** (Map pp76-8; Praça dos Restauradores).

Theatre

Teatro Nacional de Dona Maria II (Map pp76-8; ☎ 213 472 246; Rossio) Underfunding means the impressive National Theatre has a somewhat hit-and-miss schedule.

Teatro Nacional de São Carlos (Map pp76-8; ☎ 213 465 914; Rua Serpa Pinto 9) Worth visiting to see the wonderful gold-and-red interior, with opera, ballet and theatre seasons.

Teatro Municipal de São Luis (Map pp76-8; ☎ 213 225 140; Rua Antonio Maria Cardosa 38) Also offers opera, ballet and theatre.

Teatro Taborda (Map pp76-8; ☎ 218 879 484; Costa del Castelo 75; 💻) This is a cultural centre with contemporary dance, theatre and music.

Chapitô (Map pp76-8; ☎ 218 880 406; www.chapito.org; Costa do Castelo 1-7; 💻) Offers original physical theatre performances, with a theatre school attached. There's a jazz café downstairs with dentist-chair décor; there's live music Thursday to Saturday. Spectacular views and excellent restaurants are offered by both Teatro Taborda and Chapitô.

Music & Dance

Pavilhão Atlântico (Map pp74-5; ☎ 218 918 409; www.atlantico-multiusos.pt; Parque das Nações) International acts, from Moby to Madonna, play here – Portugal's largest indoor arena.

Paradise Garage (Map p79; ☎ 213 243 400; www.paradisegarage.com; Rua João Oliveira Miguens 38-48) This is one of Lisbon's chief small venues for bands, festivals and club nights.

Excellent classical concerts and ballets are held at Fundação Calouste Gulbenkian's three **concert halls** (Map pp80-1; ☎ 217 935 131; www.musica.gulbenkian.pt; Avenida de Berna) or the **Centre Cultural de Belém** (CCB; Map p81; ☎ 213 612 444; www.ccb.pt; Praça do Império, Belém) and the **Coliseu dos Recreios** (Map pp76-8; ☎ 213 240 580; Rua das Portas de Santo Antão 92). The CCB and the Coliseu dos Recreios also host bands and dance events.

A versatile exhibition venue is **Culturgest** (Map pp80-1; ☎ 217 905 155; Rua Arco do Cego).

Sport

FOOTBALL

Of Portugal's 'big three' clubs, two – SL Benfica (Sport Lisboa e Benfica) and Sporting (Sporting Club de Portugal) – are based in Lisbon. They've been rivals ever since Sporting beat Benfica 2–1 in 1907.

The season runs from September to mid-June, with most league matches on Sunday;

check the papers (especially *Bola*, the daily football paper) or ask at the turismo. Tickets cost €20 to €50 and are sold at the stadium on match day or, for higher prices, at the **ABEP ticket agency** (Map pp76-8; Praça dos Restauradores).

Estádio da Luz (Map pp74-5; ☎ 217 219 540; www.slbenfica.pt; metro Colégio Militar-Luz) SL Benfica plays at this 65,000-seat stadium in the northwestern Benfica district. Euro2004's big ones were played here.

Estádio Nacional (☎ 214 197 212; Cruz Quebrada; train from Cais do Sodré) Hosts the national Taça de Portugal (Portugal Cup) each May.

Pavilhão Atlântico (Map pp74-5) Other major sporting events are held here in Parque das Nações.

Estádio José de Alvalade (Map pp74-5; ☎ 217 514 069; metro Campo Grande, bus No 1 or 36 from Rossio) You will find sport here, just north of the university. A 54,000-seat stadium here hosted Euro2004 matches.

BULLFIGHTING

Lisbon's **Praça de Touros** (bullring; Map pp80-1; ☎ 217 932 442; Avenida da República; tickets €15-60), near Campo Pequeno metro, is normally where bullfights are staged but the ancient, Moorish-style venue is closed for long-term restoration. The season runs from May to October, with fights usually on Thursday or Sunday. Tickets are on sale outside the bullring, or at higher prices from the **ABEP ticket agency** (Map pp76-8; Praça dos Restauradores).

MARATHON RUNNING

Lisbon hosts an international **marathon** (☎ 213 616 160; www.lisbon-marathon.com) in December, with a half marathon as well, starting and finishing at Praça do Comercio. Around March another half marathon, the **Meia Maratona Cidade de Lisboa**, starts from Almada with around 35,000 runners crossing the Ponte 25 de Abril, finishing in Belém; contact the **Federação Portuguese de Atletismo** (☎ 214 146 020; www.fpatletismo.pt) for details.

SHOPPING

Shopping in Lisbon is marvellously diverse, with many charming stuck-in-time shops dealing exclusively in hats, gloves or canned fish, but also the brilliant, funky boutiques of Bairro Alto – which often open around 4pm and stay open till midnight, with DJs to blur the nightlife/shopping distinction further.

Shopaholics may like to take advantage of the Lisboa Shopping Card, which offers discounts of up to 20% in over 200 selected stores. It costs €3.5/5.5 for 24-/72-hour versions, and is available at Turismos de Lisboa.

Most city centre shops open 9am to 1pm and 3pm to 7pm Monday to Saturday (but often until 10pm or 11pm in the shopping centres).

Azulejos & Ceramics

Fábrica Sant'Ana (Map pp76-8; ☎ 213 638 292; Rua do Alecrim 95) One of Lisbon's finest azulejo factories and showrooms, this sells wonderful elaborate tiles, as well as cherubs and candlesticks.

Cerâmica Viúva Lamego (Map pp74-5; ☎ 218 852 408; www.viuvalamego.com; Largo do Intendente Pina Manique 25) Another good showroom for azulejos (including made-to-order items) and other ceramic ware.

Olaria do Desterros (Map pp74-5; ☎ 218 850 329; Rua Nova do Desterro 14) A family-run pottery factory, a few blocks west of Cerâmica Viúva Lamego. The factory (there's no obvious showroom) is at entry F in an alley, seemingly within the grounds of the Hospital do Desterro.

Museu Nacional do Azulejo (p88) Azulejos-central also sells a few azulejo souvenirs.

Museu Gulbenkian The shop next door to the main museum building (p89) sells quality souvenirs, including some attractive tiles.

Vista Alegre (Map pp76-8; ☎ 213 461 401; Largo do Chiado 20) The most famous name in ceramics. Its finely crafted products can be found at a number of Lisbon stores.

Arte Rústica (Map pp76-8; ☎ 213 421 127; Rua d'Aurea 246) Has an excellent range of more rustic ceramics.

Wine

Portuguese wine is excellent value. In most supermarkets you can buy something decent for as little as €4 a bottle (p64).

If you prefer port, have a taste at the Solar do Vinho do Porto (p107) and then head for the supermarket, or a wine speciality shop such as **Napoleão** (Map pp76-8; ☎ 218 861 108; Rua dos Fanqueiros 70) or **Manuel Tavares** (Map pp76-8; ☎ 213 424 209; Rua da Betesga 1A). Staff here can also offer recommendations.

For more on port see p64 and p364.

Handicrafts & Textiles

Santos Ofícios (Map pp76-8; ☎ 218 872 031; Rua da Madalena 87) A fascinating, chi-chi *artesanato* (handicrafts shop), stocking an eclectic range of folk art from all around Portugal.

Casa das Cortiças (Map p79; ☎ 213 425 858; Rua da Escola Politécnica 4) A dusty store specialising in cork items, with some bargain souvenirs plus useful cork mats.

Madeira House (Map pp76-8; ☎ 213 426 813; Rua Augusta 131) Hand-embroidered linen from its most famous source, Madeira, is here.

Mercado da Ribeira (Map pp76-8; ☎ 210 312 600; Ave 24 de Julho; 10am-11pm Mon-Sat, 7.30am-2pm Sun) On the 1st floor of the former central food market, the Centro de Artesanato sells high-quality handicrafts and has demonstrations by artisans and regional cuisine. The ground floor retains the flower market, and Sundays there's a collectors market (9am to 1pm).

Clothes & Jewellery

Bairro Alto has a concentration of cool boutiques selling retro-inspired clothes, unusual local design and Brazilian imports. Good places to start are Rua do Norte and Rua da Rosa. Many of the shops here open around 3pm and stay open till midnight.

Sneakers Delight (Map pp74-5; ☎ 213 479 976; Rua do Norte 30 branch Ave Infante Dom Henrique) Here trainers are treated with the reverence they deserve. DJs play at the weekend.

Speduci (Map p79; ☎ 213 431 824; Rua de S Marçal 30; noon-8pm Tue-Fri & Sat) An unusual jewellery shop with a collection of glittering, contemporary costume pieces from Italian, French and Spanish designers.

Music

Valentim de Carvalho Megastore (Map pp76-8; ☎ 213 241 570; Rua do Carmo) Lisbon's longest-established music store.

Fnac (Map pp76-8; ☎ 213 221 800; Rua Nova do Almada 110) Fnac also sells a vast array of music and audiovisual gear.

Discoteca Amália (Map pp76-8; ☎ 213 421 485; Rua de Áurea 272) Specialises in fado and cheap classical CDs.

There are plenty of gemlike vinyl and CD shops in Bairro Alto.

Shopping Centres

Huge shopping malls include:

Atrium Saldanha (Map pp80-1; Praça Duque de Saldanha) Swanky.

Centro Comercial Colombo (Map pp74-5; Avenida Colégio Militar) Colossal.

Centro Vasco da Gama (Map pp74-5) Between Gare do Oriente and Parque das Nações.

Complexo das Amoreiras (Map pp80-1; Avenida Engenheiro Duarte Pacheco; bus No 11 from Praça do Comércio) Modernist.

Galerias Monumental (Map pp80-1; Praça Duque de Saldanha)

El Corte Inglês (Map pp80-1; Avenida António Augusto de Aguiar 31) Massive and Spanish.

GETTING THERE & AWAY

Air

Aeroporto de Lisboa (Aeroporto da Portela; flight information ☎ 218 413 700) is about 4km northeast of the centre. A new international airport will open at Ota, 48km north, in 2010.

Portugália and TAP both have multiple daily flights to Lisbon from Porto and Faro, and over 20 carriers operate scheduled international services (p466).

Boat

The **Transtejo ferry line** (www.transtejo.pt) has several riverfront terminals. From the eastern end of the Terreiro do Paço terminal (Map pp76–8), swanky catamarans zip across the Tejo to Montijo (€1.65, 30 minutes) and Seixal (€1.35, 30 minutes, half-hourly weekdays, every hour or so weekends). From the main part of the terminal, called Estação do Sul e Sueste, Soflusa ferries run very frequently to Barreiro (€0.65, 30 minutes), for rail connections to the Alentejo and Algarve. From Cais do Sodre, passenger ferries go to Cacilhas (€0.60, 10 minutes, every 10 minutes all day). Car (and bicycle) ferries also go from Cais do Sodré to Cacilhas.

From Belém, ferries depart for Trafaria and Porto Brandão (€0.65, every 30 to 60 minutes), about 3.5km and 5km respectively from Costa da Caparica town.

Bus

The major long-distance bus terminal is **Arco do Cego** (Map pp80-1; ☎ 213 545 439; Avenida João Crisóstomo). From here the big carriers, **Rede Expressos** (24hr ☎ 707 223 344; www.rede-expressos.pt) and **Eva/Mundial Turismo** (☎ 213 147 710; www.eva-bus.com), run frequent services to almost every major town. Destinations with 10 or more services a day include Coimbra (€9.50, 2½ hours), Évora (€9.80, 1¾ hours),

Porto (€13.50, 3½ to four hours) and Faro (€15, 4½ to five hours). You can buy your ticket up to seven days in advance.

The other major terminal is **Gare do Oriente** (Map pp74–5), concentrating on services to the north and to Spain. On the 1st floor of this architectural stunner are bus company booths (mostly open 9am to 5.30pm Monday to Saturday, to 7pm Friday, closed lunch; smaller operators only open just before arrival or departure). At weekends you may have to buy your ticket on the bus (though it's wise to phone ahead). The biggest companies operating from here are **Renex** (☎ 218 940 285/888) and the Spanish operator **Auto-Res** (☎ 218 940 250; www.auto-res.net).

Many Renex buses take passengers 20 minutes early at Campo das Cebolas in Alfama, before Gare do Oriente.

Several regional companies with destinations in the north, including Mafrense (for Ericeira and Mafra), Barraqueiro Oeste (for Malveira and Torres Vedras) and Rodoviária do Tejo (for Peniche), operate from outside Campo Grande metro station.

Buses to Sesimbra and Costa da Caparica go from a terminal (Map pp80–1) at Praça de Espanha.

Eurolines (Map pp80-1; ☎ 218 957 398; Loja 203, Gare do Oriente; 🕑 9.30am-1pm & 2-6.30pm Mon-Fri, 9am-1pm & 2-4pm Sat) runs coaches to destinations all over Europe (p468), with all coaches serving both Arco do Cego and Gare do Oriente. You can also go to many European cities from Arco do Cego with Eurolines affiliate **Intercentro** (Map pp80-1; ☎ 213 571 745; Rua Actor Taborda 25; 🕑 Mon-Fri), which has an additional ticket office in the **Arco do Cego bus station** (Map pp80-1; ☎ 213 159 277; Arco do Cego; 🕑 8am-12.30pm & 1.30-5pm Mon-Fri, 8am-1pm Sat).

Lisbon's Busabout stop (p468) is at Parque Municipal de Campismo de Monsanto.

Information and tickets for international departures are scarce at weekends, so try and avoid that last-minute Sunday dash out of Portugal.

Car & Motorcycle

The nearest place to rent a motorbike is Cascais (see p131). For vehicle rental rates, see p474. Car-hire companies include the following:

Avis (☎ 800 201 002; www.avis.com.pt)
Europcar (☎ 808 204 050; www.europcar.pt)
Hertz (☎ 219 426 300; www.hertz.com)
Rentauto (☎ 218 966 320; www.rentauto.pt)
Sixt (☎ 707 207 007; www.e-sixt.com)

Train

Lisbon is linked by train to Portugal's major cities. See p475 for details on domestic services, and p469 on international services. Some sample 2nd-class direct journeys to/from Lisbon (Faro times include ferry connection):

Destination	Service	Price (€)	Duration (hr)	Frequency (daily)
Coimbra	Alfa	17	2	6
	IC/IN	12	2¼	7
Faro	Alfa	16	3	1
	IC	14.50	4¼	2
Porto C	Alfa	22.50	3¼	7
	IC	14	3½	4

Lisbon has four major stations plus some smaller ones. **Santa Apolónia** is the terminal for trains from northern and central Portugal, and for international services. It has a helpful **information desk** (☎ 808 208 208; 🕑 7.30am-9pm) at door No 8. The international section at door No 47 includes an international ticket desk, bank, ATM and cash-exchange machine, snack bar, car-rental agencies and a **Turismo de Lisboa desk** (🕑 10am-6pm). Left-luggage lockers are nearby.

All of Santa Apolónia's services also stop at the increasingly important **Gare do Oriente** (Map pp74–5). Ticket booths are on the 1st floor here (platforms on the 2nd) and car-rental offices, banks and shops are at street level. Left-luggage lockers are on the basement metro level.

Barreiro is the terminal for *suburbano* services to Setúbal and for long-distance services to the south of Lisbon; connecting ferries leave frequently from the pier at Terreiro do Paço where travellers buy two tickets: a €0.65 ferry ticket to Barreiro plus their onward train ticket.

Barreiro will become redundant once the North–South Railway Line (which currently reaches to the Setúbal Peninsula suburbs via the Ponte 25 de Abril) is extended to the main line south.

Rossio (☎ 213 433 747, 800 200 904) serves Queluz-Belas, Cacém (connections to Estremadura) and Sintra. Cais do Sodré is the station for Cascais and Estoril.

Modernised **Entrecampos** (Avenida 5 de Outubro) serves the northern suburbs as well as Fertagus trains across the Ponte 25 de Abril. **Entrecampos Poente,** 200m east of Entrecampos, serves the suburban line to Cacém.

GETTING AROUND

To/From the Airport

The AeroBus departs from outside Arrivals (€2.85, 30 to 45 minutes, roughly every 20 minutes from 7.45am to 9pm). It goes via Marquês Pombal, Avenida Liberdade, Restauradores, Rossio and Praça do Comércio to Cais do Sodré. You get a Bilhete Turístico, which you can use on all city buses, trams and funiculars for the rest of the day. Passengers who show their boarding pass get a free ticket.

Local bus Nos 8, 44, 45 and 83 also run from the centre but they're bad news in rush hour if you have baggage. There's also a direct bus service to/from Cascais (p130).

If you're arriving by train just to get to the airport, the quickest option is bus No 44 from Gare do Oriente (with Vasco da Gama shopping centre behind you, the stop is under the station's arches to the left).

Taxi rip-offs can occur on the airport-to-city route. You can buy a prepaid Táxi Voucher from the Turismo de Lisboa desk in Arrivals at set prices for specific destinations (eg most of central Lisbon about €14/16 per day/night and weekends). Only taxis involved in the scheme – marked with a colour sticker – will accept the vouchers.

With nonvoucher taxis, expect to pay about €8 to the city centre, plus €1.50 if your luggage needs to be placed in the boot. Avoid long queues by flagging down a taxi at Departures.

Car & Motorcycle

Lisbon can be quite stressful to drive around, thanks to heavy traffic, maverick drivers, one-way systems and tram lines, but the city is at least small. If you are used to driving in other European capitals you probably won't find it too problematic. There are two ring roads, both useful for staying out of the centre: the inner Cintura Regional Interna de Lisboa (CRIL) and the outer Cintura Regional Externa de Lisboa (CREL).

Once in the centre, parking is the main issue – spaces are scarce, parking regulations complex, pay-and-display machines often broken and car park rates expensive (about €8 to €10 per day). On Saturday afternoon and Sunday parking is normally free.

Upmarket hotels usually have their own garages. If you need to park for more than a few days, park in cheaper car parks near Parque das Nações (metro Gare do Oriente – the multistorey here costs around €4 per day) or Belém (free car parks), then catch a bus or tram to the centre. Always lock up and don't leave anything visible, even if it's worthless, and certainly not any valuables inside, as theft is a risk.

Bicycle

Traffic, trams, hills, cobbles and disgruntled drivers equal a cycling nightmare. You're better off stashing your bike with the left-luggage office at the bus station or airport and seeing the city by public transport. Better hotels and *pensões* may have a storage room. On the Lisbon-Sintra train you can take it for free on weekends or for €2.50 return on weekdays (only outside the rush hour). For more information on transporting your bike between cities, see p471.

There are two pleasant places to ride a bike in Lisbon: Parque das Nações, where you can rent from **Tejo Bike** (Map pp74-5; ☎ 218 871 976); and a 5km stretch on the Rio Tejo promenade, from 1km west of Doca de Santo Amaro to Belém and Praia d'Algés. Here you will find a bike stall run by **Tejo Bike** (Map pp74-5; 🕑 10am-8pm Jun-Sep, 10am-7pm Sat & Sun Oct-May).

The nearest place to rent a mountain bike or motorbike is **Transrent** in Cascais (p131).

Public Transport

BUS, TRAM & FUNICULAR

Companhia Carris de Ferro de Lisboa (Carris; ☎ 213 613 054; www.carris.pt) operates all transport except the metro. Its buses and trams run from about 5am or 6am to 1am; there are some night bus and tram services.

You can get a transport map, *Planta dos Transportes Públicas da Carris* (including a map of night-time services) from turismos or from Carris kiosks, which are dotted around the city. The Carris website has timetables and route details.

Individual tickets cost €1.10 on board or €0.65 if you buy a BUC (Bilhete Único de Coroa, a one-zone city-centre ticket) beforehand. These prepaid tickets are sold at Carris kiosks – most conveniently at Praça da Figueira, at the foot of the Elevador de Santa Justa, and at Santa Apolónia and Cais do Sodré train stations.

The Carris kiosks also sell a one-/five-day (€2.85/11.35) Bilhete Carris/Metro valid for buses, trams, funiculars *and* the metro.

These passes aren't great bargains unless you're planning a lot of travel outside the centre. A better deal is the Lisboa Card (p83), good for most tourist sights as well as bus, tram, funicular and metro travel.

TRAMS

Don't leave the city without riding the No 28 from Largo Martim Moniz or No 12 from Praça da Figueira through the narrow streets of the Alfama.

Two other useful lines are the No 15 from Praça da Figueira and Praça do Comércio via Alcântara to Belém, and the No 18 from Praça do Comércio via Alcântara to Ajuda. The No 15 line features space-age articulated trams with on-board machines for buying tickets and passes. Tram stops are marked by a small yellow *paragem* (stop) sign hanging from a lamppost or the overhead wires.

METRO

The expanding **metropolitano** (underground; www.metrolisboa.pt; 1-zone single/return €0.65/1.20, 2-zone single €1, caderneta – 10-ticket booklet – one/two zone €6/9; 6.30-1am) system is useful for short hops and to reach the Gare do Oriente and nearby Parque das Nações. The Santa Apolónia link from Baixa-Chiado will hopefully be finished by the end of 2005.

Buy tickets from metro ticket offices or machines. Lisboa Cards (p83) and Bilhetes Carris/Metro (above) are also valid.

Entrances are marked by a big red 'M'. Useful signs include *correspondência* (transfer between lines) and *saída* (exit to the street). There is an impressive array of contemporary art at various stations, for example, Angelo de Sousa at Baixa-Chiado, and various artists including Hundertwasser at Oriente.

Watch out for pickpockets in rush-hour crowds.

Taxi

Lisbon's *táxis* are reasonable and plentiful. Hailing one can be difficult but ranks are numerous, including at the Rossio, Praça dos Restauradores, near all stations and ferry terminals, and at top-end hotels. To call one, try **Rádio Táxis de Lisboa** (☎ 218 119 000) or **Autocoope** (☎ 217 932 756).

All taxis have meters, but rip-offs do occasionally happen (the airport route is the main culprit). If you think you've been cheated, get a receipt from the driver (and note the car's registration number and your time of departure and arrival) and talk to the tourist police.

For more about taxis and taxi fares, see p474.

AROUND LISBON

Magical Sintra, the monstrous extravagance of Mafra, sophisticated Cascais, the long beaches of Cacilhas, the beautiful natural parks near Setúbal; all these are short excursions from Lisbon.

SINTRA

pop 260,950 / elevation 280m

Sintra is *Sleeping Beauty* meets *Lord of the Rings*, a hilly, mountainous Never-Never land. Its exceptional microclimate encourages exotic vegetation, flowering and climbing around icing-sugar palaces crowned by gargoyles. There's even a cork-lined monastery deep in a wood. Even if you're only in Lisbon for the weekend, it's worth making a day trip, only 28km to the northwest. Otherwise spend at least a day or two.

On the northern slopes of the craggy Serra de Sintra, the historic centre is a Unesco World Heritage site – listed because of its unique and influential marriage between landscape and architecture. It's long been a popular getaway: the early Iberians made it a centre of cult worship; the Moors built the castle; the Middle Ages brought monasteries; after the 1755 earthquake, the nobility bolted here; then, in the 19th century, it became one of the first centres of European Romantic architecture. It was one of the few places in Portugal that Lord Byron liked, inspiring his travel epic *Childe Harold's Pilgimage* ('Lo! Cintra's glorious Eden intervenes, in variegated maze of mount and glen').

Aside from some bizarre and beautiful palaces, mansions and gardens to visit, Sintra is a lovely place to go walking, and the surrounding area is also good to explore.

The Parque Natural de Sintra-Cascais encompasses both the Serra de Sintra and nearby coastal attractions (including Cabo da Roca, Europe's most westerly point).

Orientation

There are four parts to Sintra: the historic centre (Centro Histórico), called Sintra-Vila (or Vila Velha, 'old town'); the new-town district of Estefânia, 1.5km northeast, where the railway terminates; this new town's extension, Portela de Sintra, 1km further east, where you'll find Sintra's bus station, Portela Interface (beside the Portela de Sintra train station); and São Pedro de Penaferrim, 2km southeast of Sintra-Vila.

Information

EMERGENCY

Police station (Map p119; ☎ 219 230 761; Rua João de Deus 6)

MEDICAL SERVICES

Centro de saúde (medical centre; Map p119; ☎ 219 066 680; Rua Dr Alfredo Costa 34)

MONEY

There's an ATM in the turismo building.
Totta (Map p119; Rua das Padarias 2)

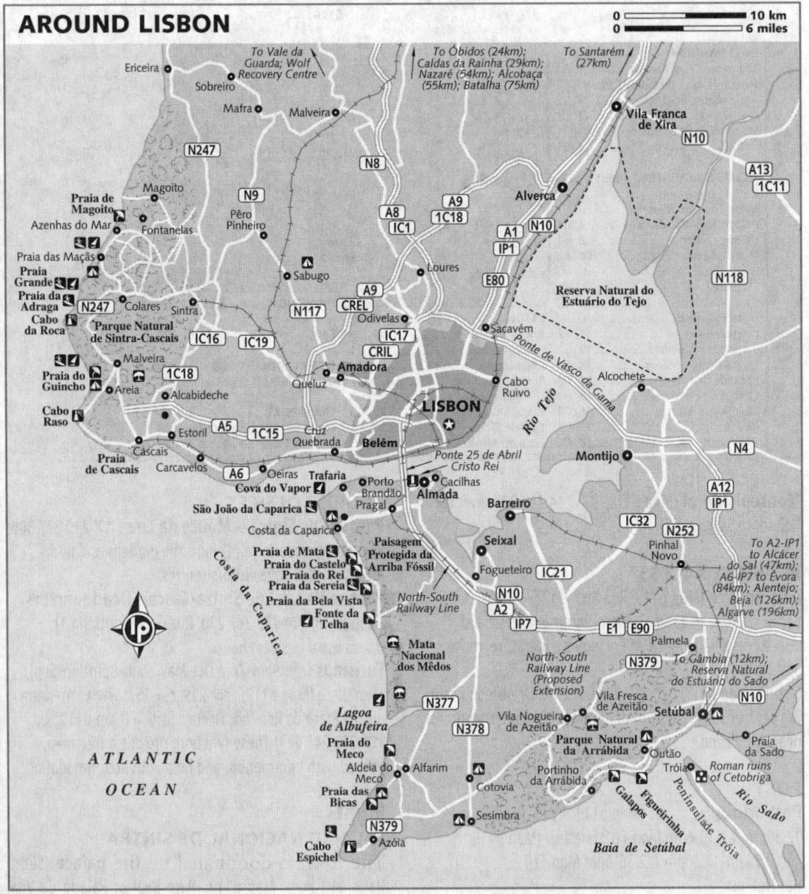

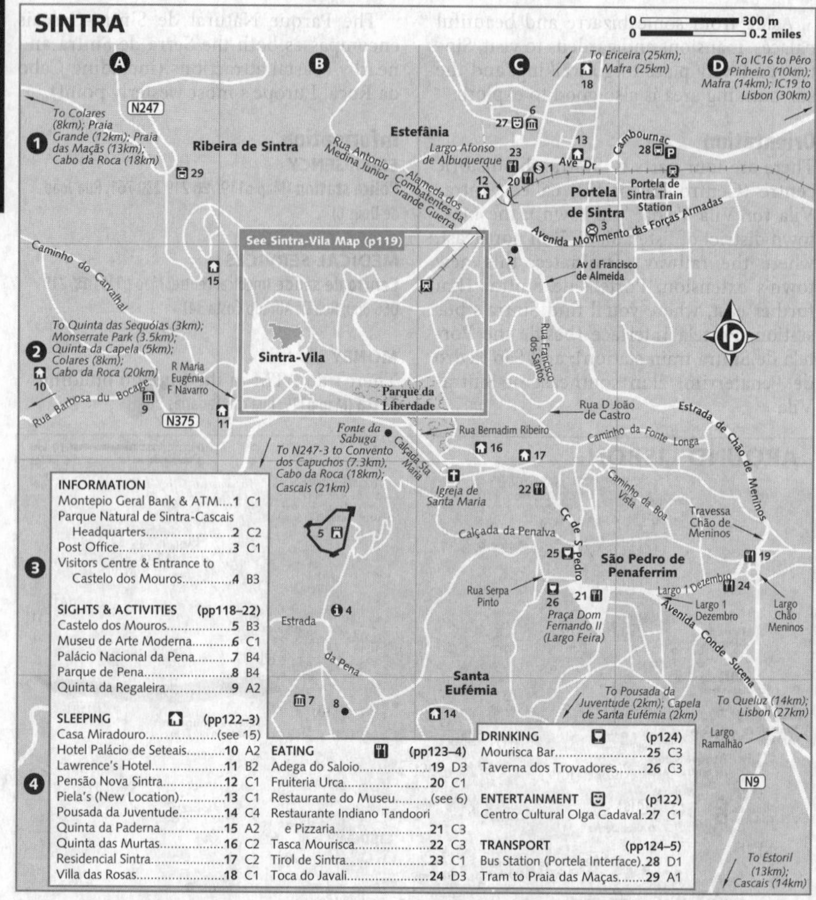

Montepio Geral (Map p118; ☎ 214 248 000; Avenida Heliodoro Salgado 42)

INTERNET ACCESS

Loja do Arco (Map p119; Rua Arco do Teixeira 2; per hr €3.50; 🕑 11am-7.30pm) Internet access, and also stocks a wide range of Portuguese literature, music and crafts.

Sabat (Map p119; ☎ 219 230 802; Rua Dr Alfredo Costa 74; per hr €3; 🕑 noon-midnight Mon-Sat) Internet access near the station.

POST

Post offices Sintra-Vila (Map p119; 🕑 9.30am-12.30pm & 2.30-6pm Mon-Fri); Estefânia (Map p118; 🕑 9.30am-12.30pm & 2.30-6pm Mon-Fri) Has NetPost.

TOURIST OFFICES

Parques de Sintra – Monte da Lua (☎ 219 237 300; www.parquesdesintra.pt) Runs the gardens and parks, most of which have visitors centres.

Parque Natural de Sintra-Cascais Headquarters (Map p118; ☎ 219 247 200; Rua Gago Coutinho 1) Opens usual business hours.

Turismos (🕑 9am-7pm Oct-May, 9am-8pm Jun-Sep); Main Office (Map p119; ☎ 219 231 157; www.cm-sintra.pt; 23 Praça da República); Train Station (Map p119; ☎ 219 241 623) These two both provide a free map, packed with information, and help with accommodation.

Sights

PALÁCIO NACIONAL DE SINTRA

The town is dominated by the **palace** (Sintra National Palace; Map p119; Paço Real or Palácio da Vila;

(☎ 219 053 340; adult/15-25/under 14 €3/1.50/free, free 10am-2pm Sun; 10am-5.30pm Thu-Tue), with its two huge white conical chimneys that loom up like Ku Klux Klan hoods. Of Moorish origins, the palace was first expanded by Dom Dinis (1261–1325), greatly enlarged by João I in the early 15th century (when the kitchens were built), adorned with Manueline additions by Manuel I in the following century, and repeatedly restored and redecorated right up to the present day. It was often occupied, as royalty went hunting in the region or took refuge from Lisbon's heat or outbreaks of plague.

A combination of three different royal residences, it houses an incredible collection of 15th- and 16th-century azulejos – some of the oldest in Portugal. It's also connected with a number of notable occasions: João I planned his 1415 Ceuta campaign here; the three-year-old Sebastião was crowned king here in 1557; and Afonso VI was imprisoned here by his brother Pedro II for nine years, and died of apoplexy in 1683 while listening to Mass in the chapel gallery.

Highlights include the delightful Sala dos Cisnes (Swan Room), with a polychrome ceiling adorned with 27 gold-collared swans. Used for plays and dancing, it was damaged in the 1755 earthquake but rebuilt as it was.

There's the Sala das Pêgas (Magpie Room), its ceiling thick with painted magpies, each holding in its beak a scroll with the words *por bem* (for good). The story goes that João I

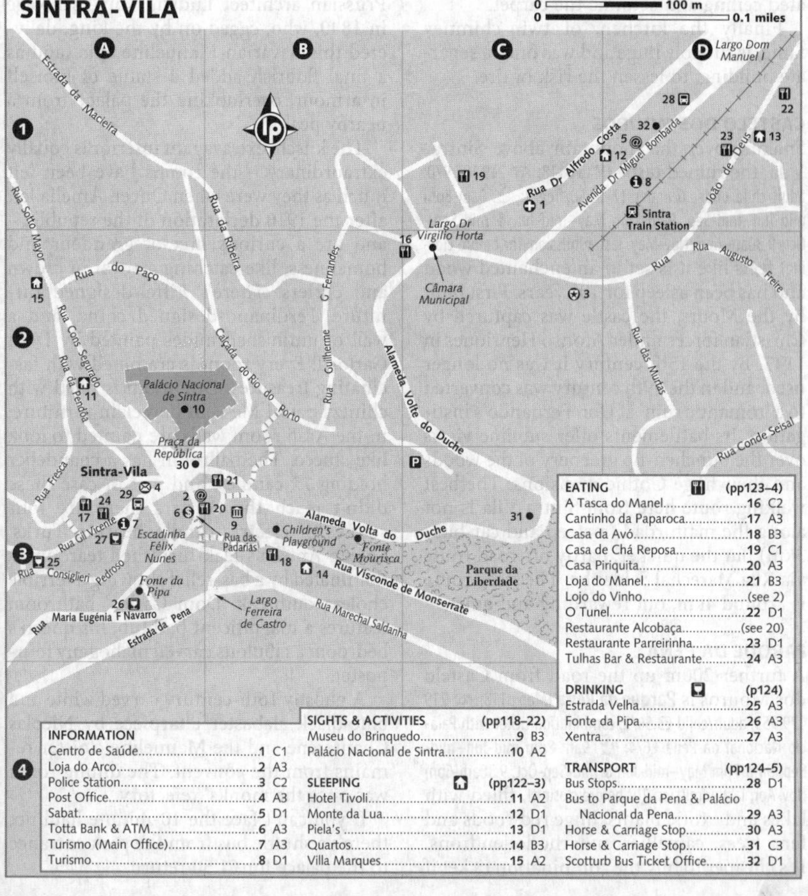

commissioned the cheeky decoration to represent the court gossip about his advances towards one of the ladies-in-waiting. Caught red-handed by his queen, *'por bem'* was the king's alleged response.

The Sala das Armas (Armoury Room, also called the Sala dos Brasões or Coat of Arms Room) carries the heraldic shields of 74 leading 16th-century families on its wooden coffered ceiling.

The Sala dos Árabes – Arab Room – was João I's bedroom, with amazing early-16th-century Manueline tiles, some of the oldest in Portugal.

Busily patterned, the Palatine chapel dates from the 14th century, but was altered in the 15th, and restored in the 1930s. You can see the Islamic influence in the decorated ceiling and ceramic tile carpet.

Finally the kitchen, of twin-chimney fame, is suitably huge and was once a separate building, to lessen the risk of fire.

CASTELO DOS MOUROS

Snaking over the mountain above Sintra-Vila, the ruined **castle** (Map p118; ☎ 219 107 970; adult/child under 6/under 17 €3.50/free/2; 🕒 9am-8pm mid-Jun–mid-Sep, 9am-7pm May–mid-Jun & mid-Sep–Oct, 9.30am-6pm Nov-May, last admission 1hr before closing) feels like it is set in an enchanted wood and has been asleep for 100 years. First built by the Moors, the castle was captured by Christian forces under Afonso Henriques in 1147. By the 15th century it was no longer used, and in the 19th century was converted to a 'romantic ruin' at Don Fernando's instigation. Its battlements offer sublime views over the bunched-up greenery of the woods and their huge Gothic mansions. The best walking route here from Sintra-Vila is not along the main road (a steep and car-busy 3km) but the quicker, partly off-road route via Rua Marechal Saldanha. The steep route is around 4km, but rewarding and quiet.

PARQUE DA PENA

A further 200m up the road from Castelo dos Mouros is **Parque da Pena** (Map p118; ☎ 219 079 955; adult/child €3.50/2, combination ticket with Palácio Nacional da Pena €6/4; 🕒 9am-8pm mid-Jun–mid-Sep, 9am-7pm May–mid-Jun & mid-Sep-Oct, 9.30am-6pm Nov-Apr, last admission 1hr before closing), filled with lakes and exotic plants, huge redwoods and fern trees, camellias and rhododendrons. It's cheaper to buy the combination ticket if you want to visit the palace too, as the only entrance is via Parque da Pena.

PALÁCIO NACIONAL DA PENA

The lavender, lemon and rose-tinted turrets and battlements of the ludicrous, magical **Palácio Nacional da Pena** (Pena National Palace; Map p118; ☎ 219 105 340; adult/child under 6/under 17 €3.50/free/2, combination ticket with Parque da Pena €6/4; 🕒 10am-6.30pm Tue-Sun, 10am-5pm Nov-May, last admission 1hr before closing) rise up from a thickly wooded Sintra peak.

There had long been a convent here, reduced to 16th-century ruins when Ferdinand of Saxe Coburg-Gotha (artist-husband of Queen Maria II) became enchanted with the site, bought it, and began restoration of the convent. He then commissioned Prussian architect Ludwig von Eschwege in 1840, who, egged on by the king, delivered this Bavarian-Manueline epic (and as a final flourish added a statue of himself in armour, overlooking the palace from a nearby peak).

The kitsch, extravagant interior is equally extraordinary – the rooms have been left much as they were when Queen Amélia left after the 1910 declaration of the republic – and are a curious mix of grandeur and homeliness, like catching a royal in crown and curlers. There's Eiffel-designed furniture, Ferdinand-designed china, and a wall of unfinished nudes painted by Dom Carlos I. Every room is crammed with fascinating treasures. One room is filled with chintzy pastel Messein porcelain furniture; in the Arab room walls are painted to look like stucco. The ballroom has a chandelier holding 72 candles, and just in case these didn't reach the corners there are four statues of electric candle–bearing Turks. Queen Amélia's teak-furnished tearoom is dominated by a bas-relief showing a terrible cholera outbreak. Dom Carlos' bathroom features a magnificent bathtub; his queen's bedroom a fabulous carved mahogany four-poster.

A ghostly 16th-century carved white and blue-black alabaster altarpiece by Nicolas Chanterène and the Manueline cloister remains from the convent. The dining room was once the monks' refectory.

If you can't face the 10-minute haul up, there's a shuttle bus from the park entrance to the palace for €1.50 return.

There's a classy **restaurant** (mains €7.90-9.50; noon-midnight) in an arched castle room, smart and white-tableclothed, with risotto, fish, pasta and a couple of vegie choices, or a cheaper terrace **café** (snacks €1.50-8) with snacks and good pastries (but slow service – go to the bar rather than waiting to be served).

Buses to the park entrance leave from Sintra train station and near the turismo (p124). A taxi will cost around €7 one way. The charming but steep woodland walk from Sintra-Vila to here is around 5km (opposite).

QUINTA DA REGALEIRA

Symbols from the Knights Templar, freemasonry, alchemy and mythology cover this mystical **villa and gardens** (Map p118; ☎ 219 106 650; adult guided/unguided visit €10/5; 10am-6pm Jun-Sep, to 4pm Mar-May, Oct & Nov, 11am-3.30pm Dec-Feb), an intensely theatrical, early-20th-century, neo-Manueline extravaganza that is one of Sintra's highlights. It was dreamed up by an opera-set designer, Italian Luigi Manini (who also designed the stunning Palace Hotel do Buçaco in the Beiras), under the orders of António Carvalho Monteiro, a Brazilian-born mining and coffee tycoon known as Monteiro dos Milhões (Moneybags Monteiro).

The villa is surprisingly small and homely inside, despite its ferociously carved fireplaces and floors of Venetian glass. By the main house is a beautiful small chapel, the **Capela da Santíssima Trindade**, with more Venetian glass mosaics. The playful gardens are brilliant to explore, with winding paths leading through exotic foliage to follies, fountains, grottoes, lakes and underground caverns. All paths seem to eventually end at the initiation well, the **Poço Iniciáto**, which plunges down 30m, looking like an inverted Tower of Babel. You walk down the nine-tiered spiral (3 x 3 – three being the magic number) to thrillingly mysterious hollowed-out underground galleries, lit by fairylights.

CONVENTO DOS CAPUCHOS

Hidden in the woods is another magical sight, a far remove from lavish palaces, the hobbit hole–like **Convento dos Capuchos** (Capuchin Monastery; ☎ 219 896 630; adult/child under 6/under 17 €3.50/free/2; 9am-8pm Jun-Oct, to 6pm Nov-May, last admission 1hr before closing). Built in 1560 to house 12 monks, its builders took Matthew's gospel literally when it said 'the way to heaven is sinuous and its doors low and narrow'. The monks lived in incredibly cramped conditions, their tiny cells having low and narrow doors in preparation for the trip to heaven. Byron mocked the monastery in his poem *Childe Harold*, referring to one recluse, Honorius, who spent an astonishing but obviously healthy 36 years here (he was 95 when he died in 1596).

Called Capuchos after the long garment the friars wore, the order was founded by St Francis of Assisi and lived by values of humility and seclusion. It's often known as the Cork Convent, because the diminutive cells are lined with cork. Visiting here is an *Alice in Wonderland* experience as you squeeze through to explore the warren of cells, chapels, kitchen and cavern. The monks lived a simple, touchingly well-ordered life in this idyllic yet spartan place, hiding away here right up until 1834 when it was abandoned.

You can walk here – the monastery is 7.3km away from Sintra-Vila (5.1km from the turn-off to Parque da Pena) along a remote, wooded road – which will bring home just how secluded this place is. There's no bus connection (taxis charge around €15 return). Admission is by guided visit only (lasting 45 minutes), usually every 15 to 30 minutes, but you don't usually have to book in advance. Visits are run in English or Portuguese – it depends who was first to book a tour.

MONSERRATE PARK

Marvellous, rambling, partly wild, **Monserrate Park** (☎ 219 107 806; www.parquesdesintra.pt; adult/child under 6/under 17 €3.50/free/2; 9am-8pm mid-Jun–mid-Sep, to 7pm May–mid-Jun & mid-Sep–Oct, 9.30am-6pm Nov-May, last admission 1hr before closing) is a romantic 30-hectare garden. The wooded hillsides feature flora ranging from roses and conifers to Chinese weeping cypress, dragon trees, eucalyptus, Himalayan rhododendrons and at least 24 species of palm. The park is over 3.5km west of Sintra-Vila – take care of traffic on the narrow road if you're walking.

The gardens, first created in the 18th century by Gerard de Visme, a wealthy English merchant, were enlarged in the 1850s by the painter William Stockdale (with help from London's Kew Gardens), who imported many plants from Australasia and Mexico. Neglected for years (the site was sold to the government in 1949 and forgotten), it's being trimmed up by Parques de Sintra but retains its aura of wild abandon.

At the heart of the gardens is a Moorish-looking **quinta** (mansion) constructed in the late 1850s by James Knowles for another wealthy Englishman, Sir Francis Cook. Previously there was a Gothic-style villa here, rented by the rich, infamous British Gothic writer William Beckford in 1794 after he fled Britain in the wake of a homosexual scandal. The *quinta* is being slowly restored to become a museum. Nearby is a lush green lawn – perfect for relaxation – irrigated with underground pipes to ensure it stays green year-round.

MUSEU DO BRINQUEDO

In the former fire station, the **Museu do Brinquedo** (Toy Museum; Map p119; ☎ 219 242 171; www.museu-do-brinquedo.pt; Rua Visconde de Monserrate; adult/child or student €3/1.50; 🕑 10am-6pm Tue-Sun) is a delightful international collection – from 3000-year-old Egyptian stone counters to Christian Dior Barbies, via tin cars, lead soldiers, Dinky toys and spooky porcelain dolls. João Arbués Moreira, an engineer by profession, began this collection (now over 20,000 pieces) more than 50 years ago when he was 14. On the 3rd floor is a toy-repair workshop, where a man sits studiously working in a glass case, beside a bizarre tray of disembodied heads.

The museum also has a café, a small shop and disabled access.

MUSEU DE ARTE MODERNA

Sintra has a world-class museum, the **Museu de Arte Moderna** (Modern Art Museum; Map p118; ☎ 219 248 170; adult/under 18 €3/free, free 10am-2pm Sun; 🕑 10am-6pm Tue-Sun). Displayed in Estefânia's splendidly cakelike former casino is business tycoon José Berardo and his associate Francisco Capelo's spectacular collection of postwar art (particularly good on pop art) including works by Warhol, Lichtenstein, Pollock, Kossoff, Klein and Nauman. There are also excellent temporary exhibitions and disabled access.

Activities

The Sintra region is increasingly popular for **mountain biking** and **walking**. A favourite walking trail is from Sintra-Vila to Castelo dos Mouros, a relatively easy 50-minute hike. You can continue to Palácio Nacional da Pena (another 20 minutes). From here you can go on to the Serra de Sintra's highest point, the 529m Cruz Alta (high cross) so-called because marked by a 16th-century cross, with amazing views all over Sintra.

Ozono Mais (☎ 219 243 673; www.ozonomais.com; Rua General Alves Roçades 10; per person around €50) offers a day's jeep tour around Sintra.

Cabra Montez (☎ 917 446 668; www.cabramontez.com), or 'mountain goat', runs trekking/mountain-biking/canoeing trips for €25/40/30 per person.

Centro Hípico O Paddock (☎ 219 283 308; Rua do Alecrim, Janas; €20 per hr; 🕑 10am-1pm & 3-6pm Tue-Sun Oct-May, 10am-1pm & 4-7pm Jun-Sep) offers horse rides around Sintra.

Festivals & Events

Sintra's major cultural venue is the Centro Cultural Olga Cadaval, beautifully converted from an old cinema.

Festival de Música (mid-June–mid-July) This classical music festival is Sintra's big cultural event.

Noites de Bailado (mid-July–end August) The equally international classical and contemporary dance festival follows, held in the lovely gardens of hotel Palácio de Seteais. Contact the turismo for details.

Sleeping

Sintra has particularly good upper-end accommodation, and is great for a stay in stately rural manor houses.

BUDGET

Pousada da juventude (☎ 219 241 210; sintra@movijovem.pt; dm €11, d with/without bathroom €30/26) In Santa Eufémia, 4km from Sintra-Vila and 2km uphill from São Pedro. Take the bus to Parque da Pena, walk 100m downhill and follow the rough forest path (by the ruined 'Casa da Lapa').

Piela's (Map p119; ☎ 219 241 691, 966 237 682; Rua João de Deus 70; s/d with shared bathroom €25/35) Long popular, with comfy, spacious doubles above a café and a genial, helpful owner. It plans to move to another building (see the Sintra Map pp76-8), with rooms en suite (prices will remain around the same).

Sintra's cheapest accommodation is in the 80 or so **quartos** (private rooms; Map p119); doubles usually cost about €35 to €45 with shared bathroom.

MID-RANGE

All rooms have their own bathroom unless stated otherwise. The turismo can advise on private apartments (€50 to €60).

Villa Marques (Map p119; ☎ 219 230 027; Rua Sotto Mayor 1; s/d with shared bathroom €35/50) A stately villa in central Sintra-Vila, with lovely views, high ceilings and a relaxing terrace that's good for sunset.

Pensão Nova Sintra (Map p118; ☎ /fax 219 230 220; Largo Afonso de Albuquerque 25; d €70) A renovated mansion above the main road offering small doubles with views and big outdoor terrace. Rooms on upper floors are better.

Monte da Lua (Map p119; ☎ /fax 219 241 029; Avenida Miguel Bombarda 51; d €50) Offers pleasant, airy rooms (with telephone), the best overlooking the wooded valley at the back.

Quinta da Paderna (Map p118; ☎ 219 235 053, 939 240 487; planeta.clix.pt/paderna; Rua da Paderna 4; s/d €70/80) A lovely private home: tucked away, quiet and leafy but central, elegantly old-fashioned, with fantastic views.

Residencial Sintra (Map p118; ☎ 219 230 738; pensao.residencial.sintra@clix.pt; Travessa dos Avelares 12; dinner €60 d/tr with view 75/90; P) In a picturesque position between Sintra-Vila and São Pedro, this is a stately, faded 1850s mansion with 10 spacious high-ceilinged rooms and wooded views. It's perfect for families, with a large terrace and rambling garden.

Quinta das Murtas (Map p118; ☎ 219 240 246; www.quinta-das-murtas.com; Rua Eduardo Van Zeller 4; tw €95; P) A grand salmon-pink manor house with charmingly pale rooms overlooking the wooded exterior. The sitting rooms are grandly stuccoed.

TOP END

Quinta da Capela (☎ 219 290 170; s/d with breakfast €130/140; 🕒 mid-Mar–mid-Oct; P) Another grand manor house, this dates from the 16th century, rebuilt in the 18th, and is an exquisite place to stay, set in a secluded valley just beyond Monserrate Park. Rooms are bright and beautiful, filled with antiques, and have great views. Gardens are populated by peacocks and gliding swans.

Lawrence's Hotel (Map p118; ☎ 219 105 500; lawrences_hotel@iol.pt; Rua Consigliéri Pedroso 38; s/d €185/240) This charming 18th-century hotel, where Lord Byron stayed in 1809, was beautifully restored by a Dutch couple. Many of the grand, chintzy rooms overlook the wooded valley. Disabled access.

Quinta das Sequóias (☎ 219 243 821; s/d €145/160; P) A superb, welcoming six-bedroom manor house adorned with art and flowers, en route to Monserrate Park. Rooms are charming, homely and gloriously comfortable, and views fantastic.

Villa das Rosas (Map p118; ☎ /fax 219 234 216; Rua António Cunha 2; d €100; P) Among several Turihab properties (a government-sponsored scheme for marketing private accommodation) in the area is this lovely old 19th-century house. It has splendid décor (azulejos in the hall and dining room) and birdcages and lemon trees in the garden.

Casa Miradouro (Map p118; ☎ 219 235 900; Rua Sotto Mayor 55; s/d €112/125) An imposing Battenberg cake of a house, built in 1890, with smart, pale, elegant rooms and excellent views.

Hotel Tivoli (Map p119; ☎ 219 237 200; www.tivolihotels.com; Praça da República; s/d €100/120; ❄ 💻) A modern, ugly building that's the only scar in the centre, but if you're inside looking out, the views are stunning. Very comfortable and service is good. Disabled access.

Hotel Palácio de Seteais (Map p118; ☎ 219 233 200; www.tivolihotels.com; s/d with breakfast €250/270; P) In a neoclassical palace, this hotel is vastly grand but feels faded for the price, despite fine murals and chandeliers. If you don't want to stay, the terrace overlooking the grounds is good for a drink.

Eating

BUDGET

O Tunel (Map p119; ☎ 219 231 286; 29 Rua Conde Fereira, Estefânia; mains €5-7.50; 🕒 daily) Brightly lit, popular with locals, simple and large, this has tasty traditional dishes in a cheery atmosphere.

Tirol de Sintra (Map p118; Largo Afonso de Albuquerque 9, Estefânia; mains €1-4.50; 🕒 daily) Big, busy café with outside tables.

Casa Piriquita (Map p119; Rua das Padarias 1-5, Sintra-Vila; 🕒 Thu-Mon) A busy café where everyone likes to sample Sintra's famous *queijadas* (sweet cheese cakes) and *travesseiros* (almond pastries) – or you can take away.

Casa da Avó (Map p119; ☎ 219 231 280; Rua Visconde de Monserrate 46, Sintra-Vila; mains €5-10; 🕒 lunch & dinner Fri-Wed) Jolly café-restaurant, simple meals.

Loja do Manel (Map p119; Rua do Arco do Teixeira, Sintra-Vila) Grocery store.

Tasca Mourisca (Map p118; Calçada de San Pedro 28, São Pedro; mains €6; 🕒 lunch & dinner Mon-Sat) Readers recommend this small restaurant with tasty mains.

A Tasca do Manel (Map p119; ☎ 219 230 215; Largo Dr Virgílio Horta 5, Estefânia; mains €5-6.50; breakfast, lunch & dinner Mon-Sat) Small, good-value, TV-and-tiles place.

Fruiteria Urca (Map p118; Largo Afonso de Albuquerque, Estefânia; daily) Tiny grocery, good for picnics.

MID-RANGE

Tulhas Bar & Restaurante (Map p119; ☎ 219 232 378; Rua Gil Vicente 4, Sintra-Vila; mains €7.75-12.90; lunch & dinner Thu-Tue) A converted grain warehouse; dark, tiled and quaint, with twisted chandeliers and a relaxing, cosy atmosphere. The *bacalhau con nata* is good.

Adega do Saloio (Map p118; ☎ 219 231 422; Travessa Chão de Meninos, São Pedro; mains €9-15, half-portions €6; Wed-Mon) Popular with locals, this has two outlets across the road from each other, both specialising in grills, but one more formal than the other. Both have bustling atmospheres and are decorated with strings of garlic.

Restaurante Indiano Tandoori e Pizzaria (Map p118; ☎ 219 244 667; Praça Dom Fernando II 3, São Pedro; mains €3.5-30) Overlooking the quiet and large square, this is an Indian restaurant also offering Italian mains, with outside seating and an interior covered in tiles and wood.

Restaurante Alcobaça (Map p119; ☎ 219 231 651; Rua das Padarias 7, Sintra-Vila; mains €5-10, menu €9; daily) This is the best-value and most traditional restaurant in the old town; a simple place, busy and bright.

Casa de Chá Reposa (Map p119; 29 Rua Conde Fereira 29; Tue-Sun) An amazing tearoom with a view, crammed with interesting things for sale. A chandelier hung with tissue paper–covered teapots dangles from the high stuccoed ceiling. Good cakes.

Restaurante do Museu (Map p118; ☎ 219 107 000; Museu de Arte Moderna, Estefânia; mains around €10; Tue-Sun) Classy museum restaurant.

Restaurante Parreirinha (Map p119; ☎ 219 231 207; Rua João de Deus 41, Estefânia; mains around €7; Mon-Sat) Justifiably popular, this local neighbourhood restaurant serves grilled fish cooked on coals outside.

TOP END

Loja do Vinho (Map p119; ☎ 219 105 860; Praça da Republica, Sintra-Vila; 9am-10.30pm, happy hour noon-2pm & 5.30-8pm) This touristy port shop is no bargain, even at happy hour, but it makes a charming port, ham, cheese and chutney stop.

Toca do Javali (Map p118; ☎ 219 233 503; Rua 1 de Dezembro 12, São Pedro; mains €10-19; lunch & dinner) This has a delightful tree-shaded courtyard – a charming spot – and provides delicious barbecued mains, including wild boar.

Drinking

Fonte da Pipa (Map p119; ☎ 219 234 437; Rua Fonte da Pipa 11-13; from around 9pm) A hip tiled bar, this has craggy, cavelike rooms and comfy seats.

Estrada Velha (Map p119; ☎ 219 234 355; Rua Consiglieri Pedroso 16) Another popular bar, this is vaguely pub-like, laid-back though busy, with jazzy music in the background.

Xentra (Map p119; ☎ 219 240 759; Rua Consiglieri Pedroso 2A) In an arched cellar bar.

Taverna dos Trovadores (Map p118; ☎ 219 233 548) In São Pedro, this upmarket tavern has live Portuguese music Friday and Saturday nights.

Mourisca Bar (Map p119; ☎ 219 235 253; Calçada de São Pedro 56) A casual local dive, where you can play snooker, darts or chess.

Getting There & Away

Buses run by **Scotturb** (Map p119; ☎ 214 699 100; www.scotturb.com) or **Mafrense** (☎ 219 230 971) leave regularly for Cascais (€2.75, 60 minutes), sometimes via Cabo da Roca (€2.75). Buses also head to Estoril (€2.75, 40 minutes), Mafra (45 minutes) and Ericeira (45 minutes). Most services leave from Sintra train station (*estação* on timetables) via the new Portela Interface terminal, in Portela de Sintra. For a useful bus service to the airport, see p130. Scotturb's useful information office, open 9am to 1pm and 2pm to 8pm is opposite the station.

Train services (€1.40, 45 minutes) run every 15 minutes between Sintra and Lisbon (Rossio or Entrecampos train stations). Bikes travel free at weekends and holidays (€2.50 return weekdays, not permitted from 7am to 10am Sintra to Lisbon, 4pm to 8pm Lisbon to Sintra).

Getting Around

BUS

From the station, it's about 15 minutes (1.5km) scenic walk into Sintra Vila – a good way to get your bearings. Or you can hop on a **bus** (☎ 214 699 127). No 433 runs regularly from Portela Interface to São Pedro (*Largo 1 Dez* on timetables; €0.65, 15 minutes, at least half-hourly 7am to 8pm) via Estefânia and Sintra-Vila. To get to Palácio Nacional da Pena (€3.50, 15 minutes), catch bus No 434, which starts from Sintra train station and goes via Sintra-Vila (every 20 to 40 minutes, from 10.20am to 5.15pm). The last one from Pena returns at 5.45pm.

For €7.50 you can buy a Day Rover, valid on all Scotturb bus routes, including the Pena service.

A one-day Train & Bus Travelcard (€9) is valid on Lisbon-Cascais/Sintra trains and all Scotturb buses. Ticket kiosks are at Portela Interface (near the car park) and opposite Sintra train station.

HORSE & CARRIAGE

These clip-clop all over the place, even as far as Monserrate (€60 return). The turismo has a full list of prices (€15 to €100). The carriages wait by the entrance to the Parque da Liberdade (on Alameda Volta do Duche) or by the *pelourinho* (pillory) below Palácio Nacional de Sintra.

TAXI & CAR

Taxis are available at the train station, or opposite the Sintra-Vila post office. They aren't metered, so check fares with the turismo. Figure on about €7 one way to Palácio Nacional da Pena, or €15 return to Convento dos Capuchos – arrange for them to pick you up after an hour. There's a 20% supplement at weekends and on holidays.

There's a free car park below Sintra-Vila (follow the signs by the *câmara municipal*, town hall, in Estefânia). Alternatively, park at Portela Interface and take the bus.

Diller (☎ 219 271 225), based in nearby Pêro Pinheiro, will deliver rental cars to Sintra for no extra charge.

WEST OF SINTRA

For a quick sun-and-sand fix, you can head 12km west of Sintra to the beaches of **Praia Grande** and **Praia das Maçãs**. Praia Grande lives up to its name, a big sandy beach with ripping breakers, which hosts heats of the European Surfing Championships. It also has a 102m-long oceanwater **swimming pool** (adult/child Mon-Fri €6/3, Sat & Sun €7/4; 🕒 Jun-Oct). **Praia das Maçãs** has a smaller beach, backed by a lively little resort. **Azenhas do Mar**, 2km further, is spectacularly set on a clifftop, and also has a small beach.

En route to the beaches, 8km west of Sintra, is the ancient ridgetop village of **Colares**. It's laid-back, with spectacular views and has been famous for its wines since the 13th century, made from the only vines in Europe to survive the 19th-century phylloxera plague, saved by deep roots and sandy soil. Call in advance to arrange a visit to **Adega Regional de Colares** (☎ 219 291 210) to taste some of its velvety reds.

Cabo da Roca (Rock Cape) is a sheer cliff of around 150m, facing the roaring sea, about 18km west of Sintra. It's Europe's westernmost point and the place to go for sunset, which is an occasion every day. Wild and wind-lashed, it's very uncommercialised, perhaps because it feels so remote; there are a couple of stalls, a café and a turismo where you can buy a certificate to show you've been here.

Sleeping

BUDGET

Senhora Maria Pereira (☎ /fax 219 290 319; Avenida Maestro Frederico de Freitas 19; d/tr with breakfast €45/50, 3-person apt €60) A kilometre before Praia Grande beach, here delightful *quartos* overlook a large rambling garden (with barbecue facilities). Three self-catering apartments are also available.

Residencial Real (☎ 219 292 002; Rua Fernão Magalhães, Praia das Maçãs; d with breakfast around €40) A faded, spacious place, this is at the northern end of the Praia Grande village, with expansive ocean views.

Camping Praia Grande (☎ 219 290 581; www.wondertur.com; Avenida Maestro Frederico de Freitas 28; adult/tent/car €2.15/4.50/4) Praia Grande's often-crowded site is 600m from the beach. It also has bungalows, apartments and luxury *quartos*.

MID-RANGE

Casal St Virginia (☎ 219 283 198; Avenida Luis Augusto Colares 19; d €63-68) German-run (most guests are German), this is a fantastic high-up house between Praia Grande and Azenhas do Mar; a dazzling place with a central wooden staircase, great sea views and lots of paintings.

Residencial Oceano (☎ 219 292 399; pensaoceano@iol.pt; Avenida Eugénio Levy 52, Praia das Maçãs; d with breakfast €40-60) By the tram terminal, small-scale Oceano has neat, modern, white-painted rooms (with telephone) on offer, some with balcony. There's a restaurant downstairs.

Hotel Arribas (☎ 219 289 050; www.hotelarribas.com; Avenida Alfredo Coelho, Praia Grande; s/d/tr/q €55/73/101/124;) A big custard-coloured carbuncle, overlooking Praia Grande. Rooms have sea views, and residents have free use of the huge oceanwater pool. Disabled access.

Hotel Miramonte (☎ 219 288 200; hotelmiramonte@viphotels.com; Avenida do Atlântico 155, Pinhal da Nazaré; s/tw/tr €50/60/70) An endearingly old-fashioned 1970s place on the Sintra-Praia das Maçãs road, 400m before the turn-off to Praia Grande; odd location but with appealing countryside views.

Eating

Restaurante Pôr do Sol (☎ 219 291 740; Rua António Brandão de Vasconcelos 25; mains around €7; daily Jul & Aug, Wed-Mon Sep-Jun) A fantastically situated, small-scale restaurant in Azenhas do Mar, at the top of the village, with good *pratos do dia* (daily specials) and wonderful views. Staff can recommend *quartos*.

Restaurante Adraga (☎ 219 280 028; Praia da Adraga; mains €6-14; lunch & dinner) This lone restaurant has big windows over the wild, rocky, sandy little beach. Decorated with lanterns and anchors, it gets packed out due to a great situation and fabulous seafood. A good lively place for families. Buses run here from Sintra and Praia Grande; the beach and restaurant are 2km from the bus stop.

There are plenty of cafés and restaurants at both Praia Grande and Praia das Maçãs.

Getting There & Away

Bus No 441 from Portela Interface goes frequently via Colares to Praia das Maçãs (€2.10, 25 minutes) and on to Azenhas do Mar (€2.10, 30 minutes), stopping at Praia Grande (€2.10, 25 minutes) three times daily (more in summer). Bus No 440 (€2.10, 35 minutes) also travels from Sintra to Azenhas do Mar.

The century-old tram service (€1; hourly; 9.30am to 6.25pm Friday, Saturday and Sunday) connecting Sintra with Praia das Maçãs should run from Ribeira de Sintra (1.5km from Sintra-Vila; take bus No 441 or 403), but check with the turismo.

Bus No 403 to Cascais runs regularly via Cabo da Roca (€2.75, 45 minutes) from outside Sintra station.

CASCAIS

pop 33,255

The stately seaside suburb of Cascais (kuhsh-*kaish*) gets busy with well-heeled, trendy Lisboêtas, large packs of golfers and plenty of convertibles. It was once a fishing village, but in 1870 the royal court came here for the summer, bringing a trail of nobility in its wake. Such patronage has left it with some grand pastel-coloured buildings, setting off the crisp-clothed clientele nicely. But it doesn't feel exclusive; it's the Estoril coast's liveliest resort, with an appealing old town and new marina, and there's an impressive beach – Praia do Guincho – nearby, though better for surfing than swimming.

Orientation & Information

The train station and nearby bus station are about 250m north of the main pedestrianised Rua Frederico Arouca.

BOOKSHOPS

Livraria Galileu (☎ 214 866 014; Avenida Valbom 24A) Good source of second-hand English, Spanish, Italian, French and German books.

EMERGENCY

Main police station (☎ 214 861 127; Rua Afonso Sanches)

Tourist police post (☎ 214 863 929; Rua Visconde da Luz) Next to the turismo.

INTERNET ACCESS

Golfino (☎ 214 840 150; Rua Sebastião J Carvalho e Melo 17; per hr €6; 9.30am-8pm Mon-Sat)

Smartprint (☎ 214 866 776; Rua Frederico Arouca 45, Loja 13; per hr €4; 10am-6pm Mon-Fri) In a shopping mall basement.

MEDICAL SERVICES

Cascais Hospital (☎ 214 827 700; Rua Padre Loureiro)

International Medical Centre (☎ 214 845 317/8; Largo Luis de Canoez) English-speaking. Pricey but fast; has 24-hour service available.

MONEY

Banco Espirito Santo (☎ 214 864 302; Largo Luís Camões 40)

Empório (214 838 769; Rua Frederico Arouca; 9am-6.30pm Mon-Fri, 10am-6.30pm Sat & Sun)

POST

Post office (☎ 214 447 320; Avenida Marginal; 8.30am-6pm Mon-Fri) Also has NetPost.

TOURIST INFORMATION

Turismo (☎ 214 868 204; www.estorilsintra.com; Rua Visconde da Luz 14; 🕒 9am-7pm Mon-Sat Sep-Jun, to 8pm Mon-Sat Jul-Aug; 10am-6pm Sun year-round) Helpful and has surf tables. Can assist with accommodation.

Sights

OLD CASCAIS

The **fish market** is a remnant of Cascais the fishing village, between Praia da Ribeira and Praia da Rainha; an auctioneer sells the day's catch in rapid-fire lingo at about 6pm Monday to Saturday.

The back lanes and alleys to the west of the *câmara municipal* (town hall) are also worth exploring. In a shady square southwest of the *câmara municipal* is the **Igreja de Nossa Senhora da Assunção**, decorated with azulejos predating the 1755 earthquake.

The **citadel** is where the royal family used to spend the summer, with a beautiful chapel. It's occupied by the military so is out of bounds, but plans are afoot to open it as a museum.

MUSEUMS

Shady, beautiful, with the feel of wilderness, **Parque Municipal da Gandarinha** is a great place to explore. With peacocks, aviaries, duck ponds and playground – it's a good place to head with kids. It also contains the delightful **Museu Condes de Castro Guimarães** (☎ 214 825 407; admission €1.60; 🕒 11am-5pm Tue-Sun). The whimsical late-19th-century mansion of

Jorge O'Neill was designed by a painter, apparently inspired by Luigi Manini's (p121) opera-set designs, and is a dreamlike mix of styles, with castle turrets and an Arabic cloister. O'Neill was Irish, hence the clover leaves inside. But they didn't bring him luck, as he had to sell up later because of bankruptcy. The interior displays the lavish furnishings installed by his successor, Count of Castro Guimarães, including 17th-century Indo-Portuguese inlaid cabinets, Oriental silk tapestries and 17th-century azulejos. A 16th-century illuminated manuscript is the most valuable exhibit, with a rare rendering of pre-earthquake Lisbon. Admission is with half-hourly guided tours. A bilingual booklet (€2.50) is available at the entrance.

The admirable **Museu do Mar** (☎ 214 825 400; admission €1.60, Sun free; 🕑 10am-5pm Tue-Sun), in Jardim da Parada, is a really interesting collection examining Cascais' history and maritime links, ranging from Roman *garum amphorae* (bottled fish sauce) and exploration of the lives of fishers – with fearsome fishwife recordings – to photos of cigar-toting King Carlos I in his element around Cascais.

Near the Museu Condes de Castro Guimarães, the colourful, spacious **Centro Cultural de Cascais** (☎ 214 848 900; Avenida Rei Humberto II de Itália; admission free; 🕑 10am-6pm Tue-Sun), in what was a barefooted Carmelite convent, hosts contemporary exhibitions and cultural events. Upstairs is an anthology of Portuguese music, gathered by famous Corsican ethnographer Michel Giacometti, where you can listen to regional folk music and see a large collection of traditional instruments, including bagpipes and a guitar made out of a tin can.

BOCA DO INFERNO

The sea seeps into an abyss in the coast at **Boca do Inferno** (Mouth of Hell), 2km west. Taxis charge about €5 return, or you can walk along the coast (about 20 minutes). Expect a mouth of small splashes unless a storm is raging.

Activities

Cascais has three relaxing sandy beach suntraps – largest and closest is **Praia da Ribeira** – tucked into little bays a few minutes' walk south of town. However, they do get busy and the water quality is not great.

The best beach is **Praia do Guincho**, 9km northwest. This long, wild beach is a surfer's and windsurfer's paradise (the site of previous World Surfing Championships) with massive crashing rollers. The strong undertow can be dangerous for swimmers and novice surfers.

John David's Watersports Centre (☎ 214 830 455; www.exclusive-divers.com; 🕑 3.30-7pm but ring ahead) at Praia da Duquesa, midway between Cascais and Estoril, rents sailboards (€25 per hour) and organises **water-skiing** jaunts (€25 per 15 minutes) and banana-boat rides (€24 per five people). It can also take you scuba-diving around the Cascais coastline and beyond.

Moana Surf School (☎ 964 449 436; www.moanasurfschool.com; Praia do Guincho; introductory 30-min lesson €20, 4 x 30-min classes €75) offers surfing courses. **Guincho Surf School** (☎ 965 059 421; Praia do Guincho) also runs surfing courses. You can also ring Pedro Barbudo, who runs the school, for a surf report.

Surfboards can be rented from **Aerial Wind e Surf** (☎ 214 836 745; Loja 129, Cascais Marina).

You can charter a yacht for six people from **Tuttamania** (☎ 934 843 636; Cascais Marina; half/full day incl skipper & insurance €225/375).

The **Guia Climbing School** (☎ 214 847 084; www.adesnivel.pt; 🕑 3-6pm Mar-Oct) is west of the Boca do Inferno, with seacliff climbs of around 10m to 20m, suitable for beginners or experienced climbers. It also has a **climbing wall** (€3; 🕑 8-11pm Mon-Fri, 4-8pm Sat).

Escola e Equitação (☎ 214 869 084; per hr around €20; 🕑 9am-noon & 3-7pm Tue-Sun, 9am-noon & 4-8pm Apr-Sep), 2km inland from Praia do Guincho, offers horse rides to the sand dunes and through forest as well as around Sintra.

Festivals & Events

Events for children are laid on every month, such as games, concerts and theatre, mainly in Portuguese, but some are suitable for foreigners too – inquire at the turismo.

Festas do Mar (end of June) Celebrates Cascais' marine ties and honours the patron saint of fishers, the Senhora dos Navegantes, with a procession and a parade of fishing boats.

Estoril Festival de Jazz (July) Held in both Cascais and Estoril.

Festival de Música da Costa do Estoril (July) Also held in both towns.

Free outdoor entertainment (July–mid-September) A programme with live bands at around 10.30pm nightly, usually at Estoril's Praia de Tamariz and/or Cascais' Praia de Moitas (en route to Estoril).

Fireworks displays (July–mid-September) Saturdays around midnight, usually over Praia de Tamariz.

Sleeping

Advance reservations are essential for summer. The prices listed here are for July (August is higher). *Quartos* cost €30 to €35 a double. Turismo staff may know of available *quartos*. Otherwise, ask at Adega do Gonçalves (p130).

BUDGET

Residencial Avenida (☎ 214 864 417; Rua da Palmeira 14; d with shared bathroom €40) So long-established that its sign is practically invisible, Avenida is a quiet spot. It's like staying in someone's flat – there are just four plainly decorated but comfortable doubles.

Residencial Parsi (☎ 214 845 744; fax 214 837 150; Rua Afonso Sanches 8; d with shared bathroom €50-60) A crumbling, characterful old building near the waterfront, this overlooks the square and is rundown. It's convenient for nightlife, but may be noisy.

Camping Orbitur do Guincho (☎ 214 870 450; www.orbitur.pt; adult/tent/car €3.50/3/3.15) In Areia, about 1km inland from Praia do Guincho and 9km from Cascais, this is a shady, large site, with restaurant, playground and disabled facilities. It gets busy in July and August. Buses run regularly to Guincho from Cascais.

MID-RANGE

Albergaria Valbom (☎ 214 865 801; albergariavalbom@mail.telepac.pt; Avenida Valbom 14; s/d €43-48/58-63) Well run but characterless, with modern, ordinary, comfortable rooms in a central location.

Residencial Solar Dom Carlos (☎ 214 828 115; www.solardomcarlos.com; Rua Latino Coelho 8; s/d/tw €45/60-70/60-70) A 16th-century former royal residence with a chapel where Dom Carlos used to pray, this is charming with large, old-fashioned rooms in a quiet leafy street. Breakfast is in a lavishly muralled room. Laundry, bike hire and parking are available.

TOP END

Casa da Pergola (☎ 214 840 040; pergolahouse@netc.pt; Avenida Valbom 13; d incl breakfast with/without balcony €125/115) A Turihab place, owned by the same family for more than 100 years, with an ornate façade, exquisite rooms, a gorgeous garden and superb breakfasts.

Hotel Albatroz (☎ 214 847 380; www.albatrozhotels.com; s/d €200/230, sea view 230/280, breakfast €15;) One of the Leading Small Hotels of the World group, this is a beautiful 19th-century building, with lavish interiors – lots of big gilded mirrors and orchids – plus huge rooms and great attention to detail. The saltwater pool overlooks the bay of Cascais.

Villa Albatroz (☎ 214 863 410; s/d €166/196, breakfast €12.50;) Run by the same group, similarly gorgeous but smaller scale with more of a contemporary feel, also overlooking the bay. Disabled access.

Hotel Baía (☎ 214 831 033; www.hotelbaia.com; Avenida Marginal; d incl breakfast €100/120;) A big, modern hotel in a prime spot, this has a covered rooftop pool and sea-view sundeck. Rooms have white bedspreads, and balconies overlooking the bay.

Hotel Apartamento Ecuador (☎ 214 826 500; hotelequador@mail.telepac.pt; Alto da Pampilheira 396; 2-person apt with breakfast & kitchen €93) A high-rise on the northern outskirts of town offering some of the most reasonably priced apartments. Disabled access.

Eating

BUDGET

Dom Pedro I (☎ 214 833 734; Beco dos Invalides 5; mains €5-8; Mon-Sat) A marvellous small restaurant unexpectedly tucked away in a small courtyard, serving great-value grilled fish. Try to get one of the few outdoor tables on the cobbled steps shaded by small trees.

A Económica (☎ 214 833 524; Rua Sebastião J C Melo 11; mains €5-10; lunch & dinner Fri-Wed) This is a no-nonsense little place, big cheap plates of Portuguese nosh are its game, though couvert extras can work out not so económica.

A Tasca (☎ 214 820 726; Rua Afonso Sanches 61; mains €3.50-7.50; lunch & dinner Mon-Sat) Tiny, with pine walls decked with wooden boats, this is a buzzy, simple little place, with TV and all the usual Portuguese menu suspects.

Somos um Regalo (☎ 214 865 487; Avenida Vasco da Gama 36; mains €1.50-9; Thu-Tue) Grilled chicken is it, and you can either eat in or you can takeaway.

Paradox (☎ 214 843 004; Avenida Costa Pinto 91; mains €4-5.20; noon-5pm Mon-Fri, to 4pm Sat) Is the paradox that this is a vegetarian restaurant in a carnivorous country, or that this is an eatery in a weirdly institutional building? Something to muse over as you chew veritable tofu.

MID-RANGE

Adega do Gonçalves (☎ 214 830 287; Rua Afonso Sanches 54; mains €7-14, tourist menu €15; ⏰ lunch & dinner Thu-Tue) Near A Tasca, this is popular, with a rustic feel, light, airy and friendly, serving up traditional Portuguese food; good fish.

Apeadeiro (☎ 214 832 731; Avenida Vasco da Gama 252; mains €6.50-11; ⏰ lunch Tue-Sun, dinner Tue-Sat) This is an airy, cut-above yet relaxed restaurant, renowned for its excellent, beautifully cooked grilled fish, with checked tablecloths, big windows and walls hung with fishing nets.

Jappa Sushi/Lucullus (☎ 214 844 709; Rua da Palmeira; mains €5.50-16; ⏰ lunch & dinner) In an airy, large, chic restaurant, sushi and Italian mains are on offer – fortunately the cuisines are not combined. A good place to go if you can't agree on what you want to eat.

Conversas na Gandarinha (☎ 214 866 402; Avenida Rei Humberto II de Itália; mains €7.10-10.90) The Centro Cultural de Cascais (p128) has this fantastic airy, pastel courtyard, where you can nibble cakes or enjoy a delightful lunch. The desserts are good.

Music Bar Restaurante (☎ 214 820 848; Largo Praia da Rainha 121; mains €8.50-17.50) Another bright restaurant, with unusually good views and large windows overlooking the sea and small beach.

Restaurante Pereira (☎ 214 831 215; Rua Bela Vista 92; mains €7.40-22) Simple, good-value and off-the-beaten-track, this is a good, unassuming restaurant with checked tablecloths and TV, serving up lots of seafood.

A cluster of appealing venues with outdoor seating is in the cobbled Largo Cidade de Vitória, including the low-key **Snack Bar O Marítimo** (☎ 214 843 988; mains €6-10; ⏰ daily), small with a matching short menu, and with some outside tables. Behind the nearby fish market is a string of upmarket fish restaurants.

TOP END

Furnas do Guincho (☎ 214 869 243; Estrada da Guincho; mains €10-16) Stunningly situated upmarket seafood restaurant about 1km along the road to Guincho, with views over the sea as you tuck into its bounty.

Bangkok (☎ 214 847 600; Rua da Bela Vista 6; mains €6-36; ⏰ lunch & dinner) The smiliest restaurant in town, this Thai restaurant is exquisitely decorated (there's a small shop where you can buy the furnishings), with green tiles, wood, scented candles and a few patio tables. As well, the food is excellent, aromatic and authentic. An elegant Thai dancer also does a turn. Try the delicious mango and sticky rice. Yum.

Drinking & Clubbing

Bars cluster around Largo Luís de Camões, and tend to be pub-like, loud and lively and stuffed with a good-time crowd that gets crazy after a game of golf.

John Bull (☎ 214 483 319; Largo Luís de Camões 4) Stuffed with comfy chairs and authentic English pub ambience, this is usually busy.

O'Neill's (☎ 214 868 230; Largo 5 de Outubro) One of the cheeriest pubs (Irish, draught Guinness, lots of wood), this has live music on Thursday to Saturday evening at around 11pm.

Coconuts (☎ 214 844 109; Avenida Rei Humberto II de Itália 7; ⏰ 11pm-4am) Cascais' most popular nightclub, this is impressive, with seven bars, two dance floors and an esplanade by the sea. It's packed with cool dressed-up locals as well as tourists, and it feels like an event.

Ferdi's Bar (☎ 214 835 784; Rua Afonzo Sanchez; ⏰ 6pm-4am Thu-Sat) People head to this small bar when everything else closes, hence it gets packed.

For a sea view with your drinks, head for outdoor Esplanada Rainha overlooking Praia da Rainha.

Shopping

Serious shoppers should head for CascaiShopping, a vast mall to get lost in, which also has a cinema (some films in English), en route to Sintra. Bus No 417 passes by regularly. Cascais also has the **Cascais Villa shopping centre** (Avenida Marginal) by the bus station.

The mercado municipal (municipal market), on the northern outskirts of town, is best on Wednesday and Saturday morning, while an open-air market – a mix of clothes, bags, antiques, junk, and so on – fills the area next to the former bullring, 1km west of town, the first and third Sunday of the month.

Getting There & Away

Buses go frequently to Sintra from both Estoril and Cascais (€2.75, 40 minutes) and to Cabo da Roca (€2.10, 30 minutes). You pay more on board the bus than at the kiosk.

Bus No 498 goes to Lisbon's airport (Day Rover €7.50, 30 minutes, hourly) via Estoril train station. At the weekend services between 8am and 6pm continue to Lisbon's Parque das Nações (last bus back at 6.55pm).

Trains from Lisbon's Cais do Sodré run to Cascais via Estoril (€1.30, 30 minutes, every 20 minutes daily). Bikes travel free on this line on weekends.

It's only 2km to Estoril, so it doesn't take long to walk the seafront route.

Getting Around

Since car parking is tricky (try near Museu do Mar), a good option is to park on the outskirts (eg at Praça de Touros) and take the busCas minibus (☎ 214 699 100; €1.10/0.80 day/single ticket) into town: it does a circular route via the centre every seven minutes from 7.30am to 9.20pm (10.20pm July to September) Monday to Thursday and Sunday, to 12.20am on Friday and Saturday.

Free bikes are available from 8am to 7pm daily at various points around town, including the train station, Hotel Baía and near Museu do Mar – you just have to show ID. Or you can rent them from **Transrent** (☎ 214 864 566; www.transrent.pt; Avenida Marginal), in the basement of Centro Comercial Cisne, for €7.50 per day. Transrent also rents scooters and motorbikes (from €16.50 and €30 per day, respectively). There's a cycle path the entire 8km length from Cascais to Guincho. Bus Nos 405 and 415 go to Guincho (€2.10, 20 minutes, seven daily).

Often waiting at the Jardim Visconde da Luz are a couple of horse carriages, which do half-hour trips to Boca do Inferno.

Among the car-rental agencies are **Auto Jardim** (☎ 214 831 073; www.autojardim.pt) and **Europcar** (☎ 214 864 419; Centre Comercial Cisne, Avenida Marginal). For a taxi, call ☎ 214 660 101.

ESTORIL

pop 23,770

Elegant as a shaken martini, Estoril (shtoe-*reel*) was where Ian Fleming hit on the idea for *Casino Royale,* as he stalked Yugoslav spy Duko Popov at its casino. It heaved with exiles and spies during WWII (if you're going to be an exile or a spy, you may as well base yourself on the Portuguese coast), and the palm-tree fringed resort has long fancied itself as the Portuguese Riviera, with Europe's biggest casino as its focus. Nowadays its gaming tables attract a more sedate, elderly clientele, also partial to a potter around the pleasant beach and several nearby golf courses.

Orientation & Information

The bus and train stations are on Avenida Marginal, opposite shady Parque do Estoril, at the top of which is the casino. The **turismo** (☎ 214 663 813; 9am-7pm Mon-Sat Sep-Jun, to 8pm Mon-Sat Jul-Aug, 10am-6pm Sun year-round) faces the train station.

Sights

The glitzy **casino** (☎ 214 667 700; www.casino-estoril.pt; Avenida Marginal; gaming room €5; 3pm-3am) will make your fortune or clean you out with everything from roulette to baccarat, French bank and blackjack, though it's free (!) to play the slot machines and bingo. Its vast **restaurant** (☎ 214 684 521;

GOLF ON THE ESTORIL COAST

Estoril has a dozen spectacular golf courses within 25km.

The closest is just 2km to the north – **Golf do Estoril**, designed by Mackenzie Ross, is one of the best-known courses in Portugal, having hosted the Portuguese Open Championship 20 times. It's 5262m long and set among eucalyptus, pine and mimosa.

Quinta da Marinha, 9km to the west, was designed by Robert Trent Jones to give both high handicappers and scratch golfers a challenge, with the course rolling over wind-blown dunes and rocky outcrops, with fantastic views.

Some 10km to the northwest is the **Penha Longa Club**, a Trent Jones Jr creation with superb views of the Serra de Sintra. It's ranked one of the best courses in Europe, and has also hosted the Portuguese Open. Nearby are **Estoril-Sol**, with one of the country's best practice areas; and **Quinta da Beloura**, designed by Rocky Roquemore, also responsible for beautiful **Belas Clube de Campo**, 22km northeast of Estoril in the Carregueira hills.

Estoril and Cascais turismos (www.estorilsintragolf.net) have full details of all courses.

floor show with/without dinner €50/15) puts on an international floor show nightly at 11pm – there is fado every Wednesday – and sometimes big, appropriately glitzy, names such as Lionel Richie. There is disabled access.

Estoril's small but pleasant Praia de Tamariz has showers, cafés and beachside bars and an ocean **swimming pool**.

Festivals & Events

Autodromo do Estoril, 9km north of Estoril, is the venue for various go-karting, motorbiking and car races – it no longer hosts Formula 1.

Feira do Artesanato (Handicrafts Fair; 6pm-midnight mid-Jun–Aug) In summer this takes place beside the casino to catch big winners.

International Naïve Painting Salon (October) The 1st-floor casino art gallery hosts what is acknowledged as the biggest and best such exhibition in Iberia.

Sleeping

Comfort Hotel São Mamede (214 659 110, reservations 800 201 166; reservas@hotelsmamede.com; Avenida Marginal 7105; s/d €55/65;) With some rooms boasting sea views, this is the best of the hotels lining this busy road, about 200m uphill from the station.

Pensao Pica Pau (214 667 140; Rua do Afonso Henriques 48; d €60) This is a low-key, charming, modern choice, near the casino. Friendly and treats its guests well, and has some rooms with balcony.

Hôtel Inglaterra (214 684 461; hotelinglaterra@mail.telepac.pt; Rua do Porto 1; d €83/122;) You can imagine the spies lingering around the lobby here at this old-world place, though it's now a Best Western and shabby – the spies have moved on and so have its better days.

Also good for seaside snores:

Pensão Residencial Smart (214 682 164; residencial.smart@clix.pt; Rua José Viana 3; s/d €50/60;) About 700m northeast of station, and smart it is indeed.

Pensão Costa (214 681 699; Rua de Olivença 2; d with bathroom €35) Basic and located near the train station.

Eating

Praia de Tamariz (214 681 010; Praia de Tamariz; mains €8.50-20; lunch & dinner) A beachfront venue with specials such as Spanish paella and lots of fresh fish, this is a tempting and relaxing dining choice.

La Villa (214 680 033; Praia do Estoril; Tue-Sat) If you want a splurge, head here, for a restaurant in a big old house with a view and classy, renowned, innovative seafood dishes.

Garrett do Estoril (214 680 365; Avenida de Nice 34; snacks €1-4) An upstanding old-fashioned *pastelaria* and tea salon on the eastern side of the park, this has lots of pastries, sandwiches and so on, wowing the formidable, small dog–toting clientele.

Getting There & Away

Bus 412 goes frequently to Cascais, or it's a pleasant 2km walk or cycle along the seafront. For details of other train and bus services, see p130.

QUELUZ

Versailles' whimsical cousin-once-removed, the powderpuff **Palácio de Queluz** (214 350 039; admission €3.50; 10am-5pm Wed-Mon, last admission 4.30pm) was once a hunting lodge, converted in the late-18th century to a royal summer residence, and is surrounded by Queen-of-Hearts formal gardens, with box hedges, tree-lined walkways, fountains (including the Fonte de Neptuno, ascribed to Italian master Bernini), statues, and an azulejo-lined canal where the royals went boating. One wing is still used to accommodate state guests.

The palace was designed by the Portuguese architect Mateus Vicente de Oliveira and French artist Jean-Baptiste Robillon for Prince Dom Pedro in the 1750s. Pedro's niece and wife, Queen Maria I, inspired the best gossip about the place – she lived here for most of her reign, going increasingly mad. Her fierce, scheming Spanish daughter-in-law, Carlota Joaquina, was just as bizarre – a match for eccentric British visitor William Beckford. On one occasion she insisted that Beckford run a race with her maid in the garden and then dance a bolero (which he did, he related, 'in a delirium of romantic delight').

Inside is like living in a chocolate box, with a mirror-lined Throne Room, marble-floored Ambassador's Room with a painted ceiling, and Pedro IV's bedroom where he slept surrounded by *Don Quixote* murals, under a circular ceiling. The palace's vast kitchens are now a palatial, fine-food restaurant, **Cozinha Velha** (214 350 740).

You've seen the palace, now live the life: part of the palace is a dazzling *pousada* (p101) so you can stay here.

Getting There & Away

Queluz (keh-*loozh*) is 5km northwest of Lisbon. Frequent trains from Rossio stop at Queluz-Belas (20 minutes).

MAFRA

pop 11,276 / elevation 250m

Palácio e Convento de Mafra is Portugal's most extravagant building, a hulking, ludicrous monastery-palace hybrid, with 1200 rooms. It was built during the 18th-century reign of wild-spending Dom João V, when Brazilian gold was burning a hole in the national coffers.

Nearby is the beautiful former royal park, Tapada de Mafra, once a hunting ground and now a fascinating place to explore, still full of wild animals and plants.

Mafra, 39km northwest of Lisbon, makes an excellent day trip from Lisbon, Sintra or Ericeira.

Orientation

The huge palace façade dominates the town. Opposite is a pleasant little square, Praça da República, where you can find cafés and restaurants. Mafra's **bus terminal** (☎ 261 816 152) is 1.5km northwest but buses also stop in front of the palace (called 'convent' on timetables). A Mafrense bus **ticket office** (Avenida Movimento Forças Armadas 22) is near the square.

Information

The **turismo** (☎ 261 817 170; Terreiro Dom João V; 🕑 9am-7pm Jun-Sep, to 6pm Oct-May) is in part of the palace. It has a picturesque (though outdated) map of the Mafra area and a bilingual *Mafra Real* booklet describing the palace and park.

Sights

PALÁCIO NACIONAL DE MAFRA

The mammoth baroque **palace** (Mafra National Palace; ☎ 261 817 550; adult/senior/child under 14/under 25 €3/free/free/1.50, 10am-2pm Sun free, 🕑 10am-5pm Wed-Mon) is a combination of palace, monastery and basilica, covering almost 4 sq km. Built from mock marble, the symmetrical structure centres on the basilica. The German architect, Friedrich Ludwig, had trained in Italy and the structure shows the influence of the Vatican palaces.

However, it is the extravagance that stuns rather than the architecture. It's worth reading *Memorial do Convento,* the magical novel by Nobel Laureate José Saramago (translated into English as *Baltazar and Blimunda*), centred on the building of the palace, to appreciate the incredible effort involved in its construction.

The building was begun in 1717, six years after Dom João V promised to build a monastery if he received an heir: a daughter, Dona Maria, was fortuitously born the same year. As gold from Brazil flowed into the king's coffers, he found ways to make it flow out again – the initial design for 13 monks was expanded to house 280 monks and 140 novices and incorporate two royal wings. No expense was spared to build its 1200 halls and rooms, more than 4700 doorways, 2500 windows and two bell towers with the world's largest collection of bells (92 in total). When the Flemish bell-founders queried the extravagant order for a carillon of bells, Dom João is said to have doubled the order and to have sent the money in advance.

Up to 20,000 artisans (including Italian carpenters and masons) worked on the monument – and a mind-boggling 45,000 in the last two years of construction, all of them kept in order by 7000 soldiers. The presence of so many outstanding artists spurred João V to establish a school of sculpture here from 1753 to 1770, which employed Portugal's most important sculptors. Though the building may have been an artistic coup, the expense of its construction and the use of such a large workforce helped destroy the country's economy.

After all this, it was only briefly used as a palace – the royal family visited it for short periods, the longest being for a year in 1807. But when the French invaded Portugal, Dom João VI and the royal family fled to Brazil, taking most of Mafra's furniture with them. When the French arrived here in 1807, they found only 20 elderly Franciscan friars. General Junot billeted his troops in the monastery, followed by Wellington and his men. From then on the palace became a favourite military haven. Even today, most of it is used as a military academy.

On the one-hour visit, escorted by a guard, the corridors (230m of them!) and countless salons and apartments are overwhelming, and it's understandable that the royal family spent so little time here – its scale and chill are by no means cosy; even huge furniture looks lost – though the 19th-century quarters feel more homely. But there are some memorable sights: 18th-century wooden pinball machines, a room filled with grotesque hunting décor (with furniture made from antlers, including a scary sofa that incorporates a mirror and boar's head), the monastery's infirmary beds on wheels so that ailing monks could be trundled out for mass, and a walled bed for mad monks (possibly sent over the edge by all those corridors).

Most impressive is the 83.6m-long barrel-vaulted baroque library, an unreal expanse, housing nearly 40,000 books from the 15th to 18th centuries. Many bound by the monks themselves, they look like the sort painted on disguised doorways to secret passages. It seems an appropriate fairytale coda to all this extravagance that they're gradually being gnawed away by rats.

When the royal family returned to Portugal, Mafra was mainly used during the hunting season. Manuel II spent his last night here before exile following the establishment of the Republic.

The central basilica, with its two bell towers, is wonderfully restrained by comparison, featuring multihued marble floors and panelling and Carrara marble statues.

Guided English-language tours usually set off at 11am and 2.30pm. A leaflet (€1) helps a bit if you catch a non-English tour.

If you're here on a Sunday, stay until 4pm to hear a **Concerto de Carrilhão**, a concert of the basilica's infamous bells (preceded by a free guided bell-tower tour at 3.15pm). The palace's **Jardim do Cerco** (Enclosed Garden; admission free; 10am-5pm) at the northern end of the palace, where the queen once picked her flowers, makes a charming place to wait.

TAPADA NACIONAL DE MAFRA

The palace's 819-hectare park and hunting ground, **Tapada Nacional de Mafra** (☎ 261 817 050 Mon-Fri, ☎/fax 261 814 240 Sat & Sun; www.tapadademafra.pt; walker €4.50-6, cyclist €10) was created in 1747 and is still partly enclosed by its original 21km perimeter wall – the king enclosed the land and stocked it with game after nabbing it from locals. It's a rolling, beautiful, varied park, full of wild boar and deer (people still hunt here).

On 11 September 2003 a fire outside the walls ignited a fire in the park, which burned for around four days, destroying around 70% of vegetation – it reopened in 2004. There has been an enormous project of replanting and the amount of natural regeneration is remarkable. The beautiful trails around Tapada allow you to interpret the landscape, visiting on the way a 350-year-old cork oak saved by a ring of people with buckets during the fire.

There are 2½-hour tours by tourist-train at 10.45am (per adult/child under 10/senior €9/5/6), which tour the park via its carriage and wildlife museums. Weekday visits are usually for schools, but you may be able to join them if there's room: call to check.

There are several different walking trails – 4km (€4.50), 7.5km (€6) or 11km. There's a mountain-bike trail of 15km, but you need

SAFE HAVEN FOR WOLVES

Some 10km northeast of Mafra is the **Centro de Recuperaçáo de Lobo Ibérico** (Iberian Wolf Recovery Centre; ☎ 261 785 037; admission free; 4-8pm Sat, Sun & holidays May-Sep, 2.30-6pm Oct-Apr), established in 1987 to provide a home for wolves trapped, snared or kept in dire conditions and no longer able to function in the wild. The centre's 17 hectares of secluded woodland provide a refuge for some 26 animals, all from the north of the country where Portugal's last Iberian wolves roam. You can adopt a wolf for an annual fee.

The best time to visit is around 5pm when the wolves emerge in the cool of dusk, though even then sightings are never guaranteed.

The centre isn't signposted. From Mafra head east to Malveira, then take the Torres Vedras road for 3km and turn off to Picão just after Vale da Guarda. At the end of the village there's a steep cobbled track to the left (opposite Picão's only café). The last part of this 1km-long track is badly potholed. Wheel-less wolf-lovers can catch one of the frequent buses from Mafra to Malveira (20 minutes) and change to a Torres Vedras bus to Vale da Guarda; the centre is 2km from the Picão turn-off.

your own bike. If you want to ride through the park, call ☎ 261 819 041 for information. Gates open between 9.30 and 10.30am as well as between 2.30 and 3.15pm daily for these visits; you can stay until 6pm.

The Tapada is about 7km north of Mafra, along the road to Gradil – it's best reached by your own transport, as buses are erratic. From Mafra, taxis charge around €7 one-way.

SOBREIRO

At the village of Sobreiro, 4km northwest of Mafra (take any Ericeira-bound bus), sculptor José Franco has created an enchanting miniature, faintly surreal **craft village** (admission free; 9.30am-around 7.30pm) of windmills, watermills and traditional shops. José Franco himself can often be seen crafting clay figures at the entrance. Kids love it here; so do adults, especially when they discover the rustic *adega* (winery) serving good red wine, snacks and meals. Ramped walkways make it accessible for wheelchair users.

Sleeping & Eating

Hotel Castelão (☎ 261 816 050; fax 261 816 059; Avenida 25 de Abril; s/d incl breakfast €50/70) If you get stuck here, this offers comfortable, bland rooms, north of the turismo.

Café-Restaurante Paris (☎ 261 815 797; Praça da República 14; mains €6-9; lunch & dinner Mon-Sat) This smartish, genteel pink place is among several café-restaurants around Praça da República and offers decent Portuguese dishes.

If you want something lighter, there are lots of nice *pastelarias* around the square too, such as buzzing **Polo Norte** (☎ 261 811 070; Praça República 15) selling local crusty Mafra bread and good traditional cakes, such as *bizarros* or *pastéis de feijão*, a concoction of eggs, sugar and almonds.

Getting There & Around

There are regular **Mafrense** (☎ 261 816 159; Avenida Dr Francisco Sá Carneiro) buses to/from Ericeira (€1.50, 20 minutes, at least hourly), Sintra (€2.50, 45 minutes) and Lisbon's Campo Grande terminal (€2.80, 75 minutes, at least hourly). Mafra's train station is 6km away with infrequent buses (taxis charge around €8); go to Malveira station instead for easier connections (20 minutes).

Taxis (☎ 261 815 512) are available in Praça da República.

SETÚBAL PENINSULA

The Setúbal Peninsula is Lisbon's playground, with the beautiful long beaches of Costa da Caparica, ex-fishing village-favourite Sesimbra further south or seafood-central Setúbal. Here are two fine nature reserves, the Reserva Natural do Estuário do Sado and the Parque Natural da Arrábida – where you can indulge in surfing, dolphin-watching, mountain biking and walking trips. The turismo calls it the Costa Azul.

CACILHAS

Above this suburb across the Rio Tejo from Lisbon, and visible from almost everywhere in Lisbon, is the **Cristo Rei** (☎ 212 751 000), a 28m-high statue of Christ with outstretched hands, on a pedestal, doing a European impression of Rio de Janeiro. Built in 1959, it was partly paid for by Portuguese women grateful for the country having been spared the horrors of WWII. A **lift** (€3; 10am-6pm Apr-Sep, to 5pm Oct-Mar) zooms you up to a platform, from where Lisbon is spread out like a patchwork before you. It's a fantastic place for photos.

Cacilhas is also famous for its many seafood restaurants: **Marisqueria Cabrinha** (☎ 212 764 732; mains €5-20; daily), near the ferry terminal, is cheery, friendly and buzzes with locals. It serves especially tasty shrimps, garlicky clams, and crab.

Getting There & Away

Ferries to Cacilhas (€0.60, 10 minutes) run frequently from Lisbon's Cais da Alfândega terminal (at the time of writing, from Cais do Sodré). A car-ferry service runs (every 20 minutes between 4.30am and 2.30am) from Cais do Sodré and back, or you can take bus No 101 from the bus station beside the Cacilhas terminal.

COSTA DA CAPARICA

This extraordinary 8km beach disappearing into the horizon on the western coast of the peninsula is, unsurprisingly, Lisbon's favourite weekend escape. The beginning of the beach is backed by restaurants and apartments – but these peter out to nothing but a backdrop of long, low sandstone cliff and pine forest. Beaches get busy in

July and August, but out of high season you can easily find a tranquil space and the water quality is good, although beware of the currents. It's a cool-feeling local rather than a foreign-tourist getaway. The town confusingly has the same name as the coastline, and is a typical cheery, tatty seaside place with lots of essential beachside tack and shops.

During the summer a narrow-gauge railway runs most of the length of the beach from Costa da Caparica town, and you can jump off at any one of 20 stops. Each stop marks a distinctive neighbourhood: the nearer beaches, including **Praia do Norte** and **Praia do São Sebastião**, tend to attract families, while the further ones are younger and trendier. **Praia do Castelo** (stop No 11 on the train) and **Praia da Bela Vista** (No 17) are gay and nudist havens.

Continuing along the coast all the way to Lagoa de Albufeira is the Paisagem Protegida da Arriba Fóssil, a protected fossilised cliff of geological importance backed by the Mata Nacional dos Mêdos (also called Pinhal do Rei), a 600-hectare pine forest originally planted by Dom João V to stop the encroaching sand dunes.

Surfing and windsurfing is big here, especially along the northern part of the coastline.

Orientation & Information

Costa da Caparica town focuses on Praça da Liberdade. West of the *praça*, pedestrianised Rua dos Pescadores, with hotels and restaurants, leads to the seaside. The main beach (called Praia do CDS, or Centro Desportivo de Surf), with cafés, bars and surfing clubs along its promenade, is a short walk north. The **bus terminal** (Avenida General Humberto Delgado) is 400m northwest of the Praça da Liberdade; additional stops are by the *praça*.

The **turismo** (☎ 212 900 071; Avenida da República 18; 🕓 9.30am-6pm Mon-Sat Jul–mid-Sep; 9.30am-1pm & 2-5.30pm Mon-Fri, 9.30am-1pm Sat mid-Sep–Jun) is just off the *praça*.

Policlínica São Filinto (☎ 212 954 064; Avenida da República 21) is a medical centre just nearby.

Activities

Among the hottest **surfing** spots are São João da Caparica, Praia da Mata and Praia da Sereia. Fonte da Telha (where the train terminates) is the best spot for **windsurfing**. Check the handy *Tabela de Marés* booklet (available at the turismo), which lists tide times, surf shops and clubs. There are plenty of water sports facilities to be found at Fonte de Telha.

Escola de Surf e Bodyboard (☎ 212 919 078; caparicasurfingclube@clix.pt; Praia do CDS; 🕓 10am-6pm Sat & Sun) is the main surfing school. Other operators include **Academia de Surf** (☎ 969 091 059; academiadesurf@mail.telepac.pt; Praia Nova), **Escola Oficial de Surf** (☎ 936 300 139; Rua dos Pescadores 17), and **Bulldog Surfshop** (☎ 212 912 036; Rua João Inácio de Alfama 22B) near Rua dos Pescadores, which also rents boards and runs courses. Weekend prices tend to be higher.

Centro de Mergulho (☎ 212 977 711, 919 390 278; Fonte da Telha; www.cabanadivers.com), with a nicely set up bar with wicker and basket chairs by the endless beach, provides diving lessons and equipment.

Sleeping

Prices quoted are for July – you'll be able to get discounts outside holiday season (usually Easter, and June to mid-September).

Residencial Copacabana (☎ 212 900 017; fax 212 913 429; Rua dos Pescadores 42; s/d €25/30) There are several cheap *pensões* along this street – this is above a busy café (noisy till midnight, but well placed for breakfast), with spacious rooms that have satellite TV.

Residencial Real (☎ 212 918 870; fax 212 918 879; Rua Mestre Manuel 18; s/d with breakfast €30/40) This has smallish, smart rooms with balconies – but look at a few before choosing as some views are better than others.

Costa da Caparica (☎ 212 903 894; adult/tent/car €4.50/3.80/4.40) There are masses of camp sites along the coast (most requiring camping-club membership), but Orbitur's site, 1km north of town is closest and best, with excellent facilities, pine wood, and only 200km from the beach.

Eating & Drinking

In Costa da Caparica town, touristy but good seafood restaurants line Rua dos Pescadores. Along the beaches are bars and restaurants galore.

Carolina do Aires (☎ 212 900 124; Avenida General Humberto Delgado; mains €6.50-13; 🕓 daily) A big shady greenhouse of a restaurant, this is recommended with good daily specials – an excellent setting for a long lunch.

Restaurante O Primoroso (☎ 212 914 383; Avenida 1 de Maio; mains €6.50-14.50; 🕑 lunch & dinner) The first of many eateries along Praia do Costa de Caparica, this is beachside, with airy outdoor seating and, of course, lots of good grilled fish.

Manuel dos Frangos (☎ 212 961 819; mains €5.25-12.50; 🕑 lunch & dinner) In Fonte da Telha, set a little back from the beach, this is a friendly, sweetly welcoming venue with a relaxed atmosphere and, of course, great fish.

Bar Waikiki (☎ 212 962 129; Praia da Sereia; snacks €2.50-7; 🕑 10.30am-7.30pm May-Sep) Nicely on its own, this is popular with surfers, on a great stretch of beach that's a surfing and parasurfing haunt – stop No 15 on the train.

Another place worth a look is **Kontiki** (☎ 212 914 391; Praia de Sao Joao).

Getting There & Away

Transportes Sul do Tejo (TST; ☎ 217 262 740; www.tsuldotejo.pt) runs regular buses (€2.10, 20 to 60 minutes) to Costa da Caparica from Lisbon's Praça de Espanha. Carris bus No 75 does a Costa da Caparica run (€3, every 15 minutes Saturday and Sunday June to September) from Campo Grande metro station; the ticket gives you one-day use of all Carris transport.

The best way to get here is a ferry to Cacilhas (every 15 minutes) from Lisbon's Cais do Sodré (or to Trafaria, half-hourly, from Belém), where bus No 135 (€2, 30 to 45 minutes, every 30 to 60 minutes) runs to Costa da Caparica town; bus Nos 124 and 194 also run here but are slower, also stopping at the train station (the ferries used to depart from Cais d'Alfândega but have been leaving from Cais do Sodré during long-term engineering works). Bus No 127 runs from Cacilhas to Fonte da Telha (50 minutes, at least hourly). Bus No 130 runs from Trafaria to Fonte da Telha (45 minutes, at least hourly) via Costa da Caparica and Pinhal do Rei (near Praia do Rei).

Another option to avoid the worst of the traffic is the Fertagus air-conditioned train across the Ponte 25 de Abril, from Entrecampos to Fogueteiro via Sete Rios and Campolide. From Campolide you can take a train direct to Sintra (€1.50).

At Pragal (14 minutes from Entrecampos, five daily), the stop nearest Costa da Caparica, buses run to town (€2.10, 25 minutes, half-hourly).

Getting Around

The train along the beach operates daily (€3.80 return, every 15 minutes June to September; weekends from Easter to May, depending on the weather) to Fonte da Telha, about 1km before the end of the county beach. Although this is the end of the line, the beaches continue along the coast.

SETÚBAL

pop 114,000

Setúbal (*shtoo*-bahl) has some great fish restaurants, the first-ever Manueline church, a castle with sweeping views, and is the closest town to the lovely beach-edged Parque Natural da Arrábida and the Reserva Natural do Estuário do Sado stretching around the Rio Sado and Estuary, stretching to near Alcácer do Sal at the southeast – home to around 30 bottlenose dolphins, and the winter abode of over 1000 flamingos. Its mud banks and marshes, lagoons, dunes and former salt pans house white storks (spring and summertime) and resident marsh harriers and little egrets.

Romans did a lot of fish-salting here, then came the Barbarians, then the Moors. The town developed after the 13th-century Christian reconquest, but only boomed after 19th-century industrialisation. Today it's Portugal's third-largest port (after Lisbon and Porto) but doesn't feel industrial; it's an untouristy, easygoing town and a good place to break your journey on the way to Évora or the Algarve.

Orientation

The mostly pedestrianised centre focuses on Praça de Bocage and Largo da Misericórdia, with most sights within easy walking distance. The bus station is about 150m from the municipal turismo. The main train station is 700m north of the centre, and there's a local station (serving only Praia da Sado, by the Rio Sado) at the eastern end of Avenida 5 de Outubro. Ferries shuttle across the Sado Estuary to the Tróia Peninsula from terminals around Doca do Comércio.

Information

EMERGENCY & MEDICAL SERVICES

Hospital (☎ 265 549 000) Near the Praça de Touros (bullring), off Avenida Dom João II.

Police station (☎ 265 522 022; Avenida 22 de Dezembro)

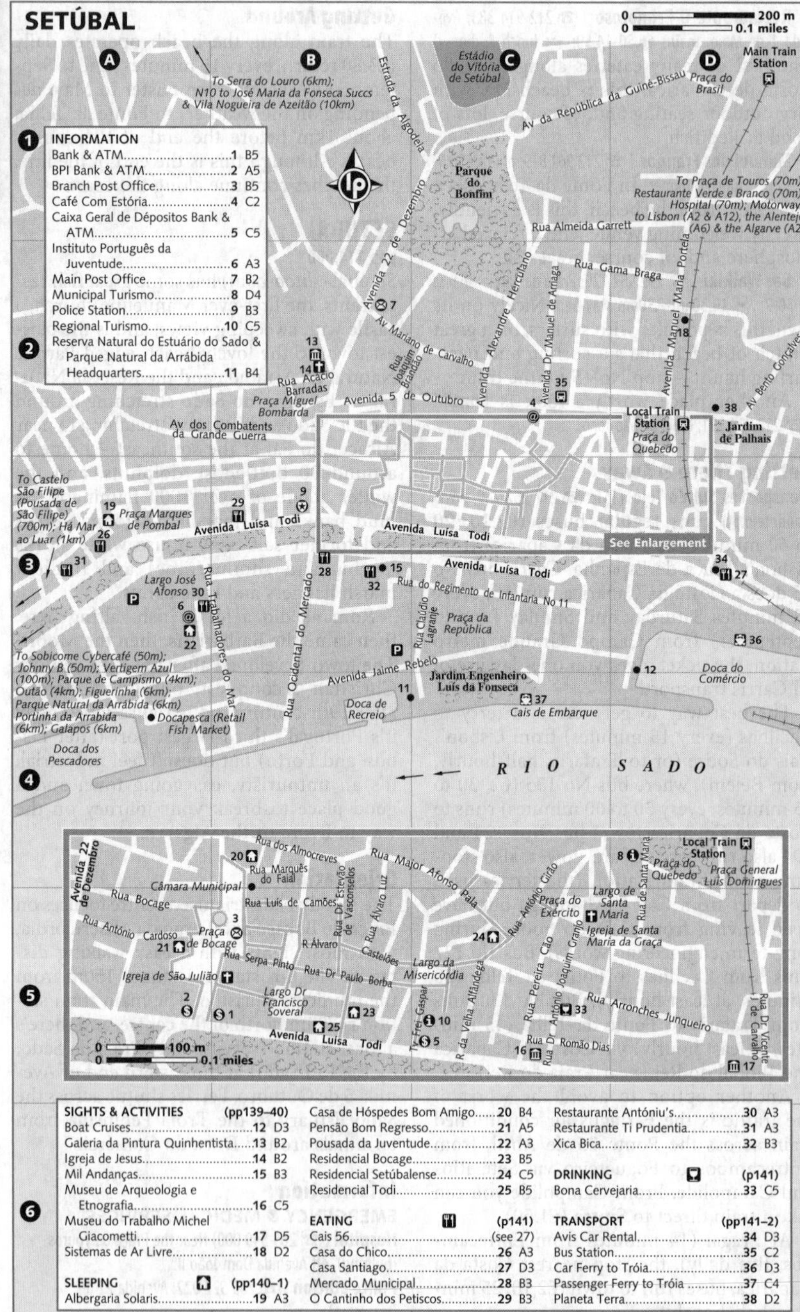
SETÚBAL
0 200 m
0 0.1 miles
A
B
C
D
1
2
3
4
5
6
INFORMATION
Bank & ATM....1 B5
BPI Bank & ATM....2 A5
Branch Post Office....3 B5
Café Com Estória....4 C2
Caixa Geral de Dépositos Bank & ATM....5 C5
Instituto Português da Juventude....6 A3
Main Post Office....7 B2
Municipal Turismo....8 D4
Police Station....9 B3
Regional Turismo....10 C5
Reserva Natural do Estuário do Sado & Parque Natural da Arrábida Headquarters....11 B4
To Serra do Louro (6km); N10 to José Maria da Fonseca Succs & Vila Nogueira de Azeitão (10km)
Estrada da Algodeia
Estádio do Vitória de Setúbal
Av da República da Guiné-Bissau
Praça do Brasil
Main Train Station
Parque do Bonfim
To Praça de Touros (70m); Restaurante Verde e Branco (70m); Hospital (70m); Motorways to Lisbon (A2 & A12), the Alentejo (A6) & the Algarve (A2)
Avenida 22 de Dezembro
Rua Almeida Garrett
Rua Gama Braga
Avenida Alexandre Herculano
Avenida Dr Manuel de Arriaga
Avenida Manuel Maria Portela
Av Mariano de Carvalho
Rua Joaquim Brandão
Av Bento Gonçalves
Rua Acácio Barradas
Praça Miguel Bombarda
Avenida 5 de Outubro
Av dos Combatentes da Grande Guerra
Local Train Station
Praça do Quebedo
Jardim de Palhais
To Castelo São Filipe (Pousada de São Filipe) (700m); Há Mar ao Luar (1km)
Praça Marques de Pombal
Avenida Luísa Todi
See Enlargement
Largo José Afonso
Rua Trabalhadores do Mar
Rua Ocidental do Mercado
Rua do Regimento de Infantaria No 11
Rua Cláudio Lagranje
Praça da República
Avenida Jaime Rebelo
Jardim Engenheiro Luís da Fonseca
Doca do Comércio
Doca de Recreio
Cais de Embarque
To Sobicome Cybercafé (50m); Johnny B (50m); Vertigem Azul (100m); Parque de Campismo (4km); Outão (4km); Figuerinha (6km); Parque Natural da Arrábida (6km) Portinha da Arrabida (6km); Galapos (6km)
Docapesca (Retail Fish Market)
Doca dos Pescadores
RIO SADO
Avenida 22 de Dezembro
Rua dos Almocreves
Rua Major Afonso Pala
Rua Marquês do Faial
Câmara Municipal
Rua Bocage
Rua Luís de Camões
Rua Dr Estevão de Vasconselos
Rua Álvaro Luz
Rua António Girão
Praça do Exército
Largo de Santa Maria
Rua de Santa Maria
Igreja de Santa Maria da Graça
Praça do Quebedo
Praça General Luís Domingues
Rua António Cardoso
Praça de Bocage
R Álvaro Castelões
Rua Serpa Pinto
Rua Dr Paulo Borba
Largo da Misericórdia
Igreja de São Julião
Largo Dr Francisco Soveral
Tv Frei Gaspar
R da Velha Alfândega
Rua Pereira Cão
Rua Dr António Joaquim Granjo
Rua Arronches Junqueiro
Rua Romão Dias
Rua Dr Vicente J de Carvalho
0 100 m
0 0.1 miles
SIGHTS & ACTIVITIES (pp139–40)
Boat Cruises....12 D3
Galeria da Pintura Quinhentista....13 B2
Igreja de Jesus....14 B2
Mil Andanças....15 B3
Museu de Arqueologia e Etnografia....16 C5
Museu do Trabalho Michel Giacometti....17 D5
Sistemas de Ar Livre....18 D2
SLEEPING (pp140–1)
Albergaria Solaris....19 A3
Casa de Hóspedes Bom Amigo....20 B4
Pensão Bom Regresso....21 A5
Pousada da Juventude....22 A3
Residencial Bocage....23 B5
Residencial Setúbalense....24 C5
Residencial Todi....25 B5
EATING (p141)
Cais 56....(see 27)
Casa do Chico....26 A3
Casa Santiago....27 D3
Mercado Municipal....28 B3
O Cantinho dos Petiscos....29 B3
Restaurante Antóniu's....30 A3
Restaurante Ti Prudentia....31 A3
Xica Bica....32 B3
DRINKING (p141)
Bona Cervejaria....33 C5
TRANSPORT (pp141–2)
Avis Car Rental....34 D3
Bus Station....35 C2
Car Ferry to Tróia....36 D3
Passenger Ferry to Tróia....37 C4
Planeta Terra....38 D2

MONEY

Caixa Geral de Dépositos (☎ 265 530 500; Avenida Luísa Todi 190)

POST

Branch post office (Praça de Bocage; 🕒 9am-12.30pm & 2.30-6pm Mon-Fri)

Main post office (☎ 265 528 620; Avenida Mariano de Carvalho; 🕒 8.30am-6.30pm Mon-Fri, 9am-12.30pm Sat) Has Netpost.

INTERNET ACCESS

Instituto Português da Juventude (IPJ; ☎ 265 532 707; Largo José Afonso; free Net access; 🕒 9am-5pm Mon-Fri) Maximum 30 minutes.

Café Com Estória (☎ 265 525 633; Avenida 5 de Outubro 35; per hr €2; 🕒 9am-8pm Mon-Thu, 10-2am Fri & Sat) A cool Internet café in Edifício Arrábida (no sign – look for the Communist flag).

Sobicome Cybercafé (1st fl, Avenida Luísa Todi 333; per hr €3; 🕒 3pm-4am) About 500m west of centre.

TOURIST OFFICES

Municipal turismo (☎ /fax 265 534 402; Praça do Quebedo; 🕒 9am-12.30pm & 2-5.30pm Mon-Fri, 9am-7pm Sat & Sun Jun-Aug) Housed in an 18th-century house.

Regional turismo (☎ 265 539 120; www.costa-azul.rts.pt; Travessa Frei Gaspar 10; 🕒 9.30am-12.30pm & 3-7pm Mon & Sat, 9.30am-7pm Tue-Fri, 9.30am-12.30pm Sun May-Sep; to 6pm Mon-Fri, closed Sun Oct-Apr) Has a glass floor revealing the remains of a Roman *garum* (fish condiment) factory. The office sells a multilingual *Artesãos e Artesanato* (Craftsmen and Handicrafts) booklet (€1.50), the booklet *Parques e Reservas Naturais* (€1.50), with an English translation, and many more.

Sights

IGREJA DE JESUS

Setúbal has an architectural treasure: the early-Gothic **Igreja de Jesus** (Praça Miguel Bombarda; admission free; 🕒 9am-1pm & 2-5pm Tue-Sat), containing the earliest known examples of Manueline decoration – extraordinary twisted pillars, like writhing snakes, that spiral upwards to the ceiling. Nebulous-seeming and organic, they are made from delicately coloured Arrábida marble. Around the altar, 18th-century dark-blue and white geometric tiles form a stunning contrast with the curling arches of the roof.

Constructed in 1491, the church was designed by Diogo de Boitac, better known for his later work on Belém's fantastical Mosteiro dos Jerónimos (p92).

GALERIA DA PINTURA QUINHENTISTA

This **gallery** (Gallery of 16th-Century Painting; Rua do Balneãrio Paula Borba; admission free; 🕒 9am-noon & 1.30-5.30pm Tue-Sat) displays the marvellous panels that were once contained in the Igreja de Jesus, just around the corner. The set of 14 panels from the Lisbon school of Jorge Afonso (sometimes attributed to the anonymous 'Master of Setúbal') and four other later panels attributed to Gregório Lopes show extraordinarily rich colours and detail. Also on show is the stained glass of the church's main window. The gallery has a fine collection of Renaissance paintings too.

MUSEU DO TRABALHO MICHEL GIACOMETTI

This **museum** (Museum of Work; Largo Defensores da República; admission free; 🕒 9.30am-6pm Tue-Sat) is set in a cavernous former sardine-canning factory. In pride of place is an entire 1920s grocery, transported from Lisbon wholesale. Portuguese rural life is the main subject, with implements collected in northern and central Portugal in 1975 by the famous Corsican ethnographer Michel Giacometti. Try to avoid being taken on a tour.

MUSEU DE ARQUEOLOGIA E ETNOGRAFIA

A nice, fusty ragbag of a **museum** (Museum of Archaeology & Ethnography; ☎ 265 239 365; Avenida Luísa Todi 162; admission free; 🕒 9am-12.30pm & 2-5.30pm Tue-Sat), this has a jumble of stuff, from Roman mosaics found nearby – Setúbal was founded by the Romans after their fishing port of Cetobriga (now Tróia), on the opposite side of the river mouth, was destroyed by an earthquake in AD 412 – to endearing 19th-century religious devotional paintings on wood, showing invalids having holy visions.

CASTELO SÃO FILIPE

Worth the 500m schlep west uphill, the **castle** (🕒 10am-9pm) was built by Filipe I in 1590 to fend off an English attack on the invincible Armada. Converted into a *pousada* in the 1960s, its ramparts are huge and impressive with wonderful views, and its chapel is fetchingly smothered in blue-and-white 18th-century azulejos depicting the life of São Filipe – you can view them through a glass wall if the door is locked. The restaurant is open to nonresidents.

Activities

BEACHES

Head west to the Parque Natural da Arrabida for long, white-sanded **Figueirinha**, **Galapos** or, best of all, **Portinho da Arrábida** overlooked by a small 17th-century fort built to protect the monks from Barbary pirates. Here there are some *quartos* right on the beach. Buses from Setúbal run in the summer to Figueirinha.

WALKING

The company **Sistemas de Ar Livre** (SAL; ☎ 265 227 685; www.sal.pt; Avenida Manuel Maria Portela 40; per person Sat/Sun €5/6; ⏰ 10am Sat & Sun Sep-Jun) organises three-hour guided walks in or near Setúbal.

Tours

Mil Andanças (☎ 265 532 996; www.mil-andancas.pt; Avenida Luísa Todi 121; half-day €27) offers jeep tours in Arrabida.

Ozono Mais (☎ 219 243 673; Rua General Alves Roçades 10; around €50) runs a jeep tour (minimum four people) to the Parque Natural da Arrábida.

Planeta Terra (☎ 265 080 176; www.planetaterra.pt; Plaça General Luis Domingues 9) organises jeep safaris into Arrábida – a half-day encompasses a nature tour and a wine cellar (€32). The Storks Route concentrates on bird-watching, history and culture (same price).

CRUISES, CANOEING & DOLPHIN-WATCHING

Plenty of companies run trips around the estuary (leaving from Doca do Comércio) and to Arrabida, mostly with the intent of spotting the local dolphins and porpoises.

Nautur (☎ 265 532 914; www.nautur.com; Rua António Feliciano Castilho; day-long cruise €40) Offers cruises with lunch – starting on the estuary, then visiting an Arrabida beach, returning to the river for dolphin spotting.

Mil Andanças (see Jeep Tours) Also runs dolphin-spotting river tours (€30 per person).

Troiacruze (☎ 265 228 482; www.troiacruze.com; Rua das Barroças 34; 5hr trip per person €20-30) Offers dolphin spotting and other cruises, eg a sailing galleon along the Sado estuary (€60 with meals).

Vertigem Azul (☎ 265 238 000; www.vertigemazul.com; Avenida Luísa Todi 375) Offers three-hour dolphin-watching tours in the Sado Estuary (with a stop for snorkelling; €25), five-hour canoeing trips in the estuary (€30); or a day's dolphin-watching and jeep tour (€60). Can be found 500m west of centre.

WINE TOURS

There are recommended free wine-cellar tours of the **José Maria da Fonseca Succs** (☎ 212 198 940; www.jmf.pt; Rua José Augusto Coelho 11; ⏰ 10am-12.30pm & 2-5pm Mon-Fri), the oldest Portuguese producer of table wine and Moscatel de Setúbal, in nearby Vila Nogueira de Azeitão. The company is now run by the sixth generation of the family. Ring ahead to arrange a visit to the house and museum. From Setúbal, buses leave frequently to Vila Nogueira de Azeitão (20 minutes).

The tourist office has a useful leaflet *Rota de Vinos da Costa Azul*, detailing all the wine producers in the area you can visit.

Sleeping

BUDGET

Pousada da juventude (☎ 265 534 431; setubal@movijovem.pt; dm €9.50, d with/without bathroom €26/23) Attached to the IPJ, this curved building is close to the busy fishing harbour. It's the usual bargain, with adequate facilities and a small adjoining café.

Residencial Todi (☎ 265 220 592; Avenida Luísa Todi 244; s/d with shared bathroom €20/30, with bathroom €25/35) This is friendly, with fraying but clean, bright and basic rooms, an easy-going atmosphere and plumb on the main drag.

Casa de Hóspedes Bom Amigo (☎ 265 526 290; 2nd fl, Rua do Concelho 7; d with/without shower €25/35) A welcoming choice, this is homely and traditional, with clean, neat rooms and lots of doilies and old-fashioned furnishings.

Pensão Bom Regresso (☎ 265 229 812; Praça de Bocage; s/d with shared bathroom €35/45) Has scruffy, overpriced rooms and a dour reception, but is saved by the location, overlooking the attractive *praça* with its pretty church. Some rooms have balcony.

Parque de campismo (☎ 265 238 318; Outão; adult/tent/car €3.20/3.80/2.50) A fairly shady site, right on the coast 4km west of Setúbal, accessible by regular bus (25 minutes).

MID-RANGE

Residencial Bocage (☎ 265 543 080; Rua de São Cristóvão 14; s/tw with breakfast €35/45; ❄) In the old-town centre, this is an upmarket choice, a small old building, with pleasant, calm spic-and-span rooms that are good value.

Albergaria Solaris (☎ 265 541 770; albergaria.solaris@netc.pt; Praça Marquês de Pombal 12; s/d with breakfast €45/55; ❄) Efficient and smart, this is a building with a tiled façade, overlooking a square – some of the comfortable, plain, businesslike rooms have small balconies.

Pousada de São Filipe (☎ 265 550 070; recepcao .sfilipe@pousada.pt; d Mon-Fri €169, Sat & Sun €178;) The most luxurious option of all within the town's hilltop castle.

Há Mar ao Luar (☎ 265 534 901; www.hamaraoluar .com; Alto San Filipe; apt/windmill €90/110) Near the castle, this is a rural tourism place, a gorgeous house that has spacious, strikingly decorated apartments with big beds, tranquil shaded terrace, sea views and even a windmill.

Residencial Setúbalense (☎ 265 525 790; Rua Major Afonso Pala 17; s/d with breakfast €50/60;)

Eating

Setúbal is packed with good fish restaurants (most with outdoor seating), especially along the western end of Avenida Luísa Todi.

BUDGET

Casa do Chico (☎ 265 239 502; Avenida Luísa Todi 490; mains €4-10; Tue-Sun) Small, friendly and modest, this is a nice little welcoming place, with TV inside and a few outside tables. Like all the restaurants along here, the name of the game is barbecued fish.

Casa Santiago (☎ 265 221 688; Avenida Luísa Todi 92; mains €3-13.50; lunch & dinner) This is bustling and down-to-earth, with a large terrace set back from the road. It specialises in *chôco frito* (deep-fried cuttlefish; grab a cuttlefish sandwich – much nicer than it sounds), but the menu also has loads of other fish fare. Go early for a lunch time space.

Cais 56 (☎ 265 238 475; Avenida Luisa Todi 56; mains €4-12; lunch & dinner Thu-Tue) This place serves tasty square pizzas as well as delicious cuttlefish sandwiches.

MID RANGE

O Cantinho dos Petiscos (☎ 265 233 280; Avenida Luísa Todi 374; mains €9-12; lunch & dinner Wed-Mon) This has a more enclosed terrace than some of the others, cheery marittime murals and small green tables and chairs, and is another recommended fish stop.

Restaurante Antóniu's (☎ 265 523 706; Rua Trabalhadores do Mar 31; mains €6-10.50; Thu-Tue) A long-popular, old-fashioned venue, serving a fantastic *arroz de marisco* (rice and seafood stew; €20 for two) or fish kebabs.

Restaurante Ti Prudentia (☎ 265 237 642; Avenida Luísa Todi 540; mains €5-10; lunch Tue-Sun, dinner Tue-Sat) Popular, with good-value barbecued fresh fish, tiled inside and has outside seating too.

TOP END

Restaurante Verde e Branco (☎ 265 526 546; Rua Maria Batista 33; mains around €9; lunch Tue-Sun Oct-Aug) Beside the Praça de Touros and famous for miles around, this traditional hotspot serves only grilled fish: simple and superb.

Pousada de São Filipe (☎ 218 442 001; mains €8.50-25.50; lunch & dinner) This restaurant has a top-of-the-world sea-view terrace, and is the town's most spectacular place to eat, with impressive traditional food too.

Xica Bia (☎ 265 522 559; Avenida Luisa Todi; mains €9-12; breakfast, lunch & dinner Mon-Sat) An upmarket, charming option near the market, this fancy place has delicious traditional food in a big arched room with exposed brickwork and wrought-iron chandeliers.

Drinking & Entertainment

Café-bars staying open until around 4am are plentiful along the western end of Avenida Luísa Todi.

Johnny B (1st fl, Avenida Luísa Todi 333; 11pm-4am Tue, Fri & Sat, daily May-Sep) Sobicome Cybercafé has a disco downstairs, named after the friendly owner; with karaoke on Tuesday and Friday evening and ladies night on Saturday.

Bona Cervejaria (☎ 967 717 505; Rua Dr Antóniu Joaquim Granjo 32; noon-2am) A German-run option, this has a range of entertainments, from Friday and Saturday transvestite shows (2am) to live fado on Tuesday evening and a stripper on Sunday at midnight.

Getting There & Away

BOAT

Car and passenger ferries to Tróia depart half-hourly to hourly daily. Note that car ferries, cruises and passenger ferries all have different departure points.

BUS

Buses run between Setúbal and Lisbon's Praça de Espanha (€3.15, 45 to 60 minutes, at least hourly) – or from Cacilhas (€2.85, 50 minutes, every 15 minutes Monday to Friday, at least every two hours Saturday and Sunday), a quick ferry-hop from Cais de Alfândega. Services also run to Évora (€5.15, 1¾ hours) and Faro (€13.40, four hours, two daily), and to Santarém (€9, three hours 20 minutes, six daily Monday to Friday, three daily Saturday and Sunday).

TRAIN

From Lisbon's Terreiro do Paço terminal you can take the ferry to Barreiro station, from where there are hourly *suburbano* trains to Setúbal (€1.30, 45 minutes, at least hourly).

Getting Around

You can rent bikes for €10/15/20 per one/two/three days from **Planeta Terra** (☎ 919 471 871; Praça General Luís Domingues 9).

Car-rental agencies include **Avis** (☎ 265 538 710; Avenida Luísa Todi 96).

SESIMBRA

pop 37,570 / elevation 60m

Once a fishing village, Sesimbra has retained something of its sedate character, with narrow cobbled streets and nets on the beach. Bustling fish restaurants and a café-lined seafront tell another story, and the small town is a favourite Lisboêta getaway. It's 30km southwest of Setúbal, sheltering under the Serra da Arrábida at the western edge of the beautiful Parque Natural da Arrábida. At weekends and holidays the place gets packed with Portuguese – it's like attending a festival with no focus. Cruises, guided walks and scuba-diving activities are on offer here, including trips to Cabo Espichel, where dinosaurs once roamed.

Orientation & Information

The **bus station** (Avenida da Liberdade) is about 250m north of the seafront. Turn right when you reach the bottom of the avenida and pass the small 17th-century Forte de Santiago (now a police station) to the helpful **turismo** (☎ 212 288 540; www.sesimbra.online.pt; Largo da Marinha; 🕑 9am-8pm Jun-Sep, 9am-12.30pm & 2-5.30pm Oct-May), set back slightly from the seafront.

Sights

CASTELO

Big coastal panoramas sit below the imposing Moorish **castle** (admission free; 🕑 7am-8pm Mon-Wed, Fri & Sat, to 7pm Sun & Thu), 200m above Sesimbra. It was taken by Dom Afonso Henriques in the 12th century, retaken by the Moors, and snatched back by Christians under Dom Sancho I the following century.

The empty ruins contain the pretty 18th-century **Igreja Santa Maria do Castelo**, with heavy gold altar and blue-and-white tiles, and its cemetery. The small **Centro de Documentação** (admission free; 🕑 9am-12.30pm & 2-5.30pm Mon & Tue, 9am-12.30pm & 1-7pm Wed & Fri, 10am-1pm & 2-6pm Sat & Sun) details the castle's history. The shady castle grounds are great for picnics.

PORTO DE ABRIGO

About 1km west of town is **Porto de Abrigo**, a busy fishing centre. Early morning and late afternoon, when fishermen auction their catch, is still a good time to catch a more traditional atmosphere.

Activities

Clube Naval de Sesimbra (☎ 212 233 451; www.naval-sesimbra.pt; Porto de Abrigo) runs three-hour coastal cruises or six-hour fishing trips.

Aquarama (☎ 212 687 266, 965 540 750; Avenida dos Náufragos; adult/child €14/8.50; 🕑 10am-6pm) runs trips to Cabo Espichel on a glass-bottomed partially submerged boat – buy tickets at their office or on the boat.

Nautilus (☎ 212 551 969; Porto de Abrigo) is an IDC PADI Dive Centre offering courses (including some for kids) and dives in the Sesimbra area. **Sersub** (☎ 964 521 006, 962 608 026; Porto de Abrigo) also runs diving courses and offers fishing trips. **Tridacna** (☎ 936 233 313; Rua da Casa Nova 2) is another diving school.

Surf Clube de Sesimbra (☎ 918 473 896, 933 237 509; www.scs.pt; Casa do Sino, Estrada Velha do Areal), based in Rotovia, offers lessons and board hire. Or you can windsurf with **O Lagoa** (☎ 212 683 109; Lagoa de Albufeira).

You can go pony trekking with **Granja Paraíso** (☎ 212 680 171; Fonte de Sesimbra), a local horse-riding school.

If this is all too low, **Falcão Azul** (☎ 212 235 452; Pocinho da Maçã 2) will take you on a helicopter tour.

Festivals

Senhor Jesus das Chagas (early May) A procession stops twice to bless the land and four times to bless the sea, carrying an image of Christ that is said to have appeared on the beach in the 16th century (usually kept in Misericórdia Church).

Cabo Espichel festival (last Sunday of September) Most spectacularly set, it celebrates an apparition of the Virgin during the 15th century – an image of the Virgin is carried through the parishes, ending at the Cape.

Sleeping

In Sesimbra, accommodation choices are not great; your best budget bets are *quartos* from €25 to €35 a double; ask at the turismo for details. Prices may be higher in August, but you'll get low-season discounts.

BUDGET

Senhora Garcia (☎ 212 233 227; Travessa Xavier da Silva 1; s/d with shared bathroom €25/35) Well-advertised *quartos* that are plain, dark and functional, but right in the centre.

Residencial Chic (☎ 212 233 110; Travessa Xavier da Silva; s/d €25/35) More cheap than chic – rooms are run-down and above a bar, but they are bright and central and in some you can glimpse the sea from the window.

Forte do Cavalo (☎ 212 288 508; www.mun-sesimbra.pt; adult/tent/car €1.70/3.70/4.75) This is the tree-shaded municipal camp site, 1km west of town, up on a hill with views over the sea. It has a restaurant.

Parque de Campismo de Valbom (☎ 212 687 545; adult/tent/car €3.15/2.70/2.70; ♿) In Cotovia, this is a smaller, well-equipped facility 5km north of Sesimbra (to get here just take any Lisbon-bound bus), with restaurant, disabled access and some shade.

MID RANGE

Residencial Náutico Club (☎ 212 233 233; www.nauticoclub.com; Avenida dos Combatentes 19; d with breakfast €75; ❄) About 500m uphill from the waterfront, this is the town's most pleasant choice, with comfortable doubles, some with terrace.

Quinta do Rio (☎ 212 189 343; fax 212 185 442; d with breakfast €40-60) Around 7km towards Setúbal is this attractive converted *quinta* set among orange groves – a really lovely, good-value place to stay. Also available are horse rides, a swimming pool and tennis court.

TOP END

Sana Park (☎ 212 289 000; sanapark.sesimbra@sanahotels.com; Avenida 25 de Abril; s/d with breakfast €83/93, with sea view €100/110) Sesimbra's smartest, a seaside property with swimming pools overlooking the sea, rooms with sea-view balconies, and health club with sauna, steam room and rooftop Jacuzzi.

Eating & Drinking

Fish restaurants abound on the waterfront: east of the fort.

Toca do Ratinho (☎ 212 232 572; Rua Plínio Mesquita 17; mains €7-11) A small, tucked-away place where you can get great barbecued fresh fish. The outside covered seating has a view down to the seafront.

O Farol (☎ 212 233 356; Largo da Marinha 4/5; mains €7.50-15; 🕑 lunch & dinner Wed-Mon) Just behind the turismo, O Farol is appealing and friendly with lots of tiles; outside seats on a small square overlook the sea. Good fish mains on offer.

Tony Bar (☎ 212 233 199; Largo de Bombaldes 19; mains €7.50-27.50; 🕑 lunch & dinner) A classy restaurant with excellent fish mains in huge portions, and good service. The swordfish with tomatoes is delicious. Inside it's cosy or there are seats on the square.

Rua da Liberdade or Largo do Município (near the market) have cheaper places like **Restaurante A Sesimbrense** (☎ 212 230 148; Rua Jorge Nunes 19; mains around €7; 🕑 lunch & dinner Thu-Tue). A short walk up from Largo de Bombaldes, this is a nice, cosy local restaurant, with more fresh fish and a local clientele.

For evening snacks and late-night drinks, trawl Avenida dos Náufragos.

Getting There & Away

Buses depart from Lisbon's Praça de Espanha (€3.15, 60 to 90 minutes, at least four to five daily), from Setúbal (€2.45, 45 minutes, at least nine daily Monday to Saturday, six Sunday) and from Cacilhas (€2.55, around 50 minutes, at least hourly). There are runs to Cabo Espichel (€1.80, 20 minutes, two daily) and more frequent runs to the village of Azóia (€1.80, 10 daily Monday to Saturday, six Sunday), about 3km before the cape.

AROUND SESIMBRA

Aldeia do Meco

This tiny village 12km northwest of Sesimbra is famous for its clustered seafood restaurants – here and in nearby Alfarim.

Eating & Sleeping

Country House (☎/fax 212 685 001; countryhouse@gep.pt; Rua Alto da Carona, Alfarim; d €45, 2-/4-person apt €60/75) A big, fairly modern whitewashed house with sloping red roofs, 1.4km north in a wooded setting, with four spacious rooms (with coffeemakers and fridge) and three apartments, most with balconies. It's 2km from the beach, and well signposted.

PARQUE NATURAL DA ARRÁBIDA

Stunning, thickly green and hilly, edged by gleamingly clean, golden beaches, the Arrábida Natural Park stretches along the southeastern coast of the Setúbal Peninsula from Setúbal to Sesimbra. Covering the 35km-long Serra da Arrábida mountain ridge, this is an area rich in Mediterranean plants from olive, pistachio and strawberry trees to lavender, thyme and camomile, and attendant butterflies, beetles and birds (especially birds of prey) and even 70 different types of seaweed. In 2004, it suffered huge fire damage, when 700 hectares were scorched, and Portugal had to appeal the EU for assistance to put out blazes across the country, but there is still much to visit.

Local honey is delicious, especially that produced in the gardens of the whitewashed, red-roofed **Convento da Arrábida** (☎ 212 180 520), a 16th-century former monastery overlooking the sea just north of Portinho (best days to visit are Tuesday or Thursday, but call ahead). Another famous product is Azeitão ewe's cheese, whose characteristic flavour owes much to lush Arrábida pastures and a variety of thistle used in the curdling process.

Public transport through the middle of the park is nonexistent – some buses serve the beach from July to September (around four daily to Figueirinha). Your best option is to rent a car or motorcycle, or take an organised trip by jeep and/or boat (p140). Be warned: parking is tricky near the beaches, even off-season.

Headquarters for both this park and the **Reserva Natural do Estuário do Sado** (☎ 265 541 140; fax 265 541 155) are on Praça da República, Setúbal. They're not much use if you don't speak Portuguese – guided walks can be arranged here, but only in Portuguese. However, you can buy a useful map of the park (€3.81).

Campimeco (☎ 212 683 394; adult/tent/car €3.15/2.70/2.70; ♿) A large camp site 3km away, above Praia das Bicas and close to several beaches. It has a great situation, right up on the clifftop, with lots of shady trees, good facilities and disabled access.

Bar do Peixe (☎ 212 684 732; Praia do Meco; mains €7-11; 🕒 lunch & dinner Wed-Mon, daily Jul & Aug) North of Praia das Bicas, right on the beach, this is a big wooden building with a seafacing terrace and a wonderful position overlooking the long sands. From July to September it holds a disco on Wednesday and Saturday. It's 500m from the bus stop.

GETTING THERE & AWAY

Buses run from Sesimbra (€1.80, 30 minutes, three to five daily).

Cabo Espichel

At strange, bleak Cabo Espichel, frighteningly tall greenery-topped cliffs drop down into the piercing blue sea, some met by swathes of beach. The only building on the cape is a huge church, the 18th-century Nossa Senhora do Cabo, flanked by two arms of desolately empty pilgrims' lodges.

It's easy to see why Wim Wenders used this spot as a location when filming *A Lisbon Story*, with its lonely, brooding, outback atmosphere. Rocks around the cape resemble prehistoric hides – an appropriate setting for dinosaurs, whose footprints have even been discovered imprinted in rock to the north, near Praia dos Lagosteiros. It's worth your while trying to catch the Cabo Espichel festival if you are visiting in September (see p142).

Buses run direct from Sesimbra (€1.80, 20 minutes, two daily), more frequently teminating at the village of Azóia (€1.80, 10 daily Monday to Saturday, six Sunday), about 3km before the cape.

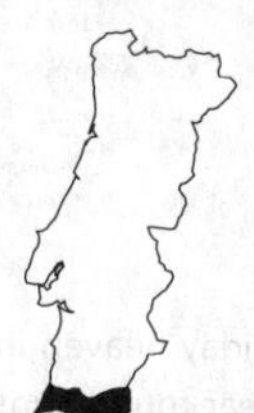

The Algarve

CONTENTS

It's holiday heaven in the Algarve – a role created by climate, geography, and personality, with year-round sunshine, long beaches, natural bays, dramatic cliffs and warm seas (the warmest in Portugal, this being the Atlantic but also the Mediterranean's next-door neighbour). In some places it's not everyone's idea of fun, as development has all but obscured the charms that inspired the development. Between Faro and Lagos, it's all apartment blocks, whitewashed villas and golf courses, providing hassle-free holiday facilities whose rowdier relatives live on the Spanish *costas* (coastal regions).

Lagos is the good-looking carnival queen of the main resorts. Praia da Rocha has the best beach on the coast – a golden, rose-tinted jewel and an apartment-block magnet, but with sophistication lurking amid the concrete. Albufeira, with a pretty town centre, is also packed with facilities, but more British- and German-centric.

Out at the Algarve's edges, it's a different story. Sagres in the southwest, balancing almost on the southwesternmost tip of Europe, is smaller and sweeter. North of here, the wild, west-facing shores have some small, appealing resorts and offer Portugal's best surfing. East of Faro, the coast is different: instead of red-streaked cliffs and long beaches, the sand lies offshore with a chain of sandy islands mainly accessible by boat. The only really built-up resort is at Monte Gordo, with the town of Tavira proving the most elegant and genteel guest at the Algarve do.

The interior offers something different, with lovely, thick-wooded hills around Monchique in the west and the lovely Rio Guardiana route in the east, culminating in the enchanting Alcoutim.

Spring or autumn are good times to visit, while July to mid-September is the busiest and priciest time as this is when most Portuguese take their holidays, as do many other Europeans.

HIGHLIGHTS

- **Seaside Frolics**
  Let yourself go in Lagos (p182)
- **Off-shore Exploration**
  Unspoilt islands in the Parque Natural da Ria Formosa (p159)
- **Old Town Strolls**
  Tavira (p160) and Silves (p176)
- **Adrenaline Rush**
  Surf-central (Carrapateira), on the wild west coast (p194)
- **Rural Escapes**
  Monchique (p197) & Alcoutim (p199)

Carrapateira
Monchique
Silves
Lagos
Alcoutim
Tavira
Parque Natural da Ria Formosa

- POPULATION: 465,000
- AREA: 5071 SQ KM

History

British expats are following a long tradition of settlement. Phoenicians came first and established trading posts about 3000 years ago, followed by the Carthaginians. Next were the Romans, typically industrious during their 400-year stay – they grew wheat, barley and grapes and built roads and palaces (check out the remains at Milreu, near Faro).

Then came the Visigoths and, in 711, the North African Moors. They stayed 500 years, but later Christians obliterated as much as they could, leaving little trace of the era. However, many place names come from this time, easily spotted by the article 'al' (eg Albufeira, Aljezur, Alcoutim). The Syrian Moors called the region in which they settled (east of Faro to Seville, Spain) al-Gharb al-Andalus (western Andalucía), which later became 'Algarve'. Another Arabic legacy is the flat-roofed house, originally used for drying almonds, figs and corn, and to escape from the night heat.

Trade boomed, particularly in nuts and dried fruit, and Silves was the mighty Moorish capital, quite independent of the large Muslim emirate to the east.

The Christian Reconquista began in the early 12th century, with the wealthy Algarve as the ultimate goal. Though Dom Sancho I captured Silves and territories to the west in 1189, the Moors returned. It was not until the first half of the 13th century that the Portuguese clawed their way back for good.

Two centuries later the Algarve had its heyday. Prince Henry the Navigator chose the appropriately end-of-the-earth Sagres as the base for his school of navigation, and had ships built and staffed in Lagos for the 15th-century exploration of Africa and Asia – seafaring triumphs that turned Portugal into a major imperial power (p26).

The Algarve coastline is 155km long, with five regions: the leeward coast (or Sotavento), from Vila Real de Santo António to Faro, largely fronted by a chain of sandy offshore *ilhas* (islands); the central coast, from Faro to Portimão, featuring the heaviest resort development; the increasingly rocky windward coast (or Barlavento), from Lagos to Sagres, culminating in the wind-scoured grandeur of the Cabo de São Vicente, Europe's southwesternmost corner; and the hilly, thickly green interior, which rises to two high mountain ranges the Serra de Monchique and the less-visited Serra do Caldeirão. The Costa do Ouro (Golden Coast) borders the Costa de Sagres (Bay of Sagres), while the Costa Vicentina stretches north of here, the windy, wild rim of a national park.

FIRE!

In the crackling summer heat, Portugal suffers annual fires that dart through the forests, attack houses and singe or kill wildlife. In 2003 massive infernos burned 5% of land, 13% of forests, and killed 18 people. In 2004 fires were even more numerous, but thankfully destroyed less. However, Portugal was forced to appeal for help from the EU – Greece, Italy and Spain sent planes to help contain the fires. Worst hit were the Parque Natural da Arrábida, near Lisbon (see p144) and the southern Algarve – particularly around Loulé, Monchique and Silves. High temperatures, forests littered with dry deadwood, and insufficient resources all add fuel to the flames. The government has been criticised for its slow approach and for failing to prevent these serious fires. It's not out of the question that some were started by arsonists. Make sure you extinguish that cigarette butt.

ALGARVE WINES

An important wine-making centre since the Romans reclined and ate grapes, the Algarve has the climate, rich soil and high-quality vines to produce full-bodied wines with low acidity and high alcohol content. The whites are dry, the reds soft and fruity and young. Although vineyards have made way for villas, there are still about 16,200 hectares around Lagoa, producing the Algarve's best-known wines. Smaller wine-producing areas are Lagos, Tavira and Portimão.

Climate

Lovely. That is, barely a winter, and sun, sun, sun almost all year round with 12/six hours' sunshine per day in a typical summer/winter. Temperatures may reach around 40°C in summer. In January and February,

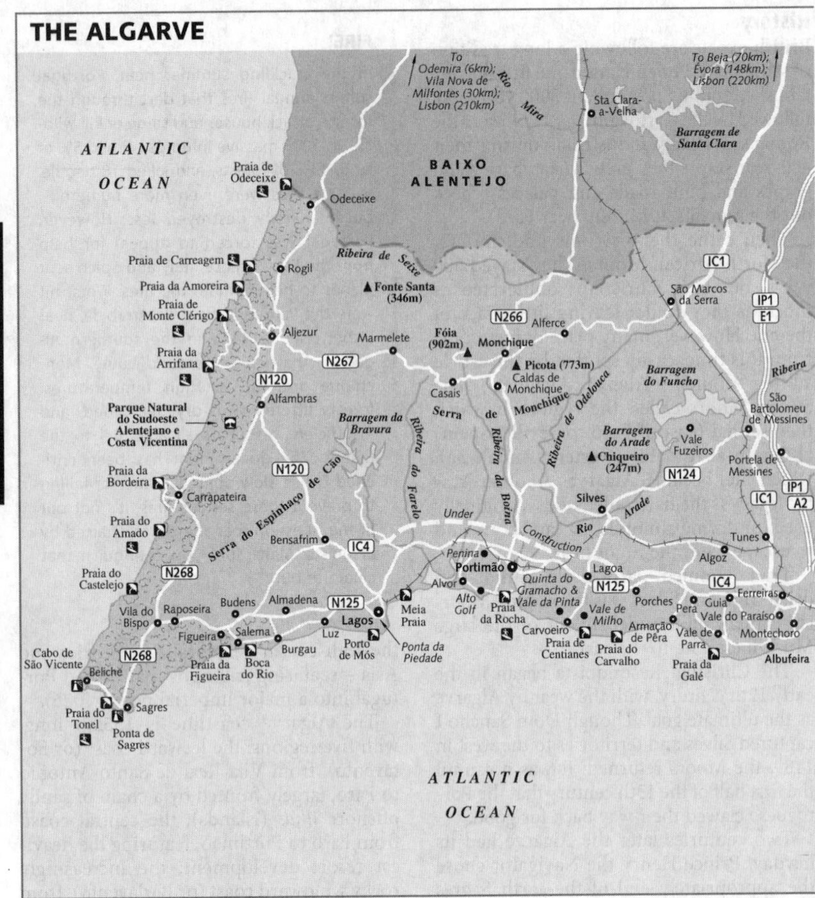

the countryside gets covered in almond blossom, while in March it's orange blossom; April is the best time for wildflowers.

Dangers & Annoyances

As this is Portugal's most touristed region, you're more vulnerable to petty theft here than elsewhere. Don't leave valuables unattended in your car or on the beach.

Swimmers should beware of dangerous ocean currents, especially on the west coast. Beaches are marked by coloured flags: chequered means it's unattended, red means don't even dip your toe in, yellow means wading is fine, but don't swim; and green means go – wade, swim. Blue is an international symbol, meaning the beach is smashing – safe, clean and with good facilities.

Orientation

One of the clearest Algarve maps, including six town maps, is published by Freytag & Berndt (1:150,000).

Information

MEDIA

Besides the English-language newspapers *Anglo-Portuguese News* (*APN*; good for job vacancies) and *The News* (www.the-news.net), there are several Algarve-specific magazines in English or German, including *Algarve Resident* (www.algarveresident.com) and *Entdecken Sie Algarve* (Dis-

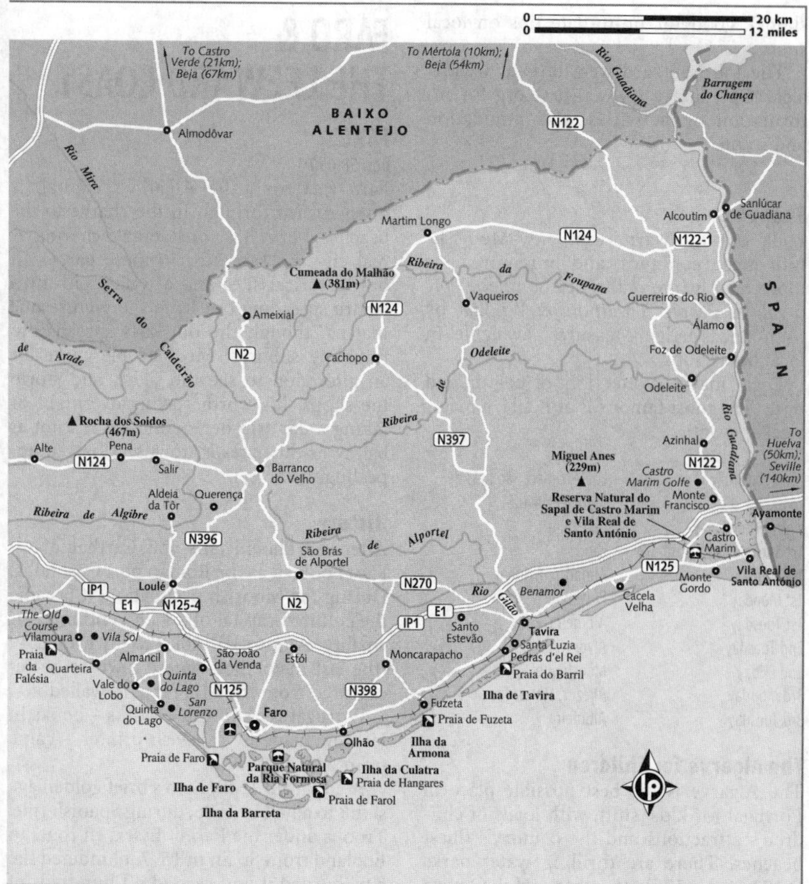

cover the Algarve). *Essential Algarve* (www.essentialalgarve.com) is a leisure and lifestyle mag.

TOURIST INFORMATION

Turismos dole out town maps, information and free leaflets, including the monthly *Algarve Guide*, which tells you what's on, the quarterly *Welcome to the Algarve*, and *Algarve Tips*. *Your Guide*, produced by the airport authority, *Aeroportos e Navegação Aérea* (ANA), is good on bar, club and hotel listings. Major towns offer a monthly *Agenda Cultural* magazine. The *Best Guide Algarve* gives the sights and activities lowdown, as well as a basic road map. *Algarve Tourist Yellow Pages* is another handy freebie, with town maps and local information. There are also privately produced *Free Maps* in resorts (often available at bars and

BUSING IT

Two big bus companies, **Eva** (☎ 289 899 740) and **Rede Expressos** (☎ 289 899 760) zip frequently between the Algarve and elsewhere in Portugal. Smaller lines include Caima, Renex and Frota Azul. If you're going to travel by bus, consider buying the Passe Turístico (€19.50), which is available from major bus stations and is good for three days of unlimited travel on most main routes between Lagos and Loulé.

shops), good for up-to-date tips on local spots.

The tourist board website is at www.rtalgarve.pt; or try www.algarve.org for information on activities, accommodation and so on.

Shopping

Look out for warm woollens, Moorish-influenced ceramics, and brassware. For more on Algarve crafts, see *Southern Portugal: Its People, Traditions & Wildlife,* by John and Madge Measures, available in local bookshops.

Local markets offer lots of colour and buzz. The most famous is at Loulé, a major weekly event:

every Saturday	Loulé, Olhão, São Brás de Alportel, Tavira
every Wednesday	Quarteira
1st Saturday of the month	Lagos
1st Sunday	Almancil, Azinhal
1st Monday	Portimão
1st Tuesday	Albufeira
2nd Tuesday	Alvor
2nd Friday	Monchique
3rd Monday	Aljezur, Silves, Tavira
3rd Tuesday	Albufeira

The Algarve for Children

The Algarve is the best possible place in Portugal for kids' stuff, with loads of children's attractions and the country's finest beaches. There are thrilling water parks (p172 and p175); the wonderful Omega and Lagos zoos (p198 and p185); and, at Silves, the imagination-firing castle (p177) and the wonderful Fábrica do Inglês (p179), with kinetic fountains and a children's playground. Near Alcoutim (p199) there's the Parque Mineiro Cova dos Mouros, an ancient mine where, if kids can't get their heads round the history, they can always ride a donkey.

Most resorts run boat trips (see individual sections for details), and many have little trains – perfect for pootling around the sights. Horse riding is another easily accessible activity (p172 and p171).

As in the rest of Portugal, children are very much welcome everywhere. See the Directory (p455) for more information on keeping little ones happy.

FARO & THE LEEWARD COAST

FARO

pop 58,050

Faro (*fah*-roo), the Algarve's capital, is often rushed through in the charge to the beaches, but it has considerable charms. A real city – a rare bird in these parts – it has historical sites and a walled old-town centre spreading out from the picturesque marina, though the outskirts spread into rambling suburbs. Most people come for an afternoon to see the sights and storm the shops. It's worth staying overnight or taking a day trip here: although it's not as balmy as other resort towns, it has an appealingly real feel.

History

After the Phoenicians and Carthaginians, Faro boomed as the Roman port Ossonoba. During the Moorish occupation, it became the cultured capital of a 11th-century principality. Afonso III took the town in 1249 (the last major Portuguese town to be recaptured from the Moors), and walled it.

Portugal's first printed works – books in Hebrew made by a Jewish printer – came from Faro in 1487.

A city from 1540, Faro's brief golden age slunk to a halt in 1596, during Spanish rule. Troops under the Earl of Essex, en route to England from Spain in 1597, plundered the city, burned it and carried off hundreds of priceless theological works from the bishop's palace, now part of the Bodleian Library in Oxford!

Battered Faro was rebuilt, poking its head over the parapet only to be shattered by an earthquake in 1722 and then almost flattened in the 1755 big one. Most of what you see today is postquake, though the historic centre largely survived. In 1834 it became the Algarve's capital.

Orientation

The town hub, Praça Dr Francisco Gomes, adjoins the marina and small garden called Jardim Manuel Bívar. The Eva bus station and the train station, both on Avenida da República, are a short walk away. The airport is about 6km west, off the N125.

THE ALGARVE

Offshore is the widest stretch of the Parque Natural da Ria Formosa. While many of the near-shore sand bars along here disappear at high tide, two of the bigger sea-facing islands – Ilha de Faro to the southwest and Ilha da Culatra to the southeast – have good beaches.

Information

BOOKSHOPS

Faro's main bookshop is **Livraria Bertrand** (☎ 289 828 147; Rua Dr Francisco Gomes 27), although souvenir shops and newsagents stock more local maps and guides.

EMERGENCY & MEDICAL SERVICES

Faro district hospital (☎ 289 891 100; Rua Leão Penedo) Over 2km northeast of the centre.

Police station (☎ 289 822 022; Rua da Polícia de Segurança Pública 32)

INTERNET ACCESS

EQInformática (☎ 289 873 731; Largo do Pé da Cruz 1; per hr €3; 🕑 9.30am-1pm & 2.30-7pm Mon-Fri, 9.30am-1pm Sat)

Instituto Português da Juventude (IPJ; Rua da Polícia de Segurança Pública 1; 🕑 9am-7pm Mon-Fri, 10am-1pm Sat) Free Internet access for up to 30 minutes. The pousada da juventude is here (p154).

LAUNDRY

Lavandaria Sólimpa (☎ 289 822 891; Rua Batista Lopes 30; 1-day wash-&-dry service per kg €1.75, min 4kg; 🕑 9am-1pm & 3-7pm Mon-Fri, 9am-1pm Sat) Calls itself self-service but isn't.

MONEY

Cota Câmbios (Rua Dr Francisco Gomes 26; 🕑 8.30am-6.30pm Mon-Fri, 10am-2pm Sat) A private exchange bureau.

Top Tours (☎ 289 895 340; faro@toptours.pt; Rua da Comunidade Lusiada; 🕑 Mon-Fri) You can change AmEx travellers cheques here.

POST

Main post office (☎ 289 892 590; Largo do Carmo; 🕑 9am-6.30pm Mon-Fri, 9am-noon Sat).

TOURIST INFORMATION

ICEP turismo (☎ 289 818 582; 🕑 8am-11.30pm) At the airport.

Municipal turismo (☎ 289 803 604; Rua da Misericórdia 8; 🕑 9.30am-1pm & 2.30-6pm Mon-Fri) The chief information office: efficient, busy and helpful.

Regional turismo administrative office (☎ 289 800 400; rtalgarve@rtalgarve.pt; Avenida 5 de Outubro 18; 🕑 8.30am-8pm Mon-Fri) Reception will provide you with a map and leaflets.

TRAVEL AGENCIES

Abreu Tours (☎ 707 201 840; www.abreu.pt; Avenida da República 124; 🕑 9am-12.30pm & 2-6pm Mon-Fri)

Tagus (☎ 289 805 483; www.viagenstagus.pt; Avenida 5 de Outubro 26C; 🕑 9.30am-7pm Mon-Fri, 10am-1pm Sat) The best student-oriented agency.

Top Tours (☎ 289 895 340; faro@toptours.pt; Rua da Comunidade Lusiada; 🕑 Mon-Fri) AmEx representative.

Sights & Activities

CIDADE VELHA

Within medieval walls, the scenic Cidade Velha (Old Town) consists of winding, peaceful cobbled streets and squares, reconstructed in a lucky-dip of styles following successive batterings – first by marauding British and then two big earthquakes.

You enter through the neoclassical **Arco da Vila**, built by order of Bishop Francisco Gomes, Faro's answer to the Marquês de Pombal (see p28), who oversaw the city's reconstruction after the 1755 earthquake. The top of the street opens into the orange tree–lined Largo da Sé, with the câmara municipal (town hall) on the left and the ancient sé (cathedral) in front of you.

The **sé** (admission €2; 🕑 10am-6pm) was completed in 1251, on what was probably the site a Roman temple, then a Visigoth cathedral and then a Moorish mosque. Only the tower gate and two chapels remain of the original Romanesque-Gothic exterior – the rest was devoured in 1755. It was rebuilt in a polygamy of Gothic, Renaissance and baroque styles, with intense gilded carving alongside elaborate tilework inside. You can climb up to the rooftop *miradouro* (lookout) with views across the pretty walled town to the sea, as well as the storks nesting in the bell towers. The cathedral buildings also house the **Museu Capitular** (closed for restoration at time of writing), and a small shrine built of bones to send a shiver down your spine and alert you to your mortality. To the right of the cathedral is the 18th-century Palácio Episcopal, with a pointy red roof and finished in multicoloured *azulejos* (hand-painted tiles), successor to the previous episcopal dwelling trashed by British troops in 1596. At the southern end of the square

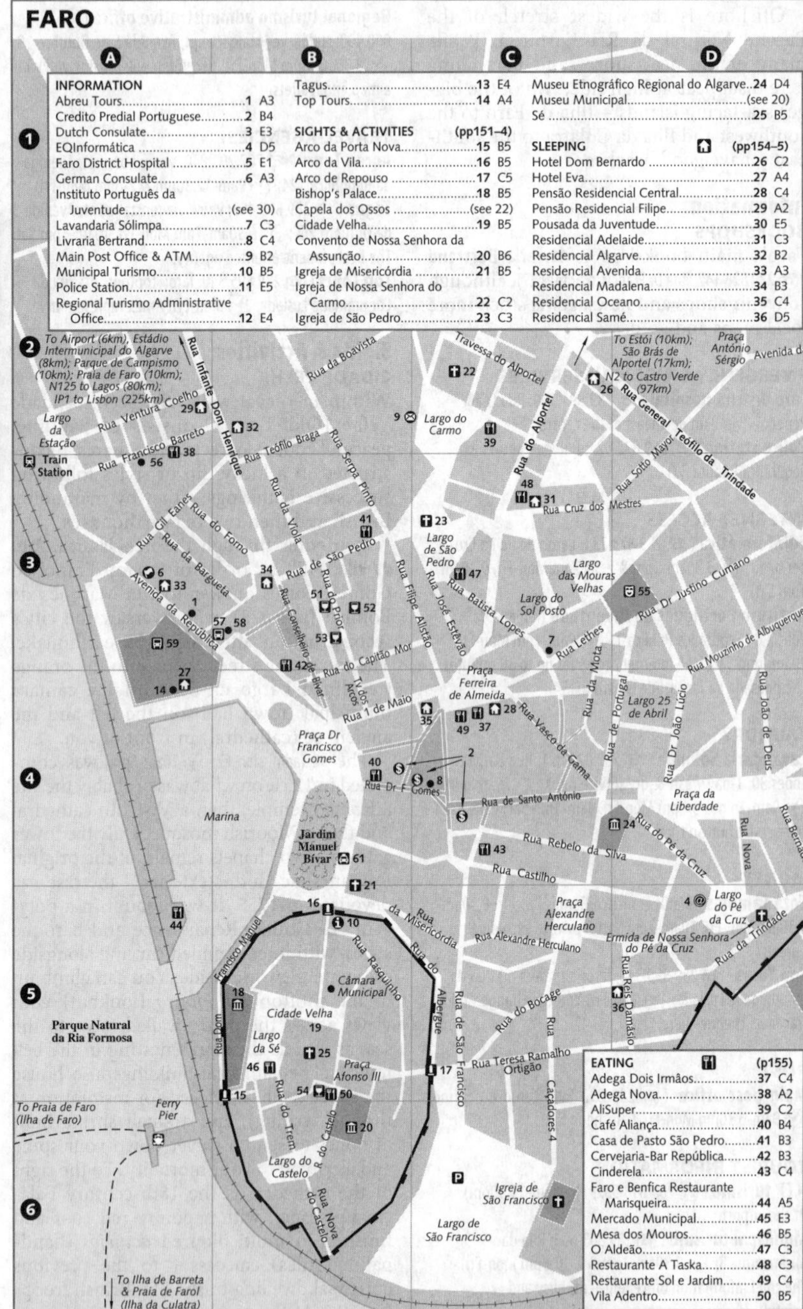
FARO
A
B
C
D
1
2
3
4
5
6
INFORMATION
Abreu Tours....1 A3
Credito Predial Portuguese....2 B4
Dutch Consulate....3 E3
EQInformática....4 D5
Faro District Hospital....5 E1
German Consulate....6 A3
Instituto Português da Juventude....(see 30)
Lavandaria Sólimpa....7 C3
Livraria Bertrand....8 C4
Main Post Office & ATM....9 B2
Municipal Turismo....10 B5
Police Station....11 E5
Regional Turismo Administrative Office....12 E4
Tagus....13 E4
Top Tours....14 A4
SIGHTS & ACTIVITIES (pp151–4)
Arco da Porta Nova....15 B5
Arco da Vila....16 B5
Arco de Repouso....17 C5
Bishop's Palace....18 B5
Capela dos Ossos....(see 22)
Cidade Velha....19 B5
Convento de Nossa Senhora da Assunção....20 B6
Igreja de Misericórdia....21 B5
Igreja de Nossa Senhora do Carmo....22 C2
Igreja de São Pedro....23 C3
Museu Etnográfico Regional do Algarve....24 D4
Museu Municipal....(see 20)
Sé....25 B5
SLEEPING (pp154–5)
Hotel Dom Bernardo....26 C2
Hotel Eva....27 A4
Pensão Residencial Central....28 C4
Pensão Residencial Filipe....29 A2
Pousada da Juventude....30 E5
Residencial Adelaide....31 C3
Residencial Algarve....32 B2
Residencial Avenida....33 A3
Residencial Madalena....34 B3
Residencial Oceano....35 C4
Residencial Samé....36 D5
To Airport (6km), Estádio Intermunicipal do Algarve (8km); Parque de Campismo (10km); Praia de Faro (10km); N125 to Lagos (80km); IP1 to Lisbon (225km)
To Estói (10km); São Brás de Alportel (17km); N2 to Castro Verde (97km)
Praça António Sérgio
Avenida da
Rua Infante Dom Henrique
Rua da Boavista
Travessa do Alportel
Rua General Teófilo da Trindade
Rua do Alportel
Largo do Carmo
Largo da Estação
Train Station
Rua Ventura Coelho
Rua Francisco Barreto
Rua Teófilo Braga
Rua Serpa Pinto
Rua da Viola
Rua Sotto Mayor
Rua Cruz dos Mestres
Rua Gil Eanes
Rua do Forno
Rua da Barqueta
Avenida da República
Rua de São Pedro
Rua do Prior
Largo de São Pedro
Rua Filipe Alistão
Rua José Estêvão
Rua Batista Lopes
Largo das Mouras Velhas
Largo do Sol Posto
Rua Dr Justino Cumano
Rua Mouzinho de Albuquerque
Rua Lethes
Rua Conselheiro de Bívar
Rua do Capitão Mor
Tv dos Arcos
Rua 1 de Maio
Praça Ferreira de Almeida
Rua Vasco da Gama
Rua da Mota
Rua de Portugal
Largo 25 de Abril
Rua Dr João Lúcio
Rua João de Deus
Praça Dr Francisco Gomes
Rua Dr F Gomes
Rua de Santo António
Praça da Liberdade
Marina
Jardim Manuel Bívar
Rua Rebelo da Silva
Rua do Pé da Cruz
Rua Nova
Rua Bernardo
Rua Castilho
Praça Alexandre Herculano
Rua Alexandre Herculano
Largo do Pé da Cruz
Ermida de Nossa Senhora do Pé da Cruz
Rua da Trindade
Rua da Misericórdia
Rua do Albergue
Rua Francisco Manuel
Rua Rasquinho
Câmara Municipal
Cidade Velha
Rua de São Francisco
Rua do Bocage
Rua Reis Damásio
Parque Natural da Ria Formosa
Rua Dom
Largo da Sé
Praça Afonso III
Rua Teresa Ramalho Ortigão
Rua Caçadores 4
Rua do Trem
R. do Castelo
Largo do Castelo
Rua Nova do Castelo
To Praia de Faro (Ilha de Faro)
Ferry Pier
Igreja de São Francisco
Largo de São Francisco
To Ilha de Barreta & Praia de Farol (Ilha da Culatra)
EATING (p155)
Adega Dois Irmãos....37 C4
Adega Nova....38 A2
AliSuper....39 C2
Café Aliança....40 B4
Casa de Pasto São Pedro....41 B3
Cervejaria-Bar República....42 B3
Cinderela....43 C4
Faro e Benfica Restaurante Marisqueira....44 A5
Mercado Municipal....45 E3
Mesa dos Mouros....46 B5
O Aldeão....47 C3
Restaurante A Taska....48 C3
Restaurante Sol e Jardim....49 C4
Vila Adentro....50 B5

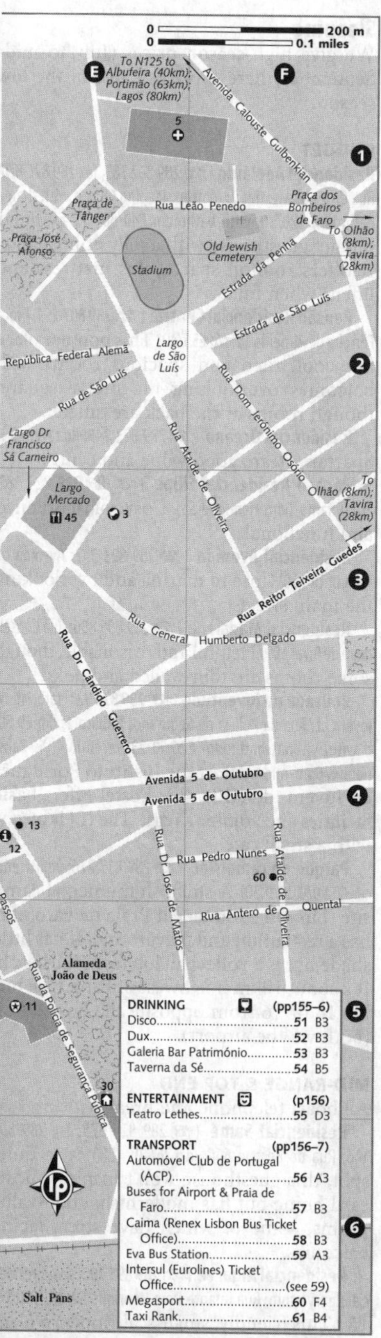

is a small 15th-century town gate, the **Arco da Porta Nova**, leading to the ferry pier.

Next to the cathedral is the stately 16th-century **Convento de Nossa Senhora da Assunção**, now housing the Museu Municipal.

From here you can leave the old town through the medieval **Arco de Repouso**, or Gate of Rest (apparently Afonso III, after taking Faro from the Moors, put his feet up and heard Mass nearby). Around the gateway are some of the town walls' oldest sections – Afonso III's improvements on the Moorish defences.

IGREJA DE NOSSA SENHORA DO CARMO & CAPELA DOS OSSOS

The twin-towered, baroque **Igreja de Nossa Senhora do Carmo** (Our Lady of Carmel; Largo do Carmo; 10am-1pm & 3-5pm Mon-Fri Oct-Apr, to 6pm Mon-Fri May-Sep, 10am-1pm Sat & Sun year-round) was completed in 1719 under João V and paid for (and gilded to death inside) with Brazilian gold. The almost-edible butterscotch façade was completed after the 1755 earthquake.

A more ghoulish attraction lies behind the church – the **Capela dos Ossos** (admission €1). This 19th-century chapel was built from the bones and skulls of over 1000 monks as a blackly reverent reminder of earthly impermanence, and the ultimate in recycling. There's a similar chapel at Évora (p210).

OTHER CHURCHES

For more dazzling woodwork, head to the frenzied 18th-century baroque interior of the **Igreja de São Francisco** (Largo de São Francisco; no fixed hr, Mass 6.30pm) with tiles depicting the life of St Francis. Its old cloisters are now Faro Infantry barracks.

The 16th-century **Igreja de Misericórdia** (Mass 9am), opposite the Arco da Vila, has a remarkable Manueline portico, the only remnant of an earlier chapel to withstand the 1755 earthquake.

At the southern end of Largo do Carmo is the 16th-century **Igreja de São Pedro** (9am-1pm & 3-7pm Mon-Fri), filled with 18th-century azulejos and fine-carved woodwork.

MUSEU MUNICIPAL

The splendid, domed 16th-century Renaissance Convento de Nossa Senhora da Assunção, in what was once the Jewish quarter, houses the **Museu Municipal** (Museu Arqueológico; ☎ 289 897 400; Largo Dom Afonso III; adult/student €2/1; 9.30-5.30pm Tue-Fri, 11.30am-5.30pm Sat & Sun Mar-Oct, 10am-6pm Tue-Fri, noon-6pm Sat & Sun Nov-Feb).

Highlights are the 3rd-century *Mosaic of the Ocean*, found in 1976 on a building site; 9th- to 13th-century domestic Islamic artefacts; and works by a notable Faro painter, Carlos Filipe Porfírio, depicting some local legends.

MUSEU ETNOGRÁFICO REGIONAL DO ALGARVE

The **Museu Etnográfico Regional do Algarve** (Algarve Regional Museum; ☎ 289 827 610; Praça da Liberdade; admission €1.50; 9am-12.30pm & 2-5.30pm Mon-Fri) has enigmatically labelled displays of ceramics, fabrics and dioramas of typical interiors. One endearing, notably well labelled exhibit is of a wooden water cart, used until the owner's death in 1974.

BEACHES

The town's beach, **Praia de Faro**, with miles of sweeping sand, windsurfing operators and some cafés, is on the Ilha de Faro, 10km away. It's crammed in July and August. Take bus No 14 or 16 from opposite the bus station (€1.20, half-hourly in summer, via the airport). Ferries go out to **Praia de Farol** (Ilha da Culatra) and **Ilha da Barreta** (aka Ilha Deserta, p157). You can also take a tour to the latter with **Animaris** (p157; www.ilha-deserta.com).

Activities

Mega Tur (☎ 289 807 648; www.megatur.pt; Rua Conselheiro de Bívar, 80; half-day €13-22, full day €29-65) offers excursions. The best choices are Silves and the Serra de Monchique, Lagos and Sagres, the Loulé market, grotto or speedboat cruises, and jeep and Rio Guadiana boat tours.

Festivals & Events

Feira de Santa Iria (mid-October) Faro's biggest traditional event, honouring St Irene with lots of fairground rides and entertainment. Held at a temporary fairground to the northeast, by the municipal fire station.

International Music Festival (May and June) A cultural highlight.

Rallye Biker (third weekend in July) One of Europe's biggest motorbike rallies. Attracts some 30,000 bikers, making for an extraordinary sight but scarce accommodation.

Sleeping

We give high-season prices (July to mid-September) here – prices halve in the low season.

BUDGET

Residencial Adelaide (☎ 289 802 383; fax 289 826 870; Rua Cruz dos Mestres 7; rooftop sleeping €8, s/d with shared bathroom €20/30, with bathroom €40/50) A popular budget guesthouse with a jolly atmosphere. It offers rooftop space (plus mattress and linen) when full.

Pensão Residencial Central (☎ 289 807 291; Praça Ferreira de Almeida 12; s/d €35/40) This popular place has cool, tiled and spacious rooms with balconies overlooking the pretty square, though rooms at the back are quieter.

Residencial Oceano (☎ 289 823 349; Rua Ivens 21) Spartan, clean, good value and central.

Pensão Residencial Filipe (☎/fax 289 824 182; Rua Infante Dom Henrique 55) Cosy, old-fashioned and functional.

Residencial Avenida (☎ 289 823 347; Avenida da República 150) Close to marina and overlooking the main street.

Residencial Madalena (☎ 289 805 806; Rua Conselheiro de Bívar 109) Helpful and reasonable, though some rooms are thin-walled and poky.

Pousada da juventude (☎ 289 826 521; faro@movijovem.pt; Rua da Polícia de Segurança Pública 1; dm €9.50, d with/without bathroom €26.50/23; reception 8am-noon & 6pm-midnight) At the Instituto Português da Juventude (IPJ), this hostel offers basic facilities and adjoins a park. The IPJ is buzzy, with a small café.

Parque de campismo (☎ 289 817 876; adult/tent/car €0.40/0.20/0.20) A smallish municipal campsite (busy in summer) at Praia de Faro, this has a restaurant and playground. It has little shade but is a volleyball lob from the beach. It's about 10km northwest of Faro; take bus No 14 or 16 from opposite the bus station (both via the airport).

MID-RANGE & TOP END

All boast telephone and breakfast.

Residencial Samé (☎ 289 824 375; fax 289 804 166; Rua do Bocage 66; s/d €26/40;) In a quiet spot, this guesthouse won't inspire a postcard home but has modernish, good-value rooms, some of which have street-facing balconies.

Residencial Algarve (☎ 289 895 700; www.residencialalgarve.com; Rua Infante Dom Henrique 52; s/d €50/60;) This friendly, small-scale modern place nirrors the 19th-century building that once ›ccupied the site. Its bright, cheerful rooms ıave small balconies.

Hotel Dom Bernardo (☎ 289 889 800; www.hotel lombernardo.cjb.net; Rua General Teófilo da Trindade 20; /d €83/100) A modern, comfortable-but-bland :entral hotel. If you pay €8 extra you get a ea view, and some rooms have a Jacuzzi.

Hotel Eva (☎ 289 001 000; www.tdhotels.pt; Avenida la República; s/d €116/136;) Faro's finest, ›verlooking the marina and the sea beyond, his hotel has rooms with balconies and iews. There's a rooftop swimming pool or more marina-gazing.

:ating

3UDGET

\dega Nova (☎ 289 813 433; Rua Francisco Barreto :4; mains €4.50-12; 🕒 lunch & dinner) You can't ;o wrong with grandma types cooking up lelicious regional staples behind a long :ounter, communal bench tables and a lofty :eiling.

Café Aliança (Rua Dr Francisco Gomes; €0.60-8; 🕒 breakfast, lunch & dinner) Head for this dog-:ared, old-fashioned place for coffee, snacks ınd people-watching from the tables spill-ng into the square.

Casa de Pasto São Pedro (☎ 289 826 743; Rua de ão Pedro 55) Cosy and stuck in time, with sim-le but good grills, this place is also worth try.

Faro's big, daily *mercado municipal* (mu-ıicipal market) is in Largo Mercado. There's n **AliSuper** (Largo do Carmo).

⁄IID-RANGE

aro e Benfica Restaurante Marisqueira (☎ 289 21 422; Marina; mains €7.50-16; 🕒 lunch & dinner) Candle-lit at night, with a marinaside set-ing, big open windows and a plant-filled errace, this classy seafood restaurant could indle something romantic.

Vilaadentro Restaurante (☎ 919 191 021; Largo fonso III 17; mains €11.70-16.50; 🕒 lunch & dinner) 'his cathedral-side, tiled restaurant with beautiful, intimate interior sets the scene or upmarket traditional Algarvian cuisine. 'here are outdoor tables as well, but for nce inside could be even nicer.

O Aldeão (☎ 289 823 339; Largo de São Pedro 54-57; ıains €11.50-14) This upmarket, fetching place ıas outdoor seating in the square, and inven-ve Algarvian and Alentejan dishes, such as teak with clams and fragrant black pork.

Restaurante A Taska (☎ 289 824 739; Rua do Alportel 38; mains €6-13; 🕒 lunch & dinner Mon-Sat) Popular with locals, this trattoria-style, high-ceilinged place serves delicious regional food and has an impressive wine list. The management run trips to Ilha Deserta, and have a good restaurant there (see p154).

Cervejaria-Bar República (☎ 289 807 312; Avenida da República 40; mains €9; 🕒 closed lunch Sat & Sun) This small, homely place has an impressively large, tasty menu of steaks and grilled fish dishes. Customers applaud the *gambas* (prawns), *bife república* (house beef) and chocolate mousse.

Mesa dos Mouros (☎ 289 878 873; Largo da Sé 10; mains around €13; 🕒 Tue-Sun) With splendid outdoor, cathedral-shaded seating, this place offers a large choice of seafood, or unusual, hearty mains such as rabbit with chestnuts.

Other good choices with mains from €6 to €12:

Cinderela (☎ 289 803 456; Tr Marques da Silva 4) Tasty seafood, rice and sardines; outdoor tables.

Adega Dois Irmãos (☎ 289 823 337; Praça Ferreira de Almeida) Founded in 1925 and specialising in traditional seafood dishes.

Restaurante Sol e Jardim (☎ 289 820 030; Praça Ferreira de Almeida 22-23) Hung with fish nets and has a garden barbecue. There's live music Friday evening.

Drinking

Faro's student-driven nightlife clusters around Rua do Prior and surrounding alleys, with bars and clubs open most days till late; they save their best moves and grooves for the weekend.

Galeria Bar Património (Rua do Prior 19) This large, cool bar in deep colours has pool tables, some Moroccan décor, lots of gilt mirrors and low lighting. We wondered if it was a gay bar, judging by the all-male, moustachioed clues; it's not – the clues just don't (necessarily) mean the same thing in Portugal.

Taverna da Sé (Praça Afonso III 26; 🕒 10am-midnight Mon-Sat) Hung with bohemian paintings, this cool, small in-crowd *taverna* is in the old town. There are some outdoor tables in the square, and it serves snacks as well as drinks.

Dux (☎ 289 812 310; Rua do Prior 38) This warehouse club is one of the town's cooler venues, playing housey sounds.

Disco (☎ 289 823 628; Rua do Prior 23) Attracting a dressed-up crowd, this smart disco is pricier and more mainstream than Dux.

Entertainment

The 30,000-seat **Estádio Intermunicipal do Algarve** is a state-of-the-art stadium built for Euro2004, at São João da Venda, 8km northwest of Faro en route to Loulé. Here you can also watch Faro's own team, SC Farense, and Loulé's Louletano. Contact the turismo for transport information.

Small Italianate theatre **Teatro Lethes** (☎ 289 820 300; Rua Lethes) hosts drama, music and dance. Built in 1874, it was once the Jesuit Colégio de Santiago Maior and is now owned by the Portuguese Cruz Vermelha (Red Cross).

Shopping

Around the central Rua de Santo António are pedestrianised shopping streets, filled with clothes and souvenir shops.

Getting There & Away

AIR

Portugália and TAP provide multiple daily Lisbon–Faro flights (40 minutes) as well as Lisbon–Porto connections (45 minutes). For details of international services, see p466.

For flight inquiries call the **airport** (☎ 289 800 800). **TAP** has a central booking office (☎ 808 205 700; Rua Dr Francisco Gomes; 🕑 9am-5.30pm Mon-Fri).

BUS

From the **Eva bus station** (☎ 289 899 760; Avenida da República 5) express coaches run to Lisbon (€15, five hours, at least hourly, one night service); some services involve changing at Vale do Paraíso, north of Albufeira. Opposite the bus station, **Caima** (☎ 289 589 602; 🕑 7.45am-11.30 & 1.30-8.30pm Mon-Fri, to 8pm Sat, 1.30-8.30pm Sun), sells tickets for the Renex Lisbon express bus (€14, four to six daily).

Buses run to Vila Real de Santo António (€3.90, 1¾ hours, six to nine daily), via Tavira (€2.45, one hour, seven to 10 daily); and to Albufeira (€3.25, 1¼ hours, at least hourly), with some going on to Portimão (€3.90, 1½ hours, seven daily weekdays, two daily weekends) and Lagos (€4.10, 1¾ hours). For Sagres, change at Lagos. There are regular buses to Olhão (€1.30, 20 minutes, every 15 minutes weekdays) and buses to São Bras de Alportel (€1.75, 35 minutes, three to six daily) via Estói (15 minutes).

Eva services run to Seville in Spain (€12, five hours, two daily) via Huelva (€7, 3½ hours). For further details, see p469.

CAR

The most direct route from Lisbon to Faro takes about five hours. A nonmotorway alternative is the often traffic-clogged N125.

Major car-rental agencies are at the airport. Local heroes include **Auto Jardim** (☎ 291 524 023) and **Rentauto** (☎ 289 818 718).

Portugal's national auto club, **Automóvel Club de Portugal** (ACP; ☎ 289 898 950; www.acp.pt Rua Francisco Barreto 26A; 🕑 9am-1pm & 2-4.30pm Mon-Fri) has an office here.

Faro's easiest parking is in Largo de São Francisco.

TRAIN

There are trains from Lisbon (€14.50 to €16, 4½ to 5½ hours, including the Tejo ferry crossing to Barreiro, five daily). You can also get to Porto (6½ to 7½ hours) usually changing at Lisbon – there are three direct trains per week via Beja (50 minutes and Coimbra (5½ hours).

Trains also run daily to Albufeira (€5 30 minutes, eight daily); Vila Real de Santo António (1¼ hours) via Olhao (20 minutes); Lagos (€4.10, 1¾ hours, eight daily) and Loulé (€5, 20 minutes).

There's a train station **information kiosk** (🕑 9am-1pm & 2-6pm).

Getting Around

TO/FROM THE AIRPORT

From June to October an AeroBus shuttle runs into town via the bus station, Jardim Manuel Bívar and Hotel Dom Bernardo (hourly 9am to 8pm Wednesday to Monday), free to airline ticket holders.

Eva (☎ 289 899 740) bus Nos 14 and 16 make the trip (€1.20, 20 minutes, half-hourly in summer, every hour or two in winter) between the airport and the bus station to about 9pm weekdays and 8pm weekends in summer.

A taxi into town costs about €9 (€10.2 after 10pm and weekends).

BICYCLE

You can rent bikes (including tandems and kids' bikes) from **Megasport** (☎/fax 289 39

044; www.megasport.pt; Rua Ataíde de Oliveira 39C; per day from €9; 10am-1pm & 3-7.30pm Mon-Fri, 10am-1pm Sat). They offer free delivery between Faro and Albufeira. Bikes can be taken on the Algarve train line (if there's space in the goods van) for €2.

BOAT

April to September, **Tavares e Guerreiro** (917 634 813; 917 761 261; 919 310 405) operates ferries from the pier next to Arco da Porta Nova to Ilha de Farol on Ilha da Culatra and Ilha da Barreta. The turismo or kiosks on the pier have details.

From the same pier, **Animaris** (www.ilha-deserta.com; €20; four daily Jun-Sep) runs trips to Ilha da Barreta through the canals of the Ria Formosa.

TAXI

Ring for a **taxi** (289 895 795) or find one on Jardim Manuel Bívar.

SÃO BRÁS DE ALPORTEL

pop 10,030 / elevation 210m

This is a quiet provincial town, 17km north of Faro, but a world away from the coast. A hot spot in the 19th-century world of cork, São Brás today doesn't have many sights, but it is untouristy and close to the olive, carob, fig and almond-wooded Barrocal region: a lush, limestone area sandwiched between the mountains and the sea, which stretches all the way from the far west Cabo de São Vicente.

Orientation & Information

Buses stop in the central Largo de São Sebastião (often called the Largo).

Turismo (Largo de São Sebastião; 9.30am-1pm & 2-5.30pm Mon-Fri)

Sights & Activities

MUSEU ETNOGRÁFICO DO TRAJO ALGARVIO

An eccentric small **museum** (289 842 618; Rua Dr José Dias Sancho 61; admission €1; 10am-noon & 2-5pm Mon-Fri, 2-5pm Sat, Sun & holidays), 200m east of the Largo (along the Tavira road), this has a very rambling collection of local costumes, handicrafts and agricultural implements. It's housed in a former cork magnate's mansion, and there are displays in the stables of the town's once buoyant cork industry.

OLD TOWN

The peaceful old town is good for an amble. Follow Rua Gago Coutinho southwards from the Largo to the 16th-century **igreja matriz** (parish church), which has breezy views of orange groves and surrounding valleys from its doorstep. Nearby, below what was once a bishop's palace (now a nursery school), is a landscaped **municipal swimming pool** (289 841 243; 10am-7pm Jun-Sep) and children's playground.

Sleeping

These all include breakfast.

Estalagem Sequeira (/fax289 843 444; Rua Dr Evaristo Gago 9; s/d €25/45) This may look boring but it's a bargain. The spruce little rooms all have telephone, and downstairs is a restaurant adjoining a pleasant courtyard.

Residencial São Brás (fax 289 842 213; Rua Luís Bívar 27; s/d €25/45) This delightful guesthouse, around the corner from Sequeira (along the Loulé road), has halls decked with plants, antiques and azulejos. Rooms are quite old-fashioned but big (more modern ones are in a back annexe).

Pousada de São Brás (289 842 305; d Mon-Fri €134, Sat & Sun €144) On a panoramic hilltop site, with a pool with a view, this renovated 1950s whitewashed stack offers deluxe rooms with terraces.

Eating

While choice isn't spectacular, you've struck gold if you like grilled chicken.

Churrasqueira Afonso (289 842 635; Estrada de Tavira 134; mains from €4; lunch & dinner Fri-Wed) Five hundred metres east of the Largo (beyond the museum), this place does great, taste-packed grilled dishes.

Restaurante A Pérola (289 843 608; Estrada de Tavira 134; mains €6-14; Fri-Wed) Near Afonso, this is a popular place filled with men eating suitably macho mains such as…grills.

Getting There & Away

Buses run from Faro (€2.75 via Estói, 35 minutes, three to six daily) and Loulé (€2.10, 25 minutes, four daily).

MILREU & ESTÓI

The Roman ruins at Milreu and the nearby charming derelict rococo Estói palace and gardens make an ideal day trip from Faro, 10km to the south.

Buses run from Faro to Estói (€2.10, 20 minutes, 11 weekdays) continuing on to São Brás de Alportel.

Milreu

The ruins of a grand Roman villa are set in beautiful countryside at **Milreu** (adult/those under 25 €1.30/0.70; 9.30am-12.30pm & 2-6pm Tue-Sun Apr-Sep, to 5pm Oct-Mar) and provide a rare opportunity to glimpse something of Roman life here. The lst-century AD ruins show the characteristic form of a peristyle villa, with a gallery of columns around a courtyard. In the surrounding rooms geometric motifs and friezes of fish were found, but have now been removed for restoration. Tantalising glimpses of the villa's former glory include the **fish mosaics** in the bathing chambers to the west of the villa's courtyard.

The remains of the bathing rooms include the **apodyterium**, or changing-room (note the arched niches and benches for clothes and postbath massage), and the **frigidarium**, which had a marble basin to hold cold water for cooling off postbath. Other luxuries were underground heating and marble sculptures (now in Faro and Lagos museums).

To the right of the entrance is the site's **nymphaerium**, or water sanctuary, a temple devoted to the cult of water. The interior was once decorated with polychrome marble slabs and its exterior with fish mosaics. In the 3rd century the Visigoths converted it into a church, adding a baptismal font and a small mausoleum.

Information sheets (€1) in various languages are available. The bus from Faro to Estói stops outside.

Palácio do Visconde de Estói

About 800m north of Milreu, this enchanting, dishevelled palace is the 18th-century version of Milreu. It's a short walk from Estói's sleepy main square. Down a palm-shaded avenue, past abandoned stables and outhouses, are the palace's delightfully overgrown, wild **gardens** (admission free; 9am-12.30pm & 2-5.30pm Tue-Sat). To add to the romance are busts of poets, rococo sculpture, and gleaming 19th-century azulejos featuring naked mythological ladies prancing – their voluptuous stone cousins bask by an ornamental pool. The palace (closed to the public), all rosy rococo overexcitement, reminiscent of Queluz palace near Lisbon (p132), is slowly being transformed into a *pousada* (upmarket inn).

OLHÃO

pop 40,800

Olhão (ol-*yowng*), the Algarve's biggest fishing port, is an industrious town with a busy waterfront. Thronging with locals and tourists it's the place to go for excellent fish restaurants. The town is also a springboard for the sandy islands of the Parque Natural da Ria Formosa, where you can find fine beaches on Ilha da Culatra and Ilha da Armona. Otherwise, Olhão is a workaday sprawl devoted to all things aquatic, including a vast precinct of docks and fish-canning factories.

Saturday is the best day for the morning **market** (Avenida 5 de Outubro) that sells fish and vegetables.

Orientation

From the small **Eva bus terminal** (Rua General Humberto Delgado), turn right (west) or, from the train station, left (east) and it's a block to the town's main avenue, Avenida da República. Turn right and 300m down the Avenida you'll reach the parish church, at the edge of the central, pedestrianised shopping zone.

At the far side of this zone is waterfront Avenida 5 de Outubro. Here is the twin-domed market and to the left (east) is the town park, Jardim Patrão Joaquim Lopes.

Information

Centro de saúde (medical centre; ☎ 289 722 153; Rua Associacao Chasfa)

Espaço Internet (Rua Teófilo Braga; 10am-9pm Mon, to 10pm Tue-Fri, to 8pm Sat) Free Internet access.

Police (☎ 289 710 770; Avenida 5 Outubro 176)

Post office (☎ 289 700 600 Avenida da República) A block north of the parish church, opposite a bank with an ATM.

Turismo (☎ 289 713 936; Largo Sebastião Martins Mestre; 9.30am-7pm May-Sep, 9.30am-noon & 1-5.30pm Mon-Fri Oct-Apr) In the centre of the pedestrian zone; from the bus station bear right at the fork beside the parish church.

Sights & Activities

BAIRRO DOS PESCADORES

Just back from the market and park is the **Bairro dos Pescadores** (Fishermen's Quarter), a knot of whitewashed, cubical houses, often with tiled fronts and flat roofs. Narrow lanes thread through the *bairro* (neighbourhood), and there's a definite Moorish influence, probably a legacy of long trade links with North Africa. Similar houses are found in Fuzeta (10km east).

BEACHES

Fine beaches nearby, oversprinkled by holiday chalets but long and wide nevertheless, include **Praia de Farol** (the best); **Praia de Hangares** on Ilha da Culatra; and **Praia de Armona** and **Praia de Fuzeta** on Ilha da Armona. There are ferries to both islands from the pier just east of Jardim Patrão Joaquim Lopes (p160). You can also reach Armona from Fuzeta, and it is less busy, but narrower.

PARQUE NATURAL DA RIA FORMOSA

The Ria Formosa Natural Park is mostly a lagoon system stretching for 60km along the Algarve coastline from just west of Faro to Cacela Velha. It encloses a vast area of *sapal* (marsh), *salinas* (salt pans), creeks and dune islands. To the west there are also two freshwater lakes, at Ludo and Quinta do Lago, a vital habitat for migrating and nesting birds. You can see a huge variety of wetland birds here, along with ducks, shorebirds, gulls and terns. This is the favoured nesting place of the little tern and rare purple gallinule (right).

You'll also find some of the Algarve's quietest, biggest beaches on the sandbank *ilhas* of Faro, Culatra, Armona and Tavira (see p150 and p160).

The **park headquarters** (☎ 289 704 134; pnrf@icn.pt; Quinta de Marim; ⌚ 9am-5.30pm) is 3km east of Olhão and has an excellent visitor centre. Try the 2.4km nature trail across the dunes.

To get to Quinta de Marim take a Tavira bus from Olhão, get off at the Cepsa petrol station, and walk seaward for 1km or take a bus to the camp site (200m before the visitor centre).

Festivals & Events

The **Festival do Marisco**, a seafood festival with food and folk music, fills the Jardim Patrão Joaquim Lopes during the second week of August.

Sleeping

There are few places to stay and they fill up quickly in summer.

GOLF & GALLINULES

The purple gallinule (aka the purple swamp-hen or sultan chicken) is one of Europe's rarest and most nattily turned-out birds, a large violet-blue water creature with red bill and legs. In Portugal, it only nests in a patch of wetland spilling into the exclusive Quinta do Lago estate (where Madonna has a villa), at the western end of the Parque Natural da Ria Formosa, 12km west of Faro.

When the estate built a freshwater lake to irrigate its São Lourenço golf course, the fortunes of the gallinule – whose numbers had dwindled to two pairs – improved dramatically. The normally shy birds, now numbering about 60, often strut around before the first golfers arrive.

There's a hide overlooking the lake, about 1km along the estate's São Lourenço Nature Trail. To reach the start of the trail, where a wooden bridge crosses the lagoon, head for roundabout 6 from the estate's entrance.

Pensão Bela Vista (☎ 289 702 538; Rua Teófilio Braga 65; d/tr €45/55) A short walk west of the turismo, this friendly and efficient place is the best among the *pensões*. It is clean and brightly tiled with a flower-filled courtyard and a warm welcome.

Pensão Bicuar (☎ 289 703 146; Rua Vasco da Gama 5; s/d €25/35) Opposite Alojamentos Vasco da Gama, this place offers trim rooms with balcony; it was being renovated at the time of research. Rua Vasco da Gama is to the left (east) of the parish church.

Alojamentos Vasco da Gama (☎ 289 703 146; Rua Vasco da Gama; s/d with shared bathroom €25/35) If Bicuar is still being renovated, give this one a try.

Camping Olhão (☎ 289 700 300; www.sbsi.pt; adult/tent/car €3.60/2.30/2.50, caravan/family bungalow €20/25; ♿) At this well-equipped, shady 800-site camp site, 2km east of Olhão and 800m off the N125, there are disabled facilities, a playground, bar and restaurant. In summer a bus runs from Jardim Patrão Joaquim Lopes.

Parque de Campismo de Fuzeta (☎ 289 793 459; fax 289 793 285; adult/tent/car €2.30/2/3.10; ⌚ year-round) This small, shady municipal site, is on the waterfront in peaceful Fuzeta, about

10km east of Olhão. You can go canoeing from the beach, and there are also ferries to the offshore islands.

Eating

Avenida 5 de Outubro is lined with excellent seafood restaurants.

Cervejaria Ria Formosa (☎ 289 702 504; Avenida 5 de Outubro 14; mains €4.75-12) On the other side of Avenida 5 de Outubro, next to the river and the small park, this popular restaurant has awning-shaded outdoor tables and tasty seafood and rice dishes.

Livramento (☎ 289 706 763; Avenida 5 de Outubro; mains €5-8.50) Opposite Cervejaria Ria Formosa, this intimate, well-known place, specialising in shellfish and decorated by fishing nets and lobster pots, is owned by and named after a famous Portuguese journalist.

Getting There & Away

BUS

Eva express buses run to Lisbon (€15, four to five hours, four to five daily), as do **Renex** (Avenida da República 101).

Buses run frequently from Faro (€1.30, 20 minutes), some continuing to the waterfront at Bairro dos Pescadores, and from Tavira (€1.85, 40 minutes, hourly).

TRAIN

There are also regular trains from Faro (10 minutes, every two hours). The other way, trains go to Fuzeta (10 minutes) and Tavira (30 minutes).

Getting Around

Ferries run out to the *ilhas* from the pier at the eastern end of Jardim Patrão Joaquim Lopes. Boats run to Ilha da Armona (€2 return, 30 minutes, at least nine daily June to mid-September, hourly July and August, four daily mid-September to May); the last trip back from Armona in July and August leaves at 8.30pm.

Boats also go to Ilha da Culatra (€2, 30 minutes) and Praia de Farol (€2.50, one hour), with six daily from June to September and four daily mid-September to May.

Ferries also run from Fuzeta to the offshore islands.

You can hire bikes from **Megasport** (☎ 289 802 136; Rua Ataide de Oliveira 39).

TAVIRA

pop 25,000

The broad mirror of the Rio Gilão runs through Tavira's centre, reflecting elegant houses on either side, and inspiring tourist brochures to call it the Venice of the Algarve. True: it's more like Venice than anywhere else on the Algarve, but this isn't difficult. Topped by castle ruins and packed with 16th- to 18th-century buildings and 37 churches, Tavira is the most genteel town on the Algarve. It's 3km from the coast, and near the beautiful, unspoilt beaches of Ilha de Tavira.

History

The Roman settlement of Balsa was just down the road, near Santa Luzia (3km west). The seven-arched bridge the Romans built at Tavira (then called Tabira) was an important link in the route between Baesuris (Castro Marim) and Ossonoba (Faro).

In the 8th century, the Moors occupied Tavira. They built the castle (probably on the site of a Roman fortress) and two mosques. In 1242 Dom Paio Peres Correia reconquered the town. Those Moors who remained were segregated into the *mouraria* (Moorish quarter) outside the town walls.

As the port closest to the Moroccan coast, it became important during the Age of Discoveries (p26), serving as a base for Portuguese expeditions to North Africa, supplying provisions (especially salt, wine and dried fish) and providing a hospital. Its maritime trade also expanded, with exports of salted fish, almonds, figs and wine to northern Europe. By 1520 it had become the Algarve's most populated settlement and was raised to the rank of city.

Decline began in the early 17th century when the North African campaign was abandoned and the Rio Gilão became so silted up that large boats couldn't enter the port. As if economic devastation wasn't enough, in 1645 came the plague, followed by the 1755 earthquake.

After briefly producing carpets in the late 18th century, Tavira found a more stable income in its tuna-fishing and canning industry, although this too declined in the 1950s when the tuna shoals sensibly moved elsewhere. Today, tourists have taken the place of fish as the biggest money-earners.

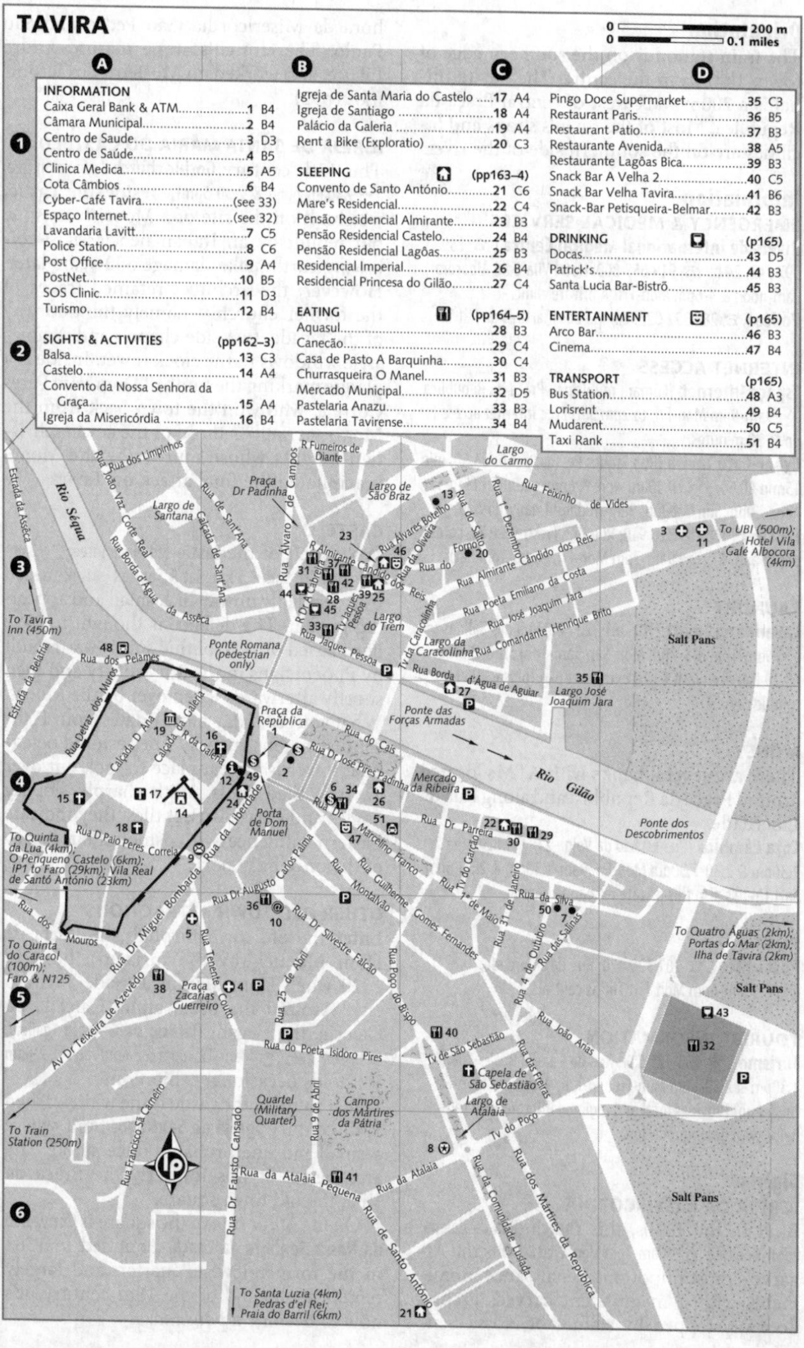

TAVIRA
0 200 m
0 0.1 miles
A
B
C
D
1
2
3
4
5
6
INFORMATION
Caixa Geral Bank & ATM 1 B4
Câmara Municipal 2 B4
Centro de Saude 3 D3
Centro de Saúde 4 B5
Clinica Medica 5 A5
Cota Câmbios 6 B4
Cyber-Café Tavira (see 33)
Espaço Internet (see 32)
Lavandaria Lavitt 7 C5
Police Station 8 C6
Post Office 9 A4
PostNet 10 B5
SOS Clinic 11 D3
Turismo 12 B4
SIGHTS & ACTIVITIES (pp162–3)
Balsa 13 C3
Castelo 14 A4
Convento da Nossa Senhora da Graça 15 A4
Igreja da Misericórdia 16 B4
Igreja de Santa Maria do Castelo 17 A4
Igreja de Santiago 18 A4
Palácio da Galeria 19 A4
Rent a Bike (Exploratio) 20 C3
SLEEPING (pp163–4)
Convento de Santo António 21 C6
Mare's Residencial 22 C4
Pensão Residencial Almirante 23 B3
Pensão Residencial Castelo 24 B4
Pensão Residencial Lagôas 25 B3
Residencial Imperial 26 B4
Residencial Princesa do Gilão 27 C4
EATING (pp164–5)
Aquasul 28 B3
Canecão 29 C4
Casa de Pasto A Barquinha 30 C4
Churrasqueira O Manel 31 B3
Mercado Municipal 32 D5
Pastelaria Anazu 33 B3
Pastelaria Tavirense 34 B4
Pingo Doce Supermarket 35 C3
Restaurant Paris 36 B5
Restaurant Patio 37 B3
Restaurante Avenida 38 A5
Restaurante Lagôas Bica 39 B3
Snack Bar A Velha 2 40 C5
Snack Bar Velha Tavira 41 B6
Snack-Bar Petisqueira-Belmar 42 B3
DRINKING (p165)
Docas 43 D5
Patrick's 44 B3
Santa Lucia Bar-Bistrõ 45 B3
ENTERTAINMENT (p165)
Arco Bar 46 B3
Cinema 47 B4
TRANSPORT (p165)
Bus Station 48 A3
Lorisrent 49 B4
Mudarent 50 C5
Taxi Rank 51 B4
Rio Séqua
Rio Gilão
Estrada da Assêca
Rua dos Limpinhos
Rua João Vaz Corte Real
Largo de Santana
Calçada de Sant'Ana
Rua de Sant'Ana
Rua Borda d'Água da Assêca
Praça Dr Padinha
Rua Álvaro de Campos
R Fumeiros de Diante
Largo de São Braz
Largo do Carmo
Rua Feixinho de Vides
Rua do Salto
Rua 1° Dezembro
Rua Álvares Botelho
Rua da Oliveira
R Almirante Cândido dos Reis
Rua Almirante Cândido dos Reis
Rua do Forno
Rua Poeta Emiliano da Costa
Rua José Joaquim Jara
Rua Comandante Henrique Brito
R Dr A Cabreira
Tv Jaques Pessoa
Rua Jaques Pessoa
Largo do Trem
Tv da Caracolinha
Largo da Caracolinha
Rua Borda d'Água de Aguiar
Largo José Joaquim Jara
To UBI (500m); Hotel Vila Galé Albocora (4km)
To Tavira Inn (450m)
Estrada da Belafria
Rua dos Pelames
Ponte Romana (pedestrian only)
Ponte das Forças Armadas
Salt Pans
Rua Detraz dos Muros
Calçada D Ana
Calçada da Galeria
R da Galeria
Praça da República
Rua do Cais
Rua Dr José Pires Padinha
Mercado da Ribeira
Rua da Liberdade
Porta de Dom Manuel
Rua Dr Marcelino Franco
Rua Dr Parreira
Tv do Garção
Ponte dos Descobrimentos
To Quinta da Lua (4km); O Penqueno Castelo (6km); IP1 to Faro (29km); Vila Real de Santó António (23km)
Rua D Paio Peres Correia
Rua Dr Miguel Bombarda
Rua Dr Augusto Carlos Palma
Rua Montalvão
Rua Guilherme Gomes Fernandes
Rua 1° de Maio
Rua 31 de Janeiro
Rua da Silva
Rua das Salinas
Rua 4 de Outubro
Rua dos Mouros
To Quatro Águas (2km); Portas do Mar (2km); Ilha de Tavira (2km)
To Quinta do Caracol (100m); Faro & N125
Rua Dr Silvestre Falcão
Rua Poço do Bispo
Rua Tenente Couto
Praça Zacarias Guerreiro
Rua 25 de Abril
Av Dr Teixeira de Azevêdo
Rua João Arias
Tv de São Sebastião
Rua das Freiras
Capela de São Sebastião
Rua do Poeta Isidoro Pires
Quartel (Military Quarter)
Campo dos Mártires da Pátria
Rua 9 de Abril
Largo de Atalaia
Tv do Poço
To Train Station (250m)
Rua Francisco Sá Carneiro
Rua Dr Fausto Cansado
Rua da Atalaia Pequena
Rua da Atalaia
Rua da Comunidade Lusíada
Rua dos Mártires da República
Rua de Santo António
To Santa Luzia (4km) Pedras d'el Rei; Praia do Barril (6km)

Orientation

The train station is on the southern edge of town, 1km from the centre. The bus terminal is a 200m walk west of central Praça da República. Most of the town's shops and facilities are on the southern side of the river.

Information

EMERGENCY & MEDICAL SERVICES

Riverside International Medical Centre (☎ 289 997 742, 24 hr ☎ 919 657 860; Hotel Vila Galé Albacora; 9am-noon & 4-6pm Mon-Fri) A private clinic.
Police (☎ 281 322 022; Campo dos Mártires da Pátria)

INTERNET ACCESS

Espaço Internet (Câmara municipal, Praça da Républica; 9am-9pm Mon-Fri, to 2pm Sat) Free Internet access for up to 30 minutes.
Cyber-Café Tavira (Rua Jaques Pessoa; per hr €3.50, min 15min €0.60; 10.30am-4pm & 6pm-midnight Mon-Sat, noon-10pm Sun Oct-Jun, 9am-midnight daily Jul-Sep)
PostNet (☎ 281 320 910; Rua Dr Silvestre Falcão, Lote 6; per 15min €1; 9am-7pm Mon-Fri, 10am-1pm Sat)

LAUNDRY

Lavandaria Lavitt (☎ 281 326 776; Rua das Salinas 6; 9am-1pm & 3-7pm Mon-Sat, 9am-1pm Sun) Charges €3.20 (service wash €3.20 extra) per 6kg (plus €3.20 for tumble dry).

MONEY

There are several banks with ATMs located around Praça da República and along Rua da Liberdade.
Cota Câmbios (Rua Estácio da Veiga 21; 8.30am-1.30pm & 2.30-7.30pm Mon-Fri, 9am-1.30pm & 2.30-6pm Sat) There's also this private exchange bureau.

POST

Post office (☎ 281 320 420; Rua da Liberdade; 8.30am-6pm Mon-Fri) This is central.

TOURIST INFORMATION

Turismo (☎ 281 322 511; Rua da Galeria 9; 10am-1.30pm & 2.30-6pm Mon-Fri Sep-Jun; 9am-7pm Mon-Fri Jul & Aug) Provides local and regional information, and helps with accommodation.

Sights

IGREJA DA MISERICÓRDIA

Built in the 1540s, this **church** (Rua da Galeria; admission free; 10am-1pm Mon, Wed & Fri) is the Algarve's most important Renaissance monument, with a magnificent carved, arched doorway topped by statues of Nossa Senhora da Misericórdia, São Pedro and São Paulo. The church's stone mason, André Pilarte, also worked on Mosteiro dos Jerónimos (p92).

IGREJA DE SANTA MARIA DO CASTELO

This 13th-century **Gothic church** (admission free; 9.30am-noon & 2.30-5pm), beside the castle, was built on the site of a Moorish mosque but rebuilt by an Italian neoclassicist following earthquake damage 500 years later. However, the architect retained traces of the former church – namely the doorway of the façade, two side chapels and Arabic-style windows in the clock tower. Inside is a plaque marking the tomb of Dom Paio Peres Correia, who won the town back from the Moors, as well as those of the seven Christian knights whose murder by the Moors precipitated the final attack on Tavira.

CASTELO

What's left of the **castle** (admission free; 8am-5pm Mon-Fri, 9am-5.30pm Sat & Sun) is surrounded by a decidedly unwar-like, small and appealing garden. The defence is thought to have been based on a Neolithic site; it was rebuilt by Phoenicians in the 8th century and then shortly afterwards taken over by the Moors. What you see today mostly dates from 17th-century reconstruction. The restored octagonal tower is a great place to look out over Tavira's tiled roofs. With sharply sloping angles and curved russet tiles, they indicate Eastern influence – a cosmopolitan legacy of the once busy port.

OTHER OLD TOWN ATTRACTIONS

Enter the old town through the Porta de Dom Manuel (by the turismo), built in 1520 when Dom Manuel I made Tavira a city. Around the back, along Calçada da Galeria, the elegant **Palácio da Galeria** (gallery; admission free; 10am-12.30pm & 2-6pm Tue-Fri, 2-6pm Sat) holds occasional exhibitions.

Just south of the castle is the whitewashed 17th-century **Igreja de Santiago**, built where a small mosque probably once stood. The area beside it was formerly the Praça da Vila, the old town square.

On the other side of the square is **Convento da Nossa Senhora da Graça**. Founded in 1568 in the former Jewish quarter, and largely rebuilt at the end of the 18th century, it's now to become a *pousada*.

Downhill from here is the **Largo da Porta do Postigo**, at the site of another old town gate and the town's Moorish quarter.

PONTE ROMANA

This seven-arched **bridge** that loops away from the Praça da República may have predated the Romans, but is so named because it linked the Roman road from Castro Marim to Tavira. The structure you see now owes its design to a 17th-century reconstruction. The latest touch-up job was in 1989, after floods knocked down one of its pillars.

PRAÇA DA REPÚBLICA

For centuries, this sociable town **square** on the riverfront served as promenade and marketplace, where slaves were traded along with less ignominious commodities such as fish and fruit. The market moved to Jardim do Coreto in 1887 to improve hygiene, only moving again in 2000 to a new riverside location. A colourful affair, the *mercado municpal* is held on Monday to Saturday mornings.

SALT PANS & QUATRO ÁGUAS

You can walk 2km east along the river, past the fascinating, snow-like **salt pans** to **Quatro Águas**. The salt pans produce tiptop table salt and in summer attract feeding birds, including flamingos. Besides being the jumping-off point for Ilha de Tavira, the seaside hub of Quatro Águas has a couple of seafood restaurants and a former tuna-canning factory – now a luxury hotel, across the river.

For information on buses to Quatro Águas, see p166.

Tours

Balsa (☎ 281 322 882; Rua Álvares Botelho 51; 🕑 daily) This ceramics shop offers bike rental and four-hour guided trips around Tavira or Ria Formosa Natural Park for €10.

Rent a Bike (Exploratio; ☎ /fax 281 321 973; exploratio@netc.pt; Rua do Forno 33) Offers four-hour trips (€25 per person, including mountain-bike hire), in and around Tavira and the Parque Natural da Ria Formosa. They can also arrange half-day walking tours.

Riosul (☎ 281 510 201; Monte Gordo) Has a pick-up point in Tavira for its jeep tours and Rio Guadiana cruises.

Festivals & Events

You can't go wrong with free sardines, and that's what you get at Tavira's biggest festival, the **Festa de Cidade**, held on 23 to 24 June. Myrtle and paper flowers decorate the streets, and the dancing and festivities carry on till late.

Sleeping

BUDGET

The turismo can recommend *quartos* (private rooms; doubles €25 to €35) and also has details of self-catering alternatives.

Pensão Residencial Lagôas (☎ 281 322 252; Rua Almirante Cândido dos Reis 24; s/d with shared bathroom €18/28, d with bathroom €38-45) A long-standing favourite, this place has bright rooms around a little courtyard decorated with plants; there are good views from a roof terrace.

Pensão Residencial Almirante (☎ 281 322 163; Rua Almirante Cândido dos Reis 51; d with shared bathroom from €25) Just across the road, this is a cosy family house full of clutter, with just six charming, old-fashioned rooms.

Residencial Princesa do Gilão (☎ /fax 281 325 171; Rua Borda d'Água de Aguiar 10; s/d €40/50) This eye-catching, modern, riverside place is laid-back and friendly. Go for a room with a small balcony overlooking the river.

Residencial Imperial (☎ 282 322 234; Rua Dr José Pires Padinha 24; s/d with breakfast €35/50) This is a cosy, efficient *residencial* with a family atmosphere and well-kept smallish rooms with cheery yellow curtains.

Ilha de Tavira (☎ 281 321 709; www.campingtavira.com; camp site per person/2 people plus tent Mon-Fri €8/11, Sat & Sun €15/20 🕑 Apr-Sep) With a great location on Ilha de Tavira (see p165), a flip-flop hop from the island's endless beach, this is the nearest camp site. It gets crowded and noisy in the high season (mid-June to mid-September). There's no car access.

MID-RANGE & TOP END

Mare's Residencial (☎ 281 325 815; maresresidencial@mail.telepac.pt; Rua Dr José Pires Padinha 134; d with breakfast €50) This attractive 24-room riverside place has dapper, snug rooms with phone, satellite TV, tiled bathrooms and small balconies overlooking the river.

Pensão Residencial Castelo (☎ 281 320 790; fax 281 320 799; Rua da Liberdade 22; s/d with breakfast €30/45, apartments with breakfast €60) This is a fine option, with smart rooms, some with castle views. There are also eight spacious, modern apartments. It has wheelchair access.

Tavira Inn (Casa do Rio; ☎ /fax 281 326 578, 917 356 623; www.tavira-inn.com; Rua Chefe António Afonso 39;

d €80, min 2 nights; Apr-Sep;) In a charming riverside spot, this place has original décor created by the owner's artist daughter, a small saltwater swimming pool and a zinging-yellow jazz bar. Children are not accepted.

Convento de Santo António (281 321 573; Rua de Santo António; r/ste from €140/225;) In an unprepossessing though quite central area, this amazing former convent has been owned by the same family since 1887. It's another world once you step inside the high walls. Antique-filled rooms lead off corridors that end in elaborate shrines. Outside, orange, apricot, lemon and banana trees shade the grounds and there is a pool with a view. Breakfast is in the cloister. Prices are usually discounted if you stay over three nights.

Quinta do Caracol (281 322 475; São Pedro; d with breakfast €75;) This 17th-century 'farmhouse of the snail' has a large, exotic garden. Its seven rooms have been converted into separate quarters with typical Algarve furnishings (all but one with a kitchenette).

Quinta da Lua (/fax 281 961 070; www.seeloud.com/go/quintadalua; Bernardinheiro, Sto Estevão; d/ste with breakfast €110/130) Set among orange groves 4km northwest of Tavira, this peaceful place has eight bright-white, airy, serene rooms with CD players. There's a large greenery-surrounded, saltwater swimming pool, hammocks in the garden and very good food.

O Pequeno Castelo (281 961 692; www.pequenocastelo.com; Poço das Bruxas, Santo Estevão; d with shared bathroom/apt per wk €360/550;) Surrounded by scenic walking country, the German-run Little Castle B&B is 6km west of Tavira. Homely rooms have a balcony; there is one apartment too.

Hotel Vila Galé Albacora (281 380 800; www.vilagale.pt; Quatro Águas; s/tw €90/112;) Four kilometres east, overlooking Ilha de Tavira, this mustard-coloured, four-star 162-room establishment was converted from a tuna-canning factory. It's an isolated, dramatic, low-rise structure with a health club. Rooms have balconies and there's disabled access. The hotel runs a private boat service to Ilha da Tavira.

Eating

BUDGET

Snack Bar A Velha 2 (281 323 661; Campo dos Martires da Pátria 1; meals €7.50; lunch & dinner Mon-Sat) Plastered with Benfica football team paraphernalia this buzzes with locals because of its bargain grilled daily specials, which come with salad and potatoes.

Snack Bar Velha Tavira (918 261 897; Rua da Atalaia Pequena; meal €7; lunch daily, dinner Jun-Sep only) Another local favourite, in an appealing cobble-floored building with arched windows, this place offers barbecued fish or meat in hefty portions.

Restaurante Lagôas Bica (281 323 843; Rua Almirante Cândido dos Reis 24; mains €5-11; lunch & dinner) Deservedly popular, here you can eat splendid food, such as fresh grilled fish (sole with orange is recommended), and down cheap bottles of decent Borba wine.

Restaurante Avenida (281 321 113; Avenida Dr Teixeira de Azevêdo; mains €4-10; lunch & dinner Wed-Mon) A local favourite with a long, long menu of fish and meat dishes.

Cafés in town include the popular hangout **Pastelaria Anazu** (Rua Jaques Pessoa; 8am-11pm Mon-Sat, 8am-8pm Sun), with outdoor tables making the most of its irresistible riverside location, and **Pastelaria Tavirense** (281 323 451; Rua Dr Marcelino Franco 17; 8am-midnight), which serves the town's scrummiest pastries.

There's a huge modern **mercado municipal** (most stalls morning only) on the eastern edge of town, and a **Pingo Doce Supermarket** across the river.

You can also try:

Churrasqueira O Manel (281 323 343; Rua Dr António Cabreira 39; mains €5-8) Great *frango no churrasco* (grilled chicken), plus takeaway.

Snack-Bar Petisqueira-Belmar (281 324 995; Rua Almirante Cândido dos Reis 16; mains €6; lunch & dinner) Cheerful, traditional and tiled, with Portuguese dishes.

MID-RANGE & TOP-END

Casa de Pasto A Barquinha (281 322 843; Rua Dr José Pires Padinha 142; mains €5-10) By the river, this restaurant has friendly service, fresh grilled fish, good prawns in garlic and unusually robust salads.

Restaurante Patio (281 323 008; Rua Dr António Cabreira 30; mains €8-12.25; lunch & dinner Mon-Sat) This fishing net–filled restaurant is cosy and recommended – best is the terrace. Try goat's cheese and honey, or tuck into cuttlefish with sweet potatoes and clams, along with excellent Portuguese wines. Silence that sweet tooth with stuffed figs.

Restaurante Paris (281 324 916; Avenida Dr Silvestre Falcão; mains €5-10; lunch & dinner Wed-Mon) This restaurant has a relaxing, low-key atmosphere and lots of excellently cooked local specialities as well as vegetarian dishes.

Aquasul (☎ 281 325 166; Rua Dr Augusto da Silva Carvalho 11; €7.50-9; 🕑 dinner Tue-Sun) With Gaudiesque broken-china tiling, Aquasul is an unusual place with fine French mains as well as pasta, pizza and home-made ice cream.

Quatro Águas (☎ 281 325 329; Quatro Águas; mains €8-15; 🕑 lunch & dinner Tue-Thu Feb-Dec) For seafood splurges, head to this renowned restaurant, which serves delicious seafood, fish and meat dishes; the octopus with bean rice is justly famous. You can eat inside or out.

Portas do Mar (☎ 281 321 255; Quatro Águas; mains €6-14) Next to Quatro Águas, this place is also good and has a river-view terrace; try tasty shrimp curry or their speciality, spaghetti with shrimp.

Canecão (☎ 281 326 278; Rua Dr José Pires Padinha 162; mains €6-11) Also with an excellent riverside situation, Canecão claims to serve the world's best *cataplanas* (types of stew). That's debatable, but try the octopus and sweet potato – it may look like alien stew but tastes quite good.

Entertainment

The main bar area in town is along Rua Almirante Cândido dos Reis and Rua Poeta Emiliano da Costa, which have relaxing, welcoming places.

Arco Bar (Rua Almirante Cândido dos Reis 67; 🕑 Tue-Sun) Run by a Portuguese-German couple, this small place attracts a mix of Portuguese and expats with its laid-back atmosphere and multicultural music.

Patrick's (Rua Dr António Cabreira 25; 🕑 from 6pm Mon-Sat) This is a cosy expat-run bar with a few outside tables on the narrow cobbled street. It serves hearty British pub grub.

Santa Lucia Bar-Bistrõ (Rua Dr António Cabreira 18) On the same pedestrianised street, Santa Lucia is lively, little and serves tapas, with a few outside tables and cheery tunes.

For a higher-velocity night, the **Docas**, an extension of the *mercado municipal,* hosts a row of newer, dancier, preclub bars that play music from hands-in-the-air house to African. The clientele is young and it is peaceful, not surprising given the police presence. The area buzzes at its highest pitch in July and August, and reduces to a barely perceptible whirr from November to March.

After that, head to **UBI** (Rua Almirante Cândido dos Reis; 🕑 midnight-6am Tue-Sun May-Sep, Sat & Sun Nov-Apr), the only nightclub, in a former factory, with an open-air bar and music until 5am.

Getting There & Around

Frequent buses (☎ 281 322 546) go to Faro (€2.45, one hour, 12/7 daily weekdays/weekends), via Olhão, and Vila Real (€2.35, 40 minutes). Buses also go to Lisbon (€15, five hours) and Huelva (Spain; €6, two hours, twice daily), with connections to Seville (€11, three hours).

Trains run daily to Faro (€1.80, 40 minutes, 12 daily) and Vila Real (€1.40, 35 minutes). A tourist train starts from Praça da Republica and visits the main sights (€2.50, 40 minutes, hourly 10am to 7pm September to May, to 8pm in June and to midnight in July and August).

Cheap local car-rental agencies include **Mudarent** (☎ 281 326 815; Rua da Silva 18D). **Lorisrent** (☎ 281 325 203, 964 079 233; Rua da Galeria 9A; 🕑 9.30am-1.30pm & 3-6.30pm Mon-Sat) charges €4/15 per day for a mountain bike/scooter; **Rent a Bike** (bikes €6 per day) and **Balsa** (p163) charge from €5/8/18 per mountain bike/tandem/scooter.

Taxis (☎ 281 321 544, 917 220 456) gather near the cinema on Rua Dr Marcelino Franco.

AROUND TAVIRA

Ilha de Tavira

Sandy islands stretch along the coast from Cacela Velha to just west of Faro, and this is one of the finest. They're all part of the Parque Natural da Ria Formosa. The huge beach at this island's eastern end, opposite Tavira, has water sports, a camp site (p163) and café-restaurants, including the world music–playing **Sunshine Bar** (☎ 963 696 561; 🕑 Tue-Sun). Off-season, it feels wonderfully remote and empty, but during July and August it's busy. Don't forget sunscreen.

West along the island is **Praia do Barril**, accessible by a miniature train that trundles over the mud flats from **Pedras d'el Rei**, a resort 4km southwest of Tavira. There are some eateries where the shuttle train stops, then sand, sand, sand as far as the eye can see.

GETTING THERE & AWAY

Ferries make the five-minute hop to the *ilha* (€1 return, from 9am to 7pm) from Quatro Águas, 2km southeast of Tavira. Times are subject to change – ask the crew when the last one runs! In July and August they usually run till midnight. From July to mid-September a boat normally runs direct from Tavira – ask at the turismo for details.

In addition, **Áqua-Taxis** (☎ 964 515 073, 917 035 207) operates 24 hours a day from July to mid-September, and until midnight May to June. The fare from Quatro Águas/Tavira to the island is €15 for six people.

A bus goes to Quatro Águas from the Tavira bus terminal July to mid-September (€0.55, nine daily). A taxi to Quatro Águas costs about €4. For Praia do Barril, take a bus from Tavira to Pedras d'el Rei (€1.40, 10 minutes, four daily weekdays), from where the little train runs regularly to the beach March to September. Off-season the timetable depends on the operating company's mood.

Cacela Velha

Enchanting, small and cobbled, Cacela Velha is a huddle of whitewashed cottages edged with bright borders, and has a pocket-sized fort, orange and olive groves and gardens blazing with colour. It's 12km east of Tavira, above a gorgeous stretch of sea, with one café-restaurant, splendid views and a meandering path down to the long, white beach.

GETTING THERE & AWAY

There's no direct bus from Tavira, but Cacela Velha is only 1km south of the N125 (2km before Vila Nova de Cacela; €1.20), which is on the Faro-Vila Real de Santo António bus route. Coming from Faro, there are two signposted turn-offs to Cacela Velha; the second is more direct.

VILA REAL DE SANTO ANTÓNIO

pop 18,000

Vila Real de Santo António has a striking riverside position, and the thriving, commercial feel of a port. The town is architecturally impressive; in five months in 1774, the Marquês de Pombal stamped the town with his hallmark gleaming grid-pattern of streets (like Lisbon's Baixa district) after the town was destroyed by floods. From here you can launch off on boat or biking trips along the Rio Guadiana (below).

Strange that Spain is just across the river, within sight but with an hour's time difference.

Orientation & Information

The seafront Avenida da República is one of the town's two main thoroughfares; the other is the pedestrianised Rua Teofílio de Braga, which leads straight from the seafront and past the main square, Praça Marquês de Pombal.

Bus station (Avenida da República) Beyond the ferry terminal, 100m east of Rua Teofílio de Braga.

Espaço Internet (free Internet access) Opposite the turismo.

MESSING ABOUT ON THE GUADIANA

You can cruise between Portugal and Spain by taking a boat along the enchanting, slow-flowing Rio Guadiana, which serves as the border for some 50km. **Riosul** (☎ 281 510 200; Monte Gordo), runs small-scale trips from Vila Real de Santo António to Foz de Odeleite at least four times weekly in summer and twice-weekly the rest of the year. The trips cost €41/20 per adult/child, including lunch and a stop for a swim.

Turismar (☎ 281 956 634, 968 831 553; adult/child aged 3 to 10 €30/15, incl lunch) has a large boat that cruises further north to Alcoutim, three times weekly between April and October, and even on to Pomarâo. Book a day ahead; tickets are available at its kiosk by the Vila Real ferry pier. They can also arrange sea trips.

Lands – Turismo na Natureza (☎ 289 817 466; www.lands.pt; Rua Bento de Jesus Caraça 22), based in Montenegro, about 2km from Faro, runs kayak tours from Foz de Odeleite; they cost €40 for a day including lunch, for groups with a maximum of 10 people. They also arrange walks around the Rio Guadiana, or bird spotting in the Parque Natural da Ria Formosa (adult/child €20/10).

The quiet back road along the river from Foz de Odeleite to Alcoutim (14km) is also popular with bikers. Along this scenic route are several villages worth visiting, including Álamo, with its Roman dam, and Guerreiros do Rio, with its small **Museu do Rio** (River Museum; ☎ 281 547 380; admission €1; 9am-12.30pm & 2-5.30pm Tue-Sat) about traditional river life.

You can rent bikes in Alcoutim or Monte Gordo (opposite). Contact operators in advance if you want to take your bike on the boat.

Train station About 400m northeast of the centre.
Turismo (☎ 281 542 100; Rua Teofílio de Braga; 🕑 10am-1.30pm & 2.30-6pm Mon-Fri Apr-Oct, 9.30am-1pm & 2-5.30pm Mon-Fri Nov-Mar) Housed in the Centro Cultural António Aleixo, a former market hall.

Sleeping

Villa Marques (☎ 281 530 420; Rua Dr José Barão; s/d €30/45) In a renovated mansion a few streets back from the waterfront, near the bus station, this place has 13 spic-and-span rooms.

Residência Matos Pereira (☎ 281 543 325; Rua Dr Sousa Martins 57; s/d €30/40) This friendly place near the turismo has quite frilly, small rooms and a family feel. There's a sunny terrace.

Residência Baixa Mar (☎ 281 543 511; Rua Teofílio de Braga 3; s/d €30/40) Though less homely than Matos Pereira, this decent guesthouse offers small rooms, some with views, and some opening onto a tiny, viewless terrace.

Parque de campismo (☎ 281 510 970; adult/tent/car €4.50/1.80/3) Frequent buses go to this mammoth municipal site outside built-up Monte Gordo, 3km west of town. It has lots of shade and neighbours the beach but is jam-packed in July and August. There are disabled facilities, a restaurant and bar.

Eating

Snack-Bar Cuca (☎ 281 513 625; Rua Dr Sousa Martins 64; mains €5-10; 🕑 lunch & dinner) Small, friendly and popular for its fresh fish, this snack bar has outside tables on the pedestrianised street.

Snack-Bar Mira (☎ 281 544 773; Rua da Princesa 59; mains €4-7; 🕑 lunch & dinner) This cheery, small place with blue-checked tablecloths has good-value daily dishes and is a winner with the locals.

Associacão Naval do Guadiano (☎ 281 513 085; Avenida da República; mains €5-10; 🕑 lunch & dinner Wed-Mon) A big blue waterfront building, this place has a terrace, views over the river and gardens, and good seafood.

Also worth tucking into, with mains around €7 to 10:

Caves do Guadiana (☎ 281 544 498; Avenida da República 90) Long-standing fave on the waterfront drag.
Pizza II (☎ 281 543 157; Rua Brazil 44) Tasty regional Algarvian cuisine.

Getting There & Away

BUS

Buses (☎ 281 511 807) run daily to Tavira (€2.35, 30 to 45 minutes, 10 to 13 daily) via Faro (€3.90, 1½ hours), some going on to Lisbon (€15, 4¾ hours, four daily). Regular buses go to Monte Gordo (€1.40, 10 minutes, six to eight daily) and Huelva (Spain; €5, 2½ hours, two daily), with connections on to Seville (€10 total from Vila Real de Santo António, 3½ hours).

BOAT

Ferries cross the river border every 40 minutes to whitewashed Ayamonte; buy tickets from the waterfront office (€1.10/4/0.60 per person/car/bike, 8.20am to 7pm).

TRAIN

Trains to Lagos (€5.50, 3½ hours, eight daily) require changes at Faro and/or Tunes. Trains run regularly to Faro (€3.30, 1¼ hours, 12 daily).

Getting Around

The nearest place to rent bikes is in Monte Gordo, from **Riosul** (☎ 281 510 201). Bikes can be delivered if you call in advance.

NOW YOU SEE ME, NOW YOU DON'T...

The Mediterranean chameleon *(Chamaeleo chamaeleon)* is a bizarre 25cm-long reptile with independently moving eyes, a tongue longer than its body and skin that mimics its environment. It only started creeping around southern Portugal about 75 years ago, and is the only chameleon found in Europe, its habitat limited to Crete and the Iberian Peninsula.

Your best chance of seeing this shy creature is on spring mornings in the Quinta de Marim area of the Parque Natural da Ria Formosa or in Monte Gordo's conifer woods, now a protected habitat for the species.

CASTRO MARIM

pop 6600

A sleepy, pretty village with a pebbled, tree-shaded centre, Castro Marim is dominated by a castle that glowers across at a pint-sized hilltop fort. It's 5km north of Vila Real de Santo António. Views from the fortifications sweep across salt pans, the bridge to Spain, and the fens and marshes of the **Reserva Natural do Sapal**, famous for its flamingos.

There are a few restaurants but nowhere to stay. It's an enjoyable stop as you head north or as a day trip from Vila Real.

Information

Odiana (☎/fax 281 531 171; www.odiana.pt; Rua Dr José Alves Moreira 3; 9.30am-1pm & 2.30-6pm) An organisation promoting the Baixo (lower) Guadiana region, it sells a good guide (€5; also available at the turismo) covering regional culture and history and suggestions for day trips.

Turismo (☎ 281 531 232; Praça 1 de Maio 2-4; 9.30am-12.30pm & 2-5.30pm Mon-Fri) Below the castle in the village centre, the turismo also offers some good local guides for sale.

Sights

CASTELO & AROUND

In the 13th century, Dom Afonso III built Castro Marim's **castle** (admission free; 8am-7pm Apr-Oct, 9am-5pm Nov-Mar) on the site of Roman and Moorish fortifications in a dramatic and strategic position for spying on the Spanish frontier. In 1319 it became the first headquarters of the religious military order known as the Order of Christ, the new version of the Knights Templar (p285). Until they moved to Tomar in 1334, the soldiers of the Order of Christ used this castle to keep watch over the estuary of the Rio Guadiana and the border with Spain, where the Moors were still in power.

The grand stretch of ruins today, however, date from the 17th century, when Dom João IV ordered the addition of vast ramparts. At the same time a smaller fort, the **Castelo de São Sebastião**, was built on a nearby hilltop (long-planned restorations to this ruin have not yet started). Much in the area was destroyed in the 1755 earthquake, but the ruins of the main fort are still pretty awesome.

Inside the wonderfully derelict castle walls is a small **Museu Arqueológico** (admission free), closed for renovations at the time of research. There's also a 14th-century church, the **Igreja de Santiago**, where Henry the Navigator, also Grand Master of the Order of Christ, is said to have prayed. The best time to see the castle is during the **Feira Mediéval**, which takes place for three days in late August or early September. There's a parade on the first day from the castle to the village, food stalls selling local products, music, and a medieval banquet.

RESERVA NATURAL DO SAPAL DE CASTRO MARIM E VILA REAL DE SANTO ANTÓNIO

Established in 1975, this nature reserve is Portugal's oldest, covering 20 sq km of marshland and salt pans bordering the Rio Guadiana north of Vila Real. Important winter visitors are greater flamingos, spoonbills, avocets and Caspian terns. In spring it's busy with white storks.

The park's **administrative office** (☎ 281 510 680; Sapal de Venta Moínhos; 9am-12.30pm & 2-5.30pm Mon-Fri) is 2km from Monte Francisco, a five-minute bus ride north of Castro Marim; get directions from the turismo at Castro Marim as there are no signs.

There are two accommodation centres in the park but they are popular with groups, so you need to book ahead. Another rewarding area for spotting the park's birdlife is around Cerro do Bufo, 2km southwest of Castro Marim. Ask staff at the park office or at Castro Marim's turismo for details.

Getting There & Away

Buses from Vila Real (eight minutes) run to Castro Marim and go on to Monte Francisco, a short distance north.

THE CENTRAL COAST

LOULÉ

pop 59,160 / elevation 160m

Snoozy Loulé (*lo*-leh) has cobbled, leafy streets hosting conferences of flat-capped men. Romans and Moors settled here, and it has an attractive old quarter and Moorish castle ruins. One of the Algarve's largest inland towns, Loulé, 16km northwest of Faro, has a weekly open-air market on Saturday, making it a popular day trip. Traditionally a handicrafts centre, the town has small shops selling lace, leather goods and ceramics.

Orientation

The bus station is about 250m north of the centre. The train station is 5km southwest (take any Quarteira-bound bus). If you're coming by car on market day (Saturday), get here early or park outside town.

Information

Bookshop (Praça da República; 9.30am-1pm & 3-6pm Mon-Fri, 9am-1pm Sat) Has an excellent range of guidebooks and maps.

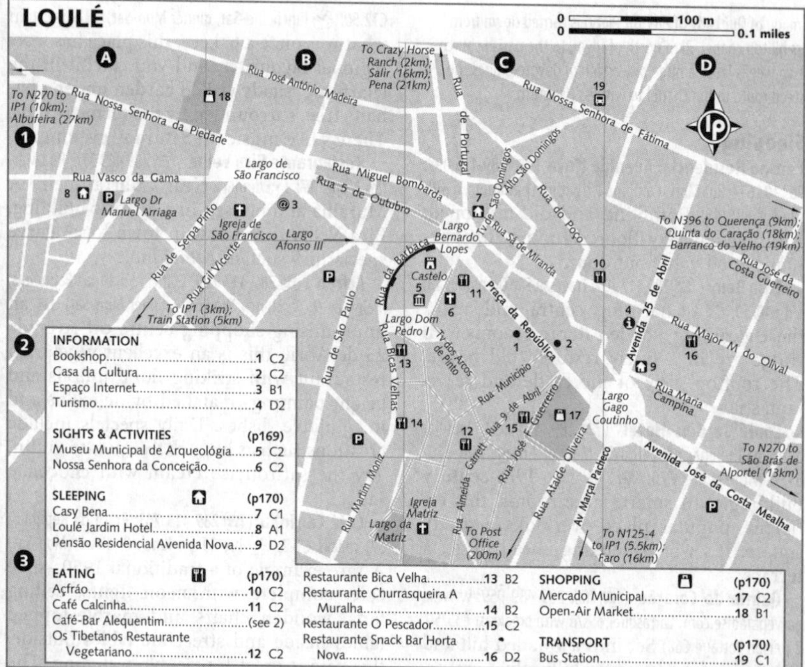

Espaço Internet (☎ 289 417 348; Largo de São Francisco; per hr €2; 9am-noon Mon-Sat, 4-11pm Sun) Provides Internet access.

Turismo (☎ 289 463 900; Avenida 25 de Abril; 9.30am-6pm Tue-Thu Oct-May, 9.30am-7pm Tue-Thu, 10am-1pm & 2-6pm Fri-Mon Jun-Sep) You can get maps of Loulé, but the staff at the museum may prove more helpful.

Sights & Activities

The restored castle ruins house the **Museu Municipal de Arqueológia** (☎ 289 400 642; Largo Dom Pedro I; admission €1; 9am-5.30pm Mon-Fri, 10am-2pm Sat), which contains well-presented fine fragments of Bronze Age and Roman ceramics. A glass floor exposes excavated Moorish ruins. The admission fee includes entry to a stretch of the castle walls and the **Cozinha Tradicional Algarvia** (9am-5.30pm Mon-Fri, 10am-2pm Sat), an evocation of a traditional Algarve kitchen, featuring a cosy hearth, archaic implements and lots of burnished copper.

Nossa Senhora da Conceição (admission free; 9.30-1pm Tue, Thu & Sat), opposite the castle, dates from the mid-17th century. It's a small chapel with a plain façade nonchalantly hiding a heavily decorated mid-18th-century interior with a magnificent gold altarpiece and blue-and-white tiles.

Crazy Horse Ranch (☎ 962 685 293; Vale do Telheiro), a few kilometres north, offers outings ranging from a two-hour trek to a two-day trip to Rocha da Pena.

Almargem (☎ 289 412 959; €2 per walk) is an environmental group that welcomes visitors on its Saturday walks of around 10km. Each year they try to cover every area of the Algarve.

Festivals & Events

Carnaval (late February or early March) Just before Lent, dozy Loulé pulls off its pyjamas and shimmies into something sexy and sequinned, with parades, tractor-drawn floats and lots of musical high jinks. Friday is the children's parade, and Saturday the big one.

Loulé International Jazz Festival (July) The town dons jazz boots on selected evenings; international and Portuguese musicians jam in the convent and castle. For information call ☎ 289 400 600.

Nossa Senhora da Piedade (Easter Sunday) Linked to ancient maternity rites, this *romaria* (religious festival) is the Algarve's most important. On Easter Sunday a 16th-century image of Our Lady of Pity (or Piety) is carried down from its hilltop chapel, 2km north of town, to the parish church. Two weeks later, a huge procession of devotees lines the steep route to the chapel to witness its return.

Sleeping

Pensão Residencial Avenida Nova (☎ 289 415 097, 963 104 614; Rua Maria Campina 1; d without bathroom/d with shower €35/45) Rambling and old-fashioned, with big, squeaky-floored rooms, this *pensão* is good value but dour.

Casa Beny (☎ 289 417 702; Travessa São Domingos 13; s/d €40/50;) Charming, central and smart, these gleaming wooden-floored rooms with fridge are in a finely restored old house. The rooftop view of the castle and sea is fantastic.

Loulé Jardim Hotel (☎ 289 413 094; loulejardim@mail.telepac.pt; Largo Dr Manuel Arriaga; s/d €50/65, d with terrace €70;) A late-19th-century building with smart, large rooms, this efficient, popular place overlooks a pretty square. It's worth booking ahead to get a terrace.

Quinta do Coração (☎/fax 289 489 959; www.algarveparadise.com; Carrasqueiro; s/d with breakfast €35/50, 2-person cottage €60) Set into a wooded hill and surrounded by majestic hilly olive groves, this remote converted farmhouse 18km north of Loulé is 1.8km off the road (down a bumpy track). It has charming rural rooms

Eating & Drinking

Restaurante O Pescador (☎ 289 462 821; Rua José F Guerreiro; mains €7) Right by the market, this is the place for a good family hubbub (especially on market days), big helpings and reasonable prices.

Os Tibetanos Restaurante Vegetariano (☎ 289 462 067; Rua Almeida Garrett 6; set menus €7.50-10; lunch & dinner Mon-Sat) A provincial cousin of the same-named restaurant in Lisbon, this garden restaurant offers unusual (for Portugal) vegetarian daily specials such as curries, rissoles and salads. The centre also houses a small shop and offers yoga lessons.

Restaurante Snack Bar Horta Nova (☎ 289 462 429; Rua Major Manuel do Olival; mains €3-10, menu €5; breakfast, lunch & dinner Mon-Sat) This restaurant offers open-air, cheap-and-cheerful dining in a large, walled garden under shady trees. They specialise in home-made pizzas and charcoal-grilled meat and fish.

Restaurante Churrasqueira A Muralha (☎ 289 412 629; Rua Martim Moniz 41; mains €6-18, 3-course lunch €12.50; lunch Tue-Sat, dinner Mon-Sat) Housed in what was once a bakery, this place has tasty regional favourites, and you can sit in the charming, shady walled garden under a banana tree, surrounded by the former ovens. There's live music on Saturday evening.

Restaurante Bica Velha (☎ 289 463 376; Rua Martim Moniz 17; dinner) Near Churrasqueira A Muralha and housed in a historic building, Bica Velha is the best in town for Algarve specialities such as *cataplana*.

Açfrão (☎ 289 417 700; Edifício Solar das Palmeiras; mains €4-9; lunch Wed-Sat, dinner Mon-Sat) In an unpromising shopping centre off Avenida 25 de Abril, this is an excellent vegetarian restaurant with striking floral murals and bright paintings matched by delicious and imaginative dishes. Daily specials include creations such as blue-cheese potato gratin. Try the saffron ice cream with chocolate sauce.

Café Calcinha (☎ 289 415 763; Praça da República 67; snacks €1-7; breakfast, lunch & dinner Mon-Sat) A rare example of a traditional 1950s-style café, complete with neon lights, ceiling fans, wooden chairs and marble-topped tables inside and streetside tables outside, this café is great for people watching. The statue outside is of António Aleixo, an early-20th-century poet who used to visit the café daily.

Café Bar Aléquentim (Rua Almeida Garrett 9A) While away the afternoon with heartfelt karaoke in this small orange-walled haunt opposite the Tibetan restaurant.

Shopping

Loulé's excellent arts and crafts – especially leather goods, brass and copperware, wooden and cane furniture – are made and sold in craft shops along Rua da Barbaca (behind the castle). The mercado municipal also has traditional craft stalls.

On Saturday morning head for the open-air market northwest of the centre, with masses of everything from clothes, shoes, toys and souvenirs.

Getting There & Away

Both Faro (15 minutes, eight daily) and Lagos trains stop at Loulé station (5km south of town). More conveniently, there are regular **bus** (☎ 289 416 655) connections from Faro (€2.10, 40 minutes, at least every two hours), Albufeira (€3, 55 minutes, three

WHERE EAGLE OWLS FLY

In the Serra do Caldeirão foothills, 21km northwest of Loulé, is the beautiful, dramatic Rocha da Pena, a 479m-high limestone outcrop – a classified site because of its rich flora and fauna. Orchids, narcissi and native cistus cover the slopes, where red foxes and Egyptian mongooses are common. Among many bird species seen here are the huge eagle owl, Bonelli's eagle and the buzzard.

There's a *centro ambiental* (environmental centre) in Pena village, and a 4.7km circular walking trail starts from Rocha, 1km from Pena.

to seven daily) and Portimão (€4.25, 1¾ hours, two to four daily). For Lisbon (€15, 4¾ hours, four daily), change at Albufeira.

ALMANCIL

It's worth making a detour here, 13km northwest of Faro and about 6km south of Loulé, to visit the marvellous **Igreja de São Lourenço de Matos** (Church of St Lourenço; admission free). The church was built on the site of a ruined chapel after local people, while digging a well, had implored the saint for help and then struck water.

The resulting baroque masterpiece, which was built by fraternal master-team Antao and Manuel Borges, is smothered in azulejos – even the ceiling is covered in them. The walls depict scenes from the life of the saint. In the earthquake of 1755, only five tiles fell from the roof.

One of the Algarve's longest-established horse-riding centres is here too: **Paraíso dos Cavalos** (☎ 289 394 189; Almancil; per hr around €20).

Buses between Albufeira (40 minutes) and Loulé (15 minutes) stop here.

ALBUFEIRA

pop 31,540

Albufeira (from the Arabic *al-buhera*, meaning 'castle on the sea') was once a scenic fishing village, which sold its soul to mass-market tourism in the 1960s. Balmy beaches are the big draw, but Albufeira also has a scenic old centre, crammed with tourist facilities, and a sparkling new marina.

It comes into its own in the evening, settling into a carnival atmosphere, with artisan stalls, buskers and live music in many bars.

The modern extension is Montechoro, apartment-block heaven, 3km to the east where 'the Strip' leads up from Praia da Oura. The jingling-jangling Strip will satisfy anyone curious about what the English seaside might look like if transferred somewhere warmer.

Prettier than some other Algarve resorts, Albufeira has tons of restaurants, family fun, tropical-cocktails nightlife, and excellent people- and *Eastenders*-watching opportunities.

Orientation

Albufeira's old town lies below the busy N526 (Avenida dos Descobrimentos). Its focal point is Largo Engenheiro Duarte Pacheco, where most of the cafés, bars and restaurants are clustered. Sprawled to the north and east is modern-day Albufeira: the market, the bus station and main police station are almost 2km north. The train station is 6km north at Ferreiras, connected to the bus station by shuttle bus.

Information

BOOKSHOPS

The kiosks around Largo Engenheiro Duarte Pacheco stock international newspapers and magazines.

Julies (☎ 289 513 773; Rua da Igreja Nova 6; 🕒 10am-4pm Mon-Fri, to 1pm Sat, to 3pm Sun) This is packed with second-hand books from English to Swahili.

EMERGENCY & MEDICAL SERVICES

Centro de saúde (medical centre; ☎ 289 585 899; 🕒 24hr) Two kilometres north of the old town.

Clioura Clinic (☎ 289 587 000; 🕒 24hr) A private clinic in Montechoro.

GNR police post (☎ 289 583 210; Avenida 25 de Abril 22) More central than the police station. Also a Gabinete de Apoio à Vítima (office to help victims). Next to Hotel Baltum.

GNR police station (☎ 289 590 790; Estrada Vale de Pedras) North of town, near the *mercado municipal*.

INTERNET ACCESS

H@ppynet (☎ 967 964 953; Rua 5 de Outubro 87B; per hr €3.50; 🕒 10am-10pm Mon-Sat)

Windcafé.com (☎ 289 513 786; 2nd fl, Centro Comercial California, Rua Cândido dos Reis 1; per hr €3.50, per 10min €1; 🕒 11am-9pm) Also has second-hand books on sale.

THE ALGARVE

MONEY

Banco Português do Atlântico (Largo Engenheiro Duarte Pacheco 23) Along and near Avenida 25 de Abril are several banks with ATMs, including this one.

POST

Post office (☎ 289 580 870; Rua 5 de Outubro; ⏲ 9am-12.30pm & 2-6pm Mon-Fri)

TOURIST INFORMATION

Turismo (☎ 289 585 279; Rua 5 de Outubro; ⏲ 9.30am-7pm Mon-Fri May-Sep, 9.30am-12.30pm & 1.30-5.30pm Oct-Apr) By a tunnel that leads to the beach.

Sights

Albufeira's pedestrianised seafront is made for seaside strolls. The town's beach, **Praia do Peneco**, through the tunnel near the turismo, is clean and scenic, but often head-to-toe with sun loungers.

For a hint of local flavour, head 400m east to **Praia dos Pescadores** (Fishermen's Beach, also called Praia dos Barcos), where you might find a remnant of Albufeira's fishing past, with fishermen mending their nets beside their high-prowed, brightly painted boats.

Further afield – both east and west of town – are numerous beautifully rugged coves and bays, though the nearest are heavily developed and often crowded. The easiest to reach is **Praia da Oura**, at the bottom of 'The Strip' 3km to the east (roughly 30 minutes on foot; follow Avenida 25 de Abril and climb the steps at the end to reach the road to the beach). It's wide and sandy, though backed by buildings.

Between Praia da Oura and **Praia da Falésia**, a wonderfully long and remote-feeling beach 10km to the east, is a string of less crowded beaches, including **Balaia** and **Olhos de Água**, whose western end is best for swimming and sunbathing. Buses run to Olhos de Água (€1.40, 10 minutes, half-hourly), mostly continuing to Praia da Falésia (20 minutes).

One of the best beaches to the west, **Praia da Galé**, about 6km away, is long and sandy, not so crowded and a centre for jet-skiing and water-skiing. It's easily accessible by car, but there's no direct bus service to this beach or the others en route, though local buses to Portimão do run along the main road about 2km above the beaches (get off at Vale de Parra).

Activities

Zebra Safari (☎ 289 583 300; www.zebrasafari.com) organises full-day jeep safaris (€45 per person including lunch) into the Algarve interior. They also offer day-long mountain-bike tours from €30 per person.

Riosul (☎ 281 510 201; www.riosul-tours.com; Monte Gordo) can whizz you off for its one-day Jeep Safari (€46), or on a cruise up the Rio Guadiana (€38, or €41 to €45 with transport from your resort).

Zoomarine (☎ 289 560 300; www.zoomarine.com; adult/child €19/11.30; ⏲ 10am-7.30pm July–mid-Sep, 10am-6pm mid-May–Jun & mid-Sep–Oct, 10am-5pm Tue-Sun Jan–mid-May & Nov, closed Dec) at Guia, 8km northwest, will satisfy all desires for aqua-entertainment, with huge swimming pools and slides, as well as lakes, an aquarium, synchronised swimming, dolphin, seal and sea lion shows. And if you tire of H2O, there are fairground rides, birds of prey and parrot performances.

Other recommendations:

Aqualand – The Big One (☎ 800 204 014; adult/child €16/13; ⏲ May-Sep) Also near Albufeira, this has a huge loop-the-loop slide and rapids.

Aqua Show (☎ 289 389 396; adult/child €18/14; ⏲ 10am-6.30pm Apr-Aug, to 5.30pm Sep-Mar) is in Vilamoura, 10km east of Albufeira, with flamingos, parrots and Europe's biggest wave pool (pools close from November to March).

Albufeira Riding Centre (☎ 289 542 870; Vale Navio Complex; 1 hr €25) This English-run centre on the road to Vilamoura offers one- to three-hour horse rides for all ages and differing abilities.

Best Day (☎ 800 204 150; www.bestday.com; Rua Alex Herculano) will whirl you away on coach tours, such as to Évora and the wine route (€45; p203).

You can play tennis at the professional-standard **Ténis da Quinta da Balaia** (☎ 289 586 575; www.quintadabalaia.pt), located 1km east of Alburfeira.

Festivals & Events

The major local shindig is **Festa da Ourada** (14 August), honouring the fishermen's patron saint, Nossa Senhora da Ourada (Our Lady of the Oracle), with a procession from the parish church along the seaside promenade and culminating in a mighty midnight fireworks display over Praia dos Pescadores.

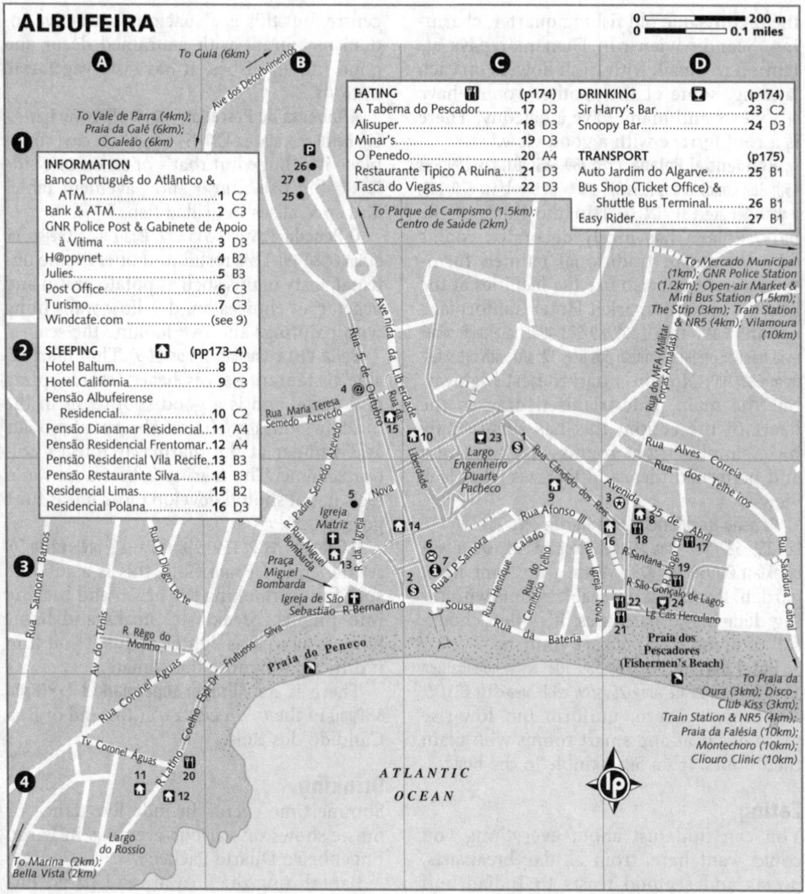

Sleeping

You'll need to book well ahead to bag accommodation in July and August. Off-season (November to March), many places close. The following prices are for July – you'll get much better prices off-season (April to June and September to October).

BUDGET

There are dozens of *quartos* (the turismo has a list), most costing around €30 a double.

Pensão Restaurante Silva (☎ 289 512 669; Rua 5 de Outubro 23; d €35) The central Silva is pleasantly small-scale and offers cheap, basic rooms.

Pensão Albufeirense Residencial (☎ 289 512 079; Rua da Liberdade 18; s/tw €30/35) Central and small, with homely, comfortable rooms.

Pensão Residencial Frentomar (☎ 289 512 005; Rua Latino Coelho 25; d €40) Tired rooms have balconies with great sea views.

Residencial Limas (☎/fax 289 514 025; Rua da Liberdade 25-27; d €40) Centrally located.

Parque de Campismo de Albufeira (☎ 289 587 629; www.roteiro-campista.pt/Faro/albufeira.htm; adult/tent/car €4.85/4.60/4.60;) Near Alpouvar, 2km north of town, this well-equipped, shady camp site has eateries, facilities for the disabled, three swimming pools, a children's playground and caravans for rent. Bus no 20 stops just nearby.

MID-RANGE & TOP END

Pensão Dianamar Residencial (☎ 289 587 801; www.dianamar.com; Rua Latino Coelho 36; s/d/tr €25/40/45) In the picturesque old fishing quarter, charming, Scandinavian-run Dianamar pays attention to detail, with fresh flowers on each landing; some of the spotless rooms have sea views and many have a balcony. There is a roof terrace with a good view.

Residencial Polana (☎ 289 583 401; fax 289 583 450; Rua Cândido dos Reis 32; s/d with breakfast €70/100, d with terrace €81;) In the thick of the bars, Polana has nicely decorated rooms with Alentejan traditional painted furniture; guests can also use the facilities at the nearby, more upmarket Hotel California.

Hotel California (☎ 289 583 400; hotelcalifornia@mail.telepac.pt; Rua Cândido dos Reis 12; s/d with breakfast from €80/100) Not on a dark desert highway, but the main pedestrianised drag in the heart of the action, this has surprisingly nice, simple, bright rooms with terracotta and patterned tiles, and terraces (that lack views).

Pensão Residencial Vila Recife (☎ 289 586 747; fax 289 587 182; Rua Miguel Bombarda 12; s/d/tr with breakfast €40/50/70;) With a pleasant front garden, Recife has agreeable rooms with tiling details and balconies; it's often chock-full of prebooked package tourists.

Hotel Baltum (☎ 289 589 102; www.hotelbaltum.com; Avenida 25 de Abril 26; s/tw with breakfast €53/75;) This modern, uniform but low-rise place has neat and smart rooms with plain tiled floors. It's a 50m amble to the beach.

Eating

You can find just about everything you could want here, from all-day breakfasts, pizzas and seafood feasts to Indian and Thai. Largo Cais Herculano forms an irresistible suntrap of outdoor tables overlooking Praia dos Pescadores.

Restaurante Tipico A Ruína (☎ 289 512 094; Largo Cais Herculano; mains €7-15; lunch & dinner) This restaurant covers all seating options, with superb sea views from the rooftop terrace, a pleasantly rustic setting and beachside outside tables. It offers tiptop seafood and fish.

Tasca do Viegas (☎ 289 514 087; Rua Largo Cais Herculano; mains €7.50-12.50; lunch & dinner Mon-Sat) With all the favourites from prawns to steaks, this place also has a sea-view roof terrace, and some outside tables.

Minar's (☎ 289 513 196; Rua Diogo Cão; mains €4.50-12; lunch Mon-Sat, dinner daily) The route here is via an unprepossessing shopping centre, but this is a spacious, attractive Indian restaurant with restrained décor and good Indian dishes. It has tasty vegetarian options.

A Taberna do Pescador (☎ 289 589 196; Travessa Cais Herculano; mains €4.80-19) This fun, cavernous place in a huge hut that's open on one side has a big fish mural and pavement tables and specialises in grilled fish.

O Penedo (☎ 289 515 072; Rua Latino Coelho 36; mains €4.80-19) This restaurant offers some unusual, tasty mains such as potato gratin and vegetarian choices amid yellow walls hung with paintings and overlooking the sea.

Bella Vista (marina; mains €4-9) This marina-side restaurant serves hearty salads, pizza and pasta, and is a good spot to sit in the outdoor squashy chairs, observe the boats and wonder at the marina architect's colour scheme. The marina is brand new and feels it, but should develop more life as time goes on.

O Galeão (☎ 289 591 918; Praia Galé; grills €2-14.50) At the end of Praia Galé, this is a sublime spot for overlooking the beach and tucking into English breakfasts, steaks and hamburgers as well as lighter mains if you find it difficult to ignore the climate.

There is an **Alisuper supermarket** (8am-8.30pm) in the town centre, at the end of Rua Cândido dos Reis.

Drinking

Summertime events include live dance or music shows on various evenings in Largo Engenheiro Duarte Pacheco.

Bars throng the area around Largo Engenheiro Duarte Pacheco and nearby Rua Cândido dos Reis. Nearly all offer happy hours (at various times of the day) and stay open until at least 4am in summer.

Snoopy Bar (Rua S Gonçalo de Lagos) This is a pleasant spot overlooking the beach.

Sir Harry's Bar (Largo Engenheiro Duarte Pacheco 37) One of the older (and pricier) British-style pubs, this is so authentic and cosy inside you can pretend you're in Britain with better weather. There's the best of British brews on tap and live music daily.

Disco-Club Kiss (nightly) This is the Algarve's most famous club, at Praia da Oura, with international poppy house DJs and usually with the addition of glitzy dancers. Saturday is ladies' night (free drinks for women).

Shopping

An open-air market, mostly selling clothes and shoes, is held on the first and third Tuesday of the month near the main bus station, located 2km north of the old town.

Getting There & Away

The bad news is that the **main bus station** (☎ 289 589 755; on Rua dos Caliços) is now 2km north of town. The good news? There's an information and ticket **Bus Shop** (☎ 289 588 122; Avenida da Liberdade). Shuttle buses go to the main bus station (free with onward bus tickets, every 15 minutes from 7am to 8pm) from outside the Bus Shop. The only buses still coming to Avenida da República are expresses to Lisbon (€14.50, 2¾ hours, six daily).

Buses run to Lagos (€3.90 to €4.30, 65 to 75 minutes, 12 daily) via Portimão; Faro (€3.35, 40 minutes, hourly); Silves (€3, 40 minutes to one hour, seven daily); and Loulé (€3, 40 minutes, 10 daily). There are two to Huelva in Spain (€9, 4¾ hours, via Faro), and on to Seville (€14, 5½ hours). Services shrink at weekends.

Trains run to Lagos (€2.90, three daily) and daily to Faro (€1.80, seven daily) – but beware of slow local services. Go to Tunes (six daily) to pick up trains to Lisbon.

Getting Around

To reach the train station, take the *estação* (station) shuttle bus (€1.40, 10 minutes, at least hourly 6.45am to 8pm) from the main bus station (above).

A major car-rental agency is **Auto Jardim** (☎ 289 580 500; Edifício Brisa, Avenida da Liberdade). **Easy Rider** (☎ 289 501 102; www.go-easyrider.com; Avenida da Liberdade 115) rents mountain bikes/scooters for €10/20 per day.

CARVOEIRO

Carvoeiro is a cluster of whitewashed buildings rising up from tawny, gold and green cliffs and backed by hills. Shops, bars and restaurants rise steeply from the small arc of beach that is the focus of the town, and beyond lie hillsides full of sprawling holiday villas. This diminutive seaside resort 5km south of Lagoa is prettier and more laid-back than many of the bigger resorts, but its size means that it gets full to bursting in summer.

Orientation & Information

Buses from Lagoa stop right by the beach, beside the turismo. The post office and several banks are on Rua dos Pescadores (the one-way road in from Lagoa).

Turismo (☎ 282 357 728; 🕑 10am-1.30pm & 2-6pm Fri-Mon, 9.30am-6pm Tue-Thu) This is the small turismo.

Sights & Activities

The town's little bite of sandy beach, **Praia do Carvoeiro** is surrounded by the steeply mounting town. About 1km east on the coastal road is the bay of **Algar Seco**, a favourite stop on the tour-bus itinerary thanks to its dramatic rock formations.

If you're looking for a stunning swimming spot, continue east along the main road, Estrada do Farol, to **Praia de Centianes**, where the secluded cliff-wrapped beach is almost as dramatic as Algar Seco. Buses heading for **Praia do Carvalho** (nine daily from Lagoa, via Carvoeiro) pass nearby – get off at Colina Sol Aparthotel, the Moorish-style clifftop hotel. The nearest water park is **Slide & Splash** (☎ 282 341 685, reservations 800 202 224; www.slidesplash.com; Estrada Nacional 125), 2km west of Lagoa.

Golfers can be choosy: there's the nine-hole **Gramacho** and 18-hole **Pinta** (☎ 282 340 900; www.pestana.com; both at Pestana Golf Resort); and the challenging **Vale de Milho** (☎ 282 358 502; www.valedemilhogolf.com; 9/18 holes €20.50/32.40; unlimited golf after 5pm €20) near Praia de Centianes, good for all levels and with some of the Algarve's best-value play. The **David Leadbetter Golf Academy** (☎ 282 340 900; www.pestanagolf.com), at the Pinta course, can arrange golfing packages.

Divers Cove (☎ 282 356 594; www.diverscove.de; Quinta do Paraiso; 🕑 9am-7pm) is a (German) family-run diving centre, providing equipment, dives and PADI certification (3hr intro €55, one-day discovery €115, 2-day scuba diver/4-day open water €215/400).

Sleeping

In July and August, it may be impossible to find a room, so call ahead. *Quartos* may require a minimum three-night stay (prices will usually be discounted the longer you stay). Prices here are for July.

Brigitte Lemieux (☎ /fax 282 356 318; Rampa da Nossa Senhora da Encarnação 4; d €55, studio €66) A Canadian woman runs some of the most attractive *quartos* and studios. Facing the sea take the steep road up to the left or east from the beach. In a pretty, whitewashed house, a double comes with a sea view, fridge and toaster. There are basement studios (no view).

O Castelo (☎ 282 357 416; casteloguesthouse@netvisao.pt; Rua do Casino 59; d €40-58) Across the other side of the bay, this place gets the sunrise view, and has spotless, well-kept rooms with sea views.

Casa von Baselli (☎ 282 357 159; Rua da Escola; d with breakfast & shared bathroom €45) Around the corner from Brigitte Lemieux, this is a cosy five-room, German-run place. There is a shared terrace, high above the bay, for breakfast and sunset.

Hotel Carvoeiro Sol (☎ 282 357 301; carvoeirosol@mail.telepac.pt; s/tw with breakfast €102/144; 🅿 ❄) Right by the beach, this modern low-rise has comfortable rooms with satellite TV and balcony. Prices plummet in winter.

Eating

There are loads of restaurants in the main part of town and along Estrada do Farol.

A Fonte Restaurante (☎ 282 356 707; Escandinhas Vai Essar 4; mains €6-15; 🕑 lunch & dinner) This Portuguese place, set off from the main street, does barbecued fish and meat mains; there is an outdoor terrace.

Mitch's Restaurant & Bar (☎ 282 356 379; Rua dos Pescadores 104; mains €9.50-17; 🕑 lunch & dinner Sun-Fri) With tall windows giving onto a greenery-filled garden, this place is well laid out and has a good atmosphere.

Getting There & Around

Buses run on weekdays from Portimão to Lagoa (€1.40, 20 minutes, half-hourly) from where there are regular connections to Carvoeiro (10 minutes).

You can rent scooters from **Scooterent** (☎ 282 356 551; Rua do Barranco; 50cc/125cc per 3 days from €50/65) on the road back to Lagoa. Several car-rental agencies are also along this road. There's a taxi rank at the bottom of Estrada do Farol.

SILVES

pop 33,830

The orange rooftops of Silves rise up from a bed of thick trees above the silted-up Rio Arade to meet a striking red-stone castle. Once the glittering Moorish capital of the Algarve, the old town is a great place to wander, with a beguiling combination of lazy cafés and history. It's 15km northeast of Portimão.

History

The Rio Arade was long an important route into the interior for the Phoenicians, Greeks and Carthaginians, who wanted the copper and iron action in the southwest of the country. With the Moorish invasion from the 8th century, the town gained prominence due to its strategic hilltop, riverside site. From the mid-11th to the mid-13th centuries, Shelb (or Xelb), as it was then known, rivalled Lisbon in prosperity and influence: according to the 12th-century Arab geographer Idrisi, it had a population of 30,000, a port and shipyards, and 'attractive buildings and well-furnished bazaars'.

Its downfall began in June 1189 when Dom Sancho I laid siege to it, supported by a horde of (mostly English) hooligan crusaders who had been persuaded (with the promise of loot) to pause in their journey to Jerusalem and give Sancho a hand. The Moors holed up inside their impregnable castle with their huge cisterns, but after three hot months of harassment they finally ran out of water and were forced to surrender. Sancho was all for mercy and honour, but the crusaders wanted the plunder they were promised, and stripped the Moors of their possessions (including the clothes on their backs) as they left, tortured those remaining and wrecked the town.

Two years later the Moors recaptured the town. It wasn't until 1249 that Christians gained control once and for all. But by then Silves was a shadow of its former self. The silting up of the river – which caused disease as well as putting a stop to maritime trade – and the increased importance of the Algarvian ports over the following centuries led to the town's steady decline. Devastation in the 1755 earthquake seemed to seal its fate. But in the 19th century local cork and dried-fruit industries revitalised Silves, hence the grand bourgeois architecture around the town. Today tourism and agriculture are the town's lifeblood.

Orientation & Information

The centre of Silves is 2km north of the train station, a mostly downhill walk on a busy highway. Buses stop on the riverfront road at the bottom of town, crossing the Rio Arade on a modern bridge slightly upriver from a picturesque 13th-century version (now for pedestrians only).

Post office (☎ 282 440 160; Rua Correira; 🕑 9am-6pm Mon-Fri) Centrally located.

Turismo (☎ 282 442 255; Rua 25 de Abril; 🕑 10am-6pm Mon-Fri Oct-Apr, 10am-6pm daily May, to 7pm Jun-Sep) It's a short climb from the bottom of town to the turismo.

Vira Opos (☎ 917 801 207; per hr €3; 🕑 2pm-2am Thu-Tue) This bar has one fast machine for Internet access.

Sights & Activities

CASTELO

The russet-coloured, Lego-like **castle** (☎ 282 445 624; adult/child under 12 €1.30/free; 🕑 9am-7pm mid-Jul–mid-Sep, to 6pm mid-Sep–mid-Jul) has great views over the town and surrounding countryside. It was restored in 1835 and you can walk around its chunky red-sandstone walls – children will love this. The walls enclose a garden and some archaeological digs that reveal the site's Roman and pre-Roman past. In the north wall you can see a treason gate (an escape route through which turncoats would sometimes let the enemy in) – typical of castles at this time. By late 2005 the site will be developed to include a historical garden, a terrace café and further excavation of the ruins. The Moorish occupation is recalled by a deep well and a rosy-coloured water cistern, 5m deep. Inside, the cistern's four vaults are supported by 10 columns. Probably built in the 11th century, the castle was abandoned by the 16th century. It is to be restored and an interior walkway installed so that visitors can walk inside the structure. This development may mean admission increases once it's all finished.

SÉ & IGREJA MISERICÓRIDIA

Just below the castle is the **sé** (cathedral; admission free; 🕑 8.30am-6.30pm daily), built in 1189 on the site of an earlier mosque, then rebuilt after the 1249 Reconquista and subsequently restored several times following earthquake damage. The stark, fortress-like building has a multiarched Portuguese-Gothic doorway, and some original Gothic touches left, including the nave and aisles and a dramatically tall, strikingly simple interior. There are several fine tombs, one of which is purported to be of Joao do Rego, who helped to settle Madeira. Nearby is the 16th-century **Igreja Misericóridia** (🕑 9am-1pm & 2-7pm), plain apart from its distinctive, fanciful Manueline doorway decorated with curious heads, pine cones, foliage and aquatic emblems.

MUSEU DE ARQUEOLOGIA

Just below the cathedral, is the impressive, well–laid-out **Museu de Arqueologia** (Archaeological Museum; ☎ 282 444 832, Rua das Portas de Loulé; adult/child under 14 €1.50/free; 🕑 9am-6pm Mon-Sat). In the centre is a well-preserved 4m-wide, 18m-deep Moorish well surrounded by a spiral staircase, which was discovered during building works. The find, together with other archaeological discoveries in the area, led to the establishment of the museum on this site; it shows prehistoric, Roman and Moorish antiquities. One wall is of glass, showing a section of the fort wall (also of Almohad origin) that is used to support the building.

MUSEU DA CORTIÇA

The award-winning **Museu da Cortiça** (Cork Museum; ☎ 282 440 480; www.fabrica-do-ingles.com; Rua Gregório Mascarenhas; adult/child 7-12 €1.50/1; 🕑 9.30am-12.45pm & 2-6.15pm) is housed in the Fábrica do Inglês (English Factory, p179). The museum, with the former workshops, machine room and press room, has excellent bilingual displays on the process and history of cork production. Cork was a major industry in Silves for 150 years, until the factory's closure in the mid-1990s, largely due to the silting-up of the Rio Arade.

HORSE RIDING & ANIMAL PARK

At **Quinta Penedo** (☎ 282 332 466; Vale Fuzeiros; one/two hr €20/35), 13km to the northeast, you can ride horses through lovely fruit farm countryside. Or there is the **Country Riding Centre** (☎ 917 976 995/992; 🕑 daily), about 4km east of Silves, left off the road to Messines (it is signposted), who offer hour-long to half-day hacks at all levels, with swimming opportunities. Lunch is included if requested.

Krazy World (☎ 282 574 134; www.krazyworld.com; adult/child €17/10; 🕑 10 am-7.30pm Jun-Aug, 10am-6pm Mar-May & Sep, Wed-Sun only Oct-Feb) is near São Bartolomeu de Messines, about 17km northwest, an animal and crocodile park with minigolf, quad-bikes and pony rides. Transport can be arranged.

Festivals & Events

For 10 days in late June the Fábrica do Inglês swills to the **Festival da Cerveja** (Beer Festival), accompanied by music, folk dance and other entertainment.

Sleeping

BUDGET

Residencial Restaurante Ponte Romana (☎ 282 443 275; Horta da Cruz; s/d €15/30) This *residencial* has a great location on the other side of the river from town, at the end of the old bridge. The riverside rooms with town and castle views across the river are a superb bargain. There's a cheery restaurant, too (right). To get here, drive over the larger bridge towards Portimão and take the first right (west) after the big bridge.

Vila Sodre (☎ /fax 282 443 441; Estrada de Messines; d with breakfast €35;) A pretty, modern blue-and-white villa 1.4km east of the newer bridge, set back from the busy road, this place is good value, with smart rooms.

Residencial Sousa (☎ 282 442 502; Rua Samoura Barros 17; s/d with shared bathroom around €15/30) A bargain-but-basic guesthouse in the centre.

MID-RANGE

Quinta da Figueirinha (☎ /fax 282 440 700; www.qdf.pt; 2-/4-/6-person apt €60/88/120;) This 36-hectare organic farm, run by kindly Dr Gerhard Zabel, produces fruit, vegetables, marzipan, marmalades and chutneys, and offers simple apartments in wonderfully remote and peaceful surroundings. Leaving Silves and crossing the bridge, take the first left in the direction of Fragura. Follow the road for around 4km – the *quinta* is signposted. You can completely self-cater or arrange breakfast, with organic produce, costing €5.

Quinta do Rio (☎ /fax 282 445 528; www.quintadorio.net; d with breakfast €52) You'll find rural tranquillity at this charming restored farmhouse set among orange groves and rolling hills, in 5 hectares of countryside. To get here, head 5.5km northeast (en route to São Bartolomeu de Messines) to Sítio São Estevão.

Eating

There are plenty of café-restaurants in the pedestrianised streets leading up to the castle or down by the river, where you'll also find a reasonable market (just west of the old pedestrian bridge).

BUDGET

Ú Monchiqueiro (☎ 282 442 142; mercado municipal; mains €4-9; lunch & dinner Thu-Tue) By the river and near the market, this restaurant serves punchy *piri-piri* chicken and has covered outdoor tables.

Suzie's Bar (☎ 282 442 107; mains €3-9; breakfast, lunch & dinner Thu-Tue) This cosy English-run café-restaurant is near the river and has outdoor tables. It serves home-made burgers, pastas, breakfasts, vegetarian fare and cakes, and has an evening bistro menu. The home-made chips are a winner.

Restaurante Ponte Romana (☎ 282 443 275; Horta da Cruz; mains €4-7) Adjoining the *residencial* (left), this friendly, large basement restaurant has novel décor – antiquated sewing-machine tables and one room with a whole wall laden with old machines – and hearty fare.

Pastelaria (Largo do Municipio; mains €1-3; daily) On the ground floor of the town hall building, this is a lovely place to sit out in the adjoining square under a warm yellow colonnade and shady trees. Inside are ajulezos of the city and wrought-iron chairs and chandeliers. The only downside is that the counter service can be slow.

MID-RANGE

Café Inglês (☎ 282 442 585; mains €4.25-12.50; 9.30am-10.30pm Tue-Thu & Sun, to 6pm Mon, to midnight Fri, 6pm-midnight Sat) Below the castle entrance, this café has a wonderful shady terrace and is everyone's favourite spot. The food is fantastic (try a delicious vegetarian salad with fruit and nuts, or home-made pizza) and you can down a pint of fresh orange juice if you've hit a thirsty patch. It has an elegant interior and in summer has occasional live jazz, Latin and 1930s Brazilian music.

Restaurante Rui (☎ 282 442 682; Rua Comendador Vilarinho 27; fish mains €6-15; lunch & dinner Wed-Mon) Situated in the old town, this deceptively simple place is Sagres' finest seafood restaurant: savour everything here from cockles, clams and crabs to sea snails, stone bass and grouper. They also serve typical Alentejan specialities such as black pork.

Tasca do Béné (☎ 282 444 767; Rua Policarpo Dias; mains €5-9; lunch & dinner Mon-Sat) Up the pedestrianised street from the river, this casual, bench-style *tasca* (tavern) serves traditional mains and has outdoor tables on the cobbled street.

Entertainment

Fábrica do Inglês (English Factory; ☎ 282 440 480; Rua Gregório Mascarenhas) In the impressive surroundings of the converted 19th-century English Museu da Cortiça (cork factory, p177), 300m northeast of the new bridge, this complex has restaurants and bars and, from July to mid-September, hosts a nightly multimedia show, featuring dancers, clowns and singers, lasers and cybernetic fountains. During the day you can press a button and walk through these; by night they are illuminated kaleidoscope-style. The ticket includes dinner and admission to the Museu da Cortiça (p177). Reservations are advised. Off-season, there's usually a weekly theme evening; check at the museum's reception. There's a big children's playground too.

Getting There & Away

Buses shuttle daily between Silves and its train station (€1.40, three to four daily), timed to meet the trains from Lagos (€1.40, 35 minutes) and Faro (€2.70, one hour, with a change at Tunes). There are buses to Albufeira (€3, 40 minutes, seven daily), and to Portimão (€2.10, 20 minutes, two to five daily) and Lagos (40 minutes). All buses leave from the riverfront, with fewer running at weekends. The **bus ticket office** (☎ 282 442 338; 🕓 8am-noon & 2-6pm Mon-Fri, 8-noon Sat & 11am-noon Sun) is on the western side of the market.

PORTIMÃO

pop 44,820

Fishing, canning and shopping are the main activities in and around this sprawling port. The town centre has recently been brushed up, with an attractive airy square facing the boat-filled waterfront as its centrepiece. The main reasons to head here are for some riverside sardines, to nose around the shops or to take a boat trip. It is 16km east of Lagos, hugging the western bank of the Rio de Arade 3km inland from Praia da Rocha.

Portimão was a ancient marine-traders' magnet, attracting the Phoenicians, Greeks and Carthaginians (Hannibal is said to have visited – maybe he was after some ceramic souvenirs). It was called Portos Magnus by the Romans and fought over by Moors and Christians. In 1189 crusaders under Dom Sancho I sailed up the Rio Arade from here to besiege Silves. Almost destroyed in the 1755 earthquake, it gained its new fishy vocation in the 19th century, and is still the Algarve's second most important port (after Olhão).

Orientation

The town's focal point is the Praça Manuel Teixeira Gomes, next to a smart riverside promenade. There's no bus station, but buses stop at various points along the riverside Avenida Guanaré (look for the Shell petrol station) and the parallel Avenida Afonso Henriques (look for the Agip station). The train station is a 15-minute walk (1.1km) north of the centre – follow the pedestrianised Rua do Comércio and its continuation, Rua Vasco da Gama. The easiest parking is a free riverside area by the Shell station.

Information

There are several banks with ATMs around the riverside Praça Manuel Teixeira Gomes.

The **Municipal turismo** (☎ 282 470 732; turismo@cm-portimao.pt; Avenida Zeca Afonso; 🕓 9am-6pm Mon-Fri, 9am-1pm Sat Jun-Aug, 9am-12.30pm & 2-5.30pm Mon-Fri Sep-May) is opposite the football stadium, about 600m west of the river.

Sights

The town's parish church, the **igreja matriz** (admission free), stands on high ground to the north of the town centre and has a 14th-century Gothic portal – all that remains of the original structure after the 1755 earthquake. Other echoes of the past can be found in the narrow streets of the **old fishing quarter**, around Largo da Barca, just before the old highway bridge.

Activities

Lots of operators along the riverside promenade offer boat trips. Most charge around €15 for a three-hour cruise along the coast, visiting caves along the way. **Arimar** (☎ 965 677 625) runs day trips in a restored fishing boat, with chances to swim, visit caves and have a barbecue on the beach. **Pirate Ship Santa Bernarda** (☎ 987 023 840; www.santa-bernarda.com; half-/full-day trips adult €25/50, child under 10 €15/25) runs cruises visiting the caves and coast on a 23m wooden sailing ship with disabled access. The full-day trip includes a beach barbecue and time to swim. Several operators also offer big-game fishing, such as **Cepemar** (☎ 282 425 866 or 917 348 414).

The nearest place to go for a gallop is at **Centro Hípico Vale de Ferro** (☎ 282 968 444; www.algarvehorseholidays.com; per hr €20), near Mexilhoeira Grande (4.2km west of Portimão), which also offers riding-holiday packages.

Liga para a Proteção da Natureza (League for the Protection of Nature; ☎ 282 968 380; donation; Sep-Jul) arranges long, easy walks on the first Saturday of each month. Meet in the square in front of the train station at 9.30am and bring a picnic.

Sleeping

Pousada da juventude (☎ 282 491 804; portimao@movijovem.pt; Lugar do Coca Maravilhas; dm/d €9.50/29;) A smashing if basic place, this hostel is set in green, tree-shaded grounds, with a restaurant and swimming pool. Renovations should be complete by June 2005 (call ahead). It's about 3km north of town. Buses (€1; green or blue line, 20 minutes, every 40 minutes 7am to 7pm) do head here; ask for the Cardosas stop. A **taxi** (☎ 282 423 645) will cost around €4. Beware the hordes of schoolchildren from July to August.

Residencial O Pátio (☎ 282 424 288; Rua Dr João Vitorino Mealha 3; s/d €20/25) This sweet place, just off the main square, has a central patio. Rooms are a bit shabby but clean and nice, with Alentejan painted furniture.

Eating

For a delicious alfresco sardine lunch, head for the strip of restaurants by the bridge, where you can buy charcoal-grilled sardines for a bargain €4.50 or so per half-dozen. Many also offer a big plate of mixed barbecued fish for two. Prices range from €4 to €11. It might be touristy, but with good reason.

Dona Barca (☎ 282 484 189; Largo da Barca; mains from €4.50) This restaurant is off the main strip, with a cluster of other terrace restaurants in the pleasant cobbled surroundings of the old fishing quarter, under the arches of the bridge; it's famous for its Algarve seafood specialities.

Simsa (☎ 282 423 057; Rua S Gonçalo; mains €14.50-17.50; dinner Tue-Sat) Cosy, deep-red and Dutch-run, Simsa is decorated by mirrors and birdcages, and has fittingly rich mains such as duck in strawberry and pepper sauce.

Café Inglesa (☎ 282 461 290; Praça Manuel T Gomes; mains €2-6; breakfast, lunch & dinner) Central to Portimão life is this large café on the main square that feels little changed since the 1950s. It has revolving cake stands, lots of snacks and outdoor tables and is a good meeting place.

Shopping

Trawl Rua do Comércio, Rua Vasco da Gama and the adjacent Rua Direita for handicrafts (especially ceramics, crystal and copper goods), shoes and cotton items. A big open-air market is held behind the train station on the first Monday of each month. A flea market also takes place on the first and third Sunday of the month (mornings only) along Avenida São João de Deus (west of Rua do Comércio).

Getting There & Away

Six daily trains connect Portimão with Tunes (via Silves) and Lagos. Change at Tunes for Lisbon.

Portimão has excellent bus connections, including the following:

Destination	Price (€)	Duration	Frequency (weekdays/ weekends)
Albufeira	3.25	45min	14/6
Cabo São Vicente	4.30	2½hr	2/0
Faro	3.90	1½ hr	7/2
Lagos	2.10	40min	19 daily
Lisbon	15	3¾hr	6/4
Loulé	4.25	1¾hr	2/4
Monchique	2.75	45min	9/5
Sagres	4.25	1¼hr	2/0
Salema	3	1hr	2/0
Silves	2.10	35min	8/5

Buses shuttle between Praia da Rocha and Portimão (€1.40 on the bus €3.30/6.60 per five/10 prepurchased tickets, at least half-hourly).

Information and tickets for Eva and Intersul (Eurolines) services are available at the **Eva office** (☎ 282 418 120; Largo do Duque 3) by the riverside. Buses either leave from outside the Restaurante Chinés Dinastia, to the right of the ticket office, or from the Shell station.

PRAIA DA ROCHA

This wonderful beach is one of the Algarve's finest. Ochre-red, gnarled and twisted cliffs back a glimmering sweep of golden sand. Take a step back, and you'll see such natural glories have led to a less scenic build up of hotels, apartment blocks, restaurants and bars of the 'Pat and Vic welcome you' variety, with a few lovely 19th-century mansions and guesthouses dotted amid the concrete – relics of Algarve's past. One of the first beaches in the Algarve to be patronised by overseas tourists in the 1950s and 1960s, Praia da Rocha's popularity continues, catering mostly to couples of all ages and families; its weekend nightlife is trendy with the Portuguese. There's a glamorous, newish marina painted weirdly autumnal colours (to match the cliffs).

Orientation

Set high above the beach, the esplanade, Avenida Tomás Cabreira, is the resort's main drag and is lined with shops, hotels and restaurants. At the eastern end is the shell of the **Fortaleza da Santa Catarina**, built in the 16th century to stop pirates and invaders from sailing up the Rio Arade to Portimão. Down below is the relatively new Marina de Portimão, with more restaurants and bars.

Information

The post office is near the turismo.

LAN Network House (☎ 282 416 435; Network House; per hr €2.50; 11am-11.30 Mon, Tue, Fri & Sat, 4pm-last client Wed & Thu, 11am-6.30pm Sun) Around the corner from Hotel Oriental, this funky place provides Internet access and rents electric bikes.

Police (🕒 9am-12.30pm & 2-5pm Mon-Fri) Next door to the turismo.

Turismo (☎ 282 419 132; 🕒 9.30am-7pm Jul & Aug, 9.30am-1pm & 2-5.30pm Mon-Fri Sep-Jun) In the centre of the esplanade, opposite Hotel Júpiter.

Activities

Travel agencies galore want to whirl you away on excursions, notably **Polotur** (☎ 282 420 800; www.polotur.pt; Rua Engenheiro José Bivar; 🕒 9.30am-6.30pm Mon-Fri, 9.30am-1pm Sat, later in summer), near the turismo, which offers jeep tours (€46) and full-day fishing trips (€65).

Marina-based **Dolphin Seafaris** (☎ 282 799 209, 919 359 359; dolphinseafaris@mail.com; €30; 🕒 Apr-Oct) offers a dolphin-spotting trip.

Sleeping

Pensão and hotel accommodation is almost impossible to find in the high season without prior reservation, though you could try asking at the turismo about *quartos*. The following prices are for May – they will go up by a quarter to a half in July, August and September.

Pensão Residencial Penguin (☎ 282 424 308; residencial.penguin@mail.telepac.pt; Rua António Feu; s/d €35/50) This charming old villa is set back from the esplanade but unfortunately close to the pulsating monster that is Discoteca Katedral. The Penguin's musty décor and elegant veranda speak of Praia da Rocha's sedate early days. Run by the same Englishwoman (now in her 80s) for over 30 years, at the time of research the Penguin was for sale, so its future was uncertain – call ahead. Some rooms have sea views.

Albergaria Vila Lido (☎ 282 241 127; fax 282 242 246; Avenida Tomás Cabreira; d with breakfast €65, d/ste with terrace & breakfast €70/80; 🕒 Mar–mid-Nov; ❄) Near the fort, this hotel was converted from a delightful 19th-century mansion and retains the feels of a gloriously elegant era, with great sea views and 10 bright rooms, eight of which have terraces.

Hotel Bela Vista (☎ 282 450 480; www.hotelbelavista.net; s/d with breakfast €75/80) This hotel lives up to its name and bags the best beach view from the middle of the esplanade. Though a bit tired-looking, it's a marvellous place – a whimsical late-19th-century, vaguely Oriental creation, with carved wooden ceilings and colourful azulejos. Only two of the 14 tile-decorated rooms lack a sea view. Rates drop by almost half in winter.

Serviceable, small-scale options:

Residencial Tursol (☎ 282 424 047; Rua António Feu)

Residencial São José (☎ 282 424 035; Rua Engenheiro Francisco Bívar).

Eating

Titanic (☎ 282 422 371; Edifício Colúmbia, rua Eng. Francisco Bivar; mains €10-24; 🕒 lunch & dinner) Swish as a liner but steady as an iceberg, this 100-seater, long-established restaurant is where you go to treat yourself to the best seafood in town, or a tasty steak.

Safari Restaurante (☎ 282 423 540; mains €5.75-20; 🕒 lunch & dinner) This smart restaurant with friendly staff and sublime views over the beach is tucked behind Discoteca Katedral. Its roast duck is delectable.

Cervejaria e Marisqueira (☎ 282 416 541; mains €5.80-14.50, 3-course menu €10; ⌚ lunch & dinner) An unusually traditional restaurant for Praia da Rocha, this popular and low-key *cervejaria* on a road opposite the casino offers decent Portuguese fare, with a hearty array of daily specials.

The marina has a row of romantic, upmarket dining and drinking spots.

Dockside (☎ 282 417 268; Marina; mains €5-15; ⌚ lunch & dinner) In a prime spot at the end of the marina, this is a classy, glassy spot with sea views.

Bella Italia (☎ 282 411 737; Marina; mains €2.50-8; ⌚ lunch & dinner) Part of a reliable Italian chain, this restaurant has glass-covered, candlelit terraces overlooking the marina or the sea and serves pizza and pasta.

Lena's Croissanteria (mains 1.50-5.50; ⌚ lunch & dinner) On the esplanade nearly opposite Hotel Bela Vista, this is a small, pleasant spot for breakfast, vegetarian dishes, ice cream and crepes.

Gelateria Bella Italia This gelateria rivals all other ice cream spots for its brilliant sea views and historic location right inside the fort.

Entertainment

Praia da Rocha bristles with bars – full of sun-kissed faces, satellite TV, live music and karaoke – often run by Irish or English expats. Dressed-up Portuguese also flock here for a big weekend splash. Classier places overlook the beach or the marina and have outdoor seating and serene views.

Bustling, but not pretty, Brit favourites are the **Celt Bar** (Rua António Feu) and adjacent **Twiins** (Rua António Feu) for their Irish atmosphere, brews and regular live music. More scenic and sedate is **Kerri's Bar** (☎ 282 483 195; Rua Jerónimo Buisel), just before the fort, for Finnish liqueurs, no TV and fairy lights.

Well-situated bars string along the front from Pensão Residencial Penguin, most with outdoor seating. Try **Pé de Vento** (⌚ 4pm-4am), a two-floor disco bar.

Monster **Discoteca Katedral** (Rua António Feu), in front of the Penguin, gets busy to pop house, to 6am nightly during summer. **Boraga Club**, nearby, is a bit cooler and gets down to funky house.

The glitzy **casino** (☎ 282 402 000; Avenida Tomás Cabreira), midway along the esplanade in Hotel Algarve, has slot machines (admission free, open from 4pm to 3am), a gambling room (admission €4, plus passport and smart attire; open from 7.30pm to 3am) and a nightly sequinned-and-feathered dinner show (€37 for dinner, €10 show only, with dinner at 8.30pm and the show at 10.30pm).

Getting There & Around

Buses shuttle to Portimão (€1.40 on the bus, €3.30/6.60 per five/10 prepurchased tickets, every 15 to 30 minutes). Buy tickets from **Hotel Júpiter** (☎ 282 415 041; Ave Tomas Cabreira). There are services to Albufeira (€7.14), Lagos (€5.50, four to six daily), Loulé (€8.60 return, one daily) and Lisbon (€15, four daily). The bus terminus in Praia da Rocha is by the fort, with another stop behind Hotel da Rocha (Rua Engenheiro José Bívar).

Citycar (☎ 282 414 398; Rua Caetano Feu) offers good car-rental deals. Next door, at **Scooterent** (☎ 282 416 998), behind the Hotel da Rocha, you can hire mountain bikes (€10 per day), and scooters (50cc/125cc from €50/65 per three days). **Luckybano** (☎ 968 157 651; Network House) rents Aerobikes (electric bikes) for €2 to €3 per hour.

THE WINDWARD COAST & COSTA VICENTINA

LAGOS

pop 25,400

Lagos (*la*-goosh) oozes life. A vibrant, sunny town, its pretty cobbled streets bristle with cafés, restaurants and bars. It's a magnet for young backpackers and surf dudes, who throng the bars as both staff and customers. But there are plenty of families around too, and the mix provides balmy holiday hedonism at its best. Apart from its enticing nightlife, there are long, sweeping beaches where you can recuperate and nearby striking, twisted coastal coves.

Aside from hedonistic charms, Lagos has historical clout, having launched many naval excursions during Portugal's extraordinary Age of Discoveries (p26).

History

Phoenicians and Greeks set up shop at this port (which later became Roman Lacobriga) at the mouth of the muddy Rio Bensafrim.

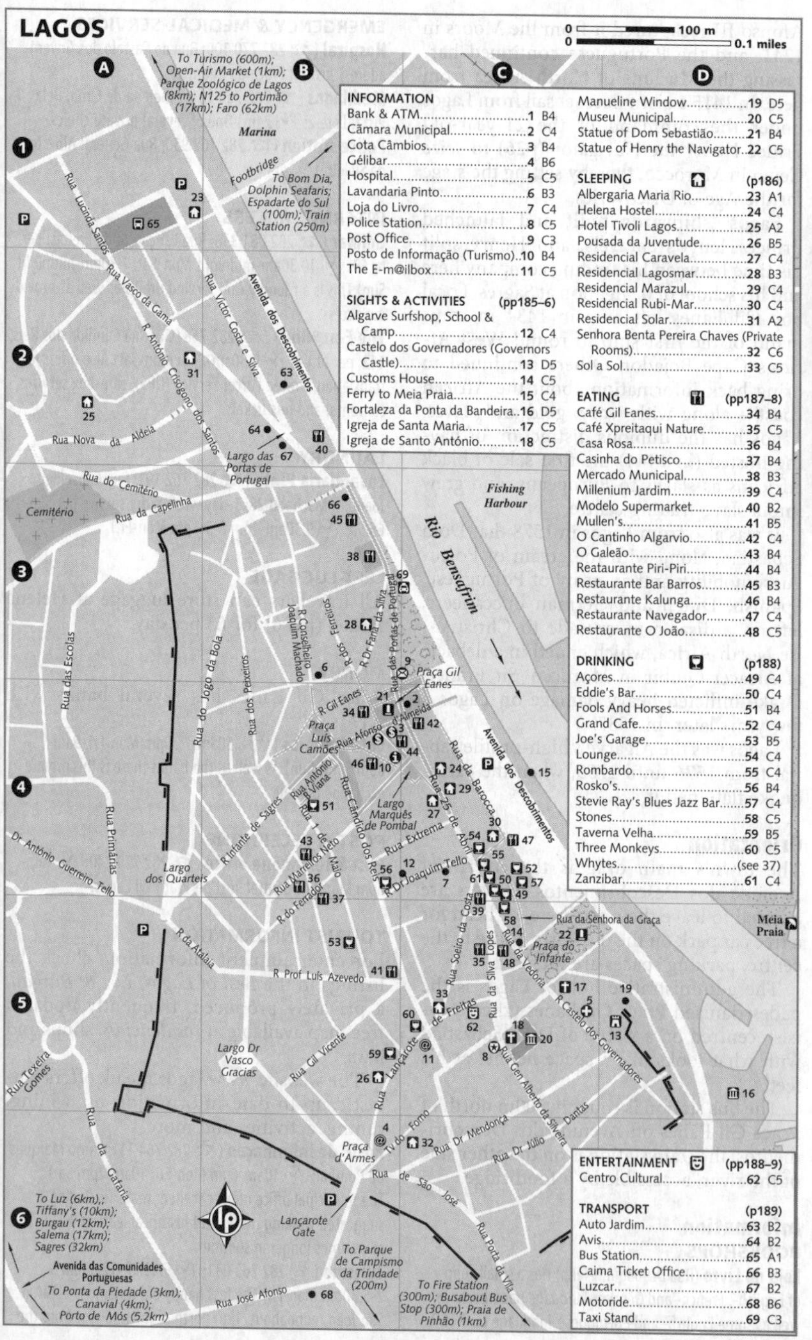
LAGOS
0 100 m
0 0.1 miles
A
B
C
D
1
2
3
4
5
6
INFORMATION
Bank & ATM....1 B4
Câmara Municipal....2 C4
Cota Câmbios....3 B4
Gélibar....4 B6
Hospital....5 C5
Lavandaria Pinto....6 B3
Loja do Livro....7 C4
Police Station....8 C5
Post Office....9 C3
Posto de Informação (Turismo)..10 B4
The E-m@ilbox....11 C5
SIGHTS & ACTIVITIES (pp185–6)
Algarve Surfshop, School & Camp....12 C4
Castelo dos Governadores (Governors Castle)....13 D5
Customs House....14 C5
Ferry to Meia Praia....15 C4
Fortaleza da Ponta da Bandeira..16 D5
Igreja de Santa Maria....17 C5
Igreja de Santo António....18 C5
Manueline Window....19 D5
Museu Municipal....20 C5
Statue of Dom Sebastião....21 B4
Statue of Henry the Navigator..22 C5
SLEEPING (p186)
Albergaria Maria Rio....23 A1
Helena Hostel....24 C4
Hotel Tivoli Lagos....25 A2
Pousada da Juventude....26 B5
Residencial Caravela....27 C4
Residencial Lagosmar....28 B3
Residencial Marazul....29 C4
Residencial Rubi-Mar....30 C4
Residencial Solar....31 A2
Senhora Benta Pereira Chaves (Private Rooms)....32 C6
Sol a Sol....33 C5
EATING (pp187–8)
Café Gil Eanes....34 B4
Café Xpreitaqui Nature....35 C5
Casa Rosa....36 B4
Casinha do Petisco....37 B4
Mercado Municipal....38 B3
Millenium Jardim....39 C4
Modelo Supermarket....40 B2
Mullen's....41 B5
O Cantinho Algarvio....42 C4
O Galeão....43 B4
Reataurante Piri-Piri....44 B4
Restaurante Bar Barros....45 B3
Restaurante Kalunga....46 B4
Restaurante Navegador....47 C4
Restaurante O João....48 C5
DRINKING (p188)
Açores....49 C4
Eddie's Bar....50 C4
Fools And Horses....51 B4
Grand Cafe....52 C4
Joe's Garage....53 B5
Lounge....54 C4
Rombardo....55 C4
Rosko's....56 B4
Stevie Ray's Blues Jazz Bar....57 C4
Stones....58 C5
Taverna Velha....59 B5
Three Monkeys....60 C5
Whytes....(see 37)
Zanzibar....61 C4
ENTERTAINMENT (pp188–9)
Centro Cultural....62 C5
TRANSPORT (p189)
Auto Jardim....63 B2
Avis....64 B2
Bus Station....65 A1
Caima Ticket Office....66 B3
Luzcar....67 B2
Motoride....68 B6
Taxi Stand....69 C3
To Turismo (600m); Open-Air Market (1km); Parque Zoológico de Lagos (8km); N125 to Portimão (17km); Faro (62km)
Marina
Footbridge
To Bom Dia, Dolphin Seafaris; Espadarte do Sul (100m); Train Station (250m)
Rua Lucinda Santos
Rua Vasco da Gama
R António Crisógono dos Santos
Rua Victor Costa e Silva
Avenida dos Descobrimentos
Rua Nova da Aldeia
Largo das Portas de Portugal
Rua do Cemitério
Cemitério
Rua da Capelinha
Fishing Harbour
Rio Bensafrim
Rua das Escolas
Rua do Jogo da Bola
Rua dos Peixeiros
R Conselheiro Joaquim Machado
R dos Ferreiros
R Dr Faria da Silva
Rua das Portas de Portugal
Praça Gil Eanes
R Gil Eanes
Praça Luís Camões
Rua Afonso d'Almeida
Rua da Barocca
Rua 25 de Abril
Rua António Viana
Rua 1 de Maio
Rua Cândido dos Reis
Largo Marquês de Pombal
Rua Extrema
R Infante de Sagres
Rua Primárias
Dr António Guerreiro Tello
Largo dos Quartéis
Rua Marreiros Neto
R do Ferrador
R Dr Joaquim Tello
Rua Soeiro da Costa
Rua da Silva Lopes
Rua da Senhora da Graça
Praça do Infante
Rua da Vedoria
R da Atalaia
R Prof Luís Azevedo
Meia Praia
Rua de Freitas
R Castelo dos Governadores
Largo Dr Vasco Gracias
Rua Gil Vicente
Rua Lançarote
Rua Gen Alberto da Silveira
Rua Teixeira Gomes
Rua da Gafaria
Tv do Forno
Rua Dr Mendonça
Rua Dr Júlio Dantas
Praça d'Armes
Rua de São José
Rua Porta da Vila
To Luz (6km),; Tiffany's (10km); Burgau (12km); Salema (17km); Sagres (32km)
Lançarote Gate
To Parque de Campismo da Trindade (200m)
Avenida das Comunidades Portuguesas
To Ponta da Piedade (3km); Canavial (4km); Porto de Mós (5.2km)
Rua José Afonso
To Fire Station (300m); Busabout Bus Stop (300m); Praia de Pinhão (1km)

THE ALGARVE

Afonso III recaptured it from the Moors in 1241, and the Portuguese continued harrassing the Muslims of North Africa from here. In 1415 a giant fleet set sail from Lagos under the command of the 21-year-old Prince Henry the Navigator (p26) to seize Ceuta in Morocco, thereby setting the stage for the Age of Discoveries.

Lagos' shipyards built and launched Prince Henry's caravels, and Henry split his time between his trading company here and his school of navigation at Sagres. Local boy Gil Eanes left here in 1434 in command of the first ship to round West Africa's Cape Bojador. Others continued to bring back information about the African coast – along with ivory, gold and slaves. Lagos has the dubious distinction of having hosted (in 1444) the first sale of black Africans as slaves to Europeans, and grew into a slave-trading centre.

It was also from Lagos in 1578 that Dom Sebastião, along with the cream of Portuguese nobility and an army of Portuguese, Spanish, Dutch and German buccaneers, left on a disastrous crusade to Christianise North Africa, which ended in a debacle at Alcácer-Quibir in Morocco. Sir Francis Drake inflicted heavy damage on Lagos a few years later, in 1587.

Lagos was the Algarve's high-profile capital from 1576 until 1755, when the earthquake flattened it.

Orientation

The town's main drag is the riverfront Avenida dos Descobrimentos. Drivers are advised to leave their cars here, or head for a free car park on the outskirts. Close to the centre, parking spaces are metered.

The administrative hub of Lagos is the pedestrianised Praça Gil Eanes (zheel *yan*-ish), centred on a statue of Dom Sebastião with what looks like a space helmet at his feet.

The bus station is roughly 500m north of Praça Gil Eanes off Avenida dos Descobrimentos; the train station is on the other side of the river, accessible by a footbridge.

Information

BOOKSHOPS

Loja do Livro (Rua Dr Joaquim Tello) Has a small supply of English-, French- and German-language paperbacks as well as some English- and Portuguese-language CD-ROMs.

EMERGENCY & MEDICAL SERVICES

Hospital (☎ 282 770 100; Rua do Castelo dos Governadores) Just off Praça do Infante.

Medilagos (☎ 282 760 181; Amejeira de Cima, Bela Vista, Lote 2; 🕑 24hr) One of several private clinics.

Police station (☎ 282 762 930; Rua General Alberto da Silveira)

INTERNET ACCESS

Gélibar (☎ 282 081 336; Rua Lançarote de Freitas; per hr €3; 🕑 10.30am-midnight Mon-Sat, 1.30pm-midnight Sun) This is a friendly café serving drinks as well as providing access.

The E-m@ilbox (☎ 282 768 950; Rua Candido dos Reis, 112; per hr €4; 🕑 9.30am-8pm Mon-Sat) Also offers fax, translation, United Parcel Service (UPS), safe-box services, car rental and bus tickets.

LAUNDRY

Lavandaria Pinto (☎ 282 762 191; Rua Conselheiro Joaquim Machado 28; 1-day wash & dry service per 5kg €6.50; 🕑 9.30am-1pm & 3-7pm Mon-Fri)

LEFT-LUGGAGE

All travellers can store luggage at Helena Hostel (p186) for €3 per day.

MONEY

Praça Gil Eanes has several banks with ATMs.

Cota Câmbios (🕑 8.30am-7.30pm Mon-Fri, 9am-6pm Sat & Sun) As well as the banks there is this private exchange bureau.

POST & TELEPHONE

Post & telephone office (☎ 282 770 240; 🕑 9am-6pm Mon-Fri) Central, just off Praça Gil Eanes.

TOURIST INFORMATION

For entertainment information, check the listings in the *Best of Lagos, Luz & Burgau*, a privately produced, frequently updated free map available at *residenciais*, shops and bars.

The website www.lagos.me.uk offers fantastic up-to-date information on wining, dining, activities and more.

Posto de informação (☎ 282 764 111; Largo Marquês de Pombal; 🕑 10am-6pm Mon-Fri, 10am-2pm Sat) The municipal office offers excellent maps (including a suggested walking route) and historical leaflets. Hours are sometimes longer in summer.

Turismo (☎ 282 763 031; 🕑 9.30am-12.30pm & 2-5.30pm Mon-Fri) The less handy old turismo is at Situo São João roundabout, 1km north of town (600m from the bus station). Follow the Avenida until you see the Galp petrol station.

Sights

IGREJA DE SANTO ANTÓNIO & MUSEU MUNICIPAL

The little **Igreja de Santo António** (Rua General Alberto da Silveira; admission €2; 9.30am-12.30pm & 2-5pm Tue-Sun), bursting with 18th- and 19th-century gilded, carved wood, is a stupendous baroque extravaganza. Beaming cherubs and ripening grapes are much in evidence. The dome and azulejo panels were installed during repairs after the 1755 earthquake.

Enter from the adjacent **Museu Municipal** (282 762 301; Rua General Alberto da Silveira), a glorious and fascinating historic mishmash. There's an entrancing haphazardness about it all, from Roman nails found locally and opium pipes from Macau to bits of the Berlin wall sharing a case with scary-looking surgical instruments.

AROUND THE TOWN

Igreja de Santa Maria (Praça do Infante; 9am-noon & 3-6pm) dates from the 15th and 16th centuries and retains a 16th-century entrance; the rest dates largely from the mid-19th century when it was restored after fire. There's a seemingly Star Trek–inspired modern mural behind the altar.

Just south of Praça do Infante is a restored section of the stout **town walls**, built (atop earlier versions) during the reigns of both Manuel I and João III in the 16th century, when the walls were enlarged to the existing outline. They extend intermittently, with at least six bastions, for about 1.5km around the central town.

Rua da Barroca once formed the boundary between the town and the sea and retains some Arabic features.

Castelo dos Governadores (in the southeast part of town at the back of the present-day hospital) was built by the Arabs. After the Reconquista in the 13th century, the Algarve's military government was established here in the 14th century. It's said that the ill-fated, evangelical Dom Sebastião attended an open-air Mass here and spoke to the assembled nobility from a small Manueline window in the castle, before leading them to a crushing defeat at Alcácer-Quibir (Morocco). A statue in Praça Gil Eanes captures Dom Sebastião's naivety but in the process turns him into a swirling pink space chick.

Near Praça do Infante is a less-than-glorious site – where slaves were auctioned off in Portugal in the 15th century. It now houses an art gallery.

FORTALEZA DA PONTA DA BANDEIRA

This little **fortress** (Avenida dos Descobrimentos; admission €2; 9.30am-12.30pm & 2-5pm Tue-Sun), at the southern end of the avenue, was built in the 17th century to protect the port. Restored, it now houses a museum on the Portuguese discoveries.

PONTA DA PIEDADE

Protruding south from Lagos, **Ponta da Piedade** (Point of Pity) is a stunning, dramatic wedge of headland. Three windswept kilometres out of town, the point is well worth a visit for its contorted, polychrome sandstone cliffs and towers, complete with lighthouse and, in spring, hundreds of nesting egrets. The surrounding area is brilliant with wild orchids in spring. On a clear day you can see east to Carvoeiro and west to Sagres.

PARQUE ZOOLÓGICO DE LAGOS

This **zoo** (282 680 100; Quinta Figueiras; adult/child €8/5; 10am-7pm Apr-Sep, 10am-5pm Oct-Mar) is a shady 3-hectare kid-pleaser, with small primates, a flight tunnel where you can observe exotic birds, lakes, and a children's farm housing domestic animals. It's near the village of Barão de São Miguel, 8km west of Lagos.

Activities

BEACHES & WATER SPORTS

Meia Praia, the vast expanse of sand to the east of town, has outlets offering sailboard rental and water-skiing lessons, plus several laid-back restaurants and beach bars. South of town the beaches – Batata, Pinhão, Dona Ana, Camilo and others – are smaller and more secluded, lapped by calm waters and punctuated with amazing grottoes, coves and towers of coloured sandstone. Avoid swimming at Batata and, to the east, at Ana. There's a ferry to Lagos beach.

Lagos is a popular surfing centre and has good facilities; surfing companies head to the west coast for the waves.

Algarve Surf Shop, School & Camp (282 767 853; surf.to/algarve; Rua Dr Joaquim Tello; equipment hire &

B&B €50/day, 1-/3-/5-day course or safari €35/90/140) will help you catch a wave.

For diving or snorkelling, contact **Blue Ocean Divers** (☎/fax 282 782 718; 964 048 002; www.blue-ocean-divers.de; Motel Ancora, Ponta da Piedade), which offers a half-day 'Snorkelling Safari' (€30), a full-day diving experience (€85) and a three-day PADI scuba course (€280). It also offers kayak safaris (€28/45 half/full day, child under 12 €14/23).

Booked through Bom Dia (below), parasailing trips cost €45 for 15 minutes of high-adrenaline thrills out at Ponta da Piedade.

BOAT TRIPS & DOLPHIN SAFARIS

Various operators have ticket stands at the marina or along the promenade opposite the marina.

The biggest operator is **Bom Dia** (☎ 282 764 670; www.bomdia.info), at the marina, which runs trips on traditional schooners, including a five-hour barbecue cruise (€37/18.50 adult/child aged 5 to 10, 10am and 2pm), with a chance to swim; a two-hour grotto trip (€17/8.50, four daily); or a full-day sail to Sagres, including lunch (€65/37, 10am). They also organise big-game fishing and offer car rental.

Espadarte do Sul (☎ 282 767 252) offers 1½-hour trips to the grottoes beneath Ponta da Piedade, a three-hour coastal cruise and day-long big-game fishing.

Southwest Charters (☎ 282 792 681; www.southwestcharters.com; Marina de Lagos) provides powerboat or yacht charters carrying eight people for €150 to €250 per half-day, €285 to €450 per full day. Larger boats and week-long rentals are available. A skipper will cost you €50/100 per half-/full day.

Local fishermen offering jaunts to the grottoes by motorboat trawl for customers along the promenade and by the Fortaleza da Ponta da Bandeira.

The marina-based **Dolphin Seafaris** (☎ 282 799 209, 919 359 359; dolphinseafaris@mail.com; €30; ⏲ Apr-Oct) offers dolphin-spotting trips.

OTHER ACTIVITIES

About 10km west of Lagos, **Tiffany's** (☎ 282 697 395; www.valegrifo.com/tiffanysriding; Vale Grifo, Almádena; ⏲ 9am-dusk) charges €25 an hour for horse riding and has other options, including a three-/five-hour trip (€60/95); the latter includes a champagne picnic. Another centre with similar activities is **Quinta Paraíso Alto** (☎ 282 687 596; Fronteira), 7km north of Lagos. Both also offer package horse-riding holidays.

Full-day bike trips can be organised through **Cycle Paths** (Eddie's Bar, Rua 25 de Abril 99) for around €30 per person, including lunch. It also does excursions to Morocco. Tickets and information are available from Eddie's Bar (p188).

Algarve Airsports Centre (☎ 914 903 384; Aeródrome de Lagos, ⏲ Mon-Sat) offers courses, lessons and trial flights.

Sleeping

BUDGET

Lagos abounds in *pensões, residenciais,* hotels, motels and so on. There are more places out on Meia Praia and south on Praia da Dona Ana. Rooms are hard to find and prices zoom upwards by about a third from July to mid-September, and may drop by half from November to March; we give July rates here. Plenty of private, unlicensed *quartos* are also on offer but similarly scarce in summer; look for *quartos* signs in shop windows or ask at the turismo for recommendations. Figure on at least €30 a double (up to €50 for fancier versions).

Senhora Benta Pereira Chaves (☎ 282 760 940, 964 159 230; ask at Travessa do Forno 13A) This charming place offers tidy, cosy rooms with balconies, and there is a flower-filled shared roof terrace.

Senhora Margarida (☎ 282 763 096, 917 628 003) Also recommended are these rooms and apartments, in different locations. They will meet you and take you to the appropriate location.

Helena Hostel (☎ 282 081 388; Rua 25 de Abril; d €45; 💻) Centrally located, these two bright, faintly crowded-feeling *quartos* are let by a mother with young children. One room has a street-facing balcony and one a terrace; both have cable TV and a fridge. Luggage can be left here by guests and nonguests.

Sol a Sol (☎ 282 761 290; Rua Lançarote de Freitas 22; s/d €25/35) This central, small hotel has rooms with small balconies and views over the town; it's a bit tired-looking but good value nonetheless.

Pousada da juventude (☎ 282 761 970; lagos@movijovem.pt; Rua Lançarote de Freitas 50; dm/d €15/42; ⏲ 24hr; 💻) One of the best in Portugal; this hostel is often packed and a great place to meet other travellers. It has a kitchen and pleasant courtyard, and the reception is helpful.

Parque de Campismo da Trindade (☎ 282 763 893; fax 282 762 885; adult/tent/car €3/3.50/4) A small site 200m south of the Lançarote gate in the town walls, this camp site is a tent-peg's throw from the sea, has lots of shade, facilities for the disabled, a playground, a restaurant, bar and snack bar.

MID-RANGE

Residencial Rubi Mar (☎ 282 763 165; rubimarlagos@yahoo.com; 2nd fl, Rua da Barroca 70; s/d with shared bathroom €30/45, d with private bathroom €50) Homely and welcoming, this guesthouse has a couple of sea-view rooms. You'll need to book well ahead in summer.

Residencial Caravela (☎ 282 763 361; Rua 25 de Abril 8; s/d €25/35) Right in the central pedestrian zone, this small place is welcoming with no-nonsense rooms.

Pensão Marazul (☎ 282 770 230; www.marinario.com; Rua 25 de Abril 13; s/d with breakfast €30/45; 💻) Also central, Marazul has comfortable, well-kept rooms with either sea views or inner balconies.

Residencial Lagosmar (☎ 282 763 722; Rua Dr Faria da Silva 13; s/d with breakfast €38/45) An endearingly small whitewashed place on a narrow street, Lagosmar has comfortable, well-furnished rooms.

Residencial Solar (☎ 282 762 477; fax 282 761 784; Rua António Crisógono dos Santos 60; d with breakfast €40-50) Near the bus station and the waterfront, but on a quiet street, this modern, peaceful place has airy white rooms with small balconies.

TOP END

Albergaria Marina Rio (☎ 282 769 859; www.marinario.com; Avenida dos Descobrimentos; r with breakfast €70, plus harbour view €83) This hotel has comfortable rooms decorated in white and cream, with balconies overlooking the yacht-filled marina; on the roof is a pool with a view and a sun terrace. It's on a slightly busy road.

Hotel Tivoli Lagos (☎ 282 790 079; www.tivolihotels.com; Rua Nova da Aldeia; s/d with breakfast €107/170; 🏊 ❄) Self-consciously classy, this is Lagos' finest hotel. Set back from the road, it offers comfort galore and its own beach club.

Eating

Lagos bulges with tasty choices, both Portuguese and international. At lunch time *pratos do dia* (daily specials) often cost around €5. Many bars also offer food.

Café Xpreitaqui Nature (☎ 282 762 758; Rua da Silva Lopes 14; salads €2-5; 🕓 10am-2am Mon-Sat) A popular meeting point, this café serves up healthy juices, smoothies, salads, breakfasts and pizzas.

Casa Rosa (☎ 966 884 317; Rua do Ferrador; dishes €2-6; 🕓 5pm-midnight) Cheapo bar-restaurant Casa Rosa serves up simple, college-days, good-value mains such as vegie stir-fry, chilli con carne or fajitas, is backpacker-packed and plays student union–style music. Surf the Net for free for 10 minutes.

Casinha do Petisco (☎ 282 084 285; Rua da Oliveira 51; mains €3-12; 🕓 lunch & dinner Mon-Sat) Nearby Casa Rosa, this snug, lively tavern is similarly popular with the youth-hostel crowd and serves traditional Portuguese dishes.

Café Gil Eanes (☎ 282 762 886; Praça Gil Eanes; mains €2-5; 🕓 breakfast, lunch & dinner Mon-Sat) An unbeatable people-watching venue, serving everything from sandwiches and salads to cocktails.

Millenium Jardim (☎ 282 762 897; Rua 25 de Abril 72; pizzas from €6; 🕓 lunch & dinner) This two-level place has a completely open front, which makes it extra bright and breezy and a good place to survey the street. Food such as pizza is served on satellite-dish–sized plates.

Mullen's (☎ 282 761 281; Rua Cândido dos Reis 86; mains €6.50-13; 🕓 dinner) A long-established *adega típica* (wine bar), this great arched tavern is filled with tiles, big barrels and unusual paintings. It serves good grilled mains and has a lively bar.

Restaurante Piri-Piri (☎ 282 763 803; Rua Lima Leitão 15; mains €8-15; 🕓 lunch & dinner) Named after everyone's favourite chilli spice, this snug place serves zippy staples of *cozinha regional* (regional cuisine), including *cataplana*, chicken piri piri and prawns in garlic.

Restaurante Navegador (☎ 282 767 162; Rua da Barroca; mains €9.50-12; 🕓 lunch & dinner Fri-Wed) With a sea view and pretty roof terrace, this smart, white-tablecloth restaurant rustles up some elaborately flambéed food, with lots of meat and fish dishes and port-based sauces.

O Cantinho Algarvio (☎ 282 761 289; Rua Afonso d'Almeida 17; mains €4.60-13; 🕓 lunch & dinner) This place has traditional local specialities such as monkfish rice or *cataplana*, tables outside on the narrow, cobbled street, and a curious grotto ledge inside that doesn't detract from its cosiness.

Restaurante Barros (☎ 282 762 276; Rua Portas de Portugal 83; mains €4.50-11; ⏲ lunch & dinner) Right by the market, this is a popular tiled place, with lots of fish and rice choices and hearty lamb stew with potatoes. There are bargain *pratos do dia*.

Restaurante O João (☎ 282 761 067; Rua da Silva Lopes 15; mains €6-9; ⏲ lunch & dinner Mon-Sat) An unpretentious, cosy nook, with arches and checked tablecloths, O João glimmers with candlelight at night. It attracts locals and tourists and serves up both Alentejan mains such as pork with clams and local favourites such as its house special, paella.

O Galeão (☎ 282 763 909; Rua da Laranjeira 1; mains €9-15 ⏲ lunch & dinner) Enjoy Portuguese fare here, including luxuries such as lobster thermidor. Watch the chefs work intensely, quietly, from an open-view kitchen.

Restaurante Kalunga (☎ 282 760 727; Rua Marquês de Pombal 26; mains from €6.50-12.30; ⏲ lunch & dinner) This cluttered 1st-floor Angolan restaurant provides something different, cooking up inviting pork with honey and chicken curry Angolan-style.

Modelo (Avenida dos Descobrimentos; ⏲ 8am-9pm) Self-caterers can stock up with groceries here at this supermarket.

Drinking

Here you can bar hop till you drop, with around 40 tourist bars at the last count. These are some of the Algarve's most diverse drinking holes, roughly divided into those popular with foreigners (complete with antipodean bar staff) and Portuguese hotspots, although the two distinctions blur (particularly later on). Most open till 2am, or 4am in summer.

Key points to underpin your night:

Taverna Velha (Rua Lançarote de Freitas 54) The snug Old Tavern is an old favourite and continues to haul in a lively crowd with its feel-good cocktail of where-it's-at popularity and singalong pop.

Eddie's Bar (Rua 25 de Abril 99) Another buzzing beer stop, this busy dark-wood bar has a good-natured, down-to-earth atmosphere.

Stevie Ray's Blues Jazz Bar (Rua da Senhora da Graça 9; admission €5; ⏲ 8pm-4am) This intimate two-level candlelit joint attracts a smart-casual older crowd, and live music (blues, jazz, oldies) every Saturday.

Fools and Horses (Rua António Barbosa Viana 7; mains €6-13.50, menu €13) For over 26 years this local boozer has offered bastions of English culture such as breakfasts, pints, pub grub and tea for two. The long opening hours are inauthentic, though.

Joe's Garage (Rua 1 de Maio 78) With a dishevelled, bar-scene-from-*Star Wars* vibe (think Aussie backpackers, not aliens), this is the kind of place where you're not sure what might happen next, though shots and dancing on the tables are likely. Staff set fire to the bar to signal closing time and chase out stragglers with chainsaws.

Grand Café (Rua Senhora da Graça) Lagos' most beautiful-people hangout, this classy bar has lots of gold leaf, kitsch, red velvet and cherubs, over which are draped dressed-up local and foreign hipsters.

Lounge (Rua da Barroca) Small and heavy on the leopardskin, Lounge plays a good range of music from – well – lounge to drum 'n' bass and Brazilian to a party crowd.

Açores (Rua Senhora da Graça 12) This Portuguese-run fun bar, with a really lively atmosphere on two levels, offers rock music and snacks with your drinks.

Three Monkeys (Rua Lançarote de Freitas) This is another partying, buzzing backpacker favourite, with Net access.

Meia Praia offers some beachfront gems just seconds from sun, swimming and sand, including **Linda's Bar** with fab food, good salads, cocktails and tunes, and **Bahia Beach Bar**, an essential hang-out. There's live music from 5pm every Sunday – a good time and place to find out about local jobs.

Other Lagos hotspots:

Zanzibar (Rua 25 de Abril) Sparkling with life, friendly and intimate.

Kuinn's (Rua Silva Lopes 5) Where dressed-up Portuguese flock to shake down to pop.

Whytes (Rua do Ferrador) Lively, small and crowded. Downstairs dance bar in summer.

Bombordo (Rua Senhora da Graça) Above a restaurant, this funky club plays lively house.

Phoenix (Rua 5 Outubro) Pop, hip hop, shots, and a bit of a cattlemarket, but fun.

Rosko's (Rua Cândido dos Reis 79) Irish, and has what's rumoured to be Lagos' best bloody Mary.

Stones (Rua 25 de Abril 101) A Salvador Dali poster, but by no means are there surreal antics; a small split-level bar.

Entertainment

Centro Cultural (☎ 282 770 450; Rua Lançarote de Freitas 7; ⏲ 10am-8pm). Lagos' main venue for classical performances, including popular fado concerts, as well as striking contemporary art exhibitions.

Getting There & Away

BUS

From the **bus station** (☎ 282 762 944; Rua Vasco da Gama) buses run to Portimão (€2.10, 20 minutes, four to eight daily) and Albufeira (express/normal €4.25/3.90, one hour, two to three daily). Connections to Sagres run regularly (€2.65, 45 minutes to one hour, about hourly on weekdays, seven daily Saturday and Sunday), via Salema (20 minutes) and some go on to Cabo de São Vicente (€3, one hour, three daily on weekdays).

Eva express buses run to Lisbon (€14.50, 7¼ hours, five to six daily). There are also regular buses to Portimão (€2.10, 20 to 35 minutes, 18 to 19 daily) and Albufeira (€3.90-4.30, one to 1½ hours, five to six daily). To get to/from Carrapateira or Monchique, change at Aljezur (€2.65, 50 minutes, one to two daily) or Portimão. Buses to Aljezur also serve Odeceixe (1½ hours). There's a frequent express service to Lisbon (€15); tickets are available from the **Caima ticket office** (☎ 282 768 931; Rua das Portas de Portugal 101; 7am-1.30pm & 3-7.15pm daily, plus 10.30pm-12.30am Sun-Fri), which can also arrange minibus transfers to Faro airport.

Buses also go to Seville (via Huelva) in Spain (€16, 5½ hours, twice daily Monday to Saturday). Busabout buses (p468) stop near the fire station.

TRAIN

Lagos is at the western end of the Algarve line, with direct regional services to Faro daily (€5, 1¾ to two hours, eight daily), via Albufeira (€4) and Loulé (€4, 1½ hours), with onward connections from Faro to Vila Real de Santo António (€6.50, 3¼ hours) via Tavira (2¼ to 2¾ hours). Trains go daily to Lisbon (all requiring a change at Tunes; €16, 5½ hours, five daily).

Getting Around

CAR, MOTORCYCLE & BICYCLE

Auto Jardim and Luzcar are local agencies offing competitive car-rental rates.

Auto Jardim (☎ 282 769 486; Rua Victor Costa e Silva 18A; 8.30am-noon & 2.30-7pm)

Avis (☎ 282 763 691; Largo das Portas de Portugal; 8.30am-noon & 2.30-7pm) An international agency, near Luzcar.

Luzcar (☎ 282 761 016; www.luzcar.com; Largo das Portas de Portugal 10; 9am-1pm & 3-6pm).

Scooterent (☎ 282 769 716; Rua Victor Costa Silva) You can hire, you've guessed it, scooters (50cc/125cc from €50/65 per three days).

Motoride (☎ 282 761 720; Rua José Afonso 23) Hires out bikes, scooters and motorcycles.

BOAT

In summer, ferries run to and fro across the estuary to the Meia Praia side from a landing just north of Praça do Infante.

TAXI

You can call for **taxis** (☎ 282 763 587) or find them on Rua das Portas de Portugal.

LAGOS TO SAGRES

West of Lagos, the coast is sharp and ragged, and much less developed, though certainly not undiscovered. Once-sleepy fishing villages set above long beaches have woken up to the benefits of tourism and get busy in the summer, but are bewitchingly calm in the off-season when they doze off again.

Luz

Just 6km west of Lagos, Luz (meaning 'light') is a small but appealing resort, packed with Brits and fronted by a sandy beach that's ideal for families. Here **Azure Seas** (☎ 282 788 304; Avenida Pescadores 34) organises bike and car rental, jeep tours and just about everything else. Buses arrive at the central Praça da República.

SLEEPING & EATING

Valverde Camping (☎ 282 789 211; fax 282 789 213; adult/tent/car €4.80/3.90/4;) This is one of the two nearest camp sites, Orbitur's typically slick ground, 3km from Luz and the beach, with shade.

Camping de Espiche (☎ 282 789 265; adult/tent/car €4.50/3.50/3;) Turiscampo-run and only 2km from Luz and also shady. Both have disabled access, bars, restaurants, playgrounds, and caravans and chalets for hire.

Bull (☎ 282 788 823; Rua Calheta 5; mains €6; lunch & dinner) There are lots of pubs and restaurants near Praça da República, including this classic mock-British pub that's more British than conversations about the weather (if you ignore the sunny outdoor tables). It serves culinary classics such as sausages and chips.

THE ALGARVE

Restaurante Atlântico (☎ 282 788 799; Avenida do Pescadores; mains €8-11; ⏰ dinner Tue-Sun) One of the most popular restaurants in the resort, this medium-sized place has indoor and outdoor seating, good international and Portuguese food and is packed with British holiday-makers.

Fortaleza da Luz (☎ 282 789 926; Rua da Igreja 3; mains €10; ⏰ lunch & dinner, barbecue closed Sun dinner) This dramatic 16th-century fort houses Luz's most spectacular restaurant, with a vaulted candlelit interior and covered sea-view terrace. Best of all is the garden overlooking the sea, with Brazilian barbecue on the menu. There's live music Sunday lunch time.

GETTING THERE & AWAY

Buses run frequently from Lagos (€1.40, 15 minutes).

Salema

This charmingly small coastal resort has an easy-going atmosphere; it's set on a wide bay 17km west of Lagos, surrounded by developments that manage not to overwhelm it. It's ideal for families, and there are several small, secluded beaches within a few kilometres – **Praia da Salema** by the village, **Praia da Figueira** to the west and **Boca do Rio** to the east.

Salema has a useful travel agency called **Horizonte** (☎/fax 282 695 920), opposite Hotel Residencial Salema. Horizonte can help with bookings for hotel and villa accommodation (often with discounts), car rental, boat or coach trips, and runs ecofriendly jeep trips within the Parque Natural do Sudoeste Alentejano e Costa Vicentina.

SLEEPING & EATING

Private rooms are plentiful along the seaside Rua dos Pescadores; expect to pay €35 or more for a double.

Senhora Silvina Maria Pedro (☎ 282 695 473; Rua dos Pescadores 91; d/apt €35/50) These charming, tiny rooms with shared bathroom are in a former fisherfolk's house with a small terrace right on the beach.

Quinta dos Carriços (☎ 282 695 201; fax 282 695 122; adult/tent/car €4/4/4) Just 1.5km north of Salema, this place is all about peace and quiet, so shhhh. (Music prohibited!) It has studios and apartments and even its own naturist camping area.

Estalagem Infante do Mar (☎ 282 690 100; www.webzip.pt/infantedomar; s/d around €65/85;) Perched high above the beach, this big modern hotel is the choice for prime comforts, views, peace and quiet.

Hotel Residencial Salema (☎ 282 695 328; www.hotel.salema.pt; s/d with breakfast €63/73) Just a few steps from the beach, Salema is a plain, comfortable, modern hotel.

A row of restaurants along the beach includes **Restaurante Atlântico** (☎ 282 695 742; mains €7-11; ⏰ lunch & dinner), which serves up an appealing range of fish dishes.

GETTING THERE & AWAY

At least six buses daily connect Lagos and Salema (€1.80, 30 minutes).

SAGRES

pop 1940

End-of-the-world Sagres is scattered across sea-carved cliffs, beyond which the ocean stretches out to meet the horizon. Nearby lies Cabo de São Vicente, a wave-lashed, rock-and-brimstone finger of land that gestures out imposingly into the nothingness of the sea.

Here dashing Prince Henry the Navigator built a new, fortified town and a semimonastic school of navigation that specialised in cartography, astronomy and ship design, steering Portugal on towards the Age of Discoveries.

At least, that's according to history and myth. Henry was, among other things, governor of the Algarve and had a residence in its primary port town, Lagos, from where most expeditions actually set sail. He certainly did put together a kind of nautical think-tank, though how much thinking actually went on out at Sagres is uncertain. He definitely had a house somewhere near Sagres, where he died in November 1460. If you want to know more about Henry, there's a thorough biography by Peter Russell (2001).

In May 1587 the English privateer Sir Francis Drake, in the course of attacking supply lines to the Spanish Armada, captured and wrecked the fortifications around Sagres. The Ponta de Sagres was refortified after the earthquake of 1755, which had left little of verifiable antiquity standing.

Paradoxically, quirky ocean currents give Sagres some of Portugal's mildest winters and Atlantic winds keep the summers cool.

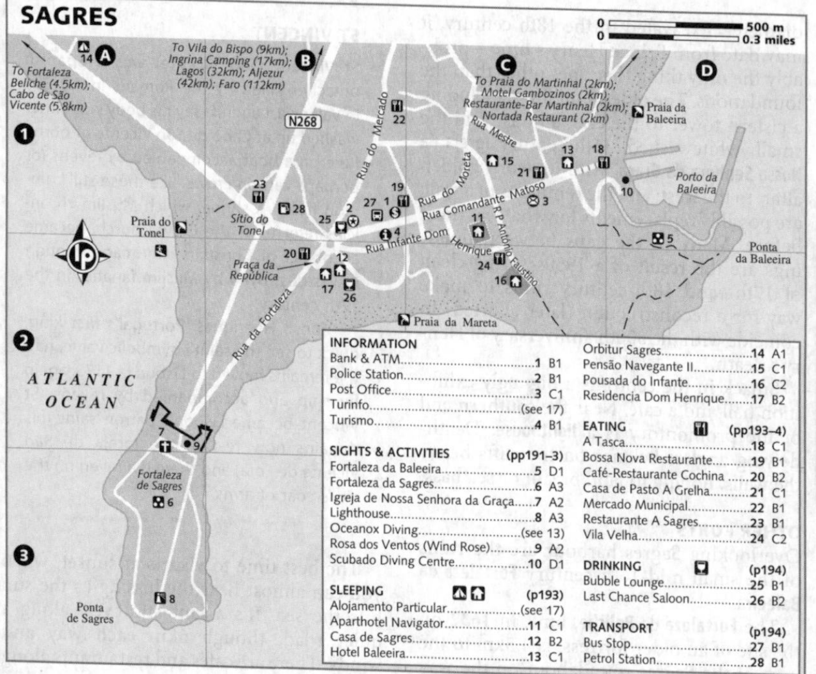

Orientation

From Vila do Bispo, the district's administrative centre at the western end of the N125, a 9km line of villas runs along the N268 to Sagres city centre.

From a roundabout at the end of the N268, roads go west for 6km to the Cabo de São Vicente, south for 1km to the Ponta de Sagres and east for 250m to little Praça da República at the head of unassuming Sagres town. One kilometre east of the square, past holiday villas and restaurants, is the port, still a centre for boat building and lobster fishing, and the marina.

Information

There's a bank and ATM just beyond the turismo, and a post office just beyond Pensão Navegante II (p193).

Turismo (☎ 282 624 873; Rua Comandante Matoso; 🕒 9.30am-12.30pm & 2-6pm Tue-Sat) Near a triangular monument, 100m east of Praça da República.

Turinfo (☎ 282 620 003; turinfo@iol.pt; Residencia Dom Henrique; Praça da República; Net access per hr €6; 🕒 10am-1pm & 2-7pm) A private tourist agency offering currency exchange, regional maps and books, excursions, bicycle hire (per 1/4/8hr €2.50/6/9.50), car rental, bus tickets, and contacts for private rooms and flats. It also has an Internet facility.

Sights

FORTALEZA DE SAGRES

Blank, hulking and prison-like, Sagres' **fortress** (adult/youth 15-25/child €3/1.50/free; 🕒 10am-8.30pm May-Sep, 10am-6.30pm Oct-Apr) has a forbidding front wall balanced by two mighty bastions. Entering is like walking through a stage set to find…nothing. Inside seems like a wasteland, dotted with a few buildings. But it's worth visiting to peer over the fierce, stunningly sheer edges and see the vast views along the coast and to the Cabo de São Vicente.

Apparently there were once short lateral walls inside the fortress as well – the flat promontory's cliffs were protection enough around the rest. In its present form it dates from 1793. Splash out on the guide (€1) that's sold at the entrance, as inside there are no labels to explain what's what.

Inside the gate is a curious, huge stone called **rosa dos ventos** (wind rose, for measuring the direction of the wind) that's 43m in diameter. Excavated in the 18th century, it may date from Prince Henry's time – probably the only thing that does other than the foundations. The oldest buildings, including a cistern tower to the east; a house and the small, whitewashed, 16th-century **Igreja da Nossa Senhora da Graça**, with its worn golden altar, to the west; and the remnants of a wall, are possibly replacements for what was there before. Many of the gaps between buildings are the result of a 1950s spring-clean of 17th- and 18th-century ruins to make way for a reconstruction (later aborted) to coincide with the 500th anniversary of Henry's death.

Smack in the centre is a big, ugly exhibition hall and a café. Near the southern end of the promontory is a **lighthouse**. Death-defying anglers balance on the cliffs below the walls, hoping to land bream or sea bass.

OTHER FORTS

Overlooking Sagres harbour are the ruins of the small mid-16th-century **Fortaleza da Baleeira**.

The **Fortaleza do Beliche**, built in 1632 on the site of an older fortress, is 4.5km to the west of the Sagres roundabout on the way to Cabo de São Vicente. Inside is a small chapel on the site of the ruined Igreja de Santa Catarina (and possibly an old convent). It was once a hotel, but sadly it's crumbling, along with the cliff, and is now off limits.

CABO DE SÃO VICENTE

A trip to **Cabo de São Vicente** (Cape St Vincent), Europe's southwesternmost point, is a must. This barren, thrusting headland is the bleak last piece of home that nervous Portuguese sailors would have seen as they launched into the unknown.

The cape – a revered place even in the time of the Phoenicians and known to the Romans as Promontorium Sacrum – takes its present name from a Spanish priest martyred by the Romans (right). The old fortifications, trashed by Sir Francis Drake in 1587, were later pulverised by the 1755 earthquake.

At the end of the cape are a wind-whipped red lighthouse (hundreds of ocean-going ships round this point every day) and a former convent. Henry the Navigator's house is believed to have been in a small castle to the right of the lighthouse.

> **ST VINCENT**
>
> St Vincent (São Vicente) was a Spanish preacher killed by the Romans in AD 304 in Valencia. Legends say his body was either washed up at Cabo de São Vicente or borne here on a boat accompanied by ravens (or perhaps carrion crows, like those still common here). A shrine, which Muslim chronicles refer to as the Crow Church, became an object of Christian pilgrimage, though it was destroyed by Muslim fanatics in the 12th century.
>
> Afonso Henriques, Portugal's first king, quick to see the saint's symbolic value, had the remains moved to Lisbon in 1173, again by ship and accompanied by ravens. St Vincent became Lisbon's patron saint (his remains now rest in the Igreja de São Vicente de Fora) and there is a raven on the city's coat of arms.

The best time to visit is at sunset, when you can almost hear the hissing as the sun hits the sea. It's a fantastic cycle along a quiet road, though 6km each way and windy. There are cafés and restaurants along the way.

Activities

There are four good beaches a short drive or long walk from Sagres: **Praia da Mareta**, just below the town; lovely **Praia do Martinhal** to the east; **Praia do Tonel** on the other side of the Ponta de Sagres; and the isolated **Praia de Beliche**, on the way to Cabo de São Vicente. **Praia da Baleeira**, adjacent to the harbour, gets polluted from all the boat traffic. Praia do Tonel is especially good for surfing.

Turinfo (p191) can arrange **jeep tours** with Horizonte to the Costa Vicentina or into the Serra de Monchique (€46 per person) or weekend guided walks in southwest Alentejo or Costa Vicentina.

The **Scubado Diving Centre** (☎ 282 624 594, 965 559 073; www.scubado-algarve.com; Porto da Baleeira; 🕑 dives at 10am & 3pm) organises diving trips (this is a great spot for shipwrecks between 12m and 30m). A dive and equipment costs €34/190/305 per one/six/10 days, while the four-day PADI open-water course goes for €280. Nondivers can ride in the boat for €5, and snorkel hire costs €10 per day.

You can also dive with **Oceanox Diving** (☎ 964 854 021; www.oceanox.net; Hotel Baleeira Complex; 3/10 dives €50/170).

Surfing is possible at all beaches except Praia do Martinhal. Praia da Baleeira is not suitable for swimmers or surfers. The **International Surf School** (☎ 914 482 407, 964 466 851 www.internationalsurfschool.com; 1-/3-/5- day €30/80/120) offers lessons.

Approximately 10km north of Sagres Julie Statham, author of *Portugal Walks*, runs **Portugal Walks** (☎ 282 698 676; www.portugalwalks.com; 37 Quinta do Montinho, Budens, Vila do Bispo), which offers all-inclusive week-long packages (€375 to €1475) for guided or unguided walks.

Sleeping

Sagres fills up in summer, though it's marginally easier to find accommodation here than in the rest of the Algarve during the high season, especially if you arrive before noon. Except at Pousada do Infante, all prices drop considerably outside summer; rates here are for July.

BUDGET

Every other house in Sagres seems to advertise private rooms or apartments. Doubles generally go for €30 and flats for €45 to €80 in high season.

Residencia Dom Henrique (☎ 282 620 003; fax 282 620 004; Praça da República; s/d with breakfast €35/40) This guesthouse offers plain but decent rooms. Those with great sea views from the back balconies cost extra.

Alojamento Particular (☎ 282 624 096; fax 282 764 775; Praça da República; s/d/tr/q €30/45/50/55) Rooms here are spacious, light and bright, with lots of pastel colours. Definitely go for a sea view and balcony.

Casa de Sagres (☎ 282 624 358; s/d with breakfast €35/50) Efficient and pretty, this place has a great, almost beachside, location, with sea views (costing more) and large, comfortable rooms. Prices sink in the off-season.

Orbitur Sagres (☎ 282 624 371; fax 282 624 445; adult/tent/car €3.30/3.50/3.80) Some 2km from town, just off the road to Cabo de São Vicente, this is a super-shaded, well-maintained site with lots of trees. You can hire bikes here.

Ingrina Camping (☎ /fax 282 639 242; adult/tent/car €4.50/4.50/3.70) About 17km northeast of Sagres, this is a much smaller site, 600m from the beach south of Raposeira, with shade, a restaurant and bike hire.

MID-RANGE & TOP END

Hotel Baleeira (☎ 282 624 212; www.sagres.net/baleeira; Rua Comandante Matoso; d with buffet breakfast €98;) Bagging the best eastern spot, this is a modernish low-rise with harbour views and comfy rooms. The pool overlooks the sea and there's a tennis court.

Aparthotel Navigator (☎ 282 624 354; www.hotel-navigator.com; Rua Infante Dom Henrique; 1-/2-/3-person apt €50/55/60;) Wonder if Prince Henry would dig his namesake…a giant, modern place with large, well-appointed apartments with sweeping views, balcony and satellite TV.

Pensão Navegante II (☎ 282 624 442; zeliafreitas@hotmail.com; Sítio da Baleeira; d with breakfast €60) This long-standing place has a faded feel, but its rooms are huge and it's easy-going.

Motel Gambozinos (☎ 282 620 160; fax 282 620 169; Praia do Martinhal; d €55, d/ste with sea view €65/75) Within earshot of the sea, this low-rise motel is among trees in a lush setting above the beach. Rooms are basic with some nice wooden furniture and strange mud-coloured murals.

Pousada do Infante (☎ 282 624 222; fax 282 624 225; d Mon-Fri €143, Sat & Sun €157;) This quite modern *pousada* has large, luscious rooms in a great setting near the clifftop. Rates drop by one third November to March.

Eating

Many of the following places close or operate shorter hours during the low season (November to April).

Restaurante A Sagres (☎ 282 624 171; Sítio do Tonel; mains €4-10; breakfast, lunch & dinner Thu-Tue) A traditional place on the way into Sagres, this is a nice, untouristy stop, with a good selection of pastries and outside seating overlooking the…road.

Casa de Pasto A Grelha (☎ 282 624 193; Rua Comandante Matoso; mains €3.70-7.50; lunch & dinner) Offers cheap, filling meals and great take-away grilled chicken.

Nortada (☎ 282 624 147; Praia da Martinhal; mains €6-10; year-round; lunch & dinner) Right on the beach, Nortada dishes up everything from pizzas to swordfish steak. There's also **Restaurante-Bar Martinhal** (☎ 282 624 032; Praia da Martinhal; mains €1-10.50; lunch & dinner) with a wooden hut on the beach and similar snacks.

Bossa Nova Restaurante (☎ 282 624 566; off Avenida Comandante Matasco; mains €4.60-9.30; lunch &

dinner) Come here for good pizzas. It's set off the main drag, behind Dromedário Bistro-Bar, with an attractive open-air dining area with wooden benches. Inside and out are big groovy canvases.

A Tasca (☎ 282 624 177; Porto da Baleeira; dishes €6.50-18, menu €18.50; lunch & dinner daily, closed Sat Nov-Apr) Overlooking the marina and out to sea, this place specialises in seafood, has a sunny seaside terrace or a cosy interior with bottles embedded in the walls.

Vila Velha (☎ 282 624 788; Rua P António Faustino; mains €8-16.75; dinner Tue-Sun) In a charming house with pine furnishing inside, this restaurant offers rich seafood mains and a good vegetarian range. The desserts are good.

Praça da República has several eateries, including **Café-Restaurante Cochina** (mains €6-12.50; breakfast, lunch & dinner), with a large menu and seats on the square.

The *mercado municipal* provides great supplies for long days on the beaches.

Drinking

Last Chance Saloon (☎ 282 624 113) In a wooden building just down the hill from the square and overlooking the sea, this bar has a great last-chance neo-saloon look about it.

Bubble Lounge (☎ 282 624 494; Rua Senhora da Graça; 4pm-2am Tue-Sun, to 3am Jul & Aug) Bright walls, beanbags, low seating, Indian lanterns and wall hangings: boho Bubble Lounge has an easy vibe and cool music. It's friendly and there is a small streetside terrace.

Getting There & Around

Buy tickets from the newsagent kiosk on Praça da República. The bus stop is north-east of the turismo. For information call ☎ 282 762 944.

Buses come from Lagos (€2.65, 50 minutes, 10 to 20 daily), via Salema, and Portimão (€4.25, 1¾ hours, three daily on weekdays). It's only 10 minutes to Cabo de São Vicente (three daily on weekdays).

Through Turinfo you can hire a car, or rent bikes (€10 per day).

For a taxi, call ☎ 282 624 501.

NORTH OF SAGRES

Heading north along the Algarve's western coast you'll find some amazing beaches, backed by beautiful wild vegetation. It's so preserved because of building restrictions imposed to protect the Parque Natural do Sudoeste Alentejano e Costa Vicentina. This extraordinary area, protected since 1995, is rarely more than 6km wide, and runs for about 120km from Burgau to Cabo de São Vicente and up nearly the entire western Algarve and Alentejo shore. Here there are at least 48 plant species found only in Portugal, and around a dozen or so found only within the park. It's home to otters, foxes and wild cats. And 200 species of birds enjoy the coastal wetlands, salt marshes and cliffs, including Portugal's last remaining ospreys. The seas are sometimes dangerous, but the area has a growing reputation for some of Europe's finest surf and attracts people from all over the world.

Carrapateira

Surf-central Carrapateira is a quiet, pretty, spread-out village, with two exhilarating beaches nearby whose lack of development, fizzing surf and strong swells attract a hippy, surf-dude crowd. The coast along here is wild, with copper-coloured and ash-grey cliffs covered in speckled yellow and green scrub, backing creamy, wide sands.

Praia da Bordeira (also known as Praia Carrapateira) is a mammoth swathe merging into dunes, 2km off the road on the northern side of the village, while the similarly stunning **Praia do Amado** (more famous for its surf) is at the southern end of the village and home to a controversial but low-key community of travellers.

Contact **Algarve Surf** (p185) for surfing courses. Or try the less official **Amado Camp** (☎ 964 432 324, 962 681 478; surfrider@europe.com; 1-week accommodation, equipment hire & lessons €300, €200 if camping; lessons per hr €35; boards per 1/2/3hr €10/18/20), run by two local brothers who are passionate and experienced surfers. They built the camp – basic but well-made three-bed wooden huts, with a communal kitchen – on family farmland, in a beautiful remote setting. They also hire out boards on both beaches from May to September.

SLEEPING & EATING

Pensão das Dunas (☎/fax 282 973 118; Rua da Padaria 9; d €25, 1-/2-room apts €40/5) A gorgeous gem with rooms overlooking a courtyard filled with brilliant flowers. It's 100m from the road at the southern end of the village. Meals are available here or next door at the tiny, no-frills **Restaurante Torres** (☎ 282

973 222; Rua da Padaria 7; mains €5-9; lunch & dinner Tue-Sun), which has simple food and a couple of outdoor tables.

Casa Fajara (282 973 123; www.casafajara.pt; d €50;) Some 500m from the village or 1.2km from Praia da Bordeira, this big modern house overlooks a valley and has rooms with shared kitchen, plus a swimming pool and tennis courts. They don't accept children under the age of six and are closed from November to March.

O Sítio do Rio (282 973 119; mains €5.50-17.50; lunch & dinner Wed-Mon) Right on the dunes near Praia da Bordeira, this fine airy place serves excellent grilled fish and meat mains with eclectic sauces, as well as a couple of vegetarian choices. It's hugely popular with Portuguese at weekends.

Restaurante do Cabrita (282 973 128; mains €2-12, tourist menu €15; lunch & dinner) Near the main N268 and also specialising in grills, this is a big, friendly restaurant.

Aljezur

Some 20km further north, Aljezur is a quiet village that straddles a river. One part, to the west, is Moorish – a collection of cottages below a ruined 10th-century hilltop castle; the other, called Igreja Nova (meaning 'new church'), is 600m up a steep hill to the east. Aljezur is close to some fantastic beaches, edged by black rocks that reach into the white-tipped, bracing sea – surfing hotspots. The countryside around, which is part of the natural park, is a tangle of yellow, mauve and green wiry gorse and heather.

ORIENTATION & INFORMATION

The high-up, pretty Largo Igreja Nova is the new town's focus, with some small cafés. Banks with ATMs, shops and restaurants can all be found on Rua 25 de Abril.

Espaço Internet (Largo Igreja Nova; 3-8pm Mon-Tue, Thu-Fri, to 10pm Sat-Sun).

Post office (282 990 160; Rua 25 de Abril; 9am-12.30pm & 2-5pm Mon-Fri)

Turismo (282 998 229; 9.30am-7pm Tue-Thu Jun-Sep, to 6pm Tue-Thu Oct-May7pm Tue-Thu Jun-Sep, 10am-1.30pm & 2.30-6pm Mon year-round) The turismo is by a small covered market, just before the bridge leading to the Lagos N120 road (Rua 25 de Abril). Buses stop near here.

SIGHTS & ACTIVITIES

Nearby wonderful, unspoilt beaches include **Praia da Arrifana** (10km southwest, near a tourist development called Vale da Telha), a dramatic curved black-cliff–backed bay with one restaurant, balmy pale sands and some big northwest swells (a surfer's delight); and **Praia de Monte Clérigo**, about 8km northwest. **Praia de Amoreira**, 6km away, is a wonderful beach where the river meets the sea.

Beginners and more experienced riders can go **horse riding** (282 991 150; per one/two hr €15/25, per half-/full day €45/70) in the natural park.

SLEEPING

The turismo in Aljezur has a list of accommodation in the area, including *quartos*.

Residencial Dom Sancho II (282 998 119; turimol@iol.pt; Largo Igreja Nova; s/d or tw with breakfast €30/45) Next to the *supermercados* in Igreja Nova, just off the main square, this guesthouse has spacious old-fashioned rooms.

Restaurante-Bar A La Reira (282 998 440; Rua 13 de Janeiro; s/d €20/25) Also in Igreja Nova, this place has big, good-value rooms opening onto a large sunny terrace with a pleasant view.

Hospedaria O Palazim (282 998 249; N120; d with breakfast around €40) This modern, hilltop place is charming, with rooms with balconies and nice views. It's 2km north of Aljezur on the Lisbon road.

In Praia da Arrifana are several *quartos.* Try the small modern ones belonging to **Senhora Odete** (282 998 789; d €30), next to A Tasquinha café, on the road above the beach. They're comfortable, with carved wooden beds, and look out onto palms and flowers.

Camping-Caravaning Vale da Telha (282 998 444; www.campingvaledatelha.netfirms.com; adult/tent/car €2.80/3/2.60;) About 2km south of Praia de Monte Clérigo, this is a shady, well-appointed site with good views and tennis courts.

Parque de Campismo Serrão (282 990 220; camping-serrao@clix.pt; adult/tent/car €4/4/2.80;) This calm, shady site is 4km north of Aljezur, then 800m down the road to Praia da Amoreira (the beach is 2.5km further). It has wheelchair access, tennis courts, a playground and apartments, plus bike rental.

EATING & DRINKING

Snack-Bar Tasca Matias (282 991 020) This friendly café (run by English-speakers), is opposite Residencial Dom Sancho II in Igreja Nova.

O Chefe Dimas (☎ 282 998 275; Aldeia Velha; mains €4-14; ⌚ lunch & dinner Thu-Tue) Next to Hospedaria O Palazim, this is the best fish restaurant around, serving deliciously scrumptious fresh fish and shellfish or monkfish rice.

Pontá Pé (☎ 282 998 104; Largo da Liberdade; mains €6.50-12; ⌚ lunch & dinner) Friendly, with wooden floors and a beamed ceiling, Pontá Pé does tasty fish dishes. Adjoining is a cheery bar with themed nights from Thursday to Sunday, from Brazilian live music to karaoke.

Comidaria o Acepipe (Largo Igreja Nova; mains €5-8; ⌚ breakfast & lunch) This small café is popular with locals for its simple mains such as grilled chicken to eat in or takeaway.

Two casual, popular places are the boat-decorated **Restaurante Ruth o Ivo** (☎ 282 998 534; Rua 25 de Abril 14; mains €4.25-12; ⌚ lunch & dinner) and **Primavera** (☎ 282 998 294; Rua 25 de Abril 67; mains around €5.50-6.80; ⌚ breakfast, lunch & dinner Mon-Sat), with a wood-sheltered streetside terrace.

In Praia da Arrifana there's a string of seafood restaurants (packed with Portuguese at weekends) on the road above the beach, where you can expect to pay around €7 for fish dishes.

At Praia da Amoreira check out **Restaurante Paraíso do Mar** (☎ 282 991 088; mains from €5-14.20; ⌚ lunch & dinner), which has a most wonderful vantage point overlooking the beach.

Odeceixe

Around here the countryside rucks up into rolling, large hills. As the Alentejo turns into the Algarve, the first coastal settlement is Odeceixe, an endearing small town clinging to the southern side of the Ribeira de Seixe valley, and so snoozy it's in danger of falling off, apart from the high season, when German, French and Portuguese visitors pack the place. The sheltered **Praia de Odeceixe**, 3.5km down the valley is a wonderful bite of sand surrounded by gorse and tree-covered cliffs.

SLEEPING

There are plenty of well-advertised *quartos* in the village, especially along Rua Nova (en route to the beach). Expect to pay at least €30 for a double. The prices quoted here are for July – you'll get bargains in the low season.

Parque de Campismo São Miguel (☎ 282 947 145; camping.sao.miguel@mail.telepac.pt; adult/tent/car €4.80/4.80/3.60) Facility-loaded and pine-shaded, this camp site is 1.5km north of Odeceixe, and has lots of shade, and appealing wooden bungalows.

Pensão Luar (☎ 282 947 194; Rua da Várzea 28; d €35) At the western edge of the village, en route to the beach, this *pensão* is an excellent bargain, with white spic-and-span modern rooms with balconies overlooking fields.

Residência do Parque (☎ 282 947 117; Rua dos Correiros 15; d with breakfast €25; ⌚ Apr-Oct) Beside the post office, this central guesthouse is a bargain off-season (double €17.50). Rooms are airy and bright, some with balconies and views, some with huge baths. The breakfast is worth getting up for. Downstairs is a hammock room, so you can lie down afterwards.

EATING

Restaurante Chaparro (☎ 282 947 304; Rua Estrada Nacional; mains €7-8.50; ⌚ lunch & dinner Mon-Sat) Opposite the post office, Chaparro has some good food and a cheery yellow interior.

Café O Retiro do Adelino (☎ 282 947 352; Rua Nova 20; mains €5-10; ⌚ lunch & dinner Tue-Sun) A large simple place with TV and outdoor tables in a small courtyard, this café will keep you in *bacalhau* (dried salt cod) and grilled meats.

There are several pleasant restaurants around Largo 1 Mai, a great spot to sit and watch the world amble by.

A Tasca da Saskia (Rua das Amoreiros; mains €2-7.60; ⌚ dinner Tue-Sun) With a small corner terrace laden with flowerpots, this arty little café off the main square provides lots of vegie options as well as other mains, such as spaghetti with shrimp.

GETTING THERE & AWAY

Buses run from Lagos to Odeceixe (€3.25, 80 minutes, five daily) via Aljezur (€2.65, 50 minutes).

One daily bus connects Vila do Bispo with Carrapateira (€3, one hour). There's a twice-weekly service to Praia de Arrifana from Aljezur.

THE INTERIOR

MONCHIQUE

pop 6975 / elevation 410m

A fiercely beautiful, lilting landscape surrounds this small, bustling hill station, set up in the forested Serra de Monchique, the Algarve's mountain range and 24km north of Portimão. It's a crisp-aired contrast to the Algarve coast, and a great region for biking, walking or horse riding. If you're not feeling that energetic, there's a balmy spa hidden in woodland and a wonderful private zoo for endangered species.

Fires regularly affect this area in the height of summer, causing widespread damage and frustration at the lack of measures to prevent the annual devastation.

Orientation & Information

Buses drop you in the central Largo dos Chorões, with a café and clunking waterwheel sculpture.

Espaço Internet (☎ 282 910 235; Largo dos Chorões; 🕓 3-9pm Mon-Thu, 11am-11pm Fri-Sun)

Turismo (☎ 282 911 189; Largo dos Chorões; 🕓 10am-1.30pm & 2.30-6pm daily Jun-Aug, Mon-Fri Sep-May) Can be helpful, but has off days.

Sights

A series of brown pedestrian signs starting near the bus station directs visitors up into the town's narrow old streets and major places of interest. The **igreja matriz** (admission free; 🕓 9am-5pm daily) has an extraordinary, star-shaped Manueline porch decorated with twisted columns looking like lengths of knotted rope, and a simple interior, with columns topped by more stoney rope and some fine chapels, including one whose vault contains beautiful 17th-century glazed tiles showing St Francis, and St Michael killing the devil.

Keep climbing and you'll eventually reach the ruined Franciscan monastery of **Nossa Senhora do Desterro**, which overlooks the town from its wooded hilltop. Built in 1632, it is to be redeveloped into a 24-room hotel.

Activities

All these require advance reservations.

The German-run **Nature Walk** (☎ 282 911 041, 964 308 767) organises one-day walking trips to nearby 773m Picota peak (€20 per person) and full-moon walks during summer.

Alternativ Tour (☎ 916 294 726, 965 004 337) offers guided walks (adult/child €30/20, including picnic); mountain-bike tours (€40/27, including picnic, €15 on your own, with a map provided); canoeing trips (€25); or combined mountain-biking and canoeing trips (€49).

Contact **Gunther** (☎ 282 913 657) for guided horse-riding (no beginners) trips. Advance notice is required.

Dutch-run **Outdoor Tours** (☎ 282 969 520, 916 736 226; www.outdoor-tours.net; based in Alvor) offers bike, canoe and walking trips in the Monchique Mountains. Among other walks, there is an easy, rewarding trail from Fóia, walking downhill to Monchique and then down to Caldas de Monchique (€29, from 9.30am to 4pm). Biking tours, also downhill (hydraulic brakes take the strain; €37, 9.30am to 2pm). They offer pick-ups from Portimão, Lagos, Carveiro and Albufeira (€4 to €8).

Sleeping

BUDGET

Residencial Estrela de Monchique (☎ 282 913 111; Rua do Porto Fundo 46; s/d €20/30) Near the bus station, this is a cheery place in the centre, with good-value rooms above a café.

Residencial Miradouro (☎ 282 912 163; Rua dos Combatentes do Ultramar; s/d with breakfast €25/35) Up steep Rua Engenheiro Duarte Pacheco (signposted to Portimão), near the bus station, this hilltop 1970s place, run with great seriousness, offers sweeping, breezy views and neat rooms, some with balcony.

MID-RANGE

Albergaria Bica-Boa (☎ 282 912 271; d with breakfast €60; 🍽) One kilometre out of town on the Lisbon road, this gorgeous four-room place overlooks a wooded valley. There's a decent restaurant here, too (with vegetarian dishes).

Quinta de São Bento (☎/fax 282 912 143; Fóia Rd; s/d with breakfast €63/78) A former holiday home of the Portuguese royal family, this is on the road to Fóia and has a balmy pool amid lush gardens.

Eating

Barlefante Tapas (Travessa das Guerreiras; mains €2.40-3.50; 🕓 noon-2am Mon-Thu, to 4am Fri-Sun) Signposted off the main drag, this is a great find, with golden-yellow walls, red-velvet alcoves, ornate mirrors, some outside tables in the narrow cobbled lane, and excellent tapas (a.k.a. sandwiches) with home-made bread. It's young Monchique's hippest haunt.

Restaurante Palmeirinha dos Chorões (☎ 282 912 588; Rua Serpa Pinto 23A; mains €5-7; ⏰ lunch & dinner) Near the turismo and offering Portuguese dishes, this restaurant has stunning views from its back window.

Restaurante Central (☎ 282 913 160; Rua da Igreja; mains €4-8; ⏰ lunch & dinner) Winning the most eccentric award, this pint-sized place is run by the characterful Nita Massano, who dishes out chicken *piri piri* when the conditions are right. The walls are smothered in a mixed array of testimonies from previous diners.

A Charrete (☎ 282 912 142; Rua Dr Samora Gil 30-34; mains €7-12, tourist menu €9.50; ⏰ lunch & dinner) Here you can feast on local specialities such as grilled boar steaks or stuffed squid, in an appealing space lined by wooden cabinets filled with grandma's china.

There are lots of restaurants on the way to Fóia offering *piri-piri* chicken. In a nice setting, about 2km from Monchique and off the main road is **Jardim das Oliveiras** (☎ 282 912 874; off Rua do Foia; mains €4-18.50; ⏰ lunch & dinner) This has regional dishes, shady trees and outside seating.

Shopping

Distinctive, locally made 'scissor chairs' – wooden folding stools – are a good buy here. Try shops along Rua Serpa Pinto, which runs from Largo dos Choróes.

Getting There & Away

Buses run from Portimão (€2.20, 45 minutes, six to eight daily).

AROUND MONCHIQUE

Fóia

The 902m Fóia peak is the Algarve's highest point, 8km west of Monchique. The road to the summit climbs through eucalyptus and pine trees and opens up vast views over the rolling hills. On the way are numerous *piri-piri* pitstops offering spicy chicken. Telecommunication towers spike the peak, but ignore them and look at the panoramic views. On clear days you can see out to the corners of the western Algarve – Cabo de São Vicente to the southwest and Odeceixe to the northwest.

A bus runs here once daily from Monchique from June to September.

Omega Parque

In a beautiful hilly setting, this marvellous, small-but-spacious **zoo** (☎ 282 911 327; www.omegaparque.com; adult/child €8/5; ⏰ 10am-5.30pm, 10am-7pm) is dedicated to endangered animal species and is a family-run labour of love. You can decide whether the sweetest is the red panda, pygmy hippo, the winsome ring-tailed lemur or Waldrapp ibis (cartoon-like birds resembling elderly men). Our favourite is the Ne Ne Hawaiian goose, so-called because of its despondent 'ne ne' cry (perhaps bemoaning its scarcity). It's the fault of humankind – all the species have been threatened due to hunting and loss of habitat.

Both children and adults will love it. There's also a café with a view. The zoo is on the N266, just before Caldas de Monchique. Buses between Portimão and Monchique stop here.

Caldas de Monchique

Caldas de Monchique is a faintly fantastical place, with a therapeutic calm, and pastel-painted buildings nestling above a delightful valley full of birdsong, eucalyptus, acacia and pine trees, 6km south of Monchique. It has been a popular spa for over two millennia – the Romans loved its 32°C, slightly sulphurous waters, which are said to be good for rheumatism and respiratory and digestive ailments. Dom João II came here for years in an unsuccessful attempt to cure his dropsy.

Floods in 1997 led to the closure of the spa hospital, after which it was redeveloped into a spa resort, and its picturesque buildings repainted pale pink, green and yellow.

ORIENTATION & INFORMATION

The hamlet is 500m below the main road. At reception (the first building on your left) you can book accommodation. Spa treatments and other luxuries are available at the spa.

SIGHTS

The most peaceful patch is a pretty, stream-side garden above the hamlet's central square. Down the valley is the spa itself and below this is the huge bottling plant where the famous Caldas waters are bottled.

Just below the central square, in a small white building, you can taste the smelly, sulphurous water. Yum. And beware – it's hot!

In the wooded valley below town, at the **Termas de Monchique Spa** (☎ 282 910 910; www.monchiquetermas.com; admission €23 hotel guests €10; 10.30am-1pm Tue, 9am-1pm Wed-Mon & 3-7pm daily) admission allows access to sauna, steam bath, gym and swimming pool with hydromassage jets. You can then indulge in special treatments, from a Cleopatra bath to a Tired Legs treatment. A 40-minute massage costs €34.

SLEEPING & EATING

There are two private places: **Restaurante & Residencial Granifóia** (☎ 282 910 500; fax 282 912 218; s/d/tw with breakfast €23/25/30;), 400m down the road from the turn-off to the hamlet, is a modern, unattractive building that has good-value rooms with nice views, while **Albergaria Lageado** (☎ 282 912 616; fax 282 911 310; s/d €40/45;) is an attractive hotel with a red-sloped roof. It provides old fashioned, appealing rooms, a small camellia-surrounded pool and a restaurant.

The three other hotels all belong to Termas de Monchique. **Hotel Termal** (s/d €50/60), located next to the spa, is the cheapest and biggest; **Pensão Central** (s/d €60/80), next to reception, has 13 beautifully furnished rooms; and **Estalagem Central** (s/d €60/80), opposite reception, is the most luxurious. The Termas also runs the self-catering **Apartmentos Turísticos D Francisco** (apt €83). You can book weekend or weeklong packages that include treatments.

The upmarket **Restaurante 1692** (mains €6-16, 4-course menu €11.50; lunch & dinner) has tables in the tree-shaded central square and a smart, vaulted interior.

GETTING THERE & AWAY

The Monchique to Portimão bus service (p198) goes via Caldas de Monchique: the bus stop is on the road above the hamlet.

ALCOUTIM

pop 3770

Alcoutim (ahl-ko-*teeng*) sits in a glorious spot above the lazy, boat-dotted Rio Guadiana, almost within spitting distance of the Spanish village of Sanlúcar de Guadiana, which rises up like a reflection on the opposite bank. What-are-you-looking-at fortresses above both villages remind one of testier times. Phoenicians, Greeks, Romans and Arabs have barricaded themselves in the hills here, and centuries of tension have bubbled across the river, which forms the Algarve's entire eastern boundary. In the 14th century, Dom Fernando I of Portugal and Don Henrique II of Castile signed a tentative peace treaty in Alcoutim. Today the best activities are riverside lazing, cobbled-street ambling, a jaunty ferry trip to Spain or a riverboat trip.

VIA ALGARVIANA

A 243km trail has been blazed across the Algarve, from Alcoutim to Cabo de São Vicente. Tested by both walkers and horse riders, the Via Algarviana is largely marked. For more details, contact the **Federação Portuguesa de Campismo Caravanismo** (☎ 218 126 890; info@fpcampismo.pt; Avenida Coronel Eduardo Galhardo 24D, 1100-007 Lisbon).

Orientation & Information

Alcoutim has a new town development 500m north of the square across the Ribeira de Cadavais stream.

Café Vila Velha (Rua da Misericordia; per hr €2; 10-2am Mon-Sat) Just off the central square; another Internet facility (when the connection's working).

Casa dos Condes (☎ 281 546 104; 9am-1pm & 2-5pm) Opposite the turismo; has free Internet access, a small display of local crafts and offers guided visits of Alcoutim.

Turismo (☎ 281 546 179; Rua 1 de Maio; 10am-1.30pm & 2.30-6pm Fri-Mon, 9.30am-6pm Tue-Thu) Behind the central square, just a few steps from the river.

Sights & Activities

The flower-ringed 14th-century **castelo** (admission €2.60; 9am-1pm & 2-5pm) has sweeping views. Inside the grounds is the small, excellent **Núcleo Museológico de Arqueologia** (archaeological museum), displaying ruined medieval castle walls and other artefacts.

You can cross the river on the small local **ferry** (€1, 9am-1pm & 2-7pm). Rent bikes or canoes from the *pousada da juventude* (p200).

The prehistoric **Parque Mineiro Cova dos Mouros** (copper mine; ☎ 281 498 505; minacovamouros.sitepac.pt; adult/child €5/4.20; 10.30am-6pm Mar-Oct,

THE ALGARVE

MONCHIQUE'S MOONSHINE

You can find commercial brands of *medronho* (a locally made firewater) everywhere in Portugal, but according to those who have suffered enough hangovers to know, the best of all is the Monchique privately made brew.

The Serra de Monchique is thick with *medronho*'s raw material – the arbutus, or strawberry tree. Its berries are collected in late autumn, fermented and then left for months before being distilled in large copper stills (for sale as souvenirs all over the Algarve).

Home-made *medronho* is usually clear and drunk neat, like schnapps. It's strong, of course, but as long as you don't mix it with other drinks it doesn't give you a hangover (say the connoisseurs). Early spring, when distilling is under way, is the best time to track down some of this brew in Monchique: ask around.

to 4.30pm Nov-Mar), 38km west of town near Vaqueiros, is over 4500 years old and includes Roman remains. You can follow a 1km walk, peer down the ancient old mine shafts and visit a reconstructed prehistoric house. For kids there are donkey rides and a nature trail, and you can also swim in the Ribeira da Foupana.

Sleeping & Eating

Private *quartos* are available (doubles around €25); ask at the turismo.

Ildo Afonso (Rua Dr João Dias; s/d €20/30) This *quarto,* with smartly decorated, bright rooms is recommended.

Pousada da juventude (☎ 281 546 004; alcoutim@movijovem.pt; dm €12.50, d €35, 4-/6-bed rooms €55/82.50; reception 🕒 8am-noon & 6pm-midnight; 🅿) One kilometre north of the square, past the new town and fire station, is this fantastically situated, well-appointed hostel, with an excellent pool and kitchen facilities, plus bikes and canoes for rent.

Estalagem do Guadiana (☎ 281 540 120; fax 281 546 647; s/d with breakfast €50/80) Below the *pousada da juventude*, this place has big rooms, big views and creature comforts in a modern building that's appealingly secluded.

Snack Bar Restaurante O Soeiro (☎ 281 546 241; Rua do Município; daily special €6; 🕒 lunch & dinner Mon-Fri) is a good choice, with a few outdoor tables overlooking the river. Both it and **Casa de Pasto O Rogério** (☎ 281 546 185; Praça da República; daily special €4; 🕒 lunch daily), a lively place on the main square, serve great lunches. They're popular with locals, so go early.

Getting There & Away

Buses from Vila Real de Santo António (€3, 1¼ hours, two daily Monday to Friday) go on to Beja (two hours) via Mértola (50 minutes).

The Alentejo

CONTENTS

Hills as rounded as sand dunes, seas of wheat, walled towns and remote prehistoric architecture, *alem Tejo* (beyond the Tejo) seems summed up by its elsewhere name. Covering almost a third of the country, olive groves, cork oaks and cattle outnumber people in a way that calls to mind the endless space of American plains. It's one of Portugal's poorest regions, but has one of its architecturally richest towns in Évora, it is scattered with prehistoric remains, and its peak and outcrops are topped by rarely visited, spectacular huddled fortified villages.

Like many places, the Alentejo has been brought closer to the rest of the world with the satellite-wired, concrete boots of modernity: the Lisbon–Estremoz motorway and Vasco da Gama bridge have made it more easily accessible, and you can watch CNN in the thick-walled, hilltop village of Monsaraz. In the southeast, the whole landscape has altered, with the new Alqueva dam flooding the countryside to make Europe's largest lake – creating new opportunities to attract young people back to the Alentejo, which seems mainly populated by the over 60s and under 10s, and bringing (it's hoped) economic salvation to this thirsty rural province.

But these leaps and bounds have not fundamentally altered anything in the province: people still meet in the village square to trade goats and dogs, there's only one dusty grocery shop and a van selling kitchenware plays a tune to announce its arrival. Most farmers wear flat caps or trilbies, and it seems obligatory that those over a certain age must sit and chat in the local square, and watch the world turn. Slooowly.

Spring is a good time to visit, when the land gets covered in wild flowers.

HIGHLIGHTS

- **Treasure Trove**
  Évora – a Unesco World Heritage city (p203)
- **Old Town Stroll**
  The walled town of Mértola, declared an open museum (p237)
- **Walled Wonders**
  Monsaraz (p217), Marvão (p235) and Castelo de Vide (p232)
- **Big, Big Stones**
  Megaliths built like they were going out of fashion around Évora (p203) and Monsaraz (p217)
- **Adrenaline Rush**
  The wild seas and long beaches near Vila Nova (p249)
- **Weird Waterworld**
  Alqueva dam – a freshly drowned landscape, boat trips and 400 islands (p205)

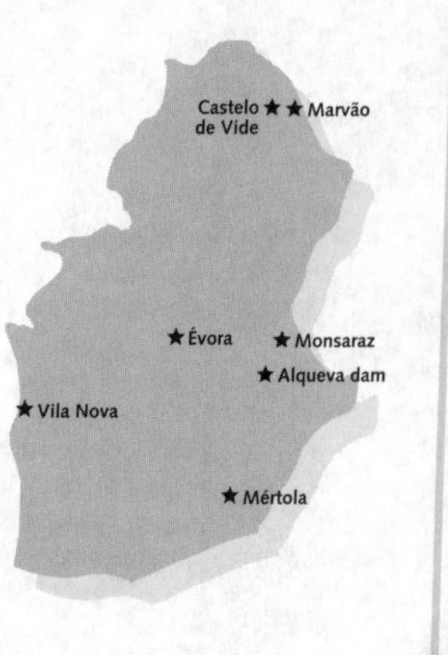

POPULATION: 767,983	AREA: 31,483 SQ KM

History

Prehistoric Alentejo was a busy place, and today's landscape is covered in megaliths. But it was the Romans who stamped and shaped the landscape, introducing vines, wheat and olives, building dams and irrigation schemes and founding huge estates called *latifúndios* (still existing today) to make the most of the region's limited rivers and poor soil.

The Moors, arriving in the early 8th century, took Roman irrigation further and introduced new crops such as citrus and rice. By 1279 they were on the run to southern Spain, or were forced to live in *mouraria* (segregated Moorish quarters) outside town walls. Many of their hilltop citadels were later reinforced by Dom Dinis, who threw a chain of spectacular fortresses along the Spanish border.

Despite Roman and Moorish development, the Alentejo remained agriculturally poor and backward, increasingly so as the Age of Discoveries led to an explosive growth in maritime trade and as seaports became sexy. Only Évora flourished, under the royal patronage of the House of Avis, but it too declined once the Spanish seized the throne in 1580.

During the 1974 revolution the Alentejo suddenly stepped into the limelight; landless rural workers who had laboured on the *latifúndios* for generations rose up in support of the communist rebellion and seized the land from its owners. Nearly 1000 estates were collectivised, although few succeeded and all were gradually reprivatised in the 1980s. Most are now back in the hands of their original owners.

Today the Alentejo, an area of gently rolling hills and plains with huge estates devoted to large-scale agriculture and grazing, remains among Europe's poorest and emptiest regions. Summers are broiling hot – with temperatures as high as 47°C. The dry heat turns into a cold blast in winter. Portugal's entry into the EU, increasing mechanisation, successive droughts and greater opportunities elsewhere have all convinced young people to head for the cities. In the last 40 years the Alentejo's population has nosedived by 45%, to just 255,000. Although its cork, olives, marble and granite are still in great demand, and the deep-water port and industrial zone of Sines is of national importance, this vast region contributes only a small fraction to the gross national product. But the huge Alqueva dam has changed the region's prospect dramatically (p205).

THE WINE ROUTE

Wines here, particularly the reds, are fat, rich and fruity. But tasting them is much more fun than reading about them, so drop in on some wineries. The Rota dos Vinhos do Alentejo (Alentejan Wine Route) splits the region into three separate areas – the Serra de São, Mamede (dark reds, full bodied, red fruit hints), Historic (around Évora, Estremoz, Borba and Monsaraz; smooth reds, fruity whites), and the Rio Guadiana (scented whites; spicy reds).

You'll see the brown signs announcing that you are on the wine trail all over the place, and can pick up the booklet that lists wineries and their details at any local tourist office. Or visit the helpful Rota dos Vinhos headquarters (p207). For details of individual wine tasting places, see p223 and p216.

ALTO ALENTEJO

ÉVORA

pop 53,755 / elevation 250m

Évora is the city that best represents Portugal's golden age, mainly because the 1755 earthquake devoured all other pretenders. It's one of those towns where the layers of history are apparent wherever you look: from the crown-like towers of a 16th-century convent that complement the capitals of the Templo Romano, to the medieval walls that clasp the centre. But besides being beautiful and historical, Évora is also full of life, a centre of Alentejan cuisine, and a university town, whose students nicely dilute the tourist population. Neolithic monuments and rustic wineries surround the town. You'll need a couple of days to get the most out of it.

History

Long and rich. The Celtic settlement of Ebora was here before the Romans arrived in 59 BC and made it a military outpost,

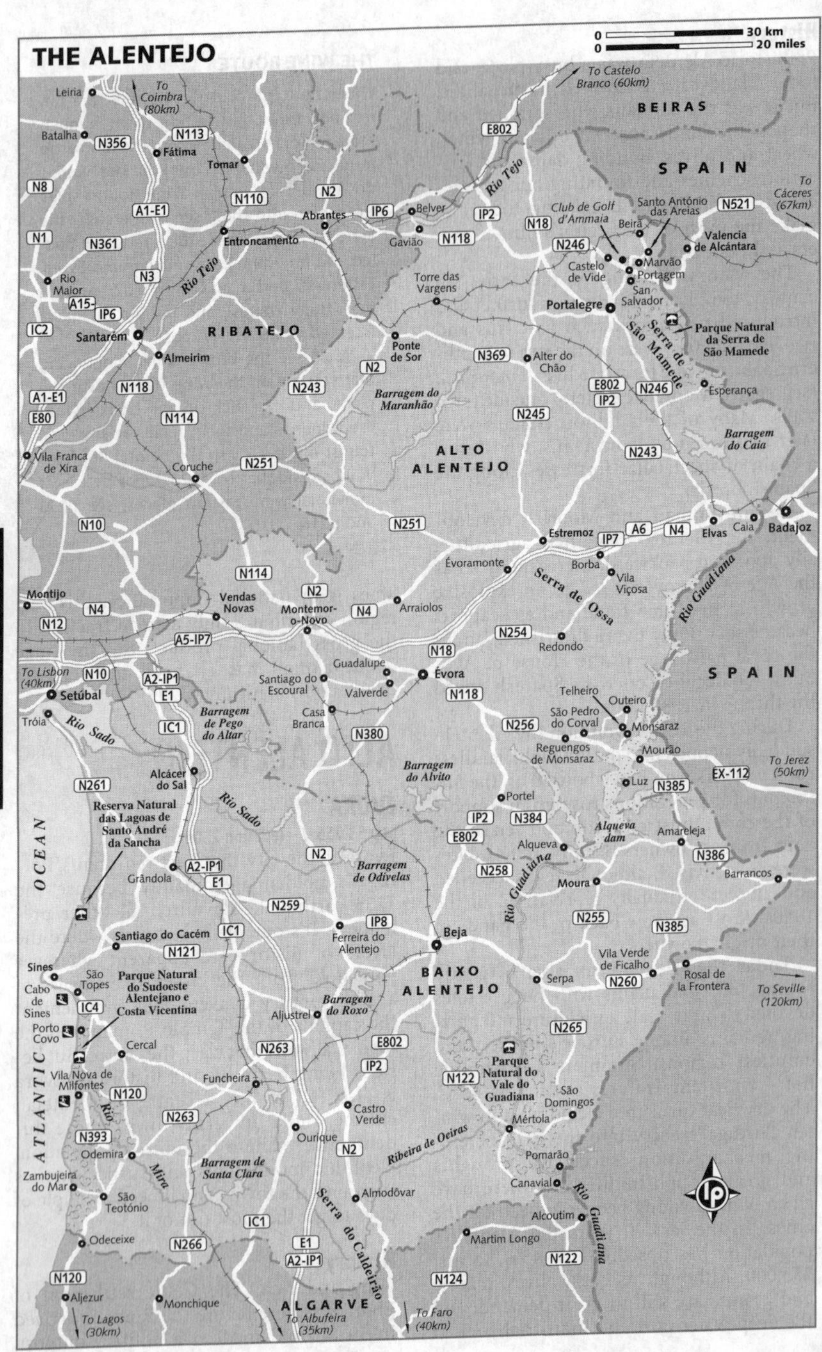
THE ALENTEJO
0 30 km
0 20 miles
To Coimbra (80km)
To Castelo Branco (60km)
BEIRAS
SPAIN
To Cáceres (67km)
RIBATEJO
ALTO ALENTEJO
BAIXO ALENTEJO
ALGARVE
ATLANTIC OCEAN
Leiria
Batalha
Fátima
Tomar
Abrantes
Entroncamento
Belver
Gavião
Rio Maior
Santarém
Almeirim
Club de Golf d'Ammaia
Santo António das Areias
Beirã
Valencia de Alcántara
Marvão
Castelo de Vide
Portagem
San Salvador
Portalegre
Torre das Vargens
Ponte de Sor
Parque Natural da Serra de São Mamede
Serra de São Mamede
Alter do Chão
Esperança
Barragem do Maranhão
Barragem do Caia
Vila Franca de Xira
Coruche
Estremoz
Elvas
Caia
Badajoz
Évoramonte
Borba
Vila Viçosa
Serra de Ossa
Rio Guadiana
Montijo
Vendas Novas
Montemor-o-Novo
Arraiolos
Redondo
To Lisbon (40km)
Setúbal
Tróia
Rio Sado
Guadalupe
Santiago do Escoural
Valverde
Évora
Casa Branca
Barragem de Pego do Altar
Telheiro
Outeiro
São Pedro do Corval
Monsaraz
Reguengos de Monsaraz
Mourão
Barragem do Alvito
Alcácer do Sal
Luz
To Jerez (50km)
Portel
Reserva Natural das Lagoas de Santo André da Sancha
Alqueva dam
Amareleja
Alqueva
Barrancos
Grândola
Barragem de Odivelas
Moura
Santiago do Cacém
Ferreira do Alentejo
Beja
Sines
São Topes
Cabo de Sines
Parque Natural do Sudoeste Alentejano e Costa Vicentina
Vila Verde de Ficalho
Serpa
Rosal de la Frontera
To Seville (120km)
Barragem do Roxo
Aljustrel
Porto Covo
Cercal
Funcheira
Parque Natural do Vale do Guadiana
Vila Nova de Milfontes
Rio Mira
Castro Verde
São Domingos
Mértola
Ourique
Ribeira de Oeiras
Odemira
Barragem de Santa Clara
Pomarão
Zambujeira do Mar
São Teotónio
Almodôvar
Canavial
Serra do Caldeirão
Alcoutim
Odeceixe
Martim Longo
Aljezur
Monchique
To Lagos (30km)
To Albufeira (35km)
To Faro (40km)
N113
N356
N8
A1-E1
N110
N2
IP6
IP2
E802
N18
N521
N1
N361
N118
N246
N3
A15-IP6
IC2
N369
N243
N246
IP2
A1-E1
E80
N114
N245
N243
N251
N10
N251
A6
N4
IP7
N114
N4
N12
A5-IP7
N254
N18
N10
A2-IP1
E1
N118
IC1
N256
N380
N261
EX-112
N385
IP2
N384
E802
N2
N258
N386
A2-IP1
E1
N259
IP8
N255
N385
IC1
N121
N260
IC4
E802
N265
N263
IP2
N122
N120
N263
N393
N2
IC1
E1
N266
A2-IP1
N122
N120
N124

DAM STATISTICS

The new 250 sq km Alqueva reservoir, Europe's largest, created by an enormous dam near Moura, is undeniably beautiful. But there is something strange and otherworldly about it: it's not so much a lake as drowned land, with islands poking out of the water and roads disappearing off into nowhere.

It is hoped that this huge water mass will save the arid Alentejo. One of Portugal's major agricultural, and poorest, regions, it employs a host of irrigation schemes and reservoirs to keep its soil from cracking. The most important source of water is the Rio Guadiana, which rises in Spain and flows through the Alentejo. Various agreements with Spain were meant to ensure that its waters were fairly shared. But successive droughts strained the arrangement. The Portuguese finally (the idea was first mooted in 1957) took matters into their own hands and started work on the giant dam to guarantee both irrigation water and electricity for years to come, flooding 2000 properties, completely rehousing one village (the now strangely antiseptic Luz), all costing €1.7 billion.

Critics say that the dam may not even fulfil its remit, that irrigation schemes will be vastly expensive, that it is an ecological disaster, and that ancient rock art has been enveloped in the waters. Local entrepreneurs are rubbing their hands at the new potential for boat and fishing trips (p217).

The dam, completed in 2002, creates an 83km-long reservoir, with a 1100km perimeter – it's Europe's largest, and big enough to affect the climate of the surrounding region. It's well worth driving to the dam for a look if you have your own transport. At the time of research there were no buses running there.

and eventually an important centre of Roman Iberia 'Ebora Liberalistas Julia'.

After a depressing spell under the Visigoths, the town got its groove back as a centre of trade under the Moors. In AD 1165 Évora's Muslim rulers were hoodwinked by a rogue Christian knight known as Giraldo Sem Pavor (Gerald the Fearless). The well embellished story goes like this: Giraldo single-handedly stormed one of the town's watchtowers by climbing up a ladder of spears driven into the walls. From there he distracted municipal sentries while his companions took the town with hardly a fight. The Moors took it back in 1192, clinging on for another 20 years or so.

The 14th to 16th centuries were Évora's golden age, when it was favoured by the Alentejo's own House of Avis, as well as by scholars and artists. Declared an archbishopric in 1540, it got its own Jesuit university in 1559.

When cardinal-king Dom Henrique, last of the Avis line, died in 1580 and Spain seized the throne, the royal court left Évora and the town began wasting away. The Marquês de Pombal's closure of the university in 1759 was the last straw. French forces plundered the town and massacred its defenders in July 1808.

Ironically, as in many other well-preserved ancient cities, it was decline itself that protected Évora's very fine old centre – economic success would have lead to far greater redevelopment. Today the population is still smaller than it was in the middle ages.

Orientation

Évora climbs a gentle hill above the Alentejo plain. Around the walled centre runs a ring road from which you can enter the town on one of several 'spoke' roads.

The town's focal point is Praça do Giraldo, 700m from the bus station to the southwest. The train station is outside the walls, 1km south of the square.

If you're driving, park outside the walls at one of the many signposted car parks (eg at the southern end of Rua da República). Except on Sunday, spaces inside the walls are limited and usually metered; pricier hotels have parking.

Information

BOOKSHOPS

Livraria Barata (☎ 266 746 146; Universidade de Évora; Mon-Fri) Well-stocked bookshop inside the university, which gives you a good excuse to visit this handsome institution.

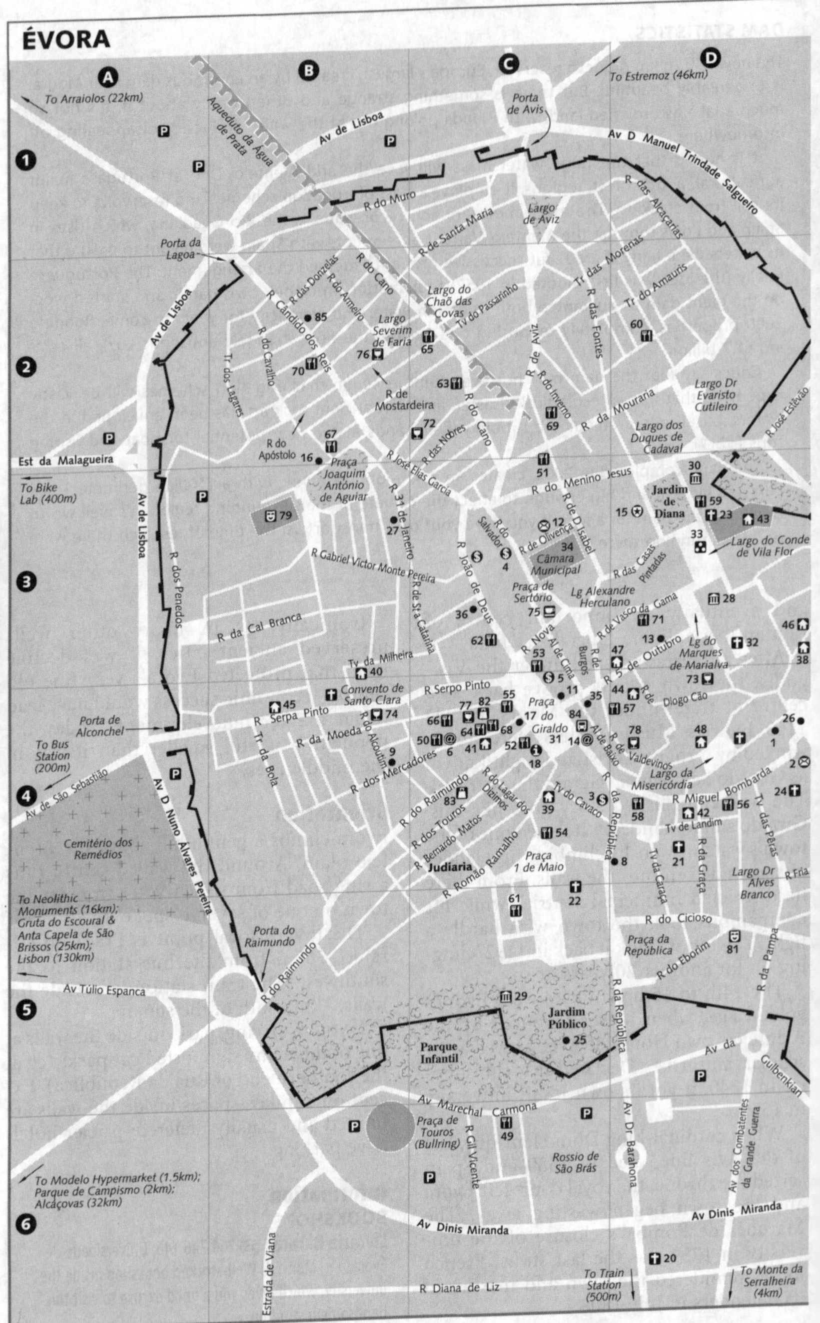
ÉVORA
A
B
C
D
1
2
3
4
5
6
To Arraiolos (22km)
To Estremoz (46km)
Aqueduto da Água de Prata
Av de Lisboa
Porta de Avis
Av D Manuel Trindade Salgueiro
R do Muro
R de Santa Maria
Largo de Aviz
R das Alcaçarias
Porta da Lagoa
R das Donzelas
R do Armeiro
R do Cano
Largo do Chaõ das Covas
Tv do Passarinho
Tr das Morenas
R das Fontes
Tr do Amauris
R Cândido dos Reis
R do Cavalho
Tr dos Lagares
Largo Severim de Faria
R de Mostardeira
R de Avis
R do Inverno
R da Mouraria
Largo Dr Evaristo Cutileiro
Largo dos Duques de Cadaval
R José Estêvão
R do Apóstolo
Praça Joaquim António de Aguiar
R José Elias Garcia
R das Nobres
Est da Malagueira
To Bike Lab (400m)
R 31 de Janeiro
R do Menino Jesus
R de D Isabel
Jardim de Diana
Largo do Conde de Vila Flor
R do Salvador
R de Olivença
Câmara Municipal
R Gabriel Victor Monte Pereira
R de Sta Catarina
R João de Deus
R dos Penedos
Praça de Sertório
Lg Alexandre Herculano
R das Casas Pintadas
R de Vasco da Gama
R da Cal Branca
Tv da Milheira
R Nova
Al de Cima
R de Burgos
R 5 de Outubro
Lg do Marques de Marialva
Convento de Santo Clara
R Serpo Pinto
R Serpa Pinto
Praça do Giraldo
R de Dilogo Cão
Porta de Alconchel
R da Moeda
R do Alcoutim
Tr da Bola
Al de Baixo
R de Valdevinos
To Bus Station (200m)
R dos Mercadores
Largo da Misericórdia
Av de São Sebastião
R do Raimundo
R do Lagar dos Dizimos
Tv do Cavaco
R Miguel Bombarda
Tv das Pêras
Av D Nuno Álvares Pereira
R dos Touros
R Bernardo Matos
R Romão Ramalho
Tv de Landim
Cemitério dos Remédios
Judiaria
Praça 1 de Maio
R da República
Tv da Caraça
R da Graça
Largo Dr Alves Branco
R Fria
To Neolithic Monuments (16km); Gruta do Escoural & Anta Capela de São Brissos (25km); Lisbon (130km)
R do Cicioso
Porta do Raimundo
Praça da República
R do Eborim
R da Pampa
Av Túlio Espanca
R do Raimundo
Jardim Público
Parque Infantil
Av da Gulbenkian
Av Marechal Carmona
Praça de Touros (Bullring)
R Gil Vicente
Rossio de São Brás
Av Dr Barahona
Av dos Combatentes da Grande Guerra
To Modelo Hypermarket (1.5km); Parque de Campismo (2km); Alcáçovas (32km)
Av Dinis Miranda
Estrada de Viana
R Diana de Liz
To Train Station (500m)
To Monte da Serralheira (4km)
THE ALENTEJO

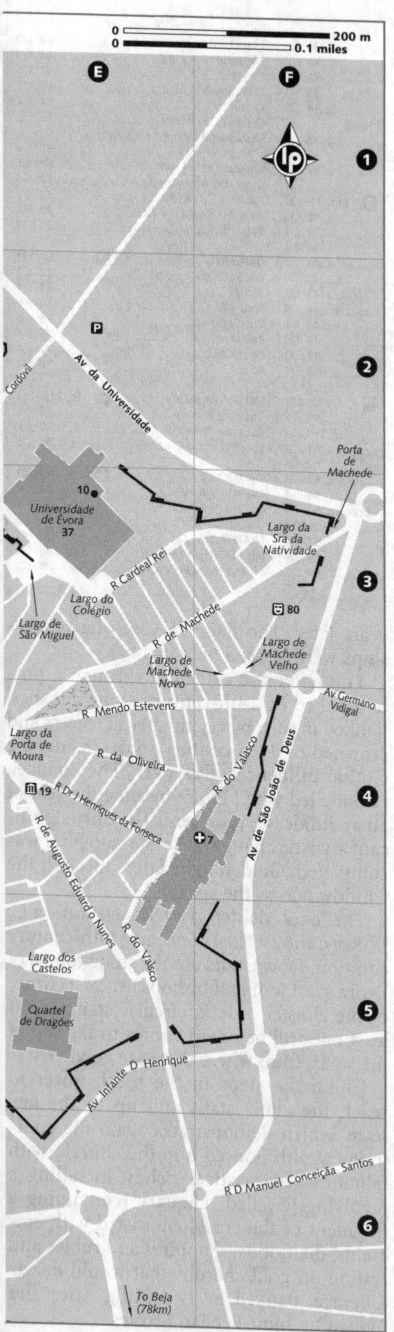

Livraria Nazareth (☎ 266 741 702; Praça do Giraldo 46) Opposite the turismo. Sells a few maps, including *Alentejo & Évora* (€4.50) and a few books in English.

EMERGENCY & MEDICAL SERVICES

Évora district hospital (☎ 266 740 100; Rua do Valasco) East of the centre.

PSP police station (☎ 266 746 977; Rua Francisco Soares Lusitano) Near the Templo Romano.

INTERNET ACCESS

Cybercenter (Rua dos Mercadores; per hr €2; 🕓 9am-midnight Mon-Fri, 2pm-midnight Sat & Sun)

Instituto Português da Juventude (IPJ; ☎ 266 737 300; ipj.evora@mail.telepac.pt; Rua da República 119) Free Internet access available

Oficin@ Bar (☎ 266 707 312; Rua da Moeda 27; per hr €3; 🕓 8pm-2am Mon-Fri, 9pm-2am Sat)

Postnet (☎ 266 730 270; Rua da Republica 1; per hr €3; 🕓 10pm-7am Mon-Fri, 9-2pm & 3-7pm Sat, from 11am Sun)

LAUNDRY

Lavandaria Olimpica (☎ 266 705 293; Largo dos Mercadores 6; 🕓 9.30am-1pm & 3.30-7pm Mon-Fri, 9am-1.30pm Sat) For one-day service visit this laundry.

MONEY

There are several banks with ATMs on and around Praça do Giraldo.

Caixa de Crédito Agricolo (Rua João de Deus)

Caixa Geral de Depósitos (Rua do Salvador)

Caixa Geral de Depósitos (Praça do Giraldo)

POST & TELEPHONE

Branch post office (☎ 266 777 570; Largo da Porta de Moura; 🕓 9am-12.30pm & 2-6.30pm Mon-Fri, 9am-12.30pm Sat).

Main post office (☎ 266 745 480; Rua de Olivença; 🕓 9am-6.30pm Mon-Fri, 9am-noon Sat)

Tabacaria Central (Rua do Raimundo 4; 🕓 10am-10pm Mon-Fri, to 8pm Sat, to 7pm Sun) Has phone booths and also sells foreign newspapers and magazines.

TOURIST INFORMATION

Rota dos Vinhos headquarters (Wine Route Office; ☎ 266 746 498; Praça Joaquim António de Aguiar 20; 🕓 9.30am-12.30pm & 2-5.30pm Mon-Fri) Head here for details of a *rota dos vinhos* (wine route) through the Alentejo with *adegas* (wineries).

Turismo (☎ 266 702 671; Praça do Giraldo 73; 🕓 9am-7pm Mon-Fri, 9.30am-12.30pm & 2-5.30pm Sat & Sun May-Sep; 9.30am-12.30pm & 2-5.30pm Oct-Apr) Has a free town map and *Historical Itineraries* leaflet (€1.05) a pack of four other themed itineraries costs €0.55. The *Alentejo Guidebook* (€7.63) only costs €5 at local newsagents and hotels!

INFORMATION

Abreu.......1 D4
Branch Post Office.......2 D4
Caixa de Crédito Agricolo Bank & ATM..3 C4
Caixa Geral de Dépositos Bank & ATM..4 C3
Caixa Geral de Dépositos Bank & ATM..5 C4
Cybercenter.......6 C4
Évora District Hospital.......7 F4
Instituto Português de Juventude.......8 D4
Lavandaria Olimpica.......9 B4
Livraria Barata.......10 E3
Livraria Nazareth.......11 C4
Main Post Office.......12 C3
Policarpo.......13 D3
Postnet.......14 C4
PSP Police Station.......15 D3
Rota dos Vinhos headquarters.......16 B2
Tabacaria Central.......17 C4
Turismo.......18 C4

SIGHTS & ACTIVITIES (pp208–10)

Capela dos Ossos.......(see 22)
Casa Cordovil.......19 E4
Ermida de São Brás.......20 D6
Galeria das Damas.......(see 29)
Igreja da Nossa Senhora da Graça.......21 D4
Igreja de São Francisco.......22 C5
Igreja de São João.......23 D3
Igreja do Carmo.......24 D4
Jardim Público.......25 C5
Largo da Porta de Moura.......26 D4
Mendes & Murteira.......27 B3
Museu de Évora.......28 D3
Palácio de Dom Manuel.......29 C5
Palácio dos Duques de Cadaval.......30 D3
Praça do Giraldo.......31 C4
Salas de Exposição do Palácio.......(see 30)
Sé.......32 D3
Templo Romano.......33 D3
Termas Romanas.......34 C3
Trans-Automóvel Club de Portugal (ACP).......35 C4
TurAventur.......36 C3
Universidade de Évora.......37 E3

SLEEPING (pp211–12)

Académica Fotocópias.......38 D3
Casa dos Teles.......39 C4
Hotel Santa Clara.......40 B3
Pensão O Giraldo.......41 C4
Pousada da Juventude.......42 D4
Pousada dos Lóios.......43 D3
Residencial Diana.......44 D4
Residencial O Alentejo.......45 B4
Residencial Policarpo.......46 D3
Residencial Riviera.......47 D3
Solar Monfalim.......48 D4

EATING (p212–13)

A Gruta.......49 C6
Adega do Neto.......50 C4
Botequim da Mouraria.......51 C3
Café Alentejo.......52 C4
Café Arcada.......53 C3
Café Restaurante Repas.......54 C4
Cafetaria Cozinha de Santo Humberto..55 C4
Casa dos Sabores.......56 D4
Chaogoiano.......57 D4
Gelataria Zoka.......58 D4
Jardim do Paço.......59 D3
Manel dos Potes.......60 D2
Mercado Municipal.......61 C5
O Antão.......62 C3
O Aqueduto.......63 C2
O Forcado.......64 C4
O Portão do Pastor.......65 C2
Restaurante Cozinha de Santo Humberto.......66 C4
Restaurante o Fialho.......67 B2
Snack-Bar Restaurante A Choupana.....68 C4
Taberna Tipica Quarta-Feira.......69 C2
Tasquina do Oliveira.......70 B2
Vasco da Gama Cafetaria.......71 D3

DRINKING (p213)

Bar Amas do Cardeal.......72 C2
Bar UÉ.......73 D4
Bota Alta.......74 B4
Cup & Cino.......75 C3
Katekero.......76 B2
Oficin@Bar.......77 C4
Praxis.......78 D4

ENTERTAINMENT (pp213–14)

Casa dos Bonecos.......79 B3
Casa dos Bonecos.......80 F3
Eborim Centro Comercial & Cinema.....81 D5

SHOPPING (p214)

Galeria Velharias.......82 C4
Oficina da Terra.......83 C4

TRANSPORT (p214)

Bus to Camp Site.......84 C4
Silvano Manuel Cégado.......85 B2

TRAVEL AGENCIES

Policarpo (☎ 266 746 970; Rua 5 de Outubro)
Abreu (☎ 266 769 180; Rua da Misericórdia 16)

Sights

PRAÇA DO GIRALDO

This **square** has seen some potent moments in Portuguese history, including the 1483 execution of Fernando, Duke of Bragança; the public burning of victims of the Inquisition in the 16th century; and fiery debates on agrarian reform in the 1970s. Nowadays it's still the city focus, hosting less-dramatic activities such as sitting in the sun and coffee drinking.

The narrow lanes to the southwest were once Évora's *judiaria* (Jewish quarter). To the southeast, Rua 5 de Outubro, climbing to the *sé* (cathedral), is lined by handsome townhouses wearing wrought-iron balconies, while side alleys pass beneath Moorish-style arches.

SÉ

Évora's **cathedral** (admission free; 9am-12.30pm & 2-5pm Tue-Sun) looks like a fortress, with two stout granite towers. Begun around 1186, during the rule of Sancho I, Afonso Henrique's son – there was probably a mosque here before. It was completed about 60 years later. The flags of Vasco da Gama's ships were blessed here in 1497.

You enter the cathedral through a portal flanked by 14th-century stone apostles, flanked in turn by asymmetrical towers and crowned by 16th-century roofs. Inside, the Gothic influence takes over. The chancel, remodelled when Évora became the seat of an archdiocese, represents the only significant stylistic change since the cathedral was completed. Golden light filters through the window across the space.

The cool **cloister** (admission with museum €3; 9am-noon & 2-4.30pm) is an early 14th-century addition. Downstairs are the stone tombs of Évora's last four archbishops. At each corner of the cloister a dark, circular staircase (at least one will be open) climbs to the top of the walls, from where there are good views.

Climb the steps in the south tower to reach the choir stalls and up to the **museum**, which demonstrates again the enormous wealth poured into the church, with fabulous ecclesiastical riches, including a revolving jewelled reliquary (containing a fragment of the cross) encrusted with emeralds, diamonds, sapphires and rubies and resting on gold cherubs that would dazzle Liberace, flanked by two Ming vases and topped by Indo-Persian textiles.

MUSEU DE ÉVORA

Adjacent to the cathedral, in what used to be the archbishop's palace (built in the 16th century), is this elegant **museum** (9.30am-12.30pm & 2-6pm Tue-Sun). Fragments of old Roman and Manueline statuary and façades line the courtyard, which has been excavated to reveal Visigothic, Roman and medieval remains. In polished rooms upstairs are former episcopal furnishings and a gallery of Flemish paintings. Most memorable is *Life of the Virgin*, a striking 13-panel series that was originally part of the cathedral's altarpiece, created by anonymous Flemish artists, most or all of them working in Portugal around 1500. Closed for renovation at the time of research, it should be open by the time you read this. Admission will cost about €2 per adult.

TEMPLO ROMANO

Opposite the museum is a complete Roman **temple** dating from the 2nd or early 3rd century. It is the best-preserved Roman monument in Portugal, probably on the Iberian Peninsula. Though it's commonly referred to as the Temple of Diana, there's no consensus about the deity to which it was dedicated. How did these 14 Corinthian columns, capped with Estremoz marble, manage to survive in such good shape for some 18 centuries? The temple was apparently walled up in the Middle Ages to form a small fortress, and then used as the town slaughterhouse. It was only rediscovered late in the 19th century. Obviously these unknowing preservation techniques worked, as the imposing colonnade is stunningly complete.

TERMAS ROMANAS

Inside the entrance hall of the *câmara municipal* (town hall) are more Roman vestiges, discovered only in 1987. These impressive Roman **baths** (admission free; 9am-5.30pm Mon-Fri), which include a *laconicum* (heated room for steam baths) with a superbly preserved 9m-diameter circular pool, would have been the largest public building in Roman Évora. The complex also includes an open-air swimming pool, discovered in 1994.

IGREJA DE SÃO JOÃO & CONVENTO DOS LÓIOS

The small, fabulous **church** (Church of St John the Evangelist; admission €3, plus Salas de Exposição do Palácio €5; 10am-12.30pm & 2-6pm Tue-Sun), which faces the Templo Romano, was founded in 1485 by one Rodrigo Afonso de Melo, count of Olivença and the first governor of Portuguese Tangier, to serve as his family's pantheon. It is still privately owned, by the Duques de Cadaval, and notably well kept.

Behind its elaborate Gothic portal is a nave lined with fantastic floor-to-ceiling *azulejos* (hand-painted tiles) produced in 1711 by one of Portugal's best-known tile-makers, António de Oliveira Bernardes. The grates in the floor expose a surprising underworld: you can see a deep Moorish cistern that predates the church, and an ossuary full of monks' bones. In the sacristy beyond are fragments of even earlier azulejos.

The former **Convento dos Lóios** to the right of the church has elegant Gothic cloisters topped by a Renaissance gallery. A national monument, the convent was converted in 1965 into a top-end *pousada* (upmarket inn; p212). If you want to wander around, wear your wealthy-guest expression – or have dinner at its upmarket restaurant.

PALÁCIO DOS DUQUES DE CADAVAL & SALAS DE EXPOSIÇÃO DO PALÁCIO

Northwest of the Igreja de São João is a 17th-century façade attached to a much older palace and castle, as revealed by the two powerful square towers that bracket it. The **Palácio dos Duques de Cadaval** (Palace of the Dukes of Cadaval) was given to the governor of Évora, Martim Afonso de Melo, by Dom João I, and it also served from time to time as a royal residence. A section of the palace still serves as the private quarters of the de Melo family; the other main occupant is the city's highway department.

The well-proportioned 1st-floor rooms are relaxing to amble around, and form the **Salas de Exposição do Palácio** (admission €3; 10am-12.30pm & 2-5pm Tue-Sun), a well laid-out, if enigmatically labelled, collection of family portraits, early illustrated manuscripts, royal documents and 16th-century religious art.

UNIVERSIDADE DE ÉVZORA

Outside the walls to the northeast is the **university**, a descendent (reopened in 1973) of the original Jesuit institution founded in 1559 (it closed when the Jesuits got shooed

THE ALENTEJO

out by Marquês de Pombal in 1759). Inside are arched, Italian Renaissance-style courtyards, a brazilwood ceiling and beautiful azulejos.

TOWN WALLS

About one-fifth of Évora's population lives within the town's old walls, some of which are built on top of 1st-century Roman fortifications. Over 3km of 14th-century walls enclose the northern part of the old town, while the bulwarks along the southern side, such as those running through the *jardim público* (public gardens), date from the 17th century.

LARGO DA PORTA DE MOURA

The so-called **Porta de Moura** (Moor's Gate) to the inner town stands beside busy **Largo da Porta de Moura**, just south of the cathedral. Among several elegant mansions around the square (and contemporary with the strange-looking, globular 16th-century Renaissance fountain in the middle of it) is **Casa Cordovil**, built in Manueline-Moorish style. Across the road to the west have a look at the extraordinary knotted Manueline stone doorway of the **Igreja do Carmo**.

IGREJA DE SÃO FRANCISCO & CAPELA DOS OSSOS

Évora's best-known **church** (Praça 1 de Maio) is a tall and huge Manueline–Gothic structure, completed around 1510 and dedicated to St Francis. Exuberant nautical motifs celebrating the Age of Discoveries deck the walls and reflect the confident, booming mood of the time. It's all topped by a cross of Christ's order and dome. Legend has it that the Portuguese navigator Gil Vicente is buried here.

What draws the crowds, though, is the **Capela dos Ossos** (Chapel of Bones; admission €1; 9am-1pm & 2.30-5.30pm Mon-Fri, from 10am Sat & Sun, to 6.30pm Jul-Aug), a mesmerising *memento mori* (reminder of death). A small room behind the altar has walls and columns lined with the bones and skulls of some 5000 people. This was the solution found by 17th-century Franciscan monks for the overflowing graveyards of several dozen churches and monasteries. There's a black humour to the way the bones and skulls have been carefully arranged in patterns, and the whole effect is strangely beautiful, if not one you would want to recreate at home. Adding a final ghoulish flourish are two hanging desiccated corpses, including one of a child. An inscription over the entrance translates as: 'We bones await yours'. A great (Addams) family day out.

The entrance is to the right of the main church entrance. It costs €0.25 extra to take photos.

JARDIM PÚBLICO

For a lovely tranquil stroll, head to the light-dappled public **gardens** (with a small outdoor café) south of the Igreja de São Francisco. Inside the walls of the 16th-century **Palácio de Dom Manuel** is the **Galeria das Damas** (Ladies' Gallery). It's an indecisive hybrid of Gothic, Manueline, neo-Moorish and Renaissance styles. There are also frequent temporary art exhibitions.

From the town walls you can see, a few blocks to the south, the crenellated, pointy-topped Arabian Gothic profile of the **Ermida de São Brás** (Chapel of St Blaise), dating from about 1490. It's possibly an early project of Diogo de Boitac, considered to be the originator of the Manueline style.

IGREJA DA NOSSA SENHORA DA GRAÇA

Down an alley off Rua da República is this curious baroque façade of the **Igreja da Nossa Senhora da Graça** (Church of Our Lady of Grace), topped by four ungainly stone giants – as if they've strayed from a mythological tale and landed up on a religious building. An early example of the Renaissance style in Portugal is found in the cloister of the 17th-century monastery next door.

AQUEDUTO DA ÁGUA DE PRATA

Jutting into the town from the northwest is the beguilingly named **Aqueduto da Água de Prata** (Aqueduct of Silver Water), designed by Francisco de Arruda (better known for Lisbon's Tower of Belém) to bring clean water to Évora, completed in the 1530s. At the end of the aqueduct, on Rua do Cano, the neighbourhood feels like a self-contained village, with houses, shops and cafés built right into its perfect arches, as if nestling against the base of a hill.

Tours

Mendes & Murteira (☎ 266 739 240; www.evora-mm.pt; Rua 31 de Janeiro 15A) This company operates out of the Barafunda boutique and offers flexible three- to four-hour tours (price negotiable) of surrounding megaliths or around the city itself with knowledgeable guides.

Oagia (☎ 963 702 392; agia@iol.pt; adult/under 12 €12/free, minimum 2 people; 🕑 10am) Oagia offers daily two-hour guided tours of Évora from outside the turismo on Praça do Giraldo.

Policarpo (☎ 266 746 970; www.policarpo-viagens.pt; Rua 5 de Outubro) Policarpo organises numerous trips, including daily 2½-hour city tours on foot (€17.50 per person), half-day minibus tours to nearby megaliths (€24) and full-day trips to nearby towns such as Estremoz (€74.50, including lunch). A minimum of four is required. Guides speak English, French, German and Italian.

TurAventur (☎ 266 743 134; www.turaventur.com; Rua João de Deus 21) TurAventur runs jeep tours to nearby megaliths and other attractions (full day including lunch adult/child under 12 €60/45, half-day €35/20), 4½-hour bike tours in surrounding countryside (four/ten people €37/30) and half-day jeep and canoeing tour (€40) or a full day including Monsaraz (€75).

Festivals & Events

Feira de São João (late June or July) Évora's biggest, bounciest annual bash, and one of the Alentejo's best country fairs.

Feira dos Ramos (Friday before Palm Sunday) Palm Fair is celebrated with a large market.

Rota de Sabores Tradicionais (February to April) A gastronomic festival, celebrating pork in February, soups in March and lamb in April – traditional restaurants throughout the city serve specialities accordingly.

Sleeping

In high season it's essential to book ahead. We list July prices – August can be more expensive. If you're interested in long-term lets, check the student-oriented notices on the door of **Académica Fotocópias** (Rua Conde da Serra 8).

BUDGET

Casa dos Teles (☎ 266 702 453; casadosteles@yahoo.com; Rua Romão Ramalho 27; s/d/apt €20/30/40) The best of the *quartos* (rooms in private houses) run by a gentlemanly English speaker; attractive rooms at the back overlook a tiny courtyard.

Pensão O Giraldo (☎ 266 705 833; Rua dos Mercadores 27; s with shared bathroom €15-25, s/d with bathroom €30/35) A popular, well run place with a variety of rooms, the best with small balconies overlooking the town. Cheaper, but less nice, rooms are in a nearby building.

Residencial O Alentejo (☎ 266 702 903; Rua Serpa Pinto 74; s/tw/tr €35/40/50) With a nice old-fashioned feel, all overlooked by the Virgin Mary, this has plain, clean rooms and well polished floors. Doors are locked at 1am.

Pousada da juventude (☎ 266 744 848; evora@movijovem.pt; Rua Miguel Bombarda 40; dm €12.50, d with toilet & shower €35) In a handsome former hotel, closed for long-term renovations at the time of research. Ring ahead.

Parque de campismo (☎ 266 705 190; fax 266 709 830; adult/tent/car €4.30/3.50/3.80) Orbitur's well equipped camp site, flat, grassy and tree-shaded, with disabled access, is 2km southwest of town. Urban Sitee bus No 5 or 8 from Praça do Giraldo, via Avenida de São Sebastião and the bus station, goes close by (€1).

MID-RANGE

Residencial Policarpo (☎/fax 266 702 424; Rua da Freiria de Baixo 16; s/d with breakfast €50/55; Ⓟ free) Run by the Policarpos for three generations, this hotel is housed in the splendid holiday home of a 16th-century count – the family was purged by the Pombals in the 18th century. Your stay will be more peaceful, amid painted ceilings, 17th-century azulejos (in room No 101), carved wooden and traditionally hand-painted Alentejan furniture.

Hotel Santa Clara (☎ 266 704 141; www.hotelsantaclara.pt; Travessa da Milheira 19; s/d with breakfast €50/63; ❄) A whitewashed building tucked away in a quiet narrow back street, this has unexciting but comfortable rooms. Prices rise by €10 from June to August and drop similarly in November and December.

Residencial Diana (☎ 266 702 008; residencialdiana@mail.telepac.pt; Rua de Diogo Cão 2; d with breakfast €50) A decent, central and recommended choice – rooms have wooden floors and high ceilings, though slightly drab décor – get a room at the back as those facing the main street are noisy.

Residencial Riviera (☎ 266 703 304; fax 266 700 467; Rua 5 de Outubro 49; s/d with breakfast €60/70; ❄) This is charming, in a central, carefully renovated building with bright rooms that have wood floors, brick arched ceilings, wooden carved beds and cable TV. Bathrooms are gleamingly tiled.

There are 10 converted *quintas* (estates) around Évora, including **Monte da Serralheira** (☎ 266 741 286; monteserralheira@mail.telepac.pt; 2-/4-person apt €50/85; 🏊), a big, blue-bordered farm, 4km south, offering self-catering or B&B,

with horses and bikes to ride. The Dutch owner is a qualified local guide.

TOP END

Solar Monfalim (☎ 266 750 000; www.monfalimtur.pt; Largo da Misericórdia 1; s/d/tr with breakfast €70/85/112; P €3 per day, ❄) A delightful former 16th-century mansion with elegant rooms and a lovely colonnaded terrace overlooking the square. This is the place to head for cherub-decorated beds. A hotel since 1892, so it has had lots of practice.

Pousada dos Lóios (☎ 266 730 070; recepcao.loios@pousadas.pt; d Mon-Fri €182, Sat & Sun €201; ❄) Occupying the former Convento dos Lóios opposite the Templo Romano, this is one of the country's most beautiful *pousadas,* stately, and centred around the pretty cloister, with uncell-like rooms in the former cells.

Eating

BUDGET

Adega do Neto (☎ 266 209 916; Rua dos Mercadores 46; mains €6.50; lunch & dinner) You will find cheap daily specials at this small, cheerful and local-packed restaurant. You can eat at tables or at the counter (great for solo travellers).

Snack-Bar Restaurante A Choupana (☎ 266 704 427; Rua dos Mercadores 16; mains €4.50-7; lunch & dinner Mon-Sat) This is a tiled, busy place where you can sit at a long bar on tall stools. There's a TV, lots of knick-knacks and bargain mains of the day. The next-door restaurant could be a granny's kitchen – cosy, tiled and doilied.

Café Restaurante Repas (☎ 266 708 540; Praça 1 de Maio 19; mains €4.50-8.75; breakfast, lunch & dinner) Nothing special cuisine-wise, but its location and outdoor seating are irresistible.

O Portão do Pastor (☎ 266 703 325; Rua do Cano 27; mains €4.75-11.50; lunch & dinner Mon-Sat) Right by the aqueduct and popular with locals and tourists alike, this is big on grilled meats.

A Gruta (☎ 266 708 186; Avenida General Humberto Delgado 2; mains €5-7, 3-course menu €15; lunch & dinner) Near the bullring, large and tiled, A Gruta specialises in grilled chicken and is packed with locals, buzzing and busy.

Café Arcada (Praça do Giraldo 10; snacks €0.75-2, meals €6.30-10; breakfast, lunch & dinner) Always busy, this barn-sized meeting place is great for coffee and cakes – there are impressive pancakes, the essential *pasteis de nata* (custard tarts) and much more.

Manel dos Potes (Rua do Amauriz 9; mains from €2; breakfast, lunch & dinner Mon-Sat) This dark, tucked away café sports huge jars of wine. Its dinginess is hip with students and it's very much a locals' hang-out.

Casa dos Sabores (☎ 266 701 030; Rua Miguel Bombordo 50; snacks €2-4; 8am-7pm) A low key new café with solid small wood tables, marble floors and nice sandwiches. You can buy local cheese and meats here, too.

Vasco da Gama Cafétaria (Rua de Vasco da Gama 10; mains €3.90-7.80; breakfast, lunch & dinner Mon-Sat) This is a cheap-and-cheerful choice.

Gelataria Zoka (Largo de São Vicente 14, Rua Miguel Bombarda; ice creams from €0.75; 8am-midnight Oct-Mar, to 1am Apr-Sep) This is heaven for ice-cream freaks.

Mercado municipal (Praça 1 de Maio; Tue-Sun) Here you can pick up fruit and vegetables and eat them in the adjacent *jardim público.* Or try **Modelo**, a hypermarket just beyond the town limits on the road to the camp site and Alcáçovas.

MID-RANGE

Taberna Típica Quarta-Feira (☎ 266 707 530; Rua do Inverno 16; mains €5-12.50; lunch & dinner Mon-Sat, tourist menu €20) A jovial spot in the heart of the Moorish quarter, this is decked with wine jars, and has robust cuisine with regional daily specials. The waiters are generous in bringing extra bits and pieces, but remember these will all be added to your bill, so if you don't want something, speak out!

O Aqueduto (☎ 266 706 373; Rua do Cano 13A; mains €10-12.50, tourist menu €18.50; lunch Tue-Sun, dinner Tue-Sat) This is a much recommended restaurant that's a cut above the rest, with inspiring food that has won prizes, and service to match.

Café Alentejo (☎ 266 706 296; Rua do Raimundo 5; mains €7-12, tourist menu €17.50; lunch & dinner Mon-Sat) With arched rooms painted in pale gold and red, and blues forming the soundtrack, this is an appealing, relaxed restaurant, with well spaced tables and traditional Alentejan specialities, featuring lots of bread, coriander and garlic.

Chaogoiano (Babo de Camarão; mains €8-11; lunch & dinner Mon-Fri, dinner Sat) Small and jolly, with white walls, white-tiled floor and a rounded roof, this welcoming place provides big portions of tasty Brazilian food and does a mean *caipirinha* (a classic Brazilian cocktail, made with sugar, limes, cachaça and crushed ice).

O Forcado (☎ 266 702 566; Rua dos Mercadores 26; mains €5.50-8; 🕑 lunch & dinner) An arched room overlooked by TV and antlers, this is a cosy, family-style traditional place serving Portuguese comfort food.

Botequim da Mouraria (☎ 266 746 775; Rua da Mouraria 16A; mains €9-11; 🕑 lunch Mon-Sat) Poke around the old Moorish quarter to find this snack bar, with some of Évora's finest food. No reservations, and there are no tables, just stools at the counter.

TOP END

Restaurante O Fialho (☎ 266 703 079; Travessa dos Mascarenhas 16; mains €14-17, specials €12-17; 🕑 lunch & dinner Mon-Sat) Smallish with wood panelling and white tablecloths, this manages to be both smart and relaxed, and is the kind of place people talk of in awed tones.

Restaurante Cozinha de Santo Humberto (☎ 266 704 251; Rua da Moeda 39; mains €9-20; 🕑 lunch Fri-Tue, dinner Fri-Wed) This is a traditional, long-established place, in a grand arched, whitewashed cellar hung with brass and ceramics. It offers a big menu of regional fare, eg the hearty, inventive *carne de porco com amêijoas* (pork and clams). There is an attached café with seats out on the *praça*.

O Antão (☎ 266 706 459; Rua João de Deus 5; mains €9.50-12; 🕑 lunch & dinner Thu-Tue) With a white, arched, leafy interior, this offers beautifully cooked rural showpieces, such as rabbit Alentejana or duck rice, and has won prizes for its cuisine.

Tasquina do Oliveira (☎ 266 752 906; Rua Cândide do Reis 45A; mains €10-15; 🕑 dinner) Snug and small, this classy restaurant serves up real quality, in the shape of mains such as *grao á alentejana* (chickpeas Alentejan style).

Jardim do Paço (☎ 266 744 300; mains €11-16, regional buffet €17.50, 3-course menu €17.50-27.50; lunch Tue-Sun, dinner Tue-Sat) Beside Igreja de São João, in the former garden of the Palácio dos Duques de Cadaval, this is a lovely setting amid orange trees – or there is an indoor hall decorated with wedding-reception chic.

Drinking

Most bars open late and don't close until at least 2am (4am at weekends). There are no cover charges at these places.

Praxis (☎ 266 707 505; Rua de Valdevinos; 🕑 midnight-6am) If you have stuff you need to shake, head to this local nightclub – and final destination for most students in town – with one big dance floor, one small; DJs play house, R&B and hip-hop: it's fun, getting busy from about 1.30am till 6am.

Oficin@ Bar (☎ 266 707 312; Rua da Moeda 27; 🕑 8pm-2am Mon-Fri, 9pm-3am Sat) Attracting all ages, this is an appealing, relaxed bar with little wooden tables in a white-arched cave-like space. It's convivial, with jazz and blues playing gently in the background.

Bar UÉ (☎ 266 706 612; Rua de Diogo Cão 21; 🕑 Mon-Sat) At the Associação de Estudantes da Universidade de Évora, this is the main central student hang-out, with a nice owner and great outdoor drinking area – relaxing in the day, and like an outdoor party in the evening. Occasional karaoke.

Bar Amas do Cardeal (☎ 266 721 133; Rua Amas do Cardeal 9A; 🕑 10pm-3am) Popular, darkly lit and weirdly decorated (suspended Barbies behind the bar, bullet holes in the DJ booth), this place attracts a chilled, eclectic crowd for post-1am drinking, and weekend dancing on the small dance floor. Regular DJs play cool and funky house.

Katekero (☎ 266 703 204; Largo Severim de Faria 1A; minimum consumption €2.50; 🕑 8am-2pm) A wholesome, dimly lit bar-dive that's popular with Évora youth. There are small tables that are good for a beer and a chat against housey Portuguese music.

Cup & Cino (☎ 916 603 896; Praç de Sertório; mains €0.70-7.45; 🕑 10-2am) Although part of a chain, this is well set on a stately square and plays ska and soul on its outdoor speakers. There are seats outside – a good place for a beer.

Bota Alta (Rua do Alcoutim) This 'high boot'-sized place has fado, meloncholy Portuguese singing, (with wine and snacks) on Thursday and Friday, and live music on Saturday.

Entertainment

CINEMA

Eborim Centro Comercial (☎ 266 703 068; Rua do Eborim) This is home to the town's cinema.

THEATRE & PUPPET THEATRE

Casa dos Bonecos (☎ 266 703 112; tickets €3, children's matinees €2) Five actors from the grand municipal Teatro Garcia de Resende studied for several years with the only surviving master of a traditional rural puppetry style called *bonecos de Santo Aleixo* (Santo Aleixo puppets). They perform this, other styles, and hand-puppet shows for children, at this little theatre off Largo de Machede Velho.

SPORT

Évora has a *praça de touros* (bullring), outside the southern walls near the *jardim público*. Three to four bullfights take place between May and October.

Shopping

The lower end of Rua 5 de Outubro has up-market *artesanatos* (handicrafts shops) with cork knick-knacks, furniture and pottery. You'll find cheaper pottery on the shady side of the *mercado municipal*. There are more up-market shops along Rua Cândido dos Reis. On the second Tuesday of each month a vast open-air market, with everything from shoes to sheep cheese, sprawls across the big Rossio de São Brás, just outside the walls on the road to the train station.

Oficina da Terra (☎ 266 746 049; www.oficinadaterra.com; Rua do Raimundo 51A; 🕑 10am-7pm Mon-Fri, 10am-3pm Sat) This is an imaginative and award-winning handicraft and clay-figure workshop and gallery. Its curious, imaginative and distorted figures are well worth a visit.

Galeria Velharias (Rua da Moeda 37) A charming small shop with lace, bric-a-brac, old bullfighting photos and antiques.

Antique market (Largo do Chão das Covas; 🕑 8am-2pm) An antique market is held near the aqueduct second Sunday of each month.

Getting There & Away

BUS

The **bus station** (☎ 266 769 410) is off Avenida de São Sebastião. Note there can be a real difference in the time you take to get to Lisbon, depending which bus you board.

Destination	Price* (€)	Duration* (hr)	Frequency (daily)
Beja	4.45/7.50	1½/1	6-8
Coimbra (via Santarem)	12.40	4¼	2
Elvas	4.90/8.50	2¼/1¼	2-4
Estremoz	3.25/6.50	1½/1	2-5
Évora	3.25/6.50	1½/1	2-5
Faro (via Albufeira)	11.80	5¼	2
Lisbon	9.80/5.75	4/2	12 Mon-Fri 6-8 Sat & Sun
Portalegre	5.15/8.80	2½/1½	3
Reguengoz de Monsaraz	2.65/5.90	1¼/¾	3-4
Vila Viçosa	4.30/6.50	1½/1	3-8

* normal/express

TRAIN

The **Évora station** (☎ 266 742 336), 500m south of the centre, is on a branch of the Lisbon–Funcheira (via Beja) train line. There are daily trains to/from Lisbon (€8.15, 2¾ hours, including Tejo ferry to Barreiro, five daily) with a change at Casa Branca. Trains also go to/from Setúbal (€6.70, 2¼ hours, five daily). There are also trains to Lagos (€12.50, six hours, two daily) via (€10.50, five hours 40 minutes).

Getting Around

CAR & BICYCLE

If you want to rent a car get in touch with Abreu or Policarpo (p208).

Évora has a branch of the **Automóvel Club de Portugal** (ACP; ☎ 266 707 533; fax 266 709 696; Alcárcova de Baixo 7).

You can rent a bike from **Bike Lab** (☎ 266 735 500; bikelab@mail.telepac.pt, Centro Comercial da Vista Alegre, Lote 14; per day €7.50-15), 800m northwest of the centre; guided bike tours also available, or from **Silvano Manuel Cágado** (☎ 266 702 424; Rua Cândido dos Reis 66; per day €7.50).

TAXI

If you want a **taxi** (☎ 266 734 734) you'll find them waiting in Praça do Giraldo and Largo da Porta de Moura. On a weekday you can expect to pay about €3 (or €4.50 with baggage) from the train station to the Praça di Giraldo.

AROUND ÉVORA

Megaliths – 'big stones' in Greek – are all over the ancient landscape that surrounds Évora. Such prehistoric structures, built around 5000 to 6000 years ago, dot the European Atlantic coast, but here in Alentejo there are an astounding amount of Neolithic remains. Dolmens (*antas* in Portuguese) were probably temples and/or tombs, covered with a large flat stone and usually built on hilltops or near water. Menhirs (individual standing stones) point to fertility rites – as phallic as skyscrapers, if smaller scale – and *cromeleques* (cromlechs, stone circles) were also places of worship.

Évora turismo's *Historical Itineraries* (€1) details many sites. Also on offer is *Guide du Megalithisme d'Evora* (€5.09), in French, which contains maps, routes and background information. Dolmen devotees can buy the *Paisagens Arqueologicas A Oeste de Évora* (€12.72), which has English summaries. The turismo and the Museu de Évora sell an English-language video, *Megalithic Enclosures* (€10.18).

You can see more of these around Reguengos de Monsaraz, Elvas and Castelo de Vide.

Sights

CROMELEQUE DOS ALMENDRES

From Guadalupe a dirt track winds through a beautiful landscape of olive and cork trees to the **Cromeleque dos Almendres** (Almendres Cromlech). This huge, spectacular oval of standing stones is the Iberian Peninsula's most important megalithic group and an extraordinary place to visit.

The site consists of a huge oval of some 95 rounded granite monoliths – some of which are engraved with symbolic markings – spread down a rough slope. They were erected over different periods, it seems with geometric and astral consideration, probably for social gatherings or sacred rituals. The setting itself is magnificent.

Just off the dirt track en route to the *cromeleque* you can follow a short path to the solitary **Menir dos Almendres**, a single phallic stone about 4m high, with some carving near the top.

ANTA GRANDE DO ZAMBUJEIRO

The **Anta Grande do Zambujeiro** (Great Dolmen of Zambujeiro), a national monument, is Europe's largest dolmen. Under a huge sheet-metal shelter in a field of wild flowers and yellow broom are seven stones, each 6m high, forming a huge chamber, more than 50m in diameter. Archaeologists removed the capstone in the 1960s. Most of the site's relics – potsherds, beads, flint tools and so on – are in the Museu de Évora.

ANTA CAPELA DE SÃO BRISSOS

Built in the 17th century from surviving stones of an *anta* (dolmen), this thick-walled whitewashed **chapel** is an unusual example of megalithic remains being recycled for Christian use – indicating acknowledgement of the stones' religious significance. It's an endearing sight, with tubby rounded walls and curved tiled roof. It's beside the Valverde-N2 road (just beyond the turn-off to São Brissos).

GRUTA DO ESCOURAL

About 2km east of the village of Santiago do Escoural (25km from Évora) is a bat-filled **cave** (☎ 266 857 000; admission €1.60; 🕒 9am-noon & 1.30-5.30pm Wed-Sun, 1.30-5.30pm Tue) with twisted rocks inside, adorned with Palaeolithic and Neolithic rock art, including a few faint ochre and black drawings of bison and engravings of horses, dating back 10,000 to 30,000 years.

Getting There & Away

There are no convenient buses to this area so your only option is to rent a car or bike (but note that about 5km of the route is rough and remote). Alternatively, you can take a guided trip (p210) or you could hire a taxi for the day (€45).

With your own wheels, head west from Évora on the old Lisbon road (N114) for 10km, then turn south for 2.8km to Guadalupe. Follow the signs from here to the Cromeleque dos Almendres (4.3km).

Return to Guadalupe and head south for 5km to Valverde, home of the Universidade de Évora's school of agriculture and the 16th-century Convento de Bom Jesus. Following the signs to Anta Grande do Zambujeiro, turn into the school's farmyard and onto a badly pot-holed track. After 1km you'll see the Great Dolmen.

Continue west from Valverde for 12km. Before joining the N2, turn right for the cave at Santiago do Escoural.

ÉVORAMONTE

pop 724 / elevation 474m

Évoramonte, a remote, walled hilltop village with a robust little 16th-century castle, demands a stop. There are views all around across the low hills. A small **turismo** is just beyond the castle.

The **castle** (admission €1.30; 🕒 10am-1pm year-round, 2-5pm Oct-May & 2.30-6.30pm Jun-Sep) dates from 1306, but was rebuilt after the 1531 earthquake. Exterior stone carving shows unwarlike small bows, the symbol of the Bragança family – the knot symbolising fidelity. The interior is neatly restored, with impressively meaty columns topped by a sinuous arched ceiling on each cavernous floor. The roof provides sweeping panoramas.

You can stay at **A Convençao** (☎ 268 959 217; Rua de Santa Maria 26; d with bathroom without/with terrace €30/35) where the two rooms have fantastic views from this peaceful spot – particularly the one with terrace. It's also an unexpectedly smart **restaurant** (mains €8-11.50; Sun-Tue) with views – you can sit in or outside – and serving traditional specialities.

Nearby are also some attractive rural tourism options including **Monte da Fazenda** (☎ 268 959 172) and **Quinta do Serafim** (☎ 268 959 360).

SÃO PEDRO DO CORVAL

Pottery lovers and present-buyers should head to this village, 5km east of Reguengoz. You'll have lots of choice – plain terracotta and bright rustic patterned plates, pots, candlesticks, jugs and floor tiles. The 32 workshops make it one of Portugal's largest pottery centres – cheap and cheerful rather than rare and refined. A good place to start is the reasonably priced **O Patalim** (☎ 266 549 117; 8.30am-noon & 1-7pm).

Buses between Requengos and Monsaraz stop here.

REGUENGOS DE MONSARAZ

pop 11,400 / elevation 200m

This modest market town, once famous for its sheep and wool production, is a stopping point and transport hub for Monsaraz. It's also close to the pottery centre of São Pedro do Corval as well as to an impressive half-dozen dolmens and menhirs (out of around 150 scattered across the surrounding plains). While you're here, enjoy some of the great local wine, Terras d'El Rei.

The rocket-like local church was designed by Antonio Dias da Silva, who was also responsible for Campo Pequeno, the Lisbon bullring.

Orientation

The bus station is 200m southwest of the central Praça da Liberdade.

Information

Espaço Internet (☎ 266 519 424; Rua do Conde de Monsaraz 32; 10am-8pm Mon-Fri, 10am-1pm & 2-8pm Sat, 1-7pm Sun) About 100m northwest of the *praça*. Free Internet access.

Turismo (☎ 266 503 315; Rua 1 de Maio; 9am-12.30pm & 2-5.30pm Mon-Fri, from 10am Sat & Sun) Just off the *praça*. On sale is *A Short Walk in the Alentejo* (€4) by locally based, award-winning novelist Robert Wilson. It's a useful detailed guide to parts of the eastern Alentejo.

Sights

There are several wineries around Reguengoz, including the award-winning **Herdade do Esporão** (☎ 266 509 280; esporao@mail.telepac.pt), a few kilometres south of town. Operating as a winery for seven centuries, with some lovely old wine cellars, it produces mostly red wines for the domestic market. It has a wine bar, restaurant and wine shop.

Sleeping & Eating

Casa da Palmeira (☎ 266 502 362; fax 266 502 513; Praça de Santo António 1; s/d with shared bathroom €15/25) A fantastic old rundown mansion 200m northwest of the main square, this has huge rooms with high ceilings.

Pensão O Gato (☎/fax 266 502 353; Praça da Liberdade 11; d €35; lunch & dinner;) This is on the main square with spacious rooms that are often booked out by business people. Its popular **restaurant** (mains €6.50-8.50) has jaunty red-and-white tablecloths and offers reliably tasty food.

Restaurante Central (☎ 266 502 219; Praça da Liberdade; mains €7-11) Central offers good Portuguese mains and keeps up a busy trade. There is a small bar-café next door with high stools, where you can choose from an array of starters, such as tasty bean or tuna salads.

Shopping

The area is rich in handicrafts, the local speciality being *mantas alentejanas*, hand-woven woollen blankets.

Tear (Loom; ☎ 266 503 710; fax 266 501 104; 9.30am-1pm & 2.30-7pm) You can watch *mantas* being made here, and they are for sale, along with beautiful ceramics, wickerware and hand-painted Alentejan furniture, only at this award-winning shop near the Adega de Cooperativa de Reguengos, on the road towards Monsaraz. The workshop and showroom, which has been converted from an old slaughterhouse, belongs to an association of young artisans founded to preserve local skills, but who also sprinkle the traditional with contemporary and adventurous ideas.

Fabrica Alentejana de Lanifícios (☎ 266 502 179; 9am-5pm Mon-Fri) Apart from Tear, this is the last remaining hand-loom producer of *mantas alentejanas*, but only produces large commissions these days (which begs the question where do all the small versions on sale come from). If you're interested in seeing how they are made, check it out; it's on the Mourão road east of town.

Getting There & Away

Buses run daily to Évora (€2.65/5.90 normal/express, 1¼ hours/45 minutes, three to eight daily), with connections on to Lisbon. There are also direct Lisbon services (€10.30, 2½ hours).

MONSARAZ

pop 977 / elevation 190m

You'll see Monsaraz from far away, a thick-walled cluster floating above the Alentejan landscape, with its castle jutting out above the rest. The narrow road towards it winds through curves of countryside, through twisted olive groves, dotted with Neolithic sites. And up in the village itself are uneven-walled cottages and black-dressed widows, and flat-capped men in the village square. The views around are startling, and you can see the olive groves planted in straight lines, following the old Roman roads.

Settled long before the Moors arrived in the 8th century, Monsaraz was recaptured by the Christians under Giraldo Sem Pavor (Gerald the Fearless) in 1167, and then given to the Knights Templar as thanks for their help. The castle was added in 1310. Now it prospers on tourism, with a few restaurants, guesthouses, and chichi foreign-run artisan shops, but it has not lost its magic or its community feel. It's at its best as it wakes up in the morning, in the quiet of the evening, or during a wintry dusk.

Neolithic megaliths are scattered throughout the landscape around Monsaraz – it is great to explore and discover these (they're signposted, but finding each one is an adventure) amid the tangles of olive groves and open fields of wild flowers. Most spectacular is Cromeleque do Xerez, which once stood 5km south of Monsaraz, moved before flooding by the massive Alqueva dam. The ensemble, including the triumphant seven-tonne phallic menhir at its centre, now forms part of a new Museu de Arqueologia de Alqueva in Telheiro (1.5km north of Monsaraz near the Convento da Orada). A remaining highlight is the Menhir de Bulhoa, another phallic stone with intriguing carved circles and lines, 4km north of Monsaraz off the Telheiro–Outeiro road. A sketch map of several other accessible megaliths is available at the Reguengez turismo.

Orientation

Coaches or cars park outside the walled village, so your arrival at one of the four arched entrances will be as it should be – on foot. From the main car park, the Porta da Alcoba leads directly onto the central Praça Dom Nuno Álvares Pereira. The main entrance, Porta da Vila, is at the north end of town (the castle is at the other end) and leads into Rua São Tiago and the parallel Rua Direita, Monsaraz's two main streets.

Information

ATM (Travessa da Misericórdia) off the main square.

Turismo (☎ 266 557 136; Praça Dom Nuno Álvares; ⌚ 10am-1pm & 2-6pm Sep-Jun, to 7pm Jul & Aug) Well stocked with regional information, including bus timetables.

Sights

IGREJA MATRIZ

The parish **church** (⌚ 9am-1pm & 2-6pm), near the turismo, was rebuilt after the 1755 earthquake and again a century later. Inside is an impressive nave and a 14th-century marble tomb carved with 14 saints. An 18th-century *pelourinho* topped by a Manueline globe stands outside. The **Igreja da Misericórdia** (⌚ 9am-1pm & 2-6pm) is opposite.

MUSEU DE ARTE SACRA

Housed in a fine Gothic building beside the parish church, this **museum** (Museum of Sacred Art; admission €0.50; ⌚ 10am-1pm & 2-6pm) houses a small collection of 14th-century wooden religious figures and 18th-century vestments and silverware. Its most famous exhibit is a rare example of a 14th-century secular fresco, a charming piece showing a good and a bad judge, the latter appropriately two-faced. Opening hours vary.

CASTELO

The castle at the southwestern end of the village was one in the chain of Dom Dinis' defensive fortresses along the Spanish border. It's now converted into a small bullring, and its ramparts offer a fine panoramic view over the Alentejan plains.

Activities

Estalgem de Monsaraz (p218) can organise a boat trip around the lake. A five-hour trip on a motor boat, with an island picnic, costs €40 per person, but they need 48 hours advance notice.

Festivals & Events

Accommodation must be booked far in advance at these times.

Bullfights (Easter Sunday) If you want to see a bullfight, this is a good time to visit.

Music festival (July in even-numbered years) Monsaraz heaves with jollity during its week-long Museu Aberto (Open Museum) music festival.

Festa de Nossa Senhora dos Passos (Second weekend of September) Bullfights and processions feature in this festival.

Sleeping

Many villagers have converted their ancient cottages to guesthouses or self-catering apartments. Unless otherwise mentioned, all the following rates include breakfast. Everywhere also has cable TV. It's essential to book ahead in high season.

BUDGET

Casa Pinto (☎ 266 557 388; Praça Dom Nuno Ávares Pereira 10; d €40) Opposite the church, this is a popular choice and has five cosy, slate-floored and comfortable rooms – you walk through the sitting room to get to them.

Casa Modesta (☎ 266 557 388; www.inoxnet.com; Rua Direita 5; s/d €30/40) Smart rooms with traditional handpainted furniture, run by a welcoming family who also have a café downstairs. Breakfast is good, with fresh orange juice.

Casa Paroquial (☎ 266 557 101; Rua Direita; d €40) This is a welcoming place, with a friendly atmosphere in a family house, and the rooms and breakfasts are nice too.

Casa Dona Antónia (☎ 266 557 142; Rua Direita 15; d/ste €45/90) Accommodation in Dona Antónia's place means four neat, large, comfy rooms; the suite is huge and includes a terrace.

Casa do Paço (☎ 266 557 306; Rua Direita; d €25, f €45) Near Dona Antónia this is attractive, with three large rooms furnished with Alentejan painted furniture, and a kitchen and lounge downstairs. For more information, contact the owner at Rua Direita 2 though she'll have probably found you first.

Casa Dom Nuno (☎ 266 557 146; fax 266 557 400; Rua José Fernandes Caeiro 6; d €55) One of several very fine Turihab properties (a government scheme for marketing private accommodation), with eight elegant doubles and offering superb terrace views.

MID-RANGE & TOP END

Estalagem de Monsaraz (☎ 266 557 112; www.estalagemdemonsaraz.com; Largo São Bartolomeu 5; s/d €67/90;) Outside the village walls, its 19 rooms are charmingly decorated with dark wood furniture and provide glorious views. You can hire bikes and they can arrange canoeing or boat trips (p217). There's a restaurant, a pool with a view, a playground and open fires in winter.

Monte Alerta (☎ 266 550 150; fax 266 557 325; Telheiro; s/d €60/75;) This gorgeous example is one of several rural alternatives close by. It's a beautifully converted, blue-bordered *quinta* and though only 2.5km from Monsaraz at Telheiro it feels wonderfully remote. In spring it's surrounded by wild flowers. Inside are family antiques and eight spacious doubles; outside are wind chimes, gardens and horses.

Convento da Orada (☎ 266 557 414; convento@conventodaorada.com; d €75) Under the same management as the Estalagem, this is 2km from Monsaraz, a beautiful, large remote convent, with the atmosphere of a retreat (with satellite TV). It also houses the new museum and now neighbours the Cromeleque do Xerez (p217). It's only a couple of kilometres from the lake. There's a huge stork's nest on the roof, also inhabited by smaller birds – like a birds' block of flats.

Eating

There's a handful of restaurants, all offering traditional Alentejan mains such as *borrego assado* (roast lamb). All close by 9pm.

Café Restaurante O Alcaide (☎ 266 557 168; Rua São Tiago 15; mains around €8; lunch & dinner Thu-Tue) This is Monsaraz' best restaurant. It is relatively smart, and you'll find good grilled fish here as well as lovely sunset views over the plains.

Café-Restaurante Lumumba (☎ 266 557 121; Rua Direita 12; mains €6.50-8.50; lunch & dinner) A popular place with a great local atmosphere that's rare in the local restaurants. TV forms a backdrop – it's a good place to watch football.

A Casa do Forno (☎ 266 557 190; Travessa da Sanabrosa; mains €7-12) You can try this airy and large place with a terrace, but food standards have slipped (not bad, just run of the mill).

Restaurante São Tiago (☎ 266 557 188; Rua São Tiago 3; mains €7-9; ⏲ lunch & dinner Thu-Tue) Close to O Alcaide, this is a lively venue with its own bar.

There are also a couple of cafés, including **Casa Modesta** (Rua Direita) with a patio, and **Pastelaria Cisterna** (Main St) just as you enter the village. Self-catering options are limited to bread and cheese from a **grocery shop** (Rua São Tiago) at the Porta da Vila end of the street; wines from **Castas & Castiços** (⏲ 10am-6pm Tue-Sun), next door; and pastries from **Pastelaria A Cisterna** (Rua Direita), also at the Porta da Vila end.

Getting There & Away

Buses run to/from Reguengos de Monsaraz (€2.10, 35 minutes, four daily on weekdays). The last bus back to Reguengos (where you can pick up connections to Évora) is at 5.20pm.

ESTREMOZ

pop 15,400 / elevation 420m

Luminescent against the hot blue sky, Estremoz (shtreh-*mozh*) is one of the three marble towns, along with nearby Borba and Vila Viçosa. Because there is so much fine marble in this region – rivalling that in Carrera, Italy – it's used all over the place: even the cobbles are rough chunks of marble.

Estremoz has a beautiful old walled city, overlooked by a castle and convent, with a small museum of lively terracotta figures. But otherwise it's a simple provincial town, with lots of elderly folk and shops selling slippers, its glowing marble splendour populated mainly by farmers in flat caps. It's famous for its earthenware pottery, preserved plums and goat's cheese, all of which you can buy (along with rabbits, orange trees and flat caps) at the great market that fills the whole huge central square on Saturday.

Orientation

The lower, newer part of town, enclosed by 17th-century ramparts, is arranged around a huge square, Rossio Marquês de Pombal (known simply as 'the Rossio'). Here you'll find most accommodation, restaurants and shops. A 10-minute climb west of the Rossio brings you to the old quarter, with its 13th-century castle (now a luxurious *pousada*) and keep.

USING YOUR MARBLES

The marble towns gleam with rosy-gold or white stone, but the effect is enhanced by the houses, which have a Hollywood-smile brightness. As if locals hadn't found enough uses for the stone stuff, with their marble doorsteps, pavements and shoes (OK, we made that last one up) a convoluted process has been cooked up to create marble paint. Marble is recrystallised limestone – so if you heat marble chips in a clay oven for three days they turn into calcium oxide which is mixed with water to become whitewash. Cheaper than paint. People take pride in the whiteness of their houses and retouch them annually.

While we're on the subject of colour, apparently the yellow borders keep away fever, while blue is the bane of flies (you can add these colours to the oxide). The blue theory may have some truth, or at least international adherents – in Rajasthan (India) local people also apply pale blue to their houses to ward off mosquitoes.

The bus station is by the disused train station, 400m east of the Rossio.

Information

Caixa Geral de Depósitos Bank (☎ 268 339 710; Rossio Marquês de Pombal 43)

Centro de saúde (medical centre; ☎ 268 332 042; Avenida 9 de Abril) At the northern end of town.

Police station (☎ 268 334 141) In the *câmara municipal*.

Post office (☎ 268 339 190; Rua 5 de Outubro; ⏲ 9am-6pm Mon-Fri) Has NetPost.

Turismo (☎ 268 333 541; fax 268 334 010; Largo da República; ⏲ 9.30am-12.30pm & 2-6pm)

Sights

LOWER TOWN

On the fringes of the Rossio are imposing old churches, former convents and, to the north, monastic buildings converted into cavalry barracks. Opposite these, by Largo General Graça, is a marble-edged water tank, called the **Lago do Gadanha** (Lake of the Scythe) after its scythe-wielding statue of Neptune. Some of the prettiest marble streets in town are south of the Rossio, off Largo da República.

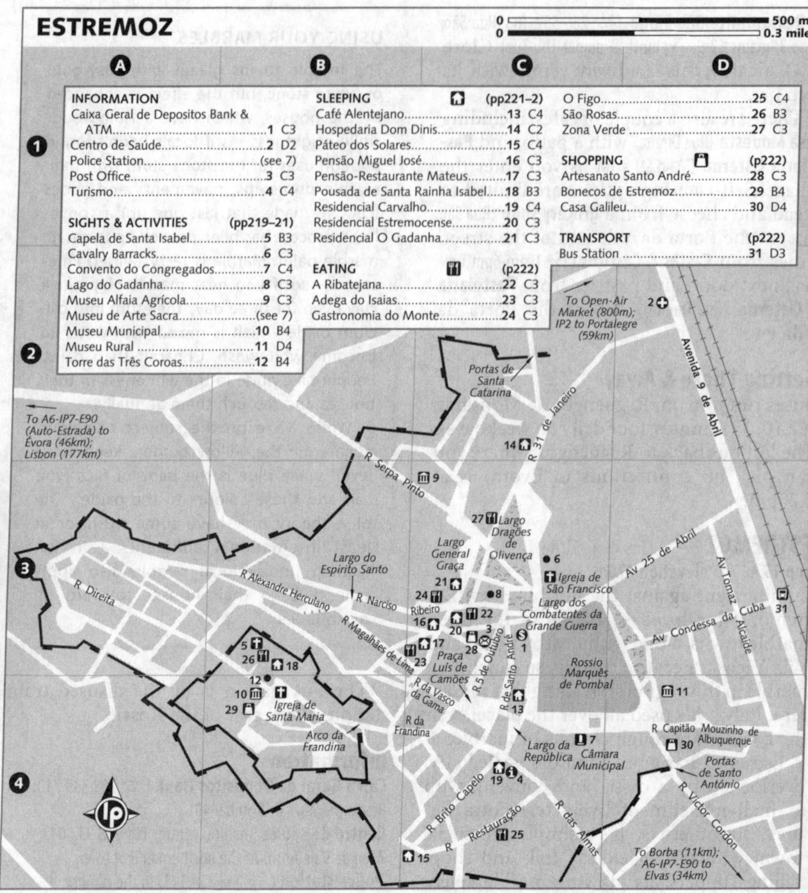

Museu de Arte Sacra

Overlooking the Rossio is the floridly bell-towered 17th-century **Convento dos Congregados**, which now leads a double life housing the police station, *câmara municipal* and the **Museu de Arte Sacra** (admission €1.10; 9.30am-noon & 2-5.30pm Tue-Sat, from 2.30pm Nov-Mar), with stately 17th- to 18th-century ecclesiastical silverware and religious statues. You also get to see the restored marble church and, best of all, a rooftop view from the bell towers themselves. The stairway to the top is lined with azulejos.

Museu Rural

This delightful one-room **museum** (☎ 268 333 541; Rossio; admission €1; 10am-12.30pm & 2-5.30pm Mon-Sat) displays the local clay figurines and implements that illustrate rural Alentejan life.

Museu Alfaia Agrícola

Old agricultural and household equipment don't sound like a must-see, but this **museum** (☎ 268 339 200; Rua Serpa Pinto; admission €1.20; 9am-12.30pm & 2-5.30pm Tue-Sun) in a cavernous old warehouse has fascinating archaic, curious implements – remnants of disappearing traditions – displayed over three floors.

UPPER TOWN

The upper town is surrounded by dramatic zigzagging ramparts and contains a gleaming white palace. The easiest way to reach it on foot is to follow narrow Rua da Frandina from Praça Luís de Camões and pass the inner castle walls through the Arco da Frandina.

Torre das Três Coroas

At the top of the upper town is the stark, glowing-white fortress-like former royal palace, now the Pousada de Santa Rainha Isabel (right). Dom Dinis built the palace in the 13th century for his new wife, Isabel of Aragon. After her death in 1336 (Dinis had died 11 years earlier) it was used as an ammunition dump. An inevitable explosion, in 1698, destroyed most of the palace and the surrounding castle, though in the 18th century João V restored the palace for use as an armoury. The 27m-high keep, the **Torre das Três Coroas** (Tower of the Three Crowns), survived and is still the dominant feature. It's so-called because it was apparently built by three kings: Sancho II, Afonso III and Dinis.

Visitors are welcome to view the public areas of the *pousada* and climb the keep, which offers a superb panorama of the old town and surrounding plains. The holes at the keep's edges were channels for boiling oil – a good way of getting rid of uninvited guests.

Capela de Santa Isabel

This richly adorned **chapel** (admission free; ⌚ 9am-11.30pm & 2-5pm Tue-Sun May-Sep) behind the keep was built in 1659. The narrow stairway up to the chapel, and the chapel itself, are lined with 18th-century azulejos, most of them featuring scenes from the saintly queen's life.

Isabel was famously generous to the poor, despite her husband's disapproval. According to one legend the king once demanded to see what she was carrying in her skirt; she let go of her apron and the bread she had hidden to donate to the poor was miraculously transformed into roses.

To visit the chapel, ask for the custodian at the Museu Municipal.

Museu Municipal

This **museum** (☎ 268 339 200; admission €1.10; ⌚ 9am-12.30pm & 2-5.30pm Tue-Sun) is in a beautiful 17th-century almshouse near the former palace. Pretty hand-painted furniture sits alongside endearing locally carved wooden figures (charming rural scenes by Joaquim Velhinho), plus a collection of typical 19th-century domestic Alentejan items. On the ground floor is an amazing display of the unique Estremoz pottery figurines – some 500 pieces covering 200 years, including lots of ladies with carnivalesque outfits, explosively floral headdresses and wind-rippled dresses. There's even an entire 19th-century Easter Parade.

Festivals & Events

The town's biggest event is the **Feira Internacional de Artesenato e Agro-Pecuária de Estremoz** (Fiape), a baskets, ceramics, vegetables and livestock bonanza, held for several days at the end of April in an open-air market area east of the bus station.

Sleeping

BUDGET

Residencial O Gadanha (☎ 268 339 110; Largo General Graça, 56; s/d €17.50/30) This is a splendid bargain, a little white-washed sprightly house, with bright, fresh, white and clean renovated rooms that overlook the square.

Residencial Carvalho (☎ 268 339 370; fax 268 322 370; Largo da República 27; s/d from €18/30) Appealingly old-fashioned accommodation.

Pensão Miguel José (☎ 268 322 326; Travessa da Levada 8; s/d with shared bathroom €15/30) This is a warren of small, plain rooms, in a quiet back street, with a gruff but homely atmosphere.

MID-RANGE

Café Alentejano (☎ 268 337 300; Rossio 14; s/d €25/40) Rooms here are notably nice, though small, with hand-painted Alentejan furniture. Some have views over the huge market square. It has a café (p222).

Residencial Estremocense (☎ 268 333 002; Travessa da Levada 19; s/d €17.50/35) Has 12 neat, modern rooms.

Hospedaria Dom Dinis (☎ 268 332 717; Rua 31 de Janeiro 46; s/d €30/50; ❄) Smart, well-kitted out accommodation.

Pensão-Restaurante Mateus (☎ 268 322 226; Rua do Almeida 41; d with/without bathroom €40/30) Cheery and welcoming, with huge rooms in an old house.

TOP END

Pousada de Santa Rainha Isabel (☎ 268 332 075; recepcao.staisobel@pousadas.pt; d Mon-Fri €182, Sat & Sun

€201) This is an aptly palatial *pousada* in the restored former palace. The fortress-like exterior sets off the inner luxury nicely – with antique furnishings, fine tapestries and views over the Alentejo plains.

Páteo dos Solares (☎ 268 338 400; fax 268 338 419; Rua Brito Capelo; s/d €140/150;) This luxurious hotel in a converted bread factory – it looks like it should have been something far more impressive – now lives up to the building, situated partly on the old city walls. There is a smart restaurant here.

Eating

Café Alentejano (☎ 268 337 300; Rossio 14; mains €6.50-11; lunch & dinner) The café here is the place to be if you wear a flat cap. It gets packed out any day of the week but especially market day. Upstairs is an attractive wood-floored, white-tableclothed restaurant, with daily specials. There are rooms upstairs (p221).

Adega do Isaias (☎ 268 322 318; Rua do Almeida 21; mains €8-14; lunch & dinner Mon-Sat) This is excellent: an award-winning, rustic *tasca* (tavern) serving Alentejan specialities as they should be. It has outdoor grills, communal bench tables and is filled with huge bulbous wine jars, fit for 40 thieves, from which your wine is served.

Gastronomia do Monte (☎ 268 083 196; Rua Narciso Ribeiro 7; €7-8.50; lunch & dinner Mon-Fri) Friendly and clean, this is a pleasant arched room with rugs and black-and-white photos on the walls; it has hearty mountain cuisine such as *bacalhau* (salt cod) with prawns and tomato.

Zona Verde (☎ 268 324 701; Largo Dragões de Olivença 86; mains €7-13; lunch & dinner Fri, Mon-Wed) This restaurant has an attractive arched interior and serves excellent regional specialities.

São Rosas (☎ 268 333 345; mains €12-17; lunch & dinner Tue-Sun) White tablecloths under whitewashed arches equal rustic meets smart, and the food is great – some unusual starters, and pork and clams, and gazpacho in summer. Just near the former palace.

O Figo (☎ 268 324 529; Rua Restauração; mains €4-11; lunch & dinner Tue-Sun) In the functional back room of a café, here you can have Alentejan comfort food such as *bacalhau á bras* (cod fried with onions and potatoes) and other hearty specialities (or rather brains and kidneys), made with homely skill.

A Ribatejana (☎ 268 323 656; Largo General Graça 41; mains €5-9; lunch & dinner Mon-Sat) If roast suckling pig is what you're after, this local institution is for you.

Shopping

The weekly Saturday market along the southern fringe of the Rossio provides a great display of Alentejan goodies and Estremoz specialities, from goat- and ewe-milk cheeses, to a unique style of unglazed, ochre-red pots. There's also a small flea market, where a crowd of Estremoz menfolk loiter.

Casa Galileu (☎ 268 323 130; Rua Victor Cordon 16) If you miss the Saturday market, come to this great place, southeast of the Rossio. It has a fine collection of locally made ceramic figures, as well as other essentials such as flat caps and cowbells.

Artesanato Santo André (☎ 268 333 360; Rua da Misericórdia 2) This is a charming shop, the size of a large cupboard, run by a genial man and packed with ceramic figurines and some pretty pieces of china.

Bonecos de Estremoz (☎ 268 339 200) For contemporary, Estremoz-style ceramic figurines visit this workshop at the back of the Museu Municipal (p221).

Getting There & Away

The **bus station** (☎ 268 322 282) is on the east side of town.

Destination	Price* (€)	Duration * (hr)	Frequency (daily)
Borba	1.60	¼	2
Elvas	3/6	1½/¾	2-4
Évora	3.25/6.50	1½/1	2-5
Évoramonte	1.80	½	2-4
Faro	13	6	1
Lisbon	9.80	2½	4-6
Portalegre	3.25/6.60	1¼/1	3-4
Vila Viçosa	2.10	¾	3 Mon-Fri

*normal/express

AROUND ESTREMOZ

Now you've visited one marble town – go for a look at the other two. Each one has its own unique character, and they are easy day trips from Estremoz.

Borba

pop 7782

The smallest of the marble towns glows with a peculiar rosy light. Its marble wealth hasn't

THE ALENTEJO

brought it many obvious riches, so its marble-lined houses and public buildings have a remarkable simplicity. This quiet small town is encircled by marble quarries (it's worth stopping en route to peer down a mine shaft) and is famous for its great red wines.

ORIENTION & INFORMATION

Borba's main square, Praça da República, is the town focus, with its ornate 18th-century marble fountain, Fonte das Bicas, a rare sojourn into fanciness. The town comes to life once a year in early November, when it hosts a huge country fair. Access the Net at **Informática** (Ave do Povo; per hr €1; 9am-1pm & 2-7pm Mon-Fri, 9am-1pm Sat). The **turismo** (268 894 113; Rua do Convento das Servas; 11am-1pm & 2-5pm) is on the outskirts of town, just off the Estremoz–Elvas road (N4).

SIGHTS

The **Adega Cooperativa de Borba** (268 894 264; Rua de San Bartolomeu; 9am-12.30pm & 2-5pm Mon-Fri) is the largest of three *adegas* in town, all producing the famous Borba full-bodied red and white *maduro* (mature) wines. Opposite is **Sovibor** (Sociedade de Vinhos de Borba; 268 894 210; 9am-12.30pm & 2-4.30pm Mon-Fri), in business since 1968, with an ornately carved portal that's worth a look even if you don't like wine. Neither place is geared for tourists but both will accept visitors.

SLEEPING & EATING

Casa de Borba (268 894 528; Rua da Cruz 5; s/d with breakfast €70/80) An aristocratic 17th-century mansion, it has high-ceilinged rooms, filled with antiques – carved beds and canopies, rich rugs and marble-topped tables. The grounds hold olive trees and vineyards.

Herdade do Monte Branco (214 830 834; montebranco@netcabo.pt; r €65) This rural option is remote, amid wooded, open hills. The converted farmhouse has self-catering apartments, but breakfast is available. Rooms are rustic and peaceful, with comfortable beds and carved furniture, and there is a lake nearby.

A Talha (268 894 473; Rua Mestre Diogo de Borba 12; mains €4-6.50; lunch & dinner Mon-Sat) Unsigned, splendid and in an arched cellar, with enormous urns indicating one of its specialities – punchy new wine. The other is delicious home-cooked food. *Bacalhau con grau* (cod with chickpeas) is delicious. To get here, walk down Rua Antonio Joaquim da Guerra (off Avenida do Povo, to the left of the large shrine). Take the first left (Rua Visconde Gião), then the first right.

GETTING THERE & AWAY

Buses daily connect Borba with Estremoz (€1.60, 15 minutes, two daily) and Vila Viçosa.

Vila Viçosa

pop 9070

Vila Viçosa is like Estremoz and Borba's more refined dowager aunt, a regal, slow-paced place that has used its marble for proper fancy stuff: marble mansions, churches (more than 20), a marble palace and convent and, of course, pearly marble squares and pavements, all shadowed by ink-green orange trees. There is a castle too, one of the few nonmarble structures. The town's royal credentials are impeccable, for here is Paço Ducal, home of the Bragança dynasty, whose kings ruled Portugal until it became a republic – Dom Carlos spent his last night here before his assassination.

The town, aesthetically all peach-glow and grandeur, is remarkably sedate, apart from during the Festa dos Capuchos (p224).

ORIENTATION & INFORMATION

The huge, sloping Praça da República is the attractive heart of town, with the *mercado municipal* and gardens 200m to the south-east. At the top of the *praça* is the 17th-century Igreja de São Bartolomeu; at the bottom is Avenida Bento de Jesus which lies at the foot of the castle. The ducal palace is 300m northwest of the *praça* (follow Rua Dr Couto Jardim). Vila Viçosa has its own **turismo** (268 881 101; www.cm-vilavicosa.pt; Praça da República 34; 9.30am-12.30pm & 2-5.30pm).

SIGHTS

Terreiro do Paço & Paço Ducal

The **palace square** covers 16,000 sq m. In the centre is a statue of Dom João IV, and it's ringed by the palace, the heavy-fronted Agostinhos Convent and graceful Chagas Nunnery.

The dukes of Bragança built their **palace** (268 980 659; adult/under 10 €5/free; 9.30am-1pm & 2-5pm Tue-Sun Oct-Mar; 9.30am-1pm & 2.30-5.30pm Tue-Fri, to 6pm Sat & Sun Apr-Sep, last admission 1hr before closing) in the early 16th century when the fourth duke, Dom Jaime, decided he had had enough of his uncomfortable hilltop castle. The wealthy Bragança family, originally from Bragança in Trás-os-Montes, had settled in Vila Viçosa in the 15th century. After the eighth duke became king in 1640, it changed from a permanent residence to just another royal palace, but the family maintained a special fondness for it and he and his successors continued to visit the palace.

The best furniture went to Lisbon after the eighth duke ascended the throne, and some went on to Brazil after the royal family fled there in 1807, but there are some stunning pieces, such as a huge 16th-century Persian rug in the Dukes Hall. Lots of royal portraits put into context the interesting background on the royal family. The private apartments hold a ghostly fascination – toiletries, knick-knacks and clothes of Dom Carlos and his wife, Marie-Amélia, are laid out as if the royal couple were about to return (Dom Carlos left one morning in 1908 and was assassinated in Lisbon that afternoon).

A Portuguese-speaking guide leads the hour-long tours – some of the guides speak English well too, but if not you can buy a guidebook (€5).

Other parts of the palace, including the 16th-century cloister, house more museums containing specific collections, which have separate admission fees (armoury/coach collection/Chinese Porcelain/treasury €2.50/1.50/2.50/2.50).

Castelo

Dom Dinis' walled hill-top castle was where the Bragança family lived before the palace was built. It has been transformed into a **Museu de Caça e Arqueologia** (Game & Hunting Museum; admission €2.50; 9.30am-1pm & 2-5pm Tue-Sun Oct-Mar; 9.30am-1pm & 2.30-5.30pm Tue-Fri, to 6pm Sat & Sun Apr-Sep), stuffed with endless unlucky animals – trophies, showing how the dukes kept themselves busy on their 20-sq-km hunting ground north of Vila Viçosa.

Surrounding the castle is a cluster of village houses and peaceful overgrown gardens. There's a 16th-century Manueline *pelourinho* (pillory – the prison used to be nearby), with sculpted frogs. It's incongruously beautiful for a whipping post. Near the castle is also the brilliantly tiled 15th-century **Igreja de Nossa Senhora da Conceição**.

FESTIVALS & EVENTS

On the second weekend of September there is the **Fiesta dos Capuchos**, with a bullfight and a *vacada* in the main square (a bull is released and locals try to jump over it to show how brave they are).

SLEEPING

Senora Maria de Conceição Paiseão (☎ 268 980 168; Rua Dr Couto Jardim 7; s/d with shared bathroom €13/22.50) The large *quartos* in this genteel place run by kindly elderly Senora Maria have beautiful Alentejan painted furniture. It can be cold outside summer months – the only heating is under Senora Maria's table.

Hospedaria Dom Carlos (☎/fax 268 980 318; Praça da República 25; s/d €20/30) This is a comfortable but bland place around the corner from Senora Maria de Conceição Paiseão, well situated on the main square.

Casa de Peixinhos (☎ 268 980 472; fax 268 881 348; s/d with breakfast €80/100) This turreted, classical 17th-century manor house, a few kilometres out on the Borba road, has rooms crammed with antiques and splendid tiling. Bathrooms are, of course, marble.

Pousada de Dom João IV (☎ 268 980 742; recepcao.djoao@pousadas.pt; d Mon-Fri €169, Sat & Sun €178;) A former royal convent that became the 'House of the Ladies of the Court', next to the ducal palace, this is wrapped around the large cloister. Large rooms have terraces overlooking the garden, and big beds just made for wallowing. Disabled access.

Hotel Convento de São Paulo (☎ 266 989 160; www.hotelconventospaulo.com; Aldeia da Serra; s/d €145/167;) A marvellously romantic huge monastery on a 600-acre estate, this has big, grand, striking rooms and a restaurant with a hugely lofty painted ceiling.

EATING

Café Restauração (☎ 268 980 256; Praça da República; mains €6.25-9.20; café daily, restaurant lunch & dinner Tue-Sun) This is the best and buzziest of several café-restaurants which sits on the square just below the turismo. It's a friendly place with outside chrome chairs. There's a café and a more formal restaurant. The photo of a local riot on the café wall was taken during the Festa dos Capuchos.

O Forno (☎ 268 999 797; Rua Cristóvão Pereira; mains €4-9; lunch & dinner Mon-Sat) Signposted off the Praça da República, this is a popular local place with a backroom that has two

TVs. Try the *bacalhau a casa* – it's fish and (home-made) chips.

Os Cucos (☎ 268 980 806; mains €5.90-8.30; lunch & dinner Mon-Sat) Hidden in the gardens near the *mercado municipal* is this popular spot, in an airy, pointed plate-glass building with garden tables. It is particularly recommended for grilled fresh fish and meat mains, with daily specialities. The fruit salad is delicious. There's a café, too. To get here head uphill from the Praça, then turn left after a block.

ENTERTAINMENT

There are classical **concerts** (admission free) in the chapel of the Ducal Palace on the last Friday of the month at 9pm year-round.

GETTING THERE & AWAY

There are **buses** (☎ 268 989 787) to/from Évora (€4.30/6.50 normal/express, 1½/one hour, three to eight daily), or Estremoz (€2.10, 35 minutes, three daily on weekdays).

ELVAS

pop 24,270 / elevation 280m

The fortifications around this frontier, walled-up town zigzag like a cartoon explosion, approached by a mammoth four-tier aqueduct. Here is 17th-century Europe's most sophisticated military architecture, featuring moats, fort and heavy walls that would indicate a certain paranoia if it weren't for Elvas' position, only 15km west of Spanish Badajoz. Inside the heavy town walls are snaking, dramatically sloping town streets that are surprisingly untouristed. It seems appropriate that a siren sounds daily at noon, but it doesn't mean the Spanish are coming – it's a fire practice. When it's for real you hear the siren twice (fire inside the walls!) or three times (fire outside the walls!).

Today Elvas is fascinating to visit, with its evocative frontier-post atmosphere, narrow medina-like streets and extraordinary, forbidding walls and buttresses. It's also possibly the European towel capital, catering to linen-hungry Spanish day-trippers.

History

In 1229, Elvas was recaptured from the Moors after 500 years of fairly peaceful occupation. The following centuries saw relentless attacks from Spain, interrupted by occasional peace treaties. Spain only succeeding in 1580, allowing Felipe II of Spain (the future Felipe I of Portugal) to set up court here for a few months. But the mighty fortifications were seldom breached: during the Wars of Succession, in 1644, the garrison held out against a nine-day Spanish siege and, in 1659, just 1000 (an epidemic had wiped out the rest) withstood an attack by a 15,000-strong Spanish army.

The fortifications saw their last action in 1811 when the Duke of Wellington used the town as the base for an attack on Badajoz during the Peninsular War.

Orientation

Considering the extent of the walls, the centre feels small. Praça da República is at its heart, with all major sights a short walk away. Those arriving by train will find themselves disembarking at Fontaínhas, 4km north of town off the Campo Maior road.

It's possible to find central parking, but not always easy; if you don't like narrow one-way streets, park on the outskirts of town (or just inside Portas de Olivença).

Information

EMERGENCY & MEDICAL SERVICES

Police station (☎ 268 622 613; Rua Isabel Maria Picão)

District hospital (☎ 268 622 225) Opposite the Pousada de Santa Luzia.

INTERNET ACCESS

O Livreiro de Elvas (☎ /fax 268 620 882; Rua de Olivença 4A; per hr €3; 🕒 9.30am-1pm & 3.30-7.15pm Mon-Fri, 9.30am-1pm Sat) As well as Net access, this sells the *Tourist Guidebook to the Planície Dourada* (€2.50).

Turismo (below) Free access.

MONEY

Banco Espirito Santo (☎ 268 939 240; Praça da República) There are many banks with ATMs around town including this one.

Cota Câmbios (Rua da Cadeia; 🕒 8.30am-1.30pm & 2.30-7.30pm Mon-Fri, 9am-1.30pm & 2.30-6pm Sat & Sun) The exchange bureau is central.

POST

Post office (☎ 268 639 030; Rua da Cadeia; 🕒 8.30am-6pm Mon-Fri, 9am-12.30pm Sat)

TOURIST INFORMATION

Turismo (☎ 268 622 236; Praça da República; 🕒 9am-6pm Mon-Fri, 10am-12.30pm & 2-5.30pm Sat & Sun

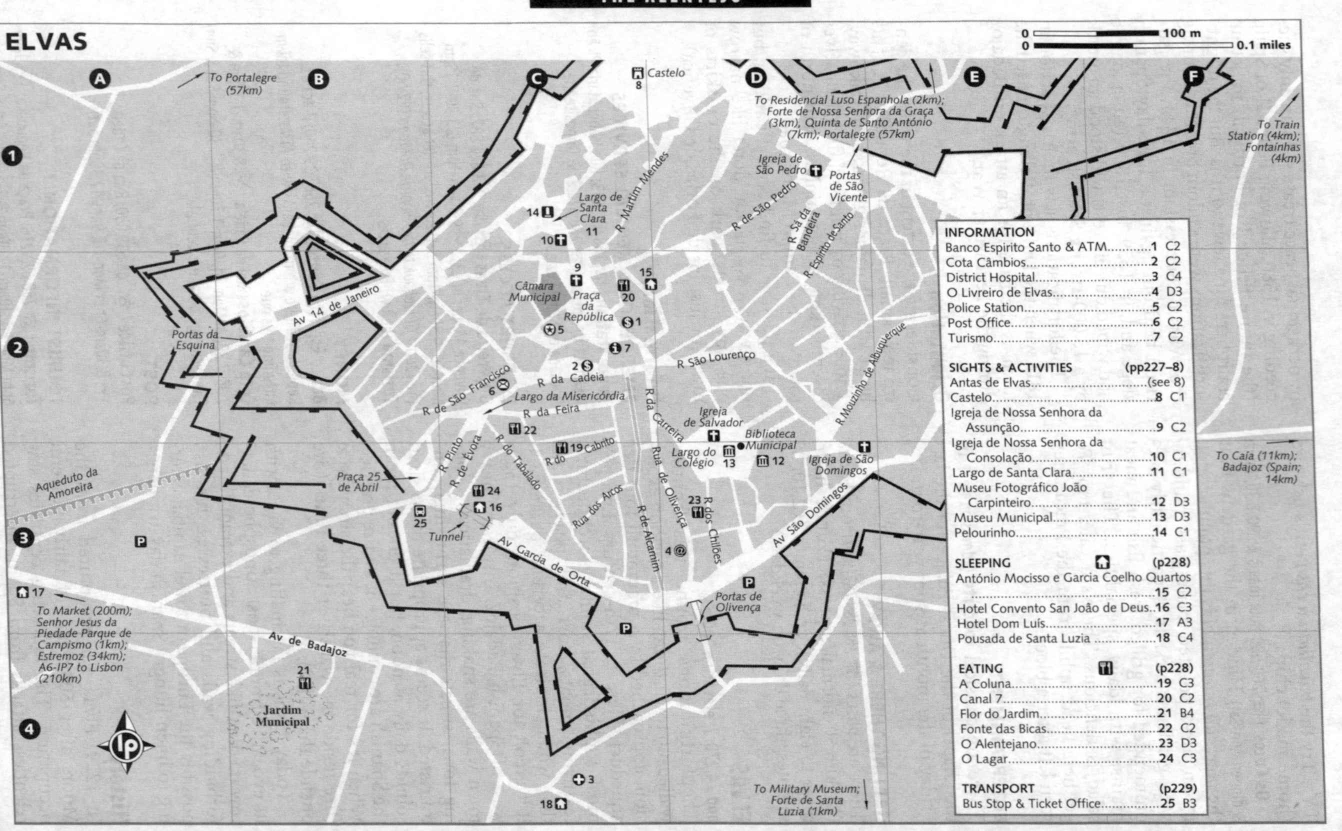
ELVAS
0 100 m
0 0.1 miles
A
B
C
D
E
F
1
2
3
4
To Portalegre (57km)
Castelo 8
To Residencial Luso Espanhola (2km); Forte de Nossa Senhora da Graça (3km), Quinta de Santo António (7km); Portalegre (57km)
To Train Station (4km); Fontaínhas (4km)
Igreja de São Pedro
Portas de São Vicente
Largo de Santa Clara
R Martim Mendes
R de São Pedro
R Sá da Bandeira
R Espírito de Santo
Câmara Municipal
Praça da República
Av 14 de Janeiro
Portas da Esquina
R São Lourenço
R da Cadeia
R de São Francisco
Largo da Misericórdia
R da Feira
R Mouzinho de Albuquerque
Igreja de Salvador
Biblioteca Municipal
Largo do Colégio
Igreja de São Domingos
R da Carreira
Rua de Olivença
R do Cabrito
R do Tabalado
R Pinto
R de Évora
Praça 25 de Abril
Aqueduto da Amoreira
Tunnel
Rua dos Arcos
R de Alcamim
R dos Chilões
Av São Domingos
Av Garcia de Orta
Portas de Olivença
To Caia (11km); Badajoz (Spain; 14km)
To Market (200m); Senhor Jesus da Piedade Parque de Campismo (1km); Estremoz (34km); A6-IP7 to Lisbon (210km)
Av de Badajoz
Jardim Municipal
To Military Museum; Forte de Santa Luzia (1km)
INFORMATION
Banco Espirito Santo & ATM............1 C2
Cota Câmbios............2 C2
District Hospital............3 C4
O Livreiro de Elvas............4 D3
Police Station............5 C2
Post Office............6 C2
Turismo............7 C2
SIGHTS & ACTIVITIES (pp227–8)
Antas de Elvas............(see 8)
Castelo............8 C1
Igreja de Nossa Senhora da Assunção............9 C2
Igreja de Nossa Senhora da Consolação............10 C1
Largo de Santa Clara............11 C1
Museu Fotográfico João Carpinteiro............12 D3
Museu Municipal............13 D3
Pelourinho............14 C1
SLEEPING (p228)
António Mocisso e Garcia Coelho Quartos............15 C2
Hotel Convento San João de Deus............16 C3
Hotel Dom Luís............17 A3
Pousada de Santa Luzia............18 C4
EATING (p228)
A Coluna............19 C3
Canal 7............20 C2
Flor do Jardim............21 B4
Fonte das Bicas............22 C2
O Alentejano............23 D3
O Lagar............24 C3
TRANSPORT (p229)
Bus Stop & Ticket Office............25 B3

May-Sep; to 5.30pm Oct-Apr) Though helpful, this only has a most rudimentary town map. It has lots of pamphlets on local attractions, and some books (though none of the latter in English). One local tourist brochure pessimistically has funeral directors listed at the back.

Sights

FORTIFICATIONS & MILITARY MUSEUM

Walls encircled Elvas as early as the 13th century, but it was in the 17th century that Flemish Jesuit engineer Cosmander designed these formidable defences, adding moats, ramparts, seven bastions, four semi-bastions and fortified gates in the style of the famous French military architect, the Marquis de Vauban. To give you an idea of the level of security: you cross a door bridge to get to the main gate; inside is a 150-sq-m square, surrounded by bastions, turrets and battlements, a covered road and three lines of trenches, some carved out of rock.

Also added was the miniature zigzag-walled **Forte de Santa Luzia**, just south of town. This now houses the **military museum** (☎ 268 628 357; ⏲ 10am-1pm & 2-5pm Oct-Mar, 10am-1pm & 3-7pm Apr-Sep). The Forte de Nossa Senhora da Graça, 3km north of town, with a similar shape, was added in the following century; it's still in use as an army base and is closed to the public.

CASTELO

You can walk around the battlements at the **castle** (admission €1.50; ⏲ 9.30am-1pm & 2.30-5.30pm) for dramatic views across the baking plains. The original castle was built by the Moors on a Roman site, and rebuilt by Dom Dinis in the 13th century, then again by Dom João II in the late 15th century. Antas de Elvas, who run archaeological tours, are based here (p228).

IGREJA DE NOSSA SENHORA DA ASSUNÇÃO

Francisco de Arruda designed this fortified, sturdy **church** (Praça da República; admission free) in the early 16th century, and it was the cathedral until Elvas lost its episcopal status in 1882. Renovated in the 17th and 18th centuries, it retains a few Manueline touches, such as the south portal. Inside is a sumptuous 18th-century organ and some pretty, but somewhat lost, 17th and 18th-century tiling.

IGREJA DE NOSSA SENHORA DA CONSOLAÇÃO

This plain **church** (admission free, donations welcome) hides a thrilling interior. There are painted marble columns under a cupola, gilded chapels and fantastic 17th-century azulejos covering the surface. The unusual octagonal design was inspired by the Knights Templar chapel, which stood on a nearby site before this church was built in the mid-16th century. It was once the church of the Dominicans, and is all that is left of the original monastery.

LARGO DE SANTA CLARA

This delightful cobbled square facing the Igreja de Nossa Senhora da Consolação has a whimsical centrepiece – a polka-dotted **pelourinho**. This pillory wasn't meant to be fun, of course; it was a symbol of municipal power: criminals would once have been chained to the metal hooks at the top.

The fancy **archway** with its own loggia at the top of the square is pure Moorish artistry, and was a flourish in the town walls that once trailed past here.

MUSEU MUNICIPAL

This excellent **museum** (Museu Thomaz Pires; Largo do Colégio; admission €0.50; ⏲ 9am-12.30pm & 2-5.30pm Mon-Fri) is jam-packed with treasures, including Neolithic artefacts, Roman mosaics, a fragment of a Visigoth altar, folk crafts, azulejos and musical instruments from the former African colonies.

AQUEDUTO DA AMOREIRA

It took an unsurprising 100 years or so to complete this breathtakingly ambitious aqueduct. Finished in 1622, these huge cylindrical buttresses and several tiers of arches stalk from 7km west of town to bring water to the marble fountain in Largo da Misericórdia. It's best seen from the Lisbon road, west of the centre.

MUSEO FOTOGRÁFICO JOÃO CARPINTEIRO

Housed in the old town cinema is this **museum** (Municipal Photography Museum João Carpinteiro; ☎ 268 636 470; Largo Luis de Camões; adult/child €2/1; ⏲ 10am-1pm & 2-5pm Oct-Mar, 10am-1pm & 3-7pm) with an impressive collection of cameras, the oldest a pocket-vest number dating from 1912. You may be followed by a guard and the museum manager during your visit, which is not very relaxing, but useful if you need to ask any questions (such as where's the exit).

Tours

Antas de Elvas (☎/fax 268 626 403; Castelo; adult/student/senior €17.50/10/10; Apr-Oct) organises half-day archaeological circuits by 4WD to several nearby megaliths twice each Wednesday, Saturday and Sunday. At the castle you can also buy *Antas de Elvas* (€5), a booklet on local megaliths in English or French, and other megalithic information.

Festivals & Events

Elvas starts to tap its blue suede shoes in late September, celebrating the **Festas do Senhor da Piedade e de São Mateus**, with everything from agricultural markets and bullfights to folk dancing and religious processions (especially the last day). Book accommodation well in advance.

Sleeping

BUDGET

António Mocisso e Garcia Coelho Quartos (☎ 268 622 126; Rua Aires Varela 15; s/d €20/30;) This is the only budget place in the town centre, and offers modern, small, thin-walled but comfortable rooms.

Residencial Luso Espanhola (☎/fax 268 623 092; Rui de Melo; s/d with breakfast €25/40) Only a short way from the town (2km north on the Portalegre road) this friendly 14-room hostelry has a faint motel look, with smallish, modern rooms and balconies that overlook quite a countryside view. There are two restaurants next door.

Senhor Jesus da Piedade Parque de Campismo (☎ 268 623 772; adult/tent/car €3/4/3; Apr–mid-Sep) On the southwestern outskirts of Elvas, off the N4 Estremoz road, is this small, basic camp site, with some big old trees. There's a municipal pool 1km away.

MID-RANGE

Hotel Dom Luís (☎ 268 622 756; fax 268 620 733; Avenida de Badajoz; s/d with breakfast €50/60;) A snappy, cheery little modern establishment, 700m from the centre, just outside the town walls, and just across the road from the aqueduct. Rooms have small windows (but you can see the aqueduct) and satellite TV.

Quinta de Santo António (☎ 268 628 406; fax 268 625 050; Estrada de Barbacena; s/d with breakfast €70/75) This beautiful, stately old house sits in lush gardens. It's 7km northwest of Elvas, with tennis courts and horses to ride.

TOP END

Pousada de Santa Luzia (☎ 268 637 470; recepcao.staluzia@pousadas.pt; Avenida de Badajoz; d with breakfast Mon-Fri €113, Sat & Sun €144;) This is a comfortable, though relatively modern and uncharacterful, *pousada* – the first in Portugal and dating from the 1940s.

Hotel Convento San João de Deus (☎ 268 639 200; d from €70) Spanish-owned, this is Elvas' finest hotel. It opened in 2004 and is a grand but not always sympathetic conversion of a 17th-century convent, which has previously hosted the military, a hospital, and firefighters. Now it has 56 impressive rooms. Suites have antique furniture and chandeliers. Disabled access.

Eating

Flor do Jardim (☎ 268 623 174; Avenida António Sardinho; mains €6-12.50; lunch & dinner) This tranquil restaurant has a peaceful terrace overlooking the park with birds tweeting around. It is a fine place for a drink as well as a meal. Next to a children's playground, it's a good family stop.

O Alentejano (☎ 268 621 925; Rua dos Chilões 29; mains €5-7) Come here for hearty, bargain Alentejan fare in a relaxed, traditional setting.

A Coluna (☎ 268 623 728; Rua do Cabrito 11; mains €5.50-7.50, tourist menu €9; lunch & dinner Wed-Mon) This whitewashed cavern is a cut above its competitors, with azulejos on the walls and lots of *bacalhau con grau* on the menu (tasty cod with chickpeas).

O Lagar (☎ 268 624 793; Rua Nova da Vedoria 7; mains €5.50-12.50; lunch & dinner Fri-Wed) O Lagar is smart and buzzing, with good regional cooking, specialising in *bacalhau*, shellfish rice and *açorda* (bread soup) with prawns.

Canal 7 (☎ 268 623 593; Rua dos Sapateiros 16; mains €4-7) This is a popular local greasy spoon, with hearty Portuguese daily specials to fill budgeting bellies.

For self-caterers there is **Fonte das Bicas** (Rua da Feira 15; 7.30am-8pm), a small supermarket.

Shopping

On alternate Mondays there's a big lively **market** around the aqueduct, just off the

Lisbon road west of town. The weeks it's not on, there is a **flea market** in Praça da República.

Getting There & Around

The bus stop and **ticket office** (☎ 268 622 875) is in Praça 25 de Abril. There are buses to Estremoz (€3, 45 minutes, three daily on weekdays), Évora (€4.90, 1¼-1¾ hours, two daily on weekdays) and Portalegre (€4, 1¼ hours, two daily on weekdays). Express coaches depart daily for Lisbon (€10.80, 3¼-3½ hours, nine daily).

Taxis (☎ 268 623 526) charge around €4 from the train station at Fontaínhas into town.

A **tourist train** (adult/child €2.50/1.50) does a circuit of the town's main sights from May to September, three daily Tuesday to Friday, and six daily on weekends.

PORTALEGRE

pop 26,110 / elevation 520m

Bunched up on a hilltop and at the foot of Serra de São Mamede – the mountain range that rears skywards from the town, Portalegre is a pretty, whitewashed, ochre-edged city. Inside the city walls, faded baroque mansions are all dressed up with no place to go – relics of its textile manufacturing heyday. In the 16th century, the town boomed through tapestry; in the 17th, silk. Bust followed, after the 1703 Treaty of Methuen brought English competition. But, even today, Portalegre stays true to its legacy of natty threads – there is a factory here producing fine tapestries using a unique technique, and an accompanying impressive museum.

It's Alto Alentejo's capital: charming, friendly, off-the-beaten-track, and handy for transport on to nearby mountaintop villages.

Orientation

Portalegre has an hourglass shape, with the new town to the northeast and the old town spread across a hilltop to the southwest. The waist is a traffic roundabout – the Rossio, which is close to the bus station, from where it's about 400m to the old town via the pedestrianised Rua 5 de Outubro.

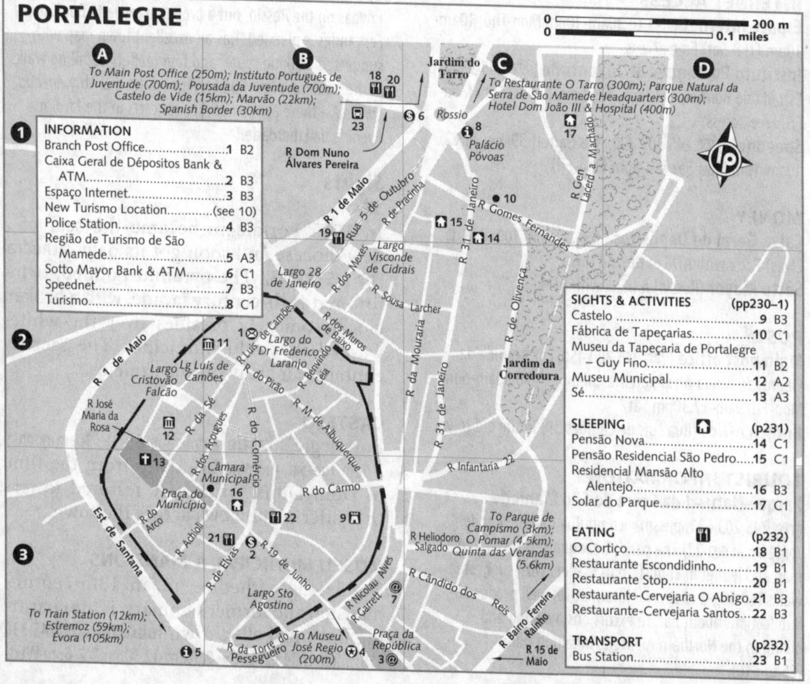

CROSSING THE SERRA DE SÃO MAMEDE

The Serra de São Mamede rises dramatically from the plains. Four peaks (Fria, Marvão, Castelo de Vide and São Mamede – the highest is 1025m) form the summit of this 40km-long range running along the Spanish border near Portalegre. The park, stretching from Castelo de Vide south to just beyond Esperança, includes all four peaks.

A combination of Atlantic forest and Mediterranean bush provides the ideal habitat for the rare trumpet narcissus and stonecrop, plus dozens of bird species – more than half of the species that breed in Portugal nest here. Keep an eye out for vultures, eagles, kites and (rare and shy) black storks.

With your own transport you can delve right into the heart of the park, to traditional villages such as Alegrete and Esperança. Buses run from Portalegre to Castelo de Vide and Marvão.

At the park's head office (below) you can make reservations for park accommodation: they have four *casas de abrigo* (shelter houses), each sleeping up to eight. Other information, including bilingual walking leaflets (€0.50), is available at the Marvão turismo (p236) and at the Centro de Interpretação in Castelo de Vide (p232). The UK's **World Walks** (☎ 01242 254353; www.worldwalks.com) offer week-long self-guided walks through the park, with accommodation, five packed lunches, car hire, one meal and a wine tasting included (€380 to €425).

Information

EMERGENCY

Hospital (☎ 245 301 000) 400m north of town.

Police station (☎ 245 300 620) Just outside Porta de Alegrete.

INTERNET ACCESS

Espaço Internet (🕑 10.30am-10pm Mon-Thu, 10am-10pm Fri & Sat) Free access.

Instituto Português de Juventude (☎ 245 330476; Estrada do Bonfim; 🕑 9am-12.30pm & 2-5.30pm Mon-Fri) Free access.

Speednet (☎ 245 309 800; Rua Garrett 39; per hr €2; 10am-1pm Mon-Sat & 3-8pm Mon-Fri)

MONEY

Caixa Geral de Depósitos (☎ 245 339 100; Rua de Elvas) Bank with ATM in the old town.

Sotto Mayor (Rossio) A bank with ATM.

POST

Main post office (☎ 245 300 450; cnr Avenida da Liberdade & Rua Alexandre Herculano; 🕑 8.30am-6pm Mon-Fri, 9am-12.30pm Sat)

Branch office (Rua Luís de Camões 39) In the old town.

TOURIST INFORMATION

Parque Natural da Serra de São Mamede (☎ 245 203 631; pnssm@icn.pt; Rua General Conde Jorge de Avilez 22) The park's headquarters has a free map and leaflet in English, plus leaflets with suggested walks (€0.50), and several informative, well produced publications about nature excursions, walking and biking in the Northern Alentejo, detailing trails (€5 to €10).

Região de Turismo de São Mamede (☎ 245 300 770; www.rtsm.pt; Estrada de Santana 25; 🕑 9am-12.30pm & 2-5.30pm Mon-Fri) The regional tourist office. Enter through the back.

Turismo (☎ 245 331 359; 🕑 10am-7pm Mon-Fri, 10am-1pm & 3-7pm Sat & Sun Jul & Aug, to 6pm Sep-Jun) Operates from the unsigned, green-shuttered Palácio Póvoas on the Rossio, but a probable move to Rua Gomes Fernandes is planned. Has an excellent town map with suggested walking route, and four leaflets detailing walks in the national park (€0.50). Pick up the monthly *Agenda Cultural* – there are sometimes concerts in the Jardim Avenida da Liberdade.

Sights

SÉ

In 1545 Portalegre became the seat of a new diocese and soon got its own **cathedral** (☎ 245 331 113). The pyramid-pointed, twin-towered 18th-century façade, with a broken clock, sombrely presides over the whitewashed Praça do Município. The sacristy contains an array of fine azulejos.

CASTELO

Portalegre's **castle** (admission €1; 🕑 10am-noon & 2-5pm Tue-Sat, morning Sun) dates from the time of Dom Dinis, with three restored towers that offer good views across the town.

MUSEU MUNICIPAL & MANSIONS

Beside the cathedral, in an 18th-century mansion and former seminary, is the charming but unlabelled town **museum** (☎ 245 330 616; adult/child €2/1; 🕑 9.30am-12.30pm & 2-6pm Wed-

Mon), with an attic-like collection of silver snuff boxes, porcelain, liturgical figures and a *Toad-of-Toad-Hall* two-seater car.

The town's former glory is recorded in stone: faded 17th-century baroque townhouses and mansions dot Rua 19 de Junho to the southeast.

MUSEU DA TAPEÇARIA DE PORTALEGRE – GUY FINO

Opened in 2001, this splendid **museum** (☎ 245 307 980; Rua da Figueira 9; admission €2; 9.30am-1pm & 2.30-6pm Thu-Tue) contains brilliant 20th-century creations from Portalegre's unique tapestry factory. It's named after the factory founder, who created an innovatory stitch. This reflects light in a certain way, enabling incredibly accurate copies of works of art. The museum shows a selection of the 6000 colours of thread used. French tapestry artist Jean Lurçat at first dismissed the technique, then the factory made a copy of one of his works – a cockerel – and asked him to identify the one made at Aubuisson, in France. He chose the more perfect Portalegre copy – you can see them juxtaposed here. The huge tapestries are vastly expensive, and the museum includes copies of works by some of the most famous names in Portuguese 20th-century art, including Almada Negreiros and Vieira de Silva.

The factory still operates from Fábriça de Tapecarias, a former Jesuit college on Rua Gomes Fernandes, just off the Rossio, producing specially commissioned works only. It is due to move when council services (including the turismo) will take over the building. It will continue operating from its new site.

MUSEU JOSÉ REGIO

This small **museum** (9.30am-12.30pm Tue-Sun) is in poet José Regio's former house, and shows his magpie-like collection of popular religious art, with around 400 Christ figures. He was also particularly keen on St António. There are lots of rustic ceramics from Coimbra, which 18th-century migrant workers used to swap for clothes.

Sleeping

BUDGET

Pousada da juventude (☎ 245 330 971; portalegre@movijovem.pt; Estrada do Bonfim; dm €9.50, d with shared bathroom €24; 8am-10am & 7pm-midnight) A big white tower block 700m north of the Rossio, labelled 'Centro de Juventude', this provides the usual not-fancy-but-fine bunks and baths; the adjacent Instituto Português da Juventude (IPJ) is the town's main youth centre.

Pensão Nova (☎ 245 331 212; fax 245 330 493; Rua 31 de Janeiro 26; d €25) A charming place in the old part of town, with characterful accommodation in pretty blue-and-white rooms.

Pensão Residencial São Pedro (☎ 245 331 212; Rua da Mouraria 14; d €25), This is another snug place in a smart house, under the same management as Pensão Nova, which is where you'll find reception.

Parque de campismo (☎/fax 245 202 848; adult/tent/car €3.50/2.90/3.40; Apr-Sep) A lovely Orbitur camp site at Quinta da Saúde, 3km northeast of town on the Estrada da Serra, high above town at 680m. It's shaded by tall pines, and there's a nearby swimming pool.

MID-RANGE

Residencial Mansão Alto Alentejo (☎ 245 202 290; marisaoa/toalentejo@netc.pt; Rua 19 de Junho 59; s/d with breakfast €35/45;) This is the most charming choice in the old town, with bright, breezy rooms and traditional painted furniture.

Solar do Parque (Solar das Avencas; ☎ 245 201 028, Parque Miguel Bombarda 11; d with breakfast €65) This 18th-century manor house is an atmospheric place, and has a lovely location just next to the park.

Quinta das Varandas (☎/fax 245 208 883; d with breakfast €65;) Some rural options along the Estrada da Serra, on spectacularly high, vineyard-clad hillsides within the Parque Natural da Serra de São Mamede, include this fabulously remote and peaceful three-roomed *quinta*, about 2.6km beyond the camp site.

Hotel Dom João III (☎ 245 330 192; fax 245 330 444; Avenida da Liberdade; d with breakfast €55) Also in town, by the garden, is this central, comfortable-but-bland hotel.

Pousada Flor da Rosa (☎ 245 997 210; Crato; d €190;) In the middle of nowhere, 21km west of Portalegre, this is strangely remote – a hotel in a medieval castle, with arches and flagstone walls. Make sure you get a room in the old building. Great for peace and quiet; it has a lovely pool.

Eating

BUDGET

Restaurante O Tarro (☎ 245 309 254; mains €7-13) At the top of Jardim do Tarro, Restaurante O Tarro has a chic indoor restaurant and a lovely outdoor terrace café overlooking the park.

Restaurante-Cervejaria Santos (☎ 245 203 066; Largo Serpa Pinto 4; mains €4-6.50; lunch & dinner Thu-Tue) On a pretty little square, this has a small outside wooden terrace under green umbrellas, and great grilled fish, as well as *migas* (pork and fried bread), *açorda* and so on.

Budget choices near the bus station include small **O Cortiço** (☎ 245 202 176; Rua Dom Nuno Álvares Pereira 17; mains €4.50-6; lunch & dinner), with good fruit salad; and the slightly nicer **Restaurante Stop** (☎ 245 201 364; Rua Dom Nuno Álvares Pereira 13; mains €5-6; lunch & dinner Sun-Fri).

MID-RANGE

Restaurante O Escondidinho (☎ 245 202 728; Traveller das Cruzes 1-3; mains €6-7.50; lunch & dinner Mon-Sat) This is a great place to eat, very popular, with tasty food – and TV, but a bit more classy than most.

Restaurante-Cervejaria O Abrigo (☎ 245 331 658; Rua de Elvas 74; mains €7-12; lunch & dinner) Inside the old town, this is a welcoming restaurant with traditional mains in a cool, simple interior.

Getting There & Around

From the **bus station** (☎ 245 330 723) services go to Lisbon (€10.80, 4½ hours), Estremoz (€4/6.80 normal/express, 80 minutes/50 minutes, three to five daily weekdays), Évora (€8.80, 1½ hours, one daily weekdays), Castelo Branco (€8, 1 hour 50 minutes, one daily), Elvas (€4, 1½ hours, two daily weekdays) and Beja (€10, four hours, one daily weekdays).

Trains from Lisbon run daily (3½ hours, two to three daily); change at Abrantes. The station is 12km south of town but shuttle buses (€1.40, 15 minutes) meet all trains.

There are **taxis** (☎ 245 202 375, 966 772 947).

CASTELO DE VIDE

pop 4145 / elevation 570m

Gleaming white houses reflect the brilliant sunlight and flowers burst with colour on the street. Housework and gardening don't get neglected in house-proud Castelo de Vide. Cobbled streets so steep that you need a handrail allow views over the village, set in the heart of a lush, hilly, olive landscape. Elderly ladies crochet on doorsteps and children play in the narrow web of streets. People chat out of upper-storey windows and, at night, the lanes are starlit. It feels like life hasn't changed much here for some years, at least in the oldest part of the village.

By the castle is a small *judiaria* – the former Jewish district, strongest here in the early 15th century after their expulsion from Spain. A small synagogue is the main memento of this era. Castle de Vide is famous for its crystal mineral water, which spouts out of various public fountains.

Orientation

At the heart of town are two parallel squares backed by the Igreja de Santa Maria da Devesa. The turismo is in a wide area in Rua Bartolomeu Álvares da Santa. Walk through the archway by the turismo to reach the southern square, Praça Dom Pedro V.

The castle, old quarter and *judiaria* lie to the northwest. Dive into the lanes behind the Igreja de Santa Maria da Devesa and follow the signs to Fonte da Vila (the old town fountain). From there it's a short, steep climb to the synagogue and castle.

Buses stop at the fountain near the post office; the train station is 4km northwest.

Information

Artitudo (☎ 245 908 085; Rua Mouzinho da Silveira, 14; per hr €3; noon-2am) Café, art gallery and bookshop providing Internet access.

Caixa Geral de Depósitos (☎ 245 339 100; Rua Elvas)

Centro de Interpretação (☎ 245 905 299; Rua de Santo Amaro 27; 9.30am-12.45pm & 2-5.45pm Mon-Fri) Parque Natural da Serra de São Mamede information centre.

Centro de saúde (Medical Centre; ☎ 245 901 105; Praça Dom Pedro V)

Open-air market Every Friday, but the biggest is the last Friday of month and located 300m east of town near the municipal sports ground (it may move to a new car park south of the centre).

Police station (☎ 245 901 314; Avenida da Aramenha)

Post office (☎ 245 900 100; Rua de Olivença; 9am-12.30 & 2-5.30pm Mon-Fri)

Turismo (☎ 245 901 361; cm.castvide@ mail.telepac.pt; Rua Buiartolomeu Álvares da Santa 81; 9am-5.30pm Oct-Apr, to 7pm May-Sep) Has town map and megaliths leaflets.

Sights

OLD TOWN & JUDIARIA

A sizable community of Jews settled here in the 12th century, then larger waves came in the 15th. At first they didn't have an exclusive district, but Dom Pedro I restricted them to specific quarters. The tiny **synagogue** (cnr Rua da Judiaria & Rua da Fonte; admission free; 8am-7pm), the oldest in Portugal, looks just like its neighbouring cottages – it was adapted from an existing building. It's divided into two levels, one for women and one for men. In the bare interior is a wooden tabernacle and Holy Ark for Torah scrolls. Following Manuel I's convert-or-leave edict, many Jews returned to Spain, though some headed to Évora.

CASTELO

Originally Castelo de Vide's inhabitants lived within the castle's sturdy outer walls; even now there remains a small inner village with a church, the 17th-century Igreja da Nossa Senhora da Alegria.

There are brilliant views from here over the town's red roofs, surrounded by green and olive hills. The **castle** (admission free; 8am-7pm May-Sep, 9am-5pm Oct-Apr), built by Dom Dinis and his brother Dom Afonso, between 1280 and 1365, is topped by a 12m-high brick tower, thought to be the oldest part. There are great views from the roof of the fine vaulted hall.

FONTE DA VILA

In a pretty square just below and east of the *judiaria* is the worn-smooth 16th-century marble **Fonte da Vila**, with a washing area. This, along with several other fountains in the village, spouts out the delicious mineral water for which Castelo de Vide is known.

ANTA DOS COURELEIROS & MENHIR DA MEADA

In the wild, boulder-strewn landscape around Castelo de Vide are dozens of ancient megaliths. The two most impressive are the Anta dos Coureleiros, 8km north of town (with three other megaliths nearby making up what's called a Parque Megalítico), and the 7m-high Menhir da Meada, 8.5km further on – supposedly the tallest menhir in the Iberian Peninsula – a large phallus for keeping the fields fertile.

Both are easily accessible by car or on foot. Turismos here and in Marvão should have *Paisagens Megalíticas Norte Alentejana* (Megalithic Landscapes North of Alentejo) a free, glossy photographic leaflet (English versions available) to help you track down these and other megaliths; follow the small wooden 'Antas' signs en route.

CIDADE DE AMMAIA

Opened in 2001, this excellent little **Roman museum** (São Salvador de Aramenha; admission €2.50; 9am-1pm & 2-5pm Mon-Fri, 10am-1pm & 2-5pm Sat & Sun) lies 7km east, en route to Marvão. From São Salvador head 700m south along the Portalegre road, then turn left following signs to Olhos d'Água restaurant.

In the 1st century AD this area was a huge Roman city called Ammaia, flourishing from the area's rich agricultural produce (especially oil, wine and cereals). Although evidence was found (and some destroyed) in the 19th century, it wasn't until 1994 that thorough digs began. Here you can see some of the finds – engraved lintels and tablets, jewellery, coins and some incredibly well-preserved glassware – and also follow paths across the fields to where the forum and spa once stood and see several impressive columns and ongoing excavations.

Activities

The **Club de Golf d'Ammaia** (☎ 245 993 755) golf course is 6km towards Marvão.

Festivals & Events

Carnaval (February/March) This is great fun, too, with everyone out to watch processions of fantastically costumed folk, many in drag.

Easter festival (March/April) Castelo de Vide's big bash is the four-day fair when hundreds of lambs go through the highs and lows of blessings and slaughter, and processions, folk dances, band music and much revelry all take place.

Sleeping

BUDGET

Casa Janeco (☎ 245 901 211; Rua da Costa 56A; s/d with shared bathroom €15/25) It's great to stay in the narrow cobbled street in the heart of town. Casa Janeco has two small rooms and the charming elderly Senhora Janeco also has a mini-apartment costing a bargain €25.

Casa Machado (☎ 245 901 515; Rua Luís de Camões 33; d €28) On the western edge of town, this is a modern place. The four rooms are spotless

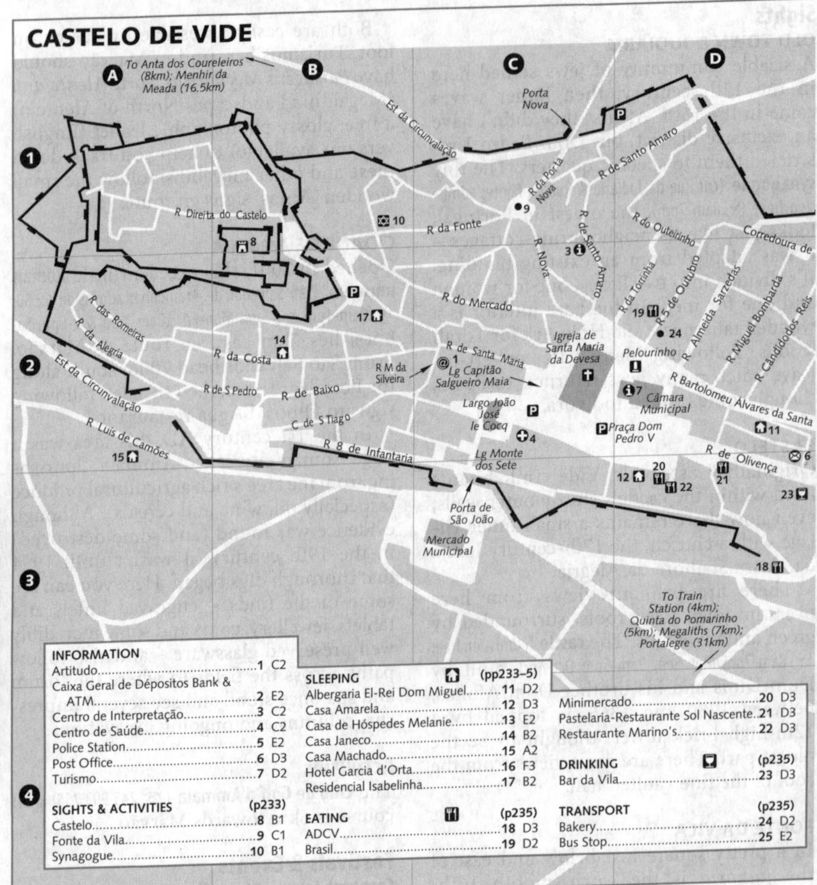

and there's a small, shared kitchen and outdoor patio. It is great for families.

Casa de Hóspedes Melanie (☎ 245 901 632; Largo do Paça Novo 3; s/d €25/35;) This efficient place on a leafy square has five plain, spacious, good-value rooms.

Residencial Isabelinha (☎ 245 901 896; Largo do Paça Novo; d with breakfast €40) Trinket-filled hallways lead to rooms overlooking the leafy square; the owner will drop prices like a shot if it's not busy.

Quinta do Pomarinho (☎ 245 901 202; www.pomarinho.com; d with shared bathroom €25-35, camping per adult/tent €4/4) A Dutch-owned old rural house 5km southwest, this is a rural, ecologically friendly farm. It also has camping and a little roundhouse.

MID-RANGE

Albergaria El-Rei Dom Miguel (☎ 245 919 191; fax 245 901 592; Rua Bartolomeu Álvares da Santa; d with breakfast €50-60) This seven-room place on the main street has charm and attention to detail – antique furniture, rooms with gleaming-white linen, balcony and smart bathrooms.

Quinta da Bela Vista (☎ 245 968 125; Póvoa e Meadas; d €80) This is an old country house 13km north of Castelo de Vide. It's been in the same family since the 1920s and is a lovely choice.

Hotel Garcia d'Orta (☎ 245 901 100; hgo@hgo.pt; Estrada de São Vicente; d with breakfast from €70;) Two hundred metres towards Marvão is this golfers' favourite. It's nicely low key and in an attractive modern building with good views.

THE ALENTEJO

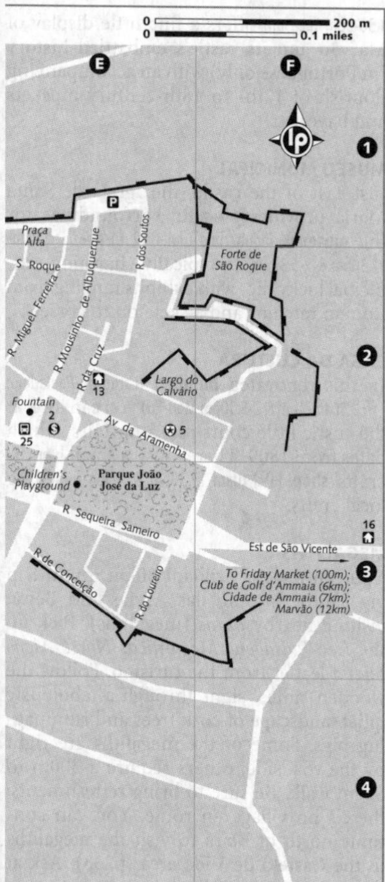

TOP END

Casa Amarela (☎ 245 905 878; Praça Dom Pedro V; d/ste with breakfast €100/125) On the main square with views over the *praça*, it has nine rooms and two suites in a beautiful, restored golden yellow house.

Eating & Drinking

Pastelaria-Restaurante Sol Nascente (☎ 245 901 789; Praça Dom Pedro V; mains €5-9; breakfast, lunch & dinner Wed-Mon) This is a pleasant central café with cheap-and-cheerful main meals, good cakes and sunny outdoor seating.

ADCV (☎ 245 905 125; Rua Alexandre Herculano; mains €5-6) Known to locals as 'Johnny's' after its genial patron (the initials stand for the local sports club), ADCV is packed with labourers at lunch and mainly men at night. Offal's on the menu, but if that sounds awful, the seafood is good too.

Restaurante Marino's (☎ 245 901 408; Praça Dom Pedro V, 6; mains €7-12, tourist menu €14.50; lunch Tue-Sat, dinner Mon-Sat) On the main square, Marino's is smart, small and slick and offers pasta and regional mains.

Brasil (☎ 245 901 407; Rua 5 de Outubrol; lunch & dinner) Bright and tiled, this is enthusiastically run, and provides lots of traditional mains as well as a meat marathon on skewers – the Brazilian portion of the menu.

Bar da Vila (☎ 245 905 433; Rua de Olivença 11; 11am-11pm) This bar has outside seating facing a garden square, well placed for watching the world go by over a beer.

Self-catering supplies are available at a **minimercado** (grocery shop; Praça Dom Pedro V).

Getting There & Away

BUS

Buses (☎ 245 901 510) run to/from Portalegre (€4.80, 20 minutes, two to three daily weekdays) and Lisbon (€12.20, 4¼ hours, two daily). Buy express tickets (and check timetables) at the **bakery** (Rua 5 de Outubro 6), just off the pillory square.

TRAIN

You can get to/from Lisbon (€8.30, four hours, twice daily) – change at Abrantes and Torre das Vargens. The station is 4km northwest of town and there are no bus links. **Taxis** (☎ 245 901 271), available from outside the turismo, charge around €4 to the station.

MARVÃO

pop 4420 / elevation 862m

At an awesome height, Marvão hovers up above blue-green, craggy hills. Its castle rears up from the rock and from it the views are stupendous, the air clear and still, so that the only sounds audible are the whirr of birds and chatter of insects. The whitewashed village is all leaning lines, orange, tiled roofs and bright flowers. There's nothing like a bit of economic stagnation for keeping development in check.

History

Marvão, a garrison town just 10km from the Spanish frontier, has unsurprisingly long been a prized possession. Romans settled here, and Christian Visigoths were on the scene when the Moors arrived in 715. It was probably the Moorish lord of Coimbra, Emir Maraun, who gave the place its present name.

In 1160 Christians took control. In 1226 the town received a municipal charter, the walls were extended to encompass the whole summit, and the castle was rebuilt by Dom Dinis.

Marvão's importance in the defence against the Castilians was highlighted during the 17th-century War of Restoration, when further defences were added. But by the 1800s it had lost its way, a garrison town without a garrison, and this lack of interest is why so many 15th and 16th buildings have been preserved. Its last action was at the centre of the tug-of-war between the Liberals and Royalists; in 1833 the Liberals used a secret entrance to seize the town, the only time Marvão has ever been captured.

Orientation

Arriving by car or bus you'll approach Portas de Ródão, one of the four village gates, opening onto Rua de Cima, which has several shops and restaurants. Drivers can park outside or enter this gate and park in Largo de Olivença, just below Rua de Cima. The castle is up at the end of Rua do Espiríto Santo.

Information

There's a bank and post office in nearby Rua do Espiríto Santo. Access the Net free at the Casa da Cultura (right). Near the castle and selling jam and local liquors is the **turismo** (☎ 245 993 886; Largo de Santa Maria; 🕒 9am-12.30pm & 2-5.30pm Sep-Jun, to 7pm Jul & Aug). Among brochures available here are walking leaflets (€0.50) describing walks and wildlife in the Parque Natural da Serra de São Mamede.

Sights

CASTELO

The formidable **castle** (admission free; 🕒 24hr), built into the rock at the western end of the village, dates from the end of the 13th century, but most of what you see today was built in the 17th century. The views from the battlements are staggering. There's a huge vaulted cistern (still full of water) near the entrance but it's swarming with little flies. At the far end, the **Núcleo Museológico Militar** (Military Museum; adult/student €1/0.80; 🕒 10am-1pm & 1.30-5pm Tue-Sun) offers a fine little display of Marvão and its castle's embattled history (in Portuguese only) with an accompanying flourish of 17th- to 18th-century muskets and bayonets.

MUSEU MUNICIPAL

Just east of the castle, the Igreja de Santa Maria provides graceful surroundings for the **museum** (adult/child under 12 €1/free; 🕒 9am-12.30pm & 2-5.30pm), a typically charming municipal lucky dip, with exhibits ranging from Roman remains and a skeleton to corsets.

CASA DA CULTURA

In this renovated **building** (Largo do Pauladino; 🕒 9.30am-1pm & 2-5.30pm Mon-Fri) you can look at the rustic little court room upstairs, which dates from 1809. There's also a small handicrafts **shop** (🕒 10am-12.30pm & 2-5pm), selling local crafts.

MEGALITHS

You can make a brilliant 30km round-trip via Santo António das Areias and Beirã, visiting nearby *antas* (megaliths). Pick up the free *Paisagens Megalíticas Norte Alentejana* leaflet from the turismo. Follow the wooden 'antas' signs through a fabulously quiet landscape of cork trees and rummaging pigs. Some of the megaliths are right by the roadside, others require a 300m to 500m walk. Be sure to bring refreshments: there's no village en route. You can continue north of Beirã to visit the megaliths in the Castelo de Vide area (p233). Ask at the turismo about bikes to rent.

Sleeping

Casa Dom Dinis (☎ 245 993 957; fax 245 993 959; Rua Dr Matos Magalhães 7; s/d with breakfast €45/53, with terrace €56) Near the turismo, the friendly Dom Dinis has cool, colourful blocky murals and imaginatively decorated rooms of varying sizes. Room 15 has a terrace.

Casa da Árvore (☎/fax 245 993 854; Rua Dr Matos Magalhães 3; d with breakfast €65) This is smart with five pretty, individually furnished rooms and adornments – including original Roman funerary stones and a João Tavares tapestry from the famous Portalegre factory. The breakfast room has a stunning view.

Casa das Portas de Ródão (☎ 245 992 160; Largo da Silveirinha 2; d €50) This two-storey, three-bedroom house right by the entrance to

Palácio do Visconde de Estói (p158), Estói

JULIA WILKINSON

CARLOS COSTA

Praia da Dona Ana (p185), Lagos

Fisherman on the Algarve's Leeward Coast (p150)

JEFF GREENBERG

JULIA WILKINSON

Igreja de Santa Maria do Castelo (p162), Tavira

DAMIEN

Óbidos (p260)

Praça do Giraldo (p208), Évora

ANDERS BL

town, with an outdoor terrace, has a rustic, country feel, with curly iron bedsteads and wood or tiled floors. There's an apartment with living room and kitchen too.

Pousada de Santa Maria (☎ 245 993 201; recepcao.stamaria@pousadas.pt; Rua 24 de Janeiro; d Mon-Fri €134, Sat & Sun €144;) Converted from two village houses, this is the most elegant and intimate option with marvellous views from some rooms.

Eating

Restaurante Casa do Povo (☎ 245 993 160; Rua de Cima; mains €4.50-8; lunch & dinner Fri-Wed) Near the main entrance, Casa do Povo has a terrace with wonderful views across the countryside below, where you can eat mains such as shark with garlic and coriander.

Restaurante O Marcelino (☎ 245 903 138; Rua de Cima 3) This modest place – its sign just says 'Bar' – has a grandmotherly cook who produces home-style mains if you arrive at the right time.

Bar-Restaurante Varanda do Alentejo (☎ 245 993 272; Praça do Pelourinho 1; mains €5.50-8; lunch & dinner) Lots of earthy Alentejan specialities on the menu here, with hearty stuff such as *bacalhau dourada* (cod, onion and potatoes). There's a terrace, and they serve sangria. They also have some *quartos* available.

Bar O Castelo (☎ 245 993 957; Rua Dr Matos Magalhães; snacks €2-3) Run by the same genial people who make Dom Denis so pleasant, this eatery just opposite serves daily specials such as pork and clams, great soups, local cheese and imaginative, humble fare such as scrambled egg with lettuce.

Getting There & Away

Two buses run daily on weekdays between Portalegre and Marvão (€2.65, 45 minutes). There are two services from Castelo de Vide, but the first requires a change of buses at Portagem, a major road junction 7.5km northeast. There are two buses daily leaving Marvão: the 7.30am to Castelo de Vide and Portalegre and the 1.10pm to Portalegre (change at Portagem for Castelo de Vide). Check the latest timetable at the turismo. Express buses run to Lisbon at 7.45am Monday to Saturday (€12.80, 4¾ hours), with an extra one on Sunday at 4.15pm, but you must tell the turismo the day before if you want to catch it or the bus won't detour here to pick you up.

The nearest train station, Marvão-Beirã, is 9km north of Marvão; it's worth a visit just to see its beautiful azulejo panels. Two trains run daily to/from Lisbon (€8.30, 4½ hours); change at Abrantes and Torre das Vargens. Taxis charge around €6 to the station. The daily Lisbon–Madrid *Talgo Lusitânia* train stops here just before 1am, en route to Valência de Alcântara, and just before 5am on the journey to Lisbon (3¼ hours). **Taxis** (☎ 245 993 272; Praça do Pelourinho) charge around €8 to Castelo de Vide.

BAIXO ALENTEJO

MÉRTOLA

pop 9800 / elevation 70m

Spectacularly set on rocky hills, high above the stately, still-life Rio Guadiana, the walled town of Mértola feels like the end of the world, or at least a last outpost. Sun-bleached buildings are crowned by a small but fierce castle, beneath which is a glowing-white, icing-sugar church, once a mosque. Long economic stagnation since medieval times meant, unusually, many traces of Islamic occupation have been left intact. Mértola's a *vila museu* (open-air museum) packed with *núcleos* (areas of historic interest), and home to a gnarled elderly population. In the heat of the day – up to 47°C – the only sound is insects buzzing. Nearby are the beautiful, bleak disused copper mines of São Domingos.

History

Mértola follows the usual pattern of settlement in this area: Phoenician traders, who sailed up the Guadiana, then Carthaginians, then Romans. Its strategic position – the northernmost port on the Guadiana, and the final destination for many Mediterranean routes – led the Romans to develop Mértola (naming it Myrtilis) as a major agricultural and mineral-exporting centre. Cereals and olive oil arrived from Beja, copper and other metals from Aljustrel and São Domingos. It was a rich merchant town.

Later the Moors, who called it Martulah and made it a regional capital, further fortified Mértola and built a mosque. Dom Sancho II and the Knights of the Order of Santiago captured the site in 1238. But then, as commercial routes shifted to the Tejo, Mértola declined. When the last steamboat

service to Vila Real de Santo António ended and the copper mines of São Domingos (the area's main employer) closed in 1965, its port days were over.

Orientation

From the bus station in the new part of town, it's about 600m southwest to the historic old walled town. Old Mértola has few right angles or horizontal surfaces, and driving into it is asking for trouble – even a donkey would struggle.

Information

Banks with ATMs can be found along Rua Dr Afonso Costa.

Caixa Geral Bank & ATM (Rua Dr Afonso Costa)
Centro de saúde (☎ 286 612 254; Cerca Carmo)
Espaço Jovem (Avenida Aureliano Mira Fernandes; per hr €0.50; 9am-9pm) The disconsolate youth centre offers Net access.
Millennium bcp Bank & ATM (Rua Dr Afonso Costa)
Police station (☎ 286 612 127; Rua Dr Afonso Costa)
Parque Natural do Vale do Guadiana headquarters (☎ 286 611 084; pnvg@icn.pt; Rua Dr Afonso Costa 40, Mértola; 9am-12.30pm & 2-5.30pm Mon-Fri Sep-Jun, 8am-2pm Jul & Aug) This is the administrative office but it supplies information on the 600-sq-km park. The offices are due to move to Largo Luís de Camões in the old town at the end of 2005.
Post office (☎ 286 610 030; Rua Alves Redol; 9am-12.30pm & 2-5.30pm)
Turismo (☎ 286 610 109; Rua Alonso Gomes 18; 9.30am-12.30pm & 2-5.30pm) The tourist office is just inside the walled town. It offers free Net access and can advise on *quartos*.

Sights

Stepping through the thick outer walls makes you feel as if you have stepped back in time. It's enchanting just to wander around the sleepy, sun-baked old-walled town.

LARGO LUÍS DE CAMÕES

This is the administrative heart of the old town, a knobbled, picturesque square lined with orange trees, with the *câmara municipal* (town hall) at its western end. To reach the *largo* (small square), enter the old town and keep to the left at the fork in the road.

The **Torre do Relógio**, a little clock tower topped with a stork's nest and overlooking the Rio Guadiana, is northeast of the square. Alongside it is a municipal building with a rooftop worthy of Van Gogh.

IGREJA MATRIZ

This striking parish **church** (admission free; Tue-Sun) – square, flat-faced and topped with little conical decorations – is best known because it was once a mosque, among the few to have survived the Reconquista. It was reconsecrated as a church in the 13th century. An unwhitewashed cavity in the wall on the right behind the altar is the former mosque's *mihrab* (prayer niche). Note also the goats, lions and other figures carved around the peculiar Gothic portal and the typically Moorish horse-shoe arch in the north door.

CASTELO & TORRE DO RIO

Above the parish church looms Mértola's fortified **castle** (admission free; 24hr), most of which dates from the 13th century. It was built upon Moorish foundations next to an Islamic residential complex and *alcáçova* (citadel), which itself overlaid the Roman forum. For centuries the castle was considered western Iberia's most impregnable fortress. From its prominent **keep** (9.30am-12.30pm & 2-5.30pm Tue-Sun) there are fabulous views – you can look down on archaeological digs outside the castle on one side, and the old town and the river on the other.

At the river's edge, near its confluence with the Ribeira de Oeiras, is the ruined, Roman-era **Torre do Rio** (River Tower), which once guarded the vital port.

MUSEUMS

All of Mértola's **museums** (1 museum adult/child €2/1, combined ticket €5/2.50; 9.30am-12.30pm & 2-5.30pm Tue-Sun) have the same opening hours.

In the cellar of the *câmara municipal* is the modest but good **Museu Romano** (Roman Museum; Largo Luís de Camões). It displays the foundations of the Roman house upon which the building rests, and also contains a small collection of pots, sculpture and other artefacts.

At the southern end of the old town, the **Museu Islâmico** (Islamic Museum) is a small but dramatic display (with atmospheric sound effects) of inscribed funerary stones, jewellery, pots and jugs from the 11th to 13th centuries.

The nearby **Museu de Arte Sacra** (Museum of Ecclesiastical Art; Largo da Misericórdia) exhibits religious statuettes from the 16th to 18th centuries and three impressive 16th-century retables, originally in the parish church, portraying the battle against the Moors.

North of the old town is the **Museu Paleocristão** (Paleo-Christian Museum; Rossio do Carmo), which is perhaps the most impressive museum of all, with a partly reconstructed line of 6th-century Roman columns and poignant funerary stones, some beautifully carved with birds, hearts and wreaths. This was the site of a huge Paleo-Christian basilica, its adjacent cemetery used over the centuries by both Roman-era Christians and medieval Moors.

CONVENTO DE SÃO FRANCISCO

This former **convent** (adult/student €1/0.50; 10am-5pm May-Sep, 2-6pm Tue-Sun Oct-Apr), across the Ribeira de Oeiras, 500m southwest of Mértola along a track, has been owned since 1980 by Dutch artist Geraldine Zwannikken and her family. They have transformed it into a nature reserve and art gallery: its grounds full of herbs, horses, rain temples and wild flowers; its former chapel exhibs Geraldine's extraordinary art; its riverside is devoted to nesting storks and lesser kestrels. On offer are occasional workshops, as well as horse rides (by prior arrangement).

PARQUE NATURAL DO VALE DO GUADIANA

Created in 1995, this zone of hills, plains and deep valleys around Serpa and Mértola shelters the Rio Guadiana, one of Portugal's largest and most important rivers. Among its rich variety of flora and fauna are several rare or endangered species, including the black stork (sightings of the shy creatures are seldom), lesser kestrel (most likely around Castro Verde), Bonelli's eagle, royal owl, grey kite, horned viper and Iberian toad. The park also has many prehistoric remains. Ask at the park headquarters (see Information) for details of walking trails (such as a walk along the mine railway track from São Domingos to Pomarão) and where to spot wildlife – they can advise you and provide you with a map.

Activities

You can rent canoes for trips down the lazy river at the Nautical Club below the Restaurante O Naútico (right).

Sleeping

Casa Janelas Verdes (☎ 286 612 145; Rua Dr Manuel Francisco Gomes 38; d €40) In the old town, this is a gorgeous Turihab, with a flower-filled terrace, lots of elderly ladies, old-fashioned rooms and a famously good breakfast.

Casa Rosmaninho (☎ 286 612 005, 963 019 341; Rua 25 de Abril 23; d €50) This is another charming Turihab, in a sweet house – one room has a Jacuzzi and another a rooftop terrace.

Pensão Oasis (☎ 286 612 404; Rua Dr Afonso Costa; d €30;) Just below the old town, this overlooks the river, but the best rooms are downstairs, opening onto a leafy garden veranda. Rooms have fridges and signs saying, 'Please do not dislocate the beds'.

Residencial Beira Rio (☎ 286 611 190; www.beirario.co.pt; Rua Dr Afonso Costa 108; s/d €35/40;) Has well-appointed, spotless rooms, several of which have large river-view terraces. Singles are a bit cramped.

There are some gorgeous rural tourism options around: try **Hospedaria Casa do Guizo** (☎ 286 655171; Monte do Guizo, Moreaness; r €40;) or ask at the turismo for further options. Ask at the park headquarters (p239) about accommodation provided within the park near the border town of Canavial, 20km southeast of Mértola.

Eating

Mértola's specialities are *javali* (wild boar) and the regional dish *migas*, a combination of pork and fried bread – great labouring fuel, but perhaps heavier than necessary for sightseeing.

Restaurante Alengarve (☎ 286 612 210; Avenida; mains €4.50-10l; ⌚ lunch & dinner Tue-Thu) The oldest restaurant in Mértola, run by the same family for years, this is a veritable place with lots of practise at traditional cuisine. A small terrace overlooks the street.

Migas (Municipal Market; mains €7.50-8.50) This is a superb little restaurant alongside the market, serving serious Alentejan specialities, such as aromatic, coriander-packed riverfish soup.

Restaurante O Naútico (☎ 286 612 596; Rua Serrão Martins 16; ⌚ Mon-Sat; mains €5.75-7.50; ⌚ lunch & dinner Mon-Sat) Above the riverside Nautical Club, this has a roof terrace and fabulous views, as well as light, nautical mains such as grilled squid or salmon.

Self-caterers and honey monsters should head to the **Municipal Market** (Praça Vasco de Gama; ⌚ 8am-4pm Mon-Sat) with lovely fresh produce, cheese, honey, nuts, fruit and vegetables.

Drinking

There are a couple of bars in the old town.

Alsafir (☎ 286 618 049; Rua dos Combatentes da Grande Guerra 9; ⌚ 9pm-4am) This bar hosts dance party nights (in an incongruous medieval setting).

Lancelote Bar Charming, with a wooden terrace attached to a white-washed blue-bordered house under the shade of an amazingly profuse tree.

Café Guadiana (☎ 286 612 186; Praça Vasco de Gama; snacks €1-4; ⌚ lunch & dinner) A café with an excellent raised vantage point on the main square, and an outside terrace for watching comings and goings.

THE ALENTEJO

Shopping

Oficina de Tecelagen (9am-12.30pm & 2-5.30pm Tue-Sun Oct-May, 10am-1pm & 3-7pm Jun-Sep) A small wool-weaving workshop, this is a good place to see craftspeople at work in a wonderfully gossipy atmosphere. You can buy products here such as rugs and ponchos. It's down some steps, just before the old town entrance.

APDM (9am-5.30pm Mon-Sat) This is just next to the Oficina de Tecelagen and sells delicious local honey, with almonds, pine nuts or walnuts, as well as stress-relieving pollen.

Getting There & Away

There are **buses** (☎ 286 611 127) to Lisbon (€11.60, 4¼ hours, one or two daily) and Vila Real de Santo António (€7.30, 1½ hours); a slower local Vila Real service (€4.55, two hours) via Alcoutim (50 minutes) runs on Monday and Friday. Services daily (normal/express, €3.90/4.80, 75 minutes/one hour) run to/from Beja.

AROUND MÉRTOLA

The ghost town of **São Domingos** consists of desolate rows of small mining cottages. Once the mine closed in the 1960s many miners emigrated or moved to Setúbal. But the village is amid beautiful countryside and next to a huge lake, where you can swim or rent a paddleboat or canoe.

The São Domingos mine itself – 150 years old in 2004, but mining has been taking place here since Roman times – is a deserted, fascinatingly eerie place to explore, with crumbling old offices and machinery. The rocks surrounding it are clouded with different colours, and the chief mine shaft is filled with deep, unnatural-seeming dark-blue water (no swimming), shot through with rust. The mines were established by a British firm, who apparently treated the workers badly, keeping them in line with a private police force.

Estalagem São Domingos is a new grand hotel, developed from part of the Mine Director's house. It was under construction at the time of research – check with Mértola turismo (p239) for details.

Best visited with your own transport, São Domingos is 15km east of Mértola.

BEJA

pop 35,830 / elevation 240m

Baixo Alentejo's principal town, Beja is easygoing, welcoming and untouristed with a walled centre and some beguiling sights. It's one of the best places to stop on your way through the Baixa, and is at the heart of the regional tourist area called Planície Dourada (Golden Plain) – meaning it's surrounded by an endless sea of wheat fields. On Saturday there's the bonus of a traditional market, spread around the castle.

BEJA'S LOVE LETTERS

A series of scandalous, passionate 17th-century love letters came from Beja, allegedly written by one of the convent's nuns, Mariana Alcoforado, to a French cavalry officer, Count Chamilly. The letters immortalised their love affair while the count was stationed here during the time of the Portuguese war with Spain. The *Letters of a Portuguese Nun* first emerged in a French translation in 1669 and later appeared in English and many other languages. Funnily enough, the originals were never found.

In 1972, three Portuguese writers, Maria Isabel Barreno, Maria Teresa Horta and Maria Velho da Costa published *The Three Marias: New Portuguese Letters*, a collection of stories, poems and letters that formed a feminist update of the letters – for which they were prosecuted under the Salazar regime.

History

The Romans founded Beja on the pinnacle of the plains. They called it Pax Julia, after Julius Caesar restored peace between the Romans and rebellious Lusitanians. It became an important agricultural centre, booming on wheat and oil.

Little evidence remains of the 400 years of subsequent Moorish rule, except for some distinctive 16th-century azulejos in the Convento de Nossa Senhora da Conceição (now the Museu Regional). The town was recaptured from the Moors in 1162.

Orientation

Beja's historic core is circled by a ring road and surrounded by modern outskirts. The train station is about 500m northeast of the town centre, the bus station 400m southeast. The main sights are all within an easy walk of each other. Drivers are advised to park near the bus station.

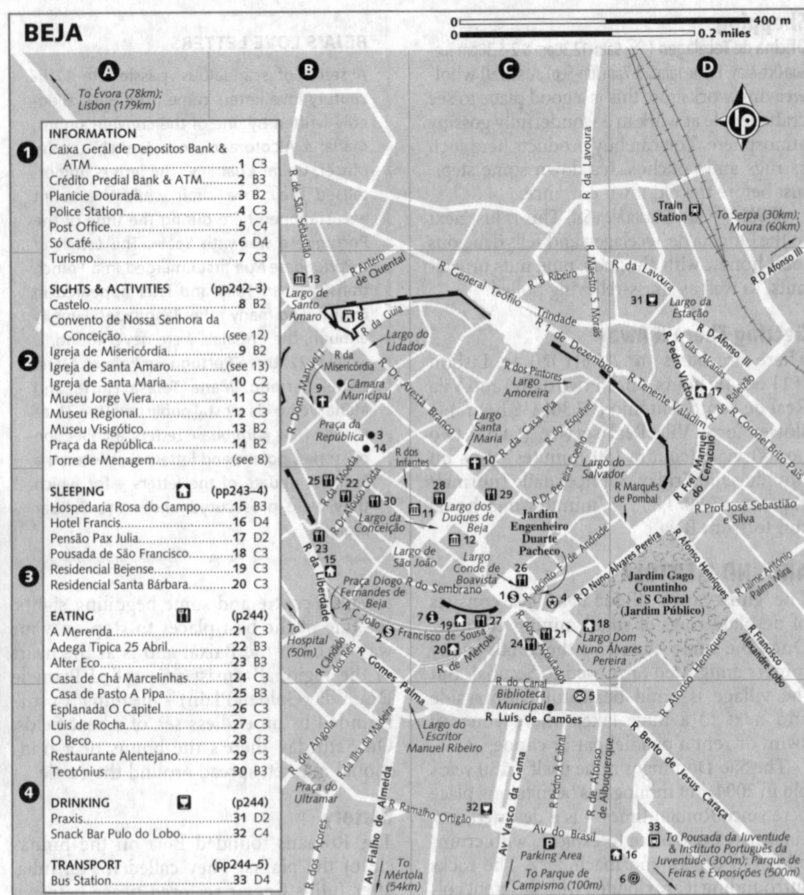

Information

There are several banks with ATMs near the turismo.

Alter Eco (☎ 284 324 102; Rua Portas de Aljustrel 29; per hr €1.5; 🕑 12.30pm-2am) Net access, but mainly food (p244).

Hospital (☎ 284 310 200; Rua Dr António Covas Lima)

Instituto Português da Juventude (IPJ; ☎ 284 325 458; Rua Acabado Janeiro; 🕑 9am-7pm Mon-Fri) Free Internet access, 300m southeast of bus station.

Planície Dourada (☎ 284 310 150; Praça da República; www.rt-planiciedourada.pt; 🕑 9am-12.30pm & 2-5.30pm) This is the regional tourism office, which will sell publications on the area if they are not available at the turismo.

Police station (☎ 284 322 022; Largo Dom Nuno Álvares Pereira)

Post office (☎ 284 311 270; Rua Luís de Camões; 🕑 8.30am-6.30pm Mon-Fri) Has NetPost.

Só Café (☎ 284 327 541; Centro Comercial Pax Júlia, Loja 16; 🕑 9-2am) Provides free Internet access, but only has one machine.

Turismo (☎ /fax 284 311 913; Rua Capitão João Francisco de Sousa 25; 🕑 10am-1pm & 2-6pm Mon-Sat) Look out for the great multilingual *Tourist Guidebook to the Planície Dourada* (€2.50) and *Nature Trails* (€1), both with suggested itineraries and maps, on sale here or at the Planície Dourada offices.

Sights

PRAÇA DA REPÚBLICA

This renovated attractive **town square** with a *pelourinho* (stone pillory) is the historic heart of the old city. Dominating the square is the 16th-century **Igreja de Misericórdia**, a hefty church with an immense porch – its crude stonework betrays its origins as a meat market. The Planície Dourada building (p242) features an elegant Manueline colonnade.

CASTELO

Dom Dinis built the **castle** (admission free; 10am-1pm & 2-6pm Tue-Sun May-Oct, 9am-noon & 1-4pm Nov-Apr) on Roman foundations in the late 13th century. There are grand views from the top of the impressive 42m-high **Torre de Menagem** (admission €1.20). The ticket office has free bilingual leaflets on Beja's culture, arts and heritage.

CONVENTO DE NOSSA SENHORA DA CONCEIÇÃO & MUSEU REGIONAL

Founded in 1459, this Franciscan **convent** (Largo da Conceição; adult/child €2/free, free 9.30-12.30 Sun; 9.30am-12.30pm & 2-5.15pm Tue-Sun) was the location for the romance between a nun and soldier that inspired *Letters of a Portuguese Nun*, which so caught the public imagination (p241). Indeed a romantic setting, it's a delicate balance between no-nonsense Gothic and Manueline flights of fancy. The interior is even more lavish than the exterior. Amazing highlights are the busily patterned rococo chapel with 17th- and 18th-century gloriously gilded woodwork, and a chapel seeming effortlessly inlaid with intricate marble. The chapterhouse is also stunning, incongruously Arabian, with a beautiful ceiling painted with wild unfurling ferns, 16th-century tiles (the oldest in the building) and a carved doorway. The cloister has some splendid 16th- and 17th-century azulejos.

Dotted around this splendour is the **Museu Regional**, displaying Roman lamps, glass bottles and stelae, and 16th-century paintings. The admission fee includes entry to the Museu Visigótico.

MUSEU VISIGÓTICO

Found just beyond the castle, the unusual Visigothic **museum** (admission €1; 9.30am-12.15pm & 2-5.15pm Tue-Sun) is housed in the former **Igreja de Santo Amaro**, parts of which date from the early 6th century when it was a Visigothic church – so it's one of Portugal's oldest standing buildings. Inside, the original columns display intriguing, beautiful carvings. The admission fee includes entry to the Museu Regional.

MUSEU JORGE VIERA

A charming, small **museum** (off Largo da Conceição; admission free; 2-8pm Tue-Sun), devoted to the work of renowned Portuguese sculptor Jorge Viera, whose monumental bulbous figures and strange creatures capture the imagination, calling to mind *Where the Wild Things Are*. Look out for his linked ellipses on Praça Diogo Fernandes de Beja.

Festivals & Events

Ovibeja agricultural fair (Mid-March) This is a huge nine-day festival, one of the largest in the south of the country, with music by day and every night a different show. Held in the Parque de Feiras e Exposições on the southeastern outskirts, it's grown from a livestock market to a music, handicrafts and cuisine bonanza.

Beja Alternative (Second half of June) For something rather different, with alternative sport competitions (skateboarding etc), new bands and street performers.

Sleeping

BUDGET

Hospedaria Rosa do Campo (284 323 578; Rua da Liberdade 12; d with breakfast €40) Charming and polished, with gleaming rooms and wooden floors, this is an excellent choice.

Pensão Pax Julia (284 322 575; Rua Pedro Victor 8; d with/without bathroom €40/30) This is a friendly place and an attractive house; frilly rooms, but good-value. Those facing the road are noisy.

Pousada da juventude (284 325 458; Rua Prof Janeiro Acabado; beja@movijovem.pt; dm €9.50, d with/without bathroom €28/23) The youth hostel next to the IPJ, 300m southeast of the bus station, is new, fresh and spick-and-span. It has a laundry and kitchen facilities, plus bikes for rent.

Parque de campismo (284 311 911; Avenida Vasco da Gama; adult/tent/car €2.13/1.57/1.57) Beja's municipal camp site is part of a somewhat desolate municipal sports area on the outskirts of town, which also houses a swimming pool and tennis courts. There's disabled access, a restaurant, and plenty of shade.

MID-RANGE

Residencial Santa Bárbara (284 312 280; fax 284 312 289; Rua de Mértola 36; d with breakfast €37.50) Briskly efficient, with neat little rooms, this is a pleasant place to stay, right in the pedestrianised town centre.

Residencial Bejense (☎ 284 311 570; Rua Capitão João de Sousa 57; d with breakfast €45) This is similarly good.

Hotel Francis (☎ 284 315 500; hotel.francis@mail.telepac.pt; Praça Fernando Lopes Graça; s/d with breakfast €55/65;) Modern, cool (in temperature), with snazzily decorated rooms with balconies, this has a sauna, Jacuzzi and health club as well as the usual frills.

TOP END

Pousada de São Francisco (☎ 284 313 580; recepcao.sfrancis@pousadas.pt; Largo Dom Nuno Álvares Pereira; d with breakfast Mon-Fri €169, Sat & Sun €178;) In a 13th-century São Francisco Convent, this *pousada* provides gorgeous rooms (formerly cells), and a dramatically vaulted restaurant.

Eating

BUDGET

O Beco (☎ 284 325 900; Rua dos Infantes; mains €4.50-7; lunch & dinner) Simple and set back from the road, this has a somewhat grey atmosphere, but is enlivened by locals tucking into grilled fish and Portuguese-style pork.

Restaurante Alentejano (☎ 284 323 849; Largo dos Duques de Beja 6; mains €4-7; lunch & dinner Sat-Thu) A popular local venue serving generous helpings of traditional mains, in a relaxed but dapper atmosphere, with TV in the background.

Casa de Chá Marcelinhas (☎ 284 321 500; Rua dos Açoutados 12; 8.30am-8pm Mon-Sat) For delicious regional pastries head to this lovely sedate tearoom, which serves typical *doces conventuais* (desserts traditionally made by nuns) and, particularly good, *pasteis de toucinho* (a delicious thin pastry and almond creation).

Luis de Rocha (☎ 284 323 179; Rua Capitão João F Sousa 63; mains €5.50-10; lunch & dinner) To hang out, head to the town hub and one of Beja's oldest cafés. It specialises in two types of cake – *trouxas de ovos* (sweet egg yolks) and *porquinho doce* (just like it sounds – 'a sweet pig'). It also serves up Alentejan staples.

Esplanada O Capitel (☎ 284 325 708; Jardim Engenheiro Duarte Pacheco; snacks €1-4; breakfast, lunch & dinner) This is a relaxing, partly open-air café, in the centre of a quiet square. The interior is all plate glass. It serves snacks.

A Merenda (☎ 284 327 726; Largo Dom Nuno Álvares Pereira 13B; lunch-time half-portions €4-4.50; breakfast, lunch & dinner) This is a plain, good-value café, popular for lunch – get there before too late or there'll be nothing left. It does great puddings.

Alter Eco (☎ 284 324 102; Rua Portas de Aljustrel 29; specials €4.50; Thu-Tue) A café-restaurant-bar on two floors of an old building, with windows overlooking the street. It has art exhibitions, comfy chairs and sofas, as well as books, music, vegie food and Net access.

MID-RANGE

Adega Tipica 25 Abril (Rua da Moeda; mains €5.50-8; lunch & dinner Tue-Sun) A cavernous, rustic *adega* serving typical food and popular at lunch, with good daily specials.

Casa de Pasto a Pipa (☎ 284 327 043; Rua da Moeda 8; mains around €7; lunch & dinner Mon-Sat) Nearby, this barn-like Alentejan tavern has a high, beamed ceiling. It is also traditional and popular.

Teotónius (☎ 284 328 010; Rua do Touro; mains €5.50-9.75, 3-course menu €12; lunch & dinner Wed-Mon) A well-regarded whitewashed arched cellar, serving good traditional mains such as *carne de porco à alentejana* (pork with clams), and less-traditional ones, such as fondue, and claiming to have the best snails in the world.

Drinking

Snack-Bar Pulo do Lobo (Avenida Vasco da Gama; daily) A café-restaurant with an outdoor terrace: a Beja favourite for a natter, a big plate of snails and an early evening beer.

Praxis (Rua General Teófilo da Trinidade; midnight-6am) Near the station, this big nightclub is the sister to the one in Évora, and equally popular for its good-time house sounds.

Getting There & Away

BUS

From the **bus station** (☎ 284 313 620) buses daily run to Évora (normal/express, €4.35/7.50, 1½/1 hours); Mértola (€3.90, 1¼ hours, two daily); Serpa (€2.45, 45 minutes, seven daily), some continuing to Moura (€4, 65 minutes, five daily). Around half this number operates on weekends. Buses run to Faro daily (€9.10, 3¼ hours, three daily) via Albufeira (€9.50, 2¼ hours), and to Lisbon (€9.80, 3¼ hours, six daily).

Buses also run to the Spanish border town of Ficalho (normal/express, €4/6.80), and on Tuesday, Thursday and Saturday to Seville (€16, 3½ hours).

TRAIN

Beja is on the Lisbon to Funcheira (near Ourique) railway line. There are three direct *intercidade* (IC) services from Lisbon (€8.50, 2½ hours, including Tejo ferry crossing to Barreiro station) and three direct *regional* (R) trains (€7, 3¼ hours).

Getting Around

Bikes are available for free use within the city from the *câmara municipal* (near Praça da República) or the turismo. Some form of ID (eg passport) must be left as a deposit.

SERPA

pop 17,915 / elevation 230m

With baked-white walls, narrow cobble-pattern streets, lots of elderly ladies, and a skyline that's a jumble of red sloped roofs, stubby towers and palm trees, Serpa is a delightful castle-topped small town. It's 30km southwest from Beja. Sitting in a wiry, olive green rural landscape, guarded by thick town walls, it also has a mighty aqueduct, a nice unawareness of tourism, and famous cheese.

Orientation

Those arriving by car must brave tight gateways into the old town and breathtakingly narrow streets (or park outside the walls).

The bus station, *mercado municipal* (municipal market) and *parque de campismo* are in the new town area, southwest of the old town. From the bus station, turn left then first right and keep walking till you see the walls.

Information

On the fourth Tuesday of the month a huge country market sprawls beside Rua de Santo António on the northeastern outskirts of town.

Bookshop (Rua do Calvario; per hr €1; 8am-8pm) A calm gallery space above a bookshop offers Net access.

C@fe (Rua Dr Eduardo Fernando de Oliveira 18; per hr €1.20; 9am-6.30pm) Provides Net access, 250m east of the *mercado municipal*.

Lavendaria Moderna (Rua das Portas de Beja; €3.20 per kg; 9am-12.30pm & 2.30-6pm Mon-Fri) Not self-service, but cheap.

Post Office (Rua dos Lagares)

Totta Bank (Praça da República) Around the corner from the turismo, with an ATM.

Turismo (☎ 284 544 727; Largo Dom Jorge de Melo 2; 9am-12.30pm & 2-5.30pm) In the centre, the tourist office has a map of the old town and sells local handicrafts.

Sights

CASTELO

You enter the small **castle** (admission free; 9am-12.30pm & 2-5.30pm) through a dramatic entrance: a heavy cracked piece of wall. Inside it feels domestic in scale. You can walk around the battlements for long views over the flat plains, the aqueduct, town walls, rooftops and orange trees, and the slow life of Serpa residents. Also inside the walls is the small **Museu de Arqueologia** (admission free; 9am-12.15pm & 2-5.15pm), housing a small collection of archaeological remnants that reveal bits of Serpa's history, which reaches back to the arrival of the Celts over 2000 years ago.

TOWN WALLS & AQUEDUTO

Walls still stand around most of the inner town. Along the west side (follow Rua dos Arcos) run the impressive remains of an 11th-century aqueduct. At the southern end is a huge 17th-century wheel pump or noria, once used for pumping water along the aqueduct to the nearby **Palácio dos Condes de Ficalho** (still used by the de Ficalho family as a holiday home).

MUSEU ETNOGRÁFICO

No traditional rural trade is left unturned in this exquisite exploration of Alentejan life found at Serpa's ethnographic **museum** (Largo do Corro; admission free; 9am-12.30pm & 2-5.30pm Tue-Sun). Beautifully presented and polished tools, used in everything from ironmongery to pottery, are on display. The accompanying booklet is only in Portuguese, so non-linguists get to play guess regarding the use of the implement.

MUSEU DO RELÓGIO

This **museum** (☎ 284 543 194; www.museudorelogio.pa-net.pt; Rua do Assento; adult/child under 10 €2/free; 2-5pm Tue-Fri, 10am-5pm Sat & Sun) houses an amazing private collection of watches and clocks, from Napoleonic gilded timepieces to Swiss cuckoo clocks, in the cool vaulted surroundings of the former Convento do Mosteirinho. Also on display are two Roman urns used to keep food cool, found during excavations.

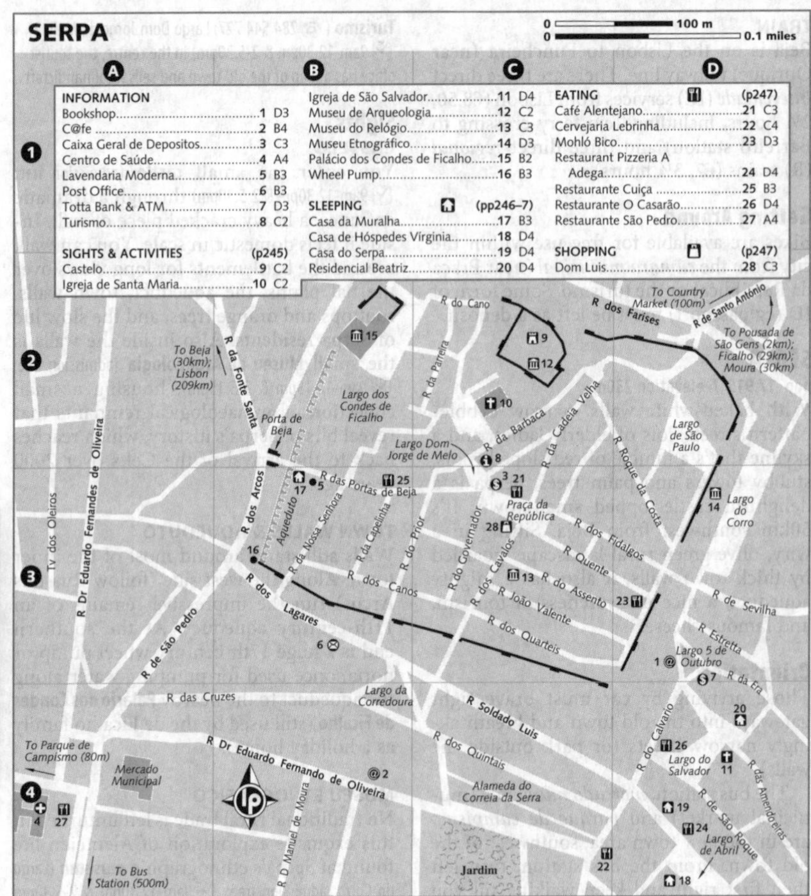

Festivals & Events

Festas de Senhora de Guadalope (March/April) Celebrations of Serpa's patron saint take place from Good Friday to the following Tuesday – there is a pilgrimage to bring the saint's image down to the parish church and on the last day a procession takes it back to the chapel on horseback. On the Tuesday everyone eats roast lamb.

Noites na Noura (July and 1st week of August) Nightly local theatre and music shows on a terrace tucked behind the aqueduct.

Sleeping

BUDGET

Residencial Beatriz (☎ 284 544 423; fax 284 543 100; Largo do Salvador 10; s/d with breakfast €29/42, 2/4-person apt €52/65;) A small modern building on a pleasant little square facing a church, this has smart rooms with big windows and mini balconies. A comfortable place.

Casa de Hóspedes Vírginia (☎ 284 549 145; Largo 25 de Abril; s/d with shared bathroom €15/25) This is a small place, which provides clean, large, thin-walled but good-value, basic rooms in a square dotted by orange trees.

Parque de campismo (☎ 284 544 290; Largo de São Pedro; adult/tent/car €2/1.80/1.50) The municipal camp site is on scrubby land 400m northeast of the bus station on the edge of town. There's a restaurant and disabled access; rates include admission to the nearby pool.

MID-RANGE

Casa do Serpa (☎ 284 549 238; www.casadeserpa.com; Adro do Salvodar 28; s/d with breakfast €35/50) A much recommended rural tourism option, run by genial hosts, in the centre of town. Lovely rooms open onto a quiet courtyard, and great breakfasts include fresh orange juice and local produce.

Casa da Muralha (☎/fax 284 543 150; Rua das Portas de Beja 43; d with breakfast €40) Nestling by the town walls – there is access to these from the house – is this Turihab property, with large whitewashed rooms with arched or beamed ceilings, filled with traditional, stately wooden furniture. They open onto a courtyard shaded by lemon and orange trees. You can rent canoes for river trips.

TOP END

Pousada de São Gens (☎ 284 540 420; recepcao.sgens@pousadas.pt; d Mon-Fri €134, Sat & Sun €144;) A modern, whitewashed, gloriously isolated building decked with balconies for overlooking the pool and vast plains, this stands on a hilltop 2km south of town, next to a dazzling white Moorish chapel.

Eating

All the local restaurants serve *tapas de queijadas de Serpa*, the salty and creamy local cheese.

BUDGET

Restaurante O Casarão (☎ 284 549 295; Largo do Salvador 20; mains from €5.50-6.50; lunch & dinner) A cheerful, simple place that's popular with locals and offers very generous servings of traditional hearty main meals with a TV accompaniment.

Restaurante Pizzeria A Adega (☎ 284 544 308, Rua do Rossio 76; mains €4-8; lunch & dinner Fri-Wed) With some outside tables on a sleepy square, this is a convivial pizzeria, good for families, that also serves Portuguese mains.

Restaurante São Pedro (☎ 284 543 186; Avenida da Paz; mains €4.75-8; lunch & dinner Mon-Sat) You'll find this place near the camp site, a simple tiled, airy restaurant, with outside tables – a good place to sit and have a snack of snails.

MID-RANGE

Mohló Bico (☎ 284 549 264; Rua Quente 1; mains €5-9; lunch & dinner Thu-Tue) This is a fine restaurant in a great arched, rustic space, with exposed brickwork, long wooden tables and huge wine urns in the front room, white tablecloths and TV in the back. Traditional food dominates the menu, with lots of fish.

Cervejaria Lebrinha (☎ 284 549 311, Rua do Calvário 6-8; mains €5-8.50; lunch & dinner Wed-Mon) This is incredibly popular and famous for its beer, with Portuguese coming from all over to sink one. Why is not clear, but it's a jolly place and the traditional mains served are a reasonable accompaniment.

Restaurante Cuiça (☎ 284 549 566; Rua das Portas de Beja 18; mains €5.50-8; lunch & dinner Mon-Sat) Inside, a café and simple restaurant merge into each other. It's a friendly, nice, cool refuge from the heat of the day, and has big salads.

Café Alentejano (☎ 284 544 335; Praça da República; mains €7-12) Across the square is this vaguely Art Deco café with outside tables. Try a locally made *queijadas de Serpa*. The restaurant upstairs has good food in an appealing, white-arched location.

Shopping

At **Dom Luis** (Praça da República; 10am-1pm & 3pm-6.30pm Wed-Sun) you can buy the cheese (€14.50 per kg) in various varieties, as well as hams. Ask for a taste.

Getting There & Away

Buses (☎ 284 544 740) run to/from Lisbon (€10, four hours, two to four daily) via Beja (€2.45, 35 minutes, two to four daily). There are no direct buses to Évora. A service goes daily to the Spanish frontier at Ficalho (€10.35, 35 minutes, one daily).

MOURA

pop 17,550 / elevation 180m

Moura has elegant buildings with fine tiling, cherubs and garlands. Well placed near water sources, and rich in ores, the town has been a farming and mining centre and a fashionable spa. It's now a beguiling backwater, with incongruously graceful buildings. It's also the nearest large town to the spectacular new lake created by the Alqueva dam, 15km to the north.

The town has some rare Moorish monuments. The Moors' 500-year occupation came to an end in 1232 after a Christian invasion. Despite the reconquest, Moorish presence in the city remained strong – they only abandoned their quarter in 1496 (after Dom Manuel's convert-or-leave edict).

The town's name comes from a legend related to the 13th-century takeover. A

Moor, Moura Salúquiyya opened the town gates to Christians disguised as Muslims. They sacked the town, and poor Moura flung herself from a tower.

Orientation

The bus station is by the defunct train station at the newer, southern end of town, around 500m from the old town and the main square, Praça Sacardo Cabral (which has the Galp petrol station on the corner). All the main places of interest are within easy walking distance.

Information

There are banks on the *praça* and along Rua Serpa Pinto directly north of the turismo.

Espaço Internet (☎ Rua 5 de Outubro 18; 🕑 10am-1pm & 2-7pm)

Post office (☎ 285 254 311; Rua da República) is east of Rua Serpa Pinto.

Turismo (☎ 285 251 375; Largo de Santa Clara; 🕑 9am-1pm & 2-5pm Mon-Fri, 10am-1pm & 2.30-5.30pm Sat & Sun) This is 400m downhill from the bus station; turn left into the first main street, Rua das Forças Armadas, and right at the end.

Sights & Activities

MUSEU MUNICIPAL

This fine tiny **museum** (☎ 285 253 978; Rua da Romeira; admission free; 🕑 9.30am-12.30pm & 2.30-5.30pm Tue-Sun), in an appealing residential quarter off a lane about 200m east of the *praça*, contains local prehistoric and Roman remains, such as 1st and 2nd-century needles, as well as Moorish funerary tablets.

LAGAR DE VARAS DO FOJO

With a system of production that would have been the similar since Roman times, the **oil press** (Rua João de Deus 20; admission free; 🕑 9.30am-12.30pm & 2.30-5.30pm Tue-Sun) recreates the oil-pressing factory that functioned here until 1941, with giant wooden and stone-wheel presses.

IGREJA DE SÃO BAPTISTA

This 16th-century **church** (admission free) has a remarkable Manueline portal. Set against the plain façade, it is a twisting, flamboyant bit of decoration, with carvings of knotted ropes, crowns and armillary spheres. Inside the church has some fine deep-blue and yellow 17th-century Sevillian azulejos. It's just outside the Jardim Dr Santiago.

JARDIM DR SANTIAGO & SPA

The **thermal spa** was at the entrance to the lovely, shady Jardim Dr Santiago, at the eastern end of Praça Sacadura Cabral, but is pretty much defunct, though pitched for redevelopment into something a bit more 21st century. Bicarbonated calcium waters, said to be good for rheumatism, burble from the richly marbled **Fonte das Três Bicas** (Fountain with Three Spouts) by the entrance to the *jardim*. The garden itself has a good view, a bandstand, and is a favourite spot for elderly men to sit and chat.

MOURARIA

The old **Moorish quarter** (Poço Árabe) lies at the western end of Praça Sacadura Cabral. It's a well-preserved tight cluster of narrow, cobbled lanes and white terraced cottages with chunky or turreted chimneys.

The **Núcleo Árabe** (Travessa da Mouraria 11; admission free; 🕑 9.30am-12.30pm & 2.30-5.30pmTue-Fri, 2.30-5.30pm Sat & Sun) just off Largo da Mouraria is a pocket collection of Moorish ceramics and other traces, such as carved stone inscriptions, centred around a 14th-century Arabic well.

CASTELO

The **castle** (admission free) above the old town has been restored, and offers fabulous views across the countryside. One of the towers is the last remnant of a Moorish fortress. Rebuilt by Dom Dinis in the 13th century and again by Dom Manuel I in 1510, the castle itself was largely destroyed by the Spanish in the 18th century. There's a ruined convent inside the walls, and due to be two museums, not yet open at the time of research.

Sleeping

Residencial Santa Comba (☎/fax 285 251 255; Praça Sacadura Cabral 34; s/d with breakfast €23/35; ❄) On the main square, this smart new place is in an old building, with clean rooms with balconies overlooking the square. Disabled access.

Residencial A Casa da Moura (☎/fax 285 251 264; Largo Dr Rodrigues Acabado 47; s/d with breakfast €23/40) In the heart of the old town near the museum is this 10-room place, clean, quiet and friendly, with sunny terraces (not attached to rooms).

Residencial Alentejana (☎ 285 250 080; Largo José Maria dos Santos 40; s/d with breakfast €25/35; ❄)

This green-shuttered house opposite the Galp petrol station near the bus station, provides comfortable, smart and well-run accommodation.

Hotel de Moura (☎ 285 251 090; fax 285 254 610; Praça Gago Coutinho; s/d €25/35) This is the most beautiful hotel in town, a grand place with sweeping staircases, polished floors, tall windows and overlooking a pretty square; but it's in a faded, forgotten-feeling state that doesn't indicate much input by its owners, Nestlé (who own the local mineral water plant).

Eating

There are plenty of café-restaurants with outside seating around Praça Sacadura Cabral, where you'll also find the *mercado municipal* in a huge glass building.

Restaurante O Guadiana (☎ 285 252 157; Rua da Latôa 1; mains €6-10; lunch & dinner Tue-Sun) Near the turismo, this is one of the best choices in town for traditional Alentejan fare.

O Trilho (☎ 285 254 261; Rua 5 de Outubro 5; €6-10; lunch & dinner Tue-Sun) Three streets east of Rua Serpa Pinto, O Trilho is another local favourite, with excellent regional mains.

Getting There & Away

Buses run to/from Beja (€4, one hour, three to five daily) via Serpa (€2.30, 40 minutes). Rede Expressos run to Lisbon (€12, four hours, daily) via Évora (€7.50, 1½ hours); the bus stop for this service is on the *praça*, near a small grocery store called Zélia, at No 36, where you can buy tickets.

COASTAL ALENTEJO

VILA NOVA DE MILFONTES

pop 3000

Vila Nova is a resort in the middle of the beautiful Parque Natural do Sudoeste Alentejano e Costa Vicentina near where long beaches line the wild sea. Scenic, small and friendly, it's a port (Hannibal is said to have sheltered here) alongside a lovely, sand-edged limb of estuary, with a small castle, pretty cobbled streets and café-filled squares. The bars and restaurants kick, in a gentle, laid-back way. You might drop by for a day and still find yourself here a week later. But in August it'll seem like most other people in Portugal had the same idea.

Orientation & Information

The main road into town from Odemira and Lisbon, Rua Custódio Bras Pacheco, is lined with restaurants, banks, shops and the post office.

Casa Amarela (Rua Dom Luis Castro e Almeida; per hr €2.5) Access the Internet here (see below).

Police station (☎ 283 998 391; Rua António Mantas)

Turismo (☎ 283 996 599; Rua António Mantas; 10am-1pm & 2-6pm) Off the main road, opposite the police station, en route to the centre of town if you're driving. Buses stop a bit further along the same road.

Beaches

Praia do Farol, the lighthouse beach just by the town, is sheltered but gets busy. Beaches over the other side of the estuary are less crowded. Be careful of the strong river currents running through the estuary. Or, with your own transport, you could head out to fantastic **Praia do Malhão**, backed by rocky dunes and covered in fragrant scrub, around 7km to the north (travel 2.5km to Bruinheras, turn left before the primary school, then travel another 3km until you see a sign to the beach where you turn left – the road is not paved all the way). The more remote parts of the beach harbour nudist and gay areas. The sea is quite wild here, but the coast is strikingly empty of development.

Activities

There are some gorgeous beaches around, both near the town and extending out along the coast. Scuba diving is organised by **Alentejo Divers** (☎ 283 996 821, 939 145 368; gitte@netc.pt; Pousadas Velhas, Apt 129), who run PADI courses about 1km beyond the Parque de Campismo Milfontes (signposted).

Sleeping

Note that prices zoom upwards in August and you'll need to book in advance.

BUDGET

Casa Amarela (☎ 283 996 632, 934 204 610; Rua Dom Luis Castro e Almeida; dm €12.50 d/tr/q €35/40/50; 💻) This is the kind of guesthouse you might find in Asia or South America, with loads of eclectic art, hammocks and cheery rooms. The charmingly genial English-speaking owner, Rui, has filled the yellow house with souvenirs from his world travels from Indian wall hangings to Vietnamese Van

Goghs. There are two shared kitchens, plus a separate apartment with a kitchen. He has also built a nearby peaceful annex centred around a large courtyard, with a bright yellow kitchen with long table, double rooms, a dorm, roof terraces and solar-heated showers.

Residencial Mil-Réis (☎ 283 998 233; fax 283 998 328; Largo do Rossio 2; d with breakfast €45) Accommodation here is in modern, well-kept rooms in a pretty house in the old town centre. It is run by an elderly couple.

Pensão do Cais (☎ 283 996 268; Rua do Cais 9; d with breakfast €45) A large communal veranda overlooks the river, and some of the slightly quaint doubles also have brilliant views.

Casa dos Arcos (☎ 283 996 264; fax 283 997 156; Rua do Cais; d with breakfast €45;) Jauntily painted in blue and white, this is a smart airy guesthouse with comfortable beds, tiled floors and small balconies. Disabled access.

Sitava Turismo (☎ 283 890 100; www.sitava.pt; adult/tent/car €3.35/3.15/2;) Near Praia do Malhão (600m), this is a superb on-its-own camp site, with supermarket, pub and restaurant and disabled facilities. It is well situated on a 50-hectare site with 8000 trees, so you should be able to find some shade.

Campiférias (☎ 283 996 409; fax 283 996 581; Rua da Praça; adult/tent/car €2.88/2.39/2.50;) A camp site 500m northwest of the turismo, this is only 800m from the beach, with disabled access and lots of shade.

Parque de Campismo Milfontes (☎ 283 996 140; fax 283 996 104; adult/tent/car €3.05/2.42/2.52;) Near Campiférias, this is an even better-equipped site, near the beach, in a pine forest, close to the beach. It offers disabled facilities and small bungalows (€20.50).

MID RANGE & TOP END

Quinta das Varandas (☎ 283 996 155; fax 283 998 102; d €45, 4-/6-person apt with breakfast €55/70) A modern, low-rise, blue-and-white apartment complex about 700m west of the turismo and near the beach. It has terraced apartments and rooms around a courtyard.

Castelo de Milfontes (☎ 283 998 231; s/d €100/130) This is a marvellously atmospheric place to stay in a 16th-century small castle, with antique furniture, suits of armour, azulejos and superb views. But if you don't have a reservation, the reception will want to wipe you off their shoe as quickly as possible.

Eating

A Telha (☎ 283 996 138; Rua do Pinhal 3; mains €5-9; lunch & dinner) Two streets north of the turismo, A Telha is popular for simple but good stuff such as barbecued chicken, served in white-walled surroundings.

Marisqueira O Pescador (☎ 283 996 338; Rua da Praça; mains €6-9; lunch & dinner Fri-Wed) This is particularly good for rice with shellfish or monkfish – usually cooked for two.

Restaurante Portinho do Canal (☎ 283 996 255; mains €6.50-10; lunch & dinner Fri-Wed) Up from the fishing harbour, this is a family-run place that has lovely views over the blue blue sea, and good grilled fish.

Restaurante A Fateixa (☎ 283 996 415; mains €6-15; lunch & dinner Thu-Tue) With a perfect setting down by the river, next to the little wooden pier, this place is great for seafood. The name means anchor, which is why there's a big one outside.

Restaurante Choupana (☎ 283 996 643; Praia do Farol; mains €7.50-15; lunch & dinner) A wooden structure right on the beach, where fish is barbecued outside, this has to be one of the nicest and best-kept restaurants around. It's more expensive than some, but matched by quality. It's pretty and carefully kept, with a great little open-air terrace where you can just stop for a drink if you prefer.

Drinking

Mabi (Largo de Santa Maria 25A; 8-2am) This is one of the town hubs. Excellent for ice cream, breakfast and coffee. Patisserie-wise, it's where it's at.

Green Island (☎ 919 176 034; Largo de Santa Maria 39) Run by a nice couple, this is a garden bar open in the summer. It will become covered to address neighbour issues, but will retain its spirit and keep serving delicious fresh-fruit juice and cocktails.

Café Azul (Rossio 20) Always lively, whatever the time of year, even if the rest of the town is dead, this is a jovial bar with a pool table and lots of papier-mâché sharks, octopuses and squid hanging from the ceiling.

Café Turco (Rua Dom João II) A hip bar with a Moorish atmosphere, pretty and partly outdoors. Only open high season.

Quebramar (Praia da Franquia) A bar-restaurant on stilts on the other town beach, this is enormously popular, open only in the high season, till late. It's undergoing a long-running battle with the authorities, though, because it's felt the structure disfigures the beach which is a protected area.

Discoteca SudWest (Estrada do Canal; midnight-6am) Just out of town, in season this is the big hip-and-happening house nightspot, so kick off your flip-flops and put on your rave shoes.

Restaurante Miramar (283 998 689; Largo Brito Pais; mains €5-8) It has a terrace next to the castle and a lovely little sea-facing square, but unfortunately the food and service is not up to scratch. It's good for a drink, though.

Getting There & Away

Vila Nova has three bus connections daily on weekdays to/from Odemira (€2.30, 20 minutes). There are buses daily from Lisbon (€11, four hours, three daily) via Setúbal (€10, three hours) and one daily from Portimão (€8.30, two hours) and Lagos. The ticket office in Vila Nova is at Largo de Santa Maria, next to Mabi.

ZAMBUJEIRA DO MAR

Whitewashed, paint-peeling, one-horse Zambujeira do Mar hangs out at the top of black basalt cliffs, above a string of creamy Atlantic-bashed beaches. The town turns into a party in August, when there is an annual market and the Festa de Nossa Senhora do Mar. The crowds give Zambujeira some uncharacteristic zip, but obscure its out-of-season charms: fresh fish in sleepy restaurants, blustering clifftop walks and a dramatic, empty coast.

There's a small **turismo** (283 961 144; 9.30am-1pm & 2-5.30pm Tue-Sat) on the main street, which closes to traffic from July to mid-September.

Sleeping & Eating

Residencial Mar-e-Sol (283 961 171, 283 961 193; Rua Miramar 17A; d €40-50) In Zambujeira's main street, this is run by a charming landlady, Dona Maria Fernanda. Rooms are spick-and-span and all have a private (though not always en suite) bathroom; there's also a shared kitchen.

Parque de Campismo Zambujeira (283 961 172; fax 283 961 320; adult/tent/car €3.50/3.50/3) This is a wooded, well-appointed site, with playground. Just 800m east of the village, it's near the beach and also has bungalows for rent.

Taverna Ti Vítoria (283 961 130; Rua da Fonte; mains €6-15; lunch & dinner Tue-Sun) Almost behind Residencial Mar-e-Sol, just off the main square, this is a traditional *churrasqueira* (grill restaurant), good for fish, and with a pleasing little terrace.

Cervejaria e Marisqueira (Rua Miramar 14; mains €9-17.50; lunch & dinner Thu-Tue) Opposite Residencial Mar-e-Sol, this has stools up at the bar, a streetside terrace and specialises in seafood.

Café-Restaurant Rita (Rua Miramar; mains €6-15; lunch & dinner Fri-Wed) This has the best position in the village, with a raised terrace overlooking the sea.

Restaurante A Barca (283 961 186; Entrada da Barca; mains €6-9.50; lunch & dinner Tue-Sun) About 2km from Zambujeira on the road to Vila Nova, this has a nice middle-of-nowhere feel about it, a pleasant small grassy garden and cooks up fine specialities such as bean stew with sea snails or fish stew with potatoes.

Festivals & Special Events

The **Festival do Sudoeste** is one of Portugal's best international contemporary music festivals. It takes place in early August. Recent years have seen PJ Harvey and Massive Attack.

Getting There & Away

In summer, Zambujeira has one to three daily connections with Vila Nova (€6, 45 minutes) and Lisbon (€11.80, 3¾ hours) – buy tickets at the **bookshop** (Rua Miramar 9). Buses also run to Odemir (40 minutes) and Beja (three hours) – for these you buy your ticket on the bus.

Estremadura & Ribatejo

CONTENTS

Within easy reach north of Lisbon, these small, wealthy regions are where the great and good built their monuments, hence the dazzling concentration of magnificent World Heritage sites: Mafra, Mosteiro de Santa Maria da Vitória (Battle Abbey), Mosteiro de Santa Maria de Alcobaça (Alcobaça Monastery), and the Convento de Cristo, headquarters of those mystical warriors, the Knights Templar.

But the regions are not just about architectural masterpieces. At Fátima is one of the Catholic world's most important sites – on the map since a 1917 vision. It's an intense manifestation of faith and an extraordinary marriage of Iberian mysticism and religious commercialism.

Along the coast is the shady, peaceful balm of the 700-year-old coastal pine forest, Pinhal de Leiria, and set up on a hilltop close by is the enchanting Óbidos, one of Portugal's most beguiling walled villages – with whitewashed blue and yellow bordered houses, covered in flowers.

The regions also provide plenty of sun, sand, sea, great fish and famed surf at appealingly small, accessible resorts along the coast – popular Lisbon getaways – from Ericeira to Peniche and Nazaré.

Most of these attractions are crammed into Estremadura (from *extrema Durii* – furthest from the Douro). However, the eastern region, Ribatejo (Tejo riverbanks), though in part an industrial powerhouse, has much to explore too. Highlights include the historic, wooded town of Tomar, the Knights Templar stomping ground, surrounded by serene countryside, and attractive Santarém, location of one of Portugal's most bizarre festivals and a bullfighting centre, overlooking agricultural plains famous for their big, bad bulls.

HIGHLIGHTS

- **Manueline Marvel**
  Mosteiro de Santa Maria da Vitória (p271)
- **Medieval Masterpiece**
  12th-century Cistercian Mosteiro de Santa Maria de Alcobaça (p269)
- **Magical Mystery Tour**
  Unesco World Heritage site Convento de Cristo, Knights Templar headquarters (p285)
- **Walled Wonder**
  The wedding-present village of Óbidos (p260)
- **Taste Sensation**
  Superb seafood at Nazaré (p266) and Peniche (p257)

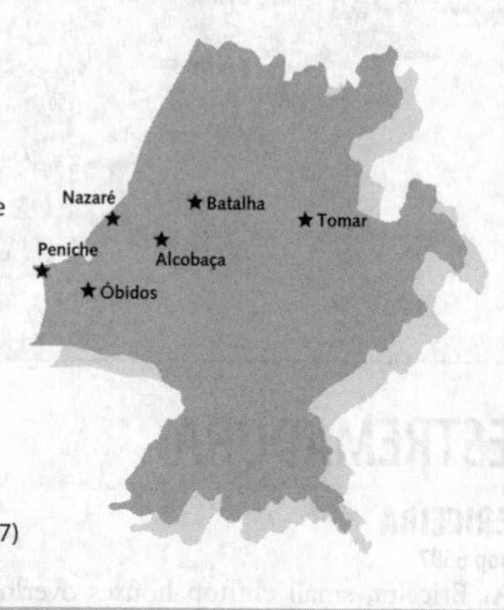

- POPULATION (RIBATEJO): 533,000
- AREA (RIBATEJO): 7500 SQ KM

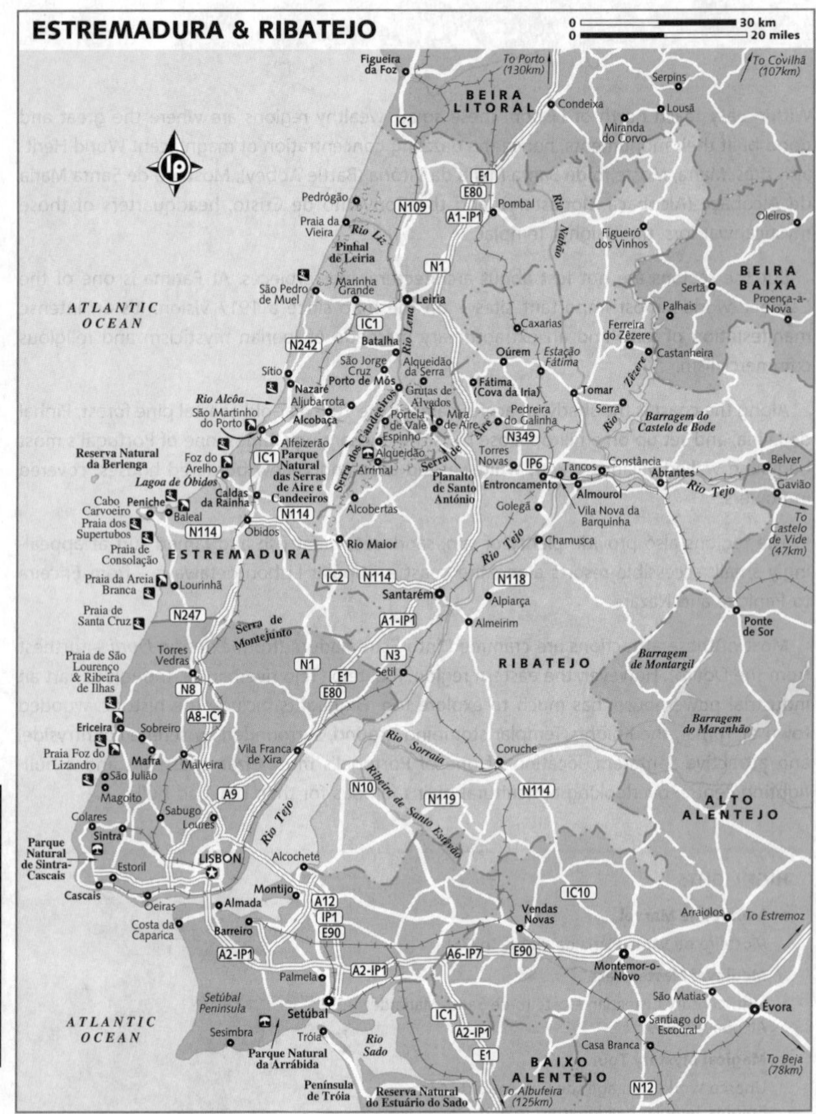

ESTREMADURA

ERICEIRA

pop 6597

At Ericeira, small clifftop houses overlook a series of sheltered white-sand beaches, with strange road-to-nowhere steps leading higgledy-piggeldy down to the rocks below. Although it's long been a popular resort and has built-up outskirts, it has kept its character, and the centre still has vestiges of the small fishing settlement it once was. It's very popular with weekending Lisboêtas, is famous for its surf, is lively on summer weekends, and has some excellent fish restaurants.

Orientation

The town's old centre is clustered around Praça da República, with a newer district to the south.

The bus station is 800m north of the *praça* (town square), off the N247 highway, but there's a bus stop at the top of town on the N247.

Information

Cyber Clube Ericeira (☎ 261 865 743; Praça da República; per hr €3; h11am-11pm)
Lavandaria Fonte do Cabo (☎ 261 864 203; Rua do Caldeira; per kg €3; 🕑 9am-1pm & 3-7pm Mon-Sat)
Millennium bcp (Praça da República) Bank with ATM.
Millennium bcp (Largo dos Condes de Ericeira)
Police station (☎ 261 863 533; Rua 5 de Outubro)
Post office (☎ 261 860 501; Rua do Paço 2; 🕑 9am-12.30pm & 2.30-6pm Mon-Fri)
Turismo (☎ 261 863 122; www.ericeira.net; Rua Dr Eduardo Burnay 46; 🕑 9.30am-midnight Jul–mid-Sep; 9.30am-7pm Mon-Fri & Sun, 9.30am-10pm Sat mid-Sep–Jun)

Sights & Activities

There are three beaches within walking distance of the *praça:* **Praia do Sul** (also called Praia da Baleia), **Praia do Norte** (also called Praia do Algodio) and **Praia de São Sebastião** to the north. Some 5km north is unspoilt **Praia de São Lourenço**, while **Praia Foz do Lizandro**, a big bite of beach, backed by a small car park and a couple of restaurants, is 3km south.

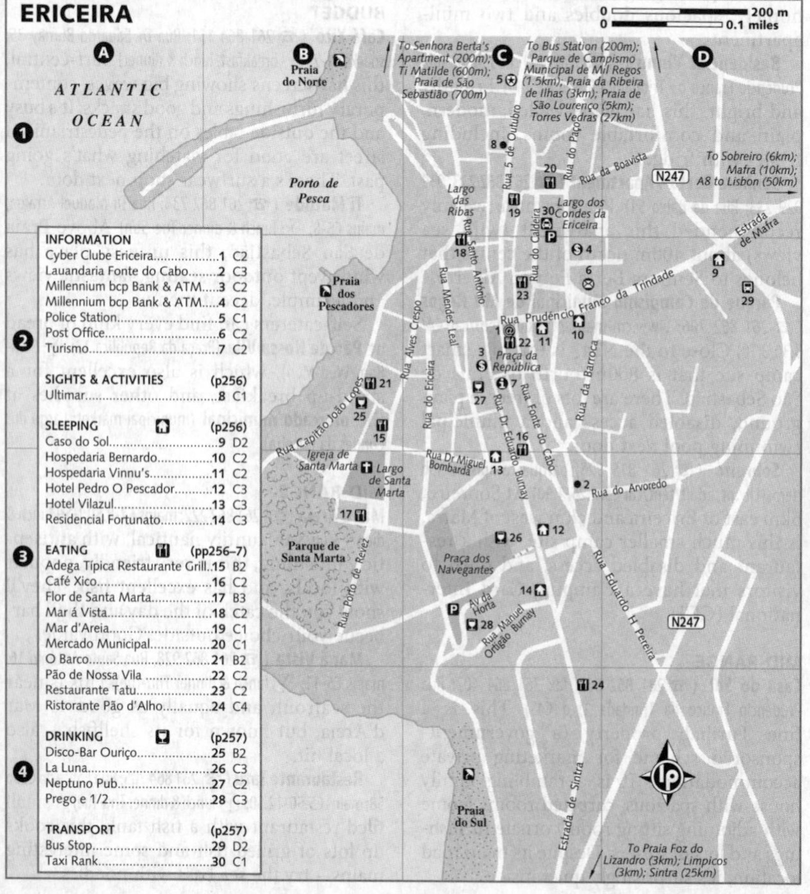

Ericeira's big attraction is **surfing**. Praia da Ribeira de Ilhas, a World Championship site, is just a few kilometres north, though the waves at the nearer Praia de São Sebastião are challenging enough for most amateurs. For more on surfing, see p454.

Ericeira Surf Clube (☎ 967 278 640; per hr 1/5/10 €15/50/80) Hires surfboards and gives lessons.

Surfada Escola (☎ 966 644 781; Complexo Turístico San Sebastião) Based at Praia de São Sebastião.

Ultimar (☎ 261 862 371; Rua 5 de Outubro 37A; per day €15; 9.30am-1pm & 3-9pm) Hires surfboards.

Sleeping

BUDGET

Hospedaria Bernardo (☎/fax 261 862 378; Rua Prudêncio Franco da Trindade 11; s/d €25/35) A super-welcoming, obliging small place with lovely homely, spacious doubles and two mini-apartments.

Residencial Vinnu's (☎/fax 261 863 830; Rua Prudêncio Franco da Trindade 19; s/d €25/45) Friendly and bright, this has white-walled, modern, plain and comfortable rooms, including triples with fridge.

Senhora Berta's Apartment (☎ 261 862 213, 919 029 233; Rua de Baixo 51) Readers have warmly recommended this apartment (with sea views) about 400m north of the centre that belongs to Senhora Berta Fontão Alberto.

Parque de Campismo Municipal de Mil Regos (☎ 261 862 706; www.cm-mafra.pt; adult/tent/car €4/3.30/3.70) Close to the N247 is this big, smart camp site that is 800m north of Praia de São Sebastião. There are lots of trees, a playground, disabled access and a municipal swimming pool next door.

Sobreiro (☎ 261 815 525; parque-campismo-sobriero@clix.pt; adult/tent/car €3/2.25/1.90) At Sobreiro, 6km east of Ericeira and 4km west of Mafra, is this much smaller camp site, with a restaurant and disabled access, and open to visitors that have a Camping Card International (CCI).

MID-RANGE

Casa do Sol (☎ 261 862 665; fax 261 864 402; Rua Prudêncio Franco da Trindade 1; d €45) This is a fine Turihab property (a government-sponsored scheme for marketing private accommodation). It is a rambling family house with spacious, carpeted rooms (some with adjoining sitting room) ornate furnishings and lots of surfers. Despite its main road location, it's surprisingly quiet inside.

Residencial Fortunato (☎/fax 261 862 829; Rua Dr Eduardo Burnay 7; s/d with breakfast €35/40) Offers good-value rooms, light and bright, with white bedspreads. The best are upstairs overlooking a small terrace, with lovely sea views.

Hotel Pedro O Pescador (☎ 261 869 121; hotelpedropescador@oninet.pt; Rua Dr Eduardo Burnay 22; s/d with breakfast €40/60) This has attractive rooms with nice wooden furniture, though unfortunately they are a bit musty.

Hotel Vilazul (☎ 261 860 000; vilazul@mail.pt; Calçada da Baleia 10; s/d with breakfast €40/60;) All things bright and businesslike at this smart-ish, though ordinary, hotel. However, the bathrooms gleam.

Eating

BUDGET

Café Xico (☎ 261 864 151; Rua Dr Eduardo Burnay 35; snacks €1-2; breakfast, lunch & dinner) Surf-central, this has screens showing big waves, contemporary furnishings and good snacks. It's busy and the outside tables on the pedestrianised street are good for watching what's going past. There's a surfwear shop next door.

Ti Matilde (☎ 261 862 734; Rua Dr Manuel Arraiga; mains €5-8; lunch & dinner Tue-Sun) Above Praia de São Sebastião, this unfussy place has windswept outdoor seating, fantastic views and a simple, decent menu.

Self-caterers can find every kind of bread at **Pão de Nossa Vila** (Praça da República 12; 8am-8pm Wed-Mon), which is also excellent for a stand-up breakfast, and other supplies at the **mercado municipal** (municipal market; Largo dos Condes da Ericeira).

MID-RANGE

Mar d'Areia (☎ 261 862 222; mains €7-8.50; lunch & dinner Mon-Sat) Jauntily nautical, with antiseptic white tiling, this is very friendly, popular with locals, and has excellent fish. They'll show you the catch of the day and then barbecue your choice outside. Good value.

Mar á Vista (☎ 261 862 928; Rua Santo António 16; mains €5-11; lunch & dinner Thu-Tue) This is near the seafront, and equally as good as Mar d'Areia, but known for its shellfish – also a local hit.

Restaurante Tatu (☎ 261 864 705; Rua Fonte do Cabo 58; mains €5.50-12.50; lunch & dinner Thu-Tue) A small tiled restaurant with a fish tank, this cooks up lots of grilled fish and some interesting mains – try the sea bass with noodles.

Ristorante Pão d'Alho (☎ 261 863 762; Estrada de Sintra 2; mains €4-13.50; ⏲ lunch & dinner Wed & Thu) The best of several pizzerias in town, this is worth seeking out. It has outdoor seating and also serves steaks, seafood and an imaginative range of salads.

Flor de Santa Marta (☎ 261 862 368; Largo de Santa Marta 4A; mains €6-7; ⏲ lunch & dinner) Pleasantly placed on a square, this tiled, tucked away place, has a tranquil atmosphere and excellent seafood.

O Barco (☎ 261 862 759; Rua Capitão João Lopes; mains €9-17; ⏲ lunch & dinner Fri-Wed) With great sea views right from the front, and some rather windswept outside tables, O Barco provides some of the town's finest seafood.

Drinking

Limipicos (☎ 261 864 121; ⏲ 9am-2am) There are a couple of bars on Lizandro beach, including this one, with outside tables overlooking the sandy expanse.

Neptuno Pub (☎ 261 862 017; Rua Mendes Leal 12) This is a friendly, cosy bar in the town centre, with *fado* (traditional singing) on Thursday nights.

La Luna (☎ 261 865 704) There's also a clutch of café-bars in the fairly modern Praça dos Navegantes, with outdoor seating, notably this one, in the corner of the upper esplanade.

Prego e 1/2 (☎ 261 863 514) On the street level, this is lively and has outside tables but is in a rather unprepossessing spot.

Late-night clubs include the **Disco-Bar Ouriço** (☎ 261 862 138; Rua Caminho Novo 9; ⏲ 11pm-6am).

Getting There & Away

There are regular buses to/from Lisbon's Campo Grande station (€4.15, 80 minutes, hourly) via Mafra (€1.50, 20 minutes) and to/from Sintra (€2.35, 45 minutes, hourly). The turismo has timetables, or call Ericeira's **bus station** (☎ 261 862 717).

Getting Around

Regular local buses to Torres Vedras go past the Parque de Campismo and Praia da Ribeira de Ilhas (€1). For Praia Foz do Lizandro (€1), take any Sintra-bound bus to a stop on the N247 above the beach.

You can rent bicycles from the **turismo** (per half-day/day €4/7.50; 9.30am-7pm Jun-Sep). **Taxis** (☎ 261 865 567) can be found in Largo Conde da Ericeira.

PENICHE

pop 25,880

The access point for the beautiful rocky nature-reserve islands of Berlenga, the walled town of Peniche is a busy fishing port. Once an island, Peniche only joined the mainland in the 16th century, when silt created a narrow isthmus. Burgeoning development around the outskirts makes the old town centre, with its excellent fish restaurants and looming, historically notorious fort, all the nicer a surprise.

Orientation

Driving into town, the main N114 turns left into Rua Alexandre Herculano, with the *turismo* (tourist office), or continues straight on for 3km round the Peniche peninsula to Cabo Carvoeiro and its lighthouse. If you are arriving by bus, you will be dropped at the market, about 20m northwest of the turismo. From the market it is a short walk south to the old town centre and fort, the harbour and Avenida do Mar, home to most of the seafood restaurants. Passenger boats for Ilha Berlenga leave from the harbour (where there's also ample free parking in Largo da Ribeira).

Information

Caixa Geral de Depósitos (☎ 261 860 400; Rua Alexandre Herculano 90) With ATM, opposite the turismo.

Espaço Internet (☎ 969 195 895; Rua Dr João de Matos Bilhau) Free Net access.

Hospital (☎ 261 863 334; Rua General Humberto Delgado) About 600m northwest of the market.

Millennium bcp & BPI (Rua António da C Bento) Also with ATM.

Police station (☎ 261 863 533; Rua Heróis Ultramar) About 400m west of the market.

Turismo (☎ /fax 262 789 571; ⏲ 9am-8pm Jul & Aug, 10am-1pm & 2-5pm Sep-Jun) In a shady public garden alongside Rua Alexandre Herculano. If you hit an off-day, they might not be much help.

Sights

FORTALEZA

Dominating the southern end of the peninsula, Peniche's imposing 16th-century **fortress** (admission free; ⏲ 10.30am-12.30pm & 2-6pm Tue-Sun) was in military use as late as the 1970s, when it was converted into a temporary home for refugees from the newly independent African colonies.

Twenty years earlier it was one of dictator Salazar's infamous jails for political prisoners. By the entrance, where prisoners once received visitors – with the stark booths with their glass partitions all preserved – is the **Núcleo-Resistência**, a grim but fascinating display about those times, including the flimsy leaflets of the resistance, education materials for schools where pupils would learn phrases such as 'Viva Salazar!', prisoners' poignant, beautifully illustrated letters to their children, and some secret ones, written in incredibly small handwriting.

Housed in another part of the fort is the **Museu Municipal** (☎ 262 780 116; admission €1.30; ⏲ 10.30am-noon & 2-6pm Tue-Sun). Outside is the desolate prison yard, and the top floor reveals the chilling, sinister interrogation chambers and cells, some used for solitary confinement. Floors below this contain a municipal mishmash, from Roman archaeological artefacts to shipwreck finds, and a strangely out-of-place, grand, recreated bedroom – that of the Peniche-born artist and politician, Paulino Montez.

LACE-MAKING SCHOOLS

Like another of Portugal's Atlantic fishing ports, Vila do Conde in the north, Peniche is famous for its exquisite bobbin lace. You can see it being made at **Escola de Rendas** (⏲ 9.30am-12.30pm & 2-5.30pm Mon-Fri) in the turismo building and **Rendibilrosa** (Rua Alexandre Herculano 68; ⏲ 9am-12.30pm & 2-5.30pm Mon-Fri), nearby.

BALEAL

About 4km to the northeast of Peniche is this small island village, connected to the mainland village of Casais do Baleal by a causeway. A fantastic sweep of sandy beach here offers some fine surfing. There are a few surf schools dotted along it, as well as restaurants. It's very popular.

Activities

Two surf camps in Baleal are German-run **Maximum Surfcamp** (☎ 262 769 295; Rua do Gualdino 7; www.maximumsurfcamp.com; week's camp €250, class €40) and **Baleal Surfcamp** (☎ 969 050 546; www.balealsurfcamp.com; week's camp €250-450, class €30, one-week class €125; surfboard hire 4hr/day €5/1), the latter with a good bar-hangout on the beach. **Peniche Surfcamp** (☎ 262 082 517; Rua do Gualdino 4; www.penichesurfcamp.com; week's camp €260-410; class €30; board rental €15) is also on the scene and offers bike hire (€10). Surfboards can also be rented from **Rip Curl Surf Shop** (☎ 262 787 206; Rua Alexandre Herculano 16).

Scuba-diving operators include **Berlenga Sub** (☎ 262 189 619; berlengasub@mail.telepac.pt; Largo da Ribeira 24) and **Mergulhão** (☎ 262 785 795; mergulhao@mail.telepac.pt), which can take you diving around the Peniche coast for about €20 or round Berlenga for €45.

For fishing trips, contact **Nautipesca** (☎ 917 588 358), which has a kiosk at the harbour.

Sleeping

Casa das Marés (☎ 262 769 371/200/255; casamares1@hotmail.com; Praia do Baleal; d with breakfast around €60-75) At the northern end of Baleal this is an imposing house – actually a row of three houses, owned by three sisters. The breezy, inviting rooms have great sea views, especially out the back, from where you can see Berlenga.

Pequena Baleia (☎ 262 769 370; Baleal Village; d with breakfast €60) A pretty, homely house in Baleal village, this looks west across the sea to Peniche.

Residencial Rimavier (☎ 262 789 459; www.ciberguia.pt/rimavier; Rua Castilho 6; d €30) This immaculate *pensão* is run by a lovely, helpful couple.

Residencial Vasco da Gama (☎ 262 781 902; Rua José Estevão 23; d with breakfast €35) This is one of the older establishments almost opposite Rimavier, with 12 smallish rooms.

Residêncial Maciel (☎ 262 784 685; Rua José Estevão 38; d with breakfast €35/40) This has six rooms that have huge bathrooms and polished, traditional décor.

Parque de campismo (☎ 262 789 529; fax 262 780 111; adult/tent/car €2.10/1.75/1.75) The small municipal camp site is 2km east of Peniche (opposite the BP station) and 500m from the beach. It has disabled facilities and is near a swimming pool, but there's not much shade.

Peniche Praia (☎ 262 783 460; fax 262 789 447; adult/tent/car €3.10/3.10/2.80; ♿) On the high, windy north side of the peninsula, 1.7km from town and the beach, and 2km from Cabo Carvoeiro, this only has 450 pitches, good facilities but no shade. It also has a few bungalows and some rooms and bikes for rent.

Eating

Mira Mar (☎ 262 781 666; Avenida do Mar 42; mains €4.50-8; ⏲ lunch & dinner Tue-Sun) Comes up with fabulous fishy goods – everything from sardines and squid to swordfish, salmon and shrimps.

Estelas (☎ 262 782 435; Rua Arq Paulino Montez 19; mains €7-19; ⌚ lunch & dinner) Near the turismo, this is a smart seafood restaurant, with lots of variations on seafood rice for two. Decorated with watery themed tiling, it's a more refined choice than most of the others restaurants.

Restaurante A Sardinha (☎ 262 781 820; Rua Vasco da Gama 81; mains €4.50-10; ⌚ lunch & dinner) This is on a narrow street parallel to Avenida do Mar, and does a roaring trade, with a bargain €7.50 tourist menu.

Trawl Peniche's Avenida do Mar for other seafood restaurants, with mains from around €5 to €10, including lively **Katekero II** (☎ 262 787 107; Avenida do Mar 70), and packed-out, tiled blue-and-white **O Canhoto** (☎ 262 784 512; Avenida do Mar) or indoors **Restaurante Beira Mar** (☎ 262 782 409; Avenida do Mar 106). Or try **Amigos do Baleal** (☎ 262 769 865; Praia do Baleal; mains €9; ⌚ lunch & dinner in season) right on the beach.

Drinking

Páteo da Lagoinha (☎ 262 789 050; Largo Bispo Mariana 24; ⌚ 6.30pm-2am Thu-Sat) Near the turismo, this is a tucked-away bar in a tree- and flower-shaded enclosed courtyard.

In Baleal you'll find several restaurants right on the beach, including **Danau Bar** (☎ 262 709 818; ⌚ lunch & dinner), a surfers' bar, open year-round and offering live music (and sometimes karaoke) at weekends. It's closed Monday in low season.

Getting There & Away

For buses out of Peniche you must go to the bus station, 400m northeast of the turismo (cross the Ponte Velha connecting the town to the isthmus). Buses run to/from Lisbon (€6.40, 1¾ hours, 12 daily) via Torres Vedras, plus to Coimbra (€9.90, 3½ hours, four daily) via Leiria (€8.90, 2½ hours). There are buses to Caldas (€2.65, 45 minutes, three to six daily) via Óbidos (€2.15, 30 minutes) and to Baleal (€1.10, 15 minutes, two to four daily).

Getting Around

Bikes can be rented from **Micro-Moto** (☎ 262 782 480; Rua António Conceição Bento 19A; per day €5), beside the market.

RESERVA NATURAL DA BERLENGA

Berlenga Grande is a spectacular, rocky and remote island, with twisting shocked-rock formations and gaping caverns. It's the only island of the Berlenga archipelago you can visit – the group consists of three tiny islands – some 280 million years old, surrounded by clear, calm, dark blue waters full of shipwrecks that are great for snorkelling and diving (see p258). It's 10km offshore from Peniche.

In the 16th century there was a monastery on Berlenga Grande, but now the most famous inhabitants are thousands of nesting sea birds (especially guillemots). The birds take priority over human visitors: the only development that has been allowed is houses for a small fishing community, a lighthouse, a shop and a restaurant-*pensão* (guesthouse). You can camp here – book at the turismo in Peniche. Paths are very clearly marked to stop day-trippers trespassing on the birds' domain.

Linked to the island by a narrow causeway is the 17th-century **Forte de São João Baptista**, rising out of the sea, now one of the country's most dramatic but barren hostels (also reserve at the Peniche turismo). In 1666, a garrison of less than 20 men withstood attack by a Spanish fleet of 14 for two days, killing 500 men – only capitulating when they ran out of provisions.

The reserve's **headquarters** (☎ 262 787 910; fax 262 787 930; Porto da Areia Norte, Estrada Marginal) are in Peniche.

Tours

Barco-Noa (☎ 262 789 997; per person €15) Runs three boat trips a day, depending on demand and weather.

Nevada (☎ 914 079 145, 914 859 054; adult/child €17/10) Organises boat trips to islands and allows four hours on the island. Two trips daily September to June; four July and August. Take a picnic if you don't want to eat at the restaurant.

TurPesca (☎ /fax 262 789 960, 963 073 818; 4-5 hr adult/child €15/10, minimum 6 people) Runs privately organised cruises on demand throughout the year. There's usually a 10am trip, plus at least two more daily during the summer, when you may have to book at least two days ahead. Tickets and information are available at the harbour in Peniche at the kiosks in Largo da Ribeira.

Sleeping & Eating

Pavilhão Mar e Sol (☎ 262 750 331; d €77; ⌚ Jun-Sep) Offers the only decent accommodation, with a restaurant. You'll need to book well ahead.

Forte de São João Baptista hostel (☎ 262 785 263; dm €7.50; ⏲ Jun-Sep) This was once a fine historic inn, but was abandoned for many years and you can feel it; it's a dramatic, but dead-basic hostel, with antiquated bathrooms: you need to bring your own sleeping bag and cooking equipment (though there is a small shop and a bar). To get a place in summer you'll have to make reservations in May. Bring a torch (the island's generator goes off at midnight).

Berlenga camp site (2/3/4-person tent €8/11.50/15; ⏲ May-Sep) There is a small rocky area for camping near the harbour, but you have to book in advance at the Peniche turismo.

There's also a small **supermarket** on the island.

Getting There & Away

Viamar (☎ 262 785 646; adult/child €17/10) does the 45-minute trip to the island once daily at 10am, returning at 4.30pm, between 15 May and 15 September (depending on the weather). During July and August there are three sailings, at 9.30am, 11.30am and 5.30pm, returning at 10.30am, 4.30pm and 6.30pm. Tickets tend to sell out quickly during this period as only 300 visitors are allowed each day.

If you're prone to seasickness, choose your day carefully – the crossing to Berlenga can be rough!

ÓBIDOS

pop 11,200 / elevation 80m

You can see why Óbidos made the ideal wedding gift. The high medieval walls stand on a limestone ridge, encircling fiercely white houses bordered in zinging blue and yellow, overflowing with lilac, flowerpots and citrus trees. Dom Dinis' wife, Dona Isabel, fell in love with it when she visited in 1228, so her husband – as he could – gave the village to her, establishing a royal custom that continued until the 19th century.

Early occupants of the hilltop included the Romans and the Visigoths, but the layout of streets is a Moorish legacy. A 16th-century aqueduct loops towards the town. Until the 15th century Óbidos overlooked the sea; the bay gradually silted up, leaving only a lagoon, so the town became landlocked.

Óbidos is an enchanting stop and gets busy with day-trippers: souvenir and craft shops await the waves – but the backstreets are surprisingly calm. If you have time, stay here to absorb the quiet of the night. It's 6km south of Caldas da Rainha.

Orientation

The town's main gate, Porta da Vila, leads directly into the main street, Rua Direita. Buses stop on the main road just outside Porta da Vila, near a small local market and the car park.

Information

Espaço Internet (☎ 262 959 037; Camara Municipal, Rua Direita; ⏲ 10am-10pm) Free Net access.

Post office (☎ 262 955 041; Rua Direita; ⏲ 9am-12.30pm & 2.30-6pm Mon-Fri)

Região de Turismo do Oeste (☎ 262 955 060; www.rt-oeste.pt; Rua Direita 45; ⏲ 10am-1pm & 2-6pm Mon-Fri) Regional tourism headquarters.

Turismo (☎ 262 959 231; ⏲ 9.30am-7.30pm May-Sep, to 5.30pm Oct-Apr) Town tourist office, just outside Porta da Vila near the bus stop.

Sights

CASTELO, WALLS & AQUEDUCT

You can walk around the unprotected **walls** for uplifting views over the countryside and ancient village. The walls date from the time of the Moors (later restored), but the **castle** itself is one of Dom Dinis' 13th-century creations. It's a stern edifice, as castles should be, with lots of towers, battlements and big gates. Converted into a palace in the 16th century, it's now a deluxe *pousada* (upmarket inn).

The **aqueduct**, west of the main gate, dates from the 16th century and is 3km long.

IGREJA DE SANTA MARIA

The town's main **church** (Rua Direita; admission free; ⏲ 9.30am-12.30pm & 2.30-7pm May-Sep, to 5pm Oct-Apr), at the northern end of the street, was built on the site of a Visigothic temple that was later converted into a mosque. Begun in the 12th century but restored several times since, it dates mostly from the Renaissance. It had its 15 minutes of fame in 1444 when 10-year-old Afonso V married his eight-year-old cousin Isabel here.

Inside, is a wonderful painted ceiling and baroque, beautiful blue-and-white 17th-century *azulejos* (hand-painted tiles). Paint-

JOSEFA DE ÓBIDOS

Josefa de Óbidos is a rarity – a recognised pre-20th-century female painter. Her accomplished paintings were unique in their personal, sympathetic interpretations of religious subjects and for their sense of innocence.

Born in 1630 in Seville (Spain) to a Portuguese painter (Baltazar Gomes Figueira), who later returned to Portugal, Josefa de Ayalla studied at the Augustine Convento de Santa Ana as a young girl. Although she later left the convent without taking the vows and settled in Óbidos (hence her nickname), she remained famously chaste and religious until her death in 1684.

Josefa left one of the finest legacies of work of any Portuguese painter. She excelled in richly coloured still lifes and detailed religious works, ignoring established iconography.

ings by the renowned 17th-century painter Josefa de Óbidos (above) are to the right of the altar There's a fine 16th-century Renaissance tomb on the left, probably carved by the French sculptor Nicolas Chanterène.

MUSEU MUNICIPAL

This **museum** (☎ 262 959 010; admission €1.50; ⏲ 10am-1pm & 2-6pm) is in the one-time town hall, which once contained the court and prison. It's now home to a haunting portrait by Josefa de Óbidos, *Faustino das Neves* (1670), which has dramatic use of light and shade. Among the other religious paintings and icons is a curious 18th-century roulette wheel, made from wood and paper. Downstairs is an incongruous display of memorabilia relating to the 19th-century Peninsular War. The museum is next to the Igreja de Santa Maria.

Festivals & Events

Óbidos celebrates **Semana Santa** (Holy Week) with religious processions and re-enactments. Its annual **festival of ancient music** is usually held during the first week of October.

Sleeping

BUDGET

There are several unofficial private rooms available.

Casa dos Castros (☎ 262 959 328; Rua Direita 41; s/d with shared bathroom €25/35) Try this friendly place with three, low-ceilinged old homely rooms, with a charming rustic feel, that unfortunately extends to the shower.

Casa Milena (☎ 919 182 563; Rua Arco da Cadeira; s/d €25/30) This is run by a nice lady and offers one double.

Óbido Sol (☎ 262 959 188; Rua Direita 40; d with shared bathroom €35) Spacious accommodation, with a huge living room and views over the hills.

Casa do Poço (☎ 262 959 358; Rua da Mouraria; d €35) An endearing, renovated place near the castle.

MID-RANGE

Casa do Relógio (☎/fax 262 959 282; Rua da Graça; d with breakfast €60) One of several Turihab options, this 18th-century house (named after its sundial) has eight splendid but small rooms, with comfortable beds and a friendly welcome.

Hospedaria Louro (☎ 262 955 100; fax 262 955 101; Casal da Canastra; d with breakfast €60; 🏊) Outside the walls 300m west of Porta da Vila, offering modern rooms, with good views, and a small, colourful garden.

Casal do Pinhão (☎/fax 262 959 078; Bairro Sra da Luz; d €60-80, apt €80-100; 🏊) A delightful rural alternative to town accommodation. It's a large family home set in tranquil pine woods 4km north (2.8km off the Caldas da Rainha road). There's plenty of space for kids to run about.

TOP END

Pousada do Castelo (☎ 262 959 105; fax 262 959 148; d €207) One of Portugal's best *pousadas*, a gloriously bleached-white convent, with characterful, comfortable rooms.

Eating & Drinking

Alcaide (☎ 262 959 220; Rua Direita; mains €6.25-14; ⏲ lunch & dinner Thu-Tue) Recommended by readers, this is an upstairs restaurant with wrought-iron chandeliers. Windows overlook the rooftops and green beyond. The cooking is classy, with mains such as tuna with onion sauce offering a taste of something different.

Adega do Ramada (☎ 262 959 462; Travessa Nossa Sra do Rosário; mains €8-10; ⏲ lunch & dinner Tue-Sun) Another great location with wooden tables and benches in the cobbled lane next to

1 de Dezembro, Ramada specialises in grills cooked on its outdoor barbecue.

O Conquistador (☎ 262 959 528; Rua Josefa Óbidos; mains €7-16; ⏰ lunch & dinner Wed-Mon) Jolly and brightly lit, this is a popular place with a terrace, offering simple traditional dishes.

Bar Lagar da Mouraria (☎ 919 937 601; Rua da Mouraria; snacks €2-8; ⏰ noon-2am) North of Igreja de Santa Maria, behind the post office, is this lovely traditional bar, with yellow walls, beams, and a flagstone floor. It's housed in a former winery, with seats around a massive old winepress. You can snack on tapas, cheese, grilled *chouriço* (spicy sausage), *morcela assada* (blood sausage) or sandwiches.

Café da Moura (Rua Josefa Óbidos; mains €1-7; ⏰ 8am-8pm) Just inside the main gate, this is a good place to watch comings and goings, and has reasonable cakes and coffee.

Café-Restaurante 1 de Dezembro (☎ 262 959 298; Largo de São Pedro; mains €2.50-12; ⏰ breakfast, lunch & dinner) In the village itself, this has a great location with outdoor seating right next to the Igreja de São Pedro, but there its advantages end as the food is not up to much.

Getting There & Away

Buses run frequently to Caldas da Rainha (€1.20, 15 minutes) and Peniche (€2.15, 45 minutes). Change at Caldas for express runs to Lisbon (see p264), but there are direct runs on weekdays (€6). Although Óbidos has a nearby train station, it's isolated, with infrequent services.

CALDAS DA RAINHA

pop 43,205 / elevation 90m

Caldas da Rainha is a back-in-time town, with the faded grandeur that is a spa-town speciality. There's a delightful, leafy, sleepy park, and several excellent art museums, including one devoted to charming local 19th-century potter Rafael Bordalo Pinheiro. It's still a ceramics centre, with artisans dotted around town.

The name means 'the Queen's Hot Springs'. Dona Leonor, wife of Dom João II, passed by this spot one day in the 1480s and saw bathers in steaming sulphuric waters in terrible conditions, inspiring her to build a more hygienic spa. Like a watery *Hello* magazine, it became a magnet for nobility and royalty, peaking in popularity in the 19th century. The spa, now Hospital Termal Rainha Dona Leonor, still provides treatment, but only for long-term patients.

Orientation

The central old town is small, though it takes a while to get to it through the sprawling outskirts and ring roads. At the old town heart is the long market square, Praça da República, with the large, shady Parque Dom Carlos I a short walk away.

The best free car parking is near the hospital, or there is pay parking in front of the park.

Information

Espaço Internet (☎ 262 839 700; Rua Diário de Noticias 33; ⏰ 9.30am-midnight Mon-Fri, 10am-10pm Sat & Sun)

General hospital (☎ 262 830 300; Rua D Leonor N Senhora Popúlo) Off Rua Diário de Notícias.

Millennium bcp (Praça da República 110)

Police station (☎ 262 832 023; off Praça da Republica)

Post office (☎ 262 840 040; Rua Eng Duarte Pacheco; ⏰ 8.30am-6.30pm Mon-Fri, 9am-12.30pm Sat)

Turismo (☎ 262 839 700; fax 262 839 726; Praça 25 de Abril; ⏰ 9am-7pm Mon-Fri, 10am-1pm & 3-7pm Sat & Sun) Next to the *câmara municipal* (town hall).

Sights

MUSEU DE CERÂMICA

The ceramics **museum** (☎ 262 840 280; Ilídio Amado; admission €2, 10am-12.30pm Sun free; ⏰ 10am-12.30pm & 2-5pm Tue-Sun Oct-May, 10am-7pm Jun-Sep) is in the former Palácio de Visconde de Sacavém, a delightful holiday mansion that the 19th-century viscount filled with beautiful azulejos from other palaces (the building exterior is azulejo covered, with dragon and wild boar gargoyles). The viscount was a patron of the arts and something of an artist himself.

Inside, Caldas da Rainha pottery reigns, with many fantastic works by Rafael Bordalo Pinheiro who was inspired by flora and fauna – Manueline-style ceramics. Most memorable are the fabulous jars and bowls (by both Pinheiro and Manuel Mafra), encrusted with animals, lobsters and snakes. The top floor is devoted to contemporary works, including intricate Manueline-style carvings by José da Silva Pedro.

MUSEU DE JOSÉ MALHOA

This huge, impressive **museum** (☎ 262 831 984; Parque Dom Carlos I; admission €2, 10am-12.30pm

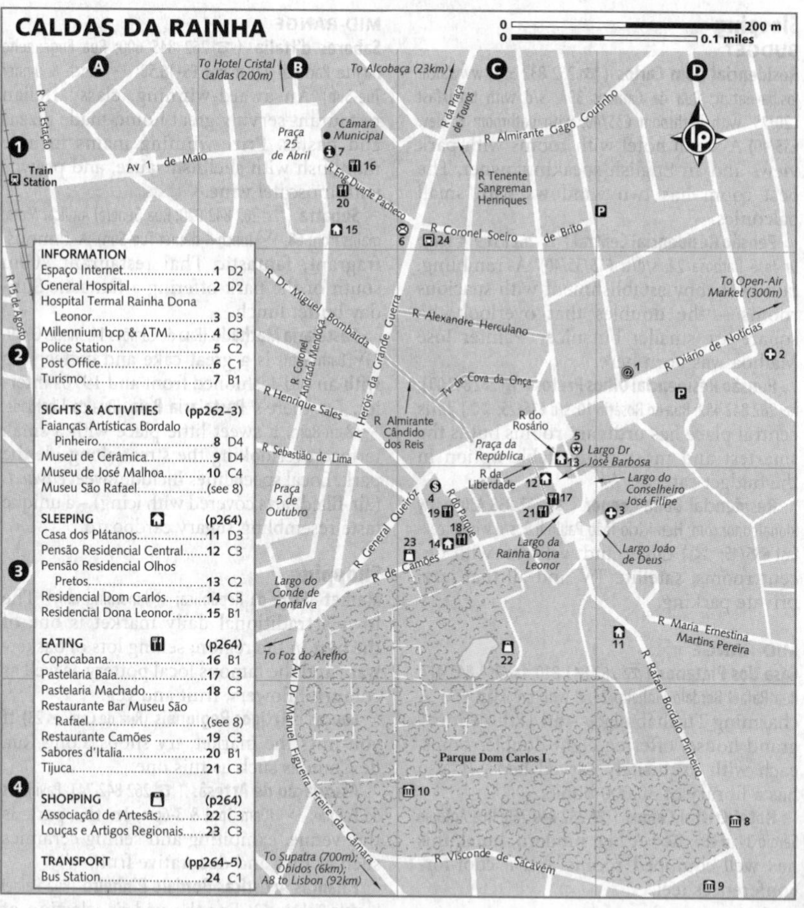

& 2-5pm Tue-Sun) was built in 1940 to house the works of the outstanding Caldas-born artist José Malhoa (1855–1933), who painted lots of local scenes, with striking portraits that capture local personalities. It also contains works by other 19th- and 20th-century Portuguese artists, notably Sousa Lopes, Silva Porto (who painted lovely rural scenes) and Columbano Bordalo Pinheiro. Among many fine sculptures, including those by Manuel Teixeira Lopes, is a set of towering historical figures by Francisco Franco. In the basement are amazing, delicately moulded ceramics and caricatures by Rafael Bordalo Pinheiro, including a large-scale, very energetic life of Christ: the bust of Pinheiro at the entrance reveals just what a jovial fellow he must have been.

FAIANÇAS ARTÍSTICAS BORDALO PINHEIRO

The original ceramics **factory** (☎ 262 839 380; Rua Rafael Bordalo Pinheiro 53), founded in 1884 by Pinheiro, is still going strong. Although you can't wander round the production workshops you can visit the charming **Museu São Rafael** (admission free; 🕐 10am-12.30pm & 2.30-4.30pm Mon-Fri), displaying some of the fantastically imaginative works created by Pinheiro and his factory craftsmen. Pinheiro turned ceramics into sculpture, and was also a caricaturist and humorist (check out his caricatures in the Museu de José Malhoa).

Sleeping

BUDGET

Residencial Dom Carlos (☎ 262 832 551; www.dcarlos.pa-net.pt; Rua de Camões 39A; s/d with breakfast €20/25, with bathroom €35/40, with bathroom & view €35/40) A small hotel with rooms with park views and an English-speaking owner. The best room has two windows with small balconies.

Pensão Residencial Central (☎ 262 831 914; Largo Dr José Barbosa 22; s/d/tr €15/35/40) A rambling, faintly shabby establishment with spacious rooms – the doubles that overlook the square are smaller but nicer. Painter José Malhoa was born here.

Pensão Residencial Olhos Pretos (☎ 262 843 001; fax 262 842 452; Rua do Rosário 10; s/d €15/25; ❄) This central place has ordinary rooms but is the smartest and most comfortable option in the budget category.

Residencial Dona Leonor (☎ 262 838 430; www.donaleonor.com; Hemiciclo João Paulo II 9; s/d with breakfast €35/45; ❄) Quiet and well-run with decent rooms, satellite TV and all that jazz; private parking.

MID-RANGE

Casa dos Plátanos (☎ 262 841 810; fax 262 843 417; Rua Rafael Bordalo Pinheiro 24; d with breakfast €75) A charming Turihab place – an 18th-century, grand house, offering eight double rooms, each with exquisitely carved beds. It also has a library of 30,000 books.

Hotel Cristal Caldas (☎ 262 840 260; Rua António Sérgio 31; d €80; P) A big, modern, hotel, this has well-equipped rooms and a cool-for-conferences feel.

Eating

BUDGET

Restaurante Camões (☎ 262 836 856; Rua do Parque 56; mains €6-8; ⏰ lunch Tue-Sun, dinner Tue-Sat) Tucked off the street by the park, this provides traditional Portuguese dishes and has good service.

Tijuca (☎ 262 824 255; Rua de Camões 89; mains €4.25-9; ⏰ lunch & dinner daily Nov-Sep, Thu-Tue Oct) This small cheery basement has a few street-side tables and a large menu of fish and meat dishes.

Copacabana (☎ 262 824 091; Rua Eng Duarte Pacheco 12; mains €5.50-13; ⏰ breakfast, lunch & dinner Mon-Sat) Copacabana has a long counter and a casual feel, and offers standard Portuguese dishes; half-portions are available.

MID-RANGE

Sabores d'Italia (☎ 262 845 600; Rua Engenheiro Duarte Pacheco 17; mains €5-16.50; ⏰ lunch & dinner Tue-Sun) An award-winning, classy Italian restaurant serving great home-made pizzas and pastas. Prize-winning mains include monkfish with shellfish sauce, and prawns with moscatel wine.

Supatra (☎ 262 842 920; Rua General Amílcar Mota; mains from €8; ⏰ lunch & dinner Tue-Sun) A famous, fragrant, fantastic Thai restaurant 700m south of the park offering a fantastic Sunday buffet lunch.

Pastelaria Machado (Rua de Camões 14; snacks €0.50-3 ⏰ 8am-8pm) is a great cake and coffee stop with an old-fashioned front and 1970s interior. Or there's **Pastelaria Baía** (Rua da Liberdade; ⏰ 8am-8pm), a sweet little place with a small terrace overlooking the street alongside the park. Local specialities include sweet *cavacas* (air-filled tarts covered with icing) – a unique taste resembling sugary cardboard.

Shopping

Market (Praça da República; ⏰ morning only) The town's traditional daily market is one of the best in the region; selling lots of basketware and the famous local pottery as well as colourful flowers, fruit and veg.

Louças e Artigos Regionais (Rua de Camões 23) If you miss the market, try shops along Rua de Camões such as this one.

Associação de Artesãs (☎ 262 842 741; Pavilhões do Parque; ⏰ 10am-1pm & 3-6pm) In the park is this venue, exhibiting and selling ceramics such as tiles and decorative fruit.

Faianças Artísticas Bordalo Pinheiro (Rua Rafael Bordalo Pinheiro 53) For the widest selection of ceramics, visit the shop based here.

There is also a big open-air market held weekly every Monday, some 300m east of the hospital.

Getting There & Away

Buses run from Peniche (€2.45, 45 minutes, six daily) via Óbidos (€1.10, 15 minutes), and Leiria (€7.30, 80 minutes, four daily). Buses run to Lisbon's Arco do Cego terminal (€6, 1¼ hours, nine daily weekdays), including three superfast runs (50 minutes) using the A8 motorway (two on weekends).

Regional trains run from Lisbon's suburban Cacém station with connections from Rossio (€5.10, two hours, seven daily) plus two *interregional* (IR) trains (€5.30, 80 minutes), continuing to Figueira da Foz (€5.30, 1½ hours) via Leiria (€3.10, 50 minutes).

FOZ DO ARELHO

Foz do Arelho, a lovely, vast expanse of sandy beach, lies alongside a lagoon, Lagoa de Óbidos, good for sailing and windsurfing. Along the seafront is a promenade (Avenida do Mar) lined with cafés and bars. The village, with a few places to stay, is 1km inland. It is the nearest beach to Caldas (8km), but is amazingly undeveloped. It's wonderfully quiet and lazy if you visit outside July to mid-September.

Escola de Vela da Lagoa (☎ 262 978 592; Rua dos Reivais 40) rents windsurfers (€14 per hour) and sailing boats (€20 per hour for a Hobie-13) and also provides courses (windsurfing, 15 hours, €90; private sailing two hours €60). Its base is 2.5km along Estrada do Nadadouro (from the village turn left towards the lagoon).

Sleeping

Residencial Pendedo Furado (☎ 262 979 610; penedo_furado@clix.pt; Rua dos Camarções 3; s/d with breakfast €30/60) Situated in the village is this smart, efficient *residencial* (guesthouse), a friendly, relaxed place with smart rooms with peaceful balconies or small terraces.

Quinta da Foz (☎ 262 979 369; Largo do Arraial; d/apt €115/115) A Turihab place just 500m from the lagoon, this has been in the same family for many years and has wonderful vaulted, romantic rooms in the grand main rambling 16th-century house, plus separate rustic apartments (minimum two-night stay) in the former outbuildings. To get here, heading into town, turn left after the Crédito Agrícola on the main street.

Parque de campismo (☎ 262 978 683; adult/tent/car €4/3.30/3.70;) This shady camp site, 2km from the beach, is run by Orbitur. It has a restaurant, bar, is shaded by trees, and has bikes for rent.

Eating

Cabana do Pescador (☎ 262 979 451; Avenida do Mar; mains €4.50-18) Most renowned of the fish restaurants, this has a central little pool and a sea-view terrace. It's very popular and the fish is superb.

Restaurante-Bar Atlântica (☎ 262 979 213; Avenida do Mar; mains €4-10; 🕑 lunch & dinner) The oldest and scruffiest of the restaurants along Avenida do Mar, Atlântica has a typically fish-heavy menu, and good views.

Getting There & Away

Buses connect Foz do Arelho with Caldas da Rainha (€1.20, 20 minutes, at least six daily on weekdays, fewer on weekends).

SÃO MARTINHO DO PORTO

pop 2644

This resort, 17km northwest of Caldas da Rainha, with warm waters ringed by a sandy beach and an almost perfectly enclosed calm bay, is ideal for families. It's one of the most popular hang-outs south of Nazaré. These charms have led to development around its fringes, but it's an attractive small place, with a market lining the seafront and cobbled centre with open-air trestle-table dining in summer.

Orientation & Information

The **turismo** (☎ 262 989 110; 🕑 9am-1pm & 3-7pm Mon-Fri May-Sep, 10am-1pm & 2-6pm Sat & Sun year-round; closed Mon Oct-Jun) is at the northern end of the ocean-side Avenida 25 de Abril (also called Avenida Marginal). The train station is about 700m to the southeast. Buses stop on Rua Conde de Avelar (a block inland), which leads to the N242.

Sleeping

Pensão Americana (☎ 262 989 170; fax 262 989 349; Rua Dom José Saldanha 2; d with breakfast €50) The most popular budget *pensão*, this is a charming place, with airy rooms. It's near the bus stop and about 300m southeast of the turismo.

Residencial Atlântica (☎ 262 980 151; fax 262 980 163; Rua Miguel Bombarda 6; s/d with breakfast €40/55) In a nice little building, with **Restaurante Carvalho** (mains €5-9) just downstairs, this has smart, plain rooms, some with balcony.

Pousada da juventude (☎ 262 999 506; smartinho@movijovem.pt; dm €9.50, d without bathroom €24) With basic dorms and some doubles, this is about 4km inland at Alfeizerão, just off the main N8 highway (buses run about four times daily).

Residencial Concha (☎ 262 989 220; Largo Vitorino Fróis; d €80) In the cobbled centre and run by the same management is the Concha, with comfortable, modern rooms with balconies.

Albergaria São Pedro (☎ 262 985 020; fax 262 985 011; Largo Vitorino Fróis; d €80) Opposite Concha is this more stately option, run by the same management again, and with similarly bright rooms. The Albergaria is open year-round, Concha only in summer.

Colina do Sol (☎ 262 989 764; www.colinadosol.net; adult/tent/car €4/3/3.50;) A well-equipped and friendly camp site 2km north of town, but only 1km from the beach, this has disabled access, children's playground, is shaded by pines and has wooden bungalows. Or there is a tiny town site **Baía Azul** (☎ 262 989 188; adult/tent/car €2.40/2.40/2.40).

Eating

Restaurante Carvalho (☎ 262 980 151; Rua Miguel Bombarda 6; mains €6-12) Attached to Pensão Atlântica, this has a big menu of traditional dishes with an outdoor canopied seating.

Snack-Bar A Cave (☎ 262 989 682; Rua Conde de Avelar 10; mains €4-8) A budget place with traditional dishes, this is tucked away right by the bus stop around the corner from Pensão Americana.

Getting There & Away

Buses run from Alcobaça (€4.65, 35 minutes, one daily) and Lisbon (€7.30, 1½ hours). Take a train from Caldas da Rainha (€1, 10 minutes, seven daily).

NAZARÉ

pop 15,320 / elevation 60m

Nazaré is a cheery, busy resort with a grid of narrow streets – the former fishing quarter – fronted by a broad sweep of beach. The town is burgeoning at the edges, but the centre is still scenic – though it gets rammed to bursting in July and August. It's also packed with black-robed widows and elderly ladies wearing traditional dress who rule the show. They're busy trading nuts and dried fruit on the beach, or touting *quartos* (private rooms), accosting newcomers along the seafront like upfront dealers.

The town's original cliff-top site was on the Promontório do Sítio, and there are swooping views from here.

Orientation

Until the 18th century the sea covered the present-day site of Nazaré; the locals lived inland at the hilltop Pederneira and the nearer Promontório do Sítio. Today, both places play second fiddle to Nazaré and its seafront Avenida da República, which is the main focus of activity. The former fisher-folk's quarter of narrow lanes now hosts restaurants and cafés.

Information

BPI (☎ 262 561 289; Avenida Vieira Guimarães) Bank with ATM.

Caixa Geral de Dépositos (☎ 262 569 050; Praça Sousa Oliveira 33) Bank with ATM.

Centro de saúde (☎ 262 551 647; Urbanizaçao Caixins) Medical centre on the eastern edge of town.

Espaço Internet (☎ 262 553 255; Centre Cultural, Avenida da República) Free Net access 200m south of town.

Hospital (☎ 262 561 140; Largo Nossa Senhora Nazaré) In Sítio.

Police station (☎ 262 551 268; Rua Sub-Vila) Near the market.

Post office (☎ 234 390 150; Avenida da Independência Nacional; 9am-12.30pm & 2.30-6pm Mon-Fri) Has NetPost.

Turismo (☎ 262 561 194; Avenida da República; 10am-1pm & 3-7pm Apr–mid-Jun; to 8pm 15-30 Jun; 10am-10pm Jul & Aug; 10am-8pm Sep; 9.30am-1pm & 2.30-6pm Oct-Mar) Comprehensive information.

Sights

The **Promontório do Sítio**, the cliff-top area 110m above the beach, is popular for its tremendous views and, among Portuguese devotees, for its religious connections. According to legend it was here that the lost statue of the Virgin, known as Nossa Senhora da Nazaré and brought back from Nazareth in the 4th century, was finally found in the 18th century.

Even more famously, it is said that an apparition of the Virgin was seen here one foggy day in 1182. Local nobleman Dom Fuas Roupinho was out hunting a deer when, with him in hot pursuit, the animal disappeared off the edge of the Sítio precipice. Dom Fuas cried out to the Virgin for help and his horse miraculously stopped just in time.

Dom Fuas built the small **Hermida da Memória** chapel on the edge of the belvedere to commemorate the event. It was later visited by a number of VIP pilgrims, including Vasco da Gama. The nearby 17th-century, baroque **Igreja de Nossa Senhora da Nazaré** replaced an earlier church, and is decorated with attractive Dutch azulejos.

From Rua do Elevador, north of the turismo, an **elevador** (funicular; €0.60; 7am-2am Jul & Aug, to midnight Sep-Jun) climbs up the hill to Sítio.

ESTREMADURA & RIBATEJO

Festivals & Events

Nossa Senhora da Nazaré romaria (8 Septempber and following weekend) This religious pilgrimage, held in Sítio, is Nazaré's big religious festival, featuring sombre processions, folk dances and bullfights.

Bullfights (July–mid-September) These take place in the *praça de touros* (bullring) almost every weekend; check with the turismo for times and ticket availability.

Sleeping

BUDGET

Hospedaria Ideal (☎ 262 551 379; Rua Adrião Batalha 96; d €25, full board €70) This is a homely, six-room place above a restaurant, with lots of regular customers, so full board is usually obligatory in August. The landlady speaks French.

Valado (☎ 262 561 111; fax 262 561 137; adult/tent/car €3.50/2.90/3.40) Orbitur's camp site is shaded by trees, has a restaurant and bar, and is 2km east of town, off the Alcobaça road.

Vale Paraíso (☎ 262 561 546; www.valeparaiso.com; adult/tent/car €4/3.20/3.20;) This camp site is 2km north off the N242 Leiria road. It's well equipped, with lots of shade, disabled access and bikes for hire. It's also security conscious. Both of these camp sites have bungalows for rent. Buses for Alcobaça and Leiria pass by.

MID-RANGE

Vila Conde Fidalgo (☎ /fax 262 552 361, 262 085 090; Avenida de Independência 21A; d €30, 2-/3-/4-person apt

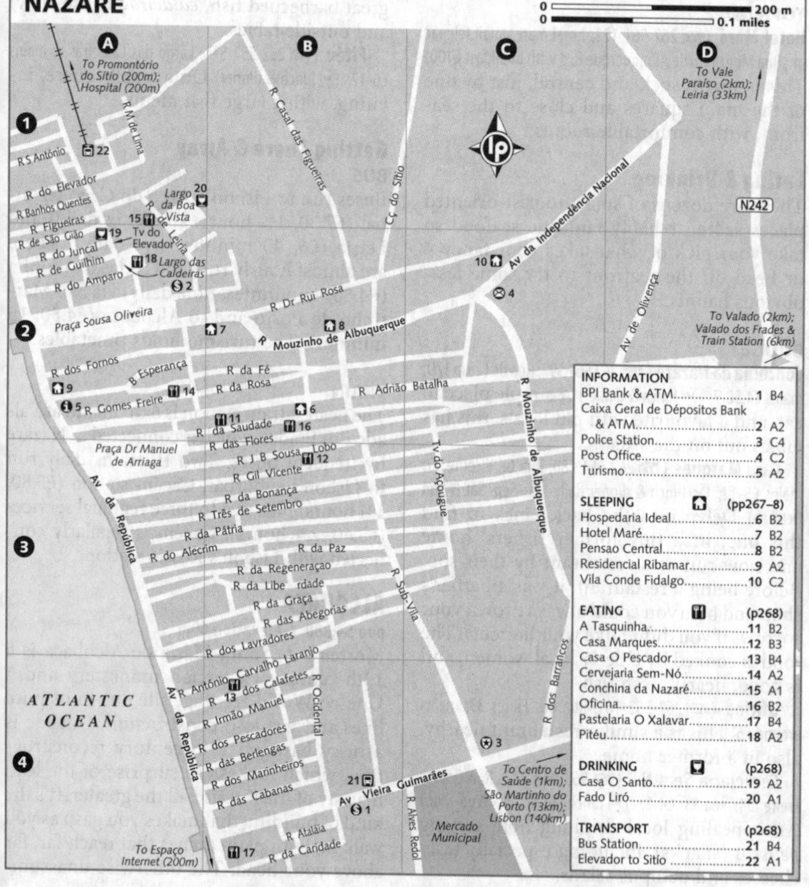

€50/60/75) A pretty little complex, with lots of courtyards and patios, decorated with broken-china mosaic, flowers and plants; this has nicely decorated rooms – the doubles are particularly airy.

Residencial Ribamar (☎ 262 551 158; fax 262 562 224; Rua Gomes Freire 9; d with breakfast €35, with sea view €45) This is right on the seafront, and is a well-run place, with comfortable if unexciting rooms. It's worth paying for the sea view.

Pensao Central (☎ 262 551 510; Rua Mouzinho Albuquerque; s/d with breakfast €45/55) Near the centre, this is quite charming, with old-fashioned rooms featuring small cubbyhole alcoves where you can retire to write your postcards.

TOP END

Hotel Maré (☎ 262 561 122; hotel.mare@mail.telepac.pt; Rua Mouzinho de Albuquerque 8; d with breakfast €100) This is smart, slick and central, just by one of the main squares and close to the seafront, with comfortable rooms.

Eating & Drinking

There are dozens of smart tourist-oriented places selling reliably fantastic seafood so take your pick of what takes your fancy – or head off the seafront to try some less-obvious haunts.

BUDGET

Conchina da Nazaré (☎ 262 561 597; Rua de Leiria 17D; mains €4.50-7; lunch & dinner) A simple place to eat, and a favourite with old locals, this has tables out on the street.

Casa Marques (☎ 262 551 680; Rua Gil Vicente 37; mains €5-12; lunch & dinner daily Mar-Sep, Sat & Sun Oct-Feb) Delve into the back lanes to find this one, in a tiny former fishers' home and now run as a restaurant by their son. Before being a restaurant, it was a barber's shop and bar (you could always drown your sorrows if you didn't like your haircut). The food is cooked by elderly local women, and is good, hearty fresh fish.

Oficina (☎ 262 552 161; Rua das Flores 33; mains around €6) This is a similar restaurant nearby, also in a former home.

Cervejaria Sem-Nó (☎ 963 940 147; Rua Gomes Freire 54; snacks €4-8; lunch & dinner Wed-Mon) An appealing local drinking hole serving *petiscos* (snacks), including especially tasty cheeses and octopus salads.

Casa O Santo (Travessa do Elevador 11; clams €3) A rustic venue where you can start the evening with beer and *ameijoas* (clams).

Fado Liró (clams €3) Near Casa O Santo is this simple, enjoyable local bar, on a quiet square.

Pastelaria O Xalavar (Avenida da República; mains €1-3; daily) This is a café with good cakes and coffee – ideal for breakfast.

MID-RANGE

A Tasquinha (☎ 262 551 945; Rua Adrião Batalha 54; mains €5-8; lunch & dinner Mon-Sat) Justifiably and massively popular, often with queues outside for tables.

Casa O Pescador (☎ 262 553 326; Rua António Carvalho Laranjo 18A; mains €5-12; lunch & dinner Jun-Sep) Tucked down a cobbled street, this has great barbecued fish, *caldeirada* (fish stew) and outside tables.

Pitéu (☎ 262 551 578; Largo das Caldeiras 8; mains €6-12; lunch & dinner) On a small square, inviting, with a large fish menu.

Getting There & Away

BUS

Buses run to Lisbon's Arco do Cego terminal (€7.30, 1¾ hours, about six daily) and Leiria (€6, 40 minutes, five daily). There are almost hourly runs to Caldas da Rainha (€4.80, 45 minutes, nine daily) via São Martinho do Porto and to Alcobaça (€4.80, 15 minutes). The turismo holds timetables.

TRAIN

The nearest train station is 6km inland at Valado dos Frades, which is connected to Nazaré by frequent buses. Two IR trains daily run to Lisbon's suburban Cacém station (€5.80, 1¾ hours) plus two to three regional services (€5.60, 2¾ hours). Cacém is regularly connected with Lisbon's Rossio station.

ALCOBAÇA

pop 54,380 / elevation 60m

Mosteiro de Santa Maria de Alcobaça is a 12th-century Cistercian monastery and a Unesco World Heritage site due to its pure lines and virtuoso construction. Outside is a fussy baroque 18th-century reconstruction, which makes the surprise of the lean majesty of the interior all the greater. It's the kind of building that makes you gasp as you walk in, with plain arches that reach far, far above your head. The otherwise unassum-

BETHUNE CARMICHAEL

Coimbra (p291)

OLIVER STREWE

Porto (p348)

CARLOS COSTA

Palace Hotel do Bucaço in the Buçaco National Forest, Luso (p305)

Quinta do Castelinho (p380) on the Rio Douro

JOHN KING

ANDERS BLOMQVIST

Torre de Menagem (p441), Bragança with Parque Natural de Montesinho (p443) in the background

Palácio de Mateus (p430), Vila Real

CARLOS COSTA

Bom Jesus do Monte (p393), near Braga

ANDERS BLOMQVIST

Ponte Romana (p435), Chaves

CARLO

ing town of Alcobaça is 26km northeast of Caldas da Rainha.

Orientation

From the bus station in the new town turn right along Avenida dos Combatentes to cross the Rio Alcôa and reach the monastery, 500m downhill. The turismo, restaurants and hotels are all near the monastery.

Information

Valuables have been stolen from cars in the monastery car park; be sure to keep them with you. There are several banks with ATMs on the *praça*.

Hospital (☎ 262 597 367; Rua Hospital) On the eastern edge of the new town, off Rua Afonso de Albuquerque.

Police station (☎ 262 595 400; Rua de Olivença)

Post office (☎ 262 590 351; Praça 25 de Abril; 8.30am-6pm Mon-Fri) Almost next door to the turismo.

Turismo (☎ 262 582 377; Praça 25 de Abril; 10am-1pm & 3-7pm Jun-Sep, 10am-1pm & 2-6pm Oct-May) This is helpful and opposite the monastery. It has useful bus timetables and free Net access for 15 minutes.

Sights

MOSTEIRO DE SANTA MARIA DE ALCOBAÇA

This **monastery** (adult/child/senior €4.50/2.25/2.25, church admission free; 9am-7pm Apr-Sep, 9am-5pm Oct-Mar) was founded in 1153 by Dom Afonso Henriques to honour a vow he'd made to St Bernard after the capture of Santarém from the Moors in 1147. The king entrusted the construction of the monastery to the monks of the Cistercian order, also giving them a huge area around Alcobaça to develop and cultivate.

Building started in 1178 and by the time the monks actually moved in, some 40 years later, the monastery estate had become one of the richest and most powerful in the country. In those early days the monastery is said to have housed 999 monks, who held Mass nonstop in shifts.

Switching from farming to teaching in the 13th century, the monks used the estate's abundant rents to carry out further enlargements and changes to the monastery to suit the fashions of the day. Towards the 17th century, the monks turned their talents to pottery and the sculpting of figures in stone, wood and clay.

Revived agricultural efforts in the 18th century made the Alcobaça area one of the most productive in the land. However, it was the monks' growing decadence that became famous, thanks to the writings of 18th-century travellers such as William Beckford who, despite his own decadence (well, he wasn't a monk), was shocked at the 'perpetual gormandising…the fat waddling monks and sleek friars with wanton eyes…'. The party ended in 1834 with the dissolution of the religious orders.

Church

Much of the original façade was altered in the 17th and 18th centuries (including the addition of wings), leaving only the main doorway and rose window unchanged.

This is modelled on the French Cistercian abbey of Clairvaux. When you step inside, the combination of Gothic simplicity and Cistercian austerity hits you immediately: the nave is a breathtaking 106m long but only 23m wide, with huge pillars and truncated columns.

Tombs of Dom Pedro & Dona Inês

Occupying the south and north transepts are two intricately carved 14th-century tombs, the church's greatest possessions, which commemorate the tragic love story of Dom Pedro and his mistress (see Love, Politics & Revenge, p270).

Although the tombs themselves were badly damaged by rampaging French troops in search of treasure in 1811, they still show extraordinary detail and are embellished with a host of figures and scenes from the life of Christ. The Wheel of Fortune at the foot of Dom Pedro's tomb and the gruesome Last Judgment scene at the head of Inês' tomb are especially amazing. The tombs are inscribed 'Até ao Fím do Mundo' (Until the End of the World) and, on Pedro's orders, placed foot to foot so that when the time comes they can rise up and see each other straightaway.

Kitchen & Refectory

The grand kitchen, described by Beckford as 'the most distinguished temple of gluttony in all Europe', owes its immense size to alterations carried out in the 18th century, including a water channel built through the middle of the room so that a tributary of the Rio Alcôa could provide a constant source of fresh fish to the monastery – they swam

> **LOVE, POLITICS & REVENGE**
>
> The gory tragedy of Dom Pedro, the son of Dom Afonso IV, who fell in love with his wife's Galician lady-in-waiting, Dona Inês de Castro, is a grandly operatic Portuguese epic tale. Even after his wife's death his father forbade him to marry Inês because of her Spanish family's potential influence. Various suspicious nobles continued to pressure the king until he finally sanctioned her murder in 1355, unaware that the two lovers had already married in secret.
>
> Two years later, when Pedro succeeded to the throne, he exacted his revenge by ripping out and eating the hearts of Inês' murderers. He then exhumed and crowned her body, and ordered the court to pay homage to his dead queen by kissing her decomposing hand.

directly into a stone basin. The water was also useful for cooking and washing.

Even now, it's not hard to imagine the scene when Beckford was led here by the abbey's grand priors ('hand in hand, all three together'). He saw 'pastry in vast abundance which a numerous tribe of lay brothers and their attendants were rolling out and puffing up into a hundred different shapes, singing all the while as blithely as larks in a corn field'.

The adjacent refectory, huge and vaulted, is where the monks ate in silence while the Bible was read to them from the pulpit. Opposite the entrance is a 14th-century *lavabo* (bathroom) embellished with a dainty hexagonal fountain. The monks had to enter through a narrow door on their way to the refectory. Those who could not fit through had to fast till they were thin enough.

Claustro do Silencio & Sala dos Reis

The beautiful Cloister of Silence dates from two eras. Dom Dinis built the intricate lower storey, with its arches and traceried stone circles, in the 14th century. The upper storey, typically Manueline in style, was added in the 16th century.

Off the northwestern corner of the cloister is the 18th-century Sala dos Reis (Kings' Room), so called because statues of practically all the kings of Portugal line the walls. Below them are azulejo friezes depicting stories relevant to the abbey's construction, including the siege of Santarém and the life of St Bernard.

MUSEU NACIONAL DO VINHO

This is one of Portugal's great wine-making regions, and this national **museum** (☎ 262 582 222; www.ivv.min-agricultura.pt; admission €1.50; 🕑 9am-12.30pm & 2-5.30pm Tue-Fri), in an atmospheric old *adega* (winery) 1.2km east of town on the Leiria road, provides a full-bodied portrait of its wine-making history. You can also sample and buy wine.

RAUL DA BERNARDA MUSEU

The oldest earthenware factory in Alcobaça (established in 1875) is also the only one geared to visitors. Its **museum** (☎ 262 590 610; fax 262 590 601; Ponte D Elias; admission free; 🕑 10am-1pm & 3-7pm Mon-Fri, 10am-7pm Sat, 10am-12.30pm & 1.30-7pm Sun), on the northern edge of town, takes you on a glazed-earthenware journey, from traditional blue-and-white to contemporary multicolour.

Sleeping

Challet Fonte Nova (☎ 262 598 300; www.challetfontenova.pt; Estrada Fonte Nova; d €110; ❄) A 19th-century grandiose chalet that would look at home on the English seaside, this has a lot of charm, with comfortable doubles of various sizes, with satellite TV and decent bathrooms with bathtubs.

Hotel de Santa Maria (☎ 262 590 160; fax 262 590 161; Rua Dr Francisco Zagalo; d with breakfast €55) This well-appointed, modern place is in a quiet spot, just above the square in front of the monastery; some rooms have monastery views.

Hotel D Inês de Castro (☎ 262 582 355; Rua Costa Veiga; s/d €60/80; ❄) A new place behind the monastery, this has identical rooms with plaid curtains and satellite TV.

Parque de campismo (☎ 262 582 265; Avenida Professor Vieira Natividade; adult/tent/car €1.90/1.25/1.25; 🕑 Feb-Dec) The small, simple municipal camp site is 500m north of the bus station. It is tree-shaded and has disabled access.

Eating & Drinking

Ti Fininho (☎ 262 596 506; Rua Frei António Brandão 34; mains €4.50-7; 🕑 lunch & dinner Thu-Tue) This is a tiny place, laden with ivy and with a snug interior. It serves simple, traditional dishes.

Pensão Restaurante Corações Unidos (☎/fax 262 582 142; Rua Frei António Brandão 39; mains €5-7.50, tourist menu €10) Near Ti Fininho, the rooms are not particularly good, but the traditional restaurant is renowned for its hearty dishes, including the local speciality, *frango a alcobaça* (chicken cooked in a pot).

Celeíro dos Frades (☎ 262 582 281; Arco de Cister; mains around €7; lunch & dinner Wed-Mon) Under the arches near the north side of the monastery, this has a trickling fountain under the arches outside and a dramatic cavern under Gothic arches inside. It's popular and has a lively bar.

Festivals & Events

The **Cistermúsica festival** (☎ 262 597 611) takes place in the second half of May, with classical concerts in the monastery and other local venues.

Getting There & Away

BUS

Buses run daily to Lisbon's Arco do Cego terminal (€8, two hours, two daily). There are runs to Nazaré (€1.40, 20 minutes, 15 daily), eight buses daily to Batalha (€2.20, 40 minutes, eight daily) and Leiria (€2.65, 50 minutes) and four to Caldas da Rainha (€6, 30 minutes). Coming from Leiria you can easily see both Batalha and Alcobaça in a day trip (best in that order).

TRAIN

The nearest train station to Alcobaça is 5km northwest at Valado dos Frades, connected to Alcobaça by regular buses (p268).

BATALHA

pop 13,330 / elevation 120m

Also founded after a battle vow, the Gothic-Manueline Mosteiro de Santa Maria da Vitória, usually known as Mosteiro da Batalha (Battle Abbey), is triumph turned into stone. The carving on the abbey is astounding, so detailed and highly wrought that the stonework seems edged in lace, as if it's been inspired by the local tablecloths. It looms, colossal and delicate, over the otherwise unobtrusive little town.

Orientation & Information

Buses stop in Largo 14 de Agosto, 200m east of the abbey. Facing the eastern end of the abbey, the **turismo** (☎ 244 765 180; 10am-1pm & 3-7pm Jun, Jul & Sep, 9am-10pm Aug, 10am-1pm & 2-6pm Oct-May) is beside a modern complex of shops and restaurants.

Sights

MOSTEIRO DE SANTA MARIA DA VITÓRIA

This **abbey** (admission cloisters & Capelas Imperfeitas adult/child/senior €3.50/2/2; 9am-2pm Sun free; 9am-6pm Apr-Sep, 9am-5pm Oct-Mar) was founded after the 1385 Battle of Aljubarrota (fought 4km south of Batalha). On one side was the 30,000-strong force under Juan I of Castile, who was claiming the Portuguese throne; on the other was the 6500-weak Portuguese army of rival claimant Dom João of Avis, commanded by Dom Nuno Álvares Pereira and supported by a few hundred English soldiers.

Defeat for João meant Portugal would slip into Spanish hands. He called on the Virgin Mary for help and vowed to build a superb abbey in return for victory. He duly won, and work on the Dominican abbey started three years later.

Most of the monument – the church, Claustro Real, Sala do Capítulo and Capela do Fundador – was completed by 1434 in flamboyant Gothic, but Manueline flamboyance steals the show, thanks to additions made in the 15th and 16th centuries. Work at Batalha only stopped in the mid-16th century when Dom João III turned his attention to expanding the Convento de Cristo in Tomar.

Exterior

The glorious ochre-limestone building bristles with pinnacles and parapets, flying buttresses and balustrades, Gothic and flamboyant carved windows, as well as octagonal chapels and massive columns, after the English perpendicular style. The western doorway positively boils over – layers of arches pack in the apostles, various angels, saints and prophets, all topped by Christ and the Evangelists.

Interior

The vast vaulted Gothic interior is plain, long and high like Alcobaça's church, warmed by light from the deep-hued stained-glass windows. To the right as you enter is the intricate **Capela do Fundador** (Founder's Chapel), a beautiful, achingly tall, star-vaulted square room, lit by an octagonal lantern. In the centre is the joint tomb of João I and his English wife, Philippa of Lancaster, whose marriage in 1387 established the special alliance that still exists between Portugal and England. The tombs of their four youngest sons line the south wall of the chapel, including that of Henry the Navigator (second from the right).

Claustro Real

Afonso Domingues, the master of works at Batalha during the late 1380s, first built the **Claustro Real** (Royal Cloisters) in a restrained Gothic style, but it's the later Manueline embellishments by the great Diogo de Boitac that really take your breath away. Every arch is a tangle of detailed stone carvings of Manueline symbols, such as armillary spheres and crosses of the Order of Christ, entwined with exotic flowers and marine motifs – ropes, pearls and shells. It's a Gothic and Manueline marriage

Claustro de Dom Afonso V

Anything would seem austere after the Claustro Real, but the simple Gothic **Cloister de Dom Afonso V** is like being plunged into cold water – sobering you up after all that frenzied decadence.

Sala do Capítulo

To the east of the Claustro Real is the early 15th-century **chapterhouse**, containing a beautiful 16th-century stained-glass window. The huge unsupported 19-sq-metre vault was considered so outrageously dangerous to build that only prisoners on death row were employed in its construction. The Sala do Capítulo contains the tomb of the unknown soldiers – one killed in Flanders in WWI, the other in Africa – now watched over by a constant guard of honour.

Capelas Imperfeitas

The roofless **Capelas Imperfeitas** (Unfinished Chapels) at the eastern end of the abbey are perhaps the most astonishing and tantalising part of Batalha. Only accessible from outside the abbey, the octagonal mausoleum with its seven chapels was commissioned by Dom Duarte (I's eldest son) in 1437. However, the later Manueline additions by the architect Mateus Fernandes overshadow everything else, including the Renaissance upper balcony.

Although Fernandes' original plan for an upper octagon supported by buttresses was never completed, the staggering ornamentation gives a hint of what might have followed, and is all the more dramatic for being open to the sky. Especially striking is the 15m-high doorway, a mass of stone-carved thistles, ivy, flowers, snails and all manner of 'scollops and twistifications', as William Beckford noted. Dom Duarte can enjoy it all for eternity; his tomb (and that of his wife) lies opposite the door.

Sleeping & Eating

Pensão Gladius (☎ 244 765 760; Praça Mouzinho de Albuquerque; d with breakfast €30) In the square right next to the abbey, this is a small, quaint place, loaded with geranium-filled window boxes, with clean modern rooms, and a café downstairs.

Residencial Casa do Outeiro (☎ 244 765 806; www.casadoouteiro.com; Largo Carvalho do Outeiro 4; s/d €45/60;) This is a great modern place up on a slight hill. It is thoughtfully run and rooms are decorated with unusual flair, the best of which have balconies providing excellent views of the abbey.

Residencial Batalha (☎ 244 767 500; Largo da Igreja; s/d with breakfast €40/50;) Small and central, this has rooms with small windows and fusty furnishings, but it's comfortable, and has a roof terrace with a view of the monastery.

Restaurante Carlos (☎ 244 768 207; Largo Goa Damão e Diu; mains €6-15; lunch & dinner Tue-Sun) This is just off the square opposite the Centro Comercial and features a menu of standard fare.

Getting There & Away

Buses come from Alcobaça (€2.30, 40 minutes, six buses daily weekdays) and Leiria (€1.30, 20 minutes) and Fátima (€1.70, three daily). There are two runs from Lisbon (€7.80, two hours).

LEIRIA

pop 102,760 / elevation 60m

A medieval castle on a thickly wooded hill seems to hover above the red roofs of Leiria (lay-*ree*-uh), a quiet town on the Rio Liz. The town has a traditional narrow-streeted old quarter with swirling cobbles that open out into bigger patterns in its small café-lined squares.

It wasn't always so quiet: Dom Afonso III convened a *cortes* (parliament) here in 1254; Dom Dinis established his main residence in the castle in the 14th century; and in 1411 the town's sizable Jewish community built Portugal's first paper mill here (Leiria was the first place to make paper in Portugal). In 1545 it was raised to the status of diocese. In 2004 it became the focus of a new fervour when several games of the European Football Championships were played here, for which the town received an enormous facelift.

It makes a fine base for visiting Alcobaça, Batalha and Fátima, or the nearby beach of São Pedro de Muel, all easily accessible by bus.

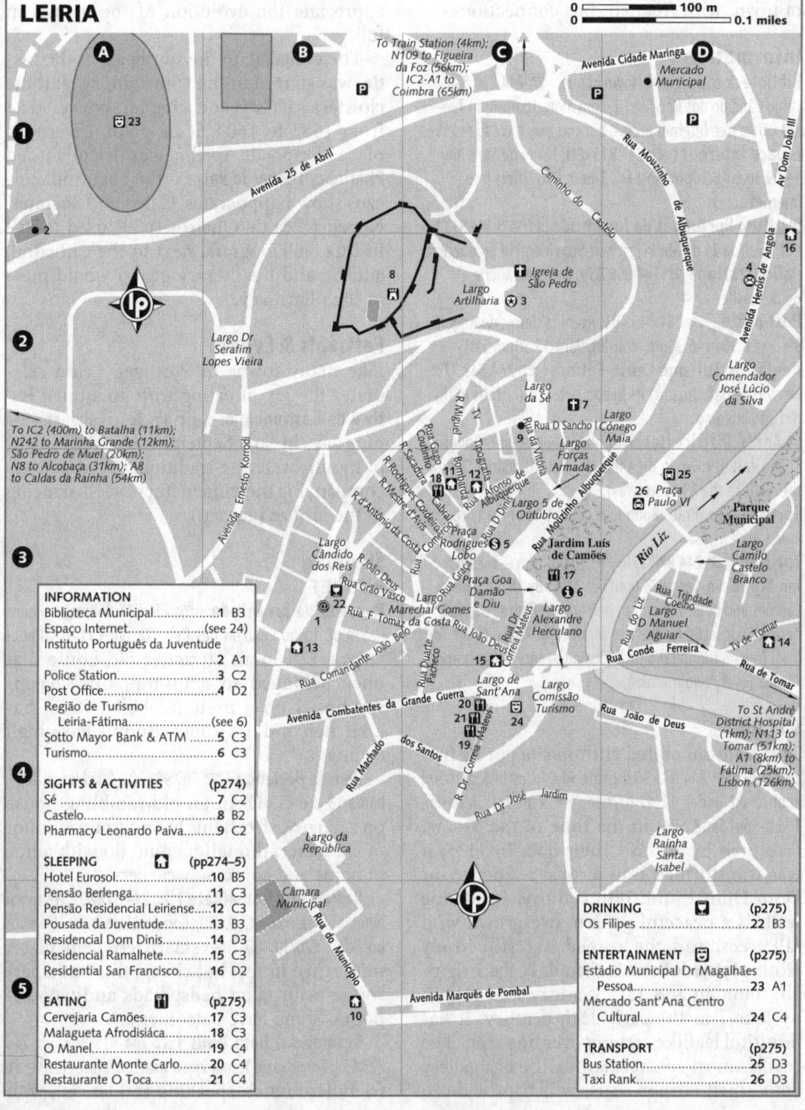

Orientation

The old town is focused on Praça Rodrigues Lobo, with hotels and restaurants nearby. The castle is perched on a wooded hilltop a short walk to the north.

There are free car parks to the north of the town, though it's fairly easy to find parking around the outskirts of the old town. The train station is 4km northwest of town, with frequent bus connections.

Information

Biblioteca municipal (town library; ☎ 244 820 850; Largo Cândido dos Reis; 1-6pm Mon, 10am-6pm Tue-Fri) Offers free Internet access, but you may have to reserve.

Espaço Internet (☎ 244 815 091; Largo de Sant'Ana; 9.30am-8.30pm Mon-Fri, 3-8pm Sat) Offers free Internet access.

Instituto Português da Juventude (IPJ; ☎ 244 813 421; Avenida 25 de Abril; 9am-9pm Mon-Fri) Free access.

Police station (☎ 244 859 859; Largo Artilharia 4) By the castle.

Post office (☎ 244 849 401; Avenida Herois de Angola 99; 8.30am-6.30pm Mon-Fri, 9am-12.30pm Sat)

Região de Turismo Leiria-Fátima (☎ 244 848 773; www.rt-leiriafatima.pt) Its headquarters is upstairs in the turismo building.

St André District Hospital (☎ 244 817 000) About 1.5km east of town in the Olhalvas–Pousos district (follow the signs to the A1 motorway).

Sotto Mayor (Praça Rodrigues Lobo) One of many central banks with ATMs.

Turismo (☎ 244 848 770; 10am-1pm & 3-7pm Jun-Sep, 10am-1pm & 2-6pm Oct-May) By Jardim Luís de Camões and helpful. You can buy an excellent town map here (€5) or settle for the free photocopy. Also pick up *Find Us!* a free multilingual booklet listing events in Leiria and Fátima (every two months).

Sights

This long-inhabited clifftop site got its first **castelo** (☎ 244 813 982; castle €1.04, castle & museum adult/child under 12 €2.07/free; 9am-5pm Mon-Fri, 10am-5pm Sat & Sun) in the time of the Moors. Captured by Afonso Henriques in 1135, it was transformed into a royal residence for Dom Dinis in the 14th century. Inside the walls is a peaceful garden, overgrown with tall trees, and the ruined but still lovely Gothic **Igreja de Nossa Senhora da Penha**, originally built in the 12th century and rebuilt by João I in the early 15th century. It has beautiful leaflike carving over one arch. The castle's most spectacular feature is a gallery with small corner seats, which provides a fantastic vantage point over the town with its red tiled roofs. The castle has been restored several times, most recently in the early 20th century by the Swiss architect Ernesto Korrodi.

In the castle keep, the **Núcleo Museológic** displays, on several floors, replicas of vicious medieval weapons, and spiky-nosed helmets. You'll need to read Portuguese to appreciate the evolution of the helmet in full.

The **cathedral**, to the southeast of the castle, was started in the 16th century, and the cloister, sacristy and chapter houses date from 1583 to 1604. It's a plain, cavernous place. Opposite is the wonderfully tiled **Pharmacy Leonardo Paiva** – the beautiful ajulezos show Hippocrates, Galen and Socrates. Novelist Eça de Queirós (p39) used to live in Rua da Tipografia next to the cathedral, and he and his literary group would meet in the pharmacy.

Festivals & Events

Like many towns in Portugal, Leiria celebrates the joy of eating with an annual **Festival de Gastronomia**. Leiria's festival lasts for nine days in early September. As well as stalls of mouth-watering traditional food and accompanying merriment, there's folk dancing in the *jardim* (garden).

Sleeping

BUDGET

Pousada da juventude (☎ 244 831 868; leiria@movijovem.pt; Largo Cândido dos Reis 7D; dm €11, d without bathroom €27) In an attractive old house that once belonged to a bishop, this charming hostel on a pretty, cobbled street has a kitchen and TV room. Rooms have high ceilings.

Pensão Berlenga (☎ 962 941 207; Rua Miguel Bombarda 13; s/d €15/30) In an old rambling house on a narrow street, this has a certain amount of character, though it could do with a lick of paint and some new carpets.

Residencial Ramalhete (☎ 244 812 802; res.ramalhete@mail.telepac.pt; Rua Dr Correia Mateus 30; s/d with breakfast €20/30; 💻) A smart, efficient place, mid-range in feel but cheap, this has smart rooms with plaid bedspreads and wooden floors. Some have balconies.

Residencial Dom Dinis (☎ 244 815 342; fax 244 823 552; Travessa de Tomar 2; s/d with breakfast €22/33) A friendly, French-speaking residencial, with modern, plain, bright rooms with bathtubs and views across the town – a pleasant surprise after the fusty tapestries and dried flowers in the reception.

Residencial San Francisco (☎ 244 823 110; Rua de San Francisco; s/d €30/40) On the 9th floor, this has small rooms with satin eiderdowns and good views.

MID-RANGE

Pensão Residencial Leiriense (☎ 244 823 054; fax 244 823 073; Rua Afonso de Albuquerque 6; d with breakfast €45) This is a charming, well-kept pension, in a cobbled street, just off Praça Rodriguez Lobo, with small peaceful rooms and good breakfasts.

Hotel Eurosol (☎ 244 849 849; Rua Dom José Alves C da Silva; s/d with breakfast €57/77;) This is businesslike, with views, mod cons and Leiria's swishest rooms.

Eating & Drinking

Cervejaria Camões (☎ 244 838 628; Jardim Luís de Camões; mains €3-15) In the *jardim*, this is a spacious café-restaurant-beerhouse, with floor-to-ceiling plate glass windows, wooden tables and chairs, and many ways of serving steak. It's a venue for live dance and music (live jazz Sunday night) and there's a bar, **Sabor Latino** (9pm-2am) upstairs.

Malagueta Afrodisiáca (☎ 244 831 607; Rua Gago Coutinho 17; mains €6-12.25; lunch & dinner) With aphrodisiac teas, and an eclectic menu from vegetarian to Mexican curry, this is tucked down a narrow street and slinkily decorated.

Restaurante Monte Carlo (☎ 244 825 406; Rua Dr Correia Mateus 32; mains €3-7, 3-course menu €8.50; lunch & dinner Mon-Sat) Along pedestrianised Rua Dr Correia Mateus are several traditional restaurants, including this family-friendly, no-nonsense popular spot with white tablecloths. It serves pork, lamb and fried fish dishes.

Restaurante A Toca (Rua Dr Correia Mateus 32; mains €3.50-9.50; lunch & dinner Mon-Fri) Also busy, with tiled walls, tableclothed tables and a big open window at the front. There's a good choice of food.

O Manel (☎ 244 832 132; Rua Dr Correia Mateus 50; mains around €7-9) The more upmarket, tiled O Manel specialises in fish and seafood, priced by the kilo.

Os Filipes (Largo Cândido dos Reis 1A; 8pm-2am) This is an appealing bar, just near the hostel. It has seats outside from where you can see down the street where, in the 19th century, Leiria's nobility lived.

Entertainment

The former market has been developed into the **Mercado Sant'Ana Centro Cultural** (☎ 244 815 091; Largo de Sant'Ana), centred around a courtyard and with an emphasis on contemporary dance. There are several cafés, a restaurant, Espaço Internet, a venue for concerts and a theatre.

Leiria hosted some of the 2004 European Football Championships in its 35,000-seat **Estádio Municipal Dr Magalhães Pessoa** (☎ 244 831 774), local team Unaio de Leiria's home ground.

Getting There & Away

BUS

From the **bus station** (☎ 244 811 507) buses run to Coimbra (€6.50, seven daily weekdays, four daily on weekends) and Fátima (€4.50/2.35 express/normal, 35 minutes/one hour), and to Tomar (€6.70, 50 minutes, four daily). Express buses run to Lisbon (€7.80, 1¼ hours, almost hourly).

TRAIN

Leiria is on the Cacém (a Lisbon suburb) to Figueira da Foz line. Two IR services run daily from Cacém (€6, 2¼ hours) to Leiria, plus a couple more regional services (€6, two to three hours), all continuing to Figueira da Foz (€3, 45 minutes). Cacém has frequent connections with Lisbon's Rossio station. Buses from the train station to town (15 minutes) cost €0.80 – take the No 1 or ask at the bus station for the next bus. A taxi will cost around €4.

PINHAL DE LEIRIA

This enchanting tall pine forest, which slices and stripes the sunlight along the coast, is more than 700 years old. It's also over 100 sq km, stretching along the coast west of Leiria. It was first planted in the reign of Dom Afonso III and expanded and shaped by Dom Dinis to serve as a barrier against the encroaching sands and also to act as a supply of timber for the maritime industry – much needed during the boat-hungry Age of Discoveries.

The aromatic **forest**, stretching from Pedrógão in the north to São Pedro de Muel in the south, is beautiful: a quiet mass of tapered trees along the coast, cut through with narrow, quiet roads. It's popular for its picnic and camp sites and for its several excellent beaches. Nearest to Leiria is **São Pedro de Muel**, with the most appealing beaches along this part of the coast (a bite of sand at São Pedro, and long empty Praia Velha nearby). To the north are two more beach resorts, **Praia da Vieira** and **Pedrógão.**

Orientation & Information

São Pedro de Muel is 20km west of Leiria. Praia da Vieira and Pedrógão are 16km to the north of São Pedro, but are becoming built up. There are some useful **turismos** Marinha Grande (☎ 244 566 644); São Pedro de Muel (☎ 244 599 633); Praia da Vieira (☎ 244 695 230).

Sleeping & Eating

Hotel Mar e Sol (☎ 244 590 000; Avenida da Liberdade 1; s/d with breakfast €33/43, with sea views €38/40) In addition to some *quartos* (look for signs near the beach), there are a few hotels in São Pedro de Muel, including this modern, seafront hotel, which has inoffensive, comfortable rooms – some have good views over the tussling sea.

Residencial Pérola do Oceano (☎ 244 599 157; s/d 20/30) This small, appealing place, nicely set on the main square, has humble rooms, some with balcony.

Hotel Cristal (☎ 244 699 060; www.hoteiscristal.pt; Avenida Marginal; d with breakfast €80; ♿) This is a flashy 100-room block in Praia da Vieira. It's just 20m from the beach and has rooms overlooking the sea.

Orbitur (☎ 244 599 168; adult/tent/car €4.30/3.50/3.80; ♿) The best camp site at São Pedro de Muel. In among the pines, it's a smart place 500m from the seaside, with disabled facilities and playground. You can rent huts here too.

Inatel (☎ 244 599 289; adult/tent/car €4.25/3.25/2) Near Orbitur, but scrubbier, this camp site is set right up above the coast. Low bushes and trees hide the tents and vans.

Parque de campismo (☎ 244 695 334; adult/tent/car €1.70/1.80/2) Praia da Vieira has a simpler, small road-side municipal camp site, a hop and skip from the beach.

Parque de campismo (☎ 244 695 403; fax 244 695 447; adult/tent/car €1.60/2.10/2.10) In the forest at nearby Pedrógão is this much smaller ground, but it's among trees and better equipped, next to the beautiful huge lake and Cabril dam.

Eating

Estrela do Mar (☎ 244 599 245; Avenida Marginal; mains €7-12; ⏲ lunch & dinner Wed-Mon) This place serves lots of really excellent fish and seafood, including a very good monkfish rice. It's set up on the cliffs above the beach, with a spectacular sea view, and outside seating.

O Pai dos Frangos (☎ 244 599 158; mains €6.50-9.50; ⏲ lunch & dinner Wed-Mon) At Praia Velha, 'The Father of the Chicken' is a lone restaurant overlooking the beach, with sea views and lots of fishing nets. There's lots of seafood and rice dishes, and specialities include lobster clams, prizewinning shellfish rice – and grilled chicken, of course.

Getting There & Away

From Leiria there are buses daily to Marinha Grande (15 minutes, two daily weekdays), from where you can pick up connections to São Pedro de Muel (ticket from Leiria €2.10). There's a daily bus to Praia da Vieira (€2.45, one daily weekdays).

FÁTIMA

pop 10,302 / elevation 320m

Fátima is an extraordinary place, fuelled by belief, and one of the most important places of pilgrimage in the Catholic world. Before 13 May 1917 no-one paid any attention to this unremarkable little place 22km southeast of Leiria, but on that day (see opposite) everything changed. It's now visited by four million pilgrims a year.

The shrine has a remarkable atmosphere, with a constant stream of devout faithful paying tribute. It's most dramatic at Fátima's key times, 12–13 May and 12–13 October, when millions of pilgrims arrive to commemorate the first apparitions. The courtyard outside the basilica is twice the size of St Peter's, and a new church is being built with room for 9000 worshippers, due to be finished in 2007.

The town itself is a shrine to cheerfully gaudy religious tat: it's packed with boarding houses and restaurants for the pilgrim massess, as well as glow-in-the-dark Virgins, Fátima T-shirts and key rings, and much, much more.

THE FÁTIMA APPARITION

On 13 May 1917 three shepherd children from Fátima – Lúcia, Francisco and Jacinta – claimed to have seen an apparition of the Virgin 'more brilliant than the sun'. Only 10-year-old Lúcia could hear what she said, including her request that they return on the 13th of each month for the next six months. The word spread and by 13 October some 70,000 devotees had gathered. What happened then has been described as the Miracle of the Sun: the sun whirled like a wheel of fire, followed by the miraculous cure of the disabilities and illnesses suffered by some spectators.

What the Virgin apparently told Lúcia must have seemed especially potent in those WWI days; her messages described the hell that resulted from 'sins of the flesh' and implored the faithful to 'pray a great deal and make many sacrifices' to secure peace. Most controversially, the Virgin claimed that if her request were heeded, 'Russia would be converted and there would be peace'. She appeared to Lucia on several occasions after this, in 1925, 1926 and 1929.

Until 2000 the third message remained secret, known only to successive popes. During an emotional ceremony that year, the visiting Pope John Paul II beatified Jacinta and Francisco, before a crowd of half a million, and revealed the third message, a prophetic vision written down by Lúcia: it predicted the attempt on the Pope's life in 1981. At the time of the attempt the Pope had insisted somewhat mysteriously that Our Lady of Fátima had saved his life; after he'd recovered, he had the bullet that wounded him welded into the crown of the Virgin's statue in Fátima.

Orientation & Information

The focus of the pilgrimages is where the apparitions occurred, Cova da Iria, just east of the A1 motorway. Where sheep once grazed there's now a vast 1km-long esplanade dominated by a huge white basilica.

Several major roads ring the area, including Avenida Dom José Alves Correia da Silva to the south, where the bus station is located. To reach the sanctuary turn right from the bus station and walk 300m, then left along Rua João Paulo II for 500m. The **turismo** (☎ 249 823 773; ⏲ 10am-1pm & 3-7pm May-Sep, 2-6pm Oct-Apr) is also on the *avenida* 300m beyond this turning. It offers 15 minutes free Net access.

Sights

Dominating the sanctuary is the 1953 **basilica**, a white triumphant building with a *praça* and colonnade reminiscent of St Peter's in Rome. It is the focus of intense devotion. Supplicants who have promised a penance – for example, in return for helping a loved one who is sick, or to signify a particularly deep conversion – even shuffle across the vast esplanade on their knees. The **Capela das Apariçoes** (Chapel of the Apparitions) marks the site where the Virgin appeared. Here devotees also kneel and shuffle or – if less in need of major help – offer flowers and light candles. There's a blazing furnace by the chapel where people can throw offerings on the fire. If they leave an offering, workers at the sanctuary collect them at the end of the day and use the profits for charity.

Inside the basilica are 15 altars dedicated to the 15 mysteries of the rosary. Attention is focused on the tombs of Blessed Francisco (died 1919 aged 11) and Blessed Jacinta (died 1920 aged 10), both victims of the flu epidemic, who were beatified in 2000. Lúcia, the third witness of the apparition, entered a convent in Coimbra in 1928 and is still alive (aged 97 in 2004). She last visited Fátima in 2000, when the Pope was here.

At the entrance of the sanctuary, to the south of the rectory, is a segment of the **Berlin Wall**, donated by a Portuguese resident of Germany and a tribute to God's part in the fall of communism, as predicted at Fátima.

Eight masses are held daily in the basilica, and seven daily in the Capela das Apariçoes. (At least two masses daily are held in English; check at the information booth by the chapel for details.)

The new **Igreja da Santissima Trinidade** (Church of the Holy Trinity) will be finished in 2007, and will cost more than €40 million. It's a great disc with a huge walkway through the centre, something like a giant ping-pong bat, if the architectural projections are to be believed.

The **Museu de Cera de Fátima** (waxwork museum; ☎ 249 539 300; www.mucefa.pt; Rua Jacinta Marto; adult/child 6-12 €4.50/2.50; 9.30am-6.30pm Mon-Sat, from 9am-6.30pm Sun Apr-Oct, 10am-5pm Mon-Fri & 9am-5.30pm Sat & Sun Nov-Mar) gives a tacky but appealingly blow-by-blow, starry-eyed account of the story of Fátima.

Sleeping

There are dozens of reasonably priced restaurants, *pensões* and boarding houses, many geared for visiting groups of hundreds.

Hotel Coracão de Fátima (☎ 249 531 433; fax 249 531 157; Rua Cônego Formigão; d with breakfast €50) Next to the post office and not far from the turismo, this popular place offers comfortable rooms and brisk, efficient service.

There are plenty of homely pilgrim lodges, east of the basilica, in the thick of the shops, including **Residencial Poeira** (☎ 249 531 419; Travessa Santo António; d with breakfast €30).

Getting There & Away

BUS

There are buses daily to Leiria (€4.80/2.10 express/normal, 25 minutes, almost hourly), to Batalha (€1.60, three daily), to Coimbra (€8.50, 1½ hours, nine daily) and to Lisbon (€8, 1½ hours, 12 daily), three of them via Santarém (€5.80, one hour). Fátima is often referred to as Cova da Iria on bus timetables.

TRAIN

Fátima is on the Lisbon–Porto line but the station is 25km from town, with few bus connections. A better bet is to get off at Caxarias, two stops to the north, which has two *intercidade* (IC; €8, 1¼ hours) and three IR direct services daily from Lisbon and the same number from Porto, plus numerous indirect services. A bus shuttles between Caxarias and Fátima (€2.20, 40 minutes, two to five times daily).

PORTO DE MÓS

pop 23,340 / elevation 260m

At the northern tip of the Parque Natural das Serras de Aire e Candeeiros, 9km south of Batalha, Porto de Mós is an appealing, untouristed small town beside the Rio Lena, dominated by a green-spiked 13th-century hilltop castle.

Once the dinosaurs (see Dinosaur Footprints, opposite) roamed here, then Porto de Mós became a major Roman settlement. The Romans used the Lena to ferry millstones hewn from a nearby quarry and, later, iron from a mine 10km south at Alqueidão da Serra, where you can still see a Roman road, fantastically cobbled and stretching up into the hills, offering a great 9km walk.

Today, the town serves as a jumping-off point for visiting the nearby caves and stunning park.

Orientation & Information

The town spreads out from a cluster of streets just below the castle to a newer area further south around the *mercado municipal* on Avenida Dr Francisco Sá Carneiro, where buses also stop. Walk west from here towards the Rio Lena and you'll hit Alameda Dom Afonso Henriques, the main road through town. The **turismo** (☎ 244 491 323; 10am-1pm & 3-7pm Tue-Sun May-Sep) is at the top of the main road in the *jardim público* (public gardens) and offers 15 minutes free Net access.

Sights

CASTELO

The green-towered **castle** (admission free; 10am-12.30pm & 2-6pm Tue-Sun May-Sep, to 5pm Oct-Apr) was originally a Moorish possession, but was conquered in 1148 by Dom Afonso Henriques. It was rebuilt in 1450. Today it hosts changing exhibitions.

MUSEU MUNICIPAL

This little **museum** (☎ 244 499 615; Travessa de São Pedro; admission free; 10am-12.30pm & 2-5.30pm Tue-Sun) is in a pink building beneath the *câmara municipal*, just off Largo Machado dos Santos, and contains a fabulous old-fashioned treasure trove. Fading labels provide sparse details on extraordinary items such as fossils of turtles and dinosaur bones, Neolithic stones, Palaeolithic flints, Roman columns and ancient azulejo fragments. In addition, there are insects, butterflies, millstones, folk costumes, old typewriters, looms, books and spinning wheels. Great fun!

Sleeping & Eating

Residencial O Filipe (☎ 244 401 455; Largo do Rossio 41; d with breakfast €40;) It may be the only *pensão* in town, but this renovated place doesn't rest on its laurels, offering 15 trim rooms, all with telephone.

Quinta de Rio Alcaide (☎ 244 402 124, 939 449 746; rioalcaide@mail.telepac.pt; d €35;) One kilometre southeast of Porto de Mós, this is fabulously set in a converted 18th-century paper mill with charming rooms and apartments, including one in a former windmill. There is a lovely pool.

Restaurante O Miguel (☎ 244 403 912; Avenida Dr Francisco Sá Carneiro 9B; mains €6-7; lunch & dinner) One of several decent restaurants near the market, this serves traditional dishes.

Esplanada Jardim (snacks €1-4) Near the turismo, a café with tables out in the garden.

Getting There & Away

One to two buses daily run to/from Leiria (€2.15, 45 minutes) via Batalha, plus three others which require a change at São Jorge Cruz, a junction on the N1 about 5km northwest of Porto de Mós. Five buses daily come from Alcobaça (€2.15, 35 minutes), also via São Jorge Cruz. You can buy tickets in the municipal market.

PARQUE NATURAL DAS SERRAS DE AIRE E CANDEEIROS

You can imagine dinosaurs roaming around this park (PNSAC for short), stretching south from Porto de Mós, a roller-coaster limestone range that rises into high plateaus and peaks and dives down into huge rocky depressions. The park is famous for its cathedral-like caves, but above ground is spectacular, too, in particular the high Planalto de Santo António (starting 2km south of the Grutas de Santo António). Sweeping hills covered in gorse and olive groves are divided by dry-stone walls and threaded by cattle trails, offering tempting walks.

Throughout the park there are over a dozen *parques de merendas* (picnic areas). There are also numerous *percursos pedestres* (walking trails), ranging from 2km to 16km, described in Portuguese-language pamphlets available from the park offices.

Information

Ecoteca (☎ 244 491 904; fax 244 403 555; 9.30am-12.30pm & 2-6pm Tue-Fri, 2.30-6pm Sat) Centro de Interpretação, in the public garden in Porto de Mós, where you can pick up information (mostly in Portuguese).

Head office (☎ 243 999 480; pnsac@icn.pt; Rua Dr Augusto César da Silva Ferreira) In Rio Maior, at the south of the park.

Sights

MIRA DE AIRE

Portugal's largest **cave system** (☎ 244 440 322; adult/child €4.50/3; 9.30am-8.30pm Jul & Aug, 9.30am-7pm Jun & Sep, 9.30am-6pm Apr & May, 9.30am-5.30pm Oct-Mar; last admission 30 min before closing), at Mira de Aire, 14km southeast of Porto de Mós, was discovered in 1947 and opened to the public in 1971. It seems the 45-minute guided tour hasn't changed much since, with groooovy psychedelically lit caverns filled with stalactites and stalagmites. The

DINOSAUR FOOTPRINTS

For years a huge quarry 10km south of Fátima yielded nothing more interesting than chunks of limestone. But when the quarry closed in 1994 a local archaeologist discovered huge footprints embedded in the sloping rock face. These, the oldest and longest sauropod tracks in the world, a trifling 175 million years old, plodded along for 147m.

The sauropods (they were those nice herbivorous dinosaurs with small heads and long necks and tails) would have been stepping through carbonated mud, later transformed into limestone. As you walk across the slope you can clearly see the large elliptical prints made by the *pes* (feet) and the smaller, half-moon prints made by the *manus* (hands).

Another major dinosaur discovery – a partial skeleton of a flesh-eating *Allosaurus fragilis* – was made in April 1999 at nearby Pombal (26km northeast of Leiria). It proved to be the same species as fossils found in the western USA, throwing into disarray the theory that the Atlantic Ocean opened only during the late Jurassic period.

You can actually follow in the footsteps of the dinosaurs, through Fátima's **Monumento Natural das Pegadas dos Dinossáurios** (☎ 249 530 160; www.pegadasdedinossaurios.org; adult/child €1.50/0.50) at Pedreira do Galinha, 9km east of the N360 running south of Fátima; follow the brown signs marked 'Pegadas da Serra de Aire'. There are special children's programmes.

last cavern, 110m down, contains a huge lake with a dramatic fountain display.

There are three buses daily except Sunday from Porto de Mós to Mira de Aire (€2.10, 30 minutes) and two that return. Two buses run daily on weekdays from Nazaré (€3.80, 1½ hours) via Alcobaça (€3, 1¼ hours) and Porto de Mós. Other services may require a change at São Jorge; check the bus schedules carefully. Buses stop in Mira de Aire town, 1km from the caves.

GRUTAS DE ALVADOS & GRUTAS DE SANTO ANTÓNIO

These **caves** (☎ 244 440 787; adult/child per cave €4.50/3, both caves €8/5; 🕑 9.30am-8.30pm Jul & Aug, 9.30am-7pm Jun & Sep, 9.30am-6pm Apr & May, 9.30am-5.30pm Oct-Mar) are about 15km southeast of Porto de Mós, and 2km and 3.5km, respectively, south of the N243 from Porto de Mós to Mira de Aire. They were discovered by workmen in 1964, and are the spiky smaller cousins of Mira de Aire with similarly disco-flavoured lighting.

There are no direct buses to the Alvados and Santo António caves. Your best bet is to hop off the Porto de Mós–Mira de Aire bus and walk (steeply uphill!) from the N243. A **taxi** (☎ 244 491 351) from Porto de Mós costs about €10 return, including an hour's wait at the caves.

Sleeping

The park operates four *centros de acolhimento* (lodging centres) in its southern section, geared to groups of four to eight. The smallest, near Alcobertas, costs around €60 per night in high season. This accommodation should be booked at least a week in advance at the **head office** (☎ 244 449 700).

The remote, basic, beautifully set **parque de campismo** (☎ 244 450 555; adult/tent €2.50/0.75 🕑 May-Sep) at Arrimal, 17km south of Porto de Mós, has only 50 pitches, and is accessible by a twice-daily bus.

RIBATEJO

SANTARÉM

pop 62,620

> A book made of stone, in which the most interesting and most poetical part of our chronicles is written
>
> *Almeida Garrett*
> Travels in My Homeland

Santarém (sang-tuh-*rayng*), the provincial capital, perches above a green sea of Ribatejan plains and the Rio Tejo valley. Such a fruitful viewpoint ensured it a rich history – chief remains of which are two beautiful churches and some impressive mansions.

The city is famous for bullfights and its numerous celebrations, especially the June agricultural fair. Its monuments, position, cafés and restaurants, and a 5000-strong student population, make it a good stop (note that everything is closed on Monday and Tuesday) even when it's not festival time – but if you get a chance to catch a festival, grab it.

History

Important to the Romans, then a legendarily impenetrable Moorish stronghold (only the site remains), Dom Afonso Henriques captured Santarém in 1147, a key success of the Reconquista. The king built the Mosteiro de Alcobaça in thanks for the victory.

Santarém became a favourite royal residence (hunting was the main draw), and its palace served as the meeting place of the *cortes* during the 13th, 14th and 15th centuries. A 400-year royal hiatus ended in 1833 – when Dom Miguel used it as his base during his brief (unsuccessful) war against his brother Pedro.

Orientation

Overlooking the Rio Tejo, Santarém commands some grand views of the Ribatejan plains. At the heart of the old town are the pedestrianised Rua Serpa Pinto and Rua Capelo e Ivens, where you will find the turismo and most of the restaurants, shops and cheap accommodation. Signposts to the Portas do Sol lookout lead visitors on a walk past most of the churches of interest.

The train station is 2.4km to the northeast, though there are regular buses to the centre. The **bus station** (Avenida do Brasil) is central.

Information

Biblioteca municipal (☎ 243 304 481; 🕑 9am-8pm Mon-Fri, 9.30am-1pm Sat) Offers free Net access.

Crédito Agricola (☎ 243 322 326; Rua Dr Teixeira Guedes 23)

Hospital (☎ 243 300 200; Avenida Bernardo Santareno Santarém) On the northern edge of town.

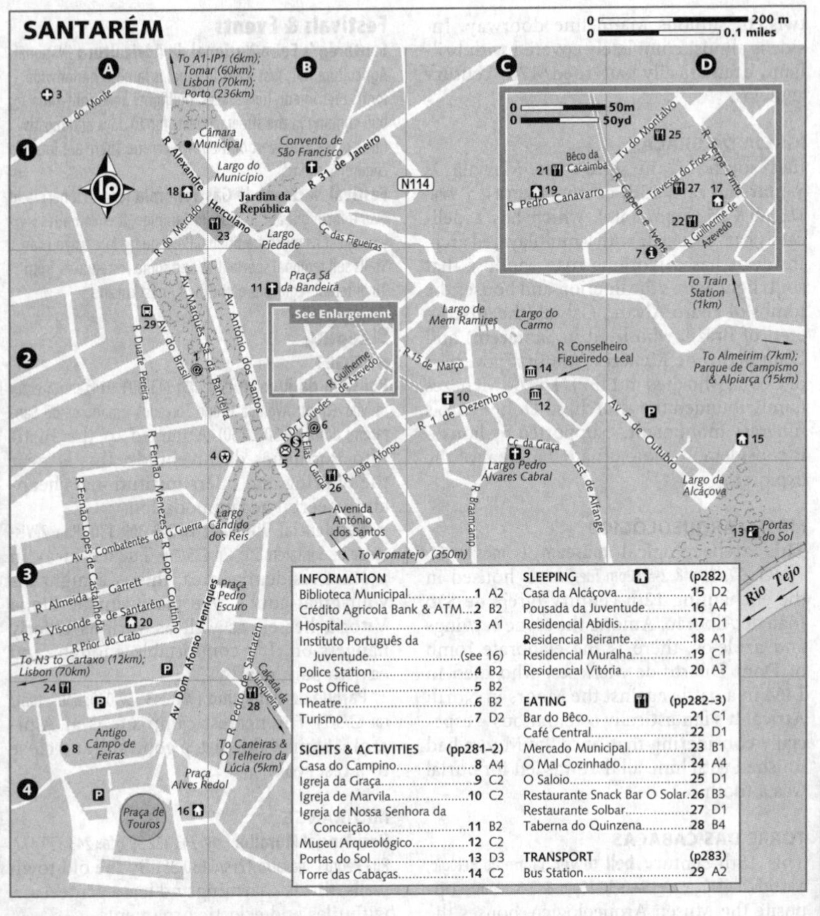

Instituto Português da Juventude (IJP; ☎ 243 333 292; Avenida Grupo Forcados Amadores de Santarém; 9am-8pm Mon-Fri) Free Internet access.

Police station (☎ 243 322 022; Campo Sá Bandeira Santarém) On the northwestern side of Largo Cândido dos Reis.

Post office (☎ 243 309 730; Rua Dr Teixeira Guedes; 8.30am-6.30pm Mon-Fri, 9am-12.30pm Sat) Has NetPost.

Turismo (☎ 243 304 437; fax 243 304 401; Rua Capelo e Ivens 63; 9am-7pm Tue-Fri, 10am-12.30pm & 2.30-5.30pm Sat & Sun, 9am-12.30pm & 2-5.30pm Mon) Has a detailed town map with multilingual descriptive text, which describes different thematic routes. There are also useful leaflets in different languages, from history to handicrafts.

Sights

IGREJA DE NOSSA SENHORA DA CONCEIÇÃO

This baroque, 17th-century Jesuit seminary **church** (9am-12.30pm & 2-5.30pm Wed-Sun), built on the site of the former royal palace, looms over the town's most impressive square, Praça Sá da Bandeira. The church now serves as the town's cathedral. Inside is a typically loopy baroque painted ceiling, bursting with angels and gold, twisted columns and gilded carved altars.

IGREJA DE MARVILA

Dating from the 12th century but with 16th-century additions, this endearing little **church** (9am-12.30pm & 2-5.30pm Wed-Sun) has a fine, twisted, sinuous Manueline doorway. Inside is almost completely covered with brilliant, dramatically patterned, 17th-century azulejos.

IGREJA DA GRAÇA

Just south of the Igreja de Marvila is Santarém's early 15th-century **church** (🕑 9am-12.30pm & 2-5.30pm Wed-Sun), which has a delicately carved façade with a multilayered arch. Inside it has a glorious rose window that spills light across the interior, and houses the tombs of Pedro Álvares Cabral (the 'discoverer' of Brazil, who lived in Santarém) and Dom Pedro de Menezes (the first governor of Ceuta, who died in 1437). The de Menezes family founded the church, so Dom Pedro's funerary monument – supported by lions – is considerably more ornate than that of the explorer.

MUSEU ARQUEOLÓGICO

This archaeological **museum** (admission €1; 🕑 9am-12.30pm & 2-5.30pm Tue-Sun) is housed in the enchanting 12th-century Igreja de São João de Alporão. Among the stone carvings and azulejos, there is the elaborate tomb of Dom Duarte de Menezes, who died in 1464 in a battle against the Moors in North Africa. It's fantastically ostentatious – especially considering that once the Moors had finished with him, all that was left for burial was a tooth.

TORRE DAS CABAÇAS

This 15th-century **bell tower** (Torre do Relógio; adult/child €1/free; 🕑 9am-12.30pm & 2-5.30pm), opposite the Museu Arqueológico, houses the imaginative, unusual **Núcleo Museológico do Tempo** (Museum of Time). With weather vanes, ancient sundials, a revolving upturned pyramid and an intricate 19th-century clock mechanism in a glass case, it's a beguiling small collection. There are good views from the top.

PORTAS DO SOL

The **Portas do Sol** (Gates of the Sun) is a garden on the site of the Moorish citadel, high up at the southeastern edge of town, and by far the town's best viewpoint. It's a lovely place for a picnic, with aviaries and a pond, and the views are amazing: you can see over the Rio Tejo and far across the plains beyond.

Festivals & Events

Santarém's Feira Nacional da Agricultura (National Agriculture Fair; first week in June) is famous nationwide for its merriment, horse races, bullfights and night-time bull-running in the streets. It lasts for 10 days and mostly takes place 2km west of the town centre. There are lots of children's events.

Festival Nacional de Gastronómia (end October) Held over a fortnight at the Casa do Campino, it encourages you to eat as much traditional Portuguese fare as you can. Stalls sell regional specialities and some restaurants from 18 different regions present their finest cuisine.

Sleeping

BUDGET

Pousada da juventude (☎ 243 391 914; santarem@movijovem.pt; Avenida Grupo Forcados Amadores de Santarém; dm/d €9.50/26.50) Attached to the Instituto Português da Juventude, this is near the bullring and offers institutional cheap-and-cheerful accommodation.

Residencial Vitória (☎ 243 309 130; Rua 2 Visconde de Santarém 21; s/d €25/40) Tucked away in a quiet residential area, this is a night-at-your-great-aunt's-type place run by Dona Vitória herself as well as various elderly hangers-on. It's comfortable enough, and easy to park nearby.

Parque de campismo (☎ 243 557 040; adult/tent/car €3/3/2) The nearest camp site is at Alpiarça, 15km to the east; a good site and close to a reservoir.

MID-RANGE

Residencial Muralha (☎ 243 322 399; fax 243 329 477; Rua Pedro Canavarro 12; s/d €30/35) By the old town walls, this is charming and has a genteel air, with tiles and eclectic ornaments.

Residencial Beirante (☎ 243 322 547; Rua Alexandre Herculano 3; s/d with breakfast €30/45) Better than it looks from the outside, this is a big two-storey affair with decent, functional rooms.

TOP END

Casa da Alcáçova (☎ 243 304 030; www.alcacova.com; Largo da Alcáçova; s/d with breakfast €110/150; 🅿) A 17th-century manor house that's inside the city walls, with superb views and eight doubles.

Eating & Drinking

As you'd expect of a student-packed agricultural town, Santarém is well off for good-value restaurants.

BUDGET

Bar do Bêco (☎ 243 322 937; Bêco da Cacaimba; snacks €1-4; breakfast, lunch & dinner Mon-Fri) A cubby-hole café, this has small tiled tables and is a popular lunch stop for its soups and sandwiches.

Restaurante Snack Bar O Solar (☎ 243 322 239; Emilio Infante da Câmara 9; mains €4.50-8; 10am-midnight Sun-Fri) With a terracotta floor and exposed brick wall, set against lace curtains, O Solar is simple yet refined, good for a snack or full lunch.

Taberna do Quinzena (☎ 243 322 804; Rua Pedro de Santarém 93; mains around €3-7; lunch & dinner Mon-Sat) This is a typical Portuguese male-dominated taverna. The walls are plastered with brightly coloured bullfighting posters to give it that air of machismo. At lunch it serves grilled mains and some snacks and salads, and in the evening just one set dish. Saloon-style swing doors mean you can make an entrance.

O Saloio (☎ 243 327 656; Travessa do Montalvo 11; mains €2.80-8; lunch & dinner Tue-Sat) A cosy, tiled, buzzing *tasca* (tavern). Great for families, with tasty food. There's some outside seating.

MID-RANGE

O Mal Cozinhado (☎ 243 323 584; Campo de Feiras; mains around €7.50-12; lunch & dinner Tue-Sun) South of town, you'll need to nose around the dark desolate area around the bullring to find it, but it's worth it; justly popular, smart but rustic, with white tablecloths, a plough hanging from the ceiling, and terracotta floor. The food is good (the name of the restaurant – 'Badly Cooked' – is a joke) Half-portions are available.

Café Central (☎ 243 322 303; Rua Guilherme de Azevedo 32; mains €4.75-13; 8am-2pm Mon-Sat) With cool chrome and Art Deco decor, and outside tables for checking out the street, this is a popular place in the heart of the town, serving a good range of traditional dishes.

Aromatejo (☎ 917 598 861; Travessa do Bairro Falco; mains €8.50-10; dinner Wed-Sun) Overlooking the Tejo, this is a garden restaurant with a fantastic river-and-rural view. It's small inside but has an outside terrace. The food is recommended, including mains such as aromatic beef and shellfish rice. It's also a bar, licensed to open till 2am.

O Telheiro da Lúcia (☎ 243 328 581) There's a culinary speciality in this region called *fataça na telha* (mullet fish grilled on a tile). The best place to try it is at this simple riverside place in Caneiras, 5km south of town, where, as well as the famous fish, you can sample Lúcia's home-baked bread. Call ahead to check availability.

Getting There & Away

BUS

Buses (☎ 243 322 001) to Lisbon (€5.50, 1¼ hours, 12 daily). Two to four buses run daily to Caldas da Rainha (€4.10, two to four daily) and Fátima (normal/express €4.30/6.50, 1¾ hours/45 minutes, five daily).

TRAIN

Very frequent IC (€5.80) and IR (€3.90) trains go to Lisbon (45 minutes). Buses run between the town and train station nine times daily (€1, 12 minutes) while **taxis** (☎ 243 322 919) charge €4 for the trip.

CASTELO DE ALMOUROL

A 10-towered castle stranded on an island looks like the setting for a chivalrous romance. This extraordinary site seems to have popped from a legend, but was built by Gualdim Pais, Grand Master of the Order of the Knights Templar, in 1171 on the site of an earlier Roman fort. It's unsurprising it caught the imagination of many excitable Age of Chivalry poets.

Sleeping & Eating

It's best to stay in nearby Constância (where poet Luís de Camões once lived), 5km east of Almourol. It has a pretty old town and riverside setting.

Casa João Chagas (☎ 249 739 403; vilapoema@mail.telepac.pt; Rua João Chagas; s/d Mon-Thu €40/45, Fri & Sat €45/50) This is an old house with modern trappings that positively gleam with cleanliness.

Casa o Palacio (☎ 249 739 224; Rua João Chagas; d €75) This is a lovely Turihab place near Casa João Chagas, on the waterfront.

João Chagas also runs **O Café da Praça**, opposite Casa o Palacio; try the fantastic *queijinhos do Céu* (sweets from heaven), still made by local nuns.

Getting There & Away

The tiny Almourol train station is 1km uphill from the castle. Four trains daily from Lisbon via Santarém (€2.10, 45 minutes), with a change at Entroncamento, stop here and at Praia do Ribatejo (€2.10, 55 minutes), the station serving Constância.

A **ferry** (☎ 249 733 062, 914 506 562) takes visitors across to the island and back for €1 per person – inquire about round-island trips.

Esplanada–Bar do Zézère (☎ 249 739 972; Esplanada) in Constância hires out bikes (€8 per day) and canoes.

TOMAR

pop 43,140 / elevation 70m

Tomar is home to the Convento de Cristo, a Unesco World Heritage site, a mysterious, rambling, extraordinary castle-monastery that could have sprung from a storybook, the hilltop headquarters of the legendary Knights Templar, in the heart of a wood.

The town itself is worth exploring. It is straddled across the Rio Nabão and its large water wheel is used for irrigating the land. The narrow grid of streets contains some fine churches, and neighbours the glorious, lush Mata Nacional dos Sete Montes (Seven Hills National Forest) spreading down from the monastery walls. Nearby you can explore charming countryside alongside the Castelo de Bode reservoir.

Orientation

The Rio Nabão neatly divides the town, with new developments largely concentrated on the east bank and the old town to the west. The monastery looks down on it all from a wooded hilltop above the town to the west.

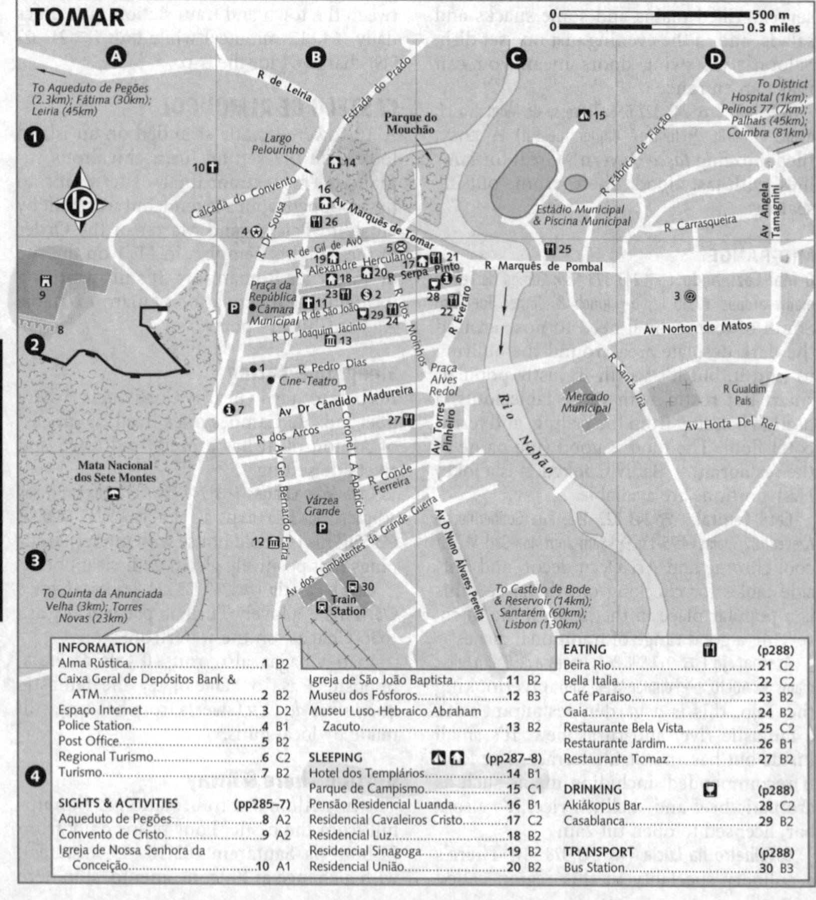

THE ORDER OF THE KNIGHTS TEMPLAR

French knights founded this religious military order in about 1119, to protect pilgrims visiting the Holy Land from marauding Muslims. The templar name came when King Baldwin of Jerusalem housed them in his palace, in what was once a Jewish temple.

The Knights became a strictly organised, semireligious gang headed by a Grand Master. Each Templar took vows of poverty and chastity, and wore white coats emblazoned with a red cross to show how holy they were – you'll see this symbol stamped in many churches. By 1139 they came under the pope's authority and were the leading defenders of the Christian crusader states in the Holy Land. In Portugal their main role was to help to expel the Moors.

Rewarded for all their good works with land, castles and titles, the order boomed, with properties all over Europe, the Mediterranean and the Holy Land. This network, and their military strength, gave them another influential role: bankers to kings and pilgrims.

By the mid-13th century, however, Christians had recaptured Portugal, and by 1300 the Knights Templar were at something of a loose end.

There was talk of merging the order with their age-old rivals, the Hospitallers (another military religious order), but in France things began to turn ugly when King Philip IV – eager for Templar wealth or afraid of Templar power – initiated an era of persecution (supported by the French pope Clement V). He arrested all of the knights, accusing many of heresy and seizing their property. In 1314, the last French Grand Maître (Master) was burned at the stake.

In Portugal, Dom Dinis followed the trend by dissolving the order in 1314, but a few years later he cannily re-established it as the Order of Christ, under the royal thumb. It was largely thanks to the order's wealth that Prince Henry the Navigator (Grand Master from 1417 to 1460) was able to fund the Age of Discoveries. Later Dom João III took the order into a humbler phase, shifting it towards monastic duties. In 1834, together with all of the other religious orders, it finally was dissolved.

The bus and train station are close together, about 500m south of the turismo. Car drivers are advised to park in the large free car park by the bus station.

Information

Alma Rústica (☎ 249 314 237; Rua do Teatro 28; ⏲ 10am-7pm Tue-Sun) A wonderful ethnographic shop selling Portuguese arts and crafts, CDs and books – if the multilingual owners are on duty they have lots of useful tips on the town.

Caixa Geral de Depósitos (☎ 249 321 975; Rua Serpa Pinto 97) Among the numerous banks with an ATM.

District hospital (☎ 249 320 100; Via da Cintura) A new hospital 1km east of town.

Espaço Internet (☎ 249 312 291; Rua Amorim Rosa; ⏲ 9.30am-10pm Mon-Sat) Free Net access.

Police station (☎ 249 329 867; Rua Dr Sousa)

Post office (☎ 249 310 400; Avenida Marquês de Tomar; ⏲ 8.30am-6pm Mon-Sat)

Regional turismo (☎ 249 329 000; fax 249 324 322; Rua Serpa Pinto 1; ⏲ Mon-Fri) Head here for information about other places in the region.

Turismo (☎/fax 249 322 427; Avenida Dr Cândido Madureira; ⏲ 10am-1pm & 2-6pm, 10am-7pm Jul & Aug) Not massively helpful but has a town map and an accommodation list with prices. It also has a small 1:5000 map (with paths marked) of the national forest.

Sights

CONVENTO DE CRISTO

Wrapped in splendour and mystique, the Knights Templar held enormous power from the 12th to 16th centuries, and partly bankrolled the Age of Discoveries. This, their headquarters, is a stony expression of magnificence combined with no-holds-barred theatricality that gave the order such an enduring fascination. It's set on wooded slopes above the town and enclosed within 12th-century walls – you almost expect dry ice to swirl around the entrance.

The **monastery** (☎ 249 313 481; adult/youth or student €4.50/2, 9am-noon Sun free; ⏲ 9am-6.30pm Jun-Sep, 9am-5.30pm Oct-May; last admission 30 min before closing) was founded in 1160 by Gualdim Pais, Grand Master of the Templars. It has a number of various chapels, cloisters and chapterhouses, added over the centuries by successive kings and Grand Masters, with amazing changing architectural styles. You can follow a short route (45 minutes) or take a more comprehensive 90-minute tour.

Charola

This 16-sided Templar **church** dominates the monastery. The interior is otherworldly in its vast height, faded colour and shapes. It doesn't feel like a church at all, more of a *Star Wars* set – appropriately enough as the knights spent much time in a self-styled crusade against the dark forces (the Moors). But this sacred centre of the building does have a circular aisle with a high altar enclosed within a central octagon. The 12th-century round design was based on the Church of the Holy Sepulchre in Jerusalem. It's said that the Knights Templar used to arrive here on horseback for Mass. Restored wall paintings date from the early 16th century. A huge funnel to the left is an ancient organ pipe (the organ itself is long gone).

Dom Manuel was responsible for tacking the nave on to the west side of the Charola and for commissioning the architect Diogo de Arruda to build a chapterhouse with a *coro alto* (choir) above it. The main western doorway into the nave – a splendid example of Spanish plateresque style (named after the ornate work of silversmiths) – is the work of Spanish architect João de Castilho, who later repeated his success at Belém's Mosteiro dos Jerónimos (p92).

Claustro do Cemitério & Claustro da Lavagem

These two serene, azulejo-decorated **cloisters** to the east of the Charola were built during the time when Prince Henry the Navigator was Grand Master of the order in the 15th century. The Claustro do Cemitério (Burial-Ground Cloisters) contains two 16th-century tombs, while the water tanks of the two-storey Claustro da Lavagem (Ablutions Cloisters) is now full of plants.

Chapterhouse

Seeming to have grown from the wall like a frenzied barnacle, the window on the western side of the **chapterhouse** is the most famous and fantastical feature of the monastery. It's the ultimate in Manueline extravagance, a celebration of the Age of Discoveries: a Medusa tangle of snaking ropes, seaweed and cork boats, on top of all which floats the Cross of the Order of Christ and the royal arms and armillary spheres of Dom Manuel. It's covered in lichen – which seems appropriate given the seaworthy themes.

Designed around 1510 by the Manueline master, Diogo de Arruda (he and his brother were also responsible for Lisbon's Torre de Belém, p93), it's best seen from the roof of the adjacent Claustro de Santa Bárbara. Follow signs to the *janela* (window).

Unfortunately obscured by the Claustro Principal is an almost equivalent window on the southern side of the chapterhouse.

Claustro Principal

The elegant Renaissance **Claustro Principal** (Great Cloisters) stand in striking contrast to the flamboyance of the monastery's Manueline architecture. Commissioned during the reign of João III, they were probably designed by the Spaniard Diogo de Torralva but were completed in 1587 by an Italian, Filippo Terzi. These foreign architects were among several responsible for introducing a delayed Renaissance style into Portugal. The Claustro Principal is arguably the country's finest expression of that style: a sober ensemble of Greek columns and Tuscan pillars, gentle arches and sinuous, spiralling staircases.

The outlines of a second chapterhouse, commissioned by João III but never finished, can be seen from the cloisters' southwestern corner.

AQUEDUTO DE PEGÕES

This immensely impressive **aqueduct**, striding towards the monastery from the northwest, was built from 1593 to 1613, to supply water to the monastery. With 180 arches, in some places double-decker, it's thought to have been designed by Italian Filippo Terzi. It's best seen just off the Leiria road, 2.3km from town.

IGREJA DE NOSSA SENHORA DA CONCEIÇÃO

Downhill from the monastery sits this strikingly simple, small, pure Renaissance **basilica**, built in the 16th century. It's believed to have been designed by Diogo de Torralva, who is also responsible for the Convento cloisters. At the time of writing it was closed for restoration.

IGREJA DE SÃO JOÃO BAPTISTA

The old town's most striking **church** (admission free; 9.30am-6pm) faces Praça da República, itself an eye-catching ensemble of 17th-century buildings. The newly restored church, now blindingly white, dates mostly from the late 15th century. It has an octagonal spire and richly ornamented Manueline doorways on its northern and western sides. Inside are 16th and 17th-century azulejos, and Gregório Lopes, one of the finest of Portugal's 16th-century artists, painted the six panels hanging inside.

MUSEU LUSO-HEBRAICO ABRAHAM ZACUTO

On a charming cobbled lane in the old town, you'll find the country's best-preserved medieval **synagogue** (Rua Dr Joaquim Jacinto 73; admission free; 10am-1pm & 2-6pm). Built between 1430 and 1460, it was used for only a few years, until Dom Manuel's convert-or-leave edict of 1496 forced most Jews to do the latter. The synagogue subsequently served as a prison, chapel, hay loft and warehouse until it was classified as a national monument in 1921.

Mostly thanks to the efforts of Luís Vasco (who comes from one of two Jewish families left in Tomar), who is often present, the small, plain building is now recreated to something like it would have been. It's named after the 15th-century Jewish mathematician and royal astrologer, who helped Vasco da Gama plan his voyages. Inside are various tombstones engraved with 13th- and 14th-century Hebraic inscriptions, as well as many touching gifts and contributions from international Jewish visitors. The upturned jars high in the wall were a device to improve acoustics. It's hoped one day to establish a museum on Jewish history next door.

MUSEU DOS FÓSFOROS

This **museum** (admission free; 2-5pm) is housed in the lovely Convento de São Francisco and is a collection of over 40,000 matchboxes. Unsurprisingly, this is the largest collection in Europe, amassed by phillumenist – a word that could have been invented for him – Aquiles da Mota Lima from the 1950s onwards.

Activities

Tomar has a generous supply of organisations that offer walking, biking, canoeing trips, rock climbing and even parachuting. Most are geared to groups, but (with advance notice) may be able to accommodate individuals. **Via Aventura** (☎/fax 249 324 464; www.aventura.web.pt; Rua Marquês de Pombal 2), which organises regular Saturday afternoon canoeing jaunts on the Rio Nabão in town and rents out canoes and bikes. Other major players include **1000 Léguas** (☎ 249 324 807; correio@1000leguas.com; 20-25 hr course €200-300) which runs canoeing and climbing courses. For horse riding contact **Coudelaria Ruy Escudeiro** (☎ 249 314 371), about 3km from town.

FESTA DOS TABULEIROS

Tomar's Festival of the Trays is a dazzling display of young women balancing top-heavy trays on their heads. It has roots in pagan fertility rites, though officially it's related to the saintly practices of 14th-century Dona Isabel (Dom Dinis' queen).

There's music, dancing and fireworks, but the festival's claim to absurdity is a procession of about 400 young white-clad women (traditionally virgins!) bearing headdresses of trays stacked as tall as they are with loaves and ears of wheat, decorated with colourful paper flowers and topped with a crown and then a cross or a white paper dove. Young male attendants (not required to be virgins), dressed in black and white, help the girls balance the load, which can weigh up to 15kg. The following day, bread and wine are blessed by the priest and handed out to local families.

The festival is held every four years; the next one is in 2007 (first weekend in July).

Festivals & Events

Festa dos Tabuleiros Tomar's most famous event is the teetering tray-spectacular (see above).

Nossa Senhora da Piedade (first Sunday in September) This is another important religious festival – the candle procession when floats decorated with paper flowers are paraded through the streets.

Sleeping

BUDGET

Residencial União (☎ 249 323 161; fax 249 321 299; Rua Serpa Pinto 94; s/d with breakfast €25/40) Smarter than Luz and on the same pedestrianised road, this has better, old-fashioned rooms and a nice courtyard out the back.

Residencial Luz (☎ 249 312 317; www.residencialluz.com; Rua Serpa Pinto 144; s/d €20/30) This quite

ESTREMADURA & RIBATEJO

threadbare place in a fine, central old building has reasonable, if drab, rooms.

Parque de campismo (☎ 249 376 421; adult/tent/car €3.15/2.75/2) Tomar's municipal camp site is next to the football stadium and municipal swimming pool, and near the huge Castelo do Bode reservoir.

Pelinos 77 (☎ 249 301 814; adult/tent/car €3/2.50/1.50;) This camp site is 7km northeast at Pelinos. It is pleasantly remote and small, with simple facilities; bus connections are poor.

MID-RANGE

Residencial Cavaleiros Cristo (☎ 249 321 203; residencialcavcristo@sapo.pt; Rua Alexandre Herculano 7; s/d 40/60;) A smart place, with nicely decorated rooms that are a real bargain off-season around 40% discounts.

Pensão Residencial Luanda (☎ 249 323 200; Avenida Marquês de Tomar 15; s/d €30/55;) A nice place run by a very jovial owner. There's a restaurant downstairs. There are some cheaper rooms on the top floor with shared bathroom.

Residencial Sinagoga (☎ 249 323 083; residencial.sinagoga@clix.pt; Rua de Gil de Avô; s/d €35/50) In a quiet residential area, rooms are biggish and old fashioned, with '70s furniture and balconies.

TOP END

Hotel dos Templários (☎ 249 321 730; www.hoteldostemplarios.pt; Largo Cândido dos Reis 1; s/d €90/105;) This is big and modern in lovely green grounds, overlooking the river. It's Tomar's smartest and where to go if you want to feel like you're at a conference.

Quinta da Anunciada Velha (☎ 249 345 218; d €65, 2-/4-person apt €80/110) Among several lovely Turihab properties in the area and the nearest to Tomar, 3km southwest of town at Cem Soldos.

Eating

Beira Rio (☎ 249 312 806; Rua Alexandre Herculano 1; mains €5.50-8; lunch & dinner Tue-Sun) With a cosy, traditional feel, this is a small snug place with simple dishes.

Restaurante Tomaz (☎ 249 312 552; Rua dos Arcos 31; mains €4-8; lunch & dinner Mon-Sat, dinner Sun Apr-Aug) A popular, bright option, this is friendly with appealing outside tables and simple food such as *bacalhau á bras* (cod fried with onions and potatoes).

Restaurante Jardim (☎ 249 312 034; Rua Silva Magalhães 39; mains €4.50-8; lunch & dinner Sun-Fri) A small, bright, tiled place; the list of local wines is almost as long as the menu.

Gaia (Rua do São João; mains €4.50-8; lunch Tue-Sun, dinner Tue-Sat) This is a vegetarian restaurant and takeaway, with mains such as tofu lasagne, as well as the rather unvegie *bacalhau*.

Bella Italia (☎ 249 322 996; Rua Everaro 91; mains €4.25-9.50; lunch & dinner Wed-Mon) The '70s metallic ceiling differentiates this place from the usual café. It's popular and serves up tasty, good pasta mains in HUGE portions.

For snacks, don't miss **Café Paraiso** (Rua de Serpa Pinto; snacks €1-4; breakfast, lunch & dinner), a key town meeting place with a cool high ceiling and outside tables.

MID-RANGE

Restaurante Bela Vista (☎ 249 312 870; Rua Fonte do Choupo 6; mains €6-9; lunch & dinner Tue-Sun) Bela Vista has a lovely position by the river; its outdoor tables are surrounded by big fern pots, shaded by wisteria and overlook the river.

Drinking

Akiákopus Bar (Rua de São João 28; 9.30pm-2am, to 4am Fri & Sat) This looks intimidating as you have to ring the doorbell, but inside it is like any [illegible] with mixed men and [illegible]den chairs and tables. [illegible] João 85; 10pm-3am Wed- [illegible] is a cool bar, which [illegible]

Entertainment

Fatias de Cá (☎ 249 314 161; www.fatiasdeca.com) A Tomar-based theatre company which presents highly innovative and entertaining performances such as *The Name of the Rose* and *Perfume* often in amazing locations (eg castles, distilleries or old palaces, including the Convento de Cristo). Performances are usually Thursday, Friday and Saturday.

Getting There & Away

From the **bus terminal** (☎ 249 312 738) there are buses daily to Lisbon (€6.50, two hours, three Saturday, four Sunday) and three to both Fátima (€5.50, 40 minutes) and Leiria (€6.70, 1¼ hours). Weekday trains run to/from Lisbon (€6.80, two hours, hourly). There are services to Santarém (€4, one hour).

The Beiras

CONTENTS

Graced by glistening mountains, a surf-caressed coastline and vital cultural hotspots, the Beiras region forms one of Portugal's most diverse landscapes. Indeed, it could be said to mirror Portugal's own multiple personalities.

The coastal region, Beira Litoral, is dominated by Coimbra – a distinguished city celebrated for its *fado* music, ancient university and atmospheric medieval heart. Around it are scattered many tempting diversions – from holy forests and hilltop fortresses to spa-towns and remote rural retreats. Here too is Conimbriga, site of some of the Iberian Peninsula's most impressive Roman ruins.

Meanwhile, Beira Litoral's refreshingly unspoilt coastline is strung with deep golden beaches, punctuated with low-key seaside settlements; the only major resort is cheerful Figueira da Foz. In the north, Aveiro presides over a complex estuary, rich in birdlife.

But move inland, and the picture changes rapidly. Straddling Beira Alta and Beira Baixa is Portugal's highest mountain range, the spectacular Serra da Estrela. Atlantic air masses tumble against this granite range, spilling their moisture and giving birth to the Rio Mondego, the longest exclusively Portuguese river. Here, too, is the country's hiking, biking and skiing heartland in the rugged Parque Natural da Serra da Estrela.

Spreading to the north and hemmed in by mountains, Beira Alta is another tough landscape populated by resilient people. This was the heartland of the Lusitani, who, under the legendary Viriato – Portugal's original national hero – so stubbornly resisted the Romans. Yet it holds pockets of exquisite Renaissance art and rich refined wines.

The region's multifaceted personality then culminates in lowland Beira Baixa, with its good-natured people, ferocious summer weather and hypnotically flat landscapes of cork oaks, olive groves and giant agricultural estates. Here lie the little-visited hilltop fortresses of Monsanto and Sortelha, lone bastions in a sea of rural quietude.

HIGHLIGHTS

- **Culture Stop**
  Ancient, fado-loving university town, Coimbra (p291)
- **Mad for Mosaics**
  Portugal's finest Roman ruins, Conimbriga (p303)
- **Country Haven**
  Hallowed forest of Buçaco (p304) and Luso spa (p304)
- **Pristine Peaks**
  Parque Natural da Serra da Estrela (p323)
- **King of the Castle**
  Medieval fortresses of Monsanto (p320) and Sortelha (p322)

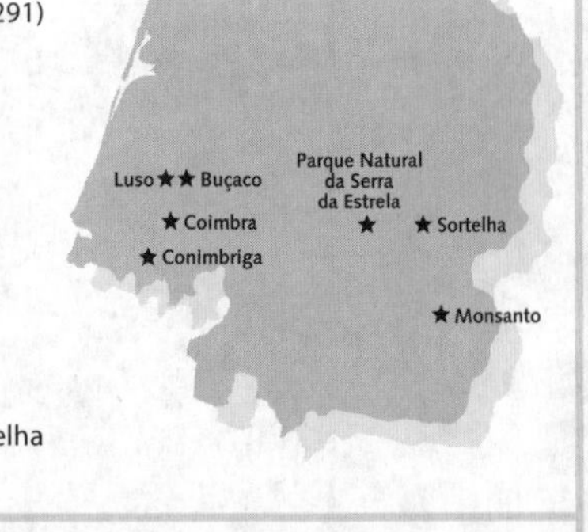

- POPULATION: 2,348,397
- AREA: 22,067 SQ KM

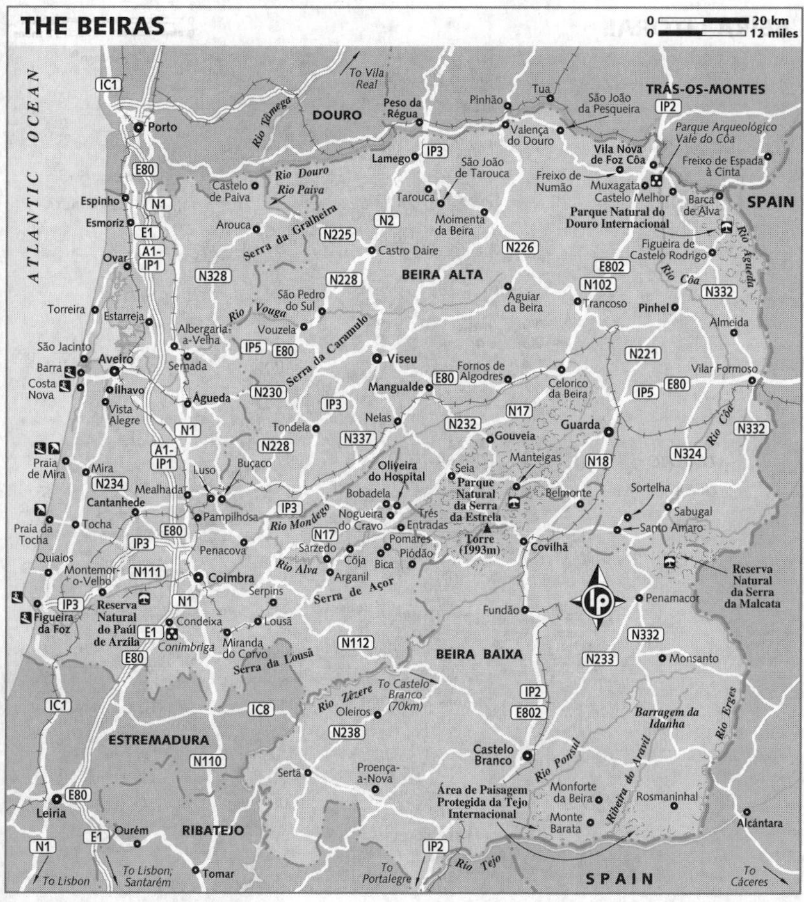

BEIRA LITORAL

Beira Litoral (coastal Beiras) rolls down from the mountains of landlocked Beira Alta and Beira Baixa to the sea. Occupying a chunky strip of the central Portuguese coast, this region is famous for its cultural capital, Coimbra, as well as its forests, spas and unique historical landscape.

COIMBRA

pop 102,000 / elevation 150m

Jewel in the Beiras' crown, the city of Coimbra (say *queem*-bra) grins and bears its international labelling as the 'Oxford of Portugal'. With a pedigree equal to any European seat of learning, the city's university was founded way back in 1290, and remains the focus of the cultural energy that earned it the title of Capital Nacional da Cultura in 2003.

Perched above the Rio Mondego midway between Lisbon and Porto, Coimbra knew glory even before the university put down its roots. And with treasures dating back as far as 850 years, you don't have to wander far to feel yourself slipping back in time.

However, Coimbra's great appeal lies in the fact that its ancient centre still teems with life. This is no museum-piece city preserved for snap-happy tourists. Ancient back lanes winding to the city's crown still channel those last-minute dashes to lectures, cafés bristle with groups bent on

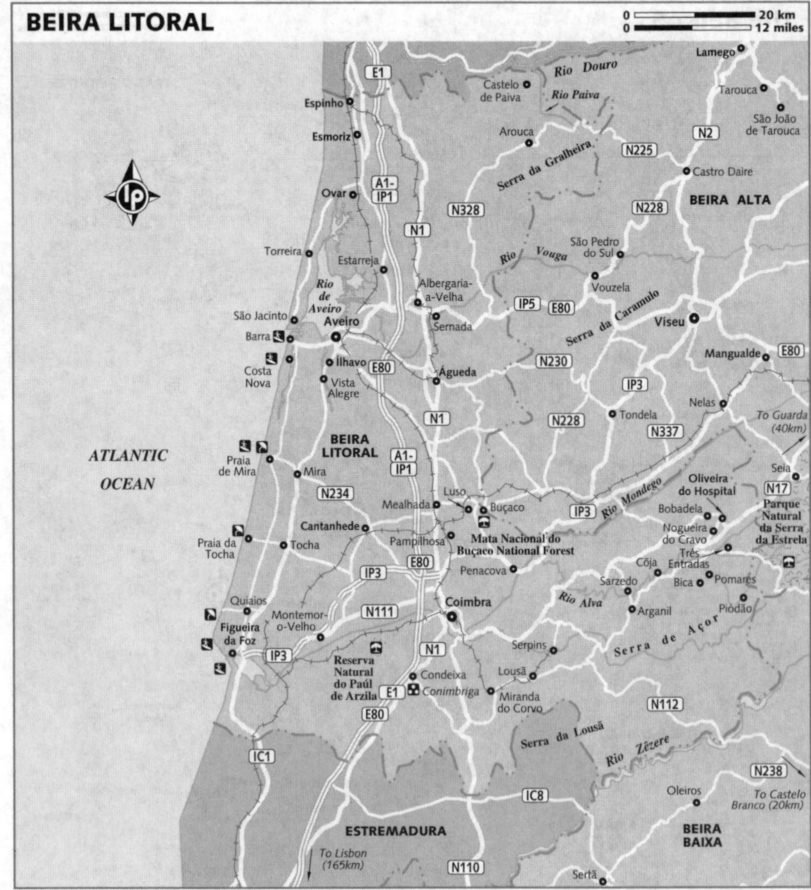

solving the world's problems, high culture is leavened with a bumptious student nightlife and the haunting sounds of fado music still echo late into the night.

Even if you visit outside university term time Coimbra has an immutable charm, and there is a wealth of excellent day-trip destinations nearby, including the stunning Roman ruins at Conimbriga (see p303).

If you're here in May, throw yourself into Coimbra's boozy student bash, Queima das Fitas (p299).

History

The Romans first gained a foothold at Conimbriga, while the Moors put their feet firmly under the table in Coimbra itself until the Christians booted them out in the 12th century. The city was Portugal's capital in 1145 but, just over a century later, Afonso III moved the capital to Lisbon.

The Universidade de Coimbra, Portugal's first university (and among the first in Europe), was actually founded in Lisbon by Dom Dinis in 1290 but settled here in 1537, attracting a steady stream of teachers, artists and intellectuals from across Europe. The 16th century was a particularly heady time thanks to Nicolas Chanterène, Jean de Rouen (João de Ruão) and other French sculptors who helped create a school of sculpture here that influenced styles all over Portugal.

Today Coimbra's university remains the country's most prestigious academic establishment. The city's prosperity, however, has traditionally come from its three Ts: tanning, textiles (although Asian competition has textile firms on the skids) and tourism.

Orientation

Compact Coimbra is best toured on foot. Crowning its steep hilltop is the university, around and below which lie a tangle of lanes that mark the boundaries of the old town.

The new town, locally called 'Baixa', sprawls at the foot of the hill and along the Rio Mondego. Hubs of activity down below include the pedestrian shopping axis of Rua Ferreira Borges and Rua Visconde

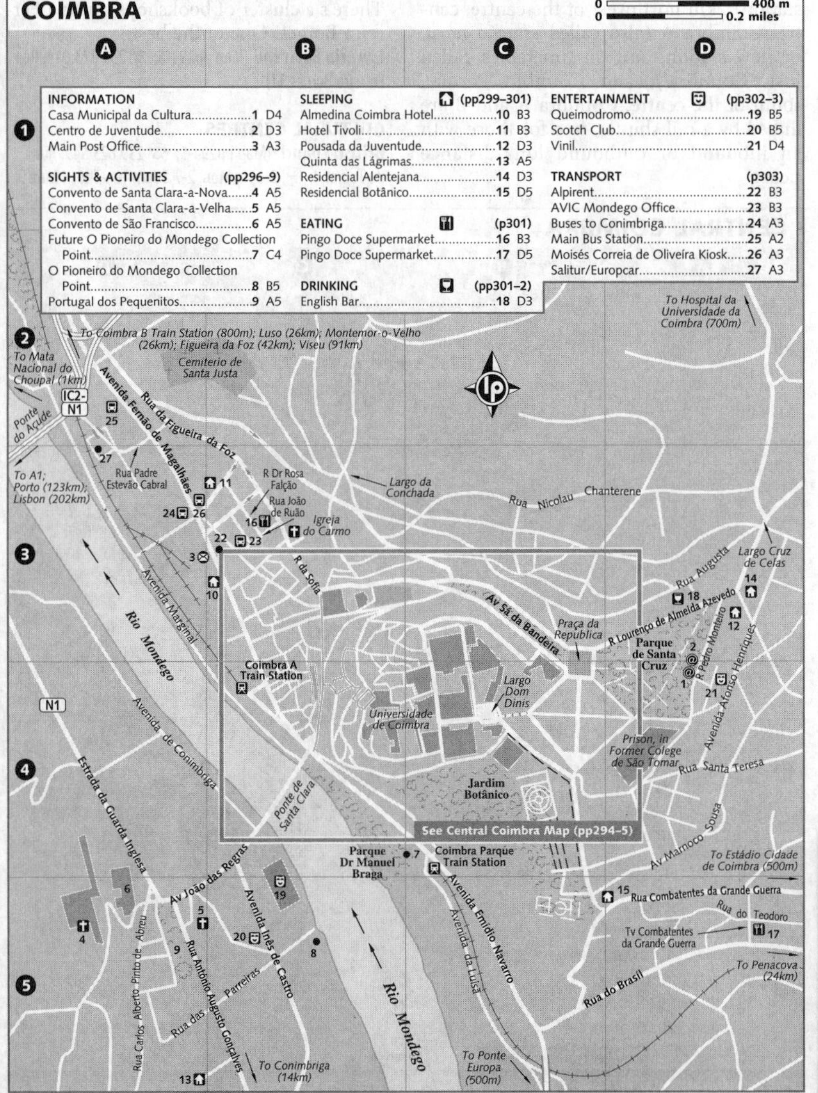

da Luz (also called the Calçada) to the west, and Praça da República to the east. Sights of interest across the river are also accessible on foot via the Ponte de Santa Clara.

From the main bus station on Avenida Fernão de Magalhães it's about 1.2km to the old centre. There are three train stations: Coimbra B (also called *estação velha,* or old station) 2km northwest of the centre; central Coimbra A (also called *estação nova,* or new station, and on timetables called just 'Coimbra'); and Coimbra Parque, south of the centre. Coimbra A and B are linked by a rail shuttle, free for those with an inbound or outbound long-distance ticket.

If you come by car, be ready for traffic jams and scarce parking. One place to leave your vehicle for a day hike around town is across the river on Avenida de Conimbriga.

Pick up a map of the city centre in any of Coimbra's tourist offices.

Information

BOOKSHOPS

There's a cluster of bookshops on Rua Ferreira Borges. One of the best:

Livraria Bertrand (Map pp294-5; ☎ 239 823 014; Rua Ferreira Borges 11)

CULTURAL CENTRES

British Council (Map pp294-5; ☎ 239 823 549; Rua de Tomar 4; 2-6pm Mon, 2-7.30pm Tue-Thu, 10am-

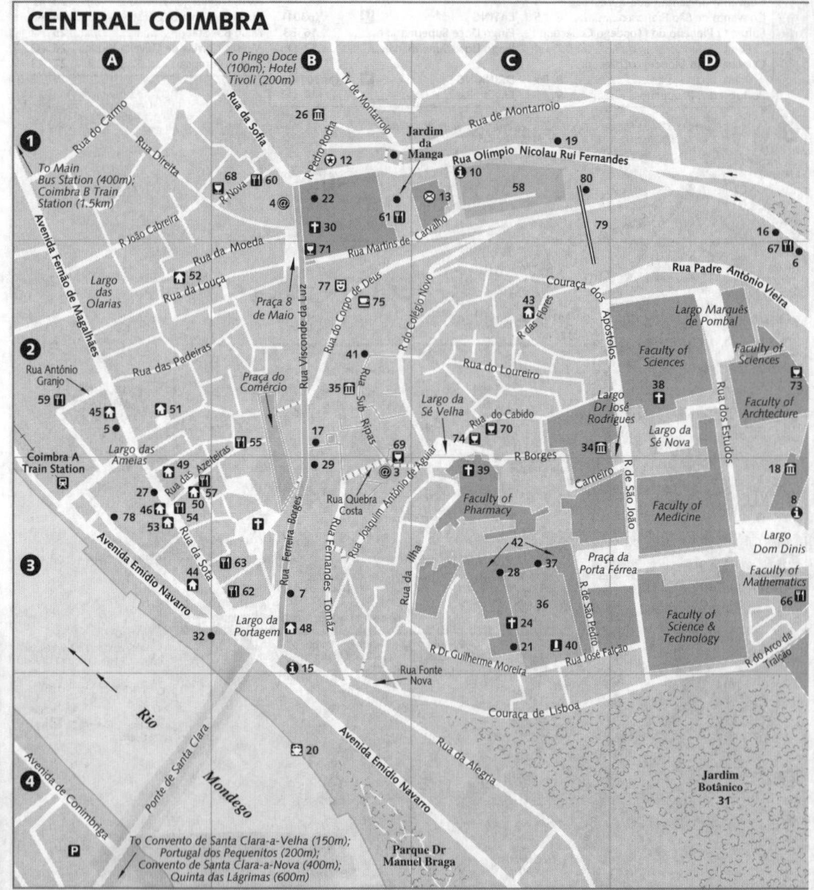

7.30pm Fri, 10am-12.30pm & 1.30-4pm Sat; closed Aug) Catch up with British newspapers at the library here.

EMERGENCY

Police Stations Rua Olímpio Nicolau Rui Fernandes (Map pp294-5; ☎ 239 822 022); Rua Venâncio Rodrigues (☎ 239 828 134; Rua Venâncio Rodrigues 25-31)

INTERNET ACCESS

Casa Municipal da Cultura (Map p293; ☎ 239 702 630; Rua Pedro Monteiro; ⏲ 10am-12.30pm & 2-6.30pm Mon-Fri, 2-6pm Sat) Limited free access at the public library. However, you must first obtain a free library card.

Centralmodem (Map pp294-5; Rua Quebra Costas; per 15 mins €0.55; ⏲ 11am-1am Mon-Fri) A handy Internet café.

Centro de Juventude (Map p293; ☎ 239 790 600; Rua Pedro Monteiro 73; ⏲ 9am-12.30pm & 2-5.30pm Mon-Fri) Free Internet access.

Esp@ço Internet (Map pp294-5; ☎ 239 824 151; Praça 8 de Maio 37; ⏲ 10am-8pm Mon-Fri, 10am-10pm Sat & Sun) Municipally sponsored space for free Internet access.

LAUNDRY

Lavandaria Lucira (Map pp294-5; ☎ 239 825 701; Avenida Sá da Bandeira 86; ⏲ 9am-1pm & 3-7pm Mon-Fri, 9am-1pm Sat) Coimbra has no self-service laundrettes but you can leave your laundry to be machine-washed & dried here.

MEDICAL SERVICES

Hospital da Universidade da Coimbra (☎ 239 400 400; Largo Professor Mota Pinto) Located 1.5km northeast of the centre.

MONEY

There are numerous banks with ATMs along Avenida Fernão de Magalhães, Avenida Emídio Navarro and Rua Ferreira Borges.

POST

Main post office (Map p293; ☎ 239 850 700; Avenida Fernão de Magalhães 223; 🕑 8.30am-6.30pm Mon-Fri) Best place for poste restante.

Branch post offices Praça da República (Map pp294-5; ☎ 239 851 820; 🕑 9am-6pm Mon-Fri); Rua Olímpio Nicolau Rui Fernandes (Map pp294-5; ☎ 239 851 870; 🕑 8.30am-6.30pm Mon-Fri & 9am-12.30pm Sat)

TOURIST INFORMATION

Good town maps as well as a very detailed bi-monthly cultural agenda, *Coimbra Viva* and other regional agendas, are available from the following four tourist offices:

Municipal turismos Largo Dom Dinis (Map pp294-5; ☎ 239 832 591; 🕑 9am-6pm Mon-Fri, 9am-12.30pm & 2-5.30pm Sat & Sun); Praça da República (Map pp294-5; ☎ 239 833 202; 🕑 10am-6.30pm Mon-Fri, 10am-1pm & 2.30pm- 6.30pm Sat & Sun); Rua Olimpio Nicolau Rui Fernandes (Map pp294-5; ☎ 239 834 038; 🕑 9am-6pm Mon-Sat) The turismo on Largo Dom Dinis was closed for renovation in 2004, but set to reopen by 2005.

Regional turismo (Map pp294-5; ☎ 239 488 120; rtc-coimbra@turismo-centro.pt; Largo da Portagem; 🕑 9am-7pm Mon-Fri mid-Jun–Sep, 9am-6pm Oct–mid-Jun; 10am-1pm & 2.30-5.30pm Sat & Sun year-round)

TRAVEL AGENCIES

Intervisa (Map pp294-5; ☎ 239 823 873; intervisacoimbra@mail.telepac.pt; Avenida Fernão de Magalhães 11)

Tagus (Map pp294-5; ☎ 239 834 999; coimbra@viagenstagus.pt; Associação Acadêmica de Coimbra, Rua Padre António Vieira) Head here for student cards and youth travel discounts.

Top Atlântico (Map pp294-5; ☎ 239 855 970; coimbra.ta@topatlantico.com; Avenida Sá da Bandeira 62)

UNIVERSITIES

Associação Acadêmica de Coimbra (AAC; Map pp294-5; ☎ 239 410 400; Rua Padre António Vieira) The university's student union has a sweaty canteen and some student-oriented shops.

Velha Universidade (Old University; Map pp294-5) The historic heart of the university campus and its most interesting part.

Sights

UPPER TOWN — Map pp294–5

Tackling the steep climb from Rua Ferreira Borges to the Velha Universidade takes you plumb into the heart of old Coimbra. Pass beneath the **Arco de Almedina** – the city's heavy-duty Moorish gateway – and up the staggered stairs known as Quebra Costa (Backbreaker). People have been gasping up this hill (and falling down it) for centuries; a local story says it was the 19th-century writer Almeida Garrett who persuaded the mayor to install the stairs.

To the left up Rua Sub Ripas is the grand Manueline doorway of the early-16th-century **Palácio de Sub Ripas**; its Renaissance windows and stone ornaments are the work of Jean de Rouen, whose workshop was nearby. Further on is the **Torre de Anto**, a tower that once formed part of the town walls.

Backtrack and climb via Largo da Sé Velha to the Museu Nacional Machado de Castro and the 'new' campus, much of it founded by the Marquês de Pombal in the 18th century. Dominating Largo da Sé Nova in front of the museum is the severe **sé nova** (new cathedral; ☎ 239 823 138; admission free; 🕑 9.30am-12.30pm & 2-6.30pm Tue-Sat), started by the Jesuits in 1598 but only completed a century later.

For a glimpse of student life, stroll along any of the alleys around the *sé velha* or below the *sé nova*. Flags and graffiti mark the cramped houses known as *repúblicas*, each housing a dozen or so students from the same region or faculty.

VELHA UNIVERSIDADE — Map pp294–5

To overdose on cultural treasures from the 16th to 18th centuries, make a beeline to the Old University. This impressive campus is set around a wide square, the **Patio das Escolas**. Here a **statue of João III** turns his back on a sweeping view of the city and the river (it was he who reestablished the university in Coimbra in 1537 and invited big-shot scholars to teach here).

The square's most prominent feature is a much-photographed 18th-century **clock tower**. This tower is nicknamed *a cabra* (the goat) because, when it chimed to mark the end of studies, the first-year undergrads would be pounced upon by swaggering elder students and then humiliated without mercy – that is, unless they leapt and jumped their way home like mountain goats to avoid them!

From the courtyard gate take the stairway on the right up to the rather grand **Sala dos Capelos** (Graduates' Hall), a former examination room hung with dark portraits of Portugal's kings and heavy patchwork-quilt-like decoration. But better yet is a catwalk that leads alongside it with excellent city views.

Back outside, take a peek to the left below the clock tower, where you'll find the entrance to the fanciful **Capela de São Miguel**, an ornate chapel with a brightly painted ceiling and a gilded baroque organ.

However, all else pales before the **Biblioteca Joanina** (João V Library) next door. A gift from João V himself in the early 18th century, its rosewood, ebony and jacaranda tables, Chinoiserie designs etched in gilt and ceilings with fine frescoes seem far too extravagant and distracting for study. Its 300,000 books, ancient and leather-bound, deal with law, philosophy and theology, though they might as well be painted onto the walls for all the hands-on study they receive now.

It costs €4 to visit all these rooms, or €2.50 to see only the library or the Sala dos Capelos (half-price for visitors aged 65 or over). With suitable identification, students and teachers from any country get a 30% discount from October to mid-March and free admission the rest of the year.

Visitors are only admitted in small numbers and on a timetable, and some rooms may be closed during degree ceremonies. The turismo may insist you book a few days ahead, but you may get in if you front up early and are prepared to wait. The **ticket office** (☎ 239 859 900; ⌚ visits 9am-7.30pm mid-Mar–Sep, 9.30am-12.30pm & 2-5.30pm Oct–mid-Mar) is near the Sala dos Capelos.

SÉ VELHA

Coimbra's chunky old **cathedral** (Map pp294-5; ☎ 239 825 273; Largo da Sé Velha; cloisters adult/under 26/student €0.75/0.50/0.50; ⌚ 10am-6pm Mon-Thu, 10am-1pm Fri, 10am-1pm & 2-6pm Sat) looks more like a fortress, and deliberately so, since it was built in the late 12th century when the Moors were still a threat.

Little has been done to it since then; even the 16th-century Renaissance doorway in the northern wall is so eroded you hardly notice it. Otherwise, what you see is pure, austere Romanesque, one of the finest Portuguese cathedrals of its time. The interior is equally simple, with the exception of a 16th-century gilded altarpiece.

MUSEU NACIONAL MACHADO DE CASTRO

Housed in a former Bishop's Palace, with a 16th-century loggia overlooking the *sé velha* and the old town, this **museum** (Map pp294-5; ☎ 239 823 727; www.ipmuseus.pt; Largo Dr José Rodrigues) houses one of Portugal's most important collections of 14th- to 16th-century sculpture. Alas, this gem closed in 2003 for renovations, with a pencilled-in date for reopening in 2006.

IGREJA DE SANTA CRUZ

From the trendy shops out on Praça 8 de Maio, this **church** (Map pp294-5; ☎ 239 822 941; adult/student/senior €2.50/1/1; ⌚ 9am-noon & 2-5.45pm Mon-Sat, 4-6pm Sun) plunges you back to Manueline and Renaissance times. Step through the Renaissance porch and flamboyant 18th-century arch to find some of the Coimbra School's finest work, including an ornate pulpit and the elaborate tombs – probably carved by Nicolas Chanterène – of Portugal's first kings, Afonso Henriques and Sancho I. The most striking Manueline work is in the restrained 1524 cloister.

At the rear of the church is the **Jardim da Manga** – once part of the cloister – and its curious fountain: a large, sugary lemon-yellow, four-buttressed affair.

EDIFÍCIO CHIADO

This sunlit confection in rippling and coiling iron opened in 1910 as a commercial emporium. Inside is this **museum** (Map pp294-5; ☎ 239 833 771; Rua Ferreira Borges; adult/student/senior €1.50/1/1; ⌚ 11am-7pm Tue-Sun), a branch of the Museu da Cidade, which now hosts exhibitions and a permanent collection of paintings, sculpture, ceramics, furniture and splendid silverware donated by local collector José Carlos Telo de Morais.

OTHER MUSEUMS

Bissaya Barreto was a local surgeon, scholar and obsessive hoarder of fine arts. His handsome late-19th-century mansion has been turned into a museum, **Casa Museu Bissaya Barreto** (Map pp294-5; ☎ 239 853 800; www.fbb.pt in Portuguese; Rua da Infantária 23; admission €2.50;

(⌚ 3-6pm Tue-Sun Easter-Oct, 3-6pm Tue-Fri Nov-Easter), jam-packed with Portuguese sculpture and painting, Chinese porcelain, old *azulejos* (hand-painted tiles) and period furniture.

Photographers can also take a look at the newly inaugurated **CAV** (Centro de Artes Visuais; Map pp294-5; ☎ 239 826 178; Pátio da Inquisição; ⌚ Tue-Sun 10am-7pm), which specialises in photographic exhibitions. It is hidden in the backstreets west of the *câmara municipal*.

AZULEJOS

Coimbra is adorned with some grand azulejos, the finest of them in the former university hospital, now home to the otherwise staid and stuffy **Museu Acadêmico** (Map pp294-5; ☎ 239 827 396; Colégio de São Jerónimo; adult/student/senior €1/0.50/0.50; ⌚ 10am-12.30pm & 2-5pm Mon-Fri), around the corner from Largo Dom Dinis.

ACROSS THE RIVER

In a kind of ecclesiastical counterweight to the university, no less than three former convents cluster together on the far side of the Rio Mondego, along with several other attractions.

Convento de Santa Clara-a-Velha

This muddy **convent** (Map p293), slowly being cleared of the river ooze that has drowned it since the 17th century, has famous connections. It was founded way back in 1330 by Dona Isabel, Dom Dinis' wife, whose tomb was later placed here beside that of the infamous Dona Inês de Castro, the brutally murdered mistress of Dom Pedro (see p270). Though the site is still a semi-quagmire, guided tours in the summer months may soon be possible. For the latest information, inquire at the tourist office.

Convento de Santa Clara-a-Nova

Dona Inês' tomb has since been moved to the Mosteiro de Santa Maria de Alcobaça (p269), while Isabel's solid-silver casket now lies in this staunch 17th-century complex, much of which now serves as an army barracks. Also adjoining the church is an unpious military exhibit, packed with guns, guns and more guns.

The hilltop convent **church** (Map p293; ☎ 239 441 674; admission cloister €1; ⌚ 9.30am-noon & 2-5pm Tue-Sun) is devoted almost entirely to the saintly Isabel's memory – aisle panels tell her life story, others show how her tomb was moved here and her clothes hang in the sacristy. Her statue here is the focus of the Festa de Rainha Santa (p299).

Convento de São Francisco

Between the two Santa Clara convents are the remains of this 18th-century **convent** (Map p293), which did duty as a soap factory in the post-Pombal era. It has since been reserved for use as a convention centre, although for the time being, it's an occasional venue for temporary exhibitions. Finding it open can be a case of pot luck.

Quinta das Lágrimas

Legend says Dona Inês met her grisly end in the gardens of this private estate. It is now a deluxe hotel (p301), although anyone can take a turn about the **gardens** (admission €0.75; ⌚ 9am-5pm), and track down the Fonte dos Amores (Lovers' Fountain), where the dastardly deed is said to have been done. Also note the tree planted by English hero the Duke of Wellington.

PARKS

A serene place to catch your breath without disturbing ghosts is the **Jardim Botânico** (Botanical Garden; Map pp294-5; ☎ 239 822 897; admission free; ⌚ 9am-8pm Apr-Sep, 9am-5.30pm Oct-Mar), in the shadow of the 16th-century Aqueduto de São Sebastião. Founded by the Marquês de Pombal, the gardens combine formal flowerbeds, meandering paths and elegant fountains. The green-fingered can also visit the lush **greenhouses** (adult/child under 6/student/senior €2/free/1.50/1.50) and the adjacent **Museu Botânico** (Botanical Museum; Map pp294-5; ☎ 239 827 625; musbot@ci.uc.pt; adult/child under 6/student/senior €2/free/1.50/1.50; ⌚ 9am-noon & 2-5pm Mon-Fri).

Activities

RIVER TRIPS

Basófias (Map pp294-5; ☎ 966 040 695; ☎ /fax 239 912 444; www.basofias.com in Portuguese; 55 min €5; ⌚ Tue-Sun May-Sep) runs boat trips on the Rio Mondego. Departures, from beside Parque Dr Manuel Braga, at 11am, 3pm, 4pm, 5pm and 6pm.

Geoaventura (☎ 914 982 651, 919 485 976; www.geoaventura.web.pt in Portuguese; Coimbra) conducts various rafting and kayaking routes, as well as archery, rock climbing and more.

O Pioneiro do Mondego (Map p293; ☎ /fax 239 478 385; Penacova; call 8am-10am, 1-3pm & 8-10pm; ⌚ Jun-Sep) rents kayaks from April to mid-October for paddling the Rio Mondego from Penacova to Coimbra, a 25km, four-hour trip costing around €15; a shorter version to Torres de Mondego, with transport back to Coimbra, costs the same. At 10am, a minibus takes you to Penacova from the boating club on the south bank of the river, although this pick-up point may shift to the eastern corner of Coimbra's Parque Dr Manuel Braga in the future.

Trans Serrano (☎ 966 217 787; ☎/fax 235 778 938; www.transserrano.com in Portuguese; Rua Forno 6, 3330-325 Góis) organises guided descents of the same stretch for about €20 per person plus lunch. Trips go year-round if there are enough participants; try to call a few days ahead.

Coimbra for Children

Portugal dos Pequenitos (Map p293; ☎ 239 801 170; Rossio de Santa Clara; adult/child under 5/child 5-13/senior €5/free/2.50/2.50; 9am-8pm Jun–mid-Sep, 10am-5pm mid-Sep–Feb, 10am-7pm Mar-May) is an impossibly cute theme park, where coachloads of kids clamber over, into and through doll's house versions of Portugal's most famous monuments, while parents clutch cameras at the ready. There's an extra charge to visit the marginally interesting mini-museums of marine life, clothing and furniture. Another way to stop your kids getting bored is to hop aboard one of the frequent river trips with Basófias (p298).

Festivals & Events

QUEIMA DAS FITAS

During the Burning of the Ribbons festival, starting on the first Thursday in May, Coimbra's students celebrate the end of the academic year with impressive gusto. The calendar includes a midnight fado (melancholy Portuguese-style blues) concert in front of the *sé velha;* a week of concerts at the so-called Queimodromo, across the Ponte de Santa Clara; and a massive parade (see 'Glug, Glug, Glug', right) from the hill top down to Portagem, with everyone in their black gowns and coloured top hats.

FESTA DA RAINHA SANTA

Held around 4 July in even-numbered years, this large festival commemorates queen-saint Isabel with a Thursday procession taking her statue from the Convento de Santa Clara-a-Nova to Igreja do Carmo and another that takes her back on the Sunday. But if pious processions aren't your bag, don't despair. The festival also coincides with the *Festa da Cidade* (Town Festival), which is all the excuse needed for a proper knees-up – especially in the form of folk music, dancing and fireworks.

GLUG, GLUG, GLUG

For European beer-consumption records, Queima das Fitas surely rivals Munich's Oktoberfest. The parade features some 100 floats, each with about 30 people on it. In their rush to sponsor individual floats, Portuguese breweries provide a free case of beer for just about every one of those people, to be consumed or given away before the parade ends. Relations between students and police are amazingly friendly, but the strain on local hospitals is heavy, with a strong emphasis on stomach-pumping; and there is a tendency for students to fall into the river.

OTHER EVENTS

Among other annual events in Coimbra are international festivals of music in July and of magic in mid-September (Coimbra is the home of Luís de Matus, Portugal's most famous magician).

There's folk music and dancing in Praça 8 de Maio and open-air fado at the Arco de Almedina and along Rua Quebra Costas from late June to mid-September, usually on Tuesday and Thursday.

Sleeping

BUDGET

Pensão Residencial Larbelo (Map pp294-5; ☎ 239 829 092; fax 239 829 094; Largo da Portagem 33; d/tr €32.50/42.50) Larbelo is bang in the centre, and boasts well-kept and rather grand wooden-floored rooms and a gruff but friendly staff. Some rooms have plaza views and all have private bathrooms.

Residencial Moeda (Map pp294-5; ☎ 239 824 784; fax 239 834 398; Rua da Moeda 81; s/d with breakfast €30/35;) Sitting above the owner's hole-in-the-wall seashell and charms shop near the Igreja de Santa Cruz, this place has good value, fresh and modern rooms with minibar.

Residencial Domus (Map pp294-5; ☎ 239 828 584; residencialdomus@sapo.pt; Rua Adelino Veiga 62; s/d/tr from €25/35/45;) A great choice, Domus is a welcoming family-run place in a quiet pedestrian shopping zone near Coimbra A. It has snug, plain rooms, some with characterful old furniture.

Pensão-Restaurante Flôr de Coimbra (Map pp294-5; 239 823 865; fax 239 821 545; Rua do Poço 5; d with shower & shared/private toilet May-Sep €25/30, Oct-Apr €20/25) An old but congenial and well-tended guesthouse a short hop from the train station.

A maze of seedy *pensões* around the station includes cheapies **Residencial Paris** (Map pp294-5; /fax 239 822 732; Rua da Sota 41; tw with/without bathroom from €30/25) and neighbouring **Pensão Lorvanense** (Map pp294-5; 239 823 481; Rua da Sota 27; d or tw €25), which are passable for budget travellers looking to stay near Coimbra A. They both have cheaper rooms without private showers.

Pousada da juventude (Map p293; 239 822 955; coimbra@movijovem.pt; Rua Dr António Henriques Seco 14; dm €11, d with toilet €30) Coimbra's pleasant suburban youth hostel is on a quiet road 500m northeast of Praça da República. From Coimbra A station take northbound bus No 46.

The nearest camping sites to be found are two stranded out near Penacova, some 25km northeast on the N110.

MID-RANGE

Rooms at the following places each have a TV, private toilet and shower/bathroom except as noted.

Residencial Botânico (Map p293; 239 714 824; fax 239 405 124; Bairro de São Jose 15; d/tr with breakfast €40/55;) This large and irreproachably kept guesthouse sits at the bottom of Alameda Dr Júlio Henriques. It has big, elegantly sparse rooms, including a few family suites.

Residencial Alentejana (Map p293; 239 825 903; residencialalentejana@hotmail.com; Rua António Henriques Seco 1; s/d/tr with breakfast €35/45/60;) Worth the uphill walk, this prominent old town house offers an eye-catching mix of handsome old high-ceilinged rooms, as well as some newer ones.

Residência Coimbra (Map pp294-5; 239 837 996; fax 239 838 124; Rua das Azeiteiras 55; s/d €30/45;) In a narrow pedestrian street squeezed full of down-to-earth cafés and restaurants, this well maintained place offers a good selection of quiet twins.

Pensão Residencial Antunes (Map pp294-5; 239 854 720; residencialantunes@mail.pt, Rua Castro Matoso 8; s/d/tr with breakfast €35/45/60; P) A few steps from the aqueduct and botanical gardens, this place offers charming, creaky old doubles with large beds and that Coimbra rarity – abundant parking.

Hotel Oslo (Map pp294-5; 239 829 071/2/3; www.hotel-oslo.web.pt; Avenida Fernão de Magalhães 25; s/d €55/75; P) This otherwise slightly bland though comfortable option redeems itself with plentiful free parking, satellite TV and a popular 5th-floor bar with views up to the university.

Almedina Coimbra Hotel (Map p293; 239 855 500; www.residencial-almedina.pt; Avenida Fernão de Magalhães 199; s/d €52/60;) This hotel offers big, bland but blissfully quiet rooms with double-glazed windows to shut out the traffic noise below.

TOP END

Hotel Astória (Map pp294-5; 239 853 020; astoria@almeidahotels.com; Avenida Emídio Navarro 21; s/d with breakfast €82/99;) The unmistakable Art Deco face of this wedge-shaped hotel contemplates the river and Largo da Portagem. It has bags of personality and professional, spiffy staff, though some of the quiet, plush rooms are a tad dog-eared. The round tower suites (from €105) also score panoramic views from the river up to the university. The restaurant has occasional fado dinner shows.

Hotel Tivoli (Map p293; 239 858 300; htcoimbra@mail.telepac.pt; Rua João Machado; d with breakfast €135; P) Central Coimbra's 'business-class' hotel has huge rooms with all the ex-

THE AUTHOR'S CHOICE

Casa Pombal Guesthouse (Map pp294-5; 239 835 175; casa.pombal@oninet.pt; Rua das Flores 18; d with/without bathroom from €46/40; closed mid-Dec–mid-Jan) The best of a limited supply of guesthouses in hilltop Coimbra, this narrow, quirky old town house has everything from bathless cubicles to eyries with huge views. It's well-equipped for travellers' needs and fluent English is spoken. Dinner (vegetarian upon request) can be served with advance notice and the room rate includes a superb buffet breakfast.

pected frills, though surrounding streets are choked with traffic.

Quinta das Lágrimas (☎ 239 802 380; geral@quintadaslagrimas.pt; Santa Clara; d/tw with breakfast from €130/155; P ⊠ ⁜ ⛾) This splendid historical palace is now one of Portugal's most enchanting upper-crust hotels. You can choose between richly furnished rooms in the old palace, or in the attached spa building, which has Scandinavian-style minimalist rooms complete with Jacuzzi. Or, for the full royal treatment, there's always the majestic 'King's Room' for a mere €375 per night. A few of its rooms look out on the garden where Dona Inês de Castro is said to have met her tragic end.

Eating

BUDGET

Bar-Restaurante ACM (Map pp294-5; ☎ 239 823 633; Rua Alexandre Herculano 21A; half-/full-portions €3.50/5; 🕑 lunch & dinner Mon-Fri, lunch Sun) ACM is Portugal's YMCA and offers plain fare and quick service.

At three plain **student canteens** (🕑 8.30am-9.30pm), anyone with a student ID card can queue for a meal for as little as €2 during term time. Downstairs behind the Centro de Juventude (see p295), another **canteen** (mains from €3; 🕑 9am-9.30pm Mon-Fri) features salads and simple meals, though its staff might ask to see student ID.

The modern town market is **Mercado Municipal Dom Pedro V** (Map pp294-5; ☎ 239 833 385; Rua Olímpio Nicolau Rui Fernandes; 🕑 Mon-Sat); it is busiest on Saturday. In Rua das Azeiteiras are several small **fruit-and-vegetable shops**, open during the day, at least on weekdays. Supermarkets include:

Pingo Doce (Map p293; Rua João de Ruão; 🕑 9am-8pm Mon-Sat); Travessa Combatentes de Grande Guerra (Map p293; Travessa Combatentes de Grande Guerra)

Minipreço (Map pp294-5; Rua António Granjo 6C; 🕑 9am-8pm Mon-Sat, 9am-1pm & 3-7pm Sun).

MID-RANGE

Restaurante Zé Manel (Map pp294-5; ☎ 239 823 790; Beco do Forno 12; mains €7-10; 🕑 lunch & dinner Mon-Fri, lunch Sat) Tucked down a nondescript little alleyway, you could easily miss this eccentric little gem, papered with knick-knacks, doodles and scribbled poems. However, it's popularity is such that you should come early or be ready to wait. Try the good *feijoada á leitão* (beans and suckling pig).

Restaurante Jardim da Manga (Map pp294-5; ☎ 239 829 156; dishes €4-9; 🕑 all day Sun-Fri) Student-friendly place reminiscent of a school canteen within, but nicely positioned at the back of an oasis of calm and pigeons – Jardim da Manga – without. It has a small menu of meaty dishes tailored to tight budgets.

Restaurante O Estudante (Map pp294-5; ☎ 239 832 699; Rua da Sota 48; half portions €6-10; 🕑 lunch & dinner Mon-Sat) Bubbly multilingual service makes this snug spot behind the Astoria a winner, and the excellent traditional dishes don't disappoint, either.

Restaurante Democrática (Map pp294-5; ☎ 239 823 784; Rua Nova; mains €4-9; 🕑 lunch & dinner Mon-Sat) If all you're after is a down-to-business, family-friendly place offering good-value standards, this backstreet favourite will fit the bill.

Tapas Bar (Map pp294-5; ☎ 239 826 048; Avenida Sá da Bandeira 80; light meals €6; 🕑 lunch & dinner) Recommended as much for the relaxed late-night bar scene as for the all-hours food – snacks from 10am, light fish and meat dishes from 8pm into the night.

Adega A Cozinha (Map pp294-5; ☎ 239 827 115; Rua das Azeiteiras 65; mains €6-8; 🕑 lunch & dinner Thu-Tue) Traditional country-feel *adega* with chunky menus scrawled on handmade paper. Meaty half-portion specials available, and good shrimp kebabs for €11.

Adega Funchal (Map pp294-5; ☎ 239 824 137; Rua das Azeiteiras 18; mains €6-10; 🕑 lunch & dinner Sun-Fri) Delicious smells fill the alleyway outside this popular spot. Owners are proud of its *chanfana carne de cabra* (goat stewed in red wine) for two. Gruff service.

Giro (☎ 239 833 020; Rua das Azeiteiras 39; mains €5-9; 🕑 all day Mon-Sat) Quick-service *churrasqueira* (grill restaurant) with platters big enough to fill any stomach.

Drinking

Bar-hopping is a common pastime around Praça da República, the epicentre of student nightlife. The big nights are Thursday to Saturday – but during university term time, any night is game.

Bar Quebra Costas (Map pp294-5; ☎ 239 821 661; Rua Quebra Costas 45-49; 🕑 Mon-Sat) In the perfect position to sip a chilled beer as you watch people puff and pant up the Quebra Costas, this old hang-out keeps folks coming with mellow alternative music and sharp art on the walls.

Centro Cultural Dom Dinis (Map pp294-5; ☎ 239 838 593; Largo Marquês de Pombal; ⏰ Mon-Sat) This cavernous bar is the best place to get in on the student scene. There's live music on Friday and Saturday (though you may be asked for student ID).

English Bar (Map p293; Rua Lourenço de Almeida Azevedo 24; ⏰ Mon-Sat) British-style pub that has light meals downstairs and a bar to knock back draught Murphy's upstairs.

Shmoo Café (Map pp294-5; Rua Corpo de Deus 68; ⏰ Mon-Sat) This slick bar lays the red light on thick, making for an intimate atmosphere that attracts a chic downtown crowd.

Café Santa Cruz (Map pp294-5; ☎ 239 833 617; Praça 8 de Maio; ⏰ all day Mon-Sat) Scooping the prize for the best people-watching patio in town, Santa Cruz also has one of the most attractive and unusual interiors. It is housed in a vaulted annexe of the Igreja de Santa Cruz, with creased leather chairs below austere arches and stained glass.

Cartola Esplanada Bar (Map pp294-5; Praça da República; ⏰ all day) This place has a great plaza-side position and a huge drinks list and, hence, is the ideal place for a spot of student-watching.

Entertainment

FADO

Soul-baring ballads filled with exquisite yearning and heavy-hearted meditations on fate can be heard late into the night in Coimbra, as listeners stare into their drinks and drown in melancholic appreciation.

If Lisbon represents the heart of Portuguese fado music, Coimbra is its head. The local style of fado is more cerebral than the Lisbon variety, with a greater emphasis on *guitarra*-led instrumental pieces. Its adherents are also staunchly protective: a fracas erupted in Coimbra in 1996 when a woman named Manuela Bravo decided to record a CD of Coimbra fado, which is traditionally sung only by men. The offending CD soon met an end as tragic as its lyrics.

You can listen to fado in several *casas de fado* (fado houses) on just about any late Friday or Saturday evening: the best is **Á Capella** (left). Alternatively, try backstreet **Bar Diligência** (Map pp294-5; ☎ 239 827 667; Rua Nova 30; ⏰ 6pm-2am), where the music is usually live from about 10.30pm; and **Boémia Bar** (Map pp294-5; ☎ 239 834 547; Rua do Cabido 6); or the large and touristy **Restaurante O Trovador** (Map pp294-5; ☎ 239 825 475; Largo da Sé Velha 15-17; ⏰ 9am-midnight Mon-Sat), where fado is sung on Friday and Saturday nights. *Casas de fado* are often restaurants too, usually with a minimum charge equivalent to a small meal or several drinks.

The AAC (student union) sometimes sponsors fado performances in the Café Santa Cruz during March, and there's also open-air fado to be found at the Arco de Almedina and along Rua Quebra Costas in summer (p299).

THE AUTHOR'S CHOICE

Á Capella (Map pp294-5; ☎ 239 833 985; www.acapella.com.pt; Rua Corpo de Deus; ⏰ 10am-2am) Coimbra is rich in doom-laden fado bars, but few are as appealing as this. Superbly set in a tiny and atmospheric 14th-century chapel, stylishly renovated so as to create a cocktail bar ambience, Á Capella rapidly fills up before the 11.30pm fado shows (from Thursday to Saturday), so try to arrive before 10.30pm. On other nights, it hosts a mixed bag of music, from Portuguese guitar to jazz. There is a minimum consumption charge of €5.

DANCING

Aside from fateful fado bars, Coimbra also rocks as a more conventional nightlife scene. So you think you can keep pace with the students? Well, let's find out. Folks swear by the DJs at **Via Latina** (Map pp294-5; ☎ 239 820 293; Rua Almeida Garrett 1; ⏰ midnight-6am Tue-Sat), which doubles as a lively pub. **Vinil** (Map p293; ☎ 239 404 047; Avenida Afonso Henriques 43; ⏰ midnight-4am Tue-Sat) is another favourite, where a mostly student crowd does the soft shake to predictable pop tunes.

On the other bank of the river is the more edgy **Scotch Club** (Map p293; ☎ 239 801 000; Santa Clara; ⏰ midnight-6am Thu-Sat), mixing things up with great Brazilian and African music and live bands. Its isolation also allows for more room to bump and grind, as well as a patio for cooling off.

SPORT

Académica is the name given to Coimbra's second-division football team and its first-division rugby team, both of which play at the newly enlarged Euro2004 stadium,

Estádio Cidade de Coimbra (☎ 239 798 300; www.gocoimbra.com; Rua Dom Manuel), 1.5km east of the centre (take bus No 7T from Coimbra A, or No 5, 7, 11 or 24 from Praça da República).

Getting There & Away

BUS

From the **main bus station** (Map p293; Avenida Fernão de Magalhães), **RBL/Rede Expressos** (☎ 239 827 081) caters for most major destinations. At least a dozen buses each go daily to Lisbon (€9.40, 2½ hours) and to Porto (€8.90, 1½ hours), and there are frequent express services to Braga (€10, 2½ hours), Évora (€12.40, 4¼ hours) and Faro (€17, 7½ hours). RBL also goes to Luso (see p304). In winter there are frequent services to Seia (€8.80, 1¾ hours), Guarda (€9.20, three hours) and also to other points around the Parque Natural da Serra da Estrela.

Joalto/AVIC (Map p293; ☎ 239 823 769; Rua João de Ruão 18; ⌚ Mon-Sat) and RBL run buses to Condeixa and Conimbriga (p304). **Moisés Correia de Oliveira** (Map p293; ☎ 239 828 263), which has a ticket kiosk on the corner outside Hotel Tivoli, and Rede Expressos have multiple daily services to Figueira da Foz (€3.15, 1¼ hours).

CAR

The local branch of the **Automóvel Club de Portugal** (ACP; Map pp294-5; ☎ 239 852 020; Avenida Emídio Navarro 6) is by Coimbra A.

Car-rental agencies that will drop off the rental car at your hotel include:

Alpirent (Map p293; ☎ 239 821 999; Avenida Fernão de Magalhães 234)
Avis (☎ 239 834 786; Coimbra A station)
Salitur/Europcar (Map p293; ☎ 239 820 594; Edifício Tricana, Rua Padre Estevão Cabral)

TRAIN

A few fast international trains stop only at Coimbra B, but most trains call at both Coimbra A (called just 'Coimbra' on timetables) and Coimbra B. International bookings must be made at Coimbra A. There's no left-luggage office at either station.

Coimbra is linked by seven daily *intercidade* (IC) trains to Lisbon (€12, 2¼ hours) and four to Porto (€8, 1¼ hours). Additional *interregional* (IR) services take 30 minutes longer and cost about €2 less. IR trains also run to Luso/Buçaco and to Figueira da Foz.

Getting Around

BICYCLE

For mountain bike rental, **Centro Velocipédico de Sangalhos** (☎ 239 824 646; Rua da Sota 23; ⌚ 9am-7pm Mon-Fri) charges €7.50 per day.

BUS

Green, university-operated Ecovia minibuses run about every 10 minutes on weekdays and Saturday morning, on two routes – one from the bus station via Avenida Sá da Bandeira and Rua Padre António Vieira to Largo Dom Dinis and on to the stadium, and the other from the hospital via Praça da República to the bus station. Tickets (purchased on board) cost €1.70/2.75 for two/four trips.

The only municipal line serving the university is the No 1 from Largo da Portagem and Coimbra A, via the Baixa. Nos 3 and 29 go from Coimbra A to Praça da República. Multiuse tickets (three/11 trips for €1.47/5) – also usable on the *elevadore* (below) – are available at the **SMTUC office** (Map pp294-5; ☎ 239 801 100; www.smtuc.pt in Portuguese; Largo do Mercado; ⌚ 7.30am-7.30pm Mon-Fri, 8am-1pm Sat) at the foot of the *elevadore*, at official kiosks and also at some *tabacarias* (tobacconist/newsagent). Tickets bought on board cost €1.30 per trip.

You may also see mini electrical buses crawling their way around pedestrian areas in the centre of Coimbra, between Baixa and Alta Coimbra and through the medieval heart of the city. These *patufinhas* are a new service also called Linha Azul. You can use the same pre-bought tickets that you would on any other SMTUC buses.

ELEVADORE DO MERCADO

The **elevadore** (Map pp294-5; ⌚ 7.30am-11.30pm Mon-Sat, 9am-11.30pm Sun) – a combination of elevator, walkway and funicular between the market and the university – can save you a tedious walk, though it's slow and fickle. See above about where to buy tickets, which you punch once for each ascent or descent. You can't buy tickets at the top.

AROUND COIMBRA

Conimbriga

Whether or not you're riveted by Roman history, the myriad mosaics and remarkably well preserved ruins of Conimbriga, 16km southwest of Coimbra, cannot fail to make a lasting impression. This extraordinary site contains by far the finest Roman ruins you'll see in Portugal, and ranks with the best-preserved sites in the whole of the Iberian Peninsula. Miss it, and you'll miss out.

HISTORY

Though Conimbriga owes its celebrity to the Romans, the site actually dates back to Celtic times (*briga* is a Celtic term for a defended area). However, when the Romans settled here in the 1st century AD it blossomed into a major city on the route from Lisbon (Olisipo) to Braga (Bracara Augusta), hosting well-to-do mansions floored with elaborate mosaics and scattered with fountains.

In the 3rd century the townsfolk, threatened by invading tribes, desperately threw up a huge defensive wall right through the town centre, abandoning the residential area. But this wasn't enough to stop the Suevi seizing the town in 468, and the inhabitants fled to nearby Aeminius (Coimbra) – thereby saving Conimbriga from destruction.

SIGHTS

Museum

First visit the small **museum** (☎ 239 944 100; Conimbriga; admission incl ruins adult/child under 14/student/teacher/senior €3/free/1.50/1.50/1.50, free admission Sunday 10am-1pm; 🕑 10am-1pm & 2-8pm Tue-Sun mid-Mar–mid-Sep, to 6pm mid-Sep–mid-Mar), to get your head around Conimbriga's history and layout. There are no English labels but the excellent displays largely speak for themselves, presenting every aspect of Roman life from mosaics to medallions. There's a café-restaurant at the back.

Ruins

The sprawling **ruins** (admission incl museum adult/child under 14/student/teacher/senior €3/free/1.50/1.50/1.50, free admission Sunday 10am-1pm; 🕑 9am-1pm & 2-8pm mid-Mar–mid-Sep, to 6pm mid-Sep–mid-Mar) tells a vivid story. On the one hand, its domesticity is obvious, with elaborate mosaics, heated baths and trickling fountains that recall many a toga-clad dalliance. But smack through the middle of this tranquil scene runs a massive defensive wall, splitting and cannibalising nearby buildings in its hasty erection to fend off raids.

It's the wall that will first draw your attention on entering, followed by the patchwork of exceptional mosaic floors below it. Here is the so-called Casa dos Repuxos (House of Fountains); though partly destroyed by the wall, it contains cool pond-gardens, fountains and truly extraordinary mosaics showing the four seasons and various hunting scenes.

The site's most important villa, on the other side of the wall, is said to have belonged to one Cantaber, whose wife and children were seized by the Suevi in an attack in 465. It's a palace of a place, with baths, pools and a sophisticated underground heating system.

Excavations continue in the outer areas. Eye-catching features include the remains of a 3km-long aqueduct, which led up to a hilltop bathing complex, and a forum, once surrounded by covered porticoes.

GETTING THERE & AWAY

You can catch a bus from Coimbra directly to the site (€1.60, 30 minutes) with **AVIC/Joalto** (☎ 239 823 769) at 9am or 9.35am (only 9.35am at weekends). Buses depart for the return trip at 1pm and 5pm (only 5pm at weekends).

They also run buses to Condeixa (€1.50) about every half-hour (less often at weekends), while **RBL** (☎ 239 855 270) has a less-frequent service. But from Condeixa to the site it's an uphill, poorly signposted 2km walk, some of it along the hard shoulder of a high-speed road.

Luso & Mata Nacional do Buçaco

The 105-hectare Buçaco (or Bussaco) National Forest, on the slopes of the Serra do Buçaco 24km northeast of Coimbra, is no ordinary forest. For centuries it's been a religious haven, a place of sanctity and peace, shut away from the outside world by a high stone wall. Even today, overrun by picnickers, it retains its mystical appeal – not to mention its botanical attractions. There are an astounding 700 different tree species, including huge Mexican cedars, giant ferns and ginkgos.

And in the midst of it all lies an extravagant palace – a royal retreat so fanciful that it brings to mind the mating of a wedding cake with a cuckoo clock.

For decades Portuguese tourists have also been coming to the prim little spa town of

Luso just to the west, to soak in its waters, a balm for everything from gout to asthma. The forest and spa make an easy day trip from Coimbra. If you want to linger, Luso has a handful of *residenciais* (guesthouses). Travellers with the wherewithal can stay at an astonishing neo-Manueline palace right in the forest.

HISTORY

The Luso and Buçaco area was probably used as a 2nd-century Christian refuge, although the earliest known hermitage was founded in the 6th century by Benedictine monks. In 1628, Carmelite monks embarked on an extensive programme of forestation, introducing exotic species, laying cobbled paths and enclosing the forest within walls. It grew so famous that in 1643 Pope Urban VIII decreed that anyone damaging the trees would be excommunicated!

The peace was briefly shattered in 1810, during the Peninsular War, when Napoleon's forces under Masséna were soundly beaten by the Anglo-Portuguese army of the future Duke of Wellington (the battle is re-enacted here every 27 September). In 1834, when religious orders throughout Portugal were abolished, the forest became state property.

ORIENTATION & INFORMATION

From Luso-Buçaco train station it's a 15-minute walk downhill (east) via Rua Dr António Granjo to the turismo and spa in the centre of Luso. Buses stop on Rua Emídio Navarro, near the turismo. By road the Portas das Ameias, the nearest gate into the forest, is 900m east of the turismo. From May to October there's a charge of €5 per car entering the forest, though walkers go in free.

The **turismo** (☎ 231 939 133; jtlb@oninet.pt; Rua Emídio Navarro 136; 🕒 9am-7pm Mon-Fri Jun-Sep, 9.30am-12.30pm & 2-6pm Oct-May, 10am-1pm & 3-5pm Sat & Sun year-round) has accommodation information, town and forest maps, and leaflets (in English) detailing flora and points of historical interest. And Internet access on a single terminal for a rather steep €5 per hour.

SIGHTS & ACTIVITIES

Forest

The aromatic forest is threaded with trails, dotted with crumbling chapels and graced with ponds and fountains. Some popular trails lead to areas of great beauty, such as the Vale dos Fetos (Valley of Ferns), but you can get enjoyably lost on more overgrown routes. Among several fine viewpoints is 545m **Cruz Alta**, reached by a path called the Via Sacra.

What most visitors come to see is the fairy-tale **Palace Hotel do Buçaco**. This unabashedly sugary-sweet cake of a building – all turrets and spires, neo-Manueline carving and azulejos with scenes from *Os Lusiados* – was built in 1907 as a royal summer residence, on the site of a 17th-century Carmelite monastery. Three years later the monarchy was abolished, so the royals hardly got a look-in. It's now a deluxe hotel (p306), though staff are surprisingly tolerant of all the gawpers. By road the hotel is 2.1km from the Portas das Ameias.

All that remains of the monastery, the Convento Santa Cruz do Buçaco, is a tiny **church** (admission €0.60; 🕒 9am-12.30pm & 2-5.30pm Tue-Sat), in the shadow of the Palace Hotel. Inside are a few cork-lined cells (in one of which Wellington spent the night before the 1810 battle) and a frieze of azulejos depicting the battle.

Museu Militar

To bone up on the Battle of Buçaco, enthusiasts will find maps, weapons and other paraphernalia in a small **military museum** (☎ 231 939 310; adult/child under 10/senior €1/free/free; 🕒 10am-noon & 2-5pm Tue-Sun), just outside the northeastern Portas da Rainha.

Spa

Just the ticket after a long walk in the forest, the **Termas de Luso** (☎ 231 937 444; Rua Alvaro; 🕒 8am-noon & 4-7pm) welcomes drop-in visitors from May to October. However, it prefers that they visit only in the afternoon. The main therapies available to day visitors are general massage (€14.40) and a kind of high-velocity shower called *duche de Vichy* plus massage (€14.90).

Other Attractions

Fill your bottle with spa water at the **Fonte de São João** (fountain), a block east of the turismo. Beside the fountain is Luso's **former casino** (☎ 231 937 417), now a venue for exhibitions, folk dancing and fado.

SLEEPING

Budget

Luso has plenty of *quartos* (private rooms); look for the signs or check the turismo's useful list. Doubles cost €15 to €40.

Pensão Alegre (☎ 231 930 256; Rua Emídio Navarro 2; s/d with breakfast from €32/35; P) This attractive 19th-century townhouse offers personal service and large doubles filled with plush drapes, decorative plaster ceilings and highly polished period furniture. Plus there's a pretty little vine-draped garden with pool.

Astória (☎ 231 939 182; Rua Emídio Navarro; s/d with breakfast €30/35) Beside the turismo, this homely place feels more like grandma's house than a guesthouse. It's filled with frilly décor and various intriguing artefacts.

Central (☎ 231 939 254; Rua Emídio Navarro; s/d with breakfast from €35/40; P) Welcoming *pensão* offering light and modern rooms, with sloping marquis floors and verandas.

Orbitur camping ground (☎ 231 930 916; www.orbitur.pt; Bairro do Comendador Melo Pimenta; adult/tent/car €3.50/2.90/3.40; year-round) This small, lush site is a pleasant walk 1.3km south of the turismo. Wooden bungalows with kitchen for four or more are also available (from €43.50).

Mid-Range & Top End

Palace Hotel do Buçaco (☎ 231 937 970; bussaco-palace@clix.pt; Mata Nacional do Buçaco; s/d/ste from €160/185/390; P) If you can afford it, why not live the fairy-tale awhile, and stay amid all the fuss and finery of this ostentatious palace. It's bound to put you in a royal mood.

Grande Hotel de Luso (☎ 231 937 937, ☎/fax 231 937 930; Rua Dr Cid de Oliveira 86; s/d with breakfast from €75/100; P) It may be a step down from a royal palace, but this mono-turreted hotel is nonetheless luxurious. It boasts tennis and squash courts and a sauna, and a large grassy garden. You can rent bikes here too.

Vila Duparchy (☎ 231 930 790; principe.santos@clix.pt; Rua José Figueiredo; s/d with breakfast €63/75; P) Alternatively, if a country manor is more your style, this one was home to French railway engineer Jean Alexis Duparchy while constructing the Beira Alta railway. The rather genteel house is cut off from the road on a woody hill top, 2km outside the centre of Luso off the EN234. English is spoken and meals are available on request.

EATING

Most *pensões* have reasonable restaurants of their own.

Varanda do Lago (☎ 231 930 888; Parque do Largo; meals €7-11; lunch & dinner Tue-Sun) Overlooking the lake, 350m west of the turismo, this pleasant glass-fronted restaurant lets you watch gaggles of geese waddling about and children playing on paddle boats as you chow down. Light meals, omelettes and snacks are all available.

Restaurante Lourenços (☎ 231 939 474; Rua Emídio Navarro; mains from €7-10; lunch & dinner Thu-Tue) On a corner just east of the turismo, this large bright place offers excellent regional specialities in a dignified setting.

Palace Hotel do Buçaco (☎ 231 937 970; bussaco-palace@clix.pt; Mata Nacional do Buçaco) Offers a blowout meal for about €40 per person plus drinks.

Salão de chá (Praça Fonte São João) This Art Deco tearoom by the Fonte de São João and perfectly capturing the spa-town atmosphere is *the* place for tea and cakes.

GETTING THERE & AWAY

Buses are the most convenient for a day trip. RBL has five services daily (only morning service at 7.30am) during the week (less at the weekend) leaving from Coimbra's main bus station (€2.45, 45 minutes). Two depart Saturday and all continue to the Palace Hotel do Buçaco (€2.65, 50 minutes). The last bus back leaves from the Palace Hotel at about 6.25pm.

The only trains depart from Coimbra A at about 7.40am and 11.45am (€1.25, 30 minutes). The last train back departs from Luso-Buçaco station just before 6pm.

Reserva Natural do Paúl de Arzila

Bird-watchers and other nature fans may wish to detour to the 535-hectare Arzila Marsh Natural Reserve, home to some 120 species of resident and migratory birds, as well as otters. There is an **on site centre** (☎ 239 980 500), from where you can take a two-hour interpretive walk. For further information, contact the **main office** (☎ 239 499 020; mpa.santosmf@icn.pt) in the Mata Nacional do Choupal, Coimbra.

PIÓDÃO

pop 225 / elevation 690m

Remote Piódão (*pyoh*-dow[n]) offers a chance to see rural Portugal at its most pristine. This tiny traditional village clings to a terraced valley in a beautiful, surprisingly remote range of vertiginous ridges, deeply cut valleys, frisky rivers and virgin woodland called the Serra de Açor (Goshawk Mountains). Until the 1970s it was reachable only on horseback or foot, and coming here still feels like slipping through a time warp.

The village is a serene, picturesque composition in schist stone and grey slate; note the many doorways with crosses over them, said to offer protection against curses and thunderstorms.

Orientation & Information

Houses descend in terraces to Largo Cónego Manuel Fernandes Nogueira – smaller than its name – and the fairy-tale parish church, the Igreja Nossa Senhora Conceição. The village **turismo** (☎ 235 732 787; 🕒 9am-noon & 1-5pm Wed-Sun Oct-May) is also here. It has a good booklet on local walks.

Festivals & Events

The area's patron saint, São Pedro do Açor, is honoured with a Mass, procession and ball, and a handicrafts fair, during the **Santos Populares no Piódão** on the last weekend in June.

Sleeping & Eating

There are *quartos* everywhere, of uneven quality and seriously overpriced at about €25 per person.

Campismo de Ponte de Trés Entradas (☎ 238 670 050; ponte3entradas@mail.telepac.pt; adult/tent/car €3/2.60/2.60; 🕒 Dec-Oct) A shady riverside site 30km from Piódão near Avô, which also has bungalows from €40 for two.

Casas da Aldeia (☎ 235 731 424; d €25, with toilet/bathroom €40/65) A private house just beyond the centre, kitted out with help from the village-improvement committee. The rooms have kitchenettes. In the same vein, village Turihab (Turismo Habitação; scheme for marketing private accommodation) properties with doubles from €35 to €40 (with breakfast) include **Casa da Padaria** (☎ 235 732 773; casa.padaria@sapo.pt) and **Casa Malhadinhas** (☎ 235 731 464).

Estalagem do Piódão (☎ 235 730 100; est.piodao@inatel.pt; s/d with breakfast €52/65; Ⓟ ⊠) This mammoth caricature of a Piódão house looms over everything on a ridge above the village. Run by Inatel, the hotel has luxurious rooms and a restaurant.

Parque de Campismo de Côja (☎ 235 729 666; coja@fpcampismo.pt; Côja; adult/tent/car €2.65/2.15/1.90; 🕒 mid-Mar–mid-Oct) A well-equipped facility near the river, 21km west on the Rio Alva, open to Camping Card International (CCI) holders (p452). It also has bungalows from €30 for four people.

Cafés around the *largo* (small square) serve pastries and toasted sandwiches. **Restaurante O Fontinha** (☎ 235 731 151; mains €5-8; 🕒 lunch & dinner), located one lane back from the *largo*, is cheap and uninspiring. If you'd like something more sophisticated, try the restaurant at the Estalagem do Piódão (left).

Getting There & Away

The only transport other than car or bicycle is a bus from Arganil that stops in the *largo* (€2.80, 1¼ hours) twice on Thursday. Buses usually leave at 7.45am and 3pm, returning immediately upon arrival, but check current times with Piódão's tourist office or by calling Arganil's **turismo** (☎ 235 204 823).

The area's breathtaking views, narrow roads and sheer drops are a lethal combination for drivers, who should also note that side roads marked '4WD' are axle-breakers for ordinary cars.

FIGUEIRA DA FOZ

pop 28,000

Poor old Figueira da Foz (fi-*guy*-ra da *fosh*). Like so many old-fashioned seaside resorts, it has developed a somewhat tacky reputation based on its candy-striped beach huts, grungy bars, ice-cream parlours and get-rich-quick casino.

But the town's original attraction never goes out of fashion: the vast golden beach that fronts this resort is one of the deepest and widest in the region. Indeed it takes a five-minute walk across creaky boardwalks simply to reach the sea. However, despite its size, Figueira's sands fill with ranks of sizzling bodies in the summer heat, and prices skyrocket with the tourist influx.

The frisky Atlantic waves also attract many a surfer. Indeed, Figueira is a regular surfing championship venue.

Orientation

Just inland from the beach and the 16th-century Forte de Santa Catarina is a knot of streets with the turismo, accommodation and restaurants and the casino. Seafront

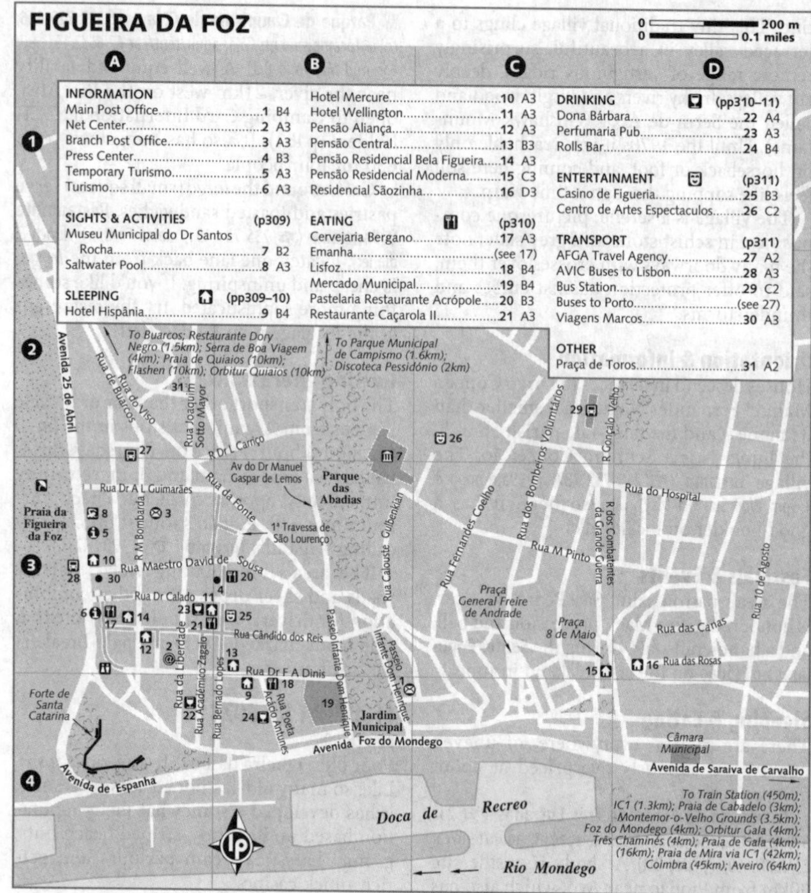

development continues clear to Buarcos, a former fishing village 3km to the north.

The train station is 1.5km east of the beach (for local transport see p311); the bus station is a tad closer. High-season parking is a headache, even in the evenings, thanks to the casino.

Information

Banks on Avenida Foz do Mondego and Praça 8 de Maio all have ATMs.

Branch post office (☎ 233 402 330; Rua Miguel Bombarda 76; 9am-12.30pm & 2-6pm Mon-Fri) Near the turismo.

Main post office (☎ 233 402 600; Passeio Infante Dom Henrique; 8.30am-6.30pm Mon-Fri, 9am-12.30pm Sat) Faces the *jardim municipal* (town garden).

Museu Municipal do Dr Santos Rocha (☎ 233 402 840; Rua Calouste Gulbenkian; 2-7.15pm Mon, 10am-7.15pm Tue-Fri, 2-6.45pm Sat) The museum library has free Internet connection, though it's often busy.

Net Center (Rua da Liberdade; per hr €1.50; 10am-10pm Mon-Sat, 3-8pm Sun) If you don't mind paying for online time, this central spot has good connections.

Press Center (Rua Bernardo Lopes 113; 9am-11pm) Newsagent stocking foreign newspapers.

Turismo (☎ 233 402 820; www.figueiraturismo.com in Portuguese; Avenida 25 de Abril; 9am-midnight daily Jun-Sep; 9am-12.30pm & 2-5.30pm Mon-Fri, 10am-12.30pm & 2.30-6.30pm Sat & Sun Oct- May) Faces the beach. During slow-starting renovations (expected to last at least until 2005) the turismo is about a block to the north.

Sights & Activities

BEACHES

Despite its size, the beach becomes packed in August, when the sun is at its hottest. For more character and some terrific surf, head north to **Buarcos**. Alfredo Farreca Rodrigues runs buses from the train station via the *mercado municipal* and the turismo to Buarcos (€0.85) every half-hour on weekdays and at least hourly at weekends, with additional services (Teimoso) from 7am to 9am weekdays.

For more seclusion, continue on around the Cabo Mondego headland to **Praia de Quiaios**, about 10km north of Figueira da Foz. AVIC services run from the bus station to Quiaios (€1.80, 30 minutes) seven times daily (less often on weekends).

South across the mouth of the Rio Mondego is **Praia de Cabedelo**, another prime surfing venue; a little further on (4km from Figueira) is **Praia de Gala**. AVIC buses to Cova run from the train station via the *mercado municipal* to Cabedelo and Gala (both €0.85) every half-hour on weekdays (less often at weekends).

MUSEU MUNICIPAL DO DR SANTOS ROCHA

This modern **museum** (☎ 233 402 840; Rua Calouste Gulbenkian; adult/child under 12/youth 12-25 €1.30/free/1; ⏲ 9.30am-5.15pm Tue-Fri, 2.15-5.15pm Sat & Sun), beside Parque das Abadias, houses a surprisingly rich collection – from Palaeolithic flint tools to African exploration and a somewhat stunted fine-arts section.

SERRA DE BOA VIAGEM

For those with wheels, this headland, found 4km north of Figueira and carpeted in pines, eucalyptus and acacias, is a fine place for panoramas, picnics and cool walks. Take the coastal road to Buarcos, turn right at the lighthouse and follow the signs to Boa Viagem.

WATER SPORTS

The Atlantic Ocean notwithstanding, you'd be surprised at the number of visitors who prefer to take their seawater in a pool. There's an open-air **saltwater pool** (⏲ 9am-around 7pm, Jun-at least Sep) a block north of the turismo. For some rugged outdoor action such as rafting and kayaking on the Rio Paiva (year-round) and Rio Minho (summer), as well as canyoning, walking and bungee jumping, contact **Capitão Dureza** (☎ 233 427 772, 919 079 852, 914 929 407; www.capitaodureza.com in Portuguese; Apartado 247, 3081-801 Figueira da Foz).

Festivals & Events

Festas da Cidade The Town Festival carries on for two weeks at the end of June, with folk music, parades and concerts at the *praça de toros* (bullring).

Mundialito de Futebol de Praia The town is mobbed for about a week in late July or August in most years for the World Beach-Football Championships.

Sleeping

Figueira brims with accommodation. Prices ratchet up to ridiculous levels in July and rise even further in August, but off-season rates can drop by half. The following places have private showers or bathrooms unless noted. The turismo has details of a few *quartos* for €20 to €25 per double. Touts may approach you at the bus or train station with their own offers.

BUDGET

Pensão Central (☎ 233 422 308; pensaocentral@figueira.net; Rua Bernardo Lopes 36; d with breakfast €40) Head up the candy-floss coloured stairway to this handsome old town house located on a pedestrian street right in the thick of things. It's just a few steps away from the casino and offers vast, fully equipped doubles with lofty windows.

Residencial Sãozinha (☎ 233 425 243; Ladeira do Monte 43; tw/d €30/40) Far from the madding crowd, this pleasant and newly done up spot is hidden away on a backstreet not far from the town hall. It has lovely neat little rooms, cable TV and personable service. Rooms have a shared shower and toilet.

Pensão Residencial Bela Figueira (☎ 233 422 728; fax 233 429 960; Rua Miguel Bombarda 13; d with/without bathroom incl breakfast from €50/40) Near the beach, snug Bela Figueira has plain, sunny rooms and two small patios to flop on after a hard day on the beach.

Pensão Aliança (☎ 233 422 197; Rua Miguel Bombarda 12; d with breakfast €60) Spacious and sparklingly clean, the rooms at this central guesthouse are worth the price tag, though they lost some character in enthusiastic renovations.

Pensão Residencial Moderna (☎ 233 422 701; Praça 8 de Maio 61; d with breakfast from €40; P) This place has a whiff of faded elegance about it, with mile-high ceilings and narrow corridors, though some rooms could use a good spring cleaning and new bathroom fittings. Pluses include a rear garden and free off-street parking.

Parque Municipal de Campismo (☎ 233 402 810; www.figueiracamping.com in Portuguese; Estrada de Tavarede; adult/tent/car €3.50/2.50/3; ⌚ year-round) This park is northeast of the centre and 2km from the beach but there's a pool nearby (and one in the works onsite), plus tennis courts and handy supermarkets a stone's throw away. Take a Casal de Areia bus (€0.85, six to 10 daily) from the train station, *mercado municipal* or Parque Abadias.

Foz do Mondego (☎ 233 402 740; foz.mondego@fpcampismo.pt; Praia de Cabedelo; adult/tent/car €3/2.40/1.90; ⌚ mid-Jan–mid-Nov) Near Cabedelo beach, 6km south of Figueira, this flat and sandy place requires a CCI (p452). It has little shade.

Orbitur Gala (☎ 233 431 492; info@orbitur.pt; Praia de Gala; adult/tent/car €4.30/3.50/3.80; ⌚ year-round) The best of a bunch of local camp sites, flat and shady Orbitur is next to a great beach. It's south of Foz do Mondego and 1km from the nearest bus stop. Bungalows here cost €60 to €92 for four to seven people in high season.

Orbitur Quiaios (☎ 233 910 499; fax 233 910 260; Praia de Quiaios; adult/tent/car €3.80/3.10/3.50; ⌚ year-round) Situated fairly close to the long Praia de Quiaios, 8km north of Figueira, this colourful camp site lacks a little shade but night-owls note that it's within walking distance of popular nightclub Flashen (p311).

For transport details to Cabedelo and Quiaios, see Beaches p309. You will find they are sandy and not nearly so shady as the others.

MID-RANGE & TOP END

Hotel Hispânia (☎ 233 422 164; fax 233 429 664; Rua Dr Francisco António Dinis 61; s/d with breakfast €35/40; 🅿) A dignified throwback to earlier days, with threadbare but reasonable-value rooms, each with a bathroom. Rates include off-street parking.

Hotel Wellington (☎ 233 426 767/8; hotelwellington@mail.telepac.pt; Rua Dr Calado 23-27; s/d with breakfast €77/88, ste €110; ❄) Good-value but run-of-the-mill hotel near the action; its modern rooms have cable TV. Off-street parking is available at a nearby car park and costs €4 per night.

Hotel Mercure (☎ 233 403 900; www.mercure.com; Avenida 25 de Abril 22; s/d €82/92; ❄ 💻) This is the only four-star hotel in town. Row upon row of balconies boast sweeping views of the vast beach, and rooms within offer a welcome touch of comfort.

Eating

Lisfoz (☎ 233 429 203; Rua Dr F A Dinis; mains €7-11; ⌚ lunch & dinner) The star dish of this popular glass-sided restaurant is its excellent *sardinha assada*, though it does plenty of other traditional fish/seafood dishes of the region.

Pastelaria Restaurante Acrópole (☎ 233 428 948; Rua Bernardo Lopes 76; dishes €4.50-7; ⌚ 6am-late Wed-Mon) For maximum mileage from your holiday funds, this casual café whips up filling burgers and omelettes for around €5. Tables spilling out onto the street make it great for people-watching, and waiters will let you nurse espressos for hours.

Restaurante Caçarola II (☎ 233 426 930; Rua Bernardo Lopes 85; mains €8-14; ⌚ 9-2am Mon-Thu, 9-4am Fri & Sat) A popular, hectic *marisqueira* (seafood restaurant) strewn with fishing tackle and dishing up good-value fish platters with intriguing names like 'dog-welks' or 'frog-fish rice'. It also has tables on the pedestrian boulevard outside.

Restaurante Dory Negro (☎ 233 421 333; Largo Caras Direitas 16, Buarcos; mains €7-10; ⌚ lunch & dinner Wed-Mon) A slap-up seafood meal is cheaper in Buarcos, and this unassuming restaurant is one of the best spots to indulge. The huge menu here includes crab, lobster, shrimps, clams and deep-sea fish. Its scrumptious *arroz de marisco* (€32 for two people), a rich stew of seafood and rice, must be booked at least a day ahead.

For simple bar snacks or a choice of 40 flavours of ice-cream from choc chip to Port (you know you want to!) on a sunny patio overlooking the sprawling beach, head for neighbouring **Cervejaria Bergano** (☎ 233 426 883; Esplanada Silva Guimarães; ⌚ 2pm-midnight Mon-Sat) and **Emanha** (☎ 233 426 567; Esplanada Silva Guimarães; ⌚ 8am-midnight) respectively.

With everything from the freshest fish to colourful crafts, the **mercado municipal** (Passeio Infante Dom Henrique; ⌚ Mon-Sat) is opposite the *jardim municipal*.

Drinking & Dancing

The best spot for a pint at sundown is the beachfront patio at **Cervejaria Bergano** (☎ 233

426 883; Esplanada Silva Guimarães). Further into town, Figueira's best bars are the grungy international-style pub **Rolls** (☎ 233 426 157; Rua Poeta Acácio Antunes 1E; ⌚ daily), which also serves up burgers, the comical beach-themed **Dona Bárbara** (☎ 233 426 060; Rua Acadêmico Zagalo 7; ⌚ daily) and **Perfumaria Pub** (☎ 233 426 442; Rua Dr Calado 37; ⌚ evenings), which has a miniscule street-side patio surrounded by a white picket fence and a smoky two-level bar within.

The big disco venues are outside the centre: **Discoteca Pessidónio** (☎ 233 435 637; Condados, Tavarede; ⌚ midnight-4am Fri & Sat) is a popular venue 2km out in Tavarede, about 400m east of the Parque Municipal de Campismo. **Flashen** (☎ 233 910 377; Praia de Quiaios; ⌚ midnight-4am Fri & Sat) is also 10km out in the sticks, but that doesn't deter its devoted following of beautiful young things.

The 'Three Chimneys' or **Três Chaminés** (☎ 233 407 920; www.3chamines.com in Portuguese; Caceira; ⌚ midnight-6am Sat, bowling 6pm-1am Mon-Thu, 6pm-3am Fri, 3pm-4am Sat, 3pm-1am Sun) is a huge industrial-looking place 4km east of town on the EN 111 towards Coimbra. The complex includes bowling, paintball and Figueira's hottest club for Latin-American rhythms.

Entertainment

Casino da Figueira (☎ 233 408 400; www.casinofigueira.pt; Rua Bernardo Lopes; ⌚ 3pm-3am) This creation in shimmering lights, acrylic and chrome often feels like the focal point of the entire resort, and crawls with cash-laden holidaymakers in search of a quick buck. The casino has roulette and slot machines, plus a sophisticated piano bar with live jazz after 11pm most nights. You're not welcome at night in beach attire, flip-flops (thongs) or sports shoes.

The venue for most big-name bands, theatre and art-house cinema is at **Centro de Artes e Espectaculos** (☎ 233 407 200; www.figueiradigital.com/cae in Portuguese) behind the museum. Check the website or pick up a schedule at the turismo.

Getting There & Away

BUS

Figueira's main terminal is served by three long-distance companies: **Moisés Correia de Oliveira** (☎ 233 426 703), **AVIC Mondego** (☎ 233 422 648) and **RBL/Rede Expressos** (in Coimbra ☎ 239 827 081). Oliveira runs multiple daily services via Montemor-o-Velho (below) to Coimbra (€3.15, 1¼ hours). Useful AVIC routes are to Mira (p312) and up to five buses daily to Aveiro (€3.85, 1½ hours). Services thin out at weekends.

Rede Expressos also has Mira (€5.90) and Aveiro (€7.20) connections, plus daily express services to Lisbon (€9.80, three hours). An AVIC express bus from Buarcos to Lisbon stops near the turismo 2pm Friday, 6pm Sunday and 6.30am Monday (€9.40, six hours); buy tickets on board or book ahead at **Viagens Marcos** (☎ 233 425 113; Rua Maestro David de Sousa 103). An express bus runs to Porto (€9) each weekday from the **AFGA travel agency** (☎ 233 402 222; Avenida Miguel Bombarda 79).

For details on transport to local beaches, see p309.

TRAIN

There are five to six daily services to Caldas da Rainha and Leiria, one of which continues directly to Lisbon (€9.50) or you can change in Caldas da Rainha. Trains to/from Coimbra (€1.55, one hour) are superior to buses, with connections every hour or two all day long.

Getting Around

AVIC (☎ 233 422 648) runs from the train station past the *mercado municipal* (€0.60) and turismo (€0.85) to Buarcos every half-hour on weekdays and at least hourly on weekends.

AROUND FIGUEIRA DA FOZ

Montemor-o-Velho

A stunning hilltop **castle** (admission free; ⌚ 10am-12.30pm & 2-5pm Tue-Sun Oct-May, 10am-8pm Tue-Sun Jun-Sep) rises like a brooding ghost above marshy fields 16km east of Figueira da Foz, on the N111 to Coimbra. Montemor-o-Velho's illustrious history has seen it serving both the Romans and the Moors, as well as being a royal retreat for rulers of the new kingdom of Portugal.

Though forbidding from afar, the castle is surprisingly tame inside – full of neatly manicured lawns and flower beds and dotted with restored towers and the charming **Igreja de Santa Maria de Alcáçova**, Manueline in outline. The views across the flat surrounding landscape are impressive, and kids will make a beeline for the unfenced battlements to stage their own battles.

The village itself is small, though there are restaurants and bus parking beneath the castle's southern and eastern walls. **Residencial Abade João** (☎ 239 689 458; fax 239 689 468; Rua dos Combatentes da Grande Guerra 15; s/d €37.50/42.50) is a beautiful old town house for anyone looking to hang their hat.

Trains between Coimbra (€1.05, 45 minutes) and Figueira da Foz (€1.15, 30 minutes) stop here every hour or two. Moisés Correia de Oliveira buses between Coimbra (€2.45, 55 minutes) and Figueira (€1.80, 30 minutes) stop 10 to 15 times daily (but just twice on Sunday).

PRAIA DE MIRA

For a few days of sunny, windblown torpor, you couldn't ask for a better stretch of the Atlantic than that between Figueira da Foz and Aveiro. In the 50km of mostly deserted coastline are two major access points to the sea, **Praia da Tocha** and **Praia de Mira**. If you fancy seafood, beer and indoor plumbing, go to Praia de Mira.

Sandwiched between a long, clean beach and a canal-fed lagoon, the colourful little village of Praia de Mira has little – aside from the candy-striped **Igreja da Nossa Senhora Conceição** on the beachfront – to distract you from the main business in hand: sun, sea and seafood. And plenty of it. You may still glimpse local fishermen hauling in their colourful *xavega* boats in summer, though they're a vanishing species.

Orientation & Information

Praia de Mira is 7km west of Mira on the N109, itself 35km north of Figueira da Foz.

Praia de Mira's axis is Avenida Cidade de Coimbra, the Mira road (N342). The erratic **turismo** (☎ 231 472 566; fax 231 458 185; Avenida da Barrinha; 🕑 9am-12.30pm & 2-5.30pm), 450m south of Avenida Cidade de Coimbra beside the lagoon, shares a wooden house with a little ethnographic exhibition.

Sleeping

Rates given here are for the high season (mid-July to August). At other times the rates drop by up to 40%, though even then they're generally overpriced. The town abounds in summer *quartos*, typically €25 to €40 per double. Watch for signs, or ask at the turismo.

Residencial Canadian Star (☎ 231 471 516; Avenida da Barrinha; d with breakfast €45) Facing the lagoon instead of the sea, this place has modest rates in comparison to those on the seafront; balconied rooms with a lagoon view cost €5 more, with the advantage of watching kids splash about in paddle boats below.

Residencial do Mar (☎ 231 471 144; residencialmar@hotmail.com; Avenida do Mar; d with breakfast €80; 🕑 closed Jan; P) An orthodox seaside holiday block. Well-kept and hospitable; all rooms have a TV and face the sea. Most have balconies.

The **pousada da juventude** has both **hostel accommodation** (☎ 231 471 199; mira@movijovem.pt; dm €10, d with toilet €27; 🕑 May-Sep) and **camping** (☎ 231 471 275; 🕑 mid-Jun–mid-Sep), although both were under renovation at the time of writing, to reopen in late 2004. Rates at the hostel include breakfast; other meals and bar service are available from mid-June to mid-September. To get here, turn left opposite the Orbitur camping site.

Parque de Campismo Municipal (☎ 231 472 173; fax 231 458 185; adult/tent/car €2.50/2.50/2.50; 🕑 May-Sep) Just steps from the wide lagoon, this is the town's cheapest and sketchiest facility 250m south of the turismo. Hot showers cost €0.80 extra.

Orbitur (☎ 231 471 234; info@orbitur.pt; adult/tent/car €3.80/3.10/3.50; 🕑 Feb-Nov) A more professional set-up, about 500m past the municipal camp site, also with tent-shaped bungalows available from €41.50. There are bikes for hire here too.

Camping Vila Caia (☎ 231 451 524; vlcaia@portugalmail.com; Lagoas; adult/tent/car €3.40/2.90/2.80; 🕑 Jan-Nov; ♿) A grassy and well-equipped, lakeside place 4km inland on the N342, which also has bungalows (from €42.50), tennis courts and a restaurant.

Parque Campismo Praia da Tocha (☎ 231 442 343; Rua dos Pescadores; adult/tent/car €2/1.60/1.60; 🕑 year-round) The next nearest camp site; a sandy, functional place within 100m of the sea, 28km south at Praia da Tocha. French spoken.

Eating

In summer there are more snack bars and cafés than you can shake a stick at, including a couple encroaching onto the beach. To the left of the beachside promenade is **Restaurante Mare Cheia** (☎ 231 472 067; Avenida do Mar; mains €6-11; 🕑 lunch & dinner) does a mean plate of sardines (€6) and other fresh seafood. Closer to the budget end, **Restaurante**

Canas (☎ 231 471 296; Avenida da Barrinha; mains €5-8; 🕑 lunch & dinner Mon-Sat) is in a no-frills setting opposite the turismo, with some outside seating.

Drinking & Entertainment

Cutting edge it's not, but every summer the local nightlife shakes off the cobwebs and splutters valiantly into action.

RX Caffé (Rua da Silva Alcaide; 🕑 11.30pm-5am Fri-Sun) This is the latest club on the scene. It tempts in a young fresh-from-the-beach crowd with live rock, and a smattering of house and alternative sounds.

Sixties Bar (Travessa Arrais Manuel Patrão; 🕑 9pm-4am) On the other hand, the Sixties Bar is an old-school Irish-flavoured pub on the first street back from the seafront.

Country Bar (Rua Padre Manuel Domingues; 🕑 10pm-4am Fri-Sun) A block south, the Country Bar is also welcoming – if you can appreciate a country-and-western soundtrack.

Contrabaixo (Rua Cidade de Viseu 28; 🕑 6pm-4am closed Mon low season) For something a tad more sophisticated, try Contrabaxio beside the canal. This is Praia de Mira's jazz headquarters and a good spot for sampling Portuguese wines, port and snacks too.

New Captain (Avenida da Barrinha; 🕑 1pm-4am Fri-Sun) Facing the lagoon, this is another popular bar. Look for the Guinness plaque.

In summer most of these places are open nightly, but don't expect the same to be true from late September to June.

Getting There & Away

Aveirense runs direct Praia de Mira buses from Aveiro's train station (€2.85, 50 minutes, three to four daily). However, most coastal transport stops inland only at Mira. AVIC Mondego comes from Aveiro around 10 times daily, from Figueira da Foz (€2.50, one hour, six daily) and Coimbra, with more limited weekend services; most of these have easy onward connections (€1.10) to Praia de Mira. Rede Expressos stops at Mira twice daily en route between Figueira da Foz and Aveiro.

If you need a **taxi** (☎ 231 471 257; Praia de Mira), they can be booked or hailed.

AVEIRO

pop 56,000

It's the nearby beaches and the bird reserve that attract most travellers to coastal Aveiro (uh-*vye*-roo), though the town itself has a rather unique atmosphere and history. It sits at the mouth of the Rio Vouga and the edge of a marshy lagoon known as the Ria, part of an extraordinary network of wetlands paralleling the seafront for 50km. Canals and humpback bridges give the town a genteel Dutch feel, and pastel-painted houses border the canals around the fish market.

History

Much of Aveiro's history revolves around the sea, salt and – more surprisingly – seaweed. The city prospered as a seaport in the early 16th century thanks to its saltpans, fishing fleet and the growing trade in *bacalhau* (salt cod). But a ferocious storm in the 1570s closed the river mouth, creating fever-breeding marshes that contributed to Aveiro's population dropping by three quarters in two centuries.

However, in 1808 the Barra Canal forged a passage back to the sea, the marshes were drained to form salt lagoons and within a century Aveiro was rich once more, its wealth reflected in a spate of Art Nouveau houses and azulejo friezes around town.

Once the harvesting of *molico* (seaweed) for use as fertiliser was another big earner for Aveiro, but this is on the decline. Many of the beautifully painted, high-prowed *moliceiro* boats moored along the canals now only carry tourists through the Ria.

Orientation

From the azulejo-clad train station it's a 1km stroll southwest down the main street, Avenida Dr Lourenço Peixinho and Rua Viana do Castelo (together called Avenida by all) to Praça Humberto Delgado (straddling the Canal Central). Nearby are the turismo and a pedestrianised centre dominated by the flashy Forum Aveiro shopping mall.

Parking is awful, and it isn't getting any better. Fight your way into the centre, past the turismo to the Largo do Rossio car park, and leave your car there for the duration. The turismo can give you a map showing other car parks.

Information

BOOKSHOPS

Livraria Bertrand (☎ 234 428 280; Avenida Dr Lourenço Peixinho 87C) The most useful bookshop.

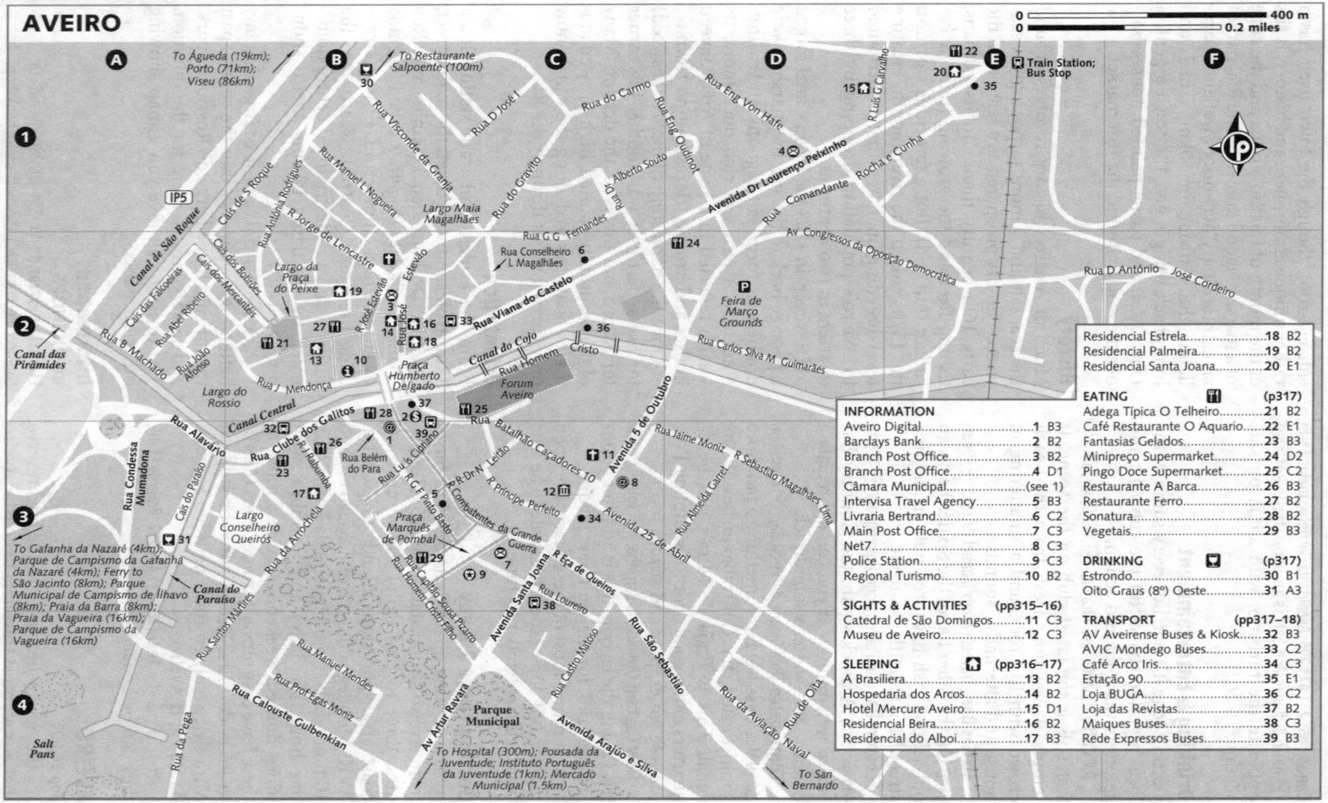

AVEIRO
0 – 400 m
0 – 0.2 miles
INFORMATION
Aveiro Digital 1 B3
Barclays Bank 2 B2
Branch Post Office 3 B2
Branch Post Office 4 D1
Câmara Municipal (see 1)
Intervisa Travel Agency 5 B3
Livraria Bertrand 6 C2
Main Post Office 7 C3
Net7 8 C3
Police Station 9 C3
Regional Turismo 10 B2
SIGHTS & ACTIVITIES (pp315–16)
Catedral de São Domingos 11 C3
Museu de Aveiro 12 C3
SLEEPING (pp316–17)
A Brasiliera 13 B2
Hospedaria dos Arcos 14 B2
Hotel Mercure Aveiro 15 D1
Residencial Beira 16 B2
Residencial do Alboi 17 B3
Residencial Estrela 18 B2
Residencial Palmeira 19 B2
Residencial Santa Joana 20 E1
EATING (p317)
Adega Típica O Telheiro 21 B2
Café Restaurante O Aquario 22 E1
Fantasias Gelados 23 B3
Minipreço Supermarket 24 D2
Pingo Doce Supermarket 25 C2
Restaurante A Barca 26 B3
Restaurante Ferro 27 B2
Sonatura 28 B2
Vegetais 29 B3
DRINKING (p317)
Estrondo 30 B1
Oito Graus (8º) Oeste 31 A3
TRANSPORT (pp317–18)
AV Aveirense Buses & Kiosk 32 B3
AVIC Mondego Buses 33 C2
Café Arco Iris 34 C3
Estação 90 35 E1
Loja BUGA 36 C2
Loja das Revistas 37 B2
Maiques Buses 38 C3
Rede Expressos Buses 39 B3
To Águeda (19km); Porto (71km); Viseu (86km)
To Restaurante Salpoente (100m)
Train Station; Bus Stop
To Gafanha da Nazaré (4km); Parque de Campismo da Gafanha da Nazaré (4km); Ferry to São Jacinto (8km); Parque Municipal de Campismo de Ílhavo (8km); Praia da Barra (8km); Praia da Vagueira (16km); Parque de Campismo da Vagueira (16km)
To Hospital (300m); Pousada da Juventude; Instituto Português da Juventude (1km); Mercado Municipal (1.5km)
To San Bernardo
Canal de São Roque
Canal das Pirâmides
Canal Central
Canal do Cojo
Canal do Paraíso
Largo do Rossio
Largo da Praça do Peixe
Largo Maia Magalhães
Praça Humberto Delgado
Praça Marquês de Pombal
Largo Conselheiro Queirós
Forum Aveiro
Feira de Março Grounds
Parque Municipal
Salt Pans
IP5
Avenida Dr Lourenço Peixinho
Rua Viana do Castelo
Avenida 5 de Outubro
Avenida 25 de Abril
Avenida Santa Joana
Avenida Arajúo e Silva
Av Artur Ravara
Rua Calouste Gulbenkian
Rua São Sebastião
Rua Clube dos Galitos
Rua Alavário
Rua Condessa Mumadona
Av Congressos da Oposição Democrática
Rua D António José Cordeiro
Rua Carlos Silva M Guimarães
Rua Batalhão Caçadores 10
Rua Eng Von Hafe
Rua Eng Oudinot
Rua do Carmo
Rua do Gravito
Rua Visconde da Granja
Rua Manuel L Nogueira
R Jorge de Lencastre
Rua Comandante Rocha e Cunha
Rua da Aviação Naval
Rua de Oita
Rua Santos Mártires
Rua da Pega
Rua Manuel Mendes
Rua Prof Egas Moniz
Rua Homem Cristo Filho
Rua Capitão Sousa Pizarro
R Eça de Queiros
Rua Loureiro
Rua Castro Matoso
R Sebastião Magalhães Lima
Rua Jaime Moniz
Rua Almeida Garret
R Combatentes da Grande Guerra
R Príncipe Perfeito
Rua da Arrochela
Cais do Paraíso
Cais de S Roque
Cais dos Botirões
Cais dos Mercantéis
Cais das Falcoeiras
Rua B Machado

EMERGENCY & MEDICAL SERVICES

Hospital (☎ 234 378 300; Avenida Artur Ravada) About 1.2km south of the town centre.

Police station (☎ 234 422 022; Praça Marquês de Pombal) A few blocks south of the Canal Central.

INTERNET ACCESS

Aveiro Digital (☎ 234 371 666; 🕑 9am-8pm Mon-Fri, 10am-7pm Sat) Aveiro pioneered municipally sponsored Internet access in Portugal, and still offers a big menu of free services in a room at the rear of the *câmara municipal* (town hall).

Instituto Português da Juventude (☎ 234 381 935; Rua das Pombas 182; 🕑 9.30am-noon & 2-5.30pm Mon-Fri) About 1km from the centre, with free Internet access.

Net7 (☎ 234 196 156; per hr €2; 🕑 9.30am-midnight Mon-Sat, 1pm-midnight Sun) For evening and weekend surfing, there's this cybercafé opposite the cathedral.

MONEY

There are banks with ATMs all along the Avenida, and a Barclays across the canal from the turismo.

POST

Main post office (☎ 234 380 840; Praça Marquês de Pombal; 🕑 8.30am-6.30pm Mon-Fri, 9am-12.30pm Sat) This is the place for poste restante.

Branch post office (Rua José Estevão 17; 🕑 9am-6pm Mon-Fri

Branch post office (Avenida Dr Lourenço Peixinho 171; 🕑 9am-6pm Mon-Fri)

TOURIST INFORMATION

Regional turismo (☎ 234 423 680; aveiro.rotadaluz@inovanet.pt; Rua João Mendonça 8; 🕑 9am-8pm Jun-Sep; 9am-7pm Mon-Fri, 9.30am-1pm & 2-5.30pm Sat Oct-May, 10am-1pm Sun Oct-May) This excellent tourist office is to be found in Art Nouveau headquarters beside the Canal Central.

TRAVEL AGENCIES

Intervisa (☎ 234 386 764; Rua Gustavo Ferreira Pinto Basto 29; 🕑 9am-6pm Mon-Fri) A reliable mainstream agency.

Sights

MUSEU DE AVEIRO

This fine, if somewhat single-minded, **museum** (☎ 234 423 297; Avenida Santa Joana Princesa; adult/child/youth 14-25/senior €1.50/free/0.75/0.75, free 10am-2pm Sun; 🕑 10am-5.30pm Tue-Sun), in the former Mosteiro de Jesus, opposite the Catedral de São Domingos, owes its finest treasures to Princesa (later beatified as Santa) Joana, daughter of Afonso V.

In 1472, 11 years after the convent was founded, Joana 'retired' here and, though forbidden to take full vows, she stayed until her death in 1490. Her tomb, a 17th-century masterpiece of marble mosaic, sits in an equally lavish baroque chancel decorated with azulejos depicting her life. The museum's paintings include a late-15th-century portrait of her, attributed to Nuno Gonçalves.

RESERVA NATURAL DAS DUNAS DE SÃO JACINTO

Stretching north from São Jacinto to Ovar, between the sea and the N327, is an excellent little 6.7-sq-km wooded nature reserve, equipped with trails and bird-watching hides. Entry is via an **interpretive centre** (☎ 234 331 282; http://camarinha.aveiro-digital.net in Portuguese; 🕑 9am-noon & 2-5pm Mon-Sat) on the N327. To minimise the impact on wildlife, you can only enter between 9am and 9.30am or between 2pm and 2.30pm, for a maximum stay of 2½ hours. There's usually a guide on hand to give a free tour, or materials available to help you make the best of a visit on your own. Book ahead if you can.

To get here, take a Forte da Barra bus from the **AV Aveirense kiosk** (☎ 234 423 513; Rua Clube dos Galitos) to the end of the line (€1.50), from where a small passenger ferry (€1 for adults) crosses to the port of São Jacinto. Children aged four to 10 and seniors go for half-price. Ask at the turismo for current timetables.

From São Jacinto port the reserve entrance is 1.3km down the Torreira road. Note that by road the entrance is 50km from Aveiro!

Activities

Though not the Costa de Prata's finest beaches, the surfing venues of **Praia da Barra** and **Costa Nova**, 13km west of Aveiro, are good for a day's outing. The prettier Costa Nova has a beachside street lined with cafés, kitsch gift shops and picturesque candy-striped cottages.

AV Aveirense buses go via Gafanha da Nazaré to Costa Nova (€1.60) about hourly from the kiosk on Rua Clube dos Galitos; the last bus back departs at about 8.15pm in summer and 6.55pm in winter.

Wilder and more remote is **Praia de São Jacinto**, on the northern side of the lagoon.

The vast beach of sand dunes is a 1.5km walk from São Jacinto port (p315), through a residential area at the back of town.

Aveirosub (☎ 234 367 666; www.aveirosub.co.pt in Portuguese; Avenida José Estevão 724, Gafanha da Nazaré) offers **scuba-diving** classes (36 sessions of 50 minutes, about half of them in the sea, for €350, or €300 for students).

From mid-June to mid-September the turismo organises daily, three-hour **motor-launch trips** (adult/child under 12/child 8-12 €8/free/5) across the Ria to Costa Nova, with a half-hour pause there. They depart at 2.30pm from the Canal Central in front of the turismo, provided there are enough passengers (at least eight).

One-hour private **moliceiros trips** (adult/child under 6/child 7-12 €7/free/3.30) around the Ria are available subject to passenger numbers; tickets are available at the turismo. Two-hour *moliceiros* trips to São Jacinto may also be on offer in July and August; ask at the turismo.

Festivals & Events

Feira de Março (March Fair) Held from late March to late April and dates back 5½ centuries. Nowadays it features everything from folk music to rock concerts.

Festa da Ria Aveiro celebrates its canals and *moliceiros* from mid-July to the end of August. Highlights include folk dancing and a *moliceiros* race.

Festas do São Paio Another *moliceiros* race features in this festival in Murtosa (on the northern side of the lagoon) in the first week of September.

Festas do Município Sees two weeks of merrymaking around 12 May in honour of Santa Joana (p315).

Sleeping

Summer accommodation is even tighter than parking here; consider booking a week or so ahead in peak season.

BUDGET

Note that apart from the pousada da juventude, the following budget options are all camp sites.

Pousada da juventude (☎ 234 420 536; aveiro@movijovem.pt; Rua das Pombas 182; dm €10, d with toilet €27; 💻) Aveiro's youth hostel is 1.5km south of the centre.

Parque Municipal de Campismo (☎ /fax 234 331 220; adult/tent/car €1.80/0.90/0.50; 🕑 Mar-Nov) Nearest and cheapest is this park at São Jacinto, 2.5km from the pier along the Torreira road.

Orbitur São Jacinto (☎ 234 838 284; info@orbitur.pt; adult/tent/car €3.50/2.90/3.40; 🕑 Feb-Nov) Around 2.5km further on, Orbitur is a very nice site with more shade, better facilities (including an ATM) and is close to the sea. There's no bus service along this road; see Reserva Natural das Dunas de São Jacinto p315 for transport details.

Parque Municipal de Campismo de Ílhavo (☎ 234 369 425; www.campingbarra.com in Portuguese; Rua Diogo Cão, Praia da Barra; adult/tent/car €2.80/3.25/3.30; 🕑 year-round) A fairly well-equipped, sandy and flat site next to the beach.

Parque de Campismo da Gafanha da Nazaré (☎ 234 366 565; fax 234 365 789; adult/tent/car €1.05/1/1.85; 🕑 year-round) Another budget option, this shady and flat site is southeast of Gafanha da Nazaré, and not a million miles from the sea. It now requires a CCI (p452).

Parque de Campismo da Vagueira (☎ 234 797 526; arliudo.ida@clix.pt; Vagueira; adult/tent/car €3.30/3/2.50; 🕑 year-round; 💻) This is one of the best camping sites in the area – there are tennis courts (€3 per hour), bikes for hire, Internet in the summer (€2.50 per hour), and nice shady, grassy pitches.

MID-RANGE & TOP END

A Brasiliera (☎ 234 428 634; Rua Tenente Resende 47; d with basin €25, with toilet & shower €30) Run by a kindly old couple, A Brasileira is a sleepy old rabbit warren of a place. It's a mite faded round the edges, but retains a certain, jumbled charm.

Hospedaria dos Arcos (☎ 234 383 130; Rua José Estevão 47; d with breakfast €37.50) This place has a just-like-grandma's-house atmosphere, with several floors of spotless, little rooms and a generous breakfast. It makes a superb retreat, though it's not a place that would welcome the kids.

Residencial Santa Joana (☎ 234 428 604; fax 234 428 602; Avenida Dr Peixinho 227; s/d €30/40) A newly remodelled spot next to the train station, with faded rooms but sparkling bathrooms and entrance.

Residencial Palmeira (☎ 234 422 521; residencial.palmeira@netc.pt; Rua da Palmeira 7; s/d with breakfast €30/35) This is another quiet, homely choice hiding in the backstreets.

Residencial do Alboi (☎ 234 380 390; www.residencial-alboi.com; Rua da Arrochela 6; s/d with breakfast €40/53; 💻) Down a quiet lane in the heart of town, this place has quiet rooms and a discernable air of dignity.

Hotel Mercure Aveiro (☎ 234 404 400; www.accorhotels.com; Rua Luís Gomes de Carvalho 23; s/d €61/68; P) Best known as the old Paloma Blanca, this hotel occupies a handsome 1930s mansion near the train station. Off-street parking costs €4 per night and breakfast is €7.50.

Two neighbouring townhouses converted into *residenciais*, bang in the centre, are the fuddy-duddy **Residential Estrela** (☎ 234 423 818; Rua José Estevão 4; d with/without shower from €35/20) offering breezy, varied rooms with old creaky furniture and no-nonsense **Residential Beira** (☎ 234 424 297; Rua José Estevão 18; d with breakfast from €45).

Eating

Fantasias Gelados (☎ 234 381 350; Rua Clube dos Galitos 23; ice creams & crepes from €1.40; 10am-7pm) You're on holiday, so don't hold back! This place offers 24 flavours of 'Fantasy Ice-creams' and dreamy crepes to get you in the vacation spirit.

Sonatura (☎ 234 424 474; Rua Clube dos Galitos 6; set meals €3.80-5; lunch Mon-Fri) Wholesome, lovingly prepared vegetarian dishes are proffered up at the self-service bar here. Even nonvegetarians will love seeing so many vegetables on a Portuguese plate, and at earthy prices.

Vegetais (☎ 234 383 555; Rua Capitão Sousa Pizarro 23; mains €5; 8.30am-10pm Mon-Thu, 8.30am-3pm Fri, noon-10pm Sun) This spic-and-span veggie option has sprung up in competition to Sonatura, and also serves decent vegetarian breakfasts.

Adega Típica O Telheiro (☎ 234 429 473; Largo Praça do Peixe 20-21; mains €8-13; lunch & dinner Sun-Fri) The *adega* (wine tavern) atmosphere – hams hanging from the ceiling, long tables, low wooden ceiling, red wine by the jug – is half the fun here. Good grilled seafood is also dished up at fair prices. Star of the 'starters' menu is the *sopa de mer*, a great warming chowder. For less formality, park yourself at the long bar and chew the fat with local bar flies.

Restaurante Ferro (☎ 234 422 214; Rua Tenente Resende 30; dishes €7-11; lunch & dinner Mon-Sat, lunch Sun) Energetic and popular, this bustling spot is great for a quick lunch stop, with lots of fish and meat dishes, plus omelettes.

Restaurante A Barca (☎ 234 426 024; Rua José Rabumba 5A; dishes €9-13; lunch & dinner Mon-Fri, lunch Sat) This restaurant has a casual atmosphere and a choice of fish, fish and more fish – all fresh from the market of course.

Café Restaurante O Aquário (☎ 234 425 014; Rua Almirante Cândido dos Reis 139; mains €4-8; lunch & dinner Mon-Sat) There's little to recommend near the train station, though this café is at least clean and cheerful, with super-fast service, long tables and a lively crowd on Sunday.

Self-caterers can choose from the **mercado municipal** (Tue-Sat) about 500m further south beyond the Pousada da Juventude, and supermarkets including **Pingo Doce** (8.30am-9pm) in the Forum Aveiro mall and **Minipreço** (9am-8pm Mon-Sat, 9am-1pm & 3-7pm Sun) on the Avenida.

Drinking

There are several good bars along the pungent Canal de São Roque beyond the fish market.

Estrondo (☎ 234 383 366; Cais de São Roque 74; Mon-Sat) This is a smart wooden-fronted bar for the well-heeled.

Restaurante Salpoente (☎ 234 382 674; Cais de São Roque 83; bar 11.30pm-3am Fri & Sat) Salpoente is a big wooden shack of a building that blasts with live music (especially rock) at weekends.

Oito Graus (8*) Oeste (☎ 234 383 169; Cais do Paraíso 19; 11.30pm-4am Fri & Sat) Another favourite, this is a popular stand-alone club surrounded by a moat of canals.

Getting There & Away

BUS

Few long-distance buses actually terminate here; there isn't even a bus station.

Rede Expressos has two to three daily services to/from Lisbon (€11.40, four hours); get tickets and timetables at the **Loja das Revistas newsagent** (Praça Humberto Delgado) and catch the bus around the corner, or book it at Intervisa (see p315).

AVIC Mondego goes up to five times a day except Sunday to Figueira da Foz (€3.35, two hours) from Rua Viana do Castelo and the train station. AV Aveirense's direct Praia de Mira services (€2.85, three to four daily) leaves from near the station, and **Maiques** (☎ 234 429 982) buses for Viseu (€5.90, 1½ hours, twice daily) leave from close to the museum. Buy tickets in nearby **Café Arco Iris** (Avenida Santa Joana).

TRAIN

Aveiro is actually within Porto's *suburbano* network, which means there are hourly commuter trains to/from Porto (€1.75, 1¼ hours); there are also four IC trains a day (€6.50, 55 minutes). Other IC links include Coimbra (€6.50, 35 minutes, four daily) and Lisbon (€13, three hours, four daily), plus additional Alfa and IR services.

Getting Around

Local bus routes converge on the Avenida and the train station. A *bilet de cidade* (city ticket) from a kiosk or *tabacaria* costs €1.10 for two journeys; from the driver they're €1.30 for just one trip. The ticket source closest to the train station is a *pastelaria* (pastry or cake shop) called **Estação 90** (Avenida Dr Lourenço Peixinho 352).

Aveiro runs a pioneering free-bike scheme, Bicicleta de Utilização Gratuita de Aveiro (BUGA). Just give your ID details at the **Loja BUGA** (10am-12.30pm & 1.30-6pm Mon-Fri, 9am-7pm Sat & Sun) kiosk beside the Canal do Cojo, take a bike and ride it as long as you like within designated town limits, and return it to the kiosk before they shut, all for free.

BEIRA BAIXA

Beira Baixa closely resembles the Alentejo, with welcoming people, fierce summers and landscapes so flat they often seem to stretch on forever. It's home to sprawling agricultural estates, pockets of farming hamlets and several stunning fortresses.

CASTELO BRANCO

pop 32,500 / elevation 360m

Castelo Branco has its proximity to the frontier, 20km to the south, to thank for brutal and repeated attacks over the centuries. Indeed its prolonged embattlement has robbed the provincial capital of Beira Baixa of much of its historic character. However, its prosperous centre is blessed with wide squares, parks and boulevards, and the city makes a good base to visit the fortress village of Monsanto and the curious hamlet of Idanha-a-Velha (p321).

Orientation

From the bus station, turn right down Rua do Saibreiro to central Alameda da Liberdade. From the train station the Alameda is 500m north on Avenida Nuno Álvares.

Information

Instituto Português da Juventude (272 348 000; Rua Dr Francisco José Palmeiro; 9am-6.30pm Mon-Fri) Free Internet access, 1km northwest of the centre.

Kryptobyte (272 323 283; Urb. Quinta Dr Beirão, Bloco 9, 30C; 10am-10pm) Games room and cyber-café 1km west of the town centre in a residential area. Bring ID.

Nisa Rato (272 327 537; Rua Pedro da Fonseca; per hr €1; 10am-1pm & 3-8pm Mon-Fri, 10am-1pm Sat) A computer shop with three Internet terminals.

Parque Natural do Tejo Internacional (272 321 445; pnti.silveiras@icn.pt; Rua Senhora da Piedade 4A) The park's headquarters is two blocks southeast of the turismo.

Post office (272 323 111; Rua da Sé; 8.30am-6.30pm Mon-Fri, 9am-12.30pm Sat)

Turismo (272 330 339; turismo.cmcb@mail.telepac.pt; 9.30am-7.30pm Mon-Fri, 9.30am-1pm & 2.30-6pm Sat & Sun) A temporary tourist booth is on the southwestern corner of the Alameda, but is likely to hop the short distance to the Alameda's centre in 2005. Everything of interest is an easy walk from here.

A STITCH IN TIME

For centuries, Castelo Branco has been famed for its exquisite *colchas* – silk-embroidered linen bedspreads or coverlets inspired by those the early Portuguese explorers brought back from India and China. These luxurious items fast became a sign of prestige and wealth, and their designs of exotic flora and fauna abound in complex symbolism (two birds symbolise lovers, trees represent families and so on).

On weekdays you can watch their painstaking production in the Museu de Francisco Tavares Proença Júnior or at the **Loja da Villa** (272 341 576, 933 498 155; Rua da Misericórdia 37; 9am-6pm Mon-Fri), a workshop in the old town. Though should you order one, you may have to wait up to a year to get your hands on it.

Meanwhile, prices are a mere snip at €1000 for a small item to €7500 for a bedspread-sized *colcha,* but if that makes your jaw drop, consider the whoppers on sale at the museum that can set you back as much as €27,500!

Sights

PALÁCIO EPISCOPAL

The Palácio Episcopal (Bishop's Palace), in the north of town, is a sober 18th-century affair housing the **Museu de Francisco Tavares Proença Júnior** (☎ 272 344 277; mftpj@ipmuseus.pt; Rua Frei Bartolomeu da Costa; adult/child under 14/student €2/free/1; ⌚ 10am-12.30pm & 2-5.30pm Tue-Sun). The museum concentrates on the history of the episcopacy, with fine 16th-century religious paintings and 18th-century portraits of various popes, kings and cardinals. But if you're a fan of embroidery you'll be wowed by the exhibition of Castelo Branco's famous *colchas* (opposite), including several 17th-century versions made in India and China.

Beside the museum is the **Jardim Episcopal** (Bishop's Garden; adult/child under 10/senior €1.50/free/free; ⌚ 9am-9pm Apr-Sep, 9am-5pm Oct-Mar), a baroque whimsy of clipped box hedges and little granite statues. Notice that the statues of the Spanish kings Felipe I and II are smaller than those of the Portuguese monarchs!

Watch your back on the bottom of the kings' stairway though as there are hidden clap-activated fountains waiting to soak passing maidens' petticoats. The attendant will show you where to clap.

CASTELO

There's little left of the castle, built by the Knights Templar in the 13th century and extended by Dom Dinis. However, the Miradouro de São Gens garden, which has supplanted the walls, offers grand views over town and countryside. The old lanes that lead back down to the town centre are very picturesque.

Sleeping

Pensão Império (☎ 272 341 720; Rua Prazeres 20; s/d/tw with breakfast €22/32/37; ❄) Best of the budget *pensões*. A friendly, very well kept spot in a backstreet near the post office, run by chirpy folks, eager to please. Top value.

Pensão Residencial Arraiana (☎ 272 341 634; Avenida 1 de Maio 18; s/d with breakfast €30/48; ❄) This less personal, more business-like spot on a busy road is a good but more jaded alternative, with minibars filled to bursting with beer.

Hotel Rainha D Amélia (☎ 272 348 800; www.bestwestern.com/pt/hotelrainhadamelia; Rua Santiago 15; s/d €61/74.50; P ⊠ ❄) Further down and around a corner from the Arraiana, is a Best Western franchise with forgettable rooms that nonetheless sport all the expected frills. It also has four rooms specially adapted for disabled visitors.

Pousada da juventude (☎ 272 323 838; Rua Dr Francisco José Palmeiro) This place, beside the Instituto Português da Juventude, was shut for renovations in 2004.

Parque Municipal de Campismo (☎ 272 322 577; adult/tent/car €1.75/1.50/1.50; Jan-Nov) About 3km from the centre of town, this dusty site has scattered trees and grassy pitches, but facilities are basic.

Eating

Restaurante O Jardim (☎ 272 342 850; Rua Figueira 29; half-portions €4.50, full portions €4.50-10; lunch & dinner Mon-Sat) Given the sheer volume of helpings (order pork and expect half a pig!), this cosy little restaurant down a backstreet across the plaza from the post office is fantastic value. Note the hundreds of lovingly collected cigarette lighters stuck to the walls.

Praça Velha (☎ 272 328 640; Largo Luís de Camões; dishes €12.50, fondue for 2 people €25; lunch & dinner Tue-Sun; P) For a proper treat, make a beeline here. Praça Velha resides in a former Knights Templar abode in the old town – low wooden ceiling, stone floors and pillars and a long buffet table heaped with platters. And the menu lives up to its grand setting. Lobster anyone?

Restaurante Zé dos Cachopos (☎ 272 345 537; Rua Emilia Oliveira Pinto 13; dishes €6-9; lunch & dinner Wed-Sun, lunch Mon) Also pretty upmarket, Zé's has a big meat menu and a comfortable ambience.

Self-caterers can find supplies, including the *queijo de ovelha* (sheep's cheese) for which this region is famous, in the **mercado municipal** (Avenida 1 de Maio) or nearby **Pingo Doce** (Avenida 1 de Maio).

Getting There & Away

BUS

Castelo Branco is on the Braga–Faro express run, which travels twice daily via Covilhã (€4.80, 50 minutes), Guarda (€7.80, 1½ hours), Viseu (€9.20, 3½ hours) and Portalegre (€8, 1½ hours). Other services include Coimbra (€9.50, 2¼ hours, three to four daily) and Lisbon (€9.40, 3½ hours, four to seven daily).

TRAIN

Castelo Branco is on the Lisbon-Guarda line, with six trains daily from Lisbon, including two IC services (€11.50, 3¼ hours), and slower regional services (€9.50, four hours).

PARQUE NATURAL DO TEJO INTERNACIONAL

One of Portugal's wildest landscapes lies along the Rio Tejo in southeastern Beira Baixa, within the watersheds of three of its tributaries, the Rio Ponsul, Ribeira do Aravil and Rio Erges. Residents include some of the country's rarest animal species: black stork, Bonelli's eagle, royal eagle, Egyptian vulture, black vulture and griffon vulture. In 2000, following a major push by the private environmental organisation Quercus (p61), a 230-sq-km *parque natural* was established here.

Information

Park headquarters is in Castelo Branco (p319), though the best source of park information is the Castelo Branco office of the private environmental organisation **Quercus** (☎ 272 324 272; quercusc.branco@mail.telepac.pt; Travessa do Espirito Santo 54, Castelo Branco).

At Castelo Branco's turismo you can buy Quercus' 250-page *Guia de Percursos Tejo Internacional,* a guide (in Portuguese) to regional geology, climate, flora and fauna, villages, trails and transport.

Quercus runs bird-watching, walking and other programmes. Basic accommodation is available at Rosmaninhal and Monte Barata; for details contact **Paulo Monteiro** (☎ 277 477 463) at Quercus.

MONSANTO

pop 200 / elevation 600m

With a reputation as Portugal's oldest settlement, the medieval fortress village of Monsanto, 48km northeast of Castelo Branco, is an achingly beautiful spot. Rising high above the surrounding landscape, its boulder-strewn castle and tiny town offer an incredible glimpse of medieval Portugal at its toughest and truest. Village life seems amazingly unaffected by the steady stream of tourists; elderly women still keep hens and goats and sit on their doorsteps, crocheting and chatting.

Orientation & Information

Monsanto is so small that you just need to follow the very steep path uphill to reach the castle.

Post office (Largo do Cruzeiro; 9am-noon Mon-Fri) Near the village entrance.

Turismo (277 314 642, 968 122 662; Rua Marquês da Gracioça; 10am-1pm & 2-6pm Sat & Sun) A little further uphill.

Sights

VILLAGE

Since Monsanto won a 1939 award as 'Portugal's most traditional village', it has been largely shielded from modernisation. Along the twisting upward path, cottages and animal sheds are built amid and carved out of towering boulders and rocky outcrops that are often topped by stone crosses. Houses near the village entrance are surprisingly grand, some sporting Manueline doorways and stone crests. Halfway to the castle you'll come across the **gruta**, a snug cavern apparently once used as a drinking den – and still used as such, judging by the half-empty glasses of beer inside.

CASTELO

This formidable stone fortress seems almost to have grown out of the boulder-littered hillside that supports it. It's a hauntingly beautiful site, populated by lizards and wildflowers. Immense vistas (marred only by mobile-phone masts) include Spain to the east and the Barragem da Idanha lake to the southwest.

There was probably a fortress here before the Romans came, but after Dom Sancho I booted out the Moors in the 12th century it was beefed up. Dom Dinis refortified it but after centuries of attacks from across the border it finally fell into ruin.

Just below the castle entrance is a plaza used for folk dances at festival time. To the right is a ruined Renaissance church and bell tower, and five stone tombs carved into the rock.

Festivals & Events

On 3 May Monsanto comes alive in the **Festa das Cruzes**, commemorating a medieval siege. The story goes that the starving villagers threw their last lonely calf over the walls, taunting their besiegers as if they had plenty to spare. And apparently, their attackers were wholly hoodwinked by the calf-chucking tactics, as they promptly abandoned the siege. These days, young girls throw baskets of flowers instead, after which there's dancing and singing beside the castle walls.

Sleeping & Eating

Adega Típica O Cruzeiro (277 314 528; Rua Fernando Namora 4; d €40) The only easily available *quartos* are at this surprisingly genteel place, which also has a rustic restaurant and daily specials for about €6 to €7.

Pousada de Monsanto (277 314 471; fax 277 314 481; d Mon-Fri €95, Sat & Sun €105) Near the village entrance is the modern, comfortable Pousada de Monsanto.

Café Jovem (277 314 590; Avenida Fernando Ramos Rocha 21; mains €7-9; lunch & dinner) Below the post office, this café cheerfully dishes up standard Portuguese fare.

Lapa da Moura (966 150 424; Rua do Castelo 15; mains €6-7; lunch & dinner) Further up the hill near the *gruta*, the small Lapa da Moura doesn't go in much for fixed menus but has good specials; just ask what's available. It has no sign – look for the knife-and-fork symbol outside. There are also souvenir shops selling home-made honey cakes, some laced with a wicked *aguardente* (alcoholic 'firewater').

Getting There & Away

On weekdays two buses run daily from Castelo Branco (€4.80, 1¾ hours); the first requires a change at Idanha-a-Nova. The return service leaves only at 6.20am (2pm on Sunday). Ask locally for the latest schedules.

IDANHA-A-VELHA

Idanha-a-Velha, a remote 15km southwest of Monsanto, is an extraordinary place with an even more extraordinary history. Once a sizable Roman city called Igaeditânia, it was pounced upon and rebuilt by the Visigoths (who erected a cathedral here), occupied by the Moors and then taken over by the Knights Templar.

So why did this much-desired enclave, once rich with gold deposits, suddenly fade into obscurity? Rats. Or some say ants. A plague of one or the other apparently drove the inhabitants out, leaving Roman and Visigothic ruins everywhere. Where was the Pied Piper when Idanha-a-Velha needed him?

Today it's a simple farming hamlet, but it has been designated one of the region's 10 Aldeias Históricas. Unfortunately, the most obvious results so far are an ugly iron walkway on top of the Roman walls and a morgue-like display gallery by the cathedral, housing Roman funerary stones. But just walking around the hamlet is an eerily memorable experience.

Information

The **turismo** (☎ 277 914 280; Rua da Sé; ⏲ 10am-12.30pm & 2-6.30pm) is built on a see-through floor over ruins of the old settlement. The office is occasionally shut if the staff are on guided visits.

Sights

From the turismo it's a short walk to the 6th-century Visigothic **cathedral**, surrounded by a jigsaw puzzle of scattered archaeological remains and undergoing heavy restoration but accessible with turismo staff. Of the frescoes within, look for the one of São Bartolomeu with what appears to be a teddy bear at his feet.

The nearby **Lagar de Varas** (admission free; ⏲ by request at turismo 10.30am-11.30am & 3-5pm) hosts an impressive olive-oil press made in the traditional way with ruddy great tree trunks providing the crushing power.

The only evidence of the Knights Templar is the **Torre des Templários**, made of massive chunks of stone and now surrounded by clucking hens. Wander round the back of the village to see the Roman bridge and walls.

After all this history it's a delight to come across the **Forno Comunitário** (communal bakery; Rua do Castelo) and discover villagers sliding trays of biscuits and enormous loaves of bread into the huge stone oven, blackened from use.

Eating

Café Lafiv (☎ 277 914 180; Rua da Amoreira 1; ⏲ daily) Near the turismo, this is the village's only café, serving little more than sandwiches and smoked sausage.

Getting There & Away

On weekdays during term-time only, there's one bus daily from Idanha-a-Nova (40 minutes). Two to three buses daily run to Idanha-a-Nova from Castelo Branco (€2.90, 55 minutes).

SORTELHA

pop 800 / elevation 760m

Sortelha is the oldest – and most atmospheric – of a string of rock fortresses guarding the frontier east of Guarda and Covilhã. It also has one of the dramatic settings, with immense fortified walls and a castle that seems to teeter on the brink of a steep drop. And inside the formidable fortifications is a lovely 12th-century walled village with Moorish origins, carved into the rocky hillside and boasting extraordinary views over a wild landscape.

Most of old Sortelha's stout granite cottages have been finely restored, but the inner village now has about half a dozen permanent residents – adding to the eerie silence.

Orientation & Information

'New' Sortelha lines the Santo Amaro–Sabugal road, along which are two restaurants and several Turihab properties. The medieval hilltop fortress is a short drive, or a 10-minute walk, up one of two lanes signposted 'castelo'.

The Liga dos Amigos de Sortelha runs an unofficial turismo and handicrafts shop a block uphill from the castle ruins, but its opening hours are unpredictable.

Sights

The entrance to the fortified old village is a grand, stone Gothic **gate**. From Largo do Corro, just inside the gate, a cobbled lane leads up to the heart of the village – a *pelourinho* (stone pillory) in front of the remains of a small **castle** to the left and the parish **church** to the right. Higher still is the **bell tower**. Climb here for a view of the entire village (but a sign begs visitors not to ring the bells), or tackle the ramparts around the village (beware precarious sections!).

Sleeping

Sortelha boasts several atmospheric Turihab properties, complete with kitchens, thick stone walls and heating. Calling a week or two ahead is essential in high season.

Casa da Cerca (☎ 963 904 449, ☎/fax 271 388 113; casadacerca@clix.pt; Largo de Santo António; s/d with breakfast €70/85; Ⓟ ✖) Situated on the main road, this is a 17th-century house with six traditional cottage rooms.

Casa do Páteo (2/4 people with kitchen €60/80) This smaller and more private place is next door to Casa da Cerca and under the same management.

Casa da Vila (Rua Direita; 1-8 people from €35-180) This delightful stone cottage has a privileged place within the village walls. It accommodates from two to eight guests, and is again owned by the same people that run Casa da Cerca and Casa do Páteo.

Casas do Campanário (☎ 271 388 198; Rua da Mesquita; double €60) Choose between a house for two people and another for up to six; ask at Bar Campanário, at the top of the village just beyond the bell tower.

Eating

Restaurante O Celta (☎ 271 388 291; mains €6.50-14; 🕑 lunch & dinner Wed-Mon) Sortelha's weddings-parties-and-anything venue, at the rear of a café of the same name on the main road, offers a bigger menu and a bit of atmosphere for marginally higher prices.

Restaurante Dom Sancho I (☎ 271 388 267; Largo do Corro) You'll find this place just inside the gate. It has an atmospheric bar downstairs and stratospheric food prices upstairs, though food is first-rate.

Café Restaurante Palmeiras (☎ 271 388 260; mains €4-6) On the main road at the northern end of the village, with zero atmosphere but lots of cheer, a few pots on the stove and a short list of specials.

LAST OF THE LYNXES

The Iberian lynx is the world's most endangered wild cat (p57), and the 218-sq-km Reserva Natural da Serra da Malcata was created in 1981 specifically to help save it. However, at the time of writing, there was debate as to whether there were actually any lynx left at all in this sprawling area of scrubby hills, oak woodland and valleys of the Rio Côa and its tributaries. The only good news for the sanctuary is that it will soon see a captive breeding programme to try to pull the species back from the brink of destruction. For more information contact the reserve's **main office** (☎ 277 394 467; rnsm@icn.pt; Rua António Nunes Ribeiro Sanches 60, 6090 Penamacor).

Getting There & Away

Getting here by public transport is hard work. A daily bus from Sabugal only runs during the school term. Regional trains on the Covilhã–Guarda line (three daily) stop at Belmonte-Manteigas station, 12km to the northwest, from where the local **taxi** (☎ 271 388 182) will collect you for about €10.

PARQUE NATURAL DA SERRA DA ESTRELA

Think of Portugal and you're unlikely to picture pristine mountains and rugged treks. However, venture into the country's heart and you'll be glad you brought along your hiking boots.

The glacially scoured plateau called the Serra da Estrela – mainland Portugal's highest mountain range, topping out at the 1993m Torre (Tower) – forms an impressive natural boundary between north and south. At higher elevations it's positively alpine, with rounded peaks, boulder-studded meadows and icy lakes. Lower down, the land furrows into stock trails, terraced fields chopped by dry-stone walls, and pine plantations.

Mountain people – some still living in traditional one-room, stone *casais* (huts) thatched with rye straw, but now mostly concentrated in valley hamlets – raise sheep, grow vegetables, and increasingly churn out traditionally made woollies, bread and distinctive cheeses for souvenir shops.

The Serra da Estrela Natural Park is – at 1011 sq km – Portugal's largest protected area and straddles the Beira Alta and Beira Baixa provinces.

If you come in winter, expect snow. There's even a modest ski run at Torre and a summer dry run at nearby Manteigas. And every weekend (and all week in July and August) Portuguese families drive here in their thousands, creating traffic jams around Torre. But for the rest of the week, and off the road at almost any time, the mountains seem blissfully empty and beg to be explored.

Information

There are park offices at Manteigas (headquarters), Seia, Gouveia and Guarda, though

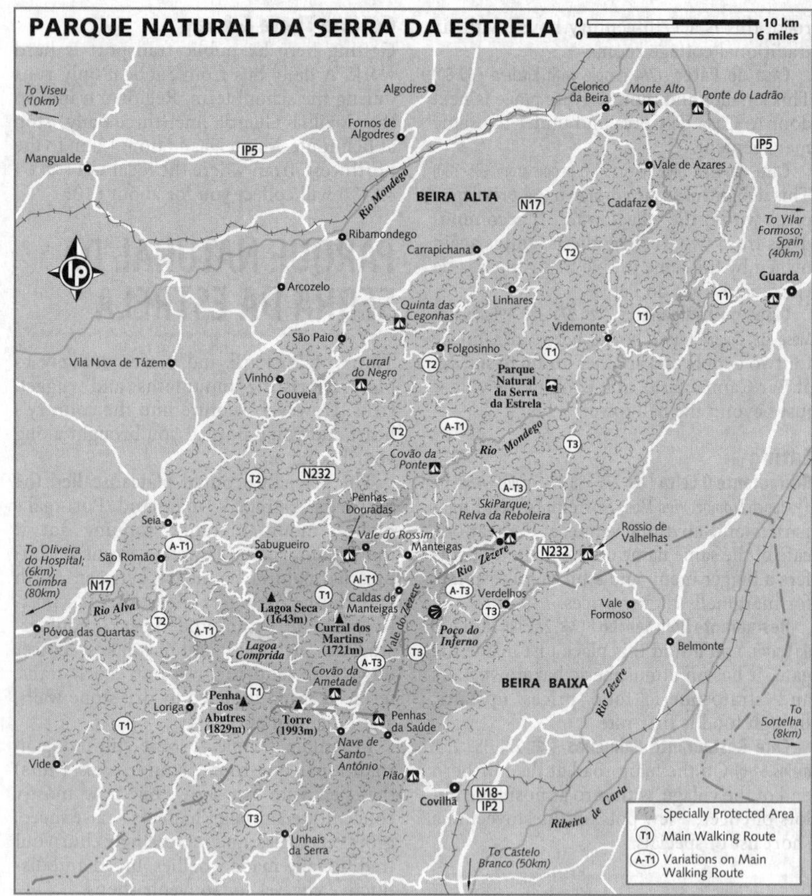

not all staff speak English. Turismos at Seia, Gouveia, Manteigas, Covilhã and Guarda also have park information.

If you're serious about exploring the park, the 1:50,000 topographic map *Carta Turística: Parque Natural da Serra da Estrela* (€5.60) includes paths, shelters and camping sites. A useful English-language booklet, *Discovering the Region of the Serra da Estrela* (€4.25), has trail profiles, walking times, historical notes and flora and fauna basics.

Flora and fauna details are in the booklet *Estrela: A Natural Approach* (€3.25). There are other books and brochures in English on geography, geology, medicinal plants and archaeology. All are available at park offices and some turismos.

Sights & Activities

FLORA & FAUNA

The park harbours many endangered or vulnerable species – especially feathered ones. These include the black stork, Montagu's harrier, chough, turtle dove and 10 species of bats.

Unusual animals also include the mountain gecko, and you may catch a glimpse of more rare birds, such as the peregrine falcon, eagle owl, black-shouldered kite and more.

The flora, too, is interesting. Popularity as medicinal remedies has put several of the park's plants in the list of endangered or vulnerable species, including mountain thrift *(Armeria transmontana)*, great yellow gentian *(Gentiana lutea)* and juniper *(Juniperus communis)*.

WALKING

Crisp air and immense vistas make this a trekking paradise. Serra da Estrela is also the only *parque natural* with a system of well-marked and mapped trails. But surprisingly few people use them, even in summer, and walkers can enjoy the feeling of having the park entirely to themselves.

In terms of when to come – wildflowers bloom in late April – the finest walking is from May to October. Winter is harsh, with snow at the higher elevations from November or December to April or May.

Whenever you come though, be prepared for extremes: scorching summer days give way to freezing nights, and chilling rainstorms blow through with little warning. Mist is a big hazard because it obscures walking routes and landmarks, and because it can stealthily chill you to the point of hypothermia. You may set out on a warm, cloudless morning and by noon find yourself fogged in and shivering, so always pack for the cold and the wet, too.

There are three main 'official' routes, plus branches and alternative trails. T1 runs the length of the park (about 90km), taking in every kind of terrain, including the summit of Torre. T2 and T3 (both around 80km) run respectively along the western and eastern slopes. All of them pass through towns and villages, each offering some accommodation. Many of the finest walks start around Manteigas (p329).

Within a zone of special protection (almost everything above 1200m altitude) camping and fires are strictly prohibited, except at designated sites, all of them on the main trails. Cutting trees and picking plants are also forbidden.

SKIING

The ski season typically runs from January to March, with the best conditions in February. For a rundown on what's available for skiers, see Torre, p330.

Sleeping

Useful bases include Seia, Gouveia, Manteigas, Covilhã and Guarda. Whereas camping sites drop their rates or close in winter, many hotels, *pensões* and *residenciais* actually raise their rates, typically from January to around April.

There are hostels at Penhas da Saúde and Guarda, and at least eight camping sites near the centre of the park. Turismo Habitação properties, concentrated on the western slopes, can be booked through turismos or Adruse, see Gouveia, p327.

EAT, DRINK & BE MERRY

The hearty, warming food of the Serra da Estrela is ideally suited to chilly mountain climes: roast lamb, roast kid and grilled trout; smoked ham, sausages and bacon; roast chestnuts and several varieties of *feijoacas* (little beans). Afterwards, put some colour back in your cheeks with a local *aguardente* made from honey or juniper berries.

The region is also famous for its heavy *pão de centeio* (rye bread), stout yellow *pão de milho* (corn bread), and the strong, creamy *queijo da serra* cheese. This delicious cheese is made in hefty rounds during the colder months. Most Serra da Estrela farming families make their own cheese, though certified cheese factories (offering tours and sales) are on the increase.

Cheese-centred regional markets are held from November to mid-April, including at Carrapichana (Monday), Fornos de Algodres (every second Monday) and Celorico da Beira (every second Friday). But go early: they're usually in full swing by sunrise and all over by 9am. Big cheese fairs are also a feature of Carnaval weekend (February or March) in Seia (Saturday), Gouveia (Sunday) and Manteigas (Monday). Good *queijo da serra* will set you back €13 per kilogram, though pure sheep's-milk cheeses cost more.

Getting There & Around

Express buses run daily from Coimbra to Seia, Guarda and Covilhã, and from Aveiro, Porto and Lisbon to Guarda and Covilhã. There are daily IC trains from Lisbon and Coimbra to Guarda (plus IR services calling at Gouveia) and from Lisbon to Covilhã (with IR services on to Guarda) – see town listings.

There are regular, though infrequent, bus services around the edges of the park but none directly across it.

THE ESTRELA MOUNTAIN DOG

The shaggy, handsome *cão da Serra da Estrela* is perfectly suited to its mountain environment: strong, fierce (thanks to wolf ancestry) and able to endure the cold, though not all are long-haired. They're all pretty big pooches: an adult can weigh up to 50kg.

Traditionally used by farmers to protect their flocks from wild animals, the breed was, until recently, in danger of dying out. Now several breeding kennels in the area work to preserve the pedigree. You may also see pups for sale along the roadside in Sabugeiro, though these probably aren't pure-bred.

Driving can be hairy, thanks to mist and wet or icy roads at high elevations, and stiff winds. The Gouveia–Manteigas N232 road is one of the most tortuous in Portugal. Be ready for traffic jams around Torre on weekends.

SEIA

pop 5700 / elevation 532m

Simple Seia (*sye*-ah), 2km from the N17/IC6 and equipped with big shops and adequate accommodation, is a useful base for weekenders seeking an easy taste of the Serra da Estrela. There is little other reason to stop here though.

Information

Espaço Internet (☎ 238 315 601; 🕒 9am-7pm Mon-Fri, 2-6pm Sat) Free Internet access. You can get here from Avenida dos Combatentes de Grande Guerra (stairs beside the Junta de Freguesia office) or Avenida Luís Vaz de Camões (stairs at left side of Cinema Teatro Jardim).

Parque Natural da Serra da Estrela office (☎ 238 310 440; fax 238 310 441; Praça da República 28; 🕒 9am-12.30pm & 2-5.30pm Mon-Fri) Small office on Praça da República (which, despite the name, is just a street), at the top of Rua Dr Simões Pereira.

Post office (☎ 238 902 111; Avenida 1 de Maio; 🕒 8.30am-12.30pm & 2-6pm Mon-Fri)

Turismo (☎ 238 317 762; fax 238 317 764; 🕒 9am-12.30pm & 2-5.30pm Mon-Sat, 9am-1pm Sun)

Sights & Activities

The **Museu do Pão** (Museum of Bread; ☎ 238 310 760; www.museudopao.pt; admission €2; 🕒 10am-6pm Tue-Sun) has all the information you'll ever need on local bread production, but its highlight is the traditional-style shop selling local goodies (including freshly ground flour and bread baked on the premises). The museum is 1km northeast of the centre on the road to Sabugeiro.

Sleeping

Estalagem de Seia (☎ 238 315 866; fax 238 315 538; Avenida Dr Afonso Costa; s/d with breakfast €55/58; P) The town's oldest building, an elegant 17th-century mansion of thickset stone, offers elegant rooms with antique furniture.

Residencial Jardim (☎ 238 311 414, 966 221 357; fax 238 310 091; Edifício Jardim II, Avenida Luís Vaz de Camões; d €35) A sparsely furnished, squeaky-clean place in a shopping complex.

Hotel Camelo (☎ 238 310 100; hotelcamelo@mail.telepac.pt; Avenida 1 de Maio 16; d Jan-Apr & Sat & Sun year-round €67, Mon-Fri Jul–mid-Sep €54, Mon-Fri other times €45; P) Luxury hotel with huge rooms, pink marble bathrooms, excellent children's play areas, tennis court and free off-street parking. All rooms face away from the street and most have views. Buffet breakfast is included in the rates.

Quinta das Mestras (☎ 238 602 988; fax 238 602 989; N510 Nogueira do Cravo-Bobadela road; d with/without shower & toilet €45/40, cabanas with shared facilities €34) A brightly coloured, renovated farmhouse and stables, 27km west of Oliveira do Hospital, this rambling place is split by a stream and surrounded by pine forest. It has peaceful private rooms, two isolated cabanas, and a small kitchen (€10 extra). Breakfast is included in the rates.

Eating

Restaurante Regional de Serra (☎ 238 312 717; Avenida dos Combatentes da Grande Guerra 14; specialities around €9; 🕒 lunch & dinner; P) Circular, banana-coloured restaurant, well known for hearty regional specialities, including *chanfana à serrana* (highland goat), plus pricey seafood – some fresh from the tank.

Restaurante Borges (☎ 238 313 010; 1st fl, Travessa do Funchal 7; mains €7.50-14; 🕒 lunch & dinner Fri-Wed) Tucked away in a tight corner off the main street, this country-style place offers good-value food; try its *arroz de feijão* (a stew of beans and rice).

Restaurante Central (☎ 238 314 433; Avenida 1 de Maio 12B; mains €6-8, daily specials €6; 🕒 lunch & dinner) If all you're after is a quick, cheap feed –

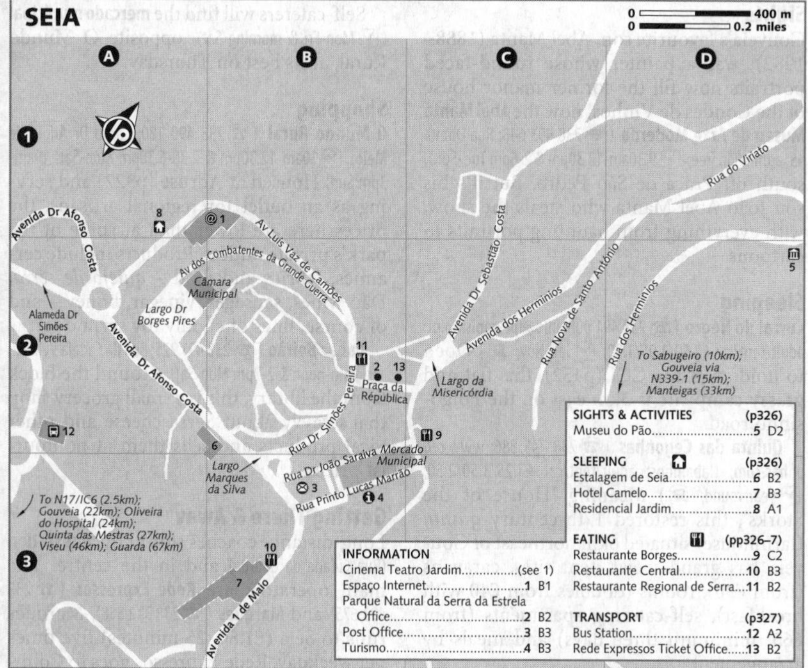

you'll do well at this plain-faced restaurant, near Hotel Carmelo.

Getting There & Away

The main long-distance carriers are **Rede Expressos** (☎ 238 313 102) and **Marques** (☎ 238 312 858). Marques goes to Gouveia (€1.80, 25 minutes), and continues to Guarda (€3.95, two hours), five times each weekday. Rede Expressos runs from Sunday to Friday via Guarda (€7.20, 1¼ hours) to Covilhã (€9, two hours), and daily to Coimbra (€8, 2¼ hours). Marques goes six times daily to Viseu (€3.25, 1½ hours), less often at weekends.

Rede Expressos also has a central **ticket office** (Rua da República 52).

GOUVEIA

pop 3800 / elevation 650m

Dozy Gouveia (goo-*vye*-ah), 5km from the N17, has a modicum more rural flavour than Seia and still has just about enough information, accommodation, food and transport to be a decent base for exploring the western side of the *parque natural*.

Orientation & Information

From the bus station, it's 450m south via Hotel de Gouveia, Avenida 1 de Maio and Rua da República to Praça de São Pedro, the town centre.

Associação de Desenvolvimento Rural da Serra da Estrela (Aduse; ☎ 238 490 180; adruse@ip.pt; Largo Dr Alípio de Melo) Among other things it organises Turihab accommodation and provides an outlet for local artisans (p328).

Municipal Library (☎ 238 490 230; Praça de São Pedro 5; ⌚ 9.30am-12.30pm & 2-6pm Mon-Fri, 9.30am-12.30pm Sat) Offers free Internet access in 30-minute chunks.

Parque Natural da Serra da Estrela office (☎ 238 492 411; fax 238 494 183; Avenida Bombeiros Voluntários 8; ⌚ 9am-12.30pm & 2-5.30pm Mon-Fri) A block south of the centre.

Post Office (☎ 238 490 070; Avenida 1 de Maio 3; ⌚ 9am-12.30pm & 2-6pm Mon-Fri) You will find this located between Praça de São Pedro and the Hotel de Gouveia.

Turismo (☎ 238 490 243; Avenida 25 de Abril; ⌚ 9am-12.30pm & 2-6pm Mon-Sat, 10am-12.30pm & 2-4pm Sun) In a building to the side of the *câmara municipal*. Has leaflets on walks in the area.

Sights

Gouveia's favourite son, Abel Manta (1888–1982), was a painter whose round-faced portraits now fill the former manor house of the Condes de Vinhós, now the **Abel Manta Museu de Arte Moderna** (☎ 238 493 648; Rua Direita 45; admission free; ⏲ 9.30am-12.30pm & 2-6pm Tue-Sun), south off Praça de São Pedro. But it's his son João Abel Manta who steals the show, with everything from haunting portraits to cartoons.

Sleeping

Curral do Negro (☎ 238 491 008; info@fpcampismo.pt; adult/tent/car €2.50/1.95/1.90; ⏲ Jan-Nov;) Open to holders of the CCI (p452), this flat and grassy camp site is 3km east on the Folgosinho road.

Quinta das Cegonhas (☎ 238 745 886; www.cegonhas.com; Nabainhos; adult/tent/car €3.25/3.50/2.50; ⏲ year-round;) Meaning 'House of the Storks', this restored 17th-century *quinta* (farmhouse) situated 6km northeast of Gouveia has grand views, tent sites, caravans (from €30), rooms (doubles from €40 with breakfast), self-catering apartments (from €65, minimum three days) and meals by arrangement.

Hotel de Gouveia (☎ 238 491 010; hoteldegouveia@hoteldegouveia.com; Avenida 1 de Maio; d Sun-Thu €50, Fri & Sat €60; P) With a mild Alpine air, this spotless and well run hotel has comfortable rooms with cable TV and a big buffet breakfast. Pity about the muzak. Private parking costs €2.25.

Casas do Toural (☎ 238 492 132, 963 023 893; Rua Direita 74; d €55-80;) If it's atmosphere you're after, try an apartment here on the street above O Mundo Rural (see right). This complex of old restored buildings has a multilayered hillside garden and tennis courts. The turismo and Adruse also have details of other Turihab places.

Eating

Restaurante O Júlio (☎ 238 498 016; Travessa do Loureiro 11A; dishes around €8.50; ⏲ lunch & dinner Wed-Mon) Gouveia's best restaurant, with cheerless but faultless service and regional specialities such as *cabrito à serrana* (mountain kid).

Bar Impérium (☎ 238 492 142; Travessa do Loureiro 1; light meals from €4.50; ⏲ lunch Tue-Sun) Across the path from O Júlio, offering cheaper lunches from the same kitchen.

Self-caterers will find the **mercado municipal** (⏲ Mon-Fri & morning Sat), opposite O Mundo Rural, at its best on Thursday.

Shopping

O Mundo Rural (☎ 238 490 180; Largo Dr Alípio de Melo; ⏲ 10am-12.30pm & 2.30-6.30pm Mon-Sat, 10am-3pm Sun) Housed at Adruse (p327) and serving as an outlet for regional artisans, the prices here are lower than at some of the park's private outlets. Products include ceramics, fabrics and food – *quiejo de serra,* Dão wines, sausages, vinegar, honey – and of course, lines of cuddly toy serra dogs.

Cabaz Beirão (☎ 238 491 225; Rua da Cadeia Velha 2; ⏲ 9am-noon & 2-7pm Mon-Sat) Around the block from the library, this is a small grocery shop that's savvy about Serra cheese and other local products and sells them at nontourist prices.

Getting There & Away

Long-distance coaches stop at the **bus station** (Rua Cidade da Guarda) and in the centre. The main operators are **Rede Expressos** (☎ 238 493 675) and **Marques** (☎ 238 312 858). Marques runs to Seia (€1.80, 25 minutes) five times per weekday. Rede Expressos goes to Coimbra (€9.20, 2¼ hours, three daily) and Lisbon. A Marques bus goes daily to Guarda (€3.45, 1½ hours), and there are also buses to Viseu (€3.60, two daily).

Gouveia is on the Beira Alta line from Lisbon to Guarda (the station is 14km north near Ribamondego) – regional trains stop five times a day between Coimbra and Guarda. A taxi between Gouveia and the station will cost around €10.

SABUGEIRO

pop 700 / elevation 1050m

Pocket-sized Sabugeiro, 12km southeast of Seia, still clings to its traditional Serra soul. It does this despite attracting tourists from far and wide thanks to its title as Portugal's highest village. To accommodate the influx of sightseers, there are a clutch of personality-less *pensões* and souvenir shops on the main road. However, Sabugeiro's true nature reveals itself the further you delve into the village. Here, chickens still roam the paths and sturdy farmer-shepherd families live in slate-roof granite houses. And outside the winter tourist season, somnolent Sabugeiro quietly goes about its business like any other far-flung Serra village.

While you're here, don't forget to stock up on the traditional local produce. Sabugeiro families manufacture and sell delicious *queijo da serra* (cheese of the mountains), smoked ham, rye bread and juniper-berry firewater. Less tasty, but very practical for the chilly mountain nights, are the fleecy slippers of Serra sheep's wool.

Sleeping & Eating

Accommodation is pricey in winter but great value the rest of the year.

Casa do Serrinho (☎ 238 314 304; Largo Nossa Senhora da Fátima; d with breakfast summer/winter about €25/35) At the top of the village, this place has a couple of neat rooms, a shared kitchen and a souvenir shop stocked high with cheese, *aguardente* (fire-water liquor) and fluffy toy dogs.

Abrigo da Montanha (☎/fax 238 315 262; d with breakfast summer/winter €35/43) Across the road from Casa do Serrinho, it has rooms with private shower. This and other places along the road also have restaurants.

You can get closer to local life in one of several dozen restored village houses that are equipped with fireplace, kitchenette and bathroom. Rates per day for two/four people start at €45/70 in midsummer (higher in winter). They fill up fast on weekends and in winter. Book through **Casas do Cruzeiro** (☎ 238 315 872; quintadocrestelo@quintadocrestelo.pt); to get there from the main road near the bottom of the hill, follow 'Turismo de Aldeia' (Village Tourism) signs to the old centre.

Getting There & Away

The only public transport is a single bus to/from Seia each Wednesday (Seia's market day), departing Sabugeiro about 8am and returning from Seia about noon. A taxi from Seia would cost around €8.

MANTEIGAS

pop 4000 / elevation 720m

Manteigas is one of the most picturesque towns in the range, set in the cathedral-like Vale do Zêzere that ascends to the foot of Torre. All around are dizzily steep, terraced hillsides clad in pine and dotted with stone *casais*, beehives and little meadows.

It's an ideal base for exploring the Serra da Estrela: centrally located, with a park office, adequate supplies, decent food and accommodation, and good walks departing in every direction.

There has been a settlement here since at least Moorish times, perhaps because of the hot springs around which the nearby spa of Caldas de Manteigas has grown (open only to those with a medical reference, sadly). Manteigas' once-thriving cloth industry has fallen on hard times, but the area has received a boost from the SkiParque down the road (p330).

Orientation & Information

From Seia or Gouveia you approach Manteigas down a near vertical switchback road, the N232. The bus from Covilhã or Guarda sets you down at the turismno on the N232. The town has no real centre; there's an ATM opposite the Galp station and more on Rua 1 de Maio (turn left as you approach the park office).

Police station (Rua Dr Esteves de Carvalho) About 200m east of the turismo.

Parque Natural da Serra da Estrela (☎ 275 980 060; pnse@icn.pt; Rua 1 de Maio 2; 🕑 9am-12.30pm & 2-5.30pm Mon-Fri) The headquarters for the natural park are across the intersection from the turismo.

Turismo (☎/fax 275 981 129; Rua Dr Esteves de Carvalho; 🕑 9.30am-noon & 2-6pm Tue-Fri, to 8pm Sat, 9.30am-noon & 3-8pm Sat)

Activities

WALKING

You could spend weeks looping in and out of Manteigas. Following are the outlines of a few modest walks. For details, and more walks, ask at the turismo or pick up *Discovering the Region of the Serra da Estrela* from the park office. Don't go without a decent topographical map, rain protection and water.

Poço do Inferno

A 7km, tree-shaded climb takes you to Poço do Inferno (Hell's Well), a waterfall in the craggy gorge of the Ribeira de Leandres. From the turismo go 500m down the N232, turn right and walk for 1km to two bridges. Take the right-hand one across the Rio Zêzere and head downstream. About 200m along, turn right on a forestry track. From here it's 1½ to two hours up to the waterfall, with an elevation change of 400m and fine views northeast.

Return the same way, or head back towards Manteigas down a roughly paved road for about 2.5km, to a pine plantation. To the right of the plantation gate, drop down a few steps past a former forestry post, descend to houses by the river, cross the bridge and climb back to Manteigas, for a total walk of about 3½ hours.

Alternatively, carry on past the plantation for a further 3.5km to Caldas de Manteigas, plus 3km along the road back to Manteigas (total 4½ hours).

Penhas Douradas & Vale do Rossim

A more demanding walk goes to Penhas Douradas, a collection of windblown holiday houses. The track climbs northwest out of town via Rua Dr Afonso Costa to join a sealed, switchback forestry road and, briefly, a wide loop of the Seia-bound N232. Branch left off the N232 almost immediately, on another forestry road to the Meteorological Observatory. From there it's a short, gentle ascent to Penhas Douradas.

You're about 700m above Manteigas here, and you mustn't miss the stunning view from a stub of rock called Fragão de Covão; just follow the signs. (You can also drive up the N232 just for the view: about 18km from Manteigas, then left at the first turning after the one marked *observatório*, and 1km to the sign for Fragão de Covão; save your oil-pan and walk the rest of the way.)

Walking back the same way makes for a return trip of about 5½ hours. Alternatively, carry on for 3.4km to the Vale do Rossim reservoir and camp site; see Sleeping, right.

Vale do Zêzere

A long day-walk or a lingering two-day trip takes you through this magnificent, glacier-scoured valley at the foot of Torre. Its only drawback: the trail is shadeless, and baking in clear summer weather.

Follow the N338 for about 3km to Caldas de Manteigas, leaving the road just below the spa, for the track up the valley. En route are typical stone *casais*. About 9km from Manteigas at Covões (where there's a shelter), a bridge takes you over the Rio Zêzere. Where the huts end, climb up to the N338; a few hundred metres along the road is a crystalline spring. About 3km along the road at a hairpin turn is the Covão da Ametade camp site (right), about 3½ hours from Manteigas.

SKIPARQUE

SkiParque (☎ 275 982 870; www.skiparque.pt in Portuguese; N232; 🕑 10am-6pm Sun-Thu, 10am-10pm Fri & Sat) is a big dry-ski run 7.5km east of Manteigas, with a lift, gear rental, snowboarding, café and camp site (below). Prices for weekday/weekend/night-time skiing start at €10/12/14.50 for two hours, and group lessons are available.

When the weather's good they also organise increasingly popular lessons in **paragliding**. It costs €50 for a one-hour lesson with an instructor, and courses are available. To further compensate for the lack of snow in summer, they organise other outdoor activities such as canoeing, rock-climbing and biking.

Sleeping

BUDGET

Vale do Rossim (☎ 275 982 899; www.a-torre.com; EN 232; adult/tent/car €2/1.75/1.50; 🕑 Jun-Sep) Situated beside a reservoir 23km from Manteigas, with free hot showers, a café-restaurant, small shop, bikes for rent and a fair amount of shade.

Relva da Reboleira (☎ 275 982 870; www.skiparque.pt; adult/tent/car €1.50/1.50/1.25; 🕑 year-round) A treeless, functional camp site at the foot of SkiParque. Hot showers cost an extra €0.50.

Rossio de Valhelhas (☎ 275 487 160; jfvalhelhas@clix.pt; Valhelhas; adult/tent/car €1.90/1.70/1.65; 🕑 May-Sep) A flat, grassy and shady municipal camp site by the N232, about 15km from Manteigas. It also charges €0.50 for hot showers.

Two bare-bones, park-run camping sites that are astonishingly cheap are **Covão da Ametade**, a popular tents-only site 13km from Manteigas at the head of the Vale do Zêzere, and **Covão da Ponte** (☎ 275 982 932), 5.4km up the N232 and 6km along an access road to the Rio Mondego. Toilets, a snack bar and (at Covão da Ponte) showers are open, and park staff on hand, in July and August; the rest of the year, campers should notify the park office at Manteigas in advance. Don't expect electricity or hot water at these sites.

MID-RANGE & TOP END

Pensão Serradalto (☎ 275 981 151; Rua 1 de Maio 15; d with breakfast €35) This professional but homely renovated house offers spotless rooms and fine valley views. It also has a café and restaurant. To get here, turn left (south) at the park office. English spoken.

Residencial Estrela (☎ 275 981 288; Rua Dr Sobral 5; d with breakfast €45) Brusque Estrela provides comfortable doubles in a boarding-house atmosphere. The neighbouring church bells go quiet at night, though they're as effective as any alarm clock again at 7am. To get here, bear right (north) at the park office.

Casa de São Roque (☎ 275 981 125, 965 357 225; Rua de Santo António 51; d with breakfast €45) A beautiful creaky old house that has been lovingly kept with antique furnishings, gauze drapes, cosy lounges and wooden floors. From the turismo take the second left beyond Pensão Serradalto.

Quinta de Leandres (inquire at Casa de São Roque; tw with bathroom or d with shower €45; P) A peaceful granite farmhouse 2km east of town, with plenty of space to breathe: including a spacious veranda, large grounds, a play frame for the kids and apple orchards. Excellent get-away-from-it-all option.

Casa das Obras (☎ 275 981 155; www.casadasobras.pt; Rua Teles de Vasconcelos; d €50) Near Residencial Estrela, this is a rather grandly renovated 18th-century town house, with all the low-ceilinged, stone-walled charm you'd expect. It also has a games room.

Pousada de São Lourenço (☎ 275 980 050; recepcao.slourenco@pousadas.pt; d €122; P) Pitching for the most stupendous view in the Beiras, this luxury modern hotel is 13km above and north of town topping the wiggly switchbacks on the N232: on a clear day, you can see all the way into Spain. The restaurant (open to nonguests) shares the views.

Eating

Restaurante São Januario (☎ 275 981 288; mains €7.50-11; lunch & dinner Tue-Sun) Sitting below Residencial Estrela, this trendy restaurant has a culinary whiz in the kitchen and a spare modern design. Its patio is a good spot for coffee or an evening tipple.

Cervejaria Central (☎ 275 982 787; grilled dishes €6-7; lunch & dinner Mon-Sat) A block back from the park office, this no-nonsense diner has a short list of lunch-time and evening grills, including fresh mountain fish, kid and more.

Monte Verde Supermercado (Rua 1 de Maio; 9am-10pm Mon-Sat, 9am-6pm Sun) will fulfil all your grocery needs. It's opposite Pensão Serradalto. **Bar-Bar** (☎ 275 982 540; Rua 1 de Maio; 8.30am-late), the circular café-bar just north of the grocery store, has munchies when everything else is closed.

Getting There & Away

On weekdays, Joalto/RBI buses leave from Guarda for Manteigas at around 11.30am and 5pm, returning from Manteigas at about 7am and 12.45pm.

To reach Manteigas from Covilhã, catch an 8.20am Guarda-bound bus and change at Vale Formoso; returning from Manteigas, catch the 7am Guarda-bound bus and change at Vale de Amoreira. During school-term time there's also a direct Covilhã–Manteigas service. All trips cost about €4 and take about 1½ hours; none run on weekends or holidays.

TORRE

Come to Torre, mainland Portugal's highest point (1993m), in winter or spring and you'll find its road signs so blasted by freezing winds that horizontal icicles barb their edges, and wire fences resemble lines of potato waffle for all the snow coating them. So reliable is the winter freeze that you'll also find a small ski 'resort' with three decrepit lifts and several beginner-grade slopes.

But snow aside, Portugal's chill pinnacle is somewhat disappointing – occupied by several ageing golf-ball radar domes, a sweaty shopping arcade smelling of cheese and smoke, and during winter, a gleeful sea of Portuguese and their cars and coaches.

A regional turismo also shivers in the arcade, though it was shut for renovation in 2004. **Ski-gear rental** (9am-4.30pm during ski season), is available from a building a few hundred metres down the Seia road, and

MOVING MOUNTAINS

Portugal's highest peak tops out at a none-too-trifling 1993m above sea level, with glacially scoured landscapes that roll compellingly away in every direction. However, these heady heights simply weren't good enough for Dom João VI, whose penchant for nice round numbers led him to erect a 7m high obelisk on Torre so Portugal could cheekily claim its highest point as 2000m exactly. And sure enough, his tactics have more or less paid off: 2000m seems to have become the 'official' height given in tourist brochures and echoed on the lips of inhabitants. Well – after all – what's a few measly metres among mountains?

includes skis, poles and boots (€18 per day), snowboards (€15 per day) or sledges (€8/10 per 30/60 minutes).

There are no bus services to Torre. A taxi costs about €20 from Covilhã, €25 from Seia or €15 from Manteigas.

PENHAS DA SAÚDE

The closest spot in which to hunker down near Torre, Penhas (about 10km from Covilhã on the N339) isn't a town but a weather-beaten collection of chalets at an elevation of about 1500m. It's uphill from a burned-out tuberculosis sanatorium (soon to be renovated as a Pousada de Portugal) and downhill from the Barragem do Viriato dam. Supplies are limited; if you're planning to go walking, do your shopping in Covilhã.

Sleeping & Eating

Pousada da juventude (☎ 275 335 375; penhas@movijovem.pt; dm summer/winter €8.50/13, d with bathroom €24/37, without bathroom €21/32; year-round; P) Penhas' enormous first-rate hostel, with perks that include a pool table and ping pong.

Pensão O Pastor (☎ 275 322 810; fax 275 314 035; d with breakfast summer/winter €40/50) This place has uninspiring, dark but homely rooms and a gift shop.

Hotel Serra da Estrela (☎ 275 310 300; hse@turistrela.pt; d with breakfast mid-Apr–Nov €75, Dec–mid-Apr €120; P) This is the top place to stay in Penhas – posh and professional, with handsome rooms as well as six-bed chalets (from €130). The same owners run the resort at Torre. They also rent mountain bikes for €12.50 per day.

There are several cafés along the N339.

Getting There & Away

At the weekends from mid-July to mid-September, and daily during August, local **Transcovilhã** (☎ 275 336 017) buses (€1.50) climb to Penhas from the kiosk on Rua António Augusto d'Aguiar in Covilhã, twice daily. Otherwise, you must take a taxi (€15), hitch, cycle or walk.

COVILHÃ

pop 35,000 / elevation 700m

Lop-sided Covilhã seems almost pinned to the side of the Serra da Estrela foothills. Indeed this steeply terraced university town is the urban centre closest to the heart of the national park, and an ideal base from which to dip into its highest reaches.

Its ironic to think that this landlocked area, so far removed from the sea, produced several of Portugal's most celebrated seaborne adventurers: not least one Pêro de Covilhã, who – disguised as a Muslim trader – journeyed far through Egypt, India and even to the holy cities of Mecca and Medina. His is the statue in Praça do Município, and the pavement beside it bears a huge map showing his travels.

Nearby Belmonte also spawned its own illustrious adventurer, Pedro Álvares Cabral, who is credited with discovering Brazil.

Orientation

From the train and long-distance bus stations it's a punishing 1.5km climb to Praça do Município, the town centre – for local transport see p334.

Street parking is dire; park well away from the centre, or use the parking garage on Rua Visconde da Coriscada.

Information

On Praça do Município are several banks with ATMs.

Police station (☎ 275 320 922; Rua António Augusto d'Aguiar)

Post office (☎ 275 320 740; 8.30am-6.30pm Mon-Fri, 9am-12.30pm Sat) Between Praça de São Pedro and Hotel de Gouveia.

PostWeb (☎ 275 310 820; Rua Comendador Campos Melo 27; per 15 min €0.60; 9am-7.30pm Mon-Fri, 9am-1pm Sat) A franchise stationery shop offering Internet access.

Regional turismo (☎ 275 319 560; turismo.estrela@mail.telepac.pt; Avenida Frei Heitor Pinto; 9am-12.30pm & 2-5.30pm Mon-Sat)

Universidade da Beira Interior The regional university is situated well south of the centre. Few of its 5000 students seem to venture into town.

Sights

The narrow, winding streets west of Praça do Município have a quiet charm, and in the midst of them is the **Igreja de Santa Maria**, with a startling façade covered in azulejos.

Covilhã, the centre of what used to be one of Europe's biggest wool-producing areas, has fallen on hard times thanks to Salazar-era neglect followed by Asian competition. Stray outside the centre and you'll see the town's ghostly mills standing empty and forlorn. On the site of the former Real Fábrica de Panos (Royal Textile Factory; founded in 1764 by the Marquês de Pombal), and now within the university, is the **Museu de Lanifícios** (Museum of Wool-Making; ☎ 275 319 700, ext 3131; adult/child under 15/youth 15-25 €2/free/1; 🕑 9.30am-noon & 2.30-6pm Tue-Sun), which looks back at this vanishing local industry. Even if yarn makes you want to yawn, this is a good little museum – the centrepiece of which is a clutch of giant-sized dyeing vats.

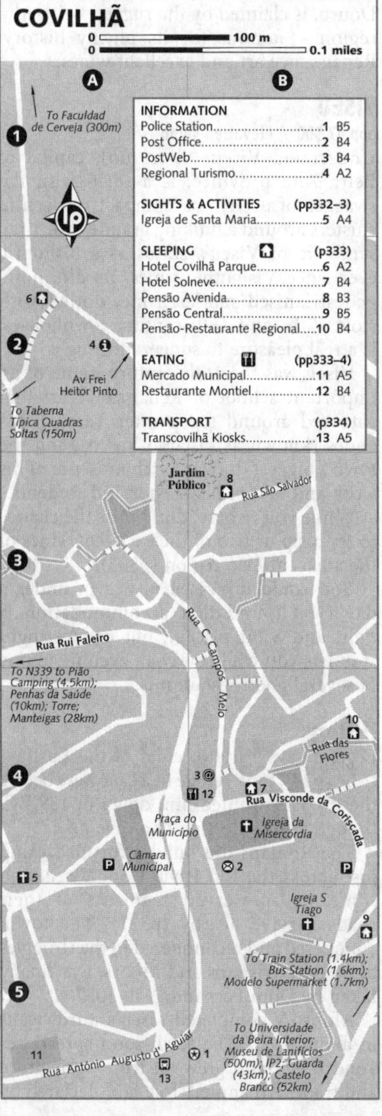

Sleeping

Hotel Solneve (☎ 275 323 001/2; solneve@mail.telepac.pt; Rua Visconde da Coriscada 126; d with breakfast €45, Fri & Sat Nov-Mar €65; 🅿 ❄ 💻) Terrific value, with everything from heated towel rails to dozens of cable TV channels, this briskly run choice is as central as you can get. It offers many rooms with photogenic views of the main square. Plus there's free Internet access, a great restaurant and off-street parking (€1.50) to boot.

Hotel Covilhã Parque (☎ 275 327 518; imb@mail.telepac.pt; Avenida Frei Heitor Pinto; d/t with breakfast €48/65, Fri & Sat Nov-Apr €60/84; ❄ 💻) Ten floors of identikit rooms peer over the city from this hotel block next to the turismo. It's big enough to have space even in peak season, and rooms on upper floors score fabulous views. Internet access costs €2 per hour.

Pensão Avenida (☎ 275 322 140; Rua São Salvador; d €28, Sat Jan-Mar €30) Homely guesthouse facing a pretty *jardim público*, with sunny, high-ceilinged old rooms, spindly old furniture and a shared shower and toilet; some rooms sleep up to five people at better rates.

Pensão-Restaurante Regional (☎/fax 275 322 596; Rua das Flores 4; s/d with breakfast €12.50/25) Tucked away in twisty disorientating little streets near the centre is this quiet place with threadbare rooms with a shared toilet, and a good-value restaurant.

Pensão Central (☎ 275 322 727; Rua Nuno Álvares Pereira 14; s/d from €10/25) Apart from old-fashioned rooms and a seriously sloping staircase, what characterises this ancient place is its similarly ancient hostess, who still has a twinkle in her eye despite immobilising arthritis (she opens the door with a long piece of string!). Get a back room, with fine views and no street noise.

Pião Camping (☎ 275 314 312; nonmembers per adult/tent/car €2.80/2.80/2.10; 🕑 year-round) Some 4km up the N339 towards Penhas da Saúde is this snug but wooded facility run by the Clube de Campismo e Caravanismo de Covilhã. Bungalows with kitchen facilities are also available, from €40 per double.

Eating

Restaurante Montiel (☎ 275 322 086; Praça do Município 33-37; daily specials around €8; 🕑 all day) This is a friendly venue for grabbing a caffeine hit, basking in the sun and indulging in flaky Portuguese pastries. The upstairs dining room serves up regional cooking: try one of a long list of succulent steer steaks on offer.

Restaurante Solneve (☎ 275 323 001/2; solneve@mail.telepac.pt; Rua Visconde da Coriscada 126; mains €8-13, specials €6; lunch & dinner Mon-Sat, Sun morning) This cavernous eatery sits below street level at the back of Hotel Solneve. Its elegant waiters proffer up quality local fare and international dishes from cordon bleu chicken to English roast. Hotel guests pay 10% less.

Pensão-Restaurante Regional (☎ 275 322 596; specials €5, mains €6-8; lunch & dinner Mon-Sat, lunch Sun) It doesn't look like much – a modest diner hidden in the knotted streets behind the main square – but this place is repeatedly recommended for its good-value *assados* (roasts) and other meaty local dishes, plus burgers and omelettes.

Self-caterers will find abundant fruit and vegetables available most mornings at the **mercado municipal** (Rua António Augusto d'Aguiar). There's a big **Modelo** supermarket a block south of the bus station (both on Eixo TCT).

Drinking

Faculdad de Cerveja (☎ 919 352 474; www.faculdadedacerveja.com in Portuguese; Rua Indústria; 5pm-4am Tue-Sat) This gritty DJ bar and club, popular with students, is named the 'Faculty of Beer'. Enough said.

Taberna Típica Quadras Soltas (☎ 275 313 683; Avenida de Santarém 39) A lower-key café-bar above the town centre that sometimes has late-night fado on weekends.

Getting There & Away

All long-distance buses run from the **main bus station** (☎ 275 336 700). Joalto and Rede Expressos go jointly to Guarda (€4, 45 minutes), and via Castelo Branco (€4.80, one hour) to Lisbon (€10, six hours), each about three times a day. Each has multiple daily services to Viseu (€8.50, 2¼ hours) and to Porto (€10.80, 4½ to 5½ hours). Rede Expressos also goes via Guarda to Seia (€9, two hours) once daily Sunday to Friday.

One daily IR (€12, 5½ hours) and two IC (€13, 4½ hours) trains run direct from Lisbon, with Porto connections.

Getting Around

Bus No 2 (Rodrigo) runs every 30 minutes from the bus and train stations, to the Transcovilhã kiosk by the police station (€0.95 from the driver, less at the kiosk). Taxis at either station charge about €4 to the centre.

BEIRA ALTA

The north side of the Serra da Estrela, and lands bouncing down towards the Douro, is claimed by the rugged Beira Alta region – famous for its plucky history, Renaissance art and excellent wines.

VISEU

pop 47,500 / elevation 480m

Underrated Viseu (vi-*zeh*-oo), capital of Beira Alta province, is a town with the swagger of a city. Its compact old centre clusters around a hulking granite cathedral, symbolic of Viseu's status as a bishopric ever since Visigothic times. Its old, now-pedestrianised market zone, dotted with stoic 17th- and 18th-century townhouses, is a real pleasure to squeeze through.

Viseu was the 16th-century home of an important school of Renaissance art that gathered around the painter Vasco Fernandes (known as O Grão Vasco), and the town's biggest draw is a rich museum of his work and that of his friends and students.

While you're here, don't miss the chance to try a sip or two of the excellent wines of the adjacent Dão region (p337).

You could do Viseu justice in under a day (you'll find that accommodation is tight and a bit pricey), but an overnight stop lets you while away an evening in one of several good restaurants.

History

Legend says Viriato, chief of the Lusitani tribe (p24), took refuge in a cave here before the Romans hunted him down in 139 BC, though there's no sign of a cave now.

The Romans did build a fortified camp just across the Rio Pavia from Viseu, and some well-preserved segments of their roads survive nearby (p337). The town, conquered and reconquered in the struggles between Christians and Moors, was finally taken by Dom Fernando I in 1057.

Afonso V completed Viseu's sturdy walls in about 1472. The town soon spread beyond them, and grew fat from agriculture and trade. An annual 'free fair' declared by

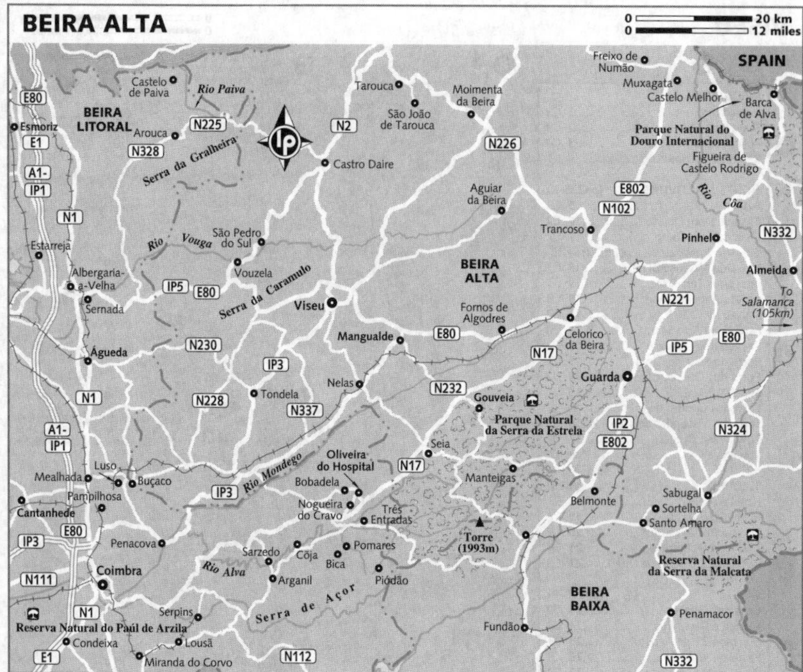

João III in 1510 carries on today as one of the region's biggest agricultural and handicrafts expositions.

Orientation

Viseu sits beside the Rio Pavia, a tributary of the Mondego. In the middle of town is Praça da República, known to all as O Rossio. From here the shopping district stretches east along Rua Formosa and Rua da Paz, and then north into the historic centre along Rua do Comércio and Rua Direita. At the town's highest point and historical heart is the cathedral.

The bus station is 500m northwest of the Rossio along Avenida Dr António José de Almeida. Drivers should avoid the old town, with its harrowing one-way lanes.

Information

Banks with ATMs line Rua Formosa.

Espaço Internet (☎ 232 427 405; Solar dos Condes de Prime; 🕑 10am-7pm Mon-Fri, 10am-1pm & 2-7pm Sat, 2-7pm Sun) Free Internet access.

Instituto Português da Juventude (IPJ; ☎ 232 483 410; Portal do Fontelo; 🕑 9am-6pm Mon-Fri) Offers free Internet access for half-hour intervals.

Main Post Office (☎ 232 424 820; Rua dos Combatentes da Grande Guerra; 🕑 8.30am-6.30pm Mon-Fri, 9am-12.30pm Sat)

Police station (☎ 232 480 380; Rua Alves Martins)

Regional turismo (☎ 232 420 950; turismo@rt-dao-lafoes.com; Avenida Calouste Gulbenkian; 🕑 9am-12.30pm & 2.30-6pm Mon-Fri, 10am-12.30pm & 2.30-5.30pm Sat, 9.30am-12.30pm Sun May-Oct) Head here for help on getting oriented.

São Teotónio Hospital (☎ 232 420 500; Avenida Dom Duarte) The district hospital, south of the centre.

Sights

AROUND THE ROSSIO

At the southern end of Praça da República (the Rossio) is the late-18th-century **Igreja dos Terceiros** (admission free), all heavy, gilded baroque, but for luminous azulejos portraying the life of St Francis.

Fine modern **azulejos** at the northern end of the Rossio depict scenes from regional life, and beyond these is the azulejo-adorned **Museu Almeida Moreira** (☎ 232 423 769; admission free; 🕑 9am-12.30pm & 2-5.30pm Mon-Fri), genteel home to the first director of the Museu de Grão Vasco.

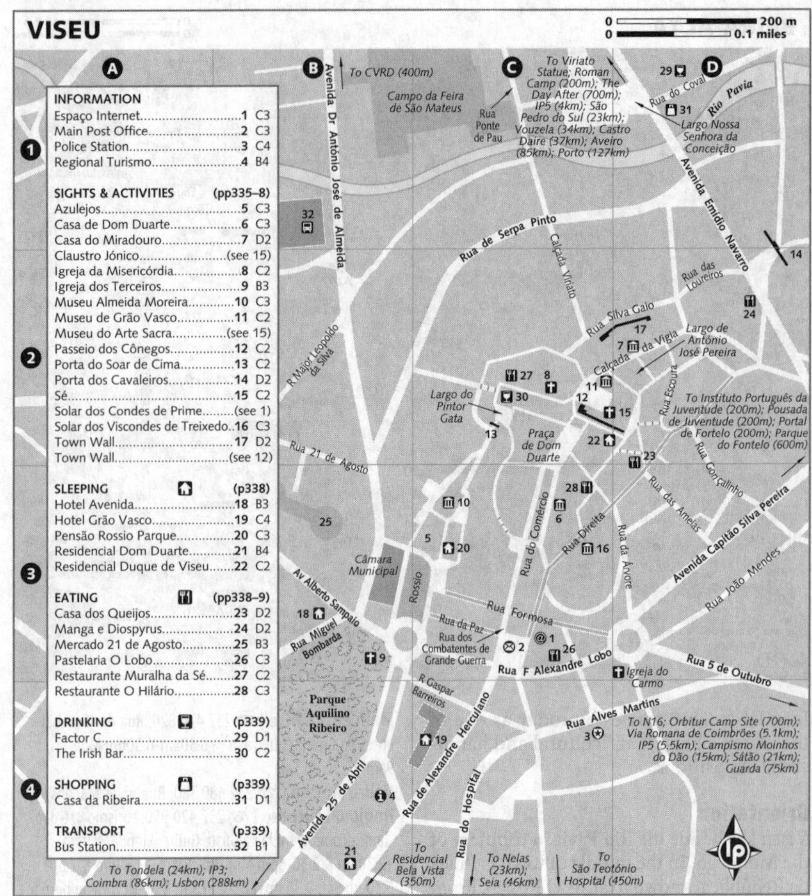

From here the grandest route into the old town is through the **Porta do Soar de Cima**, a gate set into a section of Afonso V's town walls.

SÉ

Resplendent on a rock above the town is the 13th-century granite **cathedral** (admission free; 8am-noon & 2-7pm), of which the gloomy Renaissance façade conceals a splendid 16th-century interior, including an impressive Manueline ceiling and a younger display of fabulous azulejos.

Stairs in the northern transept climb to the choir and the upper gallery of the **Claustro Jónico** (Ionian Cloister), and the overpriced **Museu do Arte Sacra** (adult/youth 14-26 €2.50/1.25; 8am-noon & 2-5pm Sun-Wed & Fri, 2-5pm Sat). However, it's worth paying just to see the side rooms' extraordinary 17th- and 18th-century azulejos that depict such monstrous and comedic scenes as naked men fighting a duel, babies being slaughtered, four-headed beasts on the rampage plus a bevy of nipple-pinching beauties. Hardly the stuff of peaceful contemplation.

The original, lower level of the cloister is one of Portugal's earliest Italian Renaissance structures. Returning to the church you pass through a Romanesque-Gothic portal, rediscovered during restoration work in 1918.

Facing the cathedral is the 1775 **Igreja da Misericórdia** – rococo, symmetrical and blindingly white outside, and neoclassical, severe and rather dull inside.

MUSEU DE GRÃO VASCO

Adjoining the cathedral is the prison-like, square granite box, known as the Paço de Três Escalões (Palace of Three Steps), probably a contemporary of the cathedral and originally built as the Bishop's Palace. In 1916 it reopened as a splendid **museum** (☎ 232 422 049; mgv@ipmuseus.pt; admission €3; ⏰ 2-6pm Tue, 10am-6pm Wed-Sun) for the works of Viseu's own Vasco Fernandes – known as O Grão Vasco, 'the Great Vasco' (1480–1543) – one of Portugal's seminal Renaissance painters, and of other bright lights in the so-called Viseu School.

Of those lights, Vasco's colleague, collaborator and rival Gaspar Vaz merits special attention. Together they spurred each other on to produce some of the best artwork ever to come out of Portugal. And despite the passing centuries, the rich colours and luminous style of their extra-realistic work has lost none of its immediacy.

AROUND THE SÉ

North of the cathedral along Rua Silva Gaio is the longest remaining stretch of the old **town walls**. At the bottom, across Avenida Emídio Navarro, is another old town gate, the **Porta dos Cavaleiros**.

South of the cathedral beneath the Passeio dos Cônegos (Curates Walk, on part of the old wall) is **Praça de Dom Duarte**, named after the Portuguese monarch (brother of Prince Henry the Navigator) who was born in Viseu. Several of the square's old mansions show off their wrought-iron balconies and genteel contours. Southward is **Casa de Dom Duarte** (Rua Dom Duarte; closed to public), a house with a beautiful Manueline window and traditionally regarded as the king's birthplace.

Rua Augusto Hilário runs southeast through Viseu's former **judiaria** (14th- to 16th-century Jewish quarter). **Rua Direita**, Viseu's most appealing street and once the most direct route to the hill top, is now a lively melee of shops, souvenir stands, restaurants and old townhouses.

MANSIONS

The most handsome of Viseu's many old townhouses is the 18th-century **Solar dos Condes de Prime** (Rua dos Andrades), also called Casa de Cimo de Vila, currently used by Espaço Internet (p335). Among other stately homes are the 18th-century **Solar dos Viscondes de Treixedo** (Rua Direita), now a bank, and the 16th-century **Casa do Miradouro** (Calçada da Vigia), just off Largo de António José Pereira. Neither are open to the public.

PARQUE DO FONTELO

A haven of woodland and open space sprawls beyond the Portal do Fontelo. Here are the 16th-century Antigo Paço Episcopal (former Bishop's Palace), being refurbished as a Solar do Dão (below), as well as the once-lovely Renaissance gardens, a stadium and recreation complex.

ROMAN & OTHER SITES

On an embankment north of the centre is a **Viriato statue**, chief of the Lusitani. Behind

WINES OF THE DÃO REGION

The velvety red wines of the Dão region (within the Rio Mondego and tributary Rio Dão, south and east of Viseu) have been cultivated here for over 2000 years, and are today among Portugal's best.

Some three-dozen Dão vineyards and producers offer multilingual cellar tours and tastings of these 'Burgundies of Portugal'. Pick up a list at the tourist office. They prefer advance bookings, but one vineyard open to drop-in visitors is **Casa da Ínsua** (☎ 232 642 222; Penalva do Castelo), 30km east of Viseu on the IP5 and N329-1.

Coordinating them all is the **Comissão Vitivinicola Regional do Dão** (CVRD; ☎ 232 410 060; cvrdao@mail.telepac.pt; Avenida Capitão Homem Ribeiro 10, Viseu), which will soon open the 16th-century Antigo Paço Episcopal (above) as a posh Solar do Dão in which to sample a range of Dão wines.

White Dão wines are also available, though the full-bodied reds are the best (and strongest). Also try the sparkling white wines of the separate, small Lafões region, northwest of Viseu.

it is the site of a **Roman military camp**, though there's little to see.

About 5km southeast of the town centre, off the N16, is the **Via Romana de Coimbrões**, a well-preserved stretch of Roman road. The turismo has a booklet on this and other regional sites of archaeological interest, from the Stone Age to the 19th century.

Festivals & Events

Viseu's biggest annual get-together is the **Feira de São Mateus** (St Matthew's Fair), a jamboree of agriculture and handicrafts, which carries on from mid-August to mid-September, augmented by folk music, traditional food, amusements and fireworks. This direct descendant of the town's old 'free fair' still takes place on the Campo da Feira de São Mateus, set aside for the event by João III in 1510. However, check with the turismo as this area may soon undergo disruptive renovations.

Sleeping

Breakfast is included in the rates of the following four places.

Residencial Duque de Viseu (☎ /fax 232 421 286; Rua das Ameias 22; s/d €20/30; ❄) This snug little place lies in the shadow of the old city walls near the cathedral. It has sunny, quiet rooms good for independent-minded travellers that don't need personable service. Not recommended for families.

Residencial Dom Duarte (☎ 232 421 980; fax 232 424 825; Rua de Alexandre Herculano 214; d from €40; ❄) More modern, with carpeted rooms, new furniture and a scattering of faux-stone decoration.

Pensão Rossio Parque (☎ 232 422 085; Rua Soar de Cima 55; d with/without bathroom from €35/30) Clapped out old timer, largely held together by gaffer tape, but as central as you could wish for.

Residencial Bela Vista (☎ 232 422 026; fax 232 428 472; Rua de Alexandre Herculano 510; d €38; P ❄) South of the centre, concrete Bela Vista is plain in the extreme, but efficient, clean and has big rooms. Does not accept credit cards.

Pousada da juventude (☎ 232 435 095; viseu@movijovem.pt; Portal do Fontelo; dm €10, d with toilet €27) Beside the IPJ is this boxy, white-washed pousada da juventude. It's poorly equipped for self-caterers, though.

Pousada da juventude (☎ 232 724 543; spedrosul@movijovem.pt; dm €12.50, d with toilet €35) There is also another place- cosier and better-equipped – hostel 22km northwest at the spa centre of São Pedro do Sul.

Orbitur (☎ 232 436 146; info@orbitur.pt; adult/tent/car €3.50/2.90/3.40; 🕑 Apr-Sep) Orbitur operates a friendly and well-forested, well-equipped camping site about 1.5km east of the Rossio on the N16. It's on the brink of the large Parque do Fontelo, great for cool woodland walks.

Campismo Moinhos do Dão (☎ 232 610 586; www.portugal-aktief.com; c/o Café Pinheiro, Tibaldinho, 3530 Mangualde; adult/tent/car €3/2.50/1.75; 🕑 Apr-Oct) This camp site offers something a little different – a no-electricity, no-frills rural place, weedy and relaxed, and built by Dutch dropouts around several restored water-mills on the Rio Dão, 15km southeast of Viseu. In addition to riverside tent sites there are 'gypsy' wagons and various cabins and pretty millhouses (available per week). To get here, follow the blue camping signs for 6km from exit 19 on the IP5, east of Viseu.

Other camp sites are located at São Pedro do Sul, 23km northwest of Viseu; Sátão, 21km northeast; Tondela, 24km southwest; Vouzela, 34km west; and Castro Daire, 37km north.

MID-RANGE & TOP END

Hotel Avenida (☎ 232 423 432; Avenida Alberto Sampaio 1; s/d/t with breakfast €35/45/52) Standing proudly on a busy corner by the Rossio, this elegant hotel has well heated rooms decorated in regal colours. The breakfast is generous.

Hotel Grão Vasco (☎ 232 423 511; hotelgraovasco@mail.telepac.pt; Rua Gaspar Barreiros; s/d with breakfast €76/86; P ❄ 💻 🏊) Top of the scale in central Viseu, this rather pompous hotel sits alone in its sizable grounds above the Rossio.

Eating

Viseu is awash in good food for any budget.

Manga e Diospyrus (Centro Comercial Acadêmico II, Loja 14E; mains €4.50-7; 🕑 lunch & dinner Mon-Thu, lunch Fri) A surprise discovery for vegetarians is this self-service gem tucked away in a shopping centre, with a good choice of creative meat alternatives and fruit juices.

Restaurante Muralha da Sé (☎ 232 437 777; Adro da Sé 24; mains €10-15; 🕑 lunch & dinner Tue-Sat & lunch Mon) Go ahead: bust your budget at this unabashedly upper-crust spot under the looming Igreja da Misericórdia with a view to the cathedral from its summer terrace.

Casa dos Queijos (☎ 232 422 643; Travessa das Escadinhas da Sé 7; pratos do dia from €4.50, mains €6.50; ⏲ lunch & dinner Mon-Sat) This stone-walled old place, hidden up some narrow stairs, gets top marks for carefully prepared *cozidos* (stews) and grilled salmon. Though you could easily drain your wallet before ever reaching the table – the shop downstairs is stacked high with tempting cheeses and good *maduro* (mature) wines.

Restaurante O Hilário (☎ 232 436 587; Rua Augusto Hilário 35; half-/full-portions €4/6; ⏲ lunch & dinner Mon-Sat) This cosy little find has a menu of imaginative meaty dishes, plus righteous prices and attentive service.

Pastelaria O Lobo (Rua Francisco Alexandre Lobo 37; ⏲ 8am-8pm) This is the place for a caffeine hit, pastry and a rather elegant uptown coffee-house atmosphere.

Self-caterers will find fruit, vegetables and other goodies at the **Mercado 21 de Agosto** (Rua 21 de Agosto; ⏲ Mon-Sat).

Drinking

A clutch of bars near the cathedral overflow onto the streets and make for a merry atmosphere on summer nights.

The Irish Bar (☎ 232 436 135; Largo Pintor Gata 8; ⏲ 9am-2am Mon-Sat) The Irish Bar has the most loyal following, and occasional live Irish music.

Factor C (☎ 232 415 808; Largo Nossa Senhora da Conceição 39-43; ⏲ 11pm-4am Mon-Sat) This place is tough to beat for good, sweaty dance fun. It has distinct rooms playing pop, rock and alternative sounds to keep everyone happy.

The Day After (☎ 232 450 645; ⏲ 11pm-7am Tue-Sun) The best visiting DJs and bands invariably head here, surely Portugal's biggest disco with 10 dance halls as well as bowling, go-karts, a restaurant and more. You'll find it on the N16 west of the Cava de Viriato.

Shopping

Handicrafts here are cheaper than in more touristy towns; check out the local basketware and lace at **Casa da Ribeira** (Largo Nossa Senhora da Conceição; ⏲ 9am-12.30pm & 2-5.30pm Mon-Sat) – a municipal space for local artisans to work and sell their products. They also stock the region's striking black pottery, wrought iron and glassware. Also look for small handicrafts shops around Rua Direita.

Getting There & Away

Operators at the bus station include the companies **RBL/Rede Expressos** (☎ 232 422 822), **Marques** (☎ 232 423 766) and **Joalto** (☎ 232 426 093).

The best connections – at least two each weekday – are to Coimbra (€7, 1¼ hours) and Lisbon (€10, four hours) with RBL; Aveiro (€5.90, 1½ hours) and Porto (€7.20, two hours) with Marques or Joalto; Braga (€9.50, three hours) with Joalto or RBL; and Guarda (€6.50, 1¼ hours) and Covilhã (€8.50, 2¼ hours) with Joalto.

Rede Expressos and Joalto each have a daily bus via Trancoso and Vila Nova de Foz Côa (€7.20) to Bragança (€10.20, 3½ hours).

GUARDA

pop 26,000 / elevation 1056m

Fria, farta, forte e feia (cold, rich, strong and ugly): such is the popular description of Portugal's highest fully fledged city. However, this granite-grey district capital and bishopric, founded in 1199 to guard the frontier, works a chilly charm on visitors, who flock here on weekends and holidays.

They come for the looming cathedral, the melancholy lanes of the old Jewish quarter and, because Guarda is also the base for exploring the untouristy northeastern corner of the Parque Natural da Serra da Estrela, and a rugged frontier zone dotted with medieval fortified towns.

Just bring a woolly hat.

Orientation

Old Guarda is perched on a steep hill, a rambling climb from the IP5 or the train station; the latter is 5km northeast of the old centre, linked by a shuttle bus.

From the bus station on Rua Dom Nuno Álvares Pereira, it's 800m northwest to Praça Luís de Camões (also called Praça Velha), heart of the old town. Most accommodation, restaurants and places of interest are near the *praça*.

Information

There are banks with ATMs all around the centre.

Á4 (☎ 271 082 551; Rua 31 de Janeiro; per 30 min €1; ⏲ 8am-10pm Mon-Fri, 8am-7pm Sat, 8am-5pm Sun) Stationers with Internet access.

Mediateca VIII Centenário (☎ 271 205 531; Praça Luís de Camões; ⏲ 9.30am-12.30 & 2-5.30pm Mon-Fri)

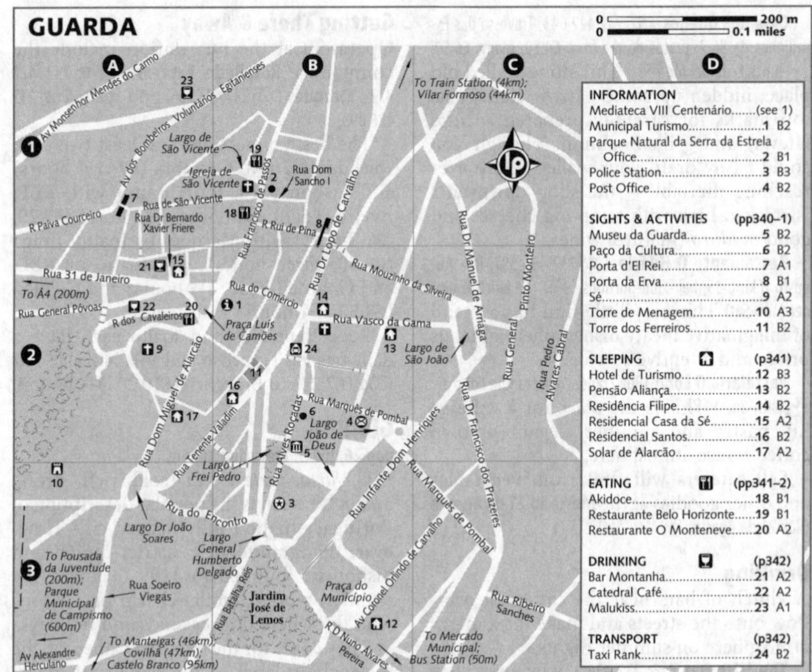

Municipal Internet shop above the turismo offering free Internet access.

Municipal turismo (☎ 271 205 530; Praça Luís de Camões; 🕑 9am-12.30pm & 2-6.30pm Mon-Sat, to 5.30pm Oct-May) In the *câmara municipal*. It too has a free Internet terminal.

Parque Natural da Serra da Estrela office (PNSE; ☎ /fax 271 225 454; Rua Dom Sancho I 3; 🕑 9am-12.30pm & 2-5.30pm Mon-Fri).

Police station (☎ 271 222 022; Rua Alves Roçadas 15)

Post office (☎ 271 221 754; Largo João de Deus; 🕑 8.30am-6pm Mon-Fri, 9am-12.30pm Sat) Southeast of the centre.

Sights

SÉ

Powerful in its sobriety, this Gothic fortress of a **cathedral** (Praça Luís de Camões; 🕑 9am-noon & 2-5pm Tue-Sat) squats heavily by a large square in the city centre. The earliest parts date from 1390 but it took 150 years to finish; it's dotted with Manueline doors and windows and Renaissance ornamentation.

The most striking feature in the immense, granite interior is a four-storey Renaissance altarpiece attributed to Jean de Rouen (João de Ruão), one of a team of 16th-century French artists who founded an influential school of sculpture at Coimbra. Also impressive are the twisted Manueline columns at each transept.

Restoration work is ongoing, and the tower was closed at the time of writing.

OLD TOWN

With its 16th- to 18th-century **mansions** and overpowering cathedral, Praça Luís de Camões is the town's centrepiece.

Little remains of Guarda's 13th-century castle except the simple **Torre de Menagem** (castle keep; closed to public), on a hilltop above the cathedral. Of the old walls and gates, the stalwart **Torre dos Ferreiros** (Blacksmiths' Tower; Rua Tenente Valadim) is still in good condition. Two other surviving gates are the **Porta d'El Rei**, the ancient steps of which you can still climb (though you'll find only broken beer bottles at the top), and the **Porta da Erva**.

Medieval atmosphere survives in the cobbled lanes and huddled houses north of the cathedral. At the heart of this area, around Rua de São Vicente, is the city's former **judiaria** (Jewish quarter). Sharp-eyed visitors will notice crosses and other symbols scratched into a few 16th-century vaulted doorframes – eg in Rua Rui de Pina and Rua Dom Sancho I – to identify the homes of *marranos* or 'New Christians' during the Inquisition (p26).

MUSEU DA GUARDA

The **museum** (☎ 271 213 460; Rua Alves Roçadas 30; admission €2, 10am-12.30pm Sun free; ⏲ 10am-12.30pm & 2-5.30pm Tue-Sun) occupies the severe 17th-century Episcopal Seminary, adjacent to the old Bishop's Palace. The museum's collection runs from Bronze Age swords to Roman coins, from Renaissance art to modern armaments.

The adjacent **Paço da Cultura** (admission free; ⏲ 2-8pm Mon-Sat) features ever-changing art exhibitions.

Festivals & Events

Guarda hosts a jazz festival called **Ciclo de Jazz de Guarda**, with several performances each week from March to May. The turismo hands out a free calendar of events.

Sleeping

Summer and weekend accommodation gets tight, so try to book ahead. There's no winter high-price season here, though Guarda is almost as close to the snow as the park's other main towns.

BUDGET

All *residência* and *pensão* rooms have a private bathroom and rates include breakfast.

Residencial Santos (☎ 271 205 400; residencial_santos@sapo.pt; Rua Tenente Valadim 14; s/d/tw €30/40/45) Santos' ultramodern interior resembles an Escher drawing with its interconnecting walkways, stairs and glass lifts that rise above its original granite walls. Plus the rooms are very comfortable and it's well run.

Residencial Casa da Sé (☎ 271 212 501; www.casa-da-se.com; Rua Augusto Gil 17; d with/without shower & toilet €42.50/33.50) This place has cosy, woody décor and azulejos in the hallways, plus many rooms have privileged views to the cathedral.

Residência Filipe (☎ 271 223 658; fax 271 221 402; Rua Vasco da Gama 9; d/t €35/45; Ⓟ) A funny mix of old and new, this guesthouse offers pretty rooms, brisk service and garage parking (€2.50).

Pensão Aliança (☎ 271 222 235; Rua Vasco da Gama 8A; d from €25; Ⓟ) Short on style but hospitable. It has dowdy rooms, but features a decent restaurant.

Parque Municipal de Campismo (☎ 271 221 200; fax 271 210 025; Rua do Estádio Municipal; adult/tent/car €1.75/1.75/1.50; ⏲ year-round) Southwest of the town centre is Guarda's own basic camp site, alongside the local park.

Pousada da juventude (☎ 271 224 482; guarda@movijovem.pt; Avenida Alexandre Herculano; dm summer/winter €8.50/11, d with toilet €22/30; Ⓟ) The rather clinical youth hostel is near the camp site.

MID-RANGE

Hotel de Turismo (☎ 271 223 366; www.hturismoguarda.com; Praça do Município; s/d €45/60; Ⓟ ⊠ ❄) A rather grand mansion-like hotel, with deluxe doubles that preserve more character than you might expect.

Solar de Alarcão (☎/fax 271 214 392; Rua Dom Miguel de Alarcão 25-27; d €75; Ⓟ) Our very firm favourite: a beautiful 17th-century granite mansion with its own courtyard and loggia, and a handful of gorgeous rooms stuffed with antique furniture and drapes. Even a Portuguese president has rested his head here.

Eating

Restaurante O Monteneve (☎ 271 212 799; Praça Luís de Camões 24; daily specials around €7, mains €7-14; ⏲ lunch & dinner Tue-Sun) Up an old granite staircase opposite the cathedral is this local institution, with bright wood-and-brick décor, excellent daily fish specials and lip-smacking desserts.

Restaurante Belo Horizonte (☎ 271 211 454; Largo de São Vicente 1; mains €7-11; ⏲ lunch & dinner Sun-Fri) Granite-fronted Belo Horizonte packs them in for lunch and dinner, with regional specialities such as *chouriçado* (a spicy sausage dish) and *cabrito grelhado* (grilled kid).

Akidoce (☎ 271 212 704; Rua Francisco de Passos 47; snacks €1.10-3.50; ⏲ all day Mon-Sat) Cheap, cheerful and open for breakfast through to late-night nibbles. Take your pick of salads, sandwiches, burgers and baguettes.

Pensão Aliança (☎ 271 222 235; Rua Vasco da Gama 8A; specials €6, mains €7.50-10; ⏲ all day) Quick-in quick-out eatery popular with locals for its good-value lunch-time specials.

Self-caterers can head to the **mercado municipal** near the bus station.

Drinking

Guarda has about a dozen central bars – all small and unlikely-looking from the outside, but welcoming enough within. Two central favourites are **Catedral Café** (Rua dos Cavaleiros 18; ⏲ 11pm-late), with frequent DJ gigs, and **Bar Montanha** (Rua Dr Bernardo Xavier Friere 13). For all-out dancing fun, try **Malukiss** (Avenida Bombeiros Voluntá rios Egitanienses).

Getting There & Away

BUS

The joint company **Joalto/RBI/Rede Expressos** (☎ 271 221 515) runs services around three times daily via Covilhã (€4, 45 minutes) to Castelo Branco (€7.80, 1¾ hours) and Lisbon (€11.40, 5½ hours); and several times daily to Viseu (€6.40, 1½ hours), Porto (€9.20, three hours) and Coimbra (€9.20, three hours).

Marques (☎ 238 312 858) goes daily via Gouveia (€4, 1½ hours) to Seia (€3.95, two hours). Rede Expressos goes to Seia (€7.20, 1¼ hours) once daily Sunday to Friday.

TRAIN

Guarda's train station is served by two lines from Lisbon. The Beira Alta line, via Coimbra, has three IC trains daily from Lisbon (€13, 4¼ hours); from Porto, change at Pampilhosa. Trains on the Beira Baixa line via Castelo Branco take an hour longer and require a change at Covilhã.

Six local trains trundle the 40km (€2.40, 50 minutes) between Guarda and the border at Vilar Formoso each day.

Getting Around

Shuttle buses run between the train station and the bus station (€0.70), with a stop at Rua Marquês de Pombal, every half-hour during the day. Call for a **taxi** (☎ 271 221 863) or board one at the rank on Rua Alves Roçadas. A taxi to the train station costs €3.50.

TRANCOSO

pop 4500 / elevation 870m

This peaceful hilltop town 43km north of Guarda offers a window onto many ages, from prehistory to the Peninsular War. Most visible is its medieval personality, with a warren of atmospheric cobbled alleyways squeezed within Dom Dinis' 13th-century walls – each sporting ornamented arcades, wrought-iron balconies and handsome granite porches.

Dinis underscored the importance of this border fortress by marrying the saintly Dona Isabel of Aragon here in 1282. But the town's favourite hero was not of royal blood. Rather, locals love to tell the story of Bandarra, a lowly 15th-century shoemaker and fortune-teller who rose above his station to put official noses out of joint foretelling the end of the Portuguese monarchy. Sure enough, shortly after Bandarra's death, the young Dom Sebastião died, heirless, in the disastrous Battle of Alcácer-Quibir in 1558. Soon afterward Portugal fell under Spanish rule.

Orientation & Information

Buses stop near the just outside the Portas d'El Rei gate.

Espaço Internet (☎ 271 829 120; ⏲ 3-7pm & 8-10.30pm Mon-Fri, 3-7pm Sat) Next to the tourist office, this has free Internet access.

Police station (Largo Luis Alberquerque)

Post office (Estrada de Lamego; ⏲ 9am-12.30pm & 2-6pm Mon-Fri) Outside the Portas do Prado gate.

Turismo (☎ 271 811 147; turismo@cm-trancoso.pt; ⏲ 9am-12.30pm & 2-5.30pm Mon-Fri, 10am-12.30pm & 2-5.30pm Sat & Sun)

Sights

The **Portas d'El Rei** (King's Gate), surmounted by the town's ancient coat of arms, has always been the town's main entrance. A guillotine-like door sealed out unwelcome visitors. The **town walls** run intact for over 1km around the medieval core. The main square is Largo Padre Francisco Ferreira (also called Largo do Pelourinho, or Largo Dom Dinis), anchored by an octagonal **pelourinho** dating from 1510.

Like many northern towns, Trancoso acquired a sizable Jewish community following the expulsion of Jews from Spain at the end of the 15th century, and much evidence remains of this period. The **old judiaria** covered roughly the southeastern third of the walled town. Among dignified reminders of that time is a former rabbinical residence called the **Casa do Gato Preto** (House of the Black Cat; Largo Luís Albuquerque), decorated with the gates of Jerusalem and other Jewish images.

On a hill in the northeastern corner is the tranquil **castelo** (castle; admission free; ⏲ 9am-5.30pm Mon-Fri, 10am-5.30pm Sat & Sun), dating from the

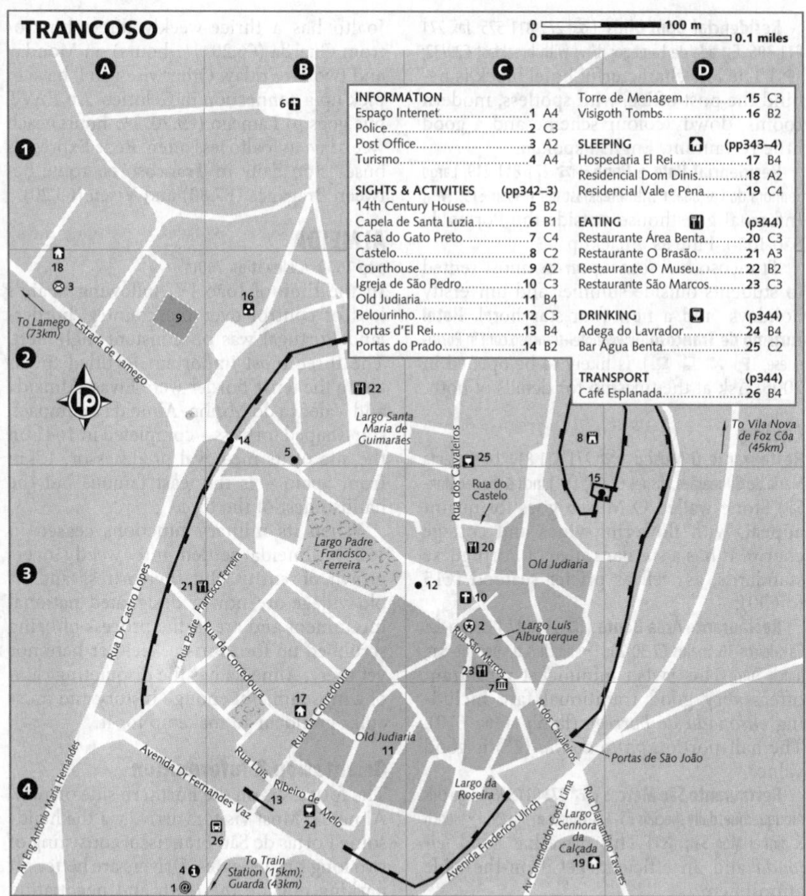

10th to 13th centuries with crenulated towers, and the impenetrable, squat, Moorish **Torre de Menagem**, with sloping walls. Kids and dogs hurtle around the courtyard: empty other than a sprinkling of wild-flowers.

To the west is a **14th-century house** typical of the time, with a big door into a storage area or shop, and a columned porch leading to living quarters (or in some cases a smaller ground-floor door opening onto interior stairs). This particular house – now appallingly neglected – served as Viscount William Beresford's regional *quartel-general* (headquarters) during the Peninsular War.

Across the road from the **Portas do Prado**, beside the courthouse, is an untended rock outcrop carved with eerie, body-shaped cavities, thought to be **Visigoth tombs** of the 7th or 8th century.

About 150m northward is Trancoso's prettiest church, the 13th-century **Capela de Santa Luzia**, with heavy Romanesque door arches and unadorned dry-stone construction. Trancoso abounds with other churches heavy with baroque make-up, most prominently the **Igreja de São Pedro**, behind the *pelourinho* on Largo Padre Francisco Ferreira.

Sleeping

Hospedaria El Rei (☎ 271 811 411; Rua da Corredoura; r from €20) This stout granite house within the walls of the old town is full of lovely old furniture and is the best bargain in town. You may find it closed until evening.

Residencial Dom Dinis (☎ 271 811 525; fax 271 811 396; Estrada de Lamego; d/tw with breakfast €29/32; 🅿) The less characterful hotel block is behind the post office, with spotless, modern rooms, dowdy colour scheme and a good little restaurant. English spoken.

Residencial Vale e Pena (☎ 271 811 219; Largo Senhora da Calçada; r with breakfast per person €15; 🅿) Informal guesthouse outside the Portas de São João. Fine as a backup.

Trancoso has some *quartos,* most rented to students outside summer and university holidays, and a new four-star hotel, **Hotel Turismo de Trancoso** (www.hotel-trancoso.com in Portuguese; 🅿), is likely to be opened in 2005. Ask at the turismo for details of both.

Eating

Restaurante O Museu (☎ 271 811 810; Largo Santa Maria de Guimarães; dishes €7-11; lunch & dinner Mon-Sat) Stone-walled O Museu goes for quaint appeal, with flowering vines and cottage charm. It has a similar range of Portuguese standards, as well as pricier seafood (€15 to €50).

Restaurante Área Benta (☎ 271 817 180; Rua dos Cavaleiros 30; mains €7.50-20; lunch & dinner Tue-Sat, lunch Sun) This swish minimalist restaurant offers very good traditional fare including *ensopada de borrego* (lamb stew; €10). The half-portion *prato do dia* (€5) is good value.

Restaurante São Marcos (☎ 271 811 326; Largo Luís Albuquerque; daily specials €5-7, 3-course menu €9; lunch & dinner Mon-Sat) This place has good *feijoada* and an efficient, get-it-on-the-table atmosphere.

Restaurante O Brasão (☎ 271 811 767; Rua Padre Francisco Ferreira; mains €5-8; lunch & dinner Sun-Fri) Expect a small meaty menu, big portions and an almost exclusively local clientele.

Drinking

Bar Água Benta (☎ 271 812 390; Rua dos Cavaleiros 36A; noon-3am Mon-Sat, 1-7pm Sun) Tucked away in the backstreets is this little café-cum-bar, with a cheerful atmosphere, international beers, and occasional live music.

Adega do Lavrador (Rua Luis Ribeiro de Melo 7A; daily) A brightly coloured and youthful *cervejaria* (beer house).

Getting There & Away

Catch buses and buy tickets at **Café Esplanada** (☎ 271 811 188), which is near the turismo. Joalto has a thrice-weekly direct bus to/from Guarda (€6.20, 1½ hours) on Monday and two on Friday. Otherwise you'll have to pick up a connection in Celorico. An EAVT bus goes to Lamego (€9.20, 1½ hours) each weekday, to Joalto less often. Rede Expressos buses stop daily in Trancoso en route between Bragança (€7.80) and Viseu (€5.20).

ALMEIDA

pop 1600 / elevation 760m

In the time of João IV, following Spain's loss of control over the country, borderland Portugal was on constant high alert. The three most important fortified towns along the tense border were Elvas, Almeida and Valença do Minho. Almeida's compact, star-shaped fortress – completed in 1641 on the site of its medieval predecessor, 15km from Spain – is the least famous but the handsomest of the three.

When its military functions ceased in 1927, Almeida settled into weedy overgrown obscurity. But the fortress and its old village are now a designated national monument and are in the process of being scrubbed up for tourism. Neither here nor yet there, Almeida has the disquieting calm of a museum, but enough history and muscular grandeur to make up for it.

Orientation & Information

The fortress is on the northern side of 'new' Almeida. Most visitors arrive via the handsome Portas de São Francisco, consisting of two long tunnel-gates. Drivers are better off parking outside the town and negotiating the inner town on foot.

The **turismo** (☎ 271 570 020; fax 271 570 021; 9am-12.30pm & 2-5.30pm, from 10am Sat & Sun) is nonetheless impressively located in an old guard-chamber within the Portas de São Francisco. Here you can get a map of the fortress, though not much else.

A bank and ATM are across Praça da República from the turismo.

Sights

The long arcaded building just inside the Portas de São Francisco is the 18th-century **Quartel das Estradas** (Infantry Barracks).

In a bastion 300m northeast of the turismo are the **casamatas** (casemates or bunkers; 9am-12.30pm & 2-5.30pm Mon-Fri, from 10am Sat & Sun), a warren of 20 underground rooms used for storage, barracks and shelter in times of siege, and in the 18th century as a prison.

The fort's **castle** was blown to smithereens during a French siege in 1810, when their own ammunition supplies exploded. You can still see the foundations, 300m northwest of the turismo, from an ugly catwalk. Below the ruins is a riding school, in the former Royal Riding Academy.

In Praça da Liberdade, on the way back, is the **Paços do Concelho** (council hall), in the former artillery barracks.

Sleeping

Casa Pátio da Figueira (☎ 271 574 773, 963 367 237; lqueiros@mail.telepac.pt; Rua Direita 48; d €75;) A restored 18th-century townhouse of chunky stone and considerable charm, at the northern end of the village, with a garden and four elegant double rooms. This road is signed 'Rua dos Combatentes Mortos Pela Patria' but nobody uses the name.

Pensão-Restaurante A Muralha (☎/fax 271 574 357; Bairro de São Pedro; d/t with breakfast €35/45; P) To pay less, you must kip outside the old town. This functional place is 300m outside the Portas de São Francisco on the Vilar Formoso road. It has quiet personality-free rooms and a large restaurant serving unsophisticated belly-filling platters.

Pousada Nossa Senhora das Neves (☎ 271 574 283; recepcao.sraneves@pousadas.pt; d weekend/midweek with breakfast €113/122; P) A deluxe but out-of-place modern *pousada* on the site of former cavalry quarters near the north bastion. Most rooms have balconies.

Eating

There are half a dozen small-time snack-bars and café-bars inside the walls.

Picadeiro D'El Rey (mains €10-20; lunch & dinner Wed-Mon) The only dedicated restaurant is this upper-crust place by the horse stables at the on the far northwestern side of the fortress.

Snack Bar 1810 (☎ 271 571 093; Rua Direita; all day Mon-Sat) More down-to-earth is this friendly bar-cum-restaurant.

4 Esquinas Bar (☎ 271 574 314; Travessa da Pereira 7; breakfast, lunch & dinner) Cosy 4 Esquinas Bar is good for baguettes and burgers.

Restaurante O Granitos (☎ 271 574 834; Largo 25 de Abril; daily specials €6; lunch & dinner) The majority of local barflies congregate here, just outside the Portas de São Francisco There's lots of hot and filling pub grub.

Getting There & Away

RBI/Redê Expressos has two Guarda–Almeida buses (about €4.80, 1¼ to two hours) each weekday, though timing leaves little time to see the fortress without spending the night. The bus stop is by the BPI bank outside the Portas de São Francisco.

The Douro

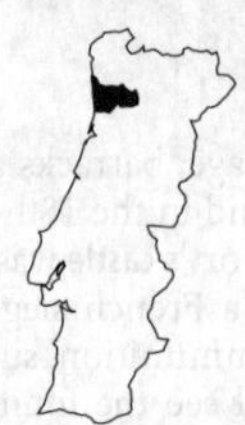

CONTENTS

Picture this: you're on deck sipping your glass of port wine, watching vine-covered hills dotted with white lodges roll past and listening to the gentle splash of the Rio Douro (River of Gold) as the boat makes its way into the heart of port-wine country. It's an idyllic image, and one that draws thousands of wandering wine lovers to the region every year.

But while the Douro region is world-famous for its production of port, it's not just the tipple that tempts travellers. In particular, Porto – Portugal's second city – has a vibrant cultural scene bubbling with nightlife, history, arts and sporting action. This is also a region rich in history, dotted with extraordinary monasteries, age-old bridges and a unique collection of Stone Age art. Although not its biggest draw, the region's coastline is also cleaning up its act, with good beaches at Vila do Conde and Vila Nova de Gaia.

But the province is, of course, dominated by Portugal's best-known river, the Douro. Rising in Spain, the Rio Douro defines part of the Spain–Portugal border before flowing 200km west to Porto. It's in the Alto Douro, from the Spanish border to Peso da Régua, that Portugal's illustrious port-wine grapes are grown, on steep terraced hills of schist that trap the region's fiery summer heat.

The river, now tamed by no less than five dams, is navigable all the way to Barca de Alva, allowing passenger cruises to slip through dramatic gorges into the epicentre of the port-wine production. Another fine way to explore the valley is on its railway; it's been hugging the riverside since 1887, stretching all the way to Pocinho. Three narrow-gauge lines also climb out of the valley from the main line, offering enchanting diversions to Amarante and into Trás-os-Montes.

This chapter includes towns from both the Beira Alta and Trás-os-Montes, which lie along the Rio Douro.

HIGHLIGHTS

- **Wining**
  A glass or three of port at Vila Nova de Gaia (p363)
- **River View**
  Porto's World Heritage–listed Ribeira district (p355)
- **Modern Art**
  Porto's Museu de Arte Contemporânea (p355)
- **Jump Aboard**
  Slow train or boat up the Douro to Peso da Régua (p358)
- **Time Travel**
  Stone Age rock art of the Vale do Côa (p382)

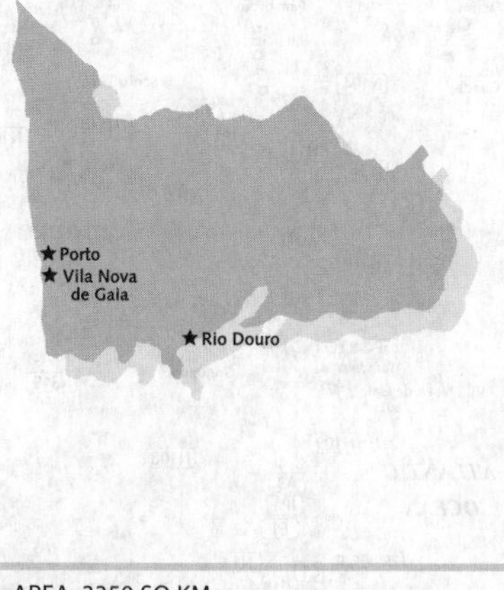

- POPULATION: 1,982,280
- AREA: 3350 SQ KM

PORTO

pop 264,000 / elevation 80m

With a brawny beauty all its own, Portugal's second-biggest city is Porto (Oporto to foreigners). Built on granite bluffs above the Rio Douro, its heart is a tangle of World Heritage-listed lanes tumbling steeply down to a medieval waterfront. It's hard not to be wooed by Porto's atmospheric riverside, dotted with old port-wine boats, pinched lanes and shadowy archways.

Dramatically straddling the river are six trademark bridges to Porto's 'other half', Vila Nova de Gaia, historic home to scores of port-wine lodges – the city's biggest attraction. Every year, vast grape harvests from the Douro valley make their way here to be matured, blended and bottled.

Despite its charms, Porto was seen as Lisbon's shy, upcountry cousin – a commercial city lacking the cosmopolitan clout of the capital. Not so any more. Its nomination as European City of Culture 2001 recognised Porto's ever-growing appetite for the finer things in life. This in turn fuelled several hugely ambitious projects, from world-class concert halls to a metro system, and the city now hosts some of the best art galleries in the country. Its cafés and bars buzz with exhibitions, poetry readings and music, and the city's nightlife is cutting-edge.

However, the biggest boost to Porto's self-confidence came courtesy of its biggest obsession – soccer. The inhabitants could hardly believe it when 2004 saw their heroic FC Porto beat off the continent's big-spenders to bring home the European Champion's League title. And within weeks they were thrust into the international spotlight as a host city for the European Football Championships (Euro2004). While, economically, the city may be paying the price for its high ambitions, its profile has rarely been higher.

You'll need a minimum of two days in Porto to soak up the atmosphere – and the port wine.

HISTORY

Porto puts the 'Portu' in 'Portugal'. In Roman times, a Lusitanian settlement on the Douro's

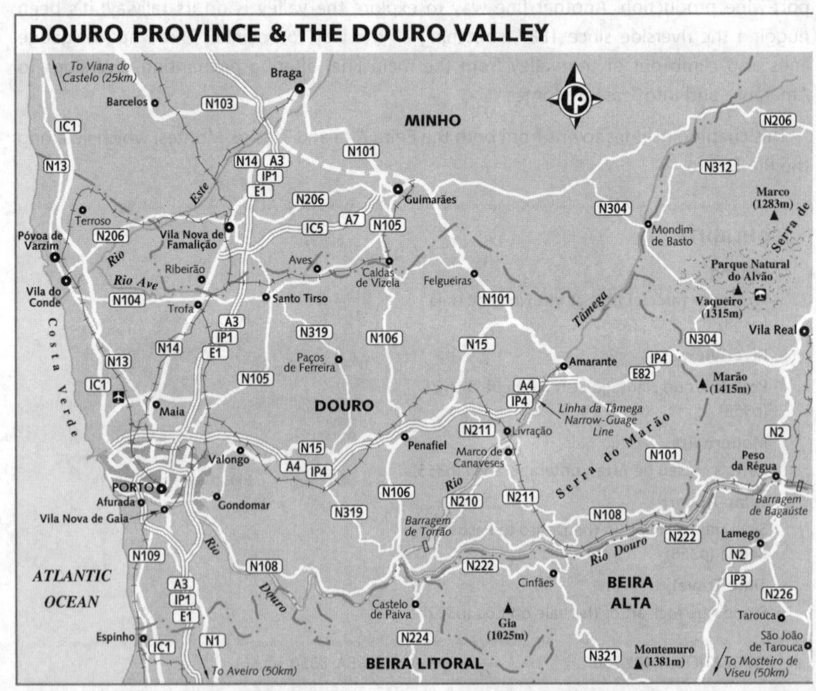

south bank was mirrored by another on the other side. These subsequently merged to become the capital of the county of Portucale, which was inherited by the British-born Henri of Burgundy in 1095 (p24). And it was from here that Henri's son and Portuguese hero Afonso Henriques launched the Reconquista, ultimately winning Portugal its status as an independent kingdom.

Porto leapt up the status ranks with the building of a cathedral in 1111 and in 1387 Dom João I married Philippa of Lancaster here: their most famous son, Henry the Navigator, was subsequently born in the city. While Henry's explorers groped around Africa for a sea route to India, British traders found a firm foothold in Porto with their trade in port wine.

Over the following centuries Porto acquired a reputation for rebelliousness. And don't think that that excludes the ladies: in 1628 a mob of maddened women attacked the minister responsible for a tax on linen. In 1757 a 'tipplers' riot' against the Marquês de Pombal's regulation of the port-wine trade was savagely put down. In 1808 Porto citizens arrested the French governor and set up their own junta. The French army, which quickly took the city back, was finally given the boot by the British under the future Duke of Wellington, but Porto radicals soon turned against British control, demanded a new liberal constitution and in 1822 got one.

Porto stood by its principles and Miguel's constitutionalist brother Pedro when the absolutist Miguel I usurped the throne in 1828. Miguel's forces laid siege to the city in 1832 after Pedro arrived from Brazil, but the liberal cause won through in the following year when Miguel's fleet was captured off Cabo São Vicente.

Demonstrations continued to erupt in Porto in support of liberals throughout the 19th century. Portugal's first republican deputy was elected from Porto in 1878.

ORIENTATION

'Old' Porto clambers haphazardly up the gorge 9km from the mouth of the Douro; 'new' Porto sprawls out to the polluted seashore at Foz do Douro. Though a separate

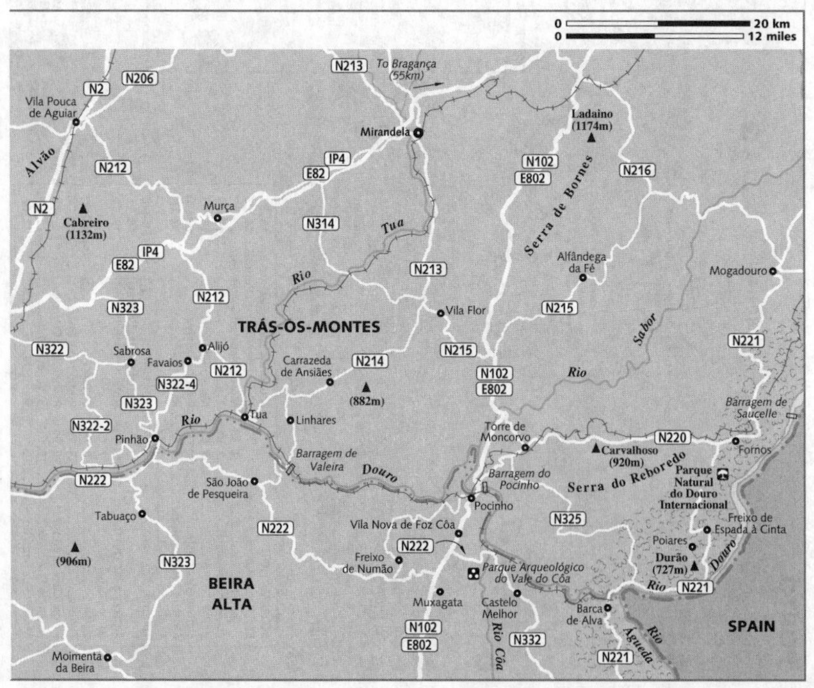

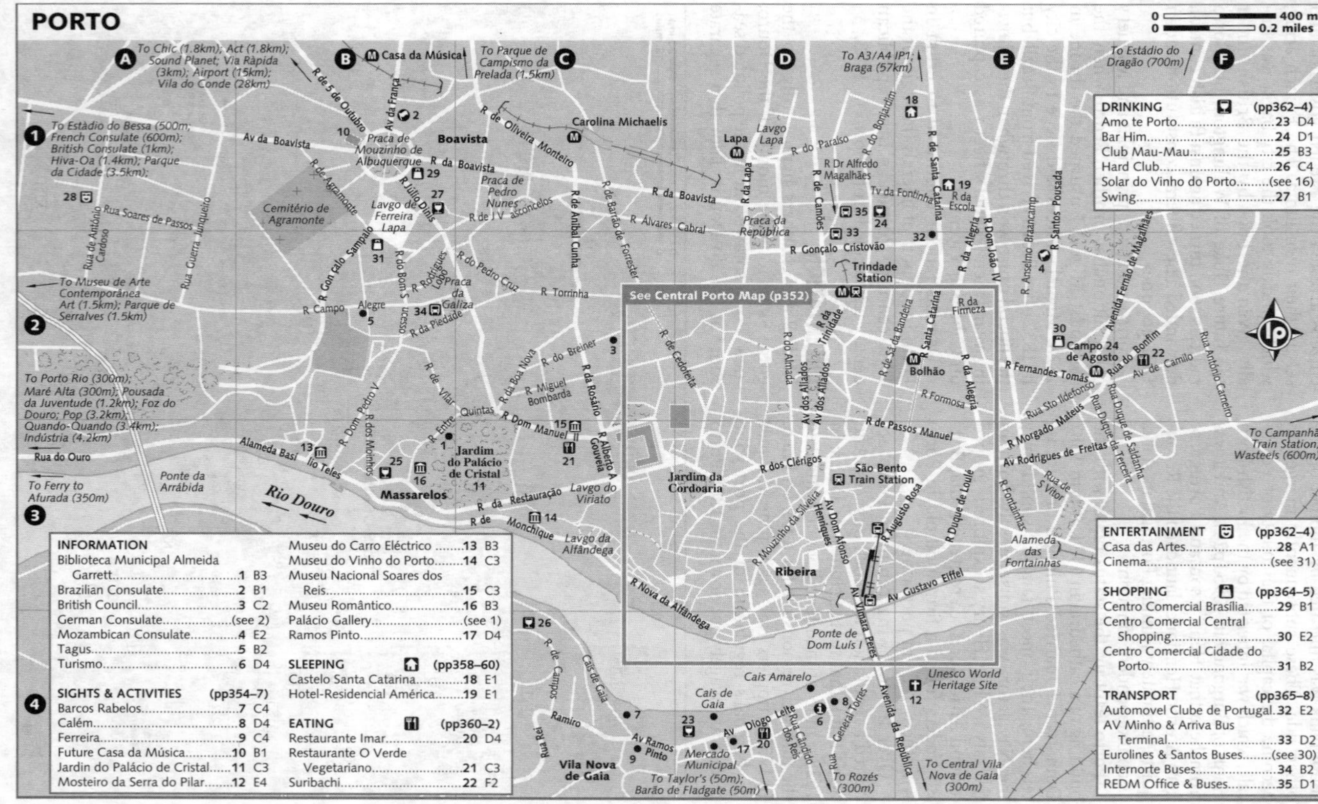
PORTO
0 400 m
0 0.2 miles
To Chic (1.8km); Act (1.8km); Sound Planet; Via Rápida (3km); Airport (15km); Vila do Conde (28km)
To Estàdio do Bessa (500m); French Consulate (600m); British Consulate (1km); Hiva-Oa (1.4km); Parque da Cidade (3.5km);
To Museu de Arte Contemporânea Art (1.5km); Parque de Serralves (1.5km)
To Porto Rio (300m); Maré Alta (300m); Pousada da Juventude (1.2km); Foz do Douro; Pop (3.2km); Quando-Quando (3.4km); Indústria (4.2km)
To Ferry to Afurada (350m)
To Parque de Campismo da Prelada (1.5km)
To A3/A4 IP1; Braga (57km)
To Estádio do Dragão (700m)
To Campanhã Train Station; Wasteels (600m)
To Taylor's (50m); Barão de Fladgate (50m)
To Rozés (300m)
To Central Vila Nova de Gaia (300m)
Casa da Música
Boavista
Carolina Michaelis
Lapa
Cemitério de Agramonte
Praca de Mouzinho de Albuquerque
Praca de Pedro Nunes
Lavgo de Ferreira Lapa
Praca da República
Trindade Station
Bolhão
Campo 24 de Agosto
See Central Porto Map (p352)
Jardim da Cordoaria
São Bento Train Station
Ribeira
Ponte de Dom Luís I
Jardim do Palácio de Cristal
Massarelos
Rio Douro
Ponte da Arrábida
Vila Nova de Gaia
Cais de Gaia
Cais Amarelo
Mercado Municipal
Unesco World Heritage Site
Av da Boavista
R da Boavista
R de Oliveira Monteiro
R de Santa Catarina
R Gonçalo Cristovão
R de Cedofeita
R dos Clérigos
R de Passos Manuel
Av dos Aliados
Av Rodrigues de Freitas
Avenida Fernão de Magalhães
Avenida da República
Av Vimara Peres
Av Gustavo Eiffel
R Nova da Alfândega
R da Restauração
Alameda Basílio Teles
Rua do Ouro
Av Diogo Leite
INFORMATION
Biblioteca Municipal Almeida Garrett....1 B3
Brazilian Consulate....2 B1
British Council....3 C2
German Consulate....(see 2)
Mozambican Consulate....4 E2
Tagus....5 B2
Turismo....6 D4
Museu do Carro Eléctrico....13 B3
Museu do Vinho do Porto....14 C3
Museu Nacional Soares dos Reis....15 C3
Museu Romântico....16 B3
Palácio Gallery....(see 1)
Ramos Pinto....17 D4
SIGHTS & ACTIVITIES (pp354–7)
Barcos Rabelos....7 C4
Calém....8 D4
Ferreira....9 C4
Future Casa da Música....10 B1
Jardin do Palácio de Cristal....11 C3
Mosteiro da Serra do Pilar....12 E4
SLEEPING (pp358–60)
Castelo Santa Catarina....18 E1
Hotel-Residencial América....19 E1
EATING (pp360–2)
Restaurante Imar....20 D4
Restaurante O Verde Vegetariano....21 C3
Suribachi....22 F2
DRINKING (pp362–4)
Amo te Porto....23 D4
Bar Him....24 D1
Club Mau-Mau....25 B3
Hard Club....26 C4
Solar do Vinho do Porto....(see 16)
Swing....27 B1
ENTERTAINMENT (pp362–4)
Casa das Artes....28 A1
Cinema....(see 31)
SHOPPING (pp364–5)
Centro Comercial Brasília....29 B1
Centro Comercial Central Shopping....30 E2
Centro Comercial Cidade do Porto....31 B2
TRANSPORT (pp365–8)
Automovel Clube de Portugal....32 E2
AV Minho & Arriva Bus Terminal....33 D2
Eurolines & Santos Buses....(see 30)
Internorte Buses....34 B2
REDM Office & Buses....35 D1

town Vila Nova de Gaia, the port-wine centre across the river, is treated as part of the city.

The city's axis is Avenida dos Aliados (called 'Aliados' by all), a handsome avenue carved out in 1915 in homage to French Art Nouveau. At its northern end are the *câmara municipal* (town hall), the main turismo, the central post office and banks.

Central hubs for city and regional buses are at Praça da Liberdade, Praça Almeida Garrett (by São Bento station) and Largo dos Lóios at the southern end of Aliados, and at Jardim da Cordoaria (or Cordoaria) about 400m west of Aliados. South of Aliados the city extends down to the riverside Ribeira district.

A lively shopping district surrounds the Mercado do Bolhão (Bolhão Market), northeast of Aliados. Another big commercial zone is Boavista, around the giant Praça de Mouzinho de Albuquerque roundabout. Here the Casa da Música (Music Hall), meant to become the city's cultural flagship, is under interminable construction.

Porto's Francisco Sá Carneiro airport is 19km northwest of the city centre. There are two train stations: Campanhã, 2km east of the centre, and central São Bento. Trindade station, just north of Aliados, is now hub of Porto's developing metro system. Intercity bus terminals are scattered all over the city; see p365 for further information.

The World Heritage zone reaches from the Torre dos Clérigos and São Bento station down to the Cais da Ribeira. Also included are the Ponte de Dom Luís I and the Mosteiro da Serra do Pilar in Vila Nova de Gaia.

You can pick up free maps of the city at any of Porto's tourist offices.

INFORMATION

Bookshops

Livraria Bertrand (Map pp352-3; ☎ 222 080 638; Centro Comercial Via Catarina, Rua Santa Catarina; ⌚ 10am-10pm) Has a selection of travel books and maps.

Livraria Latina Editora (Map pp352-3; ☎ 222 001 294; Rua Santa Catarina 2; ⌚ Mon-Sat) Well stocked with guidebooks and foreign-language novels.

Livraria Lello (Map pp352-3; ☎ 222 002 037; Rua das Carmelitas 144; ⌚ 10am-7.30pm Mon-Sat) Even if you're not after books, don't miss this Art Deco confection stacked to the rafters with new, second-hand and antique books. Open since 1919 in lavish 19th-century quarters more suited to a gentlemen's club: note the plaster painted as wood, stained-glass ceiling and unique curving staircase.

Livraria Porto Editora (Map pp352-3; ☎ 222 007 681; Praça Dona Filipa de Lencastre 42; ⌚ 9.30am-1pm & 2.30-7pm Mon-Fri, 9.30am-1pm Sat) Reference bookshop that stocks many maps including 1:25,000 military topographic maps covering Portugal (€6.40 per sheet).

Lotarias Atlânticos (Map pp352-3; Rua Sampaio Bruno; ⌚ Mon-Fri, Sat morning) One of surprisingly few newsagents selling foreign-language newspapers.

Cultural Centres

British Council (Map p350; ☎ 222 073 060; Rua do Breiner 155; ⌚ 2-8.30pm Mon & Wed, 10am-1pm & 2-8.30pm Tue & Thu, 2-7.30pm Fri, irregular hr Sat mid-Sep–mid-Jun; 2-5.30pm Mon, Wed & Fri, 10am-1pm & 2-5.30pm Tue & Thu mid-Jun–mid-Sep; closed Aug) Has a library full of English-language books and newspapers.

Emergency

Tourism police (Map pp352-3; ☎ 222 081 833; Rua Clube dos Fenianos 11; ⌚ 8-2am) The place to go for police help or enquiries is this multilingual station beside the main city turismo.

Police station (Map pp352-3; ☎ 222 006 821; Rua Augusto Rosa) South of Praça da Batalha.

Internet Access

Biblioteca Municipal Almeida Garrett (Map p350; ☎ 226 081 000; Jardim do Palácio de Cristal; ⌚ 2-6pm Mon, 10am-6pm Tue-Sat) Library with free Internet access, one-hour slots and long waits.

Laranja Mecânica (Map pp352-3; ☎ 222 010 576; Rua Santa Catarina 274, Loja V; per hr €1.40; ⌚ 10am-midnight Mon-Sat, 2-8pm Sun) The 'Clockwork Orange' has various deals for frequent users.

Portweb (Map pp352-3; ☎ 222 005 922; Praça General Humberto Delgado 291; per hr €1.20; ⌚ 10-2am Mon-Sat, 3pm-2am Sun) It has cheaper deals for as little as €0.60 for longer-term users.

Portugal Telecom (PT) Office (Map pp352-3; ☎ 225 008 436; Praça da Liberdade 62; per hr €2.50; ⌚ 8am-8pm Mon-Sat, 10am-8pm Sun) The telephone office also has a dozen pricey terminals.

Internet Resources

www.agendadoporto.pt What's-on guide to the city in Portuguese

www.portoturismo.pt The official tourist portal

www.portoxxi.com Multilingual cultural guide to Porto

Laundry

Lavandaria São Nicolau (Map p356; ☎ 222 084 621; Rua Infante Dom Henrique, Ribeira; ⌚ 8.30am-2pm Mon,

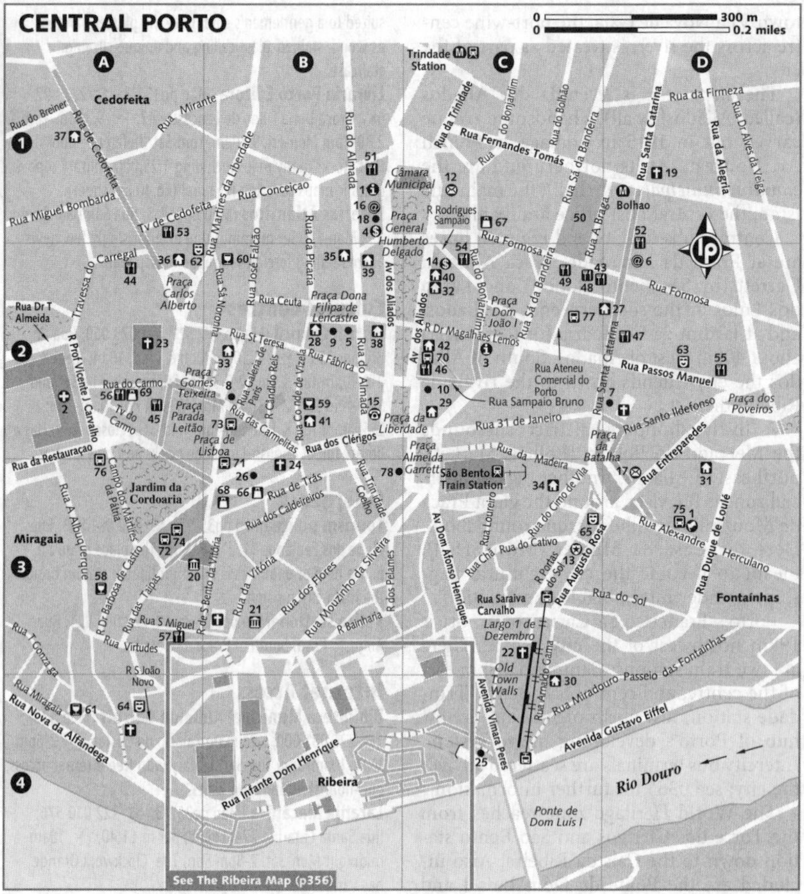

CENTRAL PORTO

See The Ribeira Map (p356)

8.30am-7.30pm Tue-Fri, 8.30am-7pm Sat) Costs €4.50 to wash and dry a 6kg load. There are also showers in this underground complex.

Medical Services

Hospital Geral de Santo António (Map pp352-3; ☎ 222 077 500; Rua Vicente José Carvalho) Some English-speaking staff.

Money

There is a 24-hour currency exchange, as well as a **bank** (🕑 8.30am-3pm Mon-Fri) and an ATM, beside the ICEP turismo in the airport arrivals hall. Plentiful ATMs pop up all along Aliados, indeed everywhere there are shops. Some private exchange bureaus are listed following:

Intercontinental (Map pp352-3; ☎ 222 005 557; Rua de Ramalho Ortigão 8; 🕑 9am-noon & 2-6.30pm Mon-Fri, 9am-noon Sat)

Portocâmbios (Map pp352-3; ☎ 222 000 238; Rua Rodrigues Sampaio 193; 🕑 9am-12.30pm & 1.30-6pm Mon-Fri, 9am-12.30pm Sat)

Top Atlântico (p353) American Express (AmEx) travellers cheques can be cashed here.

Post

Main post office (Map pp352-3; ☎ 223 400 200; Avenida dos Aliados; 🕑 8am-9pm Mon-Fri, 9am-6pm Sat, 9am-12.30pm & 2-6pm Sun) Includes poste restante and is opposite the main city turismo.

Post offices (Map pp352-3 & Map p356; Rua Ferreira Borges 67, Ribeira & Praça da Batalha; both 🕑 8.30am-6pm Mon-Fri)

INFORMATION		
Angolan Consulate	1	D3
Hospital Geral de Santo António	2	A2
ICEP Turismo	3	C2
Intercontinental	4	B1
Intervisa	5	B2
Laranja Mecânica	6	D2
Livaria Bertrand	(see 52)	
Livraria Latina Editora	7	D2
Livraria Lello	8	B2
Livraria Porto Editora	9	B2
Lotarias Atlânticos	10	C2
Main City Turismo	11	B1
Main Post Office	12	C1
Police Station	13	C3
Portocâmbios	14	C2
Portugal Telecom Office	15	B2
Portweb	16	B1
Post Office	17	D3
Top Atlântico	18	B1
Tourism Police	(see 11)	
SIGHTS & ACTIVITIES	**(pp354–7)**	
Capela das Almas	19	D1
Centro Português de Fotografia	20	A3
Igreja da Misericórdia	21	B3
Igreja de Santa Clara	22	C3
Igreja do Carmo	23	A2
Igreja dos Clérigos	24	B3
Ribeira Negra Mural	25	C4
Torre dos Clérigos	26	B3
SLEEPING	**(pp358–60)**	
Grande Hotel do Porto	27	D2
Hotel Infante de Sagres	28	B2
Hotel Peninsular	29	C2
Pensão Astória	30	C4
Pensão Aviz	31	D3
Pensão Chique	32	C2
Pensão Duas Nações	33	B2
Pensão Mondariz	34	C3
Pensão Porto Rico	35	B2
Pensão São Marino	36	A2
Pensão-Residencial Estoril	37	A1
Residencial dos Aliados	38	B2
Residencial Pão de Açucar	39	B2
Residencial Paulista	40	C2
Residencial Porto Chique	41	B2
Residencial Universal	42	C2
EATING	**(pp360–2)**	
A Pérola do Bolhão	43	C2
Adega do Carregal	44	A2
Café Ancôra Douro	45	A2
Café Embaixador	46	C2
Café Majestic	47	D2
Confeitaria do Bolhão Shop	48	C2
Confeitaria do Bolhão	49	C2
Mercado do Bolhão	50	C1
Minipreço	51	B1
Modelo	52	D1
Pão de Ló Margaridense	53	A1
Pedro dos Frangos	54	C2
Pingo Doce	55	D2
Restaurante A Tasquinha	56	A2
Restaurante O Oriente no Porto	57	A3
DRINKING	**(pp362–4)**	
Boys 'R' Us	58	A3
Gemini's	59	B2
Moinho de Vento	60	B2
Púcaros Bar	61	A4
ENTERTAINMENT	**(pp362–4)**	
Auditório Nacional Carlos Alberto	62	A2
Coliseu do Porto	63	D2
Restaurante O Fado	64	A4
Teatro Nacional de São João	65	C3
SHOPPING	**(pp364–5)**	
Artesanato dos Clérigos	66	B3
Casa Januário	67	C1
Casa Oriental	68	B3
Centro Comercial Via Caterina	(see 52)	
Garrafeira do Carmo	69	A2
TRANSPORT	**(pp365–8)**	
AeroBus Terminus	70	C2
Bus No 50	71	B3
Bus Nos 24, 41 & 56	72	A3
Bus Nos 56 & 76	73	B2
Bus Nos 93 & 96	74	A3
Paragem Atlântico Terminal	(see 75)	
Rede Expressos & RBL Buses	75	D3
Renex Buses	76	A3
Rodonorte Bus Terminal	77	C2
STCP Service Point	78	B3

Telephone

Post offices, kiosks and newsagents sell Portugal Telecom phonecards.

Portugal Telecom office (PT; Map pp352-3; ☎ 225 008 436; Praça da Liberdade 62; 🕒 8am-8pm Mon-Sat, 10am-8pm Sun) The handiest place for long-distance calls using cardphones or pay-afterward cabines.

Tourist Information

For an alternative agenda covering Portugal's hippest cultural and night life, pick up the free magazine (in Portuguese) *Difmag* from Tempo de Leitura no Porto (p362). It has listings for all major Portuguese cities including Porto.

ICEP turismo (Map pp352-3; ☎ 222 057 514; Praça Dom João I 43; 🕒 9am-7.30pm Jul & Aug; 9am-7.30pm Mon-Fri, 9.30am-3.30pm Sat & Sun Sep & Apr-Jun; 9am-7pm Mon-Fri, 9.30am-3.30pm Sat & Sun Nov-Mar). For countrywide queries visit this national turismo.

Main city turismo (Map pp352-3; ☎ 223 393 472; turismo.central@cm-porto.pt; Rua Clube dos Fenianos 25; 🕒 9am-7pm Mon-Fri Jul-Sep, 9am-5.30pm Mon-Fri Oct-Jun; 9.30am-4.30pm Sat, Sun & holidays year-round) is opposite the *câmara municipal*. It offers a detailed city map, the *Agenda do Porto* cultural calendar, the *Tourist Guide,* which bulges with practical information, and the *Museum Guide* – all free. It sells the Passe Porto, a one-/two-day tourist pass (€5/7) that is good for free bus travel, reduced museum admission and a long list of other discounts (pick up a leaflet at the turismo). The **Loja da Mobilidade** (loja.mobilidade@cm-porto.pt) desk dispenses a handy brochure, *Guia de Transportes*, and can provide details on everything from bus timetables to car parks to metro stations.

Turismo Ribeira (Map p356; ☎ 222 009 770; Rua Infante Dom Henrique 63; 🕒 9am-5.30pm Mon-Fri, 9.30am-4.30pm Sat & Sun) Maps, cultural calendars and tourist passes, as listed under the main city turismo, are also found in this smaller information centre; Airport (☎ 229 412 534, 229 432 400; 🕒 8am-11.30pm Apr-Christmas, 8am-11pm Christmas-Mar)

Travel Agencies

When booking a tour, see p357 for details of government-run Porto Tours, which acts as impartial intermediary between tour operators and travellers.

Intervisa (Map pp352-3; ☎ 222 079 200; intervisa@intervisa-viagens.pt; Praça Dona Filipa de Lencastre 1; 🕒 9am-noon & 2.30-6.30pm Mon-Fri) General travel agency.

Tagus (Map p350; ☎ 226 094 141; www.viagenstagus.pt; Rua Campo Alegre 261; 🕒 9am-6pm Mon-Fri, 10am-1pm Sat) Youth-oriented agency selling discounted tickets, rail passes and international youth and student cards.

Top Atlântico (Map pp352-3; ☎ 222 074 020; Praça General Humberto Delgado) Also Porto's AmEx representative.

Wasteels (☎ 225 194 230; porto@wasteels.pt; Rua Pinto Bessa 27-29; 🕒 9.30am-12.30pm & 1.45-6pm Mon-Fri) Another youth-oriented agency, near Campanhã train station.

DANGERS & ANNOYANCES

Porto has plenty of sketchy alleys best avoided after dark, in particular in riverside areas off Rua Nova da Alfândega and Avenida Gustavo Eiffel. Even the most central parks and squares have their share of drunks and oddballs. São Bento train station and the Ribeira district are other areas where you might not want to be alone late at night.

Stay away from the none-too-clean beach at Foz do Douro: head instead to Vila do Conde (26km to the north) or Vila Nova de Gaia's eastern coast, which has thoroughly cleaned up its act and now lays claim to over a dozen blue-flag beaches.

SIGHTS

Most major sights are found within walking distance of Porto's centre, although a full day's walking up and down the hill to the Ribeira may leave a few legs aching.

Torre & Igreja dos Clérigos

Get your bearings and bird's-eye photographs of the city atop the vertigo-inducing **Torre dos Clérigos** (Map pp352-3; Rua dos Clérigos; admission €1; 🕑 10am-1pm & 2-8pm Aug, 9.30am-1pm & 2-7pm Apr-Jul & Sep-Oct, 10am-noon & 2-5pm Nov-Mar), a 76m-high baroque tower that reverberates whenever the adjoining church's bells toll. The Italian architect Nicolau Nasoni designed the 225-step tower and the unusual oval-shaped Igreja dos Clérigos in the mid-18th century.

Sé

This hulking fortress of a **cathedral** (Map p356; ☎ 222 059 028; admission cloister €2; cathedral 🕑 8.45am-12.30pm & 2.30-7pm, cloister 9am-12.15pm & 2.30-6pm Mon-Sat, 2.30-6pm Sun, both close 1hr earlier Nov-Mar) dominates central Porto from its highest hill. It was founded in the 12th century but rebuilt a century later and extensively altered in the 18th century.

Only a Romanesque rose window and the 14th-century Gothic cloister remain from earlier incarnations. Much of the rest, inside and out, bears the baroque stamp of Nicolau Nasoni. Best of all is the upper storey of the cloister (reached via a Nasoni-designed stairway), decorated with 18th-century *azulejos* (hand-painted tiles), affording fine views.

Other Churches

Gothic **Igreja de São Francisco** (Map p356; ☎ 222 062 100; Rua Infante Dom Henrique; adult/student €3/2.50; 🕑 9am-6pm) houses the most dazzling display of baroque and over-the-top rococo gilt decoration you'll see in Portugal. Indeed barely an inch escapes unsmothered, as unworldly cherubs and sober monks alike are drowned by nearly 100kg of gold leaf dripping down the altars, pillars and from the ceiling. The sheer weight of it all can leave the visitor feeling positively claustrophobic.

Such earthly extravagance may only have driven thoughts of heaven away, for the church no longer holds services and is packed instead with tour groups.

A museum in its catacombs contains furnishings from a Franciscan monastery that once stood here, and a creepy pit full of 19th-century human bones.

The **Igreja de Santa Clara** (Map pp352-3; ☎ 222 054 837; Largo 1 de Dezembro; 🕑 9.30am-11.30am & 3-6pm Mon-Fri), east of the cathedral, was part of another Franciscan convent. Gothic in shape, with a fine Renaissance portal, its interior is also dense with carved, gilded woodwork.

Behind the rococo façade of the **Igreja da Misericórdia** (Map pp352-3; ☎ 222 074 710; Rua das Flores 15; adult/student €1.50/free; 🕑 9.30am-12.30pm & 2-5.30pm Tue-Fri, 9am-noon Sat & Sun) – now a museum – is the superb, anonymous Renaissance painting known as *Fons Vitae* (Fountain of Life), showing Dom Manuel I and his family around a fountain of blood from the crucified Christ.

Less of a must-see, the 17th-century **Igreja de São Lourenço** (Map p356; Igreja dos Grilos; ☎ 222 008 056; Largo Dr Pedro Vitorino, Ribeira; 🕑 10am-noon & 2-5pm Tue-Sat), west of the cathedral, is still of interest for its baroque façade and its prominence in any view of Porto from across the river.

Palácio da Bolsa

The pompous **Bolsa** (Stock Exchange; Map p356; ☎ 223 399 000; Rua Ferreira Borges, Ribeira; 🕑 9am-6.30pm Apr-Oct, 9am-1pm & 2-5.30pm Nov-Mar) is a splendid neoclassical monument – built from 1842 to 1910 – to Porto's past-and-present money merchants.

Just past the entrance hall is the glass-domed **Pátio das Nações** (Hall of Nations), wallpapered with international coats of arms, where the exchange once operated. But this pales beside other rooms deeper inside, and to visit these you must join one of the €5 guided tours that set off every 20 to 30 minutes, and last for 20 minutes.

You can usually join any group; tours are given in any two of Portuguese, English and French.

The highlight is a stupendous ballroom called the **Salão Árabe** (Arabian Hall), where every inch is smothered with Islamic designs and gilded stucco (18kg of gold was used): many of the Arabic inscriptions glorify Dona Maria II, who commissioned the building.

Ribeira

Don't miss the alluring riverside **Ribeira** district – a window onto the past with shadowed lanes, grimy cobbled passages, tall sugary coloured houses and *barcos rabelos* (the traditional boats used to ferry port wine) photogenically posed at the quayside for advertising or tourist jaunts. Here also are the clearest views of the sea of port warehouses across the river and the glowering Ponte de Dom Luís I. Despite the flocks of tourists it remains easy-going and surprisingly ungentrified. This is also the traditional centre of the city's nightlife.

Henry the Navigator is said to have been born (in 1394) in the handsomely renovated **Casa do Infante** (Map p356; ☎ 222 060 400; Rua Alfândega 10, Ribeira; admission free; 🕑 10am-noon & 2-5pm Tue-Sat, 2-5pm Sun), which later served as Porto's first customs house and now houses its historical archives.

Museums

Unless otherwise noted, children from four to 12 years old, students and seniors get 40% to 50% off the admission price, and children up to age four get in free.

MUSEU DE ARTE CONTEMPORÂNEA

One of the top galleries in the country, Porto's striking **Museu de Arte Contemporânea** (Fundação de Serralves; Museum of Contemporary Art; ☎ 226 156 500; www.serralves.pt; Rua Dom João de Castro 210; admission museum & park €5, 10am-2pm Sun free; 🕑 10am-7pm Tue, Wed & Fri-Sun, 10am-10pm Thu Oct-Mar; 10am-7pm Tue-Thu, 10am-10pm Fri & Sat, 10am-8pm Sun Apr-Sep) has had great success stimulating public interest in contemporary art and the environment.

The collection is packed with vitality, featuring works from the late 1960s to the present. But the building itself is of just as much interest as its contents: it's an arrestingly minimalist construction designed by the eminent Porto-based architect Álvaro Siza Vieira, full of vast whitewashed spaces and natural light. Nearby is Casa de Serralves, a pink 1930s Art Deco mansion that served as the original museum and is now an exhibition space.

Surrounding it all is the foundation's 18-hectare estate, **Parque de Serralves** (adult/child under 12/youth 14-25/senior €2.50/free/1.25/1.25; 🕑 10am-7pm Tue-Sun Oct- Mar; 10am-7pm Tue-Fri, 10am-8pm Sat & Sun Apr-Sep) filled with intriguing sculptures and other surprises. These handsome modernist gardens – now a national landmark – are worth a visit in their own right. A free museum leaflet *Passeios no Parque* maps out several walking routes around the park.

The estate and museum are 4km west of the city centre; take bus No 78 from Praça da Liberdade.

MUSEU NACIONAL SOARES DOS REIS

Porto's other must-see **art museum** (Map p350; ☎ 223 393 770; Rua Dom Manuel II 44; admission €3; 🕑 2-6pm Tue, 10am-6pm Wed-Sun) occupies the formidable neoclassical Palácio das Carrancas. During the Peninsular War (1808–14) Marshal Soult, the French commander, made his headquarters here but was evicted so suddenly by the future Duke of Wellington that he left an unfinished banquet behind.

Transformed into a museum of fine and decorative arts in 1940, its best works are from the 19th century, including sculpture by António Soares dos Reis (see especially his famous *O Desterrado,* The Exile) and António Teixeira Lopes, and the naturalistic paintings of Henrique Pousão and António Silva Porto.

CENTRO PORTUGUÊS DE FOTOGRAFIA

The muscular former prison (1796), looming grumpily over Cordoaria, is now home to the **Centro Português de Fotografia** (Portuguese Photography Centre; Map pp352-3; ☎ 226 076 310; Campo Mártires da Pátria; admission free; exhibition hall 🕑 3-6pm Tue-Fri, 3-7pm Sat & Sun). Multiple exhibitions offer a portrait of Porto and Portugal in the age of photography, but they don't even begin to occupy this massive space, with its massive walls and iron-grilled gates.

The thief José do Telhado (a legendary Robin Hood figure), the conservative party leader Pita Bezerra and the journalist João Chagas all did time here. Indeed this is

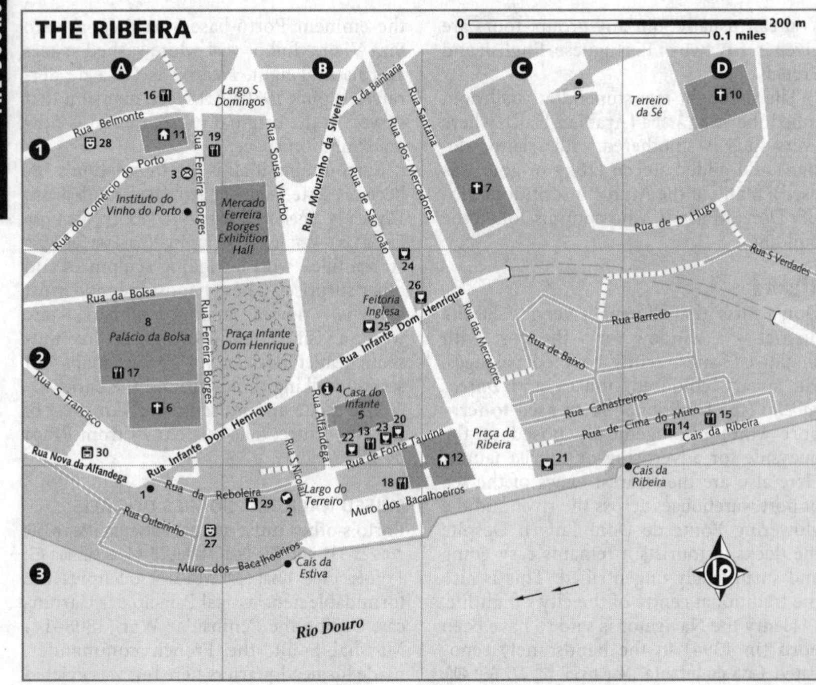

INFORMATION
- Lavandaria São Nicolau....1 A3
- Netherlands Consulate....2 B3
- Post Office....3 A1
- Turismo....4 B2

SIGHTS & ACTIVITIES (p355)
- Casa do Infante....5 B2
- CRAT....(see 29)
- Igreja de São Francisco....6 A2
- Igreja de São Lourenço....7 C1
- Palácio da Bolsa....8 A2
- Porto Tours....9 C1
- Sé....10 D1

SLEEPING (pp358–60)
- Hotel da Bolsa....11 A1
- Pestana Porto Hotel....12 C2

EATING (pp360–2)
- Casa Cardoso....13 B2
- Casa Filha da Mãe Preta....14 D2
- Don Tonho....15 D2
- Mariazinha....16 A1
- O Comercial....17 A2
- Pub-Petisqueira O Muro....18 B3
- Tempo de Leitura no Porto....19 A1

DRINKING (p362)
- Anikibóbó....20 B2
- Buraquinho....21 C2
- Está-se Bem....22 B2
- Porto Feio....23 B2
- Ribeirinha....24 B2
- Ryan's Irish Pub....25 B2
- Vinologia....26 B2

ENTERTAINMENT (p362)
- Restaurante Mal Cozinhado....27 A3
- Teatro de Belmonte....28 A1

SHOPPING (pp364–5)
- Arte Facto....29 B3

TRANSPORT (pp365–8)
- Tram 1E Terminus....30 A2

more of an architectural monument than a gallery, and it's free. Don't miss it.

The gloomy, rundown lanes south of Cordoaria were once part of Porto's *judiaria* (Jewish quarter).

MUSEU DO VINHO DO PORTO

Wine-lovers will find delight in this long-overdue **Museu do Vinho do Porto** (Port Wine Museum; Map p350; ☎ 222 076 300; Rua do Monchique 45-52; adult/student/senior Tue-Sat €1/free/free, Sat & Sun free; 🕑 noon-5pm Tue-Sun), which finally opened its doors in 2004 to showcase the history of Porto's most famous tipple.

It's an inclusive, professional museum with multilingual touch-screen computer displays, computers linked to port-wine websites, and it even has some exhibits in brail.

MUSEU DO CARRO ELÉCTRICO

The cavernous **Museu do Carro Eléctrico** (Tram Museum; Map p350; ☎ 226 158 185; http://museu-carro-electrico.stcp.pt; Alameda Basílio Teles 51; admission incl free Andante transport for 4 hr €3.50, see Getting Around, p367; 🕑 10am-noon & 2.30-5pm Mon, 9.30am-12.30pm & 2.30-6pm Tue-Fri, 3-7pm Sat & Sun) is in a former switching-house with dozens of beautifully restored old trams.

See p368 for information on Porto's surviving tram lines.

MUSEU ROMÂNTICO

The abdicated and exiled king of Sardinia, Carlos Alberto, spent his final days holed up the stately Quinta da Macieirinha in 1843. The peaceful building, beside the Jardim do Palácio de Cristal (see following), is now a 'Romantic Museum'. The **Museu Romântico** (Map p350; ☎ 226 057 033; Rua Entre Quintas 220; admission Tue-Fri €1, Sat & Sun free; 🕑 10am-12.30pm & 2-5.30pm Tue-Sat, 2-5.30pm Sun) features the king's belongings and dainty period furnishings.

Jardim do Palácio de Cristal

This leafy **park** (Map p350; main entrance Rua Dom Manuel II; 🕑 8am-9pm Apr-Sep, 8am-7pm Oct-Mar), named after a long-gone 19th-century crystal palace, is home to a striking sports pavilion, gardens and a pond, roving peacocks and a laid-lack self-service restaurant. It also boasts some terrific views down to the river. But pride of place goes to the new, high-tech Biblioteca Municipal Almeida Garrett (p351) and the adjacent **Palácio Gallery** (🕑 10am-6pm Mon-Fri).

Azulejos

Porto sports some truly stunning tilework. The largest and most exquisite is Silvestre Silvestri's panel illustrating the legend of the founding of the Carmelite order, smothering an outer wall of the **Igreja do Carmo** (Map pp352-3; ☎ 222 078 400; Praça Gomes Teixeira).

In the entrance hall of **São Bento train station** several dramatic works by Jorge Colaço (1930) depict scenes ranging from daily life to historic battles.

Another church covered from top to toe in blue tiles – in traditional style but dating from the early 20th century and undertaken by Eduardo Leite – is the **Capela das Almas** (Map pp352-3; Rua Santa Catarina). Five 18th-century panels by Vital Rifarto decorate the Gothic cloisters of the **cathedral**.

Bringing azulejos up to the modern day, **Ribeira Negra** (Map pp352–3) by Júlio Resende (1987) is a freshly designed multicoloured mural celebrating life in the old Ribeira district. It's beside the tunnel to the lower deck of the Ponte de Dom Luís I.

Pontes

Porto's most distinctive landmarks are its immense **pontes** (bridges) spanning the Rio Douro. Pride of place goes to the immense two-level Ponte de Dom Luís I to Vila Nova de Gaia, which stands above the heart of the Ribeira. A walk to Vila Nova de Gaia across either deck is a Porto highlight, offering stupendous views. However, note that the lofty upper deck has been claimed by the new metro line, so may not be walked at least until work on the line has been completed.

Other bridges are the modern Ponte da Arrábida linking Porto to the A1/IC1 Lisbon highway; the new Ponte do Infante Dom Henrique; two railway bridges, the Ponte de Dona Maria Pia (designed by Gustav Eiffel in 1876) and adjacent Ponte de São João; and the uninspiring Ponte do Freixo, linking to the A3/E1.

COURSES

CRAT (Centro Regional de Artes Tradicionais; Map p356; ☎ 223 320 201; crat@mail.telepac.pt; Rua da Reboleira 37, Porto) runs brief introductory workshops on azulejo (glazed tile) painting and stamping, aimed at tourists. Courses are available from 15 July to 15 September for three hours on Tuesday and Thursday afternoons. One lesson costs €25, and you can pick up your four freshly fired tiles two days later.

PORTO FOR CHILDREN

The best spots to let kids burn off some steam are Porto's numerous parks – in particular the Parque de Serralves (p380) has all kinds of surprises lurking in the bushes, including bizarre sculptures and mysterious recorded sounds.

If you're in town during early December, check out the Festival de Marionetas (international puppet festival), with frequent shows at the Teatro de Belmonte (p364).

TOURS

Porto Tours (Map p356; ☎ 222 000 073; www.portotours.com; Torre Medieval, Calçada Pedro Pitões 15; 🕑 9am-7pm) This is a welcome new service introduced by local government and the tourist authority, and situated next to the cathedral. It has details of all the recommended tour operators – be they for city walking tours, Douro cruises, private taxi tours or helicopter rides over the city. As well as dispensing impartial advice, it can also make the bookings for you – saving you from traipsing from agency to agency.

Diana Tours (Porto Visão; ☎ 223 771 230; www.dianatours.pt) This outfit runs a daily hop-on-hop-off city tour (€13, half-price for children aged seven to 12) that includes visit to a port-wine lodge. You can start at any of the chosen sights (eg Aliados), linger at others and then just catch the next of its buses, which run hourly except at lunch time. You can buy tickets on the bus, at travel agencies or upmarket hotels. It also has a mini train running a more limited route for €6. A range of other thematic tours is also on offer.

River Cruises

Several outfits offer cruises in ersatz *barcos rabelos,* the colourful boats once used to transport port wine from the vineyards. Cruises last 45 to 55 minutes and depart at least hourly on summer days. Board at Porto's Cais da Ribeira or Cais da Estiva, or Vila Nova de Gaia's Cais de Gaia or Cais Amarelo. Shop around – tickets cost €7.50 to €10 and kids usually go for half-price or free. The price sometimes includes a visit to a port warehouse though this is easily arranged on your own.

You can even organise dinner cruises. These outfits also have longer Douro trips; see Peso da Régua, p380.

FESTIVALS & EVENTS

There's a stream of cultural events throughout the year; check at the main tourism website (www.portoturismo.pt/en/events) for more details. There are many long-standing ones worth catching:

February/March Fantasporto (international fantasy film festival)
March/April Festival Intercéltico do Porto (festival of Celtic music)
Early May Queima das Fitas (student week)
Late May Festival Internacional de Teatro para a Infância e Juventude (international children's theatre festival)
June Festa de São João (St John's festival)
June/July Ritmos (rhythms; festival of ethnic music)
Late July Festival Internacional de Folclore (international folk festival)
Late August Noites Ritual Rock (festival of Portuguese rock)
Mid-September Desfile de Carros Eléctricos (tram parade)
October/November Grande Noite do Fado (gala evening of *fado*)
September–November Festival de Jazz do Porto (jazz festival)
Early December Festival de Marionetas (international puppet festival)

GET HAMMERED!

Porto's biggest bash is the Festa de São João (St John's Festival, also called the Festa da Cidade) on the night of 23 June, when the city erupts into all manner of merrymaking: music, competitions and riotous parties just for starters. However, one of the more bizarre customs is to pound anyone and everyone over the head with squeaky plastic mallets.

In the Ribeira, especially, you can expect the streets to ring with high-pitched squeaks and squeals all night. Everybody's fair game – so expect no mercy. Given that São João is the patron saint of lovers, it's hard to imagine what prompted such a craze – but really, who cares? Grab a hammer and join in!

SLEEPING

Unless otherwise noted, rooms in establishments listed here have a private toilet and bath or shower.

Budget

Pousada da juventude (☎ 226 177 257; porto@movijovem.pt; Rua Paulo da Gama 551; dm/d €15/42; 24hr;) Porto's top-notch youth hostel is 4km west of the centre. It has sea views, a games room, and self-caterers will be happy with a supermarket across the road. Internet costs €2.50 per hour. Take bus No 35 from Praça da Liberdade. Reservations are essential.

Pensão Astória (Map pp352-3; ☎ 222 008 175; Rua Arnaldo Gama 56; s/d with breakfast & shared bathroom from €18.50/30) A hidden gem with friendly service at the edge of the Unesco zone. Some of the character-packed old rooms (no TV) have great river and bridge views. Book well in advance.

Pensão Duas Nações (Map pp352-3; ☎ 222 081 616; www.duasnacoes.com.pt; Praça Gomes Fernandes 59; s/d without bath €12.50/20.50, with bath €16/27.50;) Cheap? You'd better believe it. This youthful spot has friendly multilingual staff and double glazing to shut out the city din. Rooms are basic but cosy.

Pensão Porto Rico (Map pp352-3; ☎ 223 394 690; fax 223 394 699; Rua do Almada 237; s/d with breakfast €22.50/30) There's little space to manoeuvre in this budget-friendly place near Aliados, but it's a characterful old place with fussy décor and an affable owner.

Pensão Mondariz (Map pp352-3; ☎ 222 005 600; Rua do Cimo de Vila 139; s without bathroom €10, d with/without toilet & shower €30/20) Tatty backstreet place with traces of Art Nouveau and a few higher rooms with rooftop views.

Residencial Porto Chique (Map pp352-3; ☎ 222 080 069; Rua Conde de Vizela 26; s without bathroom €12.50, d with/without bathroom €20/15) Pokey but liveable rooms, in a good central location.

Parque de Campismo da Prelada (☎ 228 312 616; Rua Monte dos Burgos; adult/tent/ car €3.10/2.60-4.90/2.60; year-round) Porto's shady and efficient year-round municipal facility, 4km northwest of the city centre. To get here take bus No 6 from Praça da Liberdade or bus No 50 from Jardim da Cordoaria.

Three seaside places across the river, all open year-round, are linked by a road from the Ponte da Arrábida. Bus No 57 runs to all three from Praça Almeida Garrett. Note that the beaches at these places have undergone a massive clean-up and are happily all of blue-flag standard now. So get your cozzies on.

Campismo Marisol (☎ 227 135 942; fax 227 126 351; Rua Alto das Chaquedas 82, Praia de Canide; adult/tent/car €1.50/3/2.25; year-round) This flat grassy camp site is close to the sea.

Campismo Madalena (☎ 227 122 520; info@orbitur.pt; Rua do Cerro, Praia da Madalena; adult/tent/car €4.30/3.50-4/3.80; year-round) Closer still to the sea shore is Orbitur's well-shaded and sandy camp site. It's a good deal.

Campismo Salgueiros (☎ 227 810 500; canidelo@j-f.org; Rua do Campismo, Praia de Salgueiros; adult/tent/car €1.70/1.70-2.30/1) This one is more basic and it packs campers in like sardines.

Mid-Range

Breakfast, bathroom and TV are included at all places in this section.

RIBEIRA

Hotel da Bolsa (Map p356; ☎ 222 026 768; www.hoteldabolsa.com; Rua Ferreira Borges 101; s/d with satellite TV €66/80;) Large and faultlessly managed three-star hotel behind a handsome façade a few steps above the Instituto do Vinho do Porto. Includes a few rooms with river views for an additional €15.

ALIADOS

Residencial dos Aliados (Map pp352-3; ☎ 222 004 853; www.residencialaliados.com; Rua Elísio de Melo 27; d with/without air-con €70/60;) One of Aliados' trademark Art Nouveau buildings with a grand position a short walk from the turismo, this place is well-run, helpful and good value, though street-facing rooms are noisy. Prices dip dramatically when they're not busy.

Hotel Peninsular (Map pp352-3; ☎ 222 003 012; Rua Sá da Bandeira 21; s/d with breakfast from €22/34) Centrally located place that's a surprise bargain – all azulejos, polished wood, ancient lifts and faultless service. Bring your earplugs for the front-facing rooms.

Residencial Pão de Açucar (Map pp352-3; ☎ 222 002 425; www.residencialpaodeacucar.com; Rua do Almada 262; s/d with breakfast from €38/50) Richly Art Nouveau inside, with a dizzying spiral staircase. The handsome rooms have parquet floors and quality furniture: some (costing €75 and with air-con) open onto a top-floor terrace.

Other places with honest rates, full attached bathroom and charm:

Residencial Universal (Map pp352-3; ☎ 222 006 758; hoteluniversal@sapo.pt; Avenida dos Aliados 38; s/d €50/60;) Smart friendly place bang on central Aliados. Internet access €2 per hour.

Pensão Chique (Map pp352-3; ☎ 222 009 011; fax 223 322 963; Avenida dos Aliados 206; s/d with breakfast €35/40) Plain but comfortable guesthouse with residual 1970s style and cable TV.

Residencial Paulista (Map pp352-3; ☎ 222 054 692; residencial.paulista@iol.pt; Avenida dos Aliados 214; s/d €32/37.50) Another reasonable but nondescript guesthouse on Aliados.

AROUND CORDOARIA

Pensão São Marino (Map pp352-3; ☎ 223 325 499; residencial_s.marino@clix.pt; Praça Carlos Alberto 59; s/d €38/45) Feminine, flowery rooms in a quiet building: it's good value and on an attractive square.

Pensão-Residencial Estoril (Map pp352-3; ☎ 222 002 751; www.pensaoestoril.com; Rua de Cedofeita 193; s/d €25/30) Squeezed into busy pedestrian parade, this dated but cosy family-run place also has cheaper rooms with shared facilities.

PRAÇA DA BATALHA

Pensão Aviz (Map pp352-3; ☎ 223 320 722; aviz@netc.pt; Avenida Rodrigues de Freitas 451; s/d with breakfast €33/43) Efficient, group-friendly old hotel in an otherwise droopy area. Also boasts a bar and tidy, carpeted rooms. Good value.

NORTH OF ALIADOS

Hotel-Residencial América (Map p350; ☎ 223 392 930; www.hotel-america.net; Rua Santa Catarina 1018; s/d with

THE AUTHOR'S CHOICE

Castelo Santa Catarina (Map p350; ☎ 225 095 599; www.castelosantacatarina.com.pt; Rua Santa Catarina 1347; s/d with breakfast €43/63; P) And now for something completely different: Castelo Santa Catarina is a whimsical late-19th-century pseudo-Gothic castle, a fabulously over-the-top hideaway in a palm-shaded, azulejo-smothered garden, perfect for romantic trysts and complete with its own chapel. Pick between attractive but small doubles in the castle and lighter rooms in a modern annexe.

breakfast €45/55; P) Worth the walk from the centre, this terrific place has sparklingly clean, stylish rooms, a winter garden, cable TV, generous buffet breakfast and free off-street parking. Show your guidebook for the best prices. English spoken.

Top End

Buffet breakfast is part of the package at the following establishments.

Hotel Infante de Sagres (Map pp352-3; ☎ 223 398 500; www.hotelinfantesagres.pt; Praça Dona Filipa de Lencastre 62; s/d from €180/200;) An exquisite time warp of a place with liveried doorman, crystal chandeliers, stained glass, antique furnishings and marble baths. The plush rooms are largely modern, but with all the trimmings.

Pestana Porto Hotel (Map p356; ☎ 223 402 300; pestana.porto@pestana.com; Praça da Ribeira 1; s/d with satellite TV from €118/133, with river view €140/155, ste €240;) Take a clutch of colourfully haphazard old buildings on the choicest spot of the Ribeira waterfront, lovingly renovate them into a single pristine hotel where no two of the stylish rooms are alike and many have unbeatable river views, and you get the Pestana Porto Hotel. Highly recommended.

Grande Hotel do Porto (Map pp352-3; ☎ 222 076 690; www.grandehotelporto.com; Rua Santa Catarina 197; s/d with cable TV €105/115; P) Built back in 1880, this proud old institution preserves a good deal of its grandeur though its comfortable modern rooms are less distinguished. It's well located on a busy pedestrian street.

EATING

Don't let the fact that *tripas* (tripe) is the local speciality put you off. With seafood a plenty, port wine by the barrel-load and enough cod-fish recipes for every day of the year, Porto has much to offer. Not surprisingly in a city famous for tripe, vegetarians are not always well catered for. However, there are several discreet little venues tucked away in unexpected places.

Budget

Café Embaixador (Map pp352-3; ☎ 222 054 329; Rua Sampaio Bruno 5; mains €4.50-8; all day Sun-Fri) Nothing in the Aliados neighbourhood approaches Embaixador for value, with table service downstairs and cheaper self-service on the mezzanine.

Suribachi (Map p350; ☎ 225 106 700; Rua do Bonfim 134-140; dishes €2-6; shop 9am-10pm, restaurant lunch & dinner Mon-Sat) A squeaky clean vegetarian restaurant, cheerful and contemplative, offering relief from meat and urban stress. Astonishingly cheap.

Restaurante O Oriente no Porto (Map pp352-3; ☎ 222 007 223; Rua São Miguel 19; lunch plate €4.50; lunch Mon-Sat) This vegetarian restaurant serves a peaceful macrobiotic set lunch in a centre for alternative therapies in the forlorn neighbourhood south of Cordoaria.

Confeitaria do Bolhão (Map pp352-3; ☎ 222 009 291; Rua Formosa 339; mains €3.50-9; 8am-9pm Mon-Sat) A *belle époque* café, built in 1896, and popular for its irresistible array of local sweets, including the spongy cake *pão de ló*.

Casa Cardoso (Map p356; ☎ 222 058 644; Rua de Fonte Taurina 58; half-portions €4.75-6; lunch & dinner Mon-Sat) An unflashy place popular with locals, with plenty of filling half-portions from which to pick and choose.

Pedro dos Frangos (Map pp352-3; Rua do Bonjardim 219; whole chicken €7.50; all day Wed-Mon) A hole-in-the-wall place just off Aliados that draws the crowds for good *frango no espeto* (spit-

A LOAD OF TRIPE

It's not what most of us look for on the menu, but many Porto folk can think of nothing finer than a rich stew of tripe (cow's stomach). This affection, so the story goes, dates back to 1415 when Henry the Navigator was preparing to sail for Ceuta in Morocco. Porto's loyal citizens donated their best meat, keeping the offal for themselves and earning the nickname *tripeiros* (tripe-eaters).

roasted chicken) and other cheap grills; a whole chicken is enough for two.

Café Ancôra Douro (Map pp352-3; Praça de Parada Leitão 55; ⌚ Mon-Sat) A downmarket counterpoint to Porto's posher cafés, near Cordoaria. It's a cavernous, casual place where students nurse coffees for hours and munch on crepes and light meals.

If you like *pão de ló* you can stock up at a charming little back-street bakery and confectioner's called **Pão de Ló Margaridense** (Map pp352-3; ☎ 222 001 178; Travessa de Cedofeita 20B; ⌚ 10.30am-1pm & 2-7pm Mon-Fri, 10am-1pm Sat), with its shelves lined with conserves, crockery and dusty scales.

Porto's municipal market, the **Mercado do Bolhão** (Map pp352-3; ⌚ 8am-5pm Mon-Fri, 8am-1pm Sat), brings you cheese, olives, fresh bread, strawberries and more. It's at its liveliest in the morning. Two old-school delicatessens across from the market – a branch of the **Confeitaria do Bolhão** (Map pp352-3; Rua Formosa 305) and the Art Deco **A Pérola do Bolhão** (Map pp352-3; Rua Formosa 279; ⌚ 9.30am-1pm & 3-7.30pm) – are stacked high with sausages strung like candies, nuts, dried fruit and other quality groceries.

Central supermercados include **Minipreço** (Map pp352-3; Rua Conceição; ⌚ 9am-8pm Mon-Sat), **Pingo Doce** (Map pp352-3; Rua Passos Manuel 213; ⌚ 8.30am-9pm Mon-Sat, 9am-8.30pm Sun) and **Modelo** (Map pp352-3; Centro Comercial Via Catarina, Rua Santa Catarina; ⌚ 10am-10pm).

Mid-Range

O Comercial (Map p356; ☎ 223 322 019; Palácio da Bolsa, Rua Ferreira Borges; mains €8-14; ⌚ lunch & dinner Mon-Fri, dinner only Sat) A well-hidden secret in the back of the stock-exchange building, this elegant old-world restaurant is a calming escape from the usual tourist haunts and serves excellent contemporary Portuguese cuisine.

Mariazinha (Map p356; ☎ 222 200 937; Rua Belmonte 2; mains €9-16; ⌚ Thu-Tue) A snug little eatery that wins accolades all round for jolly atmosphere, enthusiastic service and a surprise menu of gourmet food with market-fresh ingredients. While dishes are reasonably priced, the host will encourage you to try half a dozen (plus as many wines) before the night is out: hence a full meal for two could easily set you back €100.

Casa Filha da Mãe Preta (Map p356; ☎ 222 055 515; Cais da Ribeira 40; half-portions €6-9; ⌚ lunch & dinner Mon-Sat) Set beneath the old quay-front arches of the Ribeira, this is the most congenial of a long line of touristy riverside restaurants. Go early to bag an upstairs front table for views of the Douro. Don't confuse it with the old taverna of the same name, one street back.

Pub-Petisqueira O Muro (Map p356; ☎ 222 083 426; Muro dos Bacalhoeiros 88; dishes €6-13; ⌚ noon-late Tue-Sun) Escape the crowds at this rough-and-ready place on the upper riverfront walkway. It's recommended as much for its cheerful atmosphere and quirky anything-goes décor as for the well-prepared local dishes.

Restaurante A Tasquinha (Map pp352-3; ☎ 223 322 145; Rua do Carmo 23; mains €6-10; ⌚ lunch & dinner) Near Cordoaria, A Tasquinha is an attractive spot with well-prepared regional dishes and almost as many desserts as wines.

Adega do Carregal (Taberna do Carregal; Map pp352-3; ☎ 222 081 200; Travessa do Carregal; dishes €11-16; ⌚ lunch & dinner Mon-Sat) Unobtrusively tucked off a pedestrian mall close to Cordoaria, this wine-bar offers cask wines, garlicky appetisers and delicious northern specialities.

Restaurante O Verde Vegetariano (Map p350; ☎ 226 063 886; Loja 26, Basement, Edifício Crystal Park, Rua Dom Manuel II; per kilo €10; ⌚ lunch & dinner Sun-Thu, lunch Fri) This uncluttered little self-service restaurant has a varied selection of vegetarian dishes and an elegant minimalist dining area.

Café Majestic (Map pp352-3; ☎ 222 003 887; Rua Santa Catarina 112; breakfast €15, afternoon tea €9.75; ⌚ all day Mon-Sat) Porto's best-known teashop is packed with prancing cherubs, opulently gilded woodwork, leather seats and gold-braided waiters who'll serve you an elegant set breakfast, afternoon tea or any number of snacks and beverages.

THE AUTHOR'S CHOICE

Don Tonho (Map p356; ☎ 222 004 307; Cais da Ribeira 13-15; mains €10-20; ⌚ lunch & dinner) Buried under the old riverside wall below the looming Ponte Dom Luís I is this elegant upper-crust restaurant first set up by the crown prince of Portugal's pop scene, singer Rui Velosa. The traditional Portuguese selection includes superb *bacalhau* (salt cod), and the wine list is one of the best in Porto – and that's saying something!

Tempo de Leitura no Porto (Map p356; ☎ 222 010 201; Rua Ferreira Borges 86; 9-2am) In contrast, this low-lit minimalist café-cum-bar is a favourite with an artsy young crowd: there are bookcases of reading material and student magazines to browse as you drain your drink. There are sometimes fado, theatre and dance events here too.

DRINKING & ENTERTAINMENT

When it comes to having a good time, forget Porto's work-a-day image. *Portoenses* know a thing or two about partying. It's also an increasingly cultural city, with a fast-moving theatre and music scene. To keep pace, pick up the *Agenda do Porto*, a monthly cultural events brochure, at city turismos or look for listings in the *Jornal de Notícias* newspaper.

Bars & Nightclubs

Porto's clubs usually don't charge admission, but do ask you to stump up a minimum amount buying drinks: usually between €3.50 and €5 for a bar or €5 to €10 for a club.

RIBEIRA

Here's where you'll find Porto's good ol' boys bar scene. Unless indicated, all these can be found on the Ribeira map p356.

Buraquinho (Cais da Ribeira 50; admission free; 11-4am) With a privileged spot by the river, this congenial café-bar is always buzzing with a lively crowd that spills out onto the waterfront come rain or shine.

Anikibóbó (☎ 223 324 619; Rua Fonte Taurina 38; 10pm-4am Tue-Sat) This funky little place offers vanguard DJ music, an artsy crowd, exhibitions and theatre.

Está-se Bem (☎ 222 004 249; Rua Fonte Taurina 70-72; admission free; 11am-3.30pm & 9pm-4am Mon-Sat) More low-key is this little back-street bar with a smoky conspiratorial atmosphere, cheap drinks and an artsy clientele.

> **THE AUTHOR'S CHOICE**
>
> The finest place in Porto to drink port wine is the **Solar do Vinho do Porto** (Map p350; ☎ 226 097 749; Rua Entre Quintas 220; 2pm-midnight Mon-Sat, closed holidays), a posh bar with a river view terrace beside the Jardim do Palácio de Cristal. Waiters will help you choose from hundreds of varieties, from around €0.80 per glass.

Vinologia (☎ 936 057 340; www.vinologia.com in Portuguese; Rua de S. João 46; admission free; 2pm-midnight) Don't feel like dressing up for posh pub Solar do Vinho do Porto to take your pick of port wines? Then head to this more commercial alternative, which also has over 200 varieties to try.

Porto Feio (☎ 222 054 485; Rua Fonte Taurina 52-54; admission free; bar 10pm-2am Thu-Sat) A flashy bar-cum-art gallery with background music.

Ryan's Irish Pub (☎ 222 005 366; Rua Infante Dom Henrique 18; 6pm-2am) Generous drams of whisky with its good ol' Irish tunes. Follow the Guinness signs.

Ribeirinha (☎ 223 322 572; Rua de São João 70-72; 10pm-2am) This intimate little joint is the Ribeira's oldest bar and undoubtedly one of its friendliest. The light-hearted choice of music dabbles with everything from jazz and funk to pop.

Púcaros Bar (Map pp352-3; ☎ 222 087 051; Rua de Miragaia 55; Mon-Sat 10pm-2am) Low granite arches, lines of low woody tables and soft lighting distinguish this attractive cultural bar. It hosts various exhibitions, and poetry nights on Wednesdays.

MASSARELOS & RUA DO OURO

Massarelos, the riverside strip near the Jardim do Palácio de Cristal, and its westward extension, Rua do Ouro, is Porto's newest and most unusual nightlife zone. Take bus No 1 from Praça Almeida Garrett; the last bus back passes by at about 1.30am.

Clube Mau-Mau (Map p350; ☎ 226 076 660; Rua do Outeiro 4; bus stop Massarelos; club 11pm-4am Wed-Sat, restaurant 8.30pm-2am Tue-Sat) Long cherished as one of Porto's hottest clubs, Mau-Mau has held onto its trendy crowd and still attracts the hippest guest DJs. Also scores for its late-night grub.

Porto Rio (☎ 934 509 684; Rua do Ouro; 9.30pm-4am Fri & Sat) A clutch of floating bars can be found on the River Douro just west of Ponte da Arrábida, but this thumping boat-cum-club is the only bona-fide ship – sweat, oil, portholes and all.

Maré Alta (☎ 226 091 010; Rua do Ouro; bus stop Gás; 10pm-2am Wed & Thu, 10pm-4am Fri & Sat, 8pm-4am Sun) Located on a flat-bottomed barge with a dance floor, clusters of designer bean-bags and riverside tables to cool down on – this slick restaurant-cum-bar offers all kinds of up-to-date music.

VILA NOVA DE GAIA

The waterfront opposite the Ribeira has seen a mushrooming of ultra-trendy chrome-and-glass bars and nightclubs surrounded by open-air decks and designer fountains that see more than their fair share of late-night dippers cooling off from the dance floor.

Amo te Porto (Map p350; ☎ 223 701 637; www.amote.clix.pt; Avenida Ramos Pinto 220, Cais de Gaia; 10am-3am) One of the first in line, this hip DJ bar (called 'I love you Porto') looks as though it was designed by Barbie on speed. Expect a dazzling pink-and-white décor with a light-box floor, psychedelic cocktails and sugary hearts on every wall.

Hard Club (Map p350; ☎ 223 744 755; www.hard-club.com in Portuguese; Cais de Gaia 1158; 10pm-4am Wed, Fri & Sat) Set in an old tannery on the waterfront, this is one of Porto's most vanguard music haunts with the cream of visiting international and home-grown DJs. Check its website to see who's latest on the menu.

FOZ DO DOURO

There's also a brisk night scene out at the mouth of the Douro, near the beach; take bus No 1 from Praça Almeida Garrett.

Quando-Quando (☎ 226 102 797; Avenida do Brasil 60; bus stop Fonte Luz; 10.30pm-5am Tue-Sat) Funky beachfront bar at Praia dos Ingleses, with great pop, rock and vanguard music.

Indústria (☎ 226 176 806, Avenida do Brasil 843; bus stop Molhe; 11.30pm-4am Thu-Sat) An edgy beachside club with soul, funk and house, plus plenty of visiting bands and DJs. Good reputation with the in crowd.

Pop (☎ 226 183 959; www.pop-kitchen.com in Portuguese; Rua Padre Luís Cabral 1090; bus stop Castelo Foz; midnight-4am Thu-Sat) This exclusive club offers vanguard music in a slickly designed nook for the beautiful people.

BOAVISTA TO RAMALDE

Serious clubbers can follow the streaking light beams out to Ramalde, an industrial area 2km to 3km northwest of Boavista, which hosts Porto's glitzier warehouse clubs. Clubs noted here open from midnight to 6am and generally require €7.50 minimum consumption.

Swing (Map p350; ☎ 226 090 019; Praceta Engenheiro Amáro da Costa 766; midnight-4am) Closest to town is Porto's oldest and most likeably kitsch disco, which plays a mixed bag of crowd-pleasing '80s, commercial hits and house. Catch bus No 3 or 52 from Praça da Liberdade to the Bom Sucesso stop.

Chic (☎ 226 163 220; Rua Manuel Pinto de Azevedo 2; Fri & Sat) All shining metal, dazzling colours and swirling search lights without, Chic plays upbeat commercial, house and techno within. Take bus No 52 from Praça da Liberdade to the Manuel P Azevedo stop. Ramalde on metro Linha A is also nearby.

Sound Planet (☎ 226 107 232; Avenida Fontes Pereira de Melo 449; midnight-5am Thu-Sat) Head to this commercial chrome-smothered venue for mostly house music from resident DJs. Take bus No 76 from Praça da Liberdade or Cordoaria to the Fontes P Melo stop, or catch the metro to Viso.

Act (☎ 226 169 507; Rua Manuel Pinto de Azevedo 15; 11.30pm-5am Wed, Fri & Sat) This swish club hides down a driveway opposite Chic. Its vast warehouse-like interior rocks to the tune of funk, pop and house music, and features good guest DJs. Take bus No 41

GAY & LESBIAN NIGHTCLUBS

The Porto gay and lesbian scene may not match that of cosmopolitan Lisbon, but the city is increasingly studded with melting pots. Another plus for Porto is its annual summer Gay Pride march, which has been enthusiastically embraced since 2001. See p460 for more information. Clubs welcoming gay men and gay women include the following:

Boys 'R' Us (Map pp352-3; ☎ 917 549 988; Rua Dr Barbosa de Castro 63; 11pm-2am Wed & Sun, 11pm-4am Fri & Sat) This hugely popular club mixes in pumping garage sounds, raucous drag shows and a healthy dose of anything-goes mayhem.

Moinho de Vento (Map pp352-3; ☎ 222 056 883; Rua Sá Noronha 78; 11pm-4am Wed-Sun), Pulls in a mostly local crowd.

Bar Him (Map p350; ☎ 222 084 383; Rua do Bonjardim 836; 11pm-6am) For deep trance and house, try this hardcore club.

Gemini's (Map pp352-3; ☎ 223 320 136; Rua Conde de Vizela 78/80; 10pm-2am Wed, 10pm-4am Fri-Sun) One of the newer additions.

Swing (left) Gay-friendly.

from Praça da Liberdade or Cordoaria to the Manuel P Azevedo stop.

Via Rápida (☎ 226 109 427; unit 5 Rua Manuel Pinto de Azevedo 567; ⏰ midnight-7am Fri & Sat) An enormous dance floor reverberating to the sounds of house keeps the youthful clientele happy here. Catch bus No 3 from Praça da Liberdade to Manuel P Azevedo stop.

Hiva-Oa (☎ 226 179 663; Avenida Boavista 2514; admission free; ⏰ 6pm-2am) Alternatively, any age group will feel at home in this laid-back, coffee-alcohol joint. It's a Polynesian bar complete with totem poles, flowery-shirted waiters and bead curtains. Take bus No 3 from Praça da Liberdade to the Pinheiro Manso stop.

Fado

Porto has no fado tradition of its own, but you can enjoy the Lisbon or Coimbra version of 'Portugal blues' into the wee hours at smoky atmospheric haunts, **Restaurante O Fado** (Map pp352-3; ☎ 222 026 937; www.ofado.com; Largo de São João Novo 16; ⏰ 8.30pm-3.30am Mon-Sat) and **Restaurante Mal Cozinhado** (Map p356; ☎ 222 081 319; Rua Outerinho 11, Ribeira; ⏰ 8.30pm-late, show begins at 9.30pm). The food isn't the main attraction – and in any case is grossly overpriced – but there's a minimum charge, equivalent to a light meal or several drinks.

Theatre & Concert Halls

The concert hall to keep an eye on is the €100 million **Casa da Música**, a huge project taking shape at the heart of the city on Boavista roundabout. It's an enormously ambitious design pushing the boundaries of architecture. Though dogged by years of dithering and delay, the 'concrete diamond' should hopefully open its doors in 2005.

Teatro Nacional de São João (Map pp352-3; ☎ 223 401 910; www.tnsj.pt in Portuguese; Praça da Batalha) This is Porto's prime performing-arts venue, though it has no drama company of its own.

Coliseu do Porto (Map pp352-3; ☎ 223 320 385; Rua Passos Manuel 137) This venue hosts larger-scale dance, rock and other performances.

Teatro de Belmonte (Map p356; ☎ 222 083 341; www.marionetasdoporto.pt in Portuguese; Rua Belmonte 57) The place to go for puppet shows.

Other venues for classical music and drama are the **Auditório Nacional Carlos Alberto** (Map pp352-3; ☎ 223 395 050; Rua das Oliveiras 43) and **Casa das Artes** (Map p350; ☎ 226 006 153; Rua de António Cardoso 175).

Cinema

Porto has a generous supply of cinemas, often featuring subtitled English-language films. There is a multiscreen **cinema** (Map p350; ☎ 226 009 164; Centro Comercial Cidade do Porto; Rua Gonçalo Sampaio 350, Boavista).

Sport

The **Estádio do Dragão**, a flashy, new 52,000-seat stadium, hosted the opening ceremonies and first game of the 2004 European Football Championships. The ground is now home to heroes of the moment – FC Porto – whose silverware cabinet has recently been graced by not only the 2003–04 season National SuperLiga trophy, but also the 2003–04 Europeans Champions League (p37) Estádio do Dragão is northeast of the centre just off the VCI ring road (Antas metro stop on Linha A or bus No 21 from Aliados).

Porto FC's worthy cross-town rivals are the under-funded Boavista FC, who surprised everyone by seizing the national championship back in 2002. The newly spruced up **Estádio do Bessa** is Boavista's home turf and also hosted several Euro2004 matches. The stadium is west of the centre just off Avenida da Boavista (take bus No 3 from Praça da Liberdade).

Check the local edition of *Público* or *Jornal de Notícias* for upcoming fixtures.

SHOPPING

Porto boasts a diverse shopping scene from quirky delicatessens to chic fashion and endless *sapatarias* (shoe shops), and there are entire streets specialising in particular items (try Rua Galeria de Paris for fine art or Rua da Fábrica for bookshops).

Modern *centros comerciales* (shopping centres) include **Cento Comercial Via Catarina** (Map pp352-3; Rua Santa Catarina), **Centro Comercial Cidade do Porto** (Map p350; Rua Gonçalo Sampaio) and **Centro Comercial Brasília** (Map p350; Boavista).

Port & Other Wines

Few people leave Porto unladen with a few bottles of its famous tipple. It's most satisfying to buy it direct from the warehouses in Vila Nova de Gaia, but it's by no means necessary to cross the river. You'll see stockists everywhere you go. For one, **Garrafeira do Carmo** (Map pp352-3; ☎ 222 003 285; Rua do Carmo 17; ⏰ 9am-1pm & 2-7pm Mon-Sat) specialises in vintage port and high-quality wines, at reasonable prices. Other good sources are **Casa Januário** (Map pp352-3; Rua do Bonjardim 352; 9am-6pm Mon-Sat) and the photogenic **Casa Oriental** (Map pp352-3; Campo dos Mártires da Pátria 111; 9am-7.30pm Mon-Sat).

Handicrafts

Arte Facto (Map p356; Rua da Reboleira 37, Ribeira; 10am-noon & 1-6pm Tue-Fri, 1-7pm Sat & Sun) Appealing handmade textiles, puppets, toys, glass and pottery can be found at this sales outlet for CRAT (p357). Arte Facto also has exhibitions on handicrafts production and runs short handicrafts courses.

A modest shop stacked high with pottery, tiles, embroidery, copper and pewter work is **Artesanato dos Clérigos** (Map pp352-3; ☎ 222 000 257; Rua Assunção 33; 9am-12.30pm & 2.30-7.30pm Mon-Sat), behind the Torre dos Clérigos. Stalls in the **Mercado do Bolhão** sell basketry and ceramics.

Markets

See p361 for for information on good food markets. The most rewarding of Porto's many flea markets runs from 6am to noon on Saturday at Alameda das Fontaínhas, southeast of Praça da Batalha. A touristy market along the Cais da Ribeira is good for T-shirts, woolly jumpers and traditional toys. A scrawny flea market occupies a spot just north of the cathedral, daily.

GETTING THERE & AWAY

Air

International and domestic flights use **Francisco Sá Carneiro Airport** (flight information ☎ 229 412 534; www.ana-aeroportos.pt), 20km northwest of the city centre. At the time of research, it was still in the throes of a major expansion first intended for Euro2004.

Portugália and TAP have multiple daily flights to/from Lisbon. Direct international connections include one or more flights on most days to London, Madrid, Paris, Frankfurt, Amsterdam and Brussels; see p466 for details.

Be warned there is no left-luggage facility at the airport.

Bus

INTERNATIONAL

There are **Eurolines** (Map p350; ☎ 225 189 299; Centro Comercial Central Shopping, Rua Santos Pousada 200) services to/from cities all over Europe.

Northern Portugal's own international carrier is **Internorte** (Map p350; ☎ 226 052 420; www.internorte.pt in Portuguese; Praça da Galiza 96; bus No 3 or 52 from Praça da Liberdade).

Most travel agencies can book outbound buses with any of these operators (p472).

DOMESTIC

There are at least five places where you can catch long-distance buses to points within Portugal.

Renex (Map pp352-3; ☎ 222 003 395; Campo dos Mártires da Pátria 37; 24hr) is the choice for Lisbon (€13, 3½ hours), with the most direct routes and eight to 12 departures daily, including one continuing to the Algarve. Renex also goes about as often to Braga (€4.50, 1¼ hours).

Rede Expressos (☎ 222 006 954; www.rede-expressos.pt in Portuguese) departs many times a day for just about anywhere from the smoggy **Paragem Atlântico terminal** (Map pp352-3; Rua Alexandre Herculano 370). Its affiliate Rodoviária da Beira Litoral (RBL) runs from here to Coimbra (€9, 1½ hours) and other points in the Beiras.

For fast Minho connections, mainly on weekdays, three lines run from around Praceta Régulo Magauanha, off Rua Dr Alfredo Magalhães (Map p350). **REDM** (☎ 222 003 152) runs chiefly to Braga (€3.90, one hour). **AV Minho** (☎ 222 006 121) goes mainly via Vila do Conde (€2.35, 55 minutes) to Viana do Castelo (€5, 1¼ hours). **Arriva** (☎ 222 051 383) serves Guimarães (€3.90, 50 minutes).

Rodonorte (Map pp352-3; ☎ 222 005 637; Rua Ateneu Comercial do Porto 19) has multiple daily departures (fewer on Saturday) for Amarante (€4.30, one hour), Vila Real (€5.50, 1½ hours) and Bragança (€8.70, 3½ hours).

Santos (Map p350; ☎ 225 104 915; Centro Comercial Central Shopping, Rua Santos Pousada 200; bus No 6 from Praça da Liberdade) buses run to Lisbon (€11.50), Vila Real (€5.50) and Bragança (€8.70).

Car

Drivers can get information from the **Automovel Clube de Portugal** (Map p350; ☎ 222 056 732; www.acp.pt in Portuguese; Rua Gonçalo Cristóvão 2/6; 9am-12.15pm Mon-Fri). The Loja da Mobilidade at the main tourist office has a map showing all the car parks in the city. All the following companies have desks at the airport. The first three have low rates; the last four are international agencies.

Budget Castanheira (☎ 808 252 627; www.budgetportugal.com) The lowest unlimited-mileage rental rates.
Auto Jardim (☎ 229 413 661)
Sixt (☎ 229 483 752; www.sixt.pt in Portuguese)
Europcar (☎ 808 204 050; www.europcar.pt in Portuguese)
National/Guerin (☎ 800 201 078; www.guerin.pt)
Avis (☎ 800 201 002; www.avis.com.pt in Portuguese)
Hertz (☎ 800 238 238; www.hertz.com.pt in Portguese)

Train

Porto is the principal rail hub for northern Portugal. Long-distance services start at Campanhã station, 2km east of the centre. Most *suburbano*, regional and *interregional* (IR) trains start from São Bento station, though all these lines also pass through Campanhã.

For destinations on the Braga, Guimarães or Aveiro lines, or up the Douro valley as far as Marco de Canaveses, take one of the frequent *suburbano* trains (use the green ticket machines or window 7, 8 or 9 at São Bento); don't spend extra money on *interregional* (IR) or *intercidade* (IC) trains to these destinations (eg Porto-Braga costs €1.75 by *suburbano* but €6.50 by IC train).

Sample 2nd-class IR/IC fares and times for direct journeys from Porto are Viana do Castelo (IR €5.50, 1½ hours, two daily; no direct IC), Coimbra (IR €6, 1½ hours, two daily; IC €8, 1¼ hours, four daily) and Lisbon (IR €12.50, 4½ hours, two daily; IC €16.50, 3½ hours, four daily).

At São Bento you can book tickets for journeys departing from either station. Any ticket bought at São Bento for a journey starting from Campanhã entitles you to a free ride between the stations (five minutes) via *suburbano* train.

There are information points at both **São Bento** (8.30am-8pm) and **Campanhã** (9am-7pm). For telephone information call Caminhos de Ferro Portugueses' (CP) local-rates number, ☎ 808 208 208.

GETTING AROUND

To/From the Airport

A flexible bus service is **AeroBus** (☎ 808 200 166), running between Aliados and the airport via Boavista every half-hour from 6.45am to 6.15pm (7.30am to 7pm from the airport). The trip takes 25 minutes in favourable traffic. The €2.60 ticket, purchased on board, also serves as a free bus pass until midnight of the day you buy it. Arriving TAP passengers who present their boarding pass get this ticket free.

The bus will drop passengers at any train station, the Parque de Campismo da Prelada, the *pousada da juventude* or any of about three-dozen major hotels. If you're staying at one of these, it will also collect you if you call ☎ 225 071 054 by 10pm the preceding day.

Bus No 56 runs between Cordoaria and the airport (€2.05) about every half-hour from 6.30am to 8.30pm. In the evening it continues to Praça da Liberdade.

A daytime taxi costs around €20 to/from Praça da Liberdade. Taxis authorised to run *from* the airport are labelled 'Maia' and/or 'Vila Nova de Telha'; the rank is just outside the arrivals hall. Porto city taxis can take passengers *to* the airport but cannot bring any back (some do anyway, and a few overcharge).

During peak traffic time, allow an hour or more between the city centre and the airport.

Note that a branch of the Póvoa de Varzim metro line will eventually run to the airport from central Porto, though this is unlikely to be finished before 2007. When running, it will cost around €1.70 for a single into central Porto.

Bus

Porto's transport agency **STCP** (Sociedade de Transportes Colectivos do Porto; information ☎ 808 200 166; www.stcp.pt in Portuguese) operates an extensive bus system, which has central hubs at Praça da Liberdade, Praça Almeida Garrett (São Bento train station) and Cordoaria.

Maps and timetables for day and night routes are available from the city turismos and from an **STCP office** (Map pp352-3; 8am-7.30pm Mon-Fri, 8am-1pm Sat) opposite São Bento station.

Tickets are cheapest if bought in advance – from the STCP office and from many newsagents and *tabacarias*. Trips within Porto city limits cost €0.70, those to outlying areas (including Vila Nova de Gaia) cost €0.90 and longer trips (including the airport) cost €2.05; this last fare is also valid for a return. Tickets are sold singly or in discounted *cadernetas* (booklets) of 10. A ticket bought on the bus (one way to anywhere in the STCP system) costs €1.20.

Also available is a €2.10 *bilhete diário* (day pass) valid for unlimited trips within the city on buses and the tram. The city sells its own more general tourist pass, the Passe Porto, through city turismos (p353).

Note that an increasing number of STCP buses are being included in the Andante card scheme (below). At the time of writing, these included the lines: 1, 3, 6, 7, 14, 15, 19, 20, 36, 38, 39, 41 and 60. It's likely that Andante may expand to cover all bus lines in the next few years, though there were no concrete plans to do so at the time of writing.

Note that bus routes given in this chapter may change slightly as the metro system develops.

Metro

Porto's long-awaited underground system is finally a reality. In 2004 Euro2004 spurred on the inauguration of the first stretch – Linha A (blue) – from Matosinhos to the football stadium at Antas (Estádio do Dragão). This new line also passes through the CP train station at Campanhã, and central hub Trindade station, a few blocks north of the *câmara municipal*.

But that's not all. Energetic work continues to develop a total of six far-reaching lines. The network will eventually stretch north to the city limits, east to Gondomar, south to Vila Nova de Gaia, and northwest up the coast all the way to Vila do Conde and Póvoa de Varzim.

Linha D (yellow) should be next to join the action. Its estimated completion date is early 2005. When finished, it will run south across the upper deck of Ponte Dom Luís I bridge to Vila Nova da Gaia and northeast beyond the Hospital São João.

Also on the horizon are Linha C (green) north to Trofa and Linha B (red) out to Vila do Conde. Optimistic estimates suggest that initial stages will be up and running by 2005. Meanwhile the metro authority runs buses along selected parts of the network, including Vila do Conde from Viso metro station.

Two other planned lines are unlikely to materialise before 2007. However, you can keep up to date with developments on the metro's website (www.metrodoporto.pt) in Portuguese or English.

Metro trains run from 6am to 1.30am daily. For information on prices and how to get tickets, see the boxed text, below.

Funicular

Long have the people of Porto panted up the steep bank from the Ribeira to the centre of the city. But things just got easier for those who prefer to save their puff. The **Funicular dos Guindais** (8am-10pm Tue-Sun) now shuttles up and down a steep incline from Avenida Gustavo Eiffel opposite Ponte de Dom Luís I to Rua Augusto Rosa. The funicular is part of the Andante scheme (below).

Taxi

Taxi ranks are scattered throughout the centre, or you can call a **radio taxi** (☎ 225 073 900).

ANDANTE CARD

The new metro system has pushed Porto's transport system to a new level of interconnectivity. You can now purchase a rechargeable **Andante Card** (☎ 808 200 444; www.linhandante.com in Portuguese) that allows you to move smoothly between tram, metro, funicular and some bus lines (p366).

The card itself costs only €0.50 and can be reused indefinitely. Once you've purchased the card, you must charge it with travel credit according to which zones you will be travelling in. It's not as complicated as it sounds. A Z2 trip covers the whole city centre east to Campanhã train station, south to Vila Nova de Gaia and west to Foz do Douro. And each 'trip' allows you a whole hour to hop between different participating methods of transport without additional cost. Your time begins from when you first enter the vehicle or platform: just wave the card in front of a validation machine marked with Andante.

You can purchase credit in metro ticket machines and manned TIP booths at central hubs like Casa da Música and Trindade, as well as the STCP office, the funicular, the electric tram museum and a scattering of other authorised sales points.

One/two/10 'trips' in Z2 cost €0.80/1.60/7.20. Alternatively, you can choose to roam freely for 24 hours for €2.80. If you want to go further out than two zones, pick up a map and explanation of zones at any metro station.

Figure on paying around €3 across the city centre during the day, and €3.60 or more after 9pm. There's an extra charge if you leave the city limits, which includes Vila Nova de Gaia. For a customised city tour, you can hire a Mercedes **Rent-a-Cab** (☎ 222 001 530; www.rentacab.pt).

Tram

Porto's trams used to be one of its delights, but at the time of writing only two were left. However, plans to possibly expand the network once more were in the pipeline.

For the time being, the No 1E trundles from near the Igreja de São Francisco (Ribeira), via the Tram Museum (p356) out to Foz do Douro (a 25-minute trip). The No 18 goes from near the Igreja do Carmo down to Massarelos. Both run every half-hour from about 10am to 10pm daily.

The fare is €1.30 (or €0.80 with an uncharged Andante card, free with a charged one), or you can use a day pass.

AROUND PORTO

VILA NOVA DE GAIA

pop 179,000 / elevation 100m

Stray anywhere near Porto's riverside and you'll be instantly struck by the scene opposite. Crammed cheek by jowl, from the waterfront to the top of the steep slope, are more than three-score port-wine lodges, most sporting huge signs that clamour for attention. Since the mid-18th century port-wine bottlers and exporters have been obliged to maintain their lodges – basically dressed-up warehouses for pre-export storage and maturing – here.

And this enclave of historic terracotta-topped warehouses is now Porto's best-known attraction, despite not actually being in the city at all. Vila Nova de Gaia is a wholly separate municipality, and – beyond the riverbank – goes about its own business in kind of parallel universe.

But most visitors are not interested in exploring further than the stunning waterside promenade – lined with beautiful *barcos rabelos* and offering spectacular views back to Porto – and the maze of warehouses that dominate the hillside above it. Almost all of these lodges offer tours and tastings, so – depending on your alcohol tolerance – you could easily spend a whole day traipsing from one to the next.

To know your vintage port-wine from your LBV, check out the Food & Drink chapter (p62).

Information

Staff at the riverfront **turismo** (Map p350; ☎ /fax 223 751 902; Avenida Diogo Leite; 🕒 10am-7pm Mon-Sat, 2-7pm Sun Jul & Aug, 10am-6pm Mon-Sat Sep-Jun) dispense a good town map and a brochure listing the lodges open for tours. In any case you need only breathe the name of a lodge and half-a-dozen local people will simultaneously point you to it.

Sights & Activities

BARCO RABELOS

At a boatyard on Cais de Gaia at the western end of the waterfront, you can watch **barcos rabelos** being built – on a touristic scale but using traditional methods.

MOSTEIRO DA SERRA DO PILAR

There are positively stunning vistas of Porto from Gaia's severe 16th-century **monastery**, crowning the hill beside the Ponte de Dom Luís I. Because of this, the future Duke of Wellington made his headquarters here before chasing the French out of Porto in 1809.

Much of the monastery, including a striking circular cloister, now belongs to the army and there's a paltry little **military museum** (admission €0.50; 🕒 Jul-Sep). The rest of the monastery is generally shut to the public, though free guided tours can sometimes be arranged. Call ☎ 223 752 298 or inquire at the tourist office.

WINE TASTING & TOURS

About two-dozen lodges are open for tours and tastings on weekdays and Saturday. In high season (June to September) the larger ones run visitors through like clockwork and you'll wait no more than 15 minutes to join a tour. At other times they can accommodate you more or less on the spot.

Taylor's (Taylor Fladgate & Yeatman; ☎ 223 742 800; www.taylor.pt; Rua do Choupelo 250; 🕒 10am-6pm Mon-Fri Sep-Jun, 10am-6pm Mon-Sat Jul-Aug) Of the old English-run lodges, this has the best free tour and a taste of top-of-the-range (late-bottled vintage) wine.

Ramos Pinto (Map p350; ☎ 223 707 000; www.ramos pinto.pt; Avenida Ramos Pinto 380; 🕒 10am-6pm

Mon-Sat Jun & Sep, 10am-6pm daily Jul-Aug, 9am-1pm & 2-5pm Mon-Fri Oct-May) A €2 tour includes the historic old company offices and tastings.

Ferreira (Map p350; ☎ 223 746 100; Rua da Carvalhosa 19) This Portuguese-run establishment has a good tour.

Calém (Map p350; ☎ 223 746 660; Avenida Diogo Leite 26) A small, independent lodge.

Rozés (☎ 223 771 680; Rua Cândido dos Reis 526) Also small and independent.

If you can't be bothered to cross the river, you can taste all the lodges' port at the Solar do Vinho do Porto, a posh pub in Porto; see the boxed text, p362.

Eating

Restaurante Imar (Map p350 ☎ 223 792 705; Avenida Diogo Leite 56; half-portions €3-7; 🕑 lunch & dinner Tue-Sun) Located 200m west of the turismo, this no-nonsense hideaway offers regional dishes at reasonable prices.

A clutch of cheery cafés and *adegas* (wine bars) near the *mercado municipal* (municipal market) do light meals (around €4). Several lodges serve lunch in their own decidedly upper-crust restaurants. One of the best is at Taylor's, called the **Barão de Fladgate** (☎ 223 742 800; mains €10-14, set meal €24.40; 🕑 lunch & dinner Mon-Sat), with an enviable view over the warehouses to central Porto.

Getting There & Away

Bus Nos 32, 57 and 91 run between Praça Almeida Garrett in Porto and Gaia's turismo, via the lower deck of the bridge. For the Mosteiro da Serra do Pilar, take bus No 82 or 84 from Praça Almeida Garrett. Once completed, the new metro Linha D will also stop nearby. These stops are far above the lodges, although you can work your way down through narrow lanes to the riverfront.

AFURADA

To escape the city pace from Porto you could catch one of the regular local launches over to Afurada, a pretty fishing village west of Vila Nova de Gaia, its houses decked with azulejos and its cafés known locally for their hearty *caldeirada* (seafood stew).

The most scenic route is to take a tram from the Ribeira to just west of the Ponte da Arrábida. There you can catch a small ferry (€0.60) across the river to the village. It departs about every 10 minutes from 6am to midnight daily.

VILA DO CONDE

pop 25,800

Despite being a popular seaside resort, the salty-dog town of Vila do Conde retains much of its historical character as a shipbuilding port, also famous for its lace and handicrafts. Its beaches are some of the best north of Porto, and transport is easy enough to make a day trip worthwhile.

The town remains peaceful and charmingly unaffected by the activity at the beach, and offers a less touristy atmosphere than at the overdeveloped resort of Póvoa de Varzim, 4km to the north. Looming over everything is the immense hilltop Mosteiro de Santa Clara, which, along with surviving segments of a long-legged aqueduct, lends the town an air of unexpected monumentality.

Orientation & Information

Vila do Conde sits on the north side of the Rio Ave where it empties into the sea. Buses stop at the stop on the N13 (Rua 5 de Outubro), in the shadow of the monastery. From the future metro station (the old train station) it's an 800m walk west to the N13 and north to the bus stops.

Vila do Conde has two **turismos** (☎ 252 248 473; fax 252 248 422; Rua 25 de Abril 103 & Rua 5 de Outubro 207; both 🕑 9am-6pm Mon-Fri, 10am-5.30pm Sat & Sun), just 150m apart. When one is closed for lunch, the other is open. The one opposite the bus stop shares a space with a small handicrafts gallery.

The town's beach, which sees plenty of surfers and sun-worshippers, stretches north for 3km from the mouth of the river. From the turismos it's 1.2km west along Avenida 25 de Abril, Avenida Dr João Canavarro and Avenida Sacadura Cabral to the beachfront road, Avenida Brasil.

Most accommodation, cafés and bars are around Praça da República, two blocks south of the bus stop and a stone's throw from the little harbour.

Sights & Activities

MOSTEIRO DE SANTA CLARA

Over 100 nuns once lived their godly lives in the stately **Mosteiro de Santa Clara**, which peers down over the town centre. The building was founded in 1318, although only the fortified church to its left retained its severe Gothic style after rebuilding in the 18th century. Since 1944 the building has been a rather less pious reformatory for teenage boys (closed to the public).

Inside the church – accessible by a side door – are the carved tombs of Dom Afonso and his family, and the remains of a fine 18th-century cloister.

Outside, the towering **aqueduct** that dominates Vila do Conde – used to bring water to the convent from Terroso, 7km away – once had 999 arches. The church and aqueduct are now national monuments.

OTHER CHURCHES

The Manueline **igreja matriz** (parish church; Rua 25 de Abril; irregular hr) dates mostly from the early 16th century, and has an ornate doorway carved by Basque artist João de Castilho. Outside is a *pelourinho* (stone pillory) topped by the sword-wielding arm of Justice. Inside is the **Museu de Arte Sacra** (252 631 424; admission free; 10am-noon & 2-4pm Jun-Sep, 2-4pm Oct-May), a modest collection of ecclesiastical art.

Fitting only about a dozen worshippers, the tiny 17th-century **Capela da Nossa Senhora de Socorro** (Largo da Alfândega; daily), west of Praça da República, is a striking sight, with its crisp mosque-like dome. The interior is covered in azulejos as old as the church itself.

SCHOOL & MUSEUM OF LACE-MAKING

It's no accident that seafaring fingers, so deft at making nets, should also be good at lace-making. Long famous for its lace, Vila do Conde is one of the few places in Portugal with an active **school** of the art, founded in 1918.

The school, in a typical 18th-century townhouse, includes a **Museu das Rendas de Bilros** (Museum of Bobbin Lace; 252 248 470; www.mrbvc.net in Portuguese; Rua São Bento 70; admission free; 9am-noon & 2-6pm Mon-Fri), with eye-popping examples of work from around the world.

MUSEU DA CONSTRUÇÃO NAVAL

Shipbuilding has been in Vila do Conde's bones since at least the 13th century; many of the stoutest ships of the Age of Discoveries were made here.

Homage is paid to this side of the town's history at the **Museu da Construção Naval** (Museum of Shipbuilding; 252 240 740; Largo da Alfândega; admission free; 10am-6pm Tue-Sun) in the restored Royal Customs House, just west of Praça da República. The building is fitted out with an entire ship's prow, earnest exhibits on trade, spooky waxworks and interesting displays on the lovingly hand-built *nau* (a sort of pot-bellied caravel once used for cargo and naval operations), reconstructed using traditional methods.

The nau itself is across the river at a small **shipyard** (Mon-Fri summer). Recently finished, the boat will soon score its own museum in the area (ask at the turismo).

SEAFRONT

The two best beaches, broad Praia da Forno and Praia de Nossa Senhora da Guia, have calm seas suitable for young children, while surfers often ride the swells near the castelo (see below). Buses marked 'Vila do Conde' from Póvoa de Varzim stop at the station and then continue out to the beach, about every half-hour all day.

At the river mouth is the 17th-century **Castelo de São João Baptista**, once a castle but now a small, deluxe hotel (p371).

Festivals & Events

Festa de São João (23 June) The biggest religious event, when a candlelight procession winds through the streets to the beach.

Feira Nacional de Artesanato (July–August) Major handicrafts fair held last week of July and first week of August.

Sleeping

The turismo has a list of *quartos* (private rooms) and apartments, which get snapped up quickly in summer (most owners prefer long-stay guests). There are two seaside camp sites right by the sea south of town, both open year-round and equipped with a *minimercado*, café-restaurant and bar.

Parque de Campismo da Árvore (252 633 225; cnm.parque@kqnet.pt; Rua do Cabreiro, Árvore; adult/tent €5/4.50;) Tightly packed and well shaded, this camp site is 3km away from town, right next to Praia da Árvore beach.

Parque de Campismo Vila Chã (229 283 163; fax 229 280 632; Rua do Sol 150, Vila Chã; adult/tent/car €2.70/2.90-4.90/1.90) This is 7km away from town.

Residencial O Manco d'Areia (/fax 252 631 748; Praça da República 84; s/d from €35/45) Up an azulejo-clad staircase, this thoroughly renovated old town house has fresh and quiet en suite rooms, plus a few triples with shared facilities. Credit cards are not accepted.

Restaurante Le Villageois (☎/fax 252 631 119; Praça da República 94; d €30) Lively restaurant Le Villageois has a few comfortable rooms for visitors to bed down in, though breakfast isn't included; book well ahead in summer.

Pensão Patarata (☎ 252 631 894; Cais das Lavandeiras 18; d/tw €40/45) Looking over the river, off the southwest corner of the square, this place has flowery en suite rooms, a cheerful café and no-nonsense service.

Residencial Princesa do Ave (☎ 252 642 065; princesadoave@clix.pt; Rua Dr António José Sousa Pereira 261; d €40) Reliable but featureless block: pet parrots provide the only personality. Take the road left from the turismo on Rua 5 de Outubro, turn left again into Rua Conde D Mendo and keep walking for 400m.

Estalagem do Brasão (☎ 252 642 016; estalagembrazao@netcabo.pt; Avenida Dr João Canavarro; s/d/ste with breakfast €56/78/94.50; P ❄) Part modern, part old town house, this dark inn has all the comforts – from marble bathroom to cable TV – 200m west of the Rua 25 de Abril turismo.

Hotel Forte S. João Baptista (☎ 252 240 600; www.hotelfortesjoao.com; Avenida Brasil; s/d/ste 125/150/175; P ❄) Unsurpassable setting in a stylishly converted pentagonal fortress by the ocean. As exclusive as they come.

Eating

Restaurante Le Villageois (☎/fax 252 631 119; Praça da República 94; mains €8-15; ⏰ lunch & dinner Tue-Sun) Popular Le Villageois has a huge menu of well-prepared French and Portuguese dishes, a well-stocked bar and a sun-drenched patio into the bargain.

Adega Beira Rio (☎ 252 633 012; Cais das Lavandeiras 4; half-portions under €5; ⏰ lunch & dinner Mon-Sat) At lunch time this plain-faced family-run place serves good half-portions, and has whistling waiters and canaries competing with the TV.

Caximar (☎ 252 642 492; Avenida Brasil; mains €9-18, seafood platters for 2 €16-56; ⏰ lunch & dinner Tue-Sun) For special occasions or a holiday treat get stuck into a seafood platter here. Caximar sits directly on the beach, roughly 1km west of Forte S. João Baptista.

Another local favourite is the café at **Pensão Patarata** (see above; half-portions around €6; ⏰ daily).

Drinking

At the time of writing there were no discos in Vila do Conde, though welcoming bars line the riverside Cais das Lavandeiras near Pensão Patarata. Try the lively **Seca Bar** (Avenida Marqués de sa da Bandeira; ⏰ 11am-11pm Mon-Sat), whose odd name (dry bar) refers to the building's days as a cod-drying house.

Shopping

Centro de Artesanato (☎ 252 248 473; Rua 5 de Outubro 207; ⏰ 10am-7pm Mon-Fri, 10am-noon & 1.30-5.30pm Sat) Sharing space with the turismo opposite the bus stop, this is a good place for pottery, wooden toys, basketry, embroidered linen and, of course, lace. Local lacemakers sometimes work here too.

An excellent general market materialises opposite the other turismo every Friday (see p369).

Getting There & Away

Vila do Conde is 33km from Porto, a straight shot on the IC1 highway.

It will eventually be a stop on Porto's metro line to Póvoa de Varzim when that's completed – hopefully by mid-2005. Meanwhile the **metro authority** (☎ 808 200 166) runs buses (€1.20, 1¼ hours, two per hour Monday to Saturday mid-afternoon, hourly Saturday afternoon and Sunday) connecting with the metro station at Viso (this may change as work continues: check at a turismo). Buy tickets on board the bus.

AV Minho express buses stop a dozen times daily (fewer at weekends) en route between Porto (€2.20, 55 minutes) and Viana do Castelo (€2.80, one hour). Linhares also has regular services.

EASTERN DOURO

AMARANTE

pop 11,700 / elevation 150m

It is the town's patron saint, Gonçalo (p373), that lends Amarante a certain notoriety – and his namesake church and monastery dominate the town's core, beside the striking old stone bridge across the Tâmega. However, this pleasing town, straddling the Rio Tâmega, is worth visiting just for the setting. The river is dotted with rowing boats, the banks lined with willows, and balconied houses rise in tiers up the steep banks and switch-backed lanes.

Amarante is also famous for its eggy pastries – and not just the phallic cakes that

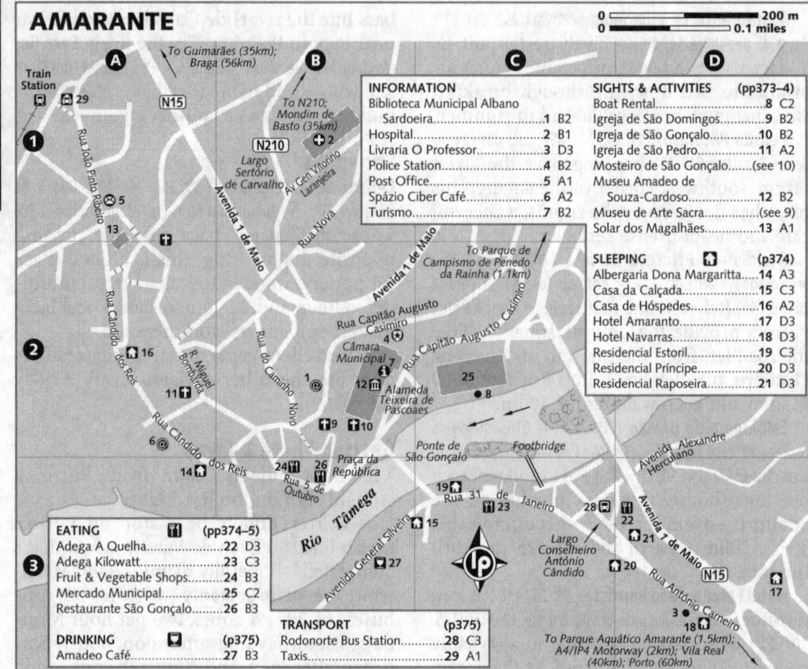

appear during the cheerful festivals of São Gonçalo.

The most appealing way to get here is on the narrow-gauge Linha da Tâmega railway (p375).

History

The town may date back as far as the 4th century BC. Gonçalo, a 13th-century hermit, is credited with everything from the founding of the town to the construction of its first bridge. His hermitage grew into the trademark church by the old bridge.

Amarante's strategic crossroad position was nearly its undoing in 1809, when the French lost their brief grip on Portugal. Marshal Soult's troops retreated to the northeast after abandoning Porto, plundering as they went. A detachment arrived here in search of a river crossing, but plucky citizens and troops held them off, allowing residents to escape to the far bank, and bringing the French to a standstill.

The French retaliated by burning much of the upper town to the ground, but it was two weeks before they managed to bluff their way across. They then withdrew quick smart and were soon in full retreat across the Minho and Trás-os-Montes.

Amarante has also suffered frequent natural invasions by the Tâmega. Little *cheia* (high-water level) plaques in Rua 31 de Janeiro and Largo Conselheiro António Cândido tell the harrowing story.

Orientation

The Tâmega flows through the middle of town, spanned by the old Ponte de São Gonçalo. On the northwest bank is Amarante's showpiece, the Igreja de São Gonçalo. In the former cloisters, the *câmara municipal* and the turismo face the market square, Alameda Teixeira de Pascoaes.

From the little train station it's an 800m walk southeast to the bridge. Nearly all coaches stop in Largo Conselheiro António Cândido, just across the river.

Information

Banks with ATMs are plentiful along Rua 5 de Outubro and Rua António Carneiro.

Biblioteca Municipal Albano Sardoeira (☎ 255 420 236; Largo de Santa Clara; ⏲ 9am-5.30 Mon-Fri, 10am-12.30pm & 2-6pm Sat) In the newly refashioned old Casa da Cerca, provides free Internet access.
Hospital (☎ 255 410 500; Largo Sertório de Carvalho) North of the centre.
Livraria O Professor (☎ 255 432 441; Rua António Carneiro; ⏲ Mon-Sat) Stocks foreign-language newspapers.
Police station (☎ 255 432 015; Rua Capitão Augusto Casimiro)
Post office (☎ 255 422 112; Rua João Pinto Ribeiro; ⏲ 8.30am-6pm Mon-Fri)
Spázio Ciber Café (☎ 255 422 652; Rua Cândido dos Reis; per hr €2.60; ⏲ 9am-2am) Has three terminals and a good little bar to keep you occupied.
Turismo (☎ 255 420 246; Alameda Teixeira de Pascoaes; ⏲ 9am-12.30pm & 2-7pm Jul–mid-Sep, 9am-12.30pm & 2-5.30pm mid-Sep–Jun) In the former cloisters of São Gonçalo.

Sights

PONTE DE SÃO GONÇALO

The granite **Ponte de São Gonçalo** is Amarante's visual centrepiece and symbol of the town's heroic defence against the French (marked by a plaque at the southeastern end). It also offers one of the best views of town. The original bridge, allegedly built at Gonçalo's urging in the 13th century, collapsed in a flood in 1763; this one was completed in 1790.

IGREJA DE SÃO GONÇALO & MOSTEIRO DE SÃO GONÇALO

The **Mosteiro de São Gonçalo** (Monastery of São Gonçalo; admission free; ⏲ 8am-6pm) and its arresting church, the **Igreja de São Gonçalo**, were founded in 1540 by João III, though only finished in 1620. Beside the church's photogenic, multi-tiered, Italian Renaissance side portal is an arcaded gallery with 17th-century statues of Dom João and the other kings who ruled while the monastery was under construction: Sebastião, Henrique and Felipe I. The bell tower was added in the 18th century.

Within the lofty interior are an impressive carved and gilded baroque altar and pulpits, an organ casing held up by fish-tailed giants, and Gonçalo's tomb in a tiny chapel to the left of the altar (see 'Patron Saint of Lonely Hearts' above, for an explanation of his worn extremities).

Through the north portal are a couple of peaceful Renaissance cloisters – one now occupied by the town hall.

PATRON SAINT OF LONELY HEARTS

São Gonçalo is the patron saint of marriage, and tradition has it that the not-so-young in search of a mate will have their wish granted within a year if they touch the statue on the outside of his tomb in Mosteiro de São Gonçalo. And sure enough – its limestone toes, fingers and face have been all but rubbed away by hopefuls.

But the saint's magic touch doesn't stop there. During the Festas de Junho (and on São Gonçalo's day, 13 January) unmarried men and women swap little phallic pastry cakes called falus de Gonçalo or bolos de Gonçalo as a sign of affection, a delightfully frank tradition that we have to assume the saintly Gonçalo inherited from more pagan times.

OTHER CHURCHES

Rising beside São Gonçalo are several impressively steep switchbacks topped by the round, 18th-century **Igreja de São Domingos** (admission free), with a tiny, peeling interior and a tiny, peeling **Museu de Arte Sacra** (☎ 255 422 050; admission €0.50; ⏲ Tue-Fri 2.30-5.30pm, 10am-12.30pm & 2.30-6.30pm) alongside. Up on Rua Miguel Bombarda, the baroque-fronted **Igreja de São Pedro** (admission free; ⏲ 2-5pm) has a nave decorated with 17th-century blue and yellow azulejos.

MUSEU AMADEO DE SOUZA-CARDOSO

In one of the monastery's cloisters is a delightfully eclectic collection of contemporary art. The **Museu Amadeo de Souza-Cardoso** (☎ 255 420 233; Alameda Teixeira de Pascoaes; adult/child under 15/student under 26/senior €1/free/0.50/0.50; ⏲ 10am-12.30pm & 2-5.30pm Tue-Sun), a surprise and a great bargain in a town of this size.

The museum is named after and dominated by Amarante's favourite son, artist Amadeo Souza-Cardoso (1889–1918). Souza-Cardoso is one of the best-known Portuguese artists of the 20th century. He abandoned naturalism for cubism and for his home-grown impressionism.

This museum is full of his sketches, cartoons, portraits and abstracts. But don't overlook the very still portraits and landscapes of António Carneiro, and Jaime Azinheira's touching *Escultura*.

SOLAR DOS MAGALHÃES
A stark and uncaptioned memento of the French stay is this burned-out skeleton of an old **manor house** situated above Rua Cândido dos Reis, near the train station.

Activities
You can potter about on the peaceful Rio Tâmega in a paddle or rowing **boat**. They're for hire in warm weather from the riverbank below the market (€5/8 per half/full hour).

After a long day mooching around monasteries, **Parque Aquático Amarante** (☎ 255 446 648; desporto@tamegaclube.com; A4 exit 15; ⏰ 10.30am-7pm Jun-Sep), a water park 2km southwest of the centre, is ideal for little kids (and big kids) to splash. It has a choice of three chutes plus swimming pools and sunbathing areas.

Festivals & Events
Held on the weekend of the first Saturday in June, **Festas de Junho** highlights include an all-night drum competition, a livestock fair, a handicrafts market, bullfights and fireworks, all rounded off with a procession in honour of the main man – São Gonçalo.

Sleeping
Not surprisingly, accommodation is hard to find during the Festas de Junho, though it's plentiful at other times.

Parque de Campismo de Penedo da Rainha (☎ 255 437 630; ccporto@sapo.pt; Lugar de Fridão; adult/tent/car €2.90/2-2.90/1.90; ⏰ Feb-Nov;) A big, shady site descending to the river and equipped with a *minimercado* and bar. Technically requires a CCI (p452). It's about 1.5km upstream from the town centre.

Casa de Hóspedes (☎ 255 423 327; 1st fl, Rua Cândido dos Reis 288; s/d/tw €20/25/32.50) A clutch of homely rooms with shared facilities are available at this hostel. It's run by one of the chattiest old dears in the north: a big plus if you speak a few words of Portuguese.

Residencial Estoril (☎ 255 431 291; Rua 31 de Janeiro 49; d facing street/river €35/40, with balcony €45) Above all else, this place offers a fabulous location jutting over the river – four of its homely rooms (two with balcony) enjoy a stunning view to São Gonçalo's bridge.

Residencial Raposeira (☎ 255 432 221; 1st fl, Largo Conselheiro António Cândido 41; d with/without shower & toilet €25/20) However, if river views are out of your league, you could do a lot worse than the cheerful rooms at this modern, bright guesthouse above a restaurant.

Residencial Príncipe (☎ 255 432 956; Largo Conselheiro António Cândido 78; s/d €15/25) Sitting across from Raposeira, this creaky old *residencial* has a mixed bag of well-worn rooms with more personality.

Albergaria Dona Margaritta (☎ 255 432 110; www.albergariadonamargaritta.pa-net.pt in Portuguese; Rua Cândido dos Reis 53; d with breakfast €50;) This faded but handsome townhouse has motherly service and is Amarante's most characterful option in its price range. If you can, bag one of the seven riverside rooms.

Casa da Calçada (☎ 255 410 830; www.casadacalcada.com; Largo do Paço 6; d with breakfast Sun-Thu €118.50, Fri & Sat €139.50;) Oozing class and boasting every creature comfort, this 16th-century nobleman's palace rises royally above the Ponte de São Gonçalo.

Hotel Navarras (☎ 255 431 036; fax 255 432 991; Rua António Carneiro; s/d with breakfast €59.50/75;) In a squeaky clean shopping centre, Navarras has smart carpeted rooms, many with big verandahs on which to catch the morning sun.

Hotel Amaranto (☎ 255 410 840; Rua Acácio Lino; www.hotelamaranto.com; d with breakfast €55;) This professional place, decorated with pastel colours and lots of pine, is equally as luxurious as Navarras.

Eating
Restaurante São Gonçalo (☎ 255 422 707; Praça da República; mains €9-10; ⏰ all day) Under the eye of Gonçalo himself, the sunny patio here is the place for coffee, pastries and light meals. You're paying for location, of course, but it's hard to begrudge that monastery view.

Adega A Quelha (☎ 255 425 786; Rua de Olivença; half-portions €4-9; ⏰ lunch & dinner Tue-Sun, lunch Mon) This chunky granite-walled place invites you to wash down local cheese and smoked ham with a jug of red wine at the bar, or sit down to some of the Douro's best food, including abundant vegetables.

Residencial Estoril (☎ 255 431 291; Rua 31 de Janeiro 49; mains €6-7; ⏰ lunch & dinner) Many *residenciais* have good little restaurants, but this cosy spot easily scoops the prize for best view in Amarante; its balcony overhangs the river with prime position in front of São Gonçalo's bridge.

Adega Kilowatt (☎ 255 433 159; Rua 31 de Janeiro 104; sandwiches €1.50; ⏰ 9am-7pm Tue-Sun) This photogenic delicatessen is hung with hams, dried corn and decorated with scrawled caricatures. It sells traditional ham sandwiches and local wine for riverside picnics.

There are several fruit-and-vegetable shops on lower Rua 5 de Outubro. The biggest days at the *mercado municipal,* east of the turismo, are Wednesday and Saturday.

Drinking

The best spot to chill out with a cold drink is in one of the bars that pop up every summer on the riverside promenade along Avenida General Silveira, opposite the monastery. Also here, the long-running **Amadeo Café** (☎ 255 431 250; Avenida General Silveira 71) is set into the old granite wall.

Getting There & Away

BUS

At the busy **Rodonorte bus station** (☎ 255 422 194; Largo Conselheiro António Cândido), buses stop at least five times daily from Porto (€4.30, one hour) en route via Vila Real (€4.60, 40 minutes) to Bragança (€8.40, 2¾ hours). Rodonorte also runs daily to Braga (€5.60, 2½ hours), Coimbra (€9, 2¾ hours) and Lisbon (€13, 5½ hours).

TRAIN

The journey on the narrow-gauge Linha da Tâmega, which runs from the Douro mainline at Livração up to Amarante, takes 25 minutes and costs €1.20 (buy tickets on board). There are six to nine trains a day, most with good connections to Porto.

LAMEGO

pop 9000 / elevation 550m

There are two attractions that commonly draw people to Lamego, a prosperous, handsome town 12km south of the Rio Douro. Firstly is its impressive religious architecture – not least the astonishing baroque stairway grandly zig-zagging its way up to the Igreja de Nossa Senhora dos Remédios. Second is the famously fragrant sparkling wine (the best of Portugal's few such wines), which grants the town unique status among connoisseurs.

Already well worth a digression from the Rio Douro trail, Lamego is also a natural base for exploring the half-ruined monasteries and medieval chapels in its environs.

Though formally in the Beira Alta, in tradition Lamego belongs to the Douro.

History

Lamego was an important centre even in the time of the Suevi, and in 1143 Portugal's first *cortes* (parliament) was convened here, in order to confirm Afonso Henriques as king of Portugal.

The little town has since grown fat thanks to its position on east–west trading routes and from its wines, already famous in the 16th century.

Orientation

The town's main axis is Avenida Visconde Guedes Teixeira (known as Jardim and shaded by lime trees) and the wide Avenida Dr Alfredo de Sousa (called Avenida and shaded by chestnut trees). Parking is free around the Avenida but not around the Jardim.

At the far end of the Avenida an immense stairway ascends to the Igreja de Nossa Senhora dos Remédios, on top of one of the two hills overlooking the town. Northwards, atop the other hill, stand the ruins of a 12th-century castle.

Information

There are several banks with ATMs found along the Jardim/Avenida and Avenida 5 de Outubro.

Hospital (☎ 254 609 980; Lugar da Franzia)

Library (☎ 254 614 013; Rua de Almacave 9; ⏲ 9.30am-12.30pm & 2-5.30pm Mon-Fri) Provides free Internet access in 30-minute chunks.

Police station (☎ 254 612 022; Rua António Osório Mota)

Post office (☎ 254 609 250; Avenida Dr Alfredo de Sousa; ⏲ 8.30am-6pm Mon-Fri)

Regional Turismo (☎ 254 612 005; douro.turismo@mail.telepac.pt; Avenida Visconde Guedes Teixeira; ⏲ 10am-12.30pm & 2-6pm Mon-Fri, 10am-12.30pm & 2-5pm Sat & Sun Jul-Sep; 9.30am-12.30pm & 2-5.30pm Mon-Fri, 10am-12.30pm Sat Oct-Jun)

Salão de Jogos (☎ 254 612 487; Avenida 5 de Octubro 109; per hr €2; ⏲ 10.30am-midnight) Unlikely looking games arcade with weekend Internet access.

Sights & Activities

IGREJA DE NOSSA SENHORA DOS REMÉDIOS

One of Portugal's best-known pilgrimage sites, this 18th-century **church** (admission free;

7.30am-8pm, 7.30am-6pm winter) is quite overshadowed by the awesome monumental stairway, resplendent with azulejos, urns, fountains and statues, that zigzags theatrically up the hill to it.

It's a dramatic sight at any time, but late summer also sees thousands of devotees arrive and ascend the steps in search of salvation and miracles during the Festas de Nossa Senhora dos Remédios (p377).

The church itself is pretty enough outside, if a tad dull inside, despite piped choral music and a blue-and-white stucco effect reminiscent of Wedgwood Jasperware.

If you can't face hauling your way up the almost 700 steps, the church is 3km by road (turn off 1km out on the Viseu road). You can make your way back down through cool winding forest paths on either side of the steps.

SÉ

Lamego's striking **cathedral** (254 612 766; Largo da Sé; admission free; 8am-1pm & 3-7pm) is older than Portugal itself, though there's little left of the 12th-century original except the base of its square belfry. The rest, including the brilliantly carved flamboyant Gothic triple portal, dates mostly from the 16th and 18th centuries. Arresting biblical frescoes seem to leap off the ceiling, and high choir stalls are the work of the 18th-century Italian architect Nicolau Nasoni, also responsible for much that's lovely about Porto's cathedral.

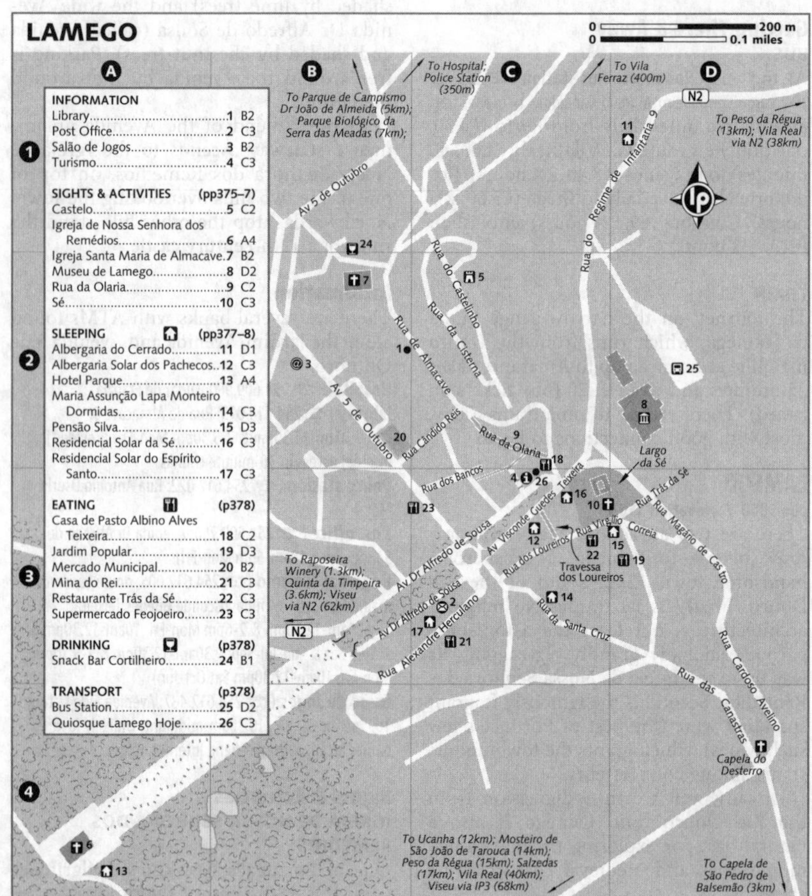

With luck you'll find the door open to the peaceful 16th-century cloisters, just around the corner.

IGREJA SANTA MARIA DE ALMACAVE

This unassuming little **church** (☎ 254 612 460; Rua da Almacave; 🕑 7.30am-noon & 4-7.30pm) is Lamego's oldest surviving building, and bits of it date back to the 12th century. The church occupies the site of a Moorish cemetery; some of its grave markers are now in the Museu de Lamego (below). On the south side is a very lovely Romanesque portal.

It's thought that an early version of the *cortes*, Portugal's proto-democratic assembly of nobles and clergy, met here from 1142 to 1144.

MUSEU DE LAMEGO

Housed in the grand, 18th-century former episcopal palace is one of Portugal's finest regional **museums** (☎ 254 600 230; adult/youth 14-25 €2/1, 10am-12.30pm Sun free; 🕑 10am-12.30pm & 2-5pm Tue-Sun). The collection features some luminous pieces, including a series of five entrancing works by the renowned 16th-century Portuguese painter Vasco Fernandes (Grão Vasco), richly worked Brussels tapestries from the same period, and an extraordinarily diverse collection of heavily gilded 17th-century chapels rescued in their entirety from the long-gone Convento das Chagas.

RUA DA OLARIA

This winding pedestrian lane – steep, narrow and lined with hole-in-the-wall shops selling everything from picturesque smoked hams to shoes – ascends the hill behind the turismo, and is one of Lamego's most atmospheric spots.

CASTELO

You can climb Rua da Olaria and double back to the **castle** (Rua do Castelinho; admission by donation; 🕑 10am-noon & 3-6pm Tue-Sun Jun-Sep, morning only Sun Oct-May), encircled by a clutch of ancient houses. What little remains – some walls and a tower – now belongs to the Boy Scouts, since their mammoth 1970s effort to clear the site after years of use as a glorified rubbish tip. You might get a quick tour from one of the Scouts. Climb to the roof for spectacular views.

RAPOSEIRA TASTING

If quaffing the region's distinctive sparkling wine in restaurants isn't enough for you, the Raposeira winery, 1.7km out on the Viseu road (N2), offers free 20-minute tours and **tastings** (🕑 10am-12.30pm & 2.30-5pm Mon-Fri May-Sep; 2.30-5pm Mon-Fri Oct-Apr); the last tour starts at 4pm.

Festivals & Events

Unsurprisingly, the Igreja de Nossa Senhora dos Remédios is the focus of Lamego's biggest shindig. The **Festa de Nossa Senhora dos Remédios** runs for several weeks from late August to mid-September. In an afternoon procession on 8 September, ox-drawn carts carry religious *tableaux vivants* (silent representation of a scene) through the streets and devotees grit their teeth before slowly ascending the stairway on their knees.

Less-pious events in the run-up include rock concerts, folk dancing, car racing, parades and at least one all-night party.

Sleeping

Parque de Campismo Dr João de Almeida (☎ 254 613 918; naturimont@oninet.pt; Serra das Meadas; adult/tent/car €2.50/2.50-3/2; 🕑 Jun-Sep) A well-equipped camping facility some 5km west of town.

Maria Assunção Lapa Monteiro (☎ 254 612 556; Rua da Santa Cruz 15; r with shared facilities €20) There are homely private rooms available for rent, including this one.

Pensão Silva (☎ 254 612 929; Rua Trás da Sé 26; d/tw €25/37.50) Surveying the back of the cathedral, this well located place has clean but vaguely melancholic old rooms with shared facilities. There's also a small patio for putting your feet up. French spoken.

Residencial Solar da Sé (☎ 254 612 060; fax 254 615 928; Avenida Visconde Guedes Teixeira 7; s/d with breakfast €24/39; ❄) Also within range of cathedral bells tolling at all hours, this place has less home-like but more comfortable rooms than Silva.

Residencial Solar do Espírito Santo (☎/fax 254 655 060; Rua Alexandre Herculano 8; d with breakfast €42; P ❄) This place offers light, modern rooms with a smattering of character.

Vila Ferraz (☎ 254 656 956; www.vilaferraz.com in Portuguese; Avenida General Alves Pedrosa; d with breakfast €60; P ❄ 🏊) Recently refashioned manor house 800m beyond the castelo, where the road splits to Regua or Resende. Every inch is packed with character and no two rooms are alike.

Quinta da Timpeira (☎ 254 612 811; quintadatimpeira@portugalmail.pt; s/d €53/65; P) An attractive modern place with tennis courts into the bargain, Quinta da Timpeira is 4km out on the Viseu road.

Hotel Parque (☎ 254 609 140; fax 254 615 203; d with breakfast €60; P) Bagging an unrivalled location in a wooded park by the Igreja de Nossa Senhora dos Remédios, this attractive hotel has tastefully decorated modern rooms with choice craftwork. The turn-off for the hotel is 1km out on the Viseu road (N2).

Albergaria Solar dos Pachecos (☎ 254 600 300; albergariasolarpachecos@clix.pt; Avenida Visconde Guedes Teixeira 27; s/d with breakfast €40/65) However, if you don't fancy clambering up a zillion stairs after a hard day's sightseeing, you may prefer this attractive guesthouse smack in the town centre, with stylishly spare décor and a buffet breakfast.

Albergaria do Cerrado (☎ 254 613 164; fax 254 615 464; Rua do Regime de Infantaria 9; s/d with breakfast €53/60; P) This place offers similar luxury, but no history or views, in a big modern building near the bus station.

Eating & Drinking

Lamego is awash with cafés to get your sugar-and-caffeine hit. There's an easy-going evening café scene under the Avenida's trees, also a nice venue for a sunny breakfast.

Restaurante Trás da Sé (☎ 254 614 075; Rua Virgílio Correia 12; half-portions €4-5, evening dishes from €5; lunch & dinner) Congratulations messages to the chef line the walls at this *adega*-style place, where the atmosphere is friendly, the menu short and simple, the food good and the *vinho maduro* (wine matured for more than a year) list long.

Casa de Pasto Albino Alves Teixeira (Rua da Olaria 1; dishes under €5; lunch & dinner) For cheap local dishes at lunch time you're spoilt for choice. Ideal for quick and satisfying belly fillers, this place packs diners into plain upstairs rooms.

Mina do Rei (☎ 254 613 353; Rua Alexandre Herculano 3; half-portions €5; lunch & dinner) The 'King's Mine' is an unabashedly touristy restaurant from the cartwheels, gourds and garlic on the walls to the rustic ceramic serving dishes. What is supposedly an old mine shaft runs from the back room: now a wine cellar.

Jardim Popular (☎ 254 609 109; Rua da Perreira; mains €8-14; lunch & dinner Tue-Sat) This conservatory-style restaurant stands in an old walled garden around the corner from Pensão Silva.

Several grocery shops on Rua da Olaria sell Lamego's famous hams and wines – perfect picnic food. Try **Supermercado Feojoeiro** (Avenida 5 de Outubro 11; 9am-12.30pm & 2-8pm Mon-Sat) or the **mercado municipal** (Mon-Fri, morning Sat) for other supplies.

Snack Bar Cortilheiro (Rua Cortes; 12.30pm-2am Tue-Sun) is an energetic youthful *cervejaria* (beerhouse) under the disapproving shadow of a sombre church and the bishop's palace.

Getting There & Away

The most appealing route to Lamego from anywhere in the Douro valley is by train to Peso da Régua (p380) and by bus or taxi from there. A **taxi** (☎ 254 321 366) from Régua costs about €10.

From Lamego's bus station, **Joalto/EAVT** (☎ 254 612 116) goes about hourly to Peso da Régua (€1.60, 20 minutes) and daily to Viseu (€4.20, 1¼ hours). **Guedes** (☎ 254 612 604) has multiple daily services to Peso da Régua and Viseu, and goes twice daily via Coimbra (€8.80, three hours) to Lisbon (€12.40, 5¾ hours).

Rodonorte buses also stop here at least twice each weekday en route between Chaves (€8.50, 2¼ hours) and Vila Real (€4.80, 55 minutes) to Lisbon. Rede Expressos stops twice daily en route between Vila Real and Viseu. **Quiosque Lamego Hoje** (☎ 254 619 447; daily), a newsagent beside the turismo, sells tickets for these services.

Getting Around

A little toy train, the **Circuito Histórico de Lamego** (☎ 254 619 220; morning & afternoon Sat & Sun all year, afternoons Mon-Fri summer only) runs a hop-on hop-off tour past the major monuments and parks of Lamego for €2.50.

AROUND LAMEGO

Sights

CAPELA DE SÃO PEDRO DE BALSEMÃO

This whimsical little 7th- to 10th-century **chapel** (admission free; 10am-12.30pm & 2-6pm Wed-Sun, 2-6pm Tue, closed 3rd weekend of month) is an extraordinary example of Visigothic architecture, with Corinthian columns, round arches and intriguing symbols scratched into the walls. Most of its ornate 14th-century additions were commissioned by the Bishop of Porto, Afonso Pires, who's buried under a slab in the floor. Check out the ancient casket dominating the entrance chamber: supported by lions and intricately engraved, it depicts the Last Supper on one side.

The chapel is tucked away in the hamlet of Balsemão, 3km southeast of Lamego above the Rio Balsemão. It's a pleasant walk from Lamego: from the 17th-century Capela do Desterro at the end of Rua da Santa Cruz, head southeast over the river and follow the road to the left. A Portuguese-speaking guide is usually on hand, and you can buy leaflets in English or French (€1).

MOSTEIRO DE SÃO JOÃO DE TAROUCA

The skeletal remains of Portugal's first Cistercian monastery, the **Mosteiro de São João de Tarouca** (☎ 254 678 766; admission free; ⏰ 10am-12.30pm & 2-6.30pm Wed-Sun, 2-5.30pm Tue Oct-Apr, 9.30am-12.30pm & 2-6pm Wed-Sun, 2.30-6pm May-Sep), founded in 1124, stand eerily in the wooded Barosa valley below the Serra de Leomil, 15km southeast of Lamego. It fell into ruin after religious orders were abolished in 1834.

Only the church, considerably altered in the 17th century, stands intact among the ghostly ruins of the monks' quarters. Its treasures include the imposing 14th-century tomb of the Conde de Barcelos (Dom Dinis' illegitimate son), carved with scenes from a boar hunt; gilded choir stalls; and 18th-century azulejos. The church's pride and joy is a luminous *São Pedro* painted by Gaspar Vaz, contemporary and colleague of Grão Vasco (p337).

A small exhibit in front of the ruins dishes out multilingual maps for €1.

From Lamego, Joalto/EAVT has eight services each weekday (fewer at weekends) to São João de Tarouca (€1.50).

PONTE DE UCANHA

Famous for its 12th-century fortified bridge, Ucanha is a lopsided little village 12km south of Lamego, off the N226 just north of Tarouca. A twisted lane leads down from the main road to the chunky **Ponte de Ucanha**, sitting squatly over the Rio Barosa. The blocky tower was added by the Abbot of Salzedas in the 15th century, probably as a tollgate: look for the stonemasons' initials visible on almost every block. The medieval stone washing enclosures under the bridge are no longer used, though village women still decorate the bridge with their laundry.

There are three Joalto/EAVT buses travelling each weekday between Lamego and Ucanha (€2).

MOSTEIRO DE SALZEDAS

Another picturesquely mouldering Cistercian monastery, the **Mosteiro de Salzedas** (☎ 254 670 627; admission free; ⏰ 9.30am-12.30pm & 2-5pm Wed-Sun, 2-5.30pm Tue) is about 3km further up the Barosa valley from Ucanha. This was one of the grandest monasteries in the land when it was built in 1168 with funds from Teresa Afonso, governess to Dom Afonso Henriques' five children. The enormous church, extensively remodelled in the 18th century, is black with decay and seems past hope of restoration, though students beaver away each summer, scraping away the moss and mopping up the puddles.

From Lamego, Joalto/EAVT runs three buses each weekday to Salzedas (€2).

PARQUE BIOLÓGICO DA SERRA DAS MEADAS

This **biological park** (☎ 254 609 600; parquebio@cm-lamego.pt; adult/child under 18/senior €1/0.50/0.50; ⏰ 10am-5pm Wed-Thu, 3-6pm Sat & Sun Jun-Sep, 2-5pm Sun Oct-May), in the hills 7km from Lamego, makes a good excursion if you've got kids and your own transport. You can see the local fauna, including deer and wild boar, at close quarters and stroll through designated walks.

PESO DA RÉGUA

pop 9500 / elevation 125m

Lamego's businesslike alter ego, the sun-bleached town of Régua abuts the Rio Douro at the western edge of the demarcated port-wine region. As the largest regional centre with river access, it grew in the 18th century into a major port-wine entrepot, though the unofficial title of 'capital of the trade' has now shifted 25km upstream to the prettier village of Pinhão.

Sat at the feet of a hulking IP3 bridge straddling the river valley, Régua remains an important transport junction, and as such, the town is commonly used as a base to visit the port-wine country, cruise the Rio Douro and ride the Corgo railway line to Vila Real.

However, the town itself offers little more than an opportunity to learn about (and drink your fill of) port wine. You can also take a stroll along the town's waterside, watch the local fishermen try their luck, and snap a shot or two of photogenic *barcos rabelos* dotting the river.

Orientation & Information

From the train station or adjacent bus stops bear right at Residencial Império into Rua dos Camilos. Carry on via Rua da Ferreirinha to reach the **turismo** (☎ 254 312 846; fax 254 322 271; Rua da Ferreirinha 505; 🕑 9am-12.30pm & 2-7pm Jul–mid-Sep, 9am-12.30pm & 2.30-6pm Mon-Fri mid-Sep–Jun), 1km west of the station. Old Régua is a steep climb above these streets. For the *cais fluvial* (river terminal) bear left at the Residencial Império.

Port-wine enthusiasts can collect an armful of brochures from the **Instituto do Vinho do Porto** (☎ 254 320 130; Rua dos Camilos 90; 🕑 8.30am-12.30pm & 2-6pm Mon-Fri). Or for a more hands-on approach, get drinking at the **Solar do Vinho do Porto** (☎ 254 320 960; Rua da Ferreirinha), a new branch of the famous Porto drinking den.

Sights & Activities

QUINTA DO CASTELINHO

If you haven't already overdosed on port wines, this **lodge** (☎ 254 320 262; 🕑 9am-7pm daily Jun-Sep, 9am-6pm Mon-Fri Feb-May & Oct-Dec, closed Jan) is the nearest to Régua, the easiest to visit and offers free tours and tastings. It also has a very good restaurant that is open Tuesday to Sunday. To reach the lodge from the train station, go 600m east on the Vila Real road, turn left and continue for 400m.

TRAIN TRIPS & RIVER CRUISES

Several companies market identical journeys along various stretches of the Rio Douro, all from or via Peso da Régua. There is a selection of popular choices:

Porto-Barca de Alva-Porto (38 hours, from €225) Weekend; boat, train and hotel.
Porto-Pinhão-Porto (11 hours, from €80) Saturday; boat and train.
Porto-Régua-Porto (11 hours, from €73) Saturday or Sunday; boat and bus/train.
Régua-Pinhão-Régua (4 hours, with/without lunch about €45/30) Saturday or Sunday; boat.
Régua-Porto (10 hours, €67) Sunday; boat.

If you're coming from Porto, visit Porto Tours (p357) for advice. There are three big operators:

Barcadouro (☎ 223 722 415; www.barcadouro.com in Portuguese)
Endouro Turismo (☎ 222 084 161; www.endouroturismo.pt)
Rota do Douro (☎ 223 759 042; www.rotadodouro.com)

Also on offer from May to October, if there are enough passengers, are Saturday-only journeys in restored steam trains along the beautiful Linha do Douro line. Trips cost €30, last about four hours and leave around 3.35pm. Telephone reservations are recommended. For more information call **UVIR** (☎ 211 021 129; lvviegas@mail.cp.pt).

Sleeping

There's little of character in town. *Residenciais* with bland but comfortable rooms include the pleasant **Residencial Império** (☎ 254 320 120; fax 254 321 457; Rua José Vasques Osório 8; d with breakfast €40; P ❄), in the high-rise just west of the train station, and plain **Don Quixote** (☎ 254 321 151; fax 254 322 802; 1st fl, Avenida Sacadura Cabral 1; d with breakfast €32.50; P ❄), 800m west of the turismo.

Eating

Restaurante O Maleiro (☎ 254 313 684; Rua dos Camilos; mains €6-12; 🕑 lunch & dinner) Situated opposite the post office, this brisk but friendly place offers a good atmosphere and meaty Portuguese standards prepared with style.

Restaurante Cacho d'Oiro (☎ 254 321 455; Rua Branca Martinho; mains €8-12; 🕑 lunch & dinner; P) This large cottage-restaurant, 150m west of the turismo, offers a wider choice and a more upmarket atmosphere than Maleiro. Splurge on *cabrito no churrasco* (grilled kid) for €12.

Getting There & Away

Joalto buses run hourly to/from Lamego (€1.60, 20 minutes); Guedes also makes the run several times a day. AV Tâmega runs to Vila Real (€2.40, 40 minutes) about hourly on weekdays and thrice daily at weekends, and Rodonorte goes four times each weekday.

There are 12 trains daily from Porto (€6.50, 2½ hours); eight go up the valley to Pinhão (€1.30, 25 minutes, nine daily) and Tua (p381). Five trains depart daily heading to Vila Real (€1.70, 55 minutes) on the narrow-gauge Corgo line.

THE ALTO DOURO

The Alto Douro (upper Douro) east of Peso da Régua is a harsh, hot landscape heavily refashioned by two millennia of pumping out wine. Terraced vineyards wrap around every precipitous, crew-cut hillside, and whitewashed port-wine *quintas* (estates) dot the valley.

Villages are small and architectural monuments rare. It's worth the trip for the panoramas, the port wine and the ride itself (scenic by train or boat): take it from Unesco, which in 2001 designated the entire Alto Douro wine-growing region a Unesco World Heritage site.

Wine isn't the only local product on offer: signs at every second gate advertise olives and honey, cheaper and better than at any tourist shop. Port-wine *quintas* offer some of the finest rural accommodation, though it gets scarce in late September and early October during the *vindima* (grape harvest).

Though not actually part of Douro province, this part of the Douro valley is included here because it's an integral part of the region and because the easiest way to get here is from Porto.

Daily trains run from Porto, with a change at Régua, up to Pinhão, Tua and Pocinho. Travellers with their own set of wheels can take the river-hugging N222 from Régua to Pinhão, beyond which the roads climb in and out of the valley. For information on river cruises, see p380.

Pinhão

pop 300 / elevation 120m

Considered the world centre of quality port-wine production, unassuming little Pinhão sits quietly 25km upriver from Peso da Régua. Encircled by hillside vineyards that seem almost to have been sewn with needle and thread rather than planted, the little village is dominated by port-wine lodges and their competing signs; even the train station has azulejos depicting the wine harvest. The town is of little interest, though you can chill out in one of the area's splendid *quintas*.

There are also several fine day-trip possibilities for itchy feet, especially by train (right).

ORIENTATION & INFORMATION

The **turismo** (☎ 254 731 932; Largo do Estação; ⌚ 10am-noon & 2-6pm Tue-Sun) is at the right-hand end of the **train station** (☎ 254 731 878). A bank with an ATM is a few minutes' walk left from the station exit.

SIGHTS & ACTIVITIES

Train Trips

The most beautiful of Portugal's narrow-gauge lines is the Linha da Tua, running from the sun-blasted backwater of Tua (13km upriver) for 52km up the Tua valley to the pretty market town of Mirandela (p445). The two-hour Pinhão–Mirandela journey (€9 return, change at Tua) is feasible as a day trip, departing about 10.30am and leaving Mirandela about 6pm.

Alternatively, take the mainline train for another hour, past dams and vineyards, to the end of the line at Pocinho (single/return €2.20/4.40), visiting the Pocinho dam and returning the same day, or travelling on up to Vila Nova de Foz Côa (p382).

Wine Tasting

Ask the tourist office about lodges open to tours and tastings. A 12km digression northeast up the N322-3 to Favaios will also reward you with the discovery of a little-known muscatel wine, one of only two produced in Portugal (the other comes from Setúbal).

SLEEPING & EATING

Pinhão isn't cheap, but it does boast some fabulous mansions and *quintas*.

Residencial Douro (☎/fax 254 732 404; Largo do Estação; d with breakfast €50; ✖) Try not to hold the price against this cheery guesthouse opposite the train station: it is one of the cheapest spots in town and has some large rooms facing a quiet rear courtyard, a sunny restaurant and a mini terrace covered with flowering vines.

Quinta de la Rosa (☎ 254 732 254; www.quintadelarosa.com; d from €75; ✖ 🏊) A lovely hillside *quinta* amid furrowed vineyards just above the river 2km west of Pinhão. Be sure to ask for a taste of its own port. Book well ahead.

Vintage House (☎ 254 730 230; www.hotelvintagehouse.com in Portuguese; s/d with breakfast €149/163; P ✖ 🏊) Jumping to the top of the luxury ladder, there's this oh-so-refined mansion perched by the river in central Pinhão. Its tranquil patio enjoys unbeatable sunset views of the river and vineyard-smothered hills. The hotel sits next to the train station, between it and the river.

Pousada de Barão de Forrester (☎ 259 959 215; recepcao.barao@pousadas.pt; d with breakfast €134; P) Alternatively, there's a rather grand Pousada de Portugal property at Alijó, 15km northeast of Pinhão.

There are two good riverside restaurant-bars:

Restaurante Veladouro (☎ 254 731 794; Mon-Sat) The closer of the two to town, this is a quaint schist building 200m from the station: turn left along the main road for 150m then left again under a railway bridge, and right at the river.

Restaurante Cais da Foz (9am-midnight) A short hop over a footbridge from Veladouro, this is another attractive riverside spot smothered in flowering vines.

Wednesday heralds a food market in the town centre.

GETTING THERE & AWAY

Regional trains run from Peso da Régua (€1.30, 25 minutes, nine daily). From Porto you must change at Régua; the quickest links (€7.50, 2½ hours, four daily) are by IC train as far as Régua.

VILA NOVA DE FOZ CÔA

pop 2800 / elevation 420m

Once remote, this whitewashed little town in the *terra quente* (hot country) of the upper Douro has been put firmly on the map with the discovery in the 1990s of thousands of mysterious Palaeolithic rock engravings – of worldwide significance – in the nearby Rio Côa valley.

The region also has some lesser historical and archaeological drawcards, and the climate is startlingly Mediterranean if you've just come from the mountains. If you come in spring, you'll also be treated to an amazing floral display as the surrounding hillsides sport the highest density of flowering almond trees in Portugal.

BLOOMING GOOD RIDE

When the almond trees are in bloom (late February to mid-March), the upper Douro valley is lovelier than ever. **Caminhos de Ferro Portugueses** (CP; ☎ 808 208 208) will take you up for a look, by special train plus coach, on a long-weekend day trip from Porto's São Bento station.

Trains chug to Freixo de Numão or Pocinho, coaches shuttle you around southern Trás-os-Montes and/or northern Beira Alta and you return by train. Tickets cost €26/19 for an adult/child under 13.

All depends, of course, on the timely arrival of the blossoms. Tickets are sold at São Bento station from the last week in January. For more information contact CP.

Orientation

Long-distance coaches stop at the bus station, from where it's 150m south to a petrol station and the turismo at Avenida Gago Coutinho. From here the town stretches eastwards along Avenida Gago Coutinho, pedestrianised Rua Dr Juiz Moutinho de Andrade and Rua Dr Júlio de Moura to the old town's centre, Praça do Município. The train station is at Pocinho, 7km north.

Information

There are ATMs outside the park office and below Residencial Marina (p384).

Espaço Internet (☎ 279 760 400; Avenida Gago Coutinho; 10am-9pm Mon-Fri, 2-6pm Sat) Free Internet access. It's behind the tourist office.

Lavandaria Alva Wipp (☎ 279 765 317; Rua de São Antonio 35; €3 per kilo; Mon-Sat) On a small street off the pedestrian boulevard.

Municipal Turismo (☎ 279 765 243; Avenida Gago Coutinho; 9am-12.30pm & 2-5.30pm) Opposite Albergaria Foz Côa.

Parque Arqueológico Office (☎ 279 768 260; www.ipa.min-cultura.pt/coa; Avenida Gago Coutinho 19A; 9am-12.30pm & 2-5.30pm) Staff here are kept busy shuttling visitors out to the rock engravings.

Police station (☎ 279 762 316; Rua Dr José Augusto Saraiva de Aguilar) A block behind the park office.

Post office (☎ 279 768 070; Avenida Dr Artur de Aguilar 6; 9am-12.30pm & 2-5.30pm Mon-Fri) Three blocks north of the park office via Largo do Rossio.

Sights & Activities

PARQUE ARQUEOLÓGICO VALE DO CÔA

Most visitors to Vila Nova da Foz Côa come for one reason: to see its world-famous gallery of rock art – see 'Rescuing Portugal's Rock Art', p383.

Although the park is an active research zone, three sites are open to visitors – Canada do Inferno from the **park office** (daily, trips Tue-Sun) in Vila Nova de Foz Côa, Ribeira de Piscos from the **Muxagata visitor centre** (☎ 279 764 298; Tue-Sun) on the western side of the valley and Penascosa from the **Castelo Melhor visitor centre** (☎ 279 713 344; Tue-Sun) on the eastern side. While Castelo Melhor has some of the most significant etchings, Canada do Inferno – which sits by the half-constructed dam – is the ideal place to understand just how close these aeons-old drawings came to disappearing.

There is also a private site (owned by the Ramos Pinto port-wine lodge) at Quinta da Ervamoira, with vineyards, wine tasting and a small museum featuring Roman and medieval artefacts. This can be included in some tours.

Visitors can front up at one of the visitor centres, from where they're taken, eight at a time in the park's own 4WDs, for a guided tour of one of the sites (one and a half hours at Canada do Inferno and Penascosa, two and a half hours at Ribeira de Piscos). Visitors with mountain bikes may go on guided bike tours in similar-sized groups. The price in either case is €5 per person.

Visitors numbers are strictly regulated, so from July to September, you'll need to book a tour well in advance or you may miss out. Also book a few weeks ahead for bicycle trips. You can make bookings through the park office (p382). Several private tour operators include park trips in their own programmes; local operators include **Ravinas do Côa** (☎ 279 762 832, 966 746 423; www.ravinasdocoa.lda.pt; Bairro Flor da Rosa 34, Vila Nova de Foz Côa) and **Impactus** (☎ 279 713 427, 962 838 261; www.impactus.pt in Portuguese; Rua da Igreja 2, Castelo Melhor).

OLD TOWN

Take a leisurely stroll down to Praça do Município to see the impressive granite *pelourinho* topped by an armillary sphere, and the elaborately carved portal of the Manueline-style parish church. Inside, the building is more befit to a banqueting hall than a church, with its chandeliers and painted ceiling. Just east off the square is the tiny Capela de Santa Quitéria, which was once the town's synagogue.

RESCUING PORTUGAL'S ROCK ART

An extraordinary Stone Age art gallery with thousands of rock engravings dating back tens of thousands of years is scattered through the rugged valley of the Rio Côa, 15km from the Spanish frontier. Yet two decades ago nobody knew they were there.

A 1989 environmental study for a hydroelectric dam that would flood the valley first revealed an array of ancient sites. Yet, it wasn't until 1992, after construction was underway, that the real discoveries began. Clusters of petroglyphs (rock engravings), mostly dating from the Upper Palaeolithic period (10,000 to 40,000 years ago), were found by rescue archaeologists. Once these finds were publicised, local people joined the search and the inventory snowballed.

Battle commenced between Electricidade de Portugal (EDP) and archaeologists who insisted the engravings were of worldwide importance. But only after an international campaign was launched was the half-built dam abandoned and the site declared a national monument. In 1998 those stubborn archaeologists got their ultimate reward when the valley was designated a Unesco World Heritage site.

Today the park encompasses the largest known array of open-air Palaeolithic art in the world. Several thousand engravings are scattered for 17km along the Côa and tributary valleys. You'll see plenty of stylised horses, aurochs (extinct ancestors of domesticated cattle) and long-horned ibex (extinct wild goat); and some later petroglyphs depict human figures too.

The pictures pose many fascinating puzzles. Some are so cluttered that it can be difficult to distinguish between the animals – yet the overlapping layers were often added many thousands of years after the first strokes were applied: a kind of Palaeolithic etch-a-sketch that generations of hunters used and reused, disregarding or adding to the work of their forebears.

Other animals are given several heads, while the very finest of drawings are so thinly drawn that they have to be studied in artificial light to be seen at all.

Put all these pieces of the puzzle together, and it adds up to one of the most dramatic archaeological discoveries in decades.

For more information, pick up the multilingual book (€10.50) sold at the ticket offices.

OTHER ATTRACTIONS

Archaeological finds from the Stone Age to the 18th century have been uncovered in the region around Freixo de Numão, 12km west of Vila Nova de Foz Côa. A good little display can be viewed at Freixo de Numão, in the **Museu da Casa Grande** (☎ 279 789 117; fax 279 789 573; adult/child under 12/youth under 26 €1.50/0.75/1; ⏰ 9am-noon & 2-6pm Tue-Sun), a baroque townhouse with Roman foundations. Some English and French are spoken here.

Free brochures provide for a **self-guided archaeological tour** of the region. Free with entrance is a leaflet on the museum and the rich Neolithic/Roman/medieval site at Prazo, about 3km west of Freixo de Numão. Guided tours are available by arrangement with the museum.

Sleeping

The large orange-brick **pousada da juventude** (☎ 279 768 190; fozcoa@movijovem.pt; Caminho Vicinal, Currauteles No 5; dm €12.50, d with toilet €35; Ⓟ) here is an 800m walk north from the town centre, or 1.4km by road. It's worth the walk, boasting a wide patio with sweeping views and a games room.

A few homes and cafés in the area around Largo do Tabulado advertise *quartos*.

Two neighbouring *residenciais* near the petrol station are the snug but gracious **Marina** (☎ 279 762 112; Avenida Gago Coutinho 2-4; d €25), with charming hosts and a front porch to kick back, and the brusque **Avenida** (☎/fax 279 762 175; Avenida Gago Coutinho 10; d €30), with larger rooms. Rooms at both have a shower and toilet; neither offers breakfast.

Albergaria Vale do Côa (☎ 279 760 010; www.albergariavaledocoa.net in Portuguese; Avenida Cidade Nova 1A; d €45; Ⓟ ❄) The only whiff of luxury in town is at this modern hotel opposite the tourist office. Some English spoken.

Eating

Blue '*restaurante*' signs pop up all around town, though the nondescript eating venues that they point to are all much of a muchness. Several *pastelarias* (pastry or cake shops) along Rua Dr Juiz Moutinho de Andrade open by 8am for breakfast.

Snack Bar-Restaurante A Marisqueira (☎ 279 762 187; Rua Dr Juiz Moutinho de Andrade; daily specials under €5; ⏰ lunch & dinner) On a sunny pedestrian boulevard, plain little A Marisqueira has a small menu of specials, and a few seafood dishes to justify its name.

There are several well-stocked fruit-and-vegetable shops on the little squares at either end of Rua Dr Juiz Moutinho de Andrade, including **A Fidalguinha Minimercado** (☎ 279 764 396; Rua Dr Juiz Montinho 11; ⏰ Mon-Sat).

Getting There & Away

Rede Expressos and Joalto buses each visit daily from Bragança (€6, 1¾ hours). Rede Expressos buses come once daily from Miranda (€5.75, 2½ hours) and four times daily via Trancoso (€4) from Viseu (€8.75, 1¾ hours).

Four daily trains run to Pocinho, at the end of the Douro valley line, from Porto (€7.50, four hours) and Peso da Régua (€3.50) through Pinhão (€2.20). A taxi between Pocinho and Vila Nova de Foz Côa costs about €5, and there are infrequent buses too (€1.15, 10 minutes).

Getting Around

There are no direct buses to Muxagata or Quinta da Ervamoira. However, a twice-daily bus passes the outskirts of Castelo Melhor (€1.40, 15 minutes), from where you can easily walk to the visitor centre. The first outward bus leaves the Foz Côa bus station at 11.45am and the last bus returns at about 5.45pm, Monday to Friday only.

The Minho

CONTENTS

It's hard to rush the Minho – the sleepy pace of the region is contagious and its distractions numerous. Tucked under the hem of Spanish Galicia, this northwestern corner of Portugal is renowned for its rich traditions, vibrant festivals and lush countryside.

But it hasn't always been such a scene of rural tranquillity. Two millennia ago, Celtiberians battled the might of Rome from their last strongholds in the Minho's hills. This too is the land that launched the bloody Reconquista against the Moors, where the kingdom of Portugal was first declared. Centuries later, the region's northern reaches resisted their Spanish neighbours.

However, after the blood soaked away and the nation made its peace with Spain, much of the Minho relaxed back into pastoral contentment. Here you'll find Portugal's liveliest traditions – vibrant country markets and a calendar full of festivals and *romarias* (religious pilgrimages). Religion holds an especially strong place in daily Minho life, and Easter in Braga, Portugal's ecclesiastical capital, is an astonishing combination of fervour and merrymaking.

The region's most popular destinations – Braga, Barcelos and Guimarães – all lie within easy reach of one another in southern Minho. Lashed by the Atlantic, the coastal region has fewer attractions, though the seafront north of the cultured resort of Viana do Castelo has good beaches and plenty of solitude.

But the region's main pull is inland, along the Rio Minho and the dreamy Rio Lima. Rural life here remains stubbornly poor and old-fashioned, with many farmers still using lyre-horned oxen to pull their carts and plough fields. In the northeastern hills, Portugal's only national park, the Parque Nacional da Peneda-Gerês is one of the best escapes in the country and proffers up a cornucopia of outdoor sports – not to mention a dense concentration of converted farmhouses for family and romantic getaways.

HIGHLIGHTS

- **Head for the Hills**
  Parque Nacional da Peneda-Gerês (p417)
- **Stairway to Heaven**
  Hillside climb to Bom Jesus do Monte (p393)
- **Bargain Buys**
  Barcelos' vast weekly market (p394)
- **Turn Back Time**
  Celtic hill settlement Citânia de Briteiros (p402)
- **Festival Frolics**
  Romaria de Nossa Senhora d'Agonia or Carnaval in seaside Viana do Castelo (p403)

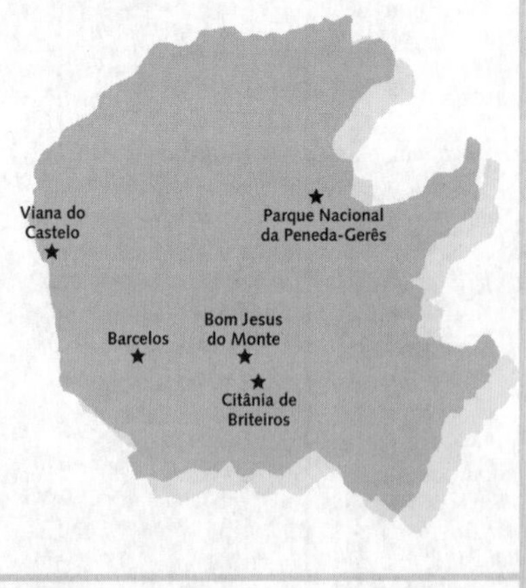

- POPULATION: 1,434,163
- AREA: 5265 SQ KM

SOUTHERN MINHO

BRAGA

pop 110,000 / elevation 200m

Portugal's spiritual heart, the proud city of Braga is choc-a-block with religious splendour. The clamorous bells of at least 35 churches ensure that the city chimes almost constantly wherever you are. And the hand of God also extends beyond the city to the area's biggest attraction, Bom Jesus do Monte, just to the east (p393).

Braga's Christian pedigree dates way back to the 6th century and from the 11th to the 18th centuries this was the seat of the archbishop, considered Primate of All Spain, or at any rate Primate of Portugal (these days the archbishop ministers as far south as Coimbra). It's an impressive record on paper, though only Braga's ancient cathedral has survived the wholesale baroque renovations that smothered the other churches in the 18th century.

But despite its ecclesiastical clout, don't come expecting a dour or overly pious city: the students of the Universidade do Minho add youthful leavening and the city's central square is one of the liveliest in northern Portugal.

History

Braga is one of Portugal's oldest settlements. A Celtic tribe first founded it, then in about 250 BC the Romans muscled in, named it Bracara Augusta and made it capital of their province Gallaecia – stretching all the way up into Spain. Braga's position at the intersection of five Roman roads helped it swell and grow fat on trade.

Braga fell to the Suevi around AD 410, and was sacked by the Visigoths 60 years later. The Visigoths' conversion to Christianity and the founding of an archbishopric in the following century put the town atop the Iberian Peninsula's ecclesiastical pecking order.

The Moors moved in around 715, sparking a long-running tug-of-war. The mounting Reconquista won the city back in 740, control returned to the southern invaders in 985 but swung back in the Christians' favour in 1040 thanks to the sweat of Fernando I, king of Castile and León. Fernando's son Alfonso VI courted help from ruthless European crusaders, and to one, Henri of Burgundy (Dom Henrique), he gave his daughter Teresa in marriage, throwing in Braga as dowry. From this marriage came Afonso Henriques, the first king of Portugal.

The archbishopric was restored in 1070, though prelates bickered with their Spanish counterparts for the next five centuries over who was Primate of All Spain. The pope finally ruled in Braga's favour. The city's subsequent prosperity was only curtailed in the 18th century, when a newly anointed Lisbon archdiocese stole its thunder.

It was from conservative Braga that the 1926 coup was launched, putting António de Oliveira Salazar in power and introducing Portugal to half a century of dictatorship.

Orientation

Praça da República is a 500m walk south of the bus station, or 1.1km east from the train station. The *praça* and the park stretching eastwards from it form the heart of Braga. The road that passes on its two long sides are together usually called Avenida Central (formerly Avenida dos Combatentes). Through traffic has been cleverly routed underground here, though this hardly alters central Braga's dire parking situation.

Information

There are banks with currency exchange desks and ATMs all along Avenida da Liberdade, Rua dos Capelistas and elsewhere in the centre. You will find that many of the *tabacarias* (tobacconists-cum-newsagents), eg by Café Vianna and outside the cathedral's west portal, stock foreign-language periodicals.

BOOKSHOPS

Livraria Bertrand (☎ 253 218 115; Rua Dom Diogo de Sousa 129-33) Limited selection of maps, guides and English-language material.

EMERGENCY & MEDICAL SERVICES

Hospital de São Marcos (☎ 253 209 000; São Lazaro) A block west of Avenida da Liberdade.

Police station (☎ 253 200 420; Rua dos Falcões)

INTERNET ACCESS

Café James Dean (Rua Santo André 85; per hr €2.40; 8am-2am Mon-Sat, 10am-midnight Sun) When that email just can't wait: there's weekend and evening access here.

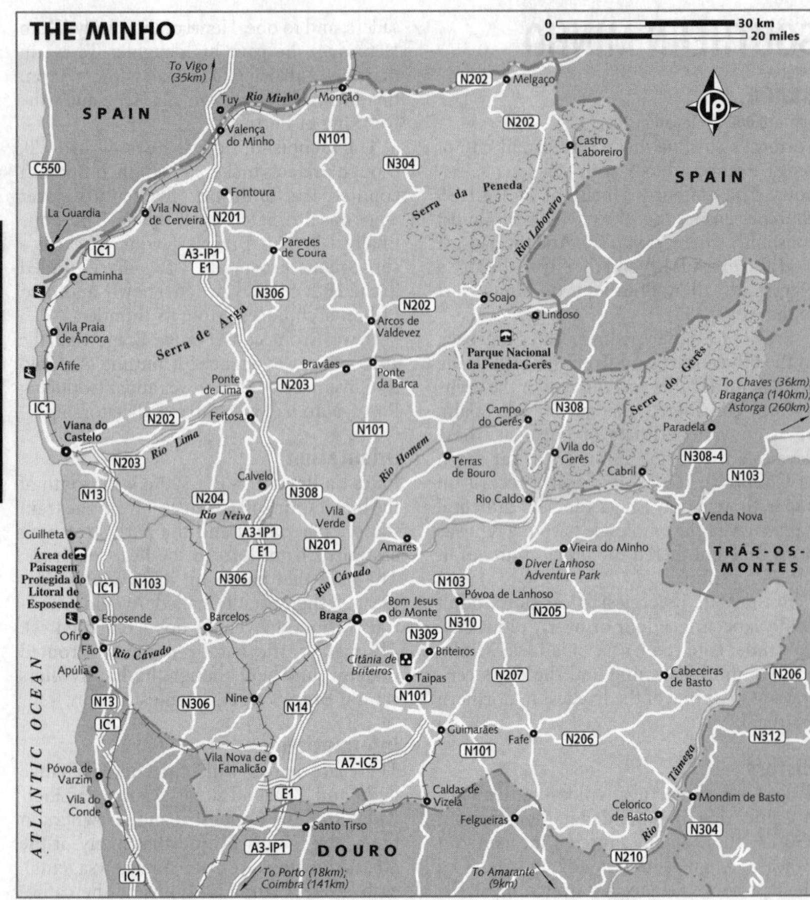

Casa da Juventude (Instituto Português da Juventude; ☎ 253 204 250; Rua de Santa Margarida; 🕒 9am-6.30pm Mon-Fri) At the southern end of the *pousada da juventude* (youth hostel), the hostel offers free Internet access.

Espaço Internet (☎ 253 267 484; Praça Conde de Agrolongo 177; 🕒 9am-7.30pm Mon-Fri, 9am-1pm Sat) More free access.

Videoteca Municipal (☎ 253 267 793; Rua do Raio; 🕒 9.30am-12.30pm & 2-6pm Mon-Sat) Free 30-minute access is available at this video archive.

LAUNDRY

Lavandaria 5 á Sec (Largo de Santa Cruz 35; per kilo €3; 🕒 9am-1.30pm & 3-8pm Mon-Fri, 9am-2pm Sat)

Lavandaria Confiança (☎ 253 216 907; Rua Dom Diogo de Sousa 46; per kilo €2.50; 🕒 9am-1.30pm & 3-8pm Mon-Fri, 9am-2pm Sat)

POST

Post office (☎ 253 606 952; Rua Gonçalo Sampaio; 🕒 8.30am-6pm Mon-Fri, 9am-12.30pm Sat) Just off Avenida da Liberdade.

TOURIST INFORMATION

Parque Nacional da Peneda-Gerês (☎ 253 203 480; pnpg@icn.pt; Quinta das Parretas; 🕒 9am-12.50pm & 2-5.30pm Mon-Fri) The park headquarters are 800m west of the town centre and reached via a tunnel under busy Avenida António Macedo.

Turismo (☎ 253 262 550; turismo@cm-braga.pt; Praça da República; 🕒 9am-7pm Mon-Fri, 9am-12.30pm & 2pm-5.30pm Sat year-round, also 9am-12.30pm & 2pm-5.30pm Sun Aug) Braga's good tourist office is in an Art Deco–style building facing the fountain. Here you'll find a free monthly what's-on brochure, *Braga Cultural*.

TRAVEL AGENCIES

AVIC (☎ 253 203 910; agbraga@avic.pt; Rua Gabriel Pereira de Castro 28; 🕑 Mon-Fri) A bus line and travel agency.

Tagus (☎ 253 215 144; Praça do Município 7; 🕑 Mon-Fri) Sells budget trips and ISIC cards.

UNIVERSITIES

Universidade do Minho (☎ 253 601 109; www.uminho.pt) Founded here in 1973. Operates from part of the Antigo Paço Episcopal on Largo do Paço, with faculties along Rua do Castelo and Rua Abade Loureira.

Sights

PRAÇA DA REPÚBLICA

A wonderful spot for bench-sitting or coffee-drinking in the sun, this broad **plaza** is the ideal place to start or finish your day. An especially mellow atmosphere descends in the evening, when coloured lights spring up and people of all ages congregate to enjoy the night air.

On the western side are two of Portugal's best venues for people-watching, Café Vianna and Café Astória, both exuding a refined *fin-de-siècle* atmosphere. And on the sprawling area in front of the cafés lies an enormous computer-controlled fountain that sprays unsuspecting bypassers with a refreshing film of water – to the delight of waiting and watching coffee-drinkers.

The square, crenellated tower behind the cafés is the **Torre de Menagem** (castle keep; Largo Terreiro do Castelo), which is all that survives of a fortified palace built in 1738.

SÉ

Braga's extraordinary **cathedral** (☎ 253 263 317; Rua Dom Diogo de Sousa; admission free; 🕑 8.30am-6.30pm May-Oct, 8.30am-5.30pm Nov-Apr) is the oldest in Portugal. It was begun way back when the archdiocese was restored in 1070 and completed in the following century. It is a rambling complex of chapels and little rooms in a jumble of architectural styles that may leave you wondering where to start.

Architectural buffs could spend half a day happily probing and distinguishing the Romanesque bits from the Gothic attachments and baroque frills. The original Romanesque style is the most interesting and survives in the cathedral's overall shape, the southern entrance and the marvellous west portal, which is carved with scenes from the medieval legend of Reynard the Fox (now sheltered inside a Gothic porch).

The most appealing external features are the filigree Manueline towers and roof. In a niche on the east wall is the lovely *Nossa Senhora do Leite* of the Virgin suckling Christ, thought to be by the 16th-century expatriate French sculptor Nicolas Chanterène.

You can enter the cathedral through the west portal, or via a courtyard and cloister lined with Gothic chapels on the north side. The church itself has a fine Manueline carved altarpiece, a tall chapel with *azulejos* (hand-painted tiles), telling the story of Braga's first bishop, and fantastic twin baroque organs held up by formidable satyrs and mermen.

To go upstairs, you must join a snail's-pace tour of the **treasury** (admission choir, chapels & treasury adult/child under 12 €2/free; 🕑 8.30am-6.30pm) – not surprisingly, a tremendous treasure-trove of ecclesiastical booty, including an iron cross that was used in 1500 to celebrate the very first Mass in Brazil. More quirkier highlights are a statue of the patron saint of shoemakers, and one of the more diminutive archbishop's 10cm high-heeled shoes!

This tour will eventually lead you to the choir stalls and an up-close look at the mesmerising organs: this alone is worth the wait. But if you'd rather skip the full tour, ask the guide to start here. Then you'll be led downstairs and into the cathedral's showpiece **Capela dos Reis** (Kings' Chapel), home to the tombs of Henri of Burgundy and Dona Teresa, parents of the first king of Portugal, Afonso Henriques.

Remember everybody else will be heading for the cathedral too, so get here early.

ANTIGO PAÇO EPISCOPAL & AROUND

Facing the cathedral is the severe **Antigo Paço Episcopal** (Archbishop's Palace; admission free; 🕑 9am-12.30pm & 2pm-7.30pm Mon-Fri). Begun in the 14th century and enlarged in the 17th and 18th centuries, it's now home to university offices and the **municipal library**. A heavily carved, painted and gilded ceiling looks down on the library's computer room; this and the azulejos lining the main stairway are well worth a peek.

Outside the spiky-topped north wing is the 17th-century **Jardim de Santa Bárbara**, with narrow paths picking their way through a sea of flowers and topiary. On sunny days, the adjacent pedestrianised streets Rua Justino Cruz and Rua Francisco Sanches fill with buskers and café tables.

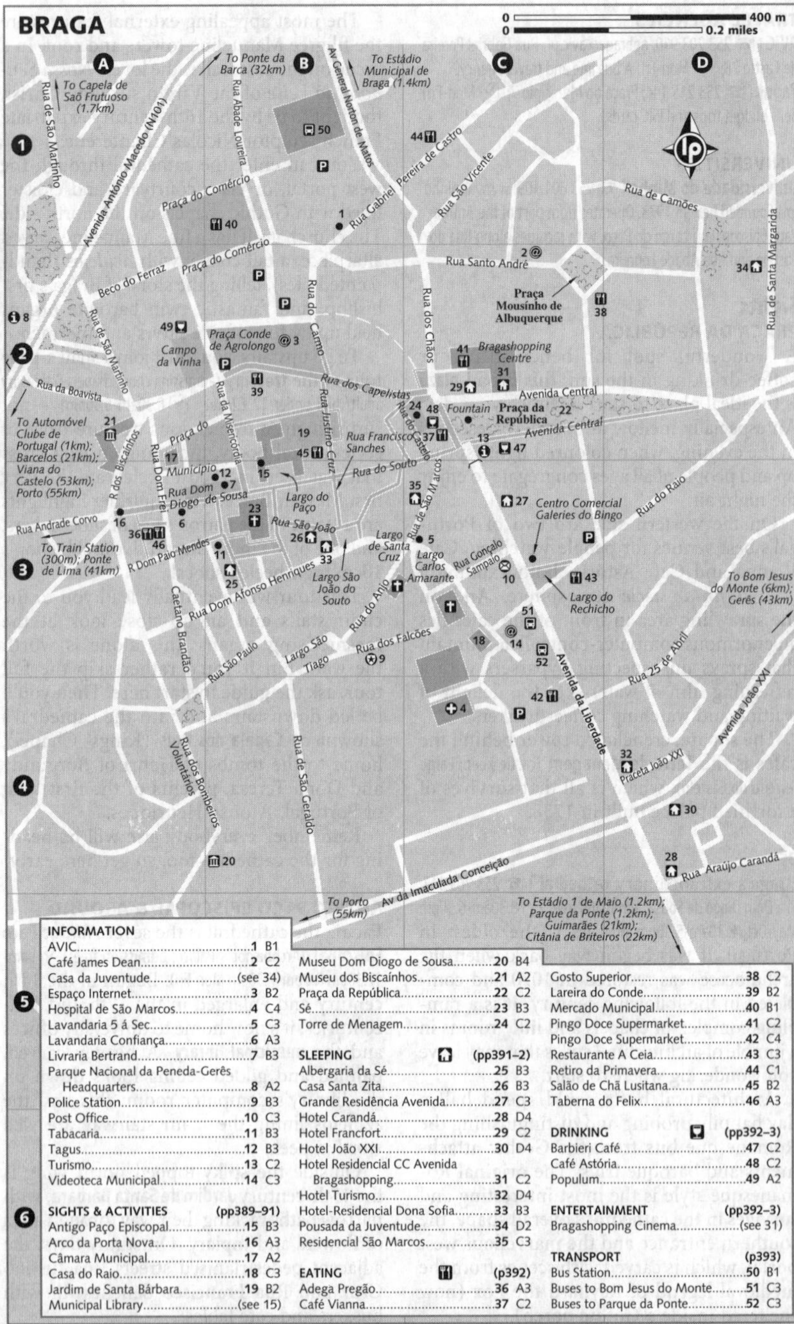
BRAGA
0 400 m
0 0.2 miles
A
B
C
D
1
2
3
4
5
6
To Ponte da Barca (32km)
To Estádio Municipal de Braga (1.4km)
To Capela de São Frutuoso (1.7km)
Rua de São Martinho
Avenida António Macedo (N101)
Rua Abade Loureira
Av General Norton de Matos
Rua Gabriel Pereira de Castro
Rua São Vicente
Rua de Camões
Praça do Comércio
Rua Santo André
Rua de Santa Margarida
Beco do Ferraz
Rua do Carmo
Rua dos Chãos
Praça Mousinho de Albuquerque
Praça Conde de Agrolongo
Campo da Vinha
Bragashopping Centre
Rua da Boavista
Rua dos Capelistas
Avenida Central
Fountain
Praça da República
To Automóvel Clube de Portugal (1km); Barcelos (21km); Viana do Castelo (53km); Porto (55km)
Praça do Município
Rua da Misericórdia
Rua Justino Cruz
Rua do Castelo
Rua Francisco Sanches
R dos Biscainhos
Rua Dom Frei
Rua Dom Diogo de Sousa
Rua do Souto
Largo do Paço
Rua de São Marcos
Rua do Raio
Centro Comercial Galeries do Bingo
Rua Andrade Corvo
Rua São João
To Train Station (300m); Ponte de Lima (41km)
R Dom Paio Mendes
Largo de Santa Cruz
Largo Carlos Amarante
Rua Gonçalo Sampaio
Largo São João do Souto
Rua Dom Afonso Henriques
Caetano Brandão
Largo do Rechicho
To Bom Jesus do Monte (6km); Gerês (43km)
Rua do Anjo
Rua dos Falcões
Largo São Tiago
Rua São Paulo
Rua 25 de Abril
Avenida João XXI
Avenida da Liberdade
Rua dos Bombeiros Voluntários
Rua de São Geraldo
Praceta João XXI
Rua Araújo Carandá
Av da Imaculada Conceição
To Porto (55km)
To Estádio 1 de Maio (1.2km); Parque da Ponte (1.2km); Guimarães (21km); Citânia de Briteiros (22km)
INFORMATION
AVIC 1 B1
Café James Dean 2 C2
Casa da Juventude (see 34)
Espaço Internet 3 B2
Hospital de São Marcos 4 C4
Lavandaria 5 á Sec 5 C3
Lavandaria Confiança 6 A3
Livraria Bertrand 7 B3
Parque Nacional da Peneda-Gerês Headquarters 8 A2
Police Station 9 B3
Post Office 10 C3
Tabacaria 11 B3
Tagus 12 B3
Turismo 13 C2
Videoteca Municipal 14 C3
SIGHTS & ACTIVITIES (pp389–91)
Antigo Paço Episcopal 15 B3
Arco da Porta Nova 16 A3
Câmara Municipal 17 A2
Casa do Raio 18 C3
Jardim de Santa Bárbara 19 B2
Municipal Library (see 15)
Museu Dom Diogo de Sousa 20 B4
Museu dos Biscaínhos 21 A2
Praça da República 22 C2
Sé 23 B3
Torre de Menagem 24 C2
SLEEPING (pp391–2)
Albergaria da Sé 25 B3
Casa Santa Zita 26 B3
Grande Residência Avenida 27 C3
Hotel Carandá 28 D4
Hotel Francfort 29 C2
Hotel João XXI 30 D4
Hotel Residencial CC Avenida Bragashopping 31 C2
Hotel Turismo 32 D4
Hotel-Residencial Dona Sofia 33 B3
Pousada da Juventude 34 D2
Residencial São Marcos 35 C3
EATING (p392)
Adega Pregão 36 A3
Café Vianna 37 C2
Gosto Superior 38 C2
Lareira do Conde 39 B2
Mercado Municipal 40 B1
Pingo Doce Supermarket 41 C2
Pingo Doce Supermarket 42 C4
Restaurante A Ceia 43 C3
Retiro da Primavera 44 C1
Salão de Chã Lusitana 45 B2
Taberna do Felix 46 A3
DRINKING (pp392–3)
Barbieri Café 47 C2
Café Astória 48 C2
Populum 49 A2
ENTERTAINMENT (pp392–3)
Bragashopping Cinema (see 31)
TRANSPORT (p393)
Bus Station 50 B1
Buses to Bom Jesus do Monte 51 C3
Buses to Parque da Ponte 52 C3

At the western end of neighbouring Praça do Município, Braga's **câmara municipal** (town hall) sports one of Portugal's finest baroque façades, designed by André Soares da Silva. A more extrovert Soares work is the **Casa do Raio** (Casa do Mexicano; Rua do Raio), its rococo face covered in azulejos.

ARCO DA PORTA NOVA

Lit like a Christmas tree at night, this puny 18th-century **arch**, west of the old centre on Rua Dom Diogo de Sousa, was for some time the city's main gate. It bears the ostentatious coat of arms of the archbishop who commissioned it, Dom José de Bragança.

MUSEU DOS BISCAÍNHOS

An 18th-century aristocrat's palace is now home to the enthusiastic **municipal museum** (☎ 253 204 650; Rua dos Biscaínhos; adult/youth 14-25/senior/child under 14 €2/1/1/free, 10am-2pm Sun free; 🕒 10am-12.15pm & 2-5.30pm Tue-Sun), with a nice collection of Roman relics and 17th- to 19th-century pottery and furnishings. A scattering of multilingual signs are designed to stimulate the visitor's imagination with a rare, guileless zeal.

The palace itself sports wonderful painted and chestnut-panelled ceilings, and 18th-century azulejos that depict hunting scenes. The ground floor is paved with deeply ribbed flagstones on which carriages would have once rattled through to the stables. The maze-like gardens at the rear also deserve a visit.

MUSEU DOM DIOGO DE SOUSA

Set to open by 2005, this major new **archaeological museum** (☎ 253 273 706; Rua dos Bombeiros Voluntários) will house exhibits for the whole of north Portugal, with a particular emphasis on the region around Braga. Check at the tourist office for details.

Festivals & Events

Braga may no longer be Portugal's religious capital, but it's still the capital of religious festivals.

Easter Week This is a truly splendid affair. The city blazes with lights and altars representing the Stations of the Cross, and the churches are bedecked with banners. The most memorable is the spooky, torch-lit Senhor Ecce Homo procession of barefoot, black-hooded penitents. Held on Maundy Thursday evening, it starts and ends at the cathedral.

Festas de São João (23 and 24 June) A pre-Christian solstice bash dressed up to look like holy days, but still bursting with pagan energy. It features medieval folk plays, processions, dancing, bonfires and illuminations. A funfair is held in the city park and mysterious little pots of basil appear everywhere. Basil is the symbol of São João (Saint John, or John the Baptist). Traditionally, people will write poems to loved ones then conceal them in little pots of basil.

Sleeping

There is definitely plenty of choice in Braga itself, although nearby Bom Jesus do Monte also offers some extra special upper-end hotels (p394).

BUDGET

Casa Santa Zita (☎ 253 618 331; Rua São João 20; s/d with breakfast & shared bathroom from €15/30) A world apart from the youth hostel, an air of palpable serenity pervades this large central hostel (look for the small tile plaque reading 'Sta Zita'). It has a wide variety of clean, spartan rooms mainly geared towards pilgrims.

Pousada da juventude (☎ 253 616 163; braga@movijovem.pt; Rua de Santa Margarida 6; dm €10, d with toilet €27; Ⓟ) Braga's nondescript but lively youth hostel is a 700m walk from the *turismo*.

Hotel Francfort (☎ 253 262 648; Avenida Central 7; d with/without shower €35/25) The best deal if you're looking to stay bang in the centre, this old-timer has big, creaky old rooms tended by ladies of a similar vintage.

Parque da Ponte (☎ 253 273 355; adult/tent/car €2/1.60/1.70; 🕒 year-round) This basic municipal camp site, 1.5km south of the centre, is really little more than a clutch of weedy caravan pitches. Bus Nos 9, 18 and 56 from Avenida da Liberdade run four services hourly (fewer at weekends) stopping at the camp site (€1.10).

MID-RANGE

Hotel Residencial CC Avenida Bragashopping (☎ 253 275 722; www.hotel-rccavenida.com; Avenida Central 27-37; s/d/t with breakfast from €33/38/40; Ⓟ ❄) Scoring top marks for convenience, if not personality, this *residencial* has a cinema, ATMs, supermarket and food court all treading on its toes. Reached by taking the lift inside the Bragashopping centre, it has well-equipped rooms and one self-catering apartment (€60).

Grande Residência Avenida (☎ 253 609 020; fax 253 609 028; 2nd fl, Avenida da Liberdade 738; d with breakfast &

with/without bathroom €45/37.50) For more character head to this great, homely spot near the plaza. It's well-run, crisply decorated and has big carpeted rooms (quiet at the back) and helpful English-speaking staff.

Residencial São Marcos (☎ 253 277 187; fax 253 277 177; Rua de São Marcos 80; s/d with breakfast €30/45;) This welcoming place has large, carpeted and rather pricey doubles with bathroom.

Hotel-Residencial Dona Sofia (☎ 253 263 160; hotel.d.sofia@sapo.pt; Largo São João do Souto 131; d €60;) Dona Sofia proudly offers English breakfast with its prim, flowery rooms and impeccable service.

Albergaria da Sé (☎ 253 214 502; fax 253 214 501; Rua Gonçalo Pereira 39; d with breakfast €55;) As the name promises, this simple guesthouse is within spitting distance of the cathedral. It also has attractive wooden floors, airy rooms and a scattering of azulejos to recommend it.

Hotel Turismo (☎ 253 206 000; www.hotelturismobraga.com; Praceta João XXI; d with breakfast Fri & Sat €70, Sun-Thu €80; P) All the mod-cons but just a modicum of character can be found at this big, business-friendly hotel south of the centre. Disabled access.

Hotel João XXI (☎ 253 616 630; reservas@hoteljoaoxxi.com; Avenida João XXI 849; s/d/tr with breakfast €35/45/55;) The big smiley face that adorns the welcome desk sets the tone here: keen to find a youthful clientele the management chose vivid colours and modern art to brighten up an otherwise bland high-rise block.

Hotel Carandá (☎ 253 614 500; www.hotelcaranda.com; Avenida da Liberdade 96; s/d with breakfast €35/44.50; P) Another plain, comfy option with parking (€3.50), and wheelchair access.

Eating

Gosto Superior (☎ 253 217 681; Praça Mousinho de Albuquerque 29; set meal €6; lunch & dinner Mon-Sat) Keen to prove to the Portuguese that 'vegetarianism is much more than eating lettuce', this excellent restaurant has succeeded where so many have failed: largely thanks to its imaginative dishes and a trendy, chilled environment.

Restaurante A Ceia (☎ 253 263 932; Largo do Rechicho 331; half-/full portions about €5/9; lunch & dinner Tue-Sun) This locally popular, easy-going *adega* (wine tavern) has highly recommended Minho specialities, such as *alheira*, a light, garlicky sausage of poultry or game – mouthwateringly good with salad and a jug or two of red *vinho verde* (young, slightly sparkling white or red wine).

Taberna do Felix (☎ 253 617 701; Praça Velha 17; dishes €6-9; dinner Mon-Sat) Situated near the Arco da Porta Nova, this very attractive country-style tavern prepares unusual Franco-Portuguese dishes; try the tapas or delicious *pataiscas* (fish fritters; €7).

Adega Pregão (☎ 253 277 249; Praça Velha 18; dishes €7; lunch & dinner Mon-Sat) Next door to Taberna on a quiet little side street, this *adega* has outdoor tables and an unpretentious menu of standard Portuguese fare, with generous helpings and a generous atmosphere. English is spoken.

Lareira do Conde (☎ 253 611 340; Praça Conde de Agrolongo 56; half-portions €4-6; lunch & dinner Thu-Tue) Great for speedy budget grills, this no-frills *churrasqueira* (grill restaurant) feeds a hungry lunch-time crowd in double-quick time.

Retiro da Primavera (☎ 253 272 482; Rua Gabriel Pereira de Castro 100; half-portions €4-6; all day Sun-Fri) Fortifying yourself before your long bus journey? Avoid the bus terminal's café and nip round the corner to this unpretentious place serving a bigger choice of good-value meat and fish dishes.

Salão de Chã Lusitana (Rua Justino Cruz 119; all day Tue-Sun) This is a good venue for a coffee-and-pastry break is Next to sweet-smelling Jardim de Santa Bárbara, this sunny glass-fronted tea shop has outdoor tables that attract buskers in summer.

The **mercado municipal** (municipal market; Praça do Comércio) buzzes on weekdays and Saturday mornings. There are **Pingo Doce** (9am-9pm) supermarkets in the Bragashopping centre (enter from Rua dos Chãos) and on Avenida da Liberdade. Several fruit-and-vegetable shops are open during the day along Rua São Marcos.

Drinking & Entertainment

BARS & CLUBS

Braga has some quirky nightspots to while away your evenings.

Barbieri Café (☎ 253 614 381; Avenida Central 42-44; minimum consumption €3; midnight-5am Fri & Sat) This can be forgiven its unsettling penchant for scissors and barber's chairs thanks to its funky Brazilian soundtrack and regular theme nights.

Populum (☎ 253 610 966; Campo da Vinha 115; 10pm-5am Thu-Sat) This is a standard club on Thursdays and Saturdays, but transforms on Fridays to cater for Latin dancers in one hall and ballroom dancing in the other!

Café Astória (☎ 253 273 944; Praça da República; ⏲ midnight-5am Fri & Sat) This is a genteel coffee house on the plaza, with a more conventional club upstairs where you can expect high-energy house and pop tracks.

CINEMA

Bragashopping Cinema (☎ 253 217 819; Avenida Central) has a very good mix of films, mostly international.

SPORT

Now home to Braga's football team, Sporting Clube de Braga, the city's new 30,000-seat Estádio Municipal de Braga was built to host the European Football Championships (Euro2004). It's 2km north of the centre off the northbound EN 101; you can buy match tickets at the **team shop** (☎ 253 271 320; Avenida da Liberdade; ⏲ 10am-1pm & 2.30-7pm Mon-Fri, 10am-1pm Sat) in the Centro Comercial Galeries do Bingo.

Getting There & Away

BUS

The following bus lines are represented at the bus station:

AVIC, Joalto and Linhares (☎ 253 216 460)
Empresa Hoteleira do Gerês (☎ 253 262 033)
REDM & Rede Expressos (☎ 253 209 401)
Rodonorte/Arriva (☎ 253 264 693)
Salvador & Renex (☎ 253 277 003)

Empresa Hoteleira do Gerês runs all day to Rio Caldo and Vila do Gerês. Other destinations with multiple daily departures from Braga:

Destination	Company	Price (€)	Duration
Arcos de Valdevez	Salvador	2.85	1¼hr
Barcelos	Linhares	1.80	50min
Coimbra	Rede Expressos	10	3hr
Guimarães	Arriva Rede Expressos	2.15	40min
Lisbon	Rede Expressos Renex	14.50	5hr
Monção	Salvador	4.70	2hr
Ponte de Lima	Rede Expressos	2.65	30min
Porto	Rede Expressos Renex	3.90-4.50	1½hr
Viana do Castelo	Rede Expressos	3.25	1¾hr

CAR & MOTORCYCLE

Braga has a branch of the **Automóvel Clube de Portugal** (ACP; ☎ 253 217 051; Avenida Conde Dom Henrique 72), and **AVIC** (☎ 253 270 302; Rua Gabriel Pereira de Castro; ⏲ 9am-6pm Mon-Fri) is an agent for Hertz should you need to rent a car.

The A3/IP1 motorway makes Braga an easy day trip from Porto. However, the N101 from Braga to Guimarães is more congested and poorly signposted.

TRAIN

Braga is at the end of a branch line from Nine, and within Porto's *suburbano* network, which means commuter trains travel every hour or two from Porto (€1.75, 1¾ hours); don't waste €6.50 on an *intercidade* (IC) train. Useful IC links include Coimbra (€9, 2¼ hours, two daily) and Lisbon (€17, 4¾ hours, two daily).

AROUND BRAGA

Bom Jesus do Monte

The goal of legions of penitent pilgrims every year, Bom Jesus is one of the country's most recognisable icons. Lying 5km east of central Braga just off the N103, this sober neoclassical church, completed in 1811, stands atop a forested hill that offers grand sunset views across Braga. However, most people don't come for the church or even the view. They come to see what lies below: the extraordinary baroque staircase, **Escadaria do Bom Jesus**.

The photogenic climb is made up of various tiered staircases, dating from different decades of the 18th century. The lowest is lined with chapels representing the Stations of the Cross, and eerily lifelike terracotta figurines. **Escadaria dos Cinco Sentidos** (The Stairway of the Five Senses) features allegorical fountains and over-the-top Old Testament figures. Highest is the **Escadaria das Três Virtudes** (Stairway of the Three Virtues), with chapels and fountains representing Faith, Hope and Charity.

You can ascend the hill by the stairs, as all pilgrims do (though you needn't go on your knees, as some do); ride the adjacent, gravity-driven **funicular** (€1; ⏲ 9am-8pm), the first on the Iberian Peninsula and in service since 1882; or drive up the twisting road.

The area around the church has become something of a resort, with sumptuous hotels, tennis courts, flower gardens and a little lake with boats for hire. It's choked with tourists on summer weekends.

SLEEPING & EATING

Accommodation here is splendid, pricey and – in summer – usually full.

Hotel do Elevador (☎ 253 603 400; www.hoteisbomjesus.web.pt; Bom Jesus do Monte; s/d with breakfast & satellite TV €75/90; P) and the adjacent **Hotel do Parque** (☎ 253 603 470; Bom Jesus do Monte; P) have the same management and room prices (which include a grand buffet breakfast). The Hotel do Elevador and its restaurant (set meal €17.50) have jaw-dropping panoramic views, while the older Hotel do Parque has the edge on *fin-de-siècle* charm.

Castello Bom Jesus (☎ 253 676 566; info@armilarworldhotels.com; N103; d with breakfast from €100; P) This Turihab property (Turismo Habitação; a scheme for marketing private accommodation), within a five-minute walk, is an over-the-top 18th-century 'castle' with whimsical gardens, gazebos, grottoes and peacocks – all peering over the city.

Casa dos Lagos (☎ 253 676 738; casadoslagosbomjesus@oninet.pt; N103; d with breakfast from €80, apt for 4 €130;) Further down the road is this altogether less fancy but just as friendly Turihab property, also with fine views.

GETTING THERE & AWAY

City bus No 2 runs to Bom Jesus (€1.10, 15 minutes) every half-hour all day (hourly on Sunday) from the bus stop closest to the town centre on Braga's Avenida da Liberdade.

BARCELOS

pop 20,600 / elevation 98m

The Minho's markets are famed, and none is more celebrated than the one in this ancient town on the banks of the Rio Cávado. Indeed the Feira de Barcelos, held every Thursday, has become so famous that tourist buses now arrive by the dozen, spilling their contents into the already brimming marketplace. Even if you don't come on a Thursday you'll find Barcelos an open-hearted town, with two good museums, several major festivals and a thriving pottery tradition.

Orientation

From the train station it's an 850m walk southwest to Campo da República (Campo da Feira), an immense shady square where the market is held. The medieval town is on the slopes above the river, southwest of the Campo.

Information

Hospital Santa Maria Maior (☎ 253 809 200; Campo da República)
Police station (☎ 253 802 570; Campo da República)
Post office (☎ 253 811 711; Avenida Dr Sidónio País; 8.30am-6.30pm Mon-Fri, 9am-12.30pm Sat)
Turismo (☎ 253 811 882; turismo@cm-barcelos.pt; Largo da Porta Nova; 9.30am-6pm Mon-Fri, 9.30am-12.30pm & 2.30-5.30pm Sat, 2.30-5.30pm Sun Mar-Oct, 9.30am-5.30pm Mon-Fri, 10am-12.30pm & 2.30-5.30pm Sat Nov-Feb) Located in the Torre de Menagem (the former castle keep), along with Centro Artesanato, a big handicrafts and souvenir shop.
Vog@Net (☎ 253 812 799; Rua Francisco Torres; per hour €1.50; 9am-midnight) A backstreet games hall with Internet access.

Sights

FEIRA DE BARCELOS

You'll need at least an hour or two to eyeball all the goods in this sprawling market. Despite attracting travellers, the **fair** (Campo da República) retains its rural soul. Villagers hawk everything from scrawny chickens to hand-embroidered linen, and Roma women bellow for business in the clothes section. Snack on sausages and home-made bread as you wander among the cow bells, handwoven baskets and carved ox yokes.

COCK-A-DOODLE-DON'T DO IT!

You've seen its colourful crest adorning a thousand souvenir stalls, but why and how did the proud Portuguese cockerel become such a national icon? Well, the story can be traced back to a humble Galician pilgrim plodding his way to Santiago de Compostela in the 16th (some say 14th) century. The exhausted traveller stopped to rest in Barcelos, only to find himself wrongfully accused of theft and swiftly condemned to be hanged.

In his last appearance at the judge's house the disgusted pilgrim declared that the roast cockerel on the judge's dinner table would stand up and crow to affirm his innocence. And wouldn't you know it – just as the judge was about to tuck in – that roasted rooster got up and crowed. The judge was so perturbed by his dinner's behaviour that he pardoned the pilgrim.

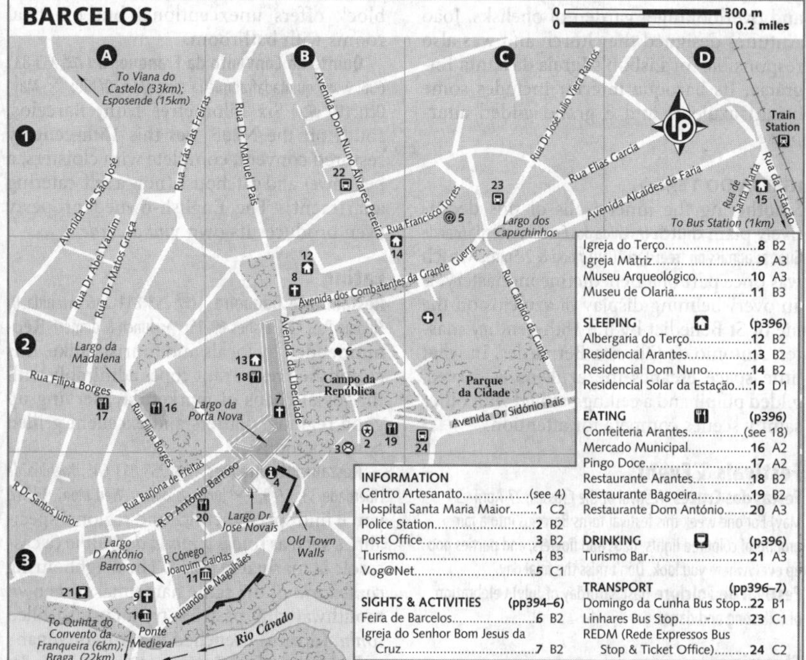

Pottery is what outsiders come to see, especially the yellow-dotted *louça de Barcelos* ware and the gaudy figurines à la Rosa Ramalho, a local potter (known as the Grandma Moses of Portuguese pottery) whose work put Barcelos on the map in the 1950s. The trademark Barcelos cockerel motif (see Cock-a-Doodle-Don't Do It!, opposite) is everywhere in pottery form of every size.

Get there early: tour buses arrive by mid-morning and the whole scene winds down after midday.

MUSEU ARQUEOLÓGICO & AROUND

On a ledge above Barcelos' 14th-century bridge over the Rio Cávado are the roofless ruins of the former palace of the counts of Barcelos and dukes of Bragança. Practically obliterated by the 1755 earthquake, it now serves as an alfresco **archaeological museum** (admission free; 9am-5.30pm).

Among the mysterious phallic stones, Roman columns and medieval caskets, the most famous item is a 14th-century stone cross, the Crucifix O Senhor do Galo, depicting the gentleman of the cockerel story and said to have been commissioned by the lucky pilgrim himself. Near the entrance is a late Gothic *pelourinho* (stone pillory) topped by a granite lantern.

Eastwards along the bluffs is a stretch of the medieval **town walls**.

Peek inside the **igreja matriz** (10am-5.30pm Tue-Fri, 10am-12.30pm & 2-5.30pm Sat & Sun), the stocky Gothic parish church behind the Museu Arqueológico, to see its 18th-century azulejos and gilded baroque chapels.

MUSEU DE OLARIA

This good **pottery museum** (253 824 741; Rua Cónego Joaquim Gaiolas; adult/youth under 26/senior/child under 14 €1.40/0.70/0.70/free, Sun morning free; 10am-5.30pm Tue-Fri, 10am-12.30pm & 2-5.30pm Sat & Sun) features ceramics in many of Portugal's regional styles, from Azores pots to Barcelos, Estremoz and Miranda do Corvo figurines, and striking pewter ware.

IGREJA DO SENHOR BOM JESUS DA CRUZ

On the corner of the Campo is this arresting **octagonal church** (Templo do Bom Jesus; admission free; 8.30am-12.30pm & 2-5.30pm), built in 1704 and overlooking a garden of obelisks. João Antunes designed the church and was also responsible for Lisbon's Igreja da Santa Engrácia. Its baroque interior includes some bright azulejos and a grand gilded altarpiece.

IGREJA DO TERÇO

Smothering the inner walls of this deceptively plain **church** (Avenida dos Combatentes da Grande Guerra; admission free; 10am-noon & 2-5pm), which was once part of a Benedictine monastery, is an overwhelming display of azulejos on the life of St Benedict by the 18th-century master, António de Oliveira Bernardes. In what little space escapes the azulejos, a carved, gilded pulpit and a ceiling painted with other saintly scenes compete for attention.

Festivals & Events

Festas das Cruzes (Festival of the Crosses; 27 April–3 May) For one week this festival turns Barcelos into a fairground of coloured lights, flags and flowers, and parties pop up everywhere you look. Don't miss the final day.

Festival de Folclore (last Saturday of July) Celebration of folk song and dance.

Sleeping

Accommodation is always tight on Wednesdays and Thursdays in the run-up to the fair.

Albergaria do Terço (253 808 380; www.arterco.com; Edifício do Terço; s/d €50/55; P) Opened in 2004, this ultra-modern mid-range option is to be found above its namesake shopping centre (take the lift round the back). The stylish, squeaky clean rooms could come straight out of an Ikea catalogue, while the bar earns brownie points with its comfy leather couches. Parking costs €2.

Residencial Solar da Estação (253 811 741; Largo Marechal Gomes da Costa 1; d with breakfast €30) This place is conveniently situated opposite the train station. In contrast to the shabby pink exterior, there are several frilly pink-and-white rooms in spotless condition, with modern fittings and wooden furniture.

Residencial Arantes (253 811 326; fax 253 821 360; Avenida da Liberdade 35; d with breakfast & with/without bathroom €42.50/27.50) Fronting Campo da República, this family-run favourite offers a mixed bag of well-kept homely rooms.

Residencial Dom Nuno (253 812 810; fax 253 816 336; Avenida Dom Nuno Álvares Pereira 76; d with breakfast from €42.50) This square modern hotel block offers unexceptional but practical rooms with bathroom.

Quinta do Convento da Franqueira (253 831 606; www.quintadafranqueira.com; s/d €70/100; May-Oct; P) Six kilometres from Barcelos, south off the N205, lies this 16th-century restored convent, complete with cloisters, a bell tower and gatehouse (now a self-catering apartment). The English-owned property even produces its own *vinho verde*.

Eating

Restaurante Bagoeira (253 811 236; Avenida Dr Sidónio Pais 495; dishes €9-15; lunch & dinner) Recommended by locals and tourists alike, this established restaurant copes admirably with the jovial chaos of market day, serving up good regional platters and excellent grilled *polvo* (octopus).

Restaurante Arantes (253 811 645; Avenida da Liberdade 33; €6-9; lunch & dinner Wed-Mon) Here you'll find speedy service and regional specialities such as *rojões á moda do Minho* (a casserole of marinated pork). The neighbouring *confeitaria* of the same name makes its own mouthwatering pastries; try a custard-filled *sonho* (dream) drenched in syrup or sugar.

Restaurante Dom António (253 812 285; Rua Dom António Barroso 85; mains around €8; lunch & dinner) Down a short passageway from the busy pedestrianised street outside, this locally popular choice has lots of good half-portions for under €5. House specialities include roast kid and grilled game meat, including wild boar and deer.

Two stops for self-caterers are the **mercado municipal** (Largo da Madalena; closed Sat afternoon, Sun) and a nearby **Pingo Doce** (Rua Filipa Borges 223) supermarket.

Drinking

Barcelos has little nightlife to speak of, but you could while away summer evenings on the riverside patio of **Turismo Bar** (Rua Duques de Bragança; 11.30am-3am).

Getting There & Away

BUS

There's a new bus terminal 1km east of the centre, but most buses pass through town on their way in and out of Barcelos. Services of **REDM/Rede Expressos** (253 814 310; Avenida Dr Sidónio Pais 445) go to/from Braga (€1.80, 50 minutes) at least hourly, and to/from Porto (€3.90, two hours) several times each weekday.

Linhares (☎ 253 811 571) has services every hour or two to Braga and Porto (€3.25, two hours) daily, and to Viana do Castelo (€2.45, 50 minutes) on weekdays. Linhares buses stop at Largo dos Capuchinhos.

Domingos da Cunha (☎ 253 815 843) buses go to Ponte de Lima (€2.45, 55 minutes) four to six times a day.

All bus services are less frequent at the weekend.

TRAIN

Barcelos station is on the Porto-Valença line. There are at least seven direct trains a day from Porto (€4, one hour) or, with a change at Nine, from Braga (€1.75, 45 minutes).

AROUND BARCELOS

Área de Paisagem Protegida do Litoral de Esposende

Embracing the Braga district's entire 18km of seashore, this protected area was set aside to safeguard its unstable sand dunes, delicate vegetation and the remnants of an ancient way of life – symbolised by the Minho's photogenic, decrepit coastal windmills.

The partnership of land and sea is illustrated by the area's agricultural fields immediately behind the dunes, watered by ocean spray and fertilised with algae and crustaceans from the sea. However, it's an area that continues to be nibbled away by the sea on one side and by humans on the other.

Attempts are being made to stabilise the dunes with fencing and plants, and access is largely restricted to elevated walkways. For more information, contact the **area office** (☎ 253 965 830; apple@icn.pt; Rua 1 de Dezembro 65, 4740-226 Esposende).

SLEEPING

Basic accommodation is available at Esposende, some 15km west of Barcelos, and at Ofir and Apúlia.

At Fão, 3km south of Esposende, there's a level, shaded **camp site** (☎ 253 815 383; cccb@esoterica.pt; Rua São João de Deus; adult/tent/car €2.90/2.60-3.15/2.25; year-round) that's open to holders of the Camping Card International (CCI; p452). There's also an attractive villa-like **pousada da juventude** (☎ 253 981 790; fozcavado@movijovem.pt; Alameda Bom Jesus; dm €11, d with toilet €30, apt for 4 €46; P) that boasts bikes for hire, a grassy garden and a games room. Apartments do not have private kitchen.

GETTING THERE & AWAY

AV Minho and AVIC buses stop at Esposende three or four times daily en route between Viana do Castelo (€2.10) and Porto. Regular buses cost €1.60 from Barcelos.

GUIMARÃES

pop 53,000 / elevation 400m

The Portuguese kingdom was born in Guimarães. That's the claim to fame that you'll see repeated everywhere you go in this historic city. And sure enough, the first true king of Portugal, Afonso Henriques, was born here in 1110 and later used the city to launch the main thrust of the Reconquista against the Moors.

Happily, the city centre more than matches its illustrious history. The large and very much lived-in historic core is chock-a-block with medieval monuments, oozing atmosphere at every turn. It's no accident that Unesco added Guimarães to its list of World Heritage sites in 2001.

But it's not all dusty treasures and national history. Guimarães also knows how to party; this is a university town, and its lively atmosphere explodes into full-scale revelry during the Festas de Cidade e Gualterianas (p400).

There's plenty to warrant a full day's sightseeing in Guimarães. For those with euros to spare, Guimarães' two Pousadas de Portugal are among the country's finest.

History

Guimarães caught the royal eye as early as AD 840 when Alfonso II of León convened a council of bishops here, but it only started to grow in the 10th century after the powerful Countess Mumadona Dias, widowed aunt of another king of León, gave it her attention, founding a monastery and building a castle built to protect it. Henri of Burgundy chose Guimarães for his court, as did his son Afonso Henriques until he shifted the capital to Coimbra in 1143.

Orientation

Old Guimarães is in the northeast of the modern city. Most points of interest lie within a demarcated tourist zone stretching south from the castle to an arc of public gardens at Alameda de São Dâmaso. Guimarães' commercial heart is Largo do Toural.

The main turismo is a 600m walk north up Avenida Dom Afonso Henriques from

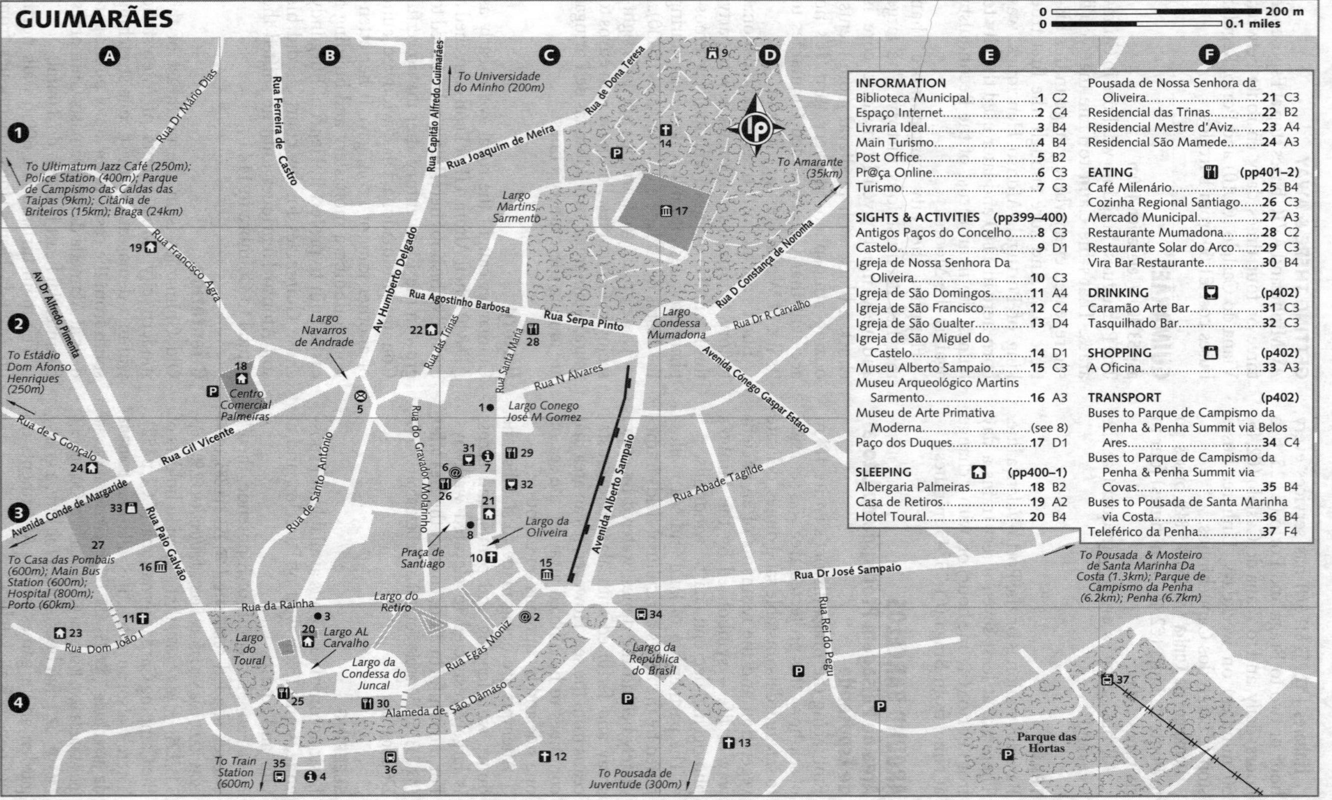
GUIMARÃES
0 200 m
0 0.1 miles
INFORMATION
Biblioteca Municipal 1 C2
Espaço Internet 2 C4
Livraria Ideal 3 B4
Main Turismo 4 B4
Post Office 5 B2
Pr@ça Online 6 C3
Turismo 7 C3
SIGHTS & ACTIVITIES (pp399–400)
Antigos Paços do Concelho 8 C3
Castelo 9 D1
Igreja de Nossa Senhora Da Oliveira 10 C3
Igreja de São Domingos 11 A4
Igreja de São Francisco 12 C4
Igreja de São Gualter 13 D4
Igreja de São Miguel do Castelo 14 D1
Museu Alberto Sampaio 15 C3
Museu Arqueológico Martins Sarmento 16 A3
Museu de Arte Primativa Moderna (see 8)
Paço dos Duques 17 D1
SLEEPING (pp400–1)
Albergaria Palmeiras 18 B2
Casa de Retiros 19 A2
Hotel Toural 20 B4
Pousada de Nossa Senhora da Oliveira 21 C3
Residencial das Trinas 22 B2
Residencial Mestre d'Aviz 23 A4
Residencial São Mamede 24 A3
EATING (pp401–2)
Café Milenário 25 B4
Cozinha Regional Santiago 26 C3
Mercado Municipal 27 A3
Restaurante Mumadona 28 C2
Restaurante Solar do Arco 29 C3
Vira Bar Restaurante 30 B4
DRINKING (p402)
Caramão Arte Bar 31 C3
Tasquilhado Bar 32 C3
SHOPPING (p402)
A Oficina 33 A3
TRANSPORT (p402)
Buses to Parque de Campismo da Penha & Penha Summit via Belos Ares 34 C4
Buses to Parque de Campismo da Penha & Penha Summit via Covas 35 B4
Buses to Pousada de Santa Marinha via Costa 36 B4
Teleférico da Penha 37 F4
To Ultimatum Jazz Café (250m); Police Station (400m); Parque de Campismo das Caldas das Taipas (9km); Citânia de Briteiros (15km); Braga (24km)
To Universidade do Minho (200m)
To Amarante (35km)
To Estádio Dom Afonso Henriques (250m)
To Casa das Pombais (600m); Main Bus Station (600m); Hospital (800m); Porto (60km)
To Train Station (600m)
To Pousada de Juventude (300m)
To Pousada & Mosteiro de Santa Marinha Da Costa (1.3km); Parque de Campismo da Penha (6.2km); Penha (6.7km)
Rua Dr Mário Dias
Rua Francisco Agra
Rua Ferreira de Castro
Av Dr Alfredo Pimenta
Rua Paio Galvão
Rua Gil Vicente
Rua de S Gonçalo
Avenida Conde de Margaride
Rua Dom João I
Rua da Rainha
Rua de Santo António
Av Humberto Delgado
Rua Capitão Alfredo Guimarães
Rua Joaquim de Meira
Rua Agostinho Barbosa
Rua das Trinas
Rua do Gravador Molarinho
Rua Santa Maria
Rua Serpa Pinto
Rua N Álvares
Rua de Dona Teresa
Rua D Constança de Noronha
Rua Dr R Carvalho
Avenida Cónego Gaspar Estaço
Avenida Alberto Sampaio
Rua Abade Tagilde
Rua Dr José Sampaio
Rua Rei do Pegu
Rua Egas Moniz
Alameda de São Dâmaso
Largo Navarros de Andrade
Centro Comercial Palmeiras
Largo do Toural
Largo AL Carvalho
Largo da Condessa do Juncal
Largo do Retiro
Praça de Santiago
Largo da Oliveira
Largo Conego José M Gomez
Largo Martins Sarmento
Largo Condessa Mumadona
Largo da República do Brasil
Parque das Hortas

the train station. It is a 1km slog up Avenida Conde de Margaride from the main bus station, which is beneath the Centro Comercial Guimarães Shopping.

Information

Numerous banks with ATMs line Largo do Toural and Rua Gil Vicente.

Biblioteca municipal (municipal library; ☎ 253 515 710; Largo Conego José M Gomez; 🕑 10am-1pm & 2-7pm Mon, 10am-12.30pm, 2-6pm & 9-11pm Tue, 10am-6pm Wed & Fri, 2-7pm Thu, 10am-1pm Sat) Free Internet access.

Espaço Internet (☎ 253 590 371; Rua Egas Moniz 29/33; 🕑 11am-1pm & 2-10pm Mon-Sat, 10am-1pm & 2-6pm Sun) More free Internet access.

Hospital (☎ 253 512 612; Rua dos Cotileros, Creixomil) Opposite the bus station.

Livraria Ideal (☎ 253 422 750; Rua da Rainha 34; 🕑 9am-1pm & 3-7pm Mon-Fri, 9am-1pm Sat) The city's best bookshop.

Main turismo (☎ 253 412 450; info@guimaraesturismo.com; Alameda de São Dâmaso 86; 🕑 9.30am-7pm Jul-Sep, 9.30am-12.30pm & 2pm-6.30pm Mon-Fri Oct-Jun) Can help with most inquiries.

Police station (☎ 253 513 334; Avenida Dr Alfredo Pimenta)

Post office (☎ 253 420 030; Largo Navarros de Andrade 27; 🕑 8.30am-6.30pm Mon-Fri, 9am-12.30pm Sat)

Pr@ça Online (☎ 253 413 518; Praça de Santiago; per hour €2; 🕑 10am-1pm & 1.30-midnight) Central Internet café and games room.

Turismo (☎ 253 518 790; Praça de Santiago; 🕑 9.30am-7pm Jul-Sep, 9.30am-6.30pm Mon-Fri, 10am-6pm Sat, 10am-1pm Sun Oct-Jun) In the old centre; more central and enthusiastic than the main turismo.

Sights

PAÇO DOS DUQUES

Recognisable by its forest of brick chimneys, the **Paço dos Duques** (Ducal Palace; ☎ 253 412 273; adult/youth under 26/senior/child under 14 €3/1.50/1.50/free, 9am-12.30pm Sun free; 🕑 9.30am-5pm Jul-Sep, 9.30am-12.30pm & 2-5pm Oct-Jun) has pushed its way into the foreground on Guimarães' hilltop. Built in 1401 by a later and equally famous Afonso (the future first Duke of Bragança), it fell into ruin after his powerful family upped sticks to the Alentejo. Pompously restored as a presidential residence for Salazar, it still contains a clutch of treasures. Skip the tedious guided tour if you can and dip in and out of the rooms, which are decorated with a huge range of paintings, tapestries, armaments and ostentatious furniture.

CASTELO & IGREJA DE SÃO MIGUEL DO CASTELO

The seven-towered **castle** (admission castle keep adult/youth under 26/senior/child under 14 €1.30/0.70/0.70/free, Sun morning free; 🕑 9.30am-5pm Jul-Sep, 9.30am-12.30pm & 2-5pm Oct-Jun), built in about 1100 and still in fine fettle, is thought to be the birthplace of the great man himself, Afonso Henriques. Climbing to the top of Countess Mumadona's keep (p397) rewards you with bird's-eye views, though the minuscule exit onto the roof will prove a squeeze for larger visitors.

Sandwiched between the palace and castle is the little Romanesque **Igreja de São Miguel do Castelo** (Church of St Michael of the Castle; admission free; 🕑 same as castle) where Afonso Henriques was probably baptised. Under its floor rest many of the king's companions-at-arms, their graves marked with worn crosses, spears and shields.

ANCIENT SQUARES & STREETS

Don't miss a lengthy stroll through Guimarães' picturesque medieval quarter. Its most important areas are **Rua Santa Maria**, its first street and the ancient route from Mumadona's monastery to the castle; the medieval ensemble of **Largo da Oliveira** and **Praça de Santiago**, best enjoyed in the early morning before café tables fill the squares; and the narrow **Rua Dom João I**, once the road to Porto, lined with balconied houses.

IGREJA DE NOSSA SENHORA DA OLIVEIRA

The beautiful Largo da Oliveira is dominated by this **convent-church** (Our Lady of the Olive Tree; admission free; 🕑 7.15am-noon & 3.30-7.30pm Tue-Sun), founded by Countess Mumadona and rebuilt four centuries later.

The odd **monument** outside the church is a Gothic canopy and cross said to mark the spot where the great Wamba the Visigoth, victorious over the Suevi, drove his spear into the ground beside an olive tree, refusing to reign unless a tree sprouted from the handle. In true legendary fashion, of course, it did just that.

Around a serene Romanesque cloister in the former convent is the **Museu Alberto Sampaio** (☎ 253 423 910; adult/youth under 26/senior/child under 14 €2/1/1/free, Sun morning free; 🕑 10am-12.30pm & 2pm-5.30pm Tue-Sun), an excellent collection of ecclesiastical art and wealth. Highlights include a 14th-century silver-gilded triptych, the tunic said to have been worn by João I at the Battle of Aljubarrota (1385) and a 16th-century silver Manueline cross. English-language notes are available in each room.

ANTIGOS PAÇOS DO CONCELHO

The building on 'legs' facing Largo da Oliveira is Guimarães' 14th-century town hall, the finest feature of which is its painted wooden ceiling. It is home to avant-garde art displays in the **Museu de Arte Primativa Moderna** (Museum of Modern Primitive Art; ☎ 253 414 186; admission free; 9am-12.30pm & 2-5.30pm Mon-Fri, 10.30am-12.30pm & 3-6pm Sat & Sun).

OTHER CHURCHES

The 13th-century **Igreja de São Francisco** (Church of St Francis of Assisi; admission free; 9.30am-noon & 3-5pm Tue-Sat, 9.30am-1pm Sun) has the most striking interior as well as boasting a lovely Renaissance cloister and 18th-century azulejos depicting scenes from the saint's life.

Meanwhile the skinny 18th-century **Igreja de São Gualter** (Church of St Walter; Largo da República do Brasil; admission free; 7.30am-noon & 3-5pm Mon-Sat, 7.30am-noon Sun), with its 19th-century twin spires and huge run-up from central Guimarães, has surely the most harmonious façade of all the city's churches.

MUSEU ARQUEOLÓGICO MARTINS SARMENTO & IGREJA DE SÃO DOMINGOS

This curious **collection** (☎ 253 415 969; Rua Paio Galvão; adult/senior €1.50/free; 10am-noon & 2-5pm Tue-Sat, 10.30am-noon & 2-5pm Sun) of mostly Celtiberian artefacts is housed in a former convent and named after the archaeologist who excavated Citânia de Briteiros (p402) in 1875. Hefty stone artefacts are dotted carelessly around the cloister of the adjacent 14th-century **Igreja de São Domingos** – look for the impressive *pedras formosas* (beautiful stones) thought to have adorned Celtiberian bathhouses in the surrounding region (not in the city).

PENHA & MOSTEIRO DE SANTA MARINHA DA COSTA

To retreat from the summer heat in Guimarães, simply head for the hills. Some 7km southeast up a twisting, cobbled road or a short ride on an ageing cable car is the wooded summit of **Penha** (617m), overlooking Guimarães and easily the highest point in the vicinity.

Its cool woods, cluttered with mossy boulders and picnic areas make it a wonderful escape from the city. Kids love losing themselves amid the massive boulders, many cut with steps, crowned with flowers and crosses, or hiding secret grottoes.

On the lower slopes of the hill lies the **Mosteiro de Santa Marinha da Costa**, 1.5km east of the town centre. It dates from 1154 when Dona Mafalda, wife of Afonso Henriques, commissioned it to honour a vow she made to the patron saint of pregnant women. Rebuilt in the 18th century, it is now a flagship Pousada de Portugal (p401). Nonguests can still snoop around the chapel and gardens.

The easiest route to the monastery is on municipal bus No 51 or 52 to São Roque (€1.10, every half-hour Monday to Saturday, hourly on Sunday), which departs from the south side of the public gardens; get off at Costa.

For the summit you can take a Mondinense bus via Covas from opposite the main turismo (€1.40, every half-hour Monday to Saturday, hourly on Sunday), or less often via Belos Ares from Largo da República do Brasil (€1.10). But the finest way to the top is on the **Teleférico da Penha** (cable car; ☎ 253 515 085; one way/return €1.50/2.50; 10.30am-6.30pm Mon-Fri, 10.30am-7.30pm Sat, Sun & holidays May-Sep, 11am-6pm Fri, 10am-7pm Sat, Sun & holidays Oct-Apr), which starts from Parque das Hortas, 600m east of the old centre.

Festivals & Events

Festas de Cidade e Gualterianas (first weekend in August) Marked by a free fair (held in Guimarães since 1452), plus folk dancing, rock concerts, bullfights, and, on the Monday, a float parade. São Gualter is the town's patron saint.

Encontros de Primavera (late May and June) Series of classical and early music concerts held at historical venues.

Jazz Festival (November; www.cm-guimaraes.pt/guimaraesjazz) A month-long festival.

Sleeping

BUDGET

Casa de Retiros (☎ 253 511 515; fax 253 511 517; Rua Francisco Agra 163; s/d/t with breakfast €20/34/45;) For bargain value at the budget end try this wholesome, Catholic missionary hostel. You must pay on arrival, stay out until 6pm and be in by 11.30pm, but at these prices the hardship is bearable.

Pousada de Juventude (☎ 253 421 380; guimaraes@movijovem.pt; Largo da Cidade; dm €12.50, d €35, apt for 4 €55) At the time of writing, a spanking new youth hostel was set to give a long-overdue boost to the city's budget scene.

Parque de Campismo da Penha (☎ 253 515 912; fax 253 515 085; adult/tent/car €2.15/1.75-3.25/1.75; ⏲ Apr-Sep) With a terrific position near the top of Penha, this is a well-equipped and densely wooded municipal camp site. Few camp sites in Portugal are so lofty. Unfortunately, the pool was more pond-like when we visited. See p400 for transport options.

Parque de Campismo das Caldas das Taipas (☎ 253 576 274; Avenida Rosas Guimarães, Taipas; adult/tent/car €2.10/1.60-2.25/1.60; ⏲ Jun-Sep) This flat but unattractive weedy patch by the Rio Ave is 9km northwest of Guimarães. There's a big swimming pool nearby, however. Take any Braga-bound bus.

MID-RANGE

All the following have private bathrooms. Prices are negotiable outside the high season.

Residencial Mestre d'Aviz (☎ 253 422 770; residencial-aviz@planetaclix.pt; Rua Dom João I 40; d with breakfast €40; ❄) Fronted by curlicue ironwork, this handsomely renovated townhouse is Guimarães' best mid-range bargain. It has slick modern touches, a stone-slab bar and minimal street traffic on the narrow old lane outside. Upper (hotter) floors have air-con.

Residencial das Trinas (☎ 253 517 358; fax 253 517 362; Rua das Trinas 29; d with breakfast €40; Ⓟ ❄) This renovated house in the historical zone offers chintzy, likeable little rooms with double-glazing and satellite TV. You won't get a better position for the price.

Residencial São Mamede (☎ 253 513 092; www.residencial-smamede.com; Rua São Gonçalo; d €35; ❄) Sitting in a high-rise above the city's traffic-jam central is this good-value, modern guesthouse. The cable TV can always help drown out the traffic noise.

Albergaria Palmeiras (☎ 253 410 324; albergariapalmeiras@oninet.pt; 4th fl, Centro Comercial Palmeiras, Rua Gil Vicente; d with breakfast €35; Ⓟ ❄) What this peaceful but plastic shopping-centre hotel lacks in character, it makes up for in comfort and practicality. Enter through the shopping centre's side entrance on Travessa dos Bimbais, then take the lift.

TOP END

Hotel Toural (☎ 253 517 184; www.hoteltoural.com; Largo AL Carvalho; s/d with breakfast €65/85; Ⓟ ❄) Big, business-friendly Toural offers large, uncluttered rooms with satellite TV and buffet breakfast. Nine rooms have an excellent view over Largo do Toural but also cop the accompanying car horns. Generally a cut above the other central options, however.

Casa das Pombais (☎ 253 412 917; pombais@solaresdeportugal.pt; Avenida de Londres; d €80; Ⓟ) This 17th-century manor house has peacocks strutting their stuff in the garden, swans in the pond and chickens freely ranging behind the rose-covered fence. However, this misleading picture of rural life survives on a busy junction surrounded by urban estates. It has just two rooms available.

Pousada de Nossa Senhora da Oliveira (☎ 253 514 157; recepcao.oliveira@pousadas.pt; Rua Santa Maria; d Sun-Thu from €134, Fri & Sat from €144; Ⓟ ❄) Sandwiched between two plazas and narrow medieval streets, this 16th-century house is in the heart of the old town. It is lovely, but be warned there is late-night revelry at weekends.

Pousada de Santa Marinha (☎ 253 511 249; recepcao.stamarinha@pousadas.pt; d Sun-Thu from €169, Fri & Sat from €186; Ⓟ ❄ 🏊) This is the real deal: history, beauty and an unbeatable location. A restored former monastery overlooking the city from the slopes of Penha, the *pousada* is now a far cry from past frugality. Guests may wander round the cloister past dribbling fountains and masterful azulejos, and sleep in now-luxurious converted monks' cells. For transport information see p400.

Eating

Cozinha Regional Santiago (☎ 253 516 669; Praça de Santiago 16; mains €7-13, half-portions €5-6.50; ⏲ Mon-Sat) An enviable location plum in the central *praça* hasn't stopped this good little restaurant from offering fair prices. You can relax in the sunny square without, or hole up in the stone-walled dining room within.

Restaurante Solar do Arco (☎ 253 513 072; Rua de Santa Maria 50; dishes around €10-18, specials €8-10; ⏲ lunch & dinner Mon-Sat; ❄) This is the place for a seafood splurge. Throw in some big stone arches, attentive service and fresh straight-from-the-market ingredients and you're set.

Restaurante Mumadona (☎ 253 416 111; Rua Serpa Pinto 260; dishes €7.50-11, half-portions €4.50-6; ⏲ lunch & dinner Mon-Sat) Snug and family-friendly, this place packs in a remarkable amount of people for its size. The menu is weighted heavily towards *bacalhau* (salt cod) and includes good-value half-portions at lunch time.

Café Milenário (Largo do Toural; all day) The quintessential after-work venue, this large, open corner café pulls in a crowd of all ages to banter over bar food, light meals and drinks.

Vira Bar Restaurant (☎ 253 518 427; Largo Condessa do Juncal 27; mains €10-17; lunch & dinner Mon-Sat) This genteel venue features vaulted ceiling and stained-glass windows. Try the speciality: *sopa de nabos* (turnip soup).

Self-caterers will like the **mercado municipal** (Rua Paio Galvão; Mon-Sat morning).

Drinking & Entertainment

BARS & CLUBS

One of a swathe of bar-hopping venues in the historic centre, the ever-popular **Tásquilhado Bar** (☎ 253 515 197; Rua de Santa Maria 42; 9.30pm-2am Wed-Sat) plays alternative sounds and has happy hour on Wednesday and Thursday lasting till midnight. Another with a more mainstream pop-and-rock bias is **Carramão Arte Bar** (☎ 253 413 815; Praça de Santiago; to 2am Mon-Sat).

For a more mellow vibe, head to **Ultimatum Jazz Café** (☎ 253 415 294; Rua Francisco Agra; 8pm-4am Tue-Sun), specialising in classical, jazz and piano-bar sounds, including live music on Thursday and Friday. There's also mainstream music from 1am Friday and Saturday nights, and a neighbouring salsa club to raise the stakes.

SPORT

Northwest of the centre, the heavily renovated Euro2004 stadium Estádio Dom Afonso Henriques is home to Guimarães' first-division football team, Vitória SC Guimarães.

Shopping

Today, as in medieval times, Guimarães is known for its linen. Other crafts contributing to its prosperity are embroidery, gold- and silversmithing and pottery. For quality work by Guimarães artisans, visit the municipal outlet **A Oficina** (☎ 253 515 250; Rua Paio Galvão 11; 9am-7pm Mon-Sat).

A big flea market takes over Praça de Santiago and Largo da Oliveira on the first Saturday of each month.

Getting There & Away

BUS

Every 30 minutes to two hours **REDM/Rede Expressos** (☎ 253 516 229) has links to Braga (€2.15, 40 minutes). **Arriva** (☎ 253 423 500) goes to Braga less often; it goes to Porto (€3.90, 50 minutes) about hourly on weekdays but less often at weekends, and to Lisbon (€13.90, five hours) daily. **Rodonorte** (☎ 253 412 646) heads for Amarante (€4.60, 50 minutes), Vila Real (€5.80, 1½ hours) and Bragança (€10.50, four hours) two or three times daily Sunday to Friday.

TRAIN

Guimarães is the terminus of a branch of Porto's wide *suburbano* network. Commuter trains potter out to Guimarães from Porto (€1.75, 1¼ hours) about 11 times daily Monday to Friday and eight daily at weekends.

AROUND GUIMARÃES

Citânia de Briteiros

One of the most evocative archaeological sites in Portugal is to be found at **Briteiros**, 15km north of Guimarães. This site is the most spectacular of a liberal scattering of northern Celtic hill settlements, called *citânias,* dating back at least 2500 years.

It's also likely that this sprawling 3.8-hectare **site** (admission incl museum €2; 9am-6pm), inhabited from about 300 BC to AD 300, was the Celtiberians' last stronghold against the invading Romans. When archaeologist Dr Martins Sarmento excavated it way back in 1875 he discovered the foundations and ruins of more than 150 rectangular, circular and elliptical stone huts, linked by paved paths and a water distribution system, cocooned by multiple protective walls.

Highlights include two reconstructed huts that evoke what it was like to have lived in the settlement, and – further back down the hill – a bathhouse with a strikingly patterned stone doorway.

Ask at the entrance for a detailed plan (€0.25), keyed to markers around the site, with information in French and English.

Some artefacts are on display in the Museu Arqueológico Martins Sarmento in Guimarães (p400), but the new **Museu da Cultura Castreja** (☎ 255 478 952; Solar da Ponte, Briteiros Salvador; 9.30am-12.30pm & 2-6pm Tue-Sun) was opened in 2004, 2km back down the hill towards Guimarães in the village of Briteiros Salvador.

GETTING THERE & AWAY

From Guimarães, Arriva buses go to within about 1km of the site (€1.60, 30 minutes);

get off between Briteiros town and Santa Leocádia. Useful departures (weekdays only) are at 7.25am, 9.35am, 12.20pm, 1.25pm and 2.25pm, with buses passing by on the return journey at about 12.05pm, 12.55pm, 2.05pm, 3.05pm and 5.05pm. Check with **Arriva** (☎ 253 423 500) or Guimarães turismo (p399) or current timetables.

From Braga, bus connections involve a change at Taipas and then finding awkwardly timed local buses from there. By car it's a scenic 15km journey via Bom Jesus do Monte.

COASTAL & NORTHERN MINHO

VIANA DO CASTELO

pop 36,500

Renowned for its multitude of good festivals, Viana is the folkloric capital of the Minho. Set by the Rio Lima estuary, a short hop from some excellent beaches, it is also the northern coast's largest, liveliest resort, an elegant town of Manueline and Renaissance houses and rococo palaces. This alone makes it worth the trip, but the town also makes a handy base for exploring the lower Lima valley.

History

The earliest evidence of a settlement sits atop Monte de Santa Luzia, overlooking the contemporary town centre. This hill bears a few paltry remains of a 4th-century Celtiberian settlement, yet there's little evidence of the Romans, Suevi, Visigoths and Moors who followed. The Romans' only lasting mark was to call their settlement Diana, which over the years became Viana.

Manueline mansions and monasteries attest to Viana's 16th-century prosperity, thanks to its sailors who fished for cod off Newfoundland. By the mid-17th century this was northern Portugal's biggest port, its merchants trading as far afield as Russia. At the same time expat British merchants were exporting shiploads of local 'red Portugal' wine to England (p64).

More riches arrived in the 18th century with the Brazilian sugar and gold trade. But with Brazil's independence and the rise of Porto as a rival port, Viana's importance stuttered and faded. Later revived as a deep-sea–fishing and industrial centre, it also cobbles together much of its living as a popular tourist destination.

Orientation

From the train station squatting at the foot of Monte de Santa Luzia, the main axis down to the river is Avenida dos Combatentes da Grande Guerra (often just called 'Avenida'). East of here is the old town, centred on Praça da República. West lies the old fishing quarter.

From the bus station it's a 2km trek southwest along Avenida Capitão Gaspar de Castro to the centre, though many regional buses stop at the station and beside Viana's riverside park, the Jardim Marginal.

Information

Foreign-language newspapers are available at many of the *tabacarias* around the centre.

BOOKSHOPS

Livraria Bertrand (☎ 258 822 838; Rua de Sacadura Cabral 32)

EMERGENCY & MEDICAL SERVICES

Hospital (☎ 258 829 081; Estrada de Santa Luzia) North of the train station.

Police station (☎ 258 822 022; Rua de Aveiro)

INTERNET ACCESS

Biblioteca municipal (☎ 258 809 302; Rua Cândido dos Reis; 🕑 9.30am-12.30pm & 1-9pm Mon-Fri, 9.30am-12.30pm Sat) Five free but slow terminals.

Instituto Português da Juventude (☎ 258 808 800; Rua do Poço 16-26; 🕑 9am-12.30pm & 2-5.30pm Mon-Fri) More free access.

Pousada da juventude (☎ 258 800 260; Rua da Argaçosa; per hr €3; 🕑 8am-midnight)

Esp@ço.net (Rua General Luis do Rego 21; per hour €1; 🕑 9am-7pm Mon-Sat) Not the same as Espaço Internet elsewhere: this one charges!

LAUNDRY

Lavandaria A Minhota (☎ 258 823 265; Rua Grande 106; 🕑 9am-12.30 & 2.30-8pm Mon-Fri, 9am-1pm & 3-8pm Sat)

Lavandaria Automática Viana (LAV; ☎ 936 546 825; Rua do Marquês 17; 🕑 9am-10pm) Self-service place in the fishing quarter.

MONEY

There are banks with ATMs on Avenida dos Combatentes and Praça da República.

POST

Post office (☎ 258 800 080; Avenida dos Combatentes; 8.30am-6pm Mon-Fri, 9am-12.30pm Sat)

TOURIST INFORMATION

Regional turismo (☎ 258 822 620; fax 258 827 873; Rua Hospital Velho; 9am-12.30pm & 2.30-6pm Mon-Sat Feb-Oct, to 5.30pm Mon-Sat Nov-Jan, Sun morning year-round) In a building that opened in 1468, rather appropriately, as a shelter for travellers. Here you can get a town map and a free what's-on monthly, *Agenda Cultura*.

Sights & Activities

PRAÇA DA REPÚBLICA

Any tour of Viana should start here: in the well-preserved zone of mansions and monuments that is the heart of the old town, and Viana's most picturesque quarter. Especially elegant is the **Chafariz**, a Renaissance fountain built in 1554 by João Lopes the Elder. It's topped with Manueline motifs of an armillary sphere and the cross of the Order of Christ. The fortress-like **Antigos Paços do Concelho** is the old town hall – another 16th-century creation.

At right angles to this is the striking former **Misericórdia** almshouse, designed in 1589 by João Lopes the Younger, its loggias supported by monster caryatids. The adjoining **Igreja de Misericórdia** (admission free; 10am-12.30pm & 2-5pm Mon-Fri Aug, 11am-12.30pm Sun year-round) was rebuilt in 1714 and is adorned with some of Portugal's finest azulejos by the master António de Oliveira Bernardes and his son Policarpo.

> **WHO'S SORRY NOW?**
>
> Picture the streets decorated with coloured sawdust, the women decked out in traditional finery of scarlet and gold, and the men drinking like there's no tomorrow. Viana's Romaria de Nossa Senhora d'Agonia (Our Lady of Sorrows) is one of the Minho's most spectacular festivals, featuring everything from emotive religious processions to firework displays and upbeat parades accompanied by deafening drums and lumbering carnival *gigantones* (giants) and *cabeçudos* (big-heads). In the main procession, statues from the Igreja de Nossa Senhora da Agonia are carried around the streets.
>
> The festival takes place for three or four days around 20 August. Accommodation is very tight at this time, so book well ahead.

IGREJA MATRIZ

This elegant **parish church** (admission free; Rua da Aurora do Lima; 9-11.30am & 3-5.30pm Mon-Fri) – also known as the *sé* – dates from the 15th century, though it has since had several reincarnations. Note its unusually sculpted Romanesque towers and Gothic doorway, carved with figures of Christ and the Evangelists.

MUSEU MUNICIPAL

The 18th-century **Palacete Barbosa Maciel** (☎ 258 820 377; Largo de São Domingos; admission €0.90; 9am-noon & 2-5pm Tue-Sun) bears striking witness to Viana's affluent past. It is home to a very impressive collection of 17th- and 18th-century ceramics (especially blue Portuguese china), azulejos and furniture.

CASTELO DE SÃO TIAGO DA BARRA

You can still scoot around the ramparts of this squat castle, a short walk west of the centre, which began life in the 15th century as a smallish fort. It was integrated into a larger fort, commissioned by Felipe II of Spain (Felipe I of Portugal) in 1592, to guard the prosperous port against pirates. The buildings inside have now been converted to office space, and the grandiose entrance is strung with washing lines!

MONTE DE SANTA LUZIA

There are two good reasons to visit Viana's 228m, eucalyptus-clad hill. One is the god's-eye **view** down the coast and up the Lima valley. The other is the fabulously over-the-top, 20th-century neo-Byzantine **Templo do Sagrado Coração de Jesus** (Temple of the Sacred Heart of Jesus; ☎ 258 823 173; admission free; 8am-7pm Apr-Sep, 8am-5pm Oct-Mar). You can get a little closer to heaven on its windy, graffiti-covered roof, via an elbow-scrapingly tight stairway (€0.50; take the entrance marked *zimbório*) or the lift (€0.80).

There's a Pousada de Portugal up here, too, behind and above the basilica. Behind that is another attraction, the poorly maintained ruins of a Celtiberian **citânia** from around the 4th century BC, though these were closed for redevelopment at the time of writing. You can also make the short walk onwards to the summit.

You can get up the mountain by car or taxi (3.5km) or on foot, a 2km climb of about 14 zillion steps – only for the penitent. The road starts by the hospital, and the steps begin about 200m up the road. An old funicular to the top has been growing rusty from disuse.

GIL EANNES

Demanding attention on the waterfront near Largo 5 de Outubro is this pioneering naval hospital ship, the *Gil Eannes* (zheel *yan*-ish). The **ship** (☎ 258 809 710; adult/child under 6 €1.50/free; 2-7pm Mon-Fri Jul-Sep, 9am-noon & 2-7pm Sat, Sun & holidays Apr-Sep, 9am-noon & 2-5.30pm Sat, Sun & holidays Oct-Mar) once provided on-the-job care for those fishing off the coast of Newfoundland. Now restored, visitors can clamber around the steep decks and cabins, though a scattering of old clinical equipment may make your hair stand on end.

It even houses a novel – if cramped – youth hostel (see Author's Choice, p406).

BEACHES

Viana's enormous arcing beach, **Praia do Cabedelo**, is one of the Minho's best, with little development to spoil its charm. It's across the river from town, and one way to get there is by passenger ferry from the pier south of Largo 5 de Outubro. The five-minute trip costs about €0.85 one way, and the ferry goes about hourly between 8.45am and 8pm daily from May to September, and to midnight between mid-July and mid-August.

Alternatively, **TransCunha** (☎ 258 829 711; Avenida dos Combatentes 127) buses go to Cabedelo (€0.60) from Largo 5 de Outubro at 7.35am, 10.15am and 12.50pm weekdays (plus weekends from July to September); the last bus back departs Cabedelo at 5.10pm. The TransCunha office has the current timetable.

There's a string of fine beaches north of Viana for 25km to Caminha, including good surfing venues at **Afife** and **Moledo**. AV Cura/Transcolvia buses (p408) depart at least hourly every day for Caminha (€1.60), with a stop en route by the Jardim Marginal. At least eight daily regional and *interregional* (IR) trains (€1.35) also make their way up the coast, though not all stop at Afife.

RIVER TRIPS

If there are enough passengers, boats run up and down the Rio Lima daily in summer, from the pier south of Largo 5 de Outubro. The most common trip takes 45 minutes (€5), but longer excursions, with lunch, are available in midsummer. For details call **Portela & Filhos** (☎ 258 842 290) or check at the pier.

Festivals & Events

Viana has a knack for celebrations. The **Romaria de Nossa Senhora d'Agonia** (www.festas-agonia.com), held in August, is the region's biggest annual bash (see Who's Sorry Now?, p404), and **Carnaval** festivities here are considered northern Portugal's best. The town also goes a little nuts in mid-May during **Semana Académica** (or Queima das Fitas), a week of student end-of-term madness similar to Coimbra's.

And that's not all. Almost every Saturday from May to September sees traditional dancing and a photogenic food market take place on Praça da República.

The town's **cultural activities office** (☎ 258 809 350; dac@nortenet.pt) has details of other annual events, which include the following:

Encontros de Viana (first week of May) A film festival.

Festival Maio (end of May) A national folk-dance extravaganza.

Canto Luso (second week of July) A gathering of singing groups from around the Portuguese-speaking world.

Jazz na Praça da Erva (first week of August) A jazz festival.

Simply Blues (third week of November) A blues festival.

Sleeping

Accommodation may be tight in summer but bargains are plentiful outside the high season. Prices given here are for July to September. The turismo keeps a list of trustworthy *quartos* (private rooms); expect to pay at least €25 for a double in summer. It also has details of several nearby cottages and manor houses, though most are hard to reach without a car. Expect to pay €65 to €90 for a double.

THE AUTHOR'S CHOICE

Provided you don't suffer from claustrophobia, why not push the boat out further and hop aboard the **Pousada da Juventude Gil Eannes** (☎ 258 821 582; naviogileannes@movijovem.pt; Gil Eannes; dm €11, s/d from €18/26). Yes – that's right – this newly opened hostel is located in the oily bowels of the old hospital ship (see p405). It has almost five dozen small berths for visitors to squeeze into. It scores well for novelty but don't expect luxury, easy access or more natural light than fits through a few portholes.

BUDGET

Pousada da juventude (☎ 258 800 260; vianacastelo@movijovem.pt; Rua da Argaçosa; dm €12.50, d with toilet €35; P) It's not often you get to choose between youth hostels in a single Portuguese city – let alone whether to sleep on dry land or floating on water. On the one hand, Viana has this nice and ordinary hostel, 1km east of the town centre, with balconies overlooking the marina. See the Author's Choice (above) for the other option.

Casa de Hóspedes Guerreiro (☎ 258 822 099; Rua Grande 4; s/d with shared facilities €19/25) This topsy-turvy boarding house has tatty but clean rooms, and is good value at the bottom of the market (no breakfast).

Orbitur (☎ 258 322 167; info@orbitur.pt; Praia do Cabedelo; adult/car €4.30/3.80, tent 3.50-5.90; year-round;) This beachside site is within walking distance of the ferry pier on the Cabedelo side, and also has bungalows for rent. It heaves with holidaymakers in summer (prices given are for the July to August high season). Next nearest are two facilities at Vila Praia de Âncora, 16km to the north.

MID-RANGE

Residencial Magalhães (☎ 258 823 293; fax 258 828 962; Rua Manuel Espregueira 62; d with breakfast & with/without bathroom from €43/38;) Carpeted and wood-panelled, this quirky old *residencial* offers both character and value. It's central but conspicuously quiet, and no two of its rooms are alike – expect everything from prim 1950s charm to garish 1970s paint jobs.

Pensão-Restaurante Dolce Vita (☎ 258 824 860; pizzaria.dolcevita@iol.pt; Rua do Poço 44; d with breakfast €40-55; ❄) The snug rooms at Dolce Vita are faultlessly spick and span, each with shower, toilet and TV. It's good value for being in the town centre. Expect hunger-inducing smells from the pizzeria below, though.

Residencial Viana Mar (☎/fax 258 828 962; Avenida dos Combatentes 215; d €35-45) This congenial place has a small bar and four floors of shipshape rooms on one of the town's busiest thoroughfares. There are also some rooms with shared facilities and no TV.

Residencial Laranjeira (☎ 258 822 261; resid.laranjeira@mail.telepac.pt; Rua General Luís do Rego 45; d with breakfast €40-50; P) This well-run place has homely rooms and décor inherited from various bygone decades. It has a good restaurant around the block (right). Off-street parking is €5 per day.

TOP END

Margarida da Praça (☎ 258 809 630; www.margaridadapraca.com; Largo 5 de Outubro 58; d with breakfast €65; P ❄) For pampering, try this shiny new hotel. It shares the best of Jardim's river views but has 12 newer, thoroughly renovated rooms, modern art on the walls and a classy restaurant below.

Pousada do Monte de Santa Luzia (Pousada de Viana do Castelo; ☎ 258 800 370; recepcao.mluzia@pousadas.pt; d with/without sea view Sun-Thu from €153/143, Fri & Sat from €175/157; P ❄) This regal place sits squarely atop Monte de Santa Luzia, peering down at the basilica's backside and beyond it to some of the best coastal views in Portugal.

Eating

Most mid-range *pensões* (guesthouses) have restaurants that welcome nonguests and offer reasonable food and prices.

Restaurante O Garfo (☎ 258 829 415; Largo 5 de Outubro 28; mains €8; lunch & dinner Sun-Fri) Hunkering down in the arches that face the docks, O Garfo is a solid, unpretentious eatery offering lots of very fresh fish dishes and more. There are tables outside in summer.

Estação Biológica (☎ 258 100 082; Estação Viana Shopping, 2nd fl; mains €5; lunch & dinner) Vegetarians, don't despair! While there are no dedicated sit-down vegie restaurants in Viana, this tiny natural-products shop does a great meat-free takeaway. You can devour it in the shopping centre's neighbouring food court, which will also cater to carnivorous friends.

Neiva Mar Marisqueira (☎ 258 820 669; Largo Infante D Henrique 1; mains €6.50-11; lunch & dinner Thu-Tue) For kick-ass shellfish platters that don't suck your wallet dry, try this unassuming little restaurant in the sketchy area near the shipyard. It has all the freshest seafood (crab, lobster, squid, you name it) at affordable prices.

Restaurante Laranjeira (☎ 258 822 258; Rua Manuel Espregueira 24; daily special €5.50, mains €5-10; lunch & dinner Sun-Fri) Good budget standby, with brisk service, a bright setting, good Portuguese standard fare and a view of the kitchen. Sunday brings traditional dishes such as *sarrabulho*, a rich pork stew.

Zip Creperia Gelataria (☎ 258 826 594; Rua Luis Jácome 17-19; crepes €1.20-2.50, pasta dishes €4-6; lunch & dinner Wed-Sat & Mon, lunch Tue) Tucked away on a side street, this funky café has an international flavour, with fresh Italian pasta dishes, a variety of ice creams and – topping them all – a fantastic range of fluffy crepes.

A Gruta Snack Bar (☎ 258 820 214; Rua Grande 87; mains €3-8; lunch & dinner Mon-Sat) This stone-walled little bistro has an economical lunch menu with good salads, a few specials and other well-prepared local dishes – all excellent washed down with a tipple or two of local *vinho verde*.

Pensão-Restaurante Dolce Vita (☎ 258 824 860; Rua do Poço 44; most dishes under €5; lunch & dinner) This popular place has a big menu of pizza and pasta dishes.

The **mercado municipal** (Avenida Capitão Gaspar de Castro; Mon-Sat morning) is northeast of the centre. Rua Grande and its eastward extension have numerous small fruit-and-vegetable shops.

Drinking & Entertainment

To hit the dance floor, your best bet is long-running bar **Glamour** (☎ 258 822 963; Rua da Bandeira 179-185), which reinvents its slick image regularly and often hosts live music. A lower-key venue is **Indian Bar** (☎ 258 828 794; Rua Nova de São Bento 131).

Or to drink and be merry in the open air, consider the greenhouse-like **Glora Café** (☎ 258 829 781; 9am-midnight) in the Jardim Marginal, with tables spilling out into the park. This is also a good spot for a chilled daytime coffee, cake and newspaper.

Alternatively, get into the sailor's spirit with a wee dram aboard **Gil Eannes Bar** (☎ 258 809 710; Gil Eannes; ⏰ noon-midnight Wed-Mon) in the ship's stern.

Shopping

A huge open-air market sprawls across the area beside the Castelo de São Tiago da Barra every Friday. One of several surf shops in town is **Scandal Surf** (☎ 258 821 727; Rua Santo António 100; ⏰ Mon-Sat).

Getting There & Away

BUS

Long-distance *expresso* buses operate from the bus station, though most lines also sell tickets at their town-centre offices. These companies include **AV Cura/Transcolvia** (☎ 258 806 830; Avenida dos Combatentes 81); **AV Minho** (☎ 258 800 341; Avenida dos Combatentes 181); **AVIC/Transcoinha** (☎ 258 829 711; Avenida dos Combatentes 217). **REDM/Rede Expressos** (☎ 258 825 047) operates from the station.

AV Cura/Transcolvia runs up the Lima valley to Ponte de Lima (€2.35, 50 minutes), Ponte da Barca (€3, 1½ hours) and Arcos de Valdevez (€3.15, 1½ hours) at least hourly every day; you can also board these services by the Jardim Marginal. Tickets are cheaper from the office. Rede Expressos has multiple weekday services to Braga (€3.60, 1¾ hours).

AV Cura coastal express buses go north to Valença (€3.50, 1¼ hours) and Monção (€4.20, 1½ hours) several times daily; AV Minho goes less often.

AV Minho goes south to Porto (€5, 2¼ hours) four times daily. AVIC/Rede Expressos each have daily expresses to Porto (€5.20/6.50), Lisbon (€14.50/13.90, 5½ hours) and destinations in the south.

Regional services are quite limited at the weekend.

TRAIN

Daily direct services from Porto include four IR/international trains (€5.50, 1½ hours) and five regional services (€5). For Braga (€4, from 1¼ hours, 12 daily), change at Nine. There are also around 10 daily trains to Valença (€2.40, 45 minutes to 1¼ hours) during the week.

VALENÇA DO MINHO

pop 5000 / elevation 60m

If only the walls of this impressive hilltop citadel could talk, they would have a deeply ironic tale to tell. Sitting above the Rio Minho frontier, just a short canon-ball shot from Spain, Valença do Minho (Valença) was built as, and long remained, a bulwark to ward off Spanish attack.

But in a final twist of fate, this fortress town now sees a large-scale Spanish invasion of a different nature every weekend. Troops of Spanish day-trippers now stream openly across from the counterpart town of Tuy – armed with wallets and aiming to buy cheap linen and towels from the shops and stalls packed tightly along the fortress's cobbled streets.

Indeed the mighty citadel has been ungracefully rechristened 'the Shopping Fortress' – even in the tourist brochures – and chances are you'll hear more Spanish spoken than Portuguese. On these days, it can feel that the fortress itself is a kind of sideshow to the bargain hunt in hand – but if you wander off the main drags and sidestep the towel touts, you can still catch a sense of the border tension that once prevailed. And when the weary troops go home loaded with loot, the silence seeps up from the riverbank and the fortress returns to sombre contemplation of its old foe – the glowering fortress of Tuy across the river.

Orientation & Information

An uninspiring new town sprawls at the foot of the fortress. From the bus station it's 800m north via Avenida Miguel Dantas (the N13) and the Largo da Trapicheira roundabout (also called Largo da Esplanada) to the **turismo** (☎ /fax 251 823 374; Avenida de Espanha; ⏰ 9.30am-12.30pm & 2-5.30pm Mon-Sat year-round, 9.30am-12.30pm Sun Jul-Aug). The train station is just east of Avenida Miguel Dantas.

From the turismo you can climb for 400m to enter the fortress through the Portas do Sol. Coming from Viana or from Spain on the N13, turn west at Largo da Trapicheira and enter through the southern gateway, the Portas da Coroada. An interchange from the A3/IP1 motorway also leads to the Portas da Coroada.

The fortress has its own **post office** (☎ 251 824 811; ⏰ 9am-12.30pm & 2pm-5.30pm Mon-Fri). There are numerous banks with ATMs in the lower town, and one off Rua Mousinho de Albuquerque in the north fortress.

Espaço Internet (☎ 251 809 588; 🕐 10am-1pm & 2-9pm Mon-Sat), by the bus station, has free Internet access.

Sights

There are actually two **fortresses**, bristling with bastions, watchtowers, massive gateways and defensive bulwarks, and joined by a single bridge. The old churches and Manueline mansions inside testify how successful the fortifications were against several sieges as late as the 19th century.

The earliest fortifications date from the 13th-century reign of Dom Afonso III, when Valença was called Contrasta. Today's muscular, well-preserved *fortaleza* (fortress) dates from the 16th century, its design inspired by the French military architect Vauban.

Press on through the gift shops and towel merchants along the cobbled lanes to the far end of the larger northern fortress, which incorporates Dom Afonso's original stronghold and contains almost everything that's of interest.

From Praça da República bear right, then left, into Rua Guilherme José da Silva. On the left, opposite the post office, is the **Casa da Eira**, with a handsome Manueline window. The 14th-century **Igreja de Santo Estevão**, with its Renaissance façade, is at the end of the street. Nearby is a 1st-century **Roman milestone** from the old Braga-Astorga road.

From the milestone continue northwards to the end of Rua José Rodrigues and the now decrepit Romanesque parish church, **Igreja de Santa Maria dos Anjos** (St Mary of the Angels), dating from 1276. At the back is a tiny **chapel** with leering carved faces and Romano-Gothic inscriptions on the outside, though this is in an appalling state of disrepair and closed to the public.

To the left of the parish church is the **Capela da Misericórdia** and beyond it the Pousada de São Teotónio (right). All around this area are picturesquely overgrown ramparts to explore, many still with cannons forlornly pointing at Tuy.

Turn right by the *pousada* and descend the atmospheric lane through one of the 13th-century **original gates**, with a trickling stream running below and an impressive echo. Keep going and you'll pass through several thick onion-skin fortress layers to the outside world.

Sleeping

Campers sometimes pitch tents below the northwestern ramparts. However, there are only two official places to stay inside the fortress, both at the northern end and with fantastic views into Spanish Galicia, and both decidedly top-end.

Casa do Poço (☎ 251 825 235; www.casadopoco.fr.fm; Travessa da Gaviarra 4; ste with breakfast €120) For a personal touch, try this gorgeously restored 18th-century house that once lodged the sick from the Misericórdia hospital. It now cares for wealthy tourists, with contemporary European art, a library, billiard room and six silk-wallpapered suites. Food (especially French cuisine) is available with advance notice.

Pousada de São Teotónio (☎ 251 800 260; recepcao.steotonio@pousadas.pt; Rua de Baluarte do Socorro; d Sun-Thu €122, Fri & Sat €134; P ❄) Perched on the outermost post of the fortress, this modern *pousada* has prime views overlooking the walls and river to Spain.

The rest of us sleep outside the walls, on the road to the Portas do Coroada. Prices listed are for the local high season (July to mid-September); outside this period they're at least a third less.

Residencial Rio Minho (☎ 251 809 240; fax 251 809 248; d with breakfast €40) Staggering out of the train station and can't wait to drop your kit? Well you won't do much better than this guesthouse and restaurant, bang in front of the exit and boasting a shady vine-hung veranda and spacious rooms.

Val Flores (☎ 251 824 106; fax 251 824 129; Centro Comercial Val Flores; d with breakfast €40) This friendly, spotless but plain *residencial*, on the road looking up at the fortress walls, is pretty good value.

Hotel Lara (☎ 251 824 348; fax 251 824 358; Avenida Dos Bombeiros; d with breakfast €50; ❄) You'll find this bigger and more professional hotel just uphill from Val Flores. Many rooms sport balconies.

Casa da Eira (☎ 251 921 905; www.casaeira.net; Laços; d with breakfast €75; P 🏊) If you've got your own wheels and want a guesthouse with more home comfort and character, seek out this Turihab property, 8km east of Valença towards Monção. Turn off the N101 towards Laços and follow the signs.

Eating

Grabbing a bite in the fortress alongside Spanish tour groups almost guarantees a jolly atmosphere.

Restaurante Monumental (☎ 251 823 557; mains €7-14; ⌚ lunch & dinner) Built into the Portas da Coroada, this spot has a barrel-vaulted ceiling, long tables and a great outdoor area under overshadowing trees – hung with lights for atmospheric evening meals.

A Gruta (☎ 251 822 270; dishes €7-10; ⌚ lunch & dinner Jun-Aug, Tue-Sun Sep-May) This snappy little bar-restaurant is built into the portal between the two fortresses. Again, you can sit in or out, in the shade of the weedy gateway, and watch troops of tourists go past loaded with their bargain buys.

Outside the fort there are several ho-hum restaurants and cafés near the *residenciais*.

Getting There & Away

BUS

There are **Courense** (☎ 251 824 175) services to Monção (€1.80, 20 minutes) about hourly on weekdays (less often at the weekend), and via Viana do Castelo (€3.40, 1¼ hours) to Porto daily. AVIC and AV Minho have similar but less frequent services.

TRAIN

Three IR/international trains run daily to Valença from Porto (€6.50, 2¼ hours) and continue on as far as Vigo in Spain.

MONÇÃO

pop 2600 / elevation 60m

The modest spa-town of Monção (mohng-*sawng*), 22km up the Rio Minho from Valença, still has sizable chunks of a sturdy, irregular fortress finished in 1306 scattered around a small, cheerful old town centre; there's plenty of good food and *vinho verde* on offer.

History

The town's most famous daughter is one Deu-la-Deu Martins, who, according to local legend, tricked a force of Castilians into calling off a siege in 1368. She scrabbled together enough flour from starving citizens to make a few loaves of bread, and in a brazen show of plenty tossed them to the Castilians with the message, 'if you need any more, just let us know'. Amazingly, it did the trick and the disheartened besiegers withdrew.

Three centuries later, as Portugal was shaking off Spanish rule, another woman brought another siege to an end. Mariana de Lencastre, Countess of Castelo Melhor, surrendered to Spanish besiegers on the condition that they honour those inside. This they did, raising their flags to the 236 defenders, the only survivors of a force of over 2000.

Orientation

From the bus station it's 600m east to the defunct train station, then two blocks north up Rua General Pimenta de Castro to the first of the town's two main squares, Praça da República. Praça Deu-la-Deu and the heart of the old town lie a block further on.

Information

Espaço Internet (☎ 251 654 913; Praça Deu-la-Deu; ⌚ 2-9pm Sun-Thu, 2-10pm Fri-Sat)

Post office (☎ 251 640 600; Praça da República; ⌚ 9am-12.30pm & 2-5.30pm Mon-Fri)

Turismo (☎ 251 652 757; Praça da República; ⌚ 9.30am-12.30pm & 2-6pm Mon-Sat) On the ground floor of the restored Casa do Curro, along with a permanent exhibit on local Alvarinho wines.

Sights & Activities

OLD MONÇÃO

In chestnut-shaded Praça Deu-la-Deu, a hand-on-breast statue of its namesake tops a **fountain** and looks hungrily down over the surrounding cafés. The Senhora da Vista bastion at the northern end offers a gentle view across the Rio Minho into Spain – a mere slingshot's throw away, close enough for the Portuguese to thumb their noses at the Spaniards. The **Capela da Misericórdia** at the square's southern end has a coffered ceiling painted with cherubs.

East of the square is the snug, cobbled old quarter. Two blocks along Rua da Glória is the pretty little Romanesque **igreja matriz**, where Deu-la-Deu is buried.

WINE-TASTING

Another good reason to visit is the wine. Alvarinho is a delicious, full-bodied variety of white *vinho verde* produced around Monção and neighbouring Melgaço. If you'd like a free tasting, either contact the **Adega Cooperativa de Monção** (☎ 251 652 167; fax 251 651 108), 1.8km south of Monção on the N101 to Arcos de Valdevez, or try asking for a few samples at the **wine exhibition** (10am-noon & 2-6pm Tue-Sun) above the tourist office.

Otherwise, the clutch of bars around Monção's principal squares will be only too happy to oblige.

Festivals & Events

Festa da Nossa Senhora das Dores (Our Lady of Sorrows; second-last Sunday in August) A big five-day celebration headed by a pious procession.

Festa de Corpo de Deus (Ninth Thursday after Easter) The town's biggest rave, held on Corpus Christi . Events include a religious procession and a medieval fair, with a re-enactment of St George and the Dragon's battle.

Sleeping

Croissanteria Raiano (☎ 251 653 534; raiano4950@hotmail.com; Praça Deu-la-Deu 34; d with shower & toilet €30) A few rooms at this chirpy café have limited views across to Spain. The waste-not-want-not décor uses the same chintzy materials on bedspreads, tablecloths and curtains. Good value.

Hospedaria Beco da Matriz (☎ 251 651 909; Beco da Matriz; d €25-30) A few steps towards the river, left of *igreja matriz,* is this newly opened *hospedaria* offering nine spotless rooms with bathroom and TV. Its unsmiling host can often be found in the small tavern behind the guesthouse, along with his dog (beware the latter's addiction to shoelaces).

Residencial Esteves (☎ 251 652 386; Rua General Pimenta de Castro; d from €30-35) Though not particularly old itself, this *residencial* gives off an air of old-fashioned comfort. It also offers good-value rooms and a friendly welcome from the two accommodating old dears that run it.

Albergaria Atlântico (☎ 251 652 355; moscosohoteis@clix.pt; Rua General Pimenta de Castro 15; d with breakfast €55;) Upper-end Atlântico has well-equipped rooms and a top-floor restaurant with rooftop views.

For Turihab properties, ask at the turismo (p410). Closest to town are two manor houses on estates producing Alvarinho wine grapes:

Casa de Rodas (☎ 251 652 105; rodas@solaresdeportugal.pt; Lugar de Rodas; d €80; P) One kilometre south of the town centre is this huge elongated manor house dating back five centuries. English and French are spoken.

Solar de Serrade (☎ 251 654 008; www.solardeserrade.pt; Mazedo; d €60-75; P) A few kilometres further on from Casa de Rodas, this typical 17th-century mansion has whimsical gardens and a few suites with four-poster beds for romantic getaways.

Eating

The pick of local specialities is fresh shad, salmon and trout from the Rio Minho, and lamprey eels in spring. But whatever you choose, be sure to wash it down with a pitcher of Alvarinho wine.

Croissanteria Raiano (☎ 251 653 534; Praça Deu-la-Deu 34; lunch about €5; lunch Mon-Fri) A few doors from the turismo, this place has a few modest lunch-time specials (with vegetables, hurray!) and snacks into the evening.

Restaurante Mané (☎ 251 652 355; mains €8-16; lunch & dinner) Calling itself a *restaurante panorâmico,* this elegant restaurant atop Hotel Atlântico does indeed have a few rooftop views, as well as slick service and a wine list far longer than the menu.

Restaurante Cabral (☎ 251 651 755; Rua 1 de Dezembro; dishes €6-10; lunch & dinner;) A popular stone-walled place for good fish and seafood creations.

Deu-La-Deu (☎ 251 652 137; Praça da República; mains €6-9; lunch & dinner) This typical local joint sees the most lunch-time traffic. It does good regional dishes such as kid à la Monção.

Getting There & Away

Salvador/Renex (☎ 251 653 881) buses go to Arcos de Valdevez (€2.85, 45 minutes) and Braga (€4.70, two hours) three to six times daily. **Courense** (☎ 251 653 881) goes to Valença (€1.80, 25 minutes) hourly on weekdays and less often at weekends, and to Viana (€4.20, 1½ hours) and Porto several times daily. **AV Minho** (☎ 251 652 917) travels this route less often.

PONTE DE LIMA

pop 2700

This handsomely restored and photogenic town by the Rio Lima springs to life every other Monday, when a vast market sprawls along the riverbank, offering everything from farm tools and wine barrels to fresh fruit, cheese and bread.

When the Romans first passed through here, the soldiers were convinced that the Rio Lima was the River Lethe – the mythical 'river of oblivion' – and that if they crossed it they'd forget everything. It was only after their leader, Decimus Junius Brutus, plunged ahead and shouted back his legionnaires'

names that they braved the waters. The Ponte Romana (Roman Bridge) after which the town is named – part of the Roman road from Braga to Astorga in Spain – supposedly marks the very spot.

If it's not market day, you too may find yourself slipping into forgetful slumber here. It's expensive to linger, though, and you can do the town justice in a day. The heartland of Turismo de Habitação (p453), the Ponte de Lima area has more country manor houses to stay in than anywhere else in Portugal.

Orientation

The bus station is 800m uphill from the town centre, though all long-distance buses loop down to within a block of the turismo, on Praça da República. Most things of interest are in the short strip between the turismo and the riverbank. The local shopping zone is Rua do Souto. Downriver, the Ponte de Nossa Senhora da Guia carries the Braga-Valença N201.

Information

There are at least three banks with ATMs on Rua Inácio Perestrelo.

Biblioteca municipal (☎ 258 900 411; Largo da Matriz; 🕑 2pm-6.30pm Mon, 10am-12.30pm & 2-6.30pm Tue-Fri, 10am-12.30pm Sat) Provides free Internet access.

Espaço Internet (☎ 258 900 400 ext 415; Avenida António Feijó; 🕑 1-8pm Mon-Fri, 10am-8pm Sat) More Internet access for all.

Hospital (☎ 258 909 500; Rua Conde de Bertiandos)

Police station (☎ 258 941 113; Rua Dr Luís da Cunha Nogueira)
Post office (☎ 258 900 700; Praça da República; 🕑 8.30am-5.30pm Mon-Fri)
Turismo (☎ 258 942 335; Praça da República; 🕑 9.30am-12.30pm & 2-5.30pm Jun-Aug, 9.30am-12.30pm & 2.30-6pm Sep-May) This well organised tourist office shares an old tower with a small handicrafts gallery. Also, on a lower floor, are glass walkways over the excavated layers of the ancient tower.

Sights

PONTE ROMANA & ARCOZELO

This is what everyone comes to see. The elegant 31-arched bridge across the Rio Lima is now pedestrian only, and takes as much as five minutes to stroll across. Most of the bridge dates from the 14th century, when the Roman structure was extended. However, the segment on the north bank by the village of **Arcozelo** is bona fide Roman (but for the road surface).

In down-at-heel Arcozelo are the extremely photogenic little **Igreja Santo António** and the unusual **Parque do Arnado**, the latter an architecturally themed park that crams in styles from all around the world. Far more typical of the area is the little **Museu Rural** (Rural Museum; 🕑 2-6pm Tue-Sun), hiding at the back of the park.

In Ponte de Lima is **Largo de Camões**, a wonderful spot to see the sun set over the bridge, featuring a fountain that resembles a giant bonbon dish.

MUSEU DOS TERCEIROS

Downriver, the 18th-century Igreja de São Francisco dos Terceiros is now a rambling **museum** (☎ 258 942 563) of ecclesiastical and folk treasures, although the highlight is the church itself, with its gilded baroque interior. The Renaissance-style **Igreja de Santo António dos Frades**, once a convent church, is adjacent to the museum. However, both church and museum are shut for renovations estimated to last until 2006.

Behind the museum, on Rua Agostinho José Taveira, stands Ponte de Lima's pride, the galleried **Teatro Diogo Bernardes** (☎ 258 900 414), built in 1893.

TOWN WALLS & TOWERS

Two crenellated towers – part of the 14th-century fortifications – face the river at the end of Rua Cardeal Saraiva. The **Torre da Cadeia Velha** (Old Prison Tower; admission free; 🕑 2-6pm Tue-Sun) now houses temporary art exhibits, plus a host of nesting pigeons in its window ledges.

Fragments of the walls survive behind and between this and the other tower, the **Torre de São Paulo**. Note the somewhat bizarre azulejo picture on its front wall entitled *Cabras são Senhor!* (They're goats m'lord!), referring to a local story in which Dom Afonso Henriques almost attacked a herd of goats, apparently mistaking them for Moors!

Behind the tower is the rather staid 15th-century **igreja matriz** (Rua Cardeal Saraiva; admission free; 🕑 daily), sporting a pretty Romanesque doorway.

Activities

WALKING

There are charming walks all round the area – through the countryside, past ancient monuments and along cobbled lanes trellised with vines. The turismo has descriptions of walks ranging from 5km to 14km, but bear in mind that construction work on the Viana–Ponte de Lima highway, set to open in March 2005, will disrupt several walks. Take a picnic – cafés and restaurants are rare.

A steep climb north of Arcozelo yields panoramic views up and down the Lima valley. A steep climb up a hill north, about 5km from Ponte de Lima, is a tiny and bizarre **chapel** (open irregular hours) dedicated to Santo Ovídio, patron saint of ears. Yes, you read that right. The interior is covered with votive wax ears, offered in hopes of, or as thanks for, the cure of an ear affliction. You can also drive up; the turning off the N202 is about 2.5km upstream of the N201 bridge.

BOATING

The **Clube Náutico** (☎ 258 944 499; 🕑 10am-1pm & 4-7pm Jul-Sep, Sat & Sun Oct-Jun), across the river and 400m downstream by the N201 bridge (you can walk via Arcozelo), rents canoes and plastic kayaks for tootling around on the river, for €3 per 1½ hours.

GOLF

Clube de Golfe de Ponte de Lima (☎ 258 743 414; Feitosa) is 2km south of Ponte de Lima near the intersection of the N201 and the N536. The 18-hole course covers the wooded slopes above town, commanding grand views, and is open to nonmembers for €48 (or €37.50 if you're staying in a Turihab property).

HORSE RIDING

Nearby places to hire horses by the hour include **Clube Equestre** (☎ 258 942 466) in Arcozelo and **Centro Equestre Vale do Lima** (☎ 258 943 834), about 1km south of Ponte de Lima off the N201, which also has an excellent restaurant.

WINE-TASTING

For a taste of both red and white varieties of *vinho verde*, as well as two brands of *aguardente* (firewater) at source, head to the **Adega Cooperativa de Ponte de Lima** (☎ 258 909 700; Rua Conde de Bertiandos; 9.30am-noon & 2-4.30pm Mon-Fri). Wine-tasting tours in English, French and Portuguese can be organised with advance warning.

Festivals & Events

Feiras Novas (New Fairs; mid-September) Held here since 1125 and one of Portugal's most ancient ongoing events. Stretching over three days, it centres on the riverfront, with a massive market and fair, and features folk dances, fireworks, brass bands and all manner of merrymaking. Book accommodation well ahead.

Vaca das Cordas (ninth Wednesday after Easter) Another centuries-old tradition. A kind of bull-running in which young men goad a hapless bull (restrained by a long rope) as it runs through the town.

Festa do Corpo de Deus (ninth Thursday after Easter) Held annually around Corpus Christi. During this more pious festival, patterns of flowers carpet the streets.

Sleeping

There are dozens of Turihab properties in the Ponte de Lima area, from humble farmhouses to enormous mansions: pick up a list at the turismo (p413).

Pousada da Juventude (☎ 258 943 797; pontelima@movijovem.pt; Rua Agostinho José Taveira; dm/d €12.50/35;) A brand spanking new dusty-pink youth hostel, a pleasant 800m walk from the centre of town along the river.

Pensão São João (☎ 258 941 288; Largo de São João; d with/without toilet & shower €35/25) Though a shade overpriced, this is the town's best lower-end choice, with bright but serviceable rooms (no TV) next to a plaza.

Residencial O Garfo (☎ /fax 258 743 147; ogarfo@clix.pt; Rua do Arrabalde; d/tw with breakfast €35/37.50; P) In a quiet setting 1.3km northeast of the centre, this squat modern block has unexceptional frilly rooms and a no-nonsense café downstairs.

Hotel Império do Minho (☎ 258 741 510; hotelimperiominho@clix.pt; Avenida dos Plátanos; d with breakfast €62.50;) Bathed in the surrounding shopping-centre's muzak, this riverside place has an outdoor pool and forgettable rooms, each with a balcony, minibar and satellite TV.

Quinta da Aldeia (☎ 258 741 355; São João da Ribeira; cottage-apartments from €60) A child-friendly Turihab manor house about 3km northeast on the N203.

Casa do Arrabalde (☎ 258 742 442; double apt €75) This restored 1770 manor house in Arcozelo is another Turihab option.

Hotel do Golfe (☎ 258 900 250; gpl@nortenet.pt; Quinta de Pias, Fornelos; d €85; P) If golf is your bag, you might be interested in this swish new hotel, 2km south of Ponte de Lima at the golf course (p413).

Eating

Restaurante A Tulha (☎ 258 942 879; Rua Formosa; mains €8-15; lunch & dinner Tue-Sun;) All dark wood, stone and red tiles inside, this tourist-friendly restaurant serves excellent meat and fish dishes with plenty of vegetables.

Restaurante Alameda (☎ 258 941 630; Largo da Feira; dishes €4-8; lunch & dinner Tue-Sun) This jovial place packs in happy customers at lunch time. Half-portions (€3 to €5) of meaty regional specialities are a bargain, and the upstairs room is nonsmoking and non-TV.

Restaurante A Carvalheira (☎ 258 742 316; N202; mains €10-15; lunch & dinner Tue-Sun; P) On the N202 at the northern end of Arcozelo, country-style A Carvalheira is a tourist scene, but it's agreed that it serves the area's best food; it sneaks a few good Brazilian specialities in among traditional Minho fare.

Restaurante Açude (☎ 258 944 158; Arcozelo; mains €12-17; lunch & dinner Tue-Sun; P) Beside the Clube Náutico, this place has lots of knotty pine, big windows onto the river, and good food.

Self-caterers can try the **Minipreço supermarket** (Rua General Norton de Matos; 9am-8pm Mon-Sat, 9am-1pm & 3-7pm Sun). The recently rebuilt **mercado municipal** (Avenida dos Plátanos; Mon-Sat) has fresh fruit and veg.

Drinking

SA Bar (Rua Formosa; 1pm-2am) This snug little bar pulls in a good crowd at weekends and whenever there's a big football match on.

Getting There & Away

Long-distance buses can be boarded on Avenida António Feijó (buy tickets on board) or at the bus station. All services thin out on Sunday.

AV Cura (☎ 258 829 348), jointly with **AV Minho** (☎ 258 743 613), goes down to Viana do Castelo (€2.35, 50 minutes, about hourly) and up to Ponte da Barca (€1.85, 25 minutes, five daily) and Arcos de Valdevez (€2.15, 50 minutes, nine daily). **Domingos da Cunha** (☎ 258 942 791) has less frequent Lima valley services, and goes to Barcelos (€2.45, 55 minutes, six daily). **REDM/Rede Expressos** (☎ 258 942 870) runs to Braga (€2.65, 30 minutes, three daily) and via Barcelos to Porto (€4.70, two hours, four daily). Slower Braga services also run hourly from Avenida António Feijó.

PONTE DA BARCA

pop 2000

Peaceful little Ponte da Barca, named after the *barca* (barge) that once ferried pilgrims and others across the Rio Lima, has a dreamy riverfront park, a handsome 16th-century bridge, a tiny old centre and appealing local walks. It's also the home of the best source of information on the Parque Nacional de Peneda-Gerês.

The town erupts in activity every other Wednesday (alternating with Arcos de Valdevez), when a huge market spreads along the riverside.

Orientation

The old town, just east of the bridge, is packed into narrow lanes on both sides of the main road, Rua Conselheiro Rocha Peixoto. Uphill and away from the river, where the main road becomes Rua António José Pereira and Rua Dr Joaquim Moreira de Barros (and eventually the N101 to Braga), is the less picturesque new town.

Information

There are no ATMs in the old town but plenty along Rua António José Pereira in the new town.

Adere-PG (Parque Nacional da Peneda-Gerês Regional Development Association) Park information (p417).

Post office (☎ 258 480 400; Rua das Fontaínhas; 9am-12.30pm & 2-5.30pm Mon-Fri)

Turismo (☎ /fax 258 820 270; Rua Plácido de Vasconcelos; 9.30am-12.30pm & 2.30-6pm Mon-Sat) The tourist office is about 300m east of the bridge down a small street, and has a town map and accommodation information. It's next door to a large workshop devoted to traditional embroidery.

Sights & Activities

You'll remember the town for its waterfront. Take a romantic stroll beneath the picturesque weeping willows lining the riverbank, and admire the lovely 10-arched **ponte** (bridge), which originally dates from 1543, across the Rio Lima.

Beside it is the old arcaded marketplace and a little garden, **Jardim dos Poetas**, dedicated to two 16th-century poet brothers, Diogo Bernardes and Agostinho da Cruz, born in Ponte da Barca.

The turismo and Adere-PG will suggest some fine **hikes** punctuated with ancient sites.

You could take a simple stroll westwards for 3.5km to Bravães, a village famous for its lovely, small Romanesque **Igreja de São Salvador**, once part of a Benedictine monastery. Its west portal is adorned with intricate carved animals, birds and human figures; its interior is adorned with simple frescoes of the Virgin and of the Crucifixion.

Festivals & Events

The **Festa de São Bartolomeu**, held from 19 to 24 August, sees folk music and dancing aplenty, not to mention parades and fireworks.

Sleeping

Parque de Campismo de Entre Ambos-os-Rios (☎ 258 588 361; Entre Ambos-os-Rios; adult/tent/car €2.05/1.80/2.30; mid-May–Sep) This basic riverside camp site is in lush surroundings, 9km upriver from town. It can be booked through Adere-PG (left). Take any Lindoso-bound bus to reach it (p422).

Pensão Restaurante Gomes (☎ 258 452 288, 258 454 016; Rua Conselheiro Rocha Peixoto 13; d with shared facilities around €20) A bargain with bags of creaky old character thrown in to boot, this place has homely old rooms, many with sloping roofs and quaint old-fashioned furnishings; they and the rooftop terrace offer privileged views of the river and bridge. Warmly recommended.

Residencial San Fernando (☎ 258 452 580; Rua Herois da India; d with breakfast €26; P) At the very top of the new town, about 800m beyond Pensão Gomes, this business-like *residencial* is not entirely devoid of character and has

THE MINHO

smart, bright rooms with more up-to-date comforts. It's good value at this price.

Casa do Correio Mor (☎/fax 258 452 129; www.laceme.pt.vu; Rua Trás do Forno 1; d €60-100; P) Lovingly restored, this 17th-century manor house is on the street above the town hall. With 10 graceful old rooms, some with four-poster beds, it's worth the price tag. Ask the staff to recount the tale of a famous robbery here back in 1821.

There are four more Turismo Rural properties within 5km of town, including the red-tiled and whitewashed villa **Quinta da Prova** (☎258 452 163; http://members.xoom.com/quintaprova/; 2-/4-bed ste €60/100) across the river. These, and others nearer the national park, can be booked through Adere-PG.

Eating

Restaurante O Emigrante (☎258 452 248; Rua António José Pereira 26; half-portions €4-6; ⏰ lunch & dinner) There's not much in the way of flashy restaurants in Ponte da Barca. However, this humble spot offers some decent meaty main dishes and a few fishy alternatives, cheery service and good value.

Pensão Restaurant Gomes (☎258 452 288; Rua Conselheiro Rocha Peixoto 13; mains about €7-12; ⏰ lunch & dinner) The sleepy service at this large place doesn't stop them serving up delicious regional fare, including the wonderful *truta á Rio Lima* (River Lima trout).

Entertainment

História Café and **Poetas Bar** (Jardim dos Poetas; ⏰ 9pm-2am Tue-Thu, 9pm-4am Fri, 3pm-4am Sat & Sun) are both snug summer bars that spill out into the pretty bridge-side Jardim dos Poetas. They both host occasional live gigs.

Getting There & Away

Arcos de Valdevez and Braga buses stop beside Restaurante Gomes in the old town, and up in the new town on Rua António José Pereira. Buses to/from Ponte de Lima and Viana do Castelo stop just west of the bridge on Rua Diogo Bernardes (N203).

AV Cura and Domingos da Cunha buses run to Arcos de Valdevez (€0.80, 10 minutes), Ponte de Lima (€1.85, 40 minutes) and Viana do Castelo (€3, 1½ hours) four to five times daily. Renex/Salvador buses pass through Ponte da Barca about hourly, travelling between Braga (€2.75, one hour) and Arcos de Valdevez.

ARCOS DE VALDEVEZ

pop 2200 / elevation 200m

Drowsy little Arcos is home to a couple of interesting old churches and several stately homes in a small, almost tourist-free old centre. It has a pleasant setting on the west bank of the Rio Vez, a tributary of the Lima. While it doesn't merit a special trip, it's a handy gateway to the northern Parque Nacional da Peneda-Gerês.

Orientation & Information

The town is centred around Praça Municipal, a block uphill (west) from the turismo. Every other Wednesday is market day, alternating with Ponte da Barca.

The bus station is almost 1km north of the town centre, but regional buses will stop on request in front of the **turismo** (☎258 510 260; Campo do Transladário; ⏰ 9.30am-12.30pm & 2.30-6pm Mon-Sat Apr-Oct, 9am-12.30pm & 2.30-5.30pm Nov-Mar), which is on the N101 just north of where it crosses the river.

A **national park office** (☎258 515 338; Rua Tomás de Figueiredo; ⏰ 9am-12.30pm & 2-5.30pm Mon-Fri) can be found two blocks west of the riverfront fountain.

Sights

To reach the churches from the turismo climb Rua AB Cerqueira for a block beyond Praça Municipal. Around to the right is the tiny, Romano-Gothic **Capela da Nossa Senhora da Conceição** (Capela da Praça; ☎258 522 311; Rua da Praça; ⏰ 10am-6pm), dating from the late 14th or early 15th century. Inside are bas-relief grave markers and a surviving fragment of once-rich frescoes.

Carry on up to the oval, oddly pretty, baroque **Igreja da Nossa Senhora da Lapa** (Largo da Lapa; ⏰ 9am-8pm), as whitewashed inside as it is outside.

Sleeping & Eating

Residencial Dona Isabel (☎258 520 380; fax 258 520 389; Rua Mário Júlio Almeida Costa; d with breakfast €40; ❄) A short hop from the tourist office, Dona Isabel has richly decorated modern rooms, irreproachable bathrooms and a bright breezy restaurant open to nonguests.

Pensão Flôr do Minho (☎258 515 216; Rua da Valeta 106-108; d with shared facilities around €20) For those on a tight budget, this somewhat grubby option is down behind Praça Municipal; take the lane down from the Capela da Nossa Senhora da Conceição. Expect bathroom queues.

Residencial Tavares (☎ 258 516 253; Largo da Lapa; d with breakfast €40) Opposite the Igreja da Nossa Senhora da Lapa, Residencial Tavares is a tightly run place with well-kept rooms and very personable service.

Hotel Ribeira (☎ 258 510 240; hotelribeira@sapo.pt; Largo dos Milagres; d with breakfast €55; P ✈ 💻) Except for its picturesque fairy-pink façade, this early 1900s town house has been largely gutted of its original character but has an excellent position by the river. It has one room adapted for wheelchair access and use.

Doçaria Central (☎ 258 515 215; Rua General Norton de Matos 47; 9am-5.30pm) Founded in 1830, this confectioners stocks local *rebuçados dos arcos* (enormous, jaw-breaking, hard-boiled sweets), effective gobstoppers for particularly big mouths. Take the street to the right of the tourist office, past the post office.

Restaurante Floresta (☎ 258 515 163; Rua Mário Júlio Almeida Costa; half-portions around €4; daily) A popular, no-frills place feeding the crowds at a frantic pace, with just a couple of daily specials and no menu. Beside Residencial Dona Isabel.

Getting There & Away

Leaving town you can flag outbound buses by the turismo and buy a ticket on board.

AV Cura (☎ 258 515 236) has at least eight daily services to Viana do Castelo (€3.10) via Ponte de Lima, with half of them going via Ponte da Barca, too. **Domingos da Cunha** (☎ 258 815 843) runs at least four times daily to Ponte da Barca (€0.80, 10 minutes) and Ponte de Lima (€2.25, 50 minutes). **Renex/Salvador** (☎ 258 521 504) runs via Ponte da Barca to Braga (€2.85, 1¼ hours) about hourly, and to Monção (€2.85, 50 minutes) five times daily during the week and twice on Saturday. All services are reduced on weekends.

PARQUE NACIONAL DA PENEDA-GERÊS

Strewn with cascades of boulders, a patchwork of scented pine forests, tangly gorse and richly coloured heather, the beautiful 703-sq-km Peneda-Gerês National Park is Portugal's first and most important protected area. It was established in 1971 to safeguard not only natural riches but a whole way of life – ancient customs and unique agricultural practices that are still visible despite the passing centuries.

The horseshoe-shaped park takes in four granite massifs that are blessed (or cursed) with more rain than anywhere else in Portugal, and its rivers and five sizable reservoirs swell and fall with the changing seasons. Within the southern park in particular, you'll find exceptional hiking through forests and over high plateaus dotted with beehives and archaeological sites. The northwest is known for its idyllic rural accommodation in far-flung cottages and stone shelters.

In the outer part of the crescent are some 115 granite villages, dwindling as their young residents leave for the cities, but offering a glimpse into a vanishing way of life. Meanwhile, the heights close to the Spanish border (especially in the Serra do Gerês, where several peaks rise over 1500m), are almost free of human activity, other than the shifting of livestock to high pastures in summer.

The park shares 80km of frontier with Spain and embraces a corresponding Spanish reserve. The main base is spa town Vila do Gerês. Portuguese day-trippers swarm up here on summer weekends, but if you go beyond the main camping areas you'll quickly give crowds the slip.

Information

An EU-assisted consultancy helping along development in the region, **Adere-PG** (Parque Nacional da Peneda-Gerês Regional Development Association; ☎ 258 452 250; www.adere-pg.pt; Largo da Misericórdia 10, Ponte da Barca; 9am-12.30pm & 2.30-6pm Mon-Fri), is the best resource on the park. Materials available include pamphlets on the park's natural, architectural and human landscapes; village-to-village walks on marked trails; and a booklet on accommodation.

Adere-PG is also the booking agent for many camp sites, shelters and rural houses in the park. Don't confuse this with a similar but independent programme called Adere-Soajo (p420).

The next most useful information sources are the gateway turismos at Vila do Gerês, Arcos de Valdevez and Ponte da Barca. Less user-friendly are park information centres at Braga, Arcos de Valdevez, Gerês and Montalegre, and the **interpretive centre** (Mon-Fri) at Lamas de Mouro.

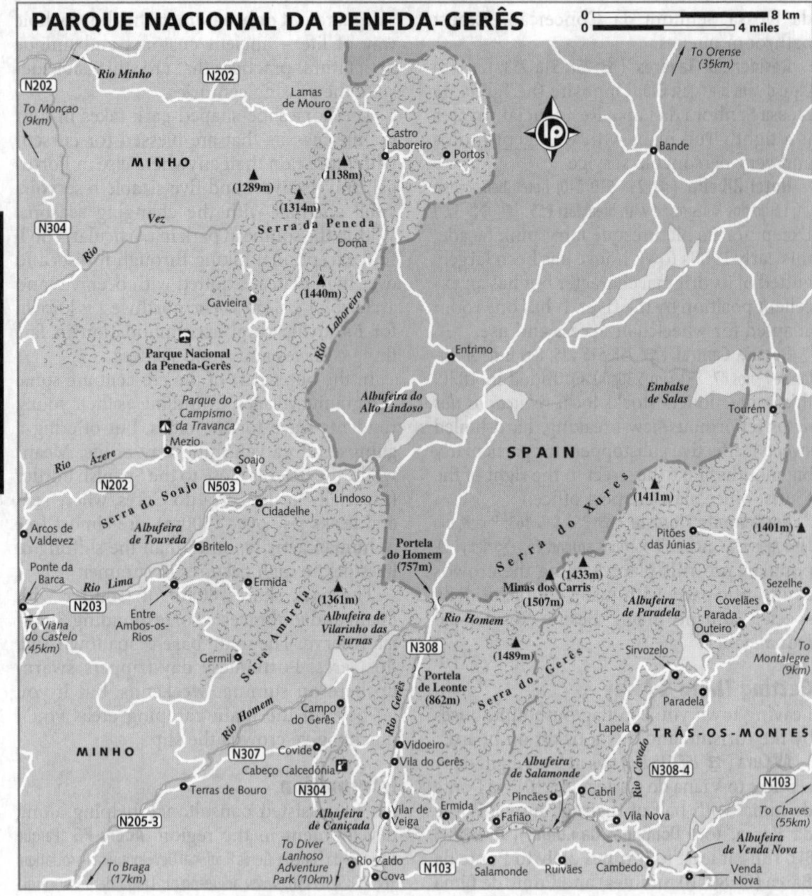

It's best to buy topographical maps at home, in Porto (p351) or in Lisbon (p461), although the Cerdeira camp site at Campo do Gerês has a few maps (p424).

Culture

Many of the park's oldest villages remain in a time warp, with oxen trundled down cobbled streets by black-clad old women, and horses shod in smoky blacksmith shops. The practice of moving livestock, and even entire villages, to high pasture for up to five months still goes on in the Serra da Peneda and Serra do Gerês.

Despite the founding of the park, and other government and private efforts, this rustic scene is fading away as young people head for the cities. Village populations are shrinking, and an astonishing 75% of local people are over 65.

Tourism may turn out to be a friend of tradition, with entrepreneurs restoring old buildings as rustic accommodation (p420). But it's an uphill battle.

Environment

WILDLIFE

The Serra da Peneda gets more rain than anywhere else in Portugal – so it's little wonder that it supports an extremely rich diversity of flora and fauna.

In the more remote areas a few wolves still roam, as do wild boar, badgers, polecats and otters. With luck, you may catch a quick glimpse of roe deer and a few wild ponies. Closer to the ground are grass snakes and the very occasional venomous black viper. Bird-fanciers can also be on the lookout for red kites, buzzards, goshawks, golden eagles and several species of owl.

But it's not just the wild animals that get all the glory here; the park's domestic animals are also of interest – and don't tend to run away so fast. In particular, primitive local breeds of long-horned cattle (the mahogany-coloured *barrosã* and darker *cachena*), goats, sheep, and the sturdy Castro Laboreiro sheepdog are all unique to the area.

In terms of flora, sheltered valleys hold stands of white oak, arbutus, laurel and cork oak. Forests of black oak, English oak and holly give way at higher elevations to birch, yew and Scots pine, and in alpine areas to juniper and sandwort. In a small patch of the Serra do Gerês grows the Gerês iris, found nowhere else in the world.

PROTECTED AREAS

The government is doing all it can to ensure that Peneda-Gerês' largely undisturbed ecosystems remain that way. The park has a high-elevation inner zone, partly set aside for research and closed to the public, and an outer buffer zone, where development is controlled. Most villages, roads, tracks and trails are in the latter area.

The most assiduously protected area is the Mata de Albergari, north of Gerês. Ironically, it's crossed by the N308 highway, which, because it serves an EU-appointed border crossing, cannot simply be closed. Satisfying both the World Conservation Union (IUCN) and the EU keeps park officials awake at night.

Motorised traffic is tolerated on a 6km stretch of road above Gerês but forbidden to linger. At checkpoints at either end, drivers get time-stamped tickets and have 15 minutes to turn them in at the other end. This stretch is patrolled daily from July to September and at weekends the rest of the year. Two side roads are also no-go areas for nonresidents: southwest down the Rio Homem valley and east from Portela do Homem into the high Serra do Gerês.

Campers must use designated sites or risk the wrath of park rangers. There are also restrictions on the type of boats in the park's *albufeiras* (reservoirs), and no boats at all are allowed on the Vilarinho das Furnas and Paradela. Even swimming is prohibited in Vilarinho das Furnas.

RURAL RETREATS

Northwest Parque Nacional da Peneda-Gerês is the ideal place to hire a remote stone cottage and relax into a blissful country break. No TVs, traffic horns or distractions here – just log fires, a few bleating goats and rolling vistas in every direction. Adere-PG (p417) is the best place to arrange rural getaways, but there are also plenty of restored houses around the tiny villages of Soajo (p420) and Lindoso (p421).

Sights & Activities

There is a scattering of **Stone Age dolmens and antas** (megaliths) on the high plateaus of the Serra da Peneda and Serra do Gerês, near Castro Laboreiro, Mezio, Paradela, Pitões das Júnias and Tourém. Not all are easily accessible, however. For details ask at Adere-PG (p417).

Mountain bikes can be hired from adventure outfits and some places to stay for around €8/13 per half-/full day. For **water sports** there are the park's reservoirs. Rio Caldo, 8km south of Vila do Gerês, is the base for the Albufeira da Caniçada; AML (below) rents single/double kayaks for €4/7 for the first hour, plus pedal boats, rowing boats and small motor boats. They'll also take you water-skiing or water-boarding. Inquire here, too, about paddling the Albufeira de Salamonde.

The park operates **horse-riding** facilities beside the Vidoeiro camp site near Vila do Gerês: Expect to pay around €50 per day.

Local outfits long involved in the park's outdoor activities:

AML (Água Montanha e Lazer; ☎ 253 391 779, 968 021 142; www.aguamontanha.com; Lugar de Paredes, 4845-024 Rio Caldo)

Diver Lanhoso (☎ 253 635 763; www.diverlanhoso.pt; off N103, Póvoa de Lanhoso) Although 10km southwest of the park, this adventure theme park makes a good trip for outdoor enthusiasts. Geared mainly towards groups, it has everything from rappelling and rock climbing to mountain biking.

Jav Sport (☎ 252 850 621; www.javsport.pt; Fafião, Cabril)

PlanAlto (☎ 253 311 807; www.planalto.com.pt; Parque de Campismo de Cerdeira, Campo do Gerês, 4840-030 Terras de Bouro)

WALKING

Scenery, crisp air and the rural panorama make walking a pleasure in Peneda-Gerês. Adere-PG has pioneered several fine, marked loop trails from 4km to 9km, described in free foldout maps available at its Ponte da Barca office.

Day walks around Vila do Gerês are popular but crowded (see p422 for details). Plan-Alto has marked some good loop trails in the Campo do Gerês area. It produces maps (p424) and organises interpretive walks.

Elsewhere in the park there's a certain amount of dead reckoning involved, although tracks of some kind (animal or vehicle) are everywhere in the populated buffer zone, nearly all within a half-day's walk of a settlement or a main road.

Sleeping

Camp sites include basic park-run sites at Entre Ambos-os-Rios, Travanca and Vidoeiro (open at least from mid-May to September), and private sites at Campo do Gerês and Cabril. For private rooms, ask at gateway turismos.

You can book restored rural houses in Soajo and Lindoso under a programme called Turismo de Aldeia, or around Arcos de Valdevez and Ponte da Barca under Adere-PG's Casas Antigas e Rústicas programme. Prices for two start at about €40 per night. Adere-PG manages 10 rustic, self-catering *casas de abrigo* (shelter houses) with four doubles in each. They're great value at €65 per night (minimum of two nights), but must be rented in full, so they're impractical for individuals. Gerês has many *pensões*, though they overflow in summer.

Shopping

Local honey is on sale everywhere. The best – unpasteurised, unadulterated and with a faint piney taste – is from small dealers; look for signs on private homes.

Getting There & Around

BUS

From Braga there are daily buses to Rio Caldo, Vila do Gerês, Campo do Gerês and, via Arcos de Valdevez, to Soajo and Lindoso. A few run on weekdays to Paradela from Montalegre in Trás-os-Montes. See the respective towns for details. No buses operate within the park.

CAR & MOTORCYCLE

Note that the back roads can be axle-breakers, even when maps suggest otherwise. There's no practical way to travel between the Peneda and Gerês sections of the park, except from outside of it – most conveniently via Spain, or back through Braga.

SOAJO

pop 500 / elevation 300m

Sturdy, remote Soajo (soo-*ahzh*-oo), high above the upper Rio Lima, is best known for its photogenic *espigueiros,* or stone granaries (below). Thanks to village enterprise and the Turismo de Aldeia, you can stay in one of Soajo's restored stone houses and look out onto a vanishing way of life. The programme has succeeded: it fills up in summer.

Orientation & Information

Soajo is 21km northeast of Ponte da Barca on the N203 and N530, or the same distance from Arcos de Valdevez via the scenic N202 and N304. Buses stop by Restaurante Videira at the intersection of these two roads. A few hundred metres down the N530 towards Lindoso are Soajo's trademark *espigueiros.*

Soajo's small main square, Largo do Eiró – with a *pelourinho* topped by what can only be described as an ancient smiley face – is down a lane in the opposite direction from the bus stop. There's an ATM below the parish council office, off the far side of the square.

The **Turismo de Aldeia office** (Adere-Soajo; ☎/fax 258 576 427; turismo.adere-soajo@sapo.pt; Largo da Cardeira, Bairros; 9am-noon & 2-7pm Mon-Fri, 9am-1pm Sat) is the village's de facto turismo; follow the signs west from the bus stop for 150m. Here you can book a room, get tips on good walks and pick up a basic map of the region.

ESPIGUEIROS

These huge slatted-granite caskets on stilts were used in the 18th and 19th centuries for storing maize and winnowed grain and protecting it from rats, and many are still in use. In clusters above their villages, grizzled with moss and topped with little crosses, they look like miniature cathedrals or giants' tombs. The brass-bellied, long-horned cows grazing around them, and the washing lines tied to them, do little to dispel their eerie appearance.

Activities

Soajo is filled with the sound of rushing water, a resource that has been painstakingly managed over the centuries. A steep **walk** above Soajo shows just how important these streams once were.

On the N304, 250m north of the bus stop, is a roofed pool for communal laundry. At a 'T' on the track directly behind it, turn left and immediately right. A path paved with immense stones and grooved by centuries of ox-cart traffic climbs though a landscape shaped by agriculture, past granite houses, *espigueiros* and superb views.

Further up are three derelict **water mills** for grinding corn, stone channels that once funnelled the stream from one mill to the next, and the reservoir that fed them. This much takes half an hour.

Above here a network of paths, often overgrown, leads to more mills and the abandoned **Branda da Portelinha**. (A *branda* was a settlement of summer houses for villagers, who drove their livestock to high pastures and lived with them all summer.)

Another walk, a steep two-hour round trip, takes you down to the **Ponte da Ladeira**, a simple medieval bridge. The path drops down to the right from the Lindoso road, about 150m down from the *espigueiros,* then forks to the right further down.

Sleeping

Village houses (for 2/8 people €40/160) Eleven houses are available for tourist accommodation under the Turismo de Aldeia scheme. Each has a fireplace or stove (with firewood in winter) and a kitchen stocked with breakfast food, including fresh bread on the doorstep each morning. Stays of more than one night are preferred at the weekend. These houses are best booked here at Soajo, though you can also book through Adere-PG in Ponte da Barca.

Casa do Adro (☎/fax 258 576 327; www.casadoadroturismorural.com; r with breakfast €43 Ⓟ) This is another available house, not in the scheme, located off Largo do Eiró by the parish church. With 300 years of history under its belt, this character-packed old manor house is a good choice. There is a minimun 3-night stay in July and August.

Parque do Campismo da Travanca (☎ 258 526 105; aderepg@mail.telepac. pt; Cabana Maior; adult/tent/car €2.05/1.80/2.30; 🕑 May-Sep) To camp in the area, try the new camp sit. It's basic and grassy and about 6km northwest of Soajo.

Eating

There are two good restaurants, both pricey.

Restaurante Videira (☎ 258 576 205; mains €7-10; 🕑 lunch Thu-Tue Jul-Sep, Sat & Sun only Oct-Jun) Situated by the bus stop, Videira has the cheerier setting and more authentic regional snacks such as ham, sausage and *pataiscas*.

Restaurante Espigueiro de Soajo (☎ 258 576 136; mains €8-10, half-portions from €5; 🕑 lunch & dinner Tue-Sun) North of the centre on the N304, this place has pleasant service and good regional food, with a bonus of outdoor seating.

Soajo also has several cafés and a *minimercado* (grocery shop), all found near the bus stop.

Getting There & Away

Salvador buses to Soajo (€2, 45 minutes) depart from Arcos de Valdevez at 5.45pm weekdays, plus 12.20pm Monday and Friday. They return at 7.40am weekdays, plus 1.20pm Monday and Friday. A taxi from Arcos costs about €14.

LINDOSO

pop 500 / elevation 380m

Lindoso (leen-*doze*-oo), across the Rio Minho from Soajo, offers a peek at what Soajo may have looked like before the tourist money rolled in – more lived-in and less prosperous, with chickens pecking on the paths, houses in an unsteady state, and cows tethered at their doors. People still keep warm at night by living upstairs from their animals.

Sights

The village and a cluster of *espigueiros* sit at the foot of a small, restored **castle** (adult/child under 11 €1/free; 🕑 at least 9am-12.30pm & 2-5.30pm Tue-Sun, closes 30-60min earlier Oct-Mar) founded in the 13th century by Afonso III. Beefed up by Dom Dinis, it was occupied by the Spanish in 1662 to 1664 and used as a military garrison until 1895. Now it's garrisoned by the national park, with a tiny exhibition on the castle and the village.

Sleeping & Eating

Lindoso has at least half a dozen restored village houses, with prices similar to those in Soajo. These must be booked through Adere-PG in Ponte da Barca (p417).

THE MINHO

Restaurante Lindoverde (☎ 258 578 010; mains €7-11 ⌚ lunch & dinner) On the N304-1, about 900m east of the turning to the village, Lindoverde also does duty as a café-bar and disco. Several cafés lurk at the village turning.

Getting There & Away

Salvador buses run to Lindoso on weekdays from Arcos de Valdevez (€2.35, one hour, departing about noon and 6.15pm) via Ponte da Barca (€2.25, departing five to 10 minutes later), and returning from Lindoso about 7.30am and 1.20pm.

VILA DO GERÊS

pop 800 / elevation 350m

If the Gerês (zh-*resh*) end of the national park has a 'centre', it's the somnolent spa town of Vila do Gerês (also known as Caldas do Gerês – *caldas* means hot springs), sandwiched tightly into the valley of the Rio Gerês. The spa and many, but not all, *pensões* close from October to April.

Orientation

The town is built on an elongated, one-way loop of road, with the *balneário* (spa centre) in the pink buildings in the middle. The original hot spring, some baths and the turismo are in the staid colonnade at the northern end. Buses stop on Avenida Manuel F Costa, just south of the *balneário*, opposite the Universal and Termas hotels.

Information

Park office (☎ 253 390 110; Centro de Educação Ambiental do Vidoeiro; ⌚ 9am-noon & 2-5.30pm Mon-Fri) About 1km north of the village on the track leading to the camp site. You can pick up leaflets (€0.60 each) here. Another small booklet on the park with a map costs €1.70.

Post office (☎ 253 351 444; ⌚ 9am-12.30pm & 2pm-5.30pm Mon-Fri) By the roundabout at the southern end of the village. There are several banks with ATMs on Avenida Manuel F Costa.

Turismo (☎ 253 391 133; fax 253 391 282; ⌚ 9.30am-12.30pm & 2.30-6pm Mon-Wed & Fri, 9.30am-12.30pm Sat year-round; also Sat afternoon, Sun morning Jul & Aug) In the colonnade.

Sights & Activities

WALKING

Miradouro Walk

About 1km up the N308 is a picnic site, which is the start of a short, popular stroll with good views to the south.

Gerês Valley

A park-maintained loop trail, the **Trilho da Preguiça**, starts on the N308 about 3km above Gerês, by a lone white house, the Casa da Preguiça. For 5km it rollercoasters through the valley's oak forests. A leaflet about the walk is available from the park office (€0.60). You can also carry on – or hitch – to the **Portela de Leonte**, 6km north of Gerês.

Further on, where the Rio Homem crosses the road (10km above Gerês), a walk east up the river takes you to a picturesque **waterfall**. (See Protected Areas, p419, for driving and parking restrictions in the Mata de Albergaria.)

An 8km walk goes southwest from the Mata de Albergaria along the Rio Homem and the Albufeira de Vilarinho das Furnas to Campo do Gerês. This route takes you along part of an ancient **Roman road** that once stretched 320km between Braga and Astorga (in Spain), and now has World Heritage status. Milestones – inscribed with the name of the emperor during whose rule they were erected – remain at miles XXIX, XXX and XXXI; the nearest to Campo do Gerês is 1km above the camp site. Others have been haphazardly collected at the Portela do Homem border post, 13km from Gerês.

Trilho da Calcedónia

A narrow, sealed road snakes over the ridge from Vila do Gerês to Campo do Gerês, offering short but spectacular, high-elevation walks from just about anywhere along its upper reaches. One of these walks is an easy, Adere PG–signposted, 3km (two-hour) loop that climbs a 912m **viewpoint** called the Cabeço Calcedónia, with views to knock your socks off.

The road is easy to find from Campo but trickier from Gerês; the turning is about 700m up the old Portelo do Homem road from Pensão Adelaide.

ERMIDA & FAFIÃO

From the picnic site above Vila Gerês (see the Miradouro Walk, left), a dirt road runs 11km southeast to Ermida, a village of smallholdings and sturdy stone houses that cling to the steep hillsides.

Casa do Criado (☎ 253 391 390; Ermida; d with breakfast €30, half-board €45) is a bucolic spot with chirpy hosts, six homely rooms (book ahead), lumpy beds and a simple restaurant.

The village also has **private rooms** (around €20), several cafés and a *minimercado*. Walkers can also continue east for 6km to Fafião village, which has rooms and a café or two.

From Fafião it's a steep 5km south on a sealed road across the Salamonde dam and up to the N103, where nearby Salamonde village is a stop for Braga-Chaves buses. A taxi between Fafião and Salamonde costs about €4.

You can drive to Ermida on a 7km sealed road from the N308 at Vilar de Veiga, and to Fafião from Salamonde, but the unpaved Ermida–Fafião road is not recommended for cars, especially after rain.

BALNEÁRIO

After a long hike, finish the day by soaking away aches and pains in the **spa** (☎ 253 391 113; www.aguasdogeres.pt; 🕑 7am-noon & 3.20-6pm Mon-Sat); buy a ticket at the entrance to the *balneário*, 150m south of the turismo. A sauna or steam bath costs about €6, a full massage €16, but there's a bewilderingly long list of treatments for those with time on their hands.

Sleeping

Private rooms are available in summer for around €25 per double; owners often approach travellers at the bus stop. Gerês also has plenty of *pensões*, though in summer you may find some are block-booked for spa patients and other visitors. Outside July and August, on the other hand, prices plummet and bargaining is in order.

BUDGET

Parque de Campismo de Vidoeiro (☎ 253 391 289; aderepg@mail.telepac.pt; Vidoeiro; adult/car €2.05/2.30; 🕑 mid-May–mid-Oct) This cool and shady hillside park-run facility next to the river is about 1km north of Gerês. Book ahead through Adere-PG (p417).

MID-RANGE

Quinta Souto-Linho (☎ 253 392 000; souto_linho@yahoo.com; d with breakfast €55; Ⓟ) This delightful gingerbread-like construction, perched above the principal southern entrance to town, is a recently renovated old mansion. It's a welcome addition to the town's mostly bland accommodation.

Pensão Baltazar (☎ 253 392 058; fax 253 392 057; N308; d from €50) This cosy, family-run place has well-kept rooms and a popular restaurant below.

Pensão da Ponte (☎ 253 391 121; Rua da Boa Vista; d with breakfast & with/without bathroom €45/30; Ⓟ) With sloping floors, erratic plumbing and a quirky *Addams Family* atmosphere, this likable old guesthouse is anything but lacking in personality. Its creaky rooms, many overlooking the gushing river alongside, are pretty good value.

Pensão Adelaide (☎ 253 390 020; www.pensaoadelaide.com.pt; d with breakfast & with/without verandah €50/45; 🕑 year-round; ❄) The big lemon-yellow place at the top of town wins for value. There are homely and smart rooms with a few nice views.

There are some more *pensões* at the lower (southern) end of town.

Grand **Hotel Universal** (☎ 253 391 143/4; www.ehgeres.com; Avenida Manuel F Costa; d with breakfast €70; Ⓟ ❄ 🏊) and the stodgier **Termas**, which is located next door, both have a long history of housing stressed-out urbanites attending the spa.

TOP END

Hotel Águas do Gerês (☎ 253 390 190; www.aguasdogeres.pt; d full board Aug/Jul & September/Oct-Jun €100/88/80; Ⓟ ⊠ ❄) For another step up the luxury ladder, try this newly fitted-out hotel, a few steps up and across the road from the spa. This place has special deals for spa users, sparkling rooms and good disabled facilities. You can hire bikes here for €5/12.50 per hour/half-day.

Eating

It may come as a surprise in Portugal to find restaurants already crowded at 11.30am and again at 6.30pm, with customers washing down huge meals with water. Don't worry, they're all spa patients, on a strict regimen.

Pensão Baltazar (N308; mains €7-11, half-portions €5-6; 🕑 lunch & dinner) Gerês' best-value restaurant, this family-run place is always brimming with customers. There's no music or unnecessary noise – just the relaxed hubbub of spa patients looking to de-stress. Its small menu always includes one daily regional special. The fare is meaty, wholesome and with *lots* of vegetables. Helpings are huge, even on the half-portions.

Restaurante Lurdes Capela (☎ 253 391 208; Avenida Manuel F Costa; dishes €5-9; 🕑 lunch & dinner) Not much to look at, this small, bustling eatery at the bottom of the village nonetheless offers good-value regional fare that attracts loyal customers who come back time and again.

Most other *pensões* do equally hearty, equally unadventurous meals. The hilltop restaurant at **Pensão Adelaide** (mains €8-12; lunch & dinner) is recommended.

Getting There & Away

Empresa Hoteleira do Gerês (253 615 896) operates 10 buses a day (fewer at weekends) from Braga to Gerês (€3.15, 1½ hours).

CAMPO DO GERÊS

pop 150 / elevation 690m

Campo do Gerês (called São João do Campo on some maps, and just Campo by nearly everybody) is barely more than a humble hamlet in the middle of nowhere, though not far from the Albufeira de Vilarinho das Furnas. It makes an excellent hiking base.

Orientation & Information

The Braga bus stops by the Museu Etnográfico, on the main road, then continues 1.5km on to the village centre. The youth hostel is 1km up a side road from the museum. About 200m before the town centre, the road to the dam branches right, northeast, with the camp site about 700m along it.

Sights

A poignant story revolves around **Vilarinho das Furnas**; this was once a remarkable democratic village, fiercely independent and with a well-organised system of shared property and decision-making. But the entire town was submerged by the reservoir in 1972, and its people relocated.

In anticipation of the end of their old way of life, villagers collected stories, memories and articles for a moving memorial. These have been fashioned into the touching **Museu Etnográfico** (253 351 888; adult/student/child under 16 €2/1/free; 10am-12.30pm & 2-5pm Tue-Fri, 10am-noon & 2-5pm Sat & Sun) in Portuguese, where the Campo road forks to the youth hostel.

In late summer and autumn when the reservoir level falls, the empty village walls rise like spectres from the water and the near shore. You can visit the spooky remains about 2.5km beyond the dam, which is a comfortable three-hour return hike from Campo or the camp site.

Activities

PlanAlto, based at the Parque Campismo de Cerdeira, has marked three loop trails around Campo do Gerês, lasting from two to five hours, and printed its own walking/orienteering maps (€1.50). Also on hand are a few military topo sheets (€7.50). Among its activities are interpretive walks, traditional games, a mountain-fitness circuit and orienteering competitions. The camp site itself has programmes linked to local festivals, such as **Desfolhada Minhota** (the harvest festival) in October and **Matança do Porco** (a slap-up pork feast) in January.

Sleeping & Eating

Parque Campismo de Cerdeira (253 351 005; www.parquecerdeira.com; adult/tent/car €4.20/3.15-4.75/3.70, 2-/4-person bungalows with kitchenette €57.50/77.50; year-round;) This camp site has oak-shaded sites, a laundry, a *minimercado,* a good restaurant and bikes to hire. There are also apartments for rent. You might be asked for a CCI in July or August; this camping card is good for a 10% discount in July and August, 15% the rest of the year. Booking ahead is definitely recommended.

Pousada da Juventude de Vilarinho das Furnas (253 351 339; vilarinho@movijovem.pt; d with/without toilet €27/24) Campo's sprawling woodland hostel began life as a dam-workers' camp and now offers a good clutch of spartan doubles (no dorms).

Albergaria Stop (253 350 040; www.albergariastop.eol.pt; d with breakfast €50; P) This peremptorily named modern guesthouse, complete with tennis courts, comfy rooms and nice little touches (heated towel racks for one), is near the turn-off for the camp site.

The road to Cerdeira is lined with signs advertising **houses** (for 4 people €40-55) for rent.

Restaurante Cerdeira (mains €6-10; lunch & dinner) The camp site's excellent restaurant offers carefully prepared local specialities such *bersame* (a pork-and-vegetable stew), as well as a more international menu of salads, omelettes, burgers and snacks.

Getting There & Away

From Braga, REDM has four daily buses (€3, 1½ hours; fewer at weekends), stopping at the museum crossroad and the village centre.

RIO CALDO

pop 1000 / elevation 160m

Just inside the park on the large Albufeira de Caniçada, Rio Caldo is a good little base for water sports on the reservoir.

English-run **AML** (Água Montanha Lazer; ☎ 253 391 779, 968 021 142; www.aguamontanha.com; Lugar de Paredes) is the place to go for boating, water-skiing and canoe rental. The shop is 100m from the N304 roundabout, but at weekends and on most summer days you're more likely to find them by the water on the other side of the bridge to Gerês. AML also has several local houses for rent for up to nine people (see the website for details and prices).

Other places to stay include the cosy **Pontes de Rio Caldo** (☎ 253 391 540; fax 253 391 195; d with breakfast from €46; P), by the reservoir near AML's shop.

EASTERN PENEDA-GERÊS

Cabril, on the eastern limb of the national park, and Montalegre, just outside it, are actually in Trás-os-Montes, but you're unlikely to visit unless you're coming in or out of the park.

Cabril

pop 700 / elevation 400m

Though it hardly looks the part, peaceful Cabril – set with its outlying hamlets in a wide, fertile bowl – is the administrative centre of Portugal's biggest *freguesia* (parish), stretching up to the Spanish border. Your best reference point is **Largo do Cruzeiro**, with its old *pelourinho*. To one side is the little **Igreja de São Lourenço**, said to have been moved five centuries ago, brick by brick, by villagers of nearby São Lourenço. Some 400m southwest is a bridge over an arm of the Albufeira de Salamonde.

SLEEPING & EATING

Parque de Campismo Outeiro Alto (☎/fax 253 659 860, 966 327 299; Eiredo; adult/small tent €2.50/2.50; year-round) This hilly woodland facility over the bridge and 800m up the Pincães road has 36 small tent sites and a patch for caravans, plus a café-bar and adjacent horse-riding centre.

Café Águia Real (☎ 253 652 188, 969 584 180; d €20, 2-bed apt with kitchenette €40) Plain and cosy, this is 300m up the Paradela road. It's often booked well ahead of time. The café does light meals and carries on in the evening as a bar.

Restaurante Ponte Nova (☎ 253 659 882; half-portions €3-4; 8am-midnight) By the bridge and overlooking the water, it does trout, *cabrito* (kid), *vitela assada* (roast veal) and other specials, from a verbal menu.

GETTING THERE & AWAY

There are no buses to Cabril. If you're not driving you could get off any Braga–Montalegre or Braga–Chaves bus at Salamonde and take a **taxi** (☎ 253 658 281, or ask at Restaurante Retiro da Cabreira), for about €10.

Drivers can cross into the park from the N103 via the Salamonde dam; a longer, but far more scenic route, is via the Venda Nova dam, 14km east of Salamonde at Cambedo.

Montalegre

pop 2000 / elevation 1000m

You're unlikely to visit chilly Montalegre unless you're en route between Chaves and the national park. Presiding over the town and the surrounding plains is a small, partially restored castle (closed to the public), part of Dom Dinis' 14th-century necklace of frontier outposts. The future Duke of Wellington rested in the castle in 1809 after chasing the French from Porto.

This is *terra fria* (cold country), with wide seasonal contrasts and long, harsh winters.

ORIENTATION

From the bus station it's 500m west on Rua General Humberto Delgado to a five-way roundabout, beside which you'll find the town hall and the turismo.

INFORMATION

Several banks around the câmara municipal have ATMs

Park information office (☎ 276 512 281; Rua do Reigoso 17; 9am-12.30pm & 2-5.30pm Mon-Fri) This gruff office is two blocks north beyond the town hall (on Rua Direita), turn right at the *pelourinho*. .

Espaço Internet (☎ 276 518 050; Rua Vitor Branco; 10am-noon & 2-6pm Mon-Fri) Free Internet access. From the turismo, turn right then left across a small square.

Post office (9am-12.30pm & 2-5.30pm Mon-Fri) is 400m northeast of the roundabout down Avenida Dom Nuno Álvares Pereira.

Turismo (☎ 276 511 010; fax 276 510 201; ⌚ 9am-12.30pm & 2-5.30pm Jul-Aug, 9am-12.30pm & 2-5.30pm Mon-Fri Sep-Jun).

SLEEPING & EATING

Residencial Fidalgo (☎ 276 512 462; Rua da Corujeira 34; d €30; P) On the Braga road, 300m south of the roundabout, this guesthouse has big and comfortable rooms; the best ones are at the back.

Quality Inn Montalegre (☎ 276 510 220; www.choicehotelsportugal.com; Rua do Avelar 2; d with breakfast from €67; P) Just southwest of the roundabout, this somewhat out-of-place luxury hotel has high-quality rooms with satellite TV. It also features a relaxing and tropically heated indoor swimming pool, sauna and gym.

Opposite the park office is the unexceptional **Café-Restaurante Ricotero** (☎ 276 512 122; Rua do Reigoso; mains €5; ⌚ lunch & dinner). Across the road is **Pizzaria Cantinho** (☎ 276 511 095; ⌚ lunch & dinner).

GETTING THERE & AWAY

REDM/AV Tâmega (☎ 276 512 131) stop at Montalegre between Braga (€4.80, 2¼ hours) and Chaves (€3.90, 1¼ hours) four times each weekday; less often at weekends. Change at Chaves for Bragança, Vila Real or Porto.

THE MINHO

Trás-os-Montes

CONTENTS

Few places in Europe offer such a sense of remoteness as Trás-os-Montes. Portugal's north-eastern province is largely ignored, even by Portuguese travellers, who consider it too far, too uncomfortable, too backward, and perhaps even too pagan. Trás-os-Montes (trahsh-oosh-*montsh*) means 'beyond the mountains', and indeed the multiple mountain ranges make it feel more walled out than walled in.

Here the climate tends to extremes too: the north is a *terra fria* (cold land) where winter temperatures may drop to freezing for months at a time, and the south, towards the Alto Douro, is a *terra quente* (hot land) where searing summers ripen olives, almonds, chestnuts, fruit, rye and the port-wine grapes of the Douro and Tua valleys.

Isolation and harsh conditions have bred a culture of rock-solid self-reliance, laced with mysterious practices and beliefs. In this vast province – almost twice the size of the Minho but with less than half the population – there are still villages where farmers plough their fields with oxen and shack up with their hens, pigs and donkeys in the humblest of granite cottages. It's these smaller villages that will stick firmest in your memory, providing you have the time and patience to reach them.

The Parque Natural do Douro Internacional, safeguarding the deep canyon of the upper Rio Douro that defines the border with Spain, is the best place in the country to see large birds of prey. And if you plunge still further off the beaten track and into the region's secluded *parques naturais* (natural parks) – Alvão, near Vila Real, and Montesinho, near Bragança – you'll be rewarded with some of the wildest walking and biking country in Portugal.

HIGHLIGHTS

- **Country Palace**
  The Palácio de Mateus (p430)
- **Piggy Ponderings**
  Statues of pigs in Bragança's lofty *cidadela* (citadel; p441)
- **Downhill Burn**
  Mountain biking in Parque Natural de Montesinho (p444)
- **Cultures Collide**
  Tiny Rio de Onor (p444) half-Portuguese, half-Spanish, but in a world of its own
- **Time Warp**
  Chaves' Roman bridge (p435), 1900 years old

- POPULATION: 270,850
- AREA: 11,772 SQ KM

WESTERN TRÁS-OS-MONTES

VILA REAL

pop 24,500 / elevation 445m

Vila Real sits above the confluence of the Rio Corgo and Rio Cabril – a lone city in a sea of rural tranquillity. Though having said that, don't expect the urban edge to bite too deep. This is essentially an unruffled laid-back university town, the pace and population of which ebbs and swells according to the academic year. Its biggest draw card is the fabulous Palácio de Mateus, which sits in the countryside just outside the city.

But most of all, Vila Real is a vital transport hub, and a springboard into the underrated hills of the Parque Natural do Alvão.

Orientation

Accommodation and food options cluster around the axis of Avenida Carvalho Araújo. The train station is about 1km across the Rio Corgo from the turismo, while the Rodonorte bus station is about 300m northwest on Rua Dom Pedro de Castro. The bus stand for AV Tâmega, Rede Expressos and Santos buses is about a further 100m northwest.

Information

ATMs are numerous in the centre.

Espaço Internet (Av 1 de Maio; 10am-7pm Mon-Fri) Free Internet in a booth around the corner from Hotel Miracorgo.

Hospital de São Pedro (259 300 500; Lordelo) Located 2km northwest of the centre.

Instituto Português da Juventude (259 309 640; Rua Dr Manuel Cardona; Mon-Fri) About 1km northeast of the centre, upstairs from the *pousada da juventude* (p431), has free Internet access; enter at the back of the building.

Parque Natural do Alvão office (259 302 830; pnal@icn.pt; Largo dos Freitas; 9am-12.30pm & 2-5.30pm Mon-Fri) Just behind the *câmara municipal* (town hall).

Police station (259 322 022; Largo Conde de Amarante)

Post office (259 330 300; Avenida Carvalho Araújo; 8.30am-6pm Mon-Fri, 9am-12.30pm Sat)

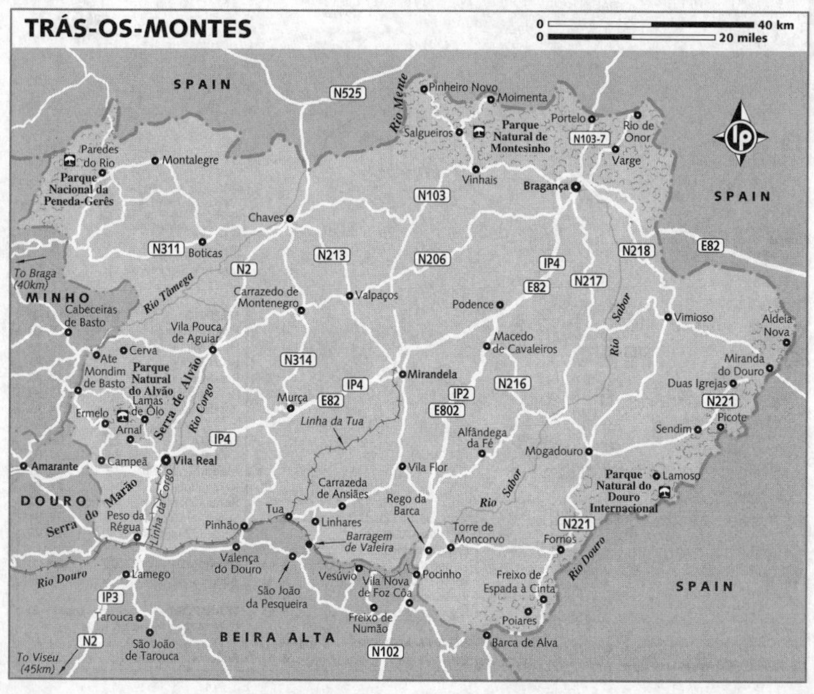

Regional turismo (☎ 259 322 819; turismarao@mail.telepac.pt; Avenida Carvalho Araújo 94; 🕑 9.30am-12.30pm & 2-5pm Mon-Sat Oct-Mar; to 7pm Mon-Fri, to 6pm Sat & Sun Apr-Sep) Located in a Manueline-designed headquarters in the town centre.

Sights

AROUND THE CENTRE

Once part of a 15th-century Dominican monastery, the Gothic cathedral or **sé** (Igreja de São Domingos; Travessa de São Domingos) is more remarkable for its age than anything else. At the time of writing it was undergoing a lengthy face-lift and was closed to the public.

Rua Central, wide enough to be a plaza, is dominated by the magnificently over-the-top baroque façade of the 17th-century **Capela Nova** (Igreja dos Clérigos), with, inside, 18th-century *azulejos* (hand-painted tiles) and large-headed cherubs with teddy-boy quiffed hair.

More baroque, and more azulejos, are on view at the **Igreja de São Pedro** (Largo de São Pedro; admission free), one block north of Capela Nova.

For a fine view across the gorge of the Rio Corgo and Rio Cabril, walk south to the **Miradouro de Trás-do-Cemitério**, just beyond a small cemetery and chapel.

PALÁCIO DE MATEUS

Famously depicted on bottles of Mateus rosé wine, this glorious baroque creation, the **Palácio de Mateus** (Solar de Mateus; ☎ 259 323 121; admission palace & gardens €6.25, gardens only €3.50;

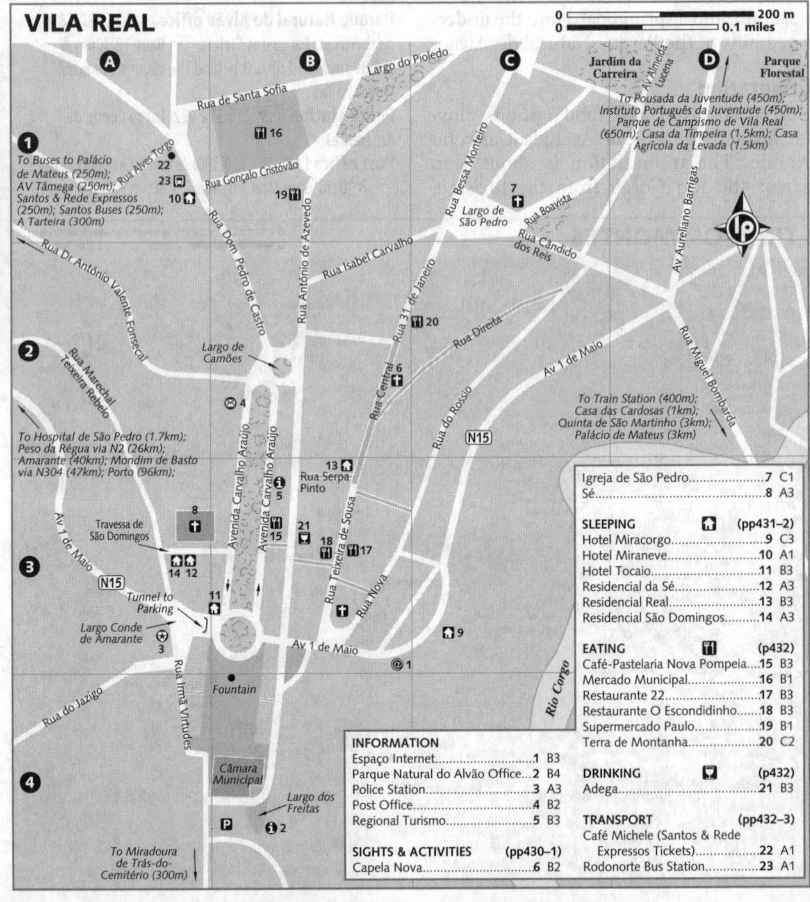

9am-7.30pm Jun-Sep, 9am-1pm & 2-6pm Oct & Mar-May, 10am-1pm & 2-5pm Nov-Feb), is the work of the ubiquitous 18th-century Italian architect Nicolau Nasoni.

Its granite wings ('advancing lobster-like towards you' wrote English critic Sacheverell Sitwell) shelter a lichen-encrusted forecourt dominated by an ornate balustraded stairway and overlooked by rooftop statues. Behind the palace is an Alice in Wonderland garden of tiny box hedges, prim statues and a fragrant cypress tunnel that's blissfully cool even on the hottest of days.

Guided tours inside will take you through several rooms, heavy with velvet drapes, quirky pictures and fussy period furnishings. But it's not all chubby cheeked cherubs and chestnut-carved ceiling. It's the final chamber that most people remember. Therein lies a collection of religious bits and bobs, including something approaching fifty macabre religious relics bought from the Vatican in the 18th-century: a bit of holy fingernail here, a saintly set of juicy eyeballs there – even a piece of Christ's cross – and each with the Vatican's oh-so-trustworthy certificate of authentication.

The palace is 3.8km east of the town centre. Useful Santos buses (€0.80, 25 minutes) include those leaving at 8.10am, 9am, 10.45am, noon, 12.30pm, 1pm and 1.30pm weekdays from the bus stand on Rua Dr António Valente Fonsecal; ask at the turismo for the latest timetable. If you ask for 'Mateus' the bus will set you down about 250m from the palace (if you don't ask, it may not stop). Return buses pass along the road in front of the palace at about 1pm and 3.25pm only. There is only one bus out on Saturday at 12.15pm but no return service, and nothing on Sundays.

As for the rosé, it's made in Porto now, but the palace does produce jams, wines and other goodies, all sold on the premises.

Festivals & Events

The **Festa de São Pedro** (28–29 June) sparks a huge market in the streets east of the turismo – a great chance to snap up the region's unusual black pottery.

Sleeping

BUDGET

Residencial Real (☎ 259 325 879; fax 259 324 613; Rua Central 5; s/d with breakfast €25/35) Nicely positioned in the middle of a pedestrian zone, above a popular *pastelaria* (pastry shop), the neatly kept rooms here are the quietest choice at night.

Pousada da juventude (☎ 259 373 193; vilareal@movijovem.pt; Rua Dr Manuel Cardona; dm €10, dm with toilet €27) This is situated at the rear of a building 200m before the camp site. below. It's not one of the country's better-equipped hostels and no meals are available, but you can use the kitchen, and the dull, high-rise residential neighbourhood does have a few cafés.

Residencial São Domingos (☎ 259 323 097; Travessa de São Domingos 33; r €23) This place has plenty of bashed-about rooms as a last resort, although it's poor value for solo travellers because there's no single rate.

Parque de Campismo de Vila Real (☎ 259 325 625, 259 324 724; Rua Dr Manuel Cardona; adult €2.75, car €1.75, tent €1.75-2.25; mid-Jan–mid-Dec) A simple, shady hillside camp site above the Rio Corgo, 1.2km northeast of the centre, with a small restaurant and an alfresco swimming pool nearby. You'll need a Camping Card International (CCI, p452).

MID-RANGE

Residencial da Sé (☎ 259 324 575; Travessa de São Domingos 19-23; d with breakfast €30) This guesthouse opposite the cathedral is a personable spot, with modest, well-kept old rooms.

Hotel Tocaio (☎ 259 371 675; fax 259 325 905; Avenida Carvalho Araújo 45; d/st with breakfast €35/40) Begging for renovation, Tocaio's characterful though decidedly weary rooms are still fair value if traffic noise doesn't bother you. Suites are worth the extra few euros.

Hotel Miraneve (☎ 259 323 153; reservas.miraneve@clix.pt; Rua Dom Pedro de Castro 17; s/d €33/45) A nice if bland option with big windows, uniform beige rooms and a generous breakfast. It cops some noise from the busy bus station below.

TOP END

Hotel Miracorgo (☎ 259 325 001; miracorgo@mail.telepac.pt; Avenida 1 de Maio 78; s/d/st with breakfast €47/68/94; P) Proper luxury is on offer here. Slick modern rooms come complete with balconies, double glazing and every creature comfort.

You can choose to dodge the centre's soulless modern hotels. Some handsome rural properties in the region offer far superior

TRÁS-OS-MONTES

deals, and they will give you a much closer insight into the bucolic pace of the surrounding countryside.

Quinta de São Martinho (☎ 259 323 986; quinta.s.martinho@clix.pt; Lugar de São Martinho, Mateus; s/d €55/65; P) Within 400m of the Palácio de Mateus is this squat granite-walled Turihab property (a government-sponsored scheme for marketing private accommodation). It is a very comfortable country house with wood-beamed ceilings and a lush little garden. It's also known for its good restaurant.

Casa das Cardosas (☎ /fax 259 331 487; Rua Central, Folhadela; s/d with breakfast €55/60; P) Highly recommended for its gardens and views, Casa das Cardosas is 600m south of the train station.

Casa da Timpeira (☎ 259 324 068; Quinta dos Azevedos, Timpeira; d with breakfast €80; P) This is a pleasant spot on the northern outskirts of Vila Real.

Casa Agrícola da Levada (☎ 259 322 190; Timpeira; d with breakfast €65, 4-person apt €110; P) Not far beyond Timpeira, this 1922 property still produces bread, honey and more traditional goodies.

Eating

While central Vila Real is short on great hotels, it's crammed with good restaurants.

Restaurante 22 (☎ 259 321 296; 1st fl, Rua Teixeira de Sousa 16; specials €4, mains €5-8; lunch & dinner Mon-Sat) Venturing through the cowboy-style swing doors and up the creaky wooden stairs takes you to this 1950s-style gem and a gimmick-free environment. The friendly staff concentrate on dishing up excellent fish and meat dishes with plenty of veg from an ever-changing menu.

Tarteira (☎ 259 375 424; Rua Dr Pedro Serra, 1st fl, Shop 12; 2-course set meal & drink €6; lunch & dinner Mon-Fri, lunch Sat) Vegetarians might want to check out this tiny little natural products shop opposite a big fountain about 500m west of the centre, where a cheerful staff serve up tofu and vegetable-heavy organic lunches.

Terra de Montanha (☎ 259 372 075; Rua 31 de Janeiro 16-18; mains €10-16; lunch & dinner Mon-Sat) Enormous wooden vats and barrels line the walls and make up cosy circular booths in this touristic but nevertheless likeable restaurant. However, the striking décor shouldn't eclipse its excellent highland dishes.

Café-Pastelaria Nova Pompeia (Avenida Carvalho Araújo 82; meals under €5; Mon-Sat) This is the best of a gaggle of cafés and *confeitarias* (patisserie or confectionary shop) spilling out onto the pavement opposite the cathedral. It has toasted sandwiches and burgers for around €3, plus light meals.

Restaurante O Escondidinho (☎ 259 325 535; Rua Teixeira de Sousa 7; dishes under €7.50; lunch & dinner) A good, but plain, little place with belly-filling regional dishes and good pasta. It's one of the few central restaurants open on Sunday evening.

Self-caterers are able to stock up on rural produce at the **mercado municipal** (municipal market; Rua de Santa Sofia; Mon-Sat), and pick up other goods at the small nearby **Supermercado Paulo** (☎ 259 378 780; Rua António Azevedo 84; Mon-Sat).

Drinking

A dusty old **adega** (wine tavern; Rua António de Azevedo 20) near the cathedral offers a certain seedy charm and a cheap slug of the local vintage. There are also a couple of popular street-side bars along Largo do Pioledo. The only central disco of note is on Friday and Saturday evenings at Hotel Miracorgo (p431).

Getting There & Away

BUS

There are several bus lines serving Vila Real, including:

AV Tâmega (☎ 259 322 928; cnr Rua Dr António Valente Fonseca & Avenida Cidade de Ourense)

Rodonorte (☎ 259 340 710; Rua Dom Pedro de Castro 19)

Santos & Rede Expressos (☎ 259 322 674) Express services leave from the Rodonorte terminal. For all others, board on the corner of Rua Dr António Valente Fonseca and Avenida Cidade de Ourense; tickets available on the bus or from Café Michele (☎ 259 375 894; Rua Dom Pedro de Castro 31; Mon-Sat).

Trás-os-Montes destinations include Chaves (€5.30, 1¼ hours) with Rodonorte or AV Tâmega; and Bragança (€7.50, two hours) with Rodonorte, Rede Expressos or Santos, all departing several times daily.

For the Minho, Rede Expressos goes to Braga (€7.20, 2¾ hours) three times daily except Saturday; and Rodonorte goes to Guimarães (€5.80, 1½ hours) several times a day.

Douro valley points include Porto (€5.50, 1½ hours, every few hours) on board AV Tâmega, Rodonorte, Rede Expressos or

Santos; Amarante (€4.60, 40 minutes, five daily) with Rodonorte; and Lamego (€4.80, 55 minutes, twice daily) with Rede Expressos. Rede also go to Coimbra (€9.20).

Weekend services tend to be less frequent or nonexistent.

TRAIN

Vila Real is at the end of the narrow-gauge Linha da Corgo from Peso da Régua (€1.70, 55 minutes), with three to four daily departures from Porto (€6.50, 3½ to four hours). A taxi between the train station and town centre costs €3.50.

PARQUE NATURAL DO ALVÃO

This 72-sq-km natural park – Portugal's smallest – straddles the 1300m-plus central ridgeline of the Serra de Alvão, between Vila Real and Mondim de Basto. In a transition zone between the humid coast and the dry interior, the park has diverse flora and fauna, but it's the harsh natural and human landscape at higher elevations that is most striking.

The Rio Ôlo, a tributary of the Rio Tâmega, rises in the park's broad granite basin. A 300m drop above Ermelo gives rise to the spectacular Fisgas de Ermelo waterfalls, the park's major tourist attraction.

Exploring the park on your own is not simple, as maps and public transport are limited. Before setting out on foot, pay a visit to one of the park offices.

Information

There are park offices in Vila Real (p429) and Mondim de Basto (p434). Both sell leaflets, with English-language inserts, on local products (including linen cloth and smoked sausages), land use, flora and fauna. Mondim de Basto's turismo is another good source of park information.

Sights

People are drawn to the 800-year-old village of **Ermelo** primarily to see its blackboard-like slate-roofed houses and traditional *espigueiros* (stone granaries), as well as an ancient chapel, sturdy granite *pelourinho* (pillory) and the staunch **Ponte de Várzea**, a Roman bridge rebuilt in medieval times. Half a dozen local linen weavers have also opened their workshops to the public here – so take a peek while you're in town.

The Ermelo turn-off is about 16km south of Mondim de Basto on the N304; you can get there from Mondim on a local Auto Mondinense/Transcovizela bus (p435). From the turn-off it is about 500m to the nearest parts of the village, though the village continues along the track for at least 1km.

About 1.3km closer to Mondim de Basto on the N304 is a turn-off to the dramatic **Fisgas de Ermelo** waterfalls. It is a shadeless 4km climb to the falls; take water and snacks. To do this as a day trip you must catch the 7am bus from Mondim de Basto. The last bus back to Mondim passes by about 6.40pm on weekdays (there's nothing late enough on weekends). Check current times at Mondim de Basto's turismo.

Another pretty destination is somnolent **Lamas de Ôlo**, with its ancient mill and photogenic thatched houses, in the heart of the park at an altitude of about 1000m.

Activities

If your feet are itching to hit some trails, you can pick up notes on a three-hour hike around the southern village of **Arnal**, south of Lamas de Ôlo and near the southern entrance to the park, in *Guia do Percurso Pedestre* (€0.40), a park leaflet with an English-language insert. The route offers views east beyond Vila Real to the Serra do Marão. While you're in Arnal, track down the slate-roofed centre for traditional handicraft techniques.

Some other walks, ranging from 2.5km to 11.5km, are outlined in a Portuguese-language booklet, *Percurso Pedestre: Mondim de Basto/Parque Natural do Alvão* (€0.56), with a rough, 1:50,000 trail map, and an even more basic version for €0.33. No other maps are available at park offices.

Basto Radical (☎ 255 382 637, 965 302 294; www.basto-radical.pt in Portuguese) is a local outfit arranging **walks**, **mountaineering** and **mountain-biking** (and bike rental) – and, outside summer season, **river trips** – with English or French-speaking guides.

Sleeping & Eating

About 2km south of Lamas de Ôlo, and sitting all alone, is the pine-shaded **Restaurante A Cabana** (☎ 259 341 745) It is known for its trout dishes, and has one double room for rent.

Ermelo has three **cafés**, where you can also inquire about private rooms.

TRÁS-OS-MONTES

An alternative (and flatter) base is at Campeã, 12km west of Vila Real. **Casa do Mineiro** (☎ 259 979 720, 917 523 575; casadacruz@mail.telepac.pt; Lugar de Trás do Vale; d €50; P) and **Casa da Cruz** (☎ 259979720, 917523575; www.geocities.com/casadacruz; 2/4/6 person €50/90/120; P) are self-catering, traditional-style rural cottages with cool granite rooms and stony simplicity. There is also the large, modern **Quality Inn** (☎ 259 979 640; www.choicehotelsportugal.com; d with breakfast €71; P) at the junction with the IP4.

Basto Radical (p433 has advice on local accommodation. And for more options, see also Mondim de Basto (right).

Getting There & Away

Transcovizela and Rodonorte jointly run buses between Vila Real and Mondim de Basto (p435), skirting the park near Ermelo. Additional villages have bus services during school term; ask at the park offices or the turismos in Vila Real or Mondim.

There are no buses to Lamas de Ôlo. A taxi costs about €20 from Mondim or €12 from Vila Real; taxis are also available at Lamas de Ôlo.

MONDIM DE BASTO

pop 6000 / elevation 200m

Sheltered deep in the park, this pretty mountain town near the intersection of the Douro, Minho and Trás-os-Montes provinces (around 30km northeast of Amarante) is made all the more special by its surroundings, its friendly people and a potent wine for which the Terras de Basto region is notorious. It's a good base from which to explore the Parque Natural do Alvão.

Orientation & Information

Buses stop behind the *mercado municipal*, from where it's 150m west to the **turismo** (☎ 255 389 370; Praça 9 de Abril; 9am-9pm Jul–mid-Sep, 9am-12.30pm & 2-5.30pm Mon-Fri mid-Sep–Jun), and what remains of the old town.

About 700m west of the turismo is a **Parque Natural do Alvão office** (☎/fax 255 381 209; pna@icn.pt; Lugar do Barrio; 9am-12.30pm & 2-5.30pm Mon-Fri).

Activities

Hikers will love the challenge of the long haul up to the Capela de Senhora da Graça on the summit of pine-clad Monte Farinha, two to three hours up and topped by a restaurant. The path starts east of town on the N312 (the turismo has a rough map). By car, turn off the N312 3.5km from Mondim in the direction of Cerva; from there it's a twisting 9.5km to the top.

SWIMMING

At Senhora da Ponte, 2km south of town on the N304, is a rocky swimming spot by a disused water mill on the Rio Cabril. Follow signs to the Parque de Campismo de Mondim de Basto and then take the track to the right.

WINE TASTING

Wine-lovers take note: the refreshing local 'Basto' *vinho verde* (semi-sparkling young wine) is produced nearby at **Quinta do Fundo** (below). Other labels come from **Quinta da Veiga** (☎ 255 361 212) in Gagos, west across the Rio Tâmega, and **Quinta d'Onega** (☎ 255 386 195) in Ate, 15km north of Mondim. Ask at the turismo for details.

Sleeping

Casa das Mourôas (☎ 255 381 394; Rua José Carvalho Camões; d with breakfast from €45; P) This delightful converted 19th-century hayloft is on the same flowery square as the turismo. It has a handful of cosy rooms and a scented vine-covered terrace. English is spoken.

Quinta do Fundo (☎ 255 381 291; fax 255 382 017; Vilar de Viando; d/ste with breakfast €50/75; P) An idyll of calm and rural relaxation, this handsome property is located 2km south on the N304. It has a tennis court and swimming pool, horses and bikes for hire, and also produces its own *vinho verde* – as testified by the vineyards enveloping the house.

Casa do Campo (☎ 255 361 231; www.casadocampo.pt; Molares, Celorico de Basto; s/d/st with breakfast €69/80/100; P) It's a long haul to this impressive, antique-filled manor house with highly extravagant if weedy topiary gardens, and a wide open lawn with pleasant views. Only for those with their own wheels: It's about 7km west of Mondim.

Quinta da Barreiro de Cima (☎ 255 386 491; Parada de Atei; d with breakfast €83, apt €130; P) You'll find this quirky old granite place about 5km to the north of Mondim. It has a few double rooms and one self-catering apartment.

Residencial Carvalho (☎ 255 381 057; Avenida Dr Augusto Brito; s/d with breakfast €15/25) West of the turismo, by the petrol station, and quite ordinary.

Residencial Arcádia (☎ 255 381 410; Avenida Dr Augusto Brito; s/d with breakfast €25/30, d with air-con €40;) Run of the mill, and south of Residencial Carvalho. Rooms aren't as cheerful as the glorious flowery front suggests.

Parque de Campismo de Mondim de Basto (☎/fax 255 381 650; mondim.basto@fpcampismo.pt; adult/car €2.65/1.90, tent €2.15-3.50) This grassy camping facility, open to CCI holders, is 1km south of town on hard ground beside the Rio Cabril.

Eating

Adega Sete Condes (☎ 255 382 342; Rua Velha; half-portions €4-6, mains €6-10; lunch & dinner Tue-Sun, lunch Mon) Tucked into a tiny corner behind the turismo with a few picnic tables outside, this granite-walled, tavern-like spot has a small menu of well-prepared traditional dishes, including *bacalhau* (salt cod) and a very tasty *feijoada* (pork and bean casserole); a half-portion is plenty.

Adega Santiago (☎ 255 386 957; Rua Velha; mains €6-9.50; lunch & dinner Mon-Sat) Another nicely renovated stone-walled eatery near Adega Sete Condes, and equally as homely as Adega Sete Condes.

Getting There & Away

A coordinated service is run by **Auto Mondinense/Transcovizela** (☎ 259 381 296) from Vila Real (€2.65, one hour) three times each weekday and once on Saturday, with a change at Avecção do Cabo.

Transcovizela runs to Mondim from Amarante train station (€3.55, 1½ hours) three times on weekdays and twice on Saturday, with a change at Fermil.

CHAVES

Literally meaning 'keys', the vital gateway town of Chaves (*shahv*-sh) has been squabbled over through the centuries by Romans, Suevi, Visigoths, Moors, French and Spanish alike. But in contrast to its often frantic history, pretty Chaves is now better known as a spot to chill out and indulge in some serious pampering in its healthy hot springs.

However, passing travellers will be more interested in Chaves' 16-arched Roman bridge, which straddles the Rio Tâmega and, amazingly, is a major traffic-bearing structure undented by time. The town's atmospheric medieval quarter, 14th-century castle keep and a muscular fortress also make it worth the detour, though you'd be smart to book ahead if you are coming in summer.

Orientation

The town centre is a 700m walk southwest of the AV Tâmega bus station, or a few blocks northeast of the Rodonorte bus stop on Rua Joaquim Delgado. The backbone of the old town is Rua de Santo António.

Information

Banks with ATMs dot Rua de Santo António, Rua Direita and Largo do Arrabalde.

District hospital (☎ 276 300 900; Avenida Francisco Sá Carneiro) Northwest of the centre.

Espaço Internet (☎ 276 340 500; 9am-12.30pm & 2-5.30pm Mon-Fri) Free Internet.

ILIC (☎ 276 332 845; Rua da Ponte 44; per hr €2; 10am-1pm & 2.30-9pm Mon-Fri, 11am-1pm & 2-6pm Sat) An IT shop with Internet access, by the Ponte Romana.

Lavandaria Popular (☎ 276 332 621; Rua do Tabolado; 9am-1pm & 3-7pm Mon-Fri, 9am-1pm Sat) Will cheerfully do your wash the same or next day (€2 per kilo).

Police station (☎ 276 322 169; Avenida Bombeiros Voluntários)

Post office (☎ 276 301 393; Largo General Silveira; 8.30am-6pm Mon-Fri, 9am-12.30pm Sat)

Regional turismo (☎ 276 340 660; rturismoatb@mail.telepac.pt; Terreiro de Cavalaria; 9.30am-12.30pm & 2-6pm Jun-Sep, Mon-Sat Oct-May) Very helpful multilingual tourist office.

Sanvitur travel agency (☎ 273 331 826; Avenida João da Cruz 38; Mon-Fri, Sat morning Apr-Oct)

Sights

PONTE ROMANA

Still taking traffic an incredible 1900 years on, Chaves' handsome bridge was completed in AD 104 by Emperor Trajan (hence its other name, Ponte Trajano). It probably served as a link on the important road between Braga and Astorga (Spain). In the middle are two engraved Roman milestones.

MUSEU DA REGIÃO FLAVIENSE

The regional archaeological-ethnographic collection is held in this **museum** (☎ 276 340 500; Praça de Luís Camões; admission incl Museu Militar adult/

TRÁS-OS-MONTES

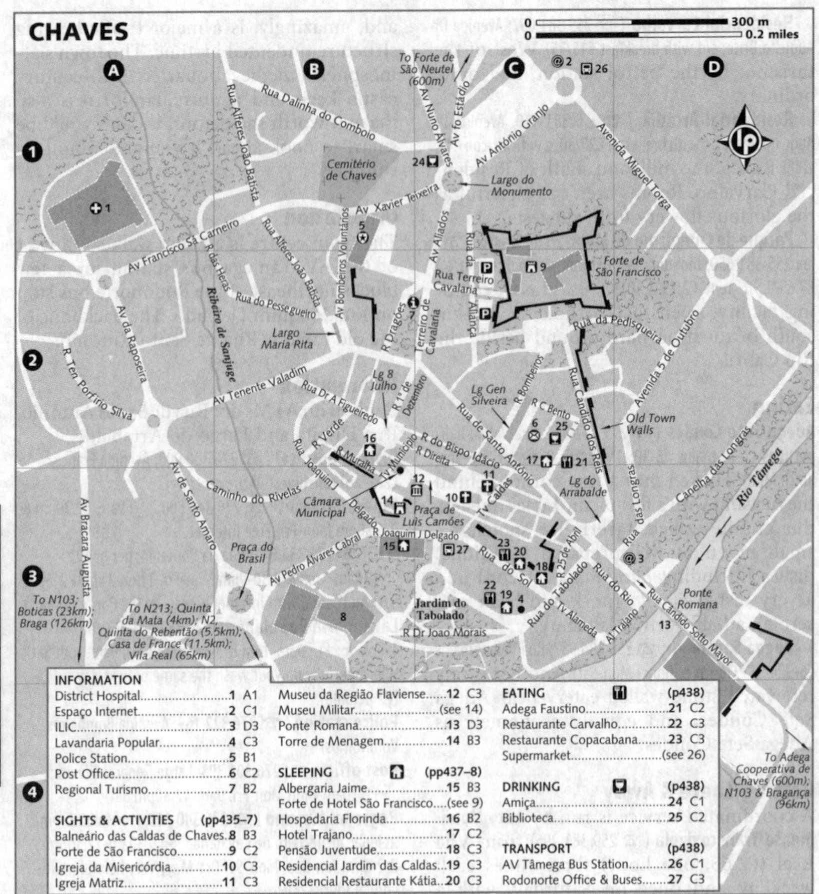

child under 18/senior €0.50/free/free; 9am-12.30pm & 2-5.30pm Tue-Fri, 2-5.30pm Sat & Sun) naturally has lots of Roman artefacts, but the most interesting items are stone menhirs and carvings, some dating back over 2500 years. There are also temporary art displays.

TORRE DE MENAGEM & MUSEU MILITAR

The stubborn-looking **Torre de Menagem** (castle keep) stands resolutely alone behind the town's main medieval square. The only major remnant of a 14th-century castle built by Dom Dinis, it was inherited first by Nuno Álvares Pereira (the Holy Constable) in 1385 (p25), then by the House of Bragança when his daughter married into their clan. Around the tower are neatly manicured gardens and a stretch of old defensive walls, with views over town and countryside.

The Torre now houses a motley collection of military gear in the **Museu Militar** (for admission see Museu da Região Flaviense, p435) and you can climb a series of creaky stairs to emerge onto the roof (usually busy with smooching couples).

FORTE DE SÃO FRANCISCO & FORTE DE SÃO NEUTEL

With two to spare, neither of Chaves' ancient fortresses get museum-piece treatment. The more impressive **Forte de São Francisco**, which was completed in 1658 around a 16th-century Franciscan convent, is now a top-end hotel (p438), though nobody minds if you snoop around inside the walls.

On the other hand, **Forte de São Neutel**, 1.2km northeast of the centre, is open only as the venue for occasional summertime concerts.

The style of both these 17th-century forts was inspired by the work of the French military architect Vauban.

CHURCHES

The 17th-century **Igreja da Misericórdia** (Praça de Luís Camões) catches the eye with its exterior porch and columns. Inside are some huge 18th-century azulejos.

Also on the square is the **igreja matriz** (parish church), Romanesque in form but thoroughly remodelled in the 16th century – though the doorway and belfry retain some original features.

Activities

The warm, salty waters of the **Balneário das Caldas de Chaves** (☎ 276 332 445; www.caldasdechaves.com.pt; Largo das Caldas) are said to be good for rheumatism, liver complaints, digestive disorders, and high blood pressure; local *residenciais* (guesthouses) are full of elderly patients. Unfortunately, the only thing available to casual visitors is a drink of the stuff, which tastes pretty awful.

If you fancy something a little tastier, such as draining a few glasses of local vintages, look especially for São Neutel (reds and sparkling whites), Flavius (sturdy reds and whites) and Vespasiano reds. The **Adega Cooperativa de Chaves** (☎ 276 322 183; Avenida Duarte), 1km southeast of the centre, is open during weekday business hours for tours and tastings. For something out of the mainstream, see Wine of the Dead (p438).

Festivals & Events

Feira de Todos Santos (All Saints Fair) Chaves' annual weeklong bash. The biggest days are 31 October and 1 November, with folk music, brass bands and market stalls in the streets.

Dia de Cidade (City Day; 8 July) Features bands, parades, fireworks and laser shows.

Sleeping

In summer, Chaves' better accommodation gets snapped up by spa patients, so book ahead. Rooms have private bathroom except as noted.

BUDGET

Hospedaria Florinda (☎ 276 333 392; fax 276 326 577; Rua dos Açougues; d/tw with breakfast €30/40; ⊠) Florinda is a charming old guesthouse distinguished by pretty, house-proud rooms and personal service.

Residencial Jardim das Caldas (☎ 276 331 189; jardimdascaldas@mail.telepac.pt; Jardim do Tabolado 5; d with breakfast €40) Facing Chaves' riverside park, this *residencial* (guesthouse) has squeaky-clean, serviceable rooms, and dazed but pleasant service.

Pensão Juventude (☎ 276 326 713; Rua do Sol 8; d €25) Accommodation here comprises eight clean, spartan rooms (with shared bathroom) above a café.

Hotel Trajano (☎ 276 301 640; info@hoteltrajano.com; Travessa Cândido dos Reis; d with breakfast from €50; ⊠) This courteous old hotel has big, simply furnished rooms that retain a certain '70s flavour.

Residencial Restaurante Kátia (☎ 276 324 446; Rua do Sol 28; d with breakfast €35) Backed up against the old town walls, this place has low-profile service and prim, well-kept rooms. It's often full.

Quinta do Rebentão (☎/fax 276 322 733; Vila Nova de Veiga; adult €2.50, car €2.50, tent €2-4; ⏲ Jan-Nov) Just off the N2 6km southwest of Chaves is a grassy, partly shaded, suburban camping facility with free hot showers and basic supplies. Bikes can be hired here.

MID-RANGE

Quinta da Mata (☎ 276 340 030; quintadamata@mail.telepac.pt; Solares de Portugal, Nantes; d with breakfast €65; P) If you've got wheels and the wherewithal (about €60 for a double), ask at the turismo about this isolated country haven, a lovingly restored 17th-century manor house 4.5km southeast off the N213, with tennis courts and sauna. It's a family friendly place, bathed in beautiful flower-filled gardens on the lush hills looking down on the city.

Casa de France (☎ 276 965 453; casadefrance@oninet.pt; N314; d with breakfast €50; P) Also attractive is this typical Transmontana house, located in the village of France, 12km south of Chaves.

TOP END

Albergaria Jaime (☎ 276 301 050; www.albergariajaime.com.pt; Rua Joaquim José Delgado; d with breakfast €98; P ⊠) Colourful old terracotta-coloured mansion that was recently remodelled to

TRÁS-OS-MONTES

contain every mod con – including cable TV. One room is adapted for wheelchairs, and there is Internet access in the separate café below the main hotel.

Forte de São Francisco Hotel (☎ 276 333 700; www.forte-s-francisco-hoteis.pt; d Sun-Thu €125, Fri & Sat €140; P) An extraordinary blend of four-star hotel and restored national monument, with faultless rooms, tennis courts, sauna – and its own church. A testament to how private enterprise can keep historical treasures in good nick.

Eating

Chaves is known for its delicious smoked *presunto* (ham) and sausages.

Adega Faustino (☎ 276 322 142; Travessa Cândido dos Reis; dishes €3-7; lunch & dinner Mon-Sat) Resembling a fire-station from without, this cavernous ex-winery is now filled with light and birdsong, with a big list of carefully prepared regional meals, from *salpicão* (small rounds of smoked ham) to pig's ear in vinaigrette sauce. There's a good selection of local wines to quaff too.

Restaurante Copacabana (☎ 276 323 570; Rua do Sol 38; dishes under €7; lunch & dinner) A warm laid-back affair with a family atmosphere, a short, meaty menu and enormous portions: perhaps a good thing that it's within waddling distance of most guesthouses.

Restaurante Carvalho (☎ 276 321 727; Jardim do Tabolado; dishes around €8; lunch & dinner Fri-Wed) This posh place delivers more than you'd expect from its position amid boisterous parkside cafés and a forest of plastic seats: the regional dishes are top-notch.

Self-caterers must settle for the **supermarket** upstairs from the AV Tâmega bus station.

Drinking

Chaves isn't the place for a wild night out, but hip bars include **Amiça** (Largo do Monumento; 11pm-late Thu-Sat), and the bar-cum-disco **Biblioteca** (Travessa Cândido dos Reis), with a tongue-in-cheek name meaning library.

Getting There & Away

From the bus station **REDM/AV Tâmega** (☎ 276 332 384) has services via Montalegre (€3.90, 80 minutes) to Braga (€5.40, 3½ hours) six times daily; to Vila Real (€5.30, 1¼ hours) three times daily; to Mirandela (€3.60) three times each weekday; via Porto (€9, 2½ hours) to Coimbra daily; and to Bragança (€7.40, 2¼ hours) twice daily.

Rodonorte (☎ 276 333 491; Rua Joaquim Delgado) goes via Vila Real and Amarante (€7.40, two hours) to Porto (€9) eight times per weekday, less often at the weekend.

AV Tâmega also has four local services each weekday to the border at Feces de Abaixo, where you can pick up Spanish buses to Orense.

WINE OF THE DEAD

From the otherwise unremarkable town of Boticas, 23km southwest of Chaves, comes the bizarrely named *vinho dos mortos* (wine of the dead), a rough red brew generously described by brochures as 'famous, tasty clarets'.

In 1809, so the story goes, villagers were so perturbed by the idea that boozy French invaders might get their sticky mitts on their wine that they buried it. Once the coast was clear, they dug their precious bottles up only to discover that the wine's taste had noticeably improved. After drinking a few bottles just to check, the improvement was notched up to the intervention of their alcohol-loving ancestors and, to this day, the townsfolk bury wine in deep cellars for up to a year.

EASTERN TRÁS-OS-MONTES

BRAGANÇA

pop 20,300 / elevation 650m

Proud Bragança is a symbol of national grit and determination, mirrored in its looming citadel – one of the most stirring sights in northern Portugal.

The name Bragança has echoed through Portuguese history since the 15th century, when its newly established duchy reminded the predatory Spaniards that it was Portuguese land, thank-you-very-much. Though the dukes of Bragança eventually moved south, their remote hometown's kudos grew as they ascended the throne in 1640 (to rule until the fall of the monarchy in 1910). However, mountains, bad roads and poor communications prolonged

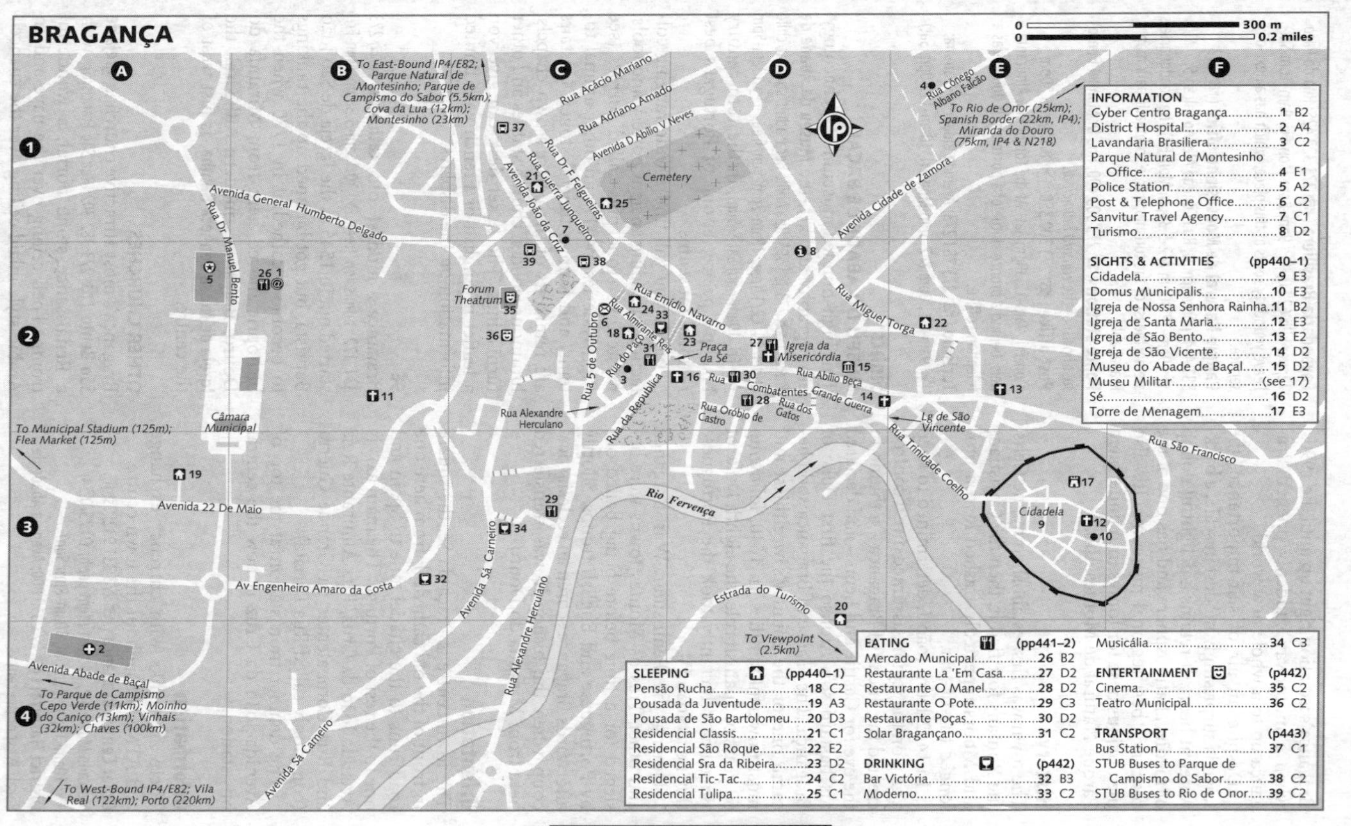
BRAGANÇA
0 300 m
0 0.2 miles
To East-Bound IP4/E82; Parque Natural de Montesinho; Parque de Campismo do Sabor (5.5km); Cova da Lua (12km); Montesinho (23km)
To Rio de Onor (25km); Spanish Border (22km, IP4); Miranda do Douro (75km, IP4 & N218)
To Municipal Stadium (125m); Flea Market (125m)
To Parque de Campismo Cepo Verde (11km); Moinho do Caniço (13km); Vinhais (32km); Chaves (100km)
To West-Bound IP4/E82; Vila Real (122km); Porto (220km)
To Viewpoint (2.5km)
Rua Acácio Mariano
Rua Adriano Amado
Avenida D Abílio V Neves
Cemetery
Rua Dr F Felgueiras
Rua Guerra Junqueiro
Avenida João da Cruz
Avenida General Humberto Delgado
Rua Dr Manuel Bento
Avenida Cidade de Zamora
Rua Cónego Albano Falcão
Forum Theatrum
Rua Emídio Navarro
Rua Almirante Reis
Rua do Paço
Rua 5 de Outubro
Praça da Sé
Igreja da Misericórdia
Rua Miguel Torga
Rua Abílio Beça
Rua Combatentes Grande Guerra
Rua dos Gatos
Rua Oróbio de Castro
Rua da República
Rua Alexandre Herculano
Lg de São Vicente
Rua Trinidade Coelho
Rua São Francisco
Cidadela
Câmara Municipal
Rio Fervença
Avenida 22 De Maio
Av Engenheiro Amaro da Costa
Avenida Sá Carneiro
Estrada do Turismo
Avenida Abade de Baçal
INFORMATION
Cyber Centro Bragança.....1 B2
District Hospital.....2 A4
Lavandaria Brasiliera.....3 C2
Parque Natural de Montesinho Office.....4 E1
Police Station.....5 A2
Post & Telephone Office.....6 C2
Sanvitur Travel Agency.....7 C1
Turismo.....8 D2
SIGHTS & ACTIVITIES (pp440–1)
Cidadela.....9 E3
Domus Municipalis.....10 E3
Igreja de Nossa Senhora Rainha.11 B2
Igreja de Santa Maria.....12 E3
Igreja de São Bento.....13 E2
Igreja de São Vicente.....14 D2
Museu do Abade de Baçal.....15 D2
Museu Militar.....(see 17)
Sé.....16 D2
Torre de Menagem.....17 E3
SLEEPING (pp440–1)
Pensão Rucha.....18 C2
Pousada da Juventude.....19 A3
Pousada de São Bartolomeu.....20 D3
Residencial Classis.....21 C1
Residencial São Roque.....22 E2
Residencial Sra da Ribeira.....23 D2
Residencial Tic-Tac.....24 C2
Residencial Tulipa.....25 C1
EATING (pp441–2)
Mercado Municipal.....26 B2
Restaurante La 'Em Casa.....27 D2
Restaurante O Manel.....28 D2
Restaurante O Pote.....29 C3
Restaurante Poças.....30 D2
Solar Bragançano.....31 C2
DRINKING (p442)
Bar Victória.....32 B3
Moderno.....33 C2
Musicália.....34 C3
ENTERTAINMENT (p442)
Cinema.....35 C2
Teatro Municipal.....36 C2
TRANSPORT (p443)
Bus Station.....37 C1
STUB Buses to Parque de Campismo do Sabor.....38 C2
STUB Buses to Rio de Onor.....39 C2

Bragança's isolation right up until the 1990s, when a motorway suddenly opened Bragança up to a whole new world.

Despite an air of self-importance, the town is surprisingly modest in scale, a backwater at heart. It retains a delightful dollop of medieval atmosphere and has one of the country's best regional museums. It's also the obvious base for forays into underrated Parque Natural de Montesinho.

History

The town was first established by the Celts, the Romans fortified it, then the Christians and Moors repeatedly trashed it in a prolonged tug-of-war.

In 1442 Dom João I, determined to keep a grip on the region, assumed direct control, created the duchy of Bragança – a thumb in the eye for Castile and León – and declared his bastard son Afonso the first Duke of Bragança. The House of Bragança soon became one of the country's wealthiest and most powerful families. In 1640, following 60 years of Spanish rule, the eighth Duke of Bragança reluctantly took the Portuguese throne as João IV.

During the Peninsular War Bragança and other Trás-os-Montes towns were besieged for a time before being bailed out by Portuguese and English troops. Shortly afterwards Bragança scored an ecclesiastical coup when the bishopric was transferred here from Miranda do Douro.

Orientation

The town centre is Praça da Sé, the square in front of the old cathedral: from here one road runs to the citadel, one to Spain and one to the rest of Portugal. The main axis is Avenida João da Cruz, Rua Almirante Reis and Rua Combatentes da Grande Guerra (commonly called Rua Direita).

The defunct train station at the top of Avenida João da Cruz is now the central bus station.

Information

There are banks with currency exchange and ATMs throughout the town centre.

Cyber Centro Bragança (☎ 273 331 932; 1st fl, Mercado Municipal; adult/student per hr €0.75/0.54; 🕙 10am-11pm Mon-Sat, 10am-8pm Sun)

District Hospital (☎ 273 310 800; Avenida Abade de Baçal) West of the centre.

Lavandaria Brasiliera (☎ 273 322 425; Rua do Paço 22; per kilo €2.50; 🕙 9am-8pm Mon-Fri, 9am-1pm Sat) Leave your dirty socks at this place, which has a next-day service.

Parque Natural de Montesinho office (☎ 273 381 444; pnm@icn.pt; Rua Cónego Albano Falcão 5; 🕙 9am-12.30pm & 2-5.30pm Mon-Fri) The headquarters are northeast of the turismo; a free schematic park map is available.

Police station (☎ 273 303 400; Rua Dr Manuel Bento) Just north of the *câmara municipal*.

Post office (☎ 273 300 350; 🕙 8.30am-5.30pm Mon-Fri, 9am-12.30pm Sat) At the top of Rua Almirante Reis, behind a bronze statue of a postman. It doubles as a telephone office.

Turismo (☎ 273 381 273; Avenida Cidade de Zamora; 🕙 9am-12.30pm & 2-5pm Mon-Fri, 10am-12.30pm Sat)

Sights

MUSEU DO ABADE DE BAÇAL

This high-minded museum of archaeology, ethnography and art, the **Museu do Abade de Baçal** (☎ 273 331 595; Rua Abílio Beça; adult/student/child under 14 €2/1/free, 10am-2pm Sun free; 🕙 10am-5pm Tue-Fri, 10am-6pm Sat & Sun), in the 16th-century bishop's palace, is one of Portugal's best regional museums.

Inside you will find a wide-ranging collection including ancient pottery and tools, mysterious stone pigs called *berrões* (see Pig Mysteries, p441) and other animal totems, and Roman funeral stones. Upstairs are remnants of the palace's own chapels, luminous wooden church statues and other furnishings. The ticket desk can give you a leaflet in English or French with limited information on the displays.

SÉ

Bragança's modest old **cathedral** (☎ 273 331 172; admission free; 🕙 10.15am-5.30pm Mon-Fri) started out in 1545 as the Igreja de São João Baptista, but got bumped up the rankings to become a cathedral in 1770 when the bishopric moved here from Miranda do Douro. Bragança's modern cathedral, the **Igreja de Nossa Senhora Rainha**, is just west of the centre.

OTHER CHURCHES

Bragança's most attractive church is **Igreja de São Bento** (☎ 273 382 302; Rua São Francisco), with a Renaissance stone portal, a wonderful trompe l'oeil ceiling over the nave and an Arabic-style inlaid ceiling over the chancel.

PIG MYSTERIES

Statues of pigs? That's right. It may sound like hogwash, but hundreds of crudely carved granite pigs or boars known as *berrões* (singular: *berrão*) are scattered around remoter parts of Trás-os-Montes and over into Spain. Some date back over 2000 years, others to the 2nd or 3rd century AD.

So what inspired generations to immortalise their pet porkers in stone? No-one knows for sure what the statues were for, but theories abound: fertility or prosperity symbols, grave guardians, offerings to Iron Age gods or simply property markers. Take your pick.

You can see these mysterious pigs in museums in Bragança, Chaves and Miranda do Douro, or *in situ* in Bragança's citadel, where there's a rather weather-beaten example pinioned by his iron-age pillory. However, the best-preserved example hogs a pedestal in the central square of tiny Murça, 30km northeast of Vila Real.

Facing little Largo de São Vicente a block westwards is the **Igreja de São Vicente**, Romanesque in origin but rebuilt in the 17th century. A chapter in Portugal's favourite – and grisliest – love story may have been played out here; tradition has it that the future Dom Pedro I secretly married Inês de Castro here around 1354 (see p269 for the whole tragic tale).

CIDADELA

Keep climbing uphill from Largo de São Vicente and you'll soon set foot inside the astonishingly well-preserved 13th-century **cidadela**. People still live in its narrow atmospheric lanes, unspoilt by the low-key handicrafts shops and cafés that have crept in.

Within the ruggedly ramparted walls is what remains of the original castle, beefed up in the 15th century by João I for the dukes of Bragança. The stout **Torre de Menagem** was garrisoned up until the early 20th century. It now houses a lacklustre **Museu Militar** (Military Museum; ☎ 273 322 378; adult/child under 10 €1.50/free, 9am-11.45am Sun free; 9am-11.45am & 2-4.45pm Fri-Wed). In front of the Torre is an extraordinary, primitive *pelourinho*, atop a granite boar similar to the *berrões* found around the province.

Squatting at the rear of the citadel is an odd pentagonal building known as the **Domus Municipalis** (Town House; admission free; 9am-4.45pm Fri-Wed), the oldest town hall in Portugal – although its precise age is a matter of scholarly disagreement – and one of the few examples of civil (nonchurch) Romanesque architecture on the Iberian Peninsula. Upstairs in an arcaded room – studded with weathered faces of man and beast and scratched with symbols of the stonemasons – Bragança's medieval town council once met.

Beside the Domus Municipalis is the early-16th-century **Igreja de Santa Maria**, with a portal covered in carved vines, and a deteriorating 18th-century trompe l'oeil ceiling.

There's a terrific view of the *cidadela* from a hilltop viewpoint near the old Mosteiro de São Bartolomeu; from the town centre cross the river on Rua Alexandre Herculano and take the first left.

FLEA MARKET

A flea market takes over the area around the municipal stadium on Avenida Abade de Baçal, west of the centre, on the 3rd, 12th and 21st of each month (or the following Monday when any of these falls on the weekend).

Festivals & Events

Bragança's biggest annual market, **Feira das Cantarinhas** (2–4 May), is a huge street fair of traditional handicrafts. (A *cantarinha* is a small terracotta pitcher.)

Sleeping

BUDGET

Pensão Rucha (☎ 273 331 672; Rua Almirante Reis 42; s/d €15/25) Filmy curtains and attractive old furniture fill this genteel gem of a guesthouse, which is top value at the budget end. Its sunny, peaceful atmosphere has no hint of hotel about it. Rooms have shared facilities.

Pousada da juventude (☎ 273 304 600; braganca@movijovem.pt; Avenida 22 de Maio; dm €12.50, d €35; P) Bragança's excellent youth hostel is in a peaceful spot about 900m west of the town centre, complete with spotless rooms, sunny café and fountain. A four-bed apartment with kitchenette (€60) and a six-bed family room (€82.50) are also available.

Residencial São Roque (☎ 273 381 481; Rua Miguel Torga; s/d with breakfast €25/35; ❄) The best thing about this ageing blocky high-rise near the turismo is its views. On one side peering over to the hilltop citadel, and on the other, commanding a privileged sweep of the Parque Natural de Montesinho.

Restaurante Poças (☎ 273 331 428; Rua Combatentes de Grande Guerra 200; per person €10) Bare-bones rooms with shared facilities.

There are two camp sites in the nearby Parque Natural de Montesinho – the Parque de Campismo do Sabor and Parque de Campismo Cepo Verde (p445).

MID-RANGE

Moinho do Caniço (☎ 273 323 577; www.braganca net.pt/moinho; Castrelos; up to 4 people €100; P) This rough-walled water mill – complete with kitchen and open fireplace – is by the river 13km west of Bragança on the N103. It's one of several delightful rural Turihab properties in the area.

Residencial Sra da Ribeira (☎ 273 300 550; fax 273 300 555; Travessa da Misericórdia; d with breakfast €35; ❄) Hidden away in an easy-to-miss alleyway, this attractive modern guesthouse has carefully colour-coordinated rooms and newly renovated fittings.

Residencial Tulipa (☎ 273 331 675; tulipaturismo@iol.pt; Rua Dr Francisco Felgueiras 8-10; d/tr with breakfast €45/50; P ❄) Uniformly spotless, unfussy modern rooms here are great value for money, and the service is courteous. There's one room adapted for disabled visitors.

Residencial Classis (☎ 273 331 631; fax 273 323 458; Avenida João da Cruz 102; s/d with breakfast €32.50/47.50; ❄) A passable *residenciais* with plain, comfortable rooms.

Residencial Tic-Tac (☎ 273 331 373; fax 273 331 673; Rua Emídio Navarro 85; d with breakfast €35) Very similar to Residencial Classis.

TOP END

Pousada de São Bartolomeu (☎ 273 331 493; recepcao.sbartolomeu@pousadas.pt; Estrada do Turismo; d Sun-Thu €134, Fri & Sat €144; P ❄ ♿) A whitewashed modern *pousada* (upmarket inn) sits proudly alone, 1.5km southeast of the centre, with every creature comfort, including balconies with citadel views to knock your socks off.

Eating

Restaurante Poças (☎ 273 331 428; Rua Combatentes de Grande Guerra 200; dishes €5-8; 🕐 lunch & dinner) A colourful multilingual joint, splashed with a two-story mural of country scenes, Restaurante Poças is a great place to tuck into well-prepared dishes with plenty of vegetables. The fresh *truta* (trout) is recommended.

Restaurante O Pote (☎ 273 333 710; Rua Alexandre Herculano 186; dishes €6-10; 🕐 lunch & dinner Mon-Sat) With a neat little café-bar downstairs and an elegant restaurant upstairs, O Pote specialises in traditional regional dishes at reasonable prices.

Solar Bragançano (☎ 274 323 875; www.solar-braganca.com; Praça da Sé 34; mains €9-20; 🕐 lunch & dinner) A 17th-century manor house on the cathedral square hosts this typical Trás-os-Montes restaurant. It boasts oak-panelled rooms, soothing music, a small garden and a seasonal menu weighted towards local game such as succulent hare and roast pheasant, best finished with a plate of creamy goat's cheese.

Restaurante La 'Em Casa (☎ 273 322 111; Rua Marquês de Pombal; mains €6-14; 🕐 lunch & dinner) Pine-panelled La 'Em consistently churns out excellent meaty dishes using mostly local produce. The veal and lamb dishes are superb.

Restaurante O Manel (☎ 273 322 480; Rua Oróbio de Castro 27-29; dishes €7-11; 🕐 lunch & dinner Mon-Sat; ❄) O Manel offers excellent food, especially fish and seafood in a calm, bright, simple setting.

The **Pousada de São Bartolomeu** (left) also has a very good upmarket restaurant. Self-caterers will find numerous **minimercados** (grocery shops) in the backstreets. It's a long walk to the new **mercado municipal** (🕐 8am-7pm Mon-Sat), behind the *câmara municipal*.

Drinking

Popular clubs include long-standing favourite **Moderno** (☎ 273 327 766; Rua Almirante Reis; 🕐 midnight-4am) and the trendy new **Musicália** (Av Sá Carneiro 121; 🕐 midnight-late Thu-Sat), which also boasts Guinness on tap. Or for a lively bar atmosphere, try **Bar Victória** (☎ 273 329 273; Av Engenheiro Amaro da Costa 23; 🕐 9.30pm-late Mon-Sat).

Entertainment

The spanking new **Teatro Municipal** (☎ 273 302 744) theatre has given the city's cultural goings-on a fantastic boost, and there's also a new multiscreen **cinema** (☎ 707 220 220; Forum Theatrum) in the shopping centre next door.

Getting There & Away

With ticket offices at the bus station are **Rede Expressos** (☎ 966 482 215), **JR Viagens e Turismo** (☎ 273 327 122), **Rodonorte** (☎ 273 300 183) and **Santos** (☎ 273 326 552), though these tend to open only around arrival or departure times. Rede Expressos bus tickets are also sold by the Sanvitur travel agency (p435).

Bragança–Miranda do Douro connections are by Santos (€5.50, one each weekday) and Rodonorte (€5.20, two each weekday). Rede Expressos and Joalto (no Bragança office) each have a daily service via Vila Nova de Foz Côa (€6) and Trancoso (€7.80) to Viseu (€10.20, 3½ hours).

Between them Rede Expressos, Rodonorte and Santos have over a dozen buses daily via Vila Real (€7.50, two hours) to Porto (€8.70, 3½ hours); Rede Expressos also has some nonstop Porto services. Rodonorte goes via Guimarães (€10.50) to Braga (€10.70, four hours, two daily).

Most of the weekend services are less frequent.

PARQUE NATURAL DE MONTESINHO

Abutting Spain with its two slatey massifs of undulating grassland and deciduous forest, the 750-sq-km natural park's main attraction is its sprinkling of 88 lean little villages – some of the most remote in the country. Hardly more than hamlets and generally housing more chickens than humans, these villages are a fast-disappearing window on the past.

There have been settlements here since the Iron Age, many sheltering in deep valleys – peaceful gems easily overlooked by the casual visitor. The harsh, remote *terra fria* inspired early Portuguese rulers to establish a system of collective land tenure and then leave the villages to their own devices. The remarkably democratic communal practices that resulted still persist today.

The park was founded in part to protect this fragile social structure, but sadly, remote villages continue to be deserted by their young. However, the peaceful little settlements retain an irresistible charm. The government has also contributed to local restoration of traditional slate-roofed stone houses, churches, forges, mills and the characteristic, charming *pombals* (dovecotes).

Villages that retain lashings of character include Pinheiro Novo, Sernande, Edroso, Santalha and Moimenta in the west, and Donai, Varge, Rio de Onor and Guadramil in the east.

The natural base from which to explore the park is Bragança. There's some accommodation at villages within the park, though public transport is dire.

Information

There are park offices at Bragança (p440) and **Vinhais** (☎ 273 771 416; Casa do Povo, Rua Dr Álvaro Leite; 9am-12.30pm & 2-5.30pm Mon-Fri). A free schematic park map is available from both offices. Brochures on flora, archaeology and handicrafts, and a booklet on park walks, are in Portuguese although staff at Bragança are more than willing to answer questions.

Sights

The most famous inhabitant of the eastern Serra de Montesinho is the rusty-coloured Iberian wolf (p56). Indeed this national park and the adjoining Spanish park together form the last major refuge for this seriously endangered animal. Other

DEVILS IN DISGUISE

Some festivals in Trás-os-Montes have a truly licentious side, a tilt towards earthier, pagan traditions.

Carnaval seems to bring these to the surface. Most of Portugal's Carnaval celebrations feature Rio-style parades and parties, but up north there's an echo of ancient rites of passage, a whiff of mischief. Witness the antics of the Caretos of Podence (near Macedo de Cavaleiros) – gangs of young men in *caretos* (leering masks) and vivid, candy-cane costumes who invade the town centre, bent on cheerfully humiliating everyone in sight. Prime targets are young women, at whom they thrust their hips and wave the cowbells hanging from their belts. Similar figures are to be seen in Varge, in the Parque Natural de Montesinho.

Saturnalian high jinks also take place in many villages around Christmas or Twelfth Night during the so-called Festa dos Rapazes (Festival of the Lads), when unmarried boys over 16 light all-night bonfires and rampage around in robes of rags and masks of brass or wood.

threatened species found here are the royal eagle and the black stork.

In vast forests of Iberian oak and chestnut, and among riverside alders, willows, poplars and hazel, there are also roe deer, otter and wild boar; in the grasslands are partridge, kite and kestrel. Above 900m the otherwise barren ground is carpeted in heather and broom in spring. Pine plantations mar the park's eastern limb, though these areas are also rich in wildlife.

RIO DE ONOR

This odd little village, with a population of 70 and an elevation 730m, is entirely unfazed by the Spanish–Portuguese border splicing it down the middle. This is one of the park's most interesting villages – not only for its beautiful stone buildings and bucket-loads of character but because it staunchly upholds the independent-minded communal lifestyle once typical of the region.

Many people still speak an ancient dialect called *mirandês,* descended almost directly from Latin (and recently recognised as Portugal's second language).

The border itself runs smack through the middle of the village and the Rio Onor trickles along perpendicular to it. The road from Bragança branches left to cross the border and right to cross the river on an old stone bridge, to the prettiest part of the village.

There is no reliable tourist accommodation, nor cafés or restaurants, in the village.

STUB bus No 5A (€1) departs from Avenida João da Cruz in Bragança at 12.33pm and about 5.50pm on weekdays but the latter returns directly to Bragança, so you'd have to stay the night in Rio de Onor. On schooldays an additional bus departs at about 2pm, which would give you two hours here. A taxi from Bragança costs €18 one way or double that for a return trip with an hour's wait.

Activities

Spring and summer are usually the best times for walking and mountain biking, though visually the park is at its best in the chilly autumn.

There are no trails specifically for self-propelled visitors, though a network of roads and dirt tracks pushes out to the furthest villages. The prettiest areas with the fewest paved roads are the watersheds of the Rio Sabor north of Soutelo and França, and the Rio Tuela between Dine and Moimenta.

The park's own schematic map shows villages, roads and tracks, camp sites and rural accommodation, but not trails. Serious walkers and bikers should talk with staff at the park offices. There are some two dozen military topographic maps that cover the park at 1:25,000, though you can only buy these in Porto (p351) or Lisbon (p73).

Park offices also sell a few booklets and leaflets on bicycle routes. The Abrigo de Montanha da Senhora da Hera (p445) has a few bikes for rent for around €6 per day for guests (€8 for nonguests).

Sleeping & Eating

Parque de Campismo do Sabor (☎ 273 331 535; N103-7 Estrada de Rabal; adult €1.50, car €2, tent €2-2.50; May-Sep) Bragança's flat, featureless but shady and quiet municipal camp site is 6km north of Bragança by the Rio Sabor. Facilities include bikes for hire, a café and a *minimercado*. You can get there on STUB bus No 7 ('Meixedo'; €1, 15 minutes), departing from Avenida João da Cruz in Bragança about 12.30pm and 1.25pm weekdays and 5.50pm Monday to Saturday. At 2pm and 5.15pm on school days you can also catch a Bragança–Portelo bus (€1.60) from the bus station.

Parque de Campismo Cepo Verde (☎ 273 999 371; adult/tent/car €3/1.80/1.80; Apr-Sep;) This is a medium-sized rural facility 12km west of Bragança near Gondesende village, with a café and shade. Rodonorte's Bragança–Vinhais bus, departing from Bragança's bus station at 11.45am and 5pm on weekdays (€1.40, 20 minutes), stops about 500m away on the N103. Villagers, if asked, may also allow free camping on common land.

There are a few self-catering rooms, notably at the tiny hamlet of Montesinho (population about 35), 23km north of Bragança. In July and August these rooms get booked out but from October to May you needn't book at all. **Dona Maria Rita** (☎ 273 919 229; 2/4 people €35/60; P) has a few cosy rooms and a kitchen complete with an old stone oven. **Senhor José Miguel Pires** (☎ 273 919 227; 2/4 people €40/60) keeps a lovely rose-covered cottage with a café below, and **Senhor Antero Pires** (☎ 273 919 248; d with/without kitchen €60/40) also has a handful of rooms. A taxi from Bragança to Montesinho costs about €15.

Elsewhere **Café Turismo** (☎ 273 919 163; França; d with breakfast €25), **Casa d'Ó Poço** (☎ 273 325 135; Espinhosela) and the very attractive **Casa dos Paulinos** (☎ 273 32 2 991; www.casadospaulinos.com; Varge) usually have rooms to rent.

Abrigo de Montanha da Senhora da Hera (☎ 273 999 414; Cova da Lua; d/tr €45/60; Feb-Dec; P) A rambling country house with rooms of all sizes (breakfast included; other meals by arrangement), and a few bikes for rent – good value and popular, so try to book ahead. It also has a **restaurant** (meals about €8; lunch & dinner) with one or two good home-style dishes. It's 12km northwest of Bragança on the N308. A Mofreita-bound bus stops here (€1.50), departing at 2pm and 5.15pm daily from Bragança's bus station.

Casa do Passal (☎ 273 323 506; www.casadopassal.no.sapo.pt; Gondesende; up to 4 people €80) In the same direction, 8km northwest of Bragança, is this schist-walled, self-catering house, good for those wishing to stay a while.

Casa dos Marrões (☎ 273 999 550; www.casadosmarroes.com; Vilarinho de Cova de Lua; d with breakfast €60; P) Also in this area is this prettily converted schist farmhouse.

For more country manor houses scattered around the area, pick up a free *Turismo no Espaço Rural* booklet from the tourist office.

The park used to operate several basic self-catering **casas de retiro** (retreat houses), which were excellent value for money. However, at the time of writing, they had been withdrawn from public use and their future was uncertain. Ask at a park office for the latest information.

Getting Around

Exploring the park is hard without a car, bike or sturdy feet. Most tracks marked on the park map are fire roads, sometimes dicey in bad weather; unsealed 'scenic' routes are marginally better. If you plan to drive on any of them, ask at the park office about current conditions.

Public buses are scarce within the park, especially on weekends, and most don't return the same day. Many school-term services disappear during summer. STUB, Bragança's municipal bus company, has routes close to Bragança; and Rodonorte covers most of the park.

MIRANDELA

pop 10,700 / elevation 270m

Mirandela is a down-to-business market town and transport junction at the epicentre of Trás-os-Montes' vast agricultural heartland. It's a good place to take the pulse of the province and on the 3rd, 14th or 25th day of the month, the region's hardy farmers stream in to market to barter fresh grapes, cherries, vegetables and more.

As a tourist you're most likely to scoot through en route to/from the Alto Douro via the lovely, narrow-gauge Linha da Tua (p381). You could step from train to bus without seeing Mirandela, but don't miss out: take a quick stroll beside the Rio Tua to the flower-bedecked bridge and stop to admire shop windows stuffed with spicy sausages and hanging hams.

Orientation

Rua Dom Afonso III runs in front of the newly combined train and bus stations. Take it to the right, then right again (north) along the river, to the town's medieval bridge and an adjacent new one. By the old bridge you can either carry on along Rua da República to the turismo and market (about 800m from the train station), or turn right and uphill on Rua Dom Manuel I to the *câmara municipal* and the old town.

Information

Banks with ATMs are located along Rua da República.

District hospital (☎ 278 260 500; Avenida Nossa Senhora do Amparo) Just across the old bridge.

Espaço Internet (☎ 278 261 924; Mercado Municipal, 1st fl; 9am-12.30pm & 2-6pm Mon-Fri, 9am-3pm Sat) Free Internet; bring ID.

Police station (☎ 278 265 416; Praça 5 de Outubro) Four blocks north of the post office.

Post office (☎ 278 200 450; Rua Dom Manuel I; 8.30am-12.30pm & 1.30-6pm Mon-Fri) Just below the *câmara municipal*.

Turismo (☎ 278 200 272; Jardim do Mercado; 9.30am-12.30pm & 2-6pm Mon-Fri, 10.30am-12.30pm & 2-3.30pm Sat) At the western end of the *mercado municipal*.

Sights

The medieval **Ponte Românica** (Romanesque bridge; 15th century) with 20 arches, each one different, has been put out to pasture as Portugal's most elegant footbridge.

Dom Dinis also built a castle and town walls in the 13th century, though all that remains is the **Porta de Santo António**, a low arch of mortared schist a block north of the post office.

Old Mirandela is centred on the *câmara municipal*, in the splendiferous **Palácio dos Távoras** (Praça do Município), built in the 17th century for António Luiz de Távora, patron of one of northeast Portugal's powerful aristocratic families. From the same period is the down-at-heel **Palácio dos Condes de Vinhais** (Praça 5 de Outubro), with its admiral's-hat pediment.

Sleeping

Pensão Praia (☎ 278 262 497; Largo 1 de Janeiro 6; s/d from €12.50/20) This creaky old place with small, rickety rooms (mostly with shared bathroom) around a skylit atrium is pretty good value at the budget end.

Pensão O Lagar (☎ 278 262 712; Rua da República 120; d with breakfast & bathroom €25) Located just beyond the market, this place has sparsely furnished rooms and a homely, boarding-house atmosphere.

Hotel Mira-Tua (☎ 278 200 140; fax 278 200 143; Rua da República 38; d with breakfast €45;) This hotel offers very comfortable, forgettable mid-range rooms with cable TV, and a piano bar downstairs.

Hotel Dom Dinis (☎ 278 260 100; hoteldondinis@mail.telepac.pt; Avenida Nossa Senhora do Amparo; s/d €95/150;) This ugly big block of a hotel dominates the skyline on the other side of the river, with large glossy rooms, each with balcony and affording spectacular panoramic views of the bridge.

Parque de Campismo des Três Rios (☎ 278 263 177; Maravilha; adult/tent/car €3/2.50/2.50, 2-/4-person bungalows €50/65; year-round;) A flat, shady, riverside camp site located 3km north of the centre on the N15. It has a restaurant and *minimercado*.

Eating

There are a few restaurants to choose from around the *mercado municipal* and the central riverfront, but plenty of photogenic delicatessens selling the local speciality, *alheira de Mirandela*, a light, garlicky sausage of poultry or game. Also keep an eye out for fresh fish dishes from the Rio Tua.

Café-Restaurante Jardim (☎ 278 265 720; Jardim do Mercado; dishes €5.50-7.50; lunch & dinner Mon-Sat, lunch Sun) A lovely spot overflowing into the gardens just a few steps from the turismo, this place is popular and frantic at lunch time, and does cheap grills.

Restaurante Acquabela (☎ 278 264 039; Parque Império; mains €8-12.50; lunch & dinner Thu-Tue;) The place to splash out on a fancy meal with an unbeatable river (and bridge) view. The restaurant hogs the end of pretty Parque Império, jutting out onto the water itself.

The **mercado municipal** hums along every morning except Sunday, trailing off into the afternoon.

Getting There & Away

BUS

With multiple daily buses, **Rede Expressos** (☎ 278 265 805), **Rodonorte** (☎ 278 262 541) and **AV Tâmega** (☎ 278 265 791) all go to Bragança (€5.20, 1¼ hours) and to Vila Real (€5.60, one hour), with Rede Expressos and AV

Tâmega continuing on to Porto (€8, 2½ hours).

Other weekday services include AV Tâmega to Chaves (€3.60) and **Santos** (☎ 278 265 471) to Bragança and Miranda do Douro (€6.30).

TRAIN

From Mirandela two daily trains take the slow and scenic, narrow-gauge Linha da Tua down to Tua (€3, 1½ hours, departing 8.26am, 3.26pm and 6.08pm) in the Douro valley; check at the turismo or the station for current times. The bright green carriages of Mirandela's suburban train, the Metro, have replaced a more photogenic ageing stock.

The train journey to Porto (€8.50, five to six hours, twice daily) requires a change of trains at both Tua and Peso da Régua.

MIRANDA DO DOURO

pop 2000 / elevation 560m

Though you'd never pick it, this sleepy town facing up to Spain across a dramatic gorge, is one of Europe's smallest cities – for despite its small population, a 'city' is what history has made it.

This is the most easterly town in Portugal, and seemingly populated by more Spaniards than Portuguese. People here speak the ancient dialect of *mirandês,* as they do across the river in rural Castilla y León.

What is there to see? Spectacular canyon views, the scattered ruins of a medieval castle, a cathedral's quirky inhabitants and an eclectic ethnographic museum. The cobbled streets of the old town, lined with blindingly whitewashed 15th- and 16th-century houses, echo with the chatter of Spanish tour groups in summer. However, the region's famous *pauliteiros* (stick dancers, right) are hard to catch.

This town would make a pleasant day trip if it were closer to anywhere else in Portugal. It's possible to see everything in a couple of hours, but the vagaries of public transport make it almost essential for nondrivers to stay longer. Don't come on Monday, when both the museum and the cathedral are shut.

History

Miranda was a vital bulwark during Portugal's first centuries of independence, and the Castilians had to be chucked out at least twice: in the early days by Dom João I, and in 1710 during the Wars of the Spanish Succession. In 1545, perhaps as a snub to the increasingly powerful House of Bragança, a diocese was created here, an oversized cathedral was built and the town was declared a *cidade* (city).

During a siege by French and Spanish troops in 1762 the castle's powder magazine blew up, pulverising most of the castle, killing 400 people and leaving almost nothing to besiege. Twenty years later, shattered Miranda lost its diocese to Bragança. No-one saw fit to rebuild the castle, and nobody paid much attention to Miranda again until the dam was built in the 1950s.

Orientation

Buses stop at Largo da Moagem, a roundabout on the N218. The new town – with handicrafts shops, *pensões,* restaurants and the *mercado municipal* – is down to the left (northeast).

Uphill (southwest) from the roundabout, past the old walls and castle ruins, are the old town and what was once the citadel. The axis is Rua da Alfândega (also called Rua Mouzinho da Albuquerque), and halfway along is central Praça de Dom João III. On Largo da Sé at the end is the cathedral.

THE STICK DANCERS

Trás-os-Montes folk customs are epitomised by the *pauliteiros* (stick dancers) of the Miranda do Douro region, who look and dance very much like England's Morris dancers. Local men deck themselves out in kilts and smocks, black waistcoats, bright flapping shawls, and black hats covered in flowers and ribbons, and do a rhythmic dance to the complex clacking of *paulitos* (short wooden sticks). It looks a bit like a sword dance, from which it may well have descended in Celtic times.

There are at least 10 *pauliteiros* groups, but they've gone big time and scoot off to appear at festivals all over Portugal. They are rarely seen in their hometowns except at local festivals. The best time to catch them in Miranda is during the Festas de Santa Bárbara (also called Festas da Cidade, or City Festival) on the third weekend in August.

Information

There are banks with ATMs located near the turismo, plus there's one beside the post office.

Parque Natural do Douro Internacional office (☎/fax 273 431 457; Palácio da Justiça, Rua do Convento; 9.30am-12.30pm & 2-5.30pm Mon-Fri) Around the block from the cathedral.

Post office (☎ 273 431 132; Largo da Sé; 9am-12.30pm & 2-5.30pm Mon-Fri)

Turismo (☎ 273 431 132; Largo da Moagem; 9am-12.30pm & 2-5.30pm Mon-Sat, until 7pm Jul-Aug) Opposite the bus stop on the N218.

Sights & Activities

MUSEU DE TERRA DE MIRANDA

A miscellany of the region's past, laid out with the guilelessness of a school project, is on show at the **municipal museum** (☎ 273 431 164; Praça de Dom João III; adult/youth 14-25/senior €1.50/0.80/0.80, 9.30-12.30pm Sun free; 9.30am-12.30pm & 2-6pm Wed-Sun, 2.30-6pm Tue Apr-Oct; 9am-12.30pm & 2-5.30pm Wed-Sun, 2-5.30pm Tue Nov-Mar). Keep your eyes peeled for the stone pig *berrão*. You'll also find 14th- and 15th-century stones with Hebrew inscriptions, rough woollen *mirandês* clothing, and – best of all – a musty collection of musical instruments, masks and wildly colourful ceremonial costumes.

OLD TOWN

The backstreets in the old town hide some dignified 15th-century **façades** on Rua da Costanilha (which runs west off Praça Dom João III) and a **Gothic gate** at the end of it.

The best thing to note about the severe 16th-century **sé** (cathedral; admission free; see Museu de Terra de Miranda), other than its disproportionate size, is a small case in one transept. Here stands the doll-like Menino Jesus da Cartolinha, a Christ child in a becoming top hat whose wardrobe is bigger than Imelda Marcos', thanks to deft local devotees. Really, it's no wonder he sports a befuddled expression faced with that choice of what to wear in the morning.

In a garden behind the cathedral are the picturesque roofless remains of the former **Bishop's Palace**, which burned down in the 18th century.

BARRAGEM DE MIRANDA

A road crawls across this 80m-high dam about 1km east of town, and on to Zamora, 55km away in Spain. Even dammed, the gorge is dramatic.

You can take a one-hour boat trip through the gorge from the **Parque Náutico** (☎ 273 432 396; per person €12; 4pm Mon-Fri, 11am & 4pm Sat & Sun), beside the dam on the Portuguese side. Outside August, call in advance to check there are enough passengers (minimum 20).

This is one of five dams on the Rio Douro along the Spanish border, the upper three for use by Portugal.

Sleeping

Rooms at the following places are uniformly tidy, spotless and equipped with shower and toilet.

Pensão Vista Bela (☎/fax 273 431 054; Rua do Mercado 63; d with breakfast from €35) Big rooms in the new town that are worth the price just to gawp at the spectacular view across the gorge.

Hospedaria Flôr do Douro (☎ 273 431 186; Rua do Mercado 7; d with breakfast €30-35) Up the street from Pensão Vista Bela and with the same panoramic views, as well as more motherly service and very cosy, well-worn rooms.

Residencial Planalto (☎ 273 431 362; reservas@hrplanalto.pt; Rua 1 de Maio 25; s/d with breakfast €25/35; P) A sunny, modern place with long rambling corridors and formal service around the corner from Flôr do Douro; all rooms have balconies.

Pensão Santa Cruz (☎ 273 431 374; Rua Abade de Baçal 61; s/d with breakfast €20/30) In the old town off the *largo* (small square) by the castle ruins you'll find this family-run spot with pretty rooms and a penchant for puppy pictures.

Hotel Turismo (☎ 273 438 030; fax 273 431 335; Rua 1 de Maio 5; s/d €25/45;) All glistening black stone and sparkling rooms with cable TV, this modern hotel opposite the turismo is a bargain. One room is adapted for disabled visitors.

Estalagem Santa Catarina (☎ 273 431 005; www.estalagemsantacatarina.pt; Largo da Pousada; d Sun-Thu from €92, Fri & Sat from €102; P) Formally a *pousada*, this luxurious modern hotel practically falls into the gorge from its prime perch, offering unimpeded views and every four-star comfort.

Parque de Campismo de Santa Luzia (☎ 273 431 273; Rua do Parque de Campismo; adult/car/tent €1.50/2/2; Jun-Sep) A modest municipal camp site at the end of a residential street, 1.8km west of Largo da Moagem across the Rio Fresno.

Eating

Most *pensões* have a restaurant of some description, open at lunch and dinner.

Restaurante–Pizzeria O Moinho (☎ 273 431 116; Rua do Mercado 47D; large pizza €5-7.50; ⏲ lunch & dinner) New-town spot with glorious unimpeded Douro views. It's a modern building but goes all out for the rustic charm with red tiles, agricultural tools and even a bale of hay topping the bar. Serves a big list of pizzas, salads and Portuguese standards.

Capa d'Houras (☎ 273 432 699; Travessa do Castelo 1; ⏲ lunch & dinner; ⊠) Look for the sinister dark-hooded monks down a street to the right of the old town entrance, and you'll find this excellent restaurant serving local specialities.

Restaurante Balbina (☎ 273 432 394; Travessa da Misericórdia 5; dishes €5-10; ⏲ lunch & dinner Mon-Sat) Around the corner from the *câmara municipal,* is this crisply decorated place with a good-value lunch-time *ementa turística* (tourist menu) for €6.50.

Drinking

Atalaia Bar (☎ 919 029 545; Largo do Castelo; ⏲ 1.30pm-5am Mon-Sat, 9.30pm-1am Sun) What little nocturnal action there is in Miranda takes place mostly in this neon-lit DJ bar.

Getting There & Away

Stopping beside the turismo are **Santos** (☎ 273 432 667) buses; **Rodonorte** (☎ 273 432 444) also stops there, and at its ticket office on Praça de Dom João III.

Santos' weekday Bragança (€5.50, 1¾ hours) services include one from Miranda via Mogadouro (€3.15, 50 minutes) and one from Vila Nova de Foz Côa (€5.75, 2¼ hours) via the train station at Pocinho (€5.50, two hours) in the Alto Douro. Santos also goes via Mogadouro, Mirandela (€6.30, 2½ hours) and Vila Real (€8, 3¼ hours) to Porto (€9.30, five hours) daily except Saturday.

Rodonorte has two buses to Bragança and one via Vila Real to Porto, daily except Saturday.

By car, the quickest road from Bragança is the N218 and N218-2, a winding 80km trip. The 80km route (N216/N221) from Macedo de Cavaleiros via Mogadouro is one of the loveliest – and wiggliest – in Portugal. It crosses a *planalto* (high plain) dotted with olive, almond and chestnut groves, with a dramatic descent into the Rio Sabor Valley.

MOGADOURO

pop 5000 / elevation 750m

Rough-and-ready, sun-bleached Mogadouro is on the map because it's home to the headquarters of the Parque Natural do Douro Internacional. Little remains of its Celtic and Moorish past, but it's a handy base for visiting the park.

Orientation & Information

Buses stop at the central Largo Trindade Coelho. Mogadouro's turismo closed in 2004, with no immediate plans to reopen. There are several banks with ATMs along Avenida Nossa Senhora do Caminho.

Park Natural do Douro Internacional (☎ 279 340 030; pndi@icn.pt; Rua de Santa Marinha 4; ⏲ 9am-12.30pm & 2-5.30pm Mon-Fri) The park's headquarters is at the southwestern end of the *largo*.

Post office (☎ 279 345 160; ⏲ 9am-12.30pm & 2-5.30pm Mon-Fri) On the *largo*.

Sights

The mighty order of the Knights Templar (p285) built a castle here in the 12th century, part of the effort to drive the Moors out. All that's left are the photogenic remains of a **tower** – now overrun by nesting birds – on a hill southwest of the park headquarters.

In the square to the south is a **pelourinho**, dating back to the 12th century. To the north is the 16th-century **igreja matriz**.

Sleeping & Eating

Hotel Trindade Coelho (☎ 279 340 010; hotelcoelho@nerba.pt; Largo Trindade Coelho; s/d with breakfast €33/45; P ⊠) This pompous modern hotel names itself after local hero, writer Trindade Coelho, who was born in the town: his moustachioed bust sits in the lobby. Inside are spacious, wooden-floored rooms some with balconies and sweeping views to the north.

Stuffy little rooms with a grandma's taste in décor are for rent upstairs at **Restaurante–Residencial A Lareira** (☎ 279 342 363; Avenida Nossa Senhora do Caminho 58; s/d with breakfast €17.50/30) and **Pensão–Restaurante Russo** (☎ 279 342 134;

Rua 15 de Outubro 10; s/d with breakfast €17.50/30), both a short walk back down Largo Trindade Coelho.

Getting There & Away

Trás-os-Montes' busiest local operator is **Santos** (☎ 279 342 537; Largo Trindade Coelho), with mostly weekday buses to Bragança (€5.25, 1½ hours), Miranda do Douro (€3.15, 50 minutes), Vila Nova de Foz Côa (€4.50, 1¾ hours), and via Mirandela (€5.25, 2¼ hours) and Vila Real (€7.25, 2½ hours) to Porto (€9.25, 3¾ hours).

From a kiosk at the other end of the Largo Trindade Coelho, Rede has daily services to Porto (€8.50) and Lisbon (€13.50).

PARQUE NATURAL DO DOURO INTERNACIONAL

If its birds of prey that get you in a flap, you'll want to check out little-visited natural Parque Natural do Douro Internacional in far-eastern Trás-os-Montes. The 852-sq-km park is Portugal's second-largest protected area, founded to protect the monumental geological landscape of the upper Rio Douro where it scores the Portugal–Spain border.

In 2002 Spain inaugurated its own 106-sq-km Parque Natural de Arribes del Duero on the other side. Together these two parks line the Douro Canyon (dammed here into a series of silent lakes), and part of the tributary Rio Águeda in the south, for over 120km.

The Douro's towering, granitic cliffs are habitat for several threatened bird species, in particular black storks and – as promised – a host of raptors, including Egyptian vultures, griffon vultures, peregrine falcons, golden eagles and Bonelli's eagles. Indeed this is probably the best place in Portugal to observe large birds of prey. Other species that put in an appearance are short-toed eagles, booted eagles, eagle owls, alpine swifts and choughs. Resident mammals include wolves, wild cats and roe deer.

Southward the valley opens out into *terra quente*, with mild winters and sizzling summers – ideal for growing grapes. In fact, the park overlaps the demarcated port-wine region.

Some 17,000 people live in 46 small communities within the park. Their ancestors include convicts banished here in medieval times, and Jews who fled the Spanish and Portuguese Inquisitions. Portugal's now-official 'second language', the ancient dialect of *mirandês*, is still widely spoken and you'll see it popping up on road signs too.

Your best bet for accommodation is Mogadouro, which has several *pensões* and a mid-range hotel to crash in (see p449).

Orientation & Information

The park's headquarters is in Mogadouro (p449), with smaller park offices in Miranda do Douro, **Figueira de Castelo Rodrigo** (☎ /fax 271 313 382; Rua Artur Costa 1) and **Freixo de Espada à Cinta** (☎ /fax 279 658 130; Largo do Outeiro). Miranda do Douro and Mogadouro are the easiest places from which to visit the park.

The park headquarters and offices sell a Portuguese-language booklet about the park, a detailed park map (€3.40), four leaflets (€0.50) on nature trails within the park, and a Portuguese-language booklet (€1) on the Egyptian vulture (the park's symbol).

Sights & Activities

The finest places to look into this yawning, green 'Grand Canyon of Portugal' – echoing with birdsong and occasionally shadowed by the flights of vultures – are sturdy **viewing platforms** at (north to south, with the nearest village in parentheses): São João das Arribas (Aldeia Nova), Fraga do Puio (Picote), Carrascalinho (Fornos), Penedo Durão (Poiares) and Santo André (Almofala).

You can do **day-walks** to the canyon's edge via these and other villages from the N221 (which runs almost the entire length of the park). In addition there are five marked trails within the park, ranging from 8km to 62km, starting from near Miranda do Douro; Duas Igrejas/Freixo de Espada à Cinta; Lamoso; Poiares/Barca de Alva; and Almofala/Vermiosa. At the time of writing, park leaflets were available for all but the Lamoso walk.

Getting There & Around

The bus company with the most local services to the park's towns and villages is **Santos** (Freixo de Espada à Cinta; ☎ 279 652 188; www.santosviagensturismo.pt).

Directory

CONTENTS

ACCOMMODATION

There's an excellent range of good-value, inviting accommodation in Portugal. Budget places provide some of Europe's cheapest rooms, while you'll find atmospheric, charming, peaceful accommodation in farms, palaces, castles, mansions and rustic townhouses – usually incredibly good value.

In tourist resorts, prices rise and fall with the seasons. July to mid-September are firmly high season (book ahead if you're visiting at this time), May to June and mid-September to October are mid-season and other times low season, when you can get some really good deals. In other places prices don't vary much. We list July prices throughout this book. Note that places in tourist areas – for example the big Algarve resorts – often close in winter, from around November to March.

All our listings are in author preference order and, where there are a number of listings, these have been divided into budget, mid-range and top end. Within these categories they are also in author preference order – although camp sites are featured at the end of the budget range.

This book categorises budget accommodation as hotels or guesthouses costing between €10 and €20 per person, as well as camp sites and hostels. You might have to share a bathroom in the cheapest places. In the middle range, you're looking at from €20 to €40 per person, and for this you'll almost always get an en suite bathroom, TV (sometimes satellite), often AC and telephone. In the Elysium of the top end you'll pay €40 to €150 per person, with the odd stratospheric place where you can chill by the pool with visiting royals or football stars.

We list rack rates for mid-range and top-end places here, but often you won't be charged the full whack – ask about special deals and packages. The websites listed on p15 also sometimes feature special offers. Most *pousadas* are cheaper during the week. They have lots of discount deals and prices.

Your bargaining power depends on what season it is and how much choice you have. If it's low season or echoingly empty,

PRACTICALITIES

Electricity

Recharge your mobile with a two-pin plug (sometimes with a third middle pin) – voltage is 220V, 50HZ.

Weights & Measures

Portugal uses the metric system. (See inside front cover for metric conversions chart.) Decimals are indicated by commas, thousands by points.

MEDIA

Freedom of expression has come on leaps and bounds since the repressive Salazar years, during which time many writers and intellectuals found their work banned or sleced. But Portugal now equals the rest of Europe for press liberty and rigour. There is also a significant foreign-language press presence – especially English-language papers in the south and Eastern European newspapers in cities – thanks to large immigrant populations. Many radio stations broadcast international music and the four main Portuguese channels import films and trashy but addictive Brazilian soap operas.

Portuguese language dailies include *Diário de Noticias, Público* and *Jornal de Noticias*. The tabloid best-seller is *Correio da Manhã*. English-language press are mostly staid Algarve offerings: the *APN, the News* (www.the-news.net), *Algarve Resident* (www.portugalresident.com). International newspapers are widely available at resorts and in cities. A publication with lots of interesting articles is *Portugal Magazine* (www.merricksmedia.co.uk).

State-owned Rádiodifusão Portuguesa (RDP) runs Antena 1, 2 and 3, with Portuguese broadcasts and evening music. For English-language radio there's the BBC World Service and Voice of America (VOA), or a few Algarve-based stations such as Kiss. Rádio Televisão Portuguesa (RTP-1 and RTP-2), Sociedade Independente (SIC) and TV Independente (TV1) pile airtime with Portuguese and Brazilian soaps, game shows and subtitled foreign movies.

Portugal uses the PAL video system, incompatible with both the French SECAM system and the North American and Japanese NTSC system.

people will usually drop prices without you even needing to ask. If you're planning to stay more than a few days, it's always worth inquiring whether lower rates are available for longer stays. If you're looking for somewhere cheaper than the room you have been shown just say so; frequently the management will show you the cheaper rooms they previously forgot to mention.

Turismos hold lists of accommodation and private *quartos*, but they overlook anywhere not registered with them – which can mean the cheapest options. The government grades accommodation with a star system that's bewildering and best ignored.

Some good sites for sizing up charismatic accommodation are www.manorhouses.pt or www.innsofportugal.pt.

Camping & Caravan Parks

Camping is massive in Portugal, with countless excellent camp sites, often in beautiful locations and near beaches. Prices usually range from about €2 to €4 per adult, around €4 per tent and €2 to €4 per car.

The swishest are run by **Orbitur** (www.orbitur.pt) but there are lots of other good companies, such as **Inatel** (www.inatel.pt). Most towns have a municipal site, which vary in quality.

To be a really happy camper, or at least a well-informed one, pick up the **Roteiro Campista** (www.roteiro-campista.pt; €5) sold at turismos and bookshops. It has details of most Portuguese camp sites, with directions.

CAMPING CARD INTERNATIONAL

The Camping Card International (CCI) can be presented instead of your passport at camp sites affiliated to the Federation Internationale de Camping et de Caravanning (FICC). It guarantees third-party insurance for any damage you may cause and is sometimes good for discounts.

Sometimes certain camp sites run by local camping clubs may be used by foreigners *only* if they have a CCI, so don't foget to pick one up before you travel.

The CCI is available to members of most national automobile clubs, except those in the USA; the RAC in the UK charges members £6.50 for a card. It is also issued by FICC affiliates such as the UK's **Camping & Caravanning Club** (☎ 024-7669 4995; www.campingandcaravanningclub.co.uk) and the **Federação Portuguesa de Campismo** (Map pp74-5; ☎ 218 126 890; www.fcmportugal.com; Avenida Coronel Eduardo Galhardo 24D, 1199-007 Lisbon).

Guesthouses

Known as *residenciais* or *pensões*, guesthouses are budget or mid-range, small-scale accommodation, with the personal feel that is lacking in larger hotels. The best are often better than the cheapest hotels. High-season *pensão* rates are usually €30 to €60 for a double.

Residenciais are often more expensive, and usually include breakfast. All these have been graded by the government. If they are called *residenciais* it means they haven't got official approval, but this does not mean they are bad. *Hospedarias* and *casas de hóspedes* are usually cheaper, with shared bathrooms.

Hostels

Portugal's 39 *pousadas da juventude* are all affiliated with Hostelling International (HI). Although the accommodation is basic, they offer excellent value and are often in lovely settings or historic buildings.

High-season beds cost €9.50 to €15. Most also offer bare doubles and some have small apartments. Bed linen and breakfast are included in the price. Many have kitchens, cafés and Internet access. Some have swimming pools, such as those in Alcoutim and Portimão.

Those at Alcoutim, Almograve, Évora, Sines, Lagos, Portimão, Aveiro, Coimbra, Guarda, Ovar, Penhas da Saúde, Côa, Viseu, Porto, Leiria, Almada, Catalazete, Lisbon, Viana do Castelo, Bragança Abrantes and Santarém have disabled facilities.

In summer you'll need to reserve, especially for doubles. Contact **Movijovem** (Map p80-1; ☎ 213 596 000; www.pousadasjuventude.pt; Avenida Duque d'Ávila 137, Lisbon).

If you don't have an HI card, you can get a guest card, which requires six stamps (€2 per time) – one from each hostel you stay at – after which you have paid for your membership.

Most hostels open 8am to midnight. Some (Almada, Braga, Bragança, Évora, Foz Côa, Fôz do Cávado, Lagos, Lisbon, Porto and Viana do Castelo) open 24 hours. They will usually let you stash your bags and return at check-in time (usually 8am to noon and 6pm to midnight).

Pousadas

In 1942 the government started the **pousadas scheme** (☎ 218 442 001; www.pousadas.pt), turning castles, monasteries and palaces into luxurious, splendid hotels, divided roughly into rural and historic options. July prices range from €132 to €238. You can pick up a comprehensive booklet listing all the pousadas, with photos, at any of the group. They offer frequent and ongoing special offers, such as reduced prices for the over 60s, or for the 18 to 30s.

Private Rooms

In coastal resorts, mostly in summer, you can often rent a private room or *quarto* in a private house. These usually have shared bathroom and are cheap, clean and might remind you of a stay with an elderly aunt. If you're not approached by an eager owner or don't spot a sign, try the local turismo – they usually have a list. You will find that prices are generally from €20 to €30 per double.

Rental Accommodation

There are plenty of villas and cottages available for rent. Try www.casadocampo.com (in Portuguese) or www.aldeiasdeportugal.pt for some houses with character, both concentrating on the north, though the former has a few southern options.

Turihab Properties

These are charming, unique properties that are part of a government scheme, either Turismo de Habitação, Turismo Rural or Agroturismo, through which you can stay in a farmhouse, manor house, country estate or rustic cottage as the owner's guest.

Divided into historic, historical or rustic categories, these properties provide some of the best bargains in Portugal: although they work out more expensive than some other options, you will usually be staying in splendidly beautiful surroundings.

A high-season double will range from €50 to €100. They often have swimming pools and usually include breakfast (often with local, deliciously fresh produce).

Look them up on www.turihab.pt or www.solaresdeportugal.pt.

ACTIVITIES

Putt, pedal, surf, dive, climb – Portugal is packed with beautiful countryside and many different ways to experience it. From high-adrenaline sports to gentle cycles, from surfing to walking trails, there is truly something for everybody.

Adrenaline Sports

High-adrenaline activities are run by **Capitao Dureza** (☎ 91 907 98 52; www.capitaodureza.com) operating from Figuera do Foz. This company will take you rafting, canyoning, mountain biking or trekking.

Trilhos (☎ 967 014 277 www.trilhos.pt; Rua da Belèm 94), based in Porto, offers climbing, whitewater rafting, trekking and canyoning.

Cycling

If you want to take it faster, Portugal has many exhilarating mountain biking (*bicyclete tudo terrano*; BTT) opportunities too. Monchique (p197) and Tavira (p160) in the Algarve, Sintra (p116) and Setúbal (p137) are all popular starting points for guided rural tours.

In the north try **PlanAlto** (☎ 253 311 807; www.planalto.com.pt; Parque de Campismo de Cerdeira, Campo do Gerês, 4840-030 Terras de Bouro), with BTT trips around the Minho and Trás-os-Montes. Parque Nacional da Peneda-Gerês is also a great area for mountain biking.

Golf

A golf Mecca, Portugal is famous for its rolling greens, and is full of championship courses. Most are along the Algarve, but the Estoril coast (p131) is big business too, and there are also courses in Beira Alta and the Minho.

Horse Riding

Lusitano thoroughbreds hail from Portugal, and experienced riders can take dressage lessons in Estremadura (p457). Apart from such exclusive equitation, there are hundreds of horse-riding centres – especially in the Algarve and Alentejo. This is a fantastic way to experience Portugal's beautiful countryside. Rates are usually around €25 per hour.

Jeep Tours

Many companies in the south offer jeep tours. These can be particularly useful for exploring national parks, such as Parque Natural da Arrábida (p144), if you don't have your own transport. Be aware that some operators are more environmentally aware than others. Also mistrust tours that promise you explorations of the 'real Algarve' – you're more like to find this hopping on a bus than in a convoy with 30 other people.

Skiing

There are basic facilities around Torre in Parque Natural da Serra da Estrela (p325), with Penhas da Saúde the major accommodation base. Snow is most reliable in February, though the season is from January to March.

Surfing

With 830km of Atlantic coast, it's unsurprising that Portugal has some of Europe's most curvaceous surf, with 30 to 40 major reefs and beaches. Most famous are the areas around Ericeira and Peniche, and Praia do Guincho near Cascais, which often host international championships. Another area famous among the global surfing community is around Carrapateira – schools and clubs head over here from Lagos and further afield to take advantage of the crashing waves. See Let's Go Surfing Now, right.

Walking

Portugal's wonderful walking potential is all the better because few people know about it. Most organised walking clubs are in the Algarve, with marked trails and regular meetings. There is a cluster of organisations around Monchique (p197) but also see Vila Real de Santo António (p166), Sagres (p190) and Serra de São Mamede (p230). Some good companions include *Algarve: Let's Walk* by Julie Statham (1999), describing 20 easy walks, and two *Discovery Walking Guides* to areas around Loulé (1999) and Silves (2000), featuring 1:25,000 map sections. *Walking in Portugal* by Bethan Davies and Ben Cole (2002) covers walks in the north and as far down as Setúbal.

There's fantastic walking in the north, where the Parque Natural da Serra da Estrela (p325) has a fine network of marked trails you are likely to have to yourself. Most demanding is Serra da Estrela with 1993m Torre, Portugal's highest peak. Or head to Parque Nacional da Peneda-Gerês (p420) for more glorious, empty hill trails.

Based in Lisbon, **Rotas do Vento** (☎ 213 950 035; www.rotasdovento.pt) offers countrywide walks. Quercus (p61) offers environmental trips.

Water Sports

Praia do Guincho, west of Sintra (p116) and Lagoa de Óbidos (p265) offer great

LET'S GO SURFING NOW...

Here's a list of Portugal's best surfing beaches.

Region	Beach	Nearest Town
North	Moledo	Caminha
	Afife	Viana do Castelo (p403)
	Esposende	Barcelos (p394)
	Póvoa de Varzim	Póvoa de Varzim
	Vila do Conde	Vila do Conde (p369)
Central	Praia da Barra, Costa Nova	Aveiro (p313)
	Praia de Mira	Praia de Mira (p312)
	Buarcos, Cabedelo	Figueira da Foz (p307)
	São Pedro de Muel,	Marinha Grande
	Nazaré	Nazaré (p266)
	Foz do Arelho	Caldas da Rainha (p262)
	Baleal, Supertubos, Consolação	Peniche (p257)
	Areia Branca	Lourinha
	Santa Cruz	Torres Vedras
	São Lourenço, Ribeira de Ilhas, Ericeira, Foz de Lisandro, São Julião	Ericeira (p254)
	Praia Grande, Praia do Guincho	Sintra (p116)
South	São Torpes, Porto Covo	Sines
	Vila Nova de Milfontes	Vila Nova de Milfontes (p249)
	Odeceixe	Odeceixe (p196)
	Carreagem, Monte Clérigo, Arrifana	Aljezur (p195)
	Praia do Amado	Carrapateira (p194)
	Tonel	Sagres (p190)
	Praia da Rocha	Portimão (p179)

The European surfing bible, *The Stormrider Guide*, has details on venues, wave types and conditions, and is published by **Low Pressure** (☎ 20 8876 5061; www.lowpressure.co.uk; €25). For more information look up the **Portuguese Surf Guide** (www.infopraias.com) or **Federação Portuguesa de Surf** (www.surfingportugal.com) – a tsunami of information on clubs, schools and events.

windsurfing. Costa da Caparica's Fonte da Telha (p135) is also popular. In the Algarve, Sagres attracts pros, while Lagos, Albufeira and Praia da Rocha cater to all.

You can also canoe along the lovely, lazy Rio Guadiana – thickly wooded on either side and forming a border between Portugal and Spain (p166).

If you want to go deeper, there's diving to be found around Sagres (p190), as well as outfits at Costa da Caparica and Berlenga Nature Reserve (p259).

BUSINESS HOURS

Most shops open from 9.30am to noon and 3pm to 7pm. Many close Saturday afternoon, except around Christmas, and Sunday. Malls open around 10am to 10pm daily. Banks usually open 8.30am to 3pm and most post offices from 9am to 12.30pm and 2.30pm to 5.30pm Monday to Friday. Government offices open 9am to noon and 2pm to 5pm or 5.30pm Monday to Friday.

Museums usually close on Monday, and open from around 10am to 12.30pm and 2pm to 5pm or 6pm Tuesday to Saturday. If Monday is a holiday, they'll often close on the Tuesday too.

CHILDREN

The great thing about Portugal for children is its manageable size and the range of sights and activities on offer. There's so much to explore and to catch the imagination, even for those with very short attention spans.

The Algarve has to be the finest kid-pleasing destination in Portugal, with endless beaches, zoos, water parks, horse riding and boat trips. Children will also be happy in Lisbon and its outlying provinces. There are trams, a huge aquarium, a toy museum, horse-drawn carriages, puppet shows, a puppet museum, castles, palaces, parks and playgrounds.

As for atmospheric, fairytale places, Portugal has these in droves. Some children enjoy visiting churches, especially if they get to light a candle. They'll enjoy the make-believe of the Knights Templar buildings at Tomar (p284) and Almourol (p283), and love clambering over castles in Sintra (p116), Castelo de Vide (p232) and Elvas (p225).

Near Fátima, north of Lisbon, you can thrill the kids with the chance to see dinosaur footprints: visit the extraordinary Monumento Natural das Pegadas dos Dinossáurios (p279) with huge dinosaur dents. Specially kid-pitched tours are available.

In the towns, hop-on hop-off tours can be good for saving small legs, and miniature resort trains often cause more excitement than you would've thought possible.

Kids will like Portugal almost as much as they like sweets, and they are welcome just about everywhere. They can even get literary: Nobel Prize winner José Saramago, the great Portuguese novelist, has written a charming children's fable *The Tale of the Unknown Island,* available in English. For an entertaining guide to travel with the little ones, packed with information and tips, turn to Lonely Planet's *Travel with Children*.

Turismos can often recommend local childcare, and branches of the youth-network **Instituto Portuguese da Juventude** (IPJ; Map p80-1; ☎ 213 522 694; Avenida da Liberdade 194, Lisbon) sometimes advertise babysitting.

Several travel operators offer specially tailored family tours, including:
Cosmos (☎ 0870 44 35 285; www.cosmos-holidays.co.uk)
JMC (☎ 0870 758 0203; www.jmc.com)
Powder Byrne (☎ 020 8246 5300; www.powderbyrne.com)

CLIMATE CHARTS

Portugal has a warm and sunny climate, with mild winters. Summer in the Algarve

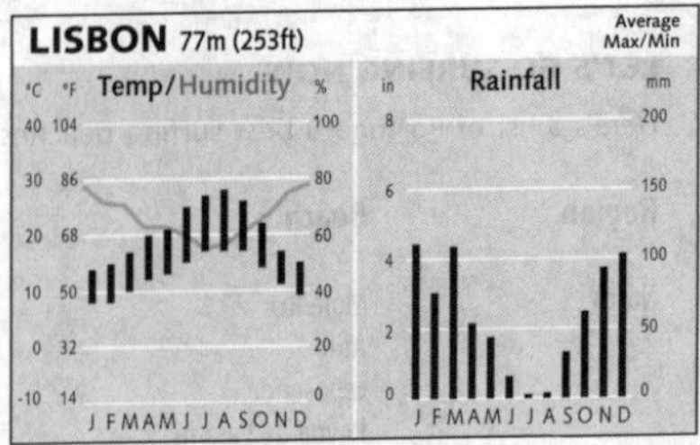

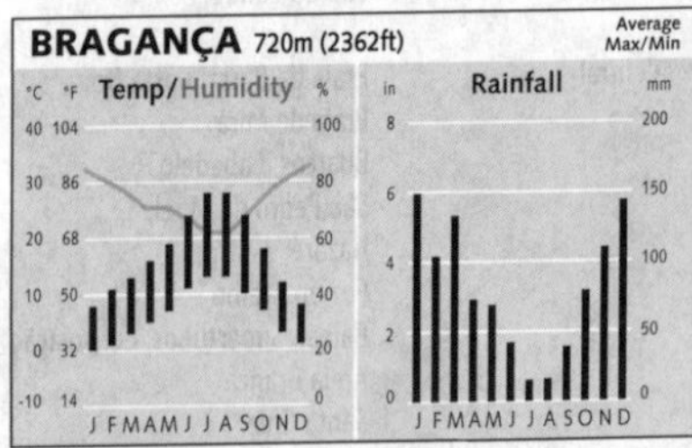

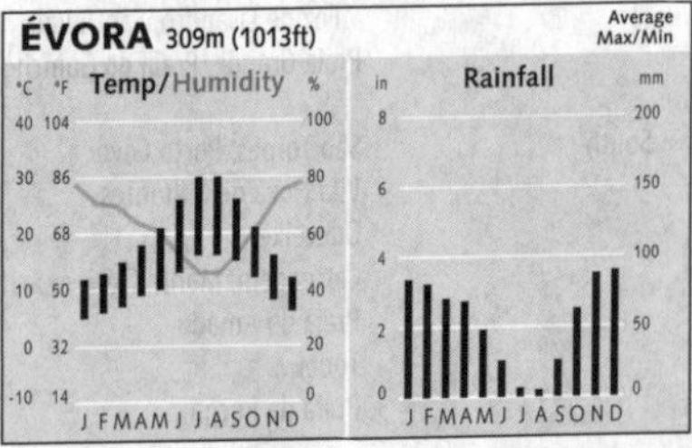

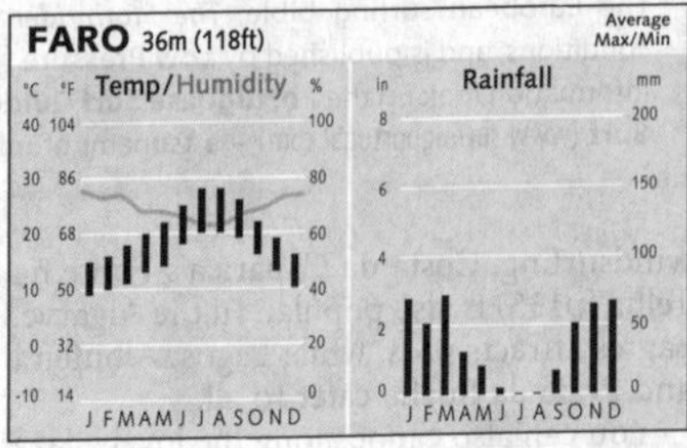

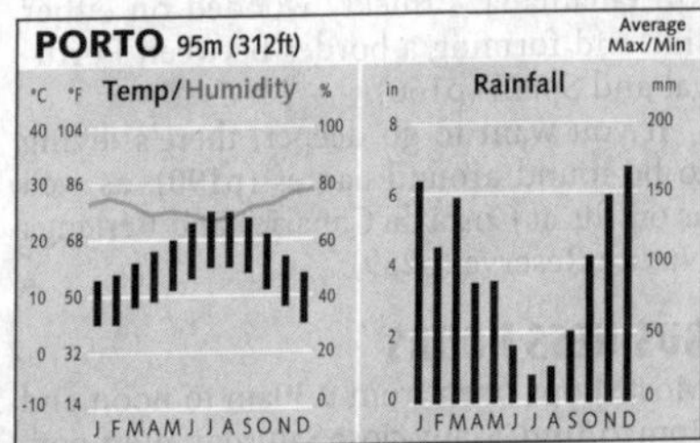

that can top 30°C. Summers are also hot in Alentejo and Alto Douro, with temperatures measured as high as 47°C in Alentejo. In the northwest weather is more mild and damp, so bring a brolly. Up to 2000mm of rain can fall annually (national average is 1100mm).

COURSES

Dance

CEM (Centro em Movimento; Centre in Motion; ☎ 218 871 917; www.c-e-m.org; Rua dos Frangueiros 150, Lisbon) Offers contemporary dance and yoga courses.

Gastronomy

Centro de Linguas (see Language) Also runs courses in Portuguese gastronomy.

Cuisineinternational.com (http://cuisineinternational.com/index2.html?/portugal/refugio/) This can be pricey, but the instruction is top notch. It's also quite a gorgeous location and you'll be pampered.

Horse Riding

Escola de Equitaçã o de Alcainça (☎ 219 662 122; Rua de São Miguel, Alcainça) There are many places to pony trek and horse ride, but this school near Mafra offers dressage lessons on Lusitano horses, and is world renowned.

Language

The following schools offer group language courses (usually around €300 for a 30- to 40-hour intensive course) and much more expensive individual lessons. Be sure to check whether there's an additional enrolment fee.

Cambridge School (www.cambridge.pt); Lisbon (Map p80-1; ☎ 213 124 600; Avenida da Liberdade, Lisbon; Porto (☎ 225 360 380; Rua Duque da Terceira 381, Porto); Coimbra (Map pp294-5; ☎ 239 834 969; Praça Da República, Coimbra)

Centro de Linguas (CIAL; www.cial.pt); Lisbon (Map p80-1; ☎ 217 940 448; Avenida da República, 41, Lisbon); Faro (☎ 289 807 611; Rua Almeida Garrett, 44 r/c, Faro)

Centro de Linguas de Lagos (☎ 282 761 070; www.centrodelinguas.com; Rua Dr Joaquim Telo 32, Lagos)

Interlingua Instituto de Linguas (☎ 282 427 690; Largo 1 de Dezembro 28, Portimão) Offers a two-hour crash course in Portuguese for €25 per person.

CUSTOMS

You can bring as much currency as you like into Portugal. Customs regulations say anyone who needs a visa must bring in at least €50 plus €10 per day, but this isn't enforced.

The duty-free allowance for travellers over 17 years old from non-EU countries is 200 cigarettes or the equivalent in tobacco, and 1L of alcohol over 22% alcohol or 2L of wine or beer. Nationals of EU countries can bring in 800 cigarettes or the equivalent, plus either 10L of spirits, 20L of fortified wine, 60L of sparkling wine or a mind-boggling 90L of still wine or 110L of beer! There's no more duty-free shopping in Portugal's airports.

DANGERS & ANNOYANCES

Crime

Compared to other European countries, Portugal's crime rate is low, but it is rising. Crime against foreigners is of the usual bag-snatching, rush-hour pickpocketing and theft-from-rental-cars variety. Take usual precautions – don't flash your cash, keep valuables in a safe place and, if you are challenged, hand it over. It's not worth taking risks.

Driving

Once behind the wheel of a car, the otherwise mild-mannered Portuguese change personality. Macho driving, such as tailgating at high speeds and overtaking on blind corners, are all too common. With the road accident rate the highest in Europe, police operate a zero-tolerance policy, which has helped limit the damage on formerly nightmare routes – for example, the cheerfully named 'highway of death' from Salamanca in Spain.

Nightclub Violence

There have been some fatal attacks in Portugal nightclubs. In 1997 an arson attack in Amarante left 13 dead. Seven were killed in Lisbon's Luanda club in 2000 after tear-gas canisters were released. In March 2001 at Kremlin in Lisbon three people opened fire after being refused entry. The same year a teenager was stabbed to death in an Albufeira disco. Although this sounds like a catalogue of incidents, in the main clubs are peaceful places.

Smoking

Very prevalent in Portugal; there are rarely nonsmoking sections in restaurants and certainly not in bars. Trains usually have a nonsmoking carriage stowed somewhere.

DISABLED TRAVELLERS

The term *deficientes* (Portuguese for disabled) gives some indication of the limited awareness of disabled needs. Public offices and agencies are required to provide access and facilities for disabled people, but private businesses are not.

Lisbon airport is accessible, while Porto and Faro airports have disabled toilets. The useful website www.allgohere.com has information on facilities offered by all airlines.

Disabled parking spaces are allotted in many places but are frequently occupied. The EU parking card entitles visitors to the same street parking concessions given to disabled residents. For details contact the **Department for Transport** (☎ 020-7944 6800; www.mobility-unit.dft.gov.uk).

Newer and larger hotels tend to have some adapted rooms, though sometimes the disabled facilities are not up to scratch. Ask at the local turismo. Most camp sites have disabled toilets (these are noted in the text). Wheelchair-accessible hostels are noted on p453.

Lisbon, with its cobbled streets and hills, is difficult for the disabled, but not impossible – the Baixa's flat grid and Belém are fine, and all the sights at Parque das Nações are accessible.

Organisations

Accessible Portugal (☎ 06 504 21 34; www.accessibleeurope.com) Based in Italy, this organisation offers a lot of helpful resources and can assist in planning tailored trips.

Cooperatia Nacional Apoio Deficientes (CNAD; Map pp74-5; ☎ 218 595 332; Praça Dr Fernando Amado, Lote 566-E, 1900 Lisbon) This is a private organisation that can help with travel needs.

Dial-a-ride Disabled Bus Service Lisbon (☎ 217 585 676); Porto (☎ 226 006 353)

Secretariado Nacional de Rehabilitação (Map p80-1; ☎ 217 929 500; www.snripd.pt; Avenida Conde Valbom, 63-1069-178 Lisbon) The national governmental organisation representing the disabled supplies information and provides links to useful operations and publishes guides (in Portuguese) that advise on barrier-free accommodation, transport, shops, restaurants and sights.

Taxi Services for Disabled Persons Braga (☎ 253 684 081); Coimbra (☎ 239 484 522).

Wheeling Around the Algarve (☎ 289 393 636; www.player.pt; Rua Casa do Povo, 1, Almancil) Another private setup, with great advice on accommodation, transport, care hire, sport and leisure facilities, and equipment.

DISCOUNT CARDS

Portugal's network of youth hostels, or *pousadas da juventude* (p453), is part of the Hostelling International (HI) network. An HI card from your hostelling association at home entitles you to the standard cheap rates.

A student card will get you reduced admission to almost all sights. Likewise those over 65 with proof of age will save €€€.

The Lisboa Card allows discounts or free admission to many attractions and free travel on public transport (p83).

EMBASSIES & CONSULATES

Portuguese Embassies & Consulates

Portuguese embassies and consulates abroad include the following:

Angola Luanda (☎ 02-33 30 27; Avenida de Portugal 50, Caixa Postal 1346, Luanda)

Australia Canberra (☎ 02-6290 1733; www.consulportugalsydney.org.au; 23 Culgoa Circuit, O'Malley, ACT 2606); Sydney (☎ 02-9262 2199; Level 9, 30 Clarence St, Sydney, NSW 2000)

Brazil Brasilia (☎ 061-321 3434; Avenida das Nações, Lote 2, CEP 70402-900, Brasilia)

Canada Ottawa (☎ 613-729 0883; www.embportugal-ottawa.org; 645 Island Park Drive, Ottawa, ON K1Y 0B8); Vancouver (☎ 604-688 6514; 700 West Pender St, Vancouver, BC V6C 1G8; also in Montreal & Toronto)

Cape Verde Cidade da Praia (☎ 62 30 32; Achada de Santo António, Cidade da Praia CP 160)

France Paris (☎ 01 47 27 35 29; www.embaixada-portugal-fr.org; 3 rue de Noisiel, 75116 Paris); Lyon (☎ 04 78 17 34 40; 71 rue Crillon, 69458 Lyon; also in Bayonne, Bordeaux, Marseille, Strasbourg & Toulouse)

Germany Berlin (☎ 030-590 06 35 00; Zimmerstrasse 56, 10117 Berlin); Düsseldorf (☎ 0211-13 87 80; Graf-Adolf-Strasse 16, 4000 Düsseldorf; also in Stuttgart, Frankfurt-am-Main & Hamburg)

Guinea-Bissau Bissau Codex (☎ 20 12 61; Avenida Cidade de Lisboa, Apartado 76, 1021 Bissau Codex)

Ireland Dublin (☎ 01-289 4416; Knock Sinna House, Knock Sinna, Fox Rock, Dublin 18)

Morocco Rabat (☎ 07-756 446; 5 rue Thami Lamdouar, Souissi, Rabat)

Mozambique Maputo (☎ 01-490 316; Avenida Julius Nyerere 720, CP 4696 Maputo)

The Netherlands The Hague (☎ 070-363 02 17; ambportugal@wxs.nl; Bazarstraat 21, 2518 AG The Hague); Rotterdam (☎ 010-411 15 40; Willemskade 18, 3016 DL Rotterdam)

New Zealand Auckland (☎ 09-309 1454; daniel@silva.co.nz; PO Box 305, 33 Garfield Street, Parnell, Auckland)

São Tomé e Príncipe São Tomé (☎ 012-21130; Avenida Marginal 12 de Julho, CP 173 São Tomé)
Spain Madrid (☎ 91 782 49 60; embaportugal@telefonica.net; Calle Pinar 1, 28006 Madrid); Barcelona (☎ 93 318 81 50; Ronda San Pedro 7, 08010 Barcelona; also in Seville & Vigo)
UK London (☎ 020-7235 5331; london@portembassy.co.uk; 11 Belgrave Square, London SWIX 8PP); London (☎ 020-7581 8722; 62 Brompton Rd, London SW3 1BJ
USA Washington DC (☎ 202-328 8610; www.portugalemb.org; 2125 Kalorama Rd NW, Washington DC 20008); New York (☎ 212-765 2980; Suite 801, 630 Fifth Ave, New York, NY 10111; also in Boston & San Francisco)

Embassies & Consulates in Portugal

Your embassy or consulate is the best first stop in any emergency. Most can provide lists of reliable local doctors, lawyers and interpreters. If your money or documents have been stolen, they might help you get a new passport or advise you on how to have funds transferred, but a free ticket home or a loan for onward travel is vastly unlikely. Most embassies no longer have mail-holding services, or reading rooms with home newspapers. Foreign embassies and consulates in Portugal include:

Angola Lisbon (Map p80-1; ☎ 217 962 124; emb.angola@mail.telepac.pt; Avenida da República 68, 1500 Lisbon); Porto (☎ 222 058 827; consulado.angola@clix.pt; Rua Alexandre Herculano 352, 4000-053 Porto)
Australia Lisbon (Map p80-1; ☎ 213 101 500; portugal.embassy.gov.au; 2nd floor, Avenida da Liberdade 200, 1250-147 Lisbon)
Brazil Lisbon (☎ 217 248 510; Estrada das Laranjeiras 144, 1949-021 Lisbon); Porto (☎ 225 430 655; cgportp@mail.telepac.pt; 1st floor, Avenida de França 20, 4050-275 Porto)
Canada Lisbon (Map p80-1; ☎ 213 164 600; lisbon@dfait-maeci.gc.ca; 3rd floor, Avenida da Liberdade 196, 1269-121 Lisbon); Faro (☎ 289 803 757; Rua Frei Lourenço de Santa Maria 1, 8000-352 Faro)
Cape Verde Lisbon (Map p81; ☎ 213 015 271; Avenida do Restelo 33, 1449-025 Lisbon)
France Lisbon (Map p79; ☎ 213 939 100; ambafrance@hotmail.com; Rua de Santos-o-Velho 5, 1249-079 Lisbon); Porto (☎ 226 094 805; Rua Eugénio de Castro 352, 4100-225 Porto)
Germany Lisbon (Map p80-1; ☎ 218 810 210; embaixada.alemanha@clix.pt; Campo dos Mártires da Pátria 38, 1169-043 Lisbon); Porto (☎ 226 052 810; 6th fl, Avenida de França 20, 4050-275 Porto; also in Faro)
Guinea-Bissau Lisbon (Map p81; ☎ 213 929 440; Rua de Alcolena, 1200-684 Lisbon)
Morocco Lisbon (☎ 213 010 842; Rua Alto do Duque 21, 1400-099 Lisbon)
Mozambique Lisbon (Map p80-1; ☎ 217 971 994; www.mozambique.mz; Avenida de Berna 7, 1050-036 Lisbon); Porto (☎ 225 077 535; Rua Santos Pousada 441, 4000-486 Porto)
The Netherlands Lisbon (Map p79; ☎ 213 914 900; nlgovlis@mail.telepac.pt; Avenida Infante Santo 43, 1399-011 Lisbon); Porto (☎ /fax 222 080 061; Rua da Reboleira 7, 4050-492 Porto; also in Faro)
New Zealand Lisbon (☎ 213 509 690; 🕘 9am-1pm Mon-Fri) There's no New Zealand embassy in Portugal. In emergencies, New Zealand citizens can call the honorary consul at this number. The nearest New Zealand embassy is Rome (☎ 06 441 71 71; nzemb.rom@ flashnet.it).
São Tomé e Príncipe Lisbon (☎ 218 461 917; op4369@mail.telepac.pt; Avenida Almirante Gago Coutinho 26, 1000-017 Lisbon)
Spain Lisbon (☎ 213 472 792; edu.lisb.es@mail.telepac.pt; Rua do Salitre 1, 1269-052 Lisbon); Porto (☎ 225 101 685; consulado.porto@oninet.pt; Rua de Dom João IV 341, 4000-302 Porto; also in Valença do Minho & Vila Real de Santo António)
UK Lisbon (Map p79; ☎ 213 961 191; Rua de São Bernardo 33, 1249-082 Lisbon); Porto (☎ 226 184 789; consular@oporto.mail.fco.gov.uk; Avenida da Boavista 3072, 4100-120 Porto; also in Portimão)
USA Lisbon (☎ 217 273 300; www.american-embassy.pt; Avenida das Forças Armadas, 1600-081 Lisbon); Porto (☎ 226 172 384; Rua Marechal Saldanha 454, 4150-652 Porto)

FESTIVALS & EVENTS

As a Catholic country that likes to party, Portugal has some thrilling festivals and special events, mostly centred on something religious, often that have grown out of previously pagan events. Some of the best:

February/March

Carnaval Sequins, feather, floats – biggest in Loulé (p169), Nazaré (p267), Ovar and Viana do Castelo (p406).

March

Ovibeja Huge Alentejan agricultural fair (p243).

March/April

Senhor Ecce Homo Braga's grand, pathos-packed Semana Santa (p391).

May

Fátima Romaris Huge pilgrimage to commemorate 1917 Virgin apparition (p277).
Festival das Cruzes In Barcelos, the folksy festival of the crosses is good for handicrafts and processions (p396).

June

Corpo de Deus Corpus Christi and time for big parties and processions in the north.

Feira Nacional da Agricultura Santarém shows its best bulls, in a livestock fair with lots of regional song and dance (p282).

Festa de Santo António Knees up for Lisbon's favorite saint (p97).

Festa de São João Porto (p358) and Braga (p391) go crazy for a week.

July

Festa dos Tabuleiros Bread-laden trays on virgins' heads in Tomar every four years (p287).

August

Romaria e Festa da Nossa Senhora da Agonia Pilgrimage, parades, folk art and fireworks in Viana do Castelo (p406).

Festival do Sudoeste The Alentejan Glastonbury, near Zambujeira, with music (previous years have included PJ Harvey and Massive Attack) and food stalls. Held in early August (p251).

September

Feiras Novas Fairs, folk and a vast riverside market on the banks of the Rio Lima, this Ponte de Lima bash dates to the 12th century (p414).

October

Fátima Part 2 (see May).

November

Feira de São Martinho Horse parades, bullfights and hearty feasts in Golegá Ribatejo.

FOOD

In this book, budget-designated places have snacks or mains from around €2 and up, mid-range around €6 to €12, and top end about €12 and up. For more tasty nuggets, see Food & Drink (p62).

GAY & LESBIAN TRAVELLERS

How out you can be depends on where you are. In Lisbon, Porto and the Algarve, acceptance has increased, while in most other areas, same-sex couples would be met with incomprehension. In this conservative Catholic country, homosexuality is still outside the norm – homophobic violence is pretty much unknown, but discrimination is reported in schools and workplaces.

Lisbon has the best gay and lesbian network and nightlife (p108). Lisbon, Porto and Leiria hold Gay Pride marches, but outside these events the gay community keeps a discreet profile. When you go to a gay bar or club, you'll usually ring a doorbell for admission.

HOLIDAYS

Banks, offices, department stores and some shops closes on the following holidays. On New Year's Day, Easter Sunday, Labour Day and Christmas Day, even turismos close.

New Year's Day 1 January

Carnaval Tuesday February/March – Day before Ash Wednesday

Good Friday March/April

Liberty Day 25 April – Celebrating 1974 revolution

Labour Day 1 May

Corpus Christi May/June – Ninth Thursday after Easter

Portugal Day 10 June – Also known as Camões and the Communities Day

Feast of the Assumption 15 August

Republic Day 5 October – Commemorating 1910 declaration of Portuguese Republic

All Saints' Day 1 November

Independence Day 1 December – Commemorating 1640 restoration of independence from Spain

Feast of the Immaculate Conception 8 December

Christmas Day 25 December

INSURANCE

Don't leave home without a travel insurance policy to cover theft, loss and medical problems. You should cover yourself for the worst case, for example, an accident or illness requiring hospitalisation and a flight home; if you can't afford that, you certainly can't afford to deal with a medical emergency abroad. Loads of policies are available; the international policies handled by youth and student travel agencies are good value.

Check the small print – some policies specifically exclude 'dangerous activities' such as scuba diving, motorcycling or even trekking. If these are in your sights, get another policy or ask about an amendment (for an extra premium) that includes them.

Make sure you keep all documentation to claim back later. Some policies ask you to call back (reverse charges) to a centre in your home country where an immediate assessment of your problem is made.

Citizens of the EU are eligible for free emergency medical treatment if they have an E111 certificate –you have to fill in a form available from the post office in your home country and get it stamped for verification.

INTERNET ACCESS

Free Net access is becoming common all over Portugal, either at local branches of the Instituto Portuguese da Juventude (IPJ) or at a growing number of municipal **Espaço Internet** (www.espacosInternet.pt). Usually you have to show some ID and then get 30 minutes free time (unless there's no one waiting). Cybercafés, common in cities and towns, charge from around €2 per hour. Many post offices have terminals for NetPost, an Internet facility payable with a special card. However, these are often out of order.

If you have your own laptop and a global modem, and your ISP offers global roaming, you may be able to log in from your hotel room – only mid-range and top-end hotels will have room phone sockets, though. Most telephone sockets in Portugal are US (RJ-II) – for those that aren't you'll need an adaptor. One problem is the faint beeps measuring calling time, which can interfere with a connection. The solution is an in-line filter. Such accessories are available from **Teleadapt** (www.teleadapt.com).

LEGAL MATTERS

Fines for illegal parking are common – if you're parked illegally you'll be towed and will have to pay around €100 to get your car back. Be aware of local road rules, as fines for other transgressions will also be enforced.

Narcotic drugs were decriminalised in 2001 in an attempt to clear up the public-health problems among drug users, and to address the issue as a social rather than a criminal one. You may be brought before a commission and subject to fines or treatment if you are caught with up to 10 doses of a drug. Drug dealing is still a serious offence and suspects may be held for many months (up to 18) before coming to trial. Bail is at the court's discretion.

LEGAL AGES

- Drinking: No minimum
- Driving: 17
- Sex (hetero/homosexual): 14/16

MAPS

Lonely Planet publishes the well-indexed, full-colour *Portugal Road Atlas* at 1:400,000.

Most current, though not indexed, is the 1:350,000 *Mapa das Estradas*, updated every June by the Automóvel Club de Portugal (p473). More or less equivalent is Michelin's 1:400,000 *Portugal, Madeira*, No 940.

Two government-mapping agencies exist: the military **Instituto Geográfico do Exército** (IGeoE; Army Geographic Institute; Map pp74-5; ☎ 218 520 063; www.igeoe.pt; Avenida Dr Alfredo Bensaúde, Lisbon); and the civilian **Instituto Geográfico Português** (IGP; Portuguese Geographic Institute; ☎ 213 819 600; fax 213 819 699; Rua Artilharia Um 107, Lisbon). IGeoE publishes 1:25,000 topographic sheets covering the entire country, plus less useful 1:50,000 and 1:250,000 series, including *Portugal Continental Mapa de Estradas*, which is precise, but not always up to date.

IGP's 1:50,000 maps tend to be more current, but lack the precision of the military publications; IGP also publishes 1:100,000, 1:200,000 and a new 1:10,000 series, including a detailed 1:10,000 *Lisbon* map

Both agencies sell maps from their Lisbon headquarters, though IGeoE is in the middle of nowhere, 2km northwest of Gare do Oriente station. Most IGeoE 1:25,000 sheets are also available at Porto's Livraria Porto Editora bookshop (p351).

National and natural park offices usually have simple park maps, though these are of little use for trekking or cycling. Other local sources for topographic maps are noted in the text. The following offer a good range of maps:

Maps Worldwide (☎ 01225-707004, www.mapsworldwide.co.uk; Datum House, Lancaster Rd, Melksham SN12 6TL, UK)

Omni Resources (☎ 336-227 8300, www.omnimap.com; 1004 South Mebane Street, PO Box 2096, Burlington, NC 27216-2096, USA)

Stanfords (☎ 020-7836 1321, www.stanfords.co.uk; 12-14 Long Acre, Covent Garden, London WC2E 9LP, UK)

MONEY

Since 1 January 2002 Portugal has used the euro, along with Austria, Belgium, Finland, France, Germany, Ireland, Italy, Luxembourg, the Netherlands and Spain. Prices jumped, but the easy conversion (100 escudos equalled half a euro) made the change-over less painful than in other countries. Some people still talk in escudos.

Banks and bureaux de change are free to set their own rates and commissions, so a low commission might mean a skewed exchange rate.

ATMs & Credit Cards

The most convenient way to get your money is from an ATM. Most banks have a Multibanco ATM, complete with annoying animated graphics, accepting Visa, Access, Mastercard, Cirrus and so on. You just need your card and PIN. Your home bank will usually charge around 1.5% per transaction. It's wise to have a back up – always a good idea, but sometimes ATMs temporarily stop accepting a certain type of card, usually a hiatus lasting a day or so. You'll be asked for a six-digit PIN, but if yours is just four-digit, that works fine.

Credit cards are taken at smarter hotels and restaurants and in larger towns, but won't be any use to pay for things in the budget arena or rural outposts.

Travellers Cheques

These are a safe way to carry money as they will be replaced if lost or stolen, but are less convenient than the card-in-machine method. Amex, Thomas Cook or Visa are most widely recognised – it's best to get them in euros. Keep a record of the ones you've cashed, in case you do mislay them. However, although they are easily exchanged, with better rates than for cash, they are poor value because commission is so high.

Tipping

If you're satisfied with the service, tip 5% to 10%. Bills at pricier restaurants may already include *serviço* (service charge). After a snack at a bar or café some shrapnel is enough. Taxi drivers are not generally tipped, but 10% for good service would be appreciated.

POST

Post offices are called **CCT** (www.ctt.pt). Ordinary mail *(correio normal)* goes in the red letter boxes, airmail *(correio azul)* goes in the blue box. Postcards and letters up to 20g cost €0.72/0.56/0.30 outside Europe/within Europe/local. International *correio azul* costs €1.75 for a 20g letter. Post to Europe takes up to five working days, and the rest of the world up to seven. Economy mail (or surface airlift) is about a third cheaper, but takes a week or so longer.

You can send post to poste restante in main post offices of cities and large towns.

Many post offices have NetPost for Internet access, but the machines are frequently out of order. If they do work, it costs €2.40 per hour, with cards costing €5.49.

SHOPPING

Home of ceramics, port, wine, lace and crazy cockerel mascots, Portugal is a splendid place to shop, not least because it moves at a relaxed pace ideal for browsing and window-shopping. Its low prices also mean more gain for less pain.

Port, Wine & Food

Port is Portugal's best-known export, and is easy to find. To hunt it to its source, visit port-wine lodges at Vila Nova de Gaia (p368), across the river from Porto, or pop into a supermarket where you'll find a good range. Lisbon, Porto and other cities have specialist shops. In Lisbon or Porto you can visit port-tasting places, then note down your favourite to buy later.

Buying wine is also popular, with some excellent wines at affordable prices. There's a wine route you can follow in the Alentejo (p203), visiting wineries, tasting and buying, and also places in Estremadura (p270) and near Setúbal (p140). Dão (p337) also has some excellent lodges where you can tour and taste.

Olive oil and honey are also good buys all over the country. Try Mértola (p241) and Serpa (p245) in Alentejo, or Parque Nacional da Peneda-Gerês in the Minho.

Linen, Cotton & Lace

Hand-embroidered linen and cotton, traditional costumes, and lacework (a speciality of coastal fishing towns) are sold at modest prices all over the country, but especially in seaside resorts such as Nazaré (p266) and Viana do Castelo (p403). Guimarães (p397) has been famous for its linen since medieval times, so it must be doing something right. Castelo Branco (p318) is a hotspot for embroidered bed covers. Bobbin lace comes from Vila do Conde (p369), Peniche (p257) and the eastern Algarve. There are also several speciality shops in Lisbon selling lacework and linen.

Music

Buy a tragic stoic soundtrack for those dramatic moments. Try the good speciality music shops, turismos and the Fado museum in Lisbon. Most towns have a selection of small music shops, all of which will have some fado. To help you choose, see p42.

Ceramics

Portugal produces beautiful ceramics, from refined tiling to rustic bowls – all bursting with brilliant colours. See p112 for where to buy the best ceramics in the capital. Caldas da Rainha (p262) is a ceramics centre, with museums devoted to its masters, as well as numerous artisans workshops and shops. Also try São Pedro do Corval (p216) which features around 30 businesses producing brightly coloured rustic ceramics. Nearby, Reguengoz de Monsaraz has some cutting-edge and traditional ceramics at a local co-op, Tear (p216).

Estremoz (p219) in the Alentejo produces unique, charming figurines – mainly saints with flowing robes – looking like they've been caught in a wind machine. There are several small shops and a wonderful workshop selling these (and other crafts), and Estremoz also hosts a fantastically thriving Saturday market where you can combine your figurine-shopping with picking up a goat.

Rugs, Jewellery & Leather

Portugal's finest carpets are produced in Arraiolos in the Alentejo – they are hand stitched and prices reflect this. More rustic *mantas* (woollen rugs and blankets) are a speciality of Regenguoz de Monsaraz (p216) and Mértola (p237) in the Alentejo.

In the Algarve, Loulé's Saturday market (p170) is a great place to buy all sorts of crafts, from brass to basketware to leather goods and every sort of souvenir.

The exquisite gold and silver filigree jewellery of the Porto area is expensive, but good value. Leather goods, especially shoes and bags, are also good buys (p364).

Icons

If you're interested in religious icons or out-and-out kitsch, Fátima (p276) rivals Disney in the merchandise stakes, with candles, miniature saints and all sort of shepherds-and-vision tableaux.

TOP FIVE BIZARRE SOUVENIRS

- Ceramics shaped like cabbages
- Barcelos Cockerel (p394)
- Port bottles shaped like shoes, swords or ships
- Canned fish (p96)
- Glow-in-the-dark Virgins (p276)

Other Handicrafts

Rush, palm and wicker basketwork pieces are appealing and cheap. They're best found in municipal markets all over the country. Tràs-os-Montes is good for woven handicrafts and tapestries and, with Beira Alta and Beira Beixa, for wrought-iron work.

In Alentejo you can buy lovely traditional hand-painted wooden furniture, such as you will see in many local hotel rooms. Monchique (p197) sells unique small wooden scissor stools.

Lisbon and Porto are also good places to buy traditional crafts from all over the country – see p112 and p364 for details.

Bargaining

Bargaining is only really done at markets, although you may sometimes be able to bargain down accommodation prices when things are quiet.

SOLO TRAVELLERS

The Portuguese tend to be friendly and welcoming, and with lots of other travellers on the road, you're unlikely to feel lonely if you're on your own. In rural areas it's odd to see a woman travelling alone, but this is likely to be put down to foreign weirdness, and unlikely to provoke anything more than a little curiosity.

Single rooms usually cost about two-thirds of the double-room price, so it's more expensive to travel alone – though youth hostels are a good bet if you're on a budget. Not only are they cheap, but they are also really good places to meet other travellers.

TELEPHONE

To call Portugal from abroad, call the **international access code** (☎ 00), then Portugal's **country code** (☎ 351), then the number. All domestic numbers have nine digits. On a public phone, it's easiest to call from a card-operated phone (coin-operated telephones have an annoying habit of munching your money). You can also call from booths in Portugal Telecom offices and post offices – pay when your call is finished.

Calls from public phones are charged per number of *impulsos* (beeps or time units) used. The price per beep is fixed (€0.06) with a phonecard, but it's the length of time units that is the key to the cost. The duration depends on destination, time of day and type of call. Coin telephones cost €0.07 per beep; hotel and café phones rack up three to six times the charges. It costs two/three beeps extra to make a domestic/international connection.

All but local calls are cheaper 9pm to 9am weekdays, all weekend and on holidays.

Local, Regional & National Calls

The cheapest way to call within Portugal is with a Portugal Telecom *cartão telefónico* (phonecard). These are available for €3/6/9 (50/100/150 beeps) from post and telephone offices and many newsagents. A youth or student card should get you a 10% discount.

A beep lasts three minutes for any local call. It last 46 seconds for a regional call (under about 50km) and 30 seconds for a national call, and lasts twice as long during the previously mentioned economy periods. Numbers starting with 800 (*linha verde*; green line) are toll free. Those starting with 808 (*linha azul*; blue line) are charged at local rates from anywhere in the country.

International Calls & Card

From Portugal Telecom, you can get a Hello CardPT or PT CARD Europe, both costing €5. You call an access number then key in the code on the back of the card. This is a cheaper way of making international calls. There are lots of competing cards offering much the same service. Note that peak and off-peak periods vary from company to company.

Directory Inquiries

Portugal's directory inquiries number is ☎ 118; operators will search by address as well as by name. International directory inquiries operator is 177. Two independent inquiry services, charged at local call rates, are **Telelista** (☎ 707 222 707; www.telelista.iol.pt) and **Páginas Amarelas** (Yellow Pages; ☎ 707 202 222; www.paginasamarelas.pt).

To make a reverse-charge call *(page no destino)* with the help of a multilingual operator, dial ☎ 171.

TIME

Portugal, like Britain, is on GMT/UTC in winter and GMT/UTC plus one hour in summer. This puts it an hour earlier than Spain year-round (a strange thought when you are crossing the border). Clocks are set forward by an hour on the last Sunday in March and back on the last Sunday in October.

TOURIST INFORMATION

Portugal's umbrella tourism organisation is **Investimentos, Comércio e Turismo de Portugal** (ICEP head office; Map pp80-1; ☎ 217 909 500; www.portugalinsite.pt; Avenida 5 de Outubro 101, 1050-051 Lisbon). There's also a Porto branch: **ICEP turismo** (Map pp352-3; ☎ 222 057 514, airport office ☎ 229 412 534, 229 432 400; Praça Dom João I 43).

Locally managed *postos de turismo* (tourist offices, usually signposted 'turismo') are everywhere, offering brochures and varying degrees of help with sights and accommodation. ICEP maintains a *regiões de turismo* (regional office) in the main town of each of its regions, and information desks at Lisbon, Porto and Faro airports. Lisbon, Porto, Coimbra and a few other towns have both municipal and ICEP turismos.

Multilingual staff at the toll-free tourist helpline **Linha Verde do Turista** (☎ 800 296 296; 🕑 9am-9pm) can provide basic – though not uniformly accurate – information on accommodation, sightseeing and so on.

Regional tourist offices include:

Alentejo Serra de São Mamede (☎ 245 300 770; www.rtsm.pt; Região de Turismo de São Mamede, Estrada de Santana 25, Portalegre); Planície Dourada (☎ 284 310 150; www.rt-planiciedourada.pt; Praça da República, Beja)

Beiras Coimbra (☎ 239 488 120; rtc-coimbra@turismo-centro.pt; Largo da Portagem); Aveiro (☎ 234 423 680; aveiro.rotadaluz@inovanet.pt; Rua João Mendonça 8); Covilhã (☎ 275 319 560; turismo.estrela@mail.telepac.pt; Avenida Frei Heitor Pinto); Viseu (☎ 232 420 950; turismo@rt-dao-lafoes.com; Avenida Calouste Gulbenkian)

Douro Lamego (☎ 254 612 005; douro.turismo@mail.telepac.pt; Avenida Visconde Guedes Teixeira)

Minho Viana do Castelo (☎ 258 822 620; fax 258 827 873; Rua Hospital Velho); Bairros (Adere-Soajo; ☎/fax 258 576 427; turismo.adere-soajo@sapo.pt; Turismo de Aldeia, Largo da Cardeira)

Trás-os-Montes Vila Real (☎ 259 322 819; turismarao@mail.telepac.pt; Avenida Carvalho Araújo 94); Chaves (☎ 276 340 660; rturismoatb@mail.telepac.pt; Terreiro de Cavalaria; 9.30am-12.30pm & 2-6pm Jun-Sep, Mon-Sat Oct-May)

VISAS

Nationals of European Union (EU) countries need no visa for any length of stay in Portugal. Those from Canada, New Zealand, the USA and (by temporary agreement) Australia can stay for up to 90 days in any half-year without a visa. Others, including nationals of South Africa, need a visa unless they're the spouse or child of an EU citizen.

The general requirements for entry into Portugal also apply to citizens of other signatories of the 1990 Schengen Convention (Austria, Belgium, Denmark, Finland, France, Germany, Greece, Iceland, Italy, Luxembourg, the Netherlands, Norway, Spain and Sweden). A visa issued by one Schengen country is generally valid for travel in all the others, but unless you're a citizen of the UK, Ireland or a Schengen country, you should check visa regulations with the consulate of each Schengen country you plan to visit. You must apply for any Schengen visa in your country of residence.

To extend a visa or 90-day period of stay after arriving in Portugal, contact the **Foreigners Registration Service** (Serviço de Estrangeiros e Fronteiras; Map p80-1; ☎ 213 585 545; Rua São Sebastião da Pedreira 15, Lisbon; 9am-3pm Mon-Fri); major tourist towns also have branches. As entry regulations are already liberal, you'll need convincing proof of employment or financial independence, or a pretty good story, if you're asking to stay longer.

WOMEN TRAVELLERS

Women travelling alone in Portugal report few serious problems. As when travelling anywhere, women should take care – be cautious about where you walk after dark and don't hitch.

If you're travelling with a male partner, people will expect him to do all the talking and ordering, and pay the bill. In some conservative pockets of the north, unmarried couples will save hassle by saying they're married.

Associação Portuguêse Apoio a Vitima (Portuguese Association for Victims; ☎ 218 884 732) Can offer assistance for rape victims.

Comissão para a Igualdade e para os Directos Mulheres (Map p80-1; Commission for the Equality & Rights of Women; ☎ 217 983 000, toll-free number ☎ 218 884 732; www.cidm.pt; Avenida da Repùblica 32) There's no specific rape-crisis hotline, but the commission operates the toll-free number for victims of violence.

WORK

The most likely kind of work you will be able to find is teaching English, if you have a TEFL qualification. Contact the British Council or the language schools listed in Courses (p457) as possible avenues of work.

Bar work is a possibility on the Algarve, particularly in Lagos. Ask around. You can also try looking in the local English press for job ads (p452).

Transport

CONTENTS

GETTING THERE & AWAY

ENTERING THE COUNTRY

Coming from within Europe, you'll have no problems entering Portugal by land, sea or air. However, if you're coming from further afield, check p465 to see if you'll need to secure a visa before arrival.

AIR

Airports & Airlines

Portugal has international airports at **Lisbon** (Airport code LIS; Map pp74-5; ☎ 218 413 500;), **Porto** (Airport code OPO; ☎ 229 412 534) and **Faro** (Airport code FAO; ☎ 289 800 800). For more information, see www.ana-aeroportos.pt. Portugal's flagship international airline is TAP Air Portugal. The main domestic airline – but with a growing menu of European connections – is PGA Portugália Airlines. Following are details of major carriers serving Portugal:

Aer Lingus (airline code EI; ☎ 217 220 511; www.aerlingus.ie; hub Dublin)
Air Berlin (airline code AB; ☎ 289 800 832; www.airberlin.com; hub Berlin)
Air France (airline code AF; ☎ 808 202 800; www.airfrance.fr; hub Paris)
Air Luxor (airline code LK; ☎ 707 500 505; www.airluxor.com; hubs Lisbon & Porto)
Alitalia (airline code AZ; ☎ 800 307 300; www.alitalia.com; hubs Milan, Rome)
British Airways (airline code BA; ☎ 808 200 125; www.britishairways.com; hub London)
British Midland/BMIbaby (airline code BD; www.bmibaby.com; hubs Cardiff, East Midlands, Manchester, Teesside)
Continental Airlines (airline code CO; ☎ 808 200 079; www.flycontinental.com; hub Houston)
Delta (airline code DL; ☎ 213 139 860; www.delta.com; hub Atlanta)
Finnair (airline code AY; ☎ 213 522 689; www.finnair.fi; hub Helsinki)
GBAirways (☎ 289 800 771; hub Londonwww.gbairways.com)
Go/easyJet Airways (airline code U2; www.easyjet.com; hubs Bristol, Liverpool, London Luton, London Stansted, Newcastle)
Grupo SATA (airport code S4; ☎ 707 227 282; www.sata.pt; hubs Lisbon, Faro & Porto)
Iberia (airline code IB; ☎ 808 261 261; www.iberia.com; hub Madfrid)
KLM (airline code KL; ☎ 204 747 747; www.klm.nl; hub Amsterdam)
Lufthansa (airline code LH; ☎ 214 245 155; www.lufthansa.com; hub Frankfurt)
Monarch Airlines (airline code ZB; ☎ 289 889 475; www.flymonarch.com; hubs London Gatwick, London Luton, Manchester)

THINGS CHANGE

The information in this chapter is particularly vulnerable to change: Prices for international travel are volatile, routes are introduced and cancelled, schedules change, special deals come and go, and rules and visa requirements are amended. You should check directly with the airline or a travel agent to make sure you understand how a fare (and ticket you may buy) works and be aware of the security requirements for international travel.

The upshot of this is that you should get opinions, quotes and advice from as many airlines and travel agents as possible before you part with your hard-earned cash. The details given in this chapter should be regarded as pointers and are not a substitute for your own careful, up-to-date research.

DEPARTURE TAX

International airport taxes, normally levied by countries of both origin and destination, are invariably included in the price of your ticket, either scheduled or charter.

PGA Portugália Airlines (www.flypga.com; airline code NI; ☎ 707 789 090; hubs Lisbon, Faro & Porto)
Regional Air Lines (www.regional.com; airline code FN; ☎ 218 425 559; hub Casablanca)
Swiss International Air Lines (www.swiss.com; airline code LX; ☎ 808 200 487; hub Zürich)
TAP Air Portugal (www.tap.pt; airline code TP; ☎ 707 205 700; hubs Lisbon, Faro & Porto)
Transavia Airlines (www.transavia.com; airline code HV; ☎ 218 925 454; hub Amsterdam)
Tunisair (www.tunisair.com.tn; airline code TU; ☎ 218 496 350; hub Tunis)
Varig (www.varig.com.br; airline code RG; ☎ 214 245 170; hub Brasilia)
Virgin Express (www.virgin-express.com; airline code VS; ☎ 808 208 082; hub Brussels)

Continental Europe

FRANCE

Carriers with multiple daily Paris–Lisbon and Paris–Porto connections include Air France, Portugália and TAP. Direct connections to Lisbon from elsewhere in France also include those from Bordeaux, Nice, Lyon and Toulouse. More expensive flights to Porto go daily from Bordeaux, and weekly from Nice. Flights to Faro are less easy to come by.

Expect to pay around €150 return for a Paris–Lisbon or Paris–Porto flight in high season. Agencies with branches around the country include:

Nouvelles Frontières (☎ 08 25 00 07 47; www.nouvelles-frontieres.fr)
OTU Voyages (☎ 08 20 81 78 17; www.otu.fr)
Voyages Wasteels (☎ 08 25 88 70 70; www.wasteels.fr).
Voyageurs du Monde (☎ 08 92 23 56 56; www.vdm.com).

SPAIN

Carriers with daily Madrid–Lisbon connections include Iberia, Portugália and TAP. Portugália, TAP and Iberia also fly Barcelona–Lisbon. Portugália also has affordable smaller aircraft flying direct to Lisbon from Bilbao, La Coruña, Málaga and Valencia.

For Porto, Portugália has daily direct flights from Madrid (about €240 return) and Barcelona (around €290 return).

Reliable Madrid-based air-fare specialists with offices throughout Spain include **Barceló Viajes** (☎ 902 116 226; www.barceloviajes.es).

ELSEWHERE IN CONTINENTAL EUROPE

An air-fare specialist with branches around Germany is **STA Travel** (☎ 01805-456 422; www.statravel.de). In Belgium go to **Usit Connections** (☎ 070-23-33-13; www.connections.be). In the Netherlands, try Amsterdam-based **Air Fair** (☎ 020-620 5121; www.airfair.nl).

The major lines from Germany are Frankfurt, Berlin and Munich to Lisbon, and Frankfurt to Porto. Other direct connections to Lisbon are from Cologne, Hamburg and Stuttgart; and to Faro from Frankfurt. Frankfurt–Lisbon return fares start at around €160 with connections. Germany also has busy charter traffic to Portugal.

From Amsterdam, there are daily flights to Lisbon and Porto, and several weekly to Faro; expect to pay from €220 return. Charter specialist **Transavia** (☎ 020-406 04 06; www.transavia.nl) also offers scheduled flights from Amsterdam to Porto, and Rotterdam to Faro.

For a similar fare, there are multiple daily flights from Brussels to Lisbon and weekend connections to Faro.

UK & Ireland

Thanks to the UK's long love affair with Portugal and its 'bucket-shop' tradition, bargains are plentiful. The UK's best-known bargain agencies and Internet-based dealers:

Expedia (www.expedia.com)
Flight Centre (www.flightcentre.co.uk)
Lastminute (www.lastminute.com)
STA Travel (☎ 0870-160 0599; www.statravel.co.uk)
Trailfinders (☎ 0845-050 5891; www.trailfinders.co.uk)

Reliable sources in Ireland:

Trailfinders (☎ 01-677 7888; www.trailfinders.ie)
Usit (☎ 0818-200 020; www.usit.ie)

Scheduled direct flights go daily to Lisbon from London Heathrow, Gatwick and Manchester. Porto flights also leave daily from Heathrow and Manchester, and less frequently from Gatwick. There's also a veritable bandwagon of flights to Faro. At the time of writing, 'no-frills' carriers to Portugal included Go/easyJet (London, Bristol, and East Midlands to Faro), BMIbaby (East Midlands to Faro) and Monarch (London and Manchester).

The best midsummer return fares for London–Lisbon start at about UK£120. The best direct fare for London–Porto is about UK£142 (but you can get as low as UK£105 with a connection). Return fares to Faro can reach as low as UK£60 booking well ahead, and even lower out of season. A standard 'no-frills' fare costs around UK£100.

Charters operate from all over the UK, mostly to Faro. A reliable charter-flight clearinghouse is **Destination Portugal** (www.destination-portugal.co.uk).

USA & Canada

The only direct air links are to Lisbon: daily from New York JFK, Newark and Los Angeles and less frequently from Boston. There are no direct flights between Canada and Portugal. If you don't mind connecting flights, return fares start at around US$650 from New York or US$1025 from Los Angeles.

Circle the Planet (☎ 800 799 8888; www.circletheplanet.com) is a leading consolidator, and you can always try your luck with **Hotwire** (www.hotwire.com). A big air-fare specialist in the USA is **STA Travel** (☎ 800 781 4040; www.statravel.com). Canada's best bargain-ticket agency is **Travel CUTS** (☎ 866 246 9762; www.travelcuts.com).

LAND

Bicycle

Bicycles can be taken on aeroplanes, but check this with the airline well in advance. Let some of the air out of the tyres to prevent them from bursting in the low-pressure baggage hold. Bikes are not allowed as baggage on either Eurolines or Busabout buses. For information on cycling in Portugal, see Getting Around (p471).

Bus

Buses are slower and less comfortable than trains, but cheaper – especially if you qualify for an under-26, student or senior discount. The two major options for European long-distance bus travel are Eurolines and Busabout.

EUROLINES

Eurolines (www.eurolines.com) is a consortium of coach operators forming Europe's largest network. A Eurolines Pass gives you unlimited travel among 35 European cities – although Madrid is currently the closest city to Portugal covered by the pass. High-season prices range from €285/240/240 (adult/under 26/senior) for a 15-day pass to €490/380/380 for a 60-day pass; low-season prices are 20% to 25% lower.

Eurolines' main Portugal offices are in **Lisbon** (Map pp74-5; ☎ 218 957 398; Loja 203, Gare do Oriente) and in **Porto** (Map p350; ☎ 225 189 299; Centro Comercial Central Shopping, Campo 24 de Agosto 125). For some European routes, Eurolines is affiliated with the three big Portuguese operators Intercentro (p114), Internorte (p365) and Eva Transportes (p156).

BUSABOUT

Busabout (www.busabout.com) is a hop-on hop-off network linking 41 European cities. Buses run from May to October, and travellers can move freely around the network using one of two passes available online from Busabout.

The Unlimited Pass is good for a set period from two weeks (€359) to six months (€1239). The Flexipass lets you choose the number of travel days you want, from eight days (€419) to 20 days (€879) that can be taken at any time during the operating season: additional days are also possible. Youth (under 26) and student-card holders pay about 10% less.

The bus stops are near camp sites, hostels or other budget accommodation, and buses pass by every two days. Stops in Portugal are in Lisbon and Lagos and details are in those sections. Each bus comes with a guide who can answer questions and make travel and accommodation arrangements.

CONTINENTAL EUROPE

France

Eurolines offers regular connections from Paris to all over Portugal, including Porto (25 hours), Lisbon (26 hours) and less often to Faro (29 hours). Expect to pay €88 to €95. Hefty surcharges apply to one-way or return tickets for most departures from July to mid-August and also on Saturday year-round.

Spain

UK–Portugal and France–Portugal Eurolines services cross to Portugal via north-west Spain. Sample fares to Lisbon include €29 from Salamanca.

From Madrid, Eurolines/Internorte runs daily via Guarda to Porto (€38 one way, 8½ hours) and also via Badajoz and Évora to Lisbon (€38, eight hours); twice weekly the Lisbon service starts from Barcelona (€77, 18 hours). The Spanish lines **AutoRes** (☎ 902 02 09 99; www.auto-res.net) and **Alsa** (☎ 913 27 05 40; www.alsa.es) each have regular Madrid–Lisbon services (€38).

From Seville, Alsa/Eurolines goes five to six times weekly via Badajoz and Évora to Lisbon (€35, seven hours).

The Portuguese carrier **Eva** (☎ 289 899 700; www.eva-bus.com) and the Spanish line **Damas** (☎ 95 925 69 00; www.damas-sa.es) operate a joint service three times weekly from Seville to Lisbon (€30 to €35, 4½ hours); with connecting buses to other cities at Ficalho.

Eurolines affiliate **Intersul** (☎ 289 899 770; Loja A, Terminal Rodoviário, Faro) runs from Seville to Lagos regularly in summer, and Eva/Damas runs a twice-daily service from Seville to Faro (€12, four to five hours), Albufeira and Lagos (€16, 4½ hours) via Huelva (p156).

Elsewhere in Continental Europe

Eurolines has services to Portugal from across Europe, typically about twice a week. Sample one-way fares from Hamburg are around €152/159/179 to Porto/Lisbon/Faro. Fares from Amsterdam or Brussels are around €134 to Lisbon or Faro.

UK

Eurolines runs several services to Portugal from Victoria coach station in London, with a stopover and change of bus in France and sometimes Spain. These include two a week to Viana do Castelo (34 hours), five to Porto (33 hours), five via Coimbra to Lisbon (35 hours) and two via Faro to Lagos (38 hours). These services cost around UK£99 one way.

Car & Motorcycle

Of over 30 roads crossing the Portugal–Spain border, the best and biggest do so near Valença do Minho (E01/A3), Chaves (N532), Bragança (E82/IP4), Guarda/Vilar Formoso (E80/IP5), Elvas (E90/A6/IP7), Serpa (N260) and Vila Real de Santo António (E1/IP1). There are no longer any border controls.

INSURANCE & DOCUMENTS

Nationals of EU countries need only their home driving licences to operate a car or motorcycle in Portugal, although holders of the UK's old, pre-EU green licences should also carry an International Driving Permit (IDP). Portugal also accepts licences issued in Brazil and the USA. Others should get an IDP through an automobile licensing department or automobile club in their home country (or at some post offices in the UK).

If you're driving your own car or motorcycle into Portugal, you'll also need vehicle registration (proof of ownership) and insurance documents. If these are in order you should be able to keep the vehicle in Portugal for up to six months.

Motor vehicle insurance with at least third-party cover is compulsory throughout the EU. Your home policy may or may not be extendable to Portugal, and the coverage of some comprehensive policies automatically drops to third-party-only outside the home country unless the insurer is notified. Though it's not a legal requirement, it's wise to carry written confirmation from your home insurer that you have the correct coverage.

If you hire a car, the rental firm will furnish you with registration and insurance papers, plus a rental contract.

UK

The quickest automobile route from the UK to Portugal is by car ferry to northern Spain with **P&O Portsmouth** (☎ 0870 520 2020; www.poferries.com) from Portsmouth to Bilbao (35 hours, twice weekly mid-March to mid-December), or **Brittany Ferries** (☎ 0870 366 5333; www.brittany-ferries.com) from Plymouth to Santander (18 hours, twice weekly from March to November). From Bilbao or Santander it's roughly 1000km to Lisbon, 800km to Porto or 1300km to Faro. Fares are wildly seasonal. A standard weekday, high-season, return ticket for a car/motorcycle with driver and one passenger (with cabin accommodation) starts at about UK£650/400, but you can usually beat this with special offers.

An alternative is to catch a ferry across the Channel (or the Eurotunnel vehicle train beneath it) to France and motor down the coast.

Train

Trains are a popular way to get around Europe – comfortable, frequent and generally on time. But unless you have a rail pass (below) the cost can be higher than flying.

There are two standard long-distance rail journeys into Portugal. Both take the *TGV Atlantique* from Paris to Irún (in Spain), where you must change trains. From there the *Sud-Expresso* crosses into Portugal at Vilar Formoso (Fuentes de Oñoro in Spain), continuing to Coimbra and Lisbon; change at Pampilhosa for Porto. The other journey runs from Irún to Madrid, with a change to the *Talgo Lusitânia*, crossing into Portugal at Marvão–Beirã and on to Lisbon. For trips to the south of Portugal, change at Lisbon (p114).

Two other important Spain–Portugal crossings are at Valença do Minho and at Caia (Caya in Spain), near Elvas.

You'll have few problems buying long-distance tickets as little as a day or two ahead, even in summer. For those intending to do a lot of European rail travel, the exhaustive *Thomas Cook European Timetable* is updated monthly and is available from **Thomas Cook Publishing** (☎ 01733-416477; www.thomascooktimetables.com) costing UK£10.50 online, plus postage.

RAIL PASSES

The following passes are available through **Rail Europe** (www.raileurope.com) and other travel agencies. Note that even with a pass you must still pay for seat and couchette reservations and express-train supplements.

The Inter-Rail Pass divides Europe into zones (zone F is Spain, Portugal and Morocco). One-zone passes are good for 16 consecutive days; the 2nd-class adult/under-26 price is €299/210. Two-zone passes are also available for 22 consecutive days (€409/289). Better-value multizone passes, good for a month, cost €559/399.

The EuroDomino Pass is good for a number of consecutive days within a specified month, in a specified country. For 2nd-class adult/under-26 travel in Portugal the cost is from €69/48 for three days to €124/103 for eight days. There's also a 1st-class option. Both passes are available to anyone resident in Europe for six months before starting their travels. You cannot use either one in your home country.

The Eurail pass and the Eurail Selectpass (both for non-European residents) are meant to be purchased from your home country but are available at a higher price from some European locations. The Eurail pass is valid for unlimited travel (1st/2nd class for those over/under 26) in 17 European countries, including Portugal. It's good for 15 days (US$588/414) to up to three months (US$1654/1160); various 'flexi' versions allow a chosen number of travel days per longer period. The Eurail Selectpass allows you to travel between three, four or five of your chosen Eurail countries (they must be directly connected by Eurail transport). You can choose from five to 10 travelling days (or up to 15 for five countries), which can be taken at any point within a two-month period. Three countries cost US$356/249 for five days, and up to US$542/379 for 10 days, while five countries cost US$438/307 for five days up to an increased total of fifteen days for US$794/556. For both these passes, there is also a 'Saver' option for those travelling in a group. For details on both of these passes see www.eurail.com.

The Iberic Rail Pass, available only to non-European residents, is also good for a specified period of 1st-class travel in Spain and Portugal during a two-month period, from three days (adult/saver US$249/219) to 10 days (US$494/429).

CONTINENTAL EUROPE

France

The daily train journey from Paris (Gare d'Austerlitz) to Lisbon takes 20 hours. A 2nd-class adult (Apex), under-26 ticket costs around €193 return for a couchette on the overnight Irún–Lisbon section. You can book directly with **SNCF** (French Railways; www.sncf.com).

Spain

The daily Paris–Lisbon train goes via Vitória, Burgos, Valladolid and Salamanca, entering Portugal at Vila Formoso. A 2nd-class one-way reserved seat from Salamanca to Lisbon costs €50.80.

The main Spain–Portugal rail route is from Madrid to Lisbon via Cáceres and the border station of Marvão-Beirã. The nightly journey on the *Talgo Lusitânia* takes 10½ hours. A 2nd-class one-way reserved seat costs €53; add on €74 for a berth in a four-person compartment or €93 in a two-person compartment.

The Badajoz–Caia–Elvas–Lisbon route (€10.20, five hours), with two regional trains a day with a change at Entroncamento, is tedious, though the scenery through the Serra de Marvão is grand. Onward Seville–Badajoz connections are by bus.

In the south, trains run west from Seville only as far as Huelva, followed by bus connections. You're better off on a bus.

UK

The fastest and most convenient route to Portugal is with Eurostar from London Waterloo to Paris via the Channel Tunnel, and then onward by *TGV* (opposite).

SEA

There are no scheduled seagoing ferries to Portugal, but many to Spain. For details on those from the UK to Spain, see Car & Motorcycle (p469).

The closest North African ferry connections are from Morocco to Spain. See **Transmediterranea** (www.trasmediterranea.net), **Euro Ferrys** (www.euroferrys.com), and **FerriMaroc** (www.ferrimaroc.com). Car ferries also run from Tangier to Gibraltar.

For details on car ferries across the Rio Guadiana from Spain, see p166.

GETTING AROUND

Note that a helpful website for schedules and prices to help you to plan your trip is www.transpor.pt.

AIR

Airlines in Portugal

Flights within mainland Portugal are expensive, and for the short distances involved, not really worth considering. Nonetheless, **PGA Portugália Airlines** (☎ 218 425 559; www.flypga.com) and **TAP Air Portugal** (☎ 707 205 700; www.tap.pt) both have multiple daily Lisbon–Porto and Lisbon–Faro flights (taking under one hour) year-round. For Porto to Faro, change in Lisbon. A high-season one-way fare (including taxes) costs around €130 for the Lisbon–Porto route or €130 for the Lisbon–Faro route, and €168 for Porto–Faro.

BICYCLE

Mountain biking is hugely popular in Portugal, although there are few dedicated bicycle paths (p115). Possible itineraries are numerous in the mountainous national/natural parks of the north (especially Parque Nacional da Peneda-Gerês), along the coast or across the Alentejo plains. Coastal trips are easiest from north to south, with the prevailing winds. More demanding is the Serra da Estrela (which serves as the Tour de Portugal's 'mountain run'). You could also try the Serra do Marão between Amarante and Vila Real.

Local bike clubs organise regular Passeio BTT trips; check their flyers at rental agencies, bike shops and turismos. Guided trips are often available in popular tourist destinations; see individual listings. For jaunts arranged from abroad, see Tours (p475).

Cobbled roads in some old-town centres may jar your teeth loose if your tyres aren't fat enough – at least 38mm in diameter.

Documents

If you're cycling around Portugal on your own bike, proof of ownership and a written description and photograph of it will help police in case it's stolen.

Information

For listings of events and bike shops, buy the bimonthly Portuguese-language *Bike Magazine,* available from larger newsagents.

For its members, the UK-based **Cyclists' Touring Club** (CTC; ☎ 0870 873 0060; www.ctc.org.uk) publishes useful and free information on cycling in Portugal, plus notes for half a dozen routes around the country. It also offers tips, maps, topoguides and other publications by mail order.

Rental

There are numerous places to rent bikes, especially in the Algarve and other touristy areas. Prices range from €7 to €15 per day. Rental outfits are noted in the text.

Transporting Your Bicycle

Boxed-up or bagged-up bicycles can be taken free on all *regional* and *interregional* trains as accompanied baggage. They can also go, unboxed, on a few suburban services on weekends or for a small charge outside the rush hour. Most domestic bus lines won't accept bikes.

BOAT

Other than river cruises along the Rio Douro from Porto (p380) and the Rio Tejo from

Lisbon, Portugal's only remaining waterborne transport is cross-river ferries. Commuter ferries include those across the Rio Tejo to/from Lisbon (p113), and across the mouth of the Rio Sado (p141).

BUS

A host of small private bus operators, most of them amalgamated into regional companies, operate a dense network of services across the country. Included among the largest companies are **Rede Expressos** (☎ 707 223 344; www.rede-expressos.pt), **Rodonorte** (www.rodonorte.pt) and the Algarve line **Eva** (www.eva-bus.com).

Bus services are of three general types: *expressos* are comfortable, fast buses between major cities, *rápidas* are quick regional buses, and *carreiras* – marked CR – stop at every crossroad (never mind that *carreiras* means something like 'in a hurry' in Portuguese). Some companies also offer a fast deluxe category called *alta qualidade.*

Even in summer you'll have little problem booking an *expresso* ticket for the same or next day. A Lisbon–Faro express bus takes four hours and costs €14.50; Lisbon–Porto takes 3½ hours for €13 or more. By contrast, local services, especially up north, can thin out to almost nothing on weekends, especially in summer when school is out.

An under-26 card should get you a discount of around 20%, at least on the long-distance services. Senior travellers can often get up to 50% off.

Don't rely on turismos for accurate timetable information. Most bus-station ticket desks will give you a little computer printout of fares and all services.

CAR & MOTORCYCLE

Portugal's modest network of *estradas* (highways) is gradually spreading across the country. Main roads are sealed and generally in good condition. And if you choose to pootle around on lesser roads you'll find most of the roads empty.

The downside is your fellow drivers. A leading Swedish road-safety investigator was quoted as saying the Portuguese 'drive like car thieves' and the prime minister described what happens on Portugal's major highways as 'civil war'. The country's per-

ROAD DISTANCES (KM)

	Aveiro	Beja	Braga	Bragança	Castelo Branco	Coimbra	Évora	Faro	Guarda	Leiria	Lisbon	Portalegre	Porto	Santarém	Setúbal	Viana do Castelo	Vila Real	Viseu
Aveiro	---																	
Beja	383	---																
Braga	129	504	---															
Bragança	287	566	185	---														
Castelo Branco	239	271	366	299	---													
Coimbra	60	329	178	314	191	---												
Évora	305	78	426	488	191	251	---											
Faro	522	166	643	732	437	468	244	---										
Guarda	163	369	260	197	102	161	291	535	---									
Leiria	126	273	244	402	179	72	195	412	233	---								
Lisbon	256	183	372	530	264	202	138	296	402	146	---							
Portalegre	276	178	403	390	93	222	100	344	193	172	219	---						
Porto	71	446	58	216	308	123	368	585	202	189	317	339	---					
Santarém	188	195	309	464	181	134	117	346	295	78	80	147	251	---				
Setúbal	299	143	420	575	316	246	105	256	406	189	47	186	362	123	---			
Viana do Castelo	144	519	56	241	382	191	441	658	275	262	387	412	73	324	435	---		
Vila Real	169	528	94	120	261	199	450	683	159	282	412	352	98	349	460	150	---	
Viseu	86	415	185	228	177	86	366	554	75	158	288	268	127	220	331	241	113	---

capita death rate from road accidents has long been one of Europe's highest – and drinking, driving and dying are hot political potatoes.

A tough law in 2001 dropped the legal blood-alcohol level to the equivalent of a single glass of wine. But the law was suspended months later following intense pressure from – you guessed it – Portugal's wine producers. Even the present limit of 0.5g/L is pretty stringent, plus there are fines up to €2500.

The good news is that 2003 saw a 10% decrease in road-death rates thanks to a zero-tolerance police crackdown on accident-prone routes and alcohol limits.

Driving can be tricky in Portugal's small walled towns, where roads may taper down to donkey-cart size before you know it, and fiendish one-way systems can force you out of your way.

Parking is often metered within city centres, but free Saturday evening and Sunday. However, car parks in central Lisbon can cost as much as €10 per day.

A common sight in larger towns is the down-and-outers who lurk around squares and car parks, wave you into the parking space you've just found for yourself, and ask for payment for this service. Of course it's a racket and of course there's no need to give them anything, but the Portuguese often do, and €0.20 might keep your car out of trouble.

For information on what to bring in the way of documents, see p469.

Accidents

If you are involved in a minor 'fender-bender' with no injuries, the easiest way for drivers to sort things out with their insurance companies is to fill out a Constat Aimable (the English version is called a European Accident Statement). There's no risk in signing this: it's just a way to exchange the relevant information and there's usually one included in rental-car documents. Make sure it includes any details that may help you prove that the accident was not your fault. To alert the police, dial ☎ 112.

Assistance

Automóvel Club de Portugal (ACP; Map pp80-1; ☎ 213 180 202; www.acp.pt in Portuguese; Rua Rosa Araújo 24, Lisbon), Portugal's national auto club, provides medical, legal and breakdown assistance for its members. Road information and maps are available to anyone at ACP offices, including the head office in Lisbon and branches at Aveiro, Braga, Bragança, Coimbra, Évora, Faro, Porto and elsewhere.

If your national auto club belongs to the Fédération Internationale de l'Automobile or the Alliance Internationale de Tourisme, you can also use ACP's emergency services and get discounts on maps and other products. Among clubs that qualify are the AA and RAC in the UK, and the Australian, New Zealand, Canadian and American Automobile Associations.

The 24-hour emergency help number is ☎ 707 509 510.

Fuel

Fuel is expensive – about €1.06 for a litre of *sem chumbo* (unleaded petrol) at the time of writing. There are plenty of self-service stations, and credit cards are accepted at most.

Highways & Toll-roads

Top of the range are *auto-estradas* (motorways), all of them *portagens* (toll-roads); the longest of these are Lisbon–Porto and Lisbon–Algarve. Toll-roads charge cars and motorcycles around €0.06 per kilometre (eg total €17.60 for Lisbon–Porto or €6.25 for Lisbon–Setúbal).

Nomenclature can be baffling. Motorway numbers prefixed with an E are Europe-wide designations. Portugal's toll-roads are prefixed with an A. Highways in the country's main network are prefixed IP *(itinerário principal)* and subsidiary ones IC *(itinerário complementar)*. Some highways have several designations, and numbers that change in mid-flow.

Numbers for the main two-lane *estradas nacionais* (national roads) have no prefix letter on some road maps, while on other maps, they're prefixed by N. If you want to get off the big roads, consider going for the really small ones, which tend to be prettier and more peaceful.

Motorail

Caminhos de Ferro Portugueses (CP; ☎ 808 208 208, www.cp.pt; 7am-11pm), which is the state railway company, offers car transport by rail with certain services on the Lisbon–Porto,

Lisbon–Guarda, Lisbon–Castelo Branco and Porto–Faro lines.

Rental

To rent a car in Portugal you must be at least 25 years old and have held your driving licence for over a year (some companies allow younger drivers at higher rates). The widest choice of car-hire companies is at Lisbon, Porto and Faro airports. Competition has driven Algarve rates lower than elsewhere.

Some of the best advance-booking rates are offered by Internet-based brokers such as **Holiday Autos** (www.holidayautos.com). Other bargains come as part of 'fly-drive' packages. The worst deals tend to be those done with international firms on arrival, though their prepaid promotional rates are competitive. Book at least a few days ahead in high season. For on-the-spot rental, domestic firms such as **Auto Jardim** (www.auto-jardim.com) have the best rates.

Renting the smallest and cheapest available car for a week in the high season costs as little as UK£125 (with tax, insurance and unlimited mileage) if booked from abroad, and a similar amount through a Portuguese firm. It can cost up to €400 if you book through Portuguese branches of international firms such as Hertz, Europcar and Aviz.

For an additional fee you can get personal insurance through the rental company, unless you're covered by your home policy (see p469). A minimum of third-party coverage is compulsory in the EU.

Rental cars are especially at risk of break-ins or petty theft in larger towns, so don't leave anything of value visible in the car. If you can unscrew the radio antenna, leave it inside the car at night; and put the wheel covers (hubcaps) in the boot (trunk) for the duration of your trip.

Motorcycles and scooters can be rented in larger cities, and all over coastal Algarve. Expect to pay from €30/60 per day for a scooter/motorcycle.

Road Rules

You may not believe it after seeing the antics of Portuguese drivers, but there are rules. To begin with, driving is on the right, overtaking is on the left and most signs use international symbols. An important rule to remember is that traffic from the right usually has priority. Portugal has lots of ambiguously marked intersections, so this is more important than you might think.

Except when marked otherwise, speed limits for cars (without a trailer) and motorcycles (without a sidecar) are 50km/h in towns and villages, 90km/h outside built-up areas and 120km/h on motorways. By law, car safety belts must be worn in the front and back seats, and children under 12 years may not ride in the front. Motorcyclists and their passengers must wear helmets, and motorcycles must have their headlights on day and night.

The police can impose steep on-the-spot fines for speeding and parking offences, so save yourself a big hassle and remember to toe the line.

HITCHING

Hitching is never entirely safe anywhere, and we don't recommend it. In any case it isn't an easy option in Portugal. Almost nobody stops on major highways, and on smaller roads drivers tend to be going short distances so you may only advance from one field to the next.

LOCAL TRANSPORT

Bus

Except in Lisbon or Porto there's little reason to take municipal buses, as most attractions are within walking distance. Most areas have regional bus services, for better or worse (see p472).

Metro

Both Lisbon and Porto now have ambitious underground systems that are still growing (see p116 and p367).

Taxi

Taxis offer pretty good value over short distances, and are plentiful in large towns and cities. Ordinary taxis are usually marked A (which stands for *aluguer*, for hire) on the door, number plate or elsewhere. They use meters and are available on the street and at taxi ranks, or by telephone for a surcharge of €0.75.

The fare on weekdays during daylight hours is about €1.90 *bandeirada* (flag fall) plus around €0.40 per kilometre, and a bit more for periods spent idling in traffic. A fare of €3 will usually get you across big-

TRANSPORT

ger towns. It's best to insist on the meter, although it's possible to negotiate a flat fare. If you have a sizable load of luggage you'll pay a further €1.50.

Rates are about 20% higher at night (9pm to 6am), on weekends and holidays. Once a taxi leaves the city limits you also pay a surcharge or higher rate.

In larger cities, including Lisbon and Porto, meterless taxis marked T (for turismo) can be hired from private companies for excursions. Rates for these are higher, but standardised; drivers are honest and polite, and speak foreign languages.

Trams

Enthusiasts for stately progress shouldn't miss the trams of Lisbon (p116) and Porto (p368), an endangered species.

TOURS

Lisbon-based **Gray Line** (☎ 213 191 090; www.grayline.com), Viana do Castelo's **AVIC** (☎ 258 806 180; www.avic.pt), Porto's **Diana Tours** (☎ 223 771 230; www.dianatours.pt), and the Algarves's **Mega Tur** (☎ 289 807 485; www.megatur.pt) all run bus tours.

Caminhos de Ferro Portugueses (CP; ☎ 808 208 208, www.cp.pt; 7am-11pm), the state railway company, organises weekend day trips up the Douro valley during almond-blossom time (p382).

Locally run adventure tours are noted under individual town listings.

If you prefer to assemble your own holiday, Portugal specialist **Destination Portugal** (www.destination-portugal.co.uk) will tell you all you need to know and can help with flights, car hire and accommodation, separately or together.

The following companies are all UK based, unless specified.

Cycling Tours

CTC (Cyclists' Touring Club; ☎ 0870 873 0060; www.ctc.org.uk) UK's biggest cycling club, with not-for-profit tours run by and for members.

Easy Rider Tours (☎ 978-463 6955, 800 488 8332; www.easyridertours.com) Based in the US and with a long menu of guided cycling and walking itineraries.

Rough Tracks (☎ 07000 560749; www.roughtracks.com) Offers one-week mountain-biking and road tours.

Saddle skedaddle (☎ 0191-265 1110; www.skedaddle.co.uk) Offers eight-day tours through isolated countryside.

Other Specialist Tours

3D Golf (☎ 0870 122 5050; www.3dgolf.com) Offers golfing packages in the Algarve.

Arblaster & Clarke (☎ 01730-893344; www.arblasterandclarke.com) Offers wine tours in the Douro.

Equitour (☎ 61 303 31 08; www.equitour.com) For riding holidays; Swiss based.

Martin Randall Travel (☎ 020-8742 3355; www.martinrandall.com) Cultural specialist that arranges first-rate escorted art and architecture tours.

Naturetrek (☎ 01962-733051; www.naturetrek.co.uk) Specialist in bird-watching and botanical tours, runs an eight-day excursion around southern Portugal.

Walking Tours

ATG Oxford (☎ 01865-315678; www.atg-oxford.co.uk) Guided walking holidays.

Headwater (☎ 01606-720099; www.headwater.com) Weeklong jaunts and self-guided tours.

Ramblers Holidays (☎ 01707-331133; www.ramblersholidays.co.uk) Guided walking holidays.

Sherpa Expeditions (☎ 020-8577 2717; www.sherpa-walking-holidays.co.uk) Good self-guided walks in the north.

Winetrails (☎ 01306-712111; www.winetrails.co.uk) Gentle rambles with fine wining and dining.

TRAIN

If you can match your itinerary and pace to a regional service, travelling with **Caminhos de Ferro Portugueses** (CP; ☎ 808 208 208, 7am-11pm; www.cp.pt), the state railway company, is cheaper than by bus. Trains are generally slower than long-distance buses, however.

Until main-line tracks are completed to Pinhal Novo, there is no direct rail link from Lisbon to the south of Portugal; for that you must first take a ferry across the Rio Tejo to Barreiro (p113).

Three of Portugal's most appealing old railway lines, on narrow-gauge tracks climbing out of the Douro valley, survive in truncated form: the Linha da Tâmega from Livração to Amarante (p375), the Linha da Corgo from Peso da Régua to Vila Real (p433) and the beautiful Linha da Tua from Tua to Mirandela (p447).

Discounts

Children under four travel free; those aged four to 12 go for half-price. A Euro26 card gets you a 30% discount on *regional* and *interrgional* services on any day, and on *intercidade* services from Monday noon to Friday noon. Travellers aged 65 and over

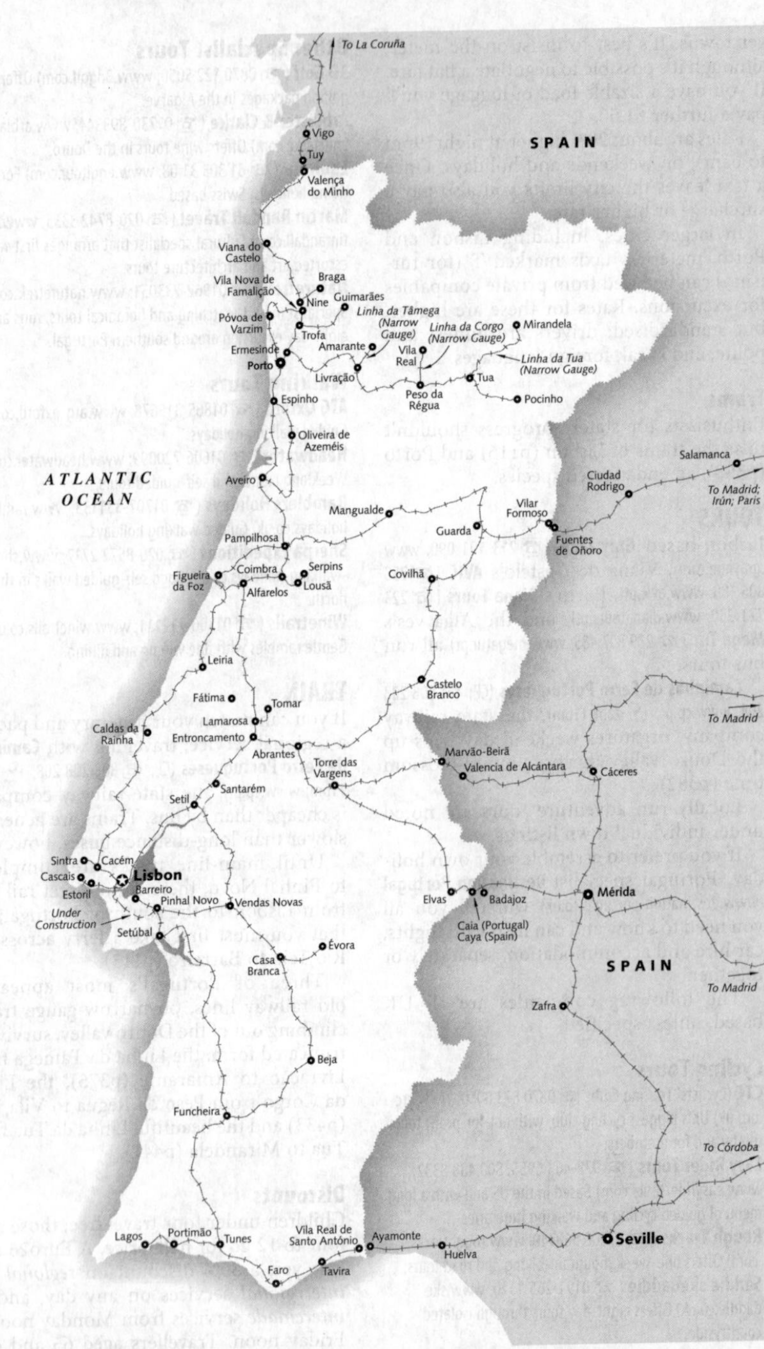

To La Coruña
SPAIN
Vigo
Tuy
Valença do Minho
Viana do Castelo
Braga
Vila Nova de Famalição
Guimarães
Nine
Linha da Tâmega (Narrow Gauge)
Póvoa de Varzim
Trofa
Linha da Corgo (Narrow Gauge)
Mirandela
Ermesinde
Amarante
Vila Real
Linha da Tua (Narrow Gauge)
Porto
Livração
Tua
Peso da Régua
Pocinho
Espinho
Oliveira de Azeméis
Salamanca
Ciudad Rodrigo
To Madrid; Irún; Paris
ATLANTIC OCEAN
Aveiro
Mangualde
Vilar Formoso
Guarda
Fuentes de Oñoro
Pampilhosa
Coimbra
Serpins
Figueira da Foz
Lousã
Alfarelos
Covilhã
Leiria
Castelo Branco
Fátima
Tomar
Lamarosa
To Madrid
Caldas da Rainha
Entroncamento
Abrantes
Marvão-Beirã
Valencia de Alcántara
Torre das Vargens
Cáceres
Santarém
Setil
Sintra
Cacém
Cascais
Lisbon
Estoril
Barreiro
Pinhal Novo
Vendas Novas
Under Construction
Elvas
Badajoz
Mérida
Caia (Portugal)
Caya (Spain)
Setúbal
Évora
Casa Branca
SPAIN
To Madrid
Zafra
Beja
Funcheira
To Córdoba
Lagos
Portimão
Tunes
Vila Real de Santo António
Ayamonte
Huelva
Seville
Faro
Tavira

can get 50% off any service by showing some ID.

Information & Reservations

Timetable and fare information is available at all stations and from CP (p475). You can book *intercidade* and Alfa tickets up to 30 days ahead, though you'll have little problem booking for the next or even the same day. Other services can only be booked 24 hours in advance. A seat reservation is mandatory on most *intercidade* and Alfa trains and the booking fee is included in the ticket price.

Types & Classes of Service

There are three main types of long-distance service: *regional* trains (marked R on timetables), which stop everywhere; reasonably fast *interregional* (IR) trains; and express trains, called *rápido* or *intercidade* (IC). Alfa Pendular is a deluxe, marginally faster and pricier IC service on the Lisbon–Coimbra–Porto main line. International services are marked IN on timetables.

Lisbon and Porto have their own *suburbano* (suburban) train networks. Lisbon's network extends predictably to Sintra, Cascais, Setúbal and up the lower Tejo Valley. Porto's network takes the definition of 'suburban' to new lengths, running all the way to Braga, Guimarães and Aveiro. There are also *suburbano* services travelling between Coimbra and Figueira da Foz. The distinction matters where long-distance services parallel the more convenient, plentiful, and considerably cheaper, *suburbanos*.

Only the Faro–Porto *Comboio Azul* and international trains like *Sud-Expresso* and *Talgo Lusitânia* have restaurant cars, though all IC and Alfa trains have aisle service and most have bars. There's a nonsmoking section somewhere on every CP train.

Train Passes

The Portuguese Railpass (US$105) gives you unlimited 1st-class travel on any four days out of 15. This is only available to travellers from outside Europe, and must be purchased before you arrive; contact **Rail Europe** (www.raileurope.com).

Special CP *bilhetes turísticos* (tourist tickets), valid for unlimited travel during seven/14/21 consecutive days, cost €110/187/275 (half-price for those aged under 12 or over 65), and are on sale at major stations. For information on other rail passes, see p470.

Health

CONTENTS

BEFORE YOU GO

Prevention is the key to staying healthy while abroad. A little planning before departure, particularly for pre-existing illnesses, will save trouble later. See your dentist before a long trip, carry a spare pair of contact lenses and glasses, and take your optical prescription with you. Bring medications in their original, clearly labelled, containers. A signed and dated letter from your physician describing your medical conditions and medications, including generic names, is also a good idea. If carrying syringes or needles, be sure to have a physician's letter documenting their medical necessity.

INSURANCE

If you're an EU citizen, an E111 form, available from health centres or, in the UK, post offices, covers you for most medical care. E111 will not cover you for nonemergencies or emergency repatriation. Citizens from other countries should find out if there is a reciprocal arrangement for free medical care between their country and the country visited. If you do need health insurance, strongly consider a policy that covers you for the worst possible scenario, such as an accident requiring an emergency flight home. Find out in advance if your insurance plan will make payments directly to providers or reimburse you later for overseas health expenditures. The former option is generally preferable, as it doesn't require you to pay out of pocket in a foreign country.

> **TRAVEL HEALTH WEBSITES**
>
> It's usually a good idea to consult your government's travel health website before departure, if one is available:
>
> **Australia** (www.smartraveller.gov.au)
> **Canada** (www.hc-sc.gc.ca/english/index.html)
> **UK** (www.doh.gov.uk)
> **United States** (www.cdc.gov/travel)

RECOMMENDED VACCINATIONS

The WHO recommends that all travellers should be covered for diphtheria, tetanus, measles, mumps, rubella and polio, regardless of their destination. Since most vaccines don't produce immunity until at least two weeks after they're given, visit a physician at least six weeks before departure.

INTERNET RESOURCES

The WHO's publication *International Travel and Health* is revised annually and is available on line at www.who.int/ith. Other useful websites include www.mdtravelhealth.com (travel health recommendations for every country; updated daily), www.fitfortravel.scot.nhs.uk (general travel advice for the layperson), www.ageconcern.org.uk (advice on travel for the elderly) and www.mariestopes.org.uk (information on women's health and contraception).

IN PORTUGAL

AVAILABILITY & COST OF HEALTH CARE

Good health care is readily available and for minor illnesses pharmacists can give valuable advice and sell over-the-counter medication. They can also advise when more specialised help is required and point you in the right direction. The standard of dental care is usually good, but it is sensible to have a dental check-up before a long trip.

TRAVELLER'S DIARRHOEA

If you develop diarrhoea, be sure to drink plenty of fluids, preferably an oral rehydration solution (eg Dioralyte). A few loose stools don't require treatment, but if you start having more than four or five stools a day, you should start taking an antibiotic (usually a quinolone drug) and an antidiarrhoeal agent (such as Loperamide). If diarrhoea is bloody, persists for more than 72 hours or is accompanied by fever, shaking, chills or severe abdominal pain you should seek medical attention.

ENVIRONMENTAL HAZARDS

Heat Exhaustion & Heat Stroke

Heat exhaustion occurs following excessive fluid loss with inadequate replacement of fluids and salt. Symptoms include headache, dizziness and tiredness. Dehydration is already happening by the time you feel thirsty – aim to drink sufficient water to produce pale, diluted urine. To treat heat exhaustion, replace lost fluids by drinking water and/or fruit juice, and cool the body with cold water and fans. Treat salt loss with salty fluids such as soup or Bovril, or add a little more table salt to foods than usual.

Heat stroke is much more serious, resulting in irrational and hyperactive behaviour and eventually loss of consciousness and death. Rapid cooling by spraying the body with water and fanning is ideal. Emergency fluid and electrolyte replacement by intravenous drip is recommended.

Insect Bites & Stings

Mosquitoes are found in most parts of Europe. They may not carry malaria but can cause irritation and infected bites. Use a DEET-based insect repellent.

Bees and wasps cause real problems only to those with a severe allergy (anaphylaxis). If you have a severe allergy to bee or wasp stings carry an 'epipen' or similar adrenaline injection.

Sand flies are found around Mediterranean beaches. They usually cause only a nasty itchy bite but can carry a rare skin disorder called cutaneous leishmaniasis.

Bed bugs lead to very itchy, lumpy bites. Spraying the mattress with crawling insect killer after changing bedding will get rid of them.

Scabies are tiny mites that live in the skin, particularly between the fingers. They cause an intensely itchy rash. Scabies is easily treated with lotion from a pharmacy; other members of the household also need treating to avoid spreading scabies between asymptomatic carriers.

Snake Bites

Avoid getting bitten – do not walk barefoot or stick your hand into holes or cracks. Half of those bitten by venomous snakes are not actually injected with poison (envenomed). If bitten by a snake, do not panic. Immobilise the bitten limb with a splint (eg a stick) and apply a bandage over the site firmly, similar to a bandage over a sprain. Do not apply a tourniquet, or cut or suck the bite. Get the victim to medical help as soon as possible so that antivenin can be given if necessary.

Jellyfish, Sea Urchins & Weever Fish

Stings from jellyfish can be painful but are not dangerous. Dousing in vinegar will deactivate any stingers which haven't 'fired'. Calamine lotion, antihistamines or analgesics may reduce the reaction and relieve the pain.

Watch for sea urchins around rocky beaches. If you get their needles embedded in your skin, immersing the limb in hot water will relieve the pain. But to avoid infection you should visit a doctor to have the needles removed.

Thankfully it is very rare to find the dangerous weever fish that inhabit shallow tidal zones along the Atlantic coast. They bury themselves in the sand with their spines protruding and inject a powerful toxin if trodden upon. Soaking the foot in very hot water breaks down the poison, but you should seek medical advice in any case, since in rare cases this can cause permanent local paralysis.

TRAVELLING WITH CHILDREN

All travellers with small children should know how to treat minor ailments and when to seek medical treatment. Make sure the children are up to date with routine vaccinations, and discuss possible travel vaccines with your doctor well before departure as some vaccines are not suitable for children under a year.

In hot moist climates any wound or break in the skin is likely to let in infection. The area should be cleaned and kept dry.

Remember to avoid contaminated food and water. If your child has vomiting or diarrhoea, lost fluid and salts must be replaced. It may be helpful to take rehydration powders for reconstituting with boiled water.

Children should be encouraged to avoid and mistrust any dogs or other mammals because of the risk of rabies and other diseases. Any bite, scratch or lick from a warm blooded, furry animal should immediately be thoroughly cleaned. If there is any possibility that the animal is infected with rabies, immediate medical assistance should be sought.

WOMEN'S HEALTH

Travelling during pregnancy is usually possible but always consult your doctor before planning your trip. The most risky times for travel are during the first 12 weeks of pregnancy and after 30 weeks.

SEXUAL HEALTH

Emergency contraception is most effective if taken within 24 hours after unprotected sex. The **International Planned Parent Federation** (www.ippf.org) can advise about the availability of contraception in different countries.

When buying condoms, look for a European CE mark, which means they have been rigorously tested, and then store them in a cool and dry place or they may crack and perish.

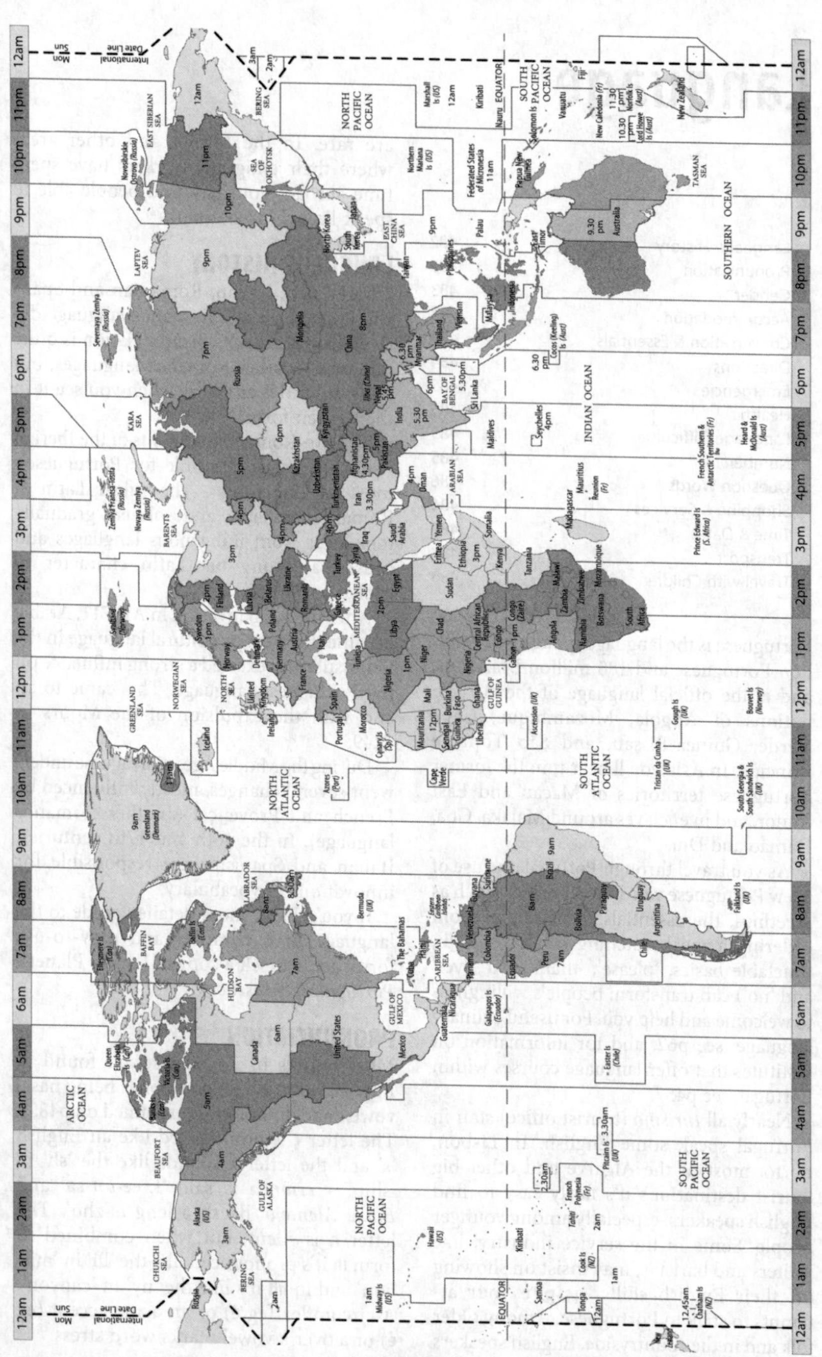
12am
1am
2am
3am
4am
5am
6am
7am
8am
9am
10am
11am
12pm
1pm
2pm
3pm
4pm
5pm
6pm
7pm
8pm
9pm
10pm
11pm
12am
International Date Line
Mon
Sun
ARCTIC OCEAN
NORTH PACIFIC OCEAN
NORTH ATLANTIC OCEAN
SOUTH ATLANTIC OCEAN
INDIAN OCEAN
SOUTH PACIFIC OCEAN
SOUTHERN OCEAN
EQUATOR
MEDITERRANEAN SEA
GULF OF MEXICO
CARIBBEAN SEA
GULF OF GUINEA
ARABIAN SEA
BAY OF BENGAL
TASMAN SEA
BERING SEA
United States
Canada
Mexico
Brazil
Russia
China
India
Australia
Mongolia
Kazakhstan
Greenland (Denmark)
New Zealand

Language

CONTENTS

Portuguese is the language spoken by 10 million Portuguese and 180 million Brazilians, and is the official language of the African nations of Angola, Mozambique, Cape Verde, Guinea-Bissau, and São Tomé e Príncipe. In Asia you'll hear it in the former Portuguese territories of Macau and East Timor, and in enclaves around Malaka, Goa, Damão and Diu.

As you travel through Portugal, the use of a few Portuguese words and phrases (such as greetings, the essentials of getting a room ordering a meal, catching a bus or train, timetable basics, 'please', 'thank you', 'yes' and 'no') can transform people's willingness to welcome and help you. For useful culinary language, see p62, and for information on institutes that offer language courses within Portugal, see p457.

Nearly all *turismo* (tourist office) staff in Portugal speak some English. In Lisbon, Porto, most of the Algarve and other big tourist destinations it's fairly easy to find English speakers, especially among younger people. Some in the service industry, like waiters and baristas, may insist on showing off their English skills, despite your attempts to stick to Portuguese. Among older folk and in the countryside, English speakers are rare. In the Minho and other areas where their emigrant workers have spent time abroad, you may find people able to speak French or German.

LANGUAGE HISTORY

Like French, Italian, Romanian and Spanish, Portuguese is a Romance language derived from Latin. Its pronunciation is quite different to other Romance languages, but the similarities are clear when you see it in the written form.

The pre-Roman inhabitants of the Iberian Peninsula are responsible for Portuguese's most striking traits – the vulgar Latin of Roman merchants and soldiers gradually took over from indigenous languages and caused a strong neo-Latin character to evolve.

After the Arab invasion in AD 711, Arabic became the prestige cultural language in the Peninsula and exerted a strong influence on the Portuguese language. This came to an end with the expulsion of the Moors in 1249.

During the Middle Ages, Portuguese underwent several changes, mostly influenced by French and Provençal (another Romance language). In the 16th and 17th centuries, Italian and Spanish were responsible for innovations in vocabulary.

If you'd like a more detailed guide to the language in a compact and easy-to-use form, get yourself a copy of Lonely Planet's *Portuguese Phrasebook*.

PRONUNCIATION

Most sounds in Portuguese are found in English, with the toughest ones being nasal vowels and diphthongs (explained on p483). The letter **ç** is pronounced like an English 's' and the letter **x** sounds like the 'sh' in 'ship' – *criança* is said 'kree-*an*-sa' and *Baixe Alentejo* 'baysh a-leng-*te*-zho'. The letter **h** is silent, but when combined to form **lh** it's pronounced like the 'lli' in 'million' and in **nh** it's like the 'ny' in 'canyon'. A circumflex (eg **ê**) or an acute accent (eg **é**) or a over a vowel marks word stress.

Vowels

In this pronunciation guide, we've used the following symbols for vowel sounds.

a as the 'u' in 'run'
ai as in 'aisle'
aw as in 'saw'
ay as in 'day'
e as in 'bet'
ee as in 'bee'
o as in 'go'
oo as in 'moon'
ow as in 'how'
oy as in 'boy'

Nasal Sounds

A characteristic feature of Portuguese is the use of nasal vowels and diphthongs (vowel combinations). Pronounce them as if you're trying to make the sound through your nose rather than your mouth. English also has nasal vowels to some extent – when you say 'sing' in English, the 'i' is nasalized by the 'ng'. In Portuguese, written vowels that have a nasal consonant after them (**m** or **n**), or a tilde over them (eg **ã**), will be nasal. In our pronunciation guide, we've used 'ng' to indicate a nasal sound.

Consonants

These symbols represent the trickier consonant sounds in Portuguese.

ly as the 'lli' in 'million'
ny as in 'canyon'
r as in 'run'
rr as in 'run' but stronger and rolled
zh as the 's' in 'pleasure'

Word Stress

Stress generally falls on the second last syllable of a word, though there are exceptions. When a word ends in **-r** or is pronounced with a nasalized vowel, the stress falls on the last syllable. Vowels marked with an accent are always stressed.

In our transliteration system, we've shown the stressed syllable with italics.

GENDER

Portuguese has masculine and feminine forms of nouns and adjectives. Alternative endings appear separated by a slash with the masculine form first. Generally, a word ending in **o** is masculine and one ending in **a** is feminine.

ACCOMMODATION

I'm looking for a ...
Procuro ... — proo·*koo*·roo·...

Where's a ...?
Onde é ...? — ongd e ...

bed and breakfast
um turismo de habitação — *oong* too·*reezh*·moo de a·bee·ta·*sowng*

camping ground
um parque de campismo — oong park·de kang·*peezh*·moo

guesthouse
uma pensão — *oo*·ma peng·*sowng*

hotel
um hotel — oong oo·*tel*

youth hostel
um pousada da juventude — oong po·*za*·da da zhoo·*veng*·tood

room
um quarto — oong *kwarr*·too

I'd like a ... room.
Queria um quarto de ... — *kree*·a oong *kwarr*·too de ...

Do you have a ... room?
Tem um quarto de ...? — teng oong *kwarr*·too de ...

double
casal — ka·*zal*

single
individual — ing·dee·vee·*dwal*

twin
duplo — *doo*·ploo

For (three) nights.
Para (três) noites. — *pa*·ra (trezh) noytsh

Does it include breakfast?
Inclui pequeno almoço? — eeng·kloo·*ee* pee·*ke*·noo al·*mo*·soo

May I see it?
Posso ver? — *po*·soo verr

I'll take the room.
Fico com ele. — *fee*·koo kom *e*·lee

I don't like it.
Não gosto. — nowng *gos*·too

I'm leaving now.
Estou indo embora agora. — shto *een*·doo em·*bo*·ra a·*go*·ra

How much is it per ...?
Quanto custa por ...? — *kwang*·too *koos*·ta porr ...

night
uma noite — *oo*·ma noyt

person
pessoa — *pso*·a

week
uma semana — *oo*·ma se·*ma*·na

MAKING A RESERVATION

(for phone or written requests)

To ...	*Para ...*
From ...	*De ...*
Date	*Data*
I'd like to book ...	*Queria fazer uma reserva ...* (see the list under 'Accommodation' for bed/room options)
in the name of ...	*no nome de ...*
for the nights of ...	*para os dias ...*
from ... to ...	*de ... até ...*
credit card ...	*cartão de credito ...*
number	*número*
expiry date	*data de vencimento*

Please confirm availability/price.
Por favor confirme a disponibilidade/o preço.

CONVERSATION & ESSENTIALS

Hello.
Bom dia. — bong *dee*·a

Hi.
Olá. — o·*la*

Good day.
Bom dia. — bong *dee*·a

Good evening.
Boa noite. — *bo*·a noyt

See you later.
Até logo. — a·*te lo*·goo

Goodbye.
Adeus. — a·*dyoos*

How are you?
Como está? — *ko*·moo shta

Fine, and you?
Tudo bem, e tu? — *too*·doo beng e too

I'm pleased to meet you.
Prazer em conhecê-lo/-la. (m/f) — pra·*zerr* eng ko·nye·*se*·loo/la

Yes.
Sim. — seeng

No.
Não. — nowng

Please.
Faz favor. — fash fa·*vorr*

Thank you (very much).
(Muito) Obrigado/a. (m/f) — (*mweeng*·too) o·bree·*ga*·doo/da

You're welcome.
De nada. — de *na*·da

Excuse me. (to get past)
Com licença. — kong lee·*seng*·sa

Excuse me. (before asking a question/making a request)
Desculpe. — des·*koolp*

What's your name?
Como se chama? — *ko*·moo se *sha*·ma

My name is ...
Chamo-me ... — *sha*·moo·me ...

Where are you from?
De onde é? — de *ong*·de e

I'm from ...
Sou (da/do/de) ... — so (da/do/de) ...

May I take a photo (of you)?
Posso tirar-lhe uma foto? — *po*·soo tee·*rarr*·lye oo·ma *fo*·too

DIRECTIONS

Where's ...?
Onde fica ...? — ongd *fee*·ka ...

Can you show me (on the map)?
Pode mostrar-me (no mapa)? — pod moos·*trarrm* (noo *ma*·pa)

What's the address?
Qual é a morada? — kwal e a moo·*ra*·da

How far is it?
Qual a distância daqui? — kwal a dees·*tan*·see·a da·*kee*

How do I get there?
Como é que eu chego ali? — *ko*·moo e ke e·oo *she*·goo a·*lee*

SIGNS

Posto de Polícia	Police Station
Pronto Socorro	Emergency Department
Aberto	Open
Encerrado	Closed
Fechado	Closed
Entrada	Entrance
Saída	Exit
Não Fumadores	No Smoking
Lavabos/WC	Toilet
Homens (H)	Men
Senhoras (S)	Women

Turn ...	*Vire ...*	veer ...
at the corner	*na esquina*	na *skee*·na
at the traffic lights	*no semáforo*	noo *sma*·foo·roo
left	*à esquerda*	a *skerr*·da
right	*à direita*	a dee·*ray*·ta
here	*aqui*	a·*kee*
there	*ali*	a·*lee*
near ...	*perto ...*	*perr*·too ...
straight ahead	*em frente*	eng frengt

north	*norte*	nort
south	*sul*	sool
east	*este*	esht
west	*oeste*	oo·*esht*

EMERGENCIES

Help!
Socorro! soo·*ko*·rroo
It's an emergency.
É uma emergência. e *oo*·ma e·merr·*zheng*·sya
I'm lost.
Estou perdido/a. (m/f) shto perr·*dee*·doo/da
Where are the toilets?
Onde ficam os lavabos? *ong*·de *fee*·kam oos la·*va*·boos
Go away!
Vai-te embora! vai·te eng·*bo*·ra

Call ...!
Chame ...! *sham* ...
a doctor
um médico oong *me*·dee·koo
an ambulance
uma ambulância *oo*·ma am·boo·*lan*·sya
the police
a polícia a poo·lee·*see*·a

HEALTH

I'm ill.
Estou doente. shto doo·*engt*
I need a doctor (who speaks English).
Preciso de um médico (que fale inglês). pre·*see*·zoo de oong *me*·dee·koo (ke fal eeng·*glesh*)
It hurts here.
Aqui dói. a·*kee* doy
I've been vomiting.
Tenho estado a vomitar. *ta*·nyo *shta*·doo a voo·mee·*tarr*
(I think) I'm pregnant.
(Acho que) Estou grávida. (*a*·shoo ke) shto *gra*·vee·da

Where's the nearest ...?
Onde fica ...is perto? *on*·de *fee*·ka ... mais *perr*·to
dentist
o dentista oo deng·*teesh*·ta
doctor
o médico oo *me*·dee·koo
hospital
o hospital oo osh·pee·*tal*
medical centre
a clínica médica a *klee*·nee·ka *me*·dee·ka
(night) phramacist
a farmácia (de serviço) a farr·*ma*·see·a (der ser·*vee*·soo)

I feel ...
Estou ... shto ...
dizzy
com tonturas kong tong·*too*·ras
nauseous
com naúseas kong *now*·shas

asthma	*asma*	*azh*·ma
diarrhea	*diarréia*	dee·a·*ray*·a
fever	*febre*	febr
pain	*dores*	dorsh

I'm allergic to ...
Sou alérgico/a à ... so a·lerr·*zhee*·koo/ka a ...
antibiotics
antibióticos ang·tee·*byo*·tee·koos
aspirin
aspirina ash·pee·*ree*·na
bees
abelhas a·*be*·lyas
peanuts
amendoins a·meng·*doyngs*
penicillin
penicilina pnee·see·*lee*·na

antiseptic
antiséptico an·tee·*sep*·tee·koo
contraceptives
anticoncepcional an·tee·kon·*sep*·syoo·nal
painkillers
analgésicos a·nal·*zhe*·zee·koos

LANGUAGE DIFFICULTIES

Do you speak English?
Fala inglês? *fa*·la eeng·*glesh*
Does anyone here speak English?
Alguém aqui fala inglês? al·*geng* a·*kee* *fa*·la eeng·*glesh*
Do you understand?
Entende? eng·*tengd*
I (don't) understand.
(Não) Entendo. (nowng) eng·*teng*·doo

Could you please ...?
Pode por favor ...? *po*·de·porr fa·*vorr* ...
repeat that
repetir isso rrpe·*teerr* *ees*·soo
speak more slowly
falar mais devagar fa·*larr* maizh dva·*garr*
write it down
escrever num papel es·kre·*verr* noom pa·*pel*

NUMBERS

0	*zero*	*ze*·roo
1	*um/uma* (m/f)	oong/*oo*·ma

LANGUAGE

2	*dois/duas* (m/f)	doys/dwash
3	*três*	tresh
4	*quatro*	*kwa*·troo
5	*cinco*	*seeng*·koo
6	*seis*	saysh
7	*sete*	set
8	*oito*	*oy*·too
9	*nove*	nov
10	*dez*	desh
11	*onze*	ongz
12	*doze*	doz
13	*treze*	trez
14	*quatorze*	ka·*torrz*
15	*quinze*	keengz
16	*dezesseis*	dze·*saysh*
17	*dezesete*	dze·*set*
18	*dezoito*	*dzoy*·too
19	*dezenove*	dze·*nov*
20	*vinte*	veengt
21	*vinte e um*	veengt e oong
22	*vinte e dois*	veengt e doysh
30	*trinta*	*treeng*·ta
40	*quarenta*	kwa·*reng*·ta
50	*cinquenta*	seeng·*kweng*·ta
60	*sessenta*	se·*seng*·ta
70	*setenta*	*steng*·ta
80	*oitenta*	oy·*teng*·ta
90	*noventa*	noo·*veng*·ta
100	*cem*	sang
200	*duzentos*	doo·*zeng*·toosh
1000	*mil*	*meel*

QUESTION WORDS

Who?
Quem? — keng

What?
(O) Quê? — (oo) ke

When?
Quando? — *kwang*·doo

Where?
Onde? — *ong*·de

Why?
Porque? — porr·*ke*

Which/What?
Qual/Quais? (sg/pl) — kwal/kwais

SHOPPING & SERVICES

What time does ... open?
A que horas abre ...? — a ke *o*·ras abr ...

I'd like to buy ...
Queria comprar ... — kree·rya kom·*prarr* ...

I'm just looking.
Estou só a olhar. — shto so a ol·*yar*

May I look at it?
Posso vê-lo/la? (m/f) — *po*·soo *ve*·loo/la

How much is it?
Quanto é? — *kwang*·too e

That's too expensive.
É muito caro. — e *mweeng*·too *ka*·roo

Can you lower the price?
Pode baixar o preço? — *po*·de ba·*sharr* oo *pre*·soo

Do you have something cheaper?
Tem uma coisa mais barata? — teng *oo*·ma *koy*·za maizh ba·*ra*·ta

I'll give you (five euros).
Dou (cinco euros). — do (*seeng*·koo *yoo*·roos)

I don't like it.
Não gosto deste. — nowng *gosh*·too desht

I'll take it.
Vou levar isso. — vo le·*var ee*·soo

Where is ...?
Onde fica ...? — *ong*·de *fee*·ka ...

an ATM
um multibanco — oom mool·tee·*bang*·koo

a bank
o banco — oo *ban*·koo

a bookstore
uma livraria — *oo*·ma lee·vra·*rya*

the ... embassy
a embaixada do/da ... — a eng·bai·*sha*·da doo/da ...

a foreign-exchange office
uma loja de câmbio — *oo*·ma *lo*·zha de *kam*·byoo

a laundrette
uma lavandaria — *oo*·ma la·vang·*dree*·a

a market
o mercado — oo merr·*ka*·doo

a pharmacy/chemist
uma farmácia — *oo*·ma far·*ma*·sya

the police station
o posto de polícia — oo *pos*·too·de poo·*lee*·see·a

the post office
o correio — oo coo·*ray*·oo

a supermarket
o supermercado — oo soo·perr·merr·*ka*·doo

Can I pay ...?
Posso pagar com ...? — *po*·soo pa·*garr* kom ...

by credit card
cartão de crédito — karr·*towng* de *kre*·dee·too

by travellers cheque
traveler cheque — *tra*·ve·ler *she*·kee

less	*menos*	*me*·noos
more	*mais*	maizh
large	*grande*	grangd
small	*pequeno/a* (m/f)	*pke*·noo/na

I want to buy ...
Quero comprar ... ke·roo kom·*prarr* ...
a phone card
um cartão telefónico oong kar·*towng* te·le·*fo*·nee·koo
stamps
selos se·loosh

Where can I ...?
Onde posso ...? on·de po·soo ...
change a travellers cheque
trocar traveler cheques troo·*karr* tra·ve·*ler she*·kes
change money
trocar dinheiro troo·*kar* dee·*nyay*·roo
check my email
ver o meu e-mail ver oo *me*·oo e·mail
get Internet access
aceder à internet a·se·*der* a een·terr·*net*

TIME & DATES

What time is it?
Que horas são? ke *o*·ras sowng
It's (ten) o'clock.
São (dez) horas. sowng (desh) *o*·ras

now	*agora*	a·*go*·ra
this morning	*esta manhã*	esh·ta ma·*nyang*
this afternoon	*esta tarde*	*esh*·ta *tard*
today	*hoje*	ozh
tonight	*esta noite*	*esh*·ta noyt
tomorrow	*amanhã*	a·ma·*nyang*
yesterday	*ontem*	*on*·teng

Monday	*segunda-feira*	*sgoon*·da·*fay*·ra
Tuesday	*terça-feira*	*terr*·sa·*fay*·ra
Wednesday	*quarta-feira*	*kwarr*·ta·*fay*·ra
Thursday	*quinta-feira*	*keeng*·ta·*fay*·ra
Friday	*sexta-feira*	*saysh*·ta·*fay*·ra
Saturday	*sábado*	*sa*·ba·doo
Sunday	*domingo*	doo·*meeng*·goo

January	*Janeiro*	zha·*nay*·roo
February	*Fevereiro*	fe·*vray*·roo
March	*Março*	*marr*·soo
April	*Abril*	a·*breel*
May	*Maio*	*ma*·yoo
June	*Junho*	*zhoo*·nyoo
July	*Julho*	*zhoo*·lyoo
August	*Agosto*	a·*gosh*·too
September	*Setembro*	*steng*·broo
October	*Outubro*	o·*too*·bro
November	*Novembro*	noo·*veng*·broo
December	*Dezembro*	*dzeng*·broo

ROAD SIGNS

Ceda a Vez	Give Way
Entrada	Entrance
Portagem	Toll
Proibido Entrar	No Entry
Rua Sem Saída	Dead End
Saída	Freeway Exit
Sentido Único	One-way

TRANSPORT

Public Transport

Which ... goes to Lisbon?	*Qual o ... que vai para Lisboa?*	kwal oo ... ke vai *pa*·ra leezh·*bo*·a
boat	*barco*	*barr*·koo
intercity bus	*camionetes*	kam·yoo·*ne*·tesh
local bus	*autocarro*	ow·too·*ka*·rroo
ferry	*ferry*	*fe*·ree
plane	*avião*	a·vee·*owng*
train	*comboio*	kom·*boy*·oo

When's the ... (bus)?	*Quando sai o ... (autocarro)?*	*kwang*·doo sai oo ... (ow·too·*ka*·rroo)
first	*primeiro*	pree·*may*·roo
next	*próximo*	*pro*·see·moo
last	*último*	*ool*·tee·moo

Is this the (bus) to ...?
Este (autocarro) vai para ...? esht (ow·to·*ka*·rroo) vai *pa*·ra ...?
What time does it leave?
Que horas sai? ke *o*·ras sai
What time does it get to ...?
Que horas chega a ...? ke *o*·ras *she*·ga a ...
Do I need to change?
Tenho de mudar de linha? te·nyoo de moo·*darr* de *lee*·nya

A ... ticket to (...)	*Um bilhete de ... para (...)*	oong bee·*lyet* de ... *pa*·ra (...)
1st-class	*primeira classe*	pree·*may*·ra klas
2nd-class	*segunda classe*	se·*goon*·da klas
one-way	*ida*	*ee*·da
round-trip	*ida e volta*	*ee*·da e *vol*·ta

the luggage check room
o balcão de guarda volume oo bal·*kowng* de *gwarr*·da voo·*loo*·me
a luggage locker
um cacifo de bagagem oong ka·*see*·foo de ba·*ga*·zheng

Is this taxi available?
Este táxi está livre? esht *tak*·see shta leevr
How much is it to ...?
Quanto custa ir a ...? *kwang*·too *koos*·ta eerr a ...

Please put the meter on.
Por favor ligue o taxímetro.
porr fa·*vorr lee*·ge oo tak·*see*·me·troo

Please take me to (this address).
Leve-me para (esta morada), por favor.
le·ve·me *pa*·ra (*esh*·ta moo·*ra*·da) porr fa·*vorr*

Private Transport

I'd like to hire a/an ...
Queria alugar ...
ke·rya a·loo·*garr* ...

4WD	*um quatro por quatro*	oom *kwa*·troo por *kwa*·troo
bicycle	*uma bicicleta*	*oo*·ma bee·see·*kle*·ta
car	*um carro*	oong *ka*·rroo
motorbike	*uma motocicleta*	*oo*·ma mo·too·see·*kle*·ta

Is this the road to ...?
Esta é a estrada para ...?
esh·ta e a es·*tra*·da *pa*·ra ...

(How long) Can I park here?
(Quanto tempo) Posso estacionar aqui?
(*kwang*·too *teng*·poo) *po*·soo es·ta·shyoo·*narr* a·*kee*

Where's a gas/petrol station?
Onde fica um posto de gasolina?
on·de *fee*·ka oong *pos*·too de ga·zoo·*lee*·na

Please fill it up.
Enche o depósito, por favor.
en·she oo de·*po*·see·too porr fa·*vorr*

I'd like ... litres.
Meta ... litros.
me·ta ... *lee*·troosh

diesel	*diesel*	*dee*·sel
LPG	*gás*	gash
unleaded	*gasolina sem chumbo*	ga·zoo·*lee*·na seng *shoom*·bo

The (car/motorbike) has broken down at ...
(O carro/A motocicleta) avariou em ...
(oo *ka*·rroo/a moo·too·see·*kle*·ta) a·*va*·ryo eng ...

The car won't start.
O carro não pega.
o *ka*·ho nowng *pe*·ga

I need a mechanic.
Preciso de um mecânico.
pre·*see*·soo de oong me·*ka*·nee·koo

I've run out of gas/petrol.
Fiquei sem gasolina.
fee·*kay* seng ga·zoo·*lee*·na

I've had an accident.
Sofri um acidente.
soo·*free* oong a·see·*dent*

TRAVEL WITH CHILDREN

I need (a/an) ...
Preciso de ...
pre·*see*·zoo de ...

Do you have (a/an) ...?
Aqui tem ...?
a·*kee* teng ...

baby change room
uma sala para mudar o bebé
oo·ma *sa*·la *pa*·ra moo·*darr* o be·*be*

baby seat
um assento de criança
oong a·*seng*·too de kree·*an*·sa

child-minding service
um serviço de ama
oong serr·*vee*·soo de *a*·ma

children's menu
um cardápio para criança
oong kar·*da*·pyo *pa*·ra kree·*an*·sa

(English-speaking) babysitter
uma ama (que fale ingles)
oo·ma *a*·ma (ke *fa*·le eeng·*glesh*)

formula (milk)
leite em pó (para bebé)
layt eng po (pa·ra be·*be*)

highchair
uma cadeira de criança
oo·ma ka·*day*·ra de kree·*an*·sa

potty
um penico
oom pe·*nee*·ko

pusher/stroller
um carrinho de bebé
oom ka·*hee*·nyoo de be·*be*

(disposable) nappies/diapers
fraldas (descartáveis)
fral·das (des·karr·*ta*·vays)

Do you mind if I breastfeed here?
Importa-se que eu amamente aqui?
een·*porr*·ta·se ke eu a·ma·*meng*·te a·*kee*

Are children allowed?
É permitida a entrada de crianças?
e perr·mee·*tee*·da a eng·*tra*·da de kree·*an*·sas

LANGUAGE

Glossary

For food and drink terms, see the Food & Drink Glossary (p69), and for general terms see the Language chapter (p482).

aberto – open
abrigo – shelter or shelter-house
Age of Discoveries – the period during the 15th and 16th centuries when Portuguese sailors explored the coast of Africa and finally charted a sea route to India
aluguer – for hire
albergaria – upmarket inn
albufeira – reservoir, lagoon
aldeia – village
alta – upper
alta qualidade – fast deluxe bus
anta – see *dolmen*
arco – arch
armazém – warehouse
armillary sphere – celestial sphere used by early astronomers and navigators to chart the stars; a common decorative motif in Manueline architecture and atop *pelourinhos*
arrabalde – outskirts, environs
arrayal, arraiais (pl) – street party
artesanato – handicrafts shop
auto-estradas – motorways
avenida – avenue
aviação – airline
azulejo – hand-painted tile, typically blue and white, used to decorate buildings

bagagem – left-luggage office
bairro – town district
baixa – lower
balneário – health resort, spa
bandarilha – spears
bandeirada – flag fall
barcos rabelos – colourful boats once used to transport port wine from vineyards
barragem – dam
beco – cul de sac
berrão, berrões (pl) – ancient stone monument shaped like a pig, found mainly in Trás-os-Montes and the adjacent part of Spain
biblioteca – library
bicyclete tudo terrano (BTT) – mountain bike
bilet de cidade – city ticket
bilhete diário – day pass
boa tarde – good afternoon
bom noite – good night

câmara municipal – city or town hall
caderneta – booklet of tickets (train)
cais fluvial – river terminal
cantarinha – small terracotta pitcher
Carnaval – Carnival; festival that takes place just before Lent
carreiras (CR) – stop at every crossroad (never mind that *carreiras* means something like 'in a hurry' in Portuguese)
cartão telefónico – plastic card used in Credifone telephones
casa de abrigo – shelter house (eg for staff and/or the public in a national/natural park)
casa de banho – toilet (literally bathroom)
casa de fado – *fado* house; a place (usually a café or restaurant) where people gather to hear *fado* music
casa de hóspedes – boarding house, usually with shared showers and toilets
casa de povo – village common house
casais – huts
castelo – castle
castro – fortified hill town
cavaleiro – horseman
CCI – Camping Card International
Celtiberians – descendants of Celts who arrived in the Iberian Peninsula around 600 BC
centro de comércio – shopping centre
centro de saúde – state-administered medical centre
centros de acolhimento – lodging centres
chegada – arrival (of bus, train etc)
cidade – town or city
cidadela – fortress
citânia – Celtic fortified village
claustro – cloisters
concelho – municipality, council
conta – bill (in a restaurant)
coro alto – choir stalls overlooking the nave in a church
correios – post office
cortes – Portugal's early parliament
couvert – cover charge added to restaurant bill to pay for sundries
CP – Caminhos de Ferro Portugueses (the Portuguese state railway company)
Credifone – card-operated public telephone
cromeleque – circle of prehistoric standing stones
cruz – cross

direita – right; abbreviated as D, dir or Dta
distrito – district
dolmen – Neolithic stone tomb (*anta* in Portuguese)

Dom, Dona – honorific titles (like Sir, Madam) given to royalty, nobility and landowners; now used more generally as a very polite form of address
dormidas – sign indicating a rooming house
duplo – room with twin beds

elevador – lift (elevator), funicular
ementa – menu
encerrado – closed or shut down (eg for repairs)
entrada – entree/starter or entrance
espigueiros – stone granaries
esplanada – terrace, seafront promenade
esquerda – left; abbreviated as E, esq or Esqa
estação – station (usually train station)
estacionamento – parking
estalagem – inn; more expensive than an *albergaria*
estradas nacionais – main two-lane national roads
expressos – comfortable, fast buses between major cities
estradas – highways

fadista – singer of *fado*
fado – traditional, melancholy Portuguese style of singing
farmácia – pharmacy
fechado – closed (eg for the day/weekend or holiday)
feira – fair
férias – holidays, vacation
festa – festival
FICC – Fédération Internationale de Camping et de Caravanning (International Camping and Caravanning Federation)
forcados – foolhardy young men who face a bull barehanded
fortaleza – fortress
FPCC – Federação Portuguesa de Campismo e Caravanismo (Portuguese Camping and Caravanning Federation)
freguesia – parish

GNR – Guarda Nacional Republicana, the national guard (the acting police force in rural towns without PSP police)
gruta – cave

hipermercado – hypermarket
horários – timetables
hospedaria – see *casa de hóspedes*

IC (intercidade) – express intercity train
ICEP – Investimentos, Comércio e Turismo de Portugal, the government's umbrella organisation for tourism
IDD – International Direct Dial
igreja – church
igreja matriz – parish church
ilha – island
infantário – children's daycare centre
IR (interregional) – fairly fast train without too many stops
itinerário complementar (IC) – subsidiary highways
itinerário principal (IP) – highways in the country's main network
IVA – Imposto sobre Valor Acrescentado, or VAT (value-added tax)

jardim – garden
jardim municipal – town garden
jardim público – public garden
judiaria – quarter in a town where Jews were once segregated
junta de turismo – see *turismo*

largo – small square
latifúndios – Roman system of large farming estates
lavabo – toilet
lavandaria – laundry
lista – see *ementa*
litoral – coastal
livraria – bookshop
Lisboêtas – Lisbon dweller
loggia – covered area or porch on the side of a building
lugar – neighbourhood, place

Manueline – elaborate Gothic/Renaissance style of art and architecture that emerged during the reign of Dom Manuel I in the 16th century
marranos - 'New Christians,' ie jews who converted during the Inquisition
menir – menhir, a standing stone monument typical of the late Neolithic Age
mercado municipal – municipal market
mesa – table
MFA – Movimento das Forçes Armadas, the military group that led the Revolution of the Carnations in 1974
minimercado – grocery shop or small supermarket
miradouro – lookout
Misericórdia – from Santa Casa da Misericórdia (Holy House of Mercy), a charitable institution founded in the 15th century to care for the poor and the sick; usually designates an old building founded by this organisation
moliceiro – high-prowed, shallow-draft boats traditionally used for harvesting seaweed in the estuaries of Beira Litoral
mosteiro – monastery
mouraria – the quarter where Moors were segregated during and after the Christian *Reconquista*
mudéjar – originally meant a Muslim under Christian rule; also used as an adjective to describe the art and architecture of the mudéjars

museu – museum
música popular – modern folk-music scene

obras – repairs

paço – palace
paisagens protegidas – protected landscape areas
parque de campismo – camp site
parque de merenda – picnic area
parque infantil – playground
parque nacional – national park
parque naturais – natural park
partida – departure (of bus, train etc)
pauliteiro – stick dancer
pega – second phase of a bullfight
pelourinho – stone pillory, often ornately carved; erected in the 13th to 18th centuries as symbols of justice and sometimes as places where criminals were punished
pensão, pensões (pl) – guesthouse, the Portuguese equivalent of a bed and breakfast (B&B), though breakfast is not always served
percursos pedestre – walking trail
peões de brega – footmen
planalto – high plain
pombal – dovecote, a structure for housing pigeons
ponte – bridge
portagem – toll road
posto de turismo – see *turismo*
pousada or Pousada de Portugal – government-run scheme of upmarket inns, often in converted castles, convents or palaces
pousada da juventude – youth hostel; usually with kitchen, common rooms and sometimes rooms with private bath
praça – square
praça de touros – bullring
praia – beach
pré-pagamento – prepayment required (as in some café-restaurants)
PSP – Polícia de Segurança Pública, the local police force

quarto de casal – room with a double bed
quarto individual – single room
quarto particular or just quarto – room in a private house
quinta – country estate or villa; in the Douro wine-growing region it often refers to a wine lodge's property

rápidas – quick regional buses
R (regional) – slow train
Reconquista – Christian reconquest of Portugal (718–1249)
recreio infantil – playground
rés do chão – ground floor (abbreviated as R/C)
reservas naturais – nature reserves
residencial, residenciais (pl) – guesthouse; slightly more expensive than a *pensão* and usually serving breakfast
retornados – refugees
ribeiro – stream
rio – river
romaria – religious pilgrimage
rua – street

sanitários – public toilets
sapataria – shoe shop
saudade – melancholy longing for better times
sé – cathedral
selos – stamps
sem chumbo – unleaded (petrol)
senhor – man
senhora – woman
senhora dona – elderly or respected woman
serra – mountain, mountain range
solar – manor house
supermercado – supermarket

tabacaria – tobacconist-cum-newsagent
talha dourada – gilded woodwork
termas – spa
terra fria – cold country
terra quente – hot country
torre de menagem – castle tower, keep
tourada – bullfight
troco – change
Turihab – short for Turismo Habitação, a scheme for marketing private accommodation (particularly in northern Portugal) in cottages, historic buildings and manor houses
turismo – tourist office

vila – town

Behind the Scenes

THIS BOOK

This 5th edition of Portugal was coordinated by Abigail Hole who also wrote the Destination Portugal, Highlights, Getting Started, Itineraries, Architecture, Lisbon & Around, Algarve, Alentejo, Estremadura & Ribatejo and Directory chapters. She was assisted by co-author Charlotte Beech who wrote the History, Culture, Environment, Beiras, Douro, Minho, Trás-os-Montes and Transport chapters. Specialist food writer Richard Sterling wrote the Food & Drink chapter. The Health chapter was adapted from material written by Dr Caroline Evans. John King and Julia Wilkinson wrote the first four editions of this guide.

THANKS from the Authors

Abigail Hole Thanks to Heather Dickson for giving me the chance to do this; Charlie, the best co-author you could have; Pedro Correira and Manuela Silva for all their restaurant help and other guidance; all the brilliant turismo staff across Portugal; readers for all their advice; Conceição Colaço in Tapada; Nestor, who returned my notebook from a service station between San Sebastian and Bilbao; Matthieu the hitchhiker, who lent me money to get to Toulouse; to Nelson in the Elvas turismo; António Serzedo of Opus Gay in Lisbon; Imogen Franks for massive help and encouragement; Carrie and Marcus for a very funny weekend in Lisbon; Sumeet and Sophia, Dad, Mum, Ant, Morag, Esther and Omi for endless support; Nolan – for sympathy and patience in Toulouse; kindred spirit David Corfield for excellent tips; special-assistant Sandi; to Tris and Sophie for hospitality at Maison Biggs. Much appreciation to all in production for their hard work. Biggest thanks to Luca, with whom I fell in love in Lisbon.

Charlotte Beech A very special *obrigada* goes to Vitor Enes in Aveiro, for all his support and insider information. Pedro Correia was also of invaluable help in exploring the Porto restaurant scene. Suzanna Vieira deserves a medal for answering a thousand questions in Aveiro, as do Anabela Pereira in Bragança, José Serra in Manteigas and Maria in Trancoso. I'm also hugely indebted to the helpful tourist offices in Porto, Braga, Coimbra, Guimarães and all around the north of the country. And thanks to all the readers who wrote in with useful comments and suggestions.

CREDITS

Portugal 5 was commissioned and developed in Lonely Planet's London office by Heather Dickson. Production was coordinated by Julia Taylor (editorial) and Natasha Velleley (cartography). Overseeing production were Charles Rawlings-Way (project manager) and Mark Griffiths (managing cartographer).

Editorial assistance was provided by Helen Yeates, Jackey Coyle, Adrienne Costanzo, John Hinman and Sarah Hassall. Cartographic assistance was provided by Andrew Smith, Emma McNicol, Louise Klep and Kelly Stanhope, with map checking by Daniel Fennessy and Wayne Murphy. The Language chapter was produced by Quentin Frayne, Meladel Mistica and Jodie Martire.

THE LONELY PLANET STORY

The story begins with a classic travel adventure: Tony and Maureen Wheeler's 1972 journey across Europe and Asia to Australia. There was no useful information about the overland trail then, so Tony and Maureen published the first Lonely Planet guidebook to meet a growing need.

From a kitchen table, Lonely Planet has grown to become the largest independent travel publisher in the world, with offices in Melbourne (Australia), Oakland (USA) and London (UK). Today Lonely Planet guidebooks cover the globe. There is an ever-growing list of books and information in a variety of media. Some things haven't changed. The main aim is still to make it possible for adventurous travellers to get out there – to explore and better understand the world.

At Lonely Planet we believe travellers can make a positive contribution to the countries they visit – if they respect their host communities and spend their money wisely. Every year 5% of company profit is donated to charities around the world.

Vicki Beale laid out the book and produced the colour pages. Katherine Marsh and Kaitlin Beckett assisted with layout. The climate charts were produced by Csanad Csutoros. The book was indexed by Julia Taylor. The back-cover map was produced by Wayne Murphy. The cover was designed by Kristin Guthrie and Annika Roojun. Thanks to Imogen Franks, Alan Murphy, Sam Trafford, Ray Thomson, Nancy Ianni, Stephanie Pearson, Kerryn Burgesss, Adriana Mammarella, Kate McDonald and Sally Darmody.

THANKS from Lonely Planet

Many thanks to the following travellers who used the last edition and wrote to us with helpful hints, useful advice and interesting anecdotes.

A Poul Alberg Ostergaard **B** Janneke Bastiaanssen, Joy Behennah, Philipp Bencze, Oth Blom, Kerry and Jim Bloodworth, Terje Børresen, Kate Botkin, Kevin Bourke, Paul Bouwman **C** Filipe Carvalho, Andrew Castellano, D Cawthraw, Ron and Sheila Corbett, James Costello, Robert Cotter **D** Katherine Daley, Annemieke Dekker, Tomara Dini, Lucie Draai, Chris and Willy Duarte-Van Selm **F** Olivia Faul, Nikki Feltham **G** David Galliford, Douglas and Isolde Gibson, Jasper Groenendaal, Janelle Groom, Vera Guerreiro **H** Toril Hagen, Susie Hargreaves, Kenneth Hay, Jolyne Hoogstraaten **J** Marianne James, Barry Johnston, Susan Jones **K** M Kamalizadeh, Jan Willem Keen, Verena Kellner, Laura Kogelman, Anatoliy Kurmanaev **L** Jacquelyn and Rick Lane, Rebecca Letven, Mark Leyland, Pauline Lockstone **M** John Macauley, John and Lynn Midgley, Sanna Miettunen **O** Luis Ortigao **P** Ben Pacitti, Elisa Pedro **R** Serena Raffaeli, Terence Reed, Ydun Ritz **S** Sally Scott, David Serisier, David Smith, ALJ Stoffels, Birgit Strozyk, Andrew Synn **T** Joshua Taylor Barnes, Katharina Tiefenböck, Andre Toledo **V** Julia Vajda, Maurits Van Der Hoofd, Daan Van Hooreweghe, Ruben Van Moppes, Maria Isabel Coutinho Vieira **W** Reto Westermann Blass, Kathleen A Williams, Frank Wilson and Lillian Wong

ACKNOWLEDGMENTS

Many thanks to the following for the use of their content:

Globe on back cover © Mountain High Maps 1993 Digital Wisdom, Inc.

SEND US YOUR FEEDBACK

We love to hear from travellers – your comments keep us on our toes and help make our books better. Our well-travelled team reads every word on what you loved or loathed about this book. Although we cannot reply individually to postal submissions, we always guarantee that your feedback goes straight to the appropriate authors, in time for the next edition. Each person who sends us information is thanked in the next edition – and the most useful submissions are rewarded with a free book.

To send us your updates – and find out about Lonely Planet events, newsletters and travel news – visit our award-winning website: **www.lonelyplanet.com/feedback**

Note: We may edit, reproduce and incorporate your comments in Lonely Planet products such as guidebooks, websites and digital products, so let us know if you don't want your comments reproduced or your name acknowledged. For a copy of our privacy policy visit www.lonelyplanet.com/privacy.

Index

000 Map pages
000 Location of colour photographs

000 Map pages
000 Location of colour photographs

INDEX

N

000 Map pages
000 Location of colour photographs

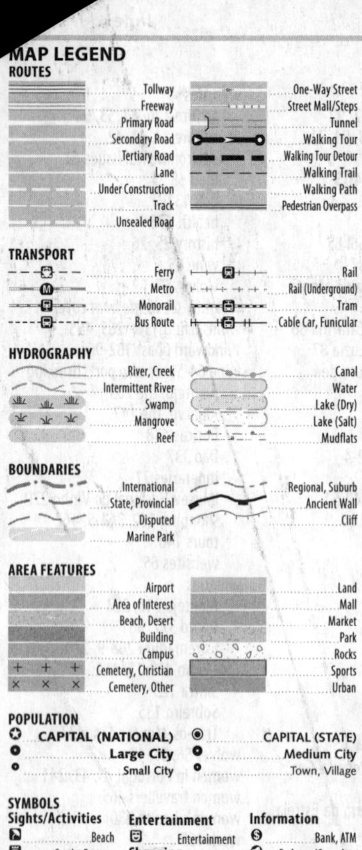

LONELY PLANET OFFICES

Australia
Head Office
Locked Bag 1, Footscray, Victoria 3011
☎ 03 8379 8000, fax 03 8379 8111
talk2us@lonelyplanet.com.au

USA
150 Linden St, Oakland, CA 94607
☎ 510 893 8555, toll free 800 275 8555
fax 510 893 8572, info@lonelyplanet.com

UK
72–82 Rosebery Ave,
Clerkenwell, London EC1R 4RW
☎ 020 7841 9000, fax 020 7841 9001
go@lonelyplanet.co.uk

Published by Lonely Planet Publications Pty Ltd
ABN 36 005 607 983

Cover photographs by Lonely Planet Images: Cockerels, typical craft work, Barcelos, Carlos Costa (front); Boat on Carvoeiro beach, Gerry Reilly (back). Many of the images in this guide are available for licensing from Lonely Planet Images: www.lonelyplanetimages.com

Printed by SNP Security Printing Pte Ltd, Singapore